ALL GLORY TO ŚRĪ GURU AND GAURĀṄGA

ŚRĪMAD BHĀGAVATAM

of

KṚṢṆA-DVAIPĀYANA VYĀSA

सत्त्वेन प्रतिलभ्याय नैष्कर्म्येण विपश्चिता ।
नमः कैवल्यनाथाय निर्वाणसुखसंविदे ॥ ११ ॥

sattvena pratilabhyāya
naiṣkarmyeṇa vipaścitā
namaḥ kaivalya-nāthāya
nirvāṇa-sukha-saṁvide
(*Śrīmad-Bhāgavatam* 8.3.11)

Books by His Divine Grace
A. C. Bhaktivedanta Swami Prabhupāda:

Bhagavad-gītā As It Is
Śrīmad-Bhāgavatam (1st to 10th Cantos)
Śrī Caitanya-Caritāmṛta (9 vols.)
Kṛṣṇa, The Supreme Personality of Godhead
Teachings of Lord Caitanya
The Nectar of Devotion
The Nectar of Instruction
Śrī Īśopaniṣad
Light of the Bhāgavata
Easy Journey to Other Planets
The Science of Self-Realization
Kṛṣṇa Consciousness: The Topmost Yoga System
Perfect Questions, Perfect Answers
Teachings of Lord Kapila, the Son of Devahuti
Transcendental Teachings of Prahlāda Mahārāja
Teachings of Queen Kuntī
Kṛṣṇa, the Reservoir of Pleasure
The Path of Perfection
Life Comes from Life
Message of Godhead
The Perfection of Yoga
Beyond Birth and Death
On the Way to Kṛṣṇa
Rāja-vidyā: The King of Knowledge
Elevation to Kṛṣṇa Consciousness
Kṛṣṇa Consciousness: The Matchless Gift
Selected Verses from the Vedic Scriptures
Back to Godhead magazine (founder)

ŚRĪMAD BHĀGAVATAM

Eighth Canto

"Withdrawal of the Cosmic Creations"

With the Original Sanskrit Text,
Its Roman Transliteration, Synonyms,
Translation and Elaborate Purports

by

His Divine Grace
A. C. Bhaktivedanta Swami Prabhupāda
Founder-*Ācārya* of the International Society for Krishna Consciousness

THE BHAKTIVEDANTA BOOK TRUST

Readers interested in the subject matter of this book are invited by The Bhaktivedanta Book Trust to correspond with its secretary at the following address:

The Bhaktivedanta Book Trust
Hare Krishna Land,
Juhu, Mumbai 400 049, India.

Website / E-mail :
www.indiabbt.com
admin@indiabbt.com

Śrīmad Bhāgavatam Eighth Canto (English)

First printing in India : 2,000 copies
Second to Seventeenth printings : 52,500 copies
Eighteenth printing, November 2018 : 7,000 copies

ISBN : 978-93-84564-10-0 (v.10)
ISBN : 978-93-84564-00-1 (18-volume set)

Published and Printed by
The Bhaktivedanta Book Trust.

SJ1K

Table of Contents

Preface

We must know the present need of human society. And what is that need? Human society is no longer bounded by geographical limits to particular countries or communities. Human society is broader than in the Middle Ages, and the world tendency is toward one state or one human society. The ideals of spiritual communism, according to *Śrīmad-Bhāgavatam,* are based more or less on the oneness of the entire human society, nay, of the entire energy of living beings. The need is felt by great thinkers to make this a successful ideology. *Śrīmad-Bhāgavatam* will fill this need in human society. It begins, therefore, with an aphorism of Vedānta philosophy, *janmādy asya yataḥ,* to establish the ideal of a common cause.

Human society, at the present moment, is not in the darkness of oblivion. It has made rapid progress in the fields of material comforts, education and economic development throughout the entire world. But there is a pinprick somewhere in the social body at large, and therefore there are large-scale quarrels, even over less important issues. There is need of a clue as to how humanity can become one in peace, friendship and prosperity with a common cause. *Śrīmad-Bhāgavatam* will fill this need, for it is a cultural presentation for the respiritualization of the entire human society.

Śrīmad-Bhāgavatam should be introduced also in the schools and colleges, for it is recommended by the great student-devotee Prahlāda Mahārāja in order to change the demoniac face of society.

kaumāra ācaret prājño
dharmān bhāgavatān iha
durlabhaṁ mānuṣaṁ janma
tad apy adhruvam artha-dam

(*Bhāg.* 7.6.1)

Disparity in human society is due to lack of principles in a godless civilization. There is God, or the Almighty One, from whom everything emanates, by whom everything is maintained and in whom everything is merged to rest. Material science has tried to find the ultimate source of creation very insufficiently, but it is a fact that there is one ultimate source of everything that be. This ultimate source is explained rationally and authoritatively in the beautiful *Bhāgavatam,* or *Śrīmad-Bhāgavatam.*

Śrīmad-Bhāgavatam is the transcendental science not only for knowing the ultimate source of everything but also for knowing our relation with Him and our duty toward perfection of the human society on the basis of this perfect knowledge. It is powerful reading matter in the Sanskrit language, and it is now rendered into English elaborately so that simply by a careful reading one will know God perfectly well, so much so that the reader will be sufficiently educated to defend himself from the onslaught of atheists. Over and above this, the reader will be able to convert others to accepting God as a concrete principle.

Śrīmad-Bhāgavatam begins with the definition of the ultimate source. It is a bona fide commentary on the *Vedānta-sūtra* by the same author, Śrīla Vyāsadeva, and gradually it develops into nine cantos up to the highest state of God realization. The only qualification one needs to study this great book of transcendental knowledge is to proceed step by step cautiously and not jump forward haphazardly as with an ordinary book. It should be gone through chapter by chapter, one after another. The reading matter is so arranged with the original Sanskrit text, its English transliteration, synonyms, translation and purports so that one is sure to become a God-realized soul at the end of finishing the first nine cantos.

The Tenth Canto is distinct from the first nine cantos because it deals directly with the transcendental activities of the Personality of Godhead, Śrī Kṛṣṇa. One will be unable to capture the effects of the Tenth Canto without going through the first nine cantos. The book is complete in twelve cantos, each independent, but it is good for all to read them in small installments one after another.

I must admit my frailties in presenting *Śrīmad-Bhāgavatam,* but still I am hopeful of its good reception by the thinkers and leaders of society on the strength of the following statement of *Śrīmad-Bhāgavatam* (1.5.11):

tad vāg visargo janatāgha-viplavo
yasmin prati-ślokam abaddhavaty api
nāmāny anantasya yaśo 'ṅkitāni yac
chṛṇvanti gāyanti gṛṇanti sādhavaḥ

"On the other hand, that literature which is full of descriptions of the transcendental glories of the name, fame, form and pastimes of the unlimited Supreme Lord is a transcendental creation meant for bringing about a revolution in the impious life of a misdirected civilization. Such transcendental literature, even though irregularly composed, is heard, sung and accepted by purified men who are thoroughly honest."

Oṁ tat sat

A. C. Bhaktivedanta Swami

Introduction

"This *Bhāgavata Purāṇa* is as brilliant as the sun, and it has arisen just after the departure of Lord Kṛṣṇa to His own abode, accompanied by religion, knowledge, etc. Persons who have lost their vision due to the dense darkness of ignorance in the age of Kali shall get light from this *Purāṇa.*" (*Śrīmad-Bhāgavatam* 1.3.43)

The timeless wisdom of India is expressed in the *Vedas,* ancient Sanskrit texts that touch upon all fields of human knowledge. Originally preserved through oral tradition, the *Vedas* were first put into writing five thousand years ago by Śrīla Vyāsadeva, the "literary incarnation of God." After compiling the *Vedas,* Vyāsadeva set forth their essence in the aphorisms known as *Vedānta-sūtras. Śrīmad-Bhāgavatam* (*Bhāgavata Purāṇa*) is Vyāsadeva's commentary on his own *Vedānta-sūtras.* It was written in the maturity of his spiritual life under the direction of Nārada Muni, his spiritual master. Referred to as "the ripened fruit of the tree of Vedic literature," *Śrīmad-Bhāgavatam* is the most complete and authoritative exposition of Vedic knowledge.

After compiling the *Bhāgavatam,* Vyāsa imparted the synopsis of it to his son, the sage Śukadeva Gosvāmī. Śukadeva Gosvāmī subsequently recited the entire *Bhāgavatam* to Mahārāja Parīkṣit in an assembly of learned saints on the bank of the Ganges at Hastināpura (now Delhi). Mahārāja Parīkṣit was the emperor of the world and was a great *rājarṣi* (saintly king). Having received a warning that he would die within a week, he renounced his entire kingdom and retired to the bank of the Ganges to fast until death and receive spiritual enlightenment. The *Bhāgavatam* begins with Emperor Parīkṣit's sober inquiry to Śukadeva Gosvāmī: "You are the spiritual master of great saints and devotees. I am therefore begging you to show the way of perfection for all persons, and especially for one who is about to die. Please let me know what a man should hear, chant, remember and worship, and also what he should not do. Please explain all this to me."

Śukadeva Gosvāmī's answer to this question, and numerous other questions posed by Mahārāja Parīkṣit, concerning everything from the nature of the self to the origin of the universe, held the assembled sages in rapt attention continuously for the seven days leading up to the king's death. The sage Sūta Gosvāmī, who was present in that assembly when Śukadeva Gosvāmī first recited *Śrīmad-Bhāgavatam,* later repeated the *Bhāgavatam* before a gathering of sages in the forest of Naimiṣāraṇya. Those sages, concerned about the spiritual welfare of the people in general, had gathered to perform a long, continuous chain of sacrifices to counteract the degrading influence of the incipient age of Kali. In response to the sages' request that he speak the essence of Vedic wisdom, Sūta Gosvāmī repeated from memory the entire eighteen thousand verses of *Śrīmad-Bhāgavatam,* as spoken by Śukadeva Gosvāmī to Mahārāja Parīkṣit.

The reader of *Śrīmad-Bhāgavatam* hears Sūta Gosvāmī relate the questions of Mahārāja Parīkṣit and the answers of Śukadeva Gosvāmī. Also, Sūta Gosvāmī sometimes responds directly to questions put by Śaunaka Ṛṣi, the spokesman for the sages gathered at Naimiṣāraṇya. One therefore simultaneously hears two dialogues: one between Mahārāja Parīkṣit and Śukadeva Gosvāmī on the bank of the Ganges, and another at Naimiṣāraṇya between Sūta Gosvāmī and the sages at Naimiṣāraṇya forest, headed by Śaunaka Ṛṣi. Futhermore, while instructing King Parīkṣit, Śukadeva Gosvāmī often relates historical episodes and gives accounts of lengthy philosophical discussions between such great souls as Nārada Muni and Vasudeva. With this understanding of the history of the *Bhāgavatam,* the reader will easily be able to follow its intermingling of dialogues and events from various sources. Since philosophical wisdom, not chronological order, is most important in the text, one need only be attentive to the subject matter of *Śrīmad-Bhāgavatam* to appreciate fully its profound message.

The translators of this edition compare the *Bhāgavatam* to sugar candy—wherever you taste it, you will find it equally sweet and relishable. Therefore, to taste the sweetness of the *Bhāgavatam,* one may begin by reading any of its volumes. After such an introductory taste, however, the serious reader is best advised to go back to the First Canto and then proceed through the *Bhāgavatam,* canto after canto, in its natural order.

This edition of the *Bhāgavatam* is the first complete English translation of this important text with an elaborate commentary, and it is the first widely available to the English-speaking public. The first twelve volumes (Canto One through Canto Ten, Part One) are the product of the scholarly and devotional effort of His Divine Grace A. C. Bhaktivedanta Swami Prabhupāda, the founder-*ācārya* of the International Society for Krishna Consciousness and the world's most distinguished teacher of Indian religious and philosophical thought. His consummate Sanskrit scholarship and intimate familiarity with Vedic culture and thought as well as the modern way of life combine to reveal to the West a magnificent exposition of this important classic. After the departure of Śrīla

Prabhupāda from this world in 1977, his monumental work of translating and annotating *Śrīmad-Bhāgavatam* has been continued by his disciples Hridayananda dāsa Goswami and Gopīparāṇadhana dāsa.

Readers will find this work of value for many reasons. For those interested in the classical roots of Indian civilization, it serves as a vast reservoir of detailed information on virtually every one of its aspects. For students of comparative philosophy and religion, the *Bhāgavatam* offers a penetrating view into the meaning of India's profound spiritual heritage. To sociologists and anthropologists, the *Bhāgavatam* reveals the practical workings of a peaceful and scientifically organized Vedic culture, whose institutions were integrated on the basis of a highly developed spiritual world view. Students of literature will discover the *Bhāgavatam* to be a masterpiece of majestic poetry. For students of psychology, the text provides important perspectives on the nature of consciousness, human behavior and the philosophical study of identity. Finally, to those seeking spiritual insight, the *Bhāgavatam* offers simple and practical guidance for attainment of the highest self-knowledge and realization of the Absolute Truth. The entire multivolume text, presented by the Bhaktivedanta Book Trust, promises to occupy a significant place in the intellectual, cultural and spiritual life of modern man for a long time to come.

—The Publishers

CHAPTER ONE

The Manus, Administrators of the Universe

First of all, let me offer my humble, respectful obeisances unto the lotus feet of my spiritual master, His Divine Grace Śrī Śrīmad Bhaktisiddhānta Sarasvatī Gosvāmī Prabhupāda. Sometime in the year 1935 when His Divine Grace was staying at Rādhā-kuṇḍa, I went to see him from Bombay. At that time, he gave me many important instructions in regard to constructing temples and publishing books. He personally told me that publishing books is more important than constructing temples. Of course, those same instructions remained within my mind for many years. In 1944 I began publishing my *Back to Godhead,* and when I retired from family life in 1958 I began publishing *Śrīmad-Bhāgavatam* in Delhi. When three parts of *Śrīmad-Bhāgavatam* had been published in India, I then started for the United States of America on the thirteenth of August, 1965.

I am continuously trying to publish books, as suggested by my spiritual master. Now, in this year, 1976, I have completed the Seventh Canto of *Śrīmad-Bhāgavatam,* and a summary of the Tenth Canto has already been published as *Kṛṣṇa, the Supreme Personality of Godhead.* Still, the Eighth Canto, Ninth Canto, Tenth Canto, Eleventh Canto and Twelfth Canto are yet to be published. On this occasion, therefore, I am praying to my spiritual master to give me strength to finish this work. I am neither a great scholar nor a great devotee; I am simply a humble servant of my spiritual master, and to the best of my ability I am trying to please him by publishing these books, with the cooperation of my disciples in America. Fortunately, scholars all over the world are appreciating these publications. Let us cooperatively publish more and more volumes of *Śrīmad-Bhāgavatam* just to please His Divine Grace Bhaktisiddhānta Sarasvatī Ṭhākura.

This First Chapter of the Eighth Canto may be summarized as a description of four Manus, namely Svāyambhuva, Svārociṣa, Uttama and Tāmasa. After hearing descriptions of the dynasty of Svāyambhuva Manu until the end of the Seventh Canto, Mahārāja Parīkṣit desired to know about other Manus. He desired to understand how the Supreme Personality of

Godhead descends—not only in the past but at the present and in the future—and how He acts in various pastimes as Manu. Since Parīkṣit Mahārāja was eager to know all this, Śukadeva Gosvāmī gradually described all the Manus, beginning with the six Manus who had appeared in the past.

The first Manu was Svāyambhuva Manu. His two daughters, namely Ākūti and Devahūti, gave birth to two sons, named Yajña and Kapila respectively. Because Śukadeva Gosvāmī had already described the activities of Kapila in the Third Canto, he now described the activities of Yajña. The original Manu, along with his wife, Śatarūpā, went into the forest to practice austerities on the bank of the River Sunandā. They practiced austerities for a hundred years, and then Manu, in a trance, formed prayers to the Supreme Personality of Godhead. Rākṣasas and *asuras* then attempted to devour him, but Yajña, accompanied by his sons the Yāmas and the demigods, killed them. Then Yajña personally took the post of Indra, the King of the heavenly planets.

The second Manu, whose name was Svārociṣa, was the son of Agni, and His sons were headed by Dyumat, Suṣeṇa and Rociṣmat. In the age of this Manu, Rocana became Indra, the ruler of the heavenly planets, and there were many demigods, headed by Tuṣita. There were also many saintly persons, such as Ūrja and Stambha. Among them was Vedaśirā, whose wife, Tuṣitā, gave birth to Vibhu. Vibhu instructed eighty-eight thousand *dṛḍha-vratas,* or saintly persons, on self-control and austerity.

Uttama, the son of Priyavrata, was the third Manu. Among his sons were Pavana, Sṛñjaya and Yajñahotra. During the reign of this Manu, the sons of Vasiṣṭha, headed by Pramada, became the seven saintly persons. The Satyas, Devaśrutas and Bhadras became the demigods, and Satyajit became Indra. From the womb of Sunṛtā, the wife of Dharma, the Lord appeared as Satyasena, and He killed all the Yakṣas and Rākṣasas who were fighting with Satyajit.

Tāmasa, the brother of the third Manu, was the fourth Manu, and he had ten sons, including Pṛthu, Khyāti, Nara and Ketu. During his reign, the Satyakas, Haris, Vīras and others were demigods, the seven great saints were headed by Jyotirdhāma, and Triśikha became Indra. Harimedhā begot a son named Hari in the womb of his wife Hariṇī. This Hari, an incarnation of God, saved the devotee Gajendra. This incident is described as *gajendra-mokṣaṇa.* At the end of this chapter, Parīkṣit Mahārāja particularly asks about this incident.

TEXT 1

श्रीराजोवाच
स्वायम्भुवस्येह गुरो वंशोऽयं विस्तराच्छ्रुतः ।
यत्र विश्वसृजां सर्गो मनूनन्यान्वदस्व नः ॥ १ ॥

śrī-rājovāca
svāyambhuvasyeha guro
vaṁśo 'yaṁ vistarāc chrutaḥ
yatra viśva-sṛjāṁ sargo
manūn anyān vadasva naḥ

śrī-rājā uvāca—the King (Mahārāja Parīkṣit) said; *svāyambhuvasya*—of the great personality Svāyambhuva Manu; *iha*—in this connection; *guro*—O my spiritual master; *vaṁśaḥ*—dynasty; *ayam*—this; *vistarāt*—extensively; *śrutaḥ*—I have heard (from you); *yatra*—wherein; *viśva-sṛjām*—of the great personalities known as the *prajāpatis,* such as Marīci; *sargaḥ*—creation, involving the birth of many sons and grandsons from the daughters of Manu; *manūn*—Manus; *anyān*—other; *vadasva*—kindly describe; *naḥ*—to us.

TRANSLATION

King Parīkṣit said: O my lord, my spiritual master, now I have fully heard from Your Grace about the dynasty of Svāyambhuva Manu. But there are also other Manus, and I want to hear about their dynasties. Kindly describe them to us.

TEXT 2

मन्वन्तरे हरेर्जन्म कर्माणि च महीयसः ।
गृणन्ति कवयो ब्रह्मंस्तानि नो वद शृण्वताम् ॥ २ ॥

manvantare harer janma
karmāṇi ca mahīyasaḥ
gṛṇanti kavayo brahmaṁs
tāni no vada śṛṇvatām

manvantare—during the change of *manvantaras* (one Manu following another); *hareḥ*—of the Supreme Personality of Godhead; *janma*—appearance; *karmāṇi*—and activities; *ca*—also; *mahīyasaḥ*—of the supremely glorified; *gṛṇanti*—describe; *kavayaḥ*—the great learned persons who have perfect intelligence; *brahman*—O learned *brāhmaṇa* (Śukadeva Gosvāmī); *tāni*—all of them; *naḥ*—to us; *vada*—please describe; *śṛṇvatām*—who are very eager to hear.

TRANSLATION

O learned brāhmaṇa, Śukadeva Gosvāmī, the great learned persons who are completely intelligent describe the activities and appearance of the Supreme Personality of Godhead during the various manvantaras. We are very eager to hear about these narrations. Kindly describe them.

PURPORT

The Supreme Personality of Godhead has different varieties of incarnations, including the *guṇa-avatāras, manvantara-avatāras, līlā-avatāras* and *yuga-avatāras,* all of which are described in the *śāstras.* Without reference to the *śāstras* there can be no question of accepting anyone as an incarnation of the Supreme Personality of Godhead. Therefore, as especially mentioned here, *gṛṇanti kavayaḥ:* the descriptions of various incarnations are accepted by great learned scholars with perfect intelligence. At the present time, especially in India, so many rascals are claiming to be incarnations, and people are being misled. Therefore, the identity of an incarnation should be confirmed by the descriptions of the *śāstras* and by wonderful activities. As described in this verse by the word *mahīyasaḥ,* the activities of an incarnation are not ordinary magic or jugglery, but are wonderful activities. Thus any incarnation of the Supreme Personality of Godhead must be supported by the statements of the *śāstra* and must actually perform wonderful activities. Parīkṣit Mahārāja was eager to hear about the Manus of different ages. There are fourteen Manus during a day of Brahmā, and the age of each Manu lasts for seventy-one *yugas.* Thus there are thousands of Manus during the life of Brahmā.

TEXT 3

यद्यस्मिन्नन्तरे ब्रह्मन्भगवान्विश्वभावनः ।
कृतवान्कुरुते कर्ता ह्यतीतेऽनागतेऽद्य वा ॥ ३ ॥

yad yasminn antare brahman
bhagavān viśva-bhāvanaḥ
kṛtavān kurute kartā
hy atīte 'nāgate 'dya vā

yat—whatever activities; *yasmin*—in a particular age; *antare*—*manvantara; brahman*—O great *brāhmaṇa; bhagavān*—the Supreme Personality of Godhead; *viśva-bhāvanaḥ*—who has created this cosmic manifestation; *kṛtavān*—has done; *kurute*—is doing; *kartā*—and will do; *hi*—indeed; *atīte*—in the past; *anāgate*—in the future; *adya*—at the present; *vā*—either.

TRANSLATION

O learned brāhmaṇa, kindly describe to us whatever activities the Supreme Personality of Godhead, who created this cosmic manifestation, has performed in the past manvantaras, is performing at present, and will perform in the future manvantaras.

PURPORT

In *Bhagavad-gītā* the Supreme Personality of Godhead said that both He and the other living entities present on the battlefield had existed in the past, they existed at present, and they would continue to exist in the future. Past, present and future always exist, both for the Supreme Personality of Godhead and for ordinary living entities. *Nityo nityānāṁ cetanaś cetanānām* . Both the Lord and the living entities are eternal and sentient, but the difference is that the Lord is unlimited whereas the living entities are limited. The Supreme Personality of Godhead is the creator of everything, and although the living entities are not created but exist with the Lord eternally, their bodies are created, whereas the Supreme Lord's body is never created. There is no difference between the Supreme Lord and His body, but the conditioned soul, although eternal, is different from his body.

TEXT 4

श्रीऋषिरुवाच
मनवोऽस्मिन्व्यतीताः षट् कल्पे स्वायम्भुवादयः ।
आद्यस्ते कथितो यत्र देवादीनां च सम्भवः ॥ ४ ॥

śrī-ṛṣir uvāca
manavo 'smin vyatītāḥ ṣaṭ
kalpe svāyambhuvādayaḥ
ādyas te kathito yatra
devādīnāṁ ca sambhavaḥ

śrī-ṛṣiḥ uvāca—the great saint Śukadeva Gosvāmī said; *manavaḥ*—Manus; *asmin*—during this period (one day of Brahmā); *vyatītāḥ*—already past; *ṣaṭ*—six; *kalpe*—in this duration of Brahmā's day; *svāyambhuva*—Svāyambhuva Manu; *ādayaḥ*—and others; *ādyaḥ*—the first one (Svāyambhuva); *te*—unto you; *kathitaḥ*—I have already described; *yatra*—wherein; *deva-ādīnām*—of all the demigods; *ca*—also; *sambhavaḥ*—the appearance.

TRANSLATION

Śukadeva Gosvāmī said: In the present kalpa there have already been six Manus. I have described to you Svāyambhuva Manu and the appearance of many demigods. In this kalpa of Brahmā, Svāyambhuva is the first Manu.

TEXT 5

आकूत्यां देवहूत्यां च दुहित्रोस्तस्य वै मनोः ।
धर्मज्ञानोपदेशार्थं भगवान्पुत्रतां गतः ॥ ५ ॥

ākūtyāṁ devahūtyāṁ ca
duhitros tasya vai manoḥ
dharma-jñānopadeśārthaṁ
bhagavān putratāṁ gataḥ

ākūtyām—from the womb of Ākūti; *devahūtyām ca*—and from the womb of Devahūti; *duhitroḥ*—of the two daughters; *tasya*—of him; *vai*—indeed; *manoḥ*—of Svāyambhuva Manu; *dharma*—religion; *jñāna*—and knowledge; *upadeśa-artham*—for instructing; *bhagavān*—the Supreme Personality of Godhead; *putratām*—sonhood under Ākūti and Devahūti; *gataḥ*—accepted.

TRANSLATION

Svāyambhuva Manu had two daughters, named Ākūti and Devahūti. From their wombs, the Supreme Personality of Godhead appeared as two sons named Yajñamūrti and Kapila respectively. These sons were entrusted with preaching about religion and knowledge.

PURPORT

Devahūti's son was known as Kapila, and Ākūti's son was known as Yajñamūrti. Both of Them taught about religion and philosophical knowledge.

TEXT 6

कृतं पुरा भगवतः कपिलस्यानुवर्णितम् ।
आख्यास्ये भगवान्यज्ञो यच्चकार कुरूद्वह ॥ ६ ॥

kṛtaṁ purā bhagavataḥ
kapilasyānuvarṇitam
ākhyāsye bhagavān yajño
yac cakāra kurūdvaha

kṛtam—already done; *purā*—before; *bhagavataḥ*—of the Supreme Personality of Godhead; *kapilasya*—Kapila, the son of Devahūti; *anuvarṇitam*—fully described; *ākhyāsye*—I shall describe now; *bhagavān*—the Supreme Personality of Godhead; *yajñaḥ*—of the name Yajñapati or Yajñamūrti; *yat*—whatever; *cakāra*—executed; *kuru-udvaha*—O best of the Kurus.

TRANSLATION

O best of the Kurus, I have already described [in the Third Canto] the activities of Kapila, the son of Devahūti. Now I shall describe the activities of Yajñapati, the son of Ākūti.

TEXT 7

विरक्तः कामभोगेषु शतरूपापतिः प्रभुः ।
विसृज्य राज्यं तपसे सभार्यो वनमाविशत् ॥ ७ ॥

viraktaḥ kāma-bhogeṣu
śatarūpā-patiḥ prabhuḥ
visṛjya rājyaṁ tapase
sabhāryo vanam āviśat

viraktaḥ—without attachment; *kāma-bhogeṣu*—in sense gratification (in *gṛhastha* life); *śatarūpā-patiḥ*—the husband of Śatarūpā, namely Svāyambhuva Manu; *prabhuḥ*—who was the master or king of the world; *visṛjya*—after renouncing totally; *rājyam*—his kingdom; *tapase*—for practicing austerities; *sa-bhāryaḥ*—with his wife; *vanam*—the forest; *āviśat*—entered.

TRANSLATION

Svāyambhuva Manu, the husband of Śatarūpā, was by nature not at all attached to enjoyment of the senses. Thus he gave up his kingdom of sense enjoyment and entered the forest with his wife to practice austerities.

PURPORT

As stated in *Bhagavad-gītā* (4.2), *evaṁ paramparā-prāptam imaṁ rājarṣayo viduḥ:* "The supreme science was thus received through the chain of disciplic succession, and the saintly kings understood it in that way." All the Manus were perfect kings. They were *rājarṣis.* In other words, although they held posts as kings of the world, they were as good as great saints. Svāyambhuva Manu, for example, was the emperor of the world, yet he had no desire for sense gratification. This is the meaning of monarchy. The king of the country or the emperor of the empire must be so trained that by nature he renounces sense gratification. It is not that because one becomes king he should unnecessarily spend money for sense gratification. As soon as kings became degraded, spending money for sense gratification, they were lost. Similarly, at the present moment, monarchy having been lost, the people have created democracy, which is also failing. Now, by the laws of nature, the time is coming when dictatorship will put the citizens into more and more difficulty. If the king or dictator individually, or the members of the government collectively, cannot maintain the state or kingdom according to the rules of *Manu-saṁhitā,* certainly their government will not endure.

TEXT 8

सुनन्दायां वर्षशतं पदैकेन भुवं स्पृशन् ।
तप्यमानस्तपो घोरमिदमन्वाह भारत ॥ ८ ॥

sunandāyāṁ varṣa-śataṁ
padaikena bhuvaṁ spṛśan
tapyamānas tapo ghoram
idam anvāha bhārata

sunandāyām—on the bank of the River Sunandā; *varṣa-śatam*—for one hundred years; *pada-ekena*—on one leg; *bhuvam*—the earth; *spṛśan*—touching; *tapyamānaḥ*—he performed austerities; *tapaḥ*—austerities; *ghoram*—very severe; *idam*—the following; *anvāha*—and spoke; *bhārata*—O scion of Bharata.

TRANSLATION

O scion of Bharata, after Svāyambhuva Manu had thus entered the forest with his wife, he stood on one leg on the bank of the River Sunandā, and in this way, with only one leg touching the earth, he performed great austerities for one hundred years. While performing these austerities, he spoke as follows.

PURPORT

Śrīla Viśvanātha Cakravartī Ṭhākura comments that the word *anvāha* means that he chanted or murmured to himself, not that he lectured to anyone.

TEXT 9

श्रीमनुरुवाच
येन चेतयते विश्वं विश्वं चेतयते न यम् ।
यो जागर्ति शयानेऽस्मिन्नायं तं वेद वेद सः ॥ ९ ॥

śrī-manur uvāca
yena cetayate viśvaṁ
viśvaṁ cetayate na yam
yo jāgarti śayāne 'smin
nāyaṁ taṁ veda veda saḥ

śrī-manuḥ uvāca—Svāyambhuva Manu chanted; *yena*—by whom (the Personality of Godhead); *cetayate*—is brought into animation; *viśvam*—the whole universe; *viśvam*—the whole universe (the material world); *cetayate*—animates; *na*—not; *yam*—He whom; *yaḥ*—He who; *jāgarti*—is always awake (watching all activities); *śayāne*—while sleeping; *asmin*—in this body; *na*—not; *ayam*—this living entity; *tam*—Him; *veda*—knows; *veda*—knows; *saḥ*—He.

TRANSLATION

Lord Manu said: The supreme living being has created this material world of animation; it is not that He was created by this material world. When everything is silent, the Supreme Being stays awake as a witness. The living entity does not know Him, but He knows everything.

PURPORT

Here is a distinction between the Supreme Personality of Godhead and the living entities. *Nityo nityānāṁ cetanaś cetanānām* . According to the Vedic version, the Lord is the supreme eternal, the supreme living being. The difference between the Supreme Being and the ordinary living being is that when this material world is annihilated, all the living entities remain silent in oblivion, in a dreaming or unconscious condition, whereas the Supreme Being stays awake as the witness of everything. This material world is created, it stays for some time, and then it is annihilated. Throughout these changes, however, the Supreme Being remains awake. In the material condition of all living entities, there are three stages of dreaming. When the material world is awake and put in working order, this is a kind of dream, a waking dream. When the living entities go to sleep, they dream again. And when unconscious at the time of annihilation, when this material world is unmanifested, they enter another stage of dreaming. At any stage in the material world, therefore, they are all dreaming. In the spiritual world, however, everything is awake.

TEXT 10

आत्मावास्यमिदं विश्वं यत् किञ्चिज्जगत्यां जगत् ।
तेन त्यक्तेन भुञ्जीथा मा गृधः कस्यस्विद्धनम् ॥ १० ॥

ātmāvāsyam idaṁ viśvaṁ
yat kiñcij jagatyāṁ jagat
tena tyaktena bhuñjīthā
mā gṛdhaḥ kasya svid dhanam

ātma—the Supersoul; *āvāsyam*—living everywhere; *idam*—this universe; *viśvam*—all universes, all places; *yat*—whatever; *kiñcit*—everything that exists; *jagatyām*—in this world, everywhere; *jagat*—everything, animate and inanimate; *tena*—by Him; *tyaktena*—allotted; *bhuñjīthāḥ*—you may enjoy; *mā*—do not; *gṛdhaḥ*—accept; *kasya svit*—of anyone else; *dhanam*—the property.

TRANSLATION

Within this universe, the Supreme Personality of Godhead in His Supersoul feature is present everywhere, wherever there are animate or inanimate beings. Therefore, one should accept only that which is allotted to him; one should not desire to infringe upon the property of others.

PURPORT

Having described the situation of the Supreme Personality of Godhead as transcendental, Svāyambhuva Manu, for the instruction of the sons and grandsons in his dynasty, is now describing all the property of the universe as belonging to the Supreme Personality of Godhead. Manu's instructions are not only for his own sons and grandsons, but for all of human society. The word "man"—or, in Sanskrit, *manuṣya*—has been derived from the name Manu, for all the members of human society are descendants of the original Manu. Manu is also mentioned in *Bhagavad-gītā* (4.1), where the Lord says:

imaṁ vivasvate yogaṁ
proktavān aham avyayam
vivasvān manave prāha
manur ikṣvākave 'bravīt

"I instructed this imperishable science of *yoga* to the sun-god, Vivasvān, and Vivasvān instructed it to Manu, the father of mankind, and Manu in turn instructed it to Ikṣvāku." Svāyambhuva Manu and Vaivasvata Manu have similar duties. Vaivasvata Manu was born of the sun-god, Vivasvān, and his son was Ikṣvāku, the King of the earth. Since Manu is understood to be the original father of humanity, human society should follow his instructions.

Svāyambhuva Manu instructs that whatever exists, not only in the spiritual world but even within this material world, is the property of the Supreme Personality of Godhead, who is present everywhere as the Superconsciousness. As confirmed in *Bhagavad-gītā* (13.3), *kṣetra-jñaṁ cāpi māṁ viddhi sarva-kṣetreṣu bhārata:* in every field—in other words, in every body—the Supreme Lord is existing as the Supersoul. The individual soul is given a body in which to live and act according to the instructions of the Supreme Person, and therefore the Supreme Person also exists within every body. We should not think that we are independent; rather, we should understand that we are allotted a certain portion of the total property of the Supreme Personality of Godhead.

This understanding will lead to perfect communism. Communists think in terms of their own nations, but the spiritual communism instructed here is not only nationwide but universal. Nothing belongs to any nation or any individual person; everything belongs to the Supreme Personality of Godhead. That is the meaning of this verse. *Ātmāvāsyam idaṁ viśvam:* whatever exists within this universe is the property of the Supreme Personality of Godhead. The modern communistic theory, and also the idea of the United Nations, can be reformed—indeed, rectified—by the understanding that everything belongs to the Supreme Personality of Godhead. The Lord is not a creation of our intelligence; rather, He has created us. *Ātmāvāsyam idaṁ viśvam. Īśāvāsyam idaṁ sarvam* . This universal communism can solve all the problems of the world.

One should learn from the Vedic literature that one's body is also not the property of the individual soul, but is given to the individual soul according to his *karma. Karmaṇā daiva-netreṇa jantur dehopapattaye* . The 8,400,000 different bodily forms are machines given to the individual soul. This is confirmed in *Bhagavad-gītā* (18.61):

īśvaraḥ sarva-bhūtānāṁ
hṛd-deśe 'rjuna tiṣṭhati
bhrāmayan sarva-bhūtāni
yantrārūḍhāni māyayā

"The Supreme Lord is situated in everyone's heart, O Arjuna, and is directing the wanderings of all living entities, who are seated as on a machine, made of the material energy." The Lord, as the Supersoul, sits in everyone's heart and observes the various desires of the individual soul. The Lord is so merciful that He gives the living entity the opportunity to enjoy varieties of desires in suitable bodies, which are nothing but machines (*yantrārūḍhāni māyayā*). These machines are manufactured by the material ingredients of the external energy, and thus the living entity enjoys or suffers according to his desires. This opportunity is given by the Supersoul.

Everything belongs to the Supreme, and therefore one should not usurp another's property. We have a tendency to manufacture many things. Especially nowadays, we are building skyscrapers and developing other material facilities. We should know, however, that the ingredients of the skyscrapers and machines cannot be manufactured by anyone but the Supreme Personality of Godhead. The whole world is nothing but a combination of the five material elements (*tejo-vāri-mṛdāṁ yathā vinimayaḥ*). A skyscraper is a transformation of earth, water and fire. Earth and water are combined and burnt into bricks by fire, and a skyscraper is essentially a tall construction of bricks. Although the bricks may be manufactured by man, the ingredients of the bricks are not. Of course, man, as a manufacturer, may accept a salary from the Supreme Personality of Godhead. That is stated here: *tena tyaktena bhuñjīthāḥ* . One may construct a big skyscraper, but neither the constructor, the merchant nor the worker can claim proprietorship. Proprietorship belongs to the person who has spent for the building. The Supreme Personality of Godhead has manufactured water, earth, air, fire and the sky, and one can use these and take a salary (*tena tyaktena bhuñjīthāḥ*). However, one cannot claim proprietorship. This is perfect communism. Our tendency to construct great buildings should be used only for constructing

His Divine Grace
A. C. Bhaktivedanta Swami Prabhupāda
Founder-Ācārya of ISKCON and greatest exponent of Kṛṣṇa consciousness in the modern world

The elephant Gajendra took a lotus in his trunk, and with great difficulty due to his painful condition, he uttered the following words: "O Lord Nārāyaṇa, master of the universe, I offer my respectful obeisances unto You." (8.3.32)

When the Lord severed its head from its body, the crocodile assumed a beautiful form as a Gandharva. Even greater was Gajendra's blessing: liberation from birth and death, and a form like the Lord's. (8.4.1–8)

With His merciful glance the Lord brought the demons and demigods back to life, and then He lifted Mount Mandara with one hand. (8.6.36–38)

When Lord Śiva saw that everyone was extremely disturbed by the poison, he became very compassionate. Thus he took all the poison in his palm and drank it. (8.7.36–42)

As the demons and demigods churned the milk ocean, a wonderful male person appeared, carrying a jug filled with nectar. He was Dhanvantari, a plenary portion of a plenary portion of Viṣṇu. (8.8.31–35).

Mohinī-mūrti beheaded Rāhu with Her razor-sharp disc. But the head did not die, for Rāhu had begun drinking the nectar. (8.9.25–26)

The demon Kālanemi, seeing the Supreme Lord on the battlefield, took up his trident and prepared to throw it at Garuḍa's head. (8.10.56)

Accompanied by his wife, Śiva went to Lord Madhusūdana's abode and begged the Lord to show him His form as a woman. (8.12.1–13)

At the sacrifice called Viśvajit, Prahlāda Mahārāja gave Bali a garland of flowers that would never fade, and Śukrācārya gave him a conchshell. (8.15.6–7)

King Indra was struck with wonder upon seeing Bali at the head of his vast army of soldiers and demon chiefs, who looked as if they would swallow the sky and burn all directions. (8.15.10–24)

After Aditi had performed the Payovrata ceremony, the Supreme Lord appeared before her, overwhelming her with ecstasy. (8.17.3–4)

In the presence of His father and mother, the Lord assumed the form of Vāmana (a *brāhmaṇa*-dwarf and celibate student) just like a theatrical actor. (8.18.12)

As Bali Mahārāja and the members of the assembly watched in stunned amazement, the unlimited Supreme Personality of Godhead, who had assumed the form of Vāmana, began increasing in size, until everything in the universe was within His body, including the earth, planetary systems, sky and oceans, as well as the birds, beasts, human beings and demigods. The Lord in His universal form thus stood before Bali Mahārāja holding a conchshell, sword, shield, flaming disc, arrow, bow, lotus and club. (8.20.21–32)

After Lord Vāmana's associates had defeated all the demons, Garuḍa arrested Bali Mahārāja with the snake-ropes of Varuṇa and brought him before the Lord. (8.21.26–27)

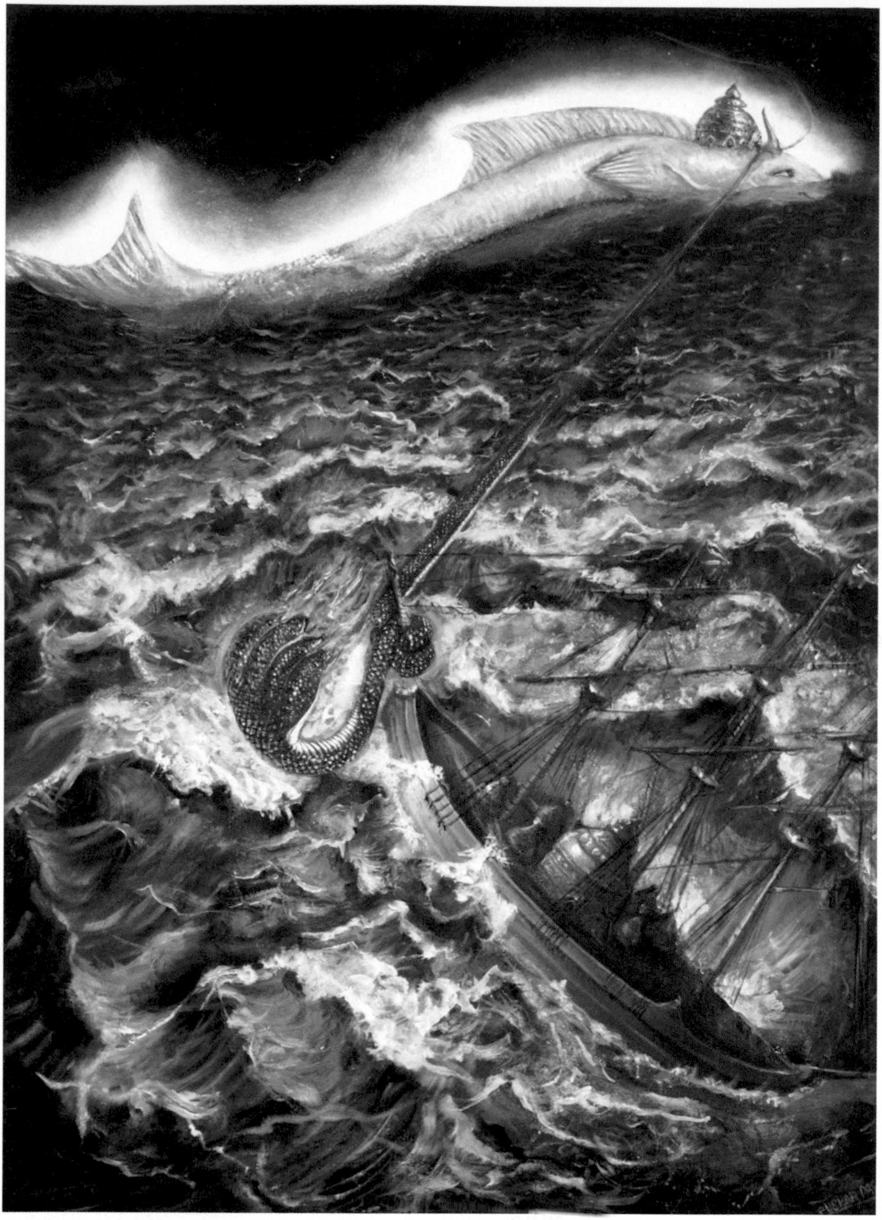

Following the instructions that the Lord had previously imparted to him, King Satyavrata anchored his boat to the great fish's horn, using the serpent Vāsuki as a rope. (8.24.45)

large and valuable temples in which to install the Deity of the Supreme Personality of Godhead. Then our desire for construction will be fulfilled.

Since all property belongs to the Supreme Personality of Godhead, everything should be offered to the Lord, and we should take only *prasāda* (*tena tyaktena bhuñjīthāḥ*). We should not fight among ourselves to take more than we need. As Nārada said to Mahārāja Yudhiṣṭhira:

yāvad bhriyeta jaṭharaṁ
tāvat svatvaṁ hi dehinām
adhikaṁ yo 'bhimanyeta
sa steno daṇḍam arhati

"One may claim proprietorship to as much wealth as required to maintain body and soul together, but one who desires proprietorship over more than that must be considered a thief, and he deserves to be punished by the laws of nature." (*Bhāg.* 7.14.8) Of course, we need to be maintained in eating, sleeping, mating and defending (*āhāra-nidra-bhaya-maithuna*), but since the Supreme Lord, the Personality of Godhead, has provided these necessities of life for the birds and bees, why not for mankind? There is no need for economic development; everything is provided. Therefore one should understand that everything belongs to Kṛṣṇa, and with this idea, one may take *prasāda.* However, if one interferes with the allotments of others, he is a thief. We should not accept more than what we actually need. Therefore, if by chance we get an abundance of money, we should always consider that it belongs to the Supreme Personality of Godhead. In Kṛṣṇa consciousness we are getting sufficient money, but we should never think that the money belongs to us; it belongs to the Supreme Personality of Godhead and should be equally distributed to the workers, the devotees. No devotee should claim that any money or property belongs to him. If one thinks that any portion of property of this huge universe belongs to anyone, he is to be considered a thief and is punishable by the laws of nature. *Daivī hy eṣā guṇa-mayī mama māyā duratyayā:* no one can surpass the vigilance of material nature or hide his intentions from material nature. If human society unlawfully claims that the property of the universe, either partially or wholly, belongs to mankind, all of human society will be cursed as a society of thieves and will be punished by the laws of nature.

TEXT 11

यं पश्यति न पश्यन्तं चक्षुर्यस्य न रिष्यति ।
तं भूतनिलयं देवं सुपर्णमुपधावत ॥ ११ ॥

yaṁ paśyati na paśyantaṁ
cakṣur yasya na riṣyati
taṁ bhūta-nilayaṁ devaṁ
suparṇam upadhāvata

yam—He who; *paśyati*—the living entity sees; *na*—not; *paśyantam*—although always seeing; *cakṣuḥ*—eye; *yasya*—whose; *na*—never; *riṣyati*—diminishes; *tam*—Him; *bhūta-nilayam*—the original source of all living entities; *devam*—the Supreme Personality of Godhead; *suparṇam*—who accompanies the living entity as a friend; *upadhāvata*—everyone should worship.

TRANSLATION

Although the Supreme Personality of Godhead constantly watches the activities of the world, no one sees Him. However, one should not think that because no one sees Him, He does not see, for His power to see is never diminished. Therefore, everyone should worship the Supersoul, who always stays with the individual soul as a friend.

PURPORT

Offering prayers to Kṛṣṇa, Śrīmatī Kuntīdevī, the mother of the Pāṇḍavas, said, *alakṣyaṁ sarva-bhūtānām antar bahir avasthitam:* "Kṛṣṇa, You reside both inside and outside of everything, yet the unintelligent conditioned souls cannot see You." In *Bhagavad-gītā* it is said that one can see the Supreme Personality of Godhead through *jñāna-cakṣuṣaḥ,* eyes of knowledge. He who opens these eyes of knowledge is called a spiritual master. Thus we offer our prayers to the spiritual master with the following *śloka:*

oṁ ajñāna-timirāndhasya
jñānāñjana-śalākayā
cakṣur unmīlitaṁ yena
tasmai śrī-gurave namaḥ

"I offer my respectful obeisances unto my spiritual master, who with the torchlight of knowledge has opened my eyes, which were blinded by the darkness of ignorance." (*Gautamīya Tantra*) The *guru's* task is to open the disciple's eyes of knowledge. When the disciple is awakened from ignorance to knowledge, he can see the Supreme Personality of Godhead everywhere because the Lord actually is everywhere. *Aṇḍāntara-stha-paramāṇu-*

cayāntara-stham. The Lord resides within this universe, He resides within the hearts of all living entities, and He resides even within the atom. Because we lack perfect knowledge, we cannot see God, but a little deliberation can help us to see God everywhere. This requires training. With a little deliberation, even the most degraded person can perceive the presence of God. If we take into account whose property is the vast ocean, whose property is the vast land, how the sky exists, how the numberless millions of stars and planets are set in the sky, who has made this universe and whose property it is, we should certainly come to the conclusion that there is a proprietor of everything. When we claim proprietorship over a certain piece of land, whether individually or for our families or nations, we should also consider how we became the proprietors. The land was there before our birth, before we came to the land. How did it become our property? Such deliberation will help us understand that there is a supreme proprietor of everything—the Supreme Personality of Godhead.

The Supreme Godhead is always awake. In the conditioned stage we forget things because we change our bodies, but because the Supreme Personality of Godhead does not change His body, He remembers past, present and future. Kṛṣṇa says in *Bhagavad-gītā* (4.1), *imaṁ vivasvate yogaṁ proktavān aham avyayam:* "I spoke this science of God—*Bhagavad-gītā*—to the sun-god at least forty million years ago." When Arjuna inquired from Kṛṣṇa how He could remember incidents that had taken place so long ago, the Lord answered that Arjuna was also present at that time. Because Arjuna is Kṛṣṇa's friend, wherever Kṛṣṇa goes, Arjuna goes. But the difference is that Kṛṣṇa remembers everything, whereas the living entity like Arjuna, being a minute particle of the Supreme Lord, forgets. Therefore it is said, the Lord's vigilance is never diminished. This is also confirmed in *Bhagavad-gītā* (15.15). *Sarvasya cāhaṁ hṛdi sanniviṣṭo mattaḥ smṛtir jñānam apohanaṁ ca:* the Supreme Personality of Godhead in His Paramātmā feature is always present within the hearts of all living entities, and from Him come memory, knowledge and forgetfulness. This is also indicated in this verse by the word *suparṇam,* which means "friend." In the *Śvetāśvatara Upaniṣad* (4.6) it is therefore said, *dvā suparṇā-sayujā sakhāyā samānaṁ vṛkṣaṁ pariṣasvajāte:* two birds are sitting on the same tree as friends. One bird is eating the fruit of the tree, and the other is simply observing. This observing bird is always present as a friend to the eating bird and giving him remembrance of things he wanted to do. Thus if we take into account the Supreme Personality of Godhead in our daily affairs, we can see Him or at least perceive His presence everywhere.

The words *cakṣur yasya na riṣyati* mean that although we cannot see Him, this does not mean that He cannot see us. Nor does He die when the cosmic manifestation is annihilated. The example is given in this connection that the sunshine is present when the sun is present, but when the sun is not present, or when we cannot see the sun, this does not mean that the sun is lost. The sun is there, but we cannot see it. Similarly, although we cannot see the Supreme Personality of Godhead in our present darkness, our lack of knowledge, He is always present, seeing our activities. As the Paramātmā, He is the witness and adviser (*upadraṣṭā* and *anumantā*). Therefore, by following the instructions of the spiritual master and studying authorized literatures, one can understand that God is present before us, seeing everything, although we have no eyes with which to see Him.

TEXT 12

न यस्याद्यन्तौ मध्यं च स्वः परो नान्तरं बहिः ।
विश्वस्यामूनि यद् यस्माद् विश्वं च तदृतं महत् ॥ १२ ॥

na yasyādy-antau madhyaṁ ca
svaḥ paro nāntaraṁ bahiḥ
viśvasyāmūni yad yasmād
viśvaṁ ca tad ṛtaṁ mahat

na—neither; *yasya*—of whom (the Supreme Personality of Godhead); *ādi*—a beginning; *antau*—end; *madhyam*—middle; *ca*—also; *svaḥ*—own; *paraḥ*—others; *na*—nor; *antaram*—inside; *bahiḥ*—outside; *viśvasya*—of the whole cosmic manifestation; *amūni*—all such considerations; *yat*—whose form; *yasmāt*—from He who is the cause of everything; *viśvam*—the whole universe; *ca*—and; *tat*—all of them; *ṛtam*—truth; *mahat*—very, very great.

TRANSLATION

The Supreme Personality of Godhead has no beginning, no end and no middle. Nor does He belong to a particular person or nation. He has no inside or outside. The dualities found within this material world, such as beginning and end, mine and theirs, are all absent from the personality of the Supreme Lord. The universe, which emanates from Him, is another feature of the Lord. Therefore the Supreme Lord is the ultimate truth, and He is complete in greatness.

PURPORT

The Supreme Personality of Godhead, Kṛṣṇa, is described in the *Brahma-saṁhitā* (5.1):

īśvaraḥ paramaḥ kṛṣṇaḥ
sac-cid-ānanda-vigrahaḥ
anādir ādir govindaḥ
sarva-kāraṇa-kāraṇam

"Kṛṣṇa, known as Govinda, is the supreme controller. He has an eternal, blissful, spiritual body. He is the origin of all. He has no other origin, for He is the prime cause of all causes." For the Lord's existence there is no cause, for He is the cause of everything. He is in everything (*mayā tatam idaṁ sarvam*), He is expanded in everything, but He is not everything. He is *acintya-bhedābheda,* simultaneously one and different. That is explained in this verse. In the material condition we have a conception of beginning, end and middle, but for the Supreme Personality of Godhead there are no such things. The universal cosmic manifestation is also the *virāṭ-rūpa* that was shown to Arjuna in *Bhagavad-gītā.* Therefore, since the Lord is present everywhere and all the time, He is the Absolute Truth and the greatest. He is complete in greatness. God is great, and how He is great is explained here.

TEXT 13

स विश्वकायः पुरुहूत ईशः
सत्यः स्वयंज्योतिरजः पुराणः ।
धत्तेऽस्य जन्माद्यजयात्मशक्त्या
तां विद्ययोदस्य निरीह आस्ते ॥ १३ ॥

sa viśva-kāyaḥ puru-hūta-īśaḥ
satyaḥ svayaṁ-jyotir ajaḥ purāṇaḥ
dhatte 'sya janmādy-ajayātma-śaktyā
tāṁ vidyayodasya nirīha āste

saḥ—that Supreme Personality of Godhead; *viśva-kāyaḥ*—the total form of the universe (the whole universe is the external body of the Supreme Personality of Godhead); *puru-hūtaḥ*—known by so many names; *īśaḥ*—the supreme controller (with full power); *satyaḥ*—the ultimate truth; *svayam*—personally; *jyotiḥ*—self-effulgent; *ajaḥ*—unborn, beginningless; *purāṇaḥ*—

the oldest; *dhatte*—He performs; *asya*—of this universe; *janma-ādi*—the creation, maintenance and annihilation; *ajayā*—by His external energy; *ātma-śaktyā*—by His personal potency; *tām*—that external material energy; *vidyayā*—by His spiritual potency; *udasya*—giving up; *nirīhaḥ*—without any desire or activity; *āste*—He is existing (untouched by the material energy).

TRANSLATION

The entire cosmic manifestation is the body of the Supreme Personality of Godhead, the Absolute Truth, who has millions of names and unlimited potencies. He is self-effulgent, unborn and changeless. He is the beginning of everything, but He has no beginning. Because He has created this cosmic manifestation by His external energy, the universe appears to be created, maintained and annihilated by Him. Nonetheless, He remains inactive in His spiritual energy and is untouched by the activities of the material energy.

PURPORT

Śrī Caitanya Mahāprabhu says in His *Śikṣāṣṭaka, nāmnām akāri bahudhā nija-sarva-śaktiḥ:* the Supreme Personality of Godhead has many names, which are all nondifferent from the Supreme Person. This is spiritual existence. By chanting the Hare Kṛṣṇa *mahā-mantra,* consisting of names of the Supreme Lord, we find that the name has all the potencies of the person. The Lord's activities are many, and according to His activities He has many names. He appeared as the son of mother Yaśodā, and also as the son of mother Devakī, and therefore He is named Devakī-nandana and Yaśodā-nandana. *Parāsya śaktir vividhaiva śrūyate:* the Lord has a multitude of energies, and therefore He acts in multifarious ways. Yet He has a particular name. The *śāstras* recommend which names we should chant, such as Hare Kṛṣṇa, Hare Kṛṣṇa, Kṛṣṇa Kṛṣṇa, Hare Hare. It is not that we have to search for some name or manufacture one. Rather, we must follow the saintly persons and the *śāstras* in chanting His holy name.

Although the material and spiritual energies both belong to the Lord, He is impossible to understand as long as we are in the material energy. And when we come to the spiritual energy, He is very easy to know. As stated in *Śrīmad-Bhāgavatam* (1.7.23): *māyāṁ vyudasya cic-chaktyā kaivalye sthita ātmani.* Although the external energy belongs to the Lord, when one is in the external energy (*mama māyā duratyayā*) He is very difficult to understand. However, when one comes to the spiritual energy, one can understand Him. Therefore in *Bhagavad-gītā* (18.55) it is said, *bhaktyā mām abhijānāti yāvān yaś cāsmi tattvataḥ:* one who wants to understand the Supreme Personality of Godhead in reality must take to the platform of *bhakti,* or Kṛṣṇa consciousness. This *bhakti* consists of various activities (*śravaṇaṁ kīrtanaṁ viṣṇoḥ smaraṇaṁ pāda-sevanam/ arcanaṁ vandanaṁ dāsyaṁ sakhyam ātma-nivedanam*), and to understand the Lord one must take to this path of devotional service. Even though the people of the world have forgotten God and may say that God is dead, this is not a fact. One can understand God when one takes to the Kṛṣṇa consciousness movement, and thus one can be happy.

TEXT 14

अथाग्रे ऋषयः कर्माणीहन्तेऽकर्महेतवे ।
ईहमानो हि पुरुषः प्रायोऽनीहां प्रपद्यते ॥ १४ ॥

athāgre ṛṣayaḥ karmāṇ-
īhante 'karma-hetave
īhamāno hi puruṣaḥ
prāyo 'nīhāṁ prapadyate

atha—therefore; *agre*—in the beginning; *ṛṣayaḥ*—all learned *ṛṣis,* saintly persons; *karmāṇi*—fruitive activities; *īhante*—execute; *akarma*—freedom from fruitive results; *hetave*—for the purpose of; *īhamānaḥ*—engaging in such activities; *hi*—indeed; *puruṣaḥ*—a person; *prāyaḥ*—almost always; *anīhām*—liberation from *karma; prapadyate*—attains.

TRANSLATION

Therefore, to enable people to reach the stage of activities that are not tinged by fruitive results, great saints first engage people in fruitive activities, for unless one begins by performing activities as recommended in the śāstras, one cannot reach the stage of liberation, or activities that produce no reactions.

PURPORT

In *Bhagavad-gītā* (3.9) Lord Kṛṣṇa advises, *yajñārthāt karmaṇo 'nyatra loko 'yaṁ karma-bandhanaḥ:* "Work done as a sacrifice for Viṣṇu has to be performed, otherwise work binds one to this material world." Generally, everyone is attracted to hard labor for becoming happy in this material world, but although various activities are going on all over the world simply for the sake of happiness, unfortunately only problems are being created from such fruitive activities. Therefore it is advised that active persons engage in activities of Kṛṣṇa consciousness, which are called *yajña,* because then they will gradually come to the platform of devotional service. *Yajña* means Lord Viṣṇu, the *yajña-puruṣa,* the enjoyer of all sacrifices (*bhoktāraṁ yajña-tapasāṁ sarva-loka-maheśvaram*). The Supreme Personality of Godhead is actually the enjoyer, and therefore if we begin our activities for His satisfaction, we will gradually lose our taste for material activities.

Sūta Gosvāmī declared to the great assembly of sages at Naimiṣāraṇya:

ataḥ pumbhir dvija-śreṣṭhā
varṇāśrama-vibhāgaśaḥ
svanuṣṭhitasya dharmasya
saṁsiddhir hari-toṣaṇam

"O best among the twice-born, it is concluded that the highest perfection one can achieve, by discharging his prescribed duties [*dharma*] according to caste divisions and order of life, is to please the Lord Hari." (*Bhāg.* 1.2.13) According to Vedic principles, everyone must act according to his classification as *brāhmaṇa, kṣatriya, vaiśya, śūdra, brahmacārī, gṛhastha, vānaprastha* or *sannyāsī.* Everyone should progress toward perfection by acting in such a way that Kṛṣṇa will be pleased (*saṁsiddhir hari-toṣaṇam*). One cannot please Kṛṣṇa by sitting idly; one must act according to the directions of the spiritual master for the sake of pleasing the Supreme Personality of Godhead, and then one will gradually come to the stage of pure devotional service. As confirmed in *Śrīmad-Bhāgavatam* (1.5.12):

naiṣkarmyam apy acyuta-bhāva-varjitaṁ
na śobhate jñānam alaṁ nirañjanam

"Knowledge of self-realization, even though freed from all material affinity, does not look well if devoid of a conception of the infallible [God]." *Jñānīs* recommend that one adopt *naiṣkarmya* by not doing anything but simply meditating and thinking of Brahman, but this is impossible unless one realizes Parabrahman, Kṛṣṇa. If there is no Kṛṣṇa consciousness, any kind of activity, be it philanthropic, political or social, simply causes *karma-bandhana,* bondage to material work.

As long as one is entangled in *karma-bandhana,* one must accept different types of bodies that spoil the human form of facility. Therefore, in *Bhagavad-gītā* (6.3) *karma-yoga* is recommended:

āruruksor muner yogaṁ
karma kāraṇam ucyate
yogārūḍhasya tasyaiva
śamaḥ kāraṇam ucyate

"For one who is a neophyte in the *yoga* system, work is said to be the means; and for one who has already attained to *yoga,* cessation of all material activities is said to be the means." Nonetheless:

karmendriyāṇi saṁyamya
ya āste manasā smaran
indriyārthān vimūḍhātmā
mithyācāraḥ sa ucyate

"One who restrains the senses and organs of action, but whose mind dwells on sense objects, certainly deludes himself and is called a pretender." (Bg. 3.6) One should act for Kṛṣṇa very seriously in order to become fully Kṛṣṇa conscious and should not sit down to imitate such great personalities as Haridāsa Ṭhākura. Śrīla Bhaktisiddhānta Sarasvatī Ṭhākura condemned such imitation. He said:

duṣṭa mana! tumi kisera vaiṣṇava?
pratiṣṭhāra tare, nirjanera ghare,
tava hari-nāma kevala kaitava

"My dear mind, what kind of devotee are you? Simply for cheap adoration, you sit in a solitary place and pretend to chant the Hare Kṛṣṇa *mahā-mantra,* but this is all cheating." Recently at Māyāpur an African devotee wanted to imitate Haridāsa Ṭhākura, but after fifteen days he became restless and went away. Do not suddenly try to imitate Haridāsa Ṭhākura. Engage yourself in Kṛṣṇa conscious activities, and gradually you will come to the stage of liberation (*muktir hitvānyathā rūpaṁ svarūpeṇa vyavasthitiḥ*).

TEXT 15

ईहते भगवानीशो न हि तत्र विसज्जते ।
आत्मलाभेन पूर्णार्थो नावसीदन्ति येऽनु तम् ॥ १५ ॥

īhate bhagavān īśo
na hi tatra visajjate
ātma-lābhena pūrṇārtho
nāvasīdanti ye 'nu tam

īhate—engages in activities of creation, maintenance and annihilation; *bhagavān*—the Supreme Personality of Godhead, Kṛṣṇa; *īśaḥ*—the supreme controller; *na*—not; *hi*—indeed; *tatra*—in such activities; *visajjate*—He becomes entangled; *ātma-lābhena*—because of His own gain; *pūrṇa-arthaḥ*—who is self-satisfied; *na*—not; *avasīdanti*—are disheartened; *ye*—persons who; *anu*—follow; *tam*—the Supreme Personality of Godhead.

TRANSLATION

The Supreme Personality of Godhead is full in opulence by His own gain, yet He acts as the creator, maintainer and annihilator of this material world. In spite of acting in that way, He is never entangled. Hence devotees who follow in His footsteps are also never entangled.

PURPORT

As stated in *Bhagavad-gītā* (3.9), *yajñārthāt karmaṇo 'nyatra loko'yaṁ karma-bandhanaḥ:* "Work done as a sacrifice for Viṣṇu has to be performed, otherwise work binds one to this material world." If we do not act in Kṛṣṇa consciousness we shall be entangled, like silkworms in cocoons. The Supreme Personality of Godhead, Kṛṣṇa, appears in order to teach us how to work so that we will not be entangled in this material world. Our real problem is that we are entangled in materialistic activities, and because we are conditioned, our struggle continues through punishment in material existence in one body after another in different forms of life. As the Lord says in *Bhagavad-gītā* (15.7):

mamaivāṁśo jīva-loke
jīva-bhūtaḥ sanātanaḥ
manaḥ ṣaṣṭhānīndriyāṇi
prakṛti-sthāni karṣati

"The living entities in this conditioned world are My eternal, fragmental parts. Due to conditioned life, they are struggling very hard with the six senses, which include the mind." The living entities are actually minute forms who are part and parcel of the Supreme Lord. The Supreme Lord is full in everything, and the small particles of the Lord are also originally qualified like Him, but because of their minute existence, they are infected by material attraction and thus entangled. We must therefore follow the instructions of the Supreme Personality of Godhead, and then, like Kṛṣṇa, who is never entangled by His material activities of creation, maintenance and annihilation, we will have nothing for which to lament (*nāvasīdanti ye 'nu tam*). Kṛṣṇa personally gives instructions in *Bhagavad-gītā,* and anyone who follows these instructions is liberated.

Following Kṛṣṇa's instructions is possible when one is a devotee, for Kṛṣṇa instructs that one should become a devotee. *Man-manā bhava mad-bhakto mad-yājī māṁ namaskuru:* "Always think of Me and become My devotee. Worship Me and offer your homage unto Me." (Bg. 18.65) Always thinking of Kṛṣṇa means chanting the Hare Kṛṣṇa *mantra,* but unless one is an initiated devotee he cannot do this. As soon as one becomes a devotee, he engages in Deity worship (*mad-yājī*). A devotee's business is to offer obeisances to the Lord and the spiritual master constantly. This principle is the recognized way to come to the platform of *bhakti.* As soon as one comes to this platform, he gradually understands the Supreme Personality of Godhead, and simply by understanding Kṛṣṇa one is liberated from material bondage.

TEXT 16

तमीहमानं निरहङ्कृतं बुधं
निराशिषं पूर्णमनन्यचोदितम् ।
नॄञ् शिक्षयन्तं निजवर्त्मसंस्थितं
प्रभुं प्रपद्येऽखिलधर्मभावनम् ॥ १६ ॥

tam īhamānaṁ nirahaṅkṛtaṁ budhaṁ
nirāśiṣaṁ pūrṇam ananya-coditam
nṝñ śikṣayantaṁ nija-vartma-saṁsthitaṁ
prabhuṁ prapadye 'khila-dharma-bhāvanam

tam—unto the same Supreme Personality of Godhead; *īhamānam*—who is acting for our benefit; *nirahaṅkṛtam*—who is without entanglement or desire for gain; *budham*—who is completely in knowledge; *nirāśiṣam*—without desires to enjoy the fruits of His activities; *pūrṇam*—who is full and therefore has no need to fulfill desires; *ananya*—by others; *coditam*—induced or inspired; *nṝn*—all of human society; *śikṣayantam*—to teach (the real path of life); *nija-vartma*—His own personal way of life; *saṁsthitam*—to establish (without deviation); *prabhum*—unto the Supreme Lord; *prapadye*—I request everyone to surrender; *akhila-dharma-bhāvanam*—who is the master of all religious principles or the occupational duties for a human being.

TRANSLATION

The Supreme Personality of Godhead, Kṛṣṇa, works just like an ordinary human being, yet He does not desire to enjoy the fruits of work. He is full in knowledge, free from material desires and diversions, and completely independent. As the supreme teacher of human society, He teaches His own way of activities, and thus He inaugurates the real path of religion. I request everyone to follow Him.

PURPORT

This is the sum and substance of our Kṛṣṇa consciousness movement. We are simply requesting human society to follow in the footsteps of the teacher of *Bhagavad-gītā.* Follow the instructions of *Bhagavad-gītā As It Is,* and your life will be successful. That is the summary of the Kṛṣṇa consciousness movement. The organizer of the Kṛṣṇa consciousness movement is teaching everyone how to follow Lord Rāmacandra, how to follow Lord Kṛṣṇa, and how to follow Śrī Caitanya Mahāprabhu. In this material world, we need a leader for a monarchy or good government. Lord Śrī Rāmacandra, by His practical example, showed how to live for the benefit of all human society. He fought with demons like Rāvaṇa, He carried out the orders of His father, and He remained the faithful husband of mother Sītā. Thus there is no comparison to Lord Rāmacandra's acting as an ideal king. Indeed, people still hanker for *rāma-rājya,* a government conducted like that of Lord Rāmacandra. Similarly, although Lord Kṛṣṇa is the Supreme Personality of Godhead, He taught His disciple and devotee Arjuna how to lead a life ending in going back home, back to Godhead (*tyaktvā dehaṁ punar janma naiti mām eti so 'rjuna*). All teachings—political, economic, social, religious, cultural and philosophical—are to be found in *Bhagavad-gītā.* One only has to follow them strictly. The Supreme Personality of Godhead also comes as Lord Caitanya just to play the part of a pure devotee. Thus the Lord teaches us in different ways just to make our lives successful, and Svāyambhuva Manu requests us to follow Him.

Svāyambhuva Manu is the leader of mankind, and he has given a book called *Manu-saṁhitā* to guide human society. Herein he directs us to follow the Supreme Personality of Godhead in His different incarnations. These incarnations are described in Vedic literature, and Jayadeva Gosvāmī has described ten important incarnations in summary (*keśava dhṛta-mīna-śarīra jaya jagad-īśa hare, keśava dhṛta-nara-hari-rūpa jaya jagad-īśa hare, keśava dhṛta-buddha-śarīra jaya jagad-īśa hare,* etc.). Svāyambhuva Manu instructs us to follow the instructions of God's incarnations, especially Kṛṣṇa's instructions of *Bhagavad-gītā As It Is.*

Appreciating *bhakti-mārga* as instructed by Śrī Caitanya Mahāprabhu, Sārvabhauma Bhaṭṭācārya thus depicted the activities of Śrī Caitanya Mahāprabhu:

vairāgya-vidyā-nija-bhakti-yoga-
śikṣārtham ekaḥ puruṣaḥ purāṇaḥ
śrī-kṛṣṇa-caitanya-śarīra-dhārī
kṛpāmbudhir yas tam ahaṁ prapadye

"Let me take shelter of the Supreme Personality of Godhead, Śrī Kṛṣṇa, who has descended in the form of Lord Caitanya Mahāprabhu to teach us real knowledge, His devotional service, and detachment from whatever does not foster Kṛṣṇa consciousness. He has descended because He is an ocean of transcendental mercy. Let me surrender unto His lotus feet." (*Caitanya-candrodaya-nāṭaka* 6.74) In this age of Kali, people cannot follow the instructions of the Supreme Personality of Godhead, and therefore the Lord Himself takes the part of Śrī Kṛṣṇa Caitanya to teach personally how to become Kṛṣṇa conscious. He asks everyone to follow Him and to become a *guru* to deliver the fallen souls of Kali-yuga.

yāre dekha, tāre kaha 'kṛṣṇa'-upadeśa
āmāra ājñāya guru hañā tāra' ei deśa

"Instruct everyone to follow the orders of Lord Śrī Kṛṣṇa as they are given in *Bhagavad-gītā* and *Śrīmad-Bhāgavatam.* In this way become a spiritual master and try to liberate everyone in this land." (Cc. *Madhya* 7.128) The coherent purpose of Lord Rāmacandra, Lord Kṛṣṇa and Lord Caitanya Mahāprabhu is to teach human society how to be happy by following the instructions of the Supreme Lord.

TEXT 17

श्रीशुक उवाच
इति मन्त्रोपनिषदं व्याहरन्तं समाहितम् ।
दृष्ट्वासुरा यातुधाना जग्धुमभ्यद्रवन् क्षुधा ॥ १७ ॥

śrī-śuka uvāca
iti mantropaniṣadaṁ
vyāharantaṁ samāhitam

dṛṣṭvāsurā yātudhānā
jagdhum abhyadravan kṣudhā

śrī-śukaḥ uvāca—Śrī Śukadeva Gosvāmī said; *iti*—thus; *mantra-upaniṣadam*—the Vedic *mantra* (uttered by Svāyambhuva Manu); *vyāharantam*—taught or chanted; *samāhitam*—concentrated the mind (without being agitated by material conditions); *dṛṣṭvā*—upon seeing (him); *asurāḥ*—the demons; *yātudhānāḥ*—the Rākṣasas; *jagdhum*—desired to devour; *abhyadravan*—running very fast; *kṣudhā*—to satisfy their appetite.

TRANSLATION

Śukadeva Gosvāmī continued: Svāyambhuva Manu was thus in a trance, chanting the mantras of Vedic instruction known as the Upaniṣads. Upon seeing him, the Rākṣasas and asuras, being very hungry, wanted to devour him. Therefore they ran after him with great speed.

TEXT 18

तांस्तथावसितान् वीक्ष्य यज्ञः सर्वगतो हरिः ।
यामैः परिवृतो देवैर्हत्वाशासत् त्रिविष्टपम् ॥ १८ ॥

tāṁs tathāvasitān vīkṣya
yajñaḥ sarva-gato hariḥ
yāmaiḥ parivṛto devair
hatvāśāsat tri-viṣṭapam

tān—the demons and Rākṣasas; *tathā*—in that way; *avasitān*—who were determined to devour Svāyambhuva Manu; *vīkṣya*—upon observing; *yajñaḥ*—Lord Viṣṇu, known as Yajña; *sarva-gataḥ*—who is seated in everyone's heart; *hariḥ*—the Supreme Personality of Godhead; *yāmaiḥ*—with His sons named the Yāmas; *parivṛtaḥ*—surrounded; *devaiḥ*—by the demigods; *hatvā*—after killing (the demons); *aśāsat*—ruled (taking the post of Indra); *tri-viṣṭapam*—the heavenly planets.

TRANSLATION

The Supreme Lord, Viṣṇu, who sits in everyone's heart, appearing as Yajñapati, observed that the Rākṣasas and demons were going to devour Svāyambhuva Manu. Thus the Lord, accompanied by His sons named the Yāmas and by all the other demigods, killed the demons and Rākṣasas. He then took the post of Indra and began to rule the heavenly kingdom.

PURPORT

The various names of the demigods—Lord Brahmā, Lord Śiva, Lord Indra and so on—are not personal names; they are names of different posts. In this regard, we understand that Lord Viṣṇu sometimes becomes Brahmā or Indra when there is no suitable person to occupy these posts.

TEXT 19

स्वारोचिषो द्वितीयस्तु मनुरग्नेः सुतोऽभवत् ।
द्युमत्सुषेणरोचिष्मत्प्रमुखास्तस्य चात्मजाः ॥ १९ ॥

svārociṣo dvitīyas tu
manur agneḥ suto 'bhavat
dyumat-suṣeṇa-rociṣmat
pramukhās tasya cātmajāḥ

svārociṣaḥ—Svārociṣa; *dvitīyaḥ*—the second; *tu*—indeed; *manuḥ*—Manu; *agneḥ*—of Agni; *sutaḥ*—the son; *abhavat*—became; *dyumat*—Dyumat; *suṣeṇa*—Suṣeṇa; *rociṣmat*—Rociṣmat; *pramukhāḥ*—beginning with them; *tasya*—of him (Svārociṣa); *ca*—also; *ātma-jāḥ*—sons.

TRANSLATION

The son of Agni named Svārociṣa became the second Manu. His several sons were headed by Dyumat, Suṣeṇa and Rociṣmat.

PURPORT

manvantaraṁ manur devā
manu-putrāḥ sureśvaraḥ
ṛṣayo 'ṁśāvatāraś ca
hareḥ ṣaḍ vidham ucyate

There are many incarnations of the Supreme Personality of Godhead. Manu, the *manu-putrāḥ* (the sons of Manu), the king of the heavenly planets, and the seven great sages are all partial incarnations of the Supreme Lord. Manu himself, his sons Priyavrata and Uttānapāda, the demigods created by Dakṣa, and the *ṛṣis* like Marīci were all partial incarnations of the Lord during the reign of Svāyambhuva Manu. During that time, the incarnation of the Lord as Yajña took charge of ruling the heavenly planets. The next Manu was Svārociṣa. The Manus and the sages and demigods are further described in the following eleven verses.

TEXT 20

तत्रेन्द्रो रोचनस्त्वासीद् देवाश्च तुषितादयः ।
ऊर्जस्तम्भादयः सप्त ऋषयो ब्रह्मवादिनः ॥ २० ॥

tatrendro rocanas tv āsīd
devāś ca tuṣitādayaḥ
ūrja-stambhādayaḥ sapta
ṛṣayo brahma-vādinaḥ

tatra—in this *manvantara; indraḥ*—Indra; *rocanaḥ*—Rocana, the son of Yajña; *tu*—but; *āsīt*—became; *devāḥ*—demigods; *ca*—also; *tuṣita-ādayaḥ*—Tuṣita and others; *ūrja*—Ūrja; *stambha*—Stambha; *ādayaḥ*—and others; *sapta*—seven; *ṛṣayaḥ*—great saints; *brahma-vādinaḥ*—all faithful devotees.

TRANSLATION

During the reign of Svārociṣa, the post of Indra was assumed by Rocana, the son of Yajña. Tuṣita and others became the principal demigods, and Ūrja, Stambha and others became the seven saints. All of them were faithful devotees of the Lord.

TEXT 21

ऋषेस्तु वेदशिरसस्तुषिता नाम पत्न्यभूत् ।
तस्यां जज्ञे ततो देवो विभुरित्यभिविश्रुतः ॥ २१ ॥

ṛṣes tu vedaśirasas
tuṣitā nāma patny abhūt
tasyāṁ jajñe tato devo
vibhur ity abhiviśrutaḥ

ṛṣeḥ—of the saintly person; *tu*—indeed; *vedaśirasaḥ*—Vedaśirā; *tuṣitā*—Tuṣitā; *nāma*—named; *patnī*—the wife; *abhūt*—begot; *tasyām*—in her (womb); *jajñe*—took birth; *tataḥ*—thereafter; *devaḥ*—the Lord; *vibhuḥ*—Vibhu; *iti*—thus; *abhiviśrutaḥ*—celebrated as.

TRANSLATION

Vedaśirā was a very celebrated ṛṣi. From the womb of his wife, whose name was Tuṣitā, came the avatāra named Vibhu.

TEXT 22

अष्टाशीतिसहस्राणि मुनयो ये धृतव्रताः ।
अन्वशिक्षन्व्रतं तस्य कौमारब्रह्मचारिणः ॥ २२ ॥

aṣṭāśīti-sahasrāṇi
munayo ye dhṛta-vratāḥ
anvaśikṣan vrataṁ tasya
kaumāra-brahmacāriṇaḥ

aṣṭāśīti—eighty-eight; *sahasrāṇi*—thousand; *munayaḥ*—great saintly persons; *ye*—those who; *dhṛta-vratāḥ*—fixed in vows; *anvaśikṣan*—took instructions; *vratam*—vows; *tasya*—from him (Vibhu); *kaumāra*—who was unmarried; *brahmacāriṇaḥ*—and fixed in the *brahmacārī* stage of life.

TRANSLATION

Vibhu remained a brahmacāri and never married throughout his life. From him, eighty-eight thousand other saintly persons took lessons on self-control, austerity and similar behavior.

TEXT 23

तृतीय उत्तमो नाम प्रियव्रतसुतो मनुः ।
पवनः सृञ्जयो यज्ञहोत्राद्यास्तत्सुता नृप ॥ २३ ॥

tṛtīya uttamo nāma
priyavrata-suto manuḥ
pavanaḥ sṛñjayo yajña-
hotrādyās tat-sutā nṛpa

tṛtīyaḥ—the third; *uttamaḥ*—Uttama; *nāma*—named; *priyavrata*—of King Priyavrata; *sutaḥ*—the son; *manuḥ*—he became the Manu; *pavanaḥ*—Pavana; *sṛñjayaḥ*—Sṛñjaya; *yajñahotra-ādyāḥ*—Yajñahotra and others; *tat-sutāḥ*—the sons of Uttama; *nṛpa*—O King.

TRANSLATION

O King, the third Manu, Uttama, was the son of King Priyavrata. Among the sons of this Manu were Pavana, Sṛñjaya and Yajñahotra.

TEXT 24

वसिष्ठतनयाः सप्त ऋषयः प्रमदादयः ।
सत्या वेदश्रुता भद्रा देवा इन्द्रस्तु सत्यजित् ॥ २४॥

vasiṣṭha-tanayāḥ sapta
ṛṣayaḥ pramadādayaḥ
satyā vedaśrutā bhadrā
devā indras tu satyajit

vasiṣṭha-tanayāḥ—the sons of Vasiṣṭha; *sapta*—seven; *ṛṣayaḥ*—the sages; *pramada-ādayaḥ*—headed by Pramada; *satyāḥ*—the Satyas; *vedaśrutāḥ*—Vedaśrutas; *bhadrāḥ*—Bhadras; *devāḥ*—demigods; *indraḥ*—the King of heaven; *tu*—but; *satyajit*—Satyajit.

TRANSLATION

During the reign of the third Manu, Pramada and other sons of Vasiṣṭha became the seven sages. The Satyas, Vedaśrutas and Bhadras became demigods, and Satyajit was selected to be Indra, the King of heaven.

TEXT 25

धर्मस्य सूनृतायां तु भगवान्पुरुषोत्तमः ।
सत्यसेन इति ख्यातो जातः सत्यव्रतैः सह ॥ २५ ॥

dharmasya sūnṛtāyāṁ tu
bhagavān puruṣottamaḥ
satyasena iti khyāto
jātaḥ satyavrataiḥ saha

dharmasya—of the demigod in charge of religion; *sūnṛtāyām*—in the womb of his wife named Sūnṛtā; *tu*—indeed; *bhagavān*—the Supreme Personality of Godhead; *puruṣa-uttamaḥ*—the Supreme Personality of Godhead; *satyasenaḥ*—Satyasena; *iti*—thus; *khyātaḥ*—celebrated; *jātaḥ*—took birth; *satyavrataiḥ*—the Satyavratas; *saha*—with.

TRANSLATION

In this manvantara, the Supreme Personality of Godhead appeared from the womb of Sūnṛtā, who was the wife of Dharma, the demigod in charge of religion. The Lord was celebrated as Satyasena, and He appeared with other demigods, known as the Satyavratas.

TEXT 26

सोऽनृतव्रतदुःशीलानसतो यक्षराक्षसान् ।
भूतद्रुहो भूतगणांश्चावधीत् सत्यजित्सखः ॥ २६ ॥

so 'nṛta-vrata-duḥśīlān
asato yakṣa-rākṣasān
bhūta-druho bhūta-gaṇāṁś
cāvadhīt satyajit-sakhaḥ

saḥ—He (Satyasena); *anṛta-vrata*—who are fond of speaking lies; *duḥśīlān*—misbehaved; *asataḥ*—miscreant; *yakṣa-rākṣasān*—Yakṣas and Rākṣasas; *bhūta-druhaḥ*—who are always against the progress of other living beings; *bhūta-gaṇān*—the ghostly living entities; *ca*—also; *avadhīt*—killed; *satyajit-sakhaḥ*—with His friend Satyajit.

TRANSLATION

Satyasena, along with His friend Satyajit, who was the King of heaven, Indra, killed all the untruthful, impious and misbehaved Yakṣas, Rākṣasas and ghostly living entities, who gave pains to other living beings.

TEXT 27

चतुर्थ उत्तमभ्राता मनुर्नाम्ना च तामसः ।
पृथुः ख्यातिर्नरः केतुरित्याद्या दश तत्सुताः ॥ २७ ॥

caturtha uttama-bhrātā
manur nāmnā ca tāmasaḥ
pṛthuḥ khyātir naraḥ ketur
ity ādyā daśa tat-sutāḥ

caturtha—the fourth Manu; *uttama-bhrātā*—the brother of Uttama; *manuḥ*—became the Manu; *nāmnā*—celebrated by the name; *ca*—also; *tāmasaḥ*—Tāmasa; *pṛthuḥ*—Pṛthu; *khyātiḥ*—Khyāti; *naraḥ*—Nara; *ketuḥ*—Ketu; *iti*—thus; *ādyāḥ*—headed by; *daśa*—ten; *tat-sutāḥ*—sons of Tāmasa Manu.

TRANSLATION

The brother of the third Manu, Uttama, was celebrated by the name Tāmasa, and he became the fourth Manu. Tāmasa had ten sons, headed by Pṛthu, Khyāti, Nara and Ketu.

TEXT 28

सत्यका हरयो वीरा देवास्त्रिशिख ईश्वरः ।
ज्योतिर्धामादयः सप्त ऋषयस्तामसेऽन्तरे ॥ २८ ॥

satyakā harayo vīrā
devās triśikha īśvaraḥ
jyotirdhāmādayaḥ sapta
ṛṣayas tāmase 'ntare

satyakāḥ—the Satyakas; *harayaḥ*—the Haris; *vīrāḥ*—the Vīras; *devāḥ*—the demigods; *triśikhaḥ*—Triśikha; *īśvaraḥ*—the King of heaven; *jyotirdhāma-ādayaḥ*—headed by the celebrated Jyotirdhāma; *sapta*—seven; *ṛṣayaḥ*—sages; *tāmase*—the reign of Tāmasa Manu; *antare*—within.

TRANSLATION

During the reign of Tāmasa Manu, among the demigods were the Satyakas, Haris and Vīras. The heavenly King, Indra, was Triśikha. The sages in saptarṣi-dhāma were headed by Jyotirdhāma.

TEXT 29

देवा वैधृतयो नाम विधृतेस्तनया नृप ।
नष्टाः कालेन यैर्वेदा विधृताः स्वेन तेजसा ॥ २९ ॥

devā vaidhṛtayo nāma
vidhṛtes tanayā nṛpa
naṣṭāḥ kālena yair vedā
vidhṛtāḥ svena tejasā

devāḥ—the demigods; *vaidhṛtayaḥ*—the Vaidhṛtis; *nāma*—by the name; *vidhṛteḥ*—of Vidhṛti; *tanayāḥ*—who were the sons; *nṛpa*—O King; *naṣṭāḥ*—were lost; *kālena*—by the influence of time; *yaiḥ*—by whom; *vedāḥ*—the *Vedas; vidhṛtāḥ*—were protected; *svena*—by their own; *tejasā*—power.

TRANSLATION

O King, in the Tāmasa manvantara the sons of Vidhṛti, who were known as the Vaidhṛtis, also became demigods. Since in course of time the Vedic authority was lost, these demigods, by their own powers, protected the Vedic authority.

PURPORT

In the Tāmasa *manvantara* there were two kinds of demigods, and one of them was known as the Vaidhṛtis. The duty of the demigods is to protect the authority of the *Vedas.* The word *devatā* refers to one who carries the authority of the *Vedas,* whereas Rākṣasas are those who defy the Vedic authority. If the authority of the *Vedas* is lost, the entire universe becomes chaotic. Therefore, it is the duty of the demigods, as well as kings and aides of governments, to give full protection to the Vedic authority; otherwise human society will be in a chaotic condition in which there cannot be peace or prosperity.

TEXT 30

तत्रापि जज्ञे भगवान्हरिण्यां हरिमेधसः ।
हरिरित्याहृतो येन गजेन्द्रो मोचितो ग्रहात् ॥ ३० ॥

tatrāpi jajñe bhagavān
hariṇyāṁ harimedhasaḥ
harir ity āhṛto yena
gajendro mocito grahāt

tatrāpi—in that period; *jajñe*—appeared; *bhagavān*—the Supreme Personality of Godhead; *hariṇyām*—in the womb of Hariṇī; *harimedhasaḥ*—begotten by Harimedhā; *hariḥ*—Hari; *iti*—thus; *āhṛtaḥ*—called; *yena*—by whom; *gaja-indraḥ*—the King of the elephants; *mocitaḥ*—was freed; *grahāt*—from the mouth of a crocodile.

TRANSLATION

Also in this manvantara, the Supreme Lord, Viṣṇu, took birth from the womb of Hariṇī, the wife of Harimedhā, and He was known as Hari. Hari saved His devotee Gajendra, the King of the elephants, from the mouth of a crocodile.

TEXT 31

श्रीराजोवाच
बादरायण एतत् ते श्रोतुमिच्छामहे वयम् ।
हरिर्यथा गजपतिं ग्राहग्रस्तममूमुचत् ॥ ३१ ॥

śrī-rājovāca
bādarāyaṇa etat te
śrotum icchāmahe vayam

harir yathā gaja-patiṁ
grāha-grastam amūmucat

śrī-rājā uvāca—King Parīkṣit said; *bādarāyaṇe*—O son of Bādarāyaṇa (Vyāsadeva); *etat*—this; *te*—from you; *śrotum icchāmahe*—desire to hear; *vayam*—we; *hariḥ*—the Lord Hari; *yathā*—the manner in which; *gaja-patim*—the King of the elephants; *grāha-grastam*—when attacked by the crocodile; *amūmucat*—delivered.

TRANSLATION

King Parīkṣit said: My lord, Bādarāyaṇi, we wish to hear from you in detail how the King of the elephants, when attacked by a crocodile, was delivered by Hari.

TEXT 32

तत्कथासु महत् पुण्यं धन्यं स्वस्त्ययनं शुभम् ।
यत्र यत्रोत्तमश्लोको भगवान्गीयते हरिः ॥ ३२ ॥

tat-kathāsu mahat puṇyaṁ
dhanyaṁ svastyayanaṁ śubham
yatra yatrottamaśloko
bhagavān gīyate hariḥ

tat-kathāsu—in those narrations; *mahat*—great; *puṇyam*—pious; *dhanyam*—glorious; *svastyayanam*—auspicious; *śubham*—all good; *yatra*—whenever; *yatra*—wherever; *uttamaślokaḥ*—the Lord, who is known as Uttamaśloka (He who is described by transcendental literature); *bhagavān*—the Supreme Personality of Godhead; *gīyate*—is glorified; *hariḥ*—the Supreme Personality of Godhead.

TRANSLATION

Any literature or narration in which the Supreme Personality of Godhead, Uttamaśloka, is described and glorified is certainly great, pure, glorious, auspicious and all good.

PURPORT

The Kṛṣṇa consciousness movement is spreading all over the world simply by describing Kṛṣṇa. We have published many books, including *Śrī Caitanya-caritāmṛta* in seventeen volumes, four hundred pages each, as well as

Bhagavad-gītā and *The Nectar of Devotion.* We are also publishing *Śrīmad-Bhāgavatam* in sixty volumes. Wherever a speaker holds discourses from these books and an audience hears him, this will create a good and auspicious situation. Therefore the preaching of Kṛṣṇa consciousness must be done very carefully by the members of the Kṛṣṇa consciousness movement, especially the *sannyāsīs.* This will create an auspicious atmosphere.

TEXT 33

श्रीसूत उवाच
परीक्षितैवं स तु बादरायणिः
प्रायोपविष्टेन कथासु चोदितः ।
उवाच विप्राः प्रतिनन्द्य पार्थिवं
मुदा मुनीनां सदसि स्म शृण्वताम् ॥ ३३ ॥

śrī-sūta uvāca
parīkṣitaivaṁ sa tu bādarāyaṇiḥ
prāyopaviṣṭena kathāsu coditaḥ
uvāca viprāḥ pratinandya pārthivaṁ
mudā munīnāṁ sadasi sma śṛṇvatām

śrī-sūtaḥ uvāca—Śrī Sūta Gosvāmī said; *parīkṣitā*—by Mahārāja Parīkṣit; *evam*—thus; *saḥ*—he; *tu*—indeed; *bādarāyaṇiḥ*—Śukadeva Gosvāmī; *prāya-upaviṣṭena*—Parīkṣit Mahārāja, who was awaiting impending death; *kathāsu*—by the words; *coditaḥ*—being encouraged; *uvāca*—spoke; *viprāḥ*—O *brāhmaṇas; pratinandya*—after congratulating; *pārthivam*—Mahārāja Parīkṣit; *mudā*—with great pleasure; *munīnām*—of great sages; *sadasi*—in the assembly; *sma*—indeed; *śṛṇvatām*—who desired to hear.

TRANSLATION

Śrī Sūta Gosvāmī said: O brāhmaṇas, when Parīkṣit Mahārāja, who was awaiting impending death, thus requested Śukadeva Gosvāmī to speak, Śukadeva Gosvāmī, encouraged by the King's words, offered respect to the King and spoke with great pleasure in the assembly of sages, who desired to hear him.

Thus end the Bhaktivedanta purports of the Eighth Canto, First Chapter, of the Śrīmad-Bhāgavatam, *entitled "The Manus, Administrators of the Universe."*

CHAPTER TWO

The Elephant Gajendra's Crisis

The Second, Third and Fourth Chapters of this canto describe how the Lord, during the reign of the fourth Manu, gave protection to the King of the elephants. As described in this Second Chapter, when the King of the elephants, along with his female elephants, was enjoying in the water, a crocodile suddenly attacked him, and the elephant surrendered to the lotus feet of the Personality of Godhead for protection.

In the midst of the ocean of milk, there is a very high and beautiful mountain that has an altitude of ten thousand *yojanas,* or eighty thousand miles. This mountain is known as Trikūṭa. In a valley of Trikūṭa there is a nice garden named Ṛtumat, which was constructed by Varuṇa, and in that area there is a very nice lake. Once the chief of the elephants, along with female elephants, went to enjoy bathing in that lake, and they disturbed the inhabitants of the water. Because of this, the chief crocodile in that water, who was very powerful, immediately attacked the elephant's leg. Thus there ensued a great fight between the elephant and the crocodile. This fight continued for one thousand years. Neither the elephant nor the crocodile died, but since they were in the water, the elephant gradually became weak whereas the power of the crocodile increased more and more. Thus the crocodile became more and more encouraged. Then the elephant, being helpless and seeing that there was no other way for his protection, sought shelter at the lotus feet of the Supreme Personality of Godhead.

TEXT 1

श्रीशुक उवाच

आसीद् गिरिवरो राजंस्त्रिकूट इति विश्रुतः ।
क्षीरोदेनावृतः श्रीमान्योजनायुतमुच्छ्रितः ॥ १ ॥

śrī-śuka uvāca
āsīd girivaro rājaṁs
trikūṭa iti viśrutaḥ
kṣīrodenāvṛtaḥ śrīmān
yojanāyutam ucchritaḥ

śrī-śukaḥ uvāca—Śrī Śukadeva Gosvāmī said; *āsīt*—there was; *giri-varaḥ*—a very big mountain; *rājan*—O King; *tri-kūṭaḥ*—Trikūṭa; *iti*—thus; *viśrutaḥ*—celebrated; *kṣīra-udena*—by the ocean of milk; *āvṛtaḥ*—surrounded; *śrīmān*—very beautiful; *yojana*—a measurement of eight miles; *ayutam*—ten thousand; *ucchritaḥ*—very high.

TRANSLATION

Śukadeva Gosvāmī said: My dear King, there is a very large mountain called Trikūṭa. It is ten thousand yojanas [eighty thousand miles] high. Being surrounded by the ocean of milk, it is very beautifully situated.

TEXTS 2-3

तावता विस्तृतः पर्यक् त्रिभिः शृङ्गैः पयोनिधिम् ।
दिशः खं रोचयन्नास्ते रौप्यायसहिरण्मयैः ॥ २ ॥
अन्यैश्च ककुभः सर्वा रत्नधातुविचित्रितैः ।
नानाद्रुमलतागुल्मैर्निर्घोषैर्निर्झराम्भसाम् ॥ ३ ॥

tāvatā vistṛtaḥ paryak
tribhiḥ śṛṅgaiḥ payo-nidhim
diśaḥ khaṁ rocayann āste
raupyāyasa-hiraṇmayaiḥ

anyaiś ca kakubhaḥ sarvā
ratna-dhātu-vicitritaiḥ
nānā-druma-latā-gulmair
nirghoṣair nirjharāmbhasām

tāvatā—in that way; *vistṛtaḥ*—length and breadth (eighty thousand miles); *paryak*—all around; *tribhiḥ*—with three; *śṛṅgaiḥ*—peaks; *payaḥ-nidhim*—situated on an island in the ocean of milk; *diśaḥ*—all directions; *kham*—the sky; *rocayan*—pleasing; *āste*—standing; *raupya*—made of silver; *ayasa*—iron; *hiraṇmayaiḥ*—and gold; *anyaiḥ*—with other peaks; *ca*—also; *kakubhaḥ*—directions; *sarvāḥ*—all; *ratna*—with jewels; *dhātu*—and minerals; *vicitritaiḥ*—decorated very nicely; *nānā*—with various; *druma-latā*—trees and creepers; *gulmaiḥ*—and shrubs; *nirghoṣaiḥ*—with the sounds of; *nirjhara*—waterfalls; *ambhasām*—of water.

TRANSLATION

The length and breadth of the mountain are of the same measurement [eighty thousand miles]. Its three principal peaks, which are made of iron, silver and gold, beautify all directions and the sky. The mountain also has other peaks, which are full of jewels and minerals and are decorated with nice trees, creepers and shrubs. The sounds of the waterfalls on the mountain create a pleasing vibration. In this way the mountain stands, increasing the beauty of all directions.

TEXT 4

स चावनिज्यमानाङ्घ्रिः समन्तात् पयऊर्मिभिः ।
करोति श्यामलां भूमिं हरिन्मरकताश्मभिः ॥ ४ ॥

sa cāvanijyamānāṅghriḥ
samantāt paya-ūrmibhiḥ
karoti śyāmalāṁ bhūmiṁ
harin-marakatāśmabhiḥ

saḥ—that mountain; *ca*—also; *avanijyamāna-aṅghriḥ*—whose foot is always washed; *samantāt*—all around; *payaḥ-ūrmibhiḥ*—by waves of milk; *karoti*—makes; *śyāmalām*—dark green; *bhūmim*—ground; *harit*—green; *marakata*—with emerald; *aśmabhiḥ*—stones.

TRANSLATION

The ground at the foot of the mountain is always washed by waves of milk that produce emeralds all around in the eight directions [north, south, east, west and the directions midway between them].

PURPORT

From *Śrīmad-Bhāgavatam* we understand that there are various oceans. Somewhere there is an ocean filled with milk, somewhere an ocean of liquor, an ocean of ghee, an ocean of oil, and an ocean of sweet water. Thus there are different varieties of oceans within this universe. The modern scientists, who have only limited experience, cannot defy these statements; they cannot give us full information about any planet, even the planet on which we live. From this verse, however, we can understand that if the valleys of some mountains are washed with milk, this produces emeralds. No one has the ability to imitate the activities of material nature as conducted by the Supreme Personality of Godhead.

TEXT 5

सिद्धचारणगन्धर्वैर्विद्याधरमहोरगैः ।
किन्नरैरप्सरोभिश्च क्रीडद्भिर्जुष्टकन्दरः ॥ ५ ॥

siddha-cāraṇa-gandharvair
vidyādhara-mahoragaiḥ
kinnarair apsarobhiś ca
krīḍadbhir juṣṭa-kandaraḥ

siddha—by the inhabitants of Siddhaloka; *cāraṇa*—the inhabitants of Cāraṇaloka; *gandharvaiḥ*—the inhabitants of Gandharvaloka; *vidyādhara*—the inhabitants of Vidyādhara-loka; *mahā-uragaiḥ*—the inhabitants of the serpent loka; *kinnaraiḥ*—the Kinnaras; *apsarobhiḥ*—the Apsarās; *ca*—and; *krīḍadbhiḥ*—who were engaged in sporting; *juṣṭa*—enjoyed; *kandaraḥ*—the caves.

TRANSLATION

The inhabitants of the higher planets—the Siddhas, Cāraṇas, Gandharvas, Vidyādharas, serpents, Kinnaras and Apsarās—go to that mountain to sport. Thus all the caves of the mountain are full of these denizens of the heavenly planets.

PURPORT

As ordinary men may play in the salty ocean, the inhabitants of the higher planetary systems go to the ocean of milk. They float in the ocean of milk and also enjoy various sports within the caves of Trikūṭa Mountain.

TEXT 6

यत्र संगीतसन्नादैर्नदद्गुहममर्षया ।
अभिगर्जन्ति हरयः श्लाघिनः परशङ्कया ॥ ६ ॥

yatra saṅgīta-sannādair
nadad-guham amarṣayā
abhigarjanti harayaḥ
ślāghinaḥ para-śaṅkayā

yatra—in that mountain (Trikūṭa); *saṅgīta*—of singing; *sannādaiḥ*—with the vibrations; *nadat*—resounding; *guham*—the caves; *amarṣayā*—because of unbearable anger or envy; *abhigarjanti*—roar; *harayaḥ*—the lions;

ślāghinaḥ—being very proud of their strength; *para-śaṅkayā*—because of suspecting another lion.

TRANSLATION

Because of the resounding vibrations of the denizens of heaven singing in the caves, the lions there, being very proud of their strength, roar with unbearable envy, thinking that another lion is roaring in that way.

PURPORT

In the higher planetary systems, there are not only different types of human beings, but also animals like lions and elephants. There are trees, and the land is made of emeralds. Such is the creation of the Supreme Personality of Godhead. Śrīla Bhaktivinoda Ṭhākura has sung in this regard, *keśava! tuyā jagata vicitra:* "My Lord Keśava, Your creation is colorful and full of varieties." Geologists, botanists and other so-called scientists speculate about other planetary systems, but being unable to estimate the varieties on other planets, they falsely imagine that all planets but this one are vacant, uninhabited, and full of dust. Although they cannot even estimate the varieties existing throughout the universe, they are very proud of their knowledge, and they are accepted as learned by persons of a similar caliber. As described in *Śrīmad-Bhāgavatam* (2.3.19), *śva-vid-varāhoṣṭra-kharaiḥ saṁstutaḥ puruṣaḥ paśuḥ:* materialistic leaders are praised by dogs, hogs, camels and asses, and they themselves are also big animals. One should not be satisfied with the knowledge imparted by a big animal. Rather, one must take knowledge from a perfect person like Śukadeva Gosvāmī. *Mahājano yena gataḥ sa panthāḥ:* our duty is to follow the instructions of the *mahājanas.* There are twelve *mahājanas,* and Śukadeva Gosvāmī is one of them.

svayambhūr nāradaḥ śambhuḥ
kumāraḥ kapilo manuḥ
prahlādo janako bhīṣmo
balir vaiyāsakir vayam

(Bhāg. 6.3.20)

Vaiyāsaki is Śukadeva Gosvāmī. Whatever he says we consider to be factual. That is perfect knowledge.

TEXT 7

नानारण्यपशुव्रातसङ्कुलद्रोण्यलङ्कृतः ।
चित्रद्रुमसुरोद्यानकलकण्ठविहङ्गमः ॥७॥

nānāraṇya-paśu-vrāta-
saṅkula-droṇy-alaṅkṛtaḥ
citra-druma-surodyāna-
kalakaṇṭha-vihaṅgamaḥ

nānā—with varieties of; *araṇya-paśu*—jungle animals; *vrāta*—with a multitude; *saṅkula*—filled; *droṇi*—with valleys; *alaṅkṛtaḥ*—very beautifully decorated; *citra*—with varieties of; *druma*—trees; *sura-udyāna*—in gardens maintained by the demigods; *kalakaṇṭha*—sweetly chirping; *vihaṅgamaḥ*—birds.

TRANSLATION

The valleys beneath Trikūṭa Mountain are beautifully decorated by many varieties of jungle animals, and in the trees, which are maintained in gardens by the demigods, varieties of birds chirp with sweet voices.

TEXT 8

सरित्सरोभिरच्छोदैः पुलिनैर्मणिवालुकैः ।
देवस्त्रीमज्जनामोदसौरभाम्ब्वनिलैर्युतः ॥ ८ ॥

sarit-sarobhir acchodaiḥ
pulinair maṇi-vālukaiḥ
deva-strī-majjanāmoda-
saurabhāmbv-anilair yutaḥ

sarit—with rivers; *sarobhiḥ*—and lakes; *acchodaiḥ*—filled with crystal-clear water; *pulinaiḥ*—beaches; *maṇi*—with small gems; *vālukaiḥ*—resembling grains of sand; *deva-strī*—of the damsels of the demigods; *majjana*—by bathing (in that water); *āmoda*—bodily fragrance; *saurabha*—very fragrant; *ambu*—with the water; *anilaiḥ*—and the air; *yutaḥ*—enriched (the atmosphere of Trikūṭa Mountain).

TRANSLATION

Trikūṭa Mountain has many lakes and rivers, with beaches covered by small gems resembling grains of sand. The water is as clear as crystal, and when the demigod damsels bathe in it, their bodies lend fragrance to the water and the breeze, thus enriching the atmosphere.

PURPORT

Even in the material world, there are many grades of living entities. The human beings on earth generally cover themselves with external fragrances to stop their bad bodily odors, but here we find that because of the bodily fragrance of the demigod damsels, the rivers, the lakes, the breeze and the entire atmosphere of Trikūṭa Mountain also become fragrant. Since the bodies of the damsels in the upper planetary systems are so beautiful, we can just imagine how beautifully formed are the bodies of the Vaikuṇṭha damsels or the damsels in Vṛndāvana, the *gopīs.*

TEXTS 9-13

तस्य द्रोण्यां भगवतो वरुणस्य महात्मनः ।
उद्यानमृतुमन्नाम आक्रीडं सुरयोषिताम् ॥ ९ ॥
सर्वतोऽलङ्कृतं दिव्यैर्नित्यपुष्पफलद्रुमैः ।
मन्दारैः पारिजातैश्च पाटलाशोकचम्पकैः ॥ १० ॥
चूतैः पियालैः पनसैराम्रैराम्रातकैरपि ।
क्रमुकैर्नारिकेलैश्च खर्जूरैर्बीजपूरकैः ॥ ११ ॥
मधुकैः शालतालैश्च तमालैरसनार्जुनैः ।
अरिष्टोडुम्बरप्लक्षैर्वटैः किंशुकचन्दनैः ॥ १२ ॥
पिचुमर्दैः कोविदारैः सरलैः सुरदारुभिः ।
द्राक्षेक्षुरम्भाजम्बुभिर्बदर्यक्षाभयामलैः ॥ १३ ॥

tasya droṇyāṁ bhagavato
varuṇasya mahātmanaḥ
udyānam ṛtuman nāma
ākrīḍaṁ sura-yoṣitām

sarvato 'laṅkṛtaṁ divyair
nitya-puṣpa-phala-drumaiḥ
mandāraiḥ pārijātaiś ca
pāṭalāśoka-campakaiḥ

cūtaiḥ piyālaiḥ panasair
āmrair āmrātakair api
kramukair nārikelaiś ca
kharjūrair bījapūrakaiḥ

madhukaiḥ śāla-tālaiś ca
tamālair asanārjunaiḥ
ariṣṭoḍumbara-plakṣair
vaṭaiḥ kiṁśuka-candanaiḥ

picumardaiḥ kovidāraiḥ
saralaiḥ sura-dārubhiḥ
drākṣekṣu-rambhā-jambubhir
badary-akṣābhayāmalaiḥ

tasya—of that mountain (Trikūṭa); *droṇyām*—in a valley; *bhagavataḥ*—of the great personality; *varuṇasya*—the demigod Varuṇa; *mahā-ātmanaḥ*—who is a great devotee of the Lord; *udyānam*—a garden; *ṛtumat*—Ṛtumat; *nāma*—of the name; *ākrīḍam*—a place of sporting pastimes; *sura-yoṣitām*—of the damsels of the demigods; *sarvataḥ*—everywhere; *alaṅkṛtam*—beautifully decorated; *divyaiḥ*—pertaining to the demigods; *nitya*—always; *puṣpa*—of flowers; *phala*—and fruits; *drumaiḥ*—by trees; *mandāraiḥ—mandāra; pārijātaiḥ-pārijāta; ca*—also; *pāṭala—pāṭala; aśoka-aśoka; campakaiḥ-campaka; cūtaiḥ-cūta* fruits; *piyālaiḥ—piyāla* fruits; *panasaiḥ—panasa* fruits; *āmraiḥ*—mangoes; *āmrātakaiḥ*—sour fruits called *āmrātaka; api*—also; *kramukaiḥ—kramuka* fruits; *nārikelaiḥ*—coconut trees; *ca*—and; *kharjūraiḥ*—date trees; *bījapūrakaiḥ*—pomegranates; *madhukaiḥ—madhuka* fruits; *śāla-tālaiḥ*—palm fruits; *ca*—and; *tamālaiḥ—tamāla* trees; *asana—asana* trees; *arjunaiḥ—arjuna* trees; *ariṣta—ariṣṭa* fruits; *uḍumbara*—big *uḍum bara* trees; *plakṣaiḥ—plakṣa* trees; *vaṭaiḥ*—banyan trees; *kiṁśuka*—red flowers with no scent; *candanaiḥ*—sandalwood trees; *picumardaiḥ—picumarda* flowers; *kovidāraiḥ—kovidāra* fruits; *saralaiḥ—sarala* trees; *sura-dārubhiḥ—sura-dāru* trees; *drākṣā*—grapes; *ikṣuḥ*—sugarcane; *rambhā*—bananas; *jambubhiḥ—jambu* fruits; *badarī—badarī* fruits; *akṣa—akṣa* fruits; *abhaya—abhaya* fruits; *āmalaiḥ—āmalakī,* a sour fruit.

TRANSLATION

In a valley of Trikūṭa Mountain there was a garden called Ṛtumat. This garden belonged to the great devotee Varuṇa and was a sporting place for the damsels of the demigods. Flowers and fruits grew there in all seasons. Among them were mandāras, pārijātas, pāṭalas, aśokas, campakas, cūtas, piyālas, panasas, mangoes, āmrātakas, kramukas, coconut trees, date trees and pomegranates. There were madhukas, palm trees, tamālas, asanas, arjunas, ariṣṭas, uḍumbaras, plakṣas, banyan trees, kiṁśukas and sandal-

wood trees. There were also picumardas, kovidāras, saralas, sura-dārus, grapes, sugarcane, bananas, jambu, badarīs, akṣas, abhayas and āmalakīs.

TEXTS 14-19

बिल्वैः कपित्थैर्जम्बीरैर्वृतो भल्लातकादिभिः ।
तस्मिन्सरः सुविपुलं लसत्काञ्चनपङ्कजम् ॥ १४ ॥
कुमुदोत्पलकह्लारशतपत्रश्रियोर्जितम् ।
मत्तषट्पदनिर्घुष्टं शकुन्तैश्च कलस्वनैः ॥ १५ ॥
हंसकारण्डवाकीर्णं चक्राह्वैः सारसैरपि ।
जलकुक्कुटकोयष्टिदात्यूहकुलकूजितम् ॥ १६ ॥
मत्स्यकच्छपसञ्चारचलत्पद्मरजःपयः ।
कदम्बवेतसनलनीपवञ्जुलकैर्वृतम् ॥ १७ ॥
कुन्दैः कुरुबकाशोकैः शिरीषैः कूटजेङ्गुदैः ।
कुब्जकैः स्वर्णयूथीभिर्नागपुन्नागजातिभिः ॥ १८ ॥
मल्लिकाशतपत्रैश्च माधवीजालकादिभिः ।
शोभितं तीरजैश्चान्यैर्नित्यर्तुभिरलं द्रुमैः ॥ १९ ॥

bilvaiḥ kapitthair jambīrair
vṛto bhallātakādibhiḥ
tasmin saraḥ suvipulaṁ
lasat-kāñcana-paṅkajam

kumudotpala-kahlāra-
śatapatra-śriyorjitam
matta-ṣaṭ-pada-nirghuṣṭaṁ
śakuntaiś ca kala-svanaiḥ

haṁsa-kāraṇḍavākīrṇaṁ
cakrāhvaiḥ sārasair api
jalakukkuṭa-koyaṣṭi-
dātyūha-kula-kūjitam

matsya-kacchapa-sañcāra-
calat-padma-rajaḥ-payaḥ
kadamba-vetasa-nala-
nīpa-vañjulakair vṛtam

kundaiḥ kurubakāśokaiḥ
śirīṣaiḥ kūṭajeṅgudaiḥ
kubjakaiḥ svarṇa-yūthībhir
nāga-punnāga-jātibhiḥ

mallikā-śatapatraiś ca
mādhavī-jālakādibhiḥ
śobhitaṁ tīra-jaiś cānyair
nityartubhir alaṁ drumaiḥ

bilvaiḥ—*bilva* trees; *kapitthaiḥ*—*kapittha* trees; *jambīraiḥ*—*jambīra* trees; *vṛtaḥ*—surrounded by; *bhallātaka-ādibhiḥ*—*bhallātaka* and other trees; *tasmin*—in that garden; *saraḥ*—a lake; *su-vipulam*—which was very large; *lasat*—shining; *kāñcana*—golden; *paṅka-jam*—filled with lotus flowers; *kumuda*—of *kumuda* flowers; *utpala*—*utpala* flowers; *kahlāra*—*kahlāra* flowers; *śatapatra*—and *śatapatra* flowers; *śriyā*—with the beauty; *ūrjitam*—excellent; *matta*—intoxicated; *ṣaṭ-pada*—bees; *nirghuṣṭam*—hummed; *śakuntaiḥ*—with the chirping of birds; *ca*—and; *kala-svanaiḥ*—whose songs were very melodious; *haṁsa*—swans; *kāraṇḍava*—*kāraṇḍavas; ākīrṇam*—crowded with; *cakrāhvaiḥ*—*cakrāvakas; sārasaiḥ*—cranes; *api*—as well as; *jalakukkuṭa*—water chickens; *koyaṣṭi*—*koyaṣṭis; dātyūha-dātyūhas; kula*—flocks of; *kūjitam*—murmured; *matsya*—of the fish; *kacchapa*—and tortoises; *sañcāra*—because of the movements; *calat*—agitating; *padma*—of the lotuses; *rajaḥ*—by the pollen; *payaḥ*—the water (was decorated); *kadamba*—*kadambas; vetasa*—*vetasas; nala*—*nalas; nīpa*—*nīpas; vañjulakaiḥ*—*vañjulakas; vṛtam*—surrounded by; *kundaiḥ*—*kundas; kurubaka*—*kurubakas; aśokaiḥ*—*aśokas; śirīṣaiḥ*—*śirīṣas; kūṭaja*—*kūṭajas; iṅgudaiḥ*—*iṅgudas; kubjakaiḥ*—*kubjakas; svarṇa-yūthībhiḥ*—*svarṇa-yūthīs; nāga*—*nāgas; punnāga*—*punnāgas; jātibhiḥ*—*jātīs; mallikā*—*mallikās; śatapatraiḥ*—*śatapatras; ca*—also; *mādhavī*—*mādhavīs; jālakādibhiḥ*—*jālakās; śobhi-tam*—adorned; *tīrajaiḥ*—growing on the banks; *ca*—and; *anyaiḥ*—others; *nitya-ṛtubhiḥ*—in all seasons; *alam*—abundantly; *drumaiḥ*—with trees (bearing flowers and fruits).

TRANSLATION

In that garden there was a very large lake filled with shining golden lotus flowers and the flowers known as kumuda, kahlāra, utpala and śatapatra, which added excellent beauty to the mountain. There were also bilva, kapittha, jambīra and bhallātaka trees. Intoxicated bumblebees

drank honey and hummed with the chirping of the birds, whose songs were very melodious. The lake was crowded with swans, kāraṇḍavas, cakrāvakas, cranes, and flocks of water chickens, dātyūhas, koyaṣṭis and other murmuring birds. Because of the agitating movements of the fish and tortoises, the water was decorated with pollen that had fallen from the lotus flowers. The lake was surrounded by kadamba flowers, vetasa flowers, nalas, nīpas, vañjulakas, kundas, kurubakas, aśokas, śirīṣas, kūṭajas, iṅgudas, kubjakas, svarṇa-yūthīs, nāgas, punnāgas, jātīs, mallikās, śatapatras, jālakās and mādhavī-latās. The banks were also abundantly adorned with varieties of trees that yielded flowers and fruits in all seasons. Thus the entire mountain stood gloriously decorated.

PURPORT

Judging from the exhaustive description of the lakes and rivers on Trikūṭa Mountain, on earth there is no comparison to their super-excellence. On other planets, however, there are many such wonders. For instance, we understand that there are two million different types of trees, and not all of them are exhibited on earth. *Śrīmad-Bhāgavatam* presents the total knowledge of the affairs of the universe. It not only describes this universe, but also takes into account the spiritual world beyond the universe. No one can challenge the *Śrīmad-Bhāgavatam's* descriptions of the material and spiritual worlds. The attempts to go from the earth to the moon have failed, but the people of earth can understand what exists on other planets. There is no need of imagination; one may take actual knowledge from *Śrīmad-Bhāgavatam* and be satisfied.

TEXT 20

तत्रैकदा तद्गिरिकाननाश्रयः
करेणुभिर्वारणयूथपश्चरन् ।
सकण्टकं कीचकवेणुवेत्रवद्
विशालगुल्मं प्ररुजन्वनस्पतीन् ॥ २० ॥

tatraikadā tad-giri-kānanāśrayaḥ
kareṇubhir vāraṇa-yūtha-paś caran
sakaṇṭakaṁ kīcaka-veṇu-vetravad
viśāla-gulmaṁ prarujan vanaspatīn

tatra—therein; *ekadā*—once upon a time; *tat-giri*—of that mountain (Trikūṭa); *kānana-āśrayaḥ*—who lives in the forest; *kareṇubhiḥ*—accompanied by female elephants; *vāraṇa-yūtha-paḥ*—the leader of the elephants; *caran*—while wandering (toward the lake); *sa-kaṇṭakam*—a place full of thorns; *kīcaka-veṇu-vetra-vat*—with plants and creepers of different names; *viśāla-gulmam*—many thickets; *prarujan*—breaking; *vanaḥ-patīn*—trees and plants.

TRANSLATION

The leader of the elephants who lived in the forest of the mountain Trikūṭa once wandered toward the lake with his female elephants. He broke many plants, creepers, thickets and trees, not caring for their piercing thorns.

TEXT 21

यद्गन्धमात्राद्धरयो गजेन्द्रा
व्याघ्रादयो व्यालमृगाः सखड्गाः ।
महोरगाश्चापि भयाद् द्रवन्ति
सगौरकृष्णाः सरभाश्चमर्यः ॥ २१ ॥

yad-gandha-mātrād dharayo gajendrā
vyāghrādayo vyāla-mṛgāḥ sakhaḍgāḥ
mahoragāś cāpi bhayād dravanti
sagaura-kṛṣṇāḥ sarabhāś camaryaḥ

yat-gandha-mātrāt—simply by the scent of that elephant; *harayaḥ*—lions; *gaja-indrāḥ*—other elephants; *vyāghra-ādayaḥ*—ferocious animals like tigers; *vyāla-mṛgāḥ*—other ferocious animals; *sakhaḍgāḥ*—rhinoceroses; *mahā-uragāḥ*—big, big serpents; *ca*—also; *api*—indeed; *bhayāt*—because of fear; *dravanti*—running away; *sa*—with; *gaura-kṛṣṇāḥ*—some of them white, some of them black; *sarabhāḥ*—*sarabhas; camaryaḥ*—also *camarīs.*

TRANSLATION

Simply by catching scent of that elephant, all the other elephants, the tigers and the other ferocious animals, such as lions, rhinoceroses, great serpents and black and white sarabhas, fled in fear. The camarī deer also fled.

TEXT 22

वृका वराहा महिषर्क्षशल्या
गोपुच्छशालावृकमर्कटाश्च ।

अन्यत्र क्षुद्रा हरिणाः शशादय-
श्चरन्त्यभीता यदनुग्रहेण ॥ २२ ॥

vṛkā varāhā mahiṣarkṣa-śalyā
gopuccha-śālāvṛka-markaṭāś ca
anyatra kṣudrā hariṇāḥ śaśādayaś
caranty abhītā yad-anugraheṇa

vṛkāḥ—foxes; *varāhāḥ*—boars; *mahiṣa*—buffalos; *ṛkṣa*—bears; *śalyāḥ*—porcupines; *gopuccha*—a type of deer; *śālāvṛka*—wolves; *markaṭāḥ*—monkeys; *ca*—and; *anyatra*—elsewhere; *kṣudrāḥ*—small animals; *hariṇāḥ*—deer; *śaśa-ādayaḥ*—rabbits and others; *caranti*—roaming (in the forest); *abhītāḥ*—without fear; *yat-anugraheṇa*—by the mercy of that elephant.

TRANSLATION

By the mercy of this elephant, animals like the foxes, wolves, buffaloes, bears, boars, gopucchas, porcupines, monkeys, rabbits, the other deer and many other small animals loitered elsewhere in the forest. They were not afraid of him.

PURPORT

All the animals were practically controlled by this elephant, yet although they could move without fear, because of respect they did not stand before him.

TEXTS 23-24

स घर्मतप्तः करिभिः करेणुभि-
र्वृतो मदच्युत्करभैरनुद्रुतः ।
गिरिं गरिम्णा परितः प्रकम्पयन्
निषेव्यमाणोऽलिकुलैर्मदाशनैः ॥ २३ ॥
सरोऽनिलं पङ्कजरेणुरूषितं
जिघ्रन्विदूरान्मदविह्वलेक्षणः ।
वृतः स्वयूथेन तृषार्दितेन तत्
सरोवराभ्यासमथागमद् द्रुतम् ॥ २४ ॥

sa gharma-taptaḥ karibhiḥ kareṇubhir
vṛto madacyut-karabhair anudrutaḥ

girim̐ garimṇā paritaḥ prakampayan
niṣevyamāṇo 'likulair madāśanaiḥ

saro 'nilam̐ paṅkaja-reṇu-rūṣitam̐
jighran vidūrān mada-vihvalekṣaṇaḥ
vṛtaḥ sva-yūthena tṛṣārditena tat
sarovarābhyāsam athāgamad drutam

saḥ—he (the leader of the elephants); *gharma-taptaḥ*—perspiring; *karibhiḥ*—by other elephants; *kareṇubhiḥ*—as well as female elephants; *vṛtaḥ*—surrounded; *mada-cyut*—liquor dripping from his mouth; *karabhaiḥ*—by small elephants; *anudrutaḥ*—was followed; *girim*—that mountain; *garimṇā*—by the weight of the body; *paritaḥ*—all around; *prakampayan*—causing to tremble; *niṣevyamāṇaḥ*—being served; *alikulaiḥ*—by the bumblebees; *mada-aśanaiḥ*—who drank honey; *saraḥ*—from the lake; *anilam*—the breeze; *paṅkaja-reṇu-rūṣitam*—carrying the dust from the lotus flowers; *jighran*—smelling; *vidūrāt*—from a distance; *mada-vihvala*—being intoxicated; *īkṣaṇaḥ*—whose vision; *vṛtaḥ*—surrounded; *sva-yūthena*—by his own associates; *tṛṣārditena*—who were afflicted by thirst; *tat*—that; *sarovara-abhyāsam*—to the bank of the lake; *atha*—thus; *agamat*—went; *drutam*—very soon.

TRANSLATION

Surrounded by the herd's other elephants, including females, and followed by the young ones, Gajapati, the leader of the elephants, made Trikūṭa Mountain tremble all around because of the weight of his body. He was perspiring, liquor dripped from his mouth, and his vision was overwhelmed by intoxication. He was being served by bumblebees who drank honey, and from a distance he could smell the dust of the lotus flowers, which was carried from the lake by the breeze. Thus surrounded by his associates, who were afflicted by thirst, he soon arrived at the bank of the lake.

TEXT 25

विगाह्य तस्मिन्नमृताम्बु निर्मलं
हेमारविन्दोत्पलरेणुरूषितम् ।
पपौ निकामं निजपुष्करोद्धृत-
मात्मानमद्भिः स्नपयन्गतक्लमः ॥ २५ ॥

vigāhya tasminn amṛtāmbu nirmalaṁ
hemāravindotpala-reṇu-rūṣitam
papau nikāmaṁ nija-puṣkaroddhṛtam
ātmānam adbhiḥ snapayan gata-klamaḥ

vigāhya—entering; *tasmin*—into the lake; *amṛta-ambu*—water as pure as nectar; *nirmalam*—crystal clear; *hema*—very cold; *aravinda-utpala*—from the lilies and lotuses; *reṇu*—with the dust; *rūṣitam*—which was mixed; *papau*—he drank; *nikāmam*—until fully satisfied; *nija*—own; *puṣkara-uddhṛtam*—drawing with his trunk; *ātmānam*—himself; *adbhiḥ*—with water; *snapayan*—bathing thoroughly; *gata-klamaḥ*—was relieved of all fatigue.

TRANSLATION

The King of the elephants entered the lake, bathed thoroughly and was relieved of his fatigue. Then, with the aid of his trunk, he drank the cold, clear, nectarean water, which was mixed with the dust of lotus flowers and water lilies, until he was fully satisfied.

TEXT 26

स पुष्करेणोद्धृतशीकराम्बुभि-
निपाययन्संस्नपयन्यथा गृही ।
घृणी करेणुः करभांश्च दुर्मदो
नाचष्ट कृच्छ्रं कृपणोऽजमायया ॥ २६ ॥

sa puṣkareṇoddhṛta-śīkarāmbubhir
nipāyayan saṁsnapayan yathā gṛhī
ghṛṇī kareṇuḥ karabhāṁś ca durmado
nācaṣṭa kṛcchraṁ kṛpaṇo 'ja-māyayā

saḥ—he (the leader of the elephants); *puṣkareṇa*—with his trunk; *uddhṛta*—by drawing out; *śīkara-ambubhiḥ*—and sprinkling the water; *nipāyayan*—causing them to drink; *saṁsnapayan*—and bathing them; *yathā*—as; *gṛhī*—a householder; *ghṛṇī*—always kind (to the members of his family); *kareṇuḥ*—to his wives, the female elephants; *karabhān*—to the children; *ca*—as well as; *durmadaḥ*—who is too attached to the members of his family; *na*—not; *ācaṣṭa*—considered; *kṛcchram*—hardship; *kṛpaṇaḥ*—being without spiritual knowledge; *aja-māyayā*—because of the influence of the external, illusory energy of the Supreme Personality of Godhead.

TRANSLATION

Like a human being who lacks spiritual knowledge and is too attached to the members of his family, the elephant, being illusioned by the external energy of Kṛṣṇa, had his wives and children bathe and drink the water. Indeed, he raised water from the lake with his trunk and sprayed it over them. He did not mind the hard labor involved in this endeavor.

TEXT 27

तं तत्र कश्चिन्नृप दैवचोदितो
ग्राहो बलीयांश्चरणे रुषाग्रहीत् ।
यदृच्छयैवं व्यसनं गतो गजो
यथाबलं सोऽतिबलो विचक्रमे ॥ २७ ॥

taṁ tatra kaścin nṛpa daiva-codito
grāho balīyāṁś caraṇe ruṣāgrahīt
yadṛcchayaivaṁ vyasanaṁ gato gajo
yathā-balaṁ so 'tibalo vicakrame

tam—him (Gajendra); *tatra*—there (in the water); *kaścit*—someone; *nṛpa*—O King; *daiva-coditaḥ*—inspired by providence; *grāhaḥ*—crocodile; *balīyān*—very powerful; *caraṇe*—his foot; *ruṣā*—angrily; *agrahīt*—captured; *yadṛcchayā*—occurring due to providence; *evam*—such; *vyasanam*—a dangerous position; *gataḥ*—having obtained; *gajaḥ*—the elephant; *yathā-balam*—according to his strength; *saḥ*—he; *ati-balaḥ*—with great endeavor; *vicakrame*—tried to get out.

TRANSLATION

By the arrangement of providence, O King, a strong crocodile was angry at the elephant and attacked the elephant's leg in the water. The elephant was certainly strong, and he tried his best to get free from this danger sent by providence.

TEXT 28

तथातुरं यूथपतिं करेणवो
विकृष्यमाणं तरसा बलीयसा ।

विचुक्रुशुर्दीनधियोऽपरे गजाः
पार्ष्णिग्रहास्तारयितुं न चाशकन् ॥ २८ ॥

tathāturaṁ yūtha-patiṁ kareṇavo
vikṛṣyamāṇaṁ tarasā balīyasā
vicukruśur dīna-dhiyo 'pare gajāḥ
pārṣṇi-grahās tārayituṁ na cāśakan

tathā—then; *āturam*—that grave condition; *yūtha-patim*—the leader of the elephants; *kareṇavaḥ*—his wives; *vikṛṣyamāṇam*—being attacked; *tarasā*—by the strength; *balīyasā*—by the strength (of the crocodile); *vicukruśuḥ*—began to cry; *dīna-dhiyaḥ*—who were less intelligent; *apare*—the other; *gajāḥ*—elephants; *pārṣṇi-grahāḥ*—grasping him from behind; *tārayitum*—to free; *na*—not; *ca*—also; *aśakan*—were able.

TRANSLATION

Thereafter, seeing Gajendra in that grave condition, his wives felt very, very sorry and began to cry. The other elephants wanted to help Gajendra, but because of the crocodile's great strength, they could not rescue him by grasping him from behind.

TEXT 29

नियुध्यतोरेवमिभेन्द्रनक्रयो-
विकर्षतोरन्तरतो बहिर्मिथः ।
समाः सहस्रं व्यगमन् महीपते
सप्राणयोश्चित्रममंसतामराः ॥ २९ ॥

niyudhyator evam ibhendra-nakrayor
vikarṣator antarato bahir mithaḥ
samāḥ sahasraṁ vyagaman mahī-pate
saprāṇayoś citram amaṁsatāmarāḥ

niyudhyatoḥ—fighting; *evam*—in this way; *ibha-indra*—of the elephant; *nakrayoḥ*—and the crocodile; *vikarṣatoḥ*—pulling; *antarataḥ*—in the water; *bahiḥ*—outside the water; *mithaḥ*—one another; *samāḥ*—years; *sahasram*—one thousand; *vyagaman*—passed; *mahī-pate*—O King; *sa-prāṇayoḥ*—both alive; *citram*—wonderful; *amaṁsata*—considered; *amarāḥ*—the demigods.

TRANSLATION

O King, the elephant and the crocodile fought in this way, pulling one another in and out of the water, for one thousand years. Upon seeing the fight, the demigods were very surprised.

TEXT 30

ततो गजेन्द्रस्य मनोबलौजसां
कालेन दीर्घेण महानभूद् व्ययः ।
विकृष्यमाणस्य जलेऽवसीदतो
विपर्ययोऽभूत् सकलं जलौकसः ॥ ३० ॥

tato gajendrasya mano-balaujasāṁ
kālena dīrgheṇa mahān abhūd vyayaḥ
vikṛṣyamāṇasya jale 'vasīdato
viparyayo 'bhūt sakalaṁ jalaukasaḥ

tataḥ—thereafter; *gaja-indrasya*—of the King of the elephants; *manaḥ*—of the strength of enthusiasm; *bala*—the physical strength; *ojasām*—and the strength of the senses; *kālena*—because of years of fighting; *dīrgheṇa*—prolonged; *mahān*—great; *abhūt*—became; *vyayaḥ*—the expenditure; *vikṛṣyamāṇasya*—who was being pulled (by the crocodile); *jale*—into the water (a foreign place); *avasīdataḥ*—reduced (mental, physical and sensory strength); *viparyayaḥ*—the opposite; *abhūt*—became; *sakalam*—all of them; *jala-okasaḥ*—the crocodile, whose home is the water.

TRANSLATION

Thereafter, because of being pulled into the water and fighting for many long years, the elephant became diminished in his mental, physical and sensual strength. The crocodile, on the contrary, being an animal of the water, increased in enthusiasm, physical strength and sensual power.

PURPORT

In the fighting between the elephant and the crocodile, the difference was that although the elephant was extremely powerful, he was in a foreign place, in the water. During one thousand years of fighting, he could not get any food, and under the circumstances his bodily strength diminished, and because his bodily strength diminished, his mind also became weak and his senses less powerful. The crocodile, however, being an animal of the water, had no difficulties. He was getting food and was therefore getting mental strength and sensual encouragement. Thus while the elephant became reduced in strength, the crocodile became more and more powerful. Now, from this we may take the lesson that in our fight with *māyā* we should not be in a position in which our strength, enthusiasm and senses will be unable to fight vigorously. Our Kṛṣṇa consciousness movement has actually declared war against the illusory energy, in which all the living entities are rotting in a false understanding of civilization. The soldiers in this Kṛṣṇa consciousness movement must always possess physical strength, enthusiasm and sensual power. To keep themselves fit, they must therefore place themselves in a normal condition of life. What constitutes a normal condition will not be the same for everyone, and therefore there are divisions of *varṇāśrama—brāhmaṇa, kṣatriya, vaiśya, śūdra, brahmacarya, gṛhastha, vānaprastha* and *sannyāsa.* Especially in this age, Kali-yuga, it is advised that no one take *sannyāsa.*

aśvamedhaṁ gavālambhaṁ
sannyāsaṁ pala-paitṛkam
devareṇa sutotpattiṁ
kalau pañca vivarjayet
(Brahma-vaivarta Purāṇa)

From this we can understand that in this age the *sannyāsa-āśrama* is forbidden because people are not strong. Śrī Caitanya Mahāprabhu showed us an example in taking *sannyāsa* at the age of twenty-four years, but even Sārvabhauma Bhaṭṭācārya advised Śrī Caitanya Mahāprabhu to be extremely careful because He had taken *sannyāsa* at an early age. For preaching we give young boys *sannyāsa,* but actually it is being experienced that they are not fit for *sannyāsa.* There is no harm, however, if one thinks that he is unfit for *sannyāsa;* if he is very much agitated sexually, he should go to the *āśrama* where sex is allowed, namely the *gṛhastha-āśrama.* That one has been found to be very weak in one place does not mean that he should stop fighting the crocodile of *māyā.* One should take shelter of the lotus feet of Kṛṣṇa, as we shall see Gajendra do, and at the same time one can be a *gṛhastha* if he is satisfied with sexual indulgence. There is no need to give up the fight. Śrī Caitanya Mahāprabhu therefore recommended, *sthāne sthitāḥ śruti-gatāṁ tanu-vāṅ-manobhiḥ.* One may stay in whichever *āśrama* is suitable for him; it is not essential that one take *sannyāsa.* If one is sexually agitated, he can enter the *gṛhastha-āśrama.* But one must continue fighting. For one who is not in a transcendental position, to take *sannyāsa* artificially is not a very great credit. If *sannyāsa* is not suitable, one may enter the *gṛhastha-āśrama* and fight *māyā* with great strength. But one should not give up the fighting and go away.

TEXT 31

इत्थं गजेन्द्रः स यदाप संकटं
प्राणस्य देही विवशो यदृच्छया।
अपारयन्नात्मविमोक्षणे चिरं
दध्याविमां बुद्धिमथाभ्यपद्यत ॥ ३१ ॥

ittham gajendraḥ sa yadāpa saṅkaṭaṁ
prāṇasya dehī vivaśo yadṛcchayā
apārayann ātma-vimokṣaṇe ciraṁ
dadhyāv imāṁ buddhim athābhyapadyata

ittham—in this way; *gaja-indraḥ*—the King of the elephants; *saḥ*—he; *yadā*—when; *āpa*—obtained; *saṅkaṭam*—such a dangerous position; *prāṇasya*—of life; *dehī*—who is embodied; *vivaśaḥ*—circumstantially helpless; *yadṛcchayā*—by the will of providence; *apārayan*—being unable; *ātma-vimokṣaṇe*—to save himself; *ciram*—for a long time; *dadhyau*—began to think seriously; *imām*—this; *buddhim*—decision; *atha*—thereupon; *abhyapadyata*—reached.

TRANSLATION

When the King of the elephants saw that he was under the clutches of the crocodile by the will of providence and, being embodied and circumstantially helpless, could not save himself from danger, he was extremely afraid of being killed. He consequently thought for a long time and finally reached the following decision.

PURPORT

Everyone in the material world is engaged in a struggle for existence. Everyone tries to save himself from danger, but when one is unable to save himself, if he is pious, he then takes shelter of the lotus feet of the Supreme Personality of Godhead. This is confirmed in *Bhagavad-gītā* (7.16):

catur-vidhā bhajante māṁ
janāḥ sukṛtino 'rjuna
ārto jijñāsur arthārthī
jñānī ca bharatarṣabha

Four kinds of pious men—namely, one who is in danger, one who is in need of money, one who is searching for knowledge and one who is inquisitive—begin to take shelter of the Supreme Personality of Godhead in order to be saved or to advance. The King of the elephants, in his condition of danger, decided to seek shelter of the lotus feet of the Lord. After considerable thought, he intelligently arrived at this correct decision. Such a decision is not reached by a sinful man. Therefore in *Bhagavad-gītā* it is said that those who are pious (*sukṛtī*) can decide that in a dangerous or awkward condition one should seek shelter of the lotus feet of Kṛṣṇa.

TEXT 32

न मामिमे ज्ञातय आतुरं गजाः
कुतः करिण्यः प्रभवन्ति मोचितुम्।
ग्राहेण पाशेन विधातुरावृतो-
ऽप्यहं च तं यामि परं परायणम् ॥ ३२ ॥

na mām ime jñātaya āturaṁ gajāḥ
kutaḥ kariṇyaḥ prabhavanti mocitum
grāheṇa pāśena vidhātur āvṛto
'py ahaṁ ca taṁ yāmi paraṁ parāyaṇam

na—not; *mām*—me; *ime*—all these; *jñātayaḥ*—friends and relatives (the other elephants); *āturam*—in my distress; *gajāḥ*—the elephant; *kutaḥ*—how; *kariṇyaḥ*—my wives; *prabhavanti*—are able; *mocitum*—to deliver (from this dangerous position); *grāheṇa*—by the crocodile; *pāśena*—by the network of ropes; *vidhātuḥ*—of providence; *āvṛtaḥ*—captured; *api*—although (I am in such a position); *aham*—I; *ca*—also; *tam*—that (Supreme Personality of Godhead); *yāmi*—take shelter of; *param*—who is transcendental; *parāyaṇam*—and who is the shelter of even the exalted demigods like Brahmā and Śiva.

TRANSLATION

The other elephants, who are my friends and relatives, could not rescue me from this danger. What then to speak of my wives? They cannot do anything. It is by the will of providence that I have been attacked by this crocodile, and therefore I shall seek shelter of the Supreme Personality of Godhead, who is always the shelter of everyone, even of great personalities.

PURPORT

This material world is described as *padaṁ padaṁ yad vipadām* , which means that at every step there is danger. A fool wrongly thinks that he is happy in this material world, but in fact he is not, for one who thinks that way is only illusioned. At every step, at every moment, there is danger. In modern civilization one thinks that if he has a nice home and a nice car his life is perfect. In the Western countries, especially in America, it is very nice to possess a good car, but as soon as one is on the road, there is danger because at any moment an accident may take place and one will be killed. The record actually shows that so many people die in such accidents. Therefore if we actually think that this material world is a very happy place, this is our ignorance. Real knowledge is that this material world is full of danger. We may struggle for existence as far as our intelligence allows and may try to take care of ourselves, but unless the Supreme Personality of Godhead, Kṛṣṇa, ultimately saves us from danger, our attempts will be useless. Therefore Prahlāda Mahārāja says:

bālasya neha śaraṇaṁ pitarau nṛsiṁha
nārtasya cāgadam udanvati majjato nauḥ
taptasya tat-pratividhir ya ihāñjaseṣṭas
tāvad vibho tanu-bhṛtāṁ tvad-upekṣitānām

(Bhāg. 7.9.19)

We may invent so many ways to be happy or to counteract the dangers of this material world, but unless our attempts are sanctioned by the Supreme Personality of Godhead, they will never make us happy. Those who try to be happy without taking shelter of the Supreme Personality of Godhead are *mūḍhas,* rascals. *Na māṁ duṣkṛtino mūḍhāḥ prapadyante narādhamāḥ* . Those who are the lowest of men refuse to take to Kṛṣṇa consciousness because they think that they will be able to protect themselves without Kṛṣṇa's care. This is their mistake. The decision of the King of the elephants, Gajendra, was correct. In such a dangerous position, he sought shelter of the Supreme Personality of Godhead.

TEXT 33

यः कश्चनेशो बलिनोऽन्तकोरगात्
प्रचण्डवेगादभिधावतो भृशम् ।
भीतं प्रपन्नं परिपाति यद्भया-
न्मृत्युः प्रधावत्यरणं तमीमहि ॥ ३३ ॥

yaḥ kaścaneśo balino 'ntakoragāt
pracaṇḍa-vegād abhidhāvato bhṛśam
bhītaṁ prapannaṁ paripāti yad-bhayān
mṛtyuḥ pradhāvaty araṇaṁ tam īmahi

yaḥ—He who (the Supreme Personality of Godhead); *kaścana*—someone; *īśaḥ*—the supreme controller; *balinaḥ*—very powerful; *antaka-uragāt*—from the great serpent of time, which brings death; *pracaṇḍa-vegāt*—whose force is fearful; *abhidhāvataḥ*—who is chasing; *bhṛśam*—endlessly (every hour and every minute); *bhītam*—one who is afraid of death; *prapannam*—who is surrendered (to the Supreme Personality of Godhead); *paripāti*—He protects; *yat-bhayāt*—from fear of the Lord; *mṛtyuḥ*—death itself; *pradhāvati*—runs away; *araṇam*—the actual shelter of everyone; *tam*—unto Him; *īmahi*—I surrender or take shelter.

TRANSLATION

The Supreme Personality of Godhead is certainly not known to everyone, but He is very powerful and influential. Therefore, although the serpent of eternal time, which is fearful in force, endlessly chases everyone, ready to swallow him, if one who fears this serpent seeks shelter of the Lord, the Lord gives him protection, for even death runs away in fear of the Lord. I therefore surrender unto Him, the great and powerful supreme authority who is the actual shelter of everyone.

PURPORT

One who is intelligent understands that there is a great and supreme authority above everything. That great authority appears in different incarnations to save the innocent from disturbances. As confirmed in *Bhagavad-gītā* (4.8), *paritrāṇāya sādhūnāṁ vināśāya ca duṣkṛtām:* the Lord appears in His various incarnations for two purposes—to annihilate the *duṣkṛtī,* the sinful, and to protect His devotees. The King of the elephants decided to surrender unto Him. This is intelligent. One must know that great Supreme Personality of Godhead and surrender unto Him. The Lord comes personally to instruct us how to be happy, and only fools and rascals do not see by intelligence this supreme authority, the Supreme Person. In the *śruti-mantra* it is said:

bhīṣāsmād vātaḥ pavate
bhīṣodeti sūryaḥ

bhīṣāsmād agniś candraś ca
mṛtyur dhāvati pañcamaḥ
(Taittirīya Upaniṣad 2.8)

It is out of fear of the Supreme Personality of Godhead that the wind is blowing, that the sun is distributing heat and light, and that death is chasing everyone. Thus there is a supreme controller, as confirmed in *Bhagavad-gītā* (9.10): *mayādhyakṣeṇa prakṛtiḥ sūyate sacarācaram.* This material manifestation is working so well because of the supreme controller. Any intelligent person, therefore, can understand that there is a supreme controller. Furthermore, the supreme controller Himself appears as Lord Kṛṣṇa, as Lord Caitanya Mahāprabhu and as Lord Rāmacandra to give us instructions and to show us by example how to surrender unto the Supreme Personality of Godhead. Yet those who are *duṣkṛtī,* the lowest of men, do not surrender (*na māṁ duṣkṛtino mūḍhāḥ prapadyante narādhamāḥ*).

In *Bhagavad-gītā* the Lord clearly says, *mṛtyuḥ sarva-haraś cāham:* "I am all-devouring death." Thus *mṛtyu,* or death, is the representative who takes everything away from the living entity who has accepted a material body. No one can say, "I do not fear death." This is a false proposition. Everyone fears death. However, one who seeks shelter of the Supreme Personality of Godhead can be saved from death. One may argue, "Does the devotee not die?" The answer is that a devotee certainly must give up his body, for the body is material. The difference is, however, that for one who surrenders to Kṛṣṇa fully and who is protected by Kṛṣṇa, the present body is his last; he will not again receive a material body to be subjected to death. This is assured in *Bhagavad-gītā* (4.9). *Tyaktvā dehaṁ punar janma naiti mām eti so'rjuna:* a devotee, after giving up his body, does not accept a material body, but returns home, back to Godhead. We are always in danger because at any moment death can take place. It is not that only Gajendra, the King of the elephants, was afraid of death. Everyone should fear death because everyone is caught by the crocodile of eternal time and may die at any moment. The best course, therefore, is to seek shelter of Kṛṣṇa, the Supreme Personality of Godhead, and be saved from the struggle for existence in this material world, in which one repeatedly takes birth and dies. To reach this understanding is the ultimate goal of life.

Thus end the Bhaktivedanta purports of the Eighth Canto, Second Chapter, of the Śrīmad-Bhāgavatam, *entitled "The Elephant Gajendra's Crisis."*

CHAPTER THREE

Gajendra's Prayers of Surrender

In this chapter, the prayers by Gajendra, the King of the elephants, are described. It appears that the King of the elephants was formerly a human being known as Indradyumna and that he learned a prayer to the Supreme Lord. Fortunately he remembered that prayer and began to chant it to himself. First he offered his respectful obeisances to the Supreme Personality of Godhead, and because of his awkward position in having been attacked by the crocodile, he expressed his inability to recite prayers nicely. Nonetheless, he tried to chant the *mantra* and expressed himself in appropriate words as follows.

"The Supreme Personality of Godhead is the cause of all causes, the original person from whom everything has emanated. He is the root cause of this cosmic manifestation, and the entire cosmos rests in Him, yet He is transcendental, for He does everything in relation to the material world through His external energy. He is eternally situated in the spiritual world—in Vaikuṇṭha or Goloka Vṛndāvana — where He engages in His eternal pastimes. The material world is a product of His external energy, or material nature, which works under His direction. It is thus that creation, maintenance and annihilation take place. The Lord exists at all times. This is extremely difficult for a nondevotee to understand. Although the transcendental Supreme Personality of Godhead is perceivable by everyone, only the pure devotees perceive His presence and activities. The Supreme Personality of Godhead is completely free from material birth, death, old age and disease. Indeed, if anyone in this material world takes shelter of Him, he also becomes situated in that transcendental position. For the satisfaction of the devotee (*paritrāṇāya sādhūnām*), the Lord appears and exhibits His activities. His appearance, disappearance and other pastimes are not at all material. One who knows this secret can enter the kingdom of God. In the Lord, all opposing elements are adjusted. The Lord is situated in everyone's heart. He is the controller of everything, He is the witness of all activities, and He is the original source of all living entities. Indeed, all living entities are parts of Him, for He is the origin of Mahā-Viṣṇu, who is the source of the living entities within this material world. The Lord can observe the activities of our senses, which can work and achieve material results because of His mercy. Although He is the original source of everything, He is untouched by any of His by-products. In this way He is like a gold mine, which is the source of gold in ornaments and yet is different from the ornaments themselves. The Lord is worshiped by the method prescribed in the *Pañcarātras.* He is the source of our knowledge, and He can give us liberation. Therefore it is our duty to understand Him according to the instructions of devotees, in particular the spiritual master. Although for us the mode of goodness is covered, by following the instructions of saintly persons and the spiritual master we can be freed from material clutches."

"The self-effulgent material form of the Supreme Personality of Godhead is adored by nondevotees, His impersonal form is adored by those advanced in spiritual knowledge, and His feature as the localized Supersoul is appreciated by *yogīs.* But His original form as a person is understood only by devotees. That Supreme Personality of Godhead is competent to dissipate the darkness of the conditioned soul through His instructions in *Bhagavad-gītā.* He is the ocean of transcendental qualities and can be understood only by liberated persons freed from the bodily concept of life. By His causeless mercy, the Lord can rescue the conditioned soul from the material clutches and enable him to return home, back to Godhead, to become His personal associate. Nonetheless, a pure devotee does not aspire to go back to Godhead; he is simply satisfied with executing his service in this material world. A pure devotee does not ask anything from the Supreme Personality of Godhead. His only prayer is to be freed from the material conception of life and to be engaged in the Lord's transcendental loving service."

In this way the King of the elephants, Gajendra, offered prayers directly to the Supreme Personality of Godhead, without mistaking Him for one of the demigods. None of the demigods came to see him, not even Brahmā or Śiva. Rather, the Supreme Personality of Godhead, Nārāyaṇa, seated on Garuḍa, personally appeared before him. Gajendra, by lifting his trunk, offered obeisances to the Lord, and the Lord immediately pulled him from the water along with the crocodile who had captured his leg. Then the Lord killed the crocodile and thus rescued Gajendra.

TEXT 1

श्रीबादरायणिरुवाच

एवं व्यवसितो बुद्ध्या समाधाय मनो हृदि।
जजाप परमं जाप्यं प्राग्जन्मन्यनुशिक्षितम् ॥ १ ॥

śrī-bādarāyaṇir uvāca
evaṁ vyavasito buddhyā
samādhāya mano hṛdi
jajāpa paramaṁ jāpyaṁ
prāg-janmany anuśikṣitam

śrī-bādarāyaṇiḥ uvāca—Śrī Śukadeva Gosvāmī said; *evam*—thus; *vyavasitaḥ*—fixed; *buddhyā*—by intelligence; *samādhāya*—for concentration; *manaḥ*—the mind; *hṛdi*—in consciousness or in the heart; *jajāpa*—he chanted; *paramam*—a supreme; *jāpyam*—*mantra* he had learned from great devotees; *prāk-janmani*—in his previous birth; *anuśikṣitam*—practiced.

TRANSLATION

Śrī Śukadeva Gosvāmī continued: Thereafter, the King of the elephants, Gajendra, fixed his mind in his heart with perfect intelligence and chanted a mantra which he had learned in his previous birth as Indradyumna and which he remembered by the grace of Kṛṣṇa.

PURPORT

Such remembrance is described in *Bhagavad-gītā* (6.43-44):

tatra taṁ buddhi-saṁyogaṁ
labhate paurva-dehikam
yatate ca tato bhūyaḥ
saṁsiddhau kuru-nandana

pūrvābhyāsena tenaiva
hriyate hy avaśo 'pi saḥ

In these verses it is assured that even if a person engaged in devotional service falls down, he is not degraded, but is placed in a position in which he will in due course of time remember the Supreme Personality of Godhead. As explained later, Gajendra was formerly King Indradyumna, and somehow or other in his next life he became King of the elephants. Now Gajendra was in danger, and although he was in a body other than that of a human being, he remembered the *stotra* he had chanted in his previous life. *Yatate ca tato bhūyaḥ saṁsiddhau kuru-nandana.* To enable one to achieve perfection, Kṛṣṇa gives one the chance to remember Him again. This is proved here, for although the King of the elephants, Gajendra, was put in danger, this was a chance for him to remember his previous devotional activities so that he could immediately be rescued by the Supreme Personality of Godhead.

It is imperative, therefore, that all devotees in Kṛṣṇa consciousness practice chanting some *mantra.* Certainly one should chant the Hare Kṛṣṇa *mantra,* which is the *mahā-mantra,* or great *mantra,* and also one should practice chanting *cintāmaṇi-prakara-sadmasu* or the Nṛsiṁha *strotra* (*ito nṛsiṁhaḥ parato nṛsiṁho yato yato yāmi tato nṛsiṁhaḥ*). Every devotee should practice in order to chant some *mantra* perfectly so that even though he may be imperfect in spiritual consciousness in this life, in his next life he will not forget Kṛṣṇa consciousness, even if he becomes an animal. Of course, a devotee should try to perfect his Kṛṣṇa consciousness in this life, for simply by understanding Kṛṣṇa and His instructions, after giving up this body one can return home, back to Godhead. Even if there is some falldown, practice of Kṛṣṇa consciousness never goes in vain. For example, Ajāmila, in his boyhood, practiced chanting the name of Nārāyaṇa under the direction of his father, but later, in his youth, he fell down and became a drunkard, woman-hunter, rogue and thief. Nonetheless, because of chanting the name of Nārāyaṇa for the purpose of calling his son, whom he had named Nārāyaṇa, he became advanced, even though he was involved in sinful activities. Therefore, we should not forget the chanting of the Hare Kṛṣṇa *mantra* under any circumstances. It will help us in the greatest danger, as we find in the life of Gajendra.

TEXT 2

श्रीगजेन्द्र उवाच

ॐ नमो भगवते तस्मै यत एतच्चिदात्मकम् ।
पुरुषायादिबीजाय परेशायाभिधीमहि ॥ २ ॥

śrī-gajendra uvāca
oṁ namo bhagavate tasmai
yata etac cid-ātmakam
puruṣāyādi-bījāya
pareśāyābhidhīmahi

śrī-gajendraḥ uvāca—Gajendra, the King of elephants, said; *oṁ*—O my Lord; *namaḥ*—I offer my respectful obeisances unto You; *bhagavate*—unto the Supreme Personality of Godhead; *tasmai*—unto Him; *yataḥ*—from whom; *etat*—this body and the material manifestation; *cit-ātmakam*—is moving due to consciousness (the spirit soul); *puruṣāya*—unto the Supreme Person; *ādi-bījāya*—who is the origin or root cause of everything; *para-īśāya*—who is supreme, transcendental and worshipable for such exalted persons as Brahmā and Śiva; *abhidhīmahi*—let me meditate upon Him.

TRANSLATION

The King of the elephants, Gajendra, said: I offer my respectful obeisances unto the Supreme Person, Vāsudeva [oṁ namo bhagavate vāsudevāya]. Because of Him this material body acts due to the presence of spirit, and He is therefore the root cause of everyone. He is worshipable for such exalted persons as Brahmā and Śiva, and He has entered the heart of every living being. Let me meditate upon Him.

PURPORT

In this verse the words *etac cid-ātmakam* are very important. The material body certainly consists only of material elements, but when one awakens to Kṛṣṇa conscious understanding, the body is no longer material but spiritual. The material body is meant for sense enjoyment, whereas the spiritual body engages in the transcendental loving service of the Lord. Therefore, a devotee who engages in the service of the Supreme Lord and who constantly thinks of Him should never be considered to have a material body. It is therefore enjoined, *guruṣu nara-matiḥ:* one should stop thinking of the spiritual master as an ordinary human being with a material body. *Arcye viṣṇau śilā-dhīḥ:* everyone knows that the Deity in the temple is made of stone, but to think that the Deity is merely stone is an offense. Similarly, to think that the body of the spiritual master consists of material ingredients is offensive. Atheists think that devotees foolishly worship a stone statue as God and an ordinary man as the *guru.* The fact is, however, that by the grace of Kṛṣṇa's omnipotence, the so-called stone statue of the Deity is directly the Supreme Personality of Godhead, and the body of the spiritual master is directly spiritual. A pure devotee who is engaged in unalloyed devotional service should be understood to be situated on the transcendental platform (*sa guṇān samatītyaitān brahma-bhūyāya kalpate*). Let us therefore offer our obeisances unto the Supreme Personality of Godhead, by whose mercy so-called material things also become spiritual when they are engaged in spiritual activity.

Oṁkāra (*praṇava*) is the symbolic sound representation of the Supreme Personality of Godhead. *Oṁ tat sad iti nirdeśo brahmaṇas tri-vidhaḥ smṛtaḥ:*

the three words *oṁ tat sat* immediately invoke the Supreme Person. Therefore Kṛṣṇa says that He is *oṁkāra* in all the Vedic *mantras* (*praṇavaḥ sarva-vedeṣu*). The Vedic *mantras* are pronounced beginning with *oṁkāra* to indicate immediately the Supreme Personality of Godhead. *Śrīmad-Bhāgavatam,* for example, begins with the words *oṁ namo bhagavate vāsudevāya.* There is no difference between the Supreme Personality of Godhead, Vāsudeva, and *oṁkāra* (*praṇava*). We should be careful to understand that *oṁkāra* does not indicate anything *nirākāra,* or formless. Indeed, this verse immediately says, *oṁ namo bhagavate.* Bhagavān is a person. Thus *oṁkāra* is the representation of the Supreme Person. *Oṁkāra* is not meant to be impersonal, as the Māyāvādī philosophers consider it to be. This is distinctly expressed here by the word *puruṣāya.* The supreme truth addressed by *oṁkāra* is *puruṣa,* the Supreme Person; He is not impersonal. Unless He is a person, how can He control the great, stalwart controllers of this universe? Lord Viṣṇu, Lord Brahmā and Lord Śiva are the supreme controllers of this universe, but Lord Viṣṇu is offered obeisances even by Lord Śiva and Lord Brahmā. Therefore this verse uses the word *pareśāya,* which indicates that the Supreme Personality of Godhead is worshiped by exalted demigods. *Pareśāya* means *parameśvara.* Lord Brahmā and Lord Śiva are *īśvaras,* great controllers, but Lord Viṣṇu is *parameśvara,* the supreme controller.

TEXT 3

यस्मिन्निदं यतश्चेदं येनेदं य इदं स्वयम् ।
योऽस्मात् परस्माच्च परस्तं प्रपद्ये स्वयम्भुवम् ॥ ३ ॥

yasminn idaṁ yataś cedaṁ
yenedaṁ ya idaṁ svayam
yo 'smāt parasmāc ca paras
taṁ prapadye svayambhuvam

yasmin—the basic platform on which; *idam*—the universe rests; *yataḥ*—the ingredients from which; *ca*—and; *idam*—the cosmic manifestation is produced; *yena*—by whom; *idam*—this cosmic manifestation is created and maintained; *yaḥ*—He who; *idam*—this material world; *svayam*—is Himself; *yaḥ*—He who; *asmāt*—from the effect (this material world); *parasmāt*—from the cause; *ca*—and; *paraḥ*—transcendental or different; *tam*—unto Him; *prapadye*—I surrender; *svayambhuvam*—unto the supreme self-sufficient.

TRANSLATION

The Supreme Godhead is the supreme platform on which everything rests, the ingredient by which everything has been produced, and the person who has created and is the only cause of this cosmic manifestation. Nonetheless, He is different from the cause and the result. I surrender unto Him, the Supreme Personality of Godhead, who is self-sufficient in everything.

PURPORT

In *Bhagavad-gītā* (9.4) the Lord says, *mayā tatam idaṁ sarvaṁ jagad avyakta-mūrtinā:* "I am the Supreme Personality of Godhead, but everything rests upon My energy, just as an earthen pot rests on the earth." The place where an earthen pot rests is also earth. Then again, the earthen pot is manufactured by a potter, whose body is a product of earth. The potter's wheel with which the pot is made is an expansion of earth, and the ingredients from which the pot are made are also earth. As confirmed in the *śruti-mantra, yato vā imāni bhūtāni jāyante. yena jātāni jīvanti yat prayanty abhisaṁviśanti.* The original cause of everything is the Supreme Personality of Godhead, and after being annihilated, everything enters into Him (*prakṛtiṁ yānti māmikām*). Thus the Supreme Lord, the Personality of Godhead—Lord Rāmacandra or Lord Kṛṣṇa—is the original cause of everything.

īśvaraḥ paramaḥ kṛṣṇaḥ
sac-cid-ānanda-vigrahaḥ
anādir ādir govindaḥ
sarva-kāraṇa-kāraṇam

"Kṛṣṇa, who is known as Govinda, is the supreme controller. He has an eternal, blissful, spiritual body. He is the origin of all. He has no other origin, for He is the prime cause of all causes." (*Brahma-saṁhitā.* 5.1) The Lord is the cause for everything, but there is no cause for Him. *Sarvaṁ khalv idaṁ brahma. Mat-sthāni sarva-bhūtāni na cāhaṁ teṣv avasthitaḥ*. Although He is everything, His personality is different from the cosmic manifestation.

TEXT 4

यः स्वात्मनीदं निजमाययार्पितं
क्वचिद् विभातं क्व च तत् तिरोहितम्।

अविद्धदृक् साक्ष्युभयं तदीक्षते
स आत्ममूलोऽवतु मां परात्परः ॥ ४ ॥

yaḥ svātmanīdaṁ nija-māyayārpitaṁ
kvacid vibhātaṁ kva ca tat tirohitam
aviddha-dṛk sākṣy ubhayaṁ tad īkṣate
sa ātma-mūlo 'vatu māṁ parāt-paraḥ

yaḥ—the Supreme Personality of Godhead who; *sva-ātmani*—in Him; *idam*—this cosmic manifestation; *nija-māyayā*—by His own potency; *arpitam*—invested; *kvacit*—sometimes, at the beginning of a *kalpa; vibhātam*—it is manifested; *kva ca*—sometimes, during dissolution; *tat*—that (manifestation); *tirohitam*—not visible; *aviddha-dṛk*—He sees everything (in all these circumstances); *sākṣī*—the witness; *ubhayam*—both (manifestation and annihilation); *tat īkṣate*—sees everything, without loss of sight; *saḥ*—that Supreme Personality of Godhead; *ātma-mūlaḥ*—self-sufficient, having no other cause; *avatu*—please give protection; *mām*—unto me; *parāt-paraḥ*—He is transcendental to transcendental, or above all transcendence.

TRANSLATION

The Supreme Personality of Godhead, by expanding His own energy, keeps this cosmic manifestation visible and again sometimes renders it invisible. He is both the supreme cause and the supreme result, the observer and the witness, in all circumstances. Thus He is transcendental to everything. May that Supreme Personality of Godhead give me protection.

PURPORT

The Supreme Personality of Godhead has multipotencies (*parāsya śaktir vividhaiva śrūyate*). Therefore, as soon as He likes, He uses one of His potencies, and by that expansion He creates this cosmic manifestation. Again, when the cosmic manifestation is annihilated, it rests in Him. Nonetheless, He is infallibly the supreme observer. Under any circumstances, the Supreme Lord is changeless. He is simply a witness and is aloof from all creation and annihilation.

TEXT 5

कालेन पञ्चत्वमितेषु कृत्स्नशो
लोकेषु पालेषु च सर्वहेतुषु ।

तमस्तदासीद् गहनं गभीरं
यस्तस्य पारेऽभिविराजते विभुः ॥ ५ ॥

kālena pañcatvam iteṣu kṛtsnaśo
lokeṣu pāleṣu ca sarva-hetuṣu
tamas tadāsīd gahanaṁ gabhīraṁ
yas tasya pāre 'bhivirājate vibhuḥ

kālena—in due course of time (after millions and millions of years); *pañcatvam*—when everything illusory is annihilated; *iteṣu*—all transformations; *kṛtsnaśaḥ*—with everything within this cosmic manifestation; *lokeṣu*—all the planets, or everything that exists; *pāleṣu*—maintainers like Lord Brahmā; *ca*—also; *sarva-hetuṣu*—all causative existences; *tamaḥ*—great darkness; *tadā*—then; *āsīt*—was; *gahanam*—very dense; *gabhīram*—very deep; *yaḥ*—the Supreme Personality of Godhead who; *tasya*—this dark situation; *pāre*—over and above; *abhivirājate*—exists or shines; *vibhuḥ*—the Supreme.

TRANSLATION

In due course of time, when all the causative and effective manifestations of the universe, including the planets and their directors and maintainers, are annihilated, there is a situation of dense darkness. Above this darkness, however, is the Supreme Personality of Godhead. I take shelter of His lotus feet.

PURPORT

From the Vedic *mantras* we understand that the Supreme Personality of Godhead is above everything. He is supreme, above all the demigods, including Lord Brahmā and Lord Śiva. He is the supreme controller. When everything disappears by the influence of His energy, the cosmic situation is one of dense darkness. The Supreme Lord, however, is the sunshine, as confirmed in the Vedic *mantras: āditya-varṇaṁ tamasaḥ parastāt.* In our daily experience, when we on earth are in the darkness of night, the sun is always luminous somewhere in the sky. Similarly, the Supreme Personality of Godhead, the supreme sun, always remains luminous, even when the entire cosmic manifestation is annihilated in due course of time.

TEXT 6

न यस्य देवा ऋषयः पदं विदु-
र्जन्तुः पुनः कोऽर्हति गन्तुमीरितुम् ।

यथा नटस्याकृतिभिर्विचेष्टतो
दुरत्ययानुक्रमणः स मावतु ॥ ६ ॥

na yasya devā ṛṣayaḥ padaṁ vidur
jantuḥ punaḥ ko 'rhati gantum īritum
yathā naṭasyākṛtibhir viceṣṭato
duratyayānukramaṇaḥ sa māvatu

na—neither; *yasya*—He of whom; *devāḥ*—the demigods; *ṛṣayaḥ*—great sages; *padam*—position; *viduḥ*—can understand; *jantuḥ*—unintelligent living beings like animals; *punaḥ*—again; *kaḥ*—who; *arhati*—is able; *gantum*—to enter into the knowledge; *īritum*—or to express by words; *yathā*—as; *naṭasya*—of the artist; *ākṛtibhiḥ*—by bodily features; *viceṣṭataḥ*—dancing in different ways; *duratyaya*—very difficult; *anukramaṇaḥ*—His movements; *saḥ*—that Supreme Personality of Godhead; *mā*—unto me; *avatu*—may give His protection.

TRANSLATION

An artist onstage, being covered by attractive dresses and dancing with different movements, is not understood by his audience; similarly, the activities and features of the supreme artist cannot be understood even by the demigods or great sages, and certainly not by those who are unintelligent like animals. Neither the demigods and sages nor the unintelligent can understand the features of the Lord, nor can they express in words His actual position. May that Supreme Personality of Godhead give me protection.

PURPORT

A similar understanding was expressed by Kuntīdevī. The Supreme Lord exists everywhere, within and without. He even exists within the heart. *Sarvasya cāhaṁ hṛdi sanniviṣṭo* . *Īśvaraḥ sarva-bhūtānāṁ hṛd-deśe 'rjuna tiṣṭhati* . Thus it is indicated that one can find the Supreme Lord within one's heart. There are many, many *yogīs* trying to find Him. *Dhyānāvasthita-tad-gatena manasā paśyanti yaṁ yoginaḥ* . Nonetheless, even great *yogīs,* demigods, saints and sages have been unable to understand the bodily features of that great artist, nor could they understand the meaning of His movements. What then is to be said of ordinary speculators like the so-called philosophers of this material world? For them He is impossible to understand.

Therefore we must accept the statements given by the Supreme when He kindly incarnates to instruct us. We must simply accept the word of Lord Rāmacandra, Lord Kṛṣṇa and Lord Śrī Caitanya Mahāprabhu and follow in Their footsteps. Then it may be possible for us to know the purpose of Their incarnations.

janma karma ca me divyam
evaṁ yo vetti tattvataḥ
tyaktvā dehaṁ punar janma
naiti mām eti so 'rjuna

(Bg. 4.9)

If by the Lord's grace one can understand Him, one will immediately be delivered, even within his material body. The material body will no longer have any function, and whatever activities take place with the body will be activities of Kṛṣṇa consciousness. In this way one may give up his body and return home, back to Godhead.

TEXT 7

दिदृक्षवो यस्य पदं सुमङ्गलं
विमुक्तसङ्गा मुनयः सुसाधवः ।
चरन्त्यलोकव्रतमव्रणं वने
भूतात्मभूताः सुहृदः स मे गतिः ॥ ७ ॥

didṛkṣavo yasya padaṁ sumaṅgalaṁ
vimukta-saṅgā munayaḥ susādhavaḥ
caranty aloka-vratam avraṇaṁ vane
bhūtātma-bhūtāḥ suhṛdaḥ sa me gatiḥ

didṛkṣavaḥ—those who desire to see (the Supreme Personality of Godhead); *yasya*—of Him; *padam*—the lotus feet; *su-maṅgalam*—all-auspicious; *vimukta-saṅgāḥ*—persons who are completely disinfected of material conditions; *munayaḥ*—great sages; *su-sādhavaḥ*—those who are highly elevated in spiritual consciousness; *caranti*—practice; *aloka-vratam*—vows of *brahmacarya, vānaprastha* or *sannyāsa; avraṇam*—without any fault; *vane*—in the forest; *bhūta-ātma-bhūtāḥ*—those who are equal to all living entities; *suhṛdaḥ*—those who are friends to everyone; *saḥ*—that same Supreme Personality of Godhead; *me*—my; *gatiḥ*—destination.

TRANSLATION

Renunciants and great sages who see all living beings equally, who are friendly to everyone and who flawlessly practice in the forest the vows of brahmacarya, vānaprastha and sannyāsa desire to see the all-auspicious lotus feet of the Supreme Personality of Godhead. May that same Supreme Personality of Godhead be my destination.

PURPORT

This verse describes the qualifications for devotees or persons highly elevated in spiritual consciousness. Devotees are always equal to everyone, seeing no distinction between lower and higher classes. *Paṇḍitāḥ sama-darśinaḥ* . They look upon everyone as a spirit soul who is part and parcel of the Supreme Lord. Thus they are competent to search for the Supreme Personality of Godhead. Understanding that the Supreme Personality of Godhead is the friend of everyone (*suhṛdaṁ sarva-bhūtānām*), they act as friends of everyone on behalf of the Supreme Lord. Making no distinction between one nation and another or one community and another, they preach Kṛṣṇa consciousness, the teachings of *Bhagavad-gītā,* everywhere. Thus they are competent to see the lotus feet of the Lord. Such preachers in Kṛṣṇa consciousness are called *paramahaṁsas.* As indicated by the word *vimukta-saṅga,* they have nothing to do with material conditions. One must take shelter of such a devotee in order to see the Supreme Personality of Godhead.

TEXTS 8-9

न विद्यते यस्य च जन्म कर्म वा
न नामरूपे गुणदोष एव वा ।
तथापि लोकाप्ययसंभवाय यः
स्वमायया तान्यनुकालमृच्छति ॥ ८ ॥
तस्मै नमः परेशाय ब्रह्मणेऽनन्तशक्तये ।
अरूपायोरुरूपाय नम आश्चर्यकर्मणे ॥ ९ ॥

na vidyate yasya ca janma karma vā
na nāma-rūpe guṇa-doṣa eva vā
tathāpi lokāpyaya-sambhavāya yaḥ
sva-māyayā tāny anukālam ṛcchati

tasmai namaḥ pareśāya
brahmaṇe 'nanta-śaktaye
arūpāyoru-rūpāya
nama āścarya-karmaṇe

na—not; *vidyate*—there is; *yasya*—of whom (the Supreme Personality of Godhead); *ca*—also; *janma*—birth; *karma*—activities; *vā*—or; *na*—nor; *nāma-rūpe*—any material name or material form; *guṇa*—qualities; *doṣaḥ*—fault; *eva*—certainly; *vā*—either; *tathāpi*—still; *loka*—of this cosmic manifestation; *apyaya*—who is the destruction; *sambhavāya*—and creation; *yaḥ*—He who; *sva-māyayā*—by His own potency; *tāni*—activities; *anukālam*—eternally; *ṛcchati*—accepts; *tasmai*—unto Him; *namaḥ*—I offer my obeisances; *para*—transcendental; *īśāya*—who is the supreme controller; *brahmaṇe*—who is the Supreme Brahman (Parabrahman); *ananta-śaktaye*—with unlimited potency; *arūpāya*—possessing no material form; *uru-rūpāya*—possessing various forms as incarnations; *namaḥ*—I offer my obeisances; *āścarya-karmaṇe*—whose activities are wonderful.

TRANSLATION

The Supreme Personality of Godhead has no material birth, activities, name, form, qualities or faults. To fulfill the purpose for which this material world is created and destroyed, He comes in the form of a human being like Lord Rāma or Lord Kṛṣṇa by His original internal potency. He has immense potency, and in various forms, all free from material contamination, He acts wonderfully. He is therefore the Supreme Brahman. I offer my respects to Him.

PURPORT

In the *Viṣṇu Purāṇa* it is said, *guṇāṁś ca doṣāṁś ca mune vyatīta samasta-kalyāṇa-guṇātmako hi.* The Supreme Personality of Godhead has no material form, qualities or faults. He is spiritual and is the only reservoir of all spiritual qualities. As stated in *Bhagavad-gītā* (4.8) by the Supreme Personality of Godhead, *paritrāṇāya sādhūnāṁ vināśāya ca duṣkṛtām.* The Lord's activities of saving the devotees and annihilating the demons are transcendental. Anyone annihilated by the Supreme Personality of Godhead gets the same result as a devotee who is protected by the Lord; both of them are transcendentally promoted. The only difference is that a devotee goes directly to the spiritual planets and becomes an associate of the Supreme Lord, whereas demons are promoted to *brahmaloka,* the impersonal effulgence of the Lord. Both of them, however, are transcendentally promoted. The Lord's killing or annihilating of the demons is not exactly like the killing of this material world. Although He appears to act within the modes of material nature, He is *nirguṇa,* above the modes of nature. His name is not material; otherwise how could one get liberation by chanting Hare Kṛṣṇa, Hare Rāma? The names of the Lord like Rāma and Kṛṣṇa are nondifferent from the person Rāma and Kṛṣṇa. Thus by chanting the Hare Kṛṣṇa *mantra* one constantly associates with Rāma and Kṛṣṇa, the Supreme Personality of Godhead, and therefore becomes liberated. A practical example is Ajāmila, who always remained transcendental to his activities simply by chanting the name Nārāyaṇa. If this was true of Ajāmila, what is to be said of the Supreme Lord? When the Lord comes to this material world, He does not become a product of matter. This is confirmed throughout *Bhagavad-gītā* (*janma-karma ca me divyam, avajānanti māṁ mūḍhāḥ mānuṣīṁ tanum āśritam*). Therefore, when the Supreme Personality of Godhead—Rāma or Kṛṣṇa—descends to act transcendentally for our benefit, we should not consider Him an ordinary human being. When the Lord comes, He does so on the basis of His spiritual potency (*sambhavāmy ātma-māyayā*). Because He is not forced to come by the material energy, He is always transcendental. One should not consider the Supreme Lord an ordinary human being. Material names and forms are contaminated, but spiritual name and spiritual form are transcendental.

TEXT 10

नम आत्मप्रदीपाय साक्षिणे परमात्मने ।
नमो गिरां विदूराय मनसश्चेतसामपि ॥ १० ॥

nama ātma-pradīpāya
sākṣiṇe paramātmane
namo girāṁ vidūrāya
manasaś cetasām api

namaḥ—I offer my respectful obeisances; *ātma-pradīpāya*—unto He who is self-effulgent or who gives enlightenment to the living entities; *sākṣiṇe*—who is situated in everyone's heart as a witness; *parama-ātmane*—unto the Supreme Soul, the Supersoul; *namaḥ*—I offer my respectful obeisances; *girām*—by words; *vidūrāya*—who is impossible to reach; *manasaḥ*—by the mind; *cetasām*—or by consciousness; *api*—even.

TRANSLATION

I offer my respectful obeisances unto the Supreme Personality of Godhead, the self-effulgent Supersoul, who is the witness in everyone's heart, who enlightens the individual soul and who cannot be reached by exercises of the mind, words or consciousness.

PURPORT

The Supreme Personality of Godhead, Kṛṣṇa, cannot be understood by the individual soul through mental, physical or intellectual exercises. It is by the grace of the Supreme Personality of Godhead that the individual soul is enlightened. Therefore, the Lord is described here as *ātma-pradīpa.* The Lord is like the sun, which illuminates everything and cannot be illuminated by anyone. Therefore, if one is serious about understanding the Supreme, one must receive enlightenment from Him, as instructed in *Bhagavad-gītā.* One cannot understand the Supreme Personality of Godhead by one's mental, physical or intellectual powers.

TEXT 11

सत्त्वेन प्रतिलभ्याय नैष्कर्म्येण विपश्चिता ।
नमः कैवल्यनाथाय निर्वाणसुखसंविदे ॥ ११ ॥

sattvena pratilabhyāya
naiṣkarmyeṇa vipaścitā
namaḥ kaivalya-nāthāya
nirvāṇa-sukha-saṁvide

sattvena—by pure devotional service; *prati-labhyāya*—unto the Supreme Personality of Godhead, who is achieved by such devotional activities; *naiṣkarmyeṇa*—by transcendental activities; *vipaścitā*—by persons who are sufficiently learned; *namaḥ*—I offer my respectful obeisances; *kaivalya-nāthāya*—unto the master of the transcendental world; *nirvāṇa*—for one completely freed from material activities; *sukha*—of happiness; *saṁvide*—who is the bestower.

TRANSLATION

The Supreme Personality of Godhead is realized by pure devotees who act in the transcendental existence of bhakti-yoga. He is the bestower of

uncontaminated happiness and is the master of the transcendental world. Therefore I offer my respect unto Him.

PURPORT

As stated in *Bhagavad-gītā,* the Supreme Personality of Godhead can be understood only by devotional service. *Bhaktyā mām abhijānāti yāvān yaś cāsmi tattvataḥ*. If one wants to know the Supreme Personality of Godhead in truth, one must take to the activities of devotional service. These activities are called *sattva* or *śuddha-sattva.* In the material world, activities of goodness, which are symptomatic of a pure *brāhmaṇa,* are appreciated. But the activities of devotional service are *śuddha-sattva;* in other words, they are on the transcendental platform. Only by devotional service can one understand the Supreme.

Devotional service is called *naiṣkarmya.* Mere negation of material activity will not endure. *Naiṣkarmyam apy acyuta-bhāva-varjitam.* Unless one performs activities with reference to Kṛṣṇa consciousness, cessation of material activities will not be helpful. In hopes of achieving *naiṣkarmya,* freedom from material action, many highly elevated *sannyāsīs* stopped their activities, yet they failed and returned to the material platform to act as materialistic persons. But once one is engaged in the spiritual activities of *bhakti-yoga,* one does not fall down. Our Kṛṣṇa consciousness movement is therefore an attempt to engage everyone always in spiritual activity, by which one becomes transcendental to material actions. The spiritual activities of *bhakti-mārga—śravaṇaṁ kīrtanaṁ viṣṇoḥ smaraṇaṁ pāda-sevanam* —lead one to understand the Supreme Personality of Godhead. Therefore, as stated here, *sattvena pratilabhyāya naiṣkarmyeṇa vipaścitā:* "The Supreme Personality of Godhead is realized by pure devotees who act in the transcendental existence of *bhakti-yoga.*"

The *Gopāla-tāpanī Upaniṣad* (15) says, *bhaktir asya bhajanaṁ tad ihāmutropādhi-nairāsyenaivāmuṣmin manasaḥ kalpanam etad eva ca naiṣkarmyam.* This is a definition of *naiṣkarmya.* One acts in *naiṣkarmya* when he fully engages in Kṛṣṇa conscious activities without material desires to enjoy, either here or in the upper planetary systems, in the present life or in a future life (*iha-amutra*). *Anyābhilāṣitā-śūnyam.* When one is freed from all contamination and he acts in devotional service under the direction of the spiritual master, one is on the platform of *naiṣkarma.* By such transcendental devotional service, the Lord is served. I offer my respectful obeisances unto Him.

TEXT 12

नमः शान्ताय घोराय मूढाय गुणधर्मिणे ।
निर्विशेषाय साम्याय नमो ज्ञानघनाय च ॥ १२ ॥

namaḥ śāntāya ghorāya
mūḍhāya guṇa-dharmiṇe
nirviśeṣāya sāmyāya
namo jñāna-ghanāya ca

namaḥ—all obeisances; *śāntāya*—unto He who is above all material qualities and completely peaceful, or unto Vāsudeva, the Supersoul in every living entity; *ghorāya*—unto the fierce forms of the Lord like Jāmadagnya and Nṛsiṁhadeva; *mūḍhāya*—the form of the Lord as an animal, such as the boar; *guṇa-dharmiṇe*—who accepts different qualities within the material world; *nirviśeṣāya*—who is without material qualities, being fully spiritual; *sāmyāya*—Lord Buddha, the form of *nirvāṇa,* wherein the material qualities stop; *namaḥ*—I offer my respectful obeisances; *jñāna-ghanāya*—who is knowledge or the impersonal Brahman; *ca*—also.

TRANSLATION

I offer my respectful obeisances to Lord Vāsudeva, who is all-pervading, to the Lord's fierce form as Lord Nṛsiṁhadeva, to the Lord's form as an animal [Lord Varāhadeva], to Lord Dattātreya, who preached impersonalism, to Lord Buddha, and to all the other incarnations. I offer my respectful obeisances unto the Lord, who has no material qualities but who accepts the three qualities goodness, passion and ignorance within this material world. I also offer my respectful obeisances unto the impersonal Brahman effulgence.

PURPORT

In the previous verses it has been described that although the Supreme Personality of Godhead has no material form, He accepts innumerable forms to favor His devotees and kill the demons. As stated in *Śrīmad-Bhāgavatam,* there are so many incarnations of the Supreme Personality of Godhead that they are like the waves of a river. The waves of a river flow incessantly, and no one can count how many waves there are. Similarly, no one can calculate when and how the different incarnations of the Lord appear according to the necessities of time, place and candidates. The Lord appears perpetually. As Kṛṣṇa says in *Bhagavad-gītā* (4.7):

yadā yadā hi dharmasya
glānir bhavati bhārata
abhyutthānam adharmasya
tadātmānaṁ sṛjāmy aham

"Whenever and wherever there is a decline in religious practice, O descendant of Bharata, and a predominant rise of irreligion—at that time I descend Myself." In the material world there is always the possibility of deviation from Kṛṣṇa consciousness, and therefore Kṛṣṇa and His devotees always act in various forms to curb such godlessness.

Even impersonalists who stress the knowledge feature of the Supreme Personality of Godhead want to merge in the effulgence of the Lord. Therefore, here the word *jñāna-ghanāya* indicates that for atheists who disbelieve in the form and existence of the Lord, all these various incarnations appear. Since the Lord comes to teach in so many forms, no one can say that there is no God. The word *jñāna-ghanāya* is especially used here to refer to those whose knowledge has become solidified by dint of their searching for the Lord through speculative philosophical understanding. Superficial knowledge is useless for understanding the Supreme Personality of Godhead, but when one's knowledge becomes extremely intense and deep, one understands Vāsudeva (*vāsudevaḥ sarvam iti sa mahātmā sudurlabhaḥ*). A *jñānī* attains this stage after many, many births. Therefore the word *jñāna-ghanāya* is used here. The word *śantāya* indicates that Lord Vāsudeva is situated in everyone's heart but does not act with the living entity. Impersonalist *jñānīs* realize Vāsudeva when they are fully mature in knowledge (*vāsudevaḥ sarvam iti sa mahātmā sudurlabhaḥ*).

TEXT 13

क्षेत्रज्ञाय नमस्तुभ्यं सर्वाध्यक्षाय साक्षिणे ।
पुरुषायात्ममूलाय मूलप्रकृतये नमः ॥ १३ ॥

kṣetra-jñāya namas tubhyaṁ
sarvādhyakṣāya sākṣiṇe
puruṣāyātma-mūlāya
mūla-prakṛtaye namaḥ

kṣetra-jñāya—unto the one who knows everything of the external body; *namaḥ*—I offer my respectful obeisances; *tubhyam*—unto You; *sarva*—everything; *adhyakṣāya*—who are superintending, managing; *sākṣiṇe*—who are the witness, Paramātmā, or *antaryāmī; puruṣāya*—the Supreme Person; *ātma-mūlāya*—who are the original source of everything; *mūla-prakṛtaye*—unto the *puruṣa-avatāra,* the origin of *prakṛti* and *pradhāna; namaḥ*—I offer my respectful obeisances.

TRANSLATION

I beg to offer my respectful obeisances unto You, who are the Supersoul, the superintendent of everything, and the witness of all that occurs. You are the Supreme Person, the origin of material nature and of the total material energy. You are also the owner of the material body. Therefore, You are the supreme complete. I offer my respectful obeisances unto You.

PURPORT

In *Bhagavad-gītā* (13.3) the Lord says, *kṣetra-jñaṁ cāpi māṁ viddhi sarva-kṣetreṣu bhārata:* "O scion of Bharata, you should understand that I am also the knower in all bodies." Every one of us is thinking, "I am this body" or "This is my body," but actually the truth is different. Our bodies are given to us by the supreme proprietor. The living entity, who is also *kṣetra-jña,* or the knower of the body, is not the body's only proprietor; the actual proprietor of the body is the Supreme Personality of Godhead, who is the supreme *kṣetra-jña.* For example, we may rent and occupy a house, but actually the owner of the house is the landlord. Similarly, we may be allotted a certain type of body as a facility with which to enjoy this material world, but the actual proprietor of the body is the Supreme Personality of Godhead. He is called *sarvādhyakṣa* because everything in the material world works under His supervision. This is confirmed in *Bhagavad-gītā* (9.10), wherein the Lord says, *mayādhyakṣeṇa prakṛtiḥ sūyate sacarācaram:* "This material nature, working under My direction, O son of Kuntī, is producing all moving and unmoving beings." From *prakṛti,* or material nature, come so many varieties of living entities, including aquatics, plants, trees, insects, birds, animals, human beings and demigods. *Prakṛti* is the mother, and the Supreme Personality of Godhead is the father (*ahaṁ bīja-pradaḥ pitā*).

Prakṛti can give us material bodies, but as spirit souls we are parts and parcels of the Supreme Personality of Godhead. This is confirmed in *Bhagavad-gītā* (15.7): *mamaivāṁśo jīva-loke jīva-bhūtaḥ sanātanaḥ.* The living entity, being part and parcel of God, is not a product of this material world. Therefore the Lord is described in this verse as *ātma-mūla,* the original source of everything. He is the seed of all existences (*bījaṁ māṁ sarva-bhūtānām*). In *Bhagavad-gītā* (14.4) the Lord says:

sarva-yoniṣu kaunteya
mūrtayaḥ sambhavanti yāḥ
tāsāṁ brahma mahad yonir
ahaṁ bīja-pradaḥ pitā

"It should be understood that all living entities, in all species of life, O son of Kuntī, are made possible by birth in this material nature, and that I am the seed-giving father." Plants, trees, insects, aquatics, demigods, beasts, birds and all other living entities are sons or parts and parcels of the Supreme Lord, but because they are struggling with different mentalities, they have been given different types of bodies (*manaḥ ṣaṣṭhānīndriyāṇi prakṛti-sthāni karṣati*). Thus they have become sons of *prakṛti,* or material nature, which is impregnated by the Supreme Personality of Godhead. Every living entity in this material world is struggling for existence, and the only salvation or relief from the cycle of birth and death in the evolutionary process is full surrender. This is indicated by the word *namaḥ,* "I offer my respectful obeisances unto You."

TEXT 14

सर्वेन्द्रियगुणद्रष्ट्रे सर्वप्रत्ययहेतवे ।
असताच्छाययोक्ताय सदाभासाय ते नमः ॥ १४ ॥

sarvendriya-guṇa-draṣṭre
sarva-pratyaya-hetave
asatā cchāyayoktāya
sad-abhasāya te namaḥ

sarva-indriya-guṇa-draṣṭre—unto the seer of all objectives pursued by the senses; *sarva-pratyaya-hetave*—who is the solution to all doubts (and without whose help one cannot solve all doubts and inabilities); *asatā*—with the manifestation of unreality or illusion; *chāyayā*—because of the resemblance; *uktāya*—called; *sat*—of reality; *ābhāsāya*—unto the reflection; *te*—unto You; *namaḥ*—I offer my respectful obeisances.

TRANSLATION

My Lord, You are the observer of all the objectives of the senses. Without Your mercy, there is no possibility of solving the problem of doubts. The material world is just like a shadow resembling You. Indeed, one accepts this material world as real because it gives a glimpse of Your existence.

PURPORT

To paraphrase this verse: "The objectives of sensual activities are actually observed by You. Without Your direction, the living entity cannot take even a step forward. As confirmed in *Bhagavad-gītā* (15.15), *sarvasya cāhaṁ hṛdi sanniviṣṭo mattaḥ smṛtir jñānam apohanaṁ ca.* You are situated in everyone's heart, and only from You come remembrance and forgetfulness. *Chāyeva yasya bhuvanāni bibharti durgā .* The living entity under the clutches of *māyā* wants to enjoy this material world, but unless You give him directions and remind him, he cannot make progress in pursuing his shadowy objective in life. The conditioned soul wrongly progresses toward the wrong objective, life after life, and he is reminded of that objective by You. In one life the conditioned soul desires to progress toward a certain objective, but after his body changes, he forgets everything. Nonetheless, my Lord, because he wanted to enjoy something of this world, You remind him of this in his next birth. *Mattaḥ smṛtir jñānam apohanaṁ ca .* Because the conditioned soul wants to forget You, by Your grace You give him opportunities, life after life, by which he can almost perpetually forget You. Therefore You are eternally the director of the conditioned souls. It is because You are the original cause of everything that everything appears real. The ultimate reality is Your Lordship, the Supreme Personality of Godhead. I offer my respectful obeisances unto You."

The word *sarva-pratyaya-hetave* is explained by Śrīla Viśvanātha Cakravartī Ṭhākura, who says that a result gives one a glimpse of its cause. For example, since an earthen pot is the result of the actions of a potter, by seeing the earthen pot one can guess at the existence of the potter. Similarly, this material world resembles the spiritual world, and any intelligent person can guess how it is acting. As explained in *Bhagavad-gītā, mayādhyakṣeṇa prakṛtiḥ sūyate sa-carācaram .* The activities of the material world suggest that behind them is the superintendence of the Lord.

TEXT 15

नमो नमस्तेऽखिलकारणाय
निष्कारणायाद्भुतकारणाय ।
सर्वागमाम्नायमहार्णवाय
नमोऽपवर्गाय परायणाय ॥ १५ ॥

namo namas te 'khila-kāraṇāya
niṣkāraṇāyādbhuta-kāraṇāya
sarvāgamāmnāya-mahārṇavāya
namo 'pavargāya parāyaṇāya

namaḥ—I offer my respectful obeisances; *namaḥ*—again I offer my respectful obeisances; *te*—unto You; *akhila-kāraṇāya*—unto the supreme cause of everything; *niṣkāraṇāya*—unto You who are causeless; *adbhuta-kāraṇāya*—the wonderful cause of everything; *sarva*—all; *āgama-āmnāya*—unto the source of the *paramparā* system of all Vedic knowledge; *mahā-arṇavāya*—the great ocean of knowledge, or the great ocean wherein all the rivers of knowledge merge; *namaḥ*—I offer my obeisances; *apavargāya*—unto You who can give deliverance or liberation; *para-ayaṇāya*—the shelter of all transcendentalists.

TRANSLATION

My Lord, You are the cause of all causes, but You Yourself have no cause. Therefore You are the wonderful cause of everything. I offer my respectful obeisances unto You, who are the shelter of the Vedic knowledge contained in the śāstras like the Pañcarātras and Vedānta-sūtra, which are Your representations, and who are the source of the paramparā system. Because it is You who can give liberation, You are the only shelter for all transcendentalists. Let me offer my respectful obeisances unto You.

PURPORT

The Supreme Personality of Godhead is described herein as the wonderful cause. He is wonderful in the sense that although there may be unlimited emanations from the Supreme Personality of Godhead (*janmādy asya yataḥ*), He always remains complete (*pūrṇasya pūrṇam ādāya pūrṇam evāvaśiṣyate*). In our experience in the material world, if we have a bank balance of one million dollars, as we withdraw money from the bank the balance gradually diminishes until it becomes nil. However, the Supreme Lord, the Personality of Godhead, is so complete that although innumerable Personalities of Godhead expand from Him, He remains the same Supreme Personality of Godhead. *Pūrṇasya pūrṇam ādāya pūrṇam evāvaśiṣyate.* Therefore He is the wonderful cause. *Govindam ādi-puruṣaṁ tam ahaṁ bhajāmi*.

īśvaraḥ paramaḥ kṛṣṇaḥ
sac-cid-ānanda-vigrahaḥ
anādir ādir govindaḥ
sarva-kāraṇa-kāraṇam

"Kṛṣṇa, who is known as Govinda, is the supreme controller. He has an eternal, blissful, spiritual body. He is the origin of all. He has no other origin, for He is the prime cause of all causes." (*Brahma-saṁhitā.* 5.1)

Even in this material world, we can understand that the sun has existed for millions of years and has given off heat and light since its creation, yet the sun still retains its power and never changes. What then is to be said of the supreme cause, *paraṁ brahma,* Kṛṣṇa? Everything emanates from Him perpetually, yet He maintains His original form (*sac-cid-ānanda-vigrahaḥ*). Kṛṣṇa personally says in *Bhagavad-gītā* (10.8), *mattaḥ sarvaṁ pravartate:* "Everything emanates from Me." Everything emanates from Kṛṣṇa eternally, yet He is the same Kṛṣṇa and does not change. Therefore He is the shelter of all transcendentalists who are eager to get free from material bondage.

Everyone must take shelter of Kṛṣṇa. It is therefore advised:

akāmaḥ sarva-kāmo vā
mokṣa-kāma udāra-dhīḥ
tīvreṇa bhakti-yogena
yajeta puruṣaṁ param

"Whether one desires everything or nothing or desires to merge into the existence of the Lord, he is intelligent only if he worships Lord Kṛṣṇa, the Supreme Personality of Godhead, by rendering transcendental loving service." (*Bhāg.* 2.3.10) *Paraṁ brahma,* the Supreme Lord, and *paraṁ dhāma,* the supreme repose, is Kṛṣṇa. Therefore anyone who desires anything—whether he be a *karmī,* a *jñānī* or a *yogī*—should try to perceive the Supreme Personality of Godhead very seriously, and all of his desires will be fulfilled. The Lord says, *ye yathā māṁ prapadyante tāṁs tathaiva bhajāmy aham:* "As the living entities surrender unto Me, I reward them accordingly." Even the *karmī* who wants everything for his enjoyment can get it from Kṛṣṇa. For Kṛṣṇa, supplying what he wants is not at all difficult. Actually, however, one should worship Kṛṣṇa, the Supreme Personality of Godhead, for the sake of getting liberation.

Vedaiś ca sarvair aham eva vedyaḥ . By studying the Vedic literature, one should understand Kṛṣṇa. As confirmed here, *sarvāgamāmnāya-mahārṇavāya.* He is the ocean, and all Vedic knowledge flows toward Him. Therefore, intelligent transcendentalists take shelter of the Supreme Personality of Godhead (*sarva-dharmān parityajya mām ekaṁ śaraṇaṁ vraja*). This is the ultimate goal.

TEXT 16

गुणारणिच्छन्नचिदुष्मपाय
तत्क्षोभविस्फूर्जितमानसाय ।
नैष्कर्म्यभावेन विवर्जितागम-
स्वयंप्रकाशाय नमस्करोमि ॥ १६ ॥

guṇāraṇi-cchanna-cid-uṣmapāya
tat-kṣobha-visphūrjita-mānasāya
naiṣkarmya-bhāvena vivarjitāgama-
svayaṁ-prakāśāya namas karomi

guṇa—by the three *guṇas,* the modes of material nature (*sattva, rajas* and *tamas*); *araṇi*—by *araṇi* wood; *channa*—covered; *cit*—of knowledge; *uṣmapāya*—unto He whose fire; *tat-kṣobha*—of the agitation of the modes of material nature; *visphūrjita*—outside; *mānasāya*—unto He whose mind; *naiṣkarmya-bhāvena*—because of the stage of spiritual understanding; *vivarjita*—in those who give up; *āgama*—Vedic principles; *svayam*—personally; *prakāśāya*—unto He who is manifest; *namaḥ karomi*—I offer my respectful obeisances.

TRANSLATION

My Lord, as the fire in araṇi wood is covered, You and Your unlimited knowledge are covered by the material modes of nature. Your mind, however, is not attentive to the activities of the modes of nature. Those who are advanced in spiritual knowledge are not subject to the regulative prin-

ciples directed in the Vedic literatures. Because such advanced souls are transcendental, You personally appear in their pure minds. Therefore I offer my respectful obeisances unto You.

PURPORT

In *Bhagavad-gītā* (10.11) it is said:

teṣām evānukampārtham
aham ajñāna-jaṁ tamaḥ
nāśayāmy ātma-bhāva-stho
jñāna-dīpena bhāsvatā

For a devotee who has taken the lotus feet of the Lord within his heart, the Lord gives spiritual enlightenment, known as *jñāna-dīpa,* by special mercy from within. This *jñāna-dīpa* is compared to the fire hidden within *araṇi* wood. To perform fire sacrifices, great sages previously did not ignite a fire directly; the fire would be invoked from *araṇi* wood. Similarly, all living entities are covered by the modes of material nature, and the fire of knowledge can be ignited only by the Supreme Personality of Godhead when one takes Him within one's heart. *Sa vai manaḥ kṛṣṇa-padāravindayoḥ*. If one takes seriously the lotus feet of Kṛṣṇa, who is seated within one's heart, the Lord eradicates all ignorance. By the torch of knowledge, one immediately understands everything properly by the special mercy of the Supreme Lord and becomes self-realized. In other words, although a devotee may externally not be very well educated, because of his devotional service the Supreme Personality of Godhead gives him enlightenment from within. If the Lord gives enlightenment from within, how can one be in ignorance? Therefore the allegation of the Māyāvādīs that the devotional path is for the unintelligent or uneducated is untrue.

yasyāsti bhaktir bhagavaty akiñcanā
sarvair guṇais tatra samāsate surāḥ
[Bhāg. 5.18.12]

If one becomes an unalloyed devotee of the Supreme Lord, he automatically manifests all good qualities. Such a devotee is above the instructions of the *Vedas.* He is a *paramahaṁsa.* Even without going through the Vedic literature, a devotee becomes pure and enlightened by the mercy of the Lord. "Therefore, my Lord," the devotee says, "I offer my respectful obeisances unto You."

TEXT 17

माद‍ृक्प्रपन्नपशुपाशविमोक्षणाय
मुक्ताय भूरिकरुणाय नमोऽलयाय ।
स्वांशेन सर्वतनुभृन्मनसि प्रतीत-
प्रत्यग्द‍ृशे भगवते बृहते नमस्ते ॥ १७ ॥

mādṛk prapanna-paśu-pāśa-vimokṣaṇāya
muktāya bhūri-karuṇāya namo 'layāya
svāṁśena sarva-tanu-bhṛn-manasi pratīta-
pratyag-dṛśe bhagavate bṛhate namas te

mādṛk—like me; *prapanna*—surrendered; *paśu*—an animal; *pāśa*—from entanglement; *vimokṣaṇāya*—unto He who releases; *muktāya*—unto the Supreme, who is untouched by the contamination of material nature; *bhūri-karuṇāya*—who are unlimitedly merciful; *namaḥ*—I offer my respectful obeisances; *alayāya*—who are never inattentive or idle (for the purpose of my deliverance); *sva-aṁśena*—by Your partial feature as Paramātmā; *sarva*—of all; *tanu-bhṛt*—the living entities embodied in material nature; *manasi*—in the mind; *pratīta*—who are acknowledged; *pratyak-dṛśe*—as the direct observer (of all activities); *bhagavate*—unto the Supreme Personality of Godhead; *bṛhate*—who are unlimited; *namaḥ*—I offer my respectful obeisances; *te*—unto You.

TRANSLATION

Since an animal such as I has surrendered unto You, who are supremely liberated, certainly You will release me from this dangerous position. Indeed, being extremely merciful, You incessantly try to deliver me. By your partial feature as Paramātmā, You are situated in the hearts of all embodied beings. You are celebrated as direct transcendental knowledge, and You are unlimited. I offer my respectful obeisances unto You, the Supreme Personality of Godhead.

PURPORT

The words *bṛhate namas te* have been explained by Śrīla Viśvanātha Cakravartī Ṭhākura: *bṛhate śrī-kṛṣṇāya.* The Supreme Personality of Godhead is Kṛṣṇa. There are many *tattvas,* such as *viṣṇu-tattva, jīva-tattva* and *śakti-tattva,* but above everything is the *viṣṇu-tattva,* which is all-pervading. This all-pervading feature of the Supreme Personality of Godhead is explained in *Bhagavad-gītā* (10.42), wherein the Lord says:

athavā bahunaitena
kiṁ jñātena tavārjuna
viṣṭabhyāham idaṁ kṛtsnam
ekāṁśena sthito jagat

"But what need is there, Arjuna, for all this detailed knowledge? With a single fragment of Myself I pervade and support this entire universe." Thus Kṛṣṇa says that the entire material world is maintained by His partial representation as Paramātmā. The Lord enters every universe as Garbhodakaśāyī Viṣṇu and then expands Himself as Kṣīrodakaśāyī Viṣṇu to enter the hearts of all living entities and even enter the atoms. *Aṇḍāntara-stha-paramāṇu-cayāntara-stham* . Every universe is full of atoms, and the Lord is not only within the universe but also within the atoms. Thus within every atom the Supreme Lord exists in His Viṣṇu feature as Paramātmā, but all the *viṣṇu-tattvas* emanate from Kṛṣṇa. As confirmed in *Bhagavad-gītā* (10.2), *aham ādir hi devānām:* Kṛṣṇa is the *ādi,* or beginning, of the *devas* of this material world—Brahmā, Viṣṇu and Maheśvara. Therefore He is described here as *bhagavate bṛhate.* Everyone is *bhagavān*—everyone possesses opulence—but Kṛṣṇa is *bṛhān bhagavān,* the possessor of unlimited opulence. *Īśvaraḥ paramaḥ kṛṣṇaḥ* . Kṛṣṇa is the origin of everyone. *Ahaṁ sarvasya prabhavaḥ* . Even Brahmā, Viṣṇu and Maheśvara come from Kṛṣṇa. *Mattaḥ parataraṁ nānyat kiñcid asti dhanañjaya:* there is no personality superior to Kṛṣṇa. Therefore Viśvanātha Cakravartī Ṭhākura says that *bhagavate bṛhate* means "unto Śrī Kṛṣṇa."

In this material world, everyone is a *paśu,* an animal, because of the bodily conception of life.

yasyātma-buddhiḥ kuṇape tri-dhātuke
sva-dhīḥ kalatrādiṣu bhauma ijya-dhīḥ
yat tīrtha-buddhiḥ salile na karhicij
janeṣv abhijñeṣu sa eva go-kharaḥ

"A human being who identifies the body made of three elements as the self, who considers the by-products of the body to be his kinsmen, who considers the land of his birth to be worshipable, and who goes to a place of pilgrimage simply to bathe rather than to meet men of transcendental knowledge there is to be considered like a cow or an ass." (*Bhāg.* 10.84.13) Practically everyone, therefore, is a *paśu,* an animal, and everyone is attacked by the crocodile of material existence. Not only the King of the elephants but every one of us is being attacked by the crocodile and is suffering the consequences.

Only Kṛṣṇa can deliver us from this material existence. Indeed, He is always trying to deliver us. *Īśvaraḥ sarva-bhūtānāṁ hṛd-deśe 'rjuna tiṣṭhati* . He is within our hearts and is not at all inattentive. His only aim is to deliver us from material life. It is not that He becomes attentive to us only when we offer prayers to Him. Even before we offer our prayers, He incessantly tries to deliver us. He is never lazy in regard to our deliverance. Therefore this verse says, *bhūri-karuṇāya namo 'layāya.* It is the causeless mercy of the Supreme Lord that He always tries to bring us back home, back to Godhead. God is liberated, and He tries to make us liberated, but although He is constantly trying, we refuse to accept His instructions (*sarva-dharmān parityajya mām ekaṁ śaraṇaṁ vraja*). Nonetheless, He has not become angry. Therefore He is described here as *bhūri-karuṇāya,* unlimitedly merciful in delivering us from this miserable material condition of life and taking us back home, back to Godhead.

TEXT 18

आत्मात्मजाप्तगृहवित्तजनेषु सक्तै-
दुष्प्रापणाय गुणसङ्गविवर्जिताय ।
मुक्तात्मभिः स्वहृदये परिभाविताय
ज्ञानात्मने भगवते नम ईश्वराय ॥ १८ ॥

ātmātma-jāpta-gṛha-vitta-janeṣu saktair
duṣprāpaṇāya guṇa-saṅga-vivarjitāya
muktātmabhiḥ sva-hṛdaye paribhāvitāya
jñānātmane bhagavate nama īśvarāya

ātma—the mind and body; *ātma-ja*—sons and daughters; *āpta*—friends and relatives; *gṛha*—home, community, society and nation; *vitta*—wealth; *janeṣu*—to various servants and assistants; *saktaiḥ*—by those who are too attached; *duṣprāpaṇāya*—unto You, who are very difficult to achieve; *guṇa-saṅga*—by the three modes of material nature; *vivarjitāya*—who are not contaminated; *mukta-ātmabhiḥ*—by persons who are already liberated; *sva-hṛdaye*—within the core of the heart; *paribhāvitāya*—unto You, who are always meditated upon; *jñāna-ātmane*—the reservoir of all enlightenment; *bhagavate*—unto the Supreme Personality of Godhead; *namaḥ*—I offer my respectful obeisances; *īśvarāya*—unto the supreme controller.

TRANSLATION

My Lord, those who are completely freed from material contamination always meditate upon You within the cores of their hearts. You are extremely difficult to attain for those like me who are too attached to mental concoction, home, relatives, friends, money, servants and assistants. You are the Supreme Personality of Godhead, uncontaminated by the modes of nature. You are the reservoir of all enlightenment, the supreme controller. I therefore offer my respectful obeisances unto You.

PURPORT

Although the Supreme Personality of Godhead comes into the material world, He is unaffected by the modes of material nature. This is confirmed in *Īśopaniṣad. Apāpa-viddham:* He is not contaminated. This same fact is described here. *Guṇa-saṅga-vivarjitāya.* Although the Supreme Personality of Godhead appears as an incarnation within this material world, He is unaffected by the modes of material nature. As stated in *Bhagavad-gītā* (9.11), *avajānanti māṁ mūḍhā mānuṣīṁ tanum āśritam:* foolish men with insufficient knowledge deride the Personality of Godhead because He appears just like a human being. Therefore the Supreme Personality of Godhead can be understood only by the *muktātmā,* the liberated soul. *Muktātmabhiḥ sva-hṛdaye paribhāvitāya:* only the liberated person can constantly think of Kṛṣṇa. Such a person is the greatest of all *yogīs.*

yoginām api sarveṣāṁ
mad-gatenāntarātmanā
śraddhāvān bhajate yo māṁ
sa me yuktatamo mataḥ

"Of all *yogīs,* he who always abides in Me with great faith, worshiping Me in transcendental loving service, is most intimately united with Me in *yoga* and is the highest of all." (Bg. 6.47)

TEXT 19

यं धर्मकामार्थविमुक्तिकामा
भजन्त इष्टां गतिमाप्नुवन्ति ।
किं चाशिषो रात्यपि देहमव्ययं
करोतु मेऽदभ्रदयो विमोक्षणम् ॥ १९ ॥

yaṁ dharma-kāmārtha-vimukti-kāmā
bhajanta iṣṭāṁ gatim āpnuvanti
kiṁ cāśiṣo rāty api deham avyayaṁ
karotu me 'dabhra-dayo vimokṣaṇam

yam—the Supreme Personality of Godhead who; *dharma-kāma-artha-vimukti-kāmāḥ*—persons who desire the four principles of religion, economic development, sense gratification and salvation; *bhajantaḥ*—by worshiping; *iṣṭām*—the objective; *gatim*—destination; *āpnuvanti*—can achieve; *kim*—what to speak of; *ca*—also; *āśiṣaḥ*—other benedictions; *rāti*—He bestows; *api*—even; *deham*—a body; *avyayam*—spiritual; *karotu*—may He bestow benediction; *me*—unto me; *adabhra-dayaḥ*—the Supreme Personality of Godhead, who is unlimitedly merciful; *vimokṣaṇam*—liberation from the present danger and from the material world.

TRANSLATION

After worshiping the Supreme Personality of Godhead, those who are interested in the four principles of religion, economic development, sense gratification and liberation obtain from Him what they desire. What then is to be said of other benedictions? Indeed, sometimes the Lord gives a spiritual body to such ambitious worshipers. May that Supreme Personality of Godhead, who is unlimitedly merciful, bestow upon me the benediction of liberation from this present danger and from the materialistic way of life.

PURPORT

Some men within this material world are *akāmī,* free from material desire, some are ambitious to get more and more material profit, and some desire fulfillment in religious life, economic development, sense gratification and finally liberation.

akāmaḥ sarva-kāmo vā
mokṣa-kāma udāra-dhīḥ
tīvreṇa bhakti-yogena
yajeta puruṣaṁ param
(Bhāg. 2.3.10)

It is recommended that whatever one's position—whether one demands no material profit, all material profit or ultimately liberation—one should offer his obedient devotional service to the Lord, and one will get what he desires. Kṛṣṇa is so kind. *Ye yathā māṁ prapadyante tāṁs tathaiva bhajāmy aham.* The Lord reciprocates. Whatever even an ordinary living entity wants, Kṛṣṇa gives. Kṛṣṇa is situated in everyone's heart, and He gives that which is desired by the living entity.

īśvaraḥ sarva-bhūtānāṁ
hṛd-deśe 'rjuna tiṣṭhati
bhrāmayan sarva-bhūtāni
yantrārūḍhāni māyayā

"The Supreme Lord is situated in everyone's heart, O Arjuna, and is directing the wanderings of all living entities, who are seated as on a machine, made of the material energy." (Bg. 18.61) The Lord gives everyone an opportunity to fulfill his ambitions. Even such a devotee as Dhruva Mahārāja wanted the material benediction of a kingdom greater than that of his father, and although he received a spiritual body, he also got the kingdom, for the Supreme Personality of Godhead does not disappoint anyone who takes shelter of His lotus feet. Therefore, since Gajendra, King of the elephants, had surrendered to the Supreme Personality of Godhead to get free from the present danger and, indirectly, from the present danger of materialistic life, why should the Supreme Personality of Godhead not fulfill his desire?

TEXTS 20-21

एकान्तिनो यस्य न कञ्चनार्थं
वाञ्छन्ति ये वै भगवत्प्रपन्नाः ।
अत्यद्भुतं तच्चरितं सुमङ्गलं
गायन्त आनन्दसमुद्रमग्नाः ॥ २० ॥
तमक्षरं ब्रह्म परं परेश-
मव्यक्तमाध्यात्मिकयोगगम्यम् ।
अतीन्द्रियं सूक्ष्ममिवातिदूर-
मनन्तमाद्यं परिपूर्णमीडे ॥ २१ ॥

ekāntino yasya na kañcanārthaṁ
vāñchanti ye vai bhagavat-prapannāḥ
aty-adbhutaṁ tac-caritaṁ sumaṅgalaṁ
gāyanta ānanda-samudra-magnāḥ

tam akṣaraṁ brahma paraṁ pareśam
avyaktam ādhyātmika-yoga-gamyam
atīndriyaṁ sūkṣmam ivātidūram
anantam ādyaṁ paripūrṇam īḍe

ekāntinaḥ—unalloyed devotees (who have no desire other than Kṛṣṇa consciousness); *yasya*—the Lord, of whom; *na*—not; *kañcana*—some; *artham*—benediction; *vāñchanti*—desire; *ye*—those devotees who; *vai*—indeed; *bhagavat-prapannāḥ*—fully surrendered unto the lotus feet of the Lord; *ati-adbhutam*—which are wonderful; *tat-caritam*—the activities of the Lord; *su-maṅgalam*—and very auspicious (to hear); *gāyantaḥ*—by chanting and hearing; *ānanda*—of transcendental bliss; *samudra*—in the ocean; *magnāḥ*—who are immersed; *tam*—unto Him; *akṣaram*—eternally existing; *brahma*—the Supreme; *param*—transcendental; *para-īśam*—the Lord of the supreme personalities; *avyaktam*—invisible or not able to be realized by the mind and senses; *ādhyātmika*—transcendental; *yoga*—by *bhakti-yoga,* devotional service; *gamyam*—obtainable (*bhaktyā mām abhijānāti*); *ati-indriyam*—beyond the perception of material senses; *sūkṣmam*—minute; *iva*—like; *ati-dūram*—very far away; *anantam*—unlimited; *ādyam*—the original cause of everything; *paripūrṇam*—completely full; *īḍe*—I offer my obeisances.

TRANSLATION

Unalloyed devotees, who have no desire other than to serve the Lord, worship Him in full surrender and always hear and chant about His activities, which are most wonderful and auspicious. Thus they always merge in an ocean of transcendental bliss. Such devotees never ask the Lord for any benediction. I, however, am in danger. Thus I pray to that Supreme Personality of Godhead, who is eternally existing, who is invisible, who is the Lord of all great personalities, such as Brahmā, and who is available only by transcendental bhakti-yoga. Being extremely subtle, He is beyond the reach of my senses and transcendental to all external realization. He is unlimited, He is the original cause, and He is completely full in everything. I offer my obeisances unto Him.

PURPORT

anyābhilāṣitā-śūnyaṁ
jñāna-karmādy-anāvṛtam

ānukūlyena kṛṣṇānu-
śīlanaṁ bhaktir uttamā

(*Bhakti-rasāmṛta-sindhu 1.1.11*)

"One should render transcendental loving service to the Supreme Lord Kṛṣṇa favorably and without desire for material profit or gain through fruitive activities or philosophical speculation. That is called pure devotional service." Unalloyed devotees have nothing to ask from the Supreme Personality of Godhead, but Gajendra, the King of the elephants, was circumstantially asking for an immediate benediction because he had no other way to be rescued. Sometimes, when there is no alternative, a pure devotee, being fully dependent on the mercy of the Supreme Lord, prays for some benediction. But in such a prayer there is also regret. One who always hears and chants about the transcendental pastimes of the Lord is always situated on a platform on which he has nothing to ask in terms of material benefits. Unless one is a completely pure devotee, one cannot enjoy the transcendental bliss derived from chanting and dancing in the ecstasy of the *saṅkīrtana* movement. Such ecstasy is not possible for an ordinary devotee. Lord Śrī Caitanya Mahāprabhu showed us how one can enjoy transcendental bliss simply by chanting, hearing and dancing in ecstasy. This is *bhakti-yoga.* Therefore the King of the elephants, Gajendra, said, *ādhyātmika-yoga-gamyam,* indicating that unless one is situated on this transcendental platform, one cannot approach the Supreme Lord. The benediction of being able to approach the Lord can be achieved after many, many births, yet Śrī Caitanya Mahāprabhu has awarded this benediction to everyone, even to the fallen souls who have no heritage of anything in spiritual life. That is actually being seen in the Kṛṣṇa consciousness movement. Therefore the path of *bhakti-yoga* is the spotless process by which to approach the Supreme Personality of Godhead. *Bhaktyāham ekayā grāhyaḥ:* only through devotional service can one approach the Supreme Lord. The Lord says in *Bhagavad-gītā* (7.1):

mayy āsakta-manāḥ pārtha
yogaṁ yuñjan mad-āśrayaḥ
asaṁśayaṁ samagraṁ māṁ
yathā jñāsyasi tac chṛṇu

"Now hear, O son of Pṛthā [Arjuna], how by practicing *yoga* in full consciousness of Me, with mind attached to Me, you can know Me in full, free from doubt." Simply by being attached to Kṛṣṇa consciousness and by thinking of the lotus feet of Kṛṣṇa constantly, one can fully understand the Supreme Personality of Godhead, without a doubt.

TEXTS 22-24

यस्य ब्रह्मादयो देवा वेदा लोकाश्चराचराः ।
नामरूपविभेदेन फल्ग्व्या च कलया कृताः ॥ २२ ॥
यथार्चिषोऽग्नेः सवितुर्गभस्तयो
निर्यान्ति संयान्त्यसकृत् स्वरोचिषः ।
तथा यतोऽयं गुणसम्प्रवाहो
बुद्धिर्मनः खानि शरीरसर्गाः ॥ २३ ॥
स वै न देवासुरमर्त्यतिर्यङ्
न स्त्री न षण्ढो न पुमान् न जन्तुः ।
नायं गुणः कर्म न सन्न चासन्
निषेधशेषो जयतादशेषः ॥ २४ ॥

yasya brahmādayo devā
vedā lokāś carācarāḥ
nāma-rūpa-vibhedena
phalgvyā ca kalayā kṛtāḥ

yathārciṣo 'gneḥ savitur gabhastayo
niryānti saṁyānty asakṛt sva-rociṣaḥ
tathā yato 'yaṁ guṇa-sampravāho
buddhir manaḥ khāni śarīra-sargāḥ

sa vai na devāsura-martya-tiryaṅ
na strī na ṣaṇḍho na pumān na jantuḥ
nāyaṁ guṇaḥ karma na san na cāsan
niṣedha-śeṣo jayatād aśeṣaḥ

yasya—of the Supreme Personality of Godhead who; *brahma-ādayaḥ*—the great demigods, headed by Lord Brahmā; *devāḥ*—and other demigods; *vedāḥ*—the Vedic knowledge; *lokāḥ*—different personalities; *cara-acarāḥ*—the moving and the nonmoving (like trees and plants); *nāma-rūpa*—of different names and different forms; *vibhedena*—by such divisions; *phalgvyā*—who are less important; *ca*—also; *kalayā*—by the parts; *kṛtāḥ*—created; *yathā*—as; *arciṣaḥ*—the sparks; *agneḥ*—of fire; *savituḥ*—from the sun; *gab-*

hastayaḥ—the shining particles; *niryānti*—emanate from; *saṁyānti*—and enter into; *asakṛt*—again and again; *sva-rociṣaḥ*—as parts and parcels; *tathā*—similarly; *yataḥ*—the Personality of Godhead from whom; *ayam*—this; *guṇa-sampravāhaḥ*—continuous manifestation of the different modes of nature; *buddhiḥ manaḥ*—the intelligence and mind; *khāni*—the senses; *śarīra*—of the body (gross and subtle); *sargāḥ*—the divisions; *saḥ*—that Supreme Personality of Godhead; *vai*—indeed; *na*—is not; *deva*—demigod; *asura*—demon; *martya*—human being; *tiryak*—bird or beast; *na*—neither; *strī*—woman; *na*—nor; *ṣaṇḍhaḥ*—neuter; *na*—neither; *pumān*—man; *na*—nor; *jantuḥ*—living being or animal; *na ayam*—nor is He; *guṇaḥ*—material quality; *karma*—fruitive activity; *na*—is not; *sat*—manifestation; *na*—nor; *ca*—also; *asat*—nonmanifestation; *niṣedha*—of the discrimination of *neti neti* ("not this, not this"); *śeṣaḥ*—He is the end; *jayatāt*—all glories unto Him; *aśeṣaḥ*—who is unlimited.

TRANSLATION

The Supreme Personality of Godhead creates His minor parts and parcels, the jīva-tattva, beginning with Lord Brahmā, the demigods and the expansions of Vedic knowledge [Sāma, Ṛg, Yajur and Atharva] and including all other living entities, moving and nonmoving, with their different names and characteristics. As the sparks of a fire or the shining rays of the sun emanate from their source and merge into it again and again, the mind, the intelligence, the senses, the gross and subtle material bodies, and the continuous transformations of the different modes of nature all emanate from the Lord and again merge into Him. He is neither demigod nor demon, neither human nor bird or beast. He is not woman, man, or neuter, nor is He an animal. He is not a material quality, a fruitive activity, a manifestation or nonmanifestation. He is the last word in the discrimination of "not this, not this," and He is unlimited. All glories to the Supreme Personality of Godhead!

PURPORT

This is a summary description of the Supreme Personality of Godhead's unlimited potency. That supreme one is acting in different phases by manifesting His parts and parcels, which are all simultaneously differently situated by His different potencies (*parāsya śaktir vividhaiva śrūyate*). Each and every potency is acting quite naturally (*svābhāvikī jñāna-bala-kriyā ca*). Therefore the Lord is unlimited. *Na tat-samaś cābhyadhikaś ca dṛśyate:*

nothing is equal to Him, nor is anything greater than Him. Although He manifests Himself in so many ways, personally He has nothing to do (*na tasya kāryaṁ karaṇaṁ ca vidyate*), for everything is done by expansions of His unlimited energies.

TEXT 25

जिजीविषे नाहमिहामुया कि-
मन्तर्बहिश्चावृतयेभयोन्या ।
इच्छामि कालेन न यस्य विप्लव-
स्तस्यात्मलोकावरणस्य मोक्षम् ॥ २५ ॥

jijīviṣe nāham ihāmuyā kim
antar bahiś cāvṛtayebha-yonyā
icchāmi kālena na yasya viplavas
tasyātma-lokāvaraṇasya mokṣam

jijīviṣe—wish to live long; *na*—not; *aham*—I; *iha*—in this life; *amuyā*—or in the next life (I do not wish to live upon being saved from this dangerous position); *kim*—what is the value; *antaḥ*—internally; *bahiḥ*—externally; *ca*—and; *āvṛtayā*—covered by ignorance; *ibha-yonyā*—in this birth as an elephant; *icchāmi*—I desire; *kālena*—because of the influence of time; *na*—there is not; *yasya*—of which; *viplavaḥ*—annihilation; *tasya*—that; *ātma-loka-āvaraṇasya*—from the covering of self-realization; *mokṣam*—liberation.

TRANSLATION

I do not wish to live anymore after I am released from the attack of the crocodile. What is the use of an elephant's body covered externally and internally by ignorance? I simply desire eternal liberation from the covering of ignorance. That covering is not destroyed by the influence of time.

PURPORT

In this material world, every living entity is covered by the darkness of ignorance. Therefore the *Vedas* enjoin that one should approach the Supreme Lord through the spiritual master, who is described and offered prayers in the *Gautamīya-tantra* as follows:

oṁ ajñāna-timirāndhasya
jñānāñjana-śalākayā

cakṣur unmīlitaṁ yena
tasmai śrī-gurave namaḥ

"I offer my respectful obeisances unto my spiritual master, who with the torchlight of knowledge has opened my eyes, which were blinded by the darkness of ignorance." Although one may struggle for existence in this material world, to live forever is impossible. One must understand, however, that this struggle for existence is due to ignorance, for otherwise every living being is an eternal part of the Supreme Lord. There is no need to live as an elephant or man, American or Indian; one should desire only to achieve liberation from the cycle of birth and death. Because of ignorance, we consider every life offered by nature to be happy and pleasing, but in the degraded life within this material world, from the life of Lord Brahmā down to that of an ant, no one can actually be happy. We are making so many plans to live happily, but there cannot be any happiness in this material world, however we may try to make a permanent settlement in this life or that.

TEXT 26

सोऽहं विश्वसृजं विश्वमविश्वं विश्ववेदसम् ।
विश्वात्मानमजं ब्रह्म प्रणतोऽस्मि परं पदम् ॥ २६ ॥

so 'haṁ viśva-sṛjaṁ viśvam
aviśvaṁ viśva-vedasam
viśvātmānam ajaṁ brahma
praṇato 'smi paraṁ padam

saḥ—that; *aham*—I (the person desiring release from material life); *viśva-sṛjam*—unto He who has created this cosmic manifestation; *viśvam*—who is Himself the whole cosmic presentation; *aviśvam*—although He is transcendental to the cosmic manifestation; *viśva-vedasam*—who is the knower or ingredient of this universal manifestation; *viśva-ātmānam*—the soul of the universe; *ajam*—who is never born, eternally existing; *brahma*—the Supreme; *praṇataḥ asmi*—I offer my respectful obeisances; *param*—who is transcendental; *padam*—the shelter.

TRANSLATION

Now, fully desiring release from material life, I offer my respectful obeisances unto that Supreme Person who is the creator of the universe, who is Himself the form of the universe and who is nonetheless transcendental

to this cosmic manifestation. He is the supreme knower of everything in this world, the Supersoul of the universe. He is the unborn, supremely situated Lord. I offer my respectful obeisances unto Him.

PURPORT

Sometimes when *bhakti-yoga,* Kṛṣṇa consciousness, is preached to the common man, people argue, "Where is Kṛṣṇa? Where is God? Can you show Him to us?" In this verse the answer is given that if we are sufficiently intelligent, we must know that there is someone who has created the entire cosmic manifestation, who has supplied and has become the ingredients for this cosmic manifestation, who is eternally existing, but who is not within the cosmic manifestation. Simply on the basis of this suggestion, one can offer respectful obeisances unto the Supreme Lord. This is the beginning of devotional life.

TEXT 27

योगरन्धितकर्माणो हृदि योगविभाविते ।
योगिनो यं प्रपश्यन्ति योगेशं तं नतोऽस्म्यहम् ॥ २७ ॥

yoga-randhita-karmāṇo
hṛdi yoga-vibhāvite
yogino yaṁ prapaśyanti
yogeśaṁ taṁ nato 'smy aham

yoga-randhita-karmāṇaḥ—persons whose reactions to fruitive activities have been burnt up by *bhakti-yoga; hṛdi*—within the core of the heart; *yoga-vibhāvite*—completely purified and clean; *yoginaḥ*—mystics who are competent; *yam*—unto the Personality of Godhead who; *prapaśyanti*—directly see; *yoga-īśam*—unto that Supreme Personality of Godhead, the master of all mystic *yoga; tam*—unto Him; *nataḥ asmi*—offering obeisances; *aham*—I.

TRANSLATION

I offer my respectful obeisances unto the Supreme, the Supersoul, the master of all mystic yoga, who is seen in the core of the heart by perfect mystics when they are completely purified and freed from the reactions of fruitive activity by practicing bhakti-yoga.

PURPORT

The King of the elephants, Gajendra, simply accepted that there must be someone who has created this cosmic manifestation and has supplied its ingredients. This should be admitted by everyone, even the most determined atheists. Why, then, do the nondevotees and atheists not admit this? The reason is that they are polluted by the reactions of their fruitive activities. One must be freed from all the dirt accumulated within the heart due to fruitive activities performed one after another. One must wash off this dirt by practicing *bhakti-yoga. Yoga-randhita-karmāṇaḥ.* As long as one is covered by material nature's modes of ignorance and passion, there is no possibility of understanding the Supreme Lord. *Tadā rajas-tamo-bhāvāḥ kāma-lobhādayaś ca ye* . When one is freed from the modes of ignorance and passion, one becomes free from the lowest qualities—*kāma* and *lobha,* lust and greed.

Nowadays there are so many *yoga* schools to encourage people in developing their lusty desires and greed through the practice of *yoga.* People are therefore very much fond of so-called *yoga* practice. The actual practice of *yoga,* however, is described here. As authoritatively stated in the *Śrīmad-Bhāgavatam* (12.13.1), *dhyānāvasthita-tad-gatena manasā paśyanti yaṁ yoginaḥ:* a *yogī* is one who always meditates on the lotus feet of the Supreme Personality of Godhead. This is also confirmed in the *Brahma-saṁhitā* (5.38):

premāñjana-cchurita-bhakti-vilocanena
santaḥ sadaiva hṛdayeṣu vilokayanti
yaṁ śyāmasundaram acintya-guṇa-svarūpaṁ
govindam ādi-puruṣaṁ tam ahaṁ bhajāmi

"I worship Govinda, the primeval Lord, who is Śyāmasundara, Kṛṣṇa Himself, with inconceivable innumerable attributes, whom the pure devotees see in their heart of hearts with the eye of devotion tinged with the salve of love." The *bhakti-yogī* constantly sees Śyāmasundara—beautiful Lord Kṛṣṇa with His blackish bodily hue. Because the King of the elephants, Gajendra, thought himself an ordinary animal, he thought himself unfit to see the Lord. In his humility, he thought that he could not practice *yoga.* In other words, how can those who are like animals in the bodily concept of life, and who have no purity of consciousness, practice *yoga*? In the present day, people who have no control over their senses, who have no understanding of philosophy and who do not follow religious principles or rules and regulations are nonetheless pretending to be *yogīs.* This is the greatest anomaly in the practice of mystic *yoga.*

TEXT 28

नमो नमस्तुभ्यमसह्यवेग-
शक्तित्रयायाखिलधीगुणाय ।
प्रपन्नपालाय दुरन्तशक्तये
कदिन्द्रियाणामनवाप्यवर्त्मने ॥ २८ ॥

namo namas tubhyam asahya-vega-
śakti-trayāyākhila-dhī-guṇāya
prapanna-pālāya duranta-śaktaye
kad-indriyāṇām anavāpya-vartmane

namaḥ—I offer my respectful obeisances; *namaḥ*—again I offer my respectful obeisances; *tubhyam*—unto You; *asahya*—formidable; *vega*—forces; *śakti-trayāya*—unto the Supreme Person, who has threefold potencies; *akhila*—of the universe; *dhī*—for the intelligence; *guṇāya*—who appears as the sense objects; *prapanna-pālāya*—unto the Supreme, who gives shelter to the surrendered; *duranta-śaktaye*—who possesses energies very difficult to overcome; *kat-indriyāṇām*—by persons unable to control their senses; *anavāpya*—who is unattainable; *vartmane*—on the path.

TRANSLATION

My Lord, You are the controller of formidable strength in three kinds of energy. You appear as the reservoir of all sense pleasure and the protector of the surrendered souls. You possess unlimited energy, but You are unapproachable by those who are unable to control their senses. I offer my respectful obeisances unto You again and again.

PURPORT

Attachment, greed and lust are three formidable forces that prevent one from concentrating upon the lotus feet of the Supreme Personality of Godhead. These forces act because the Supreme Lord does not like to be realized by nondevotees and atheists. However, when one surrenders unto the lotus feet of the Lord, these impediments are withdrawn, and one can realize the Supreme Personality of Godhead. Therefore the Lord is the protector of the surrendered soul. One cannot become a devotee until one surrenders unto the Lord's lotus feet. Then the Lord gives one the intelligence from within by which one can return home, back to Godhead.

TEXT 29

नायं वेद स्वमात्मानं यच्छक्त्याहंधिया हतम् ।
तं दुरत्ययमाहात्म्यं भगवन्तमितोऽस्म्यहम् ॥ २९ ॥

nāyaṁ veda svam ātmānaṁ
yac-chaktyāhaṁ-dhiyā hatam
taṁ duratyaya-māhātmyaṁ
bhagavantam ito 'smy aham

na—not; *ayam*—people in general; *veda*—know; *svam*—own; *ātmānam*—identity; *yat-śaktyā*—by whose influence; *aham*—I am independent; *dhiyā*—by this intelligence; *hatam*—defeated or covered; *tam*—unto Him; *duratyaya*—difficult to understand; *māhātmyam*—whose glories; *bhagavantam*—of the Supreme Personality of Godhead; *itaḥ*—taking shelter; *asmi aham*—I am.

TRANSLATION

I offer my respectful obeisances unto the Supreme Personality of Godhead, by whose illusory energy the jīva, who is part and parcel of God, forgets his real identity because of the bodily concept of life. I take shelter of the Supreme Personality of Godhead, whose glories are difficult to understand.

PURPORT

As stated in *Bhagavad-gītā,* every living entity—regardless of whether he be human, demigod, animal, bird, bee or whatever—is part and parcel of the Supreme Personality of Godhead. The Lord and the living entity are intimately related like father and son. Unfortunately, because of material contact, the living entity forgets this and wants to enjoy the material world independently, according to his own plan. This illusion (*māyā*) is very difficult to surmount. *Māyā* covers the living entity because of his willingness to forget the Supreme Personality of Godhead and make his own plan to enjoy this material world. As long as this contamination continues, the conditioned soul will be unable to understand his real identity and will perpetually continue under illusion, life after life. *Ato gṛha-kṣetra-sutāpta-vittair janasya moho 'yam ahaṁ mameti* (*SB* 5.5.8). As long as the living entity is not enlightened so that he may understand his real position, he will be attracted to materialistic life, to house, country or field, to society, sons, family, community, bank balance and so on.

Covered by all this, he will continue to think, "I am this body, and everything related to this body is mine." This materialistic conception of life is extremely difficult to surmount, but one who surrenders to the Supreme Personality of Godhead, as did Gajendra, the King of the elephants, comes to enlightenment on the Brahman platform.

brahma-bhūtaḥ prasannātmā
na śocati na kāṅkṣati
samaḥ sarveṣu bhūteṣu
mad-bhaktiṁ labhate parām

"One who is transcendentally situated at once realizes the Supreme Brahman and becomes fully joyful. He never laments nor desires to have anything; he is equally disposed toward all living entities. In that state he attains pure devotional service unto Me." (Bg. 18.54) Since a devotee is completely on the Brahman platform, he is not jealous of any other living entity (*samaḥ sarveṣu bhūteṣu*).

TEXT 30

श्रीशुक उवाच
एवं गजेन्द्रमुपवर्णितनिर्विशेषं
ब्रह्मादयो विविधलिङ्गभिदाभिमानाः ।
नैते यदोपससृपुर्निखिलात्मकत्वात्
तत्राखिलामरमयो हरिराविरासीत् ॥ ३० ॥

śrī-śuka uvāca
evaṁ gajendram upavarṇita-nirviśeṣaṁ
brahmādayo vividha-liṅga-bhidābhimānāḥ
naite yadopasasṛpur nikhilātmakatvāt
tatrākhilāmara-mayo harir avirasıt

śrī-śukaḥ uvāca—Śrī Śukadeva Gosvāmī said; *evam*—in this way; *gajendram*—unto the King of the elephants, Gajendra; *upavarṇita*—whose description; *nirviśeṣam*—not directed to any particular person (but to the Supreme, although he did not know who the Supreme is); *brahmā-ādayaḥ*—the demigods, beginning with Brahmā, Śiva, Indra and Candra; *vividha*—varieties; *liṅga-bhidā*—with separate forms; *abhimānāḥ*—considering themselves separate authorities; *na*—not; *ete*—all of them; *yadā*—when;

upasasṛpuḥ—approached; *nikhila-ātmakatvāt*—because the Supreme Personality of Godhead is the Supersoul of everyone; *tatra*—there; *akhila*—of the universe; *amara-mayaḥ*—consisting of the demigods (who are only external parts of the body); *hariḥ*—the Supreme Personality of Godhead, who can take away everything; *āvirāsīt*—appeared (before the elephant).

TRANSLATION

Śrī Śukadeva Gosvāmī continued: When the King of the elephants was describing the supreme authority, without mentioning any particular person, he did not invoke the demigods, headed by Lord Brahmā, Lord Śiva, Indra and Candra. Thus none of them approached him. However, because Lord Hari is the Supersoul, Puruṣottama, the Personality of Godhead, He appeared before Gajendra.

PURPORT

From the description of Gajendra, he apparently was aiming at the supreme authority although he did not know who the supreme authority is. He conjectured,"There is a supreme authority who is above everything." Under the circumstances, the Lord's various expansions, such as Lord Brahmā, Lord Śiva, Candra and Indra, all thought, "Gajendra is not asking our help. He is asking the help of the Supreme, who is above all of us." As Gajendra has described, the Supreme Lord has various parts and parcels, including the demigods, human beings and animals, all covered by separate forms. Although the demigods are in charge of maintaining different aspects of the universe, Gajendra thought that they were unable to rescue him. *Hariṁ vinā naiva sṛtiṁ taranti :* no one can rescue anyone from the dangers of birth, death, old age and disease. It is only the Supreme Personality of Godhead who can rescue one from the dangers of material existence. Therefore an intelligent person, to get free from this dangerous existence, approaches the Supreme Personality of Godhead, not any demigod. As confirmed in *Bhagavad-gītā* (7.20), *kāmais tais tair hṛta jñānāḥ prapadyante 'nya-devatāḥ:* those who are unintelligent approach the various demigods for temporary material benefits. Actually, however, these demigods cannot rescue the living entity from the dangers of material existence. Like other living entities, the demigods are merely external parts of the Supreme Personality of Godhead's transcendental body. As stated in the Vedic *mantras, sa ātma-aṅgāny anyā devatāḥ.* Within the body is the *ātmā,* the soul, whereas the various parts of the body like the hands and legs are external. Similarly, the *ātmā* of the entire cosmic manifestation is Nārāyaṇa, Lord Viṣṇu, and all the demigods, human beings and other living entities are parts of His body.

It may also be concluded that since a tree lives on the strength of its root and when the root is nourished with water all the parts of the tree are nourished, one should worship the Supreme Personality of Godhead, who is the original root of everything. Although the Supreme Personality of Godhead is very difficult to approach, He is very near to us because He lives within our hearts. As soon as the Lord understands that one is seeking His favor by fully surrendering, naturally He immediately takes action. Therefore although the demigods did not come to the aid of Gajendra, the Supreme Personality of Godhead immediately appeared before him because of his fervent prayer. This does not mean that the demigods were angry with Gajendra, for actually when Lord Viṣṇu is worshiped, all the other demigods are also worshiped. *Yasmin tuṣṭe jagat tuṣṭam:* if the Supreme Personality of Godhead is satisfied, everyone is satisfied.

yathā taror mūla-niṣecanena
tṛpyanti tat-skandha-bhujopaśākhāḥ
prāṇopahārāc ca yathendriyāṇāṁ
tathaiva sarvārhaṇam acyutejyā

"As pouring water on the root of a tree energizes the trunk, branches, twigs and everything else, and as supplying food to the stomach enlivens the senses and limbs of the body, so simply worshiping the Supreme Personality of Godhead through devotional service automatically satisfies the demigods, who are parts of that Supreme Personality." (*Bhāg.* 4.31.14) When the Supreme Personality of Godhead is worshiped, all the demigods are satisfied.

TEXT 31

तं तद्वदार्तमुपलभ्य जगन्निवासः
स्तोत्रं निशम्य दिविजैः सह संस्तुवद्भिः ।
छन्दोमयेन गरुडेन समुह्यमान-
श्चक्रायुधोऽभ्यगमदाशु यतो गजेन्द्रः ॥ ३१ ॥

taṁ tadvad ārtam upalabhya jagan-nivāsaḥ
stotraṁ niśamya divijaiḥ saha saṁstuvadbhiḥ
chandomayena garuḍena samuhyamānaś
cakrāyudho 'bhyagamad āśu yato gajendraḥ

tam—unto him (Gajendra); *tadvat*—in that way; *ārtam*—who was very depressed (because of being attacked by the crocodile); *upalabhya*—understanding; *jagat-nivāsaḥ*—the Lord, who exists everywhere; *stotram*—the prayer; *niśamya*—hearing; *divijaiḥ*—the denizens of the heavenly planets; *saha*—with; *saṁstuvadbhiḥ*—who were offering their prayers also; *chando-mayena*—with the speed He desired; *garuḍena*—by Garuḍa; *samuhyamānaḥ*—being carried; *cakra*—carrying His disc; *āyudhaḥ*—and other weapons, like the club; *abhyagamat*—arrived; *āśu*—immediately; *yataḥ*—where; *gajendraḥ*—the King of the elephants, Gajendra, was situated.

TRANSLATION

After understanding the awkward condition of Gajendra, who had offered his prayers, the Supreme Personality of Godhead, Hari, who lives everywhere, appeared with the demigods, who were offering prayers to Him. Carrying His disc and other weapons, He appeared there on the back of His carrier, Garuḍa, with great speed, according to His desire. Thus He appeared before Gajendra.

PURPORT

Śrīla Viśvanātha Cakravartī Ṭhākura specifically hints that since Gajendra was in such a difficult position and was praying for the mercy of the Supreme Personality of Godhead, the demigods, who could have immediately gone to his rescue, hesitated to go there. Since they considered Gajendra's prayer to be directed toward the Lord, they felt offended, and this in itself was offensive. Consequently, when the Lord went there, they also went and offered prayers to the Lord so that their offense might be excused.

TEXT 32

सोऽन्तःसरस्युरुबलेन गृहीत आर्तो
दृष्ट्वा गरुत्मति हरिं ख उपात्तचक्रम् ।
उत्क्षिप्य साम्बुजकरं गिरमाह कृच्छ्रा-
न्नारायणाखिलगुरो भगवन् नमस्ते ॥ ३२ ॥

so 'ntaḥ-sarasy urubalena gṛhīta ārto
dṛṣṭvā garutmati hariṁ kha upātta-cakram
utkṣipya sāmbuja-karaṁ giram āha kṛcchrān
nārāyaṇākhila-guro bhagavan namas te

saḥ—he (Gajendra); *antaḥ-sarasi*—in the water; *uru-balena*—with great force; *gṛhītaḥ*—who had been captured by the crocodile; *ārtaḥ*—and severely suffering; *dṛṣṭvā*—upon seeing; *garutmati*—on the back of Garuḍa; *harim*—the Lord; *khe*—in the sky; *upātta-cakram*—wielding His disc; *utkṣipya*—raising; *sa-ambuja-karam*—his trunk, along with a lotus flower; *giram-āha*—uttered the words; *kṛcchrāt*—with great difficulty (because of his precarious position); *nārāyaṇa*—O my Lord Nārāyaṇa; *akhila-guro*—O universal Lord; *bhagavan*—O Supreme Personality of Godhead; *namaḥ te*—I offer my respectful obeisances unto You.

TRANSLATION

Gajendra had been forcefully captured by the crocodile in the water and was feeling acute pain, but when he saw that Nārāyaṇa, wielding His disc, was coming in the sky on the back of Garuḍa, he immediately took a lotus flower in his trunk, and with great difficulty due to his painful condition, he uttered the following words: "O my Lord, Nārāyaṇa, master of the universe, O Supreme Personality of Godhead, I offer my respectful obeisances unto You."

PURPORT

The King of the elephants was so very eager to see the Supreme Personality of Godhead that when he saw the Lord coming in the sky, with great pain and in a feeble voice he offered respect to the Lord. A devotee does not consider a dangerous position to be dangerous, for in such a dangerous position he can fervently pray to the Lord in great ecstasy. Thus a devotee regards danger as a good opportunity. *Tat te'nukampāṁ susamīkṣamāṇaḥ.* When a devotee is in great danger, he sees that danger to be the great mercy of the Lord because it is an opportunity to think of the Lord very sincerely and with undiverted attention. *Tat te 'nukampāṁ susamīkṣamāṇo bhuñjāna evātma-kṛtaṁ vipākam* (*Bhāg.* 10.14.8). He does not accuse the Supreme Personality of Godhead for having let His devotee fall into such a dangerous condition. Rather, he considers that dangerous condition to be due to his past misdeeds and takes it as an opportunity to pray to the Lord and offer thanks for having been given such an opportunity. When a devotee lives in this way, his salvation—his going back home, back to Godhead—is guaranteed. We can see this to be true from the example of Gajendra, who anxiously prayed to the Lord and thus received an immediate chance to return home, back to Godhead.

TEXT 33

तं वीक्ष्य पीडितमजः सहसावतीर्य
सग्राहमाशु सरसः कृपयोज्जहार ।
ग्राहाद् विपाटितमुखादरिणा गजेन्द्रं
संपश्यतां हरिरमूमुचदुच्छ्रियाणाम् ॥ ३३ ॥

taṁ vīkṣya pīḍitam ajaḥ sahasāvatīrya
sa-grāham āśu sarasaḥ kṛpayojjahāra
grāhād vipāṭita-mukhād ariṇā gajendraṁ
saṁpaśyatāṁ harir amūm ucad ucchriyāṇām

tam—him (Gajendra); *vīkṣya*—after seeing (in that condition); *pīḍitam*—who was very aggrieved; *ajaḥ*—the unborn, the Supreme Personality of Godhead; *sahasā*—all of a sudden; *avatīrya*—getting down (from the back of Garuḍa); *sa-grāham*—with the crocodile; *āśu*—immediately; *sarasaḥ*—from the water; *kṛpayā*—out of great mercy; *ujjahāra*—took out; *grāhāt*—from the crocodile; *vipāṭita*—separated; *mukhāt*—from the mouth; *ariṇā*—with the disc; *gajendram*—Gajendra; *sampaśyatām*—who were looking on; *hariḥ*—the Supreme Personality of Godhead; *amūm*—him (Gajendra); *ucat*—saved; *ucchriyāṇām*—in the presence of all the demigods.

TRANSLATION

Thereafter, seeing Gajendra in such an aggrieved position, the unborn Supreme Personality of Godhead, Hari, immediately got down from the back of Garuḍa by His causeless mercy and pulled the King of the elephants, along with the crocodile, out of the water. Then, in the presence of all the demigods, who were looking on, the Lord severed the crocodile's mouth from its body with His disc. In this way He saved Gajendra, the King of the elephants.

Thus end the Bhaktivedanta purports of the Eighth Canto, Third Chapter, of the Śrīmad-Bhāgavatam, *entitled "Gajendra's Prayers of Surrender."*

CHAPTER FOUR

Gajendra Returns to the Spiritual World

This Fourth Chapter describes the previous birth of Gajendra and the crocodile. It tells how the crocodile became a Gandharva and how Gajendra became an associate of the Supreme Personality of Godhead.

There was a king on the Gandharva planet whose name was Hūhū. Once this King Hūhū was enjoying with women in the water, and while enjoying he pulled the leg of Devala Ṛṣi, who was also taking a bath in the water. Upon this, the sage became very angry and immediately cursed him to become a crocodile. King Hūhū was very sorry when cursed in that way, and he begged pardon from the sage, who in compassion gave him the benediction that he would be freed when Gajendra was delivered by the Personality of Godhead. Thus the crocodile was delivered when killed by Nārāyaṇa.

When Gajendra, by the mercy of the Lord, became one of the Lord's associates in Vaikuṇṭha, he got four hands. This achievement is called *sārūpya-mukti,* or the liberation of receiving a spiritual body exactly like that of Nārāyaṇa. Gajendra, in his previous birth, had been a great devotee of Lord Viṣṇu. His name was Indradyumna, and he was the King of the Tāmila country. Following the Vedic principles, this King retired from family life and constructed a small cottage in the Malayācala Hills, where he always worshiped the Supreme Personality of Godhead in silence. Agastya Ṛṣi, along with many disciples, once approached King Indradyumna's *āśrama,* but because the King was meditating on the Supreme Personality of Godhead, he could not receive Agastya Ṛṣi properly. Thus the *ṛṣi* became very angry and cursed the King to become a dull elephant. In accordance with this curse, the King was born as an elephant, and he forgot all about his previous activities in devotional service. Nonetheless, in his birth as an elephant, when he was dangerously attacked by the crocodile, he remembered his past life in devotional service and remembered a prayer he had learned in that life. Because of this prayer, he again received the mercy of the Lord. Thus he was immediately delivered, and he became one of the Lord's four-handed associates.

Śukadeva Gosvāmī ends this chapter by describing the good fortune of the elephant. Śukadeva Gosvāmī says that by hearing the narration of Gajendra's deliverance, one can also get the opportunity to be delivered. Śukadeva Gosvāmī vividly describes this, and thus the chapter ends.

TEXT 1

श्रीशुक उवाच
तदा देवर्षिगन्धर्वा ब्रह्मेशानपुरोगमाः ।
मुमुचुः कुसुमासारं शंसन्तः कर्म तद्धरेः ॥ १ ॥

śrī-śuka uvāca
tadā devarṣi-gandharvā
brahmeśāna-purogamāḥ
mumucuḥ kusumāsāraṁ
śaṁsantaḥ karma tad dhareḥ

śrī-śukaḥ uvāca—Śrī Śukadeva Gosvāmī said; *tadā*—at that time (when Gajendra was delivered); *deva-ṛṣi-gandharvāḥ*—the demigods, sages and Gandharvas; *brahma-īśāna-purogamāḥ*—headed by Lord Brahmā and Lord Śiva; *mumucuḥ*—showered; *kusuma-āsāram*—a covering of flowers; *śaṁsantaḥ*—while praising; *karma*—transcendental activity; *tat*—that (*gajendra-mokṣaṇa*); *hareḥ*—of the Supreme Personality of Godhead.

TRANSLATION

Śrī Śukadeva Gosvāmī said: When the Lord delivered Gajendra, King of the elephants, all the demigods, sages and Gandharvas, headed by Brahmā and Śiva, praised this activity of the Supreme Personality of Godhead and showered flowers upon both the Lord and Gajendra.

PURPORT

It is evident from this chapter that great sages like Devala Ṛṣi, Nārada Muni and Agastya Muni will sometimes curse someone. The curse of such a personality, however, is in fact a benediction. Both the crocodile, who had been a Gandharva in his previous life, and Gajendra, who had been a king named Indradyumna, were cursed, but both of them benefited. Indradyumna, in his birth as an elephant, attained salvation and became a personal associate of the Lord in Vaikuṇṭha, and the crocodile regained his status as a Gandharva. We find evidence in many places that the curse of a great saint or devotee is not a curse but a benediction.

TEXT 2

नेदुर्दुन्दुभयो दिव्या गन्धर्वा ननृतुर्जगुः ।
ऋषयश्चारणाः सिद्धास्तुष्टुवुः पुरुषोत्तमम् ॥ २ ॥

nedur dundubhayo divyā
gandharvā nanṛtur jaguḥ
ṛṣayaś cāraṇāḥ siddhās
tuṣṭuvuḥ puruṣottamam

neduḥ—vibrated; *dundubhayaḥ*—kettledrums; *divyāḥ*—in the sky of the higher planetary system; *gandharvāḥ*—residents of Gandharvaloka; *nanṛtuḥ*—danced; *jaguḥ*—and sang; *ṛṣayaḥ*—all the saintly sages; *cāraṇāḥ*—the inhabitants of the Cāraṇa planet; *siddhāḥ*—the inhabitants of the Siddha planet; *tuṣṭuvuḥ*—offered prayers; *puruṣa-uttamam*—to the Supreme Personality of Godhead, Puruṣottama, the best of males.

TRANSLATION

There was a beating of kettledrums in the heavenly planets, the inhabitants of Gandharvaloka began to dance and sing, while great sages and the inhabitants of Cāraṇaloka and Siddhaloka offered prayers to the Supreme Personality of Godhead, Puruṣottama.

TEXTS 3-4

योऽसौ ग्राहः स वै सद्यः परमाश्चर्यरूपधृक् ।
मुक्तो देवलशापेन हूहूर्गन्धर्वसत्तमः ॥ ३ ॥
प्रणम्य शिरसाधीशमुत्तमश्लोकमव्ययम् ।
अगायत यशोधाम कीर्तन्यगुणसत्कथम् ॥ ४ ॥

yo 'sau grāhaḥ sa vai sadyaḥ
paramāścarya-rūpa-dhṛk
mukto devala-śāpena
hūhūr gandharva-sattamaḥ

praṇamya śirasādhīśam
uttama-ślokam avyayam
agāyata yaśo-dhāma
kīrtanya-guṇa-sat-katham

yaḥ—he who; *asau*—that; *grāhaḥ*—became a crocodile; *saḥ*—he; *vai*—indeed; *sadyaḥ*—immediately; *parama*—very nice; *āścarya*—wonderful; *rūpa-dhṛk*—possessing the form (of his original Gandharva position); *muktaḥ*—was delivered; *devala-śāpena*—by the cursing of Devala Ṛṣi; *hūhūḥ*—whose name was formerly Hūhū; *gandharva-sattamaḥ*—the best of Gandharvaloka; *praṇamya*—offering his obeisances; *śirasā*—by the head; *adhīśam*—unto the supreme master; *uttama-ślokam*—who is worshiped by the choicest verses; *avyayam*—who is the supreme eternal; *agāyata*—he began to chant; *yaśaḥ-dhāma*—the glories of the Lord; *kīrtanya-guṇa-sat-katham*—whose transcendental pastimes and qualities are glorious.

TRANSLATION

The best of the Gandharvas, King Hūhū, having been cursed by Devala Muni, had become a crocodile. Now, having been delivered by the Supreme Personality of Godhead, he assumed a very beautiful form as a Gandharva. Understanding by whose mercy this had happened, he immediately offered his respectful obeisances with his head and began chanting prayers just suitable for the transcendental Lord, the supreme eternal, who is worshiped by the choicest verses.

PURPORT

The story of how the Gandharva had become a crocodile will be described later. The curse by which the Gandharva took this position was actually a blessing, not a curse. One should not be displeased when a saintly person curses someone, for his curse, indirectly, is a blessing. The Gandharva had the mentality of an inhabitant of the celestial planetary system, and for him to become an associate of the Supreme Lord would have taken millions of long years. However, because he was cursed by Devala Ṛṣi, he became a crocodile and in only one life was fortunate enough to see the Supreme Personality of Godhead face to face and be promoted to the spiritual world to become one of the Lord's associates. Similarly, Gajendra was also delivered by the Supreme Personality of Godhead when he was freed from the curse of Agastya Muni.

TEXT 5

सोऽनुकम्पित ईशेन परिक्रम्य प्रणम्य तम् ।
लोकस्य पश्यतो लोकं स्वमगान्मुक्तकिल्बिषः ॥ ५ ॥

so 'nukampita īśena
parikramya praṇamya tam

lokasya paśyato lokaṁ
svam agān mukta-kilbiṣaḥ

saḥ—he (King Hūhū); *anukampitaḥ*—being favored; *īśena*—by the Supreme Lord; *parikramya*—circumambulating; *praṇamya*—offering his obeisances; *tam*—unto Him; *lokasya*—all the demigods and men; *paśyataḥ*—while seeing; *lokam*—to the planet; *svam*—his own; *agāt*—went back; *mukta*—being delivered; *kilbiṣaḥ*—from the reactions of his sin.

TRANSLATION

Having been favored by the causeless mercy of the Supreme Personality of Godhead and having regained his original form, King Hūhū circumambulated the Lord and offered his obeisances. Then, in the presence of all the demigods, headed by Brahmā, he returned to Gandharvaloka. He had been freed of all sinful reactions.

TEXT 6

गजेन्द्रो भगवत्स्पर्शाद् विमुक्तोऽज्ञानबन्धनात् ।
प्राप्तो भगवतो रूपं पीतवासाश्चतुर्भुजः ॥ ६ ॥

gajendro bhagavat-sparśād
vimukto 'jñāna-bandhanāt
prāpto bhagavato rūpaṁ
pīta-vāsāś catur-bhujaḥ

gajendraḥ—the King of the elephants, Gajendra; *bhagavat-sparśāt*—because of being touched by the hand of the Supreme Personality of Godhead; *vimuktaḥ*—was immediately freed; *ajñāna-bandhanāt*—from all kinds of ignorance, especially the bodily concept of life; *prāptaḥ*—achieved; *bhagavataḥ*—of the Supreme Personality of Godhead; *rūpam*—the same bodily features; *pīta-vāsāḥ*—wearing yellow garments; *catuḥ-bhujaḥ*—and four-handed, with conchshell, disc, club and lotus.

TRANSLATION

Because Gajendra, King of the elephants, had been touched directly by the hands of the Supreme Personality of Godhead, he was immediately freed of all material ignorance and bondage. Thus he received the salvation of sārūpya-mukti, in which he achieved the same bodily features as the Lord, being dressed in yellow garments and possessing four hands.

PURPORT

If one is favored by the Supreme Personality of Godhead by having his gross body touched by the Lord, his body turns into a spiritual body, and he can go back home, back to Godhead. Gajendra assumed a spiritual body when his body was touched by the Lord. Similarly, Dhruva Mahārāja assumed his spiritual body in this way. *Arcanā-paddhati,* daily worship of the Deity, provides an opportunity to touch the body of the Supreme Personality of Godhead, and thus it enables one to be fortunate enough to get a spiritual body and go back to Godhead. Not only by touching the body of the Supreme Lord, but simply by hearing about His pastimes, chanting His glories, touching His feet and offering worship—in other words, by serving the Lord somehow or other—one is purified of material contamination. This is the result of touching the Supreme Lord. One who is a pure devotee (*anyābhilāṣitā-śūnyam*), who acts according to the *śāstra* and the words of the Supreme Personality of Godhead, certainly becomes purified. Like Gajendra, he assumes a spiritual body and returns home, back to Godhead.

TEXT 7

स वै पूर्वमभूद् राजा पाण्ड्यो द्रविडसत्तमः ।
इन्द्रद्युम्न इति ख्यातो विष्णुव्रतपरायणः ॥ ७ ॥

sa vai pūrvam abhūd rājā
pāṇḍyo draviḍa-sattamaḥ
indradyumna iti khyāto
viṣṇu-vrata-parāyaṇaḥ

saḥ—this elephant (Gajendra); *vai*—indeed; *pūrvam*—formerly; *abhūt*—was; *rājā*—a king; *pāṇḍyaḥ*—of the country known as Pāṇḍya; *draviḍa-sattamaḥ*—the best of those born in Draviḍa-deśa, South India; *indradyumnaḥ* by the name Mahārāja Indradyumna; *iti*—thus; *khyātaḥ*—celebrated; *viṣṇu-vrata-parāyaṇaḥ*—who was a first-class Vaiṣṇava, always engaged in the service of the Lord.

TRANSLATION

This Gajendra had formerly been a Vaiṣṇava and the king of the country known as Pāṇḍya, which is in the province of Draviḍa [South India]. In his previous life, he was known as Indradyumna Mahārāja.

TEXT 8

स एकदाराधनकाल आत्मवान्
गृहीतमौनव्रत ईश्वरं हरिम् ।
जटाधरस्तापस आप्लुतोऽच्युतं
समर्चयामास कुलाचलाश्रमः ॥ ८ ॥

sa ekadārādhana-kāla ātmavān
gṛhīta-mauna-vrata īśvaraṁ harim
jaṭā-dharas tāpasa āpluto 'cyutaṁ
samarcayām āsa kulācalāśramaḥ

saḥ—that Indradyumna Mahārāja; *ekadā*—once upon a time; *ārādhana-kāle*—at the time of worshiping the Deity; *ātmavān*—engaged in devotional service in meditation with great attention; *gṛhīta*—taken; *mauna-vrataḥ*—the vow of silence (not talking with anyone); *īśvaram*—the supreme controller; *harim*—the Personality of Godhead; *jaṭā-dharaḥ*—with matted locks; *tāpasaḥ*—always engaged in austerity; *āplutaḥ*—always merged in love for the Supreme Personality of Godhead; *acyutam*—the infallible Lord; *samarcayām āsa*—was worshiping; *kulācala-āśramaḥ*—he made his *āśrama* in Kulācala (the Malaya Hills).

TRANSLATION

Indradyumna Mahārāja retired from family life and went to the Malaya Hills, where he had a small cottage for his āśrama. He wore matted locks on his head and always engaged in austerities. Once, while observing a vow of silence, he was fully engaged in the worship of the Lord and absorbed in the ecstasy of love of Godhead.

TEXT 9

यदृच्छया तत्र महायशा मुनिः
समागमच्छिष्यगणैः परिश्रितः ।
तं वीक्ष्य तूष्णीमकृतार्हणादिकं
रहस्युपासीनमृषिश्चुकोप ह ॥ ९ ॥

yadṛcchayā tatra mahā-yaśā muniḥ
samāgamac chiṣya-gaṇaiḥ pariśritaḥ

taṁ vīkṣya tūṣṇīm akṛtārhaṇādikaṁ
rahasy upāsīnam ṛṣiś cukopa ha

yadṛcchayā—out of his own will (without being invited); *tatra*—there; *mahā-yaśāḥ*—very celebrated, well-known; *muniḥ*—Agastya Muni; *samāgamat*—arrived; *śiṣya-gaṇaiḥ*—by his disciples; *pariśritaḥ*—surrounded; *tam*—him; *vīkṣya*—seeing; *tūṣṇīm*—silent; *akṛta-arhaṇa-ādikam*—without offering a respectful reception; *rahasi*—in a secluded place; *upāsīnam*—sitting in meditation; *ṛṣiḥ*—the great sage; *cukopa*—became very angry; *ha*—it so happened.

TRANSLATION

While Indradyumna Mahārāja was engaged in ecstatic meditation, worshiping the Supreme Personality of Godhead, the great sage Agastya Muni arrived there, surrounded by his disciples. When the Muni saw that Mahārāja Indradyumna, who was sitting in a secluded place, remained silent and did not follow the etiquette of offering him a reception, he was very angry.

TEXT 10

तस्मा इमं शापमदादसाधु-
रयं दुरात्माकृतबुद्धिरद्य ।
विप्रावमन्ता विशतां तमिस्रं
यथा गजः स्तब्धमतिः स एव ॥ १० ॥

tasmā imaṁ śāpam adād asādhur
ayaṁ durātmākṛta-buddhir adya
viprāvamantā viśatāṁ tamisraṁ
yathā gajaḥ stabdha-matiḥ sa eva

tasmai—unto Mahārāja Indradyumna; *imam*—this; *śāpam*—curse; *adāt*—he gave; *asādhuḥ*—not at all gentle; *ayam*—this; *durātmā*—degraded soul; *akṛta*—without education; *buddhiḥ*—his intelligence; *adya*—now; *vipra*—of a *brāhmaṇa; avamantā*—insulter; *viśatām*—let him enter; *tamisram*—darkness; *yathā*—as; *gajaḥ*—an elephant; *stabdha-matiḥ*—possessing blunt intelligence; *saḥ*—he; *eva*—indeed.

TRANSLATION

Agastya Muni then spoke this curse against the King: This King Indradyumna is not at all gentle. Being low and uneducated, he has insulted a brāhmaṇa. May he therefore enter the region of darkness and receive the dull, dumb body of an elephant.

PURPORT

An elephant is very strong, it has a very big body, and it can work very hard and eat a large quantity of food, but its intelligence is not at all commensurate with its size and strength. Thus in spite of so much bodily strength, the elephant works as a menial servant for a human being. Agastya Muni thought it wise to curse the King to become an elephant because the powerful King did not receive Agastya Muni as one is obliged to receive a *brāhmaṇa.* Yet although Agastya Muni cursed Mahārāja Indradyumna to become an elephant, the curse was indirectly a benediction, for by undergoing one life as an elephant, Indradyumna Mahārāja ended the reactions for all the sins of his previous life. Immediately after the expiry of the elephant's life, he was promoted to Vaikuṇṭhaloka to become a personal associate of the Supreme Personality of Godhead, Nārāyaṇa, in a body exactly like that of the Lord. This is called *sārūpya-mukti.*

TEXTS 11-12

श्रीशुक उवाच
एवं शप्त्वा गतोऽगस्त्यो भगवान् नृप सानुगः ।
इन्द्रद्युम्नोऽपि राजर्षिर्दिष्टं तदुपधारयन् ॥ ११ ॥
आपन्नः कौञ्जरीं योनिमात्मस्मृतिविनाशिनीम् ।
हर्यर्चनानुभावेन यद्गजत्वेऽप्यनुस्मृतिः ॥ १२ ॥

śrī-śuka uvāca
evaṁ śaptvā gato 'gastyo
bhagavān nṛpa sānugaḥ
indradyumno 'pi rājarṣir
diṣṭaṁ tad upadhārayan

āpannaḥ kauñjarīṁ yonim
ātma-smṛti-vināśinīm

hary-arcanānubhāvena
yad-gajatve 'py anusmṛtiḥ

śrī-śukaḥ uvāca—Śrī Śukadeva Gosvāmī said; *evam*—thus; *śaptvā*—after cursing; *gataḥ*—left that place; *agastyaḥ*—Agastya Muni; *bhagavān*—so powerful; *nṛpa*—O King; *sa-anugaḥ*—with his associates; *indradyumnaḥ*—King Indradyumna; *api*—also; *rājarṣiḥ*—although he was a *rājarṣi; diṣṭam*—because of past deeds; *tat*—that curse; *upadhārayan*—considering; *āpannaḥ*—got; *kauñjarīm*—of an elephant; *yonim*—the species; *ātma-smṛti*—remembrance of one's identity; *vināśinīm*—which destroys; *hari*—the Supreme Personality of Godhead; *arcana-anubhāvena*—because of worshiping; *yat*—that; *gajatve*—in the body of an elephant; *api*—although; *anusmṛtiḥ*—the opportunity to remember his past devotional service.

TRANSLATION

Śukadeva Gosvāmī continued: My dear King, after Agastya Muni had thus cursed King Indradyumna, the Muni left that place along with his disciples. Since the King was a devotee, he accepted Agastya Muni's curse as welcome because it was the desire of the Supreme Personality of Godhead. Therefore, although in his next life he got the body of an elephant, because of devotional service he remembered how to worship and offer prayers to the Lord.

PURPORT

This is the unique position of a devotee of the Supreme Personality of Godhead. Although the King was cursed, he welcomed the curse because a devotee is always aware that nothing can happen without the desire of the Supreme Lord. Although the King was not at fault, Agastya Muni cursed him, and when this happened the King considered it to be due to his past misdeeds. *Tat te 'nukampāṁ susamīkṣamāṇaḥ* (*Bhāg.* 10.14.8). This is a practical example of how a devotee thinks. He regards any reverses in life as blessings of the Supreme Personality of Godhead. Therefore, instead of being agitated by such reverses, he continues his activities of devotional service, and Kṛṣṇa takes care of him and enables him to be promoted to the spiritual world, back to Godhead. If a devotee has to suffer the reactions of his past misdeeds, the Supreme Lord arranges for him to be given only a token of these reactions, and very soon he is freed from all the reactions of material contamination. One should therefore adhere to devotional service, and the Lord Himself will very soon see to one's promotion to the spiritual world. A devotee should not be disturbed by unfortunate circumstances, but must continue his regular program, depending on the Lord for everything. The word *upadhārayan,* "considering," is very significant in this verse. This word indicates that a devotee knows what is what; he understands what is happening in material, conditional life.

TEXT 13

एवं विमोक्ष्य गजयूथपमब्जनाभ-
स्तेनापि पार्षदगतिं गमितेन युक्तः ।
गन्धर्वसिद्धविबुधैरुपगीयमान-
कर्माद्भुतं स्वभवनं गरुडासनोऽगात् ॥ १३ ॥

evaṁ vimokṣya gaja-yūtha-pam abja-nābhas
tenāpi pārṣada-gatiṁ gamitena yuktaḥ
gandharva-siddha-vibudhair upagīyamāna-
karmādbhutaṁ sva-bhavanaṁ garuḍāsano 'gāt

evam—thus; *vimokṣya*—delivering; *gaja-yūtha-pam*—the King of the elephants, Gajendra; *abja-nābhaḥ*—the Supreme Personality of Godhead, from whose navel sprouts a lotus flower; *tena*—by him (Gajendra); *api*—also; *pārṣada-gatim*—the position of the Lord's associate; *gamitena*—who had already gotten; *yuktaḥ*—accompanied; *gandharva*—by the denizens of Gandharvaloka; *siddha*—the denizens of Siddhaloka; *vibudhaiḥ*—and by all great learned sages; *upagīyamāna*—were being glorified; *karma*—whose transcendental activities; *adbhutam*—all-wonderful; *sva-bhavanam*—to His own abode; *garuḍa-āsanaḥ*—sitting on the back of Garuḍa; *agāt*—returned.

TRANSLATION

Upon delivering the King of the elephants from the clutches of the crocodile, and from material existence, which resembles a crocodile, the Lord awarded him the status of sārūpya-mukti. In the presence of the Gandharvas, the Siddhas and the other demigods, who were praising the Lord for His wonderful transcendental activities, the Lord, sitting on the back of His carrier, Garuḍa, returned to His all-wonderful abode and took Gajendra with Him.

PURPORT

In this verse the word *vimokṣya* is significant. For a devotee, *mokṣa* or *mukti* —salvation—means getting the position of the Lord's associate. The impersonalists are satisfied to get the liberation of merging in the Brahman effulgence, but for a devotee, *mukti* (liberation) means not to merge in the effulgence of the Lord, but to be directly promoted to the Vaikuṇṭha planets and to become an associate of the Lord. In this regard, there is a relevant verse in *Śrīmad-Bhāgavatam* (10.14.8):

tat te 'nukampāṁ susamīkṣamāṇo
bhuñjāna evātma-kṛtaṁ vipākam
hṛd-vāg-vapurbhir vidadhan namas te
jīveta yo mukti-pade sa dāya-bhāk

"One who seeks Your compassion and thus tolerates all kinds of adverse conditions due to the *karma* of his past deeds, who engages always in Your devotional service with his mind, words and body, and who always offers obeisances unto You, is certainly a bona fide candidate for liberation." A devotee who tolerates everything in this material world and patiently executes his devotional service can become *mukti-pade sa dāya-bhāk,* a bona fide candidate for liberation. The word *dāya-bhāk* refers to a hereditary right to the Lord's mercy. A devotee must simply engage in devotional service, not caring about material situations. Then he automatically becomes a rightful candidate for promotion to Vaikuṇṭhaloka. The devotee who renders unalloyed service to the Lord gets the right to be promoted to Vaikuṇṭhaloka, just as a son inherits the property of his father.

When a devotee gets liberation, he becomes free from material contamination and engages as a servant of the Lord. This is explained in *Śrīmad-Bhāgavatam* (2.10.6): *muktir hitvānyathā rūpaṁ svarūpeṇa vyavasthitiḥ.* The word *svarūpa* refers to *sārūpya-mukti*—going back home, back to Godhead, and remaining the Lord's eternal associate, having regained a spiritual body exactly resembling that of the Lord, with four hands, holding the *śaṅkha, cakra, gadā* and *padma.* The difference between the *mukti* of the impersonalist and that of the devotee is that the devotee is immediately appointed an eternal servant of the Lord, whereas the impersonalist, although merging in the effulgence of the *brahmajyoti,* is still insecure and therefore generally falls again to this material world. *Āruhya kṛcchreṇa paraṁ padaṁ tataḥ patanty adho 'nādṛta-yuṣmad-aṅghrayaḥ* (*Bhāg.* 10.2.32). Although the impersonalist rises to the Brahman effulgence and enters into that effulgence, he has no engagement in the service of the Lord, and therefore he is again attracted to materialistic philanthropic activities. Thus he comes down to open hospitals and educational institutions, feed poor men and perform similar materialistic activities, which the impersonalist thinks are more precious than serving the Supreme Personality of Godhead. *Anādṛta-yuṣmad-aṅghrayaḥ.* The impersonalists do not think that the service of the Lord is more valuable than serving the poor man or starting a school or hospital. Although they say *brahma satyaṁ jagan mithyā*—"Brahman is real, and the material world is false"—they are nonetheless very eager to serve the false material world and neglect the service of the lotus feet of the Supreme Personality of Godhead.

TEXT 14

एतन्महाराज तवेरितो मया
कृष्णानुभावो गजराजमोक्षणम् ।
स्वर्ग्यं यशस्यं कलिकल्मषापहं
दुःस्वप्ननाशं कुरुवर्य शृण्वताम् ॥ १४ ॥

etan mahā-rāja taverito mayā
kṛṣṇānubhāvo gaja-rāja-mokṣaṇam
svargyaṁ yaśasyaṁ kali-kalmaṣāpahaṁ
duḥsvapna-nāśaṁ kuru-varya śṛṇvatām

etat—this; *mahā-rāja*—O King Parīkṣit; *tava*—unto you; *īritaḥ*—described; *mayā*—by me; *kṛṣṇa-anubhāvaḥ*—the unlimited potency of Lord Kṛṣṇa (by which He can deliver a devotee); *gaja-rāja-mokṣaṇam*—delivering the King of the elephants; *svargyam*—giving elevation to higher planetary systems; *yaśasyam*—increasing one's reputation as a devotee; *kali-kalmaṣa-apaham*—diminishing the contamination of the Kali-yuga; *duḥsvapna-nāśam*—counteracting the causes of bad dreams; *kuru-varya*—O best among the Kurus; *śṛṇvatām*—of persons who hear this narration.

TRANSLATION

My dear King Parīkṣit, I have now described the wonderful power of Kṛṣṇa, as displayed when the Lord delivered the King of the elephants. O best of the Kuru dynasty, those who hear this narration become fit to be promoted to the higher planetary systems. Simply because of hearing this narration, they gain a reputation as devotees, they are unaffected by the contamination of Kali-yuga, and they never see bad dreams.

TEXT 15

यथानुकीर्तयन्त्येतच्छ्रेयस्कामा द्विजातयः ।
शुचयः प्रातरुत्थाय दुःस्वप्नाद्युपशान्तये ॥ १५ ॥

yathānukīrtayanty etac
chreyas-kāmā dvijātayaḥ
śucayaḥ prātar utthāya
duḥsvapnādy-upaśāntaye

yathā—without deviation; *anukīrtayanti*—they chant; *etat*—this narration of the deliverance of Gajendra; *śreyaḥ-kāmāḥ*—persons who desire their own auspiciousness; *dvi-jātayaḥ*—the twice-born (*brāhmaṇas, kṣatriyas* and *vaiśyas*); *śucayaḥ*—especially the *brāhmaṇas,* who are always clean; *prātaḥ*—in the morning; *utthāya*—after getting up from sleep; *duḥsvapna-ādi*—beginning with sleeping badly at night; *upaśāntaye*—to counteract all troublesome positions.

TRANSLATION

Therefore, after getting up from bed in the morning, those who desire their own welfare—especially the brāhmaṇas, kṣatriyas, vaiśyas and in particular the brāhmaṇa Vaiṣṇavas—should chant this narration as it is, without deviation, to counteract the troubles of bad dreams.

PURPORT

Every verse in the Vedic literature, especially in the *Śrīmad-Bhāgavatam* and *Bhagavad-gītā,* is a Vedic *mantra.* Here the words *yathānukīrtayanti* are used to recommend that this literature be presented as it is. Unscrupulous persons, however, deviate from the actual narration and interpret the text in their own way with grammatical jugglery. Such deviations are to be avoided. This is a Vedic injunction supported by Śukadeva Gosvāmī, one of the *mahājanas,* or authorities. He says, *yathānukīrtayanti:* one should recite the *mantra* as it is, without deviation, for then one will be eligible to rise to the platform of all good fortune. Śukadeva Gosvāmī especially recommends that those who are *brāhmaṇas* (*śucayaḥ*) recite all these *mantras* after rising from bed in the morning.

Because of sinful activities, at night we have bad dreams, which are very troublesome. Indeed, Mahārāja Yudhiṣṭhira was obliged to see hell because of a slight deviation from devotional service to the Lord. Therefore, *duḥsvapna*

—bad dreams—occur because of sinful activities. A devotee sometimes accepts a sinful person as his disciple, and to counteract the sinful reactions he accepts from the disciple, he has to see a bad dream. Nonetheless, the spiritual master is so kind that in spite of having bad dreams due to the sinful disciple, he accepts this troublesome business for the deliverance of the victims of Kali-yuga. After initiation, therefore, a disciple should be extremely careful not to commit again any sinful act that might cause difficulties for himself and the spiritual master. Before the Deity, before the fire, before the spiritual master and before the Vaiṣṇavas, the honest disciple promises to refrain from all sinful activity. Therefore he must not again commit sinful acts and thus create a troublesome situation.

TEXT 16

इदमाह हरिः प्रीतो गजेन्द्रं कुरुसत्तम ।
शृण्वतां सर्वभूतानां सर्वभूतमयो विभुः ॥ १६ ॥

idam āha hariḥ prīto
gajendraṁ kuru-sattama
śṛṇvatāṁ sarva-bhūtānāṁ
sarva-bhūta-mayo vibhuḥ

idam—this; *āha*—said; *hariḥ*—the Supreme Personality of Godhead; *prītaḥ*—being pleased; *gajendram*—unto Gajendra; *kuru-sat-tama*—O best of the Kuru dynasty; *śṛṇvatām*—hearing; *sarva-bhūtānām*—in the presence of everyone; *sarva-bhūta-mayaḥ*—all-pervading Personality of Godhead; *vibhuḥ*—the great.

TRANSLATION

O best of the Kuru dynasty, the Supreme Personality of Godhead, the Supersoul of everyone, being thus pleased, addressed Gajendra in the presence of everyone there. He spoke the following blessings.

TEXTS 17-24

श्रीभगवानुवाच
ये मां त्वां च सरश्चेदं गिरिकन्दरकाननम् ।
वेत्रकीचकवेणूनां गुल्मानि सुरपादपान् ॥ १७ ॥

शृङ्गाणीमानि धिष्ण्यानि ब्रह्मणो मे शिवस्य च ।
क्षीरोदं मे प्रियं धाम श्वेतद्वीपं च भास्वरम् ॥ १८ ॥
श्रीवत्सं कौस्तुभं मालां गदां कौमोदकीं मम ।
सुदर्शनं पाञ्चजन्यं सुपर्णं पतगेश्वरम् ॥ १९ ॥
शेषं च मत्कलां सूक्ष्मां श्रियं देवीं मदाश्रयाम् ।
ब्रह्माणं नारदमृषिं भवं प्रह्लादमेव च ॥ २० ॥
मत्स्यकूर्मवराहाद्यैरवतारैः कृतानि मे ।
कर्माण्यनन्तपुण्यानि सूर्यं सोमं हुताशनम् ॥ २१ ॥
प्रणवं सत्यमव्यक्तं गोविप्रान् धर्ममव्ययम् ।
दाक्षायणीर्धर्मपत्नीः सोमकश्यपयोरपि ॥ २२ ॥
गङ्गां सरस्वतीं नन्दां कालिन्दीं सितवारणम् ।
ध्रुवं ब्रह्मऋषीन्सप्त पुण्यश्लोकांश्च मानवान् ॥ २३ ॥
उत्थायापररात्रान्ते प्रयताः सुसमाहिताः ।
स्मरन्ति मम रूपाणि मुच्यन्ते तेंऽहसोऽखिलात् ॥ २४ ॥

śrī-bhagavān uvāca
ye māṁ tvāṁ ca saraś cedaṁ
giri-kandara-kānanam
vetra-kīcaka-veṇūnāṁ
gulmāni sura-pādapān

śṛṅgāṇīmāni dhiṣṇyāni
brahmaṇo me śivasya ca
kṣīrodaṁ me priyaṁ dhāma
śveta-dvīpaṁ ca bhāsvaram

śrīvatsaṁ kaustubhaṁ mālāṁ
gadāṁ kaumodakīṁ mama
sudarśanaṁ pāñcajanyaṁ
suparṇaṁ patageśvaram

śeṣaṁ ca mat-kalāṁ sūkṣmāṁ
śriyaṁ devīṁ mad-āśrayām
brahmāṇaṁ nāradam ṛṣiṁ
bhavaṁ prahrādam eva ca

matsya-kūrma-varāhādyair
avatāraiḥ kṛtāni me
karmāṇy ananta-puṇyāni
sūryaṁ somaṁ hutāśanam

praṇavaṁ satyam avyaktaṁ
go-viprān dharmam avyayam
dākṣāyaṇīr dharma-patnīḥ
soma-kaśyapayor api

gaṅgāṁ sarasvatīṁ nandāṁ
kālindīṁ sita-vāraṇam
dhruvaṁ brahma-ṛṣīn sapta
puṇya-ślokāṁś ca mānavān

utthāyāpara-rātrānte
prayatāḥ susamāhitāḥ
smaranti mama rūpāṇi
mucyante te 'ṁhaso 'khilāt

śrī-bhagavān uvāca—the Supreme Personality of Godhead said; *ye*—those who; *mām*—Me; *tvām*—you; *ca*—also; *saraḥ*—lake; *ca*—also; *idam*—this; *giri*—hill (Trikūṭa Mountain); *kandara*—caves; *kānanam*—gardens; *vetra*—of cane; *kīcaka*—hollow bamboo; *veṇūnām*—and of another kind of bamboo; *gulmāni*—clusters; *sura-pādapān*—celestial trees; *śṛṅgāṇi*—the peaks; *imāni*—these; *dhiṣṇyāni*—abodes; *brahmaṇaḥ*—of Lord Brahmā; *me*—of Me; *śivasya*—of Lord Śiva; *ca*—also; *kṣīra-udam*—the ocean of milk; *me*—My; *priyam*—very dear; *dhāma*—place; *śveta-dvīpam*—known as the white island; *ca*—also; *bhāsvaram*—always brilliant with spiritual rays; *śrīvatsam*—the mark named Śrīvatsa; *kaustubham*—the Kaustubha gem; *mālām*—garland; *gadām*—club; *kaumodakīm*—known as Kaumodakī; *mama*—My; *sudarśanam*—Sudarśana disc; *pāñcajanyam*—conchshell named Pāñcajanya; *suparṇam*—Garuḍa; *pataga-īśvaram*—the king of all birds; *śeṣam*—the resting place Śeṣa Nāga; *ca*—and; *mat-kalām*—My expanded part; *sūkṣmām*—very subtle; *śriyam devīm*—the goddess of fortune; *mat-āśrayām*—all dependent upon Me; *brahmāṇam*—Lord Brahmā; *nāradam ṛṣim*—the great saint Nārada Muni; *bhavam*—Lord Śiva; *prahrādam eva ca*—as well as Prahlāda; *matsya*—the Matsya incarnation; *kūrma*—the Kūrma incarnation; *varāha*—the boar incarnation; *ādyaiḥ*—and so on; *avatāraiḥ*—

by different incarnations; *kṛtāni*—done; *me*—My; *karmāṇi*—activities; *ananta*—unlimited; *puṇyāni*—auspicious, pious; *sūryam*—the sun-god; *somam*—the moon-god; *hutāśanam*—the fire-god; *praṇavam*—the *oṁkāra mantra; satyam*—the Absolute Truth; *avyaktam*—the total material energy; *go-viprān*—the cows and *brāhmaṇas; dharmam*—devotional service; *avyayam*—never ending; *dākṣāyaṇīḥ*—the daughters of Dakṣa; *dharma-patnīḥ*—bona fide wives; *soma*—of the moon-god; *kaśyapayoḥ*—and of the great *ṛṣi* Kaśyapa; *api*—also; *gaṅgām*—the River Ganges; *sarasvatīm*—the River Sarasvatī; *nandām*—the River Nandā; *kālindīm*—the River Yamunā; *sita-vāraṇam*—the elephant Airāvata; *dhruvam*—Dhruva Mahārāja; *brahma-ṛṣīn*—great *ṛṣis; sapta*—seven; *puṇya-ślokān*—extremely pious; *ca*—and; *mānavān*—human beings; *utthāya*—getting up; *apara-rātra-ante*—at the end of the night; *prayatāḥ*—being very careful; *su-samāhitāḥ*—with concentrated minds; *smaranti*—remember; *mama*—My; *rūpāṇi*—forms; *mucyante*—are delivered; *te*—such persons; *aṁhasaḥ*—from sinful reactions; *akhilāt*—of all kinds.

TRANSLATION

The Supreme Personality of Godhead said: Freed from all sinful reactions are those who rise from bed at the end of night, early in the morning, and fully concentrate their minds with great attention upon My form; your form; this lake; this mountain; the caves; the gardens; the cane plants; the bamboo plants; the celestial trees; the residential quarters of Me, Lord Brahmā and Lord Śiva; the three peaks of Trikūṭa Mountain, made of gold, silver and iron; My very pleasing abode [the ocean of milk]; the white island, Śvetadvīpa, which is always brilliant with spiritual rays; My mark of Śrīvatsa; the Kaustubha gem; My Vaijayantī garland; My club, Kaumodakī; My Sudarśana disc and Pāñcajanya conchshell; My bearer, Garuḍa, the king of the birds; My bed, Śeṣa Nāga; My expansion of energy the goddess of fortune; Lord Brahmā; Nārada Muni; Lord Śiva; Prahlāda; My incarnations like Matsya, Kūrma and Varāha; My unlimited all-auspicious activities, which yield piety to he who hears them; the sun; the moon; fire; the mantra oṁkāra; the Absolute Truth; the total material energy; the cows and brāhmaṇas; devotional service; the wives of Soma and Kaśyapa, who are all daughters of King Dakṣa; the Rivers Ganges, Sarasvatī, Nandā and Yamunā [Kālindī]; the elephant Airāvata; Dhruva Mahārāja; the seven ṛṣis; and the pious human beings.

TEXT 25

ये मां स्तुवन्त्यनेनाङ्ग प्रतिबुध्य निशात्यये ।
तेषां प्राणात्यये चाहं ददामि विपुलां गतिम् ॥ २५ ॥

ye māṁ stuvanty anenāṅga
pratibudhya niśātyaye
teṣāṁ prāṇātyaye cāhaṁ
dadāmi vipulāṁ gatim

ye—those who; *mām*—unto Me; *stuvanti*—offer prayers; *anena*—in this way; *aṅga*—O King; *pratibudhya*—getting up; *niśa-atyaye*—at the end of night; *teṣām*—for them; *prāṇa-atyaye*—at the time of death; *ca*—also; *aham*—I; *dadāmi*—give; *vipulām*—the eternal, unlimited; *gatim*—transferral to the spiritual world.

TRANSLATION

My dear devotee, unto those who rise from bed at the end of night and offer Me the prayers offered by you, I give an eternal residence in the spiritual world at the end of their lives.

TEXT 26

श्रीशुक उवाच
इत्यादिश्य हृषीकेशः प्राध्माय जलजोत्तमम् ।
हर्षयन्विबुधानीकमारुरोह खगाधिपम् ॥ २६ ॥

śrī-śuka uvāca
ity ādiśya hṛṣīkeśaḥ
prādhmāya jalajottamam
harṣayan vibudhānīkam
āruroha khagādhipam

śrī-śukaḥ uvāca—Śrī Śukadeva Gosvāmī said; *iti*—thus; *ādiśya*—advising; *hṛṣīkeśaḥ*—the Supreme Personality of Godhead, known as Hṛṣīkeśa; *prādhmāya*—blowing; *jala-ja-uttamam*—the conchshell, the best of the aquatics; *harṣayan*—pleasing; *vibudha-anīkam*—the host of demigods, headed by Lord Brahmā and Lord Śiva; *āruroha*—got up; *khaga-adhipam*—on the back of Garuḍa.

TRANSLATION

Śrī Śukadeva Gosvāmī continued: After giving this instruction, the Lord, who is known as Hṛṣīkeśa, bugled with His Pāñcajanya conchshell, in this way pleasing all the demigods, headed by Lord Brahmā. Then He mounted the back of His carrier, Garuḍa.

Thus end the Bhaktivedanta purports of the Eighth Canto, Fourth Chapter, of the Śrīmad-Bhāgavatam, *entitled "Gajendra Returns to the Spiritual World."*

CHAPTER FIVE

The Demigods Appeal to the Lord for Protection

This chapter describes the fifth and sixth Manus, and it also describes the prayers of the demigods and the curse of Durvāsā Muni.

The brother of Tāmasa, the fourth Manu, who has previously been described, was the fifth Manu, Raivata. The sons of Raivata included Arjuna, Bali and Vindhya. During the reign of this Manu, Indra, the King of heaven, was known as Vibhu. Among the demigods were the Bhūtarayas, and among the seven *ṛṣis* were Hiraṇyaromā, Vedaśirā and Ūrdhvabāhu. The *ṛṣi* known as Śubhra, by his wife, Vikuṇṭhā, gave birth to the Supreme Personality of Godhead, Vaikuṇṭha. This Supreme Personality of Godhead manifested a Vaikuṇṭha planet at the request of Ramādevī. His power and activities are mentioned in the Third Canto.

The sixth Manu was Cākṣuṣa, the son of Cakṣu Manu. Among the sons of the sixth Manu were Pūru, Pūruṣa and Sudyumna. During the reign of this Manu, Mantradruma was Indra, the King of the heavenly planets. Among the demigods were the Āpyas, and among the seven *ṛṣis* were Haviṣmān and Vīraka. The wife of Vairāja, whose name was Devasambhūti, gave birth to Ajita, an incarnation of the Supreme Personality of Godhead. This Ajita, taking the shape of a tortoise and holding the mountain known as Mandara on His back, churned the ocean and produced nectar for the demigods.

Mahārāja Parīkṣit was very eager to hear about the churning of the ocean, and therefore Śukadeva Gosvāmī began to explain to him how the demigods, having been cursed by Durvāsā Muni, were defeated in battle by the *asuras.* When the demigods were deprived of their heavenly kingdom, they went to the assembly house of Lord Brahmā and informed Lord Brahmā of what had happened. Then Brahmā, along with all the demigods, went to the shore of the ocean of milk and offered prayers to Kṣīrodakaśāyī Viṣṇu.

TEXT 1

श्रीशुक उवाच

राजन्नुदितमेतत् ते हरेः कर्माघनाशनम् ।
गजेन्द्रमोक्षणं पुण्यं रैवतं त्वन्तरं शृणु ॥ १ ॥

śrī-śuka uvāca
rājann uditam etat te
hareḥ karmāgha-nāśanam
gajendra-mokṣaṇaṁ puṇyaṁ
raivataṁ tv antaraṁ śṛṇu

śrī-śukaḥ uvāca—Śrī Śukadeva Gosvāmī said; *rājan*—O King; *uditam*—already described; *etat*—this; *te*—unto you; *hareḥ*—of the Lord; *karma*—activity; *agha-nāśanam*—by hearing which one can be freed from all misfortune; *gajendra-mokṣaṇam*—deliverance of Gajendra, the King of the elephants; *puṇyam*—very pious to hear and describe; *raivatam*—about Raivata Manu; *tu*—but; *antaram*—in this millennium; *śṛṇu*—kindly hear from me.

TRANSLATION

Śukadeva Gosvāmī continued: O King, I have described to you the pastime of Gajendra-mokṣaṇa, which is most pious to hear. By hearing of such activities of the Lord, one can be freed from all sinful reactions. Now please listen as I describe Raivata Manu.

TEXT 2

पञ्चमो रैवतो नाम मनुस्तामससोदरः ।
बलिविन्ध्यादयस्तस्य सुता हार्जुनपूर्वकाः ॥ २ ॥

pañcamo raivato nāma
manus tāmasa-sodaraḥ
bali-vindhyādayas tasya
sutā hārjuna-pūrvakāḥ

pañcamaḥ—the fifth; *raivataḥ*—Raivata; *nama*—by the name; *manuḥ*—Manu; *tāmasa-sodaraḥ*—the brother of Tāmasa Manu; *bali*—Bali; *vindhya*—Vindhya; *ādayaḥ*—and so on; *tasya*—his; *sutāḥ*—sons; *ha*—certainly; *arjuna*—Arjuna; *pūrvakāḥ*—heading all the sons.

TRANSLATION

The brother of Tāmasa Manu was the fifth Manu, named Raivata. His sons were headed by Arjuna, Bali and Vindhya.

TEXT 3

विभुरिन्द्रः सुरगणा राजन्भूतरयादयः ।
हिरण्यरोमा वेदशिरा ऊर्ध्वबाह्वादयो द्विजाः ॥ ३ ॥

vibhur indraḥ sura-gaṇā
rājan bhūtarayādayaḥ
hiraṇyaromā vedaśirā
ūrdhvabāhv-ādayo dvijāḥ

vibhuḥ—Vibhu; *indraḥ*—the King of heaven; *sura-gaṇāḥ*—the demigods; *rājan*—O King; *bhūtaraya-ādayaḥ*—headed by the Bhūtarayas; *hiraṇyaromā*—Hiraṇyaromā; *vedaśirā*—Vedaśirā; *ūrdhvabāhu*—Ūrdhvabāhu; *ādayaḥ*—and others; *dvijāḥ*—the *brāhmaṇas* or *ṛṣis* who occupied the seven planets.

TRANSLATION

O King, in the millennium of Raivata Manu the King of heaven was known as Vibhu, among the demigods were the Bhūtarayas, and among the seven brāhmaṇas who occupied the seven planets were Hiraṇyaromā, Vedaśirā and Ūrdhvabāhu.

TEXT 4

पत्नी विकुण्ठा शुभ्रस्य वैकुण्ठैः सुरसत्तमैः ।
तयोः स्वकलया जज्ञे वैकुण्ठो भगवान्स्वयम् ॥ ४ ॥

patnī vikuṇṭhā śubhrasya
vaikuṇṭhaiḥ sura-sattamaiḥ
tayoḥ sva-kalayā jajñe
vaikuṇṭho bhagavān svayam

patnī—the wife; *vikuṇṭhā*—named Vikuṇṭhā; *śubhrasya*—of Śubhra; *vaikuṇṭhaiḥ*—with the Vaikuṇṭhas; *sura-sat-tamaiḥ*—demigods; *tayoḥ*—by Vikuṇṭhā and Śubhra; *sva-kalayā*—with plenary expansions; *jajñe*—appeared; *vaikuṇṭhaḥ*—the Lord; *bhagavān*—the Supreme Personality of Godhead; *svayam*—personally.

TRANSLATION

From the combination of Śubhra and his wife, Vikuṇṭhā, there appeared the Supreme Personality of Godhead, Vaikuṇṭha, along with demigods who were His personal plenary expansions.

TEXT 5

वैकुण्ठः कल्पितो येन लोको लोकनमस्कृतः ।
रमया प्रार्थ्यमानेन देव्या तत्प्रियकाम्यया ॥ ५ ॥

vaikuṇṭhaḥ kalpito yena
loko loka-namaskṛtaḥ
ramayā prārthyamānena
devyā tat-priya-kāmyayā

vaikuṇṭhaḥ—a Vaikuṇṭha planet; *kalpitaḥ*—was constructed; *yena*—by whom; *lokaḥ*—planet; *loka-namaskṛtaḥ*—worshiped by all people; *ramayā*—by Ramā, the goddess of fortune; *prārthyamānena*—being so requested; *devyā*—by the goddess; *tat*—her; *priya-kāmyayā*—just to please.

TRANSLATION

Just to please the goddess of fortune, the Supreme Personality of Godhead, Vaikuṇṭha, at her request, created another Vaikuṇṭha planet, which is worshiped by everyone.

PURPORT

Śrīla Viśvanātha Cakravartī Ṭhākura remarks here that this Vaikuṇṭha planet, like *Śrīmad-Bhāgavatam,* appears and is said to be born or created, but both *Śrīmad-Bhāgavatam* and Vaikuṇṭha eternally exist beyond the material universes, which are enveloped by eight kinds of coverings. As described in the Second Canto, Lord Brahmā saw Vaikuṇṭha before the creation of the universe. Vīrarāghava Ācārya mentions that this Vaikuṇṭha is within the universe. It is situated above the mountain known as Lokāloka. This planet is worshiped by everyone.

TEXT 6

तस्यानुभावः कथितो गुणाश्च परमोदयाः ।
भौमान्रेणून्स विममे यो विष्णोर्वर्णयेद् गुणान् ॥ ६ ॥

tasyānubhāvaḥ kathito
guṇāś ca paramodayāḥ
bhaumān reṇūn sa vimame
yo viṣṇor varṇayed guṇān

tasya—of the Supreme Personality of Godhead appearing as Vaikuṇṭha; *anubhāvaḥ*—great activities; *kathitaḥ*—were explained; *guṇāḥ*—transcendental qualities; *ca*—also; *parama-udayāḥ*—greatly glorious; *bhaumān*—earthly; *reṇūn*—particles; *saḥ*—someone; *vimame*—can count; *yaḥ*—such a person; *viṣṇoḥ*—of Lord Viṣṇu; *varṇayet*—can count; *guṇān*—the transcendental qualities.

TRANSLATION

Although the great activities and transcendental qualities of the Supreme Personality of Godhead's various incarnations are wonderfully described, sometimes we are unable to understand them. Yet everything is possible for Lord Viṣṇu. If one could count the atoms of the universe, then he could count the qualities of the Supreme Personality of Godhead. But no one can count the atoms of the universe, nor can anyone count the transcendental qualities of the Lord.

PURPORT

The Lord's glorious activities referred to in this connection took place after His personal bodyguards Jaya and Vijaya became Daityas, having been cursed by the great sages Sanaka, Sanātana, Sanat-kumāra and Sanandana. Jaya, as Hiraṇyākṣa, had to fight with Varāhadeva, and that same Varāhadeva is mentioned in regard to the Raivata millennium. The fighting, however, took place during the reign of the first Manu, Svāyambhuva. Therefore according to some authorities there are two Varāhas. According to others, however, Varāha appeared during the regime of Svāyambhuva Manu and stayed in the water until that of Raivata Manu. Some may doubt that this could be possible, but the answer is that everything is possible. If one could count the atoms within the universe, one could count the qualities of Lord Viṣṇu. But the atoms of the universe are impossible for anyone to count, and similarly no one can count the transcendental qualities of the Lord.

TEXT 7

षष्ठश्च चक्षुषः पुत्रश्चाक्षुषो नाम वै मनुः ।
पूरुपूरुषसुद्युम्नप्रमुखाश्चाक्षुषात्मजाः ॥ ७ ॥

ṣaṣṭhaś ca cakṣuṣaḥ putraś
cākṣuṣo nāma vai manuḥ
pūru-pūruṣa-sudyumna-
pramukhāś cākṣuṣātmajāḥ

ṣaṣṭhaḥ—the sixth; *ca*—and; *cakṣuṣaḥ*—of Cakṣu; *putraḥ*—the son; *cākṣuṣaḥ*—Cākṣuṣa; *nāma*—named; *vai*—indeed; *manuḥ*—Manu; *pūru*—Pūru; *pūruṣa*—Pūruṣa; *sudyumna*—Sudyumna; *pramukhāḥ*—headed by; *cākṣuṣa-ātma-jāḥ*—the sons of Cākṣuṣa.

TRANSLATION

The son of Cakṣu known as Cākṣuṣa was the sixth Manu. He had many sons, headed by Pūru, Pūruṣa and Sudyumna.

TEXT 8

इन्द्रो मन्त्रद्रुमस्तत्र देवा आप्यादयो गणाः ।
मुनयस्तत्र वै राजन्हविष्मद्वीरकादयः ॥ ८ ॥

indro mantradrumas tatra
devā āpyādayo gaṇāḥ
munayas tatra vai rājan
haviṣmad-vīrakādayaḥ

indraḥ—the King of heaven; *mantradrumaḥ*—known as Mantradruma; *tatra*—in that sixth *manvantara; devāḥ*—the demigods; *āpya-ādayaḥ*—the Āpyas and others; *gaṇāḥ*—that assembly; *munayaḥ*—the seven sages; *tatra*—there; *vai*—indeed; *rājan*—O King; *haviṣmat*—of the name Haviṣmān; *vīraka-ādayaḥ*—Vīraka and others.

TRANSLATION

During the reign of Cākṣuṣa Manu, the King of heaven was known as Mantradruma. Among the demigods were the Āpyas, and among the great sages were Haviṣmān and Vīraka.

TEXT 9

तत्रापि देवसम्भूत्यां वैराजस्याभवत् सुतः ।
अजितो नाम भगवानंशेन जगतः पतिः ॥ ९ ॥

tatrāpi devasambhūtyāṁ
vairājasyābhavat sutaḥ
ajito nāma bhagavān
aṁśena jagataḥ patiḥ

tatra api—again in that sixth *manvantara; devasambhūtyām*—by Devasambhūti; *vairājasya*—by her husband, Vairāja; *abhavat*—there was; *sutaḥ*—a son; *ajitaḥ nāma*—by the name Ajita; *bhagavān*—the Supreme Personality of Godhead; *aṁśena*—partially; *jagataḥ patiḥ*—the master of the universe.

TRANSLATION

In this sixth manvantara millennium, Lord Viṣṇu, the master of the universe, appeared in His partial expansion. He was begotten by Vairāja in the womb of his wife, Devasambhūti, and His name was Ajita.

TEXT 10

पयोधिं येन निर्मथ्य सुराणां साधिता सुधा।
भ्रममाणोऽम्भसि धृतः कूर्मरूपेण मन्दरः ॥ १० ॥

payodhiṁ yena nirmathya
surāṇāṁ sādhitā sudhā
bhramamāṇo 'mbhasi dhṛtaḥ
kūrma-rūpeṇa mandaraḥ

payodhim—the ocean of milk; *yena*—by whom; *nirmathya*—by churning; *surāṇām*—of the demigods; *sādhitā*—produced; *sudhā*—nectar; *bhramamāṇaḥ*—moving here and there; *ambhasi*—within the water; *dhṛtaḥ*—was staying; *kūrma-rūpeṇa*—in the form of a tortoise; *mandaraḥ*—the mountain known as Mandara.

TRANSLATION

By churning the ocean of milk, Ajita produced nectar for the demigods. In the form of a tortoise, He moved here and there, carrying on His back the great mountain known as Mandara.

TEXTS 11-12

श्रीराजोवाच

यथा भगवता ब्रह्मन्मथितः क्षीरसागरः ।
यदर्थं वा यतश्चाद्रिं दधाराम्बुचरात्मना ॥ ११ ॥
यथामृतं सुरैः प्राप्तं किञ्चान्यदभवत् ततः ।
एतद् भगवतः कर्म वदस्व परमाद्भुतम् ॥ १२ ॥

śrī-rājovāca
yathā bhagavatā brahman
mathitaḥ kṣīra-sāgaraḥ
yad-arthaṁ vā yataś cādriṁ
dadhārāmbucarātmanā

yathāmṛtaṁ suraiḥ prāptaṁ
kiṁ cānyad abhavat tataḥ
etad bhagavataḥ karma
vadasva paramādbhutam

śrī-rājā uvāca—King Parīkṣit inquired; *yathā*—as; *bhagavatā*—by the Supreme Personality of Godhead; *brahman*—O learned *brāhmaṇa; mathitaḥ*—churned; *kṣīra-sāgaraḥ*—the ocean of milk; *yat-artham*—what was the purpose; *vā*—either; *yataḥ*—wherefrom, for what reason; *ca*—and; *adrim*—the mountain (Mandara); *dadhāra*—was staying; *ambucara-ātmanā*—in the form of a tortoise; *yathā*—as; *amṛtam*—nectar; *suraiḥ*—by the demigods; *prāptam*—was achieved; *kim*—what; *ca*—and; *anyat*—other; *abhavat*—became; *tataḥ*—thereafter; *etat*—all these; *bhagavataḥ*—of the Supreme Personality of Godhead; *karma*—pastimes, activities; *vadasva*—kindly describe; *parama-adbhutam*—because they are so wonderful.

TRANSLATION

King Parīkṣit inquired: O great brāhmaṇa, Śukadeva Gosvāmī, why and how did Lord Viṣṇu churn the ocean of milk? For what reason did He stay in the water as a tortoise and hold up Mandara Mountain? How did the demigods obtain the nectar, and what other things were produced from the churning of the ocean? Kindly describe all these wonderful activities of the Lord.

TEXT 13

त्वया सङ्कथ्यमानेन महिम्ना सात्वतां पतेः ।
नातितृप्यति मे चित्तं सुचिरं तापतापितम् ॥ १३ ॥

tvayā saṅkathyamānena
mahimnā sātvatāṁ pateḥ
nātitṛpyati me cittaṁ
suciraṁ tāpa-tāpitam

tvayā—by Your Holiness; *saṅkathyamānena*—being described; *mahimnā*—by all the glories; *sātvatām pateḥ*—of the Supreme Personality of Godhead, the master of the devotees; *na*—not; *ati-tṛpyati*—is sufficiently satisfied; *me*—my; *cittam*—heart; *suciram*—for such a long time; *tāpa*—by miseries; *tāpitam*—being distressed.

TRANSLATION

My heart, which is disturbed by the three miserable conditions of material life, is not yet sated with hearing you describe the glorious activities of the Lord, the Supreme Personality of Godhead, who is the master of the devotees.

TEXT 14

श्रीसूत उवाच
सम्पृष्टो भगवानेवं द्वैपायनसुतो द्विजाः ।
अभिनन्द्य हरेर्वीर्यमभ्याचष्टुं प्रचक्रमे ॥ १४ ॥

śrī-sūta uvāca
sampṛṣṭo bhagavān evaṁ
dvaipāyana-suto dvijāḥ
abhinandya harer vīryam
abhyācaṣṭuṁ pracakrame

śrī-sūtaḥ uvāca—Śrī Sūta Gosvāmī said; *sampṛṣṭaḥ*—being questioned; *bhagavān*—Śukadeva Gosvāmī; *evam*—thus; *dvaipāyana-sutaḥ*—the son of Vyāsadeva; *dvi-jāḥ*—O *brāhmaṇas* assembled here; *abhinandya*—congratulating Mahārāja Parīkṣit; *hareḥ vīryam*—the glories of the Supreme Personality of Godhead; *abhyācaṣṭum*—to describe; *pracakrame*—endeavored.

TRANSLATION

Śrī Sūta Gosvāmī said: O learned brāhmaṇas assembled here at Naimiṣāraṇya, when Śukadeva Gosvāmī, the son of Dvaipāyana, was thus questioned by the King, he congratulated the King and then endeavored to describe further the glories of the Supreme Personality of Godhead.

TEXTS 15-16

श्रीशुक उवाच
यदा युद्धेऽसुरैर्देवा बध्यमानाः शितायुधैः ।
गतासवो निपतिता नोत्तिष्ठेरन्स्म भूरिशः ॥ १५ ॥
यदा दुर्वासः शापेन सेन्द्रा लोकास्त्रयो नृप ।
निःश्रीकाश्चाभवंस्तत्र नेशुरिज्यादयः क्रियाः ॥ १६ ॥

śrī-śuka uvāca
yadā yuddhe 'surair devā
badhyamānāḥ śitāyudhaiḥ
gatāsavo nipatitā
nottiṣṭheran sma bhūriśaḥ

yadā durvāsaḥ śāpena
sendrā lokās trayo nṛpa
niḥśrīkāś cābhavaṁs tatra
neśur ijyādayaḥ kriyāḥ

śrī-śukaḥ uvāca—Śrī Śukadeva Gosvāmī said; *yadā*—when; *yuddhe*—in the fighting; *asuraiḥ*—by the demons; *devāḥ*—the demigods; *badhyamānāḥ*—besieged; *śita-āyudhaiḥ*—by serpent weapons; *gata-āsavaḥ*—almost dead; *nipatitāḥ*—some of them having fallen; *na*—not; *uttiṣṭheran*—got up again; *sma*—so became; *bhūriśaḥ*—the majority of them; *yadā*—when; *durvāsaḥ*—of Durvāsā Muni; *śāpena*—with the curse; *sa-indrāḥ*—with Indra; *lokāḥ trayaḥ*—the three worlds; *nṛpa*—O King; *niḥśrīkāḥ*—without any material opulence; *ca*—also; *abhavan*—became; *tatra*—at that time; *neśuḥ*—could not be performed; *ijya-ādayaḥ*—sacrifices; *kriyāḥ*—ritualistic ceremonies.

TRANSLATION

Śukadeva Gosvāmī said: When the asuras, with their serpent weapons, severely attacked the demigods in a fight, many of the demigods fell and lost their lives. Indeed, they could not be revived. At that time, O King, the demigods had been cursed by Durvāsā Muni, the three worlds were poverty-stricken, and therefore ritualistic ceremonies could not be performed. The effects of this were very serious.

PURPORT

It is described that while Durvāsā Muni was passing on the road, he saw Indra on the back of his elephant and was pleased to offer Indra a garland from his own neck. Indra, however, being too puffed up, took the garland, and without respect for Durvāsā Muni, he placed it on the trunk of his carrier elephant. The elephant, being an animal, could not understand the value of the garland, and thus the elephant threw the garland between its legs and smashed it. Seeing this insulting behavior, Durvāsā Muni immediately cursed Indra to be poverty-stricken, bereft of all material opulence. Thus the demigods, afflicted on one side by the fighting demons and on the other by the curse of Durvāsā Muni, lost all the material opulences in the three worlds.

To be extremely opulent in materialistic advancement is sometimes very risky. The materially opulent person does not care about anyone, and thus he commits offenses to great personalities, such as devotees and great saints. This is the way of material opulence. As described by Śukadeva Gosvāmī, *dhana-durmadāndha:* too much wealth makes one blind. This happens even to Indra in his heavenly kingdom, and what to speak of others in this material world? When one is materially opulent, he should learn to be sober and well-behaved toward Vaiṣṇavas and saintly persons; otherwise he will fall down.

TEXTS 17-18

निशाम्यैतत् सुरगणा महेन्द्रवरुणादयः ।
नाध्यगच्छन्स्वयं मन्त्रैर्मन्त्रयन्तो विनिश्चितम् ॥ १७ ॥
ततो ब्रह्मसभां जग्मुर्मेरोर्मूर्धनि सर्वशः ।
सर्वं विज्ञापयाञ्चक्रुः प्रणताः परमेष्ठिने ॥ १८ ॥

niśāmyaitat sura-gaṇā
mahendra-varuṇādayaḥ
nādhyagacchan svayaṁ mantrair
mantrayanto viniścitam

tato brahma-sabhāṁ jagmur
meror mūrdhani sarvaśaḥ
sarvaṁ vijñāpayāṁ cakruḥ
praṇatāḥ parameṣṭhine

niśāmya—hearing; *etat*—this incident; *sura-gaṇāḥ*—all the demigods; *mahā-indra*—King Indra; *varuṇa-ādayaḥ*—Varuṇa and other demigods; *na*

—not; *adhyagacchan*—reached; *svayam*—personally; *mantraiḥ*—by deliberation; *mantrayantaḥ*—discussing; *viniścitam*—a real conclusion; *tataḥ*—thereupon; *brahma-sabhām*—to the assembly of Lord Brahmā; *jagmuḥ*—they went; *meroḥ*—of Sumeru Mountain; *mūrdhani*—on the top; *sarvaśaḥ*—all of them; *sarvam*—everything; *vijñāpayām cakruḥ*—they informed; *praṇatāḥ*—offered obeisances; *parameṣṭhine*—unto Lord Brahmā.

TRANSLATION

Lord Indra, Varuṇa and the other demigods, seeing their lives in such a state, consulted among themselves, but they could not find any solution. Then all the demigods assembled and went together to the peak of Sumeru Mountain. There, in the assembly of Lord Brahmā, they fell down to offer Lord Brahmā their obeisances, and then they informed him of all the incidents that had taken place.

TEXTS 19-20

स विलोक्येन्द्रवाय्वादीन् निःसत्त्वान्विगतप्रभान् ।
लोकानमङ्गलप्रायानसुरानयथा विभुः ॥ १९ ॥
समाहितेन मनसा संस्मरन्पुरुषं परम् ।
उवाचोत्फुल्लवदनो देवान्स भगवान्परः ॥ २० ॥

sa vilokyendra-vāyv-ādīn
niḥsattvān vigata-prabhān
lokān amaṅgala-prāyān
asurān ayathā vibhuḥ

samāhitena manasā
saṁsmaran puruṣaṁ param
uvācotphulla-vadano
devān sa bhagavān paraḥ

saḥ—Lord Brahmā; *vilokya*—looking over; *indra-vāyu-ādīn*—all the demigods, headed by Lord Indra and Vāyu; *niḥsattvān*—bereft of all spiritual potency; *vigata-prabhān*—bereft of all effulgence; *lokān*—all the three worlds; *amaṅgala-prāyān*—merged into misfortune; *asurān*—all the demons; *ayathāḥ*—flourishing; *vibhuḥ*—Lord Brahmā, the supreme within this material world; *samāhitena*—by full adjustment; *manasā*—of the mind; *saṁsmaran*—remembering again and again; *puruṣam*—the Supreme Person; *param*—transcendental; *uvāca*—said; *utphulla-vadanaḥ*—bright-faced; *devān*—unto the demigods; *saḥ*—he; *bhagavān*—the most powerful; *paraḥ*—of the demigods.

TRANSLATION

Upon seeing that the demigods were bereft of all influence and strength and that the three worlds were consequently devoid of auspiciousness, and upon seeing that the demigods were in an awkward position whereas all the demons were flourishing, Lord Brahmā, who is above all the demigods and who is most powerful, concentrated his mind on the Supreme Personality of Godhead. Thus being encouraged, he became bright-faced and spoke to the demigods as follows.

PURPORT

After hearing from the demigods the real situation, Lord Brahmā was very much concerned because the demons were unnecessarily so powerful. When demons become powerful, the entire world is placed in an awkward position because demons are simply interested in their own sense gratification and not in the welfare of the world. Demigods or devotees, however, are concerned with the welfare of all living beings. Śrīla Rūpa Gosvāmī, for example, left his ministership and went to Vṛndāvana for the benefit of the entire world (*lokānāṁ hita-kāriṇau*). This is the nature of a saintly person or demigod. Even impersonalists think of the welfare of all people. Thus Brahmā was very much concerned at seeing the demons in power.

TEXT 21

अहं भवो यूयमथोऽसुरादयो
मनुष्यतिर्यग्द्रुमघर्मजातयः ।
यस्यावतारांशकलाविसर्जिता
व्रजाम सर्वे शरणं तमव्ययम् ॥ २१ ॥

ahaṁ bhavo yūyam atho 'surādayo
manuṣya-tiryag-druma-gharma-jātayaḥ
yasyāvatārāṁśa-kalā-visarjitā
vrajāma sarve śaraṇaṁ tam avyayam

aham—I; *bhavaḥ*—Lord Śiva; *yūyam*—all of you demigods; *atho*—as well as; *asura-ādayaḥ*—demons and others; *manuṣya*—the human beings;

tiryak—the animals; *druma*—the trees and plants; *gharma-jātayaḥ*—as well as the insects and germs born of perspiration; *yasya*—of whom (the Supreme Personality of Godhead); *avatāra*—of the *puruṣa* incarnation; *aṁśa*—of His part and parcel, the *guṇa-avatāra,* Brahmā; *kalā*—of Brahmā's sons; *visarjitāḥ*—produced by the generation; *vrajāma*—we shall go; *sarve*—all of us; *śaraṇam*—unto the shelter; *tam*—unto the Supreme; *avyayam*—the inexhaustible.

TRANSLATION

Lord Brahmā said: I, Lord Śiva, all of you demigods, the demons, the living entities born of perspiration, the living beings born of eggs, the trees and plants sprouting from the earth, and the living entities born from embryos—all come from the Supreme Lord, from His incarnation of rajo-guṇa [Lord Brahmā, the guṇa-avatāra] and from the great sages [ṛṣis] who are part of me. Let us therefore go to the Supreme Lord and take shelter of His lotus feet.

PURPORT

Some creatures are born from embryos, some from perspiration, and some from seeds. In this way, all living entities emanate from the *guṇa-avatāra* of the Supreme Personality of Godhead. Ultimately, the Supreme Personality of Godhead is the shelter of all living entities.

TEXT 22

न यस्य वध्यो न च रक्षणीयो
नोपेक्षणीयादरणीयपक्षः ।
तथापि सर्गस्थितिसंयमार्थं
धत्ते रजःसत्त्वतमांसि काले ॥ २२ ॥

na yasya vadhyo na ca rakṣaṇīyo
nopekṣaṇīyādaraṇīya-pakṣaḥ
tathāpi sarga-sthiti-saṁyamārthaṁ
dhatte rajaḥ-sattva-tamāṁsi kāle

na—not; *yasya*—by whom (the Lord); *vadhyaḥ*—anyone is to be killed; *na*—nor; *ca*—also; *rakṣaṇīyaḥ*—anyone is to be protected; *na*—nor; *upekṣaṇīya*—to be neglected; *ādaraṇīya*—to be worshiped; *pakṣaḥ*—part; *tathāpi*—still; *sarga*—creation; *sthiti*—maintenance; *saṁyama*—and annihilation; *artham*—for the sake of; *dhatte*—He accepts; *rajaḥ*—passion; *sattva*—goodness; *tamāṁsi*—and ignorance; *kāle*—in due course of time.

TRANSLATION

For the Supreme Personality of Godhead there is no one to be killed, no one to be protected, no one to be neglected and no one to be worshiped. Nonetheless, for the sake of creation, maintenance and annihilation according to time, He accepts different forms as incarnations either in the mode of goodness, the mode of passion or the mode of ignorance.

PURPORT

This verse explains that the Supreme Personality of Godhead is equal to everyone. This is confirmed by the Lord Himself in *Bhagavad-gītā* (9.29):

samo 'haṁ sarva-bhūteṣu
na me dveṣyo 'sti na priyaḥ
ye bhajanti tu māṁ bhaktyā
mayi te teṣu cāpy aham

"I envy no one, nor am I partial to anyone. I am equal to all. But whoever renders service unto Me in devotion is a friend, is in Me, and I am also a friend to him." Although the Lord is impartial, He gives special attention to His devotees. Therefore the Lord says in *Bhagavad-gītā* (4.8):

paritrāṇāya sādhūnāṁ
vināśāya ca duṣkṛtām
dharma-saṁsthāpanārthāya
sambhavāmi yuge yuge

"To deliver the pious and to annihilate the miscreants, as well as to reestablish the principles of religion, I advent Myself millennium after millennium." The Lord has nothing to do with anyone's protection or destruction, but for the creation, maintenance and annihilation of this material world He apparently has to act either in goodness, in passion or in darkness. Actually, however, He is unaffected by these modes of material nature. He is the Supreme Lord of everyone. As a king sometimes punishes or rewards someone to maintain law and order, the Supreme Personality of Godhead, although having nothing to do with the activities of this material world, sometimes appears as various incarnations according to the time, place and object.

TEXT 23

अयं च तस्य स्थितिपालनक्षणः
सत्त्वं जुषाणस्य भवाय देहिनाम् ।
तस्माद् व्रजामः शरणं जगद्गुरुं
स्वानां स नो धास्यति शं सुरप्रियः ॥ २३ ॥

ayaṁ ca tasya sthiti-pālana-kṣaṇaḥ
sattvaṁ juṣāṇasya bhavāya dehinām
tasmād vrajāmaḥ śaraṇaṁ jagad-guruṁ
svānāṁ sa no dhāsyati śaṁ sura-priyaḥ

ayam—this period; *ca*—also; *tasya*—of the Supreme Personality of Godhead; *sthiti-pālana-kṣaṇaḥ*—the time for maintenance, or for establishing His rule; *sattvam*—the mode of goodness; *juṣāṇasya*—accepting (now, without waiting); *bhavāya*—for the increased development or establishment; *dehinām*—of all living entities who accept material bodies; *tasmāt*—therefore; *vrajāmaḥ*—let us take; *śaraṇam*—shelter; *jagat-gurum*—at the lotus feet of the Supreme Personality of Godhead, who is the universal teacher; *svānām*—His own persons; *saḥ*—He (the Supreme Personality of Godhead); *naḥ*—unto us; *dhāsyati*—will give; *śam*—the good fortune we need; *sura-priyaḥ*—because He is naturally very dear to the devotees.

TRANSLATION

Now is the time to invoke the mode of goodness of the living entities who have accepted material bodies. The mode of goodness is meant to establish the Supreme Lord's rule, which will maintain the existence of the creation. Therefore, this is the opportune moment to take shelter of the Supreme Personality of Godhead. Because He is naturally very kind and dear to the demigods, He will certainly bestow good fortune upon us.

PURPORT

The material world is conducted by the three modes of nature, namely *sattva-guṇa, rajo-guṇa* and *tamo-guṇa.* By *rajo-guṇa* everything material is created, by *sattva-guṇa* everything material is maintained properly, and by *tamo-guṇa,* when the creation is improperly situated, everything is destroyed.

From this verse we can understand the situation of Kali-yuga, through which we are now passing. Just before the beginning of Kali-yuga—or, in other words, at the end of Dvāpara-yuga—Lord Śrī Kṛṣṇa appeared and left

His instructions in the form of *Bhagavad-gītā,* in which He asked all living entities to surrender unto Him. Since the beginning of Kali-yuga, however, people have practically been unable to surrender to the lotus feet of Kṛṣṇa, and therefore, after some five thousand years, Kṛṣṇa came again as Śrī Caitanya Mahāprabhu just to teach the entire world how to surrender unto Him, unto Śrī Kṛṣṇa, and thus be purified.

Surrendering unto the lotus feet of Kṛṣṇa means achieving complete purification. Kṛṣṇa says in *Bhagavad-gītā* (18.66):

sarva-dharmān parityajya
mām ekaṁ śaraṇaṁ vraja
ahaṁ tvāṁ sarva-pāpebhyo
mokṣayiṣyāmi mā śucaḥ

"Abandon all varieties of religion and just surrender unto Me. I shall deliver you from all sinful reaction. Do not fear." Thus as soon as one surrenders unto the lotus feet of Kṛṣṇa, one certainly becomes free from all contamination.

Kali-yuga is full of contamination. This is described in the *Śrīmad-Bhāgavatam* (12.3.51):

kaler doṣa-nidhe rājann
asti hy eko mahān guṇaḥ
kīrtanād eva kṛṣṇasya
mukta-saṅgaḥ paraṁ vrajet

This age of Kali is full of unlimited faults. Indeed, it is just like an ocean of faults (*doṣa-nidhi*). But there is one chance, one opportunity. *Kīrtanād eva kṛṣṇasya mukta-saṅgaḥ paraṁ vrajet:* simply by chanting the Hare Kṛṣṇa *mantra,* one can be freed from the contamination of Kali-yuga and, in his original spiritual body, can return home, back to Godhead. This is the opportunity of Kali-yuga.

When Kṛṣṇa appeared, He gave His orders, and when Kṛṣṇa Himself appeared as a devotee, as Śrī Caitanya Mahāprabhu, He showed us the path by which to cross the ocean of Kali-yuga. That is the path of the Hare Kṛṣṇa movement. When Śrī Caitanya Mahāprabhu appeared, He ushered in the era for the *saṅkīrtana* movement. It is also said that for ten thousand years this era will continue. This means that simply by accepting the *saṅkīrtana* movement and chanting the Hare Kṛṣṇa *mahā-mantra,* the fallen souls of this Kali-yuga will be delivered. After the Battle of Kurukṣetra, at which *Bhagavad-gītā* was spoken, Kali-yuga continues for 432,000 years, of which only 5,000 years have passed. Thus there is still a balance of 427,000 years to come. Of these 427,000 years, the 10,000 years of the *saṅkīrtana* movement inaugurated by Śrī Caitanya Mahāprabhu 500 years ago provide the opportunity for the fallen souls of Kali-yuga to take to the Kṛṣṇa consciousness movement, chant the Hare Kṛṣṇa *mahā-mantra* and thus be delivered from the clutches of material existence and return home, back to Godhead.

Chanting of the Hare Kṛṣṇa *mahā-mantra* is potent always, but it is especially potent in this age of Kali. Therefore Śukadeva Gosvāmī, while instructing Mahārāja Parīkṣit, stressed this chanting of the Hare Kṛṣṇa *mantra.*

kaler doṣa-nidhe rājann
asti hy eko mahān guṇaḥ
kīrtanād eva kṛṣṇasya
mukta-saṅgaḥ paraṁ vrajet

"My dear King, although Kali-yuga is full of faults, there is still one good quality about this age. It is that simply by chanting the Hare Kṛṣṇa *mahā-mantra,* one can become free from material bondage and be promoted to the transcendental kingdom." (*Bhāg.* 12.3.51) Those who have accepted the task of spreading the Hare Kṛṣṇa *mahā-mantra* in full Kṛṣṇa consciousness should take this opportunity to deliver people very easily from the clutches of material existence. Our duty, therefore, is to follow the instructions of Śrī Caitanya Mahāprabhu and preach the Kṛṣṇa consciousness movement all over the world very sincerely. This is the best welfare activity for the peace and prosperity of human society.

Śrī Caitanya Mahāprabhu's movement consists of spreading *kṛṣṇa-saṅkīrtana. Paraṁ vijayate śrī-kṛṣṇa-saṅkīrtanam:* "All glories to the Śrī Kṛṣṇa *saṅkīrtana!*" Why is it so glorious? This has also been explained by Śrī Caitanya Mahāprabhu. *Ceto-darpaṇa-mārjanam:* by the chanting of the Hare Kṛṣṇa *mahā-mantra,* one's heart is cleansed. The whole difficulty is that in this age of Kali there is no *sattva-guṇa* and no clearance of the heart, and therefore people are making the mistake of identifying with their bodies. Even the big philosophers and scientists with whom we deal are practically all under the impression that they are their bodies. The other day we were discussing a prominent philosopher, Thomas Huxley, who was proud of being an Englishman. This means that he was in the bodily conception of life. Everywhere we find this same misunderstanding. As soon as one is in the bodily conception of life, one is nothing but an animal like a cat or a dog (*sa eva go-kharaḥ*). Thus the most dangerous of the dirty things within our hearts is this misidentification of the body as the self. Under the influence of this misunderstanding, one thinks, "I am this body. I am an Englishman. I am an Indian. I am an American. I am Hindu. I am Muslim." This misconception is the strongest impediment, and it must be removed. That is the instruction of *Bhagavad-gītā* and of Śrī Caitanya Mahāprabhu. Indeed, *Bhagavad-gītā* begins with this instruction:

dehino 'smin yathā dehe
kaumāraṁ yauvanaṁ jarā
tathā dehāntara-prāptir
dhīras tatra na muhyati

"As the embodied soul continually passes, in this body, from boyhood to youth to old age, the soul similarly passes into another body at death. The self-realized soul is not bewildered by such a change." (Bg. 2.13) Although the soul is within the body, nevertheless, because of misunderstanding and animal propensities one accepts the body as the self. Caitanya Mahāprabhu therefore says, *ceto-darpaṇa-mārjanam.* To cleanse the core of the heart, which is full of misunderstanding, is possible only through *śrī-kṛṣṇa-saṅkīrtana.* The leaders of the Kṛṣṇa consciousness movement should very seriously take this opportunity to be kind to the fallen souls by delivering them from the misunderstanding of materialistic life.

One cannot be happy in any way within this material world. As stated in *Bhagavad-gītā* (8.16):

ābrahma-bhuvanāl lokāḥ
punar āvartino "rjuna

"From the highest planet in this material world down to the lowest, all are places of misery wherein repeated birth and death take place." Therefore, not to speak of going to the moon, even if one is promoted to the highest planetary system, Brahmaloka, there cannot be any happiness in this material world. If one actually wants happiness, one must go to the spiritual world. The material world is characterized by a struggle for existence, and survival of the fittest is a well-known principle, but the poor souls of this material world do not know what is survival and who is fit. Survival does not mean that one should die; survival means that one should not die, but should enjoy an everlastingly blissful life of knowledge. This is survival. The Kṛṣṇa consciousness movement is meant to make every person fit for survival. Indeed, it is meant to stop the struggle for existence. The *Śrīmad-Bhāgavatam* and *Bhagavad-gītā* give definite directions on how to stop the struggle for existence and how to survive in eternal life. The *saṅkīrtana* movement, therefore, is a great opportunity.

Simply by hearing *Bhagavad-gītā* and chanting the Hare Kṛṣṇa *mahā-mantra,* one becomes completely purified. Thus the struggle for existence ceases, and one goes back home, back to Godhead.

TEXT 24

श्रीशुक उवाच
इत्याभाष्य सुरान्वेधाः सह देवैररिन्दम ।
अजितस्य पदं साक्षाज्जगाम तमसः परम् ॥ २४ ॥

śrī-śuka uvāca
ity ābhāṣya surān vedhāḥ
saha devair arindama
ajitasya padaṁ sākṣāj
jagāma tamasaḥ param

śrī-śukaḥ uvāca—Śrī Śukadeva Gosvāmī said; *iti*—thus; *ābhāṣya*—talking; *surān*—unto the demigods; *vedhāḥ*—Lord Brahmā, who is the head of this universe and who gives everyone good sense in Vedic knowledge; *saha*—with; *devaiḥ*—the demigods; *arim-dama*—O Mahārāja Parīkṣit, subduer of all kinds of enemies (such as the senses); *ajitasya*—of the Supreme Personality of Godhead; *padam*—to the place; *sākṣāt*—directly; *jagāma*—went; *tamasaḥ*—the world of darkness; *param*—transcendental to, beyond.

TRANSLATION

O Mahārāja Parīkṣit, subduer of all enemies, after Lord Brahmā finished speaking to the demigods, he took them with him to the abode of the Supreme Personality of Godhead, which is beyond this material world. The Lord's abode is on an island called Śvetadvīpa, which is situated in the ocean of mllk.

PURPORT

Mahārāja Parīkṣit is addressed here as *arindama,* "subduer of all enemies." Not only do we have enemies outside of our bodies, but within our bodies there are many enemies, such as lusty desires, anger and greed. Mahārāja Parīkṣit is specifically addressed as *arindama* because in his political life he was able to subdue all kinds of enemies, and even though he was a young king, as soon as he heard that he was going to die within seven days, he immediately left his kingdom. He did not follow the dictates of enemies within his body, such as lust, greed and anger. He was not at all angry with the *muni's* son who had cursed him. Rather, he accepted the curse and prepared for his death in the association of Śukadeva Gosvāmī. Death is inevitable; no one can surpass the force of death. Therefore Mahārāja Parīkṣit, while fully alive, wanted to hear *Śrīmad-Bhāgavatam.* He is consequently addressed here as *arindama.*

Another word, *sura-priya,* is also significant. Although Kṛṣṇa, the Supreme Personality of Godhead, is equal toward everyone, He is especially inclined toward His devotees (*ye bhajanti tu māṁ bhaktyā mayi te teṣu cāpy aham*). The devotees are all demigods. There are two kinds of men within this world. One is called the *deva,* and the other is called the *asura.* The *Padma Purāṇa* states:

dvau bhūta-sargau loke 'smin
daiva āsura eva ca
viṣṇu-bhaktaḥ smṛto daiva
āsuras tad-viparyayaḥ

Anyone who is a devotee of Lord Kṛṣṇa is called a *deva,* and others, even though they may be devotees of demigods, are called *asuras.* Rāvaṇa, for example, was a great devotee of Lord Śiva, but he is described as an *asura.* Similarly, Hiraṇyakaśipu is described as a great devotee of Lord Brahmā, yet he was also an *asura.* Therefore, only the devotee of Lord Viṣṇu is called *sura,* not *asura.* Lord Kṛṣṇa is very much pleased with His devotees, even if they are not on the topmost stage of devotional service. Even on the lower stages of devotional service one is transcendental, and if one continues with devotional life, he continues to be a *deva* or *sura.* If one continues in this way, Kṛṣṇa will always be pleased with him and will give him all instructions so that he may very easily return home, back to Godhead.

Concerning *ajitasya padam,* the abode of the Supreme Personality of Godhead in the milk ocean of this material world, Śrīla Viśvanātha Cakravartī Ṭhākura says: *padaṁ kṣīrodadhi-stha-śvetadvīpaṁ tamasaḥ prakṛteḥ param.* The island known as Śvetadvīpa, which is in the ocean of milk, is transcendental. It has nothing to do with this material world. A city government may have a rest house where the governor and important government officers stay. Such a rest house is not an ordinary house. Similarly, although Śvetadvīpa, which is in the ocean of milk, is in this material world, it is *paraṁ padam,* transcendental.

TEXT 25

तत्राद्दष्टस्वरूपाय श्रुतपूर्वाय वै प्रभुः ।
स्तुतिमब्रूत दैवीभिर्गीर्भिस्त्ववहितेन्द्रियः ॥ २५ ॥

tatrādṛṣṭa-svarūpāya
śruta-pūrvāya vai prabhuḥ
stutim abrūta daivībhir
gīrbhis tv avahitendriyaḥ

tatra—there (at the Lord's abode known as Śvetadvīpa); *adṛṣṭa-svarūpāya*—unto the Supreme Personality of Godhead, who was not seen even by Lord Brahmā; *śruta-pūrvāya*—but who was heard about from the *Vedas; vai*—indeed; *prabhuḥ*—Lord Brahmā; *stutim*—prayers derived from Vedic literature; *abrūta*—performed; *daivībhiḥ*—by prayers mentioned in the Vedic literature or offered by persons strictly following Vedic principles; *gīrbhiḥ*—by such sound vibrations or songs; *tu*—then; *avahita-indriyaḥ*—fixed in mind, without deviation.

TRANSLATION

There [at Śvetadvīpa], Lord Brahmā offered prayers to the Supreme Personality of Godhead, even though he had never seen the Supreme Lord. Simply because Lord Brahmā had heard about the Supreme Personality of Godhead from Vedic literature, with a fixed mind he offered the Lord prayers as written or approved by Vedic literature.

PURPORT

It is said that when Brahmā and the other demigods go to see the Supreme Personality of Godhead in Śvetadvīpa, they cannot directly see Him, but their prayers are heard by the Lord, and the needful action is taken. This we have seen in many instances. The word *śruta-pūrvāya* is significant. We get experience by directly seeing or by hearing. If it is not possible to see someone directly, we can hear about him from authentic sources. Sometimes people ask whether we can show them God. This is ludicrous. It is not necessary for one to see God before he can accept God. Our sensory perception is always incomplete. Therefore, even if we see God, we may not be able to understand Him. When Kṛṣṇa was on earth, many, many people saw Him but could not understand that He is the Supreme Personality of Godhead. *Avajānanti māṁ mūḍhā mānuṣīṁ tanum āśritam.* Even though the rascals and fools saw Kṛṣṇa personally, they could not understand that He is the Supreme Personality of Godhead. Even upon seeing God personally, one who is unfortunate cannot understand Him. Therefore we have to hear about God, Kṛṣṇa, from the authentic Vedic literature and from persons who understand the Vedic version properly. Even though Brahmā had not seen the Supreme Personality of Godhead before, he was confident that the Lord was there in Śvetadvīpa. Thus he took the opportunity to go there and offer prayers to the Lord.

These prayers were not ordinary concocted prayers. Prayers must be approved by Vedic literature, as indicated in this verse by the words *daivībhir gīrbhiḥ.* In our Kṛṣṇa consciousness movement we do not allow any song that has not been approved or sung by bona fide devotees. We cannot allow cinema songs to be sung in the temple. We generally sing two songs. One is *śrī-kṛṣṇa-caitanya prabhu nityānanda śrī-advaita gadādhara śrīvāsādi-gaura-bhakta-vṛnda.* This is bona fide. It is always mentioned in the *Caitanya-caritāmṛta,* and it is accepted by the *ācāryas.* The other, of course, is the *mahā-mantra*—Hare Kṛṣṇa, Hare Kṛṣṇa, Kṛṣṇa Kṛṣṇa, Hare Hare/ Hare Rāma, Hare Rāma, Rāma Rāma, Hare Hare. We may also sing the songs of Narottama dāsa Ṭhākura, Bhaktivinoda Ṭhākura and Locana dāsa Ṭhākura, but these two songs—"*śrī-kṛṣṇa-caitanya*" and the Hare Kṛṣṇa *mahā-mantra*—are sufficient to please the Supreme Personality of Godhead, although we cannot see Him. Seeing the Lord is not as important as appreciating Him from the authentic literature or the authentic statements of authorized persons.

TEXT 26

श्रीब्रह्मोवाच
अविक्रियं सत्यमनन्तमाद्यं
गुहाशयं निष्कलमप्रतर्क्यम् ।
मनोऽग्रयानं वचसानिरुक्तं
नमामहे देववरं वरेण्यम् ॥ २६ ॥

śrī-brahmovāca
avikriyaṁ satyam anantam ādyaṁ
guhā-śayaṁ niṣkalam apratarkyam
mano-'grayānaṁ vacasāniruktaṁ
namāmahe deva-varaṁ vareṇyam

śrī-brahmā uvāca—Lord Brahmā said; *avikriyam*—unto the Personality of Godhead, who never changes (as opposed to material existence); *satyam*

—the eternal supreme truth; *anantam*—unlimited; *ādyam*—the original cause of all causes; *guhā-śayam*—present in everyone's heart; *niṣkalam*—without any decrease in potency; *apratarkyam*—inconceivable, not within the jurisdiction of material arguments; *manaḥ-agrayānam*—more quick than the mind, inconceivable to mental speculation; *vacasā*—by jugglery of words; *aniruktam*—indescribable; *namāmahe*—all of us demigods offer our respectful obeisances; *deva-varam*—unto the Supreme Lord, who is not equaled or surpassed by anyone; *vareṇyam*—the supreme worshipable, who is worshiped by the Gāyatrī *mantra.*

TRANSLATION

Lord Brahmā said: O Supreme Lord, O changeless, unlimited supreme truth. You are the origin of everything. Being all-pervading, You are in everyone's heart and also in the atom. You have no material qualities. Indeed, You are inconceivable. The mind cannot catch You by speculation, and words fail to describe You. You are the supreme master of everyone, and therefore You are worshipable for everyone. We offer our respectful obeisances unto You.

PURPORT

The Supreme Personality of Godhead is not anything of material creation. Everything material must change from one form to another—for example, from earth to earthen pot and from earthen pot to earth again. All our creations are temporary, impermanent. The Supreme Personality of Godhead, however, is eternal, and similarly the living entities, who are parts of Him, are also eternal (*mamaivāṁśo jīva-loke jīva-bhūtaḥ sanātanaḥ*). The Supreme Personality of Godhead is *sanātana,* eternal, and the individual living entities are also eternal. The difference is that Kṛṣṇa, or God, is the supreme eternal, whereas the individual souls are minute, fragmental eternals. As stated in *Bhagavad-gītā* (13.3), *kṣetra-jñaṁ cāpi māṁ viddhi sarva-kṣetreṣu bhārata.* Although the Lord is a living being and the individual souls are living beings, the Supreme Lord, unlike the individual souls, is *vibhu,* all-pervading, and *ananta,* unlimited. The Lord is the cause of everything. The living entities are innumerable, but the Lord is one. No one is greater than Him, and no one is equal to Him. Thus the Lord is the supreme worshipable object, as understood from the Vedic *mantras* (*na tat-samaś cābhyadhikaś ca dṛśyate*). The Lord is supreme because no one can evaluate Him by mental speculation or jugglery of words. The Lord can travel more quickly than the mind. In the *śruti-mantras* of *Īśopaniṣad* it is said:

anejad ekaṁ manaso javīyo
nainad devā āpnuvan pūrvam arṣat
tad dhāvato 'nyān atyeti tiṣṭhat
tasminn apo mātariśvā dadhāti

"Although fixed in His abode, the Personality of Godhead is swifter than the mind and can overcome all others running. The powerful demigods cannot approach Him. Although in one place, He controls those who supply the air and rain. He surpasses all in excellence." (*Īśopaniṣad* 4) Thus the Supreme is never to be equaled by the subordinate living entities.

Because the Lord is situated in everyone's heart and the individual living entity is not, never should the individual living entity be equated with the Supreme Lord. In *Bhagavad-gītā* (15.15) the Lord says, *sarvasya cāhaṁ hṛdi sanniviṣṭaḥ:* "I am situated in everyone's heart." This does not mean, however, that everyone is equal to the Lord. In the *śruti-mantras* it is also said, *hṛdi hy ayam ātmā pratiṣṭhitaḥ.* In the beginning of *Śrīmad-Bhāgavatam* it is said, *satyaṁ paraṁ dhīmahi.* The Vedic *mantras* say, *satyaṁ jñānam anantam* and *niṣkalaṁ niṣkriyaṁ śāntaṁ niravadyam.* God is supreme. Although naturally He does not do anything, He is doing everything. As the Lord says in *Bhagavad-gītā:*

mayā tatam idaṁ sarvaṁ
jagad avyakta-mūrtinā
mat-sthāni sarva-bhūtāni
na cāhaṁ teṣv avasthitaḥ

"By Me, in My unmanifested form, this entire universe is pervaded. All beings are in Me, but I am not in them." (Bg. 9.4)

mayādhyakṣeṇa prakṛtiḥ
sūyate sacarācaram
hetunānena kaunteya
jagad viparivartate

"This material nature, working under My direction, O son of Kuntī, is producing all moving and unmoving beings. By its rule this manifestation is created and annihilated again and again." (Bg. 9.10) Thus although the Lord is silent in His abode, He is doing everything through His different energies (*parāsya śaktir vividhaiva śrūyate*).

All the Vedic *mantras,* or *śruti-mantras,* are included in this verse spoken by Lord Brahmā, for Brahmā and his followers, the Brahma-sampradāya, understand the Supreme Personality of Godhead through the *paramparā* system. We have to gain understanding through the words of our predecessors. There are twelve *mahājanas,* or authorities, of whom Brahmā is one.

svayambhūr nāradaḥ śambhuḥ
kumāraḥ kapilo manuḥ
prahlādo janako bhīṣmo
balir vaiyāsakir vayam

(Bhāg. 6.3.20)

We belong to the disciplic succession of Brahmā, and therefore we are known as the Brahma-sampradāya. As the demigods follow Lord Brahmā to understand the Supreme Personality of Godhead, we also have to follow the authorities of the *paramparā* system to understand the Lord.

TEXT 27

विपश्चितं प्राणमनोधियात्मना-
मर्थेन्द्रियाभासमनिद्रमव्रणम् ।
छायातपौ यत्र न गृध्रपक्षौ
तमक्षरं खं त्रियुगं व्रजामहे ॥ २७ ॥

vipaścitaṁ prāṇa-mano-dhiyātmanām
arthendriyābhāsam anidram avraṇam
chāyātapau yatra na gṛdhra-pakṣau
tam akṣaraṁ khaṁ tri-yugaṁ vrajāmahe

vipaścitam—unto the omniscient; *prāṇa*—how the living force is working; *manaḥ*—how the mind is working; *dhiya*—how the intelligence is working; *ātmanām*—of all living entities; *artha*—the objects of the senses; *indriya*—the senses; *ābhāsam*—knowledge; *anidram*—always awake and free from ignorance; *avraṇam*—without a material body subject to pains and pleasures; *chāyā-ātapau*—the shelter for all who are suffering from ignorance; *yatra*—wherein; *na*—not; *gṛdhra-pakṣau*—partiality toward any living being; *tam*—unto Him; *akṣaram*—infallible; *kham*—all-pervading like the sky; *tri-yugam*—appearing with six opulences in three *yugas* (Satya, Tretā and Dvāpara); *vrajāmahe*—I take shelter.

TRANSLATION

The Supreme Personality of Godhead directly and indirectly knows how everything, including the living force, mind and intelligence, is working under His control. He is the illuminator of everything and has no ignorance. He does not have a material body subject to the reactions of previous activities, and He is free from the ignorance of partiality and materialistic education. I therefore take shelter of the lotus feet of the Supreme Lord, who is eternal, all-pervading and as great as the sky and who appears with six opulences in three yugas [Satya, Tretā and Dvāpara].

PURPORT

In the beginning of *Śrīmad-Bhāgavatam* the Supreme Personality of Godhead is described in this way: *janmādy asya yato'nvayād itarataś cārtheṣv abhijñaḥ.* The Lord is the origin of all emanations, and He directly and indirectly knows everything about all the activities within His creation. Therefore the Lord is addressed here as *vipaścitam,* one who is full of all knowledge or who knows everything. The Lord is the Supreme Soul, and He knows everything about the living entities and their senses.

The word *anidram,* meaning "always awake and free from ignorance," is very important in this verse. As stated in *Bhagavad-gītā* (15.15), *mattaḥ smṛtir jñānam apohanaṁ ca:* it is the Lord who gives intelligence to everyone and who causes everyone to forget. There are millions and millions of living entities, and the Lord gives them directions. Therefore He has no time to sleep, and He is never in ignorance of our activities. The Lord is the witness of everything; He sees what we are doing at every moment. The Lord is not covered by a body resulting from *karma.* Our bodies are formed as a result of our past deeds (*karmaṇā daiva-netreṇa*), but the Supreme Personality of Godhead does not have a material body, and therefore He has no *avidyā,* ignorance. He does not sleep, but is always alert and awake.

The Supreme Lord is described as *tri-yuga* because although He appeared variously in Satya-yuga, Tretā-yuga and Dvāpara-yuga, when He appeared in Kali-yuga He never declared Himself the Supreme Personality of Godhead.

kṛṣṇa-varṇaṁ tviṣākṛṣṇaṁ
sāṅgopāṅgāstra-pārṣadam

The Lord appears in Kali-yuga as a devotee. Thus although He is Kṛṣṇa, He chants the Hare Kṛṣṇa *mantra* like a devotee. Still, *Śrīmad-Bhāgavatam* (11.5.32) recommends:

yajñaiḥ saṅkīrtana-prāyair
yajanti hi sumedhasaḥ

Śrī Caitanya Mahāprabhu, whose complexion is not black like that of Kṛṣṇa but is golden (*tviṣākṛṣṇam*), is the Supreme Personality of Godhead. He is accompanied by associates like Nityānanda, Advaita, Gadādhara and Śrīvāsa. Those who are sufficiently intelligent worship this Supreme Personality of Godhead by performing *saṅkīrtana-yajña.* In this incarnation, the Supreme Lord declares Himself not to be the Supreme Lord, and therefore He is known as Tri-yuga.

TEXT 28

अजस्य चक्रं त्वजयेर्यमाणं
मनोमयं पञ्चदशारमाशु ।
त्रिनाभि विद्युच्चलमष्टनेमि
यदक्षमाहुस्तमृतं प्रपद्ये ॥ २८ ॥

ajasya cakraṁ tv ajayeryamāṇaṁ
manomayaṁ pañcadaśāram āśu
tri-nābhi vidyuc-calam aṣṭa-nemi
yad-akṣam āhus tam ṛtaṁ prapadye

ajasya—of the living being; *cakram*—the wheel (the cycle of birth and death in this material world); *tu*—but; *ajayā*—by the external energy of the Supreme Lord; *īryamāṇam*—going around with great force; *manaḥ-mayam*—which is nothing but a mental creation depending chiefly on the mind; *pañcadaśa*—fifteen; *aram*—possessing spokes; *āśu*—very quick; *tri-nābhi*—having three naves (the three modes of material nature); *vidyut*—like electricity; *calam*—moving; *aṣṭa-nemi*—made of eight fellies (the eight external energies of the Lord—*bhūmir āpo 'nalo vāyuḥ,* etc.); *yat*—who; *akṣam*—the hub; *āhuḥ*—they say; *tam*—unto Him; *ṛtam*—the fact; *prapadye*—let us offer our respectful obeisances.

TRANSLATION

In the cycle of material activities, the material body resembles the wheel of a mental chariot. The ten senses [five for working and five for gathering knowledge] and the five life airs within the body form the fifteen spokes of the chariot's wheel. The three modes of nature [goodness, passion and ignorance] are its center of activities, and the eight ingredients

of nature [earth, water, fire, air, sky, mind, intelligence and false ego] comprise the rim of the wheel. The external, material energy moves this wheel like electrical energy. Thus the wheel revolves very quickly around its hub or central support, the Supreme Personality of Godhead, who is the Supersoul and the ultimate truth. We offer our respectful obeisances unto Him.

PURPORT

The cycle of repeated birth and death is figuratively described herein. As stated in *Bhagavad-gītā* (7.5):

apareyam itas tv anyāṁ
prakṛtiṁ viddhi me parām
jīva-bhūtāṁ mahā-bāho
yayedaṁ dhāryate jagat

The entire world is going on because the living entity, who is part and parcel of the Supreme Lord, is utilizing the material energy. Under the clutches of the material energy, the *jīvātmā* is revolving on the wheel of birth and death under the direction of the Supreme Personality of Godhead. The central point is the Supersoul. As explained in *Bhagavad-gītā* (18.61):

īśvaraḥ sarva-bhūtānāṁ
hṛd-deśe 'rjuna tiṣṭhati
bhrāmayan sarva-bhūtāni
yantrārūḍhāni māyayā

"The Supreme Lord is situated in everyone's heart, O Arjuna, and is directing the wanderings of all living entities, who are seated as on a machine, made of the material energy." The material body of the living entity is a result of the conditioned soul's activities, and because the supporter is the Supersoul, the Supersoul is the true reality. Every one of us, therefore, should offer respectful obeisances to this central reality. One should not be misguided by the activities of this material world and forget the central point, the Absolute Truth. That is the instruction given here by Lord Brahmā.

TEXT 29

य एकवर्णं तमसः परं त-
दलोकमव्यक्तमनन्तपारम् ।
आसाञ्चकारोपसुपर्णमेन-
मुपासते योगरथेन धीराः ॥ २९ ॥

ya eka-varṇaṁ tamasaḥ paraṁ tad
alokam avyaktam ananta-pāram
āsāṁ cakāropasuparṇam enam
upāsate yoga-rathena dhīrāḥ

yaḥ—the Supreme Personality of Godhead who; *eka-varṇam*—absolute, situated in pure goodness; *tamasaḥ*—to the darkness of the material world; *param*—transcendental; *tat*—that; *alokam*—who cannot be seen; *avyaktam*—not manifested; *ananta-pāram*—unlimited, beyond the measurement of material time and space; *āsām cakāra*—situated; *upa-suparṇam*—on the back of Garuḍa; *enam*—Him; *upāsate*—worship; *yoga-rathena*—by the vehicle of mystic *yoga; dhīrāḥ*—persons who are sober, undisturbed by material agitation.

TRANSLATION

The Supreme Personality of Godhead is situated in pure goodness [śuddha-sattva], and therefore He is eka-varṇa—the oṁkāra [praṇava]. Because the Lord is beyond the cosmic manifestation, which is considered to be darkness, He is not visible to material eyes. Nonetheless, He is not separated from us by time or space, but is present everywhere. Seated on His carrier, Garuḍa, He is worshiped by means of mystical yogic power by those who have achieved freedom from agitation. Let us all offer our respectful obeisances unto Him.

PURPORT

Sattvaṁ viśuddhaṁ vasudeva-śabditam (*Bhāg.* 4.3.23). In this material world, the three modes of material nature—goodness, passion and ignorance—prevail. Among these three, goodness is the platform of knowledge, and passion brings about a mixture of knowledge and ignorance, but the mode of iqnorance is full of darkness. Therefore the Supreme Personality of Godhead is beyond darkness and passion. He is on the platform where goodness or knowledge is not disturbed by passion and ignorance. This is called the *vasudeva* platform. It is on this platform of *vasudeva* that Vāsudeva, or Kṛṣṇa, can appear. Thus Kṛṣṇa appeared on this planet as the son of Vasudeva. Because the Lord is situated beyond the three modes of material nature, He is unseen by those who are dominated by these three modes. One must therefore become *dhīra,* or undisturbed by the modes of material nature. The process of *yoga* may be practiced by one who is free from the agitation of these modes. Therefore *yoga* is defined in this way: *yoga indriya-saṁyamaḥ*. As previously explained, we are disturbed by the *indriyas,* or senses. Moreover, we are agitated by the three modes of material nature, which are imposed upon us by the external energy. In conditional life, the living entity moves turbulently in the whirlpool of birth and death, but when one is situated on the transcendental platform of *viśuddha-sattva,* pure goodness, he can see the Supreme Personality of Godhead, who sits on the back of Garuḍa. Lord Brahmā offers his respectful obeisances unto that Supreme Lord.

TEXT 30

न यस्य कश्चातितितर्ति मायां
यया जनो मुह्यति वेद नार्थम् ।
तं निर्जितात्मात्मगुणं परेशं
नमाम भूतेषु समं चरन्तम् ॥ ३० ॥

na yasya kaścātititarti māyāṁ
yayā jano muhyati veda nārtham
taṁ nirjitātmātma-guṇaṁ pareśaṁ
namāma bhūteṣu samaṁ carantam

na—not; *yasya*—of whom (the Supreme Personality of Godhead); *kaśca*—anyone; *atititarti*—is able to overcome; *māyām*—the illusory energy; *yayā*—by whom (by the illusory energy); *janaḥ*—people in general; *muhyati*—become bewildered; *veda*—understand; *na*—not; *artham*—the aim of life; *tam*—unto Him (the Supreme Personality of Godhead); *nirjita*—completely controlling; *ātmā*—the living entities; *ātma-guṇam*—and His external energy; *para-īśam*—the Lord, who is transcendentally situated; *namāma*—we offer our respectful obeisances; *bhūteṣu*—unto all living beings; *samam*—equally situated, or equipoised; *carantam*—controlling or ruling them.

TRANSLATION

No one can overcome the Supreme Personality of Godhead's illusory energy [māyā], which is so strong that it bewilders everyone, making one lose the sense to understand the aim of life. That same māyā, however, is subdued by the Supreme Personality of Godhead, who rules everyone and who is equally disposed toward all living entities. Let us offer our obeisances unto Him.

PURPORT

The prowess of the Supreme Personality of Godhead, Viṣṇu, certainly controls all living entities, so much so that the living entities have forgotten the aim of life. *Na te viduḥ svārtha-gatiṁ hi viṣṇum:* the living entities have forgotten that the aim of life is to go back home, back to Godhead. The external energy of the Supreme Personality of Godhead gives all conditioned souls what appears to be an opportunity to be happy within this material world, but that is *māyā;* in other words, it is a dream that is never to be fulfilled. Thus every living being is illusioned by the external energy of the Supreme Lord. That illusory energy is undoubtedly very strong, but she is fully under the control of the transcendental person who is described in this verse as *pareśam,* the transcendental Lord. The Lord is not a part of the material creation, but is beyond the creation. Therefore, not only does He control the conditioned souls through His external energy, but He also controls the external energy itself. *Bhagavad-gītā* clearly says that the strong material energy controls everyone and that getting out of her control is extremely difficult. That controlling energy belongs to the Supreme Personality of Godhead and works under His control. The living entities, however, being subdued by the material energy, have forgotten the Supreme Personality of Godhead.

TEXT 31

इमे वयं यत्प्रिययैव तन्वा
सत्त्वेन सृष्टा बहिरन्तराविः ।
गतिं न सूक्ष्मामृषयश्च विद्महे
कुतोऽसुराद्या इतरप्रधानाः ॥ ३१ ॥

ime vayaṁ yat-priyayaiva tanvā
sattvena sṛṣṭā bahir-antar-āviḥ
gatiṁ na sūkṣmām ṛṣayaś ca vidmahe
kuto 'surādyā itara-pradhānāḥ

ime—these; *vayam*—we (the demigods); *yat*—to whom; *priyayā*—appearing very near and dear; *eva*—certainly; *tanvā*—the material body; *sattvena*—by the mode of goodness; *sṛṣṭāḥ*—created; *bahiḥ-antaḥ-āviḥ*—although fully aware, internally and externally; *gatim*—destination; *na*—not; *sūkṣmām*—very subtle; *ṛṣayaḥ*—great saintly persons; *ca*—also; *vidmahe*—

understand; *kutaḥ*—how; *asura-ādyāḥ*—the demons and atheists; *itara*—who are insignificant in their identities; *pradhānāḥ*—although they are leaders of their own societies.

TRANSLATION

Since our bodies are made of sattva-guṇa, we, the demigods, are internally and externally situated in goodness. All the great saints are also situated in that way. Therefore, if even we cannot understand the Supreme Personality of Godhead, what is to be said of those who are most insignificant in their bodily constitutions, being situated in the modes of passion and ignorance? How can they understand the Lord? Let us offer our respectful obeisances unto Him.

PURPORT

Atheists and demons cannot understand the Supreme Personality of Godhead, although He is situated within everyone. For them the Lord finally appears in the form of death, as confirmed in *Bhagavad-gītā* (*mṛtyuḥ sarva-haraś cāham*). Atheists think that they are independent, and therefore they do not care about the supremacy of the Lord, yet the Lord asserts His supremacy when He overcomes them as death. At the time of death, their attempts to use their so-called scientific knowledge and philosophical speculation to deny the supremacy of the Lord cannot work. Hiraṇyakaśipu, for example, was an exalted representative of the atheistic class of men. He always challenged the existence of God, and thus he became inimical even toward his own son. Everyone was afraid of Hiraṇyakaśipu's atheistic principles. Nonetheless, when Lord Nṛsiṁhadeva appeared in order to kill him, Hiraṇyakaśipu's atheistic principles could not save him. Lord Nṛsiṁhadeva killed Hiraṇyakaśipu and took away all his power, influence and pride. Atheistic men, however, never understand how everything they create is annihilated. The Supersoul is situated within them, but because of the predominance of the modes of passion and ignorance, they cannot understand the supremacy of the Lord. Even the demigods, the devotees, who are transcendentally situated or situated on the platform of goodness, are not fully aware of the qualities and position of the Lord. How then can the demons and atheists understand the Supreme Personality of Godhead? It is not possible. Therefore, to gain this understanding, the demigods, headed by Lord Brahmā, offered their respectful obeisances to the Lord.

TEXT 32

पादौ महीयं स्वकृतैव यस्य
चतुर्विधो यत्र हि भूतसर्गः ।
स वै महापूरुष आत्मतन्त्रः
प्रसीदतां ब्रह्म महाविभूतिः ॥ ३२ ॥

pādau mahīyaṁ sva-kṛtaiva yasya
catur-vidho yatra hi bhūta-sargaḥ
sa vai mahā-pūruṣa ātma-tantraḥ
prasīdatāṁ brahma mahā-vibhūtiḥ

pādau—His lotus feet; *mahī*—the earth; *iyam*—this; *sva-kṛta*—created by Himself; *eva*—indeed; *yasya*—of whom; *catuḥ-vidhaḥ*—of four kinds of living entities; *yatra*—wherein; *hi*—indeed; *bhūta-sargaḥ*—material creation; *saḥ*—He; *vai*—indeed; *mahā-pūruṣaḥ*—the Supreme Person; *ātma-tantraḥ*—self-sufficient; *prasīdatām*—may He be merciful to us; *brahma*—the greatest; *mahā-vibhūtiḥ*—with unlimited potency.

TRANSLATION

On this earth there are four kinds of living entities, who are all created by Him. The material creation rests on His lotus feet. He is the great Supreme Person, full of opulence and power. May He be pleased with us.

PURPORT

The word *mahī* refers to the five material elements—earth, water, air, fire and sky—which rest upon the lotus feet of the Supreme Personality of Godhead. *Mahat-padaṁ puṇya-yaśo murāreḥ.* The *mahat-tattva,* the total material energy, rests on His lotus feet, for the cosmic manifestation is but another opulence of the Lord. In this cosmic manifestation there are four kinds of living entities—*jarāyu ja* (those born from embryos), *aṇḍa ja* (those born from eggs), *sveda ja* (those born from perspiration), and *udbhij-ja* (those born from seeds). Everything is generated from the Lord, as confirmed in the *Vedānta-sūtra* (*janmādy asya yataḥ*). No one is independent, but the Supreme Soul is completely independent. *Janmādy asya yato 'nvayād itarataś cārtheṣv abhijñaḥ sva-rāṭ.* The word *sva-rāṭ* means "independent." We are dependent, whereas the Supreme Lord is completely independent. Therefore the Supreme Lord is the greatest of all. Even Lord Brahmā, who created the cosmic manifestation, is but another opulence of the Supreme Personality of Godhead. The material creation is activated by the Lord, and therefore the Lord is not a part of the material creation. The Lord exists in His original, spiritual position. The universal form of the Lord, *vairāja-mūrti,* is another feature of the Supreme Personality of Godhead.

TEXT 33

अम्भस्तु यद्रेत उदारवीर्यं
सिध्यन्ति जीवन्त्युत वर्धमानाः ।
लोकायथोऽथाखिललोकपालाः
प्रसीदतां नः स महाविभूतिः ॥ ३३ ॥

ambhas tu yad-reta udāra-vīryaṁ
sidhyanti jīvanty uta vardhamānāḥ
lokā yato 'thākhila-loka-pālāḥ
prasīdatāṁ naḥ sa mahā-vibhūtiḥ

ambhaḥ—the masses of water seen on this planet or on others; *tu*—but; *yat-retaḥ*—His semen; *udāra-vīryam*—so powerful; *sidhyanti*—are generated; *jīvanti*—live; *uta*—indeed; *vardhamānāḥ*—flourish; *lokāḥ*—all the three worlds; *yataḥ*—from which; *atha*—also; *akhila-loka-pālāḥ*—all the demigods throughout the universe; *prasīdatām*—may be pleased; *naḥ*—upon us; *saḥ*—He; *mahā-vibhūtiḥ*—a person with unlimited potency.

TRANSLATION

The entire cosmic manifestation has emerged from water, and it is because of water that all living entities endure, live and develop. This water is nothing but the semen of the Supreme Personality of Godhead. Therefore, may the Supreme Personality of Godhead, who has such great potency, be pleased with us.

PURPORT

Despite the theories of so-called scientists, the vast quantities of water on this planet and on other planets are not created by a mixture of hydrogen and oxygen. Rather, the water is sometimes explained to be the perspiration and sometimes the semen of the Supreme Personality of Godhead. It is from water that all living entities emerge, and because of water they live and grow. If there were no water, all life would cease. Water is the source of life for everyone.

Therefore, by the grace of the Supreme Personality of Godhead, we have so much water all over the world.

TEXT 34

सोमं मनो यस्य समामनन्ति
दिवौकसां यो बलमन्ध आयुः ।
ईशो नगानां प्रजनः प्रजानां
प्रसीदतां नः स महाविभूतिः ॥ ३४ ॥

somaṁ mano yasya samāmananti
divaukasāṁ yo balam andha āyuḥ
īśo nagānāṁ prajanaḥ prajānāṁ
prasīdatāṁ naḥ sa mahā-vibhūtiḥ

somam—the moon; *manaḥ*—the mind; *yasya*—of whom (of the Supreme Personality of Godhead); *samāmananti*—they say; *divaukasām*—of the denizens of the upper planetary systems; *yaḥ*—who; *balam*—the strength; *andhaḥ*—the food grains; *āyuḥ*—the duration of life; *īśaḥ*—the Supreme Lord; *nagānām*—of the trees; *prajanaḥ*—the source of breeding; *prajānām*—of all living entities; *prasīdatām*—may He be pleased; *naḥ*—upon us; *saḥ*—that Supreme Personality of Godhead; *mahā-vibhūtiḥ*—the source of all opulences.

TRANSLATION

Soma, the moon, is the source of food grains, strength and longevity for all the demigods. He is also the master of all vegetation and the source of generation for all living entities. As stated by learned scholars, the moon is the mind of the Supreme Personality of Godhead. May that Supreme Personality of Godhead, the source of all opulences, be pleased with us.

PURPORT

Soma, the predominating deity of the moon, is the source of food grains and therefore the source of strength even for the celestial beings, the demigods. He is the vital force for all vegetation. Unfortunately, modern so-called scientists, who do not fully understand the moon, describe the moon as being full of deserts. Since the moon is the source for our vegetation, how can the moon be a desert? The moonshine is the vital force for all vegetation, and therefore we cannot possibly accept that the moon is a desert.

TEXT 35

अग्निर्मुखं यस्य तु जातवेदा
जातः क्रियाकाण्डनिमित्तजन्मा ।
अन्तःसमुद्रेऽनुपचन्स्वधातून्
प्रसीदतां नः स महाविभूतिः ॥ ३५ ॥

agnir mukhaṁ yasya tu jāta-vedā
jātaḥ kriyā-kāṇḍa-nimitta-janmā
antaḥ-samudre 'nupacan sva-dhātūn
prasīdatāṁ naḥ sa mahā-vibhūtiḥ

agniḥ—fire; *mukham*—the mouth through which the Supreme Personality of Godhead eats; *yasya*—of whom; *tu*—but; *jāta-vedāḥ*—the producer of wealth or of all necessities of life; *jātaḥ*—produced; *kriyā-kāṇḍa*—ritualistic ceremonies; *nimitta*—for the sake of; *janmā*—formed for this reason; *antaḥ-samudre*—within the depths of the ocean; *anupacan*—always digesting; *sva-dhātūn*—all elements; *prasīdatām*—may be pleased; *naḥ*—upon us; *saḥ*—He; *mahā-vibhūtiḥ*—the supremely powerful.

TRANSLATION

Fire, which is born for the sake of accepting oblations in ritualistic ceremonies, is the mouth of the Supreme Personality of Godhead. Fire exists within the depths of the ocean to produce wealth, and fire is also present in the abdomen to digest food and produce various secretions for the maintenance of the body. May that supremely powerful Personality of Godhead be pleased with us.

TEXT 36

यच्चक्षुरासीत् तरणिर्देवयानं
त्रयीमयो ब्रह्मण एष धिष्ण्यम् ।
द्वारं च मुक्तेरमृतं च मृत्युः
प्रसीदतां नः स महाविभूतिः ॥ ३६ ॥

yac-cakṣur āsīt taraṇir deva-yānaṁ
trayīmayo brahmaṇa eṣa dhiṣṇyam
dvāraṁ ca mukter amṛtaṁ ca mṛtyuḥ
prasīdatāṁ naḥ sa mahā-vibhūtiḥ

yat—that which; *cakṣuḥ*—eye; *āsīt*—became; *taraṇiḥ*—the sun-god; *deva-yānam*—the predominating deity for the path of deliverance for the demigods; *trayī-mayaḥ*—for the sake of guidance in *karma-kāṇḍa* Vedic knowledge; *brahmaṇaḥ*—of the supreme truth; *eṣaḥ*—this; *dhiṣṇyam*—the place for realization; *dvāram ca*—as well as the gateway; *mukteḥ*—for liberation; *amṛtam*—the path of eternal life; *ca*—as well as; *mṛtyuḥ*—the cause of death; *prasīdatām*—may He be pleased; *naḥ*—upon us; *saḥ*—that Supreme Personality of Godhead; *mahā-vibhūtiḥ*—the all-powerful.

TRANSLATION

The sun-god marks the path of liberation, which is called arcirādi-vartma. He is the chief source for understanding of the Vedas, he is the abode where the Absolute Truth can be worshiped, he is the gateway to liberation, and he is the source of eternal life as well as the cause of death. The sun-god is the eye of the Lord. May that Supreme Lord, who is supremely opulent, be pleased with us.

PURPORT

The sun-god is considered to be the chief of the demigods. He is also considered to be the demigod who watches the northern side of the universe. He gives help for understanding the *Vedas.* As confirmed in *Brahma-saṁhitā* (5.52):

yac-cakṣur eṣa savitā sakala-grahāṇāṁ
rājā samasta-sura-mūrtir aśeṣa-tejāḥ
yasyājñayā bhramati saṁbhṛta-kāla-cakro
govindam ādi-puruṣaṁ tam ahaṁ bhajāmi

"The sun, full of infinite effulgence, is the king of all the planets and the image of the good soul. The sun is like the eye of the Supreme Lord. I adore the primeval Lord Govinda, in pursuance of whose order the sun performs his journey, mounting the wheel of time." The sun is actually the eye of the Lord. In the Vedic *mantras* it is said that unless the Supreme Personality of Godhead sees, no one can see. Unless there is sunlight, no living entity on any planet can see. Therefore the sun is considered to be the eye of the Supreme Lord. That is confirmed here by the words *yac-cakṣur āsīt* and in the *Brahma-saṁhitā* by the words *yac-cakṣur eṣa savitā.* The word *savitā* means the sun-god.

TEXT 37

प्राणादभूद् यस्य चराचराणां
प्राणः सहो बलमोजश्च वायुः ।
अन्वास्म सम्राजमिवानुगा वयं
प्रसीदतां नः स महाविभूतिः ॥ ३७ ॥

prāṇād abhūd yasya carācarāṇāṁ
prāṇaḥ saho balam ojaś ca vāyuḥ
anvāsma samrājam ivānugā vayaṁ
prasīdatāṁ naḥ sa mahā-vibhūtiḥ

prāṇāt—from the vital force; *abhūt*—generated; *yasya*—of whom; *cara-acarāṇām*—of all living entities, moving and nonmoving; *prāṇaḥ*—the vital force; *sahaḥ*—the basic principle of life; *balam*—strength; *ojaḥ*—the vital force; *ca*—and; *vāyuḥ*—the air; *anvāsma*—follow; *samrājam*—an emperor; *iva*—like; *anugāḥ*—followers; *vayam*—all of us; *prasīdatām*—may be pleased; *naḥ*—upon us; *saḥ*—He; *mahā-vibhūtiḥ*—the supremely powerful.

TRANSLATION

All living entities, moving and nonmoving, receive their vital force, their bodily strength and their very lives from the air. All of us follow the air for our vital force, exactly as servants follow an emperor. The vital force of air is generated from the original vital force of the Supreme Personality of Godhead. May that Supreme Lord be pleased with us.

TEXT 38

श्रोत्राद् दिशो यस्य हृदश्च खानि
प्रजज्ञिरे खं पुरुषस्य नाभ्याः ।
प्राणेन्द्रियात्मासुशरीरकेतः
प्रसीदतां नः स महाविभूतिः ॥ ३८ ॥

śrotrād diśo yasya hṛdaś ca khāni
prajajñire khaṁ puruṣasya nābhyāḥ
prāṇendriyātmāsu-śarīra-ketaḥ
prasīdatāṁ naḥ sa mahā-vibhūtiḥ

śrotrāt—from the ears; *diśaḥ*—different directions; *yasya*—of whom; *hṛdaḥ*—from the heart; *ca*—also; *khāni*—the holes of the body; *prajajñire*

—generated; *kham*—the sky; *puruṣasya*—of the Supreme Person; *nābhyāḥ*—from the navel; *prāṇa*—of the life force; *indriya*—senses; *ātmā*—mind; *asu*—vital force; *śarīra*—and body; *ketaḥ*—the shelter; *prasīdatām*—may be pleased; *naḥ*—upon us; *saḥ*—He; *mahā-vibhūtiḥ*—the supremely powerful.

TRANSLATION

May the supremely powerful Personality of Godhead be pleased with us. The different directions are generated from His ears, the holes of the body come from His heart, and the vital force, the senses, the mind, the air within the body, and the ether, which is the shelter of the body, come from His navel.

TEXT 39

बलान्महेन्द्रस्त्रिदशाः प्रसादा-
न्मन्योर्गिरीशो धिषणाद् विरिञ्चः ।
खेभ्यस्तुछन्दांस्यृषयो मेढ्रतः कः
प्रसीदतां नः स महाविभूतिः ॥ ३९ ॥

balān mahendras tri-daśāḥ prasādān
manyor girīśo dhiṣaṇād viriñcaḥ
khebhyas tu chandāṁsy ṛṣayo meḍhrataḥ kaḥ
prasīdatāṁ naḥ sa mahā-vibhūtiḥ

balāt—by His strength; *mahā-indraḥ*—King Indra became possible; *tri-daśāḥ*—as well as the demigods; *prasādāt*—by satisfaction; *manyoḥ*—by anger; *giri-īśaḥ*—Lord Śiva; *dhiṣaṇāt*—from sober intelligence; *viriñcaḥ*—Lord Brahmā; *khebhyaḥ*—from the bodily holes; *tu*—as well as; *chandāṁsi*—Vedic *mantras; ṛṣayaḥ*—great saintly persons; *meḍhrataḥ*—from the genitals; *kaḥ*—the *prajāpatis; prasīdatām*—may be pleased; *naḥ*—upon us; *saḥ*—He; *mahā-vibhūtiḥ*—the Supreme Personality of Godhead, who has extraordinary power.

TRANSLATION

Mahendra, the King of Heaven, was generated from the prowess of the Lord, the demigods were generated from the mercy of the Lord, Lord Śiva was generated from the anger of the Lord, and Lord Brahmā from His sober intelligence. The Vedic mantras were generated from the bodily holes of

the Lord, and the great saints and prajāpatis were generated from His genitals. May that supremely powerful Lord be pleased with us.

TEXT 40

श्रीर्वक्षसः पितरश्छाययासन्
धर्मः स्तनादितरः पृष्ठतोऽभूत् ।
द्यौर्यस्य शीर्ष्णोऽप्सरसो विहारात्
प्रसीदतां नः स महाविभूतिः ॥ ४० ॥

śrīr vakṣasaḥ pitaraś chāyayāsan
dharmaḥ stanād itaraḥ pṛṣṭhato 'bhūt
dyaur yasya śīrṣṇo 'psaraso vihārāt
prasīdatāṁ naḥ sa mahā-vibhūtiḥ

śrīḥ—the goddess of fortune; *vakṣasaḥ*—from His chest; *pitaraḥ*—the inhabitants of Pitṛloka; *chāyayā*—from His shadow; *āsan*—became possible; *dharmaḥ*—the principle of religion; *stanāt*—from His bosom; *itaraḥ*—irreligion (the opposite of *dharma*); *pṛṣṭhataḥ*—from the back; *abhūt*—became possible; *dyauḥ*—the heavenly planets; *yasya*—of whom; *śīrṣṇaḥ*—from the top of the head; *apsarasaḥ*—the inhabitants of Apsaroloka; *vihārāt*—by His sense enjoyment; *prasīdatām*—kindly be pleased; *naḥ*—upon us; *saḥ*—He (the Supreme Personality of Godhead); *mahā-vibhūtiḥ*—the greatest in all prowess.

TRANSLATION

The goddess of fortune was generated from His chest, the inhabitants of Pitṛloka from His shadow, religion from His bosom, and irreligion [the opposite of religion] from His back. The heavenly planets were generated from the top of His head, and the Apsarās from His sense enjoyment. May that supremely powerful Personality of Godhead be pleased with us.

TEXT 41

विप्रो मुखाद् ब्रह्म च यस्य गुह्यं
राजन्य आसीद् भुजयोर्बलं च ।
ऊर्वोर्विडोजोऽङ्घ्रिरवेदशूद्रौ
प्रसीदतां नः स महाविभूतिः ॥ ४१ ॥

vipro mukhād brahma ca yasya guhyaṁ
rājanya āsīd bhujayor balaṁ ca
ūrvor viḍ ojo 'ṅghrir aveda-śūdrau
prasīdatāṁ naḥ sa mahā-vibhūtiḥ

vipraḥ—the *brāhmaṇas; mukhāt*—from His mouth; *brahma*—the Vedic literatures; *ca*—also; *yasya*—of whom; *guhyam*—from His confidential knowledge; *rājanyaḥ*—the *kṣatriyas; āsīt*—became possible; *bhujayoḥ*—from His arms; *balam ca*—as well as bodily strength; *ūrvoḥ*—from the thighs; *viṭ*—*vaiśyas; ojaḥ*—and their expert productive knowledge; *aṅghriḥ*—from His feet; *aveda*—those who are beyond the jurisdiction of Vedic knowledge; *śūdrau*—the worker class; *prasīdatām*—may be pleased; *naḥ*—upon us; *saḥ*—He; *mahā-vibhūtiḥ*—the supremely powerful Personality of Godhead.

TRANSLATION

The brāhmaṇas and Vedic knowledge come from the mouth of the Supreme Personality of Godhead, the kṣatriyas and bodily strength come from His arms, the vaiśyas and their expert knowledge in productivity and wealth come from His thighs, and the śūdras, who are outside of Vedic knowledge, come from His feet. May that Supreme Personality of Godhead, who is full in prowess, be pleased with us.

TEXT 42

लोभोऽधरात् प्रीतिरुपर्यभूद् द्युति-
र्नस्तः पशव्यः स्पर्शेन कामः ।
भ्रुवोर्यमः पक्ष्मभवस्तु कालः
प्रसीदतां नः स महाविभूतिः ॥ ४२ ॥

lobho 'dharāt prītir upary abhūd dyutir
nastah paśavyah sparśena kāmah
bhruvor yamaḥ pakṣma-bhavas tu kālaḥ
prasīdatāṁ naḥ sa mahā-vibhūtiḥ

lobhaḥ—greed; *adharāt*—from the lower lip; *prītiḥ*—affection; *upari*—from the upper lip; *abhūt*—became possible; *dyutiḥ*—bodily luster; *nastaḥ*—from the nose; *paśavyaḥ*—fit for the animals; *sparśena*—by the touch; *kāmaḥ*—lusty desires; *bhruvoḥ*—from the eyebrows; *yamaḥ*—Yamarāja became possible; *pakṣma-bhavaḥ*—from the eyelashes; *tu*—but; *kālaḥ*—eternal time, which brings death; *prasīdatām*—be pleased; *naḥ*—upon us;

saḥ—He; *mahā-vibhūtiḥ*—the Supreme Personality of Godhead, who has great prowess.

TRANSLATION

Greed is generated from His lower lip, affection from His upper lip, bodily luster from His nose, animalistic lusty desires from His sense of touch, Yamarāja from His eyebrows, and eternal time from His eyelashes. May that Supreme Lord be pleased with us.

TEXT 43

द्रव्यं वयः कर्म गुणान्विशेषं
यद्योगमायाविहितान्वदन्ति ।
यद् दुर्विभाव्यं प्रबुधापबाधं
प्रसीदतां नः स महाविभूतिः ॥ ४३ ॥

dravyaṁ vayaḥ karma guṇān viśeṣaṁ
yad-yogamāyā-vihitān vadanti
yad durvibhāvyaṁ prabudhāpabādhaṁ
prasīdatāṁ naḥ sa mahā-vibhūtiḥ

dravyam—the five elements of the material world; *vayaḥ*—time; *karma*—fruitive activities; *guṇān*—the three modes of material nature; *viśeṣam*—the varieties caused by combinations of the twenty-three elements; *yat*—that which; *yoga-māyā*—by the Lord's creative potency; *vihitān*—all done; *vadanti*—all learned men say; *yat durvibhāvyam*—which is actually extremely difficult to understand; *prabudha-apabādham*—rejected by the learned, by those who are fully aware; *prasīdatām*—may be pleased; *naḥ*—upon us; *saḥ*—He; *mahā-vibhūtiḥ*—the controller of everything.

TRANSLATION

All learned men say that the five elements, eternal time, fruitive activity, the three modes of material nature, and the varieties produced by these modes are all creations of yogamāyā. This material world is therefore extremely difficult to understand, but those who are highly learned have rejected it. May the Supreme Personality of Godhead, who is the controller of everything, be pleased with us.

PURPORT

The word *durvibhāvyam* is very important in this verse. No one can understand how everything is happening in this material world by the arrangement of the Supreme Personality of Godhead through His material energies. As stated in *Bhagavad-gītā* (9.10), *mayādhyakṣeṇa prakṛtiḥ sūyate sacarācaram:* everything is actually happening under the direction of the Supreme Personality of Godhead. This much we can learn, but how it is happening is extremely difficult to understand. We cannot even understand how the affairs within our body are systematically taking place. The body is a small universe, and since we cannot understand how things are happening in this small universe, how can we understand the affairs of the bigger universe? Actually this universe is very difficult to understand, yet learned sages have advised, as Kṛṣṇa has also advised, that this material world is *duḥkhālayam aśāśvatam;* in other words, it is a place of misery and temporality. One must give up this world and go back home, back to the Personality of Godhead. Materialists may argue, "If this material world and its affairs are impossible to understand, how can we reject it?" The answer is provided by the word *prabudhāpabādham.* We have to reject this material world because it is rejected by those who are learned in Vedic wisdom. Even though we cannot understand what this material world is, we should be ready to reject it in accordance with the advice of learned persons, especially the advice of Kṛṣṇa. Kṛṣṇa says:

mām upetya punar janma
duḥkhālayam aśāśvatam
nāpnuvanti mahātmānaḥ
saṁsiddhiṁ paramāṁ gatāḥ

"After attaining Me, the great souls, who are *yogīs* in devotion, never return to this temporary world, which is full of miseries, because they have attained the highest perfection." (Bg. 8.15) One has to return home, back to Godhead, for this is the highest perfection of life. To go back to Godhead means to reject this material world. Although we cannot understand the functions of this material world and whether it is good for us or bad for us, in accordance with the advice of the supreme authority we must reject it and go back home, back to Godhead.

TEXT 44

नमोऽस्तु तस्मा उपशान्तशक्तये
स्वाराज्यलाभप्रतिपूरितात्मने ।

गुणेषु मायारचितेषु वृत्तिभि-
र्न सज्जमानाय नभस्वदूतये ॥ ४४ ॥

namo 'stu tasmā upaśānta-śaktaye
svārājya-lābha-pratipūritātmane
guṇeṣu māyā-raciteṣu vṛttibhir
na sajjamānāya nabhasvad-ūtaye

namaḥ—our respectful obeisances; *astu*—let there be; *tasmai*—unto Him; *upaśānta-śaktaye*—who does not endeavor to achieve anything else, who is free from restlessness; *svārājya*—completely independent; *lābha*—of all gains; *pratipūrita*—fully achieved; *ātmane*—unto the Supreme Personality of Godhead; *guṇeṣu*—of the material world, which is moving because of the three modes of nature; *māyā-raciteṣu*—things created by the external energy; *vṛttibhiḥ*—by such activities of the senses; *na sajjamānāya*—one who does not become attached, or one who is above material pains and pleasures; *nabhasvat*—the air; *ūtaye*—unto the Lord, who has created this material world as His pastime.

TRANSLATION

Let us offer our respectful obeisances unto the Supreme Personality of Godhead, who is completely silent, free from endeavor, and completely satisfied by His own achievements. He is not attached to the activities of the material world through His senses. Indeed, in performing His pastimes in this material world, He is just like the unattached air.

PURPORT

We can simply understand that behind the activities of material nature is the Supreme Lord, by whose indications everything takes place, although we cannot see Him. Even without seeing Him, we should offer Him our respectful obeisances. We should know that He is complete. Everything is done systematically by His energies (*parāsya śaktir vividhaiva śrūyate*), and therefore He has nothing to do (*na tasya kāryaṁ karaṇaṁ ca vidyate*). As indicated here by the word *upaśānta-śaktaye,* His different energies act, but although He sets these energies in action, He Himself has nothing to do. He is not attached to anything, for He is the Supreme Personality of Godhead. Therefore, let us offer our respectful obeisances unto Him.

TEXT 45

स त्वं नो दर्शयात्मानमस्मत्करणगोचरम् ।
प्रपन्नानां दिदृक्षूणां सस्मितं ते मुखाम्बुजम् ॥ ४५ ॥

sa tvaṁ no darśayātmānam
asmat-karaṇa-gocaram
prapannānāṁ didṛkṣūṇāṁ
sasmitaṁ te mukhāmbujam

saḥ—He (the Supreme Personality of Godhead); *tvam*—You are my Lord; *naḥ*—to us; *darśaya*—be visible; *ātmānam*—in Your original form; *asmat-karaṇa-gocaram*—appreciable by our direct senses, especially by our eyes; *prapannānām*—we are all surrendered unto You; *didṛkṣūṇām*—yet we wish to see You; *sasmitam*—smiling; *te*—Your; *mukha-ambujam*—lotuslike face.

TRANSLATION

O Supreme Personality of Godhead, we are surrendered unto You, yet we wish to see You. Please make Your original form and smiling lotus face visible to our eyes and appreciable to our other senses.

PURPORT

The devotees are always eager to see the Supreme Personality of Godhead in His original form, with His smiling lotuslike face. They are not interested in experiencing the impersonal form. The Lord has both impersonal and personal features. The impersonalists have no idea of the personal feature of the Lord, but Lord Brahmā and the members of his disciplic succession want to see the Lord in His personal form. Without a personal form there can be no question of a smiling face, which is clearly indicated here by the words *sasmitam te mukhāmbujam.* Those who are in the Vaiṣṇava *sampradāya* of Brahmā always want to see the Supreme Personality of Godhead. They are eager to realize the Lord's personal feature, not the impersonal feature. As clearly stated here, *asmat-karaṇa-gocaram:* the personal feature of the Lord can be directly perceived by our senses.

TEXT 46

तैस्तैः स्वेच्छाभूतै रूपैः काले काले स्वयं विभो ।
कर्म दुर्विषहं यन्नो भगवांस्तत् करोति हि ॥ ४६ ॥

tais taiḥ svecchā-bhūtai rūpaiḥ
kāle kāle svayaṁ vibho
karma durviṣahaṁ yan no
bhagavāṁs tat karoti hi

taiḥ—by such appearances; *taiḥ*—by such incarnations; *sva-icchā-bhūtaiḥ*—all appearing by Your personal sweet will; *rūpaiḥ*—by factual forms; *kāle kāle*—in different millenniums; *svayam*—personally; *vibho*—O Supreme; *karma*—activities; *durviṣaham*—uncommon (unable to be enacted by anyone else); *yat*—that which; *naḥ*—unto us; *bhagavān*—the Supreme Personality of Godhead; *tat*—that; *karoti*—executes; *hi*—indeed.

TRANSLATION

O Lord, O Supreme Personality of Godhead, by Your sweet will You appear in various incarnations, millennium after millennium, and act wonderfully, performing uncommon activities that would be impossible for us.

PURPORT

The Lord says in *Bhagavad-gītā* (4.7):

yadā yadā hi dharmasya
glānir bhavati bhārata
abhyutthānam adharmasya
tadātmānaṁ sṛjāmy aham

"Whenever and wherever there is a decline in religious practice, O descendant of Bharata, and a predominant rise of irreligion—at that time I descend Myself." Thus it is not imagination but a fact that the Supreme Personality of Godhead, by His sweet will, appears in different incarnations, such as Matsya, Kūrma, Varāha, Nṛsiṁha, Vāmana, Paraśurāma, Rāmacandra, Balarāma, Buddha and many other forms. Devotees are always eager to see one of the Lord's innumerable forms. It is said that just as no one can count how many waves there are in the sea, no one can count the forms of the Lord. This does not mean, however, that anyone can claim to be a form of the Lord and be acceptable as an incarnation. The incarnation of the Supreme Personality of Godhead must be accepted in terms of the descriptions found in the *śāstras.* Lord Brahmā is eager to see the incarnation of the Lord, or the original source of all incarnations; he is not eager to see an imposter. The incarnation's activities are proof of His identity. All the incarnations described in the *śāstras* act wonderfully (*keśava dhṛta-mīna-śarīra jaya jagadīśa hare*). It is only by the personal sweet will of the Supreme Personality of Godhead that He appears and disappears, and only fortunate devotees can expect to see Him face to face.

TEXT 47

क्लेशभूर्यल्पसाराणि कर्माणि विफलानि वा ।
देहिनां विषयार्तानां न तथैवार्पितं त्वयि ॥ ४७ ॥

kleśa-bhūry-alpa-sārāṇi
karmāṇi viphalāni vā
dehināṁ viṣayārtānāṁ
na tathaivārpitaṁ tvayi

kleśa—hardship; *bhūri*—very much; *alpa*—very little; *sārāṇi*—good result; *karmāṇi*—activities; *viphalāni*—frustration; *vā*—either; *dehinām*—of persons; *viṣaya-artānām*—who are eager to enjoy the material world; *na*—not; *tathā*—like that; *eva*—indeed; *arpitam*—dedicated; *tvayi*—unto Your Lordship.

TRANSLATION

Karmīs are always anxious to accumulate wealth for their sense gratification, but for that purpose they must work very hard. Yet even though they work hard, the results are not satisfying. Indeed, sometimes their work results only in frustration. But devotees who have dedicated their lives to the service of the Lord can achieve substantial results without working very hard. These results exceed the devotee's expectations.

PURPORT

We can practically see how the devotees who have dedicated their lives for the service of the Lord in the Kṛṣṇa consciousness movement are getting immense opportunities for the service of the Supreme Personality of Godhead without working very hard. The Kṛṣṇa consciousness movement actually started with only forty rupees, but now it has more than forty crores worth of property, and all this opulence has been achieved within eight or ten years. No *karmī can* expect to improve his business so swiftly, and besides that, whatever a *karmī* acquires is temporary and sometimes frustrating. In Kṛṣṇa consciousness, however, everything is encouraging and improving. The Kṛṣṇa consciousness movement is not very popular with the *karmīs* because this movement recommends that one refrain from illicit sex, meat-eating, gambling and intoxication. These are restrictions that *karmīs* very much dislike. Nonetheless, in the presence of so many enemies, this movement is progressing, going forward without impediments. If the devotees continue to spread this movement, dedicating life and soul to the lotus feet of Kṛṣṇa, no one will be able to check it. The movement will go forward without limits. Chant Hare Kṛṣṇa!

TEXT 48

नावमः कर्मकल्पोऽपि विफलायेश्वरार्पितः ।
कल्पते पुरुषस्यैव स ह्यात्मा दयितो हितः ॥ ४८ ॥

nāvamaḥ karma-kalpo 'pi
viphalāyeśvarārpitaḥ
kalpate puruṣasyaiva
sa hy ātmā dayito hitaḥ

na—not; *avamaḥ*—very little, or insignificant; *karma*—activities; *kalpaḥ*—rightly executed; *api*—even; *viphalāya*—go in vain; *īśvara-arpitaḥ*—because of being dedicated to the Supreme Personality of Godhead; *kalpate*—it is so accepted; *puruṣasya*—of all persons; *eva*—indeed; *saḥ*—the Supreme Personality of Godhead; *hi*—certainly; *ātmā*—the Supersoul, the supreme father; *dayitaḥ*—extremely dear; *hitaḥ*—beneficial.

TRANSLATION

Activities dedicated to the Supreme Personality of Godhead, even if performed in small measure, never go in vain. The Supreme Personality of Godhead, being the supreme father, is naturally very dear and always ready to act for the good of the living entities.

PURPORT

In *Bhagavad-gītā* (2.40), the Lord says *svalpam apy asya dharmasya trāyate mahato bhayāt:* this *dharma,* devotional service, is so important that even if performed to a very small, almost negligible extent, it can give one the supreme result. There are many instances in the history of the world in which even a slight service rendered to the Lord has saved a living entity from the greatest danger. Ajāmila, for example, was saved by the Supreme Personality of Godhead from the greatest danger, that of going to hell. He was saved simply because he chanted the name Nārāyaṇa at the end of his life. When Ajāmila chanted this holy name of the Lord, Nārāyaṇa, he did not chant knowingly; actually he was calling his youngest son, whose name was Nārāyaṇa. Nonetheless, Lord Nārāyaṇa took this chanting seriously, and thus Ajāmila achieved the result of *ante nārāyaṇa-smṛtiḥ,* remembering Nārāyaṇa at the end of life. If one somehow or other remembers the holy name of Nārāyaṇa, Kṛṣṇa or Rāma at the end of life, he immediately achieves the transcendental result of going back home, back to Godhead.

The Supreme Personality of Godhead is actually the only object of our love. As long as we are in this material world we have so many desires to fulfill, but when we come in touch with the Supreme Personality of Godhead, we immediately become perfect and fully satisfied, just as a child is fully satisfied when he comes to the lap of his mother. Dhruva Mahārāja went to the forest to achieve some material result by austerity and penance, but when he actually saw the Supreme Personality of Godhead he said, "I do not want any material benediction. I am completely satisfied." Even if one wants some material benefit from serving the Supreme Personality of Godhead, this can be achieved extremely easily, without hard labor. Therefore the *śāstra* recommends:

akāmaḥ sarva-kāmo vā
mokṣa-kāma udāra-dhīḥ
tīvreṇa bhakti-yogena
yajeta puruṣaṁ param

"Whether one desires everything or nothing or desires to merge into the existence of the Lord, he is intelligent only if he worships Lord Kṛṣṇa, the Supreme Personality of Godhead, by rendering transcendental loving service."(*Bh*āg. 2.3.10) Even if one has material desires, one can undoubtedly achieve what he wants by rendering service to the Lord.

TEXT 49

यथा हि स्कन्धशाखानां तरोर्मूलावसेचनम् ।
एवमाराधनं विष्णोः सर्वेषामात्मनश्च हि ॥ ४९ ॥

yathā hi skandha-śākhānāṁ
taror mūlāvasecanam
evam ārādhanaṁ viṣṇoḥ
sarveṣām ātmanaś ca hi

yathā—as; *hi*—indeed; *skandha*—of the trunk; *śākhānām*—and of the branches; *taroḥ*—of a tree; *mūla*—the root; *avasecanam*—watering; *evam*—in this way; *ārādhanam*—worship; *viṣṇoḥ*—of Lord Viṣṇu; *sarveṣām*—of everyone; *ātmanaḥ*—of the Supersoul; *ca*—also; *hi*—indeed.

TRANSLATION

When one pours water on the root of a tree, the trunk and branches of the tree are automatically pleased. Similarly, when one becomes a devotee of Lord Viṣṇu, everyone is served, for the Lord is the Supersoul of everyone.

PURPORT

As stated in the *Padma Purāṇa:*

ārādhanānāṁ sarveṣāṁ
viṣṇor ārādhanaṁ param
tasmāt parataraṁ devi
tadīyānāṁ samarcanam

"Of all types of worship, worship of Lord Viṣṇu is best, and better than the worship of Lord Viṣṇu is the worship of His devotee, the Vaiṣṇava." There are many demigods worshiped by people who are attached to material desires (*kāmais tais tair hṛta jñānāḥ prapadyante'nya-devatāḥ*). Because people are embarrassed by so many material desires, they worship Lord Śiva, Lord Brahmā, the goddess Kālī, Durgā, Gaṇeśa and Sūrya to achieve different results. However, one can achieve all these results simultaneously just by worshiping Lord Viṣṇu. As stated elsewhere in the *Bhāgavatam* (4.31.14):

yathā taror mūla-niṣecanena
tṛpyanti tat-skandha-bhujopaśākhāḥ
prāṇopahārāc ca yathendriyāṇāṁ
tathaiva sarvārhaṇam acyutejyā

"Just by pouring water on the root of a tree, one nourishes its trunk and all of its branches, fruits and flowers, and just by supplying food to the stomach, one satisfies all the limbs of the body. Similarly, by worshiping Lord Viṣṇu one can satisfy everyone." Kṛṣṇa consciousness is not a sectarian religious movement. Rather, it is meant for all-embracing welfare activities for the world. One can enter this movement without discrimination in terms of caste, creed, religion or nationality. If one is trained to worship the Supreme Personality of Godhead, Kṛṣṇa, who is the origin of *viṣṇu-tattva,* one can become fully satisfied and perfect in all respects.

TEXT 50

नमस्तुभ्यमनन्ताय दुर्वितर्क्यात्मकर्मणे ।
निर्गुणाय गुणेशाय सत्त्वस्थाय च साम्प्रतम् ॥५०॥

namas tubhyam anantāya
durvitarkyātma-karmaṇe
nirguṇāya guṇeśāya
sattva-sthāya ca sāmpratam

namaḥ—all obeisances; *tubhyam*—unto You, my Lord; *anantāya*—who are everlasting, transcending the three phases of time (past, present and future); *durvitarkya-ātma-karmaṇe*—unto You, who perform inconceivable activities; *nirguṇāya*—which are all transcendental, free from the inebriety of material qualities; *guṇa-īśāya*—unto You, who control the three modes of material nature; *sattva-sthāya*—who are in favor of the material quality of goodness; *ca*—also; *sāmpratam*—at present.

TRANSLATION

My Lord, all obeisances unto You, who are eternal, beyond time's limits of past, present and future. You are inconceivable in Your activities, You are the master of the three modes of material nature, and, being transcendental to all material qualities, You are free from material contamination. You are the controller of all three of the modes of nature, but at the present You are in favor of the quality of goodness. Let us offer our respectful obeisances unto You.

PURPORT

The Supreme Personality of Godhead controls the material activities manifested by the three modes of material nature. As stated in *Bhagavad-gītā, nirguṇaṁ guṇa-bhoktṛ ca:* the Supreme Personality of Godhead is always transcendental to the material qualities (*sattva-guṇa, rajo-guṇa* and *tamo-guṇa*), but nonetheless He is their controller. The Lord manifests Himself in three features—as Brahmā, Viṣṇu and Maheśvara—to control these three qualities. He personally takes charge of *sattva-guṇa* as Lord Viṣṇu, and He entrusts the charge of *rajo-guṇa* and *tamo-guṇa* to Lord Brahmā and Lord Śiva. Ultimately, however, He is the controller of all three *guṇas.* Lord Brahmā, expressing his appreciation, said that because Lord Viṣṇu had now taken charge of the activities of goodness, there was every hope that the demigods would be successful in fulfilling their desires. The demigods were harassed by the demons, who were infested with *tamo-guṇa.* However, as Lord Brahmā has previously described, since the time of *sattva-guṇa* had now arrived, the demigods could naturally expect to fulfill their desires. The demigods are supposedly well advanced in knowledge, yet they could not understand the knowledge of the Supreme Personality of Godhead. Therefore the Lord is addressed here as *anantāya.* Although Lord Brahmā knows past, present and future, he is unable to understand the unlimited knowledge of the Supreme Personality of Godhead.

Thus end the Bhaktivedanta purports of the Eighth Canto, Fifth Chapter, of the Śrīmad-Bhāgavatam, *entitled "The Demigods Appeal to the Lord for Protection."*

CHAPTER SIX

The Demigods and Demons Declare a Truce

This chapter describes how the Lord appeared before the demigods when they offered Him their prayers. Following the advice of the Supreme Personality of Godhead, the demigods executed a truce with the demons for the purpose of churning nectar from the sea.

Because of the prayers offered by the demigods in the previous chapter, Lord Kṣīrodakaśāyī Viṣṇu was pleased with the demigods, and thus He appeared before them. The demigods were almost blinded by His transcendental bodily effulgence. At first, therefore, they could not even see any part of His body. After some time, however, when Brahmā could see the Lord, he, along with Lord Śiva, began to offer the Lord prayers.

Lord Brahmā said: "The Supreme Personality of Godhead, being beyond birth and death, is eternal. He has no material qualities. Yet He is the ocean of unlimited auspicious qualities. He is subtler than the most subtle, He is invisible, and His form is inconceivable. He is worshipable for all the demigods. Innumerable universes exist within His form, and therefore He is never separated from these universes by time, space or circumstances. He is the chief and the *pradhāna.* Although He is the beginning, the middle and the end of the material creation, the idea of pantheism conceived by Māyāvādī philosophers has no validity. The Supreme Personality of Godhead controls the entire material manifestation through His subordinate agent, the external energy. Because of His inconceivable transcendental position, He is always the master of the material energy. The Supreme Personality of Godhead, in His various forms, is always present even within this material world, but the material qualities cannot touch Him. One can understand His position only by His instructions, as given in *Bhagavad-gītā.*" As stated in *Bhagavad-gītā* (10.10), *dadāmi buddhi-yogaṁ tam. Buddhi-yoga* means *bhakti-yoga.* Only through the process of *bhakti-yoga* can one understand the Supreme Lord.

When offered prayers by Lord Śiva and Lord Brahmā, the Supreme Personality of Godhead was pleased. Thus He gave appropriate instructions to all the demigods. The Supreme Personality of Godhead, who is known as Ajita, unconquerable, advised the demigods to make a peace proposal to the demons, so that after formulating a truce, the demigods and demons could churn the ocean of milk. The rope would be the biggest serpent, known as Vāsuki, and the churning rod would be Mandara Mountain. Poison would also be produced from the churning, but it would be taken by Lord Śiva, and so there would be no need to fear it. Many other attractive things would be generated by the churning, but the Lord warned the demigods not to be captivated by such things. Nor should the demigods be angry if there were some disturbances. After advising the demigods in this way, the Lord disappeared from the scene.

Following the instructions of the Supreme Personality of Godhead, the demigods established a peace with Mahārāja Bali, the King of the demons. Then both the demons and the demigods started for the ocean, taking Mandara Mountain with them. Because of the great heaviness of the mountain, the demigods and demons became fatigued, and some of them actually died. Then the Supreme Personality of Godhead, Viṣṇu, appeared there on the back of His carrier, Garuḍa, and by His mercy He brought these demigods and demons back to life. The Lord then lifted the mountain with one of His hands and placed it on the back of Garuḍa. The Lord sat on the mountain and was carried to the spot of the churning by Garuḍa, who placed the mountain in the middle of the sea. Then the Lord asked Garuḍa to leave that place because as long as Garuḍa was present, Vāsuki could not come there.

TEXT 1

श्रीशुक उवाच
एवं स्तुतः सुरगणैर्भगवान् हरिरीश्वरः ।
तेषामाविरभूद् राजन्सहस्रार्कोदयद्युतिः ॥ १ ॥

śrī-śuka uvāca
evaṁ stutaḥ sura gaṇair
bhagavān harir īśvaraḥ
teṣām āvirabhūd rājan
sahasrārkodaya-dyutiḥ

śrī-śukaḥ uvāca—Śrī Śukadeva Gosvāmī said; *evam*—in this way; *stutaḥ*—being worshiped by prayers; *sura-gaṇaiḥ*—by the demigods; *bhagavān*—the Supreme Personality of Godhead; *hariḥ*—the vanquisher of all inauspiciousness; *īśvaraḥ*—the supreme controller; *teṣām*—in front of Lord

Brahmā and all the demigods; *āvirabhūt*—appeared there; *rājan*—O King (Parīkṣit); *sahasra*—of thousands; *arka*—of suns; *udaya*—like the rising; *dyutiḥ*—His effulgence.

TRANSLATION

Śrī Śukadeva Gosvāmī said: O King Parīkṣit, the Supreme Personality of Godhead, Hari, being thus worshiped with prayers by the demigods and Lord Brahmā, appeared before them. His bodily effulgence resembled the simultaneous rising of thousands of suns.

TEXT 2

तेनैव सहसा सर्वे देवाः प्रतिहतेक्षणाः ।
नापश्यन्खं दिशः क्षौणीमात्मानं च कुतो विभुम् ॥ २ ॥

tenaiva sahasā sarve
devāḥ pratihatekṣaṇāḥ
nāpaśyan khaṁ diśaḥ kṣauṇīm
ātmānaṁ ca kuto vibhum

tena eva—because of this; *sahasā*—all of a sudden; *sarve*—all; *devāḥ*—the demigods; *pratihata-īkṣaṇāḥ*—their vision being blocked; *na*—not; *apaśyan*—could see; *kham*—the sky; *diśaḥ*—the directions; *kṣauṇīm*—land; *ātmānam ca*—also themselves; *kutaḥ*—and where is the question of seeing; *vibhum*—the Supreme Lord.

TRANSLATION

The vision of all the demigods was blocked by the Lord's effulgence. Thus they could see neither the sky, the directions, the land, nor even themselves, what to speak of seeing the Lord, who was present before them.

TEXTS 3-7

विरिञ्चो भगवान्दृष्ट्वा सह शर्वेण तां तनुम् ।
स्वच्छां मरकतश्यामां कञ्जगर्भारुणेक्षणाम् ॥ ३ ॥
तप्तहेमावदातेन लसत्कौशेयवाससा ।
प्रसन्नचारुसर्वाङ्गीं सुमुखीं सुन्दरभ्रुवम् ॥ ४ ॥

महामणिकिरीटेन केयूराभ्यां च भूषिताम् ।
कर्णाभरणनिर्भातकपोलश्रीमुखाम्बुजाम् ॥ ५ ॥
काञ्चीकलापवलयहारनूपुरशोभिताम् ।
कौस्तुभाभरणां लक्ष्मीं बिभ्रतीं वनमालिनीम् ॥ ६ ॥
सुदर्शनादिभिः स्वास्त्रैर्मूर्तिमद्भिरुपासिताम् ।
तुष्टाव देवप्रवरः सशर्वः पुरुषं परम् ।
सर्वामरगणैः साकं सर्वाङ्गैरवनिं गतैः ॥ ७ ॥

viriñco bhagavān dṛṣṭvā
saha śarveṇa tāṁ tanum
svacchāṁ marakata-śyāmāṁ
kañja-garbhāruṇekṣaṇām

tapta-hemāvadātena
lasat-kauśeya-vāsasā
prasanna-cāru-sarvāṅgīṁ
sumukhīṁ sundara-bhruvam

mahā-maṇi-kirīṭena
keyūrābhyāṁ ca bhūṣitām
karṇābharaṇa-nirbhāta-
kapola-śrī-mukhāmbujām

kāñcīkalāpa-valaya-
hāra-nūpura-śobhitām
kaustubhābharaṇāṁ lakṣmīṁ
bibhratīṁ vana-mālinīm

sudarśanādibhiḥ svāstrair
mūrtimadbhir upāsitām
tuṣṭāva deva-pravaraḥ
saśarvaḥ puruṣaṁ param
sarvāmara-gaṇaiḥ sākaṁ
sarvāṅgair avaniṁ gataiḥ

viriñcaḥ—Lord Brahmā; *bhagavān*—who is also addressed as *bhagavān* because of his powerful position; *dṛṣṭvā*—by seeing; *saha*—with; *śarveṇa*—Lord Śiva; *tām*—unto the Supreme Lord; *tanum*—His transcendental form; *svacchām*—without material contamination; *marakata-śyāmām*—with a bodily luster like the light of a blue gem; *kañja-garbha-aruṇa-īkṣaṇām*—with pinkish eyes like the womb of a lotus flower; *tapta-hema-avadātena*—with a luster like that of molten gold; *lasat*—shining; *kauśeya-vāsasā*—dressed in yellow silk garments; *prasanna-cāru-sarva-aṅgīm*—all the parts of whose body were graceful and very beautiful; *su-mukhīm*—with a smiling face; *sundara-bhruvam*—whose eyebrows were very beautifully situated; *mahā-maṇi-kirīṭena*—with a helmet bedecked with valuable jewels; *keyūrābhyām ca bhūṣitām*—decorated with all kinds of ornaments; *karṇa-ābharaṇa-nirbhāta*—illuminated by the rays of the jewels on His ears; *kapola*—with cheeks; *śrī-mukha-ambujām*—whose beautiful lotuslike face; *kāñcī-kalāpa-valaya*—ornaments like the belt on the waist and bangles on the hands; *hāra-nūpura*—with a necklace on the chest and ankle bells on the legs; *śobhitām*—all beautifully set; *kaustubha-ābharaṇām*—whose chest was decorated with the Kaustubha gem; *lakṣmīm*—the goddess of fortune; *bibhratīm*—moving; *vana-mālinīm*—with flower garlands; *sudarśana-ādibhiḥ*—bearing the Sudarśana *cakra* and others; *sva-astraiḥ*—with His weapons; *mūrtimadbhiḥ*—in His original form; *upāsitām*—being worshiped; *tuṣṭāva*—satisfied; *deva-pravaraḥ*—the chief of the demigods; *sa-śarvaḥ*—with Lord Śiva; *puruṣam param*—the Supreme Personality; *sarva-amara-gaṇaiḥ*—accompanied by all the demigods; *sākam*—with; *sarva-aṅgaiḥ*—with all the parts of the body; *avanim*—on the ground; *gataiḥ*—prostrated.

TRANSLATION

Lord Brahmā, along with Lord Śiva, saw the crystal-clear personal beauty of the Supreme Personality of Godhead, whose blackish body resembles a marakata gem, whose eyes are reddish like the depths of a lotus, who is dressed with garments that are yellow like molten gold, and whose entire body is attractively decorated. They saw His beautiful, smiling, lotuslike face, crowned by a helmet bedecked with valuable jewels. The Lord has attractive eyebrows, and His cheeks are adorned with earrings. Lord Brahmā and Lord Śiva saw the belt on the Lord's waist, the bangles on His arms, the necklace on His chest, and the ankle bells on His legs. The Lord is bedecked with flower garlands, His neck is decorated with the Kaustubha gem, and He carries with Him the goddess of fortune and His personal weapons, like His disc and club. When Lord Brahmā, along with Lord Śiva and the other demigods, thus saw the form of the Lord, they all immediately fell to the ground, offering their obeisances.

TEXT 8

श्रीब्रह्मोवाच
अजातजन्मस्थितिसंयमाया-
गुणाय निर्वाणसुखार्णवाय ।
अणोरणिम्नेऽपरिगण्यधाम्ने
महानुभावाय नमो नमस्ते ॥ ८ ॥

śrī-brahmovāca
ajāta-janma-sthiti-saṁyamāyā-
guṇāya nirvāṇa-sukhārṇavāya
aṇor aṇimne 'parigaṇya-dhāmne
mahānubhāvāya namo namas te

śrī-brahmā uvāca—Lord Brahmā said; *ajāta-janma-sthiti-saṁyamāya*—unto the Supreme Personality of Godhead, who is never born but whose appearance in different incarnations never ceases; *aguṇāya*—never affected by the material modes of nature (*sattva-guṇa, rajo-guṇa* and *tamo-guṇa*); *nirvāṇa-sukha-arṇavāya*—unto the ocean of eternal bliss, beyond material existence; *aṇoḥ aṇimne*—smaller than the atom; *aparigaṇya-dhāmne*—whose bodily features are never to be conceived by material speculation; *mahā-anubhāvāya*—whose existence is inconceivable; *namaḥ*—offering our obeisances; *namaḥ*—again offering our obeisances; *te*—unto You.

TRANSLATION

Lord Brahmā said: Although You are never born, Your appearance and disappearance as an incarnation never cease. You are always free from the material qualities, and You are the shelter of transcendental bliss resembling an ocean. Eternally existing in Your transcendental form, You are the supreme subtle of the most extremely subtle. We therefore offer our respectful obeisances unto You, the Supreme, whose existence is inconceivable.

PURPORT

The Lord says in *Bhagavad-gītā* (4.6):

ajo 'pi sann avyayātmā
bhūtānām īśvaro 'pi san
prakṛtiṁ svām adhiṣṭhāya
sambhavāmy ātma-māyayā

"Although I am unborn and My transcendental body never deteriorates, and although I am the Lord of all sentient beings, I still appear in every millennium in My original transcendental form." In the following verse in *Bhagavad-gītā (4.7), the Lord says:*

yadā yadā hi dharmasya
glānir bhavati bhārata
abhyutthānam adharmasya
tadātmānaṁ sṛjāmy aham

"Whenever and wherever there is a decline in religious practice, O descendant of Bharata, and a predominant rise of irreligion—at that time I descend Myself." Thus although the Supreme Lord is unborn, there is no cessation to His appearance in different forms as incarnations like Lord Kṛṣṇa and Lord Rāma. Since His incarnations are eternal, the various activities performed by these incarnations are also eternal. The Supreme Personality of Godhead does not appear because He is forced to do so by *karma* like ordinary living entities who are forced to accept a certain type of body. It is to be understood that the Lord's body and activities are all transcendental, being free from the contamination of the material modes of nature. These pastimes are transcendental bliss to the Lord. The word *apariganya-dhāmne* is very significant. There is no limit to the Lord's appearance in different incarnations. All of these incarnations are eternal, blissful and full of knowledge.

TEXT 9

रूपं तवैतत् पुरुषर्षभेज्यं
श्रेयोऽर्थिभिर्वैदिकतान्त्रिकेण ।
योगेन धातः सह नस्त्रिलोकान्
पश्याम्यमुष्मिन्नु ह विश्वमूर्तौ ॥ ९ ॥

rūpaṁ tavaitat puruṣarṣabhejyaṁ
śreyo 'rthibhir vaidika-tāntrikeṇa
yogena dhātaḥ saha nas tri-lokān
paśyāmy amuṣminn u ha viśva-mūrtau

rūpam—form; *tava*—Your; *etat*—this; *puruṣa-ṛṣabha*—O best of all personalities; *ijyam*—worshipable; *śreyaḥ*—ultimate auspiciousness; *arthibhiḥ*—by persons who desire; *vaidika*—under the direction of Vedic instructions; *tāntrikeṇa*—realized by followers of *Tantras,* like *Nārada-pañcarā-*

tra; yogena—by practice of mystic *yoga; dhātaḥ*—O supreme director; *saha*—with; *naḥ*—us (the demigods); *tri-lokān*—controlling the three worlds; *paśyāmi*—we see directly; *amuṣmin*—in You; *u*—oh; *ha*—completely manifested; *viśva-mūrtau*—in You, who have the universal form.

TRANSLATION

O best of persons, O supreme director, those who actually aspire for supreme good fortune worship this form of Your Lordship according to the Vedic Tantras. My Lord, we can see all the three worlds in You.

PURPORT

The Vedic *mantras* say: *Kasmin bhagavo vijñāte sarvam idaṁ vijñātaṁ bhavati.* When the devotee sees the Supreme Personality of Godhead by his meditation, or when he sees the Lord personally, face to face, he becomes aware of everything within this universe. Indeed, nothing is unknown to him. Everything within this material world is fully manifested to a devotee who has seen the Supreme Personality of Godhead. *Bhagavad-gītā* (4.34) therefore advises:

tad viddhi praṇipātena
paripraśnena sevayā
upadekṣyanti te jñānaṁ
jñāninas tattva-darśinaḥ

"Just try to learn the truth by approaching a spiritual master. Inquire from him submissively and render service unto him. The self-realized soul can impart knowledge unto you because he has seen the truth." Lord Brahmā is one of these self-realized authorities (*svayambhūr nāradaḥ śambhuḥ kumāraḥ kapilo manuḥ*). One must therefore accept the disciplic succession from Lord Brahmā, and then one can understand the Supreme Personality of Godhead in fullness. Here the word *viśva-mūrtau* indicates that everything exists in the form of the Supreme Personality of Godhead. One who is able to worship Him can see everything in Him and see Him in everything.

TEXT 10

त्वय्यग्र आसीत् त्वयि मध्य आसीत्
त्वय्यन्त आसीदिदमात्मतन्त्रे ।
त्वमादिरन्तो जगतोऽस्य मध्यं
घटस्य मृत्स्नेव परः परस्मात् ॥ १० ॥

tvayy agra āsīt tvayi madhya āsīt
tvayy anta āsīd idam ātma-tantre
tvam ādir anto jagato 'sya madhyaṁ
ghaṭasya mṛtsneva paraḥ parasmāt

tvayi—unto You, the Supreme Personality of Godhead; *agre*—in the beginning; *āsīt*—there was; *tvayi*—unto You; *madhye*—in the middle; *āsīt*—there was; *tvayi*—unto You; *ante*—in the end; *āsīt*—there was; *idam*—all of this cosmic manifestation; *ātma-tantre*—fully under Your control; *tvam*—Your Lordship; *ādiḥ*—beginning; *antaḥ*—end; *jagataḥ*—of the cosmic manifestation; *asya*—of this; *madhyam*—middle; *ghaṭasya*—of an earthen pot; *mṛtsnā iva*—like the earth; *paraḥ*—transcendental; *parasmāt*—because of being the chief.

TRANSLATION

My dear Lord, who are always fully independent, this entire cosmic manifestation arises from You, rests upon You and ends in You. Your Lordship is the beginning, sustenance and end of everything, like the earth, which is the cause of an earthen pot, which supports the pot, and to which the pot, when broken, finally returns.

TEXT 11

त्वं माययात्माश्रयया स्वयेदं
निर्माय विश्वं तदनुप्रविष्टः ।
पश्यन्ति युक्ता मनसा मनीषिणो
गुणव्यवायेऽप्यगुणं विपश्चितः ॥ ११ ॥

tvaṁ māyayātmāśrayayā svayedaṁ
nirmāya viśvaṁ tad-anupraviṣṭaḥ
paśyanti yuktā manasā manīṣiṇo
guṇa-vyavāye 'py aguṇaṁ vipaścitaḥ

tvam—Your Lordship; *māyayā*—by Your eternal energy; *ātma-āśrayayā*—whose existence is under Your shelter; *svayā*—emanated from Yourself; *idam*—this; *nirmāya*—for the sake of creating; *viśvam*—the entire universe; *tat*—into it; *anupraviṣṭaḥ*—You enter; *paśyanti*—they see; *yuktāḥ*—persons in touch with You; *manasā*—by an elevated mind; *manīṣiṇaḥ*—people with advanced consciousness; *guṇa*—of material qualities; *vyavāye*—in the transformation; *api*—although; *aguṇam*—still untouched by the material qualities; *vipaścitaḥ*—those who are fully aware of the truth of *śāstra.*

TRANSLATION

O Supreme, You are independent in Your self and do not take help from others. Through Your own potency, You create this cosmic manifestation and enter into it. Those who are advanced in Kṛṣṇa consciousness, who are fully in knowledge of the authoritative śāstra, and who, through the practice of bhakti-yoga, are cleansed of all material contamination, can see with clear minds that although You exist within the transformations of the material qualities, Your presence is untouched by these qualities.

PURPORT

The Lord says in *Bhagavad-gītā* (9.10):

mayādhyakṣeṇa prakṛtiḥ
sūyate sacarācaram
hetunānena kaunteya
jagad viparivartate

"This material nature, working under My direction, O son of Kuntī, is producing all moving and unmoving beings. By its rule this manifestation is created and annihilated again and again." The material energy creates, maintains and devastates the entire cosmic manifestation because of directions given by the Supreme Personality of Godhead, who enters this universe as Garbhodakaśāyī Viṣṇu but is untouched by the material qualities. In *Bhagavad-gītā* the Lord refers to *māyā,* the external energy, which creates this material world, as *mama māyā,* "My energy,"because this energy works under the full control of the Lord. These facts can be realized only by those who are well versed in Vedic knowledge and advanced in Kṛṣṇa consciousness.

TEXT 12

यथाग्निमेधस्यमृतं च गोषु
भुव्यन्नमम्बूद्यमने च वृत्तिम् ।
योगैर्मनुष्या अधियन्ति हि त्वां
गुणेषु बुद्ध्या कवयो वदन्ति ॥ १२ ॥

yathāgnim edhasy amṛtaṁ ca goṣu
bhuvy annam ambūdyamane ca vṛttim

yogair manuṣyā adhiyanti hi tvāṁ
guṇeṣu buddhyā kavayo vadanti

yathā—as; *agnim*—fire; *edhasi*—in wood; *amṛtam*—milk, which is like nectar; *ca*—and; *goṣu*—from cows; *bhuvi*—on the ground; *annam*—food grains; *ambu*—water; *udyamane*—in enterprise; *ca*—also; *vṛttim*—livelihood; *yogaiḥ*—by practice of *bhakti-yoga; manuṣyāḥ*—human beings; *adhiyanti*—achieve; *hi*—indeed; *tvām*—You; *guṇeṣu*—in the material modes of nature; *buddhyā*—by intelligence; *kavayaḥ*—great personalities; *vadanti*—say.

TRANSLATION

As one can derive fire from wood, milk from the milk bag of the cow, food grains and water from the land, and prosperity in one's livelihood from industrial enterprises, so, by the practice of bhakti-yoga, even within this material world, one can achieve Your favor or intelligently approach You. Those who are pious all affirm this.

PURPORT

Although the Supreme Personality of Godhead is *nirguṇa,* not to be found within this material world, the entire material world is pervaded by Him, as stated in *Bhagavad-gītā* (*mayā tatam idaṁ sarvam*). The material world is nothing but an expansion of the Lord's material energy, and the entire cosmic manifestation rests upon Him (*mat-sthāni sarva-bhūtāni*). Nonetheless, the Supreme Lord cannot be found here (*na cāhaṁ teṣv avasthitaḥ*). A devotee, however, can see the Supreme Personality of Godhead through the practice of *bhakti-yoga.* One ordinarily does not begin to practice *bhakti-yoga* unless he has practiced it in previous births. Moreover, one can begin *bhakti-yoga* only by the mercy of the spiritual master and Kṛṣṇa. *Guru-kṛṣṇa-prasāde pāya bhakti-latā-bīja.* The seed of devotional service is obtainable by the mercy of *guru,* the spiritual master, and Kṛṣṇa, the Supreme Personality of Godhead.

Only by the practice of *bhakti-yoga* can one achieve the favor of the Supreme Personality of Godhead and see Him face to face (*premāñjana-cchurita-bhakti-vilocanena santaḥ sadaiva hṛdayeṣu vilokayanti*). One cannot see the Lord by other methods, such as *karma, jñāna* or *yoga.* Under the direction of the spiritual master, one must cultivate *bhakti-yoga* (*śravaṇaṁ kīrtanaṁ viṣṇoḥ smaraṇaṁ pāda-sevanam*). Then, even within this material world, although the Lord is not visible, a devotee can see Him. This is confirmed in *Bhagavad-gītā* (*bhaktyā mām abhijānāti yāvān yaś cāsmi tattvataḥ*) and in *Śrīmad-Bhāgavatam* (*bhaktyāham ekayā grāhyaḥ*). Thus by devotional service one can achieve the favor of the Supreme Personality of Godhead, although He is not visible or understandable to materialistic persons.

In this verse, the cultivation of *bhakti-yoga* is compared to many material activities. By friction one can get fire from wood, by digging the earth one can get food grains and water, and by agitating the milk bag of the cow one can get nectarean milk. Milk is compared to nectar, which one can drink to become immortal. Of course, simply drinking milk will not make one immortal, but it can increase the duration of one's life. In modern civilization, men do not think milk to be important, and therefore they do not live very long. Although in this age men can live up to one hundred years, their duration of life is reduced because they do not drink large quantities of milk. This is a sign of Kali-yuga. In Kali-yuga, instead of drinking milk, people prefer to slaughter an animal and eat its flesh. The Supreme Personality of Godhead, in His instructions of *Bhagavad-gītā,* advises *go-rakṣya,* which means cow protection. The cow should be protected, milk should be drawn from the cows, and this milk should be prepared in various ways. One should take ample milk, and thus one can prolong one's life, develop his brain, execute devotional service, and ultimately attain the favor of the Supreme Personality of Godhead. As it is essential to get food grains and water by digging the earth, it is also essential to give protection to the cows and take nectarean milk from their milk bags.

The people of this age are inclined toward industrial enterprises for comfortable living, but they refuse to endeavor to execute devotional service, by which they can achieve the ultimate goal of life by returning home, back to Godhead. Unfortunately, as it is said, *na te viduḥ svārtha-gatiṁ hi viṣṇuṁ durāśayā ye bahir-artha-māninaḥ.* People without spiritual education do not know that the ultimate goal of life is to go back home, back to Godhead. Forgetting this aim of life, they are working very hard in disappointment and frustration (*moghāśā mogha-karmāṇo mogha jñānā vicetasaḥ*). The so-called *vaiśyas*—the industrialists or businessmen—are involved in big, big industrial enterprises, but they are not interested in food grains and milk. However, as indicated here, by digging for water, even in the desert, we can produce food grains; when we produce food grains and vegetables, we can give protection to the cows; while giving protection to the cows, we can draw from them abundant quantities of milk; and by getting enough milk and combining it with food grains and vegetables, we can prepare hundreds of nectarean foods.

We can happily eat this food and thus avoid industrial enterprises and joblessness.

Agriculture and cow protection are the way to become sinless and thus be attracted to devotional service. Those who are sinful cannot be attracted by devotional service. As stated in *Bhagavad-gītā* (7.28):

yeṣāṁ tv anta-gataṁ pāpaṁ
janānāṁ puṇya-karmaṇām
te dvandva-moha-nirmuktā
bhajante māṁ dṛḍha-vratāḥ

"Persons who have acted piously in previous lives and in this life, whose sinful actions are completely eradicated and who are freed from the duality of delusion, engage themselves in My service with determination." The majority of people in this age of Kali are sinful, short-living, unfortunate and disturbed (*mandāḥ sumanda-matayo manda-bhāgyā hy upadrutāḥ*). For them, Caitanya Mahāprabhu has advised:

harer nāma harer nāma
harer nāmaiva kevalam
kalau nāsty eva nāsty eva
nāsty eva gatir anyathā

"In this age of quarrel and hypocrisy the only means of deliverance is chanting the holy name of the Lord. There is no other way. There is no other way. There is no other way."

TEXT 13

तं त्वां वयं नाथ समुज्जिहानं
सरोजनाभातिचिरेप्सितार्थम् ।
दृष्ट्वा गता निर्वृतमद्य सर्वे
गजा दवार्ता इव गाङ्गमम्भः ॥ १३ ॥

taṁ tvāṁ vayaṁ nātha samujjihānaṁ
saroja-nābhāticirepsitārtham
dṛṣṭvā gatā nirvṛtam adya sarve
gajā davārtā iva gāṅgam ambhaḥ

tam—O Lord; *tvām*—Your Lordship; *vayam*—all of us; *nātha*—O master; *samujjihānam*—now appearing before us with all glories; *saroja-nābha*

—O Lord, whose navel resembles a lotus flower, or from whose navel grows a lotus flower; *ati-cira*—for an extremely long time; *īpsita*—desiring; *artham* —for the ultimate goal of life; *dṛṣṭvā*—seeing; *gatāḥ*—in our vision; *nirvṛtam* —transcendental happiness; *adya*—today; *sarve*—all of us; *gajāḥ*—elephants; *dava-artāḥ*—being afflicted in a forest fire; *iva*—like; *gāṅgam ambhaḥ*—with water from the Ganges.

TRANSLATION

Elephants afflicted by a forest fire become very happy when they get water from the Ganges. Similarly, O my Lord, from whose navel grows a lotus flower, since You have now appeared before us, we have become transcendentally happy. By seeing Your Lordship, whom we have desired to see for a very long time, we have achieved our ultimate goal in life.

PURPORT

The devotees of the Lord are always very eager to see the Supreme Lord face to face, but they do not demand that the Lord come before them, for a pure devotee considers such a demand to be contrary to devotional service. Śrī Caitanya Mahāprabhu teaches this lesson in His *Śikṣāṣṭaka. Adarśanān marma-hatāṁ karotu vā.* The devotee is always eager to see the Lord face to face, but if he is brokenhearted because he cannot see the Lord, even life after life, he will never command the Lord to appear. This is a sign of pure devotion. Therefore in this verse we find the word *ati-cira-īpsita-artham,* meaning that the devotee aspires for a long, long time to see the Lord. If the Lord, by His own pleasure, appears before the devotee, the devotee feels extremely happy, as Dhruva Mahārāja felt when he personally saw the Supreme Personality of Godhead. When Dhruva Mahārāja saw the Lord, he had no desire to ask the Lord for any benediction. Indeed, simply by seeing the Lord, Dhruva Mahārāja felt so satisfied that he did not want to ask the Lord for any benediction (*svāmin kṛtārtho 'smi varaṁ na yāce*). A pure devotee, whether able or unable to see the Lord, always engages in the Lord's devotional service, always hoping that at some time the Lord may be pleased to appear before him so that he can see the Lord face to face.

TEXT 14

स त्वं विधत्स्वाखिललोकपाला
वयं यदर्थास्तव पादमूलम् ।

समागतास्ते बहिरन्तरात्मन्
किं वान्यविज्ञाप्यमशेषसाक्षिणः ॥ १४ ॥

sa tvaṁ vidhatsvākhila-loka-pālā
vayaṁ yad arthās tava pāda-mūlam
samāgatās te bahir-antar-ātman
kiṁ vānya-vijñāpyam aśeṣa-sākṣiṇaḥ

saḥ—that; *tvam*—Your Lordship; *vidhatsva*—kindly do the needful; *akhila-loka-pālāḥ*—the demigods, directors of different departments of this universe; *vayam*—all of us; *yat*—that which; *arthāḥ*—purpose; *tava*—at Your Lordship's; *pāda-mūlam*—lotus feet; *samāgatāḥ*—we have arrived; *te*—unto You; *bahiḥ-antaḥ-ātman*—O Supersoul of everyone, O constant internal and external witness; *kim*—what; *vā*—either; *anya-vijñāpyam*—we have to inform You; *aśeṣa-sākṣiṇaḥ*—the witness and knower of everything.

TRANSLATION

My Lord, we, the various demigods, the directors of this universe, have come to Your lotus feet. Please fulfill the purpose for which we have come. You are the witness of everything, from within and without. Nothing is unknown to You, and therefore it is unnecessary to inform You again of anything.

PURPORT

As stated in *Bhagavad-gītā* (13.3), *kṣetra-jñaṁ cāpi māṁ viddhi sarva-kṣetreṣu bhārata.* The individual souls are proprietors of their individual bodies, but the Supreme Personality of Godhead is the proprietor of all bodies. Since He is the witness of everyone's body, nothing is unknown to Him. He knows what we need. Our duty, therefore, is to execute devotional service sincerely, under the direction of the spiritual master. Kṛṣṇa, by His grace, will supply whatever we need in executing our devotional service. In the Kṛṣṇa consciousness movement, we simply have to execute the order of Kṛṣṇa and *guru.* Then all necessities will be supplied by Kṛṣṇa, even if we do not ask for them.

TEXT 15

अहं गिरित्रश्च सुरादयो ये
दक्षादयोऽग्नेरिव केतवस्ते ।

किं वा विदामेश पृथग्विभाता
विधत्स्व शं नो द्विजदेवमन्त्रम् ॥ १५ ॥

ahaṁ giritraś ca surādayo ye
dakṣādayo 'gner iva ketavas te
kiṁ vā vidāmeśa pṛthag-vibhātā
vidhatsva śaṁ no dvija-deva-mantram

aham—I (Lord Brahmā); *giritraḥ*—Lord Śiva; *ca*—also; *sura-ādayaḥ*—all the demigods; *ye*—as we are; *dakṣa-ādayaḥ*—headed by Mahārāja Dakṣa; *agneḥ*—of fire; *iva*—like; *ketavaḥ*—sparks; *te*—of You; *kim*—what; *vā*—either; *vidāma*—can we understand; *īśa*—O my Lord; *pṛthak-vibhātāḥ*—independently of You; *vidhatsva*—kindly bestow upon us; *śam*—good fortune; *naḥ*—our; *dvija-deva-mantram*—the means of deliverance suitable for the *brāhmaṇas* and demigods.

TRANSLATION

I [Lord Brahmā], Lord Śiva and all the demigods, accompanied by the prajāpatis like Dakṣa, are nothing but sparks illuminated by You, who are the original fire. Since we are particles of You, what can we understand about our welfare? O Supreme Lord, please give us the means of deliverance that is suitable for the brāhmaṇas and demigods.

PURPORT

In this verse, the word *dvija-deva-mantram* is very important. The word *mantra* means "that which delivers one from the material world." Only the *dvijas* (the *brāhmaṇas*) and the *devas* (the demigods) can be delivered from material existence by the instructions of the Supreme Personality of Godhead. Whatever is spoken by the Supreme Personality of Godhead is a *mantra* and is suitable for delivering the conditioned souls from mental speculation. The conditioned souls are engaged in a struggle for existence (*manaḥ ṣaṣṭhānīndriyāṇi prakṛti-sthāni karṣati*). Deliverance from this struggle constitutes the highest benefit, but unless one gets a *mantra* from the Supreme Personality of Godhead, deliverance is impossible. The beginning *mantra* is the Gāyatrī *mantra.* Therefore, after purification, when one is qualified to become a *brāhmaṇa* (*dvija*), he is offered the Gāyatrī *mantra.* Simply by chanting the Gāyatrī *mantra,* one can be delivered. This *mantra,* however, is suitable only for the *brāhmaṇas* and demigods. In Kali-yuga, we are all in a very difficult position, in which we need a suitable *mantra* that can deliver us from the dangers of this age. Therefore the Supreme Personality of Godhead, in His incarnation as Lord Caitanya, gives us the Hare Kṛṣṇa *mantra.*

harer nāma harer nāma
harer nāmaiva kevalam
kalau nāsty eva nāsty eva
nāsty eva gatir anyathā

"In this age of quarrel and hypocrisy the only means of deliverance is chanting the holy name of the Lord. There is no other way. There is no other way. There is no other way." In His *Śikṣāṣṭaka,* Lord Caitanya says, *paraṁ vijayate śrī-kṛṣṇa-saṅkīrtanam:* "All glories to the chanting of *śrī-kṛṣṇa-saṅkīrtana!*" The *mahā-mantra*—Hare Kṛṣṇa, Hare Kṛṣṇa, Kṛṣṇa Kṛṣṇa, Hare Hare/ Hare Rāma, Hare Rāma, Rāma Rāma, Hare Hare—is directly chanted by the Lord Himself, who gives us this *mantra* for deliverance.

We cannot invent any means to be delivered from the dangers of material existence. Here, even the demigods, such as Lord Brahmā and Lord Śiva, and the *prajāpatis,* such as Dakṣa, are said to be like illuminating sparks in the presence of the Supreme Lord, who is compared to a great fire. Sparks are beautiful as long as they are in the fire. Similarly, we have to remain in the association of the Supreme Personality of Godhead and always engage in devotional service, for then we shall always be brilliant and illuminating. As soon as we fall from the service of the Lord, our brilliance and illumination will immediately be extinguished, or at least stopped for some time. When we living entities, who are like sparks of the original fire, the Supreme Lord, fall into a material condition, we must take the *mantra* from the Supreme Personality of Godhead as it is offered by Śrī Caitanya Mahāprabhu. By chanting this Hare Kṛṣṇa *mantra,* we shall be delivered from all the difficulties of this material world.

TEXT 16

श्रीशुक उवाच
एवं विरिञ्चादिभिरीडितस्तद्
विज्ञाय तेषां हृदयं यथैव ।
जगाद जीमूतगभीरया गिरा
बद्धाञ्जलीन्संवृतसर्वकारकान् ॥ १६ ॥

śrī-śuka uvāca
evaṁ viriñcādibhir īḍitas tad
vijñāya teṣāṁ hṛdayaṁ yathaiva
jagāda jīmūta-gabhīrayā girā
baddhāñjalīn saṁvṛta-sarva-kārakān

śrī-śukaḥ uvāca—Śrī Śukadeva Gosvāmī said; *evam*—thus; *viriñca-ādibhiḥ*—by all the demigods, headed by Lord Brahmā; *īḍitaḥ*—being worshiped; *tat vijñāya*—understanding the expectation; *teṣām*—of all of them; *hṛdayaṁ*—the core of the heart; *yathā*—as; *eva*—indeed; *jagāda*—replied; *jīmūta-gabhīrayā*—like the sound of clouds; *girā*—by words; *baddha-añjalīn*—unto the demigods, who stood with folded hands; *saṁvṛta*—restrained; *sarva*—all; *kārakān*—senses.

TRANSLATION

Śukadeva Gosvāmī continued: When the Lord was thus offered prayers by the demigods, headed by Lord Brahmā, He understood the purpose for which they had approached Him. Therefore, in a deep voice that resembled the rumbling of clouds, the Lord replied to the demigods, who all stood there attentively with folded hands.

TEXT 17

एक एवेश्वरस्तस्मिन्सुरकार्ये सुरेश्वरः ।
विहर्तुकामस्तानाह समुद्रोन्मथनादिभिः ॥ १७ ॥

eka eveśvaras tasmin
sura-kārye sureśvaraḥ
vihartu-kāmas tān āha
samudronmathanādibhiḥ

ekaḥ—alone; *eva*—indeed; *īśvaraḥ*—the Supreme Personality of Godhead; *tasmin*—in that; *sura-kārye*—the activities of the demigods; *sura-īśvaraḥ*—the Lord of the demigods, the Supreme Personality of Godhead; *vihartu*—to enjoy pastimes; *kāmaḥ*—desiring; *tān*—unto the demigods; *āha*—said; *samudra-unmathana-ādibhiḥ*—by activities of churning the ocean.

TRANSLATION

Although the Supreme Personality of Godhead, the master of the demigods, was capable of performing the activities of the demigods by

Himself, He wanted to enjoy pastimes in churning the ocean. Therefore He spoke as follows.

TEXT 18

श्रीभगवानुवाच
हन्त ब्रह्मन्नहो शम्भो हे देवा मम भाषितम् ।
शृणुतावहिताः सर्वे श्रेयो वः स्याद् यथा सुराः ॥ १८ ॥

śrī-bhagavān uvāca
hanta brahmann aho śambho
he devā mama bhāṣitam
śṛṇutāvahitāḥ sarve
śreyo vaḥ syād yathā surāḥ

śrī-bhagavān uvāca—the Supreme Personality of Godhead said; *hanta*—addressing them; *brahman aho*—O Lord Brahmā; *śambho*—O Lord Śiva; *he*—O; *devāḥ*—demigods; *mama*—My; *bhāṣitam*—statement; *śṛṇuta*—hear; *avahitāḥ*—with great attention; *sarve*—all of you; *śreyaḥ*—good fortune; *vaḥ*—for all of you; *syāt*—shall be; *yathā*—as; *surāḥ*—for the demigods.

TRANSLATION

The Supreme Personality of Godhead said: O Lord Brahmā, Lord Śiva and other demigods, please hear Me with great attention, for what I say will bring good fortune for all of you.

TEXT 19

यात दानवदैतेयैस्तावत् सन्धिर्विधीयताम् ।
कालेनानुगृहीतैस्तैर्यावद् वो भव आत्मनः ॥ १९ ॥

yāta dānava-daiteyais
tāvat sandhir vidhīyatām
kālenānugṛhītais tair
yāvad vo bhava ātmanaḥ

yāta—just execute; *dānava*—with the demons; *daiteyaiḥ*—and the *asuras; tāvat*—so long; *sandhiḥ*—a truce; *vidhīyatām*—execute; *kālena*—by a favorable time (or *kāvyena*—by Śukrācārya); *anugṛhītaiḥ*—receiving benedictions; *taiḥ*—with them; *yāvat*—as long as; *vaḥ*—of you; *bhavaḥ*—good fortune; *ātmanaḥ*—of yourselves.

TRANSLATION

As long as you are not flourishing, you should make a truce with the demons and asuras, who are now being favored by time.

PURPORT

One word in this verse has two readings—*kālena* and *kāvyena. Kālena* means "favored by time," and *kāvyena* means "favored by Śukrācārya," Śukrācārya being the spiritual master of the Daityas. The demons and Daityas were favored in both ways, and therefore the demigods were advised by the Supreme Lord to execute a truce for the time being, until time favored them.

TEXT 20

अरयोऽपि हि सन्धेयाः सति कार्यार्थगौरवे ।
अहिमूषिकवद् देवा ह्यर्थस्य पदवीं गतैः ॥ २० ॥

arayo 'pi hi sandheyāḥ
sati kāryārtha-gaurave
ahi-mūṣikavad devā
hy arthasya padavīṁ gataiḥ

arayaḥ—enemies; *api*—although; *hi*—indeed; *sandheyāḥ*—eligible for a truce; *sati*—being so; *kārya-artha-gaurave*—in the matter of an important duty; *ahi*—snake; *mūṣika*—mouse; *vat*—like; *devāḥ*—O demigods; *hi*—indeed; *arthasya*—of interest; *padavīm*—position; *gataiḥ*—so being.

TRANSLATION

O demigods, fulfilling one's own interests is so important that one may even have to make a truce with one's enemies. For the sake of one's self-interest, one has to act according to the logic of the snake and the mouse.

PURPORT

A snake and a mouse were once caught in a basket. Now, since the mouse is food for the snake, this was a good opportunity for the snake. However, since both of them were caught in the basket, even if the snake ate the mouse, the snake would not be able to get out. Therefore, the snake thought it wise to make a truce with the mouse and ask the mouse to make a hole in the basket so that both of them could get out. The snake's intention was that after the mouse made the hole, the snake would eat the mouse and escape from the basket through the hole. This is called the logic of the snake and the mouse.

TEXT 21

अमृतोत्पादने यत्नः क्रियतामविलम्बितम् ।
यस्य पीतस्य वै जन्तुर्मृत्युग्रस्तोऽमरो भवेत्॥ २१ ॥

amṛtotpādane yatnaḥ
kriyatām avilambitam
yasya pītasya vai jantur
mṛtyu-grasto 'maro bhavet

amṛta-utpādane—in generating nectar; *yatnaḥ*—endeavor; *kriyatām*—do; *avilambitam*—without delay; *yasya*—of which nectar; *pītasya*—anyone who drinks; *vai*—indeed; *jantuḥ*—living entity; *mṛtyu-grastaḥ*—although in imminent danger of death; *amaraḥ*—immortal; *bhavet*—can become.

TRANSLATION

Immediately endeavor to produce nectar, which a person who is about to die may drink to become immortal.

TEXTS 22-23

क्षिप्त्वा क्षीरोदधौ सर्वा वीरुत्तृणलतौषधीः ।
मन्थानं मन्दरं कृत्वा नेत्रं कृत्वा तु वासुकिम् ॥ २२ ॥
सहायेन मया देवा निर्मन्थध्वमतन्द्रिताः ।
क्लेशभाजो भविष्यन्ति दैत्या यूयं फलग्रहाः ॥ २३ ॥

kṣiptvā kṣīrodadhau sarvā
vīrut-tṛṇa-latauṣadhīḥ
manthānaṁ mandaraṁ kṛtvā
netraṁ kṛtvā tu vāsukim

sahāyena mayā devā
nirmanthadhvam atandritāḥ

kleśa-bhājo bhaviṣyanti
daityā yūyaṁ phala-grahāḥ

kṣiptvā—putting; *kṣīra-udadhau*—in the ocean of milk; *sarvāḥ*—all kinds of; *vīrut*—creepers; *tṛṇa*—grass; *latā*—vegetables; *auṣadhīḥ*—and drugs; *manthānam*—the churning rod; *mandaram*—Mandara Mountain; *kṛtvā*—making; *netram*—the churning rope; *kṛtvā*—making; *tu*—but; *vāsukim*—the snake Vāsuki; *sahāyena*—with a helper; *mayā*—by Me; *devāḥ*—all the demigods; *nirmanthadhvam*—go on churning; *atandritāḥ*—very carefully, without diversion; *kleśa-bhājaḥ*—sharetakers of sufferings; *bhaviṣyanti*—will be; *daityāḥ*—the demons; *yūyam*—but all of you; *phala-grahāḥ*—gainers of the actual result.

TRANSLATION

O demigods, cast into the ocean of milk all kinds of vegetables, grass, creepers and drugs. Then, with My help, making Mandara Mountain the churning rod and Vāsuki the rope for churning, churn the ocean of milk with undiverted attention. Thus the demons will be engaged in labor, but you, the demigods, will gain the actual result, the nectar produced from the ocean.

PURPORT

It appears that when different kinds of drugs, creepers, grass and vegetables are put into this milk and the milk is churned, as milk is churned for butter, the active principles of the vegetables and drugs mix with the milk, and the result is nectar.

TEXT 24

यूयं तदनुमोदध्वं यदिच्छन्त्यसुराः सुराः ।
न संरम्भेण सिध्यन्ति सर्वार्थाः सान्त्वया यथा ॥ २४ ॥

yūyaṁ tad anumodadhvaṁ
yad icchanty asurāḥ surāḥ
na saṁrambheṇa sidhyanti
sarvārthāḥ sāntvayā yathā

yūyam—all of you; *tat*—that; *anumodadhvam*—should accept; *yat*—whatever; *icchanti*—they desire; *asurāḥ*—the demons; *surāḥ*—O demigods; *na*—not; *saṁrambheṇa*—by being agitated in anger; *sidhyanti*—are very successful; *sarva-arthāḥ*—all desired ends; *sāntvayā*—by peaceful execution; *yathā*—as.

TRANSLATION

My dear demigods, with patience and peace everything can be done, but if one is agitated by anger, the goal is not achieved. Therefore, whatever the demons ask, agree to their proposal.

TEXT 25

न भेतव्यं कालकूटाद् विषाज्जलधिसम्भवात् ।
लोभः कार्यो न वो जातु रोषः कामस्तु वस्तुषु ॥ २५ ॥

na bhetavyaṁ kālakūṭād
viṣāj jaladhi-sambhavāt
lobhaḥ kāryo na vo jātu
roṣaḥ kāmas tu vastuṣu

na—not; *bhetavyam*—should be afraid; *kālakūṭāt*—of *kālakūṭa; viṣāt*—from the poison; *jaladhi*—from the ocean of milk; *sambhavāt*—which will appear; *lobhaḥ*—greed; *kāryaḥ*—execution; *na*—not; *vaḥ*—unto you; *jātu*—at any time; *roṣaḥ*—anger; *kāmaḥ*—lust; *tu*—and; *vastuṣu*—in the products.

TRANSLATION

A poison known as kālakūṭa will be generated from the ocean of milk, but you should not fear it. And when various products are churned from the ocean, you should not be greedy for them or anxious to obtain them, nor should you be angry.

PURPORT

It appears that by the churning process many things would be generated from the ocean of milk, including poison, valuable gems, nectar and many beautiful women. The demigods were advised, however, not to be greedy for the gems or beautiful women, but to wait patiently for the nectar. The real purpose was to get the nectar.

TEXT 26

श्रीशुक उवाच

इति देवान्समादिश्य भगवान् पुरुषोत्तमः ।
तेषामन्तर्दधे राजन्स्वच्छन्दगतिरीश्वरः ॥ २६ ॥

śrī-śuka uvāca
iti devān samādiśya
bhagavān puruṣottamaḥ
teṣām antardadhe rājan
svacchanda-gatir īśvaraḥ

śrī-śukaḥ uvāca—Śrī Śukadeva Gosvāmī said; *iti*—thus; *devān*—all the demigods; *samādiśya*—advising; *bhagavān*—the Supreme Personality of Godhead; *puruṣa-uttamaḥ*—the best of all persons; *teṣām*—from them; *antardadhe*—disappeared; *rājan*—O King; *svacchanda*—free; *gatiḥ*—whose movements; *īśvaraḥ*—the Personality of Godhead.

TRANSLATION

Śukadeva Gosvāmī continued: O King Parīkṣit, after advising the demigods in this way, the independent Supreme Personality of Godhead, the best of all living entities, disappeared from their presence.

TEXT 27

अथ तस्मै भगवते नमस्कृत्य पितामहः ।
भवश्च जग्मतुः स्वं स्वं धामोपेयुर्बलिं सुराः ॥ २७ ॥

atha tasmai bhagavate
namaskṛtya pitāmahaḥ
bhavaś ca jagmatuḥ svaṁ svaṁ
dhāmopeyur baliṁ surāḥ

atha—after this; *tasmai*—unto Him; *bhagavate*—unto the Supreme Personality of Godhead; *namaskṛtya*—offering obeisances; *pitā-mahaḥ*—Lord Brahmā; *bhavaḥ ca*—as well as Lord Śiva; *jagmatuḥ*—returned; *svam svam*—to their own; *dhāma*—abodes; *upeyuḥ*—approached; *balim*—King Bali; *surāḥ*—all the other demigods.

TRANSLATION

Then Lord Brahmā and Lord Śiva, after offering their respectful obeisances to the Lord, returned to their abodes. All the demigods then approached Mahārāja Bali.

TEXT 28

दृष्ट्वारीनप्यसंयत्ताञ्जातक्षोभान्स्वनायकान् ।
न्यषेधद् दैत्यराट् श्लोक्यः सन्धिविग्रहकालवित् ॥ २८ ॥

dṛṣṭvārīn apy asaṁyattāñ
jāta-kṣobhān sva-nāyakān
nyaṣedhad daitya-rāṭ ślokyaḥ
sandhi-vigraha-kālavit

dṛṣṭvā—observing; *arīn*—the enemies; *api*—although; *asaṁyattān*—without any endeavor to fight; *jāta-kṣobhān*—who became agitated; *sva-nāyakān*—his own captains and commanders; *nyaṣedhat*—prevented; *daitya-rāṭ*—the Emperor of the Daityas, Mahārāja Bali; *ślokyaḥ*—very respectable and prominent; *sandhi*—for making negotiations; *vigraha*—as well as for fighting; *kāla*—the time; *vit*—completely aware of.

TRANSLATION

Mahārāja Bali, a most celebrated king of the demons, knew very well when to make peace and when to fight. Thus although his commanders and captains were agitated and were about to kill the demigods, Mahārāja Bali, seeing that the demigods were coming to him without a militant attitude, forbade his commanders to kill them.

PURPORT

Vedic etiquette enjoins: *gṛhe śatrum api prāptaṁ viśvastam akutobhayam.* When enemies come to their opponent's place, they should be received in such a way that they will forget that there is animosity between the two parties. Bali Mahārāja was well conversant with the arts of peacemaking and fighting. Thus he received the demigods very well, although his commanders and captains were agitated. This kind of treatment was prevalent even during the fight between the Pāṇḍavas and the Kurus. During the day, the Pāṇḍavas and Kurus would fight with the utmost strength, and when the day was over they would go to each other's camps as friends and be received as such. During such friendly meetings, one enemy would offer anything the other enemy wanted. That was the system.

TEXT 29

ते वैरोचनिमासीनं गुप्तं चासुरयूथपैः ।
श्रिया परमया जुष्टं जिताशेषमुपागमन् ॥ २९ ॥

te vairocanim āsīnaṁ
guptaṁ cāsura-yūtha-paiḥ
śriyā paramayā juṣṭaṁ
jitāśeṣam upāgaman

te—all the demigods; *vairocanim*—unto Balirāja, the son of Virocana; *āsīnam*—sitting down; *guptam*—well protected; *ca*—and; *asura-yūtha-paiḥ*—by the commanders of the *asuras; śriyā*—by opulence; *paramayā*—supreme; *juṣṭam*—blessed; *jita-aśeṣam*—who became the proprietor of all the worlds; *upāgaman*—approached.

TRANSLATION

The demigods approached Bali Mahārāja, the son of Virocana, and sat down near him. Bali Mahārāja was protected by the commanders of the demons and was most opulent, having conquered all the universes.

TEXT 30

महेन्द्रः श्लक्ष्णया वाचा सान्त्वयित्वा महामतिः ।
अभ्यभाषत तत् सर्वं शिक्षितं पुरुषोत्तमात् ॥ ३० ॥

mahendraḥ ślakṣṇayā vācā
sāntvayitvā mahā-matiḥ
abhyabhāṣata tat sarvaṁ
śikṣitaṁ puruṣottamāt

mahā-indraḥ—the King of heaven, Indra; *ślakṣṇayā*—very mild; *vacā*—by words; *sāntvayitvā*—pleasing Bali Mahārāja very much; *mahā-matiḥ*—the most intelligent person; *abhyabhāṣata*—addressed; *tat*—that; *sarvam*—everything; *śikṣitam*—that was learned; *puruṣa-uttamāt*—from Lord Viṣṇu.

TRANSLATION

After pleasing Bali Mahārāja with mild words, Lord Indra, the King of the demigods, who was most intelligent, very politely submitted all the proposals he had learned from the Supreme Personality of Godhead, Lord Viṣṇu.

TEXT 31

तत्त्वरोचत दैत्यस्य तत्रान्ये येऽसुराधिपाः ।
शम्बरोऽरिष्टनेमिश्च ये च त्रिपुरवासिनः ॥ ३१ ॥

tat tv arocata daityasya
tatrānye ye 'surādhipāḥ
śambaro 'riṣṭanemiś ca
ye ca tripura-vāsinaḥ

tat—all those words; *tu*—but; *arocata*—were very pleasing; *daityasya*—to Bali Mahārāja; *tatra*—as well as; *anye*—others; *ye*—who were; *asura-adhipāḥ*—the chiefs of the *asuras*; *śambaraḥ*—Śambara; *ariṣṭanemiḥ*—Ariṣṭanemi; *ca*—also; *ye*—others who; *ca*—and; *tripura-vāsinaḥ*—all the residents of Tripura.

TRANSLATION

The proposals submitted by King Indra were immediately accepted by Bali Mahārāja and his assistants, headed by Śambara and Ariṣṭanemi, and by all the other residents of Tripura.

PURPORT

It appears from this verse that politics, diplomacy, the propensity to cheat, and everything that we find in this world in individual and social negotiations between two parties are also present in the upper planetary systems. The demigods went to Bali Mahārāja with the proposal to manufacture nectar, and the Daityas, the demons, immediately accepted it, thinking that since the demigods were already weak, when the nectar was produced the demons would take it from them and use it for their own purposes. The demigods, of course, had similar intentions. The only difference is that the Supreme Personality of Godhead, Lord Viṣṇu, was on the side of the demigods because the demigods were His devotees, whereas the demons did not care about Lord Viṣṇu. All over the universe there are two parties—the Viṣṇu party, or God-conscious party, and the godless party. The godless party is never happy or victorious, but the God-conscious party is always happy and victorious.

TEXT 32

ततो देवासुराः कृत्वा संविदं कृतसौहृदाः ।
उद्यमं परमं चक्रुरमृतार्थे परन्तप ॥ ३२ ॥

tato devāsurāḥ kṛtvā
saṁvidaṁ kṛta-sauhṛdāḥ
udyamaṁ paramaṁ cakrur
amṛtārthe parantapa

tataḥ—thereafter; *deva-asurāḥ*—both the demons and the demigods; *kṛtvā*—executing; *saṁvidam*—indicating; *kṛta-sauhṛdāḥ*—an armistice between them; *udyamam*—enterprise; *paramam*—supreme; *cakruḥ*—they did; *amṛta-arthe*—for the sake of nectar; *parantapa*—O Mahārāja Parīkṣit, chastiser of enemies.

TRANSLATION

O Mahārāja Parīkṣit, chastiser of enemies, the demigods and the demons thereafter made an armistice between them. Then, with great enterprise, they arranged to produce nectar, as proposed by Lord Indra.

PURPORT

The word *saṁvidam* is significant in this verse. The demigods and demons both agreed to stop fighting, at least for the time being, and endeavored to produce nectar. Śrīla Viśvanātha Cakravartī Ṭhākura notes in this connection:

saṁvid yuddhe pratijñāyām
ācāre nāmni toṣaṇe
sambhāṣaṇe kriyākāre
saṅketa-jñānayor api

The word *saṁvit* is variously used to mean "in fighting," "in promising," "for satisfying," "in addressing,""by practical action," "indication," and "knowledge."

TEXT 33

ततस्ते मन्दरगिरिमोजसोत्पाट्य दुर्मदाः ।
नदन्त उदधिं निन्युः शक्ताः परिघबाहवः ॥ ३३ ॥

tatas te mandara-girim
ojasotpāṭya durmadāḥ
nadanta udadhiṁ ninyuḥ
śaktāḥ parigha-bāhavaḥ

tataḥ—thereafter; *te*—all the demigods and demons; *mandara-girim*—Mandara Mountain; *ojasā*—with great strength; *utpāṭya*—extracting; *dur-madāḥ*—very powerful and competent; *nadanta*—cried very loudly; *udad-him*—toward the ocean; *ninyuḥ*—brought; *śaktāḥ*—very strong; *parigha-bāhavaḥ*—having long, strong arms.

TRANSLATION

Thereafter, with great strength, the demons and demigods, who were all very powerful and who had long, stout arms, uprooted Mandara Mountain. Crying very loudly, they brought it toward the ocean of milk.

TEXT 34

दूरभारोद्वहश्रान्ताः शक्रवैरोचनादयः ।
अपारयन्तस्तं वोढुं विवशा विजहुः पथि ॥ ३४ ॥

dūra-bhārodvaha-śrāntāḥ
śakra-vairocanādayaḥ
apārayantas taṁ voḍhuṁ
vivaśā vijahuḥ pathi

dūra—for a great distance; *bhāra-udvaha*—by carrying the great load; *śrāntāḥ*—being fatigued; *śakra*—King Indra; *vairocana-ādayaḥ*—and Mahārāja Bali (the son of Virocana) and others; *apārayantaḥ*—being unable; *tam*—the mountain; *voḍhum*—to bear; *vivaśāḥ*—being unable; *vijahuḥ*—gave up; *pathi*—on the way.

TRANSLATION

Because of conveying the great mountain for a long distance, King Indra, Mahārāja Bali and the other demigods and demons became fatigued. Being unable to carry the mountain, they left it on the way.

TEXT 35

निपतन्स गिरिस्तत्र बहूनमरदानवान् ।
चूर्णयामास महता भारेण कनकाचलः ॥ ३५ ॥

nipatan sa giris tatra
bahūn amara-dānavān

cūrṇayām āsa mahatā
bhāreṇa kanakācalaḥ

nipatan—falling down; *saḥ*—that; *giriḥ*—mountain; *tatra*—there; *bahūn*—many; *amara-dānavān*—demigods and demons; *cūrṇayām āsa*—were smashed; *mahatā*—by great; *bhāreṇa*—weight; *kanaka-acalaḥ*—the golden mountain known as Mandara.

TRANSLATION

The mountain known as Mandara, which was extremely heavy, being made of gold, fell and smashed many demigods and demons.

PURPORT

By constitution, gold is heavier than stone. Since Mandara Mountain was made of gold and was therefore heavier than stone, the demigods and demons could not properly carry it to the ocean of milk.

TEXT 36

तांस्तथा भग्नमनसो भग्नबाहूरुकन्धरान् ।
विज्ञाय भगवांस्तत्र बभूव गरुडध्वजः ॥ ३६ ॥

tāṁs tathā bhagna-manaso
bhagna-bāhūru-kandharān
vijñāya bhagavāṁs tatra
babhūva garuḍa-dhvajaḥ

tān—all the demigods and demons; *tathā*—thereafter; *bhagna-manasaḥ*—being brokenhearted; *bhagna-bāhu*—with broken arms; *ūru*—thighs; *kandharān*—and shoulders; *vijñāya*—knowing; *bhagavān*—the Supreme Personality of Godhead, Viṣṇu; *tatra*—there; *babhūva*—appeared; *garuḍa-dhvajaḥ*—being carried on Garuḍa.

TRANSLATION

The demigods and demons were frustrated and disheartened, and their arms, thighs and shoulders were broken. Therefore the Supreme Personality of Godhead, who knows everything, appeared there on the back of His carrier, Garuḍa.

TEXT 37

गिरिपातविनिष्पिष्टान्विलोक्यामरदानवान् ।
ईक्षया जीवयामास निर्जरान् निर्व्रणान्यथा ॥ ३७ ॥

giri-pāta-viniṣpiṣṭān
vilokyāmara-dānavān
īkṣayā jīvayām āsa
nirjarān nirvraṇān yathā

giri-pāta—because of the falling of Mandara Mountain; *viniṣpiṣṭān*—crushed; *vilokya*—observing; *amara*—the demigods; *dānavān*—and the demons; *īkṣayā*—simply by His glance; *jīvayām āsa*—brought back to life; *nirjarān*—without aggrievement; *nirvraṇān*—without bruises; *yathā*—as.

TRANSLATION

Observing that most of the demons and the demigods had been crushed by the falling of the mountain, the Lord glanced over them and brought them back to life. Thus they became free from grief, and they even had no bruises on their bodies.

TEXT 38

गिरिं चारोप्य गरुडे हस्तेनैकेन लीलया ।
आरुह्य प्रययावब्धिं सुरासुरगणैर्वृतः ॥ ३८ ॥

giriṁ cāropya garuḍe
hastenaikena līlayā
āruhya prayayāv abdhiṁ
surāsura-gaṇair vṛtaḥ

girim—the mountain; *ca*—also; *āropya*—placing; *garuḍe*—on the back of Garuḍa; *hastena*—by the hand; *ekena*—one; *līlayā*—very easily as His pastime; *āruhya*—getting on; *prayayau*—He went; *abdhim*—to the ocean of milk; *sura-asura-gaṇaiḥ*—by the demigods and *asuras; vṛtaḥ*—surrounded.

TRANSLATION

The Lord very easily lifted the mountain with one hand and placed it on the back of Garuḍa. Then, He too got on the back of Garuḍa and went to the ocean of milk, surrounded by the demigods and demons.

PURPORT

Here is proof of the omnipotence of the Supreme Personality of Godhead, who is above everyone. There are two classes of living entities—the demons and the demigods—and the Supreme Personality of Godhead is above them both. The demons believe in the "chance" theory of creation, whereas the demigods believe in creation by the hand of the Supreme Personality of Godhead. The omnipotence of the Supreme Lord is proved here, for simply with one hand He lifted Mandara Mountain, the demigods and the demons, placed them on the back of Garuḍa and brought them to the ocean of milk. Now, the demigods, the devotees, would immediately accept this incident, knowing that the Lord can lift anything, however heavy it might be. But although demons were also carried along with the demigods, demons, upon hearing of this incident, would say that it is mythological. But if God is all-powerful, why would it be difficult for Him to lift a mountain? Since He is floating innumerable planets with many hundreds and thousands of Mandara Mountains, why can't He lift one of them with His hand? This is not mythology, but the difference between the believers and the faithless is that the devotees accept the incidents mentioned in the Vedic literatures to be true, whereas the demons simply argue and label all these historical incidents mythology. Demons would prefer to explain that everything happening in the cosmic manifestation takes place by chance, but demigods, or devotees, never consider anything to be chance. Rather, they know that everything is an arrangement of the Supreme Personality of Godhead. That is the difference between the demigods and the demons.

TEXT 39

अवरोप्य गिरिं स्कन्धात् सुपर्णः पततां वरः ।
ययौ जलान्त उत्सृज्य हरिणा स विसर्जितः ॥ ३९ ॥

avaropya giriṁ skandhāt
suparṇaḥ patatāṁ varaḥ
yayau jalānta utsṛjya
hariṇā sa visarjitaḥ

avaropya—unloading; *girim*—the mountain; *skandhāt*—from his shoulder; *suparṇaḥ*—Garuḍa; *patatām*—of all the birds; *varaḥ*—the biggest or most powerful; *yayau*—went; *jala-ante*—where the water is; *utsṛjya*—placing; *hariṇā*—by the Supreme Personality of Godhead; *saḥ*—he (Garuḍa); *visarjitaḥ*—discharged from that place.

TRANSLATION

Thereafter, Garuḍa, the chief of birds, unloaded Mandara Mountain from his shoulder and brought it near the water. Then he was asked by the Lord to leave that place, and he left.

PURPORT

Garuḍa was asked by the Lord to leave that place because the snake Vāsuki, who was to be used as the rope for churning, could not go there in the presence of Garuḍa. Garuḍa, the carrier of Lord Viṣṇu, is not a vegetarian. He eats big snakes. Vāsuki, being a great snake, would be natural food for Garuḍa, the chief of birds. Lord Viṣṇu therefore asked Garuḍa to leave so that Vāsuki could be brought to churn the ocean with Mandara Mountain, which was to be used as the churning rod. These are the wonderful arrangements of the Supreme Personality of Godhead. Nothing takes place by accident. Carrying Mandara Mountain on the back of a bird and putting it in its right position might be difficult for anyone, whether demigod or demon, but for the Supreme Personality of Godhead everything is possible, as shown by this pastime. The Lord had no difficulty lifting the mountain with one hand, and Garuḍa, His carrier, carried all the demons and demigods together by the grace of the Supreme Lord. The Lord is known as Yogeśvara, the master of all mystic power, because of His omnipotence. If He likes, He can make anything lighter than cotton or heavier than the universe. Those who do not believe in the activities of the Lord cannot explain how things happen. Using words like "accident," they take shelter of ideas that are unbelievable. Nothing is accidental. Everything is done by the Supreme Personality of Godhead, as the Lord Himself confirms in *Bhagavad-gītā* (9.10). *Mayādhyakṣeṇa prakṛtiḥ sūyate sacarācaram.* Whatever actions and reactions occur within the cosmic manifestation all take place under the superintendence of the Supreme Personality of Godhead. However, because the demons do not understand the potency of the Lord, when wonderful things are done, the demons think that they are accidental.

Thus end the Bhaktivedanta purports of the Eighth Canto, Sixth Chapter, of the Śrīmad-Bhāgavatam, *entitled "The Demigods and Demons Declare a Truce."*

CHAPTER SEVEN

Lord Śiva Saves the Universe by Drinking Poison

The summary of the Seventh Chapter is as follows. As described in this chapter, the Supreme Personality of Godhead, appearing in His incarnation as a tortoise, dove deep into the ocean to carry Mandara Mountain on His back. At first the churning of the ocean produced *kālakūṭa* poison. Everyone feared this poison, but Lord Śiva satisfied them by drinking it.

With the understanding that when the nectar was generated from the churning they would share it equally, the demigods and the demons brought Vāsuki to be used as the rope for the churning rod. By the expert arrangement of the Supreme Personality of Godhead, the demons held the snake near the mouth, whereas the demigods held the tail of the great snake. Then, with great endeavor, they began pulling the snake in both directions. Because the churning rod, Mandara Mountain, was very heavy and was not held by any support in the water, it sank into the ocean, and in this way the prowess of both the demons and the demigods was vanquished. The Supreme Personality of Godhead then appeared in the form of a tortoise and supported Mandara Mountain on His back. Then the churning resumed with great force. As a result of the churning, a huge amount of poison was produced. The *prajāpatis,* seeing no one else to save them, approached Lord Śiva and offered him prayers full of truth. Lord Śiva is called Āśutoṣa because he is very pleased if one is a devotee. Therefore he easily agreed to drink all the poison generated by the churning. The goddess Durgā, Bhavānī, the wife of Lord Śiva, was not at all disturbed when Lord Śiva agreed to drink the poison, for she knew Lord Śiva's prowess. Indeed, she expressed her pleasure at this agreement. Then Lord Śiva gathered the devastating poison, which was everywhere. He took it in his hand and drank it. After he drank the poison, his neck became bluish. A small quantity of the poison dropped from his hands to the ground, and it is because of this poison that there are poisonous snakes, scorpions, toxic plants and other poisonous things in this world.

TEXT 1

श्रीशुक उवाच
ते नागराजमामन्त्र्य फलभागेन वासुकिम् ।
परिवीय गिरौ तस्मिन् नेत्रमब्धिं मुदान्विताः ।
आरेभिरे सुरायत्ता अमृतार्थे कुरूद्वह ॥ १ ॥

śrī-śuka uvāca
te nāga-rājam āmantrya
phala-bhāgena vāsukim
parivīya girau tasmin
netram abdhiṁ mudānvitāḥ
ārebhire surā yattā
amṛtārthe kurūdvaha

śrī-śukaḥ uvāca—Śrī Śukadeva Gosvāmī said; *te*—all of them (the demigods and the demons); *nāga-rājam*—the king of the Nāgas, snakes; *āmantrya*—inviting, or requesting; *phala-bhāgena*—by promising a share of the nectar; *vāsukim*—the snake Vāsuki; *parivīya*—encircling; *girau*—Mandara Mountain; *tasmin*—unto it; *netram*—the churning rope; *abdhim*—the ocean of milk; *mudā anvitāḥ*—all surcharged with great pleasure; *ārebhire*—began to act; *surāḥ*—the demigods; *yattāḥ*—with great endeavor; *amṛta-arthe*—for gaining nectar; *kuru-udvaha*—O King Parīkṣit, best of the Kurus.

TRANSLATION

Śukadeva Gosvāmī said: O best of the Kurus, Mahārāja Parīkṣit, the demigods and demons summoned Vāsuki, king of the serpents, requesting him to come and promising to give him a share of the nectar. They coiled Vāsuki around Mandara Mountain as a churning rope, and with great pleasure they endeavored to produce nectar by churning the ocean of milk.

TEXT 2

हरिः पुरस्ताज्जगृहे पूर्वं देवास्ततोऽभवन् ॥ २ ॥

hariḥ purastāj jagṛhe
pūrvaṁ devās tato 'bhavan

hariḥ—the Supreme Personality of Godhead, Ajita; *purastāt*—from the front; *jagṛhe*—took; *pūrvam*—at first; *devāḥ*—the demigods; *tataḥ*—thereafter; *abhavan*—took the front portion of Vāsuki.

TRANSLATION

The Personality of Godhead, Ajita, grasped the front portion of the snake, and then the demigods followed.

TEXT 3

तन्नैच्छन् दैत्यपतयो महापुरुषचेष्टितम् ।
न गृह्णीमो वयं पुच्छमहेरङ्गममङ्गलम् ।
स्वाध्यायश्रुतसम्पन्नाः प्रख्याता जन्मकर्मभिः ॥ ३ ॥

tan naicchan daitya-patayo
mahā-puruṣa-ceṣṭitam
na gṛhṇīmo vayaṁ puccham
aher aṅgam amaṅgalam
svādhyāya-śruta-sampannāḥ
prakhyātā janma-karmabhiḥ

tat—that arrangement; *na aicchan*—not liking; *daitya-patayaḥ*—the leaders of the demons; *mahā-puruṣa*—of the Supreme Personality of Godhead; *ceṣṭitam*—attempt; *na*—not; *gṛhṇīmaḥ*—shall take; *vayam*—all of us (the Daityas); *puccham*—the tail; *aheḥ*—of the serpent; *aṅgam*—part of the body; *amaṅgalam*—inauspicious, inferior; *svādhyāya*—with Vedic study; *śruta*—and Vedic knowledge; *sampannāḥ*—fully equipped; *prakhyātāḥ*—prominent; *janma-karmabhiḥ*—by birth and activities.

TRANSLATION

The leaders of the demons thought it unwise to hold the tail, the inauspicious portion of the snake. Instead, they wanted to hold the front, which had been taken by the Personality of Godhead and the demigods, because that portion was auspicious and glorious. Thus the demons, on the plea that they were all highly advanced students of Vedic knowledge and were all famous for their birth and activities, protested that they wanted to hold the front of the snake.

PURPORT

The demons thought that the front of the snake was auspicious and that catching hold of that portion would be more chivalrous. Moreover, Daityas must always do the opposite of the demigods. That is their nature. We have actually seen this in relation to our Kṛṣṇa consciousness movement. We are advocating cow protection and encouraging people to drink more milk and eat palatable preparations made of milk, but the demons, just to protest such proposals, are claiming that they are advanced in scientific knowledge, as described here by the words *svādhyāya-śruta-sampannāḥ.* They say that according to their scientific way, they have discovered that milk is dangerous and that the beef obtained by killing cows is very nutritious. This difference of opinion will always continue. Indeed, it has existed since days of yore. Millions of years ago, there was the same competition. The demons, as a result of their so-called Vedic study, preferred to hold the side of the snake near the mouth. The Supreme Personality of Godhead thought it wise to catch hold of the dangerous part of the snake and allow the demons to hold the tail, which was not dangerous, but because of a competitive desire, the demons thought it wise to hold the snake near the mouth. If the demigods were going to drink poison, the demons would resolve, "Why should we not share the poison and die gloriously by drinking it?"

In regard to the words *svādhyāya-śruta-sampannāḥ prakhyātā janma-karmabhiḥ,* another question may be raised. If one is actually educated in Vedic knowledge, is famous for performing prescribed activities and has been born in a great aristocratic family, why should he be called a demon? The answer is that one may be highly educated and may have been born in an aristocratic family, but if he is godless, if he does not listen to the instructions of God, then he is a demon. There are many examples in history of men like Hiraṇyakaśipu, Rāvaṇa and Kaṁsa who were well educated, who were born in aristocratic families and who were very powerful and chivalrous in fighting, but who, because of deriding the Supreme Personality of Godhead, were called Rākṣasas, or demons. One may be very well educated, but if he has no sense of Kṛṣṇa consciousness, no obedience to the Supreme Lord, he is a demon. That is described by the Lord Himself in *Bhagavad-gītā* (7.15):

na māṁ duṣkṛtino mūḍhāḥ
prapadyante narādhamāḥ
māyayāpahṛta-jñānā
āsuraṁ bhāvam āśritāḥ

"Those miscreants who are grossly foolish, lowest among mankind, whose knowledge is stolen by illusion, and who partake of the atheistic nature of demons, do not surrender unto Me." *Āsuraṁ bhāvam* refers to not accepting the existence of God or the transcendental instructions of the Personality of Godhead. *Bhagavad-gītā* clearly consists of transcendental instructions imparted directly by the Supreme Personality of Godhead. But *asuras,* instead of accepting these instructions directly, make commentaries according to their own whimsical ways and mislead everyone, without profit even for themselves. One should therefore be very careful of demoniac, godless persons. According to the words of Lord Kṛṣṇa, even if a godless demon is very well educated, he must be considered a *mūḍha, narādhama* and *māyayāpahṛta jñāna.*

TEXT 4

इति तूष्णीं स्थितान्दैत्यान् विलोक्य पुरुषोत्तमः ।
स्मयमानो विसृज्याग्रं पुच्छं जग्राह सामरः ॥ ४ ॥

iti tūṣṇīṁ sthitān daityān
vilokya puruṣottamaḥ
smayamāno visṛjyāgraṁ
pucchaṁ jagrāha sāmaraḥ

iti—thus; *tūṣṇīm*—silently; *sthitān*—staying; *daityān*—the demons; *vilokya*—seeing; *puruṣa-uttamaḥ*—the Personality of Godhead; *smayamānaḥ*—smiling; *visṛjya*—giving up; *agram*—the front portion of the snake; *puccham*—the rear portion; *jagrāha*—grasped; *sa-amaraḥ*—with the demigods.

TRANSLATION

Thus the demons remained silent, opposing the desire of the demigods. Seeing the demons and understanding their motive, the Personality of Godhead smiled. Without discussion, He immediately accepted their proposal by grasping the tail of the snake, and the demigods followed Him.

TEXT 5

कृतस्थानविभागास्त एवं कश्यपनन्दनाः ।
ममन्थुः परमं यत्ता अमृतार्थं पयोनिधिम् ॥ ५ ॥

kṛta-sthāna-vibhāgās ta
evaṁ kaśyapa-nandanāḥ
mamanthuḥ paramaṁ yattā
amṛtārthaṁ payo-nidhim

kṛta—adjusting; *sthāna-vibhāgāḥ*—the division of the places they were to hold; *te*—they; *evam*—in this way; *kaśyapa-nandanāḥ*—the sons of Kaśyapa (both the demigods and the demons); *mamanthuḥ*—churned; *paramam*—with great; *yattāḥ*—endeavor; *amṛta-artham*—for getting nectar; *payaḥ-nidhim*—the ocean of milk.

TRANSLATION

After thus adjusting how the snake was to be held, the sons of Kaśyapa, both demigods and demons, began their activities, desiring to get nectar by churning the ocean of milk.

TEXT 6

मथ्यमानेऽर्णवे सोऽद्रिरनाधारो ह्यपोऽविशत् ।
ध्रियमाणोऽपि बलिभिर्गौरवात् पाण्डुनन्दन ॥ ६ ॥

mathyamāne 'rṇave so 'drir
anādhāro hy apo 'viśat
dhriyamāṇo 'pi balibhir
gauravāt pāṇḍu-nandana

mathyamāne—while the churning was going on; *arṇave*—in the ocean of milk; *saḥ*—that; *adriḥ*—hill; *anādhāraḥ*—without being supported by anything; *hi*—indeed; *apaḥ*—in the water; *aviśat*—drowned; *dhriyamāṇaḥ*—captured; *api*—although; *balibhiḥ*—by the powerful demigods and demons; *gauravāt*—from being very heavy; *pāṇḍu-nandana*—O son of Pāṇḍu (Mahārāja Parīkṣit).

TRANSLATION

O son of the Pāṇḍu dynasty, when Mandara Mountain was thus being used as a churning rod in the ocean of milk, it had no support, and therefore although held by the strong hands of the demigods and demons, it sank into the water.

TEXT 7

ते सुनिर्विण्णमनसः परिम्लानमुखश्रियः ।
आसन् स्वपौरुषे नष्टे दैवेनातिबलीयसा ॥ ७ ॥

te sunirviṇṇa-manasaḥ
parimlāna-mukha-śriyaḥ
āsan sva-pauruṣe naṣṭe
daivenātibalīyasā

te—all of them (the demigods and demons); *sunirviṇṇa-manasaḥ*—their minds being very disappointed; *parimlāna*—dried up; *mukha-śriyaḥ*—the beauty of their faces; *āsan*—became; *sva-pauruṣe*—with their own prowess; *naṣṭe*—being lost; *daivena*—by a providential arrangement; *ati-balīyasā*—which is always stronger than anything else.

TRANSLATION

Because the mountain had been sunk by the strength of providence, the demigods and demons were disappointed, and their faces seemed to shrivel.

TEXT 8

विलोक्य विघ्नेशविधिं तदेश्वरो
दुरन्तवीर्योऽवितथाभिसन्धिः ।
कृत्वा वपुः कच्छपमद्भुतं महत्
प्रविश्य तोयं गिरिमुज्जहार ॥ ८ ॥

vilokya vighneśa-vidhiṁ tadeśvaro
duranta-vīryo 'vitathābhisandhiḥ
kṛtvā vapuḥ kacchapam adbhutaṁ mahat
praviśya toyaṁ girim ujjahāra

vilokya—observing; *vighna*—the obstruction (the sinking of the mountain); *īśa-vidhim*—by the providential arrangement; *tadā*—then; *īśvaraḥ*—the Supreme Personality of Godhead; *duranta-vīryaḥ*—inconceivably powerful; *avitatha*—infallible; *abhisandhiḥ*—whose determination; *kṛtvā*—expanding; *vapuḥ*—body; *kacchapam*—tortoise; *adbhutam*—wonderful; *mahat*—very great; *praviśya*—entering; *toyam*—the water; *girim*—the mountain (Mandara); *ujjahāra*—lifted.

TRANSLATION

Seeing the situation that had been created by the will of the Supreme, the unlimitedly powerful Lord, whose determination is infallible, took the

wonderful shape of a tortoise, entered the water, and lifted the great Mandara Mountain.

PURPORT

Here is evidence that the Supreme Personality of Godhead is the supreme controller of everything. As we have previously described, there are two classes of men — the demons and the demigods — but neither of them are supremely powerful. Everyone has experienced that hindrances are imposed upon us by the supreme power. The demons regard these hindrances as mere accidents or chance, but devotees accept them to be acts of the supreme ruler. When faced with hindrances, therefore, devotees pray to the Lord. *Tat te 'nukampāṁ susamīkṣamāṇo bhuñjāna evātma-kṛtaṁ vipākam.* Devotees endure hindrances, accepting them to be caused by the Supreme Personality of Godhead and regarding them as benedictions. Demons, however, being unable to understand the supreme controller, regard such hindrances as accidental. Here, of course, the Supreme Personality of Godhead was present personally. It was by His will that there were hindrances, and by His will those hindrances were removed. The Lord appeared as a tortoise to support the great mountain. *Kṣitir iha vipulatare tava tiṣṭhati pṛṣṭhe.* The Lord held the great mountain on His back. *Keśava dhṛta-kūrma-śarīra jaya jagadīśa hare.* Dangers can be created by the Supreme Personality of Godhead, and they can also be removed by Him. This is known to devotees, but demons cannot understand it.

TEXT 9

तमुत्थितं वीक्ष्य कुलाचलं पुनः
समुद्यता निर्मथितुं सुरासुराः ।
दधार पृष्ठेन स लक्षयोजन-
प्रस्तारिणा द्वीप इवापरो महान् ॥ ९ ॥

tam utthitaṁ vīkṣya kulācalaṁ punaḥ
samudyatā nirmathituṁ surāsurāḥ
dadhāra pṛṣṭhena sa lakṣa-yojana-
prastāriṇā dvīpa ivāparo mahān

tam — that mountain; *utthitam* — lifted; *vīkṣya* — observing; *kulācalam* — known as Mandara; *punaḥ* — again; *samudyatāḥ* — enlivened; *nirmathitum* —

to churn the ocean of milk; *sura-asurāḥ*—the demigods and the demons; *dad-hāra*—carried; *pṛṣṭhena*—by the back; *saḥ*—the Supreme Lord; *lakṣa-yojana*—one hundred thousand *yojanas* (eight hundred thousand miles); *prastāriṇā*—extending; *dvīpaḥ*—a big island; *iva*—like; *aparaḥ*—another; *mahān*—very big.

TRANSLATION

When the demigods and demons saw that Mandara Mountain had been lifted, they were enlivened and encouraged to begin churning again. The mountain rested on the back of the great tortoise, which extended for eight hundred thousand miles like a large island.

TEXT 10

सुरासुरेन्द्रैर्भुजवीर्यवेपितं
परिभ्रमन्तं गिरिमङ्ग पृष्ठतः ।
बिभ्रत् तदावर्तनमादिकच्छपो
मेनेऽङ्गकण्डूयनमप्रमेयः ॥ १० ॥

surāsurendrair bhuja-vīrya-vepitaṁ
paribhramantaṁ girim aṅga pṛṣṭhataḥ
bibhrat tad-āvartanam ādi-kacchapo
mene 'ṅga-kaṇḍūyanam aprameyaḥ

sura-asura-indraiḥ—by the leaders of the demons and the demigods; *bhuja-vīrya*—by the strength of their arms; *vepitam*—moving; *paribhraman-tam*—rotating; *girim*—the mountain; *aṅga*—O Mahārāja Parīkṣit; *pṛṣṭhataḥ*—on His back; *bibhrat*—bore; *tat*—of that; *āvartanam*—the rotating; *ādi-kacchapaḥ*—as the supreme original tortoise; *mene*—considered; *aṅga-kaṇḍūyanam*—as pleasing scratching of the body; *aprameyaḥ*—unlimited.

TRANSLATION

O King, when the demigods and demons, by the strength of their arms, rotated Mandara Mountain on the back of the extraordinary tortoise, the tortoise accepted the rolling of the mountain as a means of scratching His body, and thus He felt a pleasing sensation.

PURPORT

The Supreme Personality of Godhead is always the unlimited. Although the Supreme Personality of Godhead, in His body as a tortoise, held on His back the largest of mountains, Mandara-parvata, He did not feel any inconvenience. On the contrary, He apparently felt some itching, and thus the rotation of the mountain was certainly very pleasing.

TEXT 11

तथासुरानाविशदासुरेण
रूपेण तेषां बलवीर्यमीरयन्।
उद्दीपयन् देवगणांश्च विष्णु-
र्दैवेन नागेन्द्रमबोधरूपः ॥ ११ ॥

tathāsurān āviśad āsureṇa
rūpeṇa teṣāṁ bala-vīryam īrayan
uddīpayan deva-gaṇāṁś ca viṣṇur
daivena nāgendram abodha-rūpaḥ

tathā—thereafter; *asurān*—unto the demons; *āviśat*—entered; *āsureṇa*—by the quality of passion; *rūpeṇa*—in such a form; *teṣām*—of them; *bala-vīryam*—strength and energy; *īrayan*—increasing; *uddīpayan*—encouraging; *deva-gaṇān*—the demigods; *ca*—also; *viṣṇuḥ*—Lord Viṣṇu; *daivena*—by the feature of goodness; *nāga-indram*—unto the King of the serpents, Vāsuki; *abodha-rūpaḥ*—by the quality of ignorance.

TRANSLATION

Thereafter, Lord Viṣṇu entered the demons as the quality of passion, the demigods as the quality of goodness, and Vāsuki as the quality of ignorance to encourage them and increase their various types of strength and energy.

PURPORT

Everyone in this material world is under the different modes of material nature. There were three different parties in the churning of Mandara Mountain—the demigods, who were in the mode of goodness, the demons, who were in the mode of passion, and the snake Vāsuki, who was in the mode of ignorance. Since they were all becoming tired (Vāsuki so much so that he was almost going to die), Lord Viṣṇu, to encourage them to continue the work of churning the ocean, entered into them according to their respective modes of nature—goodness, passion and ignorance.

TEXT 12

उपर्यगेन्द्रं गिरिराडिवान्य
आक्रम्य हस्तेन सहस्त्रबाहुः ।
तस्थौ दिवि ब्रह्मभवेन्द्रमुख्यै-
रभिष्टुवद्भिः सुमनोऽभिवृष्टः ॥ १२ ॥

upary agendraṁ giri-rāḍ ivānya
ākramya hastena sahasra-bāhuḥ
tasthau divi brahma-bhavendra-mukhyair
abhiṣṭuvadbhiḥ sumano-'bhivṛṣṭaḥ

upari—on the top of; *agendram*—the big mountain; *giri-rāṭ*—the king of mountains; *iva*—like; *anyaḥ*—another; *ākramya*—catching; *hastena*—by one hand; *sahasra-bāhuḥ*—exhibiting thousands of hands; *tasthau*—situated; *divi*—in the sky; *brahma*—Lord Brahmā; *bhava*—Lord Śiva; *indra*—the King of heaven; *mukhyaiḥ*—headed by; *abhiṣṭuvadbhiḥ*—offered prayers to the Lord; *sumanaḥ*—by flowers; *abhivṛṣṭaḥ*—being showered.

TRANSLATION

Manifesting Himself with thousands of hands, the Lord then appeared on the summit of Mandara Mountain, like another great mountain, and held Mandara Mountain with one hand. In the upper planetary systems, Lord Brahmā and Lord Śiva, along with Indra, King of heaven, and other demigods, offered prayers to the Lord and showered flowers upon Him.

PURPORT

To balance Mandara Mountain while it was being pulled from both sides, the Lord Himself appeared on its summit like another great mountain. Lord Brahmā, Lord Śiva and King Indra then expanded themselves and showered flowers on the Lord.

TEXT 13

उपर्यधश्चात्मनि गोत्रनेत्रयोः
परेण ते प्राविशता समेधिताः ।

ममन्थुरब्धिं तरसा मदोत्कटा
महाद्रिणा क्षोभितनक्रचक्रम् ॥ १३ ॥

upary adhaś cātmani gotra-netrayoḥ
pareṇa te prāviśatā samedhitāḥ
mamanthur abdhiṁ tarasā madotkaṭā
mahādriṇā kṣobhita-nakra-cakram

upari—upward; *adhaḥ ca*—and downward; *ātmani*—unto the demons and demigods; *gotra-netrayoḥ*—unto the mountain and Vāsuki, who was used as a rope; *pareṇa*—the Supreme Personality of Godhead; *te*—they; *prāviśatā*—entering them; *samedhitāḥ*—sufficiently agitated; *mamanthuḥ*—churned; *abdhim*—the ocean of milk; *tarasā*—with great strength; *mada-utkaṭāḥ*—being mad; *mahā-adriṇā*—with the great Mandara Mountain; *kṣobhita*—agitated; *nakra-cakram*—all the alligators in the water.

TRANSLATION

The demigods and demons worked almost madly for the nectar, encouraged by the Lord, who was above and below the mountain and who had entered the demigods, the demons, Vāsuki and the mountain itself. Because of the strength of the demigods and demons, the ocean of milk was so powerfully agitated that all the alligators in the water were very much perturbed. Nonetheless the churning of the ocean continued in this way.

TEXT 14

अहीन्द्रसाहस्रकठोरदृङ्मुख-
श्वासाग्निधूमाहतवर्चसोऽसुराः ।
पौलोमकालेयबलील्वलादयो
दवाग्निदग्धाः सरला इवाभवन् ॥ १४ ॥

ahīndra-sāhasra-kaṭhora-dṛṅ-mukha-
śvāsāgni-dhūmāhata-varcaso 'surāḥ
pauloma-kāleya-balīlvalādayo
davāgni-dagdhāḥ saralā ivābhavan

ahīndra—of the King of serpents; *sāhasra*—by thousands; *kaṭhora*—very, very hard; *dṛk*—all directions; *mukha*—by the mouth; *śvāsa*—breathing; *agni*—fire coming out; *dhūma*—smoke; *āhata*—being affected; *var-*

casaḥ—by the rays; *asurāḥ*—the demons; *pauloma*—Pauloma; *kāleya*—Kāleya; *bali*—Bali; *ilvala*—Ilvala; *ādayaḥ*—headed by; *dava-agni*—by a forest fire; *dagdhāḥ*—burned; *saralāḥ*—*sarala* trees; *iva*—like; *abhavan*—all of them became.

TRANSLATION

Vāsuki had thousands of eyes and mouths. From his mouths he breathed smoke and blazing fire, which affected the demons, headed by Pauloma, Kāleya, Bali and Ilvala. Thus the demons, who appeared like sarala trees burned by a forest fire, gradually became powerless.

TEXT 15

देवांश्च तच्छ्वासशिखाहतप्रभान्
धूम्राम्बरस्त्रग्वरकञ्चुकाननान् ।
समभ्यवर्षन्भगवद्वशा घना
ववुः समुद्रोर्म्युपगूढवायवः ॥ १५ ॥

devāṁś ca tac-chvāsa-śikhā-hata-prabhān
dhūmrāmbara-srag-vara-kañcukānanān
samabhyavarṣan bhagavad-vaśā ghanā
vavuḥ samudrormy-upagūḍha-vāyavaḥ

devān—all the demigods; *ca*—also; *tat*—of Vāsuki; *śvāsa*—from the breathing; *śikhā*—by the flames; *hata*—being affected; *prabhān*—their bodily luster; *dhūmra*—smoky; *ambara*—dress; *srak-vara*—excellent garlands; *kañcuka*—armaments; *ānanān*—and faces; *samabhyavarṣan*—sufficiently rained; *bhagavat-vaśāḥ*—under the control of the Supreme Personality of Godhead; *ghanāḥ*—clouds; *vavuḥ*—blew; *samudra*—of the ocean of milk; *ūrmi*—from the waves; *upagūḍha*—bearing fragments of water; *vāyavaḥ*—breezes.

TRANSLATION

Because the demigods were also affected by the blazing breath of Vāsuki, their bodily lusters diminished, and their garments, garlands, weapons and faces were blackened by smoke. However, by the grace of the Supreme Personality of Godhead, clouds appeared on the sea, pouring torrents of rain, and breezes blew, carrying particles of water from the sea waves, to give the demigods relief.

TEXT 16

मथ्यमानात् तथा सिन्धोर्देवासुरवरूथपैः ।
यदा सुधा न जायेत निर्ममन्थाजितः स्वयम् ॥ १६ ॥

mathyamānāt tathā sindhor
devāsura-varūtha-paiḥ
yadā sudhā na jāyeta
nirmamanthājitaḥ svayam

mathyamānāt—sufficiently being churned; *tathā*—in this way; *sindhoḥ*—from the ocean of milk; *deva*—of the demigods; *asura*—and the demons; *varūtha-paiḥ*—by the best; *yadā*—when; *sudhā*—nectar; *na jāyeta*—did not come out; *nirmamantha*—churned; *ajitaḥ*—the Supreme Personality of Godhead, Ajita; *svayam*—personally.

TRANSLATION

When nectar did not come from the ocean of milk, despite so much endeavor by the best of the demigods and demons, the Supreme Personality of Godhead, Ajita, personally began to churn the ocean.

TEXT 17

मेघश्यामः कनकपरिधिः कर्णविद्योतविद्यु-
न्मूर्ध्नि भ्राजद्विलुलितकचः स्त्रग्धरो रक्तनेत्रः ।
जैत्रैर्दोर्भिर्जगदभयदैर्दन्दशूकं गृहीत्वा
मथ्नन् मथ्ना प्रतिगिरिरिवाशोभताथो धृताद्रिः ॥ १७ ॥

megha-śyāmaḥ kanaka-paridhiḥ karṇa-vidyota-vidyun
mūrdhni bhrājad-vilulita-kacaḥ srag-dharo rakta-netraḥ
jaitrair dorbhir jagad-abhaya-dair dandaśūkaṁ gṛhītvā
mathnan mathnā pratigirir ivāśobhatātho dhṛtādriḥ

megha-śyāmaḥ—blackish like a cloud; *kanaka-paridhiḥ*—wearing yellow garments; *karṇa*—on the ears; *vidyota-vidyut*—whose earrings shone like lightning; *mūrdhni*—on the head; *bhrājat*—gleaming; *vilulita*—disheveled; *kacaḥ*—whose hair; *srak-dharaḥ*—wearing a flower garland; *rakta-netraḥ*—with red eyes; *jaitraiḥ*—with victorious; *dorbhiḥ*—with arms; *jagat*—to the universe; *abhaya-daiḥ*—which give fearlessness; *dandaśūkam*—the snake

(Vāsuki); *gṛhītvā*—after taking; *mathnan*—churning; *mathnā*—by the churning rod (Mandara Mountain); *pratigiriḥ*—another mountain; *iva*—like; *aśobhata*—He appeared; *atho*—then; *dhṛta-adriḥ*—having taken the mountain.

TRANSLATION

The Lord appeared like a blackish cloud. He was dressed with yellow garments, His earrings shone on His ears like lightning, and His hair spread over His shoulders. He wore a garland of flowers, and His eyes were pinkish. With His strong, glorious arms, which award fearlessness throughout the universe, He took hold of Vāsuki and began churning the ocean, using Mandara Mountain as a churning rod. When engaged in this way, the Lord appeared like a beautifully situated mountain named Indranīla.

TEXT 18

निर्मथ्यमानादुदधेरभूद्विषं
महोल्बणं हालहलाह्वमग्रतः ।
सम्भ्रान्तमीनोन्मकराहिकच्छपात्
तिमिद्विपग्राहतिमिङ्गिलाकुलात् ॥ १८ ॥

nirmathyamānād udadher abhūd viṣaṁ
maholbaṇaṁ hālahalāhvam agrataḥ
sambhrānta-mīnonmakarāhi-kacchapāt
timi-dvipa-grāha-timiṅgilākulāt

nirmathyamānāt—while the activities of churning were going on; *udadheḥ*—from the ocean; *abhūt*—there was; *viṣam*—poison; *mahā-ulbaṇam*—very fierce; *hālahala-āhvam*—by the name *hālahala; agrataḥ*—at first; *sambhrānta*—agitated and going here and there; *mīna*—various kinds of fish; *unmakara*—sharks; *ahi*—different kinds of snakes; *kacchapāt*—and many kinds of tortoises; *timi*—whales; *dvipa*—water elephants; *grāha*—crocodiles; *timiṅgila*—whales that can swallow whales; *ākulāt*—being very much agitated.

TRANSLATION

The fish, sharks, tortoises and snakes were most agitated and perturbed. The entire ocean became turbulent, and even the large aquatic animals like whales, water elephants, crocodiles and timiṅgila fish [large

whales that can swallow small whales] came to the surface. While the ocean was being churned in this way, it first produced a fiercely dangerous poison called hālahala.

TEXT 19

तदुग्रवेगं दिशि दिश्युपर्यधो
विसर्पदुत्सर्पदसह्यमप्रति ।
भीताः प्रजा दुद्रुवुरङ्ग सेश्वरा
अरक्ष्यमाणाः शरणं सदाशिवम् ॥ १९ ॥

tad ugra-vegaṁ diśi diśy upary adho
visarpad utsarpad asahyam aprati
bhītāḥ prajā dudruvur aṅga seśvarā
arakṣyamāṇāḥ śaraṇaṁ sadāśivam

tat—that; *ugra-vegam*—very fierce and potent poison; *diśi diśi*—in all directions; *upari*—upward; *adhaḥ*—downward; *visarpat*—curling; *utsarpat*—going upward; *asahyam*—unbearable; *aprati*—uncontrollable; *bhītāḥ*—being very much afraid; *prajāḥ*—the residents of all the worlds; *dudruvuḥ*—moved here and there; *aṅga*—O Mahārāja Parīkṣit; *sa-īśvarāḥ*—with the Supreme Lord; *arakṣyamāṇāḥ*—not being protected; *śaraṇam*—shelter; *sadāśivam*—unto the lotus feet of Lord Śiva.

TRANSLATION

O King, when that uncontrollable poison was forcefully spreading up and down in all directions, all the demigods, along with the Lord Himself, approached Lord Śiva [Sadāśiva]. Feeling unsheltered and very much afraid, they sought shelter of him.

PURPORT

One may question that since the Supreme Personality of Godhead was personally present, why did He accompany all the demigods and people in general to take shelter of Lord Sadāśiva, instead of intervening Himself. In this connection Śrīla Madhvācārya warns:

rudrasya yaśaso 'rthāya
svayaṁ viṣṇur viṣaṁ vibhuḥ
na sañjahre samartho 'pi
vāyuṁ coce praśāntaye

Lord Viṣṇu was competent to rectify the situation, but in order to give credit to Lord Śiva, who later drank all the poison and kept it in his neck, Lord Viṣṇu did not take action.

TEXT 20

विलोक्य तं देववरं त्रिलोक्या
भवाय देव्याभिमतं मुनीनाम् ।
आसीनमद्रावपवर्गहेतो-
स्तपो जुषाणं स्तुतिभिः प्रणेमुः ॥ २० ॥

vilokya taṁ deva-varaṁ tri-lokyā
bhavāya devyābhimataṁ munīnām
āsīnam adrāv apavarga-hetos
tapo juṣāṇaṁ stutibhiḥ praṇemuḥ

vilokya—observing; *tam*—him; *deva-varam*—the best of the demigods; *tri-lokyāḥ*—of the three worlds; *bhavāya*—for the flourishing; *devyā*—with his wife, Bhavānī; *abhimatam*—accepted by; *munīnām*—great saintly persons; *āsīnam*—sitting together; *adrau*—from the top of Kailāsa Hill; *apavarga-hetoḥ*—desiring liberation; *tapaḥ*—in austerity; *juṣāṇam*—being served by them; *stutibhiḥ*—by prayers; *praṇemuḥ*—offered their respectful obeisances.

TRANSLATION

The demigods observed Lord Śiva sitting on the summit of Kailāsa Hill with his wife, Bhavānī, for the auspicious development of the three worlds. He was being worshiped by great saintly persons desiring liberation. The demigods offered him their obeisances and prayers with great respect.

TEXT 21

श्रीप्रजापतय ऊचुः

देवदेव महादेव भूतात्मन् भूतभावन ।
त्राहि नः शरणापन्नांस्त्रैलोक्यदहनाद् विषात् ॥ २१ ॥

śrī-prajāpataya ūcuḥ
deva-deva mahā-deva
bhūtātman bhūta-bhāvana

trāhi naḥ śaraṇāpannāṁs
trailokya-dahanād viṣāt

śrī-prajāpatayaḥ ūcuḥ—the *prajāpatis* said; *deva-deva*—O Lord Mahādeva, best of the demigods; *mahā-deva*—O great demigod; *bhūta-ātman*—O life and soul of everyone in this world; *bhūta-bhāvana*—O the cause of the happiness and flourishing of all of them; *trāhi*—deliver; *naḥ*—us; *śaraṇa-āpannān*—who have taken shelter at your lotus feet; *trailokya*—of the three worlds; *dahanāt*—which is causing the burning; *viṣāt*—from this poison.

TRANSLATION

The prajāpatis said: O greatest of all demigods, Mahādeva, Supersoul of all living entities and cause of their happiness and prosperity, we have come to the shelter of your lotus feet. Now please save us from this fiery poison, which is spreading all over the three worlds.

PURPORT

Since Lord Śiva is in charge of annihilation, why should he be approached for protection, which is given by Lord Viṣṇu? Lord Brahmā creates, and Lord Śiva annihilates, but both Lord Brahmā and Lord Śiva are incarnations of Lord Viṣṇu and are known as *śaktyāveśa-avatāras.* They are endowed with a special power like that of Lord Viṣṇu, who is actually all-pervading in their activities. Therefore whenever prayers for protection are offered to Lord Śiva, actually Lord Viṣṇu is indicated, for otherwise Lord Śiva is meant for destruction. Lord Śiva is one of the *īśvaras,* or the controllers known as *śaktyāveśa-avatāras.* Therefore he can be addressed as having the qualities of Lord Viṣṇu.

TEXT 22

त्वमेकः सर्वजगत ईश्वरो बन्धमोक्षयोः ।
तं त्वामर्चन्ति कुशलाः प्रपन्नार्तिहरं गुरुम् ॥ २२ ॥

tvam ekaḥ sarva-jagata
īśvaro bandha-mokṣayoḥ
taṁ tvām arcanti kuśalāḥ
prapannārti-haraṁ gurum

tvam ekaḥ—Your Lordship is indeed; *sarva-jagataḥ*—of the three worlds; *īśvaraḥ*—the controller; *bandha-mokṣayoḥ*—of both bondage and liberation;

tam—that controller; *tvām arcanti*—worship you; *kuśalāḥ*—persons who want good fortune; *prapanna-ārti-haram*—who can mitigate all the distresses of a sheltered devotee; *gurum*—you who act as a good advisor to all fallen souls.

TRANSLATION

O lord, you are the cause of bondage and liberation of the entire universe because you are its ruler. Those who are advanced in spiritual consciousness surrender unto you, and therefore you are the cause of mitigating their distresses, and you are also the cause of their liberation. We therefore worship Your Lordship.

PURPORT

Actually Lord Viṣṇu maintains and accomplishes all good fortune. If one has to take shelter of Lord Viṣṇu, why should the demigods take shelter of Lord Śiva? They did so because Lord Viṣṇu acts through Lord Śiva in the creation of the material world. Lord Śiva acts on behalf of Lord Viṣṇu. When the Lord says in *Bhagavad-gītā* (14.4) that He is the father of all living entities (*ahaṁ bīja-pradaḥ pitā*), this refers to actions performed by Lord Viṣṇu through Lord Śiva. Lord Viṣṇu is always unattached to material activities, and when material activities are to be performed, Lord Viṣṇu performs them through Lord Śiva. Lord Śiva is therefore worshiped on the level of Lord Viṣṇu. When Lord Viṣṇu is untouched by the external energy He is Lord Viṣṇu, but when He is in touch with the external energy, He appears in His feature as Lord Śiva.

TEXT 23

गुणमय्या स्वशक्त्यास्य सर्गस्थित्यप्ययान्विभो ।
धत्से यदा स्वदृग् भूमन्ब्रह्मविष्णुशिवाभिधाम् ॥ २३ ॥

guṇa-mayyā sva-śaktyāsya
sarga-sthity-apyayān vibho
dhatse yadā sva-dṛg bhūman
brahma-viṣṇu-śivābhidhām

guṇa-mayyā—acting in three modes of activity; *sva-śaktyā*—by the external energy of Your Lordship; *asya*—of this material world; *sarga-sthiti-apyayān*—creation, maintenance and annihilation; *vibho*—O lord; *dhatse*—you execute; *yadā*—when; *sva-dṛk*—you manifest yourself; *bhūman*—O great one; *brahma-viṣṇu-śiva-abhidhām*—as Lord Brahmā, Lord Viṣṇu or Lord Śiva.

TRANSLATION

O lord, you are self-effulgent and supreme. You create this material world by your personal energy, and you assume the names Brahmā, Viṣṇu and Maheśvara when you act in creation, maintenance and annihilation.

PURPORT

This prayer is actually offered to Lord Viṣṇu, the *puruṣa,* who in His incarnations as the *guṇa-avatāras* assumes the names Brahmā, Viṣṇu and Maheśvara.

TEXT 24

त्वं ब्रह्म परमं गुह्यं सदसद्भावभावनम् ।
नानाशक्तिभिराभातस्त्वमात्मा जगदीश्वरः ॥ २४ ॥

tvaṁ brahma paramaṁ guhyaṁ
sad-asad-bhāva-bhāvanam
nānā-śaktibhir ābhātas
tvam ātmā jagad-īśvaraḥ

tvam—Your Lordship; *brahma*—impersonal Brahman; *paramam*—supreme; *guhyam*—confidential; *sat-asat-bhāva-bhāvanam*—the cause of varieties of creation, its cause and effect; *nānā-śaktibhiḥ*—with varieties of potencies; *ābhātaḥ*—manifest; *tvam*—you are; *ātmā*—the Supersoul; *jagat-īśvaraḥ*—the Supreme Personality of Godhead.

TRANSLATION

You are the cause of all causes, the self-effulgent, inconceivable, impersonal Brahman, which is originally Parabrahman. You manifest various potencies in this cosmic manifestation.

PURPORT

This prayer is offered to the impersonal Brahman, which consists of the effulgent rays of Parabrahman. Parabrahman is the Supreme Personality of Godhead (*paraṁ brahma paraṁ dhāma pavitraṁ paramaṁ bhavān*). When Lord Śiva is worshiped as Parabrahman, the worship is meant for Lord Viṣṇu.

TEXT 25

त्वं शब्दयोनिर्जगदादिरात्मा
प्राणेन्द्रियद्रव्यगुणः स्वभावः ।
कालः क्रतुः सत्यमृतं च धर्म-
स्त्वय्यक्षरं यत् त्रिवृदामनन्ति ॥ २५ ॥

tvaṁ śabda-yonir jagad-ādir ātmā
prāṇendriya-dravya-guṇaḥ svabhāvaḥ
kālaḥ kratuḥ satyam ṛtaṁ ca dharmas
tvayy akṣaraṁ yat tri-vṛd-āmananti

tvam—Your Lordship; *śabda-yoniḥ*—the origin and source of Vedic literature; *jagat-ādiḥ*—the original cause of material creation; *ātmā*—the soul; *prāṇa*—the living force; *indriya*—the senses; *dravya*—the material elements; *guṇaḥ*—the three qualities; *sva-bhāvaḥ*—material nature; *kālaḥ*—eternal time; *kratuḥ*—sacrifice; *satyam*—truth; *ṛtam*—truthfulness; *ca*—and; *dharmaḥ*—two different types of religion; *tvayi*—unto you; *akṣaram*—the original syllable, *oṁkāra; yat*—that which; *tri-vṛt*—consisting of the letters *a, u* and *m; āmananti*—they say.

TRANSLATION

O lord, you are the original source of Vedic literature. You are the original cause of material creation, the life force, the senses, the five elements, the three modes and the mahat-tattva. You are eternal time, determination and the two religious systems called truth [satya] and truthfulness [ṛta]. You are the shelter of the syllable oṁ, which consists of three letters "a-u-m."

TEXT 26

अग्निर्मुखं तेऽखिलदेवतात्मा
क्षितिं विदुर्लोकभवाङ्घ्रिपङ्कजम् ।
कालं गतिं तेऽखिलदेवतात्मनो
दिशश्च कर्णौ रसनं जलेशम् ॥ २६ ॥

agnir mukhaṁ te 'khila-devatātmā
kṣitiṁ vidur loka-bhavāṅghri-paṅkajam

kālaṁ gatiṁ te 'khila-devatātmano
diśaś ca karṇau rasanaṁ jaleśam

agniḥ—fire; *mukham*—mouth; *te*—of Your Lordship; *akhila-devatā-ātmā*—the origin of all demigods; *kṣitim*—the surface of the globe; *viduḥ*—they know; *loka-bhava*—O origin of all planets; *aṅghri-paṅkajam*—your lotus feet; *kālam*—eternal time; *gatim*—progress; *te*—of Your Lordship; *akhila-devatā-ātmanaḥ*—the total aggregate of all the demigods; *diśaḥ*—all directions; *ca*—and; *karṇau*—your ears; *rasanam*—taste; *jala-īśam*—the demigod controller of the water.

TRANSLATION

O father of all planets, learned scholars know that fire is your mouth, the surface of the globe is your lotus feet, eternal time is your movement, all the directions are your ears, and Varuṇa, master of the waters, is your tongue.

PURPORT

In the *śruti-mantras* it is said, *agniḥ sarva-devatāḥ:* "Fire is the aggregate of all demigods." Agni is the mouth of the Supreme Personality of Godhead. It is through Agni, or fire, that the Lord accepts all sacrificial oblations.

TEXT 27

नाभिर्नभस्ते श्वसनं नभस्वान्
सूर्यश्च चक्षूंषि जलं स्म रेतः ।
परावरात्माश्रयणं तवात्मा
सोमो मनो द्यौर्भगवन् शिरस्ते ॥ २७ ॥

nābhir nabhas te śvasanaṁ nabhasvān
sūryaś ca cakṣūṁṣi jalaṁ sma retaḥ
parāvarātmāśrayaṇaṁ tavātmā
somo mano dyaur bhagavan śiras te

nābhiḥ—navel; *nabhaḥ*—the sky; *te*—of Your Lordship; *śvasanam*—breathing; *nabhasvān*—the air; *sūryaḥ ca*—and the sun globe; *cakṣūṁṣi*—your eyes; *jalam*—the water; *sma*—indeed; *retaḥ*—semen; *para-avara-ātma-āśrayaṇam*—the shelter of all living entities, low and high; *tava*—your;

ātmā—self; *somaḥ*—the moon; *manaḥ*—mind; *dyauḥ*—the higher planetary systems; *bhagavan*—O Your Lordship; *śiraḥ*—head; *te*—of you.

TRANSLATION

O lord, the sky is your navel, the air is your breathing, the sun is your eyes, and the water is your semen. You are the shelter of all kinds of living entities, high and low. The god of the moon is your mind, and the upper planetary system is your head.

TEXT 28

कुक्षिः समुद्रा गिरयोऽस्थिसङ्घा
रोमाणि सर्वौषधिवीरुधस्ते ।
छन्दांसि साक्षात् तव सप्त धातव-
स्त्रयीमयात्मन् हृदयं सर्वधर्मः ॥ २८ ॥

kukṣiḥ samudrā girayo 'sthi-saṅghā
romāṇi sarvauṣadhi-vīrudhas te
chandāṁsi sākṣāt tava sapta dhātavas
trayī-mayātman hṛdayaṁ sarva-dharmaḥ

kukṣiḥ—abdomen; *samudrāḥ*—the oceans; *girayaḥ*—the mountains; *asthi*—bones; *saṅghāḥ*—combination; *romāṇi*—the hairs of the body; *sarva*—all; *auṣadhi*—drugs; *vīrudhaḥ*—plants and creepers; *te*—your; *chandāṁsi*—Vedic *mantras; sākṣāt*—directly; *tava*—your; *sapta*—seven; *dhātavaḥ*—layers of the body; *trayī-maya-ātman*—O three *Vedas* personified; *hṛdayaṁ*—core of the heart; *sarva-dharmaḥ*—all kinds of religion.

TRANSLATION

O lord, you are the three Vedas personified. The seven seas are your abdomen, and the mountains are your bones. All drugs, creepers and vegetables are the hairs on your body, the Vedic mantras like Gāyatrī are the seven layers of your body, and the Vedic religious system is the core of your heart.

TEXT 29

मुखानि पञ्चोपनिषदस्तवेश
यैस्त्रिंशदष्टोत्तरमन्त्रवर्गः ।

यत् तच्छिवाख्यं परमात्मतत्त्वं
देव स्वयंज्योतिरवस्थितिस्ते ॥ २९ ॥

mukhāni pañcopaniṣadas taveśa
yais triṁśad-aṣṭottara-mantra-vargaḥ
yat tac chivākhyaṁ paramātma-tattvaṁ
deva svayaṁ-jyotir avasthitis te

mukhāni—faces; *pañca*—five; *upaniṣadaḥ*—Vedic literatures; *tava*—your; *īśa*—O lord; *yaiḥ*—by which; *triṁśat-aṣṭa-uttara-mantra-vargaḥ*—in the category of thirty-eight important Vedic *mantras; yat*—that; *tat*—as it is; *śiva-ākhyam*—celebrated by the name Śiva; *paramātma-tattvam*—which ascertain the truth about Paramātmā; *deva*—O lord; *svayam-jyotiḥ*—self-illuminated; *avasthitiḥ*—situation; *te*—of Your Lordship.

TRANSLATION

O lord, the five important Vedic mantras are represented by your five faces, from which the thirty-eight most celebrated Vedic mantras have been generated. Your Lordship, being celebrated as Lord Śiva, is self-illuminated. You are directly situated as the supreme truth, known as Paramātmā.

PURPORT

The five *mantras* mentioned in this connection are as follows: (1) *Puruṣa,* (2) *Aghora,* (3) *Sadyojāta,* (4) *Vāmadeva,* and (5) *Īśāna.* These five *mantras* are within the category of thirty-eight special Vedic *mantras* chanted by Lord Śiva, who is therefore celebrated as Śiva or Mahādeva. Another reason why Lord Śiva is called Śiva, which means "all-auspicious,"is that he is self-illuminated, exactly like Lord Viṣṇu, who is the Paramātmā. Because Lord Śiva is directly an incarnation of Lord Viṣṇu, he is situated as Lord Viṣṇu's direct representative. This fact is corroborated by a Vedic *mantra: patiṁ viśvasyātmeśvaraṁ śāśvatam śivam acyutam.* The Supersoul is called by many names, of which Maheśvara, Śiva and Acyuta are especially mentioned.

TEXT 30

छाया त्वधर्मोर्मिषु यैर्विसर्गो
नेत्रत्रयं सत्त्वरजस्तमांसि ।

सांख्यात्मनः शास्त्रकृतस्तवेक्षा
छन्दोमयो देव ऋषिः पुराणः ॥ ३० ॥

chāyā tv adharmormiṣu yair visargo
netra-trayaṁ sattva-rajas-tamāṁsi
sāṅkhyātmanaḥ śāstra-kṛtas tavekṣā
chandomayo deva ṛṣiḥ purāṇaḥ

chāyā—shadow; *tu*—but; *adharma-ūrmiṣu*—in the waves of irreligion, like *kāma, krodha, lobha* and *moha; yaiḥ*—by which; *visargaḥ*—so many varieties of creation; *netra-trayam*—three eyes; *sattva*—goodness; *rajaḥ*—passion; *tamāṁsi*—and darkness; *sāṅkhya-ātmanaḥ*—the origin of all Vedic literatures; *śāstra*—scriptures; *kṛtaḥ*—made; *tava*—by you; *īkṣā*—simply by glancing; *chandaḥ-mayaḥ*—full of Vedic verses; *deva*—O lord; *ṛṣiḥ*—all Vedic literatures; *purāṇaḥ*—and the *Purāṇas,* the supplementary *Vedas.*

TRANSLATION

O lord, your shadow is seen in irreligion, which brings about varieties of irreligious creations. The three modes of nature—goodness, passion and ignorance—are your three eyes. All the Vedic literatures, which are full of verses, are emanations from you because their compilers wrote the various scriptures after receiving your glance.

TEXT 31

न ते गिरित्राखिललोकपाल-
विरिञ्चवैकुण्ठसुरेन्द्रगम्यम् ।
ज्योतिः परं यत्र रजस्तमश्च
सत्त्वं न यद् ब्रह्म निरस्तभेदम् ॥ ३१ ॥

na te giri-trākhila-loka-pāla-
viriñca-vaikuṇṭha-surendra-gamyam
jyotiḥ paraṁ yatra rajas tamaś ca
sattvaṁ na yad brahma nirasta-bhedam

na—not; *te*—of Your Lordship; *giri-tra*—O King of the mountains; *akhila-loka-pāla*—all the directors of departments of material activities; *viriñca*—Lord Brahmā; *vaikuṇṭha*—Lord Viṣṇu; *sura-indra*—the King of heaven; *gamyam*—they can understand; *jyotiḥ*—effulgence; *param*—transcendental; *yatra*—wherein; *rajaḥ*—the mode of passion; *tamaḥ ca*—and the mode of ignorance; *sattvam*—the mode of goodness; *na*—not; *yat brahma*—which is impersonal Brahman; *nirasta-bhedam*—without distinction between demigods and human beings.

TRANSLATION

O Lord Girīśa, since the impersonal Brahman effulgence is transcendental to the material modes of goodness, passion and ignorance, the various directors of this material world certainly cannot appreciate it or even know where it is. It is not understandable even to Lord Brahmā, Lord Viṣṇu or the King of heaven, Mahendra.

PURPORT

The *brahmajyoti* is actually the effulgence of the Supreme Personality of Godhead. As stated in *Brahma-saṁhitā* (5.40):

yasya prabhā prabhavato jagad-aṇḍa-koṭi-
koṭiṣv aśeṣa-vasudhādi-vibhūti-bhinnam
tad brahma niṣkalam anantam aśeṣa-bhūtaṁ
govindam ādi-puruṣaṁ tam ahaṁ bhajāmi

"I worship Govinda, the primeval Lord, who is endowed with great power. The glowing effulgence of His transcendental form is the impersonal Brahman, which is absolute, complete and unlimited and which displays the varieties of countless planets, with their different opulences, in millions and millions of universes." Although the impersonal feature of the Absolute is an expansion of the rays of the Supreme Personality of Godhead, He does not need to take care of the impersonalists who enter the *brahmajyoti.* Kṛṣṇa says in *Bhagavad-gītā* (9.4), *mayā tatam idaṁ sarvaṁ jagad avyakta-mūrtinā:* "In My impersonal feature I pervade this entire universe." Thus the *avyakta-mūrti,* the impersonal feature, is certainly an expansion of Kṛṣṇa's energy. Māyāvādīs, who prefer to merge into this Brahman effulgence, worship Lord Śiva. The *mantras* referred to in text 29 are called *mukhāni pañcopaniṣadas taveśa.* Māyāvādīs take all these *mantras* seriously in worshiping Lord Śiva. These *mantras* are as follows: (1) *tat puruṣāya vidmahe śāntyai,* (2) *mahā-devāya dhīmahi vidyāyai,* (3) *tan no rudraḥ pratiṣṭhāyai,* (4) *pracodayāt dhṛtyai,* (5) *aghorebhyas tamā. ..,* (6) *atha ghorebhyo mohā. ..,* (7) *aghorebhyo rakṣā. ..,* (8) *aghoratarebhyo nidrā. ..,* (9) *sarvebhyaḥ sarva-vyādhyai,* (10) *sarva-sarvebhyo mṛtyave,* (11) *namas te 'stu kṣudhā. ..,* (12) *rudra-rūpebhyas tṛṣṇā. ..,* (13) *vāmadevāya rajā. ..,*

(14) *jyeṣṭhāya svāhā. ..,* (15) *śreṣṭhāya ratyai,* (16) *rudrāya kalyāṇyai,* (17) *kālāya kāmā. ..,* (18) *kala-vikaraṇāya sandhinyai,* (19) *bala-vikaraṇāya kriyā. ..,* (20) *balāya vṛddhyai,* (21) *balacchāyā. ..,* (22) *pramathanāya dhātryai,* (23) *sarva-bhūta-damanāya bhrāmaṇyai,* (24) *manaḥ-śoṣiṇyai,* (25) *unmanāya jvarā. ..,* (26) *sadyojātaṁ prapadyāmi siddhyai,* (27) *sadyojātāya vai namaḥ ṛddhyai,* (28) *bhave dityai,* (29) *abhave lakṣmyai,* (30) *nātibhave medhā. ..,* (31) *bhajasva māṁ kāntyai,* (32) *bhava svadhā. ..,* (33) *udbhavāya prabhā. ..,* (34) *īśānaḥ sarva-vidyānāṁ śaśinyai,* (35) *īśvaraḥ sarva-bhūtānām abhaya-dā. ..,* (36) *brahmādhipatir brahmaṇodhipatir brahman brahmeṣṭa-dā. ..,* (37) *śivo me astu marīcyai,* (38) *sadāśivaḥ jvālinyai.*

The impersonal Brahman is unknown even to the other directors of the material creation, including Lord Brahmā, Lord Indra and even Lord Viṣṇu. This does not mean, however, that Lord Viṣṇu is not omniscient. Lord Viṣṇu is omniscient, but He does not need to understand what is going on in His all-pervading expansion. Therefore in *Bhagavad-gītā* the Lord says that although everything is an expansion of Him (*mayā tatam idaṁ sarvam*), He does not need to take care of everything (*na cāhaṁ teṣv avasthitaḥ*), since there are various directors like Lord Brahmā, Lord Śiva and Indra.

TEXT 32

कामाध्वरत्रिपुरकालगराद्यनेक-
भूतद्रुहः क्षपयतः स्तुतये न तत् ते ।
यस्त्वन्तकाल इदमात्मकृतं स्वनेत्र-
वह्निस्फुलिङ्गशिखया भसितं न वेद ॥ ३२ ॥

kāmādhvara-tripura-kālagarādy-aneka-
bhūta-druhaḥ kṣapayataḥ stutaye na tat te
yas tv anta-kāla idam ātma-kṛtaṁ sva-netra-
vahni-sphuliṅga-śikhayā bhasitaṁ na veda

kāma-adhvara—sacrifices for sense gratification (like Dakṣa-yajña, the sacrifices performed by Dakṣa); *tripura*—the demon named Tripurāsura; *kāla-gara*—Kālagara; *ādi*—and others; *aneka*—many; *bhūta-druhaḥ*—who are meant for giving trouble to the living entities; *kṣapayataḥ*—being engaged in their destruction; *stutaye*—your prayer; *na*—not; *tat*—that; *te*—speaking to you; *yaḥ tu*—because; *anta-kāle*—at the time of annihilation; *idam*—in this material world; *ātma-kṛtam*—done by yourself; *sva-netra*—by your eyes;

vahni-sphuliṅga-śikhayā—by the sparks of fire; *bhasitam*—burned to ashes; *na veda*—I do not know how it is happening.

TRANSLATION

When annihilation is performed by the flames and sparks emanating from your eyes, the entire creation is burned to ashes. Nonetheless, you do not know how this happens. What then is to be said of your destroying the Dakṣa-yajña, Tripurāsura and the kālakūṭa poison? Such activities cannot be subject matters for prayers offered to you.

PURPORT

Since Lord Śiva considers the great acts he performs to be very unimportant, what was to be said of counteracting the strong poison produced by the churning? The demigods indirectly prayed that Lord Śiva counteract the *kālakūṭa* poison, which was spreading throughout the universe.

TEXT 33

ये त्वात्मरामगुरुभिर्हृदि चिन्तिताङ्घ्रि-
द्वन्द्वं चरन्तमुमया तपसाभितप्तम् ।
कत्थन्त उग्रपरुषं निरतं श्मशाने
ते नूनमूतिमविदंस्तव हातलज्जाः ॥ ३३ ॥

ye tv ātma-rāma-gurubhir hṛdi cintitāṅghri-
dvandvaṁ carantam umayā tapasābhitaptam
katthanta ugra-paruṣaṁ niratam śmaśāne
te nūnam ūtim avidaṁs tava hāta-lajjāḥ

ye—persons who; *tu*—indeed; *ātma-rāma-gurubhiḥ*—by those who are self-satisfied and who are considered to be spiritual masters of the world; *hṛdi*—within the heart; *cintita-aṅghri-dvandvam*—thinking of your two lotus feet; *carantam*—moving; *umayā*—with your consort, Umā; *tapasā abhitaptam*—highly advanced through practice of austerity and penance; *katthante*—criticize your acts; *ugra-paruṣam*—not a gentle person; *niratam*—always; *śmaśāne*—in the crematorium; *te*—such persons; *nūnam*—indeed; *ūtim*—such activities; *avidan*—not knowing; *tava*—your activities; *hāta-lajjāḥ*—shameless.

TRANSLATION

Exalted, self-satisfied persons who preach to the entire world think of your lotus feet constantly within their hearts. However, when persons who do not know your austerity see you moving with Umā, they misunderstand you to be lusty, or when they see you wandering in the crematorium they mistakenly think that you are ferocious and envious. Certainly they are shameless. They cannot understand your activities.

PURPORT

Lord Śiva is the topmost Vaiṣṇava (*vaiṣṇavānāṁ yathā śambhuḥ*). It is therefore said, *vaiṣṇavera kriyā-mudrā vijñe nā bujhaya.* Even the most intelligent person cannot understand what a Vaiṣṇava like Lord Śiva is doing or how he is acting. Those who are conquered by lusty desires and anger cannot estimate the glories of Lord Śiva, whose position is always transcendental. In all the activities associated with lusty desires, Lord Śiva is an implement of *ātma-rāma.* Ordinary persons, therefore, should not try to understand Lord Śiva and his activities. One who tries to criticize the activities of Lord Śiva is shameless.

TEXT 34

तत् तस्य ते सदसतोः परतः परस्य
नाञ्जः स्वरूपगमने प्रभवन्ति भूम्नः ।
ब्रह्मादयः किमुत संस्तवने वयं तु
तत्सर्गसर्गविषया अपि शक्तिमात्रम् ॥ ३४ ॥

tat tasya te sad-asatoḥ parataḥ parasya
nāñjaḥ svarūpa-gamane prabhavanti bhūmnaḥ
brahmādayaḥ kim uta saṁstavane vayaṁ tu
tat-sarga-sarga-viṣayā api śakti-mātram

tat—therefore; *tasya*—of that; *te*—of Your Lordship; *sat-asatoḥ*—of the living entities, moving and not moving; *parataḥ*—transcendentally situated; *parasya*—very difficult to understand; *na*—nor; *añjaḥ*—as it is; *svarūpa-gamane*—to approach your reality; *prabhavanti*—it is possible; *bhūmnaḥ*—O great one; *brahma-ādayaḥ*—even such persons as Lord Brahmā; *kim uta*—what to speak of others; *saṁstavane*—in offering prayers; *vayam tu*—as far as we are concerned; *tat*—of you; *sarga-sarga-viṣayāḥ*—creations of the creation; *api*—although; *śakti-mātram*—to our ability.

TRANSLATION

Even personalities like Lord Brahmā and other demigods cannot understand your position, for you are beyond the moving and nonmoving creation. Since no one can understand you in truth, how can one offer you prayers? It is impossible. As far as we are concerned, we are creatures of Lord Brahmā's creation. Under the circumstances, therefore, we cannot offer you adequate prayers, but as far as our ability allows, we have expressed our feelings.

TEXT 35

एतत् परं प्रपश्यामो न परं ते महेश्वर ।
मृडनाय हि लोकस्य व्यक्तिस्तेऽव्यक्तकर्मणः ॥ ३५ ॥

etat paraṁ prapaśyāmo
na paraṁ te maheśvara
mṛḍanāya hi lokasya
vyaktis te 'vyakta-karmaṇaḥ

etat—all these things; *param*—transcendental; *prapaśyāmaḥ*—we can see; *na*—not; *param*—the actual transcendental position; *te*—of Your Lordship; *mahā-īśvara*—O great ruler; *mṛḍanāya*—for the happiness; *hi*—indeed; *lokasya*—of all the world; *vyaktiḥ*—manifested; *te*—of Your Lordship; *avyakta-karmaṇaḥ*—whose activities are unknown to everyone.

TRANSLATION

O greatest of all rulers, your actual identity is impossible for us to understand. As far as we can see, your presence brings flourishing happiness to everyone. Beyond this, no one can appreciate your activities. We can see this much, and nothing more.

PURPORT

When the demigods offered these prayers to Lord Śiva, their inner purpose was to please him so that he would rectify the disturbing situation created by the *hālahala* poison. As stated in *Bhagavad-gītā* (7.20), *kāmais tais tair hṛta jñānāḥ prapadyante 'nya-devatāḥ:* when one worships demigods, this is certainly because of deep-rooted desires he wants fulfilled by the mercy of those demigods. People are generally attached to the worship of demigods for some motive.

TEXT 36

श्रीशुक उवाच
तद्वीक्ष्य व्यसनं तासां कृपया भृशपीडितः ।
सर्वभूतसुहृद् देव इदमाह सतीं प्रियाम् ॥ ३६ ॥

śrī-śuka uvāca
tad-vīkṣya vyasanaṁ tāsāṁ
kṛpayā bhṛśa-pīḍitaḥ
sarva-bhūta-suhṛd deva
idam āha satīṁ priyām

śrī-śukaḥ uvāca—Śrī Śukadeva Gosvāmī said; *tat*—this situation; *vīkṣya*—seeing; *vyasanam*—dangerous; *tāsām*—of all the demigods; *kṛpayā*—out of compassion; *bhṛśa-pīḍitaḥ*—greatly aggrieved; *sarva-bhūta-suhṛt*—the friend of all living entities; *devaḥ*—Mahādeva; *idam*—this; *āha*—said; *satīm*—unto Satīdevī; *priyām*—his very dear wife.

TRANSLATION

Śrīla Śukadeva Gosvāmī continued: Lord Śiva is always benevolent toward all living entities. When he saw that the living entities were very much disturbed by the poison, which was spreading everywhere, he was very compassionate. Thus he spoke to his eternal consort, Satī, as follows.

TEXT 37

श्रीशिव उवाच
अहो बत भवान्येतत् प्रजानां पश्य वैशसम् ।
क्षीरोदमथनोद्भूतात् कालकूटादुपस्थितम् ॥ ३७ ॥

śrī-śiva uvāca
aho bata bhavāny etat
prajānāṁ paśya vaiśasam
kṣīroda-mathanodbhūtāt
kālakūṭād upasthitam

śrī-śivaḥ uvāca—Śrī Śiva said; *aho bata*—how pitiable; *bhavāni*—my dear wife, Bhavānī; *etat*—this situation; *prajānām*—of all living entities; *paśya*—just see; *vaiśasam*—very dangerous; *kṣīra-uda*—of the ocean of milk; *mathana-udbhūtāt*—produced by the churning; *kālakūṭāt*—because of the production of poison; *upasthitam*—the present situation.

TRANSLATION

Lord Śiva said: My dear Bhavānī, just see how all these living entities have been placed in danger because of the poison produced from the churning of the ocean of milk.

TEXT 38

आसां प्राणपरीप्सूनां विधेयमभयं हि मे ।
एतावान्हि प्रभोरर्थो यद् दीनपरिपालनम् ॥ ३८ ॥

āsāṁ prāṇa-parīpsūnāṁ
vidheyam abhayaṁ hi me
etāvān hi prabhor artho
yad dīna-paripālanam

āsām—all of these living entities; *prāṇa-parīpsūnām*—very strongly desiring to protect their lives; *vidheyam*—something must be done; *abhayam*—safety; *hi*—indeed; *me*—by me; *etāvān*—this much; *hi*—indeed; *prabhoḥ*—of the master; *arthaḥ*—duty; *yat*—that which; *dīna-paripālanam*—to give protection to suffering humanity.

TRANSLATION

It is my duty to give protection and safety to all living entities struggling for existence. Certainly it is the duty of the master to protect his suffering dependents.

TEXT 39

प्राणैः स्वैः प्राणिनः पान्ति साधवः क्षणभङ्गुरैः ।
बद्धवैरेषु भूतेषु मोहितेष्वात्ममायया ॥ ३९ ॥

prāṇaiḥ svaiḥ prāṇinaḥ pānti
sādhavaḥ kṣaṇa-bhaṅguraiḥ
baddha-vaireṣu bhūteṣu
mohiteṣv ātma-māyayā

prāṇaiḥ—by lives; *svaiḥ*—their own; *prāṇinaḥ*—other living entities; *pānti*—protect; *sādhavaḥ*—devotees; *kṣaṇa-bhaṅguraiḥ*—temporary; *baddha-*

vaireṣu—unnecessarily engaged in animosity; *bhūteṣu*—unto living entities; *mohiteṣu*—bewildered; *ātma-māyayā*—by the external energy of the Lord.

TRANSLATION

People in general, being bewildered by the illusory energy of the Supreme Personality of Godhead, are always engaged in animosity toward one another. But devotees, even at the risk of their own temporary lives, try to save them.

PURPORT

This is the characteristic of a Vaiṣṇava. *Para-duḥkha-duḥkhī:* a Vaiṣṇava is always unhappy to see the conditioned souls unhappy. Otherwise, he would have no business teaching them how to become happy. In materialistic life, people must certainly engage in activities of animosity. Materialistic life is therefore compared to *saṁsāra-dāvānala,* a blazing forest fire that automatically takes place. Lord Śiva and his followers in the *paramparā* system try to save people from this dangerous condition of materialistic life. This is the duty of devotees following the principles of Lord Śiva and belonging to the Rudra-sampradāya. There are four Vaiṣṇava *sampradāyas,* and the Rudra-sampradāya is one of them because Lord Śiva (Rudra) is the best of the Vaiṣṇavas (*vaiṣṇavānāṁ yathā śambhuḥ*). Indeed, as we shall see, Lord Śiva drank all the poison for the benefit of humanity.

TEXT 40

पुंसः कृपयतो भद्रे सर्वात्मा प्रीयते हरिः ।
प्रीते हरौ भगवति प्रीयेऽहं सचराचरः ।
तस्मादिदं गरं भुञ्जे प्रजानां स्वस्तिरस्तु मे ॥ ४० ॥

puṁsaḥ kṛpayato bhadre
sarvātmā prīyate hariḥ
prīte harau bhagavati
prīye 'haṁ sacarācaraḥ
tasmād idaṁ garaṁ bhuñje
prajānāṁ svastir astu me

puṁsaḥ—with a person; *kṛpayataḥ*—engaged in benevolent activities; *bhadre*—O most gentle Bhavānī; *sarva-ātmā*—the Supersoul; *prīyate*—becomes pleased; *hariḥ*—the Supreme Personality of Godhead; *prīte*—because of His pleasure; *harau*—the Supreme Lord, Hari; *bhagavati*—the Personality of Godhead; *prīye*—also become pleased; *aham*—I; *sa-cara-acaraḥ*—with all others, moving and nonmoving; *tasmāt*—therefore; *idam*—this; *garam*—poison; *bhuñje*—let me drink; *prajānām*—of the living entities; *svastiḥ*—welfare; *astu*—let there be; *me*—by me.

TRANSLATION

My dear gentle wife Bhavānī, when one performs benevolent activities for others, the Supreme Personality of Godhead, Hari, is very pleased. And when the Lord is pleased, I am also pleased, along with all other living creatures. Therefore, let me drink this poison, for all the living entities may thus become happy because of me.

TEXT 41

श्रीशुक उवाच
एवमामन्त्र्य भगवान्भवानीं विश्वभावनः ।
तद् विषं जग्धुमारेभे प्रभावज्ञान्वमोदत ॥ ४१ ॥

śrī-śuka uvāca
evam āmantrya bhagavān
bhavānīṁ viśva-bhāvanaḥ
tad viṣaṁ jagdhum ārebhe
prabhāva-jñānvamodata

śrī-śukaḥ uvāca—Śrī Śukadeva Gosvāmī said; *evam*—in this way; *āmantrya*—addressing; *bhagavān*—Lord Śiva; *bhavānīm*—Bhavānī; *viśva-bhāvanah*—the well-wisher of all the universe; *tat viṣam*—that poison; *jagdhum*—to drink; *ārebhe*—began; *prabhāva-jñā*—mother Bhavānī, who perfectly knew the capability of Lord Śiva; *anvamodata*—gave her permission.

TRANSLATION

Śrīla Śukadeva Gosvāmī continued: After informing Bhavānī in this way, Lord Śiva began to drink the poison, and Bhavānī, who knew perfectly well the capabilities of Lord Śiva, gave him her permission to do so.

TEXT 42

ततः करतलीकृत्य व्यापि हालाहलं विषम् ।
अभक्षयन्महादेवः कृपया भूतभावनः ॥ ४२ ॥

tataḥ karatalī-kṛtya
vyāpi hālāhalaṁ viṣam
abhakṣayan mahā-devaḥ
kṛpayā bhūta-bhāvanaḥ

tataḥ—thereafter; *karatalī-kṛtya*—taking in his hand; *vyāpi*—widespread; *hālāhalam*—called *hālahala; viṣam*—poison; *abhakṣayat*—drank; *mahā-devaḥ*—Lord Śiva; *kṛpayā*—out of compassion; *bhūta-bhāvanaḥ*—for the welfare of all living entities.

TRANSLATION

Thereafter, Lord Śiva, who is dedicated to auspicious, benevolent work for humanity, compassionately took the whole quantity of poison in his palm and drank it.

PURPORT

Although there was such a great quantity of poison that it spread all over the universe, Lord Śiva had such great power that he reduced the poison to a small quantity so that he could hold it in his palm. One should not try to imitate Lord Śiva. Lord Śiva can do whatever he likes, but those who try to imitate Lord Śiva by smoking *gañja* and other poisonous things will certainly be killed because of such activities.

TEXT 43

तस्यापि दर्शयामास स्ववीर्यं जलकल्मषः ।
यच्चकार गले नीलं तच्च साधोर्विभूषणम् ॥ ४३ ॥

tasyāpi darśayām āsa
sva-vīryaṁ jala-kalmaṣaḥ
yac cakāra gale nīlaṁ
tac ca sādhor vibhūṣaṇam

tasya—of Lord Śiva; *api*—also; *darśayām āsa*—exhibited; *sva-vīryam*—its own potency; *jala-kalmaṣaḥ*—that poison born of the water; *yat*—which;

cakāra—made; *gale*—on the neck; *nīlam*—bluish line; *tat*—that; *ca*—also; *sādhoḥ*—of the saintly person; *vibhūṣaṇam*—ornament.

TRANSLATION

As if in defamation, the poison born from the ocean of milk manifested its potency by marking Lord Śiva's neck with a bluish line. That line, however, is now accepted as an ornament of the Lord.

TEXT 44

तप्यन्ते लोकतापेन साधवः प्रायशो जनाः ।
परमाराधनं तद्धि पुरुषस्याखिलात्मनः ॥ ४४ ॥

tapyante loka-tāpena
sādhavaḥ prāyaśo janāḥ
paramārādhanaṁ tad dhi
puruṣasyākhilātmanaḥ

tapyante—voluntarily suffer; *loka-tāpena*—because of the suffering of people in general; *sādhavaḥ*—saintly persons; *prāyaśaḥ*—almost always; *janāḥ*—such persons; *parama-ārādhanam*—the topmost method of worshiping; *tat*—that activity; *hi*—indeed; *puruṣasya*—of the Supreme Person; *akhila-ātmanaḥ*—who is the Supersoul of everyone.

TRANSLATION

It is said that great personalities almost always accept voluntary suffering because of the suffering of people in general. This is considered the highest method of worshiping the Supreme Personality of Godhead, who is present in everyone's heart.

PURPORT

Here is an explanation of how those engaged in activities for the welfare of others are very quickly recognized by the Supreme Personality of Godhead. The Lord says in *Bhagavad-gītā* (18.68-69), *ya idaṁ paramaṁ guhyaṁ mad-bhakteṣv abhidhāsyati. .. na ca tasmān manuṣyeṣu kaścin me priya-kṛttamaḥ:* "One who preaches the message of *Bhagavad-gītā* to My devotees is most dear to Me. No one can excel him in satisfying Me by worship." There are different kinds of welfare activities in this material world, but the supreme welfare activity is the spreading of Kṛṣṇa consciousness. Other welfare activities cannot be effective, for the laws of nature and the results of *karma* cannot be checked. It is by destiny, or the laws of *karma,* that one must suffer or enjoy. For instance, if one is given a court order, he must accept it, whether it brings suffering or profit. Similarly, everyone is under obligations to *karma* and it reactions. No one can change this. Therefore the *śāstra* says:

tasyaiva hetoḥ prayateta kovido
na labhyate yad bhramatām upary adhaḥ
(*Bhāg.* 1.5.18)

One should endeavor for that which is never obtained by wandering up and down the universe as a result of the reactions of *karma.* What is that? One should endeavor to become Kṛṣṇa conscious. If one tries to spread Kṛṣṇa consciousness all over the world, he should be understood to be performing the best welfare activity. The Lord is automatically very pleased with him. If the Lord is pleased with him, what is left for him to achieve? If one has been recognized by the Lord, even if he does not ask the Lord for anything, the Lord, who is within everyone, supplies him whatever he wants. This is also confirmed in *Bhagavad-gītā* (*teṣāṁ nityābhiyuktānāṁ yoga-kṣemaṁ vahāmy aham*). Again, as stated here, *tapyante loka-tāpena sādhavaḥ prāyaśo janāḥ.* The best welfare activity is raising people to the platform of Kṛṣṇa consciousness, since the conditioned souls are suffering only for want of Kṛṣṇa consciousness. The Lord Himself also comes to mitigate the suffering of humanity.

yadā yadā hi dharmasya
glānir bhavati bhārata
abhyutthānam adharmasya
tadātmānaṁ sṛjāmy aham

paritrāṇāya sādhūnāṁ
vināśāya ca duṣkṛtām
dharma-saṁsthāpanārthāya
sambhavāmi yuge yuge

"Whenever and wherever there is a decline in religious practice, O descendant of Bharata, and a predominant rise of irreligion—at that time I descend Myself. To deliver the pious and to annihilate the miscreants, as well as to reestablish the principles of religion, I advent Myself millennium after millennium." (Bg. 4.7-8) All the *śāstras* conclude, therefore, that spreading the Kṛṣṇa consciousness movement is the best welfare activity in the world.

Because of the ultimate benefit this bestows upon people in general, the Lord very quickly recognizes such service performed by a devotee.

TEXT 45

निशम्य कर्म तच्छम्भोर्देवदेवस्य मीढुषः ।
प्रजा दाक्षायणी ब्रह्मा वैकुण्ठश्च शशंसिरे ॥ ४५ ॥

niśamya karma tac chambhor
deva-devasya mīḍhuṣaḥ
prajā dākṣāyaṇī brahmā
vaikuṇṭhaś ca śaśaṁsire

niśamya—after hearing; *karma*—the act; *tat*—that; *śambhoḥ*—of Lord Śiva; *deva-devasya*—who is worshipable even for the demigods; *mīḍhuṣaḥ*—he who bestows great benedictions upon people in general; *prajāḥ*—the people in general; *dākṣāyaṇī*—Bhavānī, the daughter of Dakṣa; *brahmā*—Lord Brahmā; *vaikuṇṭhaḥ ca*—Lord Viṣṇu also; *śaśaṁsire*—praised very much.

TRANSLATION

Upon hearing of this act, everyone, including Bhavānī [the daughter of Mahārāja Dakṣa], Lord Brahmā, Lord Viṣṇu, and the people in general, very highly praised this deed performed by Lord Śiva, who is worshiped by the demigods and who bestows benedictions upon the people.

TEXT 46

प्रस्कन्नं पिबतः पाणेर्यत् किञ्चिज्जगृहुः स्म तत् ।
वृश्चिकाहिविषौषध्यो दन्दशूकाश्च येऽपरे ॥ ४६ ॥

praskannaṁ pibataḥ pāṇer
yat kiñcij jagṛhuḥ sma tat
vṛścikāhi-viṣauṣadhyo
dandaśūkāś ca ye 'pare

praskannam—scattered here and there; *pibataḥ*—of Lord Śiva while drinking; *pāṇeḥ*—from the palm; *yat*—which; *kiñcit*—very little; *jagṛhuḥ*—took the opportunity to drink; *sma*—indeed; *tat*—that; *vṛścika*—the scorpions; *ahi*—the cobras; *viṣa-auṣadhyaḥ*—poisonous drugs; *dandaśūkāḥ ca*—and animals whose bites are poisonous; *ye*—who; *apare*—other living entities.

TRANSLATION

Scorpions, cobras, poisonous drugs and other animals whose bites are poisonous took the opportunity to drink whatever little poison had fallen and scattered from Lord Śiva's hand while he was drinking.

PURPORT

Mosquitoes, jackals, dogs and other varieties of *dandaśūka,* or animals whose bites are poisonous, drank the poison of the *samudra-manthana,* the churned ocean, since it was available after it fell from the palms of Lord Śiva.

Thus end the Bhaktivedanta purports of the Eighth Canto, Seventh Chapter, of the Śrīmad-Bhāgavatam, *entitled "Lord Śiva Saves the Universe by Drinking Poison."*

CHAPTER EIGHT

The Churning of the Milk Ocean

This chapter describes how the goddess of fortune appeared during the churning of the ocean of milk and how she accepted Lord Viṣṇu as her husband. As described later in the chapter, when Dhanvantari appeared with a pot of nectar the demons immediately snatched it from him, but Lord Viṣṇu appeared as the incarnation Mohinī, the most beautiful woman in the world, just to captivate the demons and save the nectar for the demigods.

After Lord Śiva drank all the poison, both the demigods and demons took courage and resumed their activities of churning. Because of this churning, first a *surabhi* cow was produced. Great saintly persons accepted this cow to derive clarified butter from its milk and offer this clarified butter in oblations for great sacrifices. Thereafter, a horse named Uccaiḥśravā was generated. This horse was taken by Bali Mahārāja. Then there appeared Airāvata and other elephants that could go anywhere in any direction, and she-elephants also appeared. The gem known as Kaustubha was also generated, and Lord Viṣṇu took that gem and placed it on His chest. Thereafter, a *pārijāta* flower and the Apsarās, the most beautiful women in the universe, were generated. Then the goddess of fortune, Lakṣmī, appeared. The demigods, great sages, Gandharvas and others offered her their respectful worship. The goddess of fortune could not find anyone to accept as her husband. At last she selected Lord Viṣṇu to be her master. Lord Viṣṇu gave her a place to stay everlastingly at His chest. Because of this combination of Lakṣmī and Nārāyaṇa, all who were present, including the demigods and people in general, were very pleased. The demons, however, being neglected by the goddess of fortune, were very depressed. Then Vāruṇī, the goddess of drinking, was generated, and by the order of Lord Viṣṇu the demons accepted her. Then the demons and demigods, with renewed energy, began to churn again. This time a partial incarnation of Lord Viṣṇu called Dhanvantari appeared. He was very beautiful, and he carried a jug containing nectar. The demons immediately snatched the jug from Dhanvantari's hand and began to run away, and the demigods, being very morose, took shelter of Viṣṇu. After the demons snatched the jug from Dhanvantari, they began to fight among themselves. Lord Viṣṇu solaced the demigods, who therefore did not fight, but remained silent. While the fighting was going on among the demons, the Lord Himself appeared as the incarnation Mohinī, the most beautiful woman in the universe.

TEXT 1

श्रीशुक उवाच
पीते गरे वृषाङ्केण प्रीतास्तेऽमरदानवाः ।
ममन्थुस्तरसा सिन्धुं हविर्धानी ततोऽभवत् ॥ १ ॥

śrī-śuka uvāca
pīte gare vṛṣāṅkeṇa
prītās te 'mara-dānavāḥ
mamanthus tarasā sindhuṁ
havirdhānī tato 'bhavat

śrī-śukaḥ uvāca—Śrī Śukadeva Gosvāmī said; *pīte*—was drunk; *gare*—when the poison; *vṛṣa-aṅkeṇa*—by Lord Śiva, who sits on a bull; *prītāḥ*—being pleased; *te*—all of them; *amara*—the demigods; *dānavāḥ*—and the demons; *mamanthuḥ*—again began to churn; *tarasā*—with great force; *sindhum*—the ocean of milk; *havirdhānī*—the *surabhi* cow, who is the source of clarified butter; *tataḥ*—from that churning; *abhavat*—was generated.

TRANSLATION

Śukadeva Gosvāmī continued: Upon Lord Śiva's drinking the poison, both the demigods and the demons, being very pleased, began to churn the ocean with renewed vigor. As a result of this, there appeared a cow known as surabhi.

PURPORT

The *surabhi* cow is described as *havirdhānī,* the source of butter. Butter, when clarified by melting, produces ghee, or clarified butter, which is inevitably necessary for performing great ritualistic sacrifices. As stated in *Bhagavad-gītā* (18.5), *yajña-dāna-tapaḥ-karma na tyājyaṁ kāryam eva tat:* sacrifice, charity and austerity are essential to keep human society perfect in peace and prosperity. *Yajña,* the performance of sacrifice, is essential; to perform *yajña,* clarified butter is absolutely necessary; and to get clarified butter, milk is necessary. Milk is produced when there are sufficient cows. Therefore in *Bhagavad-gītā* (18.44), cow protection is recommended (*kṛṣi-go-rakṣya-vāṇijyaṁ vaiśya-karma svabhāva jam*).

TEXT 2

तामग्निहोत्रीमृषयो जगृहुर्ब्रह्मवादिनः ।
यज्ञस्य देवयानस्य मेध्याय हविषे नृप ॥ २ ॥

tām agni-hotrīm ṛṣayo
jagṛhur brahma-vādinaḥ
yajñasya deva-yānasya
medhyāya haviṣe nṛpa

tām—that cow; *agni-hotrīm*—absolutely necessary for the production of yogurt, milk and ghee to offer as oblations in the fire; *ṛṣayaḥ*—sages who perform such sacrifices; *jagṛhuḥ*—took in charge; *brahma-vādinaḥ*—because such sages know the Vedic ritualistic ceremonies; *yajñasya*—of sacrifice; *deva-yānasya*—which fulfills the desire to be elevated to the higher planetary systems and to Brahmaloka; *medhyāya*—fit for offering oblations; *haviṣe*—for the sake of pure clarified butter; *nṛpa*—O King.

TRANSLATION

O King Parīkṣit, great sages who were completely aware of the Vedic ritualistic ceremonies took charge of that surabhi cow, which produced all the yogurt, milk and ghee absolutely necessary for offering oblations into the fire. They did this just for the sake of pure ghee, which they wanted for the performance of sacrifices to elevate themselves to the higher planetary systems, up to Brahmaloka.

PURPORT

Surabhi cows are generally found on the Vaikuṇṭha planets. As described in *Brahma-saṁhitā,* Lord Kṛṣṇa, on His planet, Goloka Vṛndāvana, engages in tending the *surabhi* cows (*surabhīr abhipālayantam*). These cows are the Lord's pet animals. From the *surabhi* cows one can take as much milk as one needs, and one may milk these cows as many times as he desires. In other words, the *surabhi* cow can yield milk unlimitedly. Milk is necessary for the performance of *yajña.* Sages know how to use milk to elevate human society to the perfection of life. Since cow protection is recommended everywhere in the *śāstras,* the *brahmā vādīs* took charge of the *surabhi* cow, in which the demons were not very interested.

TEXT 3

तत उच्चैःश्रवा नाम हयोऽभूच्चन्द्रपाण्डुरः ।
तस्मिन्बलिः स्पृहां चक्रे नेन्द्र ईश्वरशिक्षया ॥ ३ ॥

tata uccaiḥśravā nāma
hayo 'bhūc candra-pāṇḍuraḥ
tasmin baliḥ spṛhāṁ cakre
nendra īśvara-śikṣayā

tataḥ—thereafter; *uccaiḥśravāḥ nāma*—by the name Uccaiḥśravā; *hayaḥ*—a horse; *abhūt*—was generated; *candra-pāṇḍuraḥ*—being as white as the moon; *tasmin*—unto it; *baliḥ*—Mahārāja Bali; *spṛhām cakre*—desired to possess; *na*—not; *indraḥ*—the King of the demigods; *īśvara-śikṣayā*—by the previous advice of the Lord.

TRANSLATION

Thereafter, a horse named Uccaiḥśravā, which was as white as the moon, was generated. Bali Mahārāja desired to possess this horse, and Indra, the King of heaven, did not protest, for he had previously been so advised by the Supreme Personality of Godhead.

TEXT 4

तत ऐरावतो नाम वारणेन्द्रो विनिर्गतः ।
दन्तैश्चतुर्भिः श्वेताद्रेर्हरन्भगवतो महिम् ॥ ४ ॥

tata airāvato nāma
vāraṇendro vinirgataḥ
dantaiś caturbhiḥ śvetādrer
haran bhagavato mahim

tataḥ—thereafter; *airāvataḥ nāma*—of the name Airāvata; *vāraṇa-indraḥ*—the king of elephants; *vinirgataḥ*—was generated; *dantaiḥ*—with its tusks; *caturbhiḥ*—four; *śveta*—white; *adreḥ*—of the mountain; *haran*—defying; *bhagavataḥ*—of Lord Śiva; *mahim*—the glories.

TRANSLATION

As the next result of the churning, the king of elephants, named Airāvata, was generated. This elephant was white, and with its four tusks

it defied the glories of Kailāsa Mountain, the glorious abode of Lord Śiva.

TEXT 5

ऐरावणादयस्त्वष्टौ दिग् गजा अभवंस्ततः ।
अभ्रमुप्रभृतयोऽष्टौ च करिण्यस्त्वभवन्नृप ॥ ५ ॥

airāvaṇādayas tv aṣṭau
dig-gajā abhavaṁs tataḥ
abhramu-prabhṛtayo 'ṣṭau ca
kariṇyas tv abhavan nṛpa

airāvaṇa-ādayaḥ—headed by Airāvaṇa; *tu*—but; *aṣṭau*—eight; *dik-gajāḥ*—elephants that could go in any direction; *abhavan*—were generated; *tataḥ*—thereafter; *abhramu-prabhṛtayaḥ*—headed by the she-elephant named Abhramu; *aṣṭau*—eight; *ca*—also; *kariṇyaḥ*—female elephants; *tu*—indeed; *abhavan*—also generated; *nṛpa*—O King.

TRANSLATION

Thereafter, O King, eight great elephants, which could go in any direction, were generated. They were headed by Airāvaṇa. Eight she-elephants, headed by Abhramu, were also generated.

PURPORT

The names of the eight elephants were Airāvaṇa, Puṇḍarīka, Vāmana, Kumuda, Añjana, Puṣpadanta, Sārvabhauma and Supratīka.

TEXT 6

कौस्तुभाख्यमभूद् रत्नं पद्मरागो महोदधेः
तस्मिन् मणौ स्पृहां चक्रे वक्षोऽलङ्करणे हरिः ।
ततोऽभवत् पारिजातः सुरलोकविभूषणम्
पूरयत्यर्थिनो योऽर्थैः शश्वद् भुवि यथा भवान्॥ ६ ॥

kaustubhākhyam abhūd ratnaṁ
padmarāgo mahodadheḥ
tasmin maṇau spṛhāṁ cakre
vakṣo-'laṅkaraṇe hariḥ

tato 'bhavat pārijātaḥ
sura-loka-vibhūṣaṇam
pūrayaty arthino yo 'rthaiḥ
śaśvad bhuvi yathā bhavān

kaustubha-ākhyam—known as Kaustubha; *abhūt*—was generated; *ratnam*—a valuable gem; *padmarāgaḥ*—another gem, named Padmarāga; *mahā-udadheḥ*—from that great ocean of milk; *tasmin*—that; *maṇau*—jewel; *spṛhām cakre*—desired to possess; *vakṣaḥ-alaṅkaraṇe*—to decorate His chest; *hariḥ*—the Lord, the Supreme Personality of Godhead; *tataḥ*—thereafter; *abhavat*—was generated; *pārijātaḥ*—the celestial flower named *pārijāta; sura-loka-vibhūṣaṇam*—which decorates the heavenly planets; *pūrayati*—fulfills; *arthinaḥ*—giving persons desiring material wealth; *yaḥ*—that which; *arthaiḥ*—by what is desired; *śaśvat*—always; *bhuvi*—on this planet; *yathā*—as; *bhavān*—Your Lordship (Mahārāja Parīkṣit).

TRANSLATION

Generated thereafter from the great ocean were the celebrated gems Kaustubha-maṇi and Padmarāga-maṇi. Lord Viṣṇu, to decorate His chest, desired to possess them. Generated next was the pārijāta flower, which decorates the celestial planets. O King, as you fulfill the desires of everyone on this planet by fulfilling all ambitions, the pārijāta fulfills the desires of everyone.

TEXT 7

ततश्चाप्सरसो जाता निष्ककण्ठ्यः सुवाससः ।
रमण्यः स्वर्गिणां वल्गुगतिलीलावलोकनैः ॥ ७ ॥

tataś cāpsaraso jātā
niṣka-kaṇṭhyaḥ suvāsasaḥ
ramaṇyaḥ svargiṇāṁ valgu-
gati-līlāvalokanaiḥ

tataḥ—thereafter; *ca*—also; *apsarasaḥ*—the residents of Apsaroloka; *jātāḥ*—were generated; *niṣka-kaṇṭhyaḥ*—decorated with golden necklaces; *su-vāsasaḥ*—dressed with fine clothing; *ramaṇyaḥ*—extremely beautiful and attractive; *svargiṇām*—of the inhabitants of the heavenly planets; *valgu-gati-līlā-avalokanaiḥ*—moving very softly, they attract everyone's heart.

TRANSLATION

Next there appeared the Apsarās [who are used as prostitutes on the heavenly planets]. They were fully decorated with golden ornaments and lockets and were dressed in fine and attractive clothing. The Apsarās move very slowly in an attractive style that bewilders the inhabitants of the heavenly planets.

TEXT 8

ततश्चाविरभूत् साक्षाच्छ्री रमा भगवत्परा ।
रञ्जयन्ती दिशः कान्त्या विद्युत् सौदामनी यथा ॥ ८ ॥

tataś cāvirabhūt sākṣāc
chrī ramā bhagavat-parā
rañjayantī diśaḥ kāntyā
vidyut saudāmanī yathā

tataḥ—thereafter; *ca*—and; *āvirabhūt*—manifested; *sākṣāt*—directly; *śrī*—the goddess of fortune; *ramā*—known as Ramā; *bhagavat-parā*—absolutely inclined to be possessed by the Supreme Personality of Godhead; *rañjayantī*—illuminating; *diśaḥ*—all directions; *kāntyā*—by luster; *vidyut*—lightning; *saudāmanī*—Saudāmanī; *yathā*—as.

TRANSLATION

Then there appeared the goddess of fortune, Ramā, who is absolutely dedicated to being enjoyed by the Supreme Personality of Godhead. She appeared like electricity, surpassing the lightning that might illuminate a marble mountain.

PURPORT

Śrī means opulence. Kṛṣṇa is the owner of all opulences.

bhoktāraṁ yajña-tapasāṁ
sarva-loka-maheśvaram
suhṛdaṁ sarva-bhūtānāṁ
jñātvā māṁ śāntim ṛcchati

This peace formula for the world is given in *Bhagavad-gītā* (5.29). When people know that the Supreme Lord, Kṛṣṇa, is the supreme enjoyer, the supreme proprietor and the most intimate well-wishing friend of all living entities, peace and prosperity will ensue all over the world. Unfortunately, the conditioned souls, being placed into illusion by the external energy of the Lord, want to fight with one another, and therefore peace is disturbed. The first prerequisite for peace is that all the wealth presented by Śrī, the goddess of fortune, be offered to the Supreme Personality of Godhead. Everyone should give up his false proprietorship over worldly possessions and offer everything to Kṛṣṇa. This is the teaching of the Kṛṣṇa consciousness movement.

TEXT 9

तस्यां चक्रुः स्पृहां सर्वे ससुरासुरमानवाः ।
रूपौदार्यवयोवर्णमहिमाक्षिप्तचेतसः ॥ ९ ॥

tasyāṁ cakruḥ spṛhāṁ sarve
sasurāsura-mānavāḥ
rūpaudārya-vayo-varṇa-
mahimākṣipta-cetasaḥ

tasyām—unto her; *cakruḥ*—did; *spṛhām*—desire; *sarve*—everyone; *sa-sura-asura-mānavāḥ*—the demigods, the demons and the human beings; *rūpa-audārya*—by the exquisite beauty and bodily features; *vayaḥ*—youth; *varṇa*—complexion; *mahimā*—glories; *ākṣipta*—agitated; *cetasaḥ*—their minds.

TRANSLATION

Because of her exquisite beauty, her bodily features, her youth, her complexion and her glories, everyone, including the demigods, the demons and the human beings, desired her. They were attracted because she is the source of all opulences.

PURPORT

Who in this world does not want to possess wealth, beauty and the social respectability that come from these opulences? People generally desire material enjoyment, material opulence and the association of aristocratic family members (*bhogaiśvarya-prasaktānām*). Material enjoyment entails money, beauty and the reputation they bring, which can all be achieved by the mercy of the goddess of fortune. The goddess of fortune, however, never remains alone. As indicated in the previous verse by the word *bhagavat-parā,* she is the property of the Supreme Personality of Godhead and is enjoyable only by Him. If one wants the favor of the goddess of fortune, mother Lakṣmī, because she is by nature *bhagavat-parā* one must keep her with Nārāyaṇa. The devotees who always engage in the service of Nārāyaṇa (*nārāyaṇa-parāyaṇa*) can easily achieve the favor of the goddess of fortune without a doubt, but materialists who try to get the favor of the goddess of fortune only to possess her for personal enjoyment are frustrated. Theirs is not a good policy. The celebrated demon Rāvaṇa, for example, wanted to deprive Rāmacandra of Lakṣmī, Sītā, and thus be victorious, but the result was just the opposite. Sītā, of course, was taken by force by Lord Rāmacandra, and Rāvaṇa and his entire material empire were vanquished. The goddess of fortune is desirable for everyone, including human beings, but one should understand that the goddess of fortune is the exclusive property of the Supreme Personality of Godhead. One cannot achieve the mercy of the goddess of fortune unless one prays both to her and to the supreme enjoyer, the Personality of Godhead.

TEXT 10

तस्या आसनमानिन्ये महेन्द्रो महदद्भुतम् ।
मूर्तिमत्यः सरिच्छ्रेष्ठा हेमकुम्भैर्जलं शुचि ॥ १० ॥

tasyā āsanam āninye
mahendro mahad-adbhutam
mūrtimatyaḥ saric-chreṣṭhā
hema-kumbhair jalaṁ śuci

tasyāḥ—for her; *āsanam*—a sitting place; *āninye*—brought; *mahā-indraḥ*—the King of heaven, Indra; *mahat*—glorious; *adbhutam*—wonderful; *mūrti-matyaḥ*—accepting forms; *sarit-śreṣṭhāḥ*—the best of various sacred waters; *hema*—golden; *kumbhaiḥ*—with waterpots; *jalam*—water; *śuci*—pure.

TRANSLATION

The King of heaven, Indra, brought a suitable sitting place for the goddess of fortune. All the rivers of sacred water, such as the Ganges and Yamunā, personified themselves, and each of them brought pure water in golden waterpots for mother Lakṣmī, the goddess of fortune.

TEXT 11

आभिषेचनिका भूमिराहरत् सकलौषधीः ।
गावः पञ्च पवित्राणि वसन्तो मधुमाधवौ ॥ ११ ॥

ābhiṣecanikā bhūmir
āharat sakalauṣadhīḥ
gāvaḥ pañca pavitrāṇi
vasanto madhu-mādhavau

ābhiṣecanikāḥ—paraphernalia required for installing the Deity; *bhūmiḥ*—the land; *āharat*—collected; *sakala*—all kinds of; *auṣadhīḥ*—drugs and herbs; *gāvaḥ*—the cows; *pañca*—five different varieties of products from the cow, namely milk, yogurt, clarified butter, cow dung and cow urine; *pavitrāṇi*—uncontaminated; *vasantaḥ*—personified springtime; *madhu-mādhavau*—flowers and fruits produced during spring, or in the months of Caitra and Vaiśākha.

TRANSLATION

The land became a person and collected all the drugs and herbs needed for installing the Deity. The cows delivered five products, namely milk, yogurt, ghee, urine and cow dung, and spring personified collected everything produced in spring, during the months of Caitra and Vaiśākha [April and May].

PURPORT

Pañca-gavya, the five products received from the cow, namely milk, yogurt, ghee, cow dung and cow urine, are required in all ritualistic ceremonies performed according to the Vedic directions. Cow urine and cow dung are uncontaminated, and since even the urine and dung of a cow are important, we can just imagine how important this animal is for human civilization. Therefore the Supreme Personality of Godhead, Kṛṣṇa, directly advocates *go-rakṣya,* the protection of cows. Civilized men who follow the system of *varṇāśrama,* especially those of the *vaiśya* class, who engage in agriculture and trade, must give protection to the cows. Unfortunately, because people in Kali-yuga are *mandāḥ,* all bad, and *sumanda-matayaḥ,* misled by false conceptions of life, they are killing cows in the thousands. Therefore they are unfortunate in spiritual consciousness, and nature disturbs them in so many ways, especially through incurable diseases like cancer and through frequent wars and among nations. As long as human society continues to allow cows to be regularly killed in slaughterhouses, there cannot be any question of peace and prosperity.

TEXT 12

ऋषयः कल्पयाञ्चक्रुराभिषेकं यथाविधि ।
जगुर्भद्राणि गन्धर्वा नट्यश्च ननृतुर्जगुः ॥ १२ ॥

ṛṣayaḥ kalpayāṁ cakrur
ābhiṣekaṁ yathā-vidhi
jagur bhadrāṇi gandharvā
naṭyaś ca nanṛtur jaguḥ

ṛṣayaḥ—the great sages; *kalpayām cakruḥ*—executed; *ābhiṣekam*—the *abhiṣeka* ceremony, which is required during the installation of the Deity; *yathā-vidhi*—as directed in the authorized scriptures; *jaguḥ*—chanted Vedic *mantras; bhadrāṇi*—all good fortune; *gandharvāḥ*—and the inhabitants of Gandharvaloka; *naṭyaḥ*—the women who were professional dancers; *ca*—also; *nanṛtuḥ*—very nicely danced on the occasion; *jaguḥ*—and sang authorized songs prescribed in the *Vedas.*

TRANSLATION

The great sages performed the bathing ceremony of the goddess of fortune as directed in the authorized scriptures, the Gandharvas chanted all-auspicious Vedic mantras, and the professional women dancers very nicely danced and sang authorized songs prescribed in the Vedas.

TEXT 13

मेघा मृदङ्गपणवमुरजानकगोमुखान् ।
व्यनादयन् शङ्खवेणुवीणास्तुमुलनिःस्वनान् ॥ १३ ॥

meghā mṛdaṅga-paṇava-
murajānaka-gomukhān
vyanādayan śaṅkha-veṇu-
vīṇās tumula-niḥsvanān

meghāḥ—personified clouds; *mṛdaṅga*—drums; *paṇava*—kettledrums; *muraja*—another kind of drum; *ānaka*—another type of drum; *gomukhān*

—a type of bugle; *vyanādayan*—vibrated; *śaṅkha*—conchshells; *veṇu*—flutes; *vīṇāḥ*—stringed instruments; *tumula*—tumultuous; *niḥsvanān*—vibration.

TRANSLATION

The clouds in personified form beat various types of drums, known as mṛdaṅgas, paṇavas, murajas and ānakas. They also blew conchshells and bugles known as gomukhas and played flutes and stringed instruments. The combined sound of these instruments was tumultuous.

TEXT 14

ततोऽभिषिषिचुर्देवीं श्रियं पद्मकरां सतीम् ।
दिग्गिभाः पूर्णकलशैः सूक्तवाक्यैर्द्विजेरितैः ॥ १४ ॥

tato 'bhiṣiṣicur devīṁ
śriyaṁ padma-karāṁ satīm
digibhāḥ pūrṇa-kalaśaiḥ
sūkta-vākyair dvijeritaiḥ

tataḥ—thereafter; *abhiṣiṣicuḥ*—poured all-auspicious water on the body; *devīm*—the goddess of fortune; *śriyam*—very beautiful; *padma-karām*—with a lotus in her hand; *satīm*—she who is most chaste, not knowing anyone but the Supreme Personality of Godhead; *digibhāḥ*—the great elephants; *pūrṇa-kalaśaiḥ*—by completely full water jugs; *sūkta-vākyaiḥ*—with Vedic *mantras; dvi-ja*—by *brāhmaṇas; īritaiḥ*—chanted.

TRANSLATION

Thereafter, the great elephants from all the directions carried big water jugs full of Ganges water and bathed the goddess of fortune, to the accompaniment of Vedic mantras chanted by learned brāhmaṇas. While thus being bathed, the goddess of fortune maintained her original style, with a lotus flower in her hand, and she appeared very beautiful. The goddess of fortune is the most chaste, for she does not know anyone but the Supreme Personality of Godhead.

PURPORT

The goddess of fortune, Lakṣmī, is described in this verse as *śriyam,* which means that she has six opulences—wealth, strength, influence, beauty, knowledge and renunciation. These opulences are received from the goddess of fortune. Lakṣmī is addressed here as *devī,* the goddess, because in Vaikuṇṭha she supplies all opulences to the Supreme Personality of Godhead and His devotees, who in this way enjoy natural life in the Vaikuṇṭha planets. The Supreme Personality of Godhead is pleased with His consort, the goddess of fortune, who carries a lotus flower in her hand. Mother Lakṣmī is described in this verse as *satī,* the supremely chaste, because she never diverts her attention from the Supreme Personality of Godhead to anyone else.

TEXT 15

समुद्रः पीतकौशेयवाससी समुपाहरत् ।
वरुणः स्रजं वैजयन्तीं मधुना मत्तषट्पदाम् ॥ १५ ॥

samudraḥ pīta-kauśeya-
vāsasī samupāharat
varuṇaḥ srajaṁ vaijayantīṁ
madhunā matta-ṣaṭpadām

samudraḥ—the ocean; *pīta-kauśeya*—yellow silk; *vāsasī*—both the upper and lower portions of a garment; *samupāharat*—presented; *varuṇaḥ*—the predominating deity of the water; *srajam*—garland; *vaijayantīm*—the most decorated and the biggest; *madhunā*—with honey; *matta*—drunken; *ṣaṭ-padām*—bumblebees, which have six legs.

TRANSLATION

The ocean, which is the source of all valuable jewels, supplied the upper and lower portions of a yellow silken garment. The predominating deity of the water, Varuṇa, presented flower garlands surrounded by six-legged bumblebees, drunken with honey.

PURPORT

When bathing the Deity in the *abhiṣeka* ceremony with various liquids, such as milk, honey, yogurt, ghee, cow dung and cow urine, it is customary to supply yellow garments. In this way the *abhiṣeka* ceremony for the goddess of fortune was performed according to the regular Vedic principles.

TEXT 16

भूषणानि विचित्राणि विश्वकर्मा प्रजापतिः ।
हारं सरस्वती पद्ममजो नागाश्च कुण्डले ॥ १६ ॥

bhūṣaṇāni vicitrāṇi
viśvakarmā prajāpatiḥ
hāraṁ sarasvatī padmam
ajo nāgāś ca kuṇḍale

bhūṣaṇāni—varieties of ornaments; *vicitrāṇi*—all very nicely decorated; *viśvakarmā prajāpatiḥ*—Viśvakarmā, one of the *prajāpatis,* the sons of Lord Brahmā who generate progeny; *hāram*—garland or necklace; *sarasvatī*—the goddess of education; *padmam*—a lotus flower; *ajaḥ*—Lord Brahmā; *nāgāḥ ca*—the inhabitants of Nāgaloka; *kuṇḍale*—two earrings.

TRANSLATION

Viśvakarmā, one of the prajāpatis, supplied varieties of decorated ornaments. The goddess of learning, Sarasvatī, supplied a necklace, Lord Brahmā supplied a lotus flower, and the inhabitants of Nāgaloka supplied earrings.

TEXT 17

ततः कृतस्वस्त्ययनोत्पलस्रजं
नदद्द्विरेफां परिगृह्य पाणिना ।
चचाल वक्त्रं सुकपोलकुण्डलं
सव्रीडहासं दधती सुशोभनम् ॥ १७ ॥

tataḥ kṛta-svastyayanotpala-srajaṁ
nadad-dvirephāṁ parigṛhya pāṇinā
cacāla vaktraṁ sukapola-kuṇḍalaṁ
savrīḍa-hāsaṁ dadhatī suśobhanam

tataḥ—thereafter; *kṛta-svastyayanā*—being worshiped regularly by all-auspicious ritualistic ceremonies; *utpala-srajam*—a garland of lotuses; *nadat*—humming; *dvirephām*—surrounded by bumblebees; *parigṛhya*—capturing; *pāṇinā*—by the hand; *cacāla*—went on; *vaktram*—face; *su-kapola-kuṇḍalam*—her cheeks decorated with earrings; *sa-vrīḍa-hāsam*—smiling with shyness; *dadhatī*—expanding; *su-śobhanam*—her natural beauty.

TEXT 20

नूनं तपो यस्य न मन्युनिर्जयो
ज्ञानं क्वचित् तच्च न सङ्गवर्जितम्।
कश्चिन्महांस्तस्य न कामनिर्जयः
स ईश्वरः किं परतोव्यपाश्रयः ॥ २० ॥

nūnaṁ tapo yasya na manyu-nirjayo
jñānaṁ kvacit tac ca na saṅga-varjitam
kaścin mahāṁs tasya na kāma-nirjayaḥ
sa īśvaraḥ kiṁ parato vyapāśrayaḥ

nūnam—certainly; *tapaḥ*—austerity; *yasya*—of someone; *na*—not; *manyu*—anger; *nirjayaḥ*—conquered; *jñānam*—knowledge; *kvacit*—in some saintly person; *tat*—that; *ca*—also; *na*—not; *saṅga-varjitam*—without the contamination of association; *kaścit*—someone; *mahān*—a very great exalted person; *tasya*—his; na—not; *kāma*—material desires; *nirjayaḥ*—conquered; *saḥ*—such a person; *īśvaraḥ*—controller; *kim*—how can he be; *parataḥ*—of others; *vyapāśrayaḥ*—under the control.

TRANSLATION

The goddess of fortune, examining the assembly, thought in this way: Someone who has undergone great austerity has not yet conquered anger. Someone possesses knowledge, but he has not conquered material desires. Someone is a very great personality, but he cannot conquer lusty desires. Even a great personality depends on something else. How, then, can he be the supreme controller?

PURPORT

Here is an attempt to find the supreme controller, or *īśvara.* Everyone may be accepted as an *īśvara,* or controller, but still such controllers are controlled by others. For example, one may have undergone severe austerities but still be under the control of anger. By a scrutinizing analysis, we find that everyone is controlled by something else. No one, therefore, can be the true controller but the Supreme Personality of Godhead, Kṛṣṇa. This is supported by the *śāstras. Īśvaraḥ paramaḥ kṛṣṇaḥ:* the supreme controller is Kṛṣṇa. Kṛṣṇa is never controlled by anyone, for He is the controller of everyone (*sarva-kāraṇa-kāraṇam*).

TEXT 21

धर्मः क्वचित् तत्र न भूतसौहृदं
त्यागः क्वचित् तत्र न मुक्तिकारणम्।
वीर्यं न पुंसोऽस्त्यजवेगनिष्कृतं
न हि द्वितीयो गुणसङ्गवर्जितः ॥ २१ ॥

dharmaḥ kvacit tatra na bhūta-sauhṛdaṁ
tyāgaḥ kvacit tatra na mukti-kāraṇam
vīryaṁ na puṁso 'sty aja-vega-niṣkṛtaṁ
na hi dvitīyo guṇa-saṅga-varjitaḥ

dharmaḥ—religion; *kvacit*—one may have full knowledge of; *tatra*—therein; *na*—not; *bhūta-sauhṛdam*—friendship with other living entities; *tyāgaḥ*—renunciation; *kvacit*—one may possess; *tatra*—therein; *na*—not; *mukti-kāraṇam*—the cause of liberation; *vīryam*—power; *na*—not; *puṁsaḥ*—of any person; *asti*—there may be; *aja-vega-niṣkṛtam*—no release from the power of time; *na*—nor; *hi*—indeed; *dvitīyaḥ*—the second one; *guṇa-saṅga-varjitaḥ*—completely freed from the contamination of the modes of nature.

TRANSLATION

Someone may possess full knowledge of religion but still not be kind to all living entities. In someone, whether human or demigod, there may be renunciation, but that is not the cause of liberation. Someone may possess great power and yet be unable to check the power of eternal time. Someone else may have renounced attachment to the material world, yet he cannot compare to the Supreme Personality of Godhead. Therefore, no one is completely freed from the influence of the material modes of nature.

PURPORT

The statement *dharmaḥ kvacit tatra na bhūta-sauhṛdam* is very important in this verse. We actually see that there are many Hindus, Muslims, Christians, Buddhists and religionists of other cults who adhere to their religious principles very nicely but are not equal to all living entities. Indeed, although they profess to be very religious, they kill poor animals. Such religion has no meaning. *Śrīmad-Bhāgavatam* (1.2.8) says:

dharmaḥ svanuṣṭhitaḥ puṁsāṁ
viṣvaksena-kathāsu yaḥ
notpādayed yadi ratiṁ
śrama eva hi kevalam

One may be very expert in following the religious principles of his own sect, but if he has no tendency to love the Supreme Personality of Godhead, his observance of religious principles is simply a waste of time. One must develop a sense of loving Vāsudeva (*vāsudevaḥ sarvam iti sa mahātmā sudurlabhaḥ*). The sign of a devotee is that he is a friend to everyone (*suhṛdaṁ sarva-bhūtānām*). A devotee will never allow a poor animal to be killed in the name of religion. This is the difference between a superficially religious person and a devotee of the Supreme Personality of Godhead.

We find that there have been many great heroes in history, but they could not escape from the cruel hands of death. Even the greatest hero cannot escape from the ruling power of the Supreme Personality of Godhead when Kṛṣṇa comes as death. That is described by Kṛṣṇa Himself: *mṛtyuḥ sarva-haraś cāham.* The Lord, appearing as death, takes away a hero's so-called power. Even Hiraṇyakaśipu could not be saved when Nṛsiṁhadeva appeared before him as death. One's material strength is nothing before the strength of the Supreme Personality of Godhead.

TEXT 22

क्वचिच्चिरायुर्न हि शीलमङ्गलं
क्वचित् तदप्यस्ति न वेद्यमायुषः ।
यत्रोभयं कुत्र च सोऽप्यमङ्गलः
सुमङ्गलः कश्च न काङ्क्षते हि माम् ॥ २२ ॥

kvacic cirāyur na hi śīla-maṅgalaṁ
kvacit tad apy asti na vedyam āyuṣaḥ
yatrobhayaṁ kutra ca so 'py amaṅgalaḥ
sumaṅgalaḥ kaśca na kāṅkṣate hi mām

kvacit—someone; *cira-āyuḥ*—has a long duration of life; *na*—not; *hi*—indeed; *śīla-maṅgalam*—good behavior or auspiciousness; *kvacit*—someone; *tat api*—although possessing good behavior; *asti*—is; *na*—not; *vedyam āyuṣaḥ*—aware of the duration of life; *yatra ubhayam*—if there are both (behavior and auspiciousness); *kutra*—somewhere; *ca*—also; *saḥ*—that person; *api*—although; *amaṅgalaḥ*—a little inauspicious in some other detail; *su-maṅgalaḥ*—auspicious in every respect; *kaśca*—someone; *na*—not; *kāṅkṣate*—desires; *hi*—indeed; *mām*—me.

TRANSLATION

Someone may have longevity but not have auspiciousness or good behavior. Someone may have both auspiciousness and good behavior, but the duration of his life is not fixed. Although such demigods as Lord Śiva have eternal life, they have inauspicious habits like living in crematoriums. And even if others are well qualified in all respects, they are not devotees of the Supreme Personality of Godhead.

TEXT 23

एवं विमृश्याव्यभिचारिसद्गुणै-
वरं निजैकाश्रयतयागुणाश्रयम् ।
वव्रे वरं सर्वगुणैरपेक्षितं
रमा मुकुन्दं निरपेक्षमीप्सितम् ॥ २३ ॥

evaṁ vimṛśyāvyabhicāri-sad-guṇair
varaṁ nijaikāśrayatayāguṇāśrayam
vavre varaṁ sarva-guṇair apekṣitaṁ
ramā mukundaṁ nirapekṣam īpsitam

evam—in this way; *vimṛśya*—after full deliberation; *avyabhicāri-sat-guṇaiḥ*—with extraordinary transcendental qualities; *varam*—superior; *nija-eka-āśrayatayā*—because of possessing all good qualities without depending on others; *aguṇa-āśrayam*—the reservoir of all transcendental qualities; *vavre*—accepted; *varam*—as a bridegroom; *sarva-guṇaiḥ*—with all transcendental qualities; *apekṣitam*—qualified; *ramā*—the goddess of fortune; *mukundam*—unto Mukunda; *nirapekṣam*—although He did not wait for her; *īpsitam*—the most desirable.

TRANSLATION

Śukadeva Gosvāmī continued: In this way, after full deliberation, the goddess of fortune accepted Mukunda as her husband because although He is independent and not in want of her, He possesses all transcendental qualities and mystic powers and is therefore the most desirable.

PURPORT

The Supreme Personality of Godhead, Mukunda, is self-sufficient. Since He is fully independent, He was not in want of the support or association of Lakṣmīdevī. Nonetheless, Lakṣmīdevī, the goddess of fortune, accepted Him as her husband.

TEXT 24

तस्यांसदेश उशतीं नवकञ्जमालां
माद्यन्मधुव्रतवरूथगिरोपघुष्टाम् ।
तस्थौ निधाय निकटे तदुरः स्वधाम
सव्रीडहासविकसन्नयनेन याता ॥ २४ ॥

tasyāṁsa-deśa uśatīṁ nava-kañja-mālāṁ
mādyan-madhuvrata-varūtha-giropaghuṣṭām
tasthau nidhāya nikaṭe tad-uraḥ sva-dhāma
savrīḍa-hāsa-vikasan-nayanena yātā

tasya—of Him (the Supreme Personality of Godhead); *aṁsa-deśe*—on the shoulders; *uśatīm*—very beautiful; *nava*—new; *kañja-mālām*—garland of lotus flowers; *mādyat*—maddened; *madhuvrata-varūtha*—of bumblebees; *girā*—with the vibrating; *upaghuṣṭām*—surrounded by their humming; *tasthau*—remained; *nidhāya*—after placing the garland; *nikaṭe*—nearby; *tat-uraḥ*—the bosom of the Lord; *sva-dhāma*—her real resort; *sa-vrīḍa-hāsa*—smiling with shyness; *vikasat*—glittering; *nayanena*—with the eyes; *yātā*—so situated.

TRANSLATION

Approaching the Supreme Personality of Godhead, the goddess of fortune placed upon His shoulders the garland of newly grown lotus flowers, which was surrounded by humming bumblebees searching for honey. Then, expecting to get a place on the bosom of the Lord, she remained standing by His side, her face smiling in shyness.

TEXT 25

तस्याः श्रियस्त्रिजगतो जनको जनन्या
वक्षोनिवासमकरोत् परमं विभूतेः ।

श्रीः स्वाः प्रजाः सकरुणेन निरीक्षणेन
यत्र स्थितैधयत साधिपतींस्त्रिलोकान् ॥ २५ ॥

tasyāḥ śriyas tri-jagato janako jananyā
vakṣo nivāsam akarot paramaṁ vibhūteḥ
śrīḥ svāḥ prajāḥ sakaruṇena nirīkṣaṇena
yatra sthitaidhayata sādhipatīṁs tri-lokān

tasyāḥ—of her; *śriyaḥ*—the goddess of fortune; *tri-jagataḥ*—of the three worlds; *janakaḥ*—the father; *jananyāḥ*—of the mother; *vakṣaḥ*—bosom; *nivāsam*—residence; *akarot*—made; *paramam*—supreme; *vibhūteḥ*—of the opulent; *śrīḥ*—the goddess of fortune; *svāḥ*—own; *prajāḥ*—descendants; *sa-karuṇena*—with favorable mercy; *nirīkṣaṇena*—by glancing over; *yatra*—wherein; *sthitā*—staying; *aidhayata*—increased; *sa-adhipatīn*—with the great directors and leaders; *tri-lokān*—the three worlds.

TRANSLATION

The Supreme Personality of Godhead is the father of the three worlds, and His bosom is the residence of mother Lakṣmī, the goddess of fortune, the proprietor of all opulences. The goddess of fortune, by her favorable and merciful glance, can increase the opulence of the three worlds, along with their inhabitants and their directors, the demigods.

PURPORT

According to the desire of Lakṣmīdevī, the goddess of fortune, the Supreme Personality of Godhead made His bosom her residence so that by her glance she could favor everyone, including the demigods and ordinary human beings. In other words, since the goddess of fortune stays on the bosom of Nārāyaṇa, she naturally sees any devotee who worships Nārāyaṇa. When the goddess of fortune understands that a devotee is in favor of devotional service to Nārāyaṇa, she is naturally inclined to bless the devotee with all opulences. The *karmīs* try to receive the favor and mercy of Lakṣmī, but because they are not devotees of Nārāyaṇa, their opulence is flickering. The opulence of devotees who are attached to the service of Nārāyaṇa is not like the opulence of *karmīs.* The opulence of devotees is as permanent as the opulence of Nārāyaṇa Himself.

TEXT 26

शङ्खतूर्यमृदङ्गानां वादित्राणां पृथुः स्वनः ।
देवानुगानां सस्त्रीणां नृत्यतां गायतामभूत् ॥ २६ ॥

śaṅkha-tūrya-mṛdaṅgānāṁ
vāditrāṇāṁ pṛthuḥ svanaḥ
devānugānāṁ sastrīṇāṁ
nṛtyatāṁ gāyatām abhūt

śaṅkha—conchshells; *tūrya*—bugles; *mṛdaṅgānām*—and of different types of drums; *vāditrāṇām*—of the musical instruments; *pṛthuḥ*—very great; *svanaḥ*—sound; *deva-anugānām*—the inhabitants of the upper planets like the Gandharvas and Cāraṇas, who follow the demigods; *sa-strīṇām*—as along with their own wives; *nṛtyatām*—engaged in dancing; *gāyatām*—singing; *abhūt*—became.

TRANSLATION

The inhabitants of Gandharvaloka and Cāraṇaloka then took the opportunity to play their musical instruments, such as conchshells, bugles and drums. They began dancing and singing along with their wives.

TEXT 27

ब्रह्मरुद्राङ्गिरोमुख्याः सर्वे विश्वसृजो विभुम् ।
ईडिरेऽवितथैर्मन्त्रैस्तल्लिङ्गैः पुष्पवर्षिणः ॥ २७ ॥

brahma-rudrāṅgiro-mukhyāḥ
sarve viśva-sṛjo vibhum
īḍire 'vitathair mantrais
tal-liṅgaiḥ puṣpa-varṣiṇaḥ

brahma—Lord Brahmā; *rudra*—Lord Śiva; *aṅgiraḥ*—the great sage Aṅgirā Muni; *mukhyāḥ*—headed by; *sarve*—all of them; *viśva-sṛjaḥ*—the directors of universal management; *vibhum*—the very great personality; *īḍire*—worshiped; *avitathaiḥ*—real; *mantraiḥ*—by chanting; *tat-liṅgaiḥ*—worshiping the Supreme Personality of Godhead; *puṣpa-varṣiṇaḥ*—throwing flowers like showers.

TRANSLATION

Lord Brahmā, Lord Śiva, the great sage Aṅgirā, and similar directors of universal management showered flowers and chanted mantras indicating the transcendental glories of the Supreme Personality of Godhead.

TEXT 28

श्रियावलोकिता देवाः सप्रजापतयः प्रजाः ।
शीलादिगुणसम्पन्ना लेभिरे निर्वृतिं पराम् ॥ २८ ॥

śriyāvalokitā devāḥ
saprajāpatayaḥ prajāḥ
śīlādi-guṇa-sampannā
lebhire nirvṛtiṁ parām

śriyā—by the goddess of fortune, Lakṣmī; *avalokitāḥ*—being seen favorably with mercy; *devāḥ*—all the demigods; *sa-prajāpatayaḥ*—with all the *prajāpatis; prajāḥ*—and their generations; *śīla-ādi-guṇa-sampannāḥ*—all blessed with good behavior and good characteristics; *lebhire*—achieved; *nirvṛtim*—satisfaction; *parām*—the ultimate.

TRANSLATION

All the demigods, along with the prajāpatis and their descendants, being blessed by Lakṣmījī's glance upon them, were immediately enriched with good behavior and transcendental qualities. Thus they were very much satisfied.

TEXT 29

निःसत्त्वा लोलुपा राजन् निरुद्योगा गतत्रपाः ।
यदा चोपेक्षिता लक्ष्म्या बभूवुर्दैत्यदानवाः ॥ २९ ॥

niḥsattvā lolupā rājan
nirudyogā gata-trapāḥ
yadā copekṣitā lakṣmyā
babhūvur daitya-dānavāḥ

niḥsattvāḥ—without strength; *lolupāḥ*—very greedy; *rājan*—O King; *nirudyogāḥ*—frustrated; *gata-trapāḥ*—shameless; *yadā*—when; *ca*—also;

upekṣitāḥ—neglected; *lakṣmyā*—by the goddess of fortune; *babhūvuḥ*—they became; *daitya-dānavāḥ*—the demons and Rākṣasas.

TRANSLATION

O King, because of being neglected by the goddess of fortune, the demons and Rākṣasas were depressed, bewildered and frustrated, and thus they became shameless.

TEXT 30

अथासीद् वारुणी देवी कन्या कमललोचना ।
असुरा जगृहुस्तां वै हरेरनुमतेन ते ॥ ३० ॥

athāsīd vāruṇī devī
kanyā kamala-locanā
asurā jagṛhus tāṁ vai
harer anumatena te

atha—thereafter (after the appearance of the goddess of fortune); *āsīt*—there was; *vāruṇī*—Vāruṇī; *devī*—the demigoddess who controls drunkards; *kanyā*—a young girl; *kamala-locanā*—lotus-eyed; *asurāḥ*—the demons; *jagṛhuḥ*—accepted; *tām*—her; *vai*—indeed; *hareḥ*—of the Supreme Personality of Godhead; *anumatena*—by the order; *te*—they (the demons).

TRANSLATION

Next appeared Vāruṇī, the lotus-eyed goddess who controls drunkards. With the permission of the Supreme Personality of Godhead, Kṛṣṇa, the demons, headed by Bali Mahārāja, took possession of this young girl.

TEXT 31

अथोदधेर्मथ्यमानात् काश्यपैरमृतार्थिभिः ।
उदतिष्ठन्महाराज पुरुषः परमाद्भुतः ॥ ३१ ॥

athodadher mathyamānāt
kāśyapair amṛtārthibhiḥ
udatiṣṭhan mahārāja
puruṣaḥ paramādbhutaḥ

atha—thereafter; *udadheḥ*—from the ocean of milk; *mathyamānāt*—while being churned; *kāśyapaiḥ*—by the sons of Kaśyapa, namely the demigods and the demons; *amṛta-arthibhiḥ*—anxious to get nectar from the churning; *udatiṣṭhat*—there appeared; *mahārāja*—O King; *puruṣaḥ*—a male person; *parama*—highly; *adbhutaḥ*—wonderful.

TRANSLATION

O King, thereafter, while the sons of Kaśyapa, both demons and demigods, were engaged in churning the ocean of milk, a very wonderful male person appeared.

TEXT 32

दीर्घपीवरदोर्दण्डः कम्बुग्रीवोऽरुणेक्षणः ।
श्यामलस्तरुणः स्रग्वी सर्वाभरणभूषितः ॥ ३२ ॥

dīrgha-pīvara-dor-daṇḍaḥ
kambu-grīvo 'ruṇekṣaṇaḥ
śyāmalas taruṇaḥ sragvī
sarvābharaṇa-bhūṣitaḥ

dīrgha—long; *pīvara*—stout and strong; *doḥ-daṇḍaḥ*—the arms; *kambu*—like a conchshell; *grīvaḥ*—the neck; *aruṇa-īkṣaṇaḥ*—reddish eyes; *śyāmalaḥ*—blackish complexion; *taruṇaḥ*—very young; *sragvī*—wearing a flower garland; *sarva*—all; *ābharaṇa*—with ornaments; *bhūṣitaḥ*—decorated.

TRANSLATION

He was strongly built; his arms were long, stout and strong; his neck, which was marked with three lines, resembled a conchshell; his eyes were reddish; and his complexion was blackish. He was very young, he was garlanded with flowers, and his entire body was fully decorated with various ornaments.

TEXT 33

पीतवासा महोरस्कः सुमृष्टमणिकुण्डलः ।
स्निग्धकुञ्चितकेशान्तसुभगः सिंहविक्रमः ।
अमृतापूर्णकलसं बिभ्रद् वलयभूषितः ॥ ३३ ॥

pīta-vāsā mahoraskaḥ
sumṛṣṭa-maṇi-kuṇḍalaḥ

snigdha-kuñcita-keśānta-
subhagaḥ siṁha-vikramaḥ
amṛtāpūrṇa-kalasaṁ
bibhrad valaya-bhūṣitaḥ

pīta-vāsāḥ—wearing yellow garments; *mahā-uraskaḥ*—his chest very broad; *su-mṛṣṭa-maṇi-kuṇḍalaḥ*—whose earrings were well polished and made of pearls; *snigdha*—polished; *kuñcita-keśa*—curling hair; *anta*—at the end; *su-bhagaḥ*—separated and beautiful; *siṁha-vikramaḥ*—strong like a lion; *amṛta*—with nectar; *āpūrṇa*—filled to the top; *kalasam*—a jar; *bibhrat*—moving; *valaya*—with bangles; *bhūṣitaḥ*—decorated.

TRANSLATION

He was dressed in yellow garments and wore brightly polished earrings made of pearls. The tips of his hair were anointed with oil, and his chest was very broad. His body had all good features, he was stout and strong like a lion, and he was decorated with bangles. In his hand he carried a jug filled to the top with nectar.

TEXT 34

स वै भगवतः साक्षाद्विष्णोरंशांशसम्भवः ।
धन्वन्तरिरिति ख्यात आयुर्वेददृगिज्यभाक् ॥ ३४ ॥

sa vai bhagavataḥ sākṣād
viṣṇor aṁśāṁśa-sambhavaḥ
dhanvantarir iti khyāta
āyur-veda-dṛg ijya-bhāk

saḥ—he; *vai*—indeed; *bhagavataḥ*—of the Supreme Personality of Godhead; *sākṣāt*—directly; *viṣṇoḥ*—of Lord Viṣṇu; *aṁśa-aṁśa-sambhavaḥ*—incarnation of the plenary portion of a plenary portion; *dhanvantariḥ*—Dhanvantari; *iti*—thus; *khyātaḥ*—celebrated; *āyuḥ-veda-dṛk*—fully conversant in the medical science; *ijya-bhāk*—one of the demigods eligible to share the benefits of sacrifices.

TRANSLATION

This person was Dhanvantari, a plenary portion of a plenary portion of Lord Viṣṇu. He was very conversant with the science of medicine, and as one of the demigods he was permitted to take a share in sacrifices.

PURPORT

Śrīla Madhvācārya remarks:

teṣāṁ satyāc cālanārthaṁ
harir dhanvantarir vibhuḥ
samartho 'py asurāṇāṁ tu
sva-hastād amucat sudhām

Dhanvantari, who was carrying the jug containing nectar, was a plenary incarnation of the Supreme Personality of Godhead, but although he was very strong, the *asuras* were able to take the jug of nectar from his hands.

TEXT 35

तमालोक्यासुराः सर्वे कलसं चामृताभृतम् ।
लिप्सन्तः सर्ववस्तूनि कलसं तरसाहरन् ॥ ३५ ॥

tam ālokyāsurāḥ sarve
kalasaṁ cāmṛtābhṛtam
lipsantaḥ sarva-vastūni
kalasaṁ tarasāharan

tam—him; *ālokya*—seeing; *asurāḥ*—the demons; *sarve*—all of them; *kalasam*—the container of nectar; *ca*—also; *amṛta-ābhṛtam*—filled with nectar; *lipsantaḥ*—desiring strongly; *sarva-vastūni*—all objects; *kalasam*—the jug; *tarasā*—immediately; *aharan*—snatched away.

TRANSLATION

Upon seeing Dhanvantari carrying the jug of nectar, the demons, desiring the jug and its contents, immediately snatched it away by force.

TEXT 36

नीयमानेऽसुरैस्तस्मिन्कलसेऽमृतभाजने ।
विषण्णमनसो देवा हरिं शरणमाययुः ॥ ३६ ॥

nīyamāne 'surais tasmin
kalase 'mṛta-bhājane
viṣaṇṇa-manaso devā
hariṁ śaraṇam āyayuḥ

nīyamāne—being carried; *asuraiḥ*—by the demons; *tasmin*—that; *kalase*—jug; *amṛta-bhājane*—containing nectar; *viṣaṇṇa-manasaḥ*—aggrieved in mind; *devāḥ*—all the demigods; *harim*—unto the Supreme Lord; *śaraṇam*—to take shelter; *āyayuḥ*—went.

TRANSLATION

When the jug of nectar was carried off by the demons, the demigods were morose. Thus they sought shelter at the lotus feet of the Supreme Personality of Godhead, Hari.

TEXT 37

इति तद्दैन्यमालोक्य भगवान्भृत्यकामकृत् ।
मा खिद्यत मिथोऽर्थं वः साधयिष्ये स्वमायया ॥ ३७ ॥

iti tad-dainyam ālokya
bhagavān bhṛtya-kāma-kṛt
mā khidyata mitho 'rthaṁ vaḥ
sādhayiṣye sva-māyayā

iti—in this way; *tat*—of the demigods; *dainyam*—moroseness; *ālokya*—seeing; *bhagavān*—the Supreme Personality of Godhead; *bhṛtya-kāma-kṛt*—who is always ready to fulfill the desires of His servants; *mā khidyata*—do not be aggrieved; *mithaḥ*—by a quarrel; *artham*—to get nectar; *vaḥ*—for all of you; *sādhayiṣye*—I shall execute; *sva-māyayā*—by My own energy.

TRANSLATION

When the Supreme Personality of Godhead, who always desires to fulfill the ambitions of His devotees, saw that the demigods were morose, He said to them, "Do not be aggrieved. By My own energy I shall bewilder the demons by creating a quarrel among them. In this way I shall fulfill your desire to have the nectar."

TEXT 38

मिथः कलिरभूत्तेषां तदर्थे तर्षचेतसाम् ।
अहं पूर्वमहं पूर्वं न त्वं न त्वमिति प्रभो ॥ ३८ ॥

mithaḥ kalir abhūt teṣāṁ
tad-arthe tarṣa-cetasām

ahaṁ pūrvam ahaṁ pūrvaṁ
na tvaṁ na tvaṁ iti prabho

mithaḥ—among themselves; *kaliḥ*—disagreement and quarrel; *abhūt*—there was; *teṣām*—of all of them; *tat-arthe*—for the sake of nectar; *tarṣa-cetasām*—bewildered in heart and soul by the illusory energy of Viṣṇu; *aham*—I; *pūrvam*—first; *aham*—I; *pūrvam*—first; *na*—not; *tvam*—you; *na*—not; *tvam*—you; *iti*—thus; *prabho*—O King.

TRANSLATION

O King, a quarrel then arose among the demons over who would get the nectar first. Each of them said, "You cannot drink it first. I must drink it first. Me first, not you!"

PURPORT

This is the symptom of demons. The first concern of a nondevotee is how to enjoy his personal sense gratification at once, whereas the devotee's first concern is to satisfy the Lord. This is the distinction between the nondevotee and the devotee. In this material world, since most people are nondevotees, they regularly compete, fight, disagree and war among themselves, for everyone wants to enjoy and satisfy his own senses. Therefore, unless such demons become Kṛṣṇa conscious and are trained to satisfy the senses of the Lord, there can be no question of peace in human society or any society, even that of the demigods. The demigods and devotees, however, always surrender to the lotus feet of the Lord, and thus the Lord is always anxious to satisfy their ambitions. While the demons fight to satisfy their own senses, devotees engage in devotional service to satisfy the senses of the Lord. The members of the Kṛṣṇa consciousness movement must be alert in regard to this point, and then their preaching of the Kṛṣṇa consciousness movement will be successful.

TEXTS 39-40

देवाः स्वं भागमर्हन्ति ये तुल्यायासहेतवः ।
सत्रयाग इवैतस्मिन्नेष धर्मः सनातनः ॥ ३९ ॥
इति स्वान्प्रत्यषेधन्वै दैतेया जातमत्सराः ।
दुर्बलाः प्रबलान् राजन् गृहीतकलसान् मुहुः ॥ ४० ॥

devāḥ svaṁ bhāgam arhanti
ye tulyāyāsa-hetavaḥ
satra-yāga ivaitasminn
eṣa dharmaḥ sanātanaḥ

iti svān pratyaṣedhan vai
daiteyā jāta-matsarāḥ
durbalāḥ prabalān rājan
gṛhīta-kalasān muhuḥ

devāḥ—the demigods; *svam bhāgam*—their own share; *arhanti*—deserve to take; *ye*—all of them who; *tulya-āyāsa-hetavaḥ*—who made an equal endeavor; *satra-yāge*—in the performance of sacrifices; *iva*—similarly; *etasmin*—in this matter; *eṣaḥ*—this; *dharmaḥ*—religion; *sanātanaḥ*—eternal; *iti*—thus; *svān*—among themselves; *pratyaṣedhan*—forbade one another; *vai*—indeed; *daiteyāḥ*—the sons of Diti; *jāta-matsarāḥ*—envious; *durbalāḥ*—weak; *prabalān*—by force; *rājan*—O King; *gṛhīta*—possessing; *kalasān*—the jug containing nectar; *muhuḥ*—constantly.

TRANSLATION

Some of the demons said, "All the demigods have taken part in churning the ocean of milk. Now, as everyone has an equal right to partake in any public sacrifice, according to the eternal religious system it is befitting that the demigods now have a share of the nectar." O King, in this way the weaker demons forbade the stronger demons to take the nectar.

PURPORT

Desiring to take the nectar, those among the demons who were less strong spoke in favor of the demigods. The weaker Daityas naturally pleaded on behalf of the demigods to stop the stronger Daityas from drinking the nectar without sharing it. In this way, disagreement and trouble arose as they forbade one another to drink the nectar.

TEXTS 41-46

एतस्मिन्नन्तरे विष्णुः सर्वोपायविदीश्वरः ।
योषिद्रूपमनिर्देश्यं दधार परमाद्भुतम् ॥ ४१ ॥
प्रेक्षणीयोत्पलश्यामं सर्वावयवसुन्दरम् ।
समानकर्णाभरणं सुकपोलोन्नसाननम् ॥ ४२ ॥

नवयौवननिर्वृत्तस्तनभारकृशोदरम् ।
मुखामोदानुरक्तालिझङ्कारोद्विग्नलोचनम् ॥ ४३ ॥
बिभ्रत् सुकेशभारेण मालामुत्फुल्लमल्लिकाम् ।
सुग्रीवकण्ठाभरणं सुभुजाङ्गदभूषितम् ॥ ४४ ॥
विरजाम्बरसंवीतनितम्बद्वीपशोभया ।
काञ्च्या प्रविलसद्वल्गुचलच्चरणनूपुरम् ॥ ४५ ॥
सव्रीडस्मितविक्षिप्तभ्रूविलासावलोकनैः ।
दैत्ययूथपचेतःसु काममुद्दीपयन् मुहुः ॥ ४६ ॥

etasminn antare viṣṇuḥ
sarvopāya-vid īśvaraḥ
yoṣid-rūpam anirdeśyaṁ
dadhāra-paramādbhutam

prekṣaṇīyotpala-śyāmaṁ
sarvāvayava-sundaram
samāna-karṇābharaṇaṁ
sukapolonnasānanam

nava-yauvana-nirvṛtta-
stana-bhāra-kṛśodaram
mukhāmodānuraktāli-
jhaṅkārodvigna-locanam

bibhrat sukeśa-bhāreṇa
mālām utphulla-mallikām
sugrīva-kaṇṭhābharaṇaṁ
su-bhujāṅgada-bhūṣitam

virajāmbara-saṁvīta-
nitamba-dvīpa-śobhayā
kāñcyā pravilasad-valgu-
calac-caraṇa-nūpuram

savrīḍa-smita-vikṣipta-
bhrū-vilāsāvalokanaiḥ
daitya-yūtha-pa-cetaḥsu
kāmam uddīpayan muhuḥ

etasmin antare—after this incident; *viṣṇuḥ*—Lord Viṣṇu; *sarva-upāya-vit*—one who knows how to deal with different situations; *īśvaraḥ*—the supreme controller; *yoṣit-rūpam*—the form of a beautiful woman; *anirdeśyam*—no one could ascertain who She was; *dadhāra*—assumed; *parama*—supremely; *adbhutam*—wonderful; *prekṣaṇīya*—pleasing to look at; *utpala-śyāmam*—blackish like a newly grown lotus; *sarva*—all; *avayava*—parts of the body; *sundaram*—very beautiful; *samāna*—equally adjusted; *karṇa-ābharaṇam*—ornaments on the ears; *su-kapola*—very beautiful cheeks; *unnasa-ānanam*—a raised nose on Her face; *nava-yauvana*—newly youthful; *nirvṛtta-stana*—breasts not agitated; *bhāra*—weight; *kṛśa*—very lean and thin; *udaram*—waist; *mukha*—face; *āmoda*—creating pleasure; *anurakta*—attracted; *ali*—bumblebees; *jhaṅkāra*—making a humming sound; *udvigna*—from anxiety; *locanam*—Her eyes; *bibhrat*—moving; *su-keśa-bhāreṇa*—by the weight of beautiful hair; *mālām*—with a flower garland; *utphulla-mallikām*—made of fully grown *mallikā* flowers; *su-grīva*—a nice neck; *kaṇṭha-ābharaṇam*—ornamented with beautiful jewelry; *su-bhuja*—very beautiful arms; *aṅgada-bhūṣitam*—decorated with bangles; *viraja-ambara*—very clean cloth; *saṁvīta*—spread; *nitamba*—breast; *dvīpa*—appearing like an island; *śobhayā*—by such beauty; *kāñcyā*—the belt on the waist; *pravilasat*—spreading over; *valgu*—very beautiful; *calat-caraṇa-nūpuram*—moving ankle bells; *sa-vrīḍa-smita*—smiling with shyness; *vikṣipta*—glancing; *bhrū-vilāsa*—activities of the eyebrows; *avalokanaiḥ*—glancing over; *daitya-yūtha-pa*—the leaders of the demons; *cetaḥsu*—in the core of the heart; *kāmam*—lusty desire; *uddīpayat*—awakening; *muhuḥ*—constantly.

TRANSLATION

The Supreme Personality of Godhead, Viṣṇu, who can counteract any unfavorable situation, then assumed the form of an extremely beautiful woman. This incarnation as a woman, Mohinī-mūrti, was most pleasing to the mind. Her complexion resembled in color a newly grown blackish lotus, and every part of Her body was beautifully situated. Her ears were equally decorated with earrings, Her cheeks were very beautiful, Her nose was raised and Her face full of youthful luster. Her large breasts made Her waist seem very thin. Attracted by the aroma of Her face and body, bumblebees hummed around Her, and thus Her eyes were restless. Her hair, which was extremely beautiful, was garlanded with mallikā flowers. Her attractively constructed neck was decorated with a necklace and other ornaments, Her arms were decorated with bangles, Her body was covered

with a clean sari, and Her breasts seemed like islands in an ocean of beauty. Her legs were decorated with ankle bells. Because of the movements of Her eyebrows as She smiled with shyness and glanced over the demons, all the demons were saturated with lusty desires, and every one of them desired to possess Her.

PURPORT

Because of the Supreme Lord's assuming the form of a beautiful woman to arouse the lusty desires of the demons, a description of Her complete beauty is given here.

Thus end the Bhaktivedanta purports of the Eighth Canto, Eighth Chapter, of the Śrīmad-Bhāgavatam, *entitled "The Churning of the Milk Ocean."*

CHAPTER NINE

The Lord Incarnates as Mohinī-mūrti

This chapter describes how the demons, being enchanted by the beauty of the Mohinī form, agreed to hand over the container of nectar to Mohinīdevī, who tactfully delivered it to the demigods.

When the demons got possession of the container of nectar, an extraordinarily beautiful young woman appeared before them. All the demons became captivated by the young woman's beauty and became attached to Her. Now, because the demons were fighting among themselves to possess the nectar, they selected this beautiful woman as a mediator to settle their quarrel. Taking advantage of their weakness in this regard, Mohinī, the incarnation of the Supreme Personality of Godhead, got the demons to promise that whatever decision She might give, they would not refuse to accept it. When the demons made this promise, the beautiful woman, Mohinī-mūrti, had the demigods and demons sit in different lines so that She could distribute the nectar. She knew that the demons were quite unfit to drink the nectar. Therefore, by cheating them She distributed all the nectar to the demigods. When the demons saw this cheating of Mohinī-mūrti, they remained silent. But one demon, named Rāhu, dressed himself like a demigod and sat down in the line of the demigods. He sat beside the sun and the moon. When the Supreme Personality of Godhead understood how Rāhu was cheating, He immediately cut off the demon's head. Rāhu, however, had already tasted the nectar, and therefore although his head was severed, he remained alive. After the demigods finished drinking the nectar, the Supreme Personality of Godhead assumed His own form. Śukadeva Gosvāmī ends this chapter by describing how powerful is the chanting of the holy names, pastimes and paraphernalia of the Supreme Personality of Godhead.

TEXT 1

श्रीशुक उवाच

तेऽन्योन्यतोऽसुराः पात्रं हरन्तस्त्यक्तसौहृदाः ।
क्षिपन्तो दस्युधर्माण आयान्तीं ददृशुः स्त्रियम् ॥ १ ॥

śrī-śuka uvāca
te 'nyonyato 'surāḥ pātraṁ
harantas tyakta-sauhṛdāḥ
kṣipanto dasyu-dharmāṇa
āyāntīṁ dadṛśuḥ striyam

śrī-śukaḥ uvāca—Śrī Śukadeva Gosvāmī said; *te*—the demons; *anyonyataḥ*—among themselves; *asurāḥ*—the demons; *pātram*—the container of nectar; *harantaḥ*—snatching from one another; *tyakta-sauhṛdāḥ*—became inimical toward one another; *kṣipantaḥ*—sometimes throwing; *dasyu-dharmāṇaḥ*—sometimes snatching like robbers; *āyāntīm*—coming forward; *dadṛśuḥ*—saw; *striyam*—a very beautiful and attractive woman.

TRANSLATION

Śukadeva Gosvāmī said: Thereafter, the demons became inimical toward one another. Throwing and snatching the container of nectar, they gave up their friendly relationship. Meanwhile, they saw a very beautiful young woman coming forward toward them.

TEXT 2

अहो रूपमहो धाम अहो अस्या नवं वयः ।
इति ते तामभिद्रुत्य पप्रच्छुर्जातहृच्छयाः ॥ २ ॥

aho rūpam aho dhāma
aho asyā navaṁ vayaḥ
iti te tām abhidrutya
papracchur jāta-hṛc-chayāḥ

aho—how wonderful; *rūpam*—Her beauty; *aho*—how wonderful; *dhāma*—Her bodily luster; *aho*—how wonderful; *asyāḥ*—of Her; *navam*—new; *vayaḥ*—beautiful age; *iti*—in this way; *te*—those demons; *tām*—unto the beautiful woman; *abhidrutya*—going before Her hastily; *papracchuḥ*—inquired from Her; *jāta-hṛt-śayāḥ*—their hearts being filled with lust to enjoy Her.

TRANSLATION

Upon seeing the beautiful woman, the demons said, "Alas, how wonderful is Her beauty, how wonderful the luster of Her body, and how won-

derful the beauty of Her youthful age!" Speaking in this way, they quickly approached Her, full of lusty desires to enjoy Her, and began to inquire from Her in many ways.

TEXT 3

का त्वं कञ्जपलाशाक्षि कुतो वा किं चिकीर्षसि।
कस्यासि वद वामोरु मथ्नतीव मनांसि नः ॥ ३ ॥

kā tvaṁ kañja-palāśākṣi
kuto vā kiṁ cikīrṣasi
kasyāsi vada vāmoru
mathnatīva manāṁsi naḥ

kā—who; *tvam*—are You; *kañja-palāśa-akṣi*—having eyes like the petals of a lotus; *kutaḥ*—from where; *vā*—either; *kim cikīrṣasi*—what is the purpose for which You have come here; *kasya*—of whom; *asi*—do You belong; *vada*—kindly tell us; *vāma-ūru*—O You whose thighs are extraordinarily beautiful; *mathnatī*—agitating; *iva*—like; *manāṁsi*—within our minds; *naḥ*—our.

TRANSLATION

O wonderfully beautiful girl, You have such nice eyes, resembling the petals of a lotus flower. Who are You? Where do You come from? What is Your purpose in coming here, and to whom do You belong? O You whose thighs are extraordinarily beautiful, our minds are becoming agitated simply because of seeing You.

PURPORT

The demons inquired from the wonderfully beautiful girl, "To whom do You belong?" A woman is supposed to belong to her father before her marriage, to her husband after her marriage, and to her grown sons in her old age. In regard to this inquiry, Śrīla Viśvanātha Cakravartī Ṭhākura says that the question "To whom do You belong?" means "Whose daughter are You?"Since the demons could understand that the beautiful girl was still unmarried, every one of them desired to marry Her. Thus they inquired, "Whose daughter are You?"

TEXT 4

न वयं त्वामरैर्दैत्यैः सिद्धगन्धर्वचारणैः ।
नास्पृष्टपूर्वां जानीमो लोकेशैश्च कुतो नृभिः ॥ ४ ॥

na vayaṁ tvāmarair daityaiḥ
siddha-gandharva-cāraṇaiḥ
nāspṛṣṭa-pūrvāṁ jānīmo
lokeśaiś ca kuto nṛbhiḥ

na—it is not; *vayam*—we; *tvā*—unto You; *amaraiḥ*—by the demigods; *daityaiḥ*—by the demons; *siddha*—by the Siddhas; *gandharva*—by the Gandharvas; *cāraṇaiḥ*—and by the Cāraṇas; *na*—not; *aspṛṣṭa-pūrvām*—never enjoyed or touched by anyone; *jānīmaḥ*—know exactly; *loka-īśaiḥ*—by the various directors of the universe; *ca*—also; *kutaḥ*—what to speak of; *nṛbhiḥ*—by human society.

TRANSLATION

What to speak of human beings, even the demigods, demons, Siddhas, Gandharvas, Cāraṇas and the various directors of the universe, the Prajāpatis, have never touched You before. It is not that we are unable to understand Your identity.

PURPORT

Even the *asuras* observed the etiquette that no one should address a married woman with lust. The great analyst Cāṇakya Paṇḍita says, *mātṛvat para-dāreṣu:* one should consider another's wife to be one's mother. The *asuras,* the demons, took it for granted that the beautiful young woman, Mohinī-mūrti, who had arrived before them, was certainly not married. Therefore they assumed that no one in the world, including the demigods, the Gandharvas, the Cāraṇas and the Siddhas, had ever touched Her. The demons knew that the young girl was unmarried, and therefore they dared to address Her. They supposed that the young girl, Mohinī-mūrti, had come there to find a husband among all those present (the Daityas, the demigods, the Gandharvas and so on).

TEXT 5

नूनं त्वं विधिना सुभ्रूः प्रेषितासि शरीरिणाम् ।
सर्वेन्द्रियमनःप्रीतिं विधातुं सघृणेन किम् ॥ ५ ॥

nūnaṁ tvaṁ vidhinā subhrūḥ
preṣitāsi śarīriṇām
sarvendriya-manaḥ-prītiṁ
vidhātuṁ saghṛṇena kim

nūnam—indeed; *tvam*—You; *vidhinā*—by Providence; *su-bhrūḥ*—O You with the beautiful eyebrows; *preṣitā*—sent; *asi*—certainly You are so; *śarīriṇām*—of all embodied living entities; *sarva*—all; *indriya*—of the senses; *manaḥ*—and of the mind; *prītim*—what is pleasing; *vidhātum*—to administer; *sa-ghṛṇena*—by Your causeless mercy; *kim*—whether.

TRANSLATION

O beautiful girl with beautiful eyebrows, certainly Providence, by His causeless mercy, has sent You to please the senses and minds of all of us. Is this not a fact?

TEXT 6

सा त्वं नः स्पर्धमानानामेकवस्तुनि मानिनि ।
ज्ञातीनां बद्धवैराणां शं विधत्स्व सुमध्यमे ॥ ६ ॥

sā tvaṁ naḥ spardhamānānām
eka-vastuni mānini
jñātīnāṁ baddha-vairāṇāṁ
śaṁ vidhatsva sumadhyame

sā—as such You are; *tvam*—Your good self; *naḥ*—of all of us demons; *spardhamānānām*—of those who are becoming increasingly inimical; *eka-vastuni*—in one subject matter (the container of nectar); *mānini*—O You who are most beautiful in Your prestigious position; *jñātīnām*—among our family members; *baddha-vairāṇām*—increasingly becoming enemies; *śam*—auspiciousness; *vidhatsva*—must execute; *su-madhyame*—O beautiful thin-waisted woman.

TRANSLATION

We are now all engaged in enmity among ourselves because of this one subject matter—the container of nectar. Although we have been born in the same family, we are becoming increasingly inimical. O thin-waisted woman, who are so beautiful in Your prestigious position, we therefore request You to favor us by settling our dispute.

PURPORT

The demons understood that the beautiful woman had attracted the attention of them all. Therefore they unanimously requested Her to become the arbiter to settle their dispute.

TEXT 7

वयं कश्यपदायादा भ्रातरः कृतपौरुषाः ।
विभजस्व यथान्यायं नैव भेदो यथा भवेत् ॥ ७ ॥

vayaṁ kaśyapa-dāyādā
bhrātaraḥ kṛta-pauruṣāḥ
vibhajasva yathā-nyāyaṁ
naiva bhedo yathā bhavet

vayam—all of us; *kaśyapa-dāyādāḥ*—descendants of Kaśyapa Muni; *bhrātaraḥ*—we are all brothers; *kṛta-pauruṣāḥ*—who are all able and competent; *vibhajasva*—just divide; *yathā-nyāyam*—according to law; *na*—not; *eva*—certainly; *bhedaḥ*—partiality; *yathā*—as; *bhavet*—should so become.

TRANSLATION

All of us, both demons and demigods, have been born of the same father, Kaśyapa, and thus we are related as brothers. But now we are exhibiting our personal prowess in dissension. Therefore we request You to settle our dispute and divide the nectar equally among us.

TEXT 8

इत्युपामन्त्रितो दैत्यैर्मायायोषिद्वपुर्हरिः ।
प्रहस्य रुचिरापाङ्गैर्निरीक्षन्निदमब्रवीत् ॥ ८ ॥

ity upāmantrito daityair
māyā-yoṣid-vapur hariḥ
prahasya rucirāpāṅgair
nirīkṣann idam abravīt

iti—thus; *upāmantritaḥ*—being fervently requested; *daityaiḥ*—by the demons; *māyā-yoṣit*—the illusory woman; *vapuḥ hariḥ*—the incarnation of the Supreme Personality of Godhead; *prahasya*—smiling; *rucira*—beautiful;

apāṅgaiḥ—by exhibiting attractive feminine features; *nirīkṣan*—looking at them; *idam*—these words; *abravīt*—said.

TRANSLATION

Having thus been requested by the demons, the Supreme Personality of Godhead, who had assumed the form of a beautiful woman, began to smile. Looking at them with attractive feminine gestures, She spoke as follows.

TEXT 9

श्रीभगवानुवाच
कथं कश्यपदायादाः पुंश्चल्यां मयि सङ्गताः ।
विश्वासं पण्डितो जातु कामिनीषु न याति हि ॥ ९ ॥

śrī-bhagavān uvāca
kathaṁ kaśyapa-dāyādāḥ
puṁścalyāṁ mayi saṅgatāḥ
viśvāsaṁ paṇḍito jātu
kāminīṣu na yāti hi

śrī-bhagavān uvāca—the Supreme Personality of Godhead in the form of Mohinī-mūrti said; *katham*—how is it so; *kaśyapa-dāyādāḥ*—you are all descendants of Kaśyapa Muni; *puṁścalyām*—unto a prostitute who agitates the minds of men; *mayi*—unto Me; *saṅgatāḥ*—you come in My association; *viśvāsam*—faith; *paṇḍitaḥ*—those who are learned; *jātu*—at any time; *kāminīṣu*—unto a woman; *na*—never; *yāti*—takes place; *hi*—indeed.

TRANSLATION

The Supreme Personality of Godhead, in the form of Mohinī, told the demons: O sons of Kaśyapa Muni, I am only a prostitute. How is it that you have so much faith in Me? A learned person never puts his faith in a woman.

PURPORT

Cāṇakya Paṇḍita, the great politician and moral instructor, said, *viśvāso naiva kartavyaḥ strīṣu rāja-kuleṣu ca:* "Never put your faith in a woman or a politician." Thus the Supreme Personality of Godhead, who was pretending to be a woman, warned the demons against putting so much faith in Her, for She had appeared as an attractive woman ultimately to cheat them. Indirectly disclosing the purpose for which She had appeared before them, She said to the sons of Kaśyapa, "How is this? You were all born of a great *ṛṣi,* yet you are putting your faith in a woman who is loitering here and there like a prostitute, unprotected by father or husband. Women in general should not be trusted, and what to speak of a woman loitering like a prostitute?" The word *kāminī* is significant in this connection. Women, especially beautiful young women, invoke the dormant lusty desires of a man. Therefore, according to *Manu-saṁhitā,* every woman should be protected, either by her husband, by her father or by her grown sons. Without such protection, a woman will be exploited. Indeed, women like to be exploited by men. As soon as a woman is exploited by a man, she becomes a common prostitute. This is explained by Mohinī-mūrti, the Supreme Personality of Godhead.

TEXT 10

सालावृकाणां स्त्रीणां च स्वैरिणीनां सुरद्विषः ।
सख्यान्याहुरनित्यानि नूत्नं नूत्नं विचिन्वताम् ॥ १० ॥

sālāvṛkāṇāṁ strīṇāṁ ca
svairiṇīnāṁ sura-dviṣaḥ
sakhyāny āhur anityāni
nūtnaṁ nūtnaṁ vicinvatām

sālāvṛkāṇām—of monkeys, jackals and dogs; *strīṇām ca*—and of women; *svairiṇīnām*—especially women who are independent; *sura-dviṣaḥ*—O demons; *sakhyāni*—friendship; *āhuḥ*—it is said; *anityāni*—temporary; *nūtnam*—new friends; *nūtnam*—new friends; *vicinvatām*—all of whom are thinking.

TRANSLATION

O demons, as monkeys, jackals and dogs are unsteady in their sexual relationships and want newer and newer friends every day, women who live independently seek new friends daily. Friendship with such a woman is never permanent. This is the opinion of learned scholars.

TEXT 11

श्रीशुक उवाच
इति ते क्ष्वेलितैस्तस्या आश्वस्तमनसोऽसुराः ।
जहसुर्भावगम्भीरं ददुश्चामृतभाजनम् ॥ ११ ॥

śrī-śuka uvāca
iti te kṣvelitais tasyā
āśvasta-manaso 'surāḥ
jahasur bhāva-gambhīraṁ
daduś cāmṛta-bhājanam

śrī-śukaḥ uvāca—Śrī Śukadeva Gosvāmī said; *iti*—thus; *te*—those demons; *kṣvelitaiḥ*—by speaking as if jokingly; *tasyāḥ*—of Mohinī-mūrti; *āśvasta*—grateful, with faith; *manasaḥ*—their minds; *asurāḥ*—all the demons; *jahasuḥ*—laughed; *bhāva-gambhīram*—although Mohinī-mūrti was full of gravity; *daduḥ*—delivered; *ca*—also; *amṛta-bhājanam*—the container of nectar.

TRANSLATION

Śrī Śukadeva Gosvāmī continued: After the demons heard the words of Mohinī-mūrti, who had spoken as if jokingly, they were all very confident. They laughed with gravity, and ultimately they delivered the container of nectar into Her hands.

PURPORT

The Personality of Godhead in His form of Mohinī was certainly not joking but talking seriously, with gravity. The demons, however, being captivated by Mohinī-mūrti's bodily features, took Her words as a joke and confidently delivered the container of nectar into Her hands. Thus Mohinī-mūrti resembles Lord Buddha, who appeared *sammohāya sura-dviṣām*—to cheat the *asuras.* The word *sura-dviṣām* refers to those who are envious of the demigods or devotees. Sometimes an incarnation of the Supreme Personality of Godhead cheats the atheists. Thus we see here that although Mohinī-mūrti was speaking factually to the *asuras,* the *asuras* took Her words to be facetious. Indeed, they were so confident of Mohinī-mūrti's honesty that they immediately delivered the container of nectar into Her hands, as if they would allow Her to do with the nectar whatever She liked, whether She distributed it, threw it away or drank it Herself without giving it to them.

TEXT 12

ततो गृहीत्वामृतभाजनं हरि-
र्बभाष ईषत्स्मितशोभया गिरा।

यद्यभ्युपेतं क्व च साध्वसाधु वा
कृतं मया वो विभजे सुधामिमाम् ॥ १२ ॥

tato gṛhītvāmṛta-bhājanaṁ harir
babhāṣa īṣat-smita-śobhayā girā
yady abhyupetaṁ kva ca sādhv asādhu vā
kṛtaṁ mayā vo vibhaje sudhām imām

tataḥ—thereafter; *gṛhītvā*—taking possession of; *amṛta-bhājanam*—the pot containing the nectar; *hariḥ*—the Supreme Personality of Godhead, Hari, in the form of Mohinī; *babhāṣa*—spoke; *īṣat*—slightly; *smita-śobhayā girā*—with smiling beauty and by words; *yadi*—if; *abhyupetam*—promised to be accepted; *kva ca*—whatever it may be; *sādhu asādhu vā*—whether honest or dishonest; *kṛtam mayā*—is done by Me; *vaḥ*—unto you; *vibhaje*—I shall give you the proper share; *sudhām*—nectar; *imām*—this.

TRANSLATION

Thereafter, the Supreme Personality of Godhead, having taken possession of the container of nectar, smiled slightly and spoke in attractive words. She said: My dear demons, if you accept whatever I may do, whether honest or dishonest, then I can take responsibility for dividing the nectar among you.

PURPORT

The Supreme Personality of Godhead cannot abide by anyone's dictation. Whatever He does is absolute. The demons, of course, were deluded by the illusory potency of the Supreme Personality of Godhead, and thus Mohinī-mūrti got them to promise that whatever She would do they would accept.

TEXT 13

इत्यभिव्याहृतं तस्या आकर्ण्यासुरपुङ्गवाः ।
अप्रमाणविदस्तस्यास्तत् तथेत्यन्वमंसत ॥ १३ ॥

ity abhivyāhṛtaṁ tasyā
ākarṇyāsura-puṅgavāḥ
apramāṇa-vidas tasyās
tat tathety anvamaṁsata

iti—thus; *abhivyāhṛtam*—the words that were spoken; *tasyāḥ*—Her; *ākarṇya*—after hearing; *asura-puṅgavāḥ*—the chiefs of the demons; *apramāṇa-vidaḥ*—because they were all foolish; *tasyāḥ*—of Her; *tat*—those words; *tathā*—let it be so; *iti*—thus; *anvamaṁsata*—agreed to accept.

TRANSLATION

The chiefs of the demons were not very expert in deciding things. Upon hearing the sweet words of Mohinī-mūrti, they immediately assented. "Yes," they answered. "What You have said is all right." Thus the demons agreed to accept Her decision.

TEXTS 14-15

अथोपोष्य कृतस्नाना हुत्वा च हविषानलम् ।
दत्त्वा गोविप्रभूतेभ्यः कृतस्वस्त्ययना द्विजैः ॥ १४ ॥
यथोपजोषं वासांसि परिधायाहतानि ते ।
कुशेषु प्राविशन्सर्वे प्रागग्रेष्वभिभूषिताः ॥ १५ ॥

athopoṣya kṛta-snānā
hutvā ca haviṣānalam
dattvā go-vipra-bhūtebhyaḥ
kṛta-svastyayanā dvijaiḥ

yathopajoṣaṁ vāsāṁsi
paridhāyāhatāni te
kuśeṣu prāviśan sarve
prāg-agreṣv abhibhūṣitāḥ

atha—thereafter; *upoṣya*—observing a fast; *kṛta-snānāḥ*—performing bathing; *hutvā*—offering oblations; *ca*—also; *haviṣā*—with clarified butter; *analam*—into the fire; *dattvā*—giving in charity; *go-vipra-bhūtebhyaḥ*—unto the cows, *brāhmaṇas* and living beings in general; *kṛta-svastyayanāḥ*—performing ritualistic ceremonies; *dvijaiḥ*—as dictated by the *brāhmaṇas; yathā-upajoṣam*—according to one's taste; *vāsāṁsi*—garments; *paridhāya*—putting on; *āhatāni*—first-class and new; *te*—all of them; *kuśeṣu*—on seats made of *kuśa* grass; *prāviśan*—sitting on them; *sarve*—all of them; *prāk-agreṣu*—facing east; *abhibhūṣitāḥ*—properly decorated with ornaments.

TRANSLATION

The demigods and demons then observed a fast. After bathing, they offered clarified butter and oblations into the fire and gave charity to the cows and to the brāhmaṇas and members of the other orders of society, namely the kṣatriyas, vaiśyas and śūdras, who were all rewarded as they deserved. Thereafter, the demigods and demons performed ritualistic ceremonies under the directions of the brāhmaṇas. Then they dressed themselves with new garments according to their own choice, decorated their bodies with ornaments, and sat facing east on seats made of kuśa grass.

PURPORT

The *Vedas* enjoin that for every ritualistic ceremony one must first become clean by bathing either in the water of the Ganges or Yamunā or in the sea. Then one may perform the ritualistic ceremony and offer clarified butter into the fire. In this verse the words *paridhāya āhatāni* are especially significant. A *sannyāsī* or a person about to perform a ritualistic ceremony should not dress himself in clothing sewn with a needle.

TEXTS 16-17

प्राङ्मुखेषूपविष्टेषु सुरेषु दितिजेषु च ।
धूपामोदितशालायां जुष्टायां माल्यदीपकैः ॥ १६ ॥
तस्यां नरेन्द्र करभोरुरुशद्दुकूल-
श्रोणीतटालसगतिर्मदविह्वलाक्षी ।
सा कूजती कनकनूपुरशिञ्जितेन
कुम्भस्तनी कलसपाणिरथाविवेश ॥ १७ ॥

prāṅ-mukheṣūpaviṣṭeṣu
sureṣu ditijeṣu ca
dhūpāmodita-śālāyāṁ
juṣṭayaṁ mālya-dīpakaiḥ

tasyāṁ narendra karabhorur uśad-dukūla-
śroṇī-taṭālasa-gatir mada-vihvalākṣī
sā kūjatī kanaka-nūpura-śiñjitena
kumbha-stanī kalasa-pāṇir athāviveśa

prāk-mukheṣu—facing east; *upaviṣṭeṣu*—were sitting on their respective seats; *sureṣu*—all the demigods; *diti-jeṣu*—the demons; *ca*—also; *dhūpa-āmodita-śālāyām*—in the arena, which was full of the smoke of incense; *juṣṭāyām*—fully decorated; *mālya-dīpakaiḥ*—with flower garlands and lamps; *tasyām*—in that arena; *nara-indra*—O King; *karabha-ūruḥ*—having thighs resembling the trunks of elephants; *uśat-dukūla*—dressed with a very beautiful sari; *śroṇī-taṭa*—because of big hips; *alasa-gatiḥ*—stepping very slowly; *mada-vihvala-akṣī*—whose eyes were restless because of youthful pride; *sā*—She; *kūjatī*—tinkling; *kanaka-nūpura*—of golden ankle bells; *śiñjitena*—with the sound; *kumbha-stanī*—a woman whose breasts were like water jugs; *kalasa-pāṇiḥ*—holding a waterpot in Her hand; *atha*—thus; *āviveśa*—entered the arena.

TRANSLATION

O King, as the demigods and demons sat facing east in an arena fully decorated with flower garlands and lamps and fragrant with the smoke of incense, that woman, dressed in a most beautiful sari, Her ankle bells tinkling, entered the arena, walking very slowly because of Her big, low hips. Her eyes were restless due to youthful pride, Her breasts were like water jugs, Her thighs resembled the trunks of elephants, and She carried a waterpot in Her hand.

TEXT 18

तां श्रीसखीं कनककुण्डलचारुकर्ण-
नासाकपोलवदनां परदेवताख्याम् ।
संवीक्ष्य संमुमुहुरुत्स्मितवीक्षणेन
देवासुरा विगलितस्तनपट्टिकान्ताम् ॥ १८ ॥

tāṁ śrī-sakhīṁ kanaka-kuṇḍala-cāru-karṇa-
nāsā-kapola-vadanāṁ para-devatākhyām
saṁvīkṣya sammumuhur utsmita-vīkṣaṇena
devāsurā vigalita-stana-paṭṭikāntām

tām—unto Her; *śrī-sakhīm*—appearing like a personal associate of the goddess of fortune; *kanaka-kuṇḍala*—with golden earrings; *cāru*—very beautiful; *karṇa*—ears; *nāsā*—nose; *kapola*—cheeks; *vadanām*—face; *para-devatā-ākhyām*—the Supreme Lord, the Personality of Godhead, appearing in that form; *saṁvīkṣya*—looking at Her; *sammumuhuḥ*—all of them became enchanted; *utsmita*—slightly smiling; *vīkṣaṇena*—glancing over them; *deva-asurāḥ*—all the demigods and demons; *vigalita-stana-paṭṭika-antām*—the border of the sari on the breasts moved slightly.

TRANSLATION

Her attractive nose and cheeks and Her ears, adorned with golden earrings, made Her face very beautiful. As She moved, Her sari's border on Her breasts moved slightly aside. When the demigods and demons saw these beautiful features of Mohinī-mūrti, who was glancing at them and slightly smiling, they were all completely enchanted.

PURPORT

Śrīla Viśvanātha Cakravartī Ṭhākura remarks here that Mohinī-mūrti is the Supreme Personality of Godhead in a feminine form and that the goddess of fortune is Her associate. This form assumed by the Personality of Godhead challenged the goddess of fortune. The goddess of fortune is beautiful, but if the Lord accepts the form of a woman, He surpasses the goddess of fortune in beauty. It is not that the goddess of fortune, being female, is the most beautiful. The Lord is so beautiful that He can excel any beautiful goddess of fortune by assuming a female form.

TEXT 19

असुराणां सुधादानं सर्पाणामिव दुर्नयम् ।
मत्वा जातिनृशंसानां न तां व्यभजदच्युतः ॥ १९ ॥

asurāṇāṁ sudhā-dānaṁ
sarpāṇām iva durnayam
matvā jāti-nṛśaṁsānāṁ
na tāṁ vyabhajad acyutaḥ

asurāṇām—of the demons; *sudhā-dānam*—giving of the nectar; *sarpāṇām*—of snakes; *iva*—like; *durnayam*—miscalculation; *matvā*—thinking like that; *jāti-nṛśaṁsānām*—of those who are by nature very envious; *na*—not; *tām*—the nectar; *vyabhajat*—delivered the share; *acyutaḥ*—the Supreme Personality of Godhead, who never falls down.

TRANSLATION

Demons are by nature crooked like snakes. Therefore, to distribute a share of the nectar to them was not at all feasible, since this would be as

dangerous as supplying milk to a snake. Considering this, the Supreme Personality of Godhead, who never falls down, did not deliver a share of nectar to the demons.

PURPORT

It is said, *sarpaḥ krūraḥ khalaḥ krūraḥ sarpāt krūrataraḥ khalaḥ:* "The snake is very crooked and envious, and so also is a person like a demon." *Mantrauṣadhi-vaśaḥ sarpaḥ khalaḥ kena nivāryate:* "One can bring a snake under control with *mantras,* herbs and drugs, but an envious and crooked person cannot be brought under control by any means." Considering this logic, the Supreme Personality of Godhead thought it unwise to distribute nectar to the demons.

TEXT 20

कल्पयित्वा पृथक् पङ्क्तीरुभयेषां जगत्पतिः ।
तांश्चोपवेशयामास स्वेषु स्वेषु च पङ्क्तिषु ॥ २० ॥

kalpayitvā pṛthak paṅktīr
ubhayeṣāṁ jagat-patiḥ
tāṁś copaveśayām āsa
sveṣu sveṣu ca paṅktiṣu

kalpayitvā—after arranging; *pṛthak paṅktīḥ*—different seats; *ubhayeṣām*—of both the demigods and the demons; *jagat-patiḥ*—the master of the universe; *tān*—all of them; *ca*—and; *upaveśayām āsa*—seated; *sveṣu sveṣu*—in their own places; *ca*—also; *paṅktiṣu*—all in order.

TRANSLATION

The Supreme Personality of Godhead as Mohinī-mūrti, the master of the universe, arranged separate lines of sitting places and seated the demigods and demons according to their positions.

TEXT 21

दैत्यान्गृहीतकलसो वञ्चयन्नुपसञ्चरैः ।
दूरस्थान् पाययामास जरामृत्युहरां सुधाम् ॥ २१ ॥

daityān gṛhīta-kalaso
vañcayann upasañcaraiḥ

dūra-sthān pāyayām āsa
jarā-mṛtyu-harāṁ sudhām

daityān—the demons; *gṛhīta-kalasaḥ*—the Lord, who bore the container of nectar; *vañcayan*—by cheating; *upasañcaraiḥ*—with sweet words; *dūra-sthān*—the demigods, who were sitting at a distant place; *pāyayām āsa*—made them drink; *jarā-mṛtyu-harām*—which can counteract invalidity, old age and death; *sudhām*—such nectar.

TRANSLATION

Taking the container of nectar in Her hands, She first approached the demons, satisfied them with sweet words and thus cheated them of their share of the nectar. Then She administered the nectar to the demigods, who were sitting at a distant place, to make them free from invalidity, old age and death.

PURPORT

Mohinī-mūrti, the Personality of Godhead, gave the demigods seats at a distance. Then She approached the demons and spoke with them very graciously, so that they thought themselves very fortunate to talk with Her. Since Mohinī-mūrti had seated the demigods at a distant place, the demons thought that the demigods would get only a little of the nectar and that Mohinī-mūrti was so pleased with the demons that She would give the demons all the nectar. The words *vañcayann upasañcaraiḥ* indicate that the Lord's whole policy was to cheat the demons simply by speaking sweet words. The Lord's intention was to distribute the nectar only to the demigods.

TEXT 22

ते पालयन्तः समयमसुराः स्वकृतं नृप ।
तूष्णीमासन्कृतस्नेहाः स्त्रीविवादजुगुप्सया ॥ २२ ॥

te pālayantaḥ samayam
asurāḥ sva-kṛtaṁ nṛpa
tūṣṇīm āsan kṛta-snehāḥ
strī-vivāda-jugupsayā

te—the demons; *pālayantaḥ*—keeping in order; *samayam*—equilibrium; *asurāḥ*—the demons; *sva-kṛtam*—made by them; *nṛpa*—O King; *tūṣṇīm āsan*—remained silent; *kṛta-snehāḥ*—because of having developed attachment to Mohinī-mūrti; *strī-vivāda*—disagreeing with a woman; *jugupsayā*—because of thinking such an action as abominable.

TRANSLATION

O King, since the demons had promised to accept whatever the woman did, whether just or unjust, now, to keep this promise, to show their equilibrium and to save themselves from fighting with a woman, they remained silent.

TEXT 23

तस्यां कृतातिप्रणयाः प्रणयापायकातराः ।
बहुमानेन चाबद्धा नोचुः किञ्चन विप्रियम् ॥ २३ ॥

tasyāṁ kṛtātipraṇayāḥ
praṇayāpāya-kātarāḥ
bahu-mānena cābaddhā
nocuḥ kiñcana vipriyam

tasyām—of Mohinī-mūrti; *kṛta-ati-praṇayāḥ*—because of staunch friendship; *praṇaya-apāya-kātarāḥ*—being afraid that their friendship with Her would be broken; *bahu-mānena*—by great respect and honor; *ca*—also; *ābaddhāḥ*—being too attached to Her; *na*—not; *ūcuḥ*—they said; *kiñcana*—even the slightest thing; *vipriyam*—by which Mohinī-mūrti might be displeased with them.

TRANSLATION

The demons had developed affection for Mohinī-mūrti and a kind of faith in Her, and they were afraid of disturbing their relationship. Therefore they showed respect and honor to Her words and did not say anything that might disturb their friendship with Her.

PURPORT

The demons were so captivated by the tricks and friendly words of Mohinī-mūrti that although the demigods were served first, the demons were pacified merely by sweet words. The Lord said to the demons, "The demigods are very miserly and are excessively anxious to take the nectar first. So let them have it first. Since you are not like them you can wait a little longer. You are all heroes and are so pleased with Me. It is better for you to wait until after the demigods drink."

TEXT 24

देवलिङ्गप्रतिच्छन्नः स्वर्भानुर्देवसंसदि ।
प्रविष्टः सोममपिबच्चन्द्रार्काभ्यां च सूचितः ॥ २४ ॥

deva-liṅga-praticchannaḥ
svarbhānur deva-saṁsadi
praviṣṭaḥ somam apibac
candrārkābhyāṁ ca sūcitaḥ

deva-liṅga-praticchannaḥ—covering himself with the dress of a demigod; *svarbhānuḥ*—Rāhu (who attacks and eclipses the sun and moon); *deva-saṁsadi*—in the group of the demigods; *praviṣṭaḥ*—having entered; *somam*—the nectar; *apibat*—drank; *candra-arkābhyām*—by both the moon and the sun; *ca*—and; *sūcitaḥ*—was pointed out.

TRANSLATION

Rāhu, the demon who causes eclipses of the sun and moon, covered himself with the dress of a demigod and thus entered the assembly of the demigods and drank nectar without being detected by anyone, even by the Supreme Personality of Godhead. The moon and the sun, however, because of permanent animosity toward Rāhu, understood the situation. Thus Rāhu was detected.

PURPORT

The Supreme Personality of Godhead, Mohinī-mūrti, was able to bewilder all the demons, but Rāhu was so clever that he was not bewildered. Rāhu could understand that Mohinī-mūrti was cheating the demons, and therefore he changed his dress, disguised himself as a demigod, and sat down in the assembly of the demigods. Here one may ask why the Supreme Personality of Godhead could not detect Rāhu. The reason is that the Lord wanted to show the effects of drinking nectar. This will be revealed in the following verses. The moon and sun, however, were always alert in regard to Rāhu. Thus when Rāhu entered the assembly of the demigods, the moon and sun immediately detected him, and then the Supreme Personality of Godhead also became aware of him.

TEXT 25

चक्रेण क्षुरधारेण जहार पिबतः शिरः ।
हरिस्तस्य कबन्धस्तु सुधयाप्लावितोऽपतत् ॥ २५ ॥

cakreṇa kṣura-dhāreṇa
jahāra pibataḥ śiraḥ
haris tasya kabandhas tu
sudhayāplāvito 'patat

cakreṇa—by the disc; *kṣura-dhāreṇa*—which was sharp like a razor; *jahāra*—cut off; *pibataḥ*—while drinking nectar; *śiraḥ*—the head; *hariḥ*—the Supreme Personality of Godhead; *tasya*—of that Rāhu; *kabandhaḥ tu*—but the headless body; *sudhayā*—by the nectar; *aplāvitaḥ*—without being touched; *apatat*—immediately fell dead.

TRANSLATION

The Supreme Personality of Godhead, Hari, using His disc, which was sharp like a razor, at once cut off Rāhu's head. When Rāhu's head was severed from his body, the body, being untouched by the nectar, could not survive.

PURPORT

When the Personality of Godhead, Mohinī-mūrti, severed Rāhu's head from his body, the head remained alive although the body died. Rāhu had been drinking nectar through his mouth, and before the nectar entered his body, his head was cut off. Thus Rāhu's head remained alive whereas the body died. This wonderful act performed by the Lord was meant to show that nectar is miraculous ambrosia.

TEXT 26

शिरस्त्वमरतां नीतमजो ग्रहमचीक्लृपत् ।
यस्तु पर्वणि चन्द्रार्कावभिधावति वैरधीः ॥ २६ ॥

śiras tv amaratāṁ nītam
ajo graham acīkḷpat
yas tu parvaṇi candrārkāv
abhidhāvati vaira-dhīḥ

śiraḥ—the head; *tu*—of course; *amaratām*—immortality; *nītam*—having obtained; *ajaḥ*—Lord Brahmā; *graham*—as one of the planets; *acīkḷpat*—recognized; *yaḥ*—the same Rāhu; *tu*—indeed; *parvaṇi*—during the periods of the full moon and dark moon; *candra-arkau*—both the moon and the sun; *abhidhāvati*—chases; *vaira-dhīḥ*—because of animosity.

TRANSLATION

Rāhu's head, however, having been touched by the nectar, became immortal. Thus Lord Brahmā accepted Rāhu's head as one of the planets. Since Rāhu is an eternal enemy of the moon and the sun, he always tries to attack them on the nights of the full moon and the dark moon.

PURPORT

Since Rāhu had become immortal, Lord Brahmā accepted him as one of the *grahas,* or planets, like the moon and the sun. Rāhu, however, being an eternal enemy of the moon and sun, attacks them periodically during the nights of the full moon and the dark moon.

TEXT 27

पीतप्रायेऽमृते देवैर्भगवान् लोकभावनः ।
पश्यतामसुरेन्द्राणां स्वं रूपं जगृहे हरिः ॥ २७ ॥

pīta-prāye 'mṛte devair
bhagavān loka-bhāvanaḥ
paśyatām asurendrāṇāṁ
svaṁ rūpaṁ jagṛhe hariḥ

pīta-prāye—when almost finished being drunk; *amṛte*—the nectar; *devaiḥ*—by the demigods; *bhagavān*—the Supreme Personality of Godhead as Mohinī-mūrti; *loka-bhāvanaḥ*—the maintainer and well-wisher of the three worlds; *paśyatām*—in the presence of; *asura-indrāṇām*—all the demons, with their chiefs; *svam*—own; *rūpam*—form; *jagṛhe*—manifested; *hariḥ*—the Supreme Personality of Godhead.

TRANSLATION

The Supreme Personality of Godhead is the best friend and well-wisher of the three worlds. Thus when the demigods had almost finished drinking the nectar, the Lord, in the presence of all the demons, disclosed His original form.

TEXT 28

एवं सुरासुरगणाः समदेशकाल-
हेत्वर्थकर्ममतयोऽपि फले विकल्पाः ।
तत्रामृतं सुरगणाः फलमञ्जसापु-
र्यत्पादपङ्कजरजःश्रयणान्न दैत्याः ॥ २८ ॥

evaṁ surāsura-gaṇāḥ sama-deśa-kāla-
hetv-artha-karma-matayo 'pi phale vikalpāḥ
tatrāmṛtaṁ sura-gaṇāḥ phalam añjasāpur
yat-pāda-paṅkaja-rajaḥ-śrayaṇān na daityāḥ

evam—thus; *sura*—the demigods; *asura-gaṇāḥ*—and the demons; *sama*—equal; *deśa*—place; *kāla*—time; *hetu*—cause; *artha*—objective; *karma*—activities; *matayaḥ*—ambition; *api*—although one; *phale*—in the result; *vikalpāḥ*—not equal; *tatra*—thereupon; *amṛtam*—nectar; *sura-gaṇāḥ*—the demigods; *phalam*—the result; *añjasā*—easily, totally or directly; *āpuḥ*—achieved; *yat*—because of; *pāda-paṅkaja*—of the lotus feet of the Supreme Personality of Godhead; *rajaḥ*—of the saffron dust; *śrayaṇāt*—because of receiving benedictions or taking shelter; *na*—not; *daityāḥ*—the demons.

TRANSLATION

The place, the time, the cause, the purpose, the activity and the ambition were all the same for both the demigods and the demons, but the demigods achieved one result and the demons another. Because the demigods are always under the shelter of the dust of the Lord's lotus feet, they could very easily drink the nectar and get its result. The demons, however, not having sought shelter at the lotus feet of the Lord, were unable to achieve the result they desired.

PURPORT

In *Bhagavad-gītā* (4.11) it is said, *ye yathā māṁ prapadyante tāṁs tathaiva bhajāmy aham:* the Supreme Personality of Godhead is the supreme judge who rewards or punishes different persons according to their surrender unto His lotus feet. Therefore it can actually be seen that although *karmīs* and *bhaktas* may work in the same place, at the same time, with the same energy and with the same ambition, they achieve different results. The *karmīs* transmigrate through different bodies in the cycle of birth and death, sometimes going upward and sometimes downward, thus suffering the results of their actions in the *karma-cakra,* the cycle of birth and death. The devotees, however, because of fully surrendering at the lotus feet of the Lord, are never baffled in their attempts. Although externally they work almost like the *karmīs,* the devotees go back home, back to Godhead, and achieve success in every effort. The demons or atheists have faith in their own endeavors, but although they work very hard day and night, they cannot get any more than their destiny. The devotees, however, can surpass the reactions of *karma* and achieve wonderful results, even without effort. It is also said, *phalena paricīyate:* one's success or defeat in any activity is understood by its result. There are many *karmīs* in the dress of devotees, but the Supreme Personality of Godhead can detect their purpose. The *karmīs* want to use the property of the Lord for their selfish sense gratification, but a devotee endeavors to use the Lord's property for God's service. Therefore a devotee is always distinct from the *karmīs,* although the *karmīs* may dress like devotees. As confirmed in *Bhagavad-gītā* (3.9), *yajñārthāt karmaṇo 'nyatra loko 'yaṁ karma-bandhanaḥ.* One who works for Lord Viṣṇu is free from this material world, and after giving up his body he goes back home, back to Godhead. A *karmī,* however, although externally working like a devotee, is entangled in his nondevotional activity, and thus he suffers the tribulations of material existence. Thus from the results achieved by the *karmīs* and devotees, one can understand the presence of the Supreme Personality of Godhead, who acts differently for the *karmīs* and *jñānīs* than for the devotees. The author of *Śrī Caitanya-caritāmṛta* therefore says:

kṛṣṇa-bhakta—niṣkāma, ataeva 'śānta'
bhukti-mukti-siddhi-kāmī—sakali 'aśānta'

The *karmīs* who desire sense gratification, the *jñānīs* who aspire for the liberation of merging into the existence of the Supreme, and the *yogīs* who seek material success in mystic power are all restless, and ultimately they are baffled. But the devotee, who does not expect any personal benefit and whose only ambition is to spread the glories of the Supreme Personality of Godhead, is blessed with all the auspicious results of *bhakti-yoga,* without hard labor.

TEXT 29

यद् युज्यतेऽसुवसुकर्ममनोवचोभि-
र्देहात्मजादिषु नृभिस्तदसत् पृथक्त्वात् ।

तैरेव सद् भवति यत् क्रियतेऽपृथक्त्वात्
सर्वस्य तद् भवति मूलनिषेचनं यत् ॥ २९ ॥

yad yujyate 'su-vasu-karma-mano-vacobhir
dehātmajādiṣu nṛbhis tad asat pṛthaktvāt
tair eva sad bhavati yat kriyate 'pṛthaktvāt
sarvasya tad bhavati mūla-niṣecanaṁ yat

yat—whatever; *yujyate*—is performed; *asu*—for the protection of one's life; *vasu*—protection of wealth; *karma*—activities; *manaḥ*—by the acts of the mind; *vacobhiḥ*—by the acts of words; *deha-ātma-ja-ādiṣu*—for the sake of one's personal body or family, etc., with reference to the body; *nṛbhiḥ*—by the human beings; *tat*—that; *asat*—impermanent, transient; *pṛthaktvāt*—because of separation from the Supreme Personality of Godhead; *taiḥ*—by the same activities; *eva*—indeed; *sat bhavati*—becomes factual and permanent; *yat*—which; *kriyate*—is performed; *apṛthaktvāt*—because of nonseparation; *sarvasya*—for everyone; *tat bhavati*—becomes beneficial; *mūla-niṣecanam*—exactly like pouring water on the root of a tree; *yat*—which.

TRANSLATION

In human society there are various activities performed for the protection of one's wealth and life by one's words, one's mind and one's actions, but they are all performed for one's personal or extended sense gratification with reference to the body. All these activities are baffled because of being separate from devotional service. But when the same activities are performed for the satisfaction of the Lord, the beneficial results are distributed to everyone, just as water poured on the root of a tree is distributed throughout the entire tree.

PURPORT

This is the distinction between materialistic activities and activities performed in Kṛṣṇa consciousness. The entire world is active, and this includes the *karmīs,* the *jñānīs,* the *yogīs* and the *bhaktas.* However, all activities except those of the *bhaktas,* the devotees, end in bafflement and a waste of time and energy. *Moghāśā mogha-karmāṇo mogha jñānā vicetasaḥ:* if one is not a devotee, his hopes, his activities and his knowledge are all baffled. A nondevotee works for his personal sense gratification or for the sense gratification of his family, society, community or nation, but because all such activities are separate from the Supreme Personality of Godhead, they are considered *asat.* The word *asat* means bad or temporary, and *sat* means permanent and good. Activities performed for the satisfaction of Kṛṣṇa are permanent and good, but *asat* activity, although sometimes celebrated as philanthropy, altruism, nationalism, this "ism" or that "ism," will never produce any permanent result and is therefore all bad. Even a little work done in Kṛṣṇa consciousness is a permanent asset and is all-good because it is done for Kṛṣṇa, the all-good Supreme Personality of Godhead, who is everyone's friend (*suhṛdaṁ sarva-bhūtānām*). The Supreme Personality of Godhead is the only enjoyer and proprietor of everything (*bhoktāraṁ yajña-tapasāṁ sarva-loka-maheśvaram*). Therefore any activity performed for the Supreme Lord is permanent. As a result of such activities, the performer is immediately recognized. *Na ca tasmān manuṣyeṣu kaścin me priya-kṛttamaḥ.* Such a devotee, because of full knowledge of the Supreme Personality of Godhead, is immediately transcendental, although he may superficially appear to be engaged in materialistic activities. The only distinction between materialistic activity and spiritual activity is that material activity is performed only to satisfy one's own senses whereas spiritual activity is meant to satisfy the transcendental senses of the Supreme Personality of Godhead. By spiritual activity everyone factually benefits, whereas by materialistic activity no one benefits and instead one becomes entangled in the laws of *karma.*

Thus ends the Bhaktivedanta purports of the Eighth Canto, Ninth Chapter, of the Śrīmad-Bhāgavatam, *entitled "The Lord Incarnates as Mohinī-mūrti."*

CHAPTER TEN

The Battle Between the Demigods and the Demons

The summary of Chapter Ten is as follows. Because of envy, the fight between the demons and the demigods continued. When the demigods were almost defeated by demoniac maneuvers and became morose, Lord Viṣṇu appeared among them.

Both the demigods and the demons are expert in activities involving the material energy, but the demigods are devotees of the Lord, whereas the demons are just the opposite. The demigods and demons churned the ocean of milk to get nectar from it, but the demons, not being devotees of the Lord, could derive no profit. After feeding nectar to the demigods, Lord Viṣṇu returned to His abode on the back of Garuḍa, but the demons, being most aggrieved, again declared war against the demigods. Bali Mahārāja, the son of Virocana, became the commander in chief of the demons. In the beginning of the battle, the demigods prepared to defeat the demons. Indra, King of heaven, fought with Bali, and other demigods, like Vāyu, Agni and Varuṇa, fought against other leaders of the demons. In this fight the demons were defeated, and to save themselves from death they began to manifest many illusions through material maneuvers, killing many soldiers on the side of the demigods. The demigods, finding no other recourse, surrendered again to the Supreme Personality of Godhead, Viṣṇu, who then appeared and counteracted all the illusions presented by the jugglery of the demons. Heroes among the demons such as Kālanemi, Mālī, Sumālī and Mālyavān fought the Supreme Personality of Godhead and were all killed by the Lord. The demigods were thus freed from all dangers.

TEXT 1

श्रीशुक उवाच

इति दानवदैतेया नाविन्दन्नमृतं नृप ।
युक्ताः कर्मणि यत्ताश्च वासुदेवपराङ्मुखाः ॥ १ ॥

śrī-śuka uvāca
iti dānava-daiteyā
nāvindann amṛtaṁ nṛpa
yuktāḥ karmaṇi yattāś ca
vāsudeva-parāṅmukhāḥ

śrī-śukaḥ uvāca—Śrī Śukadeva Gosvāmī said; *iti*—thus; *dānava-daiteyāḥ*—the *asuras* and the demons; *na*—not; *avindan*—achieved (the desired result); *amṛtam*—nectar; *nṛpa*—O King; *yuktāḥ*—all being combined; *karmaṇi*—in the churning; *yattāḥ*—engaged with full attention and effort; *ca*—and; *vāsudeva*—of the Supreme Personality of Godhead, Kṛṣṇa; *parāṅ-mukhāḥ*—because of being nondevotees.

TRANSLATION

Śukadeva Gosvāmī said: O King, the demons and Daityas all engaged with full attention and effort in churning the ocean, but because they were not devotees of Vāsudeva, the Supreme Personality of Godhead, Kṛṣṇa, they were not able to drink the nectar.

TEXT 2

साधयित्वामृतं राजन्पाययित्वा स्वकान्सुरान् ।
पश्यतां सर्वभूतानां ययौ गरुडवाहनः ॥ २ ॥

sādhayitvāmṛtaṁ rājan
pāyayitvā svakān surān
paśyatāṁ sarva-bhūtānāṁ
yayau garuḍa-vāhanaḥ

sādhayitvā—after executing; *amṛtam*—generation of the nectar; *rājan*—O King; *pāyayitvā*—and feeding; *svakān*—to His own devotees; *surān*—to the demigods; *paśyatām*—in the presence of; *sarva-bhūtānām*—all living entities; *yayau*—went away; *garuḍa-vāhanaḥ*—the Supreme Personality of Godhead, carried by Garuḍa.

TRANSLATION

O King, after the Supreme Personality of Godhead had brought to completion the affairs of churning the ocean and feeding the nectar to the demigods, who are His dear devotees, He left the presence of them all and was carried by Garuḍa to His own abode.

TEXT 3

सपत्नानां परामृद्धिं दृष्ट्वा ते दितिनन्दनाः ।
अमृष्यमाणा उत्पेतुर्देवान्प्रत्युद्यतायुधाः ॥ ३ ॥

sapatnānāṁ parām ṛddhiṁ
dṛṣṭvā te diti-nandanāḥ
amṛṣyamāṇā utpetur
devān pratyudyatāyudhāḥ

sapatnānām—of their rivals, the demigods; *parām*—the best; *ṛddhim*—opulence; *dṛṣṭvā*—observing; *te*—all of them; *diti-nandanāḥ*—the sons of Diti, the Daityas; *amṛṣyamāṇāḥ*—being intolerant; *utpetuḥ*—ran toward (just to create a disturbance); *devān*—the demigods; *pratyudyata-āyudhāḥ*—their weapons raised.

TRANSLATION

Seeing the victory of the demigods, the demons became intolerant of their superior opulence. Thus they began to march toward the demigods with raised weapons.

TEXT 4

ततः सुरगणाः सर्वे सुधया पीतयैधिताः ।
प्रतिसंयुयुधुः शस्त्रैर्नारायणपदाश्रयाः ॥ ४ ॥

tataḥ sura-gaṇāḥ sarve
sudhayā pītayaidhitāḥ
pratisaṁyuyudhuḥ śastrair
nārāyaṇa-padāśrayāḥ

tataḥ—thereafter; *sura-gaṇāḥ*—the demigods; *sarve*—all of them; *sudhayā*—by the nectar; *pītayā*—which had been drunk; *edhitāḥ*—being enlivened by such drinking; *pratisaṁyuyudhuḥ*—they counterattacked the demons; *śastraiḥ*—by regular weapons; *nārāyaṇa-pada-āśrayāḥ*—their real weapon being shelter at the lotus feet of Nārāyaṇa.

TRANSLATION

Thereafter, being enlivened because of drinking the nectar, the demigods, who are always at the shelter of the lotus feet of Nārāyaṇa, used their various weapons to counterattack the demons in a fighting spirit.

TEXT 5

तत्र दैवासुरो नाम रणः परमदारुणः ।
रोधस्युदन्वतो राजंस्तुमुलो रोमहर्षणः ॥ ५ ॥

tatra daivāsuro nāma
raṇaḥ parama-dāruṇaḥ
rodhasy udanvato rājaṁs
tumulo roma-harṣaṇaḥ

tatra—there (at the beach of the ocean of milk); *daiva*—the demigods; *asuraḥ*—the demons; *nāma*—as they are celebrated; *raṇaḥ*—fighting; *parama*—very much; *dāruṇaḥ*—fierce; *rodhasi*—on the beach of the sea; *udanvataḥ*—of the ocean of milk; *rājan*—O King; *tumulaḥ*—tumultuous; *roma-harṣaṇaḥ*—hair standing on the body.

TRANSLATION

O King, a fierce battle on the beach of the ocean of milk ensued between the demigods and the demons. The fighting was so terrible that simply hearing about it would make the hair on one's body stand on end.

TEXT 6

तत्रान्योन्यं सपत्नास्ते संरब्धमनसो रणे ।
समासाद्यासिभिर्बाणैर्निजघ्नुर्विविधायुधैः ॥ ६ ॥

tatrānyonyaṁ sapatnās te
saṁrabdha-manaso raṇe
samāsādyāsibhir bāṇair
nijaghnur vividhāyudhaiḥ

tatra—thereupon; *anyonyam*—one another; *sapatnāḥ*—all of them becoming fighters; *te*—they; *saṁrabdha*—very angry; *manasaḥ*—within their minds; *raṇe*—in that battle; *samāsādya*—getting the opportunity to fight between themselves; *asibhiḥ*—with swords; *bāṇaiḥ*—with arrows; *nijaghnuḥ*—began to beat one another; *vividha-āyudhaiḥ*—with varieties of weapons.

TRANSLATION

Both parties in that fight were extremely angry at heart, and in enmity they beat one another with swords, arrows and varieties of other weapons.

PURPORT

There are always two kinds of men in this universe, not only on this planet but also in higher planetary systems. All the kings dominating planets like the sun and moon also have enemies like Rāhu. It is because of occasional attacks upon the sun and moon by Rāhu that eclipses take place. The fighting between the demons and demigods is perpetual; it cannot be stopped unless intelligent persons from both sides take to Kṛṣṇa consciousness.

TEXT 7

शङ्खतूर्यमृदङ्गानां भेरीडमरिणां महान् ।
हस्त्यश्वरथपत्तीनां नदतां निस्वनोऽभवत् ॥ ७ ॥

śaṅkha-tūrya-mṛdaṅgānāṁ
bherī-ḍamariṇāṁ mahān
hasty-aśva-ratha-pattīnāṁ
nadatāṁ nisvano 'bhavat

śaṅkha—of conchshells; *tūrya*—of big bugles; *mṛdaṅgānām*—and of drums; *bherī*—of bugles; *ḍamariṇām*—of kettledrums; *mahān*—great and tumultuous; *hasti*—of elephants; *aśva*—of horses; *ratha-pattīnām*—of fighters on chariots or on the ground; *nadatām*—all of them making sounds together; *nisvanaḥ*—a tumultuous sound; *abhavat*—so became.

TRANSLATION

The sounds of the conchshells, bugles, drums, bherīs and ḍamarīs [kettledrums], as well as the sounds made by the elephants, horses and soldiers, who were both on chariots and on foot, were tumultuous.

TEXT 8

रथिनो रथिभिस्तत्र पत्तिभिः सह पत्तयः ।
हया हयैरिभाश्चेभैः समसज्जन्त संयुगे ॥ ८ ॥

rathino rathibhis tatra
pattibhiḥ saha pattayaḥ
hayā hayair ibhāś cebhaiḥ
samasajjanta saṁyuge

rathinaḥ—fighters on chariots; *rathibhiḥ*—with the charioteers of the enemy; *tatra*—in the battlefield; *pattibhiḥ*—with the infantry soldiers; *saha*—with; *pattayaḥ*—the infantry of the enemy soldiers; *hayāḥ*—the horses; *hayaiḥ*—with the enemy's soldiers; *ibhāḥ*—the soldiers fighting on the backs of elephants; *ca*—and; *ibhaiḥ*—with the enemy's soldiers on the backs of elephants; *samasajjanta*—began to fight together on an equal level; *saṁyuge*—on the battlefield.

TRANSLATION

On that battlefield, the charioteers fought with the opposing charioteers, the infantry soldiers with the opposing infantry, the soldiers on horseback with the opposing soldiers on horseback, and the soldiers on the backs of elephants with the enemy soldiers on elephants. In this way, the fighting took place between equals.

TEXT 9

उष्ट्रैः केचिदिभैः केचिदपरे युयुधुः खरैः ।
केचिद् गौरमुखैर्ऋक्षैर्द्वीपिभिर्हरिभिर्भटाः ॥ ९ ॥

uṣṭraiḥ kecid ibhaiḥ kecid
apare yuyudhuḥ kharaiḥ
kecid gaura-mukhair ṛkṣair
dvīpibhir haribhir bhaṭāḥ

uṣṭraiḥ—on the backs of camels; *kecit*—some persons; *ibhaiḥ*—on the backs of elephants; *kecit*—some persons; *apare*—others; *yuyudhuḥ*—engaged in fighting; *kharaiḥ*—on the backs of asses; *kecit*—some persons; *gaura-mukhaiḥ*—on white-faced monkeys; *ṛkṣaiḥ*—on red-faced monkeys; *dvīpibhiḥ*—on the backs of tigers; *haribhiḥ*—on the backs of lions; *bhaṭāḥ*—all the soldiers engaged in this way.

TRANSLATION

Some soldiers fought on the backs of camels, some on the backs of elephants, some on asses, some on white-faced and red-faced monkeys, some on tigers and some on lions. In this way, they all engaged in fighting.

TEXTS 10-12

गृध्रैः कङ्कैर्बकैरन्ये श्येनभासैस्तिमिङ्गिलैः ।
शरभैर्महिषैः खड्गैर्गोवृषैर्गवयारुणैः ॥ १० ॥
शिवाभिराखुभिः केचित् कृकलासैः शशैर्नरैः ।
बस्तैरेके कृष्णसारैर्हंसैरन्ये च सूकरैः ॥ ११ ॥
अन्ये जलस्थलखगैः सत्त्वैर्विकृतविग्रहैः ।
सेनयोरुभयो राजन्विविशुस्तेऽग्रतोऽग्रतः ॥ १२ ॥

gṛdhraiḥ kaṅkair bakair anye
śyena-bhāsais timiṅgilaiḥ
śarabhair mahiṣaiḥ khaḍgair
go-vṛṣair gavayāruṇaiḥ

śivābhir ākhubhiḥ kecit
kṛkalāsaiḥ śaśair naraiḥ
bastair eke kṛṣṇa-sārair
haṁsair anye ca sūkaraiḥ

anye jala-sthala-khagaiḥ
sattvair vikṛta-vigrahaiḥ
senayor ubhayo rājan
viviśus te 'grato 'grataḥ

gṛdhraiḥ—on the backs of vultures; *kaṅkaiḥ*—on the backs of eagles; *bakaiḥ*—on the backs of ducks; *anye*—others; *śyena*—on the backs of hawks; *bhāsaiḥ*—on the backs of *bhāsas; timiṅgilaiḥ*—on the backs of big fish known as *timiṅgilas; śarabhaiḥ*—on the backs of *śarabhas; mahiṣaiḥ*—on the backs of buffalo; *khaḍgaiḥ*—on the backs of rhinoceroses; *go*—on the backs of cows; *vṛṣaiḥ*—on the backs of bulls; *gavaya-aruṇaiḥ*—on the backs of *gavayas* and *aruṇas; śivābhiḥ*—on the backs of jackals; *ākhubhiḥ*—on the backs of big rats; *kecit*—some persons; *kṛkalāsaiḥ*—on the backs of big lizards; *śaśaiḥ*—on the backs of big rabbits; *naraiḥ*—on the backs of human beings; *bastaiḥ*—on the backs of goats; *eke*—some; *kṛṣṇa-sāraiḥ*—on the backs of black deer; *haṁsaiḥ*—on the backs of swans; *anye*—others; *ca*—also; *sūkaraiḥ*—on the backs of boars; *anye*—others; *jala-sthala-khagaiḥ*—animals moving on the water, on land and in the sky; *sattvaiḥ*—by creatures being used as vehicles; *vikṛta*—are deformed; *vigrahaiḥ*—by such animals whose bodies; *senayoḥ*—

of the two parties of soldiers; *ubhayoḥ*—of both; *rājan*—O King; *viviśuḥ*—entered; *te*—all of them; *agrataḥ agrataḥ*—going forward face to face.

TRANSLATION

O King, some soldiers fought on the backs of vultures, eagles, ducks, hawks and bhāsa birds. Some fought on the backs of timiṅgilas, which can devour huge whales, some on the backs of śarabhas, and some on buffalo, rhinoceroses, cows, bulls, jungle cows and aruṇas. Others fought on the backs of jackals, rats, lizards, rabbits, human beings, goats, black deer, swans and boars. In this way, mounted on animals of the water, land and sky, including animals with deformed bodies, both armies faced each other and went forward.

TEXTS 13-15

चित्रध्वजपटै राजन्नातपत्रैः सितामलैः ।
महाधनैर्वज्रदण्डैर्व्यजनैर्बार्हचामरैः ॥ १३ ॥
वातोद्धूतोत्तरोष्णीषैरर्चिर्भिर्वर्मभूषणैः ।
स्फुरद्भिर्विशदैः शस्त्रैः सुतरां सूर्यरश्मिभिः ॥ १४ ॥
देवदानववीराणां ध्वजिन्यौ पाण्डुनन्दन ।
रेजतुर्वीरमालाभिर्यादसामिव सागरौ ॥ १५ ॥

citra-dhvaja-paṭai rājann
ātapatraiḥ sitāmalaiḥ
mahā-dhanair vajra-daṇḍair
vyajanair bārha-cāmaraiḥ

vātoddhūtottaroṣṇīṣair
arcirbhir varma-bhūṣaṇaiḥ
sphuradbhir viśadaiḥ śastraiḥ
sutarāṁ sūrya-raśmibhiḥ

deva-dānava-vīrāṇāṁ
dhvajinyau pāṇḍu-nandana
rejatur vīra-mālābhir
yādasām iva sāgarau

citra-dhvaja-paṭaiḥ—with very nicely decorated flags and canopies; *rājan*—O King; *ātapatraiḥ*—with umbrellas for protection from the sunshine; *sita-*

amalaiḥ—most of them very clean and white; *mahā-dhanaiḥ*—by very valuable; *vajra-daṇḍaiḥ*—with rods made of valuable jewels and pearls; *vyajanaiḥ*—with fans; *bārha-cāmaraiḥ*—with other fans made of peacock feathers; *vāta-uddhūta*—flapping with the breeze; *uttara-uṣṇīṣaiḥ*—with upper and lower garments; *arcirbhiḥ*—by the effulgence; *varma-bhūṣaṇaiḥ*—with ornaments and shields; *sphuradbhiḥ*—shining; *viśadaiḥ*—sharp and clean; *śastraiḥ*—with weapons; *sutarām*—excessively; *sūrya-raśmibhiḥ*—with the dazzling illumination of the sunshine; *deva-dānava-vīrāṇām*—of all the heroes of the parties of both the demons and the demigods; *dhvajinyau*—the two parties of soldiers, each one bearing his own flag; *pāṇḍu-nandana*—O descendant of Mahārāja Pāṇḍu; *rejatuḥ*—distinctly recognized; *vīra-mālābhiḥ*—with garlands used by heroes; *yādasām*—of aquatics; *iva*—just like; *sāgarau*—two oceans.

TRANSLATION

O King, O descendant of Mahārāja Pāṇḍu, the soldiers of both the demigods and demons were decorated by canopies, colorful flags, and umbrellas with handles made of valuable jewels and pearls. They were further decorated by fans made of peacock feathers and by other fans also. The soldiers, their upper and lower garments waving in the breeze, naturally looked very beautiful, and in the light of the glittering sunshine their shields, ornaments and sharp, clean weapons appeared dazzling. Thus the ranks of soldiers seemed like two oceans with bands of aquatics.

TEXTS 16-18

वैरोचनो बलिः संख्ये सोऽसुराणां चमूपतिः ।
यानं वैहायसं नाम कामगं मयनिर्मितम् ॥ १६ ॥
सर्वसाङ्ग्रामिकोपेतं सर्वाश्चर्यमयं प्रभो ।
अप्रतर्क्यमनिर्देश्यं दृश्यमानमदर्शनम् ॥ १७ ॥
आस्थितस्तद् विमानाग्र्यं सर्वानीकाधिपैर्वृतः ।
बालव्यजनछत्राग्र्यै रेजे चन्द्र इवोदये ॥ १८ ॥

vairocano baliḥ saṅkhye
so 'surāṇāṁ camū-patiḥ
yānaṁ vaihāyasaṁ nāma
kāma-gaṁ maya-nirmitam

sarva-sāṅgrāmikopetaṁ
sarvāścaryamayaṁ prabho
apratarkyam anirdeśyaṁ
dṛśyamānam adarśanam

āsthitas tad vimānāgryaṁ
sarvānīkādhipair vṛtaḥ
bāla-vyajana-chatrāgryai
reje candra ivodaye

vairocanaḥ—the son of Virocana; *baliḥ*—Mahārāja Bali; *saṅkhye*—in the battle; *saḥ*—he, so celebrated; *asurāṇām*—of the demons; *camū-patiḥ*—commander in chief; *yānam*—airplane; *vaihāyasam*—called Vaihāyasa; *nāma*—by the name; *kāma-gam*—able to fly anywhere he desired; *maya-nirmitam*—made by the demon Maya; *sarva*—all; *sāṅgrāmika-upetam*—equipped with all kinds of weapons required for fighting with all different types of enemies; *sarva-āścarya-mayam*—wonderful in every respect; *prabho*—O King; *apratarkyam*—inexplicable; *anirdeśyam*—indescribable; *dṛśyamānam*—sometimes visible; *adarśanam*—sometimes not visible; *āsthitaḥ*—being seated on such; *tat*—that; *vimāna-agryam*—excellent airplane; *sarva*—all; *anīka-adhipaiḥ*—by the commanders of soldiers; *vṛtaḥ*—surrounded; *bāla-vyajana-chatra-agryaiḥ*—protected by beautifully decorated umbrellas and the best of *cāmaras; reje*—brilliantly situated; *candraḥ*—the moon; *iva*—like; *udaye*—at the time of rising in the evening.

TRANSLATION

For that battle the most celebrated commander in chief, Mahārāja Bali, son of Virocana, was seated on a wonderful airplane named Vaihāyasa. O King, this beautifully decorated airplane had been manufactured by the demon Maya and was equipped with weapons for all types of combat. It was inconceivable and indescribable. Indeed, it was sometimes visible and sometimes not. Seated in this airplane under a beautiful protective umbrella and being fanned by the best of cāmaras, Mahārāja Bali, surrounded by his captains and commanders, appeared just like the moon rising in the evening, illuminating all directions.

TEXTS 19-24

तस्यासन्सर्वतो यानैर्यूथानां पतयोऽसुराः ।
नमुचिः शम्बरो बाणो विप्रचित्तिरयोमुखः ॥ १९ ॥

द्विमूर्धा कालनाभोऽथ प्रहेतिर्हेतिरिल्वलः ।
शकुनिर्भूतसंतापो वज्रदंष्ट्रो विरोचनः ॥ २० ॥
हयग्रीवः शङ्कुशिराः कपिलो मेघदुन्दुभिः ।
तारकश्चक्रदृक् शुम्भो निशुम्भो जम्भ उत्कलः ॥ २१ ॥
अरिष्टोऽरिष्टनेमिश्च मयश्च त्रिपुराधिपः ।
अन्ये पौलोमकालेया निवातकवचादयः ॥ २२ ॥
अलब्धभागाः सोमस्य केवलं क्लेशभागिनः ।
सर्व एते रणमुखे बहुशो निर्जितामराः ॥ २३ ॥
सिंहनादान्विमुञ्चन्तः शङ्खान्दध्मुर्महारवान् ।
दृष्ट्वा सपत्नानुत्सिक्तान्बलभित् कुपितो भृशम् ॥ २४ ॥

tasyāsan sarvato yānair
yūthānāṁ patayo 'surāḥ
namuciḥ śambaro bāṇo
vipracittir ayomukhaḥ

dvimūrdhā kālanābho 'tha
prahetir hetir ilvalaḥ
śakunir bhūtasantāpo
vajradaṁṣṭro virocanaḥ

hayagrīvaḥ śaṅkuśirāḥ
kapilo meghadundubhiḥ
tārakaś cakradṛk śumbho
niśumbho jambha utkalaḥ

ariṣṭo 'riṣṭanemiś ca
mayaś ca tripurādhipaḥ
anye pauloma-kāleyā
nivātakavacādayaḥ

alabdha-bhāgāḥ somasya
kevalaṁ kleśa-bhāginaḥ
sarva ete raṇa-mukhe
bahuśo nirjitāmarāḥ

siṁha-nādān vimuñcantaḥ
śaṅkhān dadhmur mahā-ravān

dṛṣṭvā sapatnān utsiktān
balabhit kupito bhṛśam

tasya—of him (Mahārāja Bali); *āsan*—situated; *sarvataḥ*—all around; *yānaiḥ*—by different vehicles; *yūthānām*—of the soldiers; *patayaḥ*—the commanders; *asurāḥ*—demons; *namuciḥ*—Namuci; *śambaraḥ*—Śambara; *bāṇaḥ*—Bāṇa; *vipracittiḥ*—Vipracitti; *ayomukhaḥ*—Ayomukha; *dvimūrdhā*—Dvimūrdhā; *kālanābhaḥ*—Kālanābha; *atha*—also; *prahetiḥ*—Praheti; *hetiḥ*—Heti; *ilvalaḥ*—Ilvala; *śakuniḥ*—Śakuni; *bhūtasantāpaḥ*—Bhūtasantāpa; *vajra-daṁṣṭraḥ*—Vajradaṁṣṭra; *virocanaḥ*—Virocana; *hayagrīvaḥ*—Hayagrīva; *śaṅkuśirāḥ*—Śaṅkuśirā; *kapilaḥ*—Kapila; *megha-dundubhiḥ*—Meghadundubhi; *tārakaḥ*—Tāraka; *cakradṛk*—Cakradṛk; *śumbhaḥ*—Śumbha; *niśumbhaḥ*—Niśumbha; *jambhaḥ*—Jambha; *utkalaḥ*—Utkala; *ariṣṭaḥ*—Ariṣṭa; *ariṣṭanemiḥ*—Ariṣṭanemi; *ca*—and; *mayaḥ ca*—and Maya; *tripurād-hipaḥ*—Tripurādhipa; *anye*—others; *pauloma-kāleyāḥ*—the sons of Puloma and the Kāleyas; *nivātakavaca-ādayaḥ*—Nivātakavaca and other demons; *al-abdha-bhāgāḥ*—all unable to take a share; *somasya*—of the nectar; *kevalam*—merely; *kleśa-bhāginaḥ*—the demons took a share of the labor; *sarve*—all of them; *ete*—the demons; *raṇa-mukhe*—in the front of the battle; *bahuśaḥ*—by excessive strength; *nirjita-amarāḥ*—being very troublesome to the demigods; *siṁha-nādān*—vibrations like those of lions; *vimuñcantaḥ*—uttering; *śaṅkhān*—conchshells; *dadhmuḥ*—blew; *mahā-ravān*—making a tumultuous sound; *dṛṣṭvā*—after seeing; *sapatnān*—their rivals; *utsiktān*—ferocious; *balabhit*—(Lord Indra) being afraid of the strength; *kupitaḥ*—having become angry; *bhṛśam*—extremely.

TRANSLATION

Surrounding Mahārāja Bali on all sides were the commanders and captains of the demons, sitting on their respective chariots. Among them were the following demons: Namuci, Śambara, Bāṇa, Vipracitti, Ayomukha, Dvimūrdhā, Kālanābha, Praheti, Heti, Ilvala, Śakuni, Bhūtasantāpa, Vajradaṁṣṭra, Virocana, Hayagrīva, Śaṅkuśirā, Kapila, Meghadundubhi, Tāraka, Cakradṛk, Śumbha, Niśumbha, Jambha, Utkala, Ariṣṭa, Ariṣṭanemi, Tripurādhipa, Maya, the sons of Puloma, the Kāleyas and Nivātakavaca. All of these demons had been deprived of their share of the nectar and had shared merely in the labor of churning the ocean. Now, they fought against the demigods, and to encourage their armies, they made a tumultuous sound like the roaring of lions and blew loudly on conchshells. Balabhit,

Lord Indra, upon seeing this situation of his ferocious rivals, became extremely angry.

TEXT 25

ऐरावतं दिक्करिणमारूढः शुशुभे स्वराट्।
यथा स्रवत्प्रस्रवणमुदयाद्रिमहर्पतिः ॥ २५ ॥

airāvataṁ dik-kariṇam
ārūḍhaḥ śuśubhe sva-rāṭ
yathā sravat-prasravaṇam
udayādrim ahar-patiḥ

airāvatam—Airāvata; *dik-kariṇam*—the great elephant who could go everywhere; *ārūḍhaḥ*—mounted on; *śuśubhe*—became very beautiful to see; *sva-rāṭ*—Indra; *yathā*—just as; *sravat*—flowing; *prasravaṇam*—waves of wine; *udaya-adrim*—on Udayagiri; *ahaḥ-patiḥ*—the sun.

TRANSLATION

Sitting on Airāvata, an elephant who can go anywhere and who holds water and wine in reserve for showering, Lord Indra looked just like the sun rising from Udayagiri, where there are reservoirs of water.

PURPORT

On the top of the mountain called Udayagiri are large lakes from which water continuously pours in waterfalls. Similarly, Indra's carrier, Airāvata, holds water and wine in reserve and showers it in the direction of Lord Indra. Thus Indra, King of heaven, sitting on the back of Airāvata, appeared like the brilliant sun rising above Udayagiri.

TEXT 26

तस्यासन्सर्वतो देवा नानावाहध्वजायुधाः।
लोकपालाः सहगणैर्वाय्वग्निवरुणादयः ॥ २६ ॥

tasyāsan sarvato devā
nānā-vāha-dhvajāyudhāḥ
lokapālāḥ saha-gaṇair
vāyv-agni-varuṇādayaḥ

tasya—of Lord Indra; *āsan*—situated; *sarvataḥ*—all around; *devāḥ*—all the demigods; *nānā-vāha*—with varieties of carriers; *dhvaja-āyudhāḥ*—and with flags and weapons; *loka-pālāḥ*—all the chiefs of various higher planetary systems; *saha*—with; *gaṇaiḥ*—their associates; *vāyu*—the demigod controlling air; *agni*—the demigod controlling fire; *varuṇa*—the demigod controlling water; *ādayaḥ*—all of them surrounding Lord Indra.

TRANSLATION

Surrounding Lord Indra, King of heaven, were the demigods, seated on various types of vehicles and decorated with flags and weapons. Present among them were Vāyu, Agni, Varuṇa and other rulers of various planets, along with their associates.

TEXT 27

तेऽन्योन्यमभिसंसृत्य क्षिपन्तो मर्मभिर्मिथः ।
आह्वयन्तो विशन्तोऽग्रे युयुधुर्द्वन्द्वयोधिनः ॥ २७ ॥

te 'nyonyam abhisaṁsṛtya
kṣipanto marmabhir mithaḥ
āhvayanto viśanto 'gre
yuyudhur dvandva-yodhinaḥ

te—all of them (the demigods and the demons); *anyonyam*—one another; *abhisaṁsṛtya*—having come forward face to face; *kṣipantaḥ*—chastising one another; *marmabhiḥ mithaḥ*—with much pain to the cores of the hearts of one another; *āhvayantaḥ*—addressing one another; *viśantaḥ*—having entered the battlefield; *agre*—in front; *yuyudhuḥ*—fought; *dvandva-yodhinaḥ*—two combatants chose each other.

TRANSLATION

The demigods and demons came before each other and reproached one another with words piercing to the heart. Then they drew near and began fighting face to face in pairs.

TEXT 28

युयोध बलिरिन्द्रेण तारकेण गुहोऽस्यत ।
वरुणो हेतिनायुध्यन्मित्रो राजन्प्रहेतिना ॥ २८ ॥

yuyodha balir indreṇa
tārakeṇa guho 'syata
varuṇo hetināyudhyan
mitro rājan prahetinā

yuyodha—fought; *baliḥ*—Mahārāja Bali; *indreṇa*—with King Indra; *tārakeṇa*—with Tāraka; *guhaḥ*—Kārttikeya; *asyata*—engaged in fighting; *varuṇaḥ*—the demigod Varuṇa; *hetinā*—with Heti; *ayudhyat*—fought one another; *mitraḥ*—the demigod Mitra; *rājan*—O King; *prahetinā*—with Praheti.

TRANSLATION

O King, Mahārāja Bali fought with Indra, Kārttikeya with Tāraka, Varuṇa with Heti, and Mitra with Praheti.

TEXT 29

यमस्तु कालनाभेन विश्वकर्मा मयेन वै ।
शम्बरो युयुधे त्वष्ट्रा सवित्रा तु विरोचनः ॥ २९ ॥

yamas tu kālanābhena
viśvakarmā mayena vai
śambaro yuyudhe tvaṣṭrā
savitrā tu virocanaḥ

yamaḥ—Yamarāja; *tu*—indeed; *kālanābhena*—with Kālanābha; *viśvakarmā*—Viśvakarmā; *mayena*—with Maya; *vai*—indeed; *śambaraḥ*—Śambara; *yuyudhe*—fought; *tvaṣṭrā*—with Tvaṣṭā; *savitrā*—with the sun-god; *tu*—indeed; *virocanaḥ*—the demon Virocana.

TRANSLATION

Yamarāja fought with Kālanābha, Viśvakarmā with Maya Dānava, Tvaṣṭā with Śambara, and the sun-god with Virocana.

TEXTS 30-31

अपराजितेन नमुचिरश्विनौ वृषपर्वणा ।
सूर्यो बलिसुतैर्देवो बाणज्येष्ठैः शतेन च ॥ ३० ॥

राहुणा च तथा सोमः पुलोम्ना युयुधेऽनिलः ।
निशुम्भशुम्भयोर्देवी भद्रकाली तरस्विनी ॥ ३१ ॥

aparājitena namucir
aśvinau vṛṣaparvaṇā
sūryo bali-sutair devo
bāṇa-jyeṣṭhaiḥ śatena ca

rāhuṇā ca tathā somaḥ
pulomnā yuyudhe 'nilaḥ
niśumbha-śumbhayor devī
bhadrakālī tarasvinī

aparājitena—with the demigod Aparājita; *namuciḥ*—the demon Namuci; *aśvinau*—the Aśvinī brothers; *vṛṣaparvaṇā*—with the demon Vṛṣaparvā; *sūryaḥ*—the sun-god; *bali-sutaiḥ*—with the sons of Bali; *devaḥ*—the god; *bāṇa-jyeṣṭhaiḥ*—the chief of whom is Bāṇa; *śatena*—numbering one hundred; *ca*—and; *rāhuṇā*—by Rāhu; *ca*—also; *tathā*—as well as; *somaḥ*—the moon-god; *pulomnā*—Pulomā; *yuyudhe*—fought; *anilaḥ*—the demigod Anila, who controls air; *niśumbha*—the demon Niśumbha; *śumbhayoḥ*—with Śumbha; *devī*—the goddess Durgā; *bhadrakālī*—Bhadra Kālī; *tarasvinī*—extremely powerful.

TRANSLATION

The demigod Aparājita fought with Namuci, and the two Aśvinī-kumāra brothers fought with Vṛṣaparvā. The sun-god fought with the one hundred sons of Mahārāja Bali, headed by Bāṇa, and the moon-god fought with Rāhu. The demigod controlling air fought with Pulomā, and Śumbha and Niśumbha fought the supremely powerful material energy, Durgādevī, who is called Bhadra Kālī.

TEXTS 32-34

वृषाकपिस्तु जम्भेन महिषेण विभावसुः ।
इल्वलः सह वातापिर्ब्रह्मपुत्रैररिन्दम ॥ ३२ ॥
कामदेवेन दुर्मर्ष उत्कलो मातृभिः सह ।
बृहस्पतिश्चोशनसा नरकेण शनैश्चरः ॥ ३३ ॥

मरुतो निवातकवचैः कालेयैर्वसवोऽमराः ।
विश्वेदेवास्तु पौलोमै रुद्राः क्रोधवशैः सह ॥ ३४ ॥

vṛṣākapis tu jambhena
mahiṣeṇa vibhāvasuḥ
ilvalaḥ saha vātāpir
brahma-putrair arindama

kāmadevena durmarṣa
utkalo mātṛbhiḥ saha
bṛhaspatiś cośanasā
narakeṇa śanaiścaraḥ

maruto nivātakavacaiḥ
kāleyair vasavo 'marāḥ
viśvedevās tu paulomai
rudrāḥ krodhavaśaiḥ saha

vṛṣākapiḥ—Lord Śiva; *tu*—indeed; *jambhena*—with Jambha; *mahiṣeṇa*—with Mahiṣāsura; *vibhāvasuḥ*—the fire-god; *ilvalaḥ*—the demon Ilvala; *saha vātāpiḥ*—with his brother, Vātāpi; *brahma-putraiḥ*—with the sons of Brahmā, such as Vasiṣṭha; *arim-dama*—O Mahārāja Parīkṣit, suppressor of enemies; *kāmadevena*—with Kāmadeva; *durmarṣaḥ*—Durmarṣa; *utkalaḥ*—the demon Utkala; *mātṛbhiḥ saha*—with the demigoddesses known as the Mātṛkās; *bṛhaspatiḥ*—the demigod Bṛhaspati; *ca*—and; *uśanasā*—with Śukrācārya; *narakeṇa*—with the demon known as Naraka; *śanaiścaraḥ*—the demigod Śani, or Saturn; *marutaḥ*—the demigods of air; *nivātakavacaiḥ*—with the demon Nivātakavaca; *kāleyaiḥ*—with the Kālakeyas; *vasavaḥ amarāḥ*—the Vasus fought; *viśvedevāḥ*—the Viśvedeva demigods; *tu*—indeed; *paulomaiḥ*—with the Paulomas; *rudrāḥ*—the eleven Rudras; *krodhavaśaiḥ saha*—with the Krodhavaśa demons.

TRANSLATION

O Mahārāja Parīkṣit, suppressor of enemies [Arindama], Lord Śiva fought with Jambha, and Vibhāvasu fought with Mahiṣāsura. Ilvala, along with his brother Vātāpi, fought the sons of Lord Brahmā. Durmarṣa fought with Cupid, the demon Utkala with the Mātṛkā demigoddesses, Bṛhaspati with Śukrācārya, and Śanaiścara [Saturn] with Narakāsura. The Maruts fought Nivātakavaca, the Vasus fought the Kālakeya demons, the

Viśvedeva demigods fought the Pauloma demons, and the Rudras fought the Krodhavaśa demons, who were victims of anger.

TEXT 35

त एवमाजावसुराः सुरेन्द्रा
द्वन्द्वेन संहत्य च युध्यमानाः ।
अन्योन्यमासाद्य निजघ्नुरोजसा
जिगीषवस्तीक्ष्णशरासितोमरैः ॥ ३५ ॥

ta evam ājāv asurāḥ surendrā
dvandvena saṁhatya ca yudhyamānāḥ
anyonyam āsādya nijaghnur ojasā
jigīṣavas tīkṣṇa-śarāsi-tomaraiḥ

te—all of them; *evam*—in this way; *ājau*—on the battlefield; *asurāḥ*—the demons; *sura-indrāḥ*—and the demigods; *dvandvena*—two by two; *saṁhatya*—mixing together; *ca*—and; *yudhyamānāḥ*—engaged in fighting; *anyonyam*—with one another; *āsādya*—approaching; *nijaghnuḥ*—slashed with weapons and killed; *ojasā*—with great strength; *jigīṣavaḥ*—everyone desiring victory; *tīkṣṇa*—sharp; *śara*—with arrows; *asi*—with swords; *tomaraiḥ*—with lances.

TRANSLATION

All of these demigods and demons assembled on the battlefield with a fighting spirit and attacked one another with great strength. All of them desiring victory, they fought in pairs, hitting one another severely with sharpened arrows, swords and lances.

TEXT 36

भुशुण्डिभिश्चक्रगदर्ष्टिपट्टिशैः
शक्त्युल्मुकैः प्रासपरश्वधैरपि ।
निस्त्रिंशभल्लैः परिघैः समुद्गरैः
सभिन्दिपालैश्च शिरांसि चिच्छिदुः ॥ ३६ ॥

bhuśuṇḍibhiś cakra-gadarṣṭi-paṭṭiśaiḥ
śakty-ulmukaiḥ prāsa-paraśvadhair api

nistriṁśa-bhallaiḥ parighaiḥ samudgaraiḥ
sabhindipālaiś ca śirāṁsi cicchiduḥ

bhuśuṇḍibhiḥ—with weapons called *bhuśuṇḍi; cakra*—with discs; *gadā*—with clubs; *ṛṣṭi*—with the weapons called *ṛṣṭi; paṭṭiśaiḥ*—with the weapons called *paṭṭiśa; śakti*—with the *śakti* weapons; *ulmukaiḥ*—with the weapons called *ulmukas; prāsa*—with the *prāsa* weapons; *paraśvadhaiḥ*—with the weapons called *paraśvadha; api*—also; *nistriṁśa*—with *nistriṁśas; bhallaiḥ*—with lances; *parighaiḥ*—with the weapons named *parighas; samudgaraiḥ*—with the weapons known as *mudgara; sa-bhindipālaiḥ*—with the *bhindipāla* weapons; *ca*—also; *śirāṁsi*—heads; *cicchiduḥ*—cut off.

TRANSLATION

They severed one another's heads, using weapons like bhuśuṇḍis, cakras, clubs, ṛṣṭis, paṭṭiśas, śaktis, ulmukas, prāsas, paraśvadhas, nistriṁśas, lances, parighas, mudgaras and bhindipālas.

TEXT 37

गजास्तुरङ्गाः सरथाः पदातयः
सारोहवाहा विविधा विखण्डिताः ।
निकृत्तबाहूरुशिरोधराङ्घ्रय-
श्छिन्नध्वजेष्वासतनुत्रभूषणाः ॥ ३७ ॥

gajās turaṅgāḥ sarathāḥ padātayaḥ
sāroha-vāhā vividhā vikhaṇḍitāḥ
nikṛtta-bāhūru-śirodharāṅghrayaś
chinna-dhvajeṣvāsa-tanutra-bhūṣaṇāḥ

gajāḥ—elephants; *turaṅgāḥ*—horses; *sa-rathāḥ*—with chariots; *padātayaḥ*—infantry soldiers; *sāroha-vāhāḥ*—carriers with the riders; *vividhāḥ*—varieties; *vikhaṇḍitāḥ*—cut to pieces; *nikṛtta-bāhu*—cut off arms; *ūru*—thighs; *śirodhara*—necks; *aṅghrayaḥ*—legs; *chinna*—cut up; *dhvaja*—flags; *iṣvāsa*—bows; *tanutra*—armor; *bhūṣaṇāḥ*—ornaments.

TRANSLATION

The elephants, horses, chariots, charioteers, infantry soldiers and various kinds of carriers, along with their riders, were slashed to pieces. The

arms, thighs, necks and legs of the soldiers were severed, and their flags, bows, armor and ornaments were torn apart.

TEXT 38

तेषां पदाघातरथाङ्गचूर्णिता-
दायोधनादुल्बण उत्थितस्तदा ।
रेणुर्दिशः खं द्युमणिं च छादयन्
न्यवर्ततासृक्स्त्रुतिभिः परिप्लुतात् ॥ ३८ ॥

teṣāṁ padāghāta-rathāṅga-cūrṇitād
āyodhanād ulbaṇa utthitas tadā
reṇur diśaḥ khaṁ dyumaṇiṁ ca chādayan
nyavartatāsṛk-srutibhiḥ pariplutāt

teṣām—of all the people engaged on the battlefield; *padāghāta*—because of beating on the ground by the legs of the demons and demigods; *ratha-aṅga*—and by the wheels of the chariots; *cūrṇitāt*—which was made into pieces of dust; *āyodhanāt*—from the battlefield; *ulbaṇaḥ*—very forceful; *utthitaḥ*—rising; *tadā*—at that time; *reṇuḥ*—the dust particles; *diśaḥ*—all directions; *kham*—outer space; *dyumaṇim*—up to the sun; *ca*—also; *chādayan*—covering all of space up to that; *nyavartata*—dropped floating in the air; *asṛk*—of blood; *srutibhiḥ*—by particles; *pariplutāt*—because of being widely sprinkled.

TRANSLATION

Because of the impact on the ground of the legs of the demons and demigods and the wheels of the chariots, particles of dust flew violently into the sky and made a dust cloud that covered all directions of outer space, as far as the sun. But when the particles of dust were followed by drops of blood being sprinkled all over space, the dust cloud could no longer float in the sky.

PURPORT

The cloud of dust covered the entire horizon, but when drops of blood sprayed up as far as the sun, the dust cloud could no longer float in the sky. A point to be observed here is that although the blood is stated to have reached the sun, it is not said to have reached the mooṇ Apparently, therefore, as stated elsewhere in *Śrīmad-Bhāgavatam,* the sun, not the moon, is the planet nearest the earth. We have already discussed this point in many places. The sun is first, then the moon, then Mars, Jupiter and so on. The sun is supposed to be 93,000,000 miles above the surface fo the earth, and from the *Śrīmad-Bhāgavatam* we understand that the moon is 1,600,000 miles above the sun. Therefore the distance between the earth and the moon would be about 95,000,000 miles. So if a space capsule were traveling at the speed of 18,000 miles per hour, how could it reach the moon in four days? At that speed, going to the moon would take at least seven months. That a space capsule on a moon excursion has reached the moon in four days is therefore impossible.

TEXT 39

शिरोभिरुद्धूतकिरीटकुण्डलैः
संरम्भदृग्भिः परिदष्टदच्छदैः ।
महाभुजैः साभरणैः सहायुधैः
सा प्रास्तृता भूः करभोरुभिर्बभौ ॥ ३९ ॥

śirobhir uddhūta-kirīṭa-kuṇḍalaiḥ
saṁrambha-dṛgbhiḥ paridaṣṭa-dacchadaiḥ
mahā-bhujaiḥ sābharaṇaiḥ sahāyudhaiḥ
sā prāstṛtā bhūḥ karabhorubhir babhau

śirobhiḥ—by the heads; *uddhūta*—separated, scattered from; *kirīṭa*—having their helmets; *kuṇḍalaiḥ*—and earrings; *saṁrambha-dṛgbhiḥ*—eyes staring in anger (although the heads were severed from their bodies); *paridaṣṭa*—having been bitten by the teeth; *dacchadaiḥ*—the lips; *mahā-bhujaiḥ*—with big arms; *sa-ābharaṇaiḥ*—decorated with ornaments; *saha-āyudhaiḥ*—and with weapons in their hands, although the hands were severed; *sā*—that battlefield; *prāstṛtā*—scattered; *bhūḥ*—the warfield; *karabha-ūrubhiḥ*—and with thighs and legs resembling the trunks of elephants; *babhau*—it so became.

TRANSLATION

In the course of the battle, the warfield became strewn with the severed heads of heroes, their eyes still staring and their teeth still pressed against their lips in anger. Helmets and earrings were scattered from these severed heads. Similarly, many arms, decorated with ornaments and clutch-

ing various weapons, were strewn here and there, as were many legs and thighs, which resembled the trunks of elephants.

TEXT 40

कबन्धास्तत्र चोत्पेतुः पतितस्वशिरोऽक्षिभिः ।
उद्यतायुधदोर्दण्डैराधावन्तो भटान् मृधे ॥ ४० ॥

kabandhās tatra cotpetuḥ
patita-sva-śiro-'kṣibhiḥ
udyatāyudha-dordaṇḍair
ādhāvanto bhaṭān mṛdhe

kabandhāḥ—trunks (bodies without heads); *tatra*—there (on the battlefield); *ca*—also; *utpetuḥ*—generated; *patita*—fallen; *sva-śiraḥ-akṣibhiḥ*—by the eyes in one's head; *udyata*—raised; *āyudha*—equipped with weapons; *dordaṇḍaiḥ*—the arms of whom; *ādhāvantaḥ*—rushing toward; *bhaṭān*—the soldiers; *mṛdhe*—on the battlefield.

TRANSLATION

Many headless trunks were generated on that battlefield. With weapons in their arms, those ghostly trunks, which could see with the eyes in the fallen heads, attacked the enemy soldiers.

PURPORT

It appears that the heroes who died on the battlefield immediately became ghosts, and although their heads had been severed from their bodies, new trunks were generated, and these new trunks, seeing with the eyes in the severed heads, began to attack the enemy. In other words, many ghosts were generated to join the fight, and thus new trunks appeared on the battlefield.

TEXT 41

बलिर्महेन्द्रं दशभिस्त्रिभिरैरावतं शरैः ।
चतुर्भिश्चतुरो वाहानेकेनारोहमार्च्छयत् ॥ ४१ ॥

balir mahendraṁ daśabhis
tribhir airāvataṁ śaraiḥ

caturbhiś caturo vāhān
ekenāroham ārcchayat

baliḥ—Mahārāja Bali; *mahā-indram*—the King of heaven; *daśabhiḥ*—with ten; *tribhiḥ*—with three; *airāvatam*—Airāvata, carrying Indra; *śaraiḥ*—by arrows; *caturbhiḥ*—by four arrows; *caturaḥ*—the four; *vāhān*—mounted soldiers; *ekena*—by one; *āroham*—the driver of the elephants; *ārcchayat*—attacked.

TRANSLATION

Mahārāja Bali then attacked Indra with ten arrows and attacked Airāvata, Indra's carrier elephant, with three arrows. With four arrows he attacked the four horsemen guarding Airāvata's legs, and with one arrow he attacked the driver of the elephant.

PURPORT

The word *vāhān* refers to the soldiers on horseback who protected the legs of the carrier elephants. According to the system of military arrangement, the legs of the elephant bearing the commander were also protected.

TEXT 42

स तानापततः शक्रस्तावद्भिः शीघ्रविक्रमः ।
चिच्छेद निशितैर्भल्लैरसम्प्राप्तान्हसन्निव ॥ ४२ ॥

sa tān āpatataḥ śakras
tāvadbhiḥ śīghra-vikramaḥ
ciccheda niśitair bhallair
asamprāptān hasann iva

saḥ—he (Indra); *tān*—arrows; *āpatataḥ*—while moving toward him and falling down; *śakraḥ*—Indra; *tāvadbhiḥ*—immediately; *śīghra-vikramaḥ*—was practiced to oppress very soon; *ciccheda*—cut to pieces; *niśitaiḥ*—very sharp; *bhallaiḥ*—with another type of arrow; *asamprāptān*—the enemy's arrows not being received; *hasan iva*—as if smiling.

TRANSLATION

Before Bali Mahārāja's arrows could reach him, Indra, King of heaven, who is expert in dealing with arrows, smiled and counteracted the arrows with arrows of another type, known as bhalla, which were extremely sharp.

TEXT 43

तस्य कर्मोत्तमं वीक्ष्य दुर्मर्षः शक्तिमाददे ।
तां ज्वलन्तीं महोल्काभां हस्तस्थामच्छिनद्धरिः ॥ ४३ ॥

tasya karmottamaṁ vīkṣya
durmarṣaḥ śaktim ādade
tāṁ jvalantīṁ maholkābhāṁ
hasta-sthām acchinad dhariḥ

tasya—of King Indra; *karma-uttamam*—the very expert service in military art; *vīkṣya*—after observing; *durmarṣaḥ*—being in a very angry mood; *śaktim*—the *śakti* weapon; *ādade*—took up; *tām*—that weapon; *jvalantīm*—blazing fire; *mahā-ulkā-ābhām*—appearing like a great firebrand; *hasta-sthām*—while still in the hand of Bali; *acchinat*—cut to pieces; *hariḥ*—Indra.

TRANSLATION

When Bali Mahārāja saw the expert military activities of Indra, he could not restrain his anger. Thus he took up another weapon, known as śakti, which blazed like a great firebrand. But Indra cut that weapon to pieces while it was still in Bali's hand.

TEXT 44

ततः शूलं ततः प्रासं ततस्तोमरमृष्टयः ।
यद् यच्छस्त्रं समादद्यात्सर्वं तदच्छिनद् विभुः ॥ ४४ ॥

tataḥ śūlaṁ tataḥ prāsaṁ
tatas tomaram ṛṣṭayaḥ
yad yac chastraṁ samādadyāt
sarvaṁ tad acchinad vibhuḥ

tataḥ—thereafter; *śūlam*—lance; *tataḥ*—thereafter; *prāsam*—the *prāsa* weapon; *tataḥ*—thereafter; *tomaram*—the *tomara* weapon; *ṛṣṭayaḥ*—the *ṛṣṭi* weapons; *yat yat*—whatever and whichever; *śastram*—weapon; *samādadyāt*—Bali Mahārāja tried to use; *sarvam*—all of them; *tat*—those same weapons; *acchinat*—cut to pieces; *vibhuḥ*—the great Indra.

TRANSLATION

Thereafter, one by one, Bali Mahārāja used a lance, prāsa, tomara, ṛṣṭis and other weapons, but whatever weapons he took up, Indra immediately cut them to pieces.

TEXT 45

ससर्जाथासुरीं मायामन्तर्धानगतोऽसुरः ।
ततः प्रादुरभूच्छैलः सुरानीकोपरि प्रभो ॥ ४५ ॥

sasarjāthāsurīṁ māyām
antardhāna-gato 'suraḥ
tataḥ prādurabhūc chailaḥ
surānīkopari prabho

sasarja—released; *atha*—now; *āsurīm*—demoniac; *māyām*—illusion; *antardhāna*—out of vision; *gataḥ*—having gone; *asuraḥ*—Bali Mahārāja; *tataḥ*—thereafter; *prādurabhūt*—there appeared; *śailaḥ*—a big mountain; *sura-anīka-upari*—above the heads of the soldiers of the demigods; *prabho*—O my lord.

TRANSLATION

My dear King, Bali Mahārāja then disappeared and resorted to demoniac illusions. A giant mountain, generated from illusion, then appeared above the heads of the demigod soldiers.

TEXT 46

ततो निपेतुस्तरवो दह्यमाना दवाग्निना ।
शिलाः सटङ्कशिखराश्चूर्णयन्त्यो द्विषद्बलम् ॥ ४६ ॥

tato nipetus taravo
dahyamānā davāgninā
śilāḥ saṭaṅka-śikharāś
cūrṇayantyo dviṣad-balam

tataḥ—from that great mountain; *nipetuḥ*—began to fall; *taravaḥ*—large trees; *dahyamānāḥ*—blazing in fire; *dava-agninā*—by the forest fire; *śilāḥ*—and stones; *sa-ṭaṅka-śikharāḥ*—having edges with points as sharp as stone picks; *cūrṇayantyaḥ*—smashing; *dviṣat-balam*—the strength of the enemies.

TRANSLATION

From that mountain fell trees blazing in a forest fire. Chips of stone, with sharp edges like picks, also fell and smashed the heads of the demigod soldiers.

TEXT 47

महोरगाः समुत्पेतुर्दन्दशूकाः सवृश्चिकाः ।
सिंहव्याघ्रवराहाश्च मर्दयन्तो महागजाः ॥ ४७ ॥

mahoragāḥ samutpetur
dandaśūkāḥ savṛścikāḥ
siṁha-vyāghra-varāhāś ca
mardayanto mahā-gajāḥ

mahā-uragāḥ—big serpents; *samutpetuḥ*—fell upon them; *dandaśūkāḥ*—other poisonous animals and insects; *sa-vṛścikāḥ*—with scorpions; *siṁha*—lions; *vyāghra*—tigers; *varāhāḥ ca*—and forest boars; *mardayantaḥ*—smashing; *mahā-gajāḥ*—great elephants.

TRANSLATION

Scorpions, large snakes and many other poisonous animals, as well as lions, tigers, boars and great elephants, all began falling upon the demigod soldiers, crushing everything.

TEXT 48

यातुधान्यश्च शतशः शूलहस्ता विवाससः ।
छिन्धि भिन्धीति वादिन्यस्तथा रक्षोगणाः प्रभो ॥ ४८ ॥

yātudhānyaś ca śataśaḥ
śūla-hastā vivāsasaḥ
chindhi bhindhīti vādinyas
tathā rakṣo-gaṇāḥ prabho

yātudhānyaḥ—carnivorous female demons; *ca*—and; *śataśaḥ*—hundreds upon hundreds; *śūla-hastāḥ*—every one of them with a trident in hand; *vivāsasaḥ*—completely naked; *chindhi*—cut to pieces; *bhindhi*—pierce; *iti*—thus; *vādinyaḥ*—talking; *tathā*—in that way; *rakṣaḥ-gaṇāḥ*—a band of Rākṣasas (a type of demon); *prabho*—O my King.

TRANSLATION

O my King, many hundreds of male and female carnivorous demons, completely naked and carrying tridents in their hands, then appeared, crying the slogans "Cut them to pieces! Pierce them!"

TEXT 49

ततो महाघना व्योम्नि गम्भीरपरुषस्वनाः ।
अङ्गारान्मुमुचुर्वातैराहताः स्तनयित्नवः ॥ ४९ ॥

tato mahā-ghanā vyomni
gambhīra-paruṣa-svanāḥ
aṅgārān mumucur vātair
āhatāḥ stanayitnavaḥ

tataḥ—thereafter; *mahā-ghanāḥ*—big clouds; *vyomni*—in the sky; *gambhīra-paruṣa-svanāḥ*—making very deep rumbling sounds; *aṅgārān*—embers; *mumucuḥ*—released; *vātaiḥ*—by the strong winds; *āhatāḥ*—harassed; *stanayitnavaḥ*—with the sound of thunder.

TRANSLATION

Fierce clouds, harassed by strong winds, then appeared in the sky. Rumbling very gravely with the sound of thunder, they began to shower live coals.

TEXT 50

सृष्टो दैत्येन सुमहान्वह्निः श्वसनसारथिः ।
सांवर्तक इवात्युग्रो विबुधध्वजिनीमधाक् ॥ ५० ॥

sṛṣṭo daityena sumahān
vahniḥ śvasana-sārathiḥ
sāṁvartaka ivātyugro
vibudha-dhvajinīm adhāk

sṛṣṭaḥ—created; *daityena*—by the demon (Bali Mahārāja); *su-mahān*—very great, devastating; *vahniḥ*—a fire; *śvasana-sārathiḥ*—being carried by the blasting wind; *sāṁvartakaḥ*—the fire named Sāṁvartaka, which appears during the time of dissolution; *iva*—just like; *ati*—very much; *ugraḥ*—terrible; *vibudha*—of the demigods; *dhvajinīm*—the soldiers; *adhāk*—burned to ashes.

TRANSLATION

A great devastating fire created by Bali Mahārāja began burning all the soldiers of the demigods. This fire, accompanied by blasting winds, seemed as terrible as the Sāṁvartaka fire, which appears at the time of dissolution.

TEXT 51

ततः समुद्र उद्वेलः सर्वतः प्रत्यदृश्यत ।
प्रचण्डवातैरुद्धूततरङ्गावर्तभीषणः ॥ ५१ ॥

tataḥ samudra udvelaḥ
sarvataḥ pratyadṛśyata
pracaṇḍa-vātair uddhūta-
taraṅgāvarta-bhīṣaṇaḥ

tataḥ—thereafter; *samudraḥ*—the sea; *udvelaḥ*—being agitated; *sarvataḥ*—everywhere; *pratyadṛśyata*—appeared before everyone's vision; *pracaṇḍa*—fierce; *vātaiḥ*—by the winds; *uddhūta*—agitated; *taraṅga*—of the waves; *āvarta*—whirling water; *bhīṣaṇaḥ*—ferocious.

TRANSLATION

Thereafter, whirlpools and sea waves, agitated by fierce blasts of wind, appeared everywhere, before everyone's vision, in a furious flood.

TEXT 52

एवं दैत्यैर्महामायैरलक्ष्यगतिभीरणे ।
सृज्यमानासु मायासु विषेदुः सुरसैनिकाः ॥ ५२ ॥

evaṁ daityair mahā-māyair
alakṣya-gatibhī raṇe
sṛjyamānāsu māyāsu
viṣeduh sura-sainikāḥ

evam—thus; *daityaiḥ*—by the demons; *mahā-māyaiḥ*—who were expert in creating illusions; *alakṣya-gatibhiḥ*—but invisible; *raṇe*—in the fight; *sṛjyamānāsu māyāsu*—because of the creation of such an illusory atmosphere; *viṣeduḥ*—became morose; *sura-sainikāḥ*—the soldiers of the demigods.

TRANSLATION

While this magical atmosphere in the fight was being created by the invisible demons, who were expert in such illusions, the soldiers of the demigods became morose.

TEXT 53

न तत्प्रतिविधिं यत्र विदुरिन्द्रादयो नृप ।
ध्यातः प्रादुरभूत् तत्र भगवान्विश्वभावनः ॥ ५३ ॥

na tat-pratividhiṁ yatra
vidur indrādayo nṛpa
dhyātaḥ prādurabhūt tatra
bhagavān viśva-bhāvanaḥ

na—not; *tat-pratividhim*—the counteraction of such an illusory atmosphere; *yatra*—wherein; *viduḥ*—could understand; *indra-ādayaḥ*—the demigods, headed by Indra; *nṛpa*—O King; *dhyātaḥ*—being meditated upon; *prādurabhūt*—appeared there; *tatra*—in that place; *bhagavān*—the Supreme Personality of Godhead; *viśva-bhāvanaḥ*—the creator of the universe.

TRANSLATION

O King, when the demigods could find no way to counteract the activities of the demons, they wholeheartedly meditated upon the Supreme Personality of Godhead, the creator of the universe, who then immediately appeared.

TEXT 54

ततः सुपर्णांसकृताङ्घ्रिपल्लवः
पिशङ्गवासा नवकञ्जलोचनः ।
अदृश्यताष्टायुधबाहुरुल्लस-
च्छ्रीकौस्तुभानर्घ्यकिरीटकुण्डलः ॥ ५४ ॥

tataḥ suparṇāṁsa-kṛtāṅghri-pallavaḥ
piśaṅga-vāsā nava-kañja-locanaḥ
adṛśyatāṣṭāyudha-bāhur ullasac-
chrī-kaustubhānarghya-kirīṭa-kuṇḍalaḥ

tataḥ—thereafter; *suparṇa-aṁsa-kṛta-aṅghri-pallavaḥ*—the Supreme Personality of Godhead, whose lotus feet spread over the two shoulders of

Garuḍa; *piśaṅga-vāsāḥ*—whose dress is yellow; *nava-kañja-locanaḥ*—and whose eyes are just like the petals of a newly blossomed lotus; *adṛśyata*—became visible (in the presence of the demigods); *aṣṭa-āyudha*—equipped with eight kinds of weapons; *bāhuḥ*—arms; *ullasat*—brilliantly exhibiting; *śrī*—the goddess of fortune; *kaustubha*—the Kaustubha gem; *anarghya*—of incalculable value; *kirīṭa*—helmet; *kuṇḍalaḥ*—having earrings.

TRANSLATION

The Supreme Personality of Godhead, whose eyes resemble the petals of a newly blossomed lotus, sat on the back of Garuḍa, spreading His lotus feet over Garuḍa's shoulders. Dressed in yellow, decorated by the Kaustubha gem and the goddess of fortune, and wearing an invaluable helmet and earrings, the Supreme Lord, holding various weapons in His eight hands, became visible to the demigods.

TEXT 55

तस्मिन्प्रविष्टेऽसुरकूटकर्मजा
माया विनेशुर्महिना महीयसः ।
स्वप्नो यथा हि प्रतिबोध आगते
हरिस्मृतिः सर्वविपद्विमोक्षणम् ॥ ५५ ॥

tasmin praviṣṭe 'sura-kūṭa-karmajā
māyā vineśur mahinā mahīyasaḥ
svapno yathā hi pratibodha āgate
hari-smṛtiḥ sarva-vipad-vimokṣaṇam

tasmin praviṣṭe—upon the entrance of the Supreme Personality of Godhead; *asura*—of the demons; *kūṭa-karma-jā*—because of the illusory, magical activities; *māyā*—the false manifestations; *vineśuḥ*—were immediately curbed; *mahinā*—by the superior power; *mahīyasaḥ*—of the Supreme Personality of Godhead, who is greater than the greatest; *svapnaḥ*—dreams; *yathā*—as; *hi*—indeed; *pratibodhe*—when awakening; *āgate*—has arrived; *hari-smṛtiḥ*—remembrance of the Supreme Personality of Godhead; *sarva-vipat*—of all kinds of dangerous situations; *vimokṣaṇam*—immediately vanquishes.

TRANSLATION

As the dangers of a dream cease when the dreamer awakens, the illusions created by the jugglery of the demons were vanquished by the transcendental

prowess of the Supreme Personality of Godhead as soon as He entered the battlefield. Indeed, simply by remembrance of the Supreme Personality of Godhead, one becomes free from all dangers.

TEXT 56

दृष्ट्वा मृधे गरुडवाहमिभारिवाह
आविध्य शूलमहिनोदथ कालनेमिः ।
तल्लीलया गरुडमूर्ध्नि पतद् गृहीत्वा
तेनाहनन्नृप सवाहमरिं त्र्यधीशः ॥ ५६ ॥

dṛṣṭvā mṛdhe garuḍa-vāham ibhāri-vāha
āvidhya śūlam ahinod atha kālanemiḥ
tal līlayā garuḍa-mūrdhni patad gṛhītvā
tenāhanan nṛpa savāham ariṁ tryadhīśaḥ

dṛṣṭvā—seeing; *mṛdhe*—on the battlefield; *garuḍa-vāham*—the Supreme Personality of Godhead, carried by Garuḍa; *ibhāri-vāhaḥ*—the demon, who was carried by a big lion; *āvidhya*—whirling around; *śūlam*—trident; *ahinot*—discharged at him; *atha*—thus; *kālanemiḥ*—the demon Kālanemi; *tat*—such an attack by the demon against the Supreme Lord; *līlayā*—very easily; *garuḍa-mūrdhni*—on the head of His carrier, Garuḍa; *patat*—while falling down; *gṛhītvā*—after taking it immediately, without difficulty; *tena*—and by the same weapon; *ahanat*—killed; *nṛpa*—O King; *sa-vāham*—with his carrier; *arim*—the enemy; *tri-adhīśaḥ*—the Supreme Personality of Godhead, the proprietor of the three worlds.

TRANSLATION

O King, when the demon Kālanemi, who was carried by a lion, saw that the Supreme Personality of Godhead, carried by Garuḍa, was on the battlefield, the demon immediately took his trident, whirled it and discharged it at Garuḍa's head. The Supreme Personality of Godhead, Hari, the master of the three worlds, immediately caught the trident, and with the very same weapon he killed the enemy Kālanemi, along with his carrier, the lion.

PURPORT

In this regard, Śrīla Madhvācārya says:

kālanemy-ādayaḥ sarve
kariṇā nihatā api

śukreṇojjīvitāḥ santaḥ
punas tenaiva pātitāḥ

"Kālanemi and all the other demons were killed by the Supreme Personality of Godhead, Hari, and when Śukrācārya, their spiritual master, brought them back to life, they were again killed by the Supreme Personality of Godhead."

TEXT 57

माली सुमाल्यतिबलौ युधि पेततुर्य-
च्चक्रेण कृत्तशिरसावथ माल्यवांस्तम् ।
आहत्य तिग्मगदयाहनदण्डजेन्द्रं
तावच्छिरोऽच्छिनदरेर्नदतोऽरिणाद्यः ॥ ५७ ॥

mālī sumāly atibalau yudhi petatur yac-
cakreṇa kṛtta-śirasāv atha mālyavāṁs tam
āhatya tigma-gadayāhanad aṇḍajendraṁ
tāvac chiro 'cchinad arer nadato 'riṇādyaḥ

mālī sumālī—two demons named Mālī and Sumālī; *ati-balau*—very powerful; *yudhi*—on the battlefield; *petatuḥ*—fell down; *yat-cakreṇa*—by whose disc; *kṛtta-śirasau*—their heads having been cut off; *atha*—thereupon; *mālyavān*—Mālyavān; *tam*—the Supreme Personality of Godhead; *āhatya*—attacking; *tigma-gadayā*—with a very sharp club; *ahanat*—attempted to attack, kill; *aṇḍa-ja-indram*—Garuḍa, the king of all the birds, who are born from eggs; *tāvat*—at that time; *śiraḥ*—the head; *acchinat*—cut off; *areḥ*—of the enemy; *nadataḥ*—roaring like a lion; *ariṇā*—by the disc; *ādyaḥ*—the original Personality of Godhead.

TRANSLATION

Thereafter, two very powerful demons named Mālī and Sumālī were killed by the Supreme Lord, who severed their heads with His disc. Then Mālyavān, another demon, attacked the Lord. With his sharp club, the demon, who was roaring like a lion, attacked Garuḍa, the lord of the birds, who are born from eggs. But the Supreme Personality of Godhead, the original person, used His disc to cut off the head of that enemy also.

Thus end the Bhaktivedanta purports of the Eighth Canto, Tenth Chapter, of the Śrīmad-Bhāgavatam, *entitled "The Battle Between the Demigods and the Demons."*

CHAPTER ELEVEN

King Indra Annihilates the Demons

As described in this chapter, the great saint Nārada Muni, being very compassionate to the demons who had been killed by the demigods, forbade the demigods to continue killing. Then Śukrācārya, by his mystic power, renewed the lives of all the demons.

Having been graced by the Supreme Personality of Godhead, the demigods began fighting the demons again, with renewed energy. King Indra released his thunderbolt against Bali, and when Bali fell, his friend Jambhāsura attacked Indra, who then cut off Jambhāsura's head with his thunderbolt. When Nārada Muni learned that Jambhāsura had been killed, he informed Jambhāsura's relatives Namuci, Bala and Pāka, who then went to the battlefield and attacked the demigods. Indra, King of heaven, severed the heads of Bala and Pāka and released the weapon known as *kuliśa,* the thunderbolt, against Namuci's shoulder. The thunderbolt, however, returned unsuccessful, and thus Indra became morose. At that time, an unseen voice came from the sky. The voice declared, "A dry or wet weapon cannot kill Namuci." Hearing this voice, Indra began to think of how Namuci could be killed. He then thought of foam, which is neither moist nor dry. Using a weapon of foam, he was able to kill Namuci. Thus Indra and the other demigods killed many demons. Then, at the request of Lord Brahmā, Nārada went to the demigods and forbade them to kill the demons any longer. All the demigods then returned to their abodes. Following the instructions of Nārada, whatever demons remained alive on the battlefield took Bali Mahārāja to Asta Mountain. There, by the touch of Śukrācārya's hand, Bali Mahārāja regained his senses and consciousness, and those demons whose heads and bodies had not been completely lost were brought back to life by the mystic power of Śukrācārya.

TEXT 1

श्रीशुक उवाच

अथो सुराः प्रत्युपलब्धचेतसः
परस्य पुंसः परयानुकम्पया।

जघ्नुर्भृशं शक्रसमीरणादय-
स्तांस्तान्रणे यैरभिसंहताः पुरा ॥ १ ॥

śrī-śuka uvāca
atho surāḥ pratyupalabdha-cetasaḥ
parasya puṁsaḥ parayānukampayā
jaghnur bhṛśaṁ śakra-samīraṇādayas
tāṁs tān raṇe yair abhisaṁhatāḥ purā

śrī-śukaḥ uvāca—Śrī Śukadeva Gosvāmī said; *atho*—thereafter; *surāḥ*—all the demigods; *pratyupalabdha-cetasaḥ*—being enlivened again by revival of their consciousness; *parasya*—of the Supreme; *puṁsaḥ*—of the Personality of Godhead; *parayā*—supreme; *anukampayā*—by the mercy; *jaghnuḥ*—began to beat; *bhṛśam*—again and again; *śakra*—Indra; *samīraṇa*—Vāyu; *ādayaḥ*—and others; *tān tān*—to those demons; *raṇe*—in the fight; *yaiḥ*—by whom; *abhisaṁhatāḥ*—they were beaten; *purā*—before.

TRANSLATION

Śukadeva Gosvāmī said: Thereafter, by the supreme grace of the Supreme Personality of Godhead, Śrī Hari, all the demigods, headed by Indra and Vāyu, were brought back to life. Being enlivened, the demigods began severely beating the very same demons who had defeated them before.

TEXT 2

वैरोचनाय संरब्धो भगवान्पाकशासनः ।
उदयच्छद् यदा वज्रं प्रजा हा हेति चुक्रुशुः ॥ २ ॥

vairocanāya saṁrabdho
bhagavān pāka-śāsanaḥ
udayacchad yadā vajraṁ
prajā hā heti cukruśuḥ

vairocanāya—unto Bali Mahārāja (just to kill him); *samrabdhaḥ*—being very angry; *bhagavān*—the most powerful; *pāka-śāsanaḥ*—Indra; *udayac-chat*—took in his hand; *yadā*—at which time; *vajram*—the thunderbolt; *prajāḥ*—all the demons; *hā hā*—alas, alas; *iti*—thus; *cukruśuḥ*—began to resound.

TRANSLATION

When the most powerful Indra became angry and took his thunderbolt in hand to kill Mahārāja Bali, the demons began lamenting, "Alas, alas!"

TEXT 3

वज्रपाणिस्तमाहेदं तिरस्कृत्य पुरःस्थितम् ।
मनस्विनं सुसम्पन्नं विचरन्तं महामृधे ॥ ३ ॥

vajra-pāṇis tam āhedaṁ
tiraskṛtya puraḥ-sthitam
manasvinaṁ susampannaṁ
vicarantaṁ mahā-mṛdhe

vajra-pāṇiḥ—Indra, who always carries in his hand the thunderbolt; *tam*—unto Bali Mahārāja; *āha*—addressed; *idam*—in this way; *tiraskṛtya*—chastising him; *puraḥ-sthitam*—standing before him; *manasvinam*—very sober and tolerant; *su-sampannam*—well equipped with paraphernalia for fighting; *vicarantam*—moving; *mahā-mṛdhe*—on the great battlefield.

TRANSLATION

Sober and tolerant and well equipped with paraphernalia for fighting, Bali Mahārāja moved before Indra on the great battlefield. King Indra, who always carries the thunderbolt in his hand, rebuked Bali Mahārāja as follows.

TEXT 4

नटवन्मूढ मायाभिर्मायेशान् नो जिगीषसि ।
जित्वा बालान् निबद्धाक्षान् नटो हरति तद्धनम् ॥ ४ ॥

naṭavan mūḍha māyābhir
māyeśān no jigīṣasi
jitvā bālān nibaddhākṣān
naṭo harati tad-dhanam

naṭa-vat—like a cheater or rogue; *mūḍha*—you rascal; *māyābhiḥ*—by exhibiting illusions; *māyā-īśān*—unto the demigods, who can control all such illusory manifestations; *naḥ*—unto us; *jigīṣasi*—you are trying to become victorious; *jitvā*—conquering; *bālān*—small children; *nibaddha-akṣān*—by binding the eyes; *naṭaḥ*—a cheater; *harati*—takes away; *tat-dhanam*—the property in the possession of a child.

TRANSLATION

Indra said: O rascal, as a cheater sometimes binds the eyes of a child and takes away his possessions, you are trying to defeat us by displaying some mystic power, although you know that we are the masters of all such mystic powers.

TEXT 5

आरुरुक्षन्ति मायाभिरुत्सिसृप्सन्ति ये दिवम् ।
तान्दस्यून्विधुनोम्यज्ञान्पूर्वस्माच्च पदादधः ॥ ५ ॥

āurukṣanti māyābhir
utsisṛpsanti ye divam
tān dasyūn vidhunomy ajñān
pūrvasmāc ca padād adhaḥ

āurukṣanti—persons who desire to come to the upper planetary systems; *māyābhiḥ*—by so-called mystic power or material advancement of science; *utsisṛpsanti*—or want to be liberated by such false attempts; *ye*—such persons who; *divam*—the higher planetary system known as Svargaloka; *tān*—such rogues and ruffians; *dasyūn*—such thieves; *vidhunomi*—I force to go down; *ajñān*—rascals; *pūrvasmāt*—previous; *ca*—also; *padāt*—from the position; *adhaḥ*—downward.

TRANSLATION

Those fools and rascals who want to ascend to the upper planetary system by mystic power or mechanical means, or who endeavor to cross even the upper planets and achieve the spiritual world or liberation, I cause to be sent to the lowest region of the universe.

PURPORT

There are undoubtedly different planetary systems for different persons. As stated in *Bhagavad-gītā* (14.18), *ūrdhvaṁ gacchanti sattva-sthāḥ:* persons in the mode of goodness can go to the upper planets. Those in the modes of darkness and passion, however, are not allowed to enter the higher planets. The word *divam* refers to the higher planetary system known as Svargaloka. Indra, King of the higher planetary system, has the power to push down any conditioned soul attempting to go from the lower to the higher planets without proper qualifications. The modern attempt to go to the moon is also an attempt by inferior men to go to Svargaloka by artificial, mechanical means. This attempt cannot be successful. From this statement of Indra it appears that anyone attempting to go to the higher planetary systems by mechanical means, which are here called *māyā,* is condemned to go the hellish planets in the lower portion of the universe. To go to the higher planetary system, one needs sufficient good qualities. A sinful person situated in the mode of ignorance and addicted to drinking, meat-eating and illicit sex will never enter the higher planets by mechanical means.

TEXT 6

सोऽहं दुर्मायिनस्तेऽद्य वज्रेण शतपर्वणा ।
शिरो हरिष्ये मन्दात्मन्घटस्व ज्ञातिभिः सह ॥ ६ ॥

so 'haṁ durmāyinas te 'dya
vajreṇa śata-parvaṇā
śiro hariṣye mandātman
ghaṭasva jñātibhiḥ saha

saḥ—I am the same powerful person; *aham*—I; *durmāyinaḥ*—of you, who can perform so much jugglery with illusions; *te*—of you; *adya*—today; *vajreṇa*—by the thunderbolt; *śata-parvaṇā*—which has hundreds of sharp edges; *śiraḥ*—the head; *hariṣye*—I shall separate; *manda-ātman*—O you with a poor fund of knowledge; *ghaṭasva*—just try to exist on this battlefield; *jñātibhiḥ saha*—with your relatives and assistants.

TRANSLATION

Today, with my thunderbolt, which has hundreds of sharp edges, I, the same powerful person, shall sever your head from your body. Although you can produce so much jugglery through illusion, you are endowed with a poor fund of knowledge. Now, try to exist on this battlefield with your relatives and friends.

TEXT 7

श्रीबलिरुवाच

सङ्ग्रामे वर्तमानानां कालचोदितकर्मणाम् ।
कीर्तिर्जयोऽजयो मृत्युः सर्वेषां स्युरनुक्रमात् ॥ ७ ॥

śrī-balir uvāca
saṅgrāme vartamānānāṁ
kāla-codita-karmaṇām
kīrtir jayo 'jayo mṛtyuḥ
sarveṣāṁ syur anukramāt

śrī-baliḥ uvāca—Bali Mahārāja said; *saṅgrāme*—in the battlefield; *vartamānānām*—of all persons present here; *kāla-codita*—influenced by the course of time; *karmaṇām*—for persons engaged in fighting or any other activities; *kīrtiḥ*—reputation; *jayaḥ*—victory; *ajayaḥ*—defeat; *mṛtyuḥ*—death; *sarveṣām*—of all of them; *syuḥ*—must be done; *anukramāt*—one after another.

TRANSLATION

Bali Mahārāja replied: All those present on this battlefield are certainly under the influence of eternal time, and according to their prescribed activities, they are destined to receive fame, victory, defeat and death, one after another.

PURPORT

If one is victorious on the battlefield, he becomes famous; and if one is not victorious but is defeated, he may die. Both victory and defeat are possible, whether on such a battlefield as this or on the battlefield of the struggle for existence. Everything takes place according to the laws of nature (*prakṛteḥ kriyamāṇāni guṇaiḥ karmāṇi sarvaśaḥ*). Since everyone, without exception, is subject to the modes of material nature, whether one is victorious or defeated he is not independent, but is under the control of material nature. Bali Mahārāja, therefore, was very sensible. He knew that the fighting was arranged by eternal time and that under time's influence one must accept the results of one's own activities. Therefore even though Indra threatened that he would now kill Bali Mahārāja by releasing the thunderbolt, Bali Mahārāja was not at all afraid. This is the spirit of a *kṣatriya: yuddhe cāpy apalāyanam* (Bg. 18.43). A *kṣatriya* must be tolerant in all circumstances, especially on the battlefield. Thus Bali Mahārāja asserted that he was not at all afraid of death, although he was threatened by such a great personality as the King of heaven.

TEXT 8

तदिदं कालरशनं जगत् पश्यन्ति सूरयः ।
न हृष्यन्ति न शोचन्ति तत्र यूयमपण्डिताः ॥ ८ ॥

tad idaṁ kāla-raśanaṁ
jagat paśyanti sūrayaḥ
na hṛṣyanti na śocanti
tatra yūyam apaṇḍitāḥ

tat—therefore; *idam*—this whole material world; *kāla-raśanam*—is moving because of time eternal; *jagat*—moving forward (this whole universe); *paśyanti*—observe; *sūrayaḥ*—those who are intelligent by admission of the truth; *na*—not; *hṛṣyanti*—become jubilant; *na*—nor; *śocanti*—lament; *tatra*—in such; *yūyam*—all of you demigods; *apaṇḍitāḥ*—not very learned (having forgotten that you are working under eternal time).

TRANSLATION

Seeing the movements of time, those who are cognizant of the real truth neither rejoice nor lament for different circumstances. Therefore, because you are jubilant due to your victory, you should be considered not very learned.

PURPORT

Bali Mahārāja knew that Indra, King of heaven, was extremely powerful, certainly more powerful than he himself. Nonetheless, Bali Mahārāja challenged Indra by saying that Indra was not a very learned person. In *Bhagavad-gītā* (2.11) Kṛṣṇa rebuked Arjuna by saying:

aśocyān anvaśocas tvaṁ
prajñā-vādāṁś ca bhāṣase
gatāsūn agatāsūṁś ca
nānuśocanti paṇḍitāḥ

"While speaking learned words, you are mourning for what is not worthy of grief. Those who are wise lament neither for the living nor the dead." Thus as Kṛṣṇa challenged Arjuna by saying that he was not a *paṇḍita,* or a learned person, Bali Mahārāja also challenged King Indra and his associates. In this material world, everything happens under the influence of time. Consequently, for a learned person who sees how things are taking place, there is no question of being sorry or happy because of the waves of material nature. After all, since we are being carried away by these waves, what is the meaning of being jubilant or morose? One who is fully conversant with the laws of nature is never jubilant or morose because of nature's activities. In *Bhagavad-gītā* (2.14), Kṛṣṇa advises that one be tolerant: *tāṁs titikṣasva bhārata.* Following this advice of Kṛṣṇa's, one should not be morose or unhappy because of circumstantial changes. This is the symptom of a devotee. A devotee carries out his duty in Kṛṣṇa consciousness and is never unhappy in awkward circumstances. He has full faith that in such circumstances, Kṛṣṇa protects His devotee. Therefore a devotee never deviates from his prescribed duty of devotional service. The material qualities of jubilation and moroseness are present even in the demigods, who are very highly situated in the upper planetary system. Therefore, when one is undisturbed by the so-called favorable and unfavorable circumstances of this material world, he should be understood to be *brahma-bhūta,* or self-realized. As stated in *Bhagavad-gītā* (18.54), *brahma-bhūtaḥ prasannātmā na śocati na kāṅkṣati:* "One who is transcendentally situated at once realizes the Supreme Brahman and becomes fully joyful." When one is undisturbed by material circumstances, he should be understood to be on the transcendental stage, above the reactions of the three modes of material nature.

TEXT 9

न वयं मन्यमानानामात्मानं तत्र साधनम् ।
गिरो वः साधुशोच्यानां गृह्णीमो मर्मताडनाः ॥ ९ ॥

na vayaṁ manyamānānām
ātmānaṁ tatra sādhanam
giro vaḥ sādhu-śocyānāṁ
gṛhṇīmo marma-tāḍanāḥ

na—not; *vayam*—we; *manyamānānām*—who are considering; *ātmānam*—the self; *tatra*—in victory or defeat; *sādhanam*—the cause; *giraḥ*—the words; *vaḥ*—of you; *sādhu-śocyānām*—who are to be pitied by the saintly persons; *gṛhṇīmaḥ*—accept; *marma-tāḍanāḥ*—which afflict the heart.

TRANSLATION

You demigods think that your own selves are the cause of your attaining fame and victory. Because of your ignorance, saintly persons feel sorry for you. Therefore, although your words afflict the heart, we do not accept them.

TEXT 10

श्रीशुक उवाच
इत्याक्षिप्य विभुं वीरो नाराचैर्वीरमर्दनः ।
आकर्णपूर्णैरहनदाक्षेपैराहतं पुनः ॥ १० ॥

śrī-śuka uvāca
ity ākṣipya vibhuṁ vīro
nārācair vīra-mardanaḥ
ākarṇa-pūrṇair ahanad
ākṣepair āha taṁ punaḥ

śrī-śukaḥ uvāca—Śrī Śukadeva Gosvāmī said; *iti*—thus; *ākṣipya*—chastising; *vibhum*—unto King Indra; *vīraḥ*—the valiant Bali Mahārāja; *nārācaiḥ*—by the arrows named *nārācas; vīra-mardanaḥ*—Bali Mahārāja, who could subdue even great heros; *ākarṇa-pūrṇaiḥ*—drawn up to his ear; *ahanat*—attacked; *ākṣepaiḥ*—by words of chastisement; *āha*—said; *tam*—unto him; *punaḥ*—again.

TRANSLATION

Śukadeva Gosvāmī said: After thus rebuking Indra, King of heaven, with sharp words, Bali Mahārāja, who could subdue any other hero, drew back to his ear the arrows known as nārācas and attacked Indra with these arrows. Then he again chastised Indra with strong words.

TEXT 11

एवं निराकृतो देवो वैरिणा तथ्यवादिना ।
नामृष्यत् तदधिक्षेपं तोत्राहत इव द्विपः ॥ ११ ॥

evaṁ nirākṛto devo
vairiṇā tathya-vādinā
nāmṛṣyat tad-adhikṣepaṁ
totrāhata iva dvipaḥ

evam—thus; *nirākṛtaḥ*—being defeated; *devaḥ*—King Indra; *vairiṇā*—by his enemy; *tathya-vādinā*—who was competent to speak the truth; *na*—not; *amṛṣyat*—lamented; *tat*—of him (Bali); *adhikṣepam*—the chastisement; *totra*—by the scepter or rod; *āhataḥ*—being beaten; *iva*—just like; *dvipaḥ*—an elephant.

TRANSLATION

Since Mahārāja Bali's rebukes were truthful, King Indra did not at all become sorry, just as an elephant beaten by its driver's rod does not become agitated.

TEXT 12

प्राहरत् कुलिशं तस्मा अमोघं परमर्दनः ।
सयानो न्यपतद् भूमौ छिन्नपक्ष इवाचलः ॥ १२ ॥

prāharat kuliśaṁ tasmā
amoghaṁ para-mardanaḥ
sayāno nyapatad bhūmau
chinna-pakṣa ivācalaḥ

prāharat—inflicted; *kuliśam*—thunderbolt scepter; *tasmai*—unto him (Bali Mahārāja); *amogham*—infallible; *para-mardanaḥ*—Indra, who is expert in defeating the enemy; *sa-yānaḥ*—with his airplane; *nyapatat*—fell down; *bhūmau*—on the ground; *chinna-pakṣaḥ*—whose wings have been taken away; *iva*—like; *acalaḥ*—a mountain.

TRANSLATION

When Indra, the defeater of enemies, released his infallible thunderbolt scepter at Bali Mahārāja with a desire to kill him, Bali Mahārāja indeed fell to the ground with his airplane, like a mountain with its wings cut off.

PURPORT

In many descriptions in Vedic literature it is found that mountains also fly in the sky with wings. When such mountains are dead, they fall to the ground, where they stay as very large dead bodies.

TEXT 13

सखायं पतितं दृष्ट्वा जम्भो बलिसखः सुहृत् ।
अभ्ययात् सौहृदं सख्युर्हतस्यापि समाचरन् ॥ १३ ॥

sakhāyaṁ patitaṁ dṛṣṭvā
jambho bali-sakhaḥ suhṛt
abhyayāt sauhṛdaṁ sakhyur
hatasyāpi samācaran

sakhāyam—his intimate friend; *patitam*—having fallen; *dṛṣṭvā*—after seeing; *jambhaḥ*—the demon Jambha; *bali-sakhaḥ*—a very intimate friend of Bali Mahārāja; *suhṛt*—and constant well-wisher; *abhyayāt*—appeared on the scene; *sauhṛdam*—very compassionate friendship; *sakhyuḥ*—of his friend; *hatasya*—who was injured and fallen; *api*—although; *samācaran*—just to perform friendly duties.

TRANSLATION

When the demon Jambhāsura saw that his friend Bali had fallen, he appeared before Indra, the enemy, just to serve Bali Mahārāja with friendly behavior.

TEXT 14

स सिंहवाह आसाद्य गदामुद्यम्य रंहसा ।
जत्रावताडयच्छक्रं गजं च सुमहाबलः ॥ १४ ॥

sa siṁha-vāha āsādya
gadām udyamya raṁhasā
jatrāv atāḍayac chakraṁ
gajaṁ ca sumahā-balaḥ

saḥ—Jambhāsura; *siṁha-vāhaḥ*—being carried by a lion; *āsādya*—coming before King Indra; *gadām*—his club; *udyamya*—taking up; *raṁhasā*—with great force; *jatrau*—on the base of the neck; *atāḍayat*—hit; *śakram*—Indra; *gajam ca*—as well as his elephant; *su-mahā-balaḥ*—the greatly powerful Jambhāsura.

TRANSLATION

The greatly powerful Jambhāsura, carried by a lion, approached Indra and forcefully struck him on the shoulder with his club. He also struck Indra's elephant.

TEXT 15

गदाप्रहारव्यथितो भृशं विह्वलितो गजः ।
जानुभ्यां धरणीं स्पृष्ट्वा कश्मलं परमं ययौ ॥ १५ ॥

gadā-prahāra-vyathito
bhṛśaṁ vihvalito gajaḥ

jānubhyāṁ dharaṇīṁ spṛṣṭvā
kaśmalaṁ paramaṁ yayau

gadā-prahāra-vyathitaḥ—being aggrieved because of the blow from Jambhāsura's club; *bhṛśam*—very much; *vihvalitaḥ*—upset; *gajaḥ*—the elephant; *jānubhyām*—with its two knees; *dharaṇīm*—the earth; *spṛṣṭvā*—touching; *kaśmalam*—unconsciousness; *paramam*—ultimate; *yayau*—entered.

TRANSLATION

Being beaten by Jambhāsura's club, Indra's elephant was confused and aggrieved. Thus it touched its knees to the ground and fell unconscious.

TEXT 16

ततो रथो मातलिना हरिभिर्दशशतैर्वृतः ।
आनीतो द्विपमुत्सृज्य रथमारुरुहे विभुः ॥ १६ ॥

tato ratho mātalinā
haribhir daśa-śatair vṛtaḥ
ānīto dvipam utsṛjya
ratham āruruhe vibhuḥ

tataḥ—thereafter; *rathaḥ*—chariot; *mātalinā*—by his chariot driver named Mātali; *haribhiḥ*—with horses; *daśa-śataiḥ*—by ten times one hundred (one thousand); *vṛtaḥ*—yoked; *ānītaḥ*—being brought in; *dvipam*—the elephant; *utsṛjya*—keeping aside; *ratham*—the chariot; *āruruhe*—got up; *vibhuḥ*—the great Indra.

TRANSLATION

Thereafter, Mātali, Indra's chariot driver, brought Indra's chariot, which was drawn by one thousand horses. Indra then left his elephant and got onto the chariot.

TEXT 17

तस्य तत् पूजयन् कर्म यन्तुर्दानवसत्तमः ।
शूलेन ज्वलता तं तु स्मयमानोऽहनन्मृधे ॥ १७ ॥

tasya tat pūjayan karma
yantur dānava-sattamaḥ

śūlena jvalatā taṁ tu
smayamāno 'hanan mṛdhe

tasya—of Mātali; *tat*—that service (bringing the chariot before Indra); *pūjayan*—appreciating; *karma*—such service to the master; *yantuḥ*—of the chariot driver; *dānava-sat-tamaḥ*—the best of the demons, namely Jambhāsura; *śūlena*—by his trident; *jvalatā*—which was blazing fire; *tam*—Mātali; *tu*—indeed; *smayamānaḥ*—smiling; *ahanat*—struck; *mṛdhe*—in the battle.

TRANSLATION

Appreciating Mātali's service, Jambhāsura, the best of the demons, smiled. Nonetheless, he struck Mātali in the battle with a trident of blazing fire.

TEXT 18

सेहे रुजं सुदुर्मर्षां सत्त्वमालम्ब्य मातलिः ।
इन्द्रो जम्भस्य संक्रुद्धो वज्रेणापाहरच्छिरः ॥ १८ ॥

sehe rujaṁ sudurmarṣāṁ
sattvam ālambya mātaliḥ
indro jambhasya saṅkruddho
vajreṇāpāharac chiraḥ

sehe—tolerated; *rujam*—the pain; *su-durmarṣām*—intolerable; *sattvam*—patience; *ālambya*—taking shelter of; *mātaliḥ*—the charioteer Mātali; *indraḥ*—King Indra; *jambhasya*—of the great demon Jambha; *saṅkruddhaḥ*—being very angry at him; *vajreṇa*—with his thunderbolt; *apāharat*—separated; *śiraḥ*—the head.

TRANSLATION

Although the pain was extremely severe, Mātali tolerated it with great patience. Indra, however, became extremely angry at Jambhāsura. He struck Jambhāsura with his thunderbolt and thus severed his head from his body.

TEXT 19

जम्भं श्रुत्वा हतं तस्य ज्ञातयो नारदादृषेः ।
नमुचिश्च बलः पाकस्तत्रापेतुस्त्वरान्विताः ॥ १९ ॥

jambhaṁ śrutvā hataṁ tasya
jñātayo nāradād ṛṣeḥ
namuciś ca balaḥ pākas
tatrāpetus tvarānvitāḥ

jambham—Jambhāsura; *śrutvā*—after hearing; *hatam*—had been killed; *tasya*—his; *jñātayaḥ*—friends and relatives; *nāradāt*—from the source Nārada; *ṛṣeḥ*—from the great saint; *namuciḥ*—the demon Namuci; *ca*—also; *balaḥ*—the demon Bala; *pākaḥ*—the demon Pāka; *tatra*—there; *āpetuḥ*—immediately arrived; *tvarā-anvitāḥ*—with great haste.

TRANSLATION

When Nārada Ṛṣi informed Jambhāsura's friends and relatives that Jambhāsura had been killed, the three demons named Namuci, Bala and Pāka arrived on the battlefield in great haste.

TEXT 20

वचोभिः परुषैरिन्द्रमर्दयन्तोऽस्य मर्मसु ।
शरैरवाकिरन् मेघा धाराभिरिव पर्वतम् ॥ २० ॥

vacobhiḥ paruṣair indram
ardayanto 'sya marmasu
śarair avākiran meghā
dhārābhir iva parvatam

vacobhiḥ—with harsh words; *paruṣaiḥ*—very rough and cruel; *indram*—King Indra; *ardayantaḥ*—chastising, piercing; *asya*—of Indra; *marmasu*—in the heart, etc.; *śaraiḥ*—with arrows; *avākiran*—covered all around; *meghāḥ*—clouds; *dhārābhiḥ*—with showers of rain; *iva*—just as; *parvatam*—a mountain.

TRANSLATION

Rebuking Indra with harsh, cruel words that were piercing to the heart, these demons showered him with arrows, just as torrents of rain wash a great mountain.

TEXT 21

हरीन्दशशतान्याजौ हर्यश्वस्य बलः शरैः ।
तावद्भिरर्दयामास युगपल्लघुहस्तवान् ॥ २१ ॥

harīn daśa-śatāny ājau
haryaśvasya balaḥ śaraiḥ
tāvadbhir ardayām āsa
yugapal laghu-hastavān

harīn—horses; *daśa-śatāni*—ten times one hundred (one thousand); *ājau*—on the battlefield; *haryaśvasya*—of King Indra; *balaḥ*—the demon Bala; *śaraiḥ*—with arrows; *tāvadbhiḥ*—with so many; *ardayām āsa*—put into tribulation; *yugapat*—simultaneously; *laghu-hastavān*—with quick handling.

TRANSLATION

Quickly handling the situation on the battlefield, the demon Bala put all of Indra's one thousand horses into tribulation by simultaneously piercing them all with an equal number of arrows.

TEXT 22

शताभ्यां मातलिं पाको रथं सावयवं पृथक् ।
सकृत्सन्धानमोक्षेण तदद्भुतमभूद् रणे ॥ २२ ॥

śatābhyāṁ mātaliṁ pāko
rathaṁ sāvayavaṁ pṛthak
sakṛt sandhāna-mokṣeṇa
tad adbhutam abhūd raṇe

śatābhyām—with two hundred arrows; *mātalim*—unto the chariot driver Mātali; *pākaḥ*—the demon named Pāka; *ratham*—the chariot; *sa-avayavam*—with all paraphernalia; *pṛthak*—separately; *sakṛt*—once, at one time; *sandhāna*—by yoking the arrows to the bow; *mokṣeṇa*—and releasing; *tat*—such an action; *adbhutam*—wonderful; *abhūt*—so became; *raṇe*—on the battlefield.

TRANSLATION

Pāka, another demon, attacked both the chariot, with all its paraphernalia, and the chariot driver, Mātali, by fitting two hundred arrows to his bow and releasing them all simultaneously. This was indeed a wonderful act on the battlefield.

TEXT 23

नमुचिः पञ्चदशभिः स्वर्णपुङ्खैर्महेषुभिः ।
आहत्य व्यनदत्संख्ये सतोय इव तोयदः ॥ २३ ॥

namuciḥ pañca-daśabhiḥ
svarṇa-puṅkhair maheṣubhiḥ
āhatya vyanadat saṅkhye
satoya iva toyadaḥ

namuciḥ—the demon named Namuci; *pañca-daśabhiḥ*—with fifteen; *svarṇa-puṅkhaiḥ*—with golden feathers attached; *mahā-iṣubhiḥ*—very powerful arrows; *āhatya*—piercing; *vyanadat*—resounded; *saṅkhye*—on the battlefield; *sa-toyaḥ*—bearing water; *iva*—like; *toya-daḥ*—a cloud that delivers rain.

TRANSLATION

Then Namuci, another demon, attacked Indra and injured him with fifteen very powerful golden-feathered arrows, which roared like a cloud full of water.

TEXT 24

सर्वतः शरकूटेन शक्रं सरथसारथिम् ।
छादयामासुरसुराः प्रावृट्सूर्यमिवाम्बुदाः ॥ २४ ॥

sarvataḥ śara-kūṭena
śakraṁ saratha-sārathim
chādayām āsur asurāḥ
prāvṛṭ-sūryam ivāmbudāḥ

sarvataḥ—all around; *śara-kūṭena*—by a dense shower of arrows; *śakram*—Indra; *sa-ratha*—with his chariot; *sārathim*—and with his chariot driver; *chādayām āsuḥ*—covered; *asurāḥ*—all the demons; *prāvṛṭ*—in the rainy season; *sūryam*—the sun; *iva*—like; *ambu-dāḥ*—clouds.

TRANSLATION

Other demons covered Indra, along with his chariot and chariot driver, with incessant showers of arrows, just as clouds cover the sun in the rainy season.

TEXT 25

अलक्षयन्तस्तमतीव विह्वला
विचुक्रुशुर्देवगणाः सहानुगाः ।

अनायकाः शत्रुबलेन निर्जिता
वणिक्पथा भिन्ननवो यथार्णवे ॥ २५ ॥

alakṣayantas tam atīva vihvalā
vicukruśur deva-gaṇāḥ sahānugāḥ
anāyakāḥ śatru-balena nirjitā
vaṇik-pathā bhinna-navo yathārṇave

alakṣayantaḥ—being unable to see; *tam*—King Indra; *atīva*—fiercely; *vihvalāḥ*—bewildered; *vicukruśuḥ*—began to lament; *deva-gaṇāḥ*—all the demigods; *saha-anugāḥ*—with their followers; *anāyakāḥ*—without any captain or leader; *śatru-balena*—by the superior power of their enemies; *nirjitāḥ*—oppressed severely; *vaṇik-pathāḥ*—traders; *bhinna-navaḥ*—whose ship is wrecked; *yathā arṇave*—as in the middle of the ocean.

TRANSLATION

The demigods, being severely oppressed by their enemies and being unable to see Indra on the battlefield, were very anxious. Having no captain or leader, they began lamenting like traders in a wrecked vessel in the midst of the ocean.

PURPORT

From this statement it appears that in the upper planetary system there is shipping and that traders there engage in navigation as their occupational duty. Sometimes, as on this planet, these traders are shipwrecked in the middle of the ocean. It appears that even in the upper planetary system, such calamities occasionally take place. The upper planetary system in the creation of the Lord is certainly not vacant or devoid of living entities. From *Śrīmad-Bhāgavatam* we understand that every planet is full of living entities, just as earth is. There is no reason to accept that on other planetary systems there are no living beings.

TEXT 26

ततस्तुराषाडिषुबद्धपञ्जराद्
विनिर्गतः साश्वरथध्वजाग्रणीः ।
बभौ दिशः खं पृथिवीं च रोचयन्
स्वतेजसा सूर्य इव क्षपात्यये ॥ २६ ॥

tatas turāṣāḍ iṣu-baddha-pañjarād
vinirgataḥ sāśva-ratha-dhvajāgraṇīḥ
babhau diśaḥ khaṁ pṛthivīṁ ca rocayan
sva-tejasā sūrya iva kṣapātyaye

tataḥ—thereafter; *turāṣāṭ*—another name of Indra; *iṣu-baddha-pañjarāt*—from the cage of the network of arrows; *vinirgataḥ*—being released; *sa*—with; *aśva*—horses; *ratha*—chariot; *dhvaja*—flag; *agraṇīḥ*—and chariot driver; *babhau*—became; *diśaḥ*—all directions; *kham*—the sky; *pṛthivīm*—the earth; *ca*—and; *rocayan*—pleasing everywhere; *sva-tejasā*—by his personal effulgence; *sūryaḥ*—the sun; *iva*—like; *kṣapā-atyaye*—at the end of night.

TRANSLATION

Thereafter, Indra released himself from the cage of the network of arrows. Appearing with his chariot, flag, horses and chariot driver and thus pleasing the sky, the earth and all directions, he shone effulgently like the sun at the end of night. Indra was bright and beautiful in the vision of everyone.

TEXT 27

निरीक्ष्य पृतनां देवः परैरभ्यर्दितां रणे ।
उदयच्छद् रिपुं हन्तुं वज्रं वज्रधरो रुषा ॥ २७॥

nirīkṣya pṛtanāṁ devaḥ
parair abhyarditāṁ raṇe
udayacchad ripuṁ hantuṁ
vajraṁ vajra-dharo ruṣā

nirīkṣya—after observing; *pṛtanām*—his own soldiers; *devaḥ*—the demigod Indra; *paraiḥ*—by the enemies; *abhyarditām*—put into great difficulties or oppressed; *raṇe*—in the battlefield; *udayacchat*—took up; *ripum*—the enemies; *hantum*—to kill; *vajram*—the thunderbolt; *vajra-dharaḥ*—the carrier of the thunderbolt; *ruṣā*—in great anger.

TRANSLATION

When Indra, who is known as Vajra-dhara, the carrier of the thunderbolt, saw his own soldiers so oppressed by the enemies on the battlefield, he became very angry. Thus he took up his thunderbolt to kill the enemies.

TEXT 28

स तेनैवाष्टधारेण शिरसी बलपाकयोः ।
ज्ञातीनां पश्यतां राजञ्जहार जनयन्भयम् ॥ २८ ॥

sa tenaivāṣṭa-dhāreṇa
śirasī bala-pākayoḥ
jñātīnāṁ paśyatāṁ rājañ
jahāra janayan bhayam

saḥ—he (Indra); *tena*—by that; *eva*—indeed; *aṣṭa-dhāreṇa*—by the thunderbolt; *śirasī*—the two heads; *bala-pākayoḥ*—of the two demons known as Bala and Pāka; *jñātīnām paśyatām*—while their relatives and soldiers were watching; *rājan*—O King; *jahāra*—(Indra) cut off; *janayan*—creating; *bhayam*—fear (among them).

TRANSLATION

O King Parīkṣit, King Indra used his thunderbolt to cut off the heads of both Bala and Pāka in the presence of all their relatives and followers. In this way he created a very fearful atmosphere on the battlefield.

TEXT 29

नमुचिस्तद्वधं दृष्ट्वा शोकामर्षरुषान्वितः ।
जिघांसुरिन्द्रं नृपते चकार परमोद्यमम् ॥ २९ ॥

namucis tad-vadhaṁ dṛṣṭvā
śokāmarṣa-ruṣānvitaḥ
jighāṁsur indraṁ nṛpate
cakāra paramodyamam

namuciḥ—the demon Namuci; *tat*—of those two demons; *vadham*—the massacre; *dṛṣṭvā*—after seeing; *śoka-amarṣa*—lamentation and grief; *ruṣā-anvitaḥ*—being very angry at this; *jighāṁsuḥ*—wanted to kill; *indram*—King Indra; *nṛ-pate*—O Mahārāja Parīkṣit; *cakāra*—made; *parama*—a great; *udyamam*—endeavor.

TRANSLATION

O King, when Namuci, another demon, saw the killing of both Bala and Pāka, he was full of grief and lamentation. Thus he angrily made a great attempt to kill Indra.

TEXT 30

अश्मसारमयं शूलं घण्टावद्धेमभूषणम् ।
प्रगृह्याभ्यद्रवत् क्रुद्धो हतोऽसीति वितर्जयन् ।
प्राहिणोद् देवराजाय निनदन् मृगराडिव ॥ ३० ॥

aśmasāramayaṁ śūlaṁ
ghaṇṭāvad dhema-bhūṣaṇam
pragṛhyābhyadravat kruddho
hato 'sīti vitarjayan
prāhiṇod deva-rājāya
ninadan mṛga-rāḍ iva

aśmasāra-mayam—made of steel; *śūlam*—a spear; *ghaṇṭā-vat*—bound with bells; *hema-bhūṣaṇam*—decorated with ornaments of gold; *pragṛhya*—taking in his hand; *abhyadravat*—forcefully went; *kruddhaḥ*—in an angry mood; *hataḥ asi iti*—now you are killed; *vitarjayan*—roaring like that; *prāhiṇot*—struck; *deva-rājāya*—unto King Indra; *ninadan*—resounding; *mṛga-rāṭ*—a lion; *iva*—like.

TRANSLATION

Being angry and roaring like a lion, the demon Namuci took up a steel spear, which was bound with bells and decorated with ornaments of gold. He loudly cried, "Now you are killed!" Thus coming before Indra to kill him, Namuci released his weapon.

TEXT 31

तदापतद् गगनतले महाजवं
विचिच्छिदे हरिरिषुभिः सहस्रधा ।
तमाहनन्नृप कुलिशेन कन्धरे
रुषान्वितस्त्रिदशपतिः शिरो हरन् ॥ ३१ ॥

tadāpatad gagana-tale mahā-javaṁ
vicicchide harir iṣubhiḥ sahasradhā
tam āhanan nṛpa kuliśena kandhare
ruṣānvitas tridaśa-patiḥ śiro haran

tadā—at that time; *apatat*—falling like a meteor; *gagana-tale*—beneath the sky or on the ground; *mahā-javam*—extremely powerful; *vicicchide*—

cut to pieces; *hariḥ*—Indra; *iṣubhiḥ*—by his arrows; *sahasradhā*—into thousands of pieces; *tam*—that Namuci; *āhanat*—struck; *nṛpa*—O King; *kuliśena*—with his thunderbolt; *kandhare*—on the shoulder; *ruṣā-anvitaḥ*—being very angry; *tridaśa-patiḥ*—Indra, the King of the demigods; *śiraḥ*—the head; *haran*—to separate.

TRANSLATION

O King, when Indra, King of heaven, saw this very powerful spear falling toward the ground like a blazing meteor, he immediately cut it to pieces with his arrows. Then, being very angry, he struck Namuci's shoulder with his thunderbolt to cut off Namuci's head.

TEXT 32

न तस्य हि त्वचमपि वज्र ऊर्जितो
बिभेद यः सुरपतिनौजसेरितः ।
तदद्भुतं परमतिवीर्यवृत्रभित्
तिरस्कृतो नमुचिशिरोधरत्वचा ॥ ३२ ॥

na tasya hi tvacam api vajra ūrjito
bibheda yaḥ sura-patinaujaseritaḥ
tad adbhutaṁ param ativīrya-vṛtra-bhit
tiraskṛto namuci-śirodhara-tvacā

na—not; *tasya*—of him (Namuci); *hi*—indeed; *tvacam api*—even the skin; *vajraḥ*—the thunderbolt; *ūrjitaḥ*—very powerful; *bibheda*—could pierce; *yaḥ*—the weapon which; *sura-patinā*—by the king of the demigods; *ojasā*—very forcefully; *īritaḥ*—had been released; *tat*—therefore; *adbhutam param*—it was extraordinarily wonderful; *ativīrya-vṛtra-bhit*—so powerful that it could pierce the body of the very powerful Vṛtrāsura; *tiraskṛtaḥ*—(now in the future) which had been repelled; *namuci-śirodhara-tvacā*—by the skin of Namuci's neck.

TRANSLATION

Although King Indra hurled his thunderbolt at Namuci with great force, it could not even pierce his skin. It is very wonderful that the famed thunderbolt that had pierced the body of Vṛtrāsura could not even slightly injure the skin of Namuci's neck.

TEXT 33

तस्मादिन्द्रोऽबिभेच्छत्रोर्वज्रः प्रतिहतो यतः ।
किमिदं दैवयोगेन भूतं लोकविमोहनम् ॥ ३३ ॥

tasmād indro 'bibhec chatror
vajraḥ pratihato yataḥ
kim idaṁ daiva-yogena
bhūtaṁ loka-vimohanam

tasmāt—therefore; *indraḥ*—the King of heaven; *abibhet*—became very fearful; *śatroḥ*—from the enemy (Namuci); *vajraḥ*—the thunderbolt; *pratihataḥ*—was unable to hit and returned; *yataḥ*—because; *kim idam*—what is this; *daiva-yogena*—by some superior force; *bhūtam*—it has happened; *loka-vimohanam*—so wonderful to the people in general.

TRANSLATION

When Indra saw the thunderbolt return from the enemy, he was very much afraid. He began to wonder whether this had happened because of some miraculous superior power.

PURPORT

Indra's thunderbolt is invincible, and therefore when Indra saw that it had returned without doing any injury to Namuci, he was certainly very much afraid.

TEXT 34

येन मे पूर्वमद्रीणां पक्षच्छेदः प्रजात्यये ।
कृतो निविशतां भारैः पतत्त्रैः पततां भुवि ॥ ३४ ॥

yena me pūrvam adrīṇāṁ
pakṣa-cchedaḥ prajātyaye
kṛto niviśatāṁ bhāraiḥ
patattraiḥ patatāṁ bhuvi

yena—by the same thunderbolt; *me*—by me; *pūrvam*—formerly; *adrīṇām*—of the mountains; *pakṣa-cchedaḥ*—the cutting of the wings; *prajā-atyaye*—when there was killing of the people in general; *kṛtaḥ*—was done; *niviśatām*—of those mountains which entered; *bhāraiḥ*—by the great weight; *patattraiḥ*—by wings; *patatām*—falling; *bhuvi*—on the ground.

TRANSLATION

Indra thought: Formerly, when many mountains flying in the sky with wings would fall to the ground and kill people, I cut their wings with this same thunderbolt.

TEXT 35

तपःसारमयं त्वाष्ट्रं वृत्रो येन विपाटितः ।
अन्ये चापि बलोपेताः सर्वास्त्रैरक्षतत्वचः ॥ ३५ ॥

tapaḥ-sāramayaṁ tvāṣṭraṁ
vṛtro yena vipāṭitaḥ
anye cāpi balopetāḥ
sarvāstrair akṣata-tvacaḥ

tapaḥ—austerities; *sāra-mayam*—greatly powerful; *tvāṣṭram*—performed by Tvaṣṭā; *vṛtraḥ*—Vṛtrāsura; *yena*—by which; *vipāṭitaḥ*—was killed; *anye*—others; *ca*—also; *api*—indeed; *bala-upetāḥ*—very powerful persons; *sarva*—all kinds; *astraiḥ*—by weapons; *akṣata*—without being injured; *tvacaḥ*—their skin.

TRANSLATION

Vṛtrāsura was the essence of the austerities undergone by Tvaṣṭā, yet the thunderbolt killed him. Indeed, not only he but also many other stalwart heroes, whose very skin could not be injured even by all kinds of weapons, were killed by the same thunderbolt.

TEXT 36

सोऽयं प्रतिहतो वज्रो मया मुक्तोऽसुरेऽल्पके ।
नाहं तदाददे दण्डं ब्रह्मतेजोऽप्यकारणम् ॥ ३६ ॥

so 'yaṁ pratihato vajro
mayā mukto 'sure 'lpake
nāhaṁ tad ādade daṇḍaṁ
brahma-tejo 'py akāraṇam

saḥ ayam—therefore, this thunderbolt; *pratihataḥ*—repelled; *vajraḥ*—thunderbolt; *mayā*—by me; *muktaḥ*—released; *asure*—unto that demon; *alpake*—less important; *na*—not; *aham*—I; *tat*—that; *ādade*—hold;

daṇḍam—it is now just like a rod; *brahma-tejaḥ*—as powerful as a *brahmāstra; api*—although; *akāraṇam*—now it is useless.

TRANSLATION

But now, although the same thunderbolt has been released against a less important demon, it has been ineffectual. Therefore, although it was as good as a brahmāstra, it has now become useless like an ordinary rod. I shall therefore hold it no longer.

TEXT 37

इति शक्रं विषीदन्तमाह वागशरीरिणी ।
नायं शुष्कैरथो नार्द्रैर्वधमर्हति दानवः ॥ ३७ ॥

iti śakraṁ viṣīdantam
āha vāg aśarīriṇī
nāyaṁ śuṣkair atho nārdrair
vadham arhati dānavaḥ

iti—in this way; *śakram*—unto Indra; *viṣīdantam*—lamenting; *āha*—spoke; *vāk*—a voice; *aśarīriṇī*—without any body, or from the sky; *na*—not; *ayam*—this; *śuṣkaiḥ*—by anything dry; *atho*—also; *na*—nor; *ārdraiḥ*—by anything moist; *vadham*—annihilation; *arhati*—is befitting; *dānavaḥ*—this demon (Namuci).

TRANSLATION

Śukadeva Gosvāmī continued: While the morose Indra was lamenting in this way, an ominous, unembodied voice said from the sky, "This demon Namuci is not to be annihilated by anything dry or moist."

TEXT 38

मयास्मै यद् वरो दत्तो मृत्युर्नैवार्द्रशुष्कयोः ।
अतोऽन्यश्चिन्तनीयस्ते उपायो मघवन् रिपोः ॥ ३८ ॥

mayāsmai yad varo datto
mṛtyur naivārdra-śuṣkayoḥ
ato 'nyaś cintanīyas te
upāyo maghavan ripoḥ

mayā—by me; *asmai*—unto him; *yat*—because; *varaḥ*—a benediction; *dattaḥ*—has been granted; *mṛtyuḥ*—death; *na*—not; *eva*—indeed; *ārdra*—by either a moist; *śuṣkayoḥ*—or by a dry medium; *ataḥ*—therefore; *anyaḥ*—something else, another; *cintanīyaḥ*—has to be thought of; *te*—by you; *upāyaḥ*—means; *maghavan*—O Indra; *ripoḥ*—of your enemy.

TRANSLATION

The voice also said, "O Indra, because I have given this demon the benediction that he will never be killed by any weapon that is dry or moist, you have to think of another way to kill him."

TEXT 39

तां दैवीं गिरमाकर्ण्य मघवान्सुसमाहितः ।
ध्यायन् फेनमथापश्यदुपायमुभयात्मकम् ॥ ३९ ॥

tāṁ daivīṁ giram ākarṇya
maghavān susamāhitaḥ
dhyāyan phenam athāpaśyad
upāyam ubhayātmakam

tām—that; *daivīm*—ominous; *giram*—voice; *ākarṇya*—after hearing; *maghavān*—Lord Indra; *su-samāhitaḥ*—becoming very careful; *dhyāyan*—meditating; *phenam*—appearance of foam; *atha*—thereafter; *apaśyat*—he saw; *upāyam*—the means; *ubhaya-ātmakam*—simultaneously dry and moist.

TRANSLATION

After hearing the ominous voice, Indra, with great attention, began to meditate on how to kill the demon. He then saw that foam would be the means, for it is neither moist nor dry.

TEXT 40

न शुष्केण न चार्द्रेण जहार नमुचेः शिरः ।
तं तुष्टुवुर्मुनिगणा माल्यैश्चावाकिरन्विभुम् ॥ ४० ॥

na śuṣkeṇa na cārdreṇa
jahāra namuceḥ śiraḥ

taṁ tuṣṭuvur muni-gaṇā
mālyaiś cāvākiran vibhum

na—neither; *śuṣkeṇa*—by dry means; *na*—nor; *ca*—also; *ārdreṇa*—by a moist weapon; *jahāra*—he separated; *namuceḥ*—of Namuci; *śiraḥ*—the head; *tam*—him (Indra); *tuṣṭuvuḥ*—satisfied; *muni-gaṇāḥ*—all the sages; *mālyaiḥ*—with flower garlands; *ca*—also; *avākiran*—covered; *vibhum*—that great personality.

TRANSLATION

Thus Indra, King of heaven, severed Namuci's head with a weapon of foam, which was neither dry nor moist. Then all the sages satisfied Indra, the exalted personality, by showering flowers and garlands upon him, almost covering him.

PURPORT

In this regard, the *śruti-mantras* say, *apāṁ phenena namuceḥ śira indro 'dārayat:* Indra killed Namuci with watery foam, which is neither moist nor dry.

TEXT 41

गन्धर्वमुख्यौ जगतुर्विश्वावसुपरावसू ।
देवदुन्दुभयो नेदुर्नर्तक्यो ननृतुर्मुदा ॥ ४१ ॥

gandharva-mukhyau jagatur
viśvāvasu-parāvasū
deva-dundubhayo nedur
nartakyo nanṛtur mudā

gandharva-mukhyau—the two chiefs of the Gandharvas; *jagatuḥ*—began to sing nice songs; *viśvāvasu*—named Viśvāvasu; *parāvasū*—named Parāvasu; *deva-dundubhayaḥ*—the kettledrums beaten by the demigods; *neduḥ*—made their sound; *nartakyaḥ*—the dancers known as Apsarās; *nanṛtuḥ*—began to dance; *mudā*—in great happiness.

TRANSLATION

Viśvāvasu and Parāvasu, the two chiefs of the Gandharvas, sang in great happiness. The kettledrums of the demigods sounded, and the Apsarās danced in jubilation.

TEXT 42

अन्येऽप्येवं प्रतिद्वन्द्वान्वाय्वग्निवरुणादयः ।
सूदयामासुरसुरान् मृगान्केसरिणो यथा ॥ ४२ ॥

anye 'py evaṁ pratidvandvān
vāyv-agni-varuṇādayaḥ
sūdayām āsur asurān
mṛgān kesariṇo yathā

anye—others; *api*—also; *evam*—in this way; *pratidvandvān*—the opposing party of belligerants; *vāyu*—the demigod known as Vāyu; *agni*—the demigod known as Agni; *varuṇa-ādayaḥ*—the demigod known as Varuṇa and others; *sūdayām āsuḥ*—began to kill vigorously; *asurān*—all the demons; *mṛgān*—deer; *kesariṇaḥ*—lions; *yathā*—just as.

TRANSLATION

Vāyu, Agni, Varuṇa and other demigods began killing the demons who opposed them, just as lions kill deer in a forest.

TEXT 43

ब्रह्मणा प्रेषितो देवान्देवर्षिर्नारदो नृप ।
वारयामास विबुधान्दृष्ट्वा दानवसंक्षयम् ॥ ४३ ॥

brahmaṇā preṣito devān
devarṣir nārado nṛpa
vārayām āsa vibudhān
dṛṣṭvā dānava-saṅkṣayam

brahmaṇā—by Lord Brahmā; *preṣitaḥ*—sent; *devān*—unto the demigods; *deva-ṛṣiḥ*—the great sage of the heavenly planets; *nāradaḥ*—Nārada Muni; *nṛpa*—O King; *vārayām āsa*—forbade; *vibudhān*—all the demigods; *dṛṣṭvā*—after seeing; *dānava-saṅkṣayam*—the total annihilation of the demons.

TRANSLATION

O King, when Lord Brahmā saw the imminent total annihilation of the demons, he sent a message with Nārada, who went before the demigods to make them stop fighting.

TEXT 44

श्रीनारद उवाच
भवद्भिरमृतं प्राप्तं नारायणभुजाश्रयैः ।
श्रिया समेधिताः सर्व उपारमत विग्रहात् ॥ ४४ ॥

śrī-nārada uvāca
bhavadbhir amṛtaṁ prāptaṁ
nārāyaṇa-bhujāśrayaiḥ
śriyā samedhitāḥ sarva
upāramata vigrahāt

śrī-nāradaḥ uvāca—Nārada Muni prayed to the demigods; *bhavadbhiḥ*—by all of you; *amṛtam*—nectar; *prāptam*—has been obtained; *nārāyaṇa*—of the Supreme Personality of Godhead; *bhuja-āśrayaiḥ*—being protected by the arms; *śriyā*—by all fortune; *samedhitāḥ*—have flourished; *sarve*—all of you; *upāramata*—now cease; *vigrahāt*—from this fighting.

TRANSLATION

The great sage Nārada said: All of you demigods are protected by the arms of Nārāyaṇa, the Supreme Personality of Godhead, and by His grace you have gotten the nectar. By the grace of the goddess of fortune, you are glorious in every way. Therefore, please stop this fighting.

TEXT 45

श्रीशुक उवाच
संयम्य मन्युसंरम्भं मानयन्तो मुनेर्वचः ।
उपगीयमानानुचरैर्ययुः सर्वे त्रिविष्टपम् ॥ ४५ ॥

śrī-śuka uvāca
saṁyamya manyu-saṁrambhaṁ
mānayanto muner vacaḥ
upagīyamānānucarair
yayuḥ sarve triviṣṭapam

śrī-śukaḥ uvāca—Śrī Śukadeva Gosvāmī said; *saṁyamya*—controlling; *manyu*—of anger; *saṁrambham*—the aggravation; *mānayantaḥ*—accepting; *muneḥ vacaḥ*—the words of Nārada Muni; *upagīyamāna*—being praised; *anucaraiḥ*—by their followers; *yayuḥ*—returned; *sarve*—all of the demigods; *triviṣṭapam*—to the heavenly planets.

TRANSLATION

Śrī Śukadeva Gosvāmī said: Accepting the words of Nārada, the demigods gave up their anger and stopped fighting. Being praised by their followers, they returned to their heavenly planets.

TEXT 46

येऽवशिष्टा रणे तस्मिन् नारदानुमतेन ते ।
बलिं विपन्नमादाय अस्तं गिरिमुपागमन् ॥ ४६ ॥

ye 'vaśiṣṭā raṇe tasmin
nāradānumatena te
baliṁ vipannam ādāya
astaṁ girim upāgaman

ye—some of the demons who; *avaśiṣṭāḥ*—remained; *raṇe*—in the fight; *tasmin*—in that; *nārada-anumatena*—by the order of Nārada; *te*—all of them; *balim*—Mahārāja Bali; *vipannam*—in reverses; *ādāya*—taking; *astam*—named Asta; *girim*—to the mountain; *upāgaman*—went.

TRANSLATION

Following the order of Nārada Muni, whatever demons remained on the battlefield took Bali Mahārāja, who was in a precarious condition, to the hill known as Astagiri.

TEXT 47

तत्राविनष्टावयवान् विद्यमानशिरोधरान् ।
उशना जीवयामास संजीवन्या स्वविद्यया ॥ ४७ ॥

tatrāvinaṣṭāvayavān
vidyamāna-śirodharān
uśanā jīvayām āsa
sañjīvanyā sva-vidyayā

tatra—on that hill; *avinaṣṭa-avayavān*—the demons who had been killed but whose bodily parts had not been lost; *vidyamāna-śirodharān*—whose heads were still existing on their bodies; *uśanāḥ*—Śukrācārya; *jīvayām āsa*—brought to life; *sañjīvanyā*—by the Sañjīvanī *mantra; sva-vidyayā*—by his own achievement.

TRANSLATION

There, on that hill, Śukrācārya brought to life all the dead demoniac soldiers who had not lost their heads, trunks and limbs. He achieved this by his own mantra, known as Sañjīvanī.

TEXT 48

बलिश्चोशनसा स्पृष्टः प्रत्यापन्नेन्द्रियस्मृतिः ।
पराजितोऽपि नाखिद्यल्लोकतत्त्वविचक्षणः ॥ ४८ ॥

baliś cośanasā spṛṣṭaḥ
pratyāpannendriya-smṛtiḥ
parājito 'pi nākhidyal
loka-tattva-vicakṣaṇaḥ

baliḥ—Mahārāja Bali; *ca*—also; *uśanasā*—by Śukrācārya; *spṛṣṭaḥ*—being touched; *pratyāpanna*—was brought back; *indriya-smṛtiḥ*—realization of the actions of the senses and memory; *parājitaḥ*—he was defeated; *api*—although; *na akhidyat*—he did not lament; *loka-tattva-vicakṣaṇaḥ*—because he was very experienced in universal affairs.

TRANSLATION

Bali Mahārāja was very experienced in universal affairs. When he regained his senses and memory by the grace of Śukrācārya, he could understand everything that had happened. Therefore, although he had been defeated, he did not lament.

PURPORT

It is significant that Bali Mahārāja is here said to be very experienced. Although defeated, he was not at all sorry, for he knew that nothing can take place without the sanction of the Supreme Personality of Godhead. Since he was a devotee, he accepted his defeat without lamentation. As stated by the Supreme Personality of Godhead in *Bhagavad-gītā* (2.47), *karmaṇy evādhikāras te mā phaleṣu kadācana.* Everyone in Kṛṣṇa consciousness should execute his duty, without regard for victory or defeat. One must execute his duty as ordered by Kṛṣṇa or His representative, the spiritual master. *Ānukūlyena kṛṣṇānuśīlanaṁ bhaktir uttamā.* In first-class devotional service, one always abides by the orders and will of Kṛṣṇa.

Thus end the Bhaktivedanta purports of the Eighth Canto, Eleventh Chapter, of the Śrīmad-Bhāgavatam, *entitled "King Indra Annihilates the Demons."*

CHAPTER TWELVE

The Mohinī-mūrti Incarnation Bewilders Lord Śiva

This chapter describes how Lord Śiva was bewildered upon seeing the beautiful Mohinī-mūrti incarnation of the Supreme Personality of Godhead and how he later came to his senses. When Lord Śiva heard about the pastimes performed by the Supreme Personality of Godhead, Hari, in the form of an attractive woman, he mounted his bull and went to see the Lord. Accompanied by his wife, Umā, and his servants, the *bhūta-gaṇa,* or ghosts, he approached the lotus feet of the Lord. Lord Śiva offered obeisances to the Supreme Lord as the all-pervading Lord, the universal form, the supreme controller of creation, the Supersoul, the resting place for everyone, and the completely independent cause of all causes. Thus he offered prayers giving truthful descriptions of the Lord. Then he expressed his desire. The Supreme Personality of Godhead is very kind to His devotees. Therefore, to fulfill the desire of His devotee Lord Śiva, He expanded His energy and manifested Himself in the form of a very beautiful and attractive woman. Upon seeing this form, even Lord Śiva was captivated. Later, by the grace of the Lord, he controlled himself. This demonstrates that by the power of the Lord's external energy, everyone is captivated by the form of woman in this material world. Again, however, by the grace of the Supreme Personality of Godhead, one can overcome the influence of *māyā.* This was evinced by Lord Śiva, the topmost devotee of the Lord. First he was captivated, but later, by the grace of the Lord, he restrained himself. It is declared in this connection that only a pure devotee can restrain himself from the attractive feature of *māyā.* Otherwise, once a living entity is trapped by the external feature of *māyā,* he cannot overcome it. After Lord Śiva was graced by the Supreme Lord, he circumambulated the Lord along with his wife, Bhavānī, and his companions, the ghosts. Then he left for his own abode. Śukadeva Gosvāmī concludes this chapter by describing the transcendental qualities of Uttamaśloka, the Supreme Personality of Godhead, and by declaring that one can glorify the Lord by nine kinds of devotional service, beginning with *śravaṇaṁ kīrtanaṁ.*

TEXTS 1-2

श्रीबादरायणिरुवाच
वृषध्वजो निशम्येदं योषिद्रूपेण दानवान् ।
मोहयित्वा सुरगणान्हरिः सोममपाययत् ॥ १ ॥
वृषमारुह्य गिरिशः सर्वभूतगणैर्वृतः ।
सह देव्या ययौ द्रष्टुं यत्रास्ते मधुसूदनः ॥ २ ॥

śrī-bādarāyaṇir uvāca
vṛṣa-dhvajo niśamyedaṁ
yoṣid-rūpeṇa dānavān
mohayitvā sura-gaṇān
hariḥ somam apāyayat

vṛṣam āruhya giriśaḥ
sarva-bhūta-gaṇair vṛtaḥ
saha devyā yayau draṣṭuṁ
yatrāste madhusūdanaḥ

śrī-bādarāyaṇiḥ uvāca—Śrī Śukadeva Gosvāmī said; *vṛṣa-dhvajaḥ*—Lord Śiva, who is carried by a bull; *niśamya*—hearing; *idam*—this (news); *yoṣit-rūpeṇa*—by assuming the form of a woman; *dānavān*—the demons; *mohayitvā*—enchanting; *sura-gaṇān*—unto the demigods; *hariḥ*—the Supreme Personality of Godhead; *somam*—nectar; *apāyayat*—caused to drink; *vṛṣam*—the bull; *āruhya*—mounting; *giriśaḥ*—Lord Śiva; *sarva*—all; *bhūta-gaṇaiḥ*—by the ghosts; *vṛtaḥ*—surrounded; *saha devyā*—with Umā; *yayau*—went; *draṣṭum*—to see; *yatra*—where; *āste*—stays; *madhusūdanaḥ*—Lord Viṣṇu.

TRANSLATION

Śukadeva Gosvāmī said: The Supreme Personality of Godhead, Hari, in the form of a woman, captivated the demons and enabled the demigods to drink the nectar. After hearing of these pastimes, Lord Śiva, who is carried by a bull, went to the place where Madhusūdana, the Lord, resides. Accompanied by his wife, Umā, and surrounded by his companions, the ghosts, Lord Śiva went there to see the Lord's form as a woman.

TEXT 3

सभाजितो भगवता सादरं सोमया भवः ।
सूपविष्ट उवाचेदं प्रतिपूज्य स्मयन्हरिम् ॥ ३ ॥

sabhājito bhagavatā
sādaraṁ somayā bhavaḥ
sūpaviṣṭa uvācedaṁ
pratipūjya smayan harim

sabhājitaḥ—well received; *bhagavatā*—by the Supreme Personality of Godhead, Viṣṇu; *sa-ādaram*—with great respect (as befitting Lord Śiva); *sa-umayā*—with Umā; *bhavaḥ*—Lord Śambhu (Lord Śiva); *su-upaviṣṭaḥ*—being comfortably situated; *uvāca*—said; *idam*—this; *pratipūjya*—offering respect; *smayan*—smiling; *harim*—unto the Lord.

TRANSLATION

The Supreme Personality of Godhead welcomed Lord Śiva and Umā with great respect, and after being seated comfortably, Lord Śiva duly worshiped the Lord and smilingly spoke as follows.

TEXT 4

श्रीमहादेव उवाच
देवदेव जगद्व्यापिञ्जगदीश जगन्मय ।
सर्वेषामपि भावानां त्वमात्मा हेतुरीश्वरः ॥ ४ ॥

śrī-mahādeva uvāca
deva-deva jagad-vyāpiñ
jagad-īśa jagan-maya
sarveṣām api bhāvānāṁ
tvam ātmā hetur īśvaraḥ

śrī-mahādevaḥ uvāca—Lord Śiva (Mahādeva) said; *deva-deva*—O best demigod among the demigods; *jagat-vyāpin*—O all-pervading Lord; *jagat-īśa*—O master of the universe; *jagat-maya*—O my Lord, who are transformed by Your energy into this creation; *sarveṣām api*—all kinds of; *bhāvānām*—situations; *tvam*—You; *ātmā*—the moving force; *hetuḥ*—because of this; *īśvaraḥ*—the Supreme Lord, Parameśvara.

TRANSLATION

Lord Mahādeva said: O chief demigod among the demigods, O all-pervading Lord, master of the universe, by Your energy You are transformed into the creation. You are the root and efficient cause of everything. You are not material. Indeed, You are the Supersoul or supreme living force of everything. Therefore, You are Parameśvara, the supreme controller of all controllers.

PURPORT

The Supreme Personality of Godhead, Viṣṇu, resides within the material world as the *sattva-guṇa-avatāra.* Lord Śiva is the *tamo-guṇa-avatāra,* and Lord Brahmā is the *rajo-guṇa-avatāra,* but although Lord Viṣṇu is among them, He is not in the same category. Lord Viṣṇu is *deva-deva,* the chief of all the demigods. Since Lord Śiva is in this material world, the energy of the Supreme Lord, Viṣṇu, includes Lord Śiva. Lord Viṣṇu is therefore called *jagad-vyāpī,* "the all-pervading Lord." Lord Śiva is sometimes called Maheśvara, and so people think that Lord Śiva is everything. But here Lord Śiva addresses Lord Viṣṇu as Jagad-īśa, "the master of the universe." Lord Śiva is sometimes called Viśveśvara, but here he addresses Lord Viṣṇu as Jagan-maya, indicating that even Viśveśvara is under Lord Viṣṇu's control. Lord Viṣṇu is the master of the spiritual world, yet He controls the material world also, as stated in *Bhagavad-gītā* (*mayādhyakṣeṇa prakṛtiḥ sūyate sacarācaram*). Lord Brahmā and Lord Śiva are also sometimes called *īśvara,* but the supreme *īśvara* is Lord Viṣṇu, Lord Kṛṣṇa. As stated in *Brahma-saṁhitā, īśvaraḥ paramaḥ kṛṣṇaḥ:* the Supreme Lord is Kṛṣṇa, Lord Viṣṇu. Everything in existence works in proper order because of Lord Viṣṇu. *Aṇḍāntara-stha-paramāṇu-cayāntara-stham.* Even *paramāṇu,* the small atoms, work because of Lord Viṣṇu's presence within them.

TEXT 5

आद्यन्तावस्य यन्मध्यमिदमन्यदहं बहिः ।
यतोऽव्ययस्य नैतानि तत् सत्यं ब्रह्म चिद् भवान् ॥ ५ ॥

ādy-antāv asya yan madhyam
idam anyad ahaṁ bahiḥ
yato 'vyayasya naitāni
tat satyaṁ brahma cid bhavān

ādi—the beginning; *antau*—and the end; *asya*—of this manifested cosmos or of anything material or visible; *yat*—that which; *madhyam*—between the beginning and the end, the sustenance; *idam*—this cosmic manifestation; *anyat*—anything other than You; *aham*—the wrong mental conception; *bahiḥ*—outside of You; *yataḥ*—because of; *avyayasya*—the inexhaustible; *na*—not; *etāni*—all these differences; *tat*—that; *satyam*—the Absolute Truth; *brahma*—the Supreme; *cit*—spiritual; *bhavān*—Your Lordship.

TRANSLATION

The manifest, the unmanifest, false ego and the beginning, maintenance and annihilation of this cosmic manifestation all come from You, the Supreme Personality of Godhead. But because You are the Absolute Truth, the supreme absolute spirit soul, the Supreme Brahman, such changes as birth, death and sustenance do not exist in You.

PURPORT

According to the Vedic *mantras, yato vā imāni bhūtāni jāyante:* everything is an emanation of the Supreme Personality of Godhead. As stated by the Lord Himself in *Bhagavad-gītā* (7.4):

bhūmir āpo 'nalo vāyuḥ
khaṁ mano buddhir eva ca
ahaṅkāra itīyaṁ me
bhinnā prakṛtir aṣṭadhā

"Earth, water, fire, air, ether, mind, intelligence and false ego—all together these eight comprise My separated material energies." In other words, the ingredients of the cosmic manifestation also consist of the energy of the Supreme Personality of Godhead. This does not mean, however, that because the ingredients come from Him, He is no longer complete. *Pūrṇasya pūrṇam ādāya pūrṇam evāvaśiṣyate:* "Because He is the complete whole, even though so many complete units emanate from Him, He remains the complete balance." Thus the Lord is called *avyaya,* inexhaustible. Unless we accept the Absolute Truth as *acintya-bhedābheda,* simultaneously one and different, we cannot have a clear conception of the Absolute Truth. The Lord is the root of everything. *Aham ādir hi devānām:* He is the original cause of all the *devas,* or demigods. *Ahaṁ sarvasya prabhavaḥ:* everything emanates from Him. In all cases—nominative, objective, positive, negative and so on—whatever we may conceive of in this entire cosmic manifestation is in fact the Supreme Lord.

For Him there are no such distinctions as "this is mine, and this belongs to someone else," because He is everything. He is therefore called *avyaya*—changeless and inexhaustible. Because the Supreme Lord is *avyaya,* He is the Absolute Truth, the fully spiritual Supreme Brahman.

TEXT 6

तवैव चरणाम्भोजं श्रेयस्कामा निराशिषः ।
विसृज्योभयतः सङ्गं मुनयः समुपासते ॥ ६ ॥

tavaiva caraṇāmbhojaṁ
śreyas-kāmā nirāśiṣaḥ
visṛjyobhayataḥ saṅgaṁ
munayaḥ samupāsate

tava—Your; *eva*—indeed; *caraṇa-ambhojam*—lotus feet; *śreyaḥ-kāmāḥ*—persons desiring the ultimate auspiciousness, the ultimate goal of life; *nirāśiṣaḥ*—without material desire; *visṛjya*—giving up; *ubhayataḥ*—in this life and the next; *saṅgam*—attachment; *munayaḥ*—great sages; *samupāsate*—worship.

TRANSLATION

Pure devotees or great saintly persons who desire to achieve the highest goal in life and who are completely free from all material desires for sense gratification engage constantly in the transcendental service of Your lotus feet.

PURPORT

One is in the material world when he thinks, "I am this body, and everything with reference to my body is mine." *Ato gṛha-kṣetra-sutāpta-vittair janasya moho 'yam ahaṁ mameti.* This is the symptom of material life. In the materialistic conception of life, one thinks, "This is my house, this is my land, this is my family, this is my state," and so on. But those who are *munayaḥ,* saintly persons following in the footsteps of Nārada Muni, simply engage in the transcendental loving service of the Lord without any personal desire for sense gratification. *Anyābhilāṣitā-śūnyaṁ jñāna-karmādy-anāvṛtam.* Either in this life or in the next, the only concern of such saintly devotees is to serve the Supreme Personality of Godhead. Thus they are also absolute because they have no other desires. Being freed from the dualities of material desire, they are called *śreyas-kāmāḥ.* In other words, they are not concerned with *dharma* (religiosity), *artha* (economic development), or *kāma* (sense gratification). The only concern of such devotees is *mokṣa,* liberation. This *mokṣa* does not refer to becoming one with the Supreme like the Māyāvādī philosophers. Caitanya Mahāprabhu explained that real *mokṣa* means taking shelter of the lotus feet of the Personality of Godhead. The Lord clearly explained this fact while instructing Sārvabhauma Bhaṭṭācārya. Sārvabhauma Bhaṭṭācārya wanted to correct the word *mukti-pade* in *Śrīmad-Bhāgavatam,* but Caitanya Mahāprabhu informed him that there is no need to correct any word in *Śrīmad-Bhāgavatam.* He explained that *mukti-pade* refers to the lotus feet of the Supreme Personality of Godhead, Viṣṇu, who offers *mukti* and is therefore called Mukunda. A pure devotee is not concerned with material things. He is not concerned with religiosity, economic development or sense gratification. He is interested only in serving the lotus feet of the Lord.

TEXT 7

त्वं ब्रह्म पूर्णममृतं विगुणं विशोक-
मानन्दमात्रमविकारमनन्यदन्यत् ।
विश्वस्य हेतुरुदयस्थितिसंयमाना-
मात्मेश्वरश्च तदपेक्षतयानपेक्षः ॥ ७ ॥

tvaṁ brahma pūrṇam amṛtaṁ viguṇaṁ viśokam
ānanda-mātram avikāram ananyad anyat
viśvasya hetur udaya-sthiti-saṁyamānām
ātmeśvaraś ca tad-apekṣatayānapekṣaḥ

tvam—Your Lordship; *brahma*—the all-pervading Absolute Truth; *pūrṇam*—fully complete; *amṛtam*—never to be vanquished; *viguṇam*—spiritually situated, free from the material modes of nature; *viśokam*—without lamentation; *ānanda-mātram*—always in transcendental bliss; *avikāram*—changeless; *ananyat*—separated from everything; *anyat*—yet You are everything; *viśvasya*—of the cosmic manifestation; *hetuḥ*—the cause; *udaya*—of the beginning; *sthiti*—maintenance; *saṁyamānām*—and of all the directors controlling the various departments of the cosmic manifestation; *ātma-īśvaraḥ*—the Supersoul giving direction to everyone; *ca*—also; *tat-apekṣatayā*—everyone depends upon You; *anapekṣaḥ*—always fully independent.

TRANSLATION

My Lord, You are the Supreme Brahman, complete in everything. Being completely spiritual, You are eternal, free from the material modes of nature, and full of transcendental bliss. Indeed, for You there is no question of lamentation. Since You are the supreme cause, the cause of all causes, nothing can exist without You. Yet we are different from You in a relationship of cause and effect, for in one sense the cause and effect are different. You are the original cause of creation, manifestation and annihilation, and You bestow benedictions upon all living entities. Everyone depends upon You for the results of his activities, but You are always independent.

PURPORT

The Supreme Personality of Godhead says in *Bhagavad-gītā* (9.4):

mayā tatam idaṁ sarvaṁ
jagad avyakta-mūrtinā
mat-sthāni sarva-bhūtāni
na cāhaṁ teṣv avasthitaḥ

"By Me, in My unmanifested form, this entire universe is pervaded. All beings are in Me, but I am not in them." This explains the philosophy of simultaneous oneness and difference, known as *acintya-bhedābheda.* Everything is the Supreme Brahman, the Personality of Godhead, yet the Supreme Person is differently situated from everything. Indeed, because the Lord is differently situated from everything material, He is the Supreme Brahman, the supreme cause, the supreme controller. *Īśvaraḥ paramaḥ kṛṣṇaḥ sac-cid-ānanda-vigrahaḥ.* The Lord is the supreme cause, and His form has nothing to do with the material modes of nature. The devotee prays: "As Your devotee is completely free from all desires, Your Lordship is also completely free from desires. You are fully independent. Although all living entities engage in Your service, You do not depend on the service of anyone. Although this material world is created complete by You, everything depends on Your sanction. As stated in *Bhagavad-gītā, mattaḥ smṛtir jñānam apohanaṁ ca:* remembrance, knowledge and forgetfulness come from You. Nothing can be done independently, yet You act independently of the service rendered by Your servants. The living entities depend on Your mercy for liberation, but when You want to give them liberation, You do not depend on anyone else. Indeed, by Your causeless mercy, You can give liberation to anyone. Those who receive Your mercy are called *kṛpā-siddha.* To reach the platform of perfection takes many, many lives (*bahūnāṁ janmanām ante jñānavān māṁ prapadyate*). Nonetheless, even without undergoing severe austerities, one can attain perfection by Your mercy. Devotional service should be unmotivated and free from impediments (*ahaituky apratihatā yayātmā suprasīdati*). This is the position of *nirāśiṣaḥ,* or freedom from expectations for results. A pure devotee continuously offers transcendental loving service to You, but You may nonetheless offer mercy to anyone, without depending on his service."

TEXT 8

एकस्त्वमेव सदसद् द्वयमद्वयं च
स्वर्णं कृताकृतमिवेह न वस्तुभेदः ।
अज्ञानतस्त्वयि जनैर्विहितो विकल्पो
यस्माद् गुणव्यतिकरो निरुपाधिकस्य ॥ ८ ॥

ekas tvam eva sad asad dvayam advayaṁ ca
svarṇaṁ kṛtākṛtam iveha na vastu-bhedaḥ
ajñānatas tvayi janair vihito vikalpo
yasmād guṇa-vyatikaro nirupādhikasya

ekaḥ—the only one; *tvam*—Your Lordship; *eva*—indeed; *sat*—which is existing, as the effect; *asat*—which is nonexistent, as the cause; *dvayam*—both of them; *advayam*—without duality; *ca*—and; *svarṇam*—gold; *kṛta*—manufactured into different forms; *ākṛtam*—the original source of gold (the gold mine); *iva*—like; *iha*—in this world; *na*—not; *vastu-bhedaḥ*—difference in the substance; *ajñānataḥ*—only because of ignorance; *tvayi*—unto You; *janaiḥ*—by the general mass of people; *vihitaḥ*—it should be done; *vikalpaḥ*—differentiation; *yasmāt*—because of; *guṇa-vyatikaraḥ*—free from the differences created by the material modes of nature; *nirupādhikasya*—without any material designation.

TRANSLATION

My dear Lord, Your Lordship alone is the cause and the effect. Therefore, although You appear to be two, You are the absolute one. As there is no difference between the gold of a golden ornament and the gold in a mine, there is no difference between cause and effect; both of them are the same. Only because of ignorance do people concoct differences and dualities. You are free from material contamination, and since the entire

cosmos is caused by You and cannot exist without You, it is an effect of Your transcendental qualities. Thus the conception that Brahman is true and the world false cannot be maintained.

PURPORT

Śrīla Viśvanātha Cakravartī Ṭhākura says that the living entities are representations of the Supreme Personality of Godhead's marginal potency whereas the various bodies accepted by the living entities are products of the material energy. Thus the body is considered material, and the soul is considered spiritual. The origin of them both, however, is the same Supreme Personality of Godhead. As the Lord explains in *Bhagavad-gītā* (7.4-5):

bhūmir āpo 'nalo vāyuḥ
khaṁ mano buddhir eva ca
ahaṅkāra itīyaṁ me
bhinnā prakṛtir aṣṭadhā

apareyam itas tv anyāṁ
prakṛtiṁ viddhi me parām
jīva-bhūtāṁ mahā-bāho
yayedaṁ dhāryate jagat

"Earth, water, fire, air, ether, mind, intelligence and false ego—all together these eight comprise My separated material energies. But besides this inferior nature, O mighty-armed Arjuna, there is a superior energy of Mine, which consists of all living entities who are struggling with material nature and are sustaining the universe." Thus both matter and the living entities are manifestations of energy of the Supreme Lord. Since the energy and the energetic are not different and since the material and marginal energies are both energies of the supreme energetic, the Supreme Lord, ultimately the Supreme Personality of Godhead is everything. In this regard, the example may be given of gold that has not been molded and gold that has been molded into various ornaments. A gold earring and the gold in a mine are different only as cause and effect; otherwise they are the same. The *Vedānta-sūtra* describes that Brahman is the cause of everything. *Janmādy asya yataḥ.* Everything is born of the Supreme Brahman, from which everything emanates as different energies. None of these energies, therefore, should be considered false. The Māyāvādīs' differentiation between Brahman and *māyā* is only due to ignorance.

Śrīmad Vīrarāghava Ācārya, in his *Bhāgavata-candra-candrikā,* describes the Vaiṣṇava philosophy as follows. The cosmic manifestation is described as *sat* and *asat,* as *cit* and *acit.* Matter is *acit,* and the living force is *cit,* but their origin is the Supreme Personality of Godhead, in whom there is no difference between matter and spirit. According to this conception, the cosmic manifestation, consisting of both matter and spirit, is not different from the Supreme Personality of Godhead. *Idaṁ hi viśvaṁ bhagavān ivetaraḥ:* "This cosmic manifestation is also the Supreme Personality of Godhead, although it appears different from Him." In *Bhagavad-gītā* (9.4) the Lord says:

mayā tatam idaṁ sarvaṁ
jagad avyakta-mūrtinā
mat-sthāni sarva-bhūtāni
na cāhaṁ teṣv avasthitaḥ

"By Me, in My unmanifested form, this entire universe is pervaded. All beings are in Me, but I am not in them." Thus although someone may say that the Supreme Person is different from the cosmic manifestation, actually He is not. The Lord says, *mayā tatam idaṁ sarvam:* "In My impersonal feature I am spread throughout the world." Therefore, this world is not different from Him. The difference is a difference in names. For example, whether we speak of gold earrings, gold bangles or gold necklaces, ultimately they are all gold. In a similar way, all the different manifestations of matter and spirit are ultimately one in the Supreme Personality of Godhead. *Ekam evādvitīyaṁ brahma.* This is the Vedic version (*Chāndogya Upaniṣad* 6.2.1). There is oneness because everything emanates from the Supreme Brahman. The example already given is that there is no difference between a golden earring and the gold mine as it is. The Vaiśeṣika philosophers, however, because of their Māyāvāda conception, create differences. They say, *brahma satyaṁ jagan mithyā:* "The Absolute Truth is real, and the cosmic manifestation is false." But why should the *jagat* be considered *mithyā*? The *jagat* is an emanation from Brahman. Therefore the *jagat* is also truth.

Vaiṣṇavas, therefore, do not consider the *jagat* to be *mithyā;* rather, they regard everything as reality in connection with the Supreme Personality of Godhead.

anāsaktasya viṣayān
yathārham upayuñjataḥ
nirbandhaḥ kṛṣṇa-sambandhe
yuktaṁ vairāgyam ucyate

prāpañcikatayā buddhyā
hari-sambandhi-vastunaḥ
mumukṣubhiḥ parityāgo
vairāgyaṁ phalgu kathyate

"Things should be accepted for the Lord's service and not for one's personal sense gratification. If one accepts something without attachment and accepts it because it is related to Kṛṣṇa, one's renunciation is called *yuktaṁ vairāgyam.* Whatever is favorable for the rendering of service to the Lord should be accepted and should not be rejected as a material thing."(*Bhakti-rasāmṛta-sindhu* 1.2.255-256) The *jagat* should not be rejected as *mithyā.* It is truth, and the truth is realized when everything is engaged in the service of the Lord. A flower accepted for one's sense gratification is material, but when the same flower is offered to the Supreme Personality of Godhead by a devotee, it is spiritual. Food taken and cooked for oneself is material, but food cooked for the Supreme Lord is spiritual *prasāda.* This is a question of realization. Actually, everything is given by the Supreme Personality of Godhead, and therefore everything is spiritual, but those who are not advanced in proper knowledge make distinctions because of the interactions of the three modes of material nature. In this regard, Śrīla Jīva Gosvāmī says that although the sun is the only light, the sunshine, which is exhibited in seven colors, and darkness, which is the absence of sunshine, are not different from the sun, for without the existence of the sun such differentiations cannot exist. There may be varied nomenclature because of different conditions, but they are all the sun. The *Purāṇas* therefore say:

eka-deśa-sthitasyāgner
jyotsnā vistāriṇī yathā
parasya brahmaṇaḥ śaktis
tathedam akhilaṁ jagat

"Just as the illumination of a fire, which is situated in one place, is spread all over, the energies of the Supreme Personality of Godhead, Parabrahman, are spread all over this universe." (*Viṣṇu Purāṇa* 1.22.53) Materially, we can directly perceive the sunshine spreading itself according to different names and activities, but ultimately the sun is one. Similarly, *sarvaṁ khalv idaṁ brahma:* everything is an expansion of the Supreme Brahman. Therefore, the Supreme Lord is everything, and He is one without differentiation. There is no existence separate from the Supreme Personality of Godhead.

TEXT 9

त्वां ब्रह्म केचिदवयन्त्युत धर्ममेके
एके परं सदसतोः पुरुषं परेशम् ।
अन्येऽवयन्ति नवशक्तियुतं परं त्वां
केचिन्महापुरुषमव्ययमात्मतन्त्रम् ॥ ९ ॥

tvāṁ brahma kecid avayanty uta dharmam eke
eke paraṁ sad-asatoḥ puruṣaṁ pareśam
anye 'vayanti nava-śakti-yutaṁ paraṁ tvāṁ
kecin mahā-puruṣam avyayam ātma-tantram

tvām—You; *brahma*—the supreme truth, the Absolute Truth, Brahman; *kecit*—some people, namely the group of Māyāvādīs known as the Vedāntists; *avayanti*—consider; *uta*—certainly; *dharmam*—religion; *eke*—some others; *eke*—some others; *param*—transcendental; *sat-asatoḥ*—to both cause and effect; *puruṣam*—the Supreme person; *pareśam*—the supreme controller; *anye*—others; *avayanti*—describe; *nava-śakti-yutam*—endowed with nine potencies; *param*—transcendental; *tvām*—unto You; *kecit*—some; *mahā-puruṣam*—the Supreme Personality of Godhead; *avyayam*—without loss of energy; *ātma-tantram*—supremely independent.

TRANSLATION

Those who are known as the impersonalist Vedāntists regard You as the impersonal Brahman. Others, known as the Mīmāṁsaka philosophers, regard You as religion. The Sāṅkhya philosophers regard You as the transcendental person who is beyond prakṛti and puruṣa and who is the controller of even the demigods. The followers of the codes of devotional service known as the Pañcarātras regard You as being endowed with nine different potencies. And the Patañjala philosophers, the followers of Patañjali Muni, regard You as the supreme independent Personality of Godhead, who has no equal or superior.

TEXT 10

नाहं परायुर्ऋषयो न मरीचिमुख्या
जानन्ति यद्विरचितं खलु सत्त्वसर्गाः ।
यन्मायया मुषितचेतस ईश दैत्य-
मर्त्यादयः किमुत शश्वदभद्रवृत्ताः ॥ १० ॥

nāhaṁ parāyur ṛṣayo na marīci-mukhyā
jānanti yad-viracitaṁ khalu sattva-sargāḥ
yan-māyayā muṣita-cetasa īśa daitya-
martyādayaḥ kim uta śaśvad-abhadra-vṛttāḥ

na—neither; *aham*—I; *para-āyuḥ*—that personality who lives for millions and millions of years (Lord Brahmā); *ṛṣayaḥ*—the seven *ṛṣis* of the seven planets; *na*—nor; *marīci-mukhyāḥ*—headed by Marīci Ṛṣi; *jānanti*—know; *yat*—by whom (the Supreme Lord); *viracitam*—this universe, which has been created; *khalu*—indeed; *sattva-sargāḥ*—although born in the mode of material goodness; *yat-māyayā*—by the influence of whose energy; *muṣita-cetasaḥ*—their hearts are bewildered; *īśa*—O my Lord; *daitya*—the demons; *martya-ādayaḥ*—the human beings and others; *kim uta*—what to speak of; *śaśvat*—always; *abhadra-vṛttāḥ*—influenced by the base qualities of material nature.

TRANSLATION

O my Lord, I, who am considered to be the best of the demigods, and Lord Brahmā and the great ṛṣis, headed by Marīci, are born of the mode of goodness. Nonetheless, we are bewildered by Your illusory energy and cannot understand what this creation is. Aside from us, what is to be said of others, like the demons and human beings, who are in the base modes of material nature [rajo-guṇa and tamo-guṇa]? How will they know You?

PURPORT

Factually speaking, even those who are situated in the material mode of goodness cannot understand the position of the Supreme Personality of Godhead. What then is to be said of those who are situated in *rajo-guṇa* and *tamo-guṇa,* the base qualities of material nature? How can we even imagine the Supreme Personality of Godhead? There are so many philosophers trying to understand the Absolute Truth, but since they are situated in the base qualities of material nature and are addicted to so many bad habits, like drinking, meat-eating, illicit sex and gambling, how can they conceive of the Supreme Personality of Godhead? For them it is impossible. For the present day, the *pāñcarātrikī-vidhi* as enunciated by Nārada Muni is the only hope. Śrīla Rūpa Gosvāmī, therefore, has quoted the following verse from the *Brahma-yāmala:*

śruti-smṛti-purāṇādi-
pañcarātra-vidhiṁ vinā

aikāntikī harer bhaktir
utpātāyaiva kalpate

"Devotional service of the Lord that ignores the authorized Vedic literatures like the *Upaniṣads, Purāṇas* and *Nārada-pañcarātra* is simply an unnecessary disturbance in society." (*Bhakti-rasāmṛta-sindhu* 1.2.101) Those who are very advanced in knowledge and are situated in the mode of goodness follow the Vedic instructions of the *śruti* and *smṛti* and other religious scriptures, including the *pāñcarātrikī-vidhi.* Without understanding the Supreme Personality of Godhead in this way, one only creates a disturbance. In this age of Kali, so many *gurus* have sprung up, and because they do not refer to the *śruti-smṛti-purāṇādi-pañcarātrika-vidhi,* they are creating a great disturbance in the world in regard to understanding the Absolute Truth. However, those who follow the *pāñcarātrikī-vidhi* under the guidance of a proper spiritual master can understand the Absolute Truth. It is said, *pañcarātrasya kṛtsnasya vaktā tu bhagavān svayam:* the *pañcarātra* system is spoken by the Supreme Personality of Godhead, just like *Bhagavad-gītā. Vāsudeva-śaraṇā vidur añjasaiva:* the truth can be understood only by one who has taken shelter of the lotus feet of Vāsudeva.

bahūnāṁ janmanām ante
jñānavān māṁ prapadyate
vāsudevaḥ sarvam iti
sa mahātmā sudurlabhaḥ

"After many births and deaths, he who is actually in knowledge surrenders unto Me, knowing Me to be the cause of all causes and all that is. Such a great soul is very rare." (Bg. 7.19) Only those who have surrendered to the lotus feet of Vāsudeva can understand the Absolute Truth.

vāsudeve bhagavati
bhakti-yogaḥ prayojitaḥ
janayaty āśu vairāgyaṁ
jñānaṁ ca yad ahaitukam

"By rendering devotional service unto the Personality of Godhead, Śrī Kṛṣṇa, one immediately acquires causeless knowledge and detachment from the world."(*Bhā*g. 1.2.7) Therefore, Vāsudeva, Bhagavān Śrī Kṛṣṇa, personally teaches in *Bhagavad-gītā:*

sarva-dharmān parityajya
mām ekaṁ śaraṇaṁ vraja

"Abandon all varieties of religion and just surrender unto Me." (Bg. 18.66)

bhaktyā mām abhijānāti
yāvān yaś cāsmi tattvataḥ

"One can understand the Supreme Personality as He is only by devotional service." (Bg. 18.55) The Supreme Personality of Godhead is not properly understood even by Lord Śiva or Lord Brahmā, what to speak of others, but He can be understood by the process of *bhakti-yoga.*

mayy āsakta-manāḥ pārtha
yogaṁ yuñjan mad-āśrayaḥ
asaṁśayaṁ samagraṁ māṁ
yathā jñāsyasi tac chṛṇu

(*Bg.* 7.1)

If one practices *bhakti-yoga* by taking shelter of Vāsudeva, Kṛṣṇa, simply by hearing Vāsudeva speak about Himself, one can understand everything about Him. Indeed, one can understand Him completely (*samagram*).

TEXT 11

स त्वं समीहितमदः स्थितिजन्मनाशं
भूतेहितं च जगतो भवबन्धमोक्षौ ।
वायुर्यथा विशति खं च चराचराख्यं
सर्वं तदात्मकतयावगमोऽवरुन्त्से ॥ ११ ॥

sa tvaṁ samīhitam adaḥ sthiti-janma-nāśaṁ
bhūtehitaṁ ca jagato bhava-bandha-mokṣau
vāyur yathā viśati khaṁ ca carācarākhyaṁ
sarvaṁ tad-ātmakatayāvagamo 'varuntse

saḥ—Your Lordship; *tvam*—the Supreme Personality of Godhead; *samīhitam*—which has been created (by You); *adaḥ*—of this material cosmic manifestation; *sthiti-janma-nāśam*—creation, maintenance and annihilation; *bhūta*—of the living entities; *īhitam ca*—and the different activities or endeavors; *jagataḥ*—of the whole world; *bhava-bandha-mokṣau*—in being implicated and being liberated from material complications; *vāyuḥ*—the air; *yathā*—as; *viśati*—enters; *kham*—in the vast sky; *ca*—and; *cara-acara-ākhyam*—and everything, moving and nonmoving; *sarvam*—everything; *tat*—that; *ātmakatayā*—because of Your presence; *avagamaḥ*—everything is known to You; *avaruntse*—You are all-pervading and therefore know everything.

TRANSLATION

My Lord, You are the supreme knowledge personified. You know everything about this creation and its beginning, maintenance and annihilation, and You know all the endeavors made by the living entities, by which they are either implicated in this material world or liberated from it. As the air enters the vast sky and also enters the bodies of all moving and nonmoving entities, You are present everywhere, and therefore You are the knower of all.

PURPORT

As stated in the *Brahma-saṁhitā:*

eko 'py asau racayituṁ jagad-aṇḍa-koṭiṁ
yac-chaktir asti jagad-aṇḍa-cayā yad-antaḥ
aṇḍāntara-stha-paramāṇu-cayāntara-sthaṁ
govindam ādi-puruṣaṁ tam ahaṁ bhajāmi

"I worship the Personality of Godhead, Govinda, who by one of His plenary portions enters the existence of every universe and every atomic particle and thus manifests His infinite energy unlimitedly throughout the material creation." (*Bs.* 5.35)

ānanda-cinmaya-rasa-pratibhāvitābhis
tābhir ya eva nija-rūpatayā kalābhiḥ
goloka eva nivasaty akhilātma-bhūto
govindam ādi-puruṣaṁ tam ahaṁ bhajāmi

"I worship Govinda, the primeval Lord, who resides in His own realm, Goloka, with Rādhā, who resembles His own spiritual figure and who embodies the ecstatic potency [*hlādinī*]. Their companions are Her confidantes, who embody extensions of Her bodily form and who are imbued and permeated with ever-blissful spiritual *rasa.*" (*Bs.* 5.37)

Although Govinda is always present in His abode (*goloka eva nivasati*), He is simultaneously present everywhere. Nothing is unknown to Him, and nothing can be hidden from Him. The example given here compares the Lord to the air, which is within the vast sky and within every body but still is different from everything.

TEXT 12

अवतारा मया दृष्टा रममाणस्य ते गुणैः ।
सोऽहं तद् द्रष्टुमिच्छामि यत् ते योषिद्वपुर्धृतम् ॥ १२ ॥

avatārā mayā dṛṣṭā
ramamāṇasya te guṇaiḥ
so 'haṁ tad draṣṭum icchāmi
yat te yoṣid-vapur dhṛtam

avatārāḥ—incarnations; *mayā*—by me; *dṛṣṭāḥ*—have been seen; *ramamāṇasya*—while You demonstrate Your various pastimes; *te*—of You; *guṇaiḥ*—by the manifestations of transcendental qualities; *saḥ*—Lord Śiva; *aham*—I; *tat*—that incarnation; *draṣṭum icchāmi*—wish to see; *yat*—which; *te*—of You; *yoṣit-vapuḥ*—the body of a woman; *dhṛtam*—was accepted.

TRANSLATION

My Lord, I have seen all kinds of incarnations You have exhibited by Your transcendental qualities, and now that You have appeared as a beautiful young woman, I wish to see that form of Your Lordship.

PURPORT

When Lord Śiva approached Lord Viṣṇu, Lord Viṣṇu inquired about the purpose for Lord Śiva's coming there. Now Lord Śiva discloses his desire. He wanted to see the recent incarnation of Mohinī-mūrti, which Lord Viṣṇu had assumed to distribute the nectar generated from the churning of the ocean of milk.

TEXT 13

येन सम्मोहिता दैत्याः पायिताश्चामृतं सुराः ।
तद् दिदृक्षव आयाताः परं कौतूहलं हि नः ॥ १३ ॥

yena sammohitā daityāḥ
pāyitāś cāmṛtaṁ surāḥ
tad didṛkṣava āyātāḥ
paraṁ kautūhalaṁ hi naḥ

yena—by such an incarnation; *sammohitāḥ*—were captivated; *daityāḥ*—the demons; *pāyitāḥ*—were fed; *ca*—also; *amṛtam*—nectar; *surāḥ*—the demigods; *tat*—that form; *didṛkṣavaḥ*—desiring to see; *āyātāḥ*—we have come here; *param*—very much; *kautūhalam*—great eagerness; *hi*—indeed; *naḥ*—of ourselves.

TRANSLATION

My Lord, we have come here desiring to see that form of Your Lordship which You showed to the demons to captivate them completely and in this way enable the demigods to drink nectar. I am very eager to see that form.

TEXT 14

श्रीशुक उवाच
एवमभ्यर्थितो विष्णुर्भगवान् शूलपाणिना ।
प्रहस्य भावगम्भीरं गिरिशं प्रत्यभाषत ॥ १४ ॥

śrī-śuka uvāca
evam abhyarthito viṣṇur
bhagavān śūla-pāṇinā
prahasya bhāva-gambhīraṁ
giriśaṁ pratyabhāṣata

śrī-śukaḥ uvāca—Śrī Śukadeva Gosvāmī said; *evam*—in this way; *abhyarthitaḥ*—being requested; *viṣṇuḥ bhagavān*—Lord Viṣṇu, the Supreme Personality of Godhead; *śūla-pāṇinā*—by Lord Śiva, who carries a trident in his hand; *prahasya*—laughing; *bhāva-gambhīram*—with serious gravity; *giriśam*—unto Lord Śiva; *pratyabhāṣata*—replied.

TRANSLATION

Śukadeva Gosvāmī said: When Lord Viṣṇu was thus requested by Lord Śiva, who carries a trident in his hand, He smiled with gravity and replied to Lord Śiva as follows.

PURPORT

The Supreme Personality of Godhead, Viṣṇu, is known as Yogeśvara. *Yatra yogeśvaraḥ kṛṣṇaḥ.* Mystic *yogīs* want to acquire some power by practicing the *yoga* system, but Kṛṣṇa, the Supreme Personality of Godhead, is known as the Supreme Lord of all mystic power. Lord Śiva wanted to see the Mohinī-mūrti, which was captivating the entire world, and Lord Viṣṇu was gravely thinking of how to captivate Lord Śiva also. Therefore the word *bhāva-*

gambhīram is used here. The illusory, material energy is represented by Durgādevī, who is the wife of Giriśa, or Lord Śiva. Durgādevī could not captivate Lord Śiva's mind, but now that Lord Śiva wanted to see Lord Viṣṇu's feminine form, Lord Viṣṇu, by His mystic power, would assume a form that would captivate even Lord Śiva. Therefore Lord Viṣṇu was grave and at the same time was smiling.

TEXT 15

श्रीभगवानुवाच

कौतूहलाय दैत्यानां योषिद्वेषो मया धृतः ।
पश्यता सुरकार्याणि गते पीयूषभाजने ॥ १५ ॥

śrī-bhagavān uvāca
kautūhalāya daityānāṁ
yoṣid-veṣo mayā dhṛtaḥ
paśyatā sura-kāryāṇi
gate pīyūṣa-bhājane

śrī-bhagavān uvāca—the Supreme Personality of Godhead said; *kautūhalāya*—for the bewildering; *daityānām*—of the demons; *yoṣit-veṣaḥ*—the form of a beautiful woman; *mayā*—by Me; *dhṛtaḥ*—assumed; *paśyatā*—seeing that it is necessary for Me; *sura-kāryāṇi*—for executing the interests of the demigods; *gate*—having been taken away; *pīyūṣa-bhājane*—the jug of nectar.

TRANSLATION

The Supreme Personality of Godhead said: When the demons took away the jug of nectar, I assumed the form of a beautiful woman to bewilder them by directly cheating them and thus to act in the interest of the demigods.

PURPORT

When the Supreme Personality of Godhead assumed the form of the beautiful woman Mohinī-mūrti, the demons were certainly captivated, but the demigods present were not. In other words, those who maintain a demoniac mentality are bewildered by the beauty of a woman, but those who are advanced in Kṛṣṇa consciousness, or even those on the platform of goodness, are not bewildered. The Supreme Personality of Godhead knew that because Lord Śiva is not an ordinary person, he cannot be bewildered even by the most beautiful woman. Cupid himself tried to invoke Lord Śiva's lusty desires in the presence of Pārvatī, but Lord Śiva was never agitated. Rather, the blazing fire from Lord Śiva's eyes turned Cupid to ashes. Therefore, Lord Viṣṇu had to think twice about what kind of beautiful form would bewilder even Lord Śiva. Consequently He was smiling gravely, as stated in the previous verse (*prahasya bhāva-gambhīram*). A beautiful woman generally cannot induce Lord Śiva to be lusty, but Lord Viṣṇu was considering whether there was any form of woman who could enchant him.

TEXT 16

तत्तेऽहं दर्शयिष्यामि दिदृक्षोः सुरसत्तम ।
कामिनां बहु मन्तव्यं सङ्कल्पप्रभवोदयम् ॥ १६ ॥

tat te 'haṁ darśayiṣyāmi
didṛkṣoḥ sura-sattama
kāminām bahu mantavyaṁ
saṅkalpa-prabhavodayam

tat—that; *te*—unto you; *aham*—I; *darśayiṣyāmi*—shall show; *didṛkṣoḥ*—desirous of seeing; *sura-sattama*—O best of the demigods; *kāminām*—of persons who are very lusty; *bahu*—very much; *mantavyam*—an object of adoration; *saṅkalpa*—lusty desires; *prabhava-udayam*—causing to be strongly aroused.

TRANSLATION

O best of the demigods, I shall now show you My form that is very much appreciated by those who are lusty. Since you want to see that form, I shall reveal it in your presence.

PURPORT

Lord Śiva's desiring to see Lord Viṣṇu reveal the most attractive and beautiful form of a woman was certainly a joking affair. Lord Śiva knew that he could not be agitated by any so-called beautiful woman. "The Daityas may have been bewildered,"he thought, "but since even the demigods could not be agitated, what to speak of me, who am the best of all the demigods?"However, because Lord Śiva wanted to see Lord Viṣṇu's form as a woman, Lord Viṣṇu decided to impersonate a woman and show him a form that would immediately put him in an ocean of lusty desires. In effect, therefore, Lord Viṣṇu told Lord Śiva, "I will show you My form as a woman, and if you become agitated by lusty desires, do not blame Me." The attractive features of a woman are appreciated by those who are affected by lusty desires, but those who are above such desires, who are on the platform of Kṛṣṇa consciousness, are very difficult to bewilder. Nonetheless, by the supreme desire of the Personality of Godhead, everything can be done. This was to be a test of whether Lord Śiva could remain unagitated.

TEXT 17

श्रीशुक उवाच
इति ब्रुवाणो भगवांस्तत्रैवान्तरधीयत।
सर्वतश्चारयंश्चक्षुर्भव आस्ते सहोमया ॥ १७ ॥

śrī-śuka uvāca
iti bruvāṇo bhagavāṁs
tatraivāntaradhīyata
sarvataś cārayaṁś cakṣur
bhava āste sahomayā

śrī-śukaḥ uvāca—Śrī Śukadeva Gosvāmī said; *iti*—thus; *bruvāṇaḥ*—while speaking; *bhagavān*—Lord Viṣṇu, the Supreme Personality of Godhead; *tatra*—there; *eva*—immediately; *antaradhīyata*—disappeared from the vision of Lord Śiva and his associates; *sarvataḥ*—everywhere; *cārayan*—moving; *cakṣuḥ*—the eyes; *bhavaḥ*—Lord Śiva; *āste*—remained; *saha-umayā*—with his wife, Umā.

TRANSLATION

Śukadeva Gosvāmī continued: After speaking in this way, the Supreme Personality of Godhead, Viṣṇu, immediately disappeared, and Lord Śiva remained there with Umā, looking for Him all around with moving eyes.

TEXT 18

ततो ददर्शोपवने वरस्त्रियं
विचित्रपुष्पारुणपल्लवद्रुमे ।
विक्रीडतीं कन्दुकलीलया लसद्-
दुकूलपर्यस्तनितम्बमेखलाम् ॥ १८ ॥

tato dadarśopavane vara-striyaṁ
vicitra-puṣpāruṇa-pallava-drume
vikrīḍatīṁ kanduka-līlayā lasad-
dukūla-paryasta-nitamba-mekhalām

tataḥ—thereafter; *dadarśa*—Lord Śiva saw; *upavane*—in a nice forest; *vara-striyam*—a very beautiful woman; *vicitra*—of many varieties; *puṣpa*—flowers; *aruṇa*—pink; *pallava*—leaves; *drume*—in the midst of the trees; *vikrīḍatīm*—engaged in playing; *kanduka*—with a ball; *līlayā*—by pastimes of playing; *lasat*—shining; *dukūla*—by a sari; *paryasta*—covered; *nitamba*—on her hips; *mekhalām*—dressed with a belt.

TRANSLATION

Thereafter, in a nice forest nearby, full of trees with reddish-pink leaves and varieties of flowers, Lord Śiva saw a beautiful woman playing with a ball. Her hips were covered with a shining sari and ornamented with a belt.

TEXT 19

आवर्तनोद्वर्तनकम्पितस्तन-
प्रकृष्टहारोरुभरैः पदे पदे ।
प्रभज्यमानामिव मध्यतश्चलत्-
पदप्रवालं नयतीं ततस्ततः ॥ १९ ॥

āvartanodvartana-kampita-stana-
prakṛṣṭa-hāroru-bharaiḥ pade pade
prabhajyamānām iva madhyataś calat-
pada-pravālaṁ nayatīṁ tatas tataḥ

āvartana—by the falling down; *udvartana*—and springing up; *kampita*—trembling; *stana*—of the two breasts; *prakṛṣṭa*—beautiful; *hāra*—and of garlands; *uru-bharaiḥ*—because of the heavy load; *pade pade*—at every step; *prabhajyamānām iva*—as if breaking; *madhyataḥ*—in the middle portion of the body; *calat*—moving like that; *pada-pravālam*—feet reddish like coral; *nayatīm*—moving; *tataḥ tataḥ*—here and there.

TRANSLATION

Because the ball was falling down and bouncing up, as She played with it Her breasts trembled, and because of the weight of those breasts and

Her heavy flower garlands, Her waist appeared to be all but breaking at every step, as Her two soft feet, which were reddish like coral, moved here and there.

TEXT 20

दिक्षु भ्रमत्कन्दुकचापलैर्भृशं
प्रोद्विग्नतारायतलोललोचनाम् ।
स्वकर्णविभ्राजितकुण्डलोल्लसत्-
कपोलनीलालकमण्डिताननाम् ॥ २० ॥

dikṣu bhramat-kanduka-cāpalair bhṛśaṁ
prodvigna-tārāyata-lola-locanām
sva-karṇa-vibhrājita-kuṇḍalollasat-
kapola-nīlālaka-maṇḍitānanām

dikṣu—in all directions; *bhramat*—moving; *kanduka*—of the ball; *cāpalaiḥ*—restlessness; *bhṛśam*—now and then; *prodvigna*—full of anxieties; *tāra*—eyes; *āyata*—broad; *lola*—restless; *locanām*—with such eyes; *sva-karṇa*—on Her own two ears; *vibhrājita*—illuminating; *kuṇḍala*—earrings; *ullasat*—shining; *kapola*—cheeks; *nīla*—bluish; *alaka*—with hair; *maṇḍita*—was decorated; *ānanām*—face.

TRANSLATION

The woman's face was decorated by broad, beautiful, restless eyes, which moved as the ball bounced here and there from Her hand. The two brilliant earrings on Her ears decorated Her shining cheeks like bluish reflections, and the hair scattered on Her face made Her even more beautiful to see.

TEXT 21

श्लथद् दुकूलं कबरीं च विच्युतां
सन्नह्यतीं वामकरेण वल्गुना ।
विनिघ्नतीमन्यकरेण कन्दुकं
विमोहयन्तीं जगदात्ममायया ॥ २१ ॥

ślathad dukūlaṁ kabarīṁ ca vicyutāṁ
sannahyatīṁ vāma-kareṇa valgunā

vinighnatīm anya-kareṇa kandukaṁ
vimohayantīṁ jagad-ātma-māyayā

ślathat—slipping or slackening; *dukūlam*—the sari; *kabarīm ca*—and the hair on the head; *vicyutām*—being slackened and scattered; *sannahyatīm*—trying to bind; *vāma-kareṇa*—with the left hand; *valgunā*—very beautifully attractive; *vinighnatīm*—striking; *anya-kareṇa*—with the right hand; *kandukam*—the ball; *vimohayantīm*—in this way captivating everyone; *jagat*—the whole world; *ātma-māyayā*—by the spiritual potency, the internal energy.

TRANSLATION

As She played with the ball, the sari covering Her body became loose, and Her hair scattered. She tried to bind Her hair with Her beautiful left hand, and at the same time She played with the ball by striking it with Her right hand. This was so attractive that the Supreme Lord, by His internal potency, in this way captivated everyone.

PURPORT

In *Bhagavad-gītā* (7.14) it is said, *daivī hy eṣā guṇa-mayī mama māyā duratyayā:* the external potency of the Supreme Personality of Godhead is extremely strong. Indeed, everyone is fully captivated by her activities. Lord Śambhu (Śiva) was not to be captivated by the external potency, but because Lord Viṣṇu wanted to captivate Him also, He exhibited His internal potency to act the way that His external potency acts to captivate ordinary living entities. Lord Viṣṇu can captivate anyone, even such a strong personality as Lord Śambhu.

TEXT 22

तां वीक्ष्य देव इति कन्दुकलीलयेषद्-
व्रीडास्फुटस्मितविसृष्टकटाक्षमुष्टः ।
स्त्रीप्रेक्षणप्रतिसमीक्षणविह्वलात्मा
नात्मानमन्तिक उमां स्वगणांश्च वेद ॥ २२ ॥

tāṁ vīkṣya deva iti kanduka-līlayeṣad-
vrīḍāsphuṭa-smita-visṛṣṭa-kaṭākṣa-muṣṭaḥ
strī-prekṣaṇa-pratisamīkṣaṇa-vihvalātmā
nātmānam antika umāṁ sva-gaṇāṁś ca veda

tām—Her; *vīkṣya*—after observing; *devaḥ*—Lord Śambhu; *iti*—in this way; *kanduka-līlayā*—by playing with the ball; *īṣat*—slight; *vrīḍā*—by bashfulness; *asphuṭa*—not very distinct; *smita*—with smiling; *visṛṣṭa*—sent; *kaṭākṣa-muṣṭaḥ*—defeated by the glances; *strī-prekṣaṇa*—by glancing at that beautiful woman; *pratisamīkṣaṇa*—and by constantly being watched by Her; *vihvala-ātmā*—whose mind was agitated; *na*—not; *ātmānam*—himself; *antike*—(situated) nearby; *umām*—his wife, mother Umā; *sva-gaṇān ca*—and his associates; *veda*—Lord Śiva could understand.

TRANSLATION

While Lord Śiva observed the beautiful woman playing with the ball, She sometimes glanced at him and slightly smiled in bashfulness. As he looked at the beautiful woman and She watched him, he forgot both himself and Umā, his most beautiful wife, as well as his associates nearby.

PURPORT

The material bondage of this world is that a beautiful woman can captivate a handsome man and that a handsome man can captivate a beautiful woman. Such are the affairs that began when Lord Śiva observed the beautiful girl playing with the ball. In such activities, the influence of Cupid is very prominent. As both parties move their eyebrows and glance at one another, their lusty desires increase more and more. Such reciprocations of lusty desire took place between Lord Śiva and the beautiful woman, even though Umā and Lord Śiva's associates were by Lord Śiva's side. Such is the attraction between man and woman in the material world. Lord Śiva was supposed to be above all this attraction, but he was victimized by the captivating power of Lord Viṣṇu. Ṛṣabhadeva thus explains the nature of lusty attraction:

puṁsaḥ striyā mithunī-bhāvam etaṁ
tayor mitho hṛdaya-granthim āhuḥ
ato gṛha-kṣetra-sutāpta-vittair
janasya moho 'yam ahaṁ mameti

"The attraction between male and female is the basic principle of material existence. On the basis of this misconception, which ties together the hearts of the male and female, one becomes attracted to his body, home, property, children, relatives and wealth. In this way one increases life's illusions and thinks in terms of 'I and mine.' "(*Bhā*g. 5.5.8) When a man and woman exchange feelings of lust, both of them are victimized, and thus they are bound to this material world in various ways.

TEXT 23

तस्याः कराग्रात् स तु कन्दुको यदा
गतो विदूरं तमनुव्रजत्स्त्रियाः ।
वासः ससूत्रं लघु मारुतोऽहरद्
भवस्य देवस्य किलानुपश्यतः ॥ २३ ॥

tasyāḥ karāgrāt sa tu kanduko yadā
gato vidūraṁ tam anuvrajat-striyāḥ
vāsaḥ sasūtraṁ laghu māruto 'harad
bhavasya devasya kilānupaśyataḥ

tasyāḥ—of the beautiful woman; *kara-agrāt*—from the hand; *saḥ*—that; *tu*—but; *kandukaḥ*—the ball; *yadā*—when; *gataḥ*—had gone; *vidūram*—far off; *tam*—that ball; *anuvrajat*—began to follow; *striyāḥ*—of that woman; *vāsaḥ*—the covering dress; *sa-sūtram*—with the belt; *laghu*—because of being very fine; *mārutaḥ*—the breeze; *aharat*—blew away; *bhavasya*—while Lord Śiva; *devasya*—the chief demigod; *kila*—indeed; *anupaśyataḥ*—was always looking.

TRANSLATION

When the ball leaped from Her hand and fell at a distance, the woman began to follow it, but as Lord Śiva observed these activities, a breeze suddenly blew away the fine dress and belt that covered her.

TEXT 24

एवं तां रुचिरापाङ्गीं दर्शनीयां मनोरमाम् ।
दृष्ट्वा तस्यां मनश्चक्रे विषज्जन्त्यां भवः किल ॥ २४ ॥

evaṁ tāṁ rucirāpāṅgīṁ
darśanīyāṁ manoramām
dṛṣṭvā tasyāṁ manaś cakre
viṣajjantyāṁ bhavaḥ kila

evam—in this way; *tām*—Her; *rucira-apāṅgīm*—possessing all attractive features; *darśanīyām*—pleasing to see; *manoramām*—beautifully formed; *dṛṣṭvā*—seeing; *tasyām*—upon Her; *manaḥ cakre*—thought; *viṣajjantyām*—to be attracted by him; *bhavaḥ*—Lord Śiva; *kila*—indeed.

TRANSLATION

Thus Lord Śiva saw the woman, every part of whose body was beautifully formed, and the beautiful woman also looked at him. Therefore, thinking that She was attracted to him, Lord Śiva became very much attracted to Her.

PURPORT

Lord Śiva was observing every part of the woman's body, and She was also glancing at him with restless eyes. Thus Śiva thought that She was also attracted to him, and now he wanted to touch Her.

TEXT 25

तयापहृतविज्ञानस्तत्कृतस्मरविह्वलः ।
भवान्या अपि पश्यन्त्या गतह्रीस्तत्पदं ययौ ॥ २५ ॥

tayāpahṛta-vijñānas
tat-kṛta-smara-vihvalaḥ
bhavānyā api paśyantyā
gata-hrīs tat-padaṁ yayau

tayā—by Her; *apahṛta*—taken away; *vijñānaḥ*—good sense; *tat-kṛta*—done by Her; *smara*—by the smiling; *vihvalaḥ*—having become mad for Her; *bhavānyāḥ*—while Bhavānī, the wife of Lord Śiva; *api*—although; *paśyantyāḥ*—was seeing all these incidents; *gata-hrīḥ*—bereft of all shame; *tat-padam*—to the place where She was situated; *yayau*—went.

TRANSLATION

Lord Śiva, his good sense taken away by the woman because of lusty desires to enjoy with Her, became so mad for Her that even in the presence of Bhavānī he did not hesitate to approach Her.

TEXT 26

सा तमायान्तमालोक्य विवस्त्रा व्रीडिता भृशम् ।
निलीयमाना वृक्षेषु हसन्ती नान्वतिष्ठत ॥ २६ ॥

sā tam āyāntam ālokya
vivastrā vrīḍitā bhṛśam

nilīyamānā vṛkṣeṣu
hasantī nānvatiṣṭhata

sā—that woman; *tam*—Lord Śiva; *āyāntam*—who was coming near; *ālokya*—seeing; *vivastrā*—She was naked; *vrīḍitā*—very bashful; *bhṛśam*—so much; *nilīyamānā*—was hiding; *vṛkṣeṣu*—among the trees; *hasantī*—smiling; *na*—not; *anvatiṣṭhata*—stood in one place.

TRANSLATION

The beautiful woman was already naked, and when She saw Lord Śiva coming toward Her, She became extremely bashful. Thus She kept smiling, but She hid Herself among the trees and did not stand in one place.

TEXT 27

तामन्वगच्छद् भगवान् भवः प्रमुषितेन्द्रियः ।
कामस्य च वशं नीतः करेणुमिव यूथपः ॥ २७ ॥

tām anvagacchad bhagavān
bhavaḥ pramuṣitendriyaḥ
kāmasya ca vaśaṁ nītaḥ
kareṇum iva yūthapaḥ

tām—Her; *anvagacchat*—followed; *bhagavān*—Lord Śiva; *bhavaḥ*—known as Bhava; *pramuṣita-indriyaḥ*—whose senses were agitated; *kāmasya*—of lusty desires; *ca*—and; *vaśam*—victimized; *nītaḥ*—having become; *kareṇum*—a female elephant; *iva*—just as; *yūthapaḥ*—a male elephant.

TRANSLATION

His senses being agitated, Lord Śiva, victimized by lusty desires, began to follow Her, just as a lusty elephant follows a she-elephant.

TEXT 28

सोऽनुव्रज्यातिवेगेन गृहीत्वानिच्छतीं स्त्रियम् ।
केशबन्ध उपानीय बाहुभ्यां परिषस्वजे ॥ २८ ॥

so 'nuvrajyātivegena
gṛhītvānicchatīṁ striyam
keśa-bandha upānīya
bāhubhyāṁ pariṣasvaje

saḥ—Lord Śiva; *anuvrajya*—following Her; *ati-vegena*—with great speed; *gṛhītvā*—catching; *anicchatīm*—although She was not willing to be caught; *striyam*—the woman; *keśa-bandhe*—on the cluster of hair; *upānīya*—dragging Her near; *bāhubhyām*—with his arms; *pariṣasvaje*—embraced Her.

TRANSLATION

After following Her with great speed, Lord Śiva caught Her by the braid of Her hair and dragged Her near him. Although She was unwilling, he embraced Her with his arms.

TEXTS 29-30

सोपगूढा भगवता करिणा करिणी यथा ।
इतस्ततः प्रसर्पन्ती विप्रकीर्णशिरोरुहा ॥ २९ ॥
आत्मानं मोचयित्वाङ्ग सुरर्षभभुजान्तरात् ।
प्राद्रवत्सा पृथुश्रोणी माया देवविनिर्मिता ॥ ३० ॥

sopagūḍhā bhagavatā
kariṇā kariṇī yathā
itas tataḥ prasarpantī
viprakīrṇa-śiroruhā

ātmānaṁ mocayitvāṅga
surarṣabha-bhujāntarāt
prādravat sā pṛthu-śroṇī
māyā deva-vinirmitā

sā—the woman; *upagūḍhā*—being captured and embraced; *bhagavatā*—by Lord Śiva; *kariṇā*—by a male elephant; *kariṇī*—a she-elephant; *yathā*—as; *itaḥ tataḥ*—here and there; *prasarpantī*—swirling like a snake; *viprakīrṇa*—scattered; *śiroruhā*—all the hair on Her head; *ātmānam*—Herself; *mocayitvā*—releasing; *aṅga*—O King; *sura-ṛṣabha*—of the best of the demigods (Lord Śiva); *bhuja-antarāt*—from the entanglement in the midst of the arms; *prādravat*—began to run very fast; *sā*—She; *pṛthu-śroṇī*—bearing very large hips; *māyā*—internal potency; *deva-vinirmitā*—exhibited by the Supreme Personality of Godhead.

TRANSLATION

Being embraced by Lord Śiva like a female elephant embraced by a male, the woman, whose hair was scattered, swirled like a snake. O King,

this woman, who had large, high hips, was a woman of yogamāyā presented by the Supreme Personality of Godhead. She released Herself somehow or other from the fond embrace of Lord Śiva's arms and ran away.

TEXT 31

तस्यासौ पदवीं रुद्रो विष्णोरद्भुतकर्मणः ।
प्रत्यपद्यत कामेन वैरिणेव विनिर्जितः ॥ ३१ ॥

tasyāsau padavīṁ rudro
viṣṇor adbhuta-karmaṇaḥ
pratyapadyata kāmena
vairiṇeva vinirjitaḥ

tasya—of He who is the Supreme Lord; *asau*—Lord Śiva; *padavīm*—the place; *rudraḥ*—Lord Śiva; *viṣṇoḥ*—of Lord Viṣṇu; *adbhuta-karmaṇaḥ*—of He who acts very wonderfully; *pratyapadyata*—began to follow; *kāmena*—by lusty desire; *vairiṇā iva*—as if by an enemy; *vinirjitaḥ*—being harassed.

TRANSLATION

As if harassed by an enemy in the form of lusty desires, Lord Śiva followed the path of Lord Viṣṇu, who acts very wonderfully and who had taken the form of Mohinī.

PURPORT

Lord Śiva cannot be victimized by *māyā.* Therefore it is to be understood that Lord Śiva was being thus harassed by Lord Viṣṇu's internal potency. Lord Viṣṇu can perform many wonderful activities through His various potencies.

parāsya śaktir vividhaiva śrūyate
svābhāvikī jñāna-bala-kriyā ca
(*Śvetāśvatara Upaniṣad* 6.8)

The Supreme Lord has various potencies, by which He can act very efficiently. To do anything expertly, He doesn't even need to contemplate. Since Lord Śiva was being harassed by the woman, it is to be understood that this was being done not by a woman but by Lord Viṣṇu Himself.

TEXT 32

तस्यानुधावतो रेतश्चस्कन्दामोघरेतसः ।
शुष्मिणो यूथपस्येव वासितामनुधावतः ॥ ३२ ॥

tasyānudhāvato retaś
caskandāmogha-retasaḥ
śuṣmiṇo yūthapasyeva
vāsitām anudhāvataḥ

tasya—of him (Lord Śiva); *anudhāvataḥ*—who was following; *retaḥ*—the semen; *caskanda*—discharged; *amogha-retasaḥ*—of that person whose discharge of semen never goes in vain; *śuṣmiṇaḥ*—mad; *yūthapasya*—of a male elephant; *iva*—just like; *vāsitām*—to a female elephant able to conceive pregnancy; *anudhāvataḥ*—following.

TRANSLATION

Just as a maddened bull elephant follows a female elephant who is able to conceive pregnancy, Lord Śiva followed the beautiful woman and discharged semen, even though his discharge of semen never goes in vain.

TEXT 33

यत्र यत्रापतन्मह्यां रेतस्तस्य महात्मनः ।
तानि रूप्यस्य हेम्नश्च क्षेत्राण्यासन्महीपते ॥ ३३ ॥

yatra yatrāpatan mahyāṁ
retas tasya mahātmanaḥ
tāni rūpyasya hemnaś ca
kṣetrāṇy āsan mahī-pate

yatra—wherever; *yatra*—and wherever; *apatat*—fell; *mahyām*—on the surface of the world; *retaḥ*—the semen; *tasya*—of him; *mahā-ātmanaḥ*—of the great personality (Lord Śiva); *tāni*—all those places; *rūpyasya*—of silver; *hemnaḥ*—of gold; *ca*—and; *kṣetrāṇi*—mines; *āsan*—became; *mahī-pate*—O King.

TRANSLATION

O King, wheresoever on the surface of the globe fell the semen of the great personality of Lord Śiva, mines of gold and silver later appeared.

PURPORT

Śrīla Viśvanātha Cakravartī Ṭhākura comments that those who seek gold and silver can worship Lord Śiva for material opulences. Lord Śiva lives under a *bael* tree and does not even construct a house in which to dwell, but although he is apparently poverty-stricken, his devotees are sometimes opulently endowed with large quantities of silver and gold. Parīkṣit Mahārāja later asks about this, and Śukadeva Gosvāmī replies.

TEXT 34

सरित्सरःसु शैलेषु वनेषूपवनेषु च ।
यत्र क्व चासन्नृषयस्तत्र संनिहितो हरः ॥ ३४ ॥

sarit-saraḥsu śaileṣu
vaneṣūpavaneṣu ca
yatra kva cāsann ṛṣayas
tatra sannihito haraḥ

sarit—near the shores of the rivers; *saraḥsu*—and near the lakes; *śaileṣu*—near the mountains; *vaneṣu*—in the forests; *upavaneṣu*—in the gardens or small forests; *ca*—also; *yatra*—wherever; *kva*—anywhere; *ca*—also; *āsan*—were exiting; *ṛṣayaḥ*—great sages; *tatra*—there; *sannihitaḥ*—was present; *haraḥ*—Lord Śiva.

TRANSLATION

Following Mohinī, Lord Śiva went everywhere—near the shores of the rivers and lakes, near the mountains, near the forests, near the gardens, and wherever there lived great sages.

PURPORT

Śrīla Viśvanātha Cakravartī Ṭhākura remarks that Mohinī-mūrti dragged Lord Śiva to so many places, especially to where the great sages lived, to instruct the sages that their Lord Śiva had become mad for a beautiful woman. Thus although they were all great sages and saintly persons, they should not think themselves free, but should remain extremely cautious about beautiful women. No one should think himself liberated in the presence of a beautiful woman. The *śāstras* enjoin:

mātrā svasrā duhitrā vā
nāviviktāsano bhavet
balavān indriya-grāmo
vidvāṁsam api karṣati

"One should not stay in a solitary place with a woman, even if she be his mother, sister or daughter, for the senses are so uncontrollably powerful that in the presence of a woman one may become agitated, even if he is very learned and advanced."(*Bhāg.* 9.19.17)

TEXT 35

स्कन्ने रेतसि सोऽपश्यदात्मानं देवमायया।
जडीकृतं नृपश्रेष्ठ संन्यवर्तत कश्मलात् ॥ ३५ ॥

skanne retasi so 'paśyad
ātmānaṁ deva-māyayā
jaḍīkṛtaṁ nṛpa-śreṣṭha
sannyavartata kaśmalāt

skanne—when fully discharged; *retasi*—the semen; *saḥ*—Lord Śiva; *apaśyat*—saw; *ātmānam*—his own self; *deva-māyayā*—by the *māyā* of the Supreme Personality of Godhead; *jaḍīkṛtam*—had become victimized as a fool; *nṛpa-śreṣṭha*—O best of kings (Mahārāja Parīkṣit); *sannyavartata*—restrained himself further; *kaśmalāt*—from illusion.

TRANSLATION

O Mahārāja Parīkṣit, best of kings, when Lord Śiva had fully discharged semen, he could see how he himself had been victimized by the illusion created by the Supreme Personality of Godhead. Thus he restrained himself from any further māyā.

PURPORT

Once one is agitated by lusty desires upon seeing a woman, those desires increase more and more, but when semen is discharged in the act of sex, the lusty desires diminish. The same principle acted upon Lord Śiva. He was allured by the beautiful woman Mohinī-mūrti, but when his semen had been fully discharged, he came to his senses and realized how he had been victimized as soon as he saw the woman in the forest. If one is trained to protect his semen by observing celibacy, naturally he is not attracted by the beauty of a woman. If one can remain a *brahmacārī,* he saves himself so much trouble in material existence. Material existence means enjoying the pleasure of sexual intercourse (*yan maithunādi-gṛhamedhi-sukham*). If one is educated about sex life and is trained to protect his semen, he is saved from the danger of material existence.

TEXT 36

अथावगतमाहात्म्य आत्मनो जगदात्मनः ।
अपरिज्ञेयवीर्यस्य न मेने तदुहाद्भुतम् ॥ ३६ ॥

athāvagata-māhātmya
ātmano jagad-ātmanaḥ
aparijñeya-vīryasya
na mene tad u hādbhutam

atha—thus; *avagata*—being fully convinced about; *māhātmyaḥ*—the greatness; *ātmanaḥ*—of himself; *jagat-ātmanaḥ*—and of the Supreme Personality of Godhead; *aparijñeya-vīryasya*—who has unlimited potency; *na*—not; *mene*—did consider; *tat*—the miraculous activities of the Supreme Personality of Godhead in bewildering him; *u ha*—certainly; *adbhutam*—as wonderful.

TRANSLATION

Thus Lord Śiva could understand his position and that of the Supreme Personality of Godhead, who has unlimited potencies. Having reached this understanding, he was not at all surprised by the wonderful way Lord Viṣṇu had acted upon him.

PURPORT

The Supreme Personality of Godhead is known as all-powerful because no one can excel Him in any activity. In *Bhagavad-gītā* (7.7) the Lord says, *mattaḥ parataraṁ nānyat kiñcid asti dhanañjaya:* "O conqueror of wealth, there is no truth superior to Me." No one can equal the Lord or be greater than Him, for He is the master of everyone. As stated in *Caitanya-caritāmṛta* (*Ādi* 5.142), *ekale īśvara kṛṣṇa, āra saba bhṛtya.* The Supreme Personality of Godhead, Kṛṣṇa, is the only master of everyone, including even Lord Śiva, what to speak of others. Lord Śiva was already aware of the supreme power of Lord Viṣṇu, but when he was actually put into bewilderment, he felt proud to have such an exalted master.

TEXT 37

तमविक्लवमव्रीडमालक्ष्य मधुसूदनः ।
उवाच परमप्रीतो बिभ्रत्स्वां पौरुषीं तनुम् ॥ ३७ ॥

taṁ aviklavam avrīḍam
ālakṣya madhusūdanaḥ
uvāca parama-prīto
bibhrat svāṁ pauruṣīṁ tanum

tam—him (Lord Śiva); *aviklavam*—without being agitated by the incident that had taken place; *avrīḍam*—without being ashamed; *ālakṣya*—seeing; *madhu-sūdanaḥ*—the Supreme Personality of Godhead, who is known as Madhusūdana, the killer of the demon Madhu; *uvāca*—said; *parama-prītaḥ*—being very pleased; *bibhrat*—assuming; *svām*—His own; *pauruṣīm*—original; *tanum*—form.

TRANSLATION

Seeing Lord Śiva unagitated and unashamed, Lord Viṣṇu [Madhusūdana] was very pleased. Thus He resumed His original form and spoke as follows.

PURPORT

Although Lord Śiva was aghast at the potency of Lord Viṣṇu, he did not feel ashamed. Rather, he was proud to be defeated by Lord Viṣṇu. Nothing is hidden from the Supreme Personality of Godhead, for He is in everyone's heart. Indeed, the Lord says in *Bhagavad-gītā* (15.15), *sarvasya cāhaṁ hṛdi sanniviṣṭo mattaḥ smṛtir jñānam apohanaṁ ca:* "I am seated in everyone's heart, and from Me come remembrance, knowledge and forgetfulness." Whatever happened had taken place under the direction of the Supreme Personality of Godhead, and therefore there was no cause to be sorry or ashamed. Although Lord Śiva is never defeated by anyone, when defeated by Lord Viṣṇu he felt proud that he had such an exalted and powerful master.

TEXT 38

श्रीभगवानुवाच
दिष्ट्या त्वं विबुधश्रेष्ठ स्वां निष्ठामात्मना स्थितः ।
यन्मे स्त्रीरूपया स्वैरं मोहितोऽप्यङ्ग मायया ॥ ३८ ॥

śrī-bhagavān uvāca
diṣṭyā tvaṁ vibudha-śreṣṭha
svāṁ niṣṭhām ātmanā sthitaḥ
yan me strī-rūpayā svairaṁ
mohito 'py aṅga māyayā

śrī-bhagavān uvāca—the Supreme Personality of Godhead said; *diṣṭyā*—all auspiciousness; *tvam*—unto you; *vibudha-śreṣṭha*—O best of all the demigods; *svām*—in your own; *niṣṭhām*—fixed situation; *ātmanā*—of your own self; *sthitaḥ*—you are situated; *yat*—as; *me*—Mine; *strī-rūpayā*—appearance like a woman; *svairam*—sufficiently; *mohitaḥ*—enchanted; *api*—in spite of; *aṅga*—O Lord Śiva; *māyayā*—by My potency.

TRANSLATION

The Supreme Personality of Godhead said: O best of the demigods, although you have been amply harassed because of My potency in assuming the form of a woman, you are established in your position. Therefore, may all good fortune be upon you.

PURPORT

Since Lord Śiva is the best of the demigods, he is the best of all devotees (*vaiṣṇavānāṁ yathā śambhuḥ*). His exemplary character was therefore praised by the Supreme Personality of Godhead, who gave His benediction by saying, "May all good fortune be upon you." When a devotee becomes a little proud, the Supreme Lord sometimes exhibits His supreme power to dissipate the devotee's misunderstanding. After being amply harassed by Lord Viṣṇu's potency, Lord Śiva resumed his normal, unagitated condition. This is the position of a devotee. A devotee should not be agitated under any circumstances, even in the worst reverses. As confirmed in *Bhagavad-gītā* (6.22), *yasmin sthito na duḥkhena guruṇāpi vicālyate:* because of his full faith in the Supreme Personality of Godhead, a devotee is never agitated, even in the greatest trials. This pridelessness is possible only for the first-class devotees, of whom Lord Śambhu is one.

TEXT 39

को नु मेऽतितरेन्मायां विषक्तस्त्वदृते पुमान् ।
तांस्तान्विसृजतीं भावान्दुस्तरामकृतात्मभिः ॥ ३९ ॥

ko nu me 'titaren māyāṁ
viṣaktas tvad-ṛte pumān
tāṁs tān visṛjatīṁ bhāvān
dustarām akṛtātmabhiḥ

kaḥ—what; *nu*—indeed; *me*—My; *atitaret*—can surpass; *māyām*—illusory energy; *viṣaktaḥ*—attached to material sense enjoyment; *tvat-ṛte*—

except for you; *pumān*—person; *tān*—such conditions; *tān*—unto the materially attached persons; *visṛjatīm*—in surpassing; *bhāvān*—reactions of material activities; *dustarām*—very difficult to surmount; *akṛta-ātmabhiḥ*—by persons unable to control their senses.

TRANSLATION

My dear Lord Śambhu, who within this material world but you can surpass My illusory energy? People are generally attached to sense enjoyment and conquered by its influence. Indeed, the influence of material nature is very difficult for them to surmount.

PURPORT

Of the three chief demigods—Brahmā, Viṣṇu and Maheśvara—all but Viṣṇu are under the influence of *māyā.* In *Caitanya-caritāmṛta,* they are described as *māyī,* which means "under *māyā's* influence." But even though Lord Śiva associates with *māyā,* he is not influenced. The living entities are affected by *māyā,* but although Lord Śiva apparently associates with *māyā,* he is not affected. In other words, all living entities within this material world except for Lord Śiva are swayed by *māyā.* Lord Śiva is therefore neither *viṣṇu-tattva* nor *jīva-tattva.* He is between the two.

TEXT 40

सेयं गुणमयी माया न त्वामभिभविष्यति ।
मया समेता कालेन कालरूपेण भागशः ॥ ४० ॥

seyaṁ guṇa-mayī māyā
na tvām abhibhaviṣyati
mayā sametā kālena
kāla-rūpeṇa bhāgaśaḥ

sā—that insurmountable; *iyam*—this; *guṇa-mayī*—consisting of the three modes of material nature; *māyā*—illusory energy; *na*—not; *tvām*—you; *abhibhaviṣyati*—will be able to bewilder in the future; *mayā*—with Me; *sametā*—joined; *kālena*—eternal time; *kāla-rūpeṇa*—in the form of time; *bhāgaśaḥ*—with her different parts.

TRANSLATION

The material, external energy [māyā], who cooperates with Me in creation and who is manifested in the three modes of nature, will not be able to bewilder you any longer.

PURPORT

When Lord Śiva was present, his wife, Durgā, was also there. Durgā works in cooperation with the Supreme Personality of Godhead in creating the cosmic manifestation. The Lord says in *Bhagavad-gītā* (9.10), *mayādhyakṣeṇa prakṛtiḥ sūyate sacarācaram:* "The material energy [*prakṛti*] works under My direction, O son of Kuntī, and is producing all moving and unmoving beings." *Prakṛti* is Durgā.

sṛṣṭi-sthiti-pralaya-sādhana-śaktir ekā
chāyeva yasya bhuvanāni bibharti durgā

The entire cosmos is created by Durgā in cooperation with Lord Viṣṇu in the form of *kāla,* time. *Sa īkṣata lokān nu sṛjā. Sa imāl lokān asṛjata.* This is the version of the *Vedas* (*Aitareya Upaniṣad* 1.1.1-2). *Māyā* happens to be the wife of Lord Śiva, and thus Lord Śiva is in association with *māyā,* but Lord Viṣṇu here assures Lord Śiva that this *māyā* will no longer be able to captivate him.

TEXT 41

श्रीशुक उवाच
एवं भगवता राजन् श्रीवत्साङ्केन सत्कृतः ।
आमन्त्र्य तं परिक्रम्य सगणः स्वालयं ययौ ॥ ४१ ॥

śrī-śuka uvāca
evaṁ bhagavatā rājan
śrīvatsāṅkena sat-kṛtaḥ
āmantrya taṁ parikramya
sagaṇaḥ svālayaṁ yayau

śrī-śukaḥ uvāca—Śrī Śukadeva Gosvāmī said; *evam*—thus; *bhagavatā*—by the Supreme Personality of Godhead; *rājan*—O King; *śrīvatsa-aṅkena*—who always carries the mark of Śrīvatsa on His breast; *sat-kṛtaḥ*—being very much applauded; *āmantrya*—taking permission from; *tam*—Him; *parikramya*—circumambulating; *sa-gaṇaḥ*—with his associates; *sva-ālayam*—to his own abode; *yayau*—went back.

TRANSLATION

Śukadeva Gosvāmī said: O King, having thus been praised by the Supreme Personality, who bears the mark of Śrīvatsa on His chest, Lord

Śiva circumambulated Him. Then, after taking permission from Him, Lord Śiva returned to his abode, Kailāsa, along with his associates.

PURPORT

Śrīla Viśvanātha Cakravartī Ṭhākura remarks that when Lord Śiva was offering obeisances unto Lord Viṣṇu, Lord Viṣṇu arose and embraced him. Therefore the word *śrīvatsāṅkena* is used here. The mark of Śrīvatsa adorns the chest of Lord Viṣṇu, and therefore when Lord Viṣṇu embraced Lord Śiva while being circumambulated, the Śrīvatsa mark touched Lord Śiva's bosom.

TEXT 42

आत्मांशभूतां तां मायां भवानीं भगवान्भवः ।
संमतामृषिमुख्यानां प्रीत्याचष्टाथ भारत ॥ ४२ ॥

ātmāṁśa-bhūtāṁ tāṁ māyāṁ
bhavānīṁ bhagavān bhavaḥ
sammatām ṛṣi-mukhyānāṁ
prītyācaṣṭātha bhārata

ātma-aṁśa-bhūtām—a potency of the Supreme Soul; *tām*—unto her; *māyām*—the illusory energy; *bhavānīm*—who is the wife of Lord Śiva; *bhagavān*—the powerful; *bhavaḥ*—Lord Śiva; *sammatām*—accepted; *ṛṣi-mukhyānām*—by the great sages; *prītyā*—in jubilation; *ācaṣṭa*—began to address; *atha*—then; *bhārata*—O Mahārāja Parīkṣit, descendant of Bharata.

TRANSLATION

O descendant of Bharata Mahārāja, Lord Śiva, in jubilation, then addressed his wife, Bhavānī, who is accepted by all authorities as the potency of Lord Viṣṇu.

TEXT 43

अयि व्यपश्यस्त्वमजस्य मायां
परस्य पुंसः परदेवतायाः ।
अहं कलानामृषभोऽपि मुह्ये
ययावशोऽन्ये किमुतास्वतन्त्राः ॥ ४३ ॥

ayi vyapaśyas tvam ajasya māyāṁ
parasya puṁsaḥ para-devatāyāḥ
ahaṁ kalānām ṛṣabho 'pi muhye
yayāvaśo 'nye kim utāsvatantrāḥ

ayi—oh; *vyapaśyaḥ*—have seen; *tvam*—you; *ajasya*—of the unborn; *māyām*—the illusory energy; *parasya puṁsaḥ*—of the Supreme Person; *para-devatāyāḥ*—the Absolute Truth; *aham*—myself; *kalānām*—of plenary portions; *ṛṣabhaḥ*—the chief; *api*—although; *muhye*—became bewildered; *yayā*—by her; *avaśaḥ*—imperceptibly; *anye*—others; *kim uta*—what to speak of; *asvatantrāḥ*—fully dependent on *māyā.*

TRANSLATION

Lord Śiva said: O Goddess, you have now seen the illusory energy of the Supreme Personality of Godhead, who is the unborn master of everyone. Although I am one of the principal expansions of His Lordship, even I was illusioned by His energy. What then is to be said of others, who are fully dependent on māyā?

TEXT 44

यं मामपृच्छस्त्वमुपेत्य योगात्
समासहस्रान्त उपारतं वै ।
स एष साक्षात् पुरुषः पुराणो
न यत्र कालो विशते न वेदः ॥ ४४ ॥

yaṁ mām apṛcchas tvam upetya yogāt
samā-sahasrānta upāratam vai
sa eṣa sākṣāt puruṣaḥ purāṇo
na yatra kālo viśate na vedaḥ

yam—about whom; *mām*—from me; *apṛcchaḥ*—inquired; *tvam*—you; *upetya*—coming near me; *yogāt*—from performing mystic *yoga; samā*—years; *sahasra-ante*—at the end of one thousand; *upāratam*—ceasing; *vai*—indeed; *saḥ*—He; *eṣaḥ*—here is; *sākṣāt*—directly; *puruṣaḥ*—the Supreme Person; *purāṇaḥ*—the original; *na*—not; *yatra*—where; *kālaḥ*—eternal time; *viśate*—can enter; *na*—nor; *vedaḥ*—the *Vedas.*

TRANSLATION

When I finished performing mystic yoga for one thousand years, you asked me upon whom I was meditating. Now, here is that Supreme Person to whom time has no entrance and who the Vedas cannot understand.

PURPORT

Eternal time enters anywhere and everywhere, but it cannot enter the kingdom of god. Nor can the *Vedas* understand the Supreme Personality of Godhead. This is an indication of the Lord's being omnipotent, omnipresent and omniscient.

TEXT 45

श्रीशुक उवाच
इति तेऽभिहितस्तात विक्रमः शार्ङ्गधन्वनः ।
सिन्धोर्निर्मथने येन धृतः पृष्ठे महाचलः ॥ ४५ ॥

śrī-śuka uvāca
iti te 'bhihitas tāta
vikramaḥ śārṅga-dhanvanaḥ
sindhor nirmathane yena
dhṛtaḥ pṛṣṭhe mahācalaḥ

śrī-śukaḥ uvāca—Śrī Śukadeva Gosvāmī said; *iti*—thus; *te*—unto you; *abhihitaḥ*—explained; *tāta*—my dear King; *vikramaḥ*—prowess; *śārṅga-dhanvanaḥ*—of the Supreme Personality of Godhead, who carries the Śārṅga bow; *sindhoḥ*—of the ocean of milk; *nirmathane*—in the churning; *yena*—by whom; *dhṛtaḥ*—was held; *pṛṣṭhe*—on the back; *mahā-acalaḥ*—the great mountain.

TRANSLATION

Śukadeva Gosvāmī said: My dear King, the person who bore the great mountain on His back for the churning of the ocean of milk is the same Supreme Personality of Godhead, known as Śārṅga-dhanvā. I have now described to you His prowess.

TEXT 46

एतन्मुहुः कीर्तयतोऽनुशृण्वतो
न रिष्यते जातु समुद्यमः क्वचित् ।

यदुत्तमश्लोकगुणानुवर्णनं
समस्तसंसारपरिश्रमापहम् ॥ ४६ ॥

etan muhuḥ kīrtayato 'nuśṛṇvato
na riṣyate jātu samudyamaḥ kvacit
yad uttamaśloka-guṇānuvarṇanaṁ
samasta-saṁsāra-pariśramāpaham

etat—this narration; *muhuḥ*—constantly; *kīrtayataḥ*—of one who chants; *anuśṛṇvataḥ*—and also hears; *na*—not; *riṣyate*—annihilated; *jātu*—at any time; *samudyamaḥ*—the endeavor; *kvacit*—at any time; *yat*—because; *uttamaśloka*—of the Supreme Personality of Godhead; *guṇa-anuvarṇanam*—describing the transcendental qualities; *samasta*—all; *saṁsāra*—of material existence; *pariśrama*—misery; *apaham*—finishing.

TRANSLATION

The endeavor of one who constantly hears or describes this narration of the churning of the ocean of milk will never be fruitless. Indeed, chanting the glories of the Supreme Personality of Godhead is the only means to annihilate all sufferings in this material world.

TEXT 47

असदविषयमङ्घ्रिं भावगम्यं प्रपन्ना-
नमृतममरवर्यानाशयत् सिन्धुमथ्यम् ।
कपटयुवतिवेषो मोहयन्यः सुरारीं-
स्तमहमुपसृतानां कामपूरं नतोऽस्मि ॥ ४७ ॥

asad-aviṣayam aṅghriṁ bhāva-gamyaṁ prapannān
amṛtam amara-varyān āśayat sindhu-mathyam
kapaṭa-yuvati-veṣo mohayan yaḥ surārīṁs
tam aham upasṛtānāṁ kāma-pūraṁ nato 'smi

asat-aviṣayam—not understood by the atheists; *aṅghrim*—unto the lotus feet of the Supreme Personality of Godhead; *bhāva-gamyam*—understood by devotees; *prapannān*—fully surrendered; *amṛtam*—the nectar; *amara-varyān*—only unto the demigods; *āśayat*—gave to drink; *sindhu-mathyam*—produced from the ocean of milk; *kapaṭa-yuvati-veṣaḥ*—appearing as a false young girl; *mohayan*—captivating; *yaḥ*—He who; *sura-arīn*—the enemies of the demigods; *tam*—unto Him; *aham*—I; *upasṛtānām*—of the devotees; *kāma-pūram*—who fulfills all desires; *nataḥ asmi*—I offer my respectful obeisances.

TRANSLATION

Assuming the form of a young woman and thus bewildering the demons, the Supreme Personality of Godhead distributed to His devotees, the demigods, the nectar produced from the churning of the ocean of milk. Unto that Supreme Personality of Godhead, who always fulfills the desires of His devotees, I offer my respectful obeisances.

PURPORT

The instruction of this narration concerning the churning of the milk ocean is clearly manifested by the Supreme Personality of Godhead. Although He is equal to everyone, because of natural affection He favors His devotees. The Lord says in *Bhagavad-gītā* (9.29):

samo 'haṁ sarva-bhūteṣu
na me dveṣyo 'sti na priyaḥ
ye bhajanti tu māṁ bhaktyā
mayi te teṣu cāpy aham

"I envy no one, nor am I partial to anyone. I am equal to all. But whoever renders service unto Me in devotion is a friend, is in Me, and I am also a friend to him." This partiality of the Supreme Personality of Godhead is natural. A person cares for his children not because of partiality but in a reciprocation of love. The children depend on the father's affection, and the father affectionately maintains the children. Similarly, because devotees do not know anything but the lotus feet of the Lord, the Lord is always prepared to give protection to His devotees and fulfill their desires. He therefore says, *kaunteya pratijānīhi na me bhaktaḥ praṇaśyati:* "O son of Kuntī, declare it boldly that My devotee never perishes."

Thus end the Bhaktivedanta purports of the Eighth Canto, Twelfth Chapter, of the Śrīmad-Bhāgavatam*, entitled "The Mohinī-mūrti Incarnation Bewilders Lord Śiva."*

CHAPTER THIRTEEN

Description of Future Manus

Of the fourteen Manus, six Manus have already been described. Now, this chapter will consecutively describe each Manu from the seventh to the fourteenth.

The seventh Manu, who is the son of Vivasvān, is known as Śrāddhadeva. He has ten sons, named Ikṣvāku, Nabhaga, Dhṛṣṭa, Śaryāti, Nariṣyanta, Nābhāga, Diṣṭa, Tarūṣa, Pṛṣadhra and Vasumān. In this *manvantara,* or reign of Manu, among the demigods are the Ādityas, Vasus, Rudras, Viśvedevas, Maruts, Aśvinī-kumāras and Ṛbhus. The king of heaven, Indra, is known as Purandara, and the seven sages are known as Kaśyapa, Atri, Vasiṣṭha, Viśvāmitra, Gautama, Jamadagni and Bharadvāja. During this period of Manu, the Supreme Personality of Godhead Viṣṇu appears from the womb of Aditi in His incarnation as the son of Kaśyapa.

In the period of the eighth Manu, the Manu is Sāvarṇi. His sons are headed by Nirmoka, and among the demigods are the Sutapās. Bali, the son of Virocana, is Indra, and Gālava and Paraśurāma are among the seven sages. In this age of Manu, the incarnation of the Supreme Personality of Godhead appears as Sārvabhauma, the son of Devaguhya and Sarasvatī.

In the period of the ninth Manu, the Manu is Dakṣa-sāvarṇi. His sons are headed by Bhūtaketu, and among the demigods are the Marīcigarbhas. Adbhuta is Indra, and among the seven sages is Dyutimān. In this period of Manu, the incarnation Ṛṣabha is born of Āyuṣmān and Ambudhārā.

In the period of the tenth Manu, the Manu is Brahma-sāvarṇi. Among his sons is Bhūriṣeṇa, and the seven sages are Haviṣmān and others. Among the demigods are the Suvāsanas, and Śambhu is Indra. The incarnation in this period of Manu is Viṣvaksena, who is a friend of Śambhu and who is born from the womb of Viṣūcī in the house of a *brāhmaṇa* named Viśvasraṣṭā.

In the period of the eleventh Manu, the Manu is Dharma-sāvarṇi, who has ten sons, headed by Satyadharma. Among the demigods are the Vihaṅgamas, Indra is known as Vaidhṛta, and the seven sages are Aruṇa and others. In this *manvantara,* the incarnation is Dharmasetu, who is born of Vaidhṛtā and Āryaka.

In the period of the twelfth Manu, the Manu is Rudra-sāvarṇi, whose sons are headed by Devavān. The demigods are the Haritas and others, Indra is Ṛtadhāmā, and the seven sages are Tapomūrti and others. The incarnation in this *manvantara* is Sudhāmā, or Svadhāmā, who is born from the womb of Sunṛtā. His father's name is Satyasahā.

In the period of the thirteenth Manu, the Manu is Deva-sāvarṇi. Among his sons is Citrasena, the demigods are the Sukarmās and others, Indra is Divaspati, and Nirmoka is among the sages. The *manvantara-avatāra* is Yogeśvara, who is born of Devahotra and Bṛhatī.

In the period of the fourteenth Manu, the Manu is Indra-sāvarṇi. Among his sons are Uru and Gambhīra, the demigods are the Pavitras and others, Indra is Śuci, and among the sages are Agni and Bāhu. The incarnation of this *manvantara* is known as Bṛhadbhānu. He is born of Satrāyaṇa from the womb of Vitānā.

The total duration of the periods ruled by these Manus is calculated to be one thousand *catur-yugas,* or 4,300,000 times 1,000 years.

TEXT 1

श्रीशुक उवाच
मनुर्विवस्वतः पुत्रः श्राद्धदेव इति श्रुतः ।
सप्तमो वर्तमानो यस्तदपत्यानि मे शृणु ॥ १ ॥

śrī-śuka uvāca
manur vivasvataḥ putraḥ
śrāddhadeva iti śrutaḥ
saptamo vartamāno yas
tad-apatyāni me śṛṇu

śrī-śukaḥ uvāca—Śrī Śukadeva Gosvāmī said; *manuḥ*—Manu; *vivasvataḥ*—of the sun-god; *putraḥ*—son; *śrāddhadevaḥ*—as Śrāddhadeva; *iti*—thus; *śrutaḥ*—known, celebrated; *saptamaḥ*—seventh; *vartamānaḥ*—at the present moment; *yaḥ*—he who; *tat*—his; *apatyāni*—children; *me*—from me; *śṛṇu*—just hear.

TRANSLATION

Śukadeva Gosvāmī said: The present Manu, who is named Śrāddhadeva, is the son of Vivasvān, the predominating deity on the sun planet.

Śrāddhadeva is the seventh Manu. Now please hear from me as I describe his sons.

TEXTS 2-3

इक्ष्वाकुर्नभगश्चैव धृष्टः शर्यातिरेव च ।
नरिष्यन्तोऽथ नाभागः सप्तमो दिष्ट उच्यते ॥ २ ॥
तरूषश्च पृषध्रश्च दशमो वसुमान्स्मृतः ।
मनोर्वैवस्वतस्यैते दशपुत्राः परन्तप ॥ ३ ॥

ikṣvākur nabhagaś caiva
dhṛṣṭaḥ śaryātir eva ca
nariṣyanto 'tha nābhāgaḥ
saptamo diṣṭa ucyate

tarūṣaś ca pṛṣadhraś ca
daśamo vasumān smṛtaḥ
manor vaivasvatasyaite
daśa-putrāḥ parantapa

ikṣvākuḥ—Ikṣvāku; *nabhagaḥ*—Nabhaga; *ca*—also; *eva*—indeed; *dhṛṣṭaḥ*—Dhṛṣṭa; *śaryātiḥ*—Śaryāti; *eva*—certainly; *ca*—also; *nariṣyantaḥ*—Nariṣyanta; *atha*—as well as; *nābhāgaḥ*—Nābhāga; *saptamaḥ*—the seventh one; *diṣṭaḥ*—Diṣṭa; *ucyate*—is so celebrated; *tarūṣaḥ ca*—and Tarūṣa; *pṛṣadhraḥ ca*—and Pṛṣadhra; *daśamaḥ*—the tenth one; *vasumān*—Vasumān; *smṛtaḥ*—known; *manoḥ*—of Manu; *vaivasvatasya*—of Vaivasvata; *ete*—all these; *daśa-putrāḥ*—ten sons; *parantapa*—O King.

TRANSLATION

O King Parīkṣit, among the ten sons of Manu are Ikṣvāku, Nabhaga, Dhṛṣṭa, Śaryāti, Nariṣyanta and Nābhāga. The seventh son is known as Diṣṭa. Then come Tarūṣa and Pṛṣadhra, and the tenth son is known as Vasumān.

TEXT 4

आदित्या वसवो रुद्रा विश्वेदेवा मरुद्गणाः ।
अश्विनावृभवो राजन्निन्द्रस्तेषां पुरन्दरः ॥ ४ ॥

ādityā vasavo rudrā
viśvedevā marud-gaṇāḥ
aśvināv ṛbhavo rājann
indras teṣāṁ purandaraḥ

ādityāḥ—the Ādityas; *vasavaḥ*—the Vasus; *rudrāḥ*—the Rudras; *viśvedevāḥ*—the Viśvedevas; *marut-gaṇāḥ*—and the Maruts; *aśvinau*—the two Aśvinī brothers; *ṛbhavaḥ*—the Ṛbhus; *rājan*—O King; *indraḥ*—the king of heaven; *teṣām*—of them; *purandaraḥ*—Purandara.

TRANSLATION

In this manvantara, O King, the Ādityas, the Vasus, the Rudras, the Viśvedevas, the Maruts, the two Aśvinī-kumāra brothers and the Ṛbhus are the demigods. Their head king [Indra] is Purandara.

TEXT 5

कश्यपोऽत्रिर्वसिष्ठश्च विश्वामित्रोऽथ गौतमः ।
जमदग्निर्भरद्वाज इति सप्तर्षयः स्मृताः ॥ ५ ॥

kaśyapo 'trir vasiṣṭhaś ca
viśvāmitro 'tha gautamaḥ
jamadagnir bharadvāja
iti saptarṣayaḥ smṛtāḥ

kaśyapaḥ—Kaśyapa; *atriḥ*—Atri; *vasiṣṭhaḥ*—Vasiṣṭha; *ca*—and; *viśvāmitraḥ*—Viśvāmitra; *atha*—as well as; *gautamaḥ*—Gautama; *jamadagniḥ*—Jamadagni; *bharadvājaḥ*—Bharadvāja; *iti*—thus; *sapta-ṛṣayaḥ*—the seven sages; *smṛtāḥ*—celebrated.

TRANSLATION

Kaśyapa, Atri, Vasiṣṭha, Viśvāmitra, Gautama, Jamadagni and Bharadvāja are known as the seven sages.

TEXT 6

अत्रापि भगवज्जन्म कश्यपाददितेरभूत् ।
आदित्यानामवरजो विष्णुर्वामनरूपधृक् ॥ ६ ॥

atrāpi bhagavaj-janma
kaśyapād aditer abhūt

ādityānām avarajo
viṣṇur vāmana-rūpa-dhṛk

atra—in this Manu's reign; *api*—certainly; *bhagavat-janma*—appearance of the Supreme Personality of Godhead; *kaśyapāt*—by Kaśyapa Muni; *aditeḥ*—of mother Aditi; *abhūt*—became possible; *ādityānām*—of the Ādityas; *avara-jaḥ*—the youngest; *viṣṇuḥ*—Lord Viṣṇu Himself; *vāmana-rūpa-dhṛk*—appearing as Lord Vāmana.

TRANSLATION

In this manvantara, the Supreme Personality of Godhead appeared as the youngest of all the Ādityas, known as Vāmana, the dwarf. His father was Kaśyapa and His mother Aditi.

TEXT 7

संक्षेपतो मयोक्तानि सप्तमन्वन्तराणि ते ।
भविष्याण्यथ वक्ष्यामि विष्णोः शक्त्यान्वितानि च ॥ ७ ॥

saṅkṣepato mayoktāni
sapta-manvantarāṇi te
bhaviṣyāṇy atha vakṣyāmi
viṣṇoḥ śaktyānvitāni ca

saṅkṣepataḥ—in brief; *mayā*—by me; *uktāni*—explained; *sapta*—seven; *manu-antarāṇi*—changes of Manu; *te*—unto you; *bhaviṣyāṇi*—the future Manus; *atha*—also; *vakṣyāmi*—I shall speak; *viṣṇoḥ*—of Lord Viṣṇu; *śaktyā anvitāni*—empowered by the energy; *ca*—also.

TRANSLATION

I have briefly explained to you the position of the seven Manus. Now I shall describe the future Manus, along with the incarnations of Lord Viṣṇu.

TEXT 8

विवस्वतश्च द्वे जाये विश्वकर्मसुते उभे ।
संज्ञा छाया च राजेन्द्र ये प्रागभिहिते तव ॥ ८ ॥

vivasvataś ca dve jāye
viśvakarma-sute ubhe

saṁjñā chāyā ca rājendra
ye prāg abhihite tava

vivasvataḥ—of Vivasvān; *ca*—also; *dve*—two; *jāye*—wives; *viśvakarma-sute*—the two daughters of Viśvakarmā; *ubhe*—both of them; *saṁjñā*—Saṁjñā; *chāyā*—Chāyā; *ca*—and; *rāja-indra*—O King; *ye*—both of whom; *prāk*—before; *abhihite*—described; *tava*—unto you.

TRANSLATION

O King, I have previously described [in the Sixth Canto] the two daughters of Viśvakarmā, named Saṁjñā and Chāyā, who were the first two wives of Vivasvān.

TEXT 9

तृतीयां वडवामेके तासां संज्ञासुतास्त्रयः ।
यमो यमी श्राद्धदेवश्छायायाश्च सुताञ्छृणु ॥ ९ ॥

tṛtīyāṁ vaḍavām eke
tāsāṁ saṁjñā-sutās trayaḥ
yamo yamī śrāddhadevaś
chāyāyāś ca sutāñ chṛṇu

tṛtīyām—the third wife; *vaḍavām*—Vaḍavā; *eke*—some people; *tāsām*—of all three wives; *saṁjñā-sutāḥ trayaḥ*—three issues of Saṁjñā; *yamaḥ*—one son named Yama; *yamī*—Yamī, a daughter; *śrāddhadevaḥ*—Śrāddhadeva, another son; *chāyāyāḥ*—of Chāyā; *ca*—and; *sutān*—the sons; *śṛṇu*—just hear about.

TRANSLATION

It is said that the sun-god had a third wife, named Vaḍavā. Of the three wives, the wife named Saṁjñā had three children-Yama, Yamī and Śrāddhadeva. Now let me describe the children of Chāyā.

TEXT 10

सावर्णिस्तपती कन्या भार्या संवरणस्य या ।
शनैश्चरस्तृतीयोऽभूदश्विनौ वडवात्मजौ ॥ १० ॥

sāvarṇis tapatī kanyā
bhāryā saṁvaraṇasya yā

śanaiścaras tṛtīyo 'bhūd
aśvinau vaḍavātmajau

sāvarṇiḥ—Sāvarṇi; *tapatī*—Tapatī; *kanyā*—the daughter; *bhāryā*—the wife; *saṁvaraṇasya*—of King Saṁvaraṇa; *yā*—she who; *śanaiścaraḥ*—Śanaiścara; *tṛtīyaḥ*—the third issue; *abhūt*—took birth; *aśvinau*—the two Aśvinī-kumāras; *vaḍavā-ātma-jau*—the sons of the wife known as Vaḍavā.

TRANSLATION

Chāyā had a son named Sāvarṇi and a daughter named Tapatī, who later became the wife of King Saṁvaraṇa. Chāyā's third child is known as Śanaiścara [Saturn]. Vaḍavā gave birth to two sons, namely the Aśvinī brothers.

TEXT 11

अष्टमेऽन्तर आयाते सावर्णिर्भविता मनुः ।
निर्मोकविरजस्काद्याः सावर्णितनया नृप ॥ ११ ॥

aṣṭame 'ntara āyāte
sāvarṇir bhavitā manuḥ
nirmoka-virajaskādyāḥ
sāvarṇi-tanayā nṛpa

aṣṭame—the eighth; *antare*—Manu's period; *āyāte*—when arrived; *sāvarṇiḥ*—Sāvarṇi; *bhavitā*—will become; *manuḥ*—the eighth Manu; *nirmoka*—Nirmoka; *virajaska-ādyāḥ*—Virajaska and others; *sāvarṇi*—of Sāvarṇi; *tanayāḥ*—the sons; *nṛpa*—O King.

TRANSLATION

O King, when the period of the eighth Manu arrives, Sāvarṇi will become the Manu. Nirmoka and Virajaska will be among his sons.

PURPORT

The present reign is that of Vaivasvata Manu. According to astronomical calculations, we are now in the twenty-eighth *yuga* of Vaivasvata Manu. Each Manu lives for seventy-one *yugas,* and fourteen such Manus rule in one day of Lord Brahmā. We are now in the period of Vaivasvata Manu, the seventh Manu, and the eighth Manu will come into existence after many millions of years. But Śukadeva Gosvāmī, having heard from authorities, foretells that the eighth Manu will be Sāvarṇi and that Nirmoka and Virajaska will be among his sons. *Śāstra* can foretell what will happen millions and millions of years in the future.

TEXT 12

तत्र देवाः सुतपसो विरजा अमृतप्रभाः ।
तेषां विरोचनसुतो बलिरिन्द्रो भविष्यति ॥ १२ ॥

tatra devāḥ sutapaso
virajā amṛtaprabhāḥ
teṣāṁ virocana-suto
balir indro bhaviṣyati

tatra—in that period of Manu; *devāḥ*—the demigods; *sutapasaḥ*—the Sutapās; *virajāḥ*—the Virajas; *amṛtaprabhāḥ*—the Amṛtaprabhas; *teṣām*—of them; *virocana-sutaḥ*—the son of Virocana; *baliḥ*—Mahārāja Bali; *indraḥ*—the king of heaven; *bhaviṣyati*—will become.

TRANSLATION

In the period of the eighth Manu, among the demigods will be the Sutapās, the Virajas and the Amṛtaprabhas. The king of the demigods, Indra, will be Bali Mahārāja, the son of Virocana.

TEXT 13

दत्त्वेमां याचमानाय विष्णवे यः पदत्रयम् ।
राद्धमिन्द्रपदं हित्वा ततः सिद्धिमवाप्स्यति ॥ १३ ॥

dattvemāṁ yācamānāya
viṣṇave yaḥ pada-trayam
rāddham indra-padaṁ hitvā
tataḥ siddhim avāpsyati

dattvā—giving in charity; *imām*—this entire universe; *yācamānāya*—who was begging from him; *viṣṇave*—unto Lord Viṣṇu; *yaḥ*—Bali Mahārāja; *pada-trayam*—three paces of land; *rāddham*—achieved; *indra-padam*—the post of Indra; *hitvā*—giving up; *tataḥ*—thereafter; *siddhim*—perfection; *avāpsyati*—will achieve.

TRANSLATION

Bali Mahārāja gave a gift of three paces of land to Lord Viṣṇu, and because of this charity he lost all the three worlds. Later, however, when Lord Viṣṇu is pleased because of Bali's giving everything to Him, Bali Mahārāja will achieve the perfection of life.

PURPORT

In *Bhagavad-gītā* (7.3) it is stated, *manuṣyāṇāṁ sahasreṣu kaścid yatati siddhaye:* out of many millions of people, one may attempt to achieve success in life. This success is explained here. *Rāddham indra-padaṁ hitvā tataḥ siddhim avāpsyati. Siddhi* consists of achieving the favor of Lord Viṣṇu, not the *yoga-siddhis.* The *yoga-siddhis—aṇimā, laghimā, mahimā, prāpti, prākāmya, īśitva, vaśitva* and *kāmāvasāyitā*—are temporary. The ultimate *siddhi* is to achieve the favor of Lord Viṣṇu.

TEXT 14

योऽसौ भगवता बद्धः प्रीतेन सुतले पुनः ।
निवेशितोऽधिके स्वर्गादधुनास्ते स्वराडिव ॥ १४ ॥

yo 'sau bhagavatā baddhaḥ
prītena sutale punaḥ
niveśito 'dhike svargād
adhunāste sva-rāḍ iva

yaḥ—Bali Mahārāja; *asau*—he; *bhagavatā*—by the Personality of Godhead; *baddhaḥ*—bound; *prītena*—because of favor; *sutale*—in the kingdom of Sutala; *punaḥ*—again; *niveśitaḥ*—situated; *adhike*—more opulent; *svargāt*—than the heavenly planets; *adhunā*—at the present moment; *āste*—is situated; *sva-rāṭ iva*—equal to the position of Indra.

TRANSLATION

With great affection, the Personality of Godhead bound Bali and then installed him in the kingdom of Sutala, which is more opulent than the heavenly planets. Mahārāja Bali now resides on that planet and is more comfortably situated than Indra.

TEXTS 15-16

गालवो दीप्तिमान्रामो द्रोणपुत्रः कृपस्तथा ।
ऋष्यशृङ्गः पितास्माकं भगवान्बादरायणः ॥ १५ ॥
इमे सप्तर्षयस्तत्र भविष्यन्ति स्वयोगतः ।
इदानीमासते राजन् स्वे स्व आश्रममण्डले ॥ १६ ॥

gālavo dīptimān rāmo
droṇa-putraḥ kṛpas tathā
ṛṣyaśṛṅgaḥ pitāsmākaṁ
bhagavān bādarāyaṇaḥ

ime saptarṣayas tatra
bhaviṣyanti sva-yogataḥ
idānīm āsate rājan
sve sva āśrama-maṇḍale

gālavaḥ—Gālava; *dīptimān*—Dīptimān; *rāmaḥ*—Paraśurāma; *droṇa-putraḥ*—the son of Droṇācārya, namely Aśvatthāmā; *kṛpaḥ*—Kṛpācārya; *tathā*—as well; *ṛṣyaśṛṅgaḥ*—Ṛṣyaśṛṅga; *pitā asmākam*—our father; *bhagavān*—the incarnation of Godhead; *bādarāyaṇaḥ*—Vyāsadeva; *ime*—all of them; *sapta-ṛṣayaḥ*—the seven sages; *tatra*—in the eighth *manvantara; bhaviṣyanti*—will become; *sva-yogataḥ*—as a result of their service to the Lord; *idānīm*—at the present moment; *āsate*—they are all existing; *rājan*—O King; *sve sve*—in their own; *āśrama-maṇḍale*—different hermitages.

TRANSLATION

O King, during the eighth manvantara, the great personalities Gālava, Dīptimān, Paraśurāma, Aśvatthāmā, Kṛpācārya, Ṛṣyaśṛṅga and our father, Vyāsadeva, the incarnation of Nārāyaṇa, will be the seven sages. For the present, they are all residing in their respective āśramas.

TEXT 17

देवगुह्यात्सरस्वत्यां सार्वभौम इति प्रभुः ।
स्थानं पुरन्दराद्धृत्वा बलये दास्यतीश्वरः ॥ १७ ॥

devaguhyāt sarasvatyāṁ
sārvabhauma iti prabhuḥ

sthānaṁ purandarād dhṛtvā
balaye dāsyatīśvaraḥ

devaguhyāt—from His father, Devaguhya; *sarasvatyām*—in the womb of Sarasvatī; *sārvabhaumaḥ*—Sārvabhauma; *iti*—thus; *prabhuḥ*—the master; *sthānam*—place; *purandarāt*—from Lord Indra; *hṛtvā*—taking away by force; *balaye*—unto Bali Mahārāja; *dāsyati*—will give; *īśvaraḥ*—the master.

TRANSLATION

In the eighth manvantara, the greatly powerful Personality of Godhead Sārvabhauma will take birth. His father will be Devaguhya, and His mother will be Sarasvatī. He will take the kingdom away from Purandara [Lord Indra] and give it to Bali Mahārāja.

TEXT 18

नवमो दक्षसावर्णिर्मनुर्वरुणसम्भवः ।
भूतकेतुर्दीप्तकेतुरित्याद्यास्तत्सुता नृप ॥ १८ ॥

navamo dakṣa-sāvarṇir
manur varuṇa-sambhavaḥ
bhūtaketur dīptaketur
ity ādyās tat-sutā nṛpa

navamaḥ—ninth; *dakṣa-sāvarṇiḥ*—Dakṣa-sāvarṇi; *manuḥ*—the Manu; *varuṇa-sambhavaḥ*—born as the son of Varuṇa; *bhūtaketuḥ*—Bhūtaketu; *dīptaketuḥ*—Dīptaketu; *iti*—thus; *ādyāḥ*—and so on; *tat*—his; *sutāḥ*—sons; *nṛpa*—O King.

TRANSLATION

O King, the ninth Manu will be Dakṣa-sāvarṇi, who is born of Varuṇa. Among his sons will be Bhūtaketu, and Dīptaketu.

TEXT 19

पारामरीचिगर्भाद्या देवा इन्द्रोऽद्भुतः स्मृतः ।
द्युतिमत्प्रमुखास्तत्र भविष्यन्त्यृषयस्ततः ॥ १९ ॥

pārā-marīcigarbhādyā
devā indro 'dbhutaḥ smṛtaḥ

dyutimat-pramukhās tatra
bhaviṣyanty ṛṣayas tataḥ

pārā—the Pāras; *marīcigarbha*—the Marīcigarbhas; *ādyāḥ*—like that; *devāḥ*—the demigods; *indraḥ*—the king of heaven; *adbhutaḥ*—Adbhuta; *smṛtaḥ*—known; *dyutimat*—Dyutimān; *pramukhāḥ*—headed by; *tatra*—in that ninth period of Manu; *bhaviṣyanti*—will become; *ṛṣayaḥ*—the seven *ṛṣis;* *tataḥ*—then.

TRANSLATION

In this ninth manvantara, the Pāras and Marīcigarbhas will be among the demigods. The king of heaven, Indra, will be named Adbhuta, and Dyutimān will be among the seven sages.

TEXT 20

आयुष्मतोऽम्बुधारायामृषभो भगवत्कला ।
भविता येन संराद्धां त्रिलोकीं भोक्ष्यतेऽद्भुतः ॥ २० ॥

āyuṣmato 'mbudhārāyām
ṛṣabho bhagavat-kalā
bhavitā yena saṁrāddhāṁ
tri-lokīṁ bhokṣyate 'dbhutaḥ

āyuṣmataḥ—of the father, Āyuṣmān; *ambudhārāyām*—in the womb of the mother, Ambudhārā; *ṛṣabhaḥ*—Ṛṣabha; *bhagavat-kalā*—a partial incarnation of the Supreme Personality of Godhead; *bhavitā*—will be; *yena*—by whom; *saṁrāddhām*—all-opulent; *tri-lokīm*—the three worlds; *bhokṣyate*—will enjoy; *adbhutaḥ*—the Indra of the name Adbhuta.

TRANSLATION

Ṛṣabhadeva, a partial incarnation of the Supreme Personality of Godhead, will take birth from his father, Āyuṣmān, and his mother, Ambudhārā. He will enable the Indra named Adbhuta to enjoy the opulence of the three worlds.

TEXT 21

दशमो ब्रह्मसावर्णिरुपश्लोकसुतो मनुः ।
तत्सुता भूरिषेणाद्या हविष्मत्प्रमुखा द्विजाः ॥ २१ ॥

daśamo brahma-sāvarṇir
upaśloka-suto manuḥ
tat-sutā bhūriṣeṇādyā
haviṣmat pramukhā dvijāḥ

daśamaḥ—the tenth Manu; *brahma-sāvarṇiḥ*—Brahma-sāvarṇi; *upaśloka-sutaḥ*—born of Upaśloka; *manuḥ*—will be Manu; *tat-sutāḥ*—his sons; *bhūriṣeṇa-ādyāḥ*—Bhūriṣeṇa and others; *haviṣmat*—Haviṣmān; *pramukhāḥ*—headed by; *dvijāḥ*—the seven sages.

TRANSLATION

The son of Upaśloka known as Brahma-sāvarṇi will be the tenth Manu. Bhūriṣeṇa will be among his sons, and the brāhmaṇas headed by Haviṣmān will be the seven sages.

TEXT 22

हविष्मान्सुकृतः सत्यो जयो मूर्तिस्तदा द्विजाः ।
सुवासनविरुद्धाद्या देवाः शम्भुः सुरेश्वरः ॥ २२ ॥

haviṣmān sukṛtaḥ satyo
jayo mūrtis tadā dvijāḥ
suvāsana-viruddhādyā
devāḥ śambhuḥ sureśvaraḥ

haviṣmān—Haviṣmān; *sukṛtaḥ*—Sukṛta; *satyaḥ*—Satya; *jayaḥ*—Jaya; *mūrtiḥ*—Mūrti; *tadā*—at that time; *dvijāḥ*—the seven sages; *suvāsana*—the Suvāsanas; *viruddha*—the Viruddhas; *ādyāḥ*—and so on; *devāḥ*—the demigods; *śambhuḥ*—Śambhu; *sura-īśvaraḥ*—Indra, king of the demigods.

TRANSLATION

Haviṣmān, Sukṛta, Satya, Jaya, Mūrti and others will be the seven sages, the Suvāsanas and Viruddhas will be among the demigods, and Śambhu will be their king, Indra.

TEXT 23

विष्वक्सेनो विषूच्यां तु शम्भोः सख्यं करिष्यति ।
जातः स्वांशेन भगवान्गृहे विश्वसृजो विभुः ॥ २३ ॥

viṣvakseno viṣūcyāṁ tu
śambhoḥ sakhyaṁ kariṣyati
jātaḥ svāṁśena bhagavān
gṛhe viśvasṛjo vibhuḥ

viṣvaksenaḥ—Viṣvaksena; *viṣūcyām*—in the womb of Viṣūcī; *tu*—then; *śambhoḥ*—of Śambhu; *sakhyam*—friendship; *kariṣyati*—will create; *jātaḥ*—being born; *sva-aṁśena*—by a plenary portion; *bhagavān*—the Supreme Personality of Godhead; *gṛhe*—in the home; *viśvasṛjaḥ*—of Viśvasraṣṭā; *vibhuḥ*—the supremely powerful Lord.

TRANSLATION

In the home of Viśvasraṣṭā, a plenary portion of the Supreme Personality of Godhead will appear from the womb of Viṣūcī as the incarnation known as Viṣvaksena. He will make friends with Śambhu.

TEXT 24

मनुर्वै धर्मसावर्णिरेकादशम आत्मवान् ।
अनागतास्तत्सुताश्च सत्यधर्मादयो दश ॥ २४ ॥

manur vai dharma-sāvarṇir
ekādaśama ātmavān
anāgatās tat-sutāś ca
satyadharmādayo daśa

manuḥ—the Manu; *vai*—indeed; *dharma-sāvarṇiḥ*—Dharma-sāvarṇi; *ekādaśamaḥ*—eleventh; *ātmavān*—the controller of the senses; *anāgatāḥ*—will come in the future; *tat*—his; *sutāḥ*—sons; *ca*—and; *satyadharma-ādayaḥ*—Satyadharma and others; *daśa*—ten.

TRANSLATION

In the eleventh manvantara, the Manu will be Dharma-sāvarṇi, who will be extremely learned in spiritual knowledge. From him there will come ten sons, headed by Satyadharma.

TEXT 25

विहङ्गमाः कामगमा निर्वाणरुचयः सुराः ।
इन्द्रश्च वैधृतस्तेषामृषयश्चारुणादयः ॥ २५ ॥

vihaṅgamāḥ kāmagamā
nirvāṇarucayaḥ surāḥ
indraś ca vaidhṛtas teṣām
ṛṣayaś cāruṇādayaḥ

vihaṅgamāḥ—the Vihaṅgamas; *kāmagamāḥ*—the Kāmagamas; *nirvāṇarucayaḥ*—the Nirvāṇarucis; *surāḥ*—the demigods; *indraḥ*—the king of heaven, Indra; *ca*—also; *vaidhṛtaḥ*—Vaidhṛta; *teṣām*—of them; *ṛṣayaḥ*—the seven sages; *ca*—also; *aruṇa-ādayaḥ*—headed by Aruṇa.

TRANSLATION

The Vihaṅgamas, Kāmagamas, Nirvāṇarucis and others will be the demigods. The king of the demigods, Indra, will be Vaidhṛta, and the seven sages will be headed by Aruṇa.

TEXT 26

आर्यकस्य सुतस्तत्र धर्मसेतुरिति स्मृतः ।
वैधृतायां हरेरंशस्त्रिलोकीं धारयिष्यति ॥ २६ ॥

āryakasya sutas tatra
dharmasetur iti smṛtaḥ
vaidhṛtāyāṁ harer aṁśas
tri-lokīṁ dhārayiṣyati

āryakasya—of Āryaka; *sutaḥ*—the son; *tatra*—in that period (the eleventh *manvantara*); *dharmasetuḥ*—Dharmasetu; *iti*—thus; *smṛtaḥ*—celebrated; *vaidhṛtāyām*—from the mother, Vaidhṛtā; *hareḥ*—of the Supreme Personality of Godhead; *aṁśaḥ*—a partial incarnation; *tri-lokīm*—the three worlds; *dhārayiṣyati*—will rule.

TRANSLATION

The son of Āryaka known as Dharmasetu, a partial incarnation of the Supreme Personality of Godhead, will appear from the womb of Vaidhṛtā, the wife of Āryaka, and will rule the three worlds.

TEXT 27

भविता रुद्रसावर्णी राजन्द्वादशमो मनुः ।
देववानुपदेवश्च देवश्रेष्ठादयः सुताः ॥ २७ ॥

bhavitā rudra-sāvarṇī
rājan dvādaśamo manuḥ
devavān upadevaś ca
devaśreṣṭhādayaḥ sutāḥ

bhavitā—will appear; *rudra-sāvarṇiḥ*—Rudra-sāvarṇi; *rājan*—O King; *dvādaśamaḥ*—the twelfth; *manuḥ*—Manu; *devavān*—Devavān; *upadevaḥ*—Upadeva; *ca*—and; *devaśreṣṭha*—Devaśreṣṭha; *ādayaḥ*—such persons; *sutāḥ*—sons of the Manu.

TRANSLATION

O King, the twelfth Manu will be named Rudra-sāvarṇi. Devavān, Upadeva and Devaśreṣṭha will be among his sons.

TEXT 28

ऋतधामा च तत्रेन्द्रो देवाश्च हरितादयः ।
ऋषयश्च तपोमूर्तिस्तपस्व्याग्नीध्रकादयः ॥ २८ ॥

ṛtadhāmā ca tatrendro
devāś ca haritādayaḥ
ṛṣayaś ca tapomūrtis
tapasvy āgnīdhrakādayaḥ

ṛtadhāmā—Ṛtadhāmā; *ca*—also; *tatra*—in that period; *indraḥ*—the king of heaven; *devāḥ*—the demigods; *ca*—and; *harita-ādayaḥ*—headed by the Haritas; *ṛṣayaḥ ca*—and the seven sages; *tapomūrtiḥ*—Tapomūrti; *tapasvī*—Tapasvī; *āgnīdhraka*—Āgnīdhraka; *ādayaḥ*—and so on.

TRANSLATION

In this manvantara, the name of Indra will be Ṛtadhāmā, and the demigods will be headed by the Haritas. Among the sages will be Tapomūrti, Tapasvī and Āgnīdhraka.

TEXT 29

स्वधामाख्यो हरेरंशः साधयिष्यति तन्मनोः ।
अन्तरं सत्यसहसः सुनृतायाः सुतो विभुः ॥ २९ ॥

svadhāmākhyo harer aṁśaḥ
sādhayiṣyati tan-manoḥ

antaraṁ satyasahasaḥ
sunṛtāyāḥ suto vibhuḥ

svadhāmā-ākhyaḥ—Svadhāmā; *hareḥ aṁśaḥ*—a partial incarnation of the Supreme Personality of Godhead; *sādhayiṣyati*—will rule; *tat-manoḥ*—of that Manu; *antaram*—the *manvantara; satyasahasaḥ*—of Satyasahā; *sunṛtāyāḥ*—of Sunṛtā; *sutaḥ*—the son; *vibhuḥ*—most powerful.

TRANSLATION

From the mother named Sunṛtā and the father named Satyasahā will come Svadhāmā, a partial incarnation of the Supreme Personality of Godhead. He will rule that manvantara.

TEXT 30

मनुस्त्रयोदशो भाव्यो देवसावर्णिरात्मवान् ।
चित्रसेनविचित्राद्या देवसावर्णिदेहजाः ॥ ३० ॥

manus trayodaśo bhāvyo
deva-sāvarṇir ātmavān
citrasena-vicitrādyā
deva-sāvarṇi-dehajāḥ

manuḥ—the Manu; *trayodaśaḥ*—thirteenth; *bhāvyaḥ*—will become; *deva-sāvarṇiḥ*—Deva-sāvarṇi; *ātmavān*—well advanced in spiritual knowledge; *citrasena*—Citrasena; *vicitra-ādyāḥ*—and others, like Vicitra; *deva-sāvarṇi*—of Deva-sāvarṇi; *deha-jāḥ*—sons.

TRANSLATION

The thirteenth Manu will be named Deva-sāvarṇi, and he will be very advanced in spiritual knowledge. Among his sons will be Citrasena and Vicitra.

TEXT 31

देवाः सुकर्मसुत्रामसंज्ञा इन्द्रो दिवस्पतिः ।
निर्मोकतत्त्वदर्शाद्या भविष्यन्त्यृषयस्तदा ॥ ३१ ॥

devāḥ sukarma-sutrāma-
saṁjñā indro divaspatiḥ

nirmoka-tattvadarśādyā
bhaviṣyanty ṛṣayas tadā

devāḥ—the demigods; *sukarma*—the Sukarmās; *sutrāma-saṁjñāḥ*—and the Sutrāmas; *indraḥ*—the king of heaven; *divaspatiḥ*—Divaspati; *nirmoka*—Nirmoka; *tattvadarśa-ādyāḥ*—and others, like Tattvadarśa; *bhaviṣyanti*—will become; *ṛṣayaḥ*—the seven sages; *tadā*—at that time.

TRANSLATION

In the thirteenth manvantara, the Sukarmās and Sutrāmās will be among the demigods, Divaspati will be the king of heaven, and Nirmoka and Tattvadarśa will be among the seven sages.

TEXT 32

देवहोत्रस्य तनय उपहर्ता दिवस्पतेः ।
योगेश्वरो हरेरंशो बृहत्यां सम्भविष्यति ॥ ३२ ॥

devahotrasya tanaya
upahartā divaspateḥ
yogeśvaro harer aṁśo
bṛhatyāṁ sambhaviṣyati

devahotrasya—of Devahotra; *tanayaḥ*—the son; *upahartā*—the benefactor; *divaspateḥ*—of Divaspati, the Indra at that time; *yoga-īśvaraḥ*—Yogeśvara, the master of mystic powers; *hareḥ aṁśaḥ*—a partial representation of the Supreme Personality of Godhead; *bṛhatyām*—in the womb of his mother, Bṛhatī; *sambhaviṣyati*—will appear.

TRANSLATION

The son of Devahotra known as Yogeśvara will appear as a partial incarnation of the Supreme Personality of Godhead. His mother's name will be Bṛhatī. He will perform activities for the welfare of Divaspati.

TEXT 33

मनुर्वा इन्द्रसावर्णिश्चतुर्दशम एष्यति ।
उरुगम्भीरबुधाद्या इन्द्रसावर्णिवीर्यजाः ॥ ३३ ॥

manur vā indra-sāvarṇiś
caturdaśama eṣyati

uru-gambhīra-budhādyā
indra-sāvarṇi-vīryajāḥ

manuḥ—the Manu; *vā*—either; *indra-sāvarṇiḥ*—Indra-sāvarṇi; *catur-daśamaḥ*—fourteenth; *eṣyati*—will become; *uru*—Uru; *gambhīra*—Gambhīra; *budha-ādyāḥ*—and others, such as Budha; *indra-sāvarṇi*—of Indra-sāvarṇi; *vīrya-jāḥ*—born of the semen.

TRANSLATION

The name of the fourteenth Manu will be Indra-sāvarṇi. He will have sons like Uru, Gambhīra and Budha.

TEXT 34

पवित्राश्चाक्षुषा देवाः शुचिरिन्द्रो भविष्यति ।
अग्निर्बाहुः शुचिः शुद्धो मागधाद्यास्तपस्विनः ॥ ३४ ॥

pavitrāś cākṣuṣā devāḥ
śucir indro bhaviṣyati
agnir bāhuḥ śuciḥ śuddho
māgadhādyās tapasvinaḥ

pavitrāḥ—the Pavitras; *cākṣuṣāḥ*—the Cākṣuṣas; *devāḥ*—the demigods; *śuciḥ*—Śuci; *indraḥ*—the king of heaven; *bhaviṣyati*—will become; *agniḥ*—Agni; *bāhuḥ*—Bāhu; *śuciḥ*—Śuci; *śuddhaḥ*—Śuddha; *māgadha*—Māgadha; *ādyāḥ*—and so on; *tapasvinaḥ*—the sages.

TRANSLATION

The Pavitras and Cākṣuṣas will be among the demigods, and Śuci will be Indra, the king of heaven. Agni, Bāhu, Śuci, Śuddha, Māgadha and others of great austerity will be the seven sages.

TEXT 35

सत्रायणस्य तनयो बृहद्भानुस्तदा हरिः ।
वितानायां महाराज क्रियातन्तून्वितायिता ॥ ३५ ॥

satrāyaṇasya tanayo
bṛhadbhānus tadā hariḥ
vitānāyāṁ mahārāja
kriyā-tantūn vitāyitā

satrāyaṇasya—of Satrāyaṇa; *tanayaḥ*—the son; *bṛhadbhānuḥ*—Bṛhadbhānu; *tadā*—at that time; *hariḥ*—the Supreme Personality of Godhead; *vitānāyām*—in the womb of Vitānā; *mahā-rāja*—O King; *kriyā-tantūn*—all spiritual activities; *vitāyitā*—will perform.

TRANSLATION

O King Parīkṣit, in the fourteenth manvantara the Supreme Personality of Godhead will appear from the womb of Vitānā, and His father's name will be Satrāyaṇa. This incarnation will be celebrated as Bṛhadbhānu, and He will administer spiritual activities.

TEXT 36

राजंश्चतुर्दशैतानि त्रिकालानुगतानि ते ।
प्रोक्तान्येभिर्मितः कल्पो युगसाहस्रपर्ययः ॥ ३६ ॥

rājaṁś caturdaśaitāni
tri-kālānugatāni te
proktāny ebhir mitaḥ kalpo
yuga-sāhasra-paryayaḥ

rājan—O King; *caturdaśa*—fourteen; *etāni*—all these; *tri-kāla*—the three periods of time (past, present and future); *anugatāni*—covering; *te*—to you; *proktāni*—described; *ebhiḥ*—by these; *mitaḥ*—estimated; *kalpaḥ*—one day of Brahmā; *yuga-sāhasra*—one thousand cycles of four *yugas; paryayaḥ*—consisting of.

TRANSLATION

O King, I have now described to you the fourteen Manus appearing in the past, present and future. The total duration of time ruled by these Manus is one thousand yuga cycles. This is called a kalpa, or one day of Lord Brahmā.

Thus end the Bhaktivedanta purports of the Eighth Canto, Thirteenth Chapter, of the Śrīmad-Bhāgavatam, *entitled "Description of Future Manus."*

CHAPTER FOURTEEN

The System of Universal Management

This chapter describes the duties allotted to Manu by the Supreme Personality of Godhead. All the Manus, as well as their sons, the sages, the demigods and the Indras, act under the orders of various incarnations of the Supreme Personality of Godhead. At the end of every *catur-yuga,* consisting of Satya-yuga, Dvāpara-yuga, Tretā-yuga and Kali-yuga, the sages, acting under the orders of the Supreme Personality of Godhead, distribute the Vedic knowledge and thus reinstate eternal religious principles. Manu's duty is to reestablish the system of religion. Manu's sons execute Manu's orders, and thus the entire universe is maintained by Manu and his descendants. The Indras are various rulers of the heavenly planets. Assisted by the demigods, they rule the three worlds. The Supreme Personality of Godhead also appears as incarnations in different *yugas.* He appears as Sanaka, Sanātana, Yājñavalkya, Dattātreya and others, and thus He gives instructions in spiritual knowledge, prescribed duties, principles of mystic *yoga,* and so on. As Marīci and others, He creates progeny; as the king, He punishes the miscreants; and in the form of time, He annihilates the creation. One may argue, "If the all-powerful Supreme Personality of Godhead can do anything simply by His will, why has He arranged for so many personalities to manage?" How and why He does this cannot be understood by those who are under the clutches of *māyā.*

TEXT 1

श्रीराजोवाच
मन्वन्तरेषु भगवन्यथा मन्वादयस्त्विमे ।
यस्मिन्कर्मणि ये येन नियुक्तास्तद्वदस्व मे ॥ १ ॥

śrī-rājovāca
manvantareṣu bhagavan
yathā manv-ādayas tv ime
yasmin karmaṇi ye yena
niyuktās tad vadasva me

śrī-rājā uvāca—King Parīkṣit said; *manvantareṣu*—in the reign of each Manu; *bhagavan*—O great sage; *yathā*—as; *manu-ādayaḥ*—the Manus and others; *tu*—but; *ime*—these; *yasmin*—in which; *karmaṇi*—activities; *ye*—which persons; *yena*—by whom; *niyuktāḥ*—appointed; *tat*—that; *vadasva*—kindly describe; *me*—to me.

TRANSLATION

Mahārāja Parīkṣit inquired: O most opulent Śukadeva Gosvāmī, please explain to me how Manu and the others in each manvantara are engaged in their respective duties, and by whose order they are so engaged.

TEXT 2

श्रीऋषिरुवाच
मनवो मनुपुत्राश्च मुनयश्च महीपते ।
इन्द्राः सुरगणाश्चैव सर्वे पुरुषशासनाः ॥ २ ॥

śrī-ṛṣir uvāca
manavo manu-putrāś ca
munayaś ca mahī-pate
indrāḥ sura-gaṇāś caiva
sarve puruṣa-śāsanāḥ

śrī-ṛṣiḥ uvāca—Śrī Śukadeva Gosvāmī said; *manavaḥ*—all the Manus; *manu-putrāḥ*—all the sons of Manu; *ca*—and; *munayaḥ*—all the great sages; *ca*—and; *mahī-pate*—O King; *indrāḥ*—all the Indras; *sura-gaṇāḥ*—the demigods; *ca*—and; *eva*—certainly; *sarve*—all of them; *puruṣa-śāsanāḥ*—under the rule of the Supreme person.

TRANSLATION

Śukadeva Gosvāmī said: The Manus, the sons of Manu, the great sages, the Indras and all the demigods, O King, are appointed by the Supreme Personality of Godhead in His various incarnations such as Yajña.

TEXT 3

यज्ञादयो याः कथिताः पौरुष्यस्तनवो नृप ।
मन्वादयो जगद्यात्रां नयन्त्याभिः प्रचोदिताः ॥ ३ ॥

yajñādayo yāḥ kathitāḥ
pauruṣyas tanavo nṛpa
manv-ādayo jagad-yātrāṁ
nayanty ābhiḥ pracoditāḥ

yajña-ādayaḥ—the Lord's incarnation known as Yajña and others; *yāḥ*—who; *kathitāḥ*—already spoken of; *pauruṣyaḥ*—of the Supreme Person; *tanavaḥ*—incarnations; *nṛpa*—O King; *manu-ādayaḥ*—the Manus and others; *jagat-yātrām*—universal affairs; *nayanti*—conduct; *ābhiḥ*—by the incarnations; *pracoditāḥ*—being inspired.

TRANSLATION

O King, I have already described to you various incarnations of the Lord, such as Yajña. The Manus and others are chosen by these incarnations, under whose direction they conduct the universal affairs.

PURPORT

The Manus execute the orders of the Supreme Personality of Godhead in His various incarnations.

TEXT 4

चतुर्युगान्ते कालेन ग्रस्ताञ्छ्रुतिगणान्यथा ।
तपसा ऋषयोऽपश्यन्यतो धर्मः सनातनः ॥ ४ ॥

catur-yugānte kālena
grastāñ chruti-gaṇān yathā
tapasā ṛṣayo 'paśyan
yato dharmaḥ sanātanaḥ

catuḥ-yuga-ante—at the end of every four *yugas* (Satya, Dvāpara, Tretā and Kali); *kālena*—in due course of time; *grastān*—lost; *śruti-gaṇān*—the Vedic instruction; *yathā*—as; *tapasā*—by austerity; *ṛṣayaḥ*—great saintly persons; *apaśyan*—by seeing misuse; *yataḥ*—wherefrom; *dharmaḥ*—occupational duties; *sanātanaḥ*—eternal.

TRANSLATION

At the end of every four yugas, the great saintly persons, upon seeing that the eternal occupational duties of mankind have been misused, reestablish the principles of religion.

PURPORT

In this verse, the words *dharmaḥ* and *sanātanaḥ* are very important. *Sanātana* means "eternal," and *dharma* means "occupational duties." From Satya-yuga to Kali-yuga, the principles of religion and occupational duty gradually deteriorate. In Satya-yuga, the religious principles are observed in full, without deviation. In Tretā-yuga, however, these principles are somewhat neglected, and only three fourths of the religious duties continue. In Dvāpara-yuga only half of the religious principles continue, and in Kali-yuga only one fourth of the religious principles, which gradually disappear. At the end of Kali-yuga, the principles of religion, or the occupational duties of humanity, are almost lost. Indeed, in this Kali-yuga we have passed through only five thousand years, yet the decline of *sanātana-dharma* is very prominent. The duty of saintly persons, therefore, is to take up seriously the cause of *sanātana-dharma* and try to reestablish it for the benefit of the entire human society. The Kṛṣṇa consciousness movement has been started according to this principle. As stated in *Śrīmad-Bhāgavatam* (12.3.51):

kaler doṣa-nidhe rājann
asti hy eko mahān guṇaḥ
kīrtanād eva kṛṣṇasya
mukta-saṅgaḥ paraṁ vrajet

The entire Kali-yuga is full of faults. It is like an unlimited ocean of faults. But the Kṛṣṇa consciousness movement is very authorized. Therefore, following in the footsteps of Śrī Caitanya Mahāprabhu, who five hundred years ago inaugurated the movement of *saṅkīrtana, kṛṣṇa-kīrtana,* we are trying to introduce this movement, according to superior orders, all over the world. Now, if the inaugurators of this movement strictly follow the regulative principles and spread this movement for the benefit of all human society, they will certainly usher in a new way of life by reestablishing *sanātana-dharma,* the eternal occupational duties of humanity. The eternal occupational duty of the human being is to serve Kṛṣṇa. *Jīvera 'svarūpa' haya—kṛṣṇera 'nitya-dāsa.'*. This is the purport of *sanātana-dharma. Sanātana* means *nitya,* or "eternal," and *kṛṣṇa-dāsa* means "servant of Kṛṣṇa." The eternal occupational duty of the human being is to serve Kṛṣṇa. This is the sum and substance of the Kṛṣṇa consciousness movement.

TEXT 5

ततो धर्मं चतुष्पादं मनवो हरिणोदिताः ।
युक्ताः सञ्चारयन्त्यद्धा स्वे स्वे काले महीं नृप ॥ ५ ॥

tato dharmaṁ catuṣpādaṁ
manavo hariṇoditāḥ
yuktāḥ sañcārayanty addhā
sve sve kāle mahīṁ nṛpa

tataḥ—thereafter (at the end of Kali-yuga); *dharmam*—the religious principle; *catuḥ-pādam*—in four parts; *manavaḥ*—all the Manus; *hariṇā*—by the Supreme Personality of Godhead; *uditāḥ*—being instructed; *yuktāḥ*—being engaged; *sañcārayanti*—reestablish; *addhā*—directly; *sve sve*—in their own; *kāle*—time; *mahīm*—within this world; *nṛpa*—O King.

TRANSLATION

Thereafter, O King, the Manus, being fully engaged according to the instructions of the Supreme Personality of Godhead, directly reestablish the principles of occupational duty in its full four parts.

PURPORT

Dharma, or occupational duty, can be established in its full four parts as explained in *Bhagavad-gītā.* In *Bhagavad-gītā* (4.1) the Lord says:

imaṁ vivasvate yogaṁ
proktavān aham avyayam
vivasvān manave prāha
manur ikṣvākave 'bravīt

"I instructed this imperishable science of *yoga* to the sun-god, Vivasvān, and Vivasvān instructed it to Manu, the father of mankind, and Manu in turn instructed it to Ikṣvāku." This is the process of disciplic succession. Following the same process, the Kṛṣṇa consciousness movement is teaching the principles of *Bhagavad-gītā* as it is, without deviation, all over the world. If the fortunate people of this time accept the instructions of Lord Kṛṣṇa, they will certainly be happy in Śrī Caitanya Mahāprabhu's mission. Caitanya Mahāprabhu wanted everyone, at least in India, to become a preacher of this mission. In other words, one should become a *guru* and preach the Lord's instructions all over the world for the peace and prosperity of humanity.

TEXT 6

पालयन्ति प्रजापाला यावदन्तं विभागशः ।
यज्ञभागभुजो देवा ये च तत्रान्विताश्च तैः ॥ ६ ॥

pālayanti prajā-pālā
yāvad antaṁ vibhāgaśaḥ
yajña-bhāga-bhujo devā
ye ca tatrānvitāś ca taiḥ

pālayanti—execute the order; *prajā-pālāḥ*—the rulers of the world, namely the sons and grandsons of Manu; *yāvat antam*—unto the end of Manu's reign; *vibhāgaśaḥ*—in divisions; *yajña-bhāga-bhujaḥ*—the enjoyers of the result of *yajñas; devāḥ*—the demigods; *ye*—others; *ca*—also; *tatra anvitāḥ*—engaged in that business; *ca*—also; *taiḥ*—by them.

TRANSLATION

To enjoy the results of sacrifices [yajñas], the rulers of the world, namely the sons and grandsons of Manu, discharge the orders of the Supreme Personality of Godhead until the end of Manu's reign. The demigods also share the results of these sacrifices.

PURPORT

As stated in *Bhagavad-gītā* (4.2):

evaṁ paramparā-prāptam
imaṁ rājarṣayo viduḥ

'This supreme science was thus received through the chain of disciplic succession, and the saintly kings understood it in that way." This *paramparā* system extends from Manu to Ikṣvāku and from Ikṣvāku to his sons and grandsons. The rulers of the world in the line of hierarchy execute the order of the Supreme Personality of Godhead in the *paramparā* system. Anyone interested in peaceful life must participate in this *paramparā* system and perform *yajñas.* As Gauḍīya Vaiṣṇavas in the *paramparā* system of Śrī Caitanya Mahāprabhu, we must perform *saṅkīrtana-yajña* all over the world (*yajñaiḥ saṅkīrtana-prāyair yajanti hi sumedhasaḥ*). Śrī Caitanya Mahāprabhu is the incarnation of the Supreme Personality of Godhead in this age of Kali, and He will be easily satisfied if the *saṅkīrtana* movement is spread vigorously all over the world. This will also make people happy without a doubt.

TEXT 7

इन्द्रो भगवता दत्तां त्रैलोक्यश्रियमूर्जिताम् ।
भुञ्जानः पाति लोकांस्त्रीन् कामं लोके प्रवर्षति ॥ ७ ॥

indro bhagavatā dattāṁ
trailokya-śriyam ūrjitām
bhuñjānaḥ pāti lokāṁs trīn
kāmaṁ loke pravarṣati

indraḥ—the King of heaven; *bhagavatā*—by the Supreme Personality of Godhead; *dattām*—given; *trailokya*—of the three worlds; *śriyam ūrjitām*—the great opulences; *bhuñjānaḥ*—enjoying; *pāti*—maintains; *lokān*—all the planets; *trīn*—within the three worlds; *kāmam*—as much as necessary; *loke*—within the world; *pravarṣati*—pours rain.

TRANSLATION

Indra, King of heaven, receiving benedictions from the Supreme Personality of Godhead and thus enjoying highly developed opulences, maintains the living entities all over the three worlds by pouring sufficient rain on all the planets.

TEXT 8

ज्ञानं चानुयुगं ब्रूते हरिः सिद्धस्वरूपधृक् ।
ऋषिरूपधरः कर्म योगं योगेशरूपधृक् ॥ ८ ॥

jñānaṁ cānuyugaṁ brūte
hariḥ siddha-svarūpa-dhṛk
ṛṣi-rūpa-dharaḥ karma
yogaṁ yogeśa-rūpa-dhṛk

jñānam—transcendental knowledge; *ca*—and; *anuyugam*—according to the age; *brūte*—explains; *hariḥ*—the Supreme Personality of Godhead; *siddha-svarūpa-dhṛk*—assuming the form of liberated persons like Sanaka and Sanātana; *ṛṣi-rūpa-dharaḥ*—assuming the form of great saintly persons like Yājñavalkya; *karma*—*karma; yogam*—the mystic *yoga* system; *yoga-īśa-rūpa-dhṛk*—by assuming the form of a great *yogī* like Dattātreya.

TRANSLATION

In every yuga, the Supreme Personality of Godhead, Hari, assumes the form of Siddhas such as Sanaka to preach transcendental knowledge, He assumes the form of great saintly persons such as Yājñavalkya to teach the way of karma, and He assumes the form of great yogīs such as Dattātreya to teach the system of mystic yoga.

PURPORT

For the benefit of all human society, not only does the Lord assume the form of Manu as an incarnation to rule the universe properly, but He also assumes the forms of a teacher, *yogī, jñānī* and so on, for the benefit of human society. The duty of human society, therefore, is to accept the path of action enunciated by the Supreme Lord. In the present age, the sum and substance of all Vedic knowledge is to be found in *Bhagavad-gītā,* which is personally taught by the Supreme Personality of Godhead, and the same Supreme Godhead, assuming the form of Śrī Caitanya Mahāprabhu, expands the teachings of *Bhagavad-gītā* all over the world. In other words, the Supreme Personality of Godhead, Hari, is so kind and merciful to human society that He is always anxious to take the fallen souls back home, back to Godhead.

TEXT 9

सर्गं प्रजेशरूपेण दस्यून्हन्यात् स्वराड्वपुः ।
कालरूपेण सर्वेषामभावाय पृथग्गुणः ॥ ९ ॥

sargaṁ prajeśa-rūpeṇa
dasyūn hanyāt svarāḍ-vapuḥ
kāla-rūpeṇa sarveṣām
abhāvāya pṛthag guṇaḥ

sargam—creation of progeny; *prajā-īśa-rūpeṇa*—in the form of the Prajāpati Marīci and others; *dasyūn*—thieves and rogues; *hanyāt*—kills; *sva-rāṭ-vapuḥ*—in the form of the king; *kāla-rūpeṇa*—in the form of time; *sarveṣām*—of everything; *abhāvāya*—for the annihilation; *pṛthak*—different; *guṇaḥ*—possessing qualities.

TRANSLATION

In the form of Prajāpati Marīci, the Supreme Personality of Godhead creates progeny; becoming the king, He kills the thieves and rogues; and in the form of time, He annihilates everything. All the different qualities of material existence should be understood to be qualities of the Supreme Personality of Godhead.

TEXT 10

स्तूयमानो जनैरेभिर्मायया नामरूपया ।
विमोहितात्मभिर्नानादर्शनैर्न च दृश्यते ॥ १० ॥

stūyamāno janair ebhir
māyayā nāma-rūpayā
vimohitātmabhir nānā-
darśanair na ca dṛśyate

stūyamānaḥ—being sought; *janaiḥ*—by people in general; *ebhiḥ*—by all of them; *māyayā*—under the influence of *māyā; nāma-rūpayā*—possessing different names and forms; *vimohita*—bewildered; *ātmabhiḥ*—by illusion; *nānā*—various; *darśanaiḥ*—by philosophical approaches; *na*—not; *ca*—and; *dṛśyate*—the Supreme Personality of Godhead can be found.

TRANSLATION

People in general are bewildered by the illusory energy, and therefore they try to find the Absolute Truth, the Supreme Personality of Godhead, through various types of research and philosophical speculation. Nonetheless, they are unable to see the Supreme Lord.

PURPORT

Whatever actions and reactions take place for the creation, maintenance and annihilation of this material world are actually brought about by the one Supreme Person. There are many varieties of philosophers trying to search for the ultimate cause under different names and forms, but they are unable to find the Supreme Personality of Godhead, Kṛṣṇa, who explains in *Bhagavad-gītā* that He is the origin of everything and the cause of all causes (*ahaṁ sarvasya prabhavaḥ*). This inability is due to the illusory energy of the Supreme Lord. Devotees, therefore, accept the Supreme Personality of Godhead as He is and remain happy simply by chanting the glories of the Lord.

TEXT 11

एतत् कल्पविकल्पस्य प्रमाणं परिकीर्तितम् ।
यत्र मन्वन्तराण्याहुश्चतुर्दश पुराविदः ॥ ११ ॥

etat kalpa-vikalpasya
pramāṇaṁ parikīrtitam
yatra manvantarāṇy āhuś
caturdaśa purāvidaḥ

etat—all these; *kalpa*—in one day of Lord Brahmā; *vikalpasya*—of the changes in a *kalpa,* such as the change of Manus; *pramāṇam*—evidences;

parikīrtitam—described (by me); *yatra*—wherein; *manvantarāṇi*—periods of Manu; *āhuḥ*—said; *caturdaśa*—fourteen; *purā-vidaḥ*—learned scholars.

TRANSLATION

In one kalpa, or one day of Brahmā, there take place the many changes called vikalpas. O King, all of these have been previously described to you by me. Learned scholars who know the past, present and future have ascertained that in one day of Brahmā there are fourteen Manus.

Thus end the Bhaktivedanta purports of the Eighth Canto, Fourteenth Chapter, of the Śrīmad-Bhāgavatam, *entitled "The System of Universal Management."*

CHAPTER FIFTEEN

Bali Mahārāja Conquers the Heavenly Planets

This chapter describes how Bali, after performing the Viśvajit-yajña, received the benediction of a chariot and various kinds of paraphernalia for war, with which he attacked the King of heaven. All the demigods, being afraid of him, left the heavenly planets and went away, following the instructions of their *guru.*

Mahārāja Parīkṣit wanted to understand how Lord Vāmanadeva, on the plea of taking three paces of land from Bali Mahārāja, took everything away from him and arrested him. Śukadeva Gosvāmī responded to this inquiry with the following explanation. In the fight between the demons and the demigods, as described in the Eleventh Chapter of this canto, Bali was defeated, and he died in the fight, but by the grace of Śukrācārya he regained his life. Thus he engaged himself in the service of Śukrācārya, his spiritual master. The descendants of Bhṛgu, being pleased with him, engaged him in the Viśvajit-yajña. When this *yajña* was performed, from the fire of *yajña* came a chariot, horses, a flag, a bow, armor and two quivers of arrows. Mahārāja Prahlāda, Bali Mahārāja's grandfather, gave Bali an eternal garland of flowers, and Śukrācārya gave him a conchshell. Bali Mahārāja, after offering obeisances to Prahlāda, the *brāhmaṇas* and his spiritual master, Śukrācārya, equipped himself to fight with Indra and went to Indrapurī with his soldiers. Blowing his conchshell, he attacked the outskirts of Indra's kingdom. When Indra saw Bali Mahārāja's prowess, he went to his own spiritual master, Bṛhaspati, told him about Bali's strength, and inquired about his duty. Bṛhaspati informed the demigods that because Bali had been endowed with extraordinary power by the *brāhmaṇas,* the demigods could not fight with him. Their only hope was to gain the favor of the Supreme Personality of Godhead. Indeed, there was no alternative. Under the circumstances, Bṛhaspati advised the demigods to leave the heavenly planets and keep themselves somewhere invisible. The demigods followed his orders, and Bali Mahārāja, along with his associates, gained the entire kingdom of Indra. The descendants of Bhṛgu Muni, being very affectionate to their disciple Bali Mahārāja, engaged him in performing one hundred *aśvamedha-yajñas.* In this way, Bali enjoyed the opulences of the heavenly planets.

TEXTS 1-2

श्रीराजोवाच
बलेः पदत्रयं भूमेः कस्माद्धरिरयाचत ।
भूत्वेश्वरः कृपणवल्लब्धार्थोऽपि बबन्ध तम् ॥ १ ॥
एतद् वेदितुमिच्छामो महत् कौतूहलं हि नः ।
याच्ञेश्वरस्य पूर्णस्य बन्धनं चाप्यनागसः ॥ २ ॥

śrī-rājovāca
baleḥ pada-trayaṁ bhūmeḥ
kasmād dharir ayācata
bhūtveśvaraḥ kṛpaṇa-val
labdhārtho 'pi babandha tam

etad veditum icchāmo
mahat kautūhalaṁ hi naḥ
yācñeśvarasya pūrṇasya
bandhanaṁ cāpy anāgasaḥ

śrī-rājā uvāca—the King said; *baleḥ*—of Bali Mahārāja; *pada-trayam*—three steps; *bhūmeḥ*—of land; *kasmāt*—why; *hariḥ*—the Supreme Personality of Godhead (in the form of Vāmana); *ayācata*—begged; *bhūtva-īśvaraḥ*—the proprietor of all the universe; *kṛpaṇa-vat*—like a poor man; *labdha-arthaḥ*—He got the gift; *api*—although; *babandha*—arrested; *tam*—him (Bali); *etat*—all this; *veditum*—to understand; *icchāmaḥ*—we desire; *mahat*—very great; *kautūhalam*—eagerness; *hi*—indeed; *naḥ*—our; *yācñā*—begging; *īśvarasya*—of the Supreme Personality of Godhead; *pūrṇasya*—who is full in everything; *bandhanam*—arresting; *ca*—also; *api*—although; *anāgasaḥ*—of he who was faultless.

TRANSLATION

Mahārāja Parīkṣit inquired: The Supreme Personality of Godhead is the proprietor of everything. Why did He beg three paces of land from Bali Mahārāja like a poor man, and when He got the gift for which He had begged, why did He nonetheless arrest Bali Mahārāja? I am very much anxious to know the mystery of these contradictions.

TEXT 3

श्रीशुक उवाच
पराजितश्रीरसुभिश्च हापितो
हीन्द्रेण राजन्भृगुभिः स जीवितः ।
सर्वात्मना तानभजद् भृगून्बलिः
शिष्यो महात्मार्थनिवेदनेन ॥ ३ ॥

śrī-śuka uvāca
parājita-śrīr asubhiś ca hāpito
hīndreṇa rājan bhṛgubhiḥ sa jīvitaḥ
sarvātmanā tān abhajad bhṛgūn baliḥ
śiṣyo mahātmārtha-nivedanena

śrī-śukaḥ uvāca—Śrī Śukadeva Gosvāmī said; *parājita*—being defeated; *śrīḥ*—opulences; *asubhiḥ ca*—of life also; *hāpitaḥ*—deprived; *hi*—indeed; *indreṇa*—by King Indra; *rājan*—O King; *bhṛgubhiḥ*—by the descendants of Bhṛgu Muni; *saḥ*—he (Bali Mahārāja); *jīvitaḥ*—brought back to life; *sarva-ātmanā*—in full submission; *tān*—them; *abhajat*—worshiped; *bhṛgūn*—the descendants of Bhṛgu Muni; *baliḥ*—Mahārāja Bali; *śiṣyaḥ*—a disciple; *mahātmā*—the great soul; *artha-nivedanena*—by giving them everything.

TRANSLATION

Śukadeva Gosvāmī said: O King, when Bali Mahārāja lost all his opulence and died in the fight, Śukrācārya, a descendant of Bhṛgu Muni, brought him back to life. Because of this, the great soul Bali Mahārāja became a disciple of Śukrācārya and began to serve him with great faith, offering everything he had.

TEXT 4

तं ब्राह्मणा भृगवः प्रीयमाणा
अयाजयन्विश्वजिता त्रिणाकम् ।
जिगीषमाणं विधिनाभिषिच्य
महाभिषेकेण महानुभावाः ॥ ४ ॥

taṁ brāhmaṇā bhṛgavaḥ prīyamāṇā
ayājayan viśvajitā tri-ṇākam

jigīṣamāṇaṁ vidhinābhiṣicya
mahābhiṣekeṇa mahānubhāvāḥ

tam—upon him (Bali Mahārāja); *brāhmaṇāḥ*—all the *brāhmaṇas; bhṛgavaḥ*—the descendants of Bhṛgu Muni; *prīyamāṇāḥ*—being very pleased; *ayājayan*—engaged him in performing a sacrifice; *viśvajitā*—known as Viśvajit; *tri-nākam*—the heavenly planets; *jigīṣamāṇam*—desiring to conquer; *vidhinā*—according to regulative principles; *abhiṣicya*—after purifying; *mahā-abhiṣekeṇa*—by bathing him in a great *abhiṣeka* ceremony; *mahā-anubhāvāḥ*—the exalted *brāhmaṇas.*

TRANSLATION

The brāhmaṇa descendants of Bhṛgu Muni were very pleased with Bali Mahārāja, who desired to conquer the kingdom of Indra. Therefore, after purifying him and properly bathing him according to regulative principles, they engaged him in performing the yajña known as Viśvajit.

TEXT 5

ततो रथः काञ्चनपट्टनद्धो
हयाश्च हर्यश्वतुरङ्गवर्णाः ।
ध्वजश्च सिंहेन विराजमानो
हुताशनादास हविर्भिरिष्टात् ॥ ५ ॥

tato rathaḥ kāñcana-paṭṭa-naddho
hayāś ca haryaśva-turaṅga-varṇāḥ
dhvajaś ca siṁhena virājamāno
hutāśanād āsa havirbhir iṣṭāt

tataḥ—thereafter; *rathaḥ*—a chariot; *kāñcana*—with gold; *paṭṭa*—and silk garments; *naddhaḥ*—wrapped; *hayāḥ ca*—horses also; *haryaśva-turaṅga-varṇāḥ*—exactly of the same color as the horses of Indra (yellow); *dhvajaḥ ca*—a flag also; *siṁhena*—with the mark of a lion; *virājamānaḥ*—existing; *huta-aśanāt*—from the blazing fire; *āsa*—there was; *havirbhiḥ*—by offerings of clarified butter; *iṣṭāt*—worshiped.

TRANSLATION

When ghee [clarified butter] was offered in the fire of sacrifice, there appeared from the fire a celestial chariot covered with gold and silk. There

also appeared yellow horses like those of Indra, and a flag marked with a lion.

TEXT 6

धनुश्च दिव्यं पुरटोपनद्धं
तूणावरिक्तौ कवचं च दिव्यम्।
पितामहस्तस्य ददौ च माला-
मम्लानपुष्पां जलजं च शुक्रः ॥ ६ ॥

dhanuś ca divyaṁ puraṭopanaddhaṁ
tūṇāv ariktau kavacaṁ ca divyam
pitāmahas tasya dadau ca mālām
amlāna-puṣpāṁ jalajaṁ ca śukraḥ

dhanuḥ—a bow; *ca*—also; *divyam*—uncommon; *puraṭa-upanaddham*—covered with gold; *tūṇau*—two quivers; *ariktau*—infallible; *kavacam ca*—and armor; *divyam*—celestial; *pitāmahaḥ tasya*—his grandfather, namely Prahlāda Mahārāja; *dadau*—gave; *ca*—and; *mālām*—a garland; *amlāna-puṣpām*—made of flowers that do not fade away; *jala jam*—a conchshell (which is born in water); *ca*—as well as; *śukraḥ*—Śukrācārya.

TRANSLATION

A gilded bow, two quivers of infallible arrows, and celestial armor also appeared. Bali Mahārāja's grandfather Prahlāda Mahārāja offered Bali a garland of flowers that would never fade, and Śukrācārya gave him a conchshell.

TEXT 7

एवं स विप्रार्जितयोधनार्थ-
स्तैः कल्पितस्वस्त्ययनोऽथ विप्रान् ।
प्रदक्षिणीकृत्य कृतप्रणामः
प्रह्रादमामन्त्र्य नमश्चकार ॥ ७ ॥

evaṁ sa viprārjita-yodhanārthas
taiḥ kalpita-svastyayano 'tha viprān
pradakṣiṇī-kṛtya kṛta-praṇāmaḥ
prahrādam āmantrya namaś-cakāra

evam—in this way; *saḥ*—he (Bali Mahārāja); *vipra-arjita*—gained by the grace of the *brāhmaṇas; yodhana-arthaḥ*—possessing equipment for fighting; *taiḥ*—by them (the *brāhmaṇas*); *kalpita*—advice; *svastyayanaḥ*—ritualistic performance; *atha*—as; *viprān*—all the *brāhmaṇas* (Śukrācārya and others); *pradakṣiṇī-kṛtya*—circumambulating; *kṛta-praṇāmaḥ*—offered his respectful obeisances; *prahrādam*—unto Prahlāda Mahārāja; *āmantrya*—addressing; *namaḥ-cakāra*—offered him obeisances.

TRANSLATION

When Mahārāja Bali had thus performed the special ritualistic ceremony advised by the brāhmaṇas and had received, by their grace, the equipment for fighting, he circumambulated the brāhmaṇas and offered them obeisances. He also saluted Prahlāda Mahārāja and offered obeisances to him.

TEXTS 8-9

अथारुह्य रथं दिव्यं भृगुदत्तं महारथः ।
सुस्रग्धरोऽथ संनह्य धन्वी खड्गी धृतेषुधिः ॥ ८ ॥
हेमाङ्गदलसद्बाहुः स्फुरन्मकरकुण्डलः ।
रराज रथमारूढो धिष्ण्यस्थ इव हव्यवाट् ॥ ९ ॥

athāruhya rathaṁ divyaṁ
bhṛgu-dattaṁ mahārathaḥ
susrag-dharo 'tha sannahya
dhanvī khaḍgī dhṛteṣudhiḥ

hemāṅgada-lasad-bāhuḥ
sphuran-makara-kuṇḍalaḥ
rarāja ratham ārūḍho
dhiṣṇya-stha iva havyavāṭ

atha—thereupon; *āruhya*—getting on; *ratham*—the chariot; *divyam*—celestial; *bhṛgu-dattam*—given by Śukrācārya; *mahā-rathaḥ*—Bali Mahārāja, the great charioteer; *su-srak-dharaḥ*—decorated with a nice garland; *atha*—thus; *sannahya*—covering his body with armor; *dhanvī*—equipped with a bow; *khaḍgī*—taking a sword; *dhṛta-iṣudhiḥ*—taking a quiver of arrows; *hema-aṅgada-lasat-bāhuḥ*—decorated with golden bangles on his arms;

sphurat-makara-kuṇḍalaḥ—decorated with brilliant earrings resembling sapphires; *rarāja*—was illuminating; *ratham ārūḍhaḥ*—getting on the chariot; *dhiṣṇya-sthaḥ*—situated on the altar of sacrifice; *iva*—like; *havya-vāṭ*—worshipable fire.

TRANSLATION

Then, after getting on the chariot given by Śukrācārya, Bali Mahārāja, decorated with a nice garland, put protective armor on his body, equipped himself with a bow, and took up a sword and a quiver of arrows. When he sat down on the seat of the chariot, his arms decorated with golden bangles and his ears with sapphire earrings, he shone like a worshipable fire.

TEXTS 10-11

तुल्यैश्वर्यबलश्रीभिः स्वयूथैर्दैत्ययूथपैः ।
पिबद्भिरिव खं दृग्भिर्दहद्भिः परिधीनिव ॥ १० ॥
वृतो विकर्षन् महतीमासुरीं ध्वजिनीं विभुः ।
ययाविन्द्रपुरीं स्वृद्धां कम्पयन्निव रोदसी ॥ ११ ॥

tulyaiśvarya-bala-śrībhiḥ
sva-yūthair daitya-yūthapaiḥ
pibadbhir iva khaṁ dṛgbhir
dahadbhiḥ paridhīn iva

vṛto vikarṣan mahatīm
āsurīṁ dhvajinīṁ vibhuḥ
yayāv indra-purīṁ svṛddhāṁ
kampayann iva rodasī

tulya-aiśvarya—equal in opulence; *bala*—strength; *śrībhiḥ*—and in beauty; *sva-yūthaiḥ*—by his own men; *daitya-yūtha-paiḥ*—and by the chiefs of the demons; *pibadbhiḥ*—drinking; *iva*—as if; *kham*—the sky; *dṛgbhiḥ*—with the sight; *dahadbhiḥ*—burning; *paridhīn*—all directions; *iva*—as if; *vṛtaḥ*—surrounded; *vikarṣan*—attracting; *mahatīm*—very great; *āsurīm*—demoniac; *dhvajinīm*—soldiers; *vibhuḥ*—most powerful; *yayau*—went; *indra-purīm*—to the capital of King Indra; *su-ṛddhām*—very opulent; *kampayan*—causing to tremble; *iva*—as if; *rodasī*—the complete surface of the world.

TRANSLATION

When he assembled with his own soldiers and the demon chiefs, who were equal to him in strength, opulence and beauty, they appeared as if they would swallow the sky and burn all directions with their vision. After thus gathering the demoniac soldiers, Bali Mahārāja departed for the opulent capital of Indra. Indeed, he seemed to make the entire surface of the world tremble.

TEXT 12

रम्यामुपवनोद्यानैः श्रीमद्भिर्नन्दनादिभिः ।
कूजद्विहङ्गमिथुनैर्गायन्मत्तमधुव्रतैः ।
प्रवालफलपुष्पोरुभारशाखामरद्रुमैः ॥ १२ ॥

ramyām upavanodyānaiḥ
śrīmadbhir nandanādibhiḥ
kūjad-vihaṅga-mithunair
gāyan-matta-madhuvrataiḥ
pravāla-phala-puṣporu-
bhāra-śākhāmara-drumaiḥ

ramyām—very pleasing; *upavana*—with orchards; *udyānaiḥ*—and gardens; *śrīmadbhiḥ*—very beautiful to see; *nandana-ādibhiḥ*—such as Nandana; *kūjat*—chirping; *vihaṅga*—birds; *mithunaiḥ*—with pairs; *gāyat*—singing; *matta*—mad; *madhu-vrataiḥ*—with bees; *pravāla*—of leaves; *phala-puṣpa*—fruits and flowers; *uru*—very great; *bhāra*—bearing the weight; *śākhā*—whose branches; *amara-drumaiḥ*—with eternal trees.

TRANSLATION

King Indra's city was full of pleasing orchards and gardens, such as the Nandana garden. Because of the weight of the flowers, leaves and fruit, the branches of the eternally existing trees were bending down. The gardens were visited by pairs of chirping birds and singing bees. The entire atmosphere was celestial.

TEXT 13

हंससारसचक्राह्वकारण्डवकुलाकुलाः ।
नलिन्यो यत्र क्रीडन्ति प्रमदाः सुरसेविताः ॥ १३ ॥

haṁsa-sārasa-cakrāhva-
kāraṇḍava-kulākulāḥ
nalinyo yatra krīḍanti
pramadāḥ sura-sevitāḥ

haṁsa—of swans; *sārasa*—cranes; *cakrāhva*—birds known as *cakravākas; kāraṇḍava*—and water fowl; *kula*—by groups; *ākulāḥ*—congested; *nalinyaḥ*—lotus flowers; *yatra*—where; *krīḍanti*—enjoyed sporting; *pramadāḥ*—beautiful women; *sura-sevitāḥ*—protected by the demigods.

TRANSLATION

Beautiful women protected by the demigods sported in the gardens, which had lotus ponds full of swans, cranes, cakravākas and ducks.

TEXT 14

आकाशगङ्गया देव्या वृतां परिखभूतया ।
प्राकारेणाग्निवर्णेन साट्टालेनोन्नतेन च ॥ १४ ॥

ākāśa-gaṅgayā devyā
vṛtāṁ parikha-bhūtayā
prākāreṇāgni-varṇena
sāṭṭālenonnatena ca

ākāśa-gaṅgayā—by Ganges water known as Ākāśa-gaṅgā; *devyā*—the always-worshipable goddess; *vṛtām*—surrounded; *parikha-bhūtayā*—as a trench; *prākāreṇa*—by ramparts; *agni-varṇena*—resembling fire; *sa-aṭṭālena*—with places for fighting; *unnatena*—very high; *ca*—and.

TRANSLATION

The city was surrounded by trenches full of Ganges water, known as Ākāśa-gaṅgā, and by a high wall, which was the color of fire. Upon this wall were parapets for fighting.

TEXT 15

रुक्मपट्टकपाटैश्च द्वारैः स्फटिकगोपुरैः ।
जुष्टां विभक्तप्रपथां विश्वकर्मविनिर्मिताम् ॥ १५ ॥

rukma-paṭṭa-kapāṭaiś ca
dvāraiḥ sphaṭika-gopuraiḥ
juṣṭāṁ vibhakta-prapathāṁ
viśvakarma-vinirmitām

rukma-paṭṭa—possessing plates made of gold; *kapāṭaiḥ*—the doors of which; *ca*—and; *dvāraiḥ*—with entrances; *sphaṭika-gopuraiḥ*—with gates made of excellent marble; *juṣṭām*—linked; *vibhakta-prapathām*—with many different public roads; *viśvakarma-vinirmitām*—constructed by Viśvakarmā, the heavenly architect.

TRANSLATION

The doors were made of solid gold plates, and the gates were of excellent marble. These were linked by various public roads. The entire city had been constructed by Viśvakarmā.

TEXT 16

सभाचत्वररथ्याढ्यां विमानैर्न्यर्बुदैर्युताम् ।
शृङ्गाटकैर्मणिमयैर्वज्रविद्रुमवेदिभिः ॥ १६ ॥

sabhā-catvara-rathyāḍhyāṁ
vimānair nyārbudair yutām
śṛṅgāṭakair maṇimayair
vajra-vidruma-vedibhiḥ

sabhā—with assembly houses; *catvara*—courtyards; *rathya*—and public roads; *āḍhyām*—opulent; *vimānaiḥ*—by airplanes; *nyārbudaiḥ*—not less than ten *crores* (one hundred million); *yutām*—endowed; *śṛṅga-āṭakaiḥ*—with crossroads; *maṇi-mayaiḥ*—made of pearls; *vajra*—made of diamonds; *vidruma*—and coral; *vedibhiḥ*—with places to sit.

TRANSLATION

The city was full of courtyards, wide roads, assembly houses, and not less than one hundred million airplanes. The crossroads were made of pearl, and there were sitting places made of diamond and coral.

TEXT 17

यत्र नित्यवयोरूपाः श्यामा विरजवाससः ।
भ्राजन्ते रूपवन्नार्यो ह्यर्चिर्भिरिव वह्नयः ॥ १७ ॥

yatra nitya-vayo-rūpāḥ
śyāmā viraja-vāsasaḥ
bhrājante rūpavan-nāryo
hy arcirbhir iva vahnayaḥ

yatra—in that city; *nitya-vayaḥ-rūpāḥ*—who were ever beautiful and young; *śyāmāḥ*—possessing the quality of *śyāmā; viraja-vāsasaḥ*—always dressed with clean garments; *bhrājante*—glitter; *rūpa-vat*—well decorated; *nāryaḥ*—women; *hi*—certainly; *arcirbhiḥ*—with many flames; *iva*—like; *vahnayaḥ*—fires.

TRANSLATION

Everlastingly beautiful and youthful women, who were dressed with clean garments, glittered in the city like fires with flames. They all possessed the quality of śyāmā.

PURPORT

Śrīla Viśvanātha Cakravartī Ṭhākura gives a hint of the quality of the *śyāmā* woman.

śīta-kāle bhaved uṣṇā
uṣma-kāle suśītalāḥ
stanau sukaṭhinau yāsāṁ
tāḥ śyāmāḥ parikīrtitāḥ

A woman whose body is very warm during the winter and cool during the summer and who generally has very firm breasts is called *śyāmā.*

TEXT 18

सुरस्त्रीकेशविभ्रष्टनवसौगन्धिकस्त्रजाम् ।
यत्रामोदमुपादाय मार्ग आवाति मारुतः ॥ १८ ॥

sura-strī-keśa-vibhraṣṭa-
nava-saugandhika-srajām
yatrāmodam upādāya
mārga āvāti mārutaḥ

sura-strī—of the women of the demigods; *keśa*—from the hair; *vibhraṣṭa*—fallen; *nava-saugandhika*—made of fresh, fragrant flowers; *srajām*—of the flower garlands; *yatra*—wherein; *āmodam*—the fragrance; *upādāya*—carrying; *mārge*—on the roads; *āvāti*—blows; *mārutaḥ*—the breeze.

TRANSLATION

The breezes blowing in the streets of the city bore the fragrance of the flowers falling from the hair of the women of the demigods.

TEXT 19

हेमजालाक्षनिर्गच्छद्धूमेनागुरुगन्धिना ।
पाण्डुरेण प्रतिच्छन्नमार्गे यान्ति सुरप्रियाः ॥ १९ ॥

hema-jālākṣa-nirgacchad-
dhūmenāguru-gandhinā
pāṇḍureṇa praticchanna-
mārge yānti sura-priyāḥ

hema-jāla-akṣa—from dainty little windows made of networks of gold; *nirgacchat*—emanating; *dhūmena*—by smoke; *aguru-gandhinā*—fragrant due to burning incense known as *aguru; pāṇḍureṇa*—very white; *praticcha-nna*—covered; *mārge*—on the street; *yānti*—pass; *sura-priyāḥ*—beautiful public women known as Apsarās, celestial girls.

TRANSLATION

Apsarās passed on the streets, which were covered with the white, fragrant smoke of aguru incense emanating from windows with golden filigree.

TEXT 20

मुक्तावितानैर्मणिहेमकेतुभि-
र्नानापताकावलभीभिरावृताम् ।
शिखण्डिपारावतभृङ्गनादितां
वैमानिकस्त्रीकलगीतमङ्गलाम् ॥ २० ॥

muktā-vitānair maṇi-hema-ketubhir
nānā-patākā-valabhībhir āvṛtām
śikhaṇḍi-pārāvata-bhṛṅga-nāditāṁ
vaimānika-strī-kala-gīta-maṅgalām

muktā-vitānaiḥ—by canopies decorated with pearls; *maṇi-hema-ketubhiḥ*—with flags made with pearls and gold; *nānā-patākā*—possessing various kinds of flags; *valabhībhiḥ*—with the domes of the palaces; *āvṛtām*—covered; *śikhaṇḍi*—of birds like peacocks; *pārāvata*—pigeons; *bhṛṅga*—bees; *nāditām*—vibrated by the respective sounds; *vaimānika*—getting on airplanes; *strī*—of women; *kala-gīta*—from the choral singing; *maṅgalām*—full of auspiciousness.

TRANSLATION

The city was shaded by canopies decorated with pearls, and the domes of the palaces had flags of pearl and gold. The city always resounded with the vibrations of peacocks, pigeons and bees, and above the city flew airplanes full of beautiful women who constantly chanted auspicious songs that were very pleasing to the ear.

TEXT 21

मृदङ्गशङ्खानकदुन्दुभिस्वनैः
सतालवीणामुरजेष्टवेणुभिः ।
नृत्यैः सवाद्यैरुपदेवगीतकै-
र्मनोरमां स्वप्रभया जितप्रभाम् ॥ २१ ॥

mṛdaṅga-śaṅkhānaka-dundubhi-svanaiḥ
satāla-vīṇā-murajeṣṭa-veṇubhiḥ
nṛtyaiḥ savādyair upadeva-gītakair
manoramāṁ sva-prabhayā jita-prabhām

mṛdaṅga—of drums; *śaṅkha*—conchshells; *ānaka-dundubhi*—and kettledrums; *svanaiḥ*—by the sounds; *sa-tāla*—in perfect tune; *vīṇā*—a stringed instrument; *muraja*—a kind of drum; *iṣṭa-veṇubhiḥ*—accompanied by the very nice sound of the flute; *nṛtyaiḥ*—with dancing; *sa-vādyaiḥ*—with concert instruments; *upadeva-gītakaiḥ*—with singing by the secondary demigods like the Gandharvas; *manoramām*—beautiful and pleasing; *sva-prabhayā*—by its own brilliance; *jita-prabhām*—the personification of beauty was conquered.

TRANSLATION

The city was filled with the sounds of mṛdaṅgas, conchshells, kettledrums, flutes and well-tuned stringed instruments all playing in concert.

There was constant dancing and the Gandharvas sang. The combined beauty of Indrapurī defeated beauty personified.

TEXT 22

यां न व्रजन्त्यधर्मिष्ठाः खला भूतद्रुहः शठाः ।
मानिनः कामिनो लुब्धा एभिर्हीना व्रजन्ति यत्॥ २२ ॥

yāṁ na vrajanty adharmiṣṭhāḥ
khalā bhūta-druhaḥ śaṭhāḥ
māninaḥ kāmino lubdhā
ebhir hīnā vrajanti yat

yām—in the streets of the city; *na*—not; *vrajanti*—pass; *adharmiṣṭhāḥ*—irreligious persons; *khalāḥ*—envious persons; *bhūta-druhaḥ*—persons violent toward other living entities; *śaṭhāḥ*—cheaters; *māninaḥ*—falsely prestigious; *kāminaḥ*—lusty; *lubdhāḥ*—greedy; *ebhiḥ*—these; *hīnāḥ*—completely devoid of; *vrajanti*—walk; *yat*—on the street.

TRANSLATION

No one who was sinful, envious, violent toward other living entities, cunning, falsely proud, lusty or greedy could enter that city. The people who lived there were all devoid of these faults.

TEXT 23

तां देवधानीं स वरूथिनीपति-
र्बहिः समन्ताद् रुरुधे पृतन्यया ।
आचार्यदत्तं जलजं महास्वनं
दध्मौ प्रयुञ्जन्भयमिन्द्रयोषिताम् ॥ २३ ॥

tāṁ deva-dhānīṁ sa varūthinī-patir
bahiḥ samantād rurudhe pṛtanyayā
ācārya-dattaṁ jalajaṁ mahā-svanaṁ
dadhmau prayuñjan bhayam indra-yoṣitām

tām—that; *deva-dhānīm*—place where Indra lived; *saḥ*—he (Bali Mahārāja); *varūthinī-patiḥ*—the commander of the soldiers; *bahiḥ*—outside; *samantāt*—in all directions; *rurudhe*—attacked; *pṛtanyayā*—by soldiers;

ācārya-dattam—given by Śukrācārya; *jala-jam*—the conchshell; *mahā-svanam*—a loud sound; *dadhmau*—resounded; *prayuñjan*—creating; *bhayam*—fear; *indra-yoṣitām*—of all the ladies protected by Indra.

TRANSLATION

Bali Mahārāja, who was the commander of numberless soldiers, gathered his soldiers outside this abode of Indra and attacked it from all directions. He sounded the conchshell given him by his spiritual master, Śukrācārya, thus creating a fearful situation for the women protected by Indra.

TEXT 24

मघवांस्तमभिप्रेत्य बलेः परममुद्यमम् ।
सर्वदेवगणोपेतो गुरुमेतदुवाच ह ॥ २४ ॥

maghavāṁs tam abhipretya
baleḥ paramam udyamam
sarva-deva-gaṇopeto
gurum etad uvāca ha

maghavān—Indra; *tam*—the situation; *abhipretya*—understanding; *baleḥ*—of Bali Mahārāja; *paramam udyamam*—great enthusiasm; *sarva-deva-gaṇa*—by all the demigods; *upetaḥ*—accompanied; *gurum*—unto the spiritual master; *etat*—the following words; *uvāca*—said; *ha*—indeed.

TRANSLATION

Seeing Bali Mahārāja's indefatigable endeavor and understanding his motive, King Indra, along with the other demigods, approached his spiritual master, Bṛhaspati, and spoke as follows.

TEXT 25

भगवन्नुद्यमो भूयान्बलेर्नः पूर्ववैरिणः ।
अविषह्यमिमं मन्ये केनासीत्तेजसोर्जितः ॥ २५ ॥

bhagavann udyamo bhūyān
baler naḥ pūrva-vairiṇaḥ
aviṣahyam imaṁ manye
kenāsīt tejasorjitaḥ

bhagavan—O my lord; *udyamaḥ*—enthusiasm; *bhūyān*—great; *baleḥ*—of Bali Mahārāja; *naḥ*—our; *pūrva-vairiṇaḥ*—past enemy; *aviṣahyam*—unbearable; *imam*—this; *manye*—I think; *kena*—by whom; *āsīt*—got; *tejasā*—prowess; *ūrjitaḥ*—achieved.

TRANSLATION

My lord, our old enemy Bali Mahārāja now has new enthusiasm, and he has obtained such astonishing power that we think that perhaps we cannot resist his prowess.

TEXT 26

नैनं कश्चित् कुतो वापि प्रतिव्योढुमधीश्वरः ।
पिबन्निव मुखेनेदं लिहन्निव दिशो दश ।
दहन्निव दिशो दृग्भिः संवर्ताग्निरिवोत्थितः ॥ २६ ॥

nainaṁ kaścit kuto vāpi
prativyoḍhum adhīśvaraḥ
pibann iva mukhenedaṁ
lihann iva diśo daśa
dahann iva diśo dṛgbhiḥ
saṁvartāgnir ivotthitaḥ

na—not; *enam*—this arrangement; *kaścit*—anyone; *kutaḥ*—from anywhere; *vā api*—either; *prativyoḍhum*—to counteract; *adhīśvaraḥ*—capable; *piban iva*—as if drinking; *mukhena*—by the mouth; *idam*—this (world); *lihan iva*—as if licking up; *diśaḥ daśa*—all ten directions; *dahan iva*—as if burning; *diśaḥ*—all directions; *dṛgbhiḥ*—by his vision; *saṁvarta-agniḥ*—the fire known as *saṁvarta; iva*—like; *utthitaḥ*—now arisen.

TRANSLATION

No one anywhere can counteract this military arrangement of Bali's. It now appears that Bali is trying to drink up the entire universe with his mouth, lick up the ten directions with his tongue, and raise fire in every direction with his eyes. Indeed, he has arisen like the annihilating fire known as saṁvartaka.

TEXT 27

ब्रूहि कारणमेतस्य दुर्धर्षत्वस्य मद्रिपोः ।
ओजः सहो बलं तेजो यत एतत्समुद्यमः ॥ २७ ॥

brūhi kāraṇam etasya
durdharṣatvasya mad-ripoḥ
ojaḥ saho balaṁ tejo
yata etat samudyamaḥ

brūhi—kindly inform us; *kāraṇam*—the cause; *etasya*—of all this; *durdharṣatvasya*—of the formidableness; *mat-ripoḥ*—of my enemy; *ojaḥ*—prowess; *sahaḥ*—energy; *balam*—strength; *tejaḥ*—influence; *yataḥ*—wherefrom; *etat*—all this; *samudyamaḥ*—endeavor.

TRANSLATION

Kindly inform me. What is the cause for Bali Mahārāja's strength, endeavor, influence and victory? How has he become so enthusiastic?

TEXT 28

श्रीगुरुरुवाच
जानामि मघवञ्छत्रोरुन्नतेरस्य कारणम् ।
शिष्यायोपभृतं तेजो भृगुभिर्ब्रह्मवादिभिः ॥ २८ ॥

śrī-gurur uvāca
jānāmi maghavañ chatror
unnater asya kāraṇam
śiṣyāyopabhṛtaṁ tejo
bhṛgubhir brahma-vādibhiḥ

śrī-guruḥ uvāca—Bṛhaspati said; *jānāmi*—I know; *maghavan*—O Indra; *śatroḥ*—of the enemy; *unnateḥ*—of the elevation; *asya*—of him; *kāraṇam*—the cause; *śiṣyāya*—unto the disciple; *upabhṛtam*—endowed; *tejaḥ*—power; *bhṛgubhiḥ*—by the descendants of Bhṛgu; *brahma-vādibhiḥ*—all-powerful *brāhmaṇas.*

TRANSLATION

Bṛhaspati, the spiritual master of the demigods, said: O Indra, I know the cause for your enemy's becoming so powerful. The brāhmaṇa descen-

dants of Bhṛgu Muni, being pleased by Bali Mahārāja, their disciple, endowed him with such extraordinary power.

PURPORT

Bṛhaspati, the spiritual master of the demigods, informed Indra, "Ordinarily, Bali and his forces could not achieve such strength, but it appears that the *brāhmaṇa* descendants of Bhṛgu Muni, being pleased with Bali Mahārāja, endowed them with this spiritual power." In other words, Bṛhaspati informed Indra that Bali Mahārāja's prowess was not his own but that of his exalted *guru,* Śukrācārya. We sing in our daily prayers, *yasya prasādād bhagavat-prasādo yasyāprasādān na gatiḥ kuto 'pi*. By the pleasure of the spiritual master, one can get extraordinary power, especially in spiritual advancement. The blessings of the spiritual master are more powerful than one's personal endeavor for such advancement. Narottama dāsa Ṭhākura therefore says:

guru-mukha-padma-vākya, cittete kariyā aikya,
āra nā kariha mane āśā

Especially for spiritual advancement, one should carry out the bona fide order of the spiritual master. By the *paramparā* system, one can thus be endowed with the original spiritual power coming from the Supreme Personality of Godhead (*evaṁ paramparā-prāptam imaṁ rājarṣayo viduḥ*).

TEXT 29

ओजस्विनं बलिं जेतुं न समर्थोऽस्ति कश्चन ।
भवद्विधो भवान्वापि वर्जयित्वेश्वरं हरिम् ।
विजेष्यति न कोऽप्येनं ब्रह्मतेजःसमेधितम् ।
नास्य शक्तः पुरः स्थातुं कृतान्तस्य यथा जनाः ॥ २९ ॥

ojasvinaṁ baliṁ jetuṁ
na samartho 'sti kaścana
bhavad-vidho bhavān vāpi
varjayitveśvaraṁ harim
vijeṣyati na ko 'py enaṁ
brahma-tejaḥ-samedhitam
nāsya śaktaḥ puraḥ sthātuṁ
kṛtāntasya yathā janāḥ

ojasvinam—so powerful; *balim*—Bali Mahārāja; *jetum*—to conquer; *na*—not; *samarthaḥ*—able; *asti*—is; *kaścana*—anyone; *bhavat-vidhaḥ*—like you; *bhavān*—you yourself; *vā api*—either; *varjayitvā*—excepting; *īśvaram*—the supreme controller; *harim*—the Supreme Personality of Godhead; *vijeṣyati*—will conquer; *na*—not; *kaḥ api*—anyone; *enam*—him (Bali Mahārāja); *brahma-tejaḥ-samedhitam*—now empowered with *brahma-tejas,* extraordinary spiritual power; *na*—not; *asya*—of him; *śaktaḥ*—is able; *puraḥ*—in front; *sthātum*—to stay; *kṛta-antasya*—of Yamarāja; *yathā*—as; *janāḥ*—people.

TRANSLATION

Neither you nor your men can conquer the most powerful Bali. Indeed, no one but the Supreme Personality of Godhead can conquer him, for he is now equipped with the supreme spiritual power [brahma-tejas]. As no one can stand before Yamarāja, no one can now stand before Bali Mahārāja.

TEXT 30

तस्मान्निलयमुत्सृज्य यूयं सर्वे त्रिविष्टपम् ।
यात कालं प्रतीक्षन्तो यतः शत्रोर्विपर्ययः ॥ ३० ॥

tasmān nilayam utsṛjya
yūyaṁ sarve tri-viṣṭapam
yāta kālaṁ pratīkṣanto
yataḥ śatror viparyayaḥ

tasmāt—therefore; *nilayam*—not visible; *utsṛjya*—giving up; *yūyam*—you; *sarve*—all; *tri-viṣṭapam*—the heavenly kingdom; *yāta*—go somewhere else; *kālam*—time; *pratīkṣantaḥ*—waiting for; *yataḥ*—whereof; *śatroḥ*—of your enemy; *viparyayaḥ*—the reverse condition arrives.

TRANSLATION

Therefore, waiting until the situation of your enemies is reversed, you should all leave this heavenly planet and go elsewhere, where you will not be seen.

TEXT 31

एष विप्रबलोदर्कः सम्प्रत्यूर्जितविक्रमः ।
तेषामेवापमानेन सानुबन्धो विनङ्क्ष्यति ॥ ३१ ॥

eṣa vipra-balodarkaḥ
sampraty ūrjita-vikramaḥ
teṣām evāpamānena
sānubandho vinaṅkṣyati

eṣaḥ—this (Bali Mahārāja); *vipra-bala-udarkaḥ*—flourishing because of the brahminical power invested in him; *samprati*—at the present moment; *ūrjita-vikramaḥ*—extremely powerful; *teṣām*—of the same *brāhmaṇas; eva*—indeed; *apamānena*—by insult; *sa-anubandhaḥ*—with friends and assistants; *vinaṅkṣyati*—will be vanquished.

TRANSLATION

Bali Mahārāja has now become extremely powerful because of the benedictions given him by the brāhmaṇas, but when he later insults the brāhmaṇas, he will be vanquished, along with his friends and assistants.

PURPORT

Bali Mahārāja and Indra were enemies. Therefore, when Bṛhaspati, the spiritual master of the demigods, predicted that Bali Mahārāja would be vanquished when he insulted the *brāhmaṇas* by whose grace he had become so powerful, Bali Mahārāja's enemies were naturally anxious to know when that opportune moment would come. To pacify King Indra, Bṛhaspati assured him that the time would certainly come, for Bṛhaspati could see that in the future Bali Mahārāja would defy the orders of Śukrācārya in order to pacify Lord Viṣṇu, Vāmanadeva. Of course, to advance in Kṛṣṇa consciousness, one can take all risks. To please Vāmanadeva, Bali Mahārāja risked defying the orders of his spiritual master, Śukrācārya. Because of this, he would lose all his property, yet because of devotional service to the Lord, he would get more than he expected, and in the future, in the eighth *manvantara,* he would occupy the throne of Indra again.

TEXT 32

एवं सुमन्त्रितार्थास्ते गुरुणार्थानुदर्शिना ।
हित्वा त्रिविष्टपं जग्मुर्गीर्वाणाः कामरूपिणः ॥ ३२ ॥

evaṁ sumantritārthās te
guruṇārthānudarśinā
hitvā tri-viṣṭapaṁ jagmur
gīrvāṇāḥ kāma-rūpiṇaḥ

evam—thus; *su-mantrita*—being well advised; *arthāḥ*—about duties; *te*—they (the demigods); *guruṇā*—by their spiritual master; *artha-anudarśinā*—whose instructions were quite befitting; *hitvā*—giving up; *tri-viṣṭapam*—the heavenly kingdom; *jagmuḥ*—went; *gīrvāṇāḥ*—the demigods; *kāma-rūpiṇaḥ*—who could assume any form they liked.

TRANSLATION

Śukadeva Gosvāmī continued: The demigods, being thus advised by Bṛhaspati for their benefit, immediately accepted his words. Assuming forms according to their desire, they left the heavenly kingdom and scattered, without being observed by the demons.

PURPORT

The word *kāma-rūpiṇaḥ* indicates that the demigods, the inhabitants of the heavenly planets, can assume any form they desire. Thus it was not at all difficult for them to remain incognito before the eyes of the demons.

TEXT 33

देवेष्वथ निलीनेषु बलिर्वैरोचनः पुरीम् ।
देवधानीमधिष्ठाय वशं निन्ये जगत्त्रयम् ॥ ३३ ॥

deveṣv atha nilīneṣu
balir vairocanaḥ purīm
deva-dhānīm adhiṣṭhāya
vaśaṁ ninye jagat-trayam

deveṣu—all the demigods; *atha*—in this way; *nilīneṣu*—when they disappeared; *baliḥ*—Bali Mahārāja; *vairocanaḥ*—the son of Virocana; *purīm*—the heavenly kingdom; *deva-dhānīm*—the residence of the demigods; *adhiṣṭhāya*—taking possession of; *vaśam*—under control; *ninye*—brought; *jagat-trayam*—the three worlds.

TRANSLATION

When the demigods had disappeared, Bali Mahārāja, the son of Virocana, entered the heavenly kingdom, and from there he brought the three worlds under his control.

TEXT 34

तं विश्वजयिनं शिष्यं भृगवः शिष्यवत्सलाः ।
शतेन हयमेधानामनुव्रतमयाजयन् ॥ ३४ ॥

taṁ viśva-jayinaṁ śiṣyaṁ
bhṛgavaḥ śiṣya-vatsalāḥ
śatena hayamedhānām
anuvratam ayājayan

tam—unto him (Bali Mahārāja); *viśva-jayinam*—the conqueror of the entire universe; *śiṣyam*—because of his being a disciple; *bhṛgavaḥ*—the *brāhmaṇas,* descendants of Bhṛgu like Śukrācārya; *śiṣya-vatsalāḥ*—being very pleased with the disciple; *śatena*—by one hundred; *haya-medhānām*—sacrifices known as *aśvamedha; anuvratam*—following the instruction of the *brāhmaṇas; ayājayan*—caused to execute.

TRANSLATION

The brāhmaṇa descendants of Bhṛgu, being very pleased with their disciple, who had conquered the entire universe, now engaged him in performing one hundred aśvamedha sacrifices.

PURPORT

We have seen in the dispute between Mahārāja Pṛthu and Indra that when Mahārāja Pṛthu wanted to perform one hundred *aśvamedha-yajñas,* Indra wanted to impede him, for it is because of such great sacrifices that Indra was made King of heaven. Here the *brāhmaṇa* descendants of Bhṛgu decided that although Mahārāja Bali was situated on the throne of Indra, he would not be able to stay there unless he performed such sacrifices. Therefore they advised Mahārāja Bali to perform at least as many *aśvamedha-yajñas* as Indra. The word *ayājayan* indicates that all the *brāhmaṇas* induced Bali Mahārāja to perform such sacrifices.

TEXT 35

ततस्तदनुभावेन भुवनत्रयविश्रुताम् ।
कीर्तिं दिक्षु वितन्वानः स रेज उडुराडिव ॥ ३५ ॥

tatas tad-anubhāvena
bhuvana-traya-viśrutām
kīrtiṁ dikṣu-vitanvānaḥ
sa reja uḍurāḍ iva

tataḥ—thereafter; *tat-anubhāvena*—because of performing such great sacrifices; *bhuvana-traya*—throughout the three worlds; *viśrutām*—celebrated; *kīrtim*—reputation; *dikṣu*—in all directions; *vitanvānaḥ*—spreading; *saḥ*—he (Bali Mahārāja); *reje*—became effulgent; *uḍurāṭ*—the moon; *iva*—like.

TRANSLATION

When Bali Mahārāja performed these sacrifices, he gained a great reputation in all directions, throughout the three worlds. Thus he shone in his position, like the brilliant moon in the sky.

TEXT 36

बुभुजे च श्रियं स्वृद्धां द्विजदेवोपलम्भिताम् ।
कृतकृत्यमिवात्मानं मन्यमानो महामनाः ॥ ३६ ॥

bubhuje ca śriyaṁ svṛddhāṁ
dvija-devopalambhitām
kṛta-kṛtyam ivātmānaṁ
manyamāno mahāmanāḥ

bubhuje—enjoyed; *ca*—also; *śriyam*—opulence; *su-ṛddhām*—prosperity; *dvija*—of the *brāhmaṇas; deva*—as good as the demigods; *upalambhitām*—achieved because of the favor; *kṛta-kṛtyam*—very satisfied by his activities; *iva*—like that; *ātmānam*—himself; *manyamānaḥ*—thinking; *mahā-manāḥ*—the great-minded.

TRANSLATION

Because of the favor of the brāhmaṇas, the great soul Bali Mahārāja, thinking himself very satisfied, became very opulent and prosperous and began to enjoy the kingdom.

PURPORT

The *brāhmaṇas* are called *dvija-deva,* and *kṣatriyas* are generally called *nara-deva.* The word *deva* actually refers to the Supreme Personality of Godhead. The *brāhmaṇas* guide human society in becoming happy by satisfying Lord Viṣṇu, and according to their advice, the *kṣatriyas,* who are called *nara-deva,* keep law and order so that other people, namely the *vaiśyas* and *śūdras,* may properly follow regulative principles. In this way, people are gradually elevated to Kṛṣṇa consciousness.

Thus end the Bhaktivedanta purports of the Eighth Canto, Fifteenth Chapter, of the Śrīmad-Bhāgavatam, *entitled "Bali Mahārāja Conquers the Heavenly Planets."*

CHAPTER SIXTEEN

Executing the Payo-vrata Process of Worship

As described in this chapter, because Aditi, the mother of the demigods, was very afflicted, her husband, Kaśyapa Muni, told her how to observe vows in austerities for the benefit of her sons.

Since the demigods were not visible in the heavenly kingdom, their mother, Aditi, because of separation from them, was very much aggrieved. One day after many, many years, the great sage Kaśyapa emerged from a trance of meditation and returned to his *āśrama*. He saw that the *āśrama* was no longer beautiful and that his wife was very morose. Everywhere in the *āśrama*, he saw signs of lamentation. The great sage therefore inquired from his wife about the well-being of the *āśrama* and asked her why she looked so morose. After Aditi informed Kaśyapa Muni about the *āśrama's* well-being, she told him that she was lamenting for the absence of her sons. She then requested him to tell her how her sons could return and reoccupy their positions. She wanted all good fortune for her sons. Moved by Aditi's request, Kaśyapa Muni instructed her in the philosophy of self-realization, the difference between matter and spirit, and how to be unaffected by material loss. But when he saw that Aditi was not satisfied even after he had given these instructions, he advised her to worship Vāsudeva, Janārdana. He assured her that only Lord Vāsudeva could satisfy her and fulfill all her desires. When Aditi then expressed her desire to worship Lord Vāsudeva, Prajāpati Kaśyapa told her about a process of worship known as *payo-vrata*, which is executed in twelve days. Lord Brahmā had instructed him how to satisfy Lord Kṛṣṇa by this process, and thus he advised his wife to observe this vow and its regulative principles.

TEXT 1

श्रीशुक उवाच

एवं पुत्रेषु नष्टेषु देवमातादितिस्तदा ।
हृते त्रिविष्टपे दैत्यैः पर्यतप्यदनाथवत् ॥ १ ॥

śrī-śuka uvāca
evaṁ putreṣu naṣṭeṣu
deva-mātāditis tadā
hṛte tri-viṣṭape daityaiḥ
paryatapyad anāthavat

śrī-śukaḥ uvāca—Śrī Śukadeva Gosvāmī said; *evam*—in this way; *putreṣu*—when her sons; *naṣṭeṣu*—disappearing from their position; *deva-mātā*—the mother of the demigods; *aditiḥ*—Aditi; *tadā*—at that time; *hṛte*—because of being lost; *tri-viṣṭape*—the kingdom of heaven; *daityaiḥ*—by the influence of the demons; *paryatapyat*—began to lament; *anātha-vat*—as if she had no protector.

TRANSLATION

Śukadeva Gosvāmī said: O King, when Aditi's sons, the demigods, had thus disappeared from heaven and the demons had occupied their places, Aditi began lamenting, as if she had no protector.

TEXT 2

एकदा कश्यपस्तस्या आश्रमं भगवानगात्।
निरुत्सवं निरानन्दं समाधेर्विरतश्चिरात् ॥ २ ॥

ekadā kaśyapas tasyā
āśramaṁ bhagavān agāt
nirutsavaṁ nirānandaṁ
samādher virataś cirāt

ekadā—one day; *kaśyapaḥ*—the great sage Kaśyapa Muni; *tasyāḥ*—of Aditi; *āśramam*—to the shelter; *bhagavān*—greatly powerful; *agāt*—went; *nirutsavam*—without enthusiasm; *nirānandam*—without jubilation; *samādheḥ*—his trance; *virataḥ*—stopping; *cirāt*—after a long time.

TRANSLATION

After many, many days, the great powerful sage Kaśyapa Muni arose from a trance of meditation and returned home to see the āśrama of Aditi neither jubilant nor festive.

TEXT 3

स पत्नीं दीनवदनां कृतासनपरिग्रहः ।
सभाजितो यथान्यायमिदमाह कुरूद्वह ॥ ३ ॥

sa patnīṁ dīna-vadanāṁ
kṛtāsana-parigrahaḥ
sabhājito yathā-nyāyam
idam āha kurūdvaha

saḥ—Kaśyapa Muni; *patnīm*—unto his wife; *dīna-vadanām*—having a dry face; *kṛta-āsana-parigrahaḥ*—after accepting a sitting place; *sabhājitaḥ*—being honored by Aditi; *yathā-nyāyam*—according to time and place; *idam āha*—spoke as follows; *kuru-udvaha*—O Mahārāja Parīkṣit, the best of the Kurus.

TRANSLATION

O best of the Kurus, when Kaśyapa Muni had been properly received and welcomed, he took his seat and then spoke as follows to his wife, Aditi, who was very morose.

TEXT 4

अप्यभद्रं न विप्राणां भद्रे लोकेऽधुनागतम् ।
न धर्मस्य न लोकस्य मृत्योश्छन्दानुवर्तिनः ॥ ४ ॥

apy abhadraṁ na viprāṇāṁ
bhadre loke 'dhunāgatam
na dharmasya na lokasya
mṛtyoś chandānuvartinaḥ

api—whether; *abhadram*—ill fortune; *na*—not; *viprāṇām*—of the *brāhmaṇas; bhadre*—O most gentle Aditi; *loke*—in this world; *adhunā*—at the present moment; *āgatam*—has come; *na*—not; *dharmasya*—of religious principles; *na*—not; *lokasya*—of the people in general; *mṛtyoḥ*—death; *chanda-anuvartinaḥ*—who are followers of the whims of death.

TRANSLATION

O most gentle one, I wonder whether anything inauspicious has now taken place in regard to religious principles, the brāhmaṇas or the people in general, who are subject to the whims of death.

PURPORT

There are prescribed duties for all the inhabitants of this material world, especially for the *brāhmaṇas* but also for the people in general, who are subject to the whims of death. Kaśyapa Muni wondered whether the regulative principles, which are meant for the well-being of everyone, had been disobeyed. He accordingly continued his inquiries for seven verses.

TEXT 5

अपि वाकुशलं किञ्चिद् गृहेषु गृहमेधिनि ।
धर्मस्यार्थस्य कामस्य यत्र योगो ह्ययोगिनाम् ॥ ५ ॥

api vākuśalaṁ kiñcid
gṛheṣu gṛha-medhini
dharmasyārthasya kāmasya
yatra yogo hy ayoginām

api—I am wondering; *vā*—either; *akuśalam*—inauspiciousness; *kiñcit*—some; *gṛheṣu*—at home; *gṛha-medhini*—O my wife, who are attached to household life; *dharmasya*—of the principles of religion; *arthasya*—of the economic condition; *kāmasya*—of satisfaction of desires; *yatra*—at home; *yogaḥ*—the result of meditation; *hi*—indeed; *ayoginām*—even of those who are not transcendentalists.

TRANSLATION

O my wife, who are very much attached to household life, if the principles of religion, economic development and satisfaction of the senses are properly followed in household life, one's activities are as good as those of a transcendentalist. I wonder whether there have been any discrepancies in following these principles.

PURPORT

In this verse, Aditi has been addressed by her husband, Kaśyapa Muni, as *gṛha-medhini,* which means "one who is satisfied in household life for sense gratification." Generally, those who are in household life pursue sense gratification in the field of activities performed for material results. Such *gṛhamedhīs* have only one aim in life—sense gratification. Therefore it is said, *yan maithunādi-gṛhamedhi-sukhaṁ hi tuccham:* the householder's life is based on sense gratification, and therefore the happiness derived from it is very meager. Nonetheless, the Vedic process is so comprehensive that even in householder life one can adjust his activities according to the regulative principles of *dharma, artha, kāma* and *mokṣa.* One's aim should be to achieve liberation, but because one cannot at once give up sense gratification, in the *śāstras* there are injunctions prescribing how to follow the principles of religion, economic development and sense gratification. As explained in *Śrīmad-Bhāgavatam* (1.2.9), *dharmasya hy āpavargyasya nārtho 'rthāyopakalpate:* "All occupational engagements are certainly meant for ultimate liberation. They should never be performed for material gain." Those who are in household life should not think that religion is meant to improve the process of the householder's sense gratification. Household life is also meant for advancement in spiritual understanding, by which one can ultimately gain liberation from the material clutches. One should remain in household life with the aim of understanding the ultimate goal of life (*tattva jijñāsā*). Then household life is as good as the life of a *yogī.* Kaśyapa Muni therefore inquired from his wife whether the principles of religion, economic development and sense gratification were being properly followed in terms of the śāstric injunctions. As soon as one deviates from the injunctions of the *śāstra,* the purpose of household life is immediately lost in confusion.

TEXT 6

अपि वातिथयोऽभ्येत्य कुटुम्बासक्तया त्वया ।
गृहादपूजिता याताः प्रत्युत्थानेन वा क्वचित् ॥ ६ ॥

api vātithayo 'bhyetya
kuṭumbāsaktayā tvayā
gṛhād apūjitā yātāḥ
pratyutthānena vā kvacit

api—whether; *vā*—either; *atithayaḥ*—guests who come without an invitation; *abhyetya*—coming to the home; *kuṭumba-āsaktayā*—who were too attached to the family members; *tvayā*—by you; *gṛhāt*—from the house; *apūjitāḥ*—without being properly welcomed; *yātāḥ*—went away; *pratyutthānena*—by standing up; *vā*—either; *kvacit*—sometimes.

TRANSLATION

I wonder whether because of being too attached to the members of your family, you failed to properly receive uninvited guests, who therefore were not welcomed and went away.

PURPORT

It is the duty of a householder to receive guests, even if a guest be an enemy. When a guest comes to one's home, one should properly receive him by standing up and offering him a seat. It is enjoined, *gṛhe śatrum api prāptaṁ viśvastam akutobhayam:* if even an enemy comes to one's home, one should receive him in such a way that the guest will forget that his host is an enemy. According to one's position, one should properly receive anyone who comes to one's home. At least a seat and a glass of water should be offered, so that the guest will not be displeased. Kaśyapa Muni inquired from Aditi whether disrespect had been shown to such guests, or *atithis.* The word *atithi* refers to one who comes without an invitation.

TEXT 7

गृहेषु येष्वतिथयो नार्चिताः सलिलैरपि ।
यदि निर्यान्ति ते नूनं फेरुराजगृहोपमाः ॥ ७ ॥

gṛheṣu yeṣv atithayo
nārcitāḥ salilair api
yadi niryānti te nūnaṁ
pherurāja-gṛhopamāḥ

gṛheṣu—at home; *yeṣu*—which; *atithayaḥ*—uninvited guests; *na*—not; *arcitāḥ*—welcomed; *salilaiḥ api*—even by offering a glass of water; *yadi*—if; *niryānti*—they go away; *te*—such household life; *nūnam*—indeed; *pheru-rāja*—of jackals; *gṛha*—the homes; *upamāḥ*—like.

TRANSLATION

Homes from which guests go away without having been received even with an offering of a little water are like those holes in the field which are the homes of jackals.

PURPORT

In a field there may be holes made by snakes and mice, but when there are very big holes, it may be supposed that jackals live there. Certainly no one goes to take shelter in such homes. Thus the homes of human beings where *atithis,* uninvited guests, are not properly received are like the homes of jackals.

TEXT 8

अप्यग्नयस्तु वेलायां न हुता हविषा सति ।
त्वयोद्विग्नधिया भद्रे प्रोषिते मयि कर्हिचित् ॥ ८ ॥

apy agnayas tu velāyāṁ
na hutā haviṣā sati
tvayodvigna-dhiyā bhadre
proṣite mayi karhicit

api—whether; *agnayaḥ*—fires; *tu*—indeed; *velāyām*—in the fire sacrifice; *na*—not; *hutāḥ*—offered; *haviṣā*—by ghee; *sati*—O chaste woman; *tvayā*—by you; *udvigna-dhiyā*—because of some anxiety; *bhadre*—O auspicious woman; *proṣite*—was away from home; *mayi*—when I; *karhicit*—sometimes.

TRANSLATION

O chaste and auspicious woman, when I left home for other places, were you in so much anxiety that you did not offer oblations of ghee into the fire?

TEXT 9

यत्पूजया कामदुघान्याति लोकान्गृहान्वितः ।
ब्राह्मणोऽग्निश्च वै विष्णोः सर्वदेवात्मनो मुखम् ॥ ९ ॥

yat-pūjayā kāma-dughān
yāti lokān gṛhānvitaḥ
brāhmaṇo 'gniś ca vai viṣṇoḥ
sarva-devātmano mukham

yat-pūjayā—by worshiping the fire and *brāhmaṇas; kāma-dughān*—which fulfill one's desires; *yāti*—one goes; *lokān*—to the destination of the higher planetary system; *gṛha-anvitaḥ*—a person attached to household life; *brāhmaṇaḥ*—the *brāhmaṇas; agniḥ ca*—and the fire; *vai*—indeed; *viṣṇoḥ*—of Lord Viṣṇu; *sarva-deva-ātmanaḥ*—the soul of all the demigods; *mukham*—the mouth.

TRANSLATION

By worshiping the fire and the brāhmaṇas, a householder can achieve the desired goal of residing in the higher planets, for the sacrificial fire and

the brāhmaṇas are to be considered the mouth of Lord Viṣṇu, who is the Supersoul of all the demigods.

PURPORT

According to the Vedic system, a fire sacrifice is held in order to offer oblations of ghee, grains, fruits, flowers and so on, so that Lord Viṣṇu may eat and be satisfied. The Lord says in *Bhagavad-gītā* (9.26):

patraṁ puṣpaṁ phalaṁ toyaṁ
yo me bhaktyā prayacchati
tad ahaṁ bhakty-upahṛtam
aśnāmi prayatātmanaḥ

"If one offers Me with love and devotion a leaf, a flower, fruit or water, I will accept it." Therefore, all these items may be offered in the sacrificial fire, and Lord Viṣṇu will be satisfied. Similarly, *brāhmaṇa-bhojana,* feeding of the *brāhmaṇas,* is also recommended, for when the *brāhmaṇas* eat sumptuous remnants of food after *yajña,* this is another way that Lord Viṣṇu Himself eats. Therefore the Vedic principles recommend that in every festival or ceremony one offer oblations to the fire and give sumptuous food for the *brāhmaṇas* to eat. By such activities, a householder may be elevated to the heavenly planets and similar places in the higher planetary systems.

TEXT 10

अपि सर्वे कुशलिनस्तव पुत्रा मनस्विनि ।
लक्षयेऽस्वस्थमात्मानं भवत्या लक्षणैरहम् ॥ १० ॥

api sarve kuśalinas
tava putrā manasvini
lakṣaye 'svastham ātmānaṁ
bhavatyā lakṣaṇair aham

api—whether; *sarve*—all; *kuśalinaḥ*—in full auspiciousness; *tava*—your; *putrāḥ*—sons; *manasvini*—O great-minded lady; *lakṣaye*—I see; *asvastham*—not in tranquillity; *ātmānam*—the mind; *bhavatyāḥ*—of you; *lakṣaṇaiḥ*—by symptoms; *aham*—I.

TRANSLATION

O great-minded lady, are all your sons faring well? Seeing your withered face, I can perceive that your mind is not tranquil. How is this so?

TEXT 11

श्रीअदितिरुवाच
भद्रं द्विजगवां ब्रह्मन्धर्मस्यास्य जनस्य च ।
त्रिवर्गस्य परं क्षेत्रं गृहमेधिन्गृहा इमे ॥ ११ ॥

śrī-aditir uvāca
bhadraṁ dvija-gavāṁ brahman
dharmasyāsya janasya ca
tri-vargasya paraṁ kṣetraṁ
gṛhamedhin gṛhā ime

śrī-aditiḥ uvāca—Śrīmatī Aditi said; *bhadram*—all auspiciousness; *dvija-gavām*—of the *brāhmaṇas* and the cows; *brahman*—O *brāhmaṇa; dharmasya asya*—of the religious principles mentioned in *śāstra; janasya*—of the people in general; *ca*—and; *tri-vargasya*—of the three processes of elevation (*dharma, artha* and *kāma*); *param*—the supreme; *kṣetram*—field; *gṛhamedhin*—O my husband, who are attached to household life; *gṛhāḥ*—your home; *ime*—all these things.

TRANSLATION

Aditi said: O my respected brāhmaṇa husband, all is well with the brāhmaṇas, the cows, religion and the welfare of other people. O master of the house, the three principles of dharma, artha and kāma flourish in household life, which is consequently full of good fortune.

PURPORT

In household life one can develop the three principles of religion, economic development and sense gratification according to the regulations given in the *śāstras,* but to attain liberation one must give up household life and place himself in the transcendental renounced order. Kaśyapa Muni was not in the renounced order of life. Therefore he is addressed here once as *brahman* and another time as *gṛhamedhin.* Aditi, his wife, assured him that as far as household life was concerned, everything was going nicely, and the *brāhmaṇas* and cows were being honored and protected. In other words, there were no disturbances; household life was duly progressing.

TEXT 12

अग्नयोऽतिथयो भृत्या भिक्षवो ये च लिप्सवः ।
सर्वं भगवतो ब्रह्मन्ननुध्यानान्न रिष्यति ॥ १२ ॥

agnayo 'tithayo bhṛtyā
bhikṣavo ye ca lipsavaḥ
sarvaṁ bhagavato brahmann
anudhyānān na riṣyati

agnayaḥ—worshiping the fires; *atithayaḥ*—receiving the guests; *bhṛtyāḥ*—satisfying the servants; *bhikṣavaḥ*—pleasing the beggars; *ye*—all of them who; *ca*—and; *lipsavaḥ*—as they desire (are taken care of); *sarvam*—all of them; *bhagavataḥ*—of you, my lord; *brahman*—O *brāhmaṇa; anudhyānāt*—from always thinking; *na riṣyati*—nothing is missed (everything is properly done).

TRANSLATION

O beloved husband, the fires, guests, servants and beggars are all being properly cared for by me. Because I always think of you, there is no possibility that any of the religious principles will be neglected.

TEXT 13

को नु मे भगवन्कामो न सम्पद्येत मानसः ।
यस्या भवान्प्रजाध्यक्ष एवं धर्मान्प्रभाषते ॥ १३ ॥

ko nu me bhagavan kāmo
na sampadyeta mānasaḥ
yasyā bhavān prajādhyakṣa
evaṁ dharmān prabhāṣate

kaḥ—what; *nu*—indeed; *me*—my; *bhagavan*—O lord; *kāmaḥ*—desire; *na*—not; *sampadyeta*—can be fulfilled; *mānasaḥ*—within my mind; *yasyāḥ*—of me; *bhavān*—your good self; *prajā-adhyakṣaḥ*—Prajāpati; *evam*—thus; *dharmān*—religious principles; *prabhāṣate*—talks.

TRANSLATION

O my lord, since you are a Prajāpati and are personally my instructor in the principles of religion, where is the possibility that all my desires will not be fulfilled?

TEXT 14

तवैव मारीच मनःशरीरजाः
प्रजा इमाः सत्त्वरजस्तमोजुषः ।
समो भवांस्तास्वसुरादिषु प्रभो
तथापि भक्तं भजते महेश्वरः ॥ १४ ॥

tavaiva mārīca manaḥ-śarīrajāḥ
prajā imāḥ sattva-rajas-tamo-juṣaḥ
samo bhavāṁs tāsv asurādiṣu prabho
tathāpi bhaktaṁ bhajate maheśvaraḥ

tava—your; *eva*—indeed; *mārīca*—O son of Marīci; *manaḥ-śarīra-jāḥ*—born either of your body or of your mind (all the demons and demigods); *prajāḥ*—born of you; *imāḥ*—all of them; *sattva-rajaḥ-tamaḥ-juṣaḥ*—infected with *sattva-guṇa, rajo-guṇa* or *tamo-guṇa; samaḥ*—equal; *bhavān*—your good self; *tāsu*—to every one of them; *asura-ādiṣu*—beginning with the *asuras; prabho*—O my lord; *tathā api*—still; *bhaktam*—unto the devotees; *bhajate*—takes care of; *mahā-īśvaraḥ*—the Supreme Personality of Godhead, the supreme controller.

TRANSLATION

O son of Marīci, because you are a great personality you are equal toward all the demons and demigods, who are born either from your body or from your mind and who possess one or another of the three qualities —sattva-guṇa, rajo-guṇa or tamo-guṇa. But although the Supreme Personality of Godhead, the supreme controller, is equal toward all living entities, He is especially favorable to the devotees.

PURPORT

In *Bhagavad-gītā* (9.29) the Lord says:

samo 'haṁ sarva-bhūteṣu
na me dveṣyo 'sti na priyaḥ
ye bhajanti tu māṁ bhaktyā
mayi te teṣu cāpy aham

Although the Supreme Personality of Godhead is equal toward everyone, He is especially inclined toward those who engage in His devotional service. The Lord says, *kaunteya pratijānīhi na me bhaktaḥ praṇaśyati:* "My dear son of

Kuntī, please declare that My devotee will never be vanquished." Elsewhere, Kṛṣṇa also says:

ye yathā māṁ prapadyante
tāṁs tathaiva bhajāmy aham
mama vartmānuvartante
manuṣyāḥ pārtha sarvaśaḥ

(Bg. 4.11)

Actually, everyone is trying to please the Supreme Personality of Godhead in various ways, but according to their methods of approach, the Supreme Lord endows them with different benedictions. Thus Aditi appealed to her husband by saying that since even the supreme controller favors His devotees and since Indra, Kaśyapa's devoted son, was in difficulty, Kaśyapa should bestow his favor upon Indra.

TEXT 15

तस्मादीश भजन्त्या मे श्रेयश्चिन्तय सुव्रत ।
हृतश्रियो हृतस्थानान्सपत्नैः पाहि नः प्रभो ॥ १५ ॥

tasmād īśa bhajantyā me
śreyaś cintaya suvrata
hṛta-śriyo hṛta-sthānān
sapatnaiḥ pāhi naḥ prabho

tasmāt—therefore; *īśa*—O powerful controller; *bhajantyāḥ*—of your servitor; *me*—me; *śreyaḥ*—auspiciousness; *cintaya*—just consider; *su-vrata*—O most gentle one; *hṛta-śriyaḥ*—bereft of all opulence; *hṛta-sthānān*—bereft of a residence; *sapatnaiḥ*—by the competitors; *pāhi*—please protect; *naḥ*—us; *prabho*—O my lord.

TRANSLATION

Therefore, most gentle lord, kindly favor your maidservant. We have now been deprived of our opulence and residence by our competitors, the demons. Kindly give us protection.

PURPORT

Aditi, the mother of the demigods, appealed to Kaśyapa Muni to give the demigods protection. When we speak of the demigods, this also includes their mother.

TEXT 16

परैर्विवासिता साहं मग्ना व्यसनसागरे ।
ऐश्वर्यं श्रीर्यशः स्थानं हृतानि प्रबलैर्मम ॥ १६ ॥

parair vivāsitā sāhaṁ
magnā vyasana-sāgare
aiśvaryaṁ śrīr yaśaḥ sthānaṁ
hṛtāni prabalair mama

paraiḥ—by our enemies; *vivāsitā*—taken away from our residential quarters; *sā*—the same; *aham*—I; *magnā*—drowned; *vyasana-sāgare*—in an ocean of trouble; *aiśvaryam*—opulence; *śrīḥ*—beauty; *yaśaḥ*—reputation; *sthānam*—place; *hṛtāni*—all taken away; *prabalaiḥ*—very powerful; *mama*—my.

TRANSLATION

The demons, our formidably powerful enemies, have taken away our opulence, our beauty, our fame and even our residence. Indeed, we have now been exiled, and we are drowning in an ocean of trouble.

TEXT 17

यथा तानि पुनः साधो प्रपद्येरन् ममात्मजाः ।
तथा विधेहि कल्याणं धिया कल्याणकृत्तम ॥ १७ ॥

yathā tāni punaḥ sādho
prapadyeran mamātmajāḥ
tathā vidhehi kalyāṇaṁ
dhiyā kalyāṇa-kṛttama

yathā—as; *tāni*—all of our lost things; *punaḥ*—again; *sādho*—O great saintly person; *prapadyeran*—can regain; *mama*—my; *ātmajāḥ*—offspring (sons); *tathā*—so; *vidhehi*—kindly do; *kalyāṇam*—auspiciousness; *dhiyā*—by consideration; *kalyāṇa-kṛt-tama*—O you who are the best person to act for our welfare.

TRANSLATION

O best of sages, best of all those who grant auspicious benedictions, please consider our situation and bestow upon my sons the benedictions by which they can regain what they have lost.

TEXT 18

श्रीशुक उवाच
एवमभ्यर्थितोऽदित्या कस्तामाह स्मयन्निव ।
अहो मायाबलं विष्णोः स्नेहबद्धमिदं जगत् ॥ १८ ॥

śrī-śuka uvāca
evam abhyarthito 'dityā
kas tām āha smayann iva
aho māyā-balaṁ viṣṇoḥ
sneha-baddham idaṁ jagat

śrī-śukaḥ uvāca—Śrī Śukadeva Gosvāmī said; *evam*—in this way; *abhyarthitaḥ*—being requested; *adityā*—by Aditi; *kaḥ*—Kaśyapa Muni; *tām*—unto her; *āha*—said; *smayan*—smiling; *iva*—just like; *aho*—alas; *māyā-balam*—the influence of the illusory energy; *viṣṇoḥ*—of Lord Viṣṇu; *sneha-baddham*—influenced by this affection; *idam*—this; *jagat*—whole world.

TRANSLATION

Śukadeva Gosvāmī continued: When Kaśyapa Muni was thus requested by Aditi, he slightly smiled. "Alas," he said, "how powerful is the illusory energy of Lord Viṣṇu, by which the entire world is bound by affection for children!"

PURPORT

Kaśyapa Muni was surely sympathetic to his wife's affliction, yet he was surprised at how the whole world is influenced by affection.

TEXT 19

क्व देहो भौतिकोऽनात्मा क्व चात्मा प्रकृतेः परः ।
कस्य के पतिपुत्राद्या मोह एव हि कारणम् ॥ १९ ॥

kva deho bhautiko 'nātmā
kva cātmā prakṛteḥ paraḥ
kasya ke pati-putrādyā
moha eva hi kāraṇam

kva—where is; *dehaḥ*—this material body; *bhautikaḥ*—made of five elements; *anātmā*—not the spirit soul; *kva*—where is; *ca*—also; *ātmā*—the spirit soul; *prakṛteḥ*—to the material world; *paraḥ*—transcendental; *kasya*—of whom; *ke*—who is; *pati*—husband; *putra-ādyāḥ*—or son and so on; *mohaḥ*—illusion; *eva*—indeed; *hi*—certainly; *kāraṇam*—cause.

TRANSLATION

Kaśyapa Muni continued: What is this material body, made of five elements? It is different from the spirit soul. Indeed, the spirit soul is completely different from the material elements from which the body is made. But because of bodily attachment, one is regarded as a husband or son. These illusory relationships are caused by misunderstanding.

PURPORT

The spirit soul (*ātmā* or *jīva*) is certainly different from the body, which is a combination of five material elements. This is a simple fact, but it is not understood unless one is spiritually educated. Kaśyapa Muni met his wife, Aditi, in the heavenly planets, but the same misconception extends throughout the entire universe and is also here on earth. There are different grades of living entities, but all of them are more or less under the impression of the bodily conception of life. In other words, all living entities in this material world are more or less devoid of spiritual education. The Vedic civilization, however, is based on spiritual education, and spiritual education is the special basis on which *Bhagavad-gītā* was spoken to Arjuna. In the beginning of *Bhagavad-gītā,* Kṛṣṇa instructed Arjuna to understand that the spirit soul is different from the body.

dehino 'smin yathā dehe
kaumāraṁ yauvanaṁ jarā
tathā dehāntara-prāptir
dhīras tatra na muhyati

"As the embodied soul continually passes, in this body, from boyhood to youth to old age, the soul similarly passes into another body at death. The self-realized soul is not bewildered by such a change." (Bg. 2.13) Unfortunately, this spiritual education is completely absent from modern human civilization. No one understands his real self-interest, which lies with the spirit soul, not with the material body. Education means spiritual education. To work hard in the bodily conception of life, without spiritual education, is to live like an animal. *Nāyaṁ deho deha-bhājāṁ nṛ-loke kaṣṭān kāmān arhate viḍ-bhujāṁ ye* (*Bhāg.* 5.5.1). People are working so hard simply for bodily comforts, without education regarding the spirit soul. Thus they are living in a very risky civilization, for it is a fact that the spirit soul has to transmigrate from one body to another (*tathā dehāntara-prāptiḥ*). Without spiritual education, people are kept in dark ignorance and do not know what will happen to them after the annihilation of the present body. They are working blindly, and blind leaders are directing them. *Andhā yathāndhair upanīyamānās te 'pīśa-tantryām uru-dāmni baddhāḥ* (*Bhāg.* 7.5.31). A foolish person does not know that he is completely under the bondage of material nature and that after death material nature will impose upon him a certain type of body, which he will have to accept. He does not know that although in his present body he may be a very important man, he may next get the body of an animal or tree because of his ignorant activities in the modes of material nature. Therefore the Kṛṣṇa consciousness movement is trying to give the true light of spiritual existence to all living entities. This movement is not very difficult to understand, and people must take advantage of it, for it will save them from the risky life of irresponsibility.

TEXT 20

उपतिष्ठस्व पुरुषं भगवन्तं जनार्दनम् ।
सर्वभूतगुहावासं वासुदेवं जगद्गुरुम् ॥ २० ॥

upatiṣṭhasva puruṣaṁ
bhagavantaṁ janārdanam
sarva-bhūta-guhā-vāsaṁ
vāsudevaṁ jagad-gurum

upatiṣṭhasva—just try to worship; *puruṣam*—the Supreme Person; *bhagavantam*—the Personality of Godhead; *janārdanam*—who can kill all the enemies; *sarva-bhūta-guhā-vāsam*—living within the core of the heart of everyone; *vāsudevam*—Vāsudeva, Kṛṣṇa, who is all-pervading and is the son of Vasudeva; *jagat-gurum*—the spiritual master and teacher of the whole world.

TRANSLATION

My dear Aditi, engage in devotional service to the Supreme Personality of Godhead, who is the master of everything, who can subdue everyone's enemies, and who sits within everyone's heart. Only that Supreme Person—Kṛṣṇa, or Vāsudeva—can bestow all auspicious benedictions upon everyone, for He is the spiritual master of the universe.

PURPORT

With these words, Kaśyapa Muni tried to pacify his wife. Aditi made her appeal to her material husband. Of course, that is nice, but actually a material relative cannot do anything good for anyone. If anything good can be done, it is done by the Supreme Personality of Godhead, Vāsudeva. Therefore, Kaśyapa Muni advised his wife, Aditi, to begin worshiping Lord Vāsudeva, who is situated in everyone's heart. He is the friend of everyone and is known as Janārdana because He can kill all enemies. There are three modes of material nature—goodness, passion and ignorance—and above material nature, transcendental to material nature, is another existence, which is called *śuddha-sattva.* In the material world, the mode of goodness is considered the best, but because of material contamination, even the mode of goodness is sometimes overpowered by the modes of passion and ignorance. But when one transcends the competition between these modes and engages himself in devotional service, he rises above the three modes of material nature. In that transcendental position, one is situated in pure consciousness. *Sattvaṁ viśuddhaṁ vasudeva-śabditam* (*Bhā*g. 4.3.23). Above material nature is the position called *vasudeva,* or freedom from material contamination. Only in that position can one perceive the Supreme Personality of Godhead, Vāsudeva. Thus the *vasudeva* condition fulfills a spiritual necessity. *Vāsudevaḥ sarvam iti sa mahātmā sudurlabhaḥ* . When one realizes Vāsudeva, the Supreme Personality of Godhead, he becomes most exalted.

Paramātmā (Vāsudeva) is situated in everyone's heart, as confirmed in *Bhagavad-gītā.* The Lord says:

teṣāṁ satata-yuktānāṁ
bhajatāṁ prīti-pūrvakam
dadāmi buddhi-yogaṁ taṁ
yena mām upayānti te

"To those who are constantly devoted and who worship Me with love, I give the understanding by which they can come to Me." (Bg. 10.10)

īśvaraḥ sarva-bhūtānāṁ
hṛd-deśe 'rjuna tiṣṭhati

"The Supreme Lord is situated in everyone's heart, O Arjuna." (Bg. 18.61)

bhoktāraṁ yajña-tapasāṁ
sarva-loka-maheśvaram

suhṛdaṁ sarva-bhūtānāṁ
jñātvā māṁ śāntim ṛcchati

"The sages, knowing Me as the ultimate purpose of all sacrifices and austerities, the Supreme Lord of all planets and demigods and the benefactor and well-wisher of all living entities, attains peace from the pangs of material miseries." (Bg. 5.29)

Whenever one is perplexed, let him take shelter of the lotus feet of Vāsudeva, Kṛṣṇa, who will give the devotee intelligence to help him surpass all difficulties and return home, back to Godhead. Kaśyapa Muni advised his wife to seek shelter at the lotus feet of Vāsudeva, Kṛṣṇa, so that all her problems would be very easily solved. Thus Kaśyapa Muni was an ideal spiritual master. He was not so foolish that he would present himself as an exalted personality, as good as God. He was actually a bona fide *guru* because he advised his wife to seek shelter at the lotus feet of Vāsudeva. One who trains his subordinate or disciple to worship Vāsudeva is the truly bona fide spiritual master. The word *jagad-gurum* is very important in this regard. Kaśyapa Muni did not falsely declare himself to be *jagad-guru,* although he actually was *jagad-guru* because he advocated the cause of Vāsudeva. Actually, Vāsudeva is *jagad-guru,* as clearly stated here (*vāsudevaṁ jagad-gurum*). One who teaches the instructions of Vāsudeva, *Bhagavad-gītā,* is as good as *vāsudevaṁ jagad-gurum.* But when one who does not teach this instruction—as it is—declares himself *jagad-guru,* he simply cheats the public. Kṛṣṇa is *jagad-guru,* and one who teaches the instruction of Kṛṣṇa as it is, on behalf of Kṛṣṇa, may be accepted as *jagad-guru.* One who manufactures his own theories cannot be accepted; he becomes *jagad-guru* falsely.

TEXT 21

स विधास्यति ते कामान्हरिर्दीनानुकम्पनः ।
अमोघा भगवद्भक्तिर्नेतरेति मतिर्मम ॥ २१ ॥

sa vidhāsyati te kāmān
harir dīnānukampanaḥ
amoghā bhagavad-bhaktir
netareti matir mama

saḥ—he (Vāsudeva); *vidhāsyati*—will undoubtedly fulfill; *te*—your; *kāmān*—desires; *hariḥ*—the Supreme Personality of Godhead; *dīna*—unto the poor; *anukampanaḥ*—very merciful; *amoghā*—infallible; *bhagavat-bhaktiḥ*—devotional service unto the Supreme Personality of Godhead; *na*—not; *itarā*—anything but *bhagavad-bhakti; iti*—thus; *matiḥ*—opinion; *mama*—my.

TRANSLATION

The Supreme Personality of Godhead, who is very merciful to the poor, will fulfill all of your desires, for devotional service unto Him is infallible. Any method other than devotional service is useless. That is my opinion.

PURPORT

There are three kinds of men, who are called *akāma, mokṣa-kāma* and *sarva-kāma.* One who tries to get liberation from this material world is called *mokṣa-kāma,* one who wants to enjoy this material world to its fullest extent is called *sarva-kāma,* and one who has fulfilled all his desires and has no further material desires is called *akāma.* A *bhakta* has no desire. *Sarvopādhi-vinirmuktaṁ tat-paratvena nirmalam*. He is purified and free from material desires. The *mokṣa-kāmī* wants to achieve liberation by merging into the existence of the Supreme Brahman, and because of this desire to merge into the existence of the Lord, he is not yet pure. And since those who want liberation are impure, what to speak of the *karmīs,* who have so many desires to fulfill? Nonetheless, the *śāstra* says:

akāmaḥ sarva-kāmo vā
mokṣa-kāma udāra-dhīḥ
tīvreṇa bhakti-yogena
yajeta puruṣaṁ param

"Whether one desires everything or nothing or desires to merge into the existence of the Lord, he is intelligent only if he worships Lord Kṛṣṇa, the Supreme Personality of Godhead, by rendering transcendental loving service." (*Bhāg.* 2.3.10)

Kaśyapa Muni saw that his wife, Aditi, had some material desires for the welfare of her sons, but still he advised her to render devotional service to the Supreme Personality of Godhead. In other words, everyone, regardless of whether he is a *karmī, jñānī, yogī* or *bhakta,* should invariably take shelter of the lotus feet of Vāsudeva and render transcendental loving service unto Him so that all his desires will be duly fulfilled. Kṛṣṇa is *dīna-anukampana:* He is very merciful to everyone. Therefore if one wants to fulfill his material desires,

Kṛṣṇa helps him. Of course, sometimes if a devotee is very sincere, the Lord, as a special favor to him, refuses to fulfill his material desires and directly blesses him with pure, unalloyed devotional service. It is said in *Caitanya-caritāmṛta* (*Madhya* 22.38-39):

kṛṣṇa kahe,—'āmā bhaje, māge viṣaya-sukha
amṛta chāḍi' viṣa māge,—ei baḍa mūrkha
āmi—vijña, ei mūrkhe 'viṣaya' kene diba?
sva-caraṇāmṛta diyā 'viṣaya' bhulāiba

"Kṛṣṇa says, 'If one engages in My transcendental loving service but at the same time wants the opulence of material enjoyment, he is very, very foolish. Indeed, he is just like a person who gives up ambrosia to drink poison. Since I am very intelligent, why should I give this fool material prosperity? Instead I shall induce him to take the nectar of the shelter of My lotus feet and make him forget illusory material enjoyment.' " If a devotee maintains some material desire and at the same time very sincerely desires to engage at the lotus feet of Kṛṣṇa, Kṛṣṇa may directly give him unalloyed devotional service and take away all his material desires and possessions. This is the Lord's special favor to devotees. Otherwise, if one takes to Kṛṣṇa's devotional service but still has material desires to fulfill, he may become free from all material desires, as Dhruva Mahārāja did, but this may take some time. However, if a very sincere devotee wants only Kṛṣṇa's lotus feet, Kṛṣṇa directly gives him the position of *śuddha-bhakti,* unalloyed devotional service.

TEXT 22

श्रीअदितिरुवाच
केनाहं विधिना ब्रह्मन्नुपस्थास्ये जगत्पतिम् ।
यथा मे सत्यसङ्कल्पो विदध्यात् स मनोरथम् ॥ २२ ॥

śrī-aditir uvāca
kenāhaṁ vidhinā brahmann
upasthāsye jagat-patim
yathā me satya-saṅkalpo
vidadhyāt sa manoratham

śrī-aditiḥ uvāca—Śrīmatī Aditi began to pray; *kena*—by which; *aham*—I; *vidhinā*—by regulative principles; *brahman*—O *brāhmaṇa; upasthāsye*—can please; *jagat-patim*—the Lord of the universe, Jagannātha; *yathā*—by which; *me*—my; *satya-saṅkalpaḥ*—desire may actually be fulfilled; *vidadhyāt*—may fulfill; *saḥ*—He (the Supreme Lord); *manoratham*—ambitions or desires.

TRANSLATION

Śrīmatī Aditi said: O brāhmaṇa, tell me the regulative principles by which I may worship the supreme master of the world so that the Lord will be pleased with me and fulfill all my desires.

PURPORT

It is said, "Man proposes, God disposes." Thus a person may desire many things, but unless these desires are fulfilled by the Supreme Personality of Godhead, they cannot be fulfilled. Fulfillment of desire is called *satya-saṅkalpa.* Here the word *satya-saṅkalpa* is very important. Aditi placed herself at the mercy of her husband so that he would give her directions by which to worship the Supreme Personality of Godhead so that all her desires would be fulfilled. A disciple must first decide that he should worship the Supreme Lord, and then the spiritual master will give the disciple correct directions. One cannot dictate to the spiritual master, just as a patient cannot demand that his physician prescribe a certain type of medicine. Here is the beginning of worship of the Supreme Personality of Godhead. As confirmed in *Bhagavad-gītā* (7.16):

catur-vidhā bhajante māṁ
janāḥ sukṛtino 'rjuna
ārto jijñāsur arthārthī
jñānī ca bharatarṣabha

"O best among the Bhāratas, four kinds of pious men render devotional service unto Me—the distressed, the desirer of wealth, the inquisitive, and he who is searching for knowledge of the Absolute." Aditi was *ārta,* a person in distress. She was very much aggrieved because her sons, the demigods, were bereft of everything. Thus she wanted to take shelter of the Supreme Personality of Godhead under the direction of her husband, Kaśyapa Muni.

TEXT 23

आदिश त्वं द्विजश्रेष्ठ विधिं तदुपधावनम् ।
आशु तुष्यति मे देवः सीदन्त्याः सह पुत्रकैः ॥ २३ ॥

ādiśa tvaṁ dvija-śreṣṭha
vidhiṁ tad-upadhāvanam

āśu tuṣyati me devaḥ
sīdantyāḥ saha putrakaiḥ

ādiśa—just instruct me; *tvam*—O my husband; *dvija-śreṣṭha*—O best of the *brāhmaṇas; vidhim*—the regulative principles; *tat*—the Lord; *upadhāvanam*—the process of worshiping; *āśu*—very soon; *tuṣyati*—becomes satisfied; *me*—unto me; *devaḥ*—the Lord; *sīdantyāḥ*—now lamenting; *saha*—with; *putrakaiḥ*—all my sons, the demigods.

TRANSLATION

O best of the brāhmaṇas, kindly instruct me in the perfect method of worshiping the Supreme Personality of Godhead in devotional service, by which the Lord may very soon be pleased with me and save me, along with my sons, from this most dangerous condition.

PURPORT

Sometimes less intelligent men ask whether one has to approach a *guru* to be instructed in devotional service for spiritual advancement. The answer is given here—indeed, not only here, but also in *Bhagavad-gītā,* where Arjuna accepted Kṛṣṇa as his *guru* (*śiṣyas te 'haṁ śādhi māṁ tvāṁ prapannam*). The *Vedas* also instruct, *tad-vijñānārthaṁ sa guruṁ evābhigacchet:* one must accept a *guru* for proper direction if one is seriously inclined toward advancement in spiritual life. The Lord says that one must worship the *ācārya,* who is the representative of the Supreme Personality of Godhead (*ācāryaṁ māṁ vijānīyāt*). One should definitely understand this. In *Caitanya-caritāmṛta* it is said that the *guru* is the manifestation of the Supreme Personality of Godhead. Therefore, according to all the evidence given by the *śāstra* and by the practical behavior of devotees, one must accept a *guru.* Aditi accepted her husband as her *guru,* so that he would direct her how to advance in spiritual consciousness, devotional service, by worshiping the Supreme Lord.

TEXT 24

श्रीकश्यप उवाच
एतन्मे भगवान्पृष्टः प्रजाकामस्य पद्मजः ।
यदाह ते प्रवक्ष्यामि व्रतं केशवतोषणम् ॥ २४ ॥

śrī-kaśyapa uvāca
etan me bhagavān pṛṣṭaḥ
prajā-kāmasya padmajaḥ

yad āha te pravakṣyāmi
vrataṁ keśava-toṣaṇam

śrī-kaśyapaḥ uvāca—Kaśyapa Muni said; *etat*—this; *me*—by me; *bhagavān*—the most powerful; *pṛṣṭaḥ*—when he was requested; *prajā-kāmasya*—desiring offspring; *padma-jaḥ*—Lord Brahmā, who was born of a lotus flower; *yat*—whatever; *āha*—he said; *te*—unto you; *pravakṣyāmi*—I shall explain; *vratam*—in the form of worship; *keśava-toṣaṇam*—by which Keśava, the Supreme Personality of Godhead, is satisfied.

TRANSLATION

Śrī Kaśyapa Muni said: When I desired offspring, I placed inquiries before Lord Brahmā, who is born from a lotus flower. Now I shall explain to you the same process Lord Brahmā instructed me, by which Keśava, the Supreme Personality of Godhead, is satisfied.

PURPORT

Here the process of devotional service is further explained. Kaśyapa Muni wanted to instruct Aditi in the same process recommended to him by Brahmā for satisfying the Supreme Personality of Godhead. This is valuable. The *guru* does not manufacture a new process to instruct the disciple. The disciple receives from the *guru* an authorized process received by the *guru* from his *guru.* This is called the system of disciplic succession (*evaṁ paramparā-prāptam imaṁ rājarṣayo viduḥ*). This is the bona fide Vedic system of receiving the process of devotional service, by which the Supreme Personality of Godhead is pleased. Therefore, to approach a bona fide *guru,* or spiritual master, is essential. The bona fide spiritual master is he who has received the mercy of his *guru,* who in turn is bona fide because he has received the mercy of his *guru.* This is called the *paramparā* system. Unless one follows this *paramparā* system, the *mantra* one receives will be chanted for no purpose. Nowadays there are so many rascal *gurus* who manufacture their *mantras* as a process for material advancement, not spiritual advancement. Still, the *mantra* cannot be successful if it is manufactured. *Mantras* and the process of devotional service have special power, provided they are received from the authorized person.

TEXT 25

फाल्गुनस्यामले पक्षे द्वादशाहं पयोव्रतम् ।
अर्चयेदरविन्दाक्षं भक्त्या परमयान्वितः ॥ २५ ॥

phālgunasyāmale pakṣe
dvādaśāhaṁ payo-vratam
arcayed aravindākṣaṁ
bhaktyā paramayānvitaḥ

phālgunasya—of the month of Phālguna (February and March); *amale*—during the bright; *pakṣe*—fortnight; *dvādaśa-aham*—for twelve days, ending with Dvādaśī, the day after Ekādaśī; *payaḥ-vratam*—accepting the vow of taking only milk; *arcayet*—one should worship; *aravinda-akṣam*—the lotus-eyed Supreme Personality of Godhead; *bhaktyā*—with devotion; *paramayā*—unalloyed; *anvitaḥ*—surcharged.

TRANSLATION

In the bright fortnight of the month of Phālguna [February and March], for twelve days ending with Dvādaśī, one should observe the vow of subsisting only on milk and should worship the lotus-eyed Supreme Personality of Godhead with all devotion.

PURPORT

Worshiping the Supreme Lord Viṣṇu with devotion means following *arcana-mārga.*

śravaṇaṁ kīrtanaṁ viṣṇoḥ
smaraṇaṁ pāda-sevanam
arcanaṁ vandanaṁ dāsyaṁ
sakhyam ātma-nivedanam

One should install the Deity of Lord Viṣṇu or Kṛṣṇa and worship Him nicely by dressing Him, decorating Him with flower garlands, and offering Him all kinds of fruits, flowers and cooked food, nicely prepared with ghee, sugar and grains. One should also offer a flame, incense and so on, while ringing a bell, as prescribed. This is called worship of the Lord. Here it is recommended that one observe the vow of subsisting only by drinking milk. This is called *payo-vrata.* As we generally perform devotional service on Ekādaśī by not eating grains, it is generally recommended that on Dvādaśī one not consume anything but milk. *Payo-vrata* and *arcana* devotional service to the Supreme Lord should be performed with a pure devotional attitude (*bhaktyā*). Without *bhakti,* one cannot worship the Supreme Personality of Godhead. *Bhaktyā mām abhijānāti yāvān yaś cāsmi tattvataḥ* . If one wants to know the Supreme Personality of Godhead and be directly connected with Him, knowing what He wants to eat and how He is satisfied, one must take to the process of *bhakti.* As recommended here also, *bhaktyā paramayānvitaḥ:* one should be surcharged with unalloyed devotional service.

TEXT 26

सिनीवाल्यां मृदालिप्य स्नायात् क्रोडविदीर्णया।
यदि लभ्येत वै स्रोतस्येतं मन्त्रमुदीरयेत् ॥ २६ ॥

sinīvālyāṁ mṛdālipya
snāyāt kroḍa-vidīrṇayā
yadi labhyeta vai srotasy
etaṁ mantram udīrayet

sinīvālyām—on the dark-moon day; *mṛdā*—with dirt; *ālipya*—smearing the body; *snāyāt*—one should bathe; *kroḍa-vidīrṇayā*—dug up by the tusk of a boar; *yadi*—if; *labhyeta*—it is available; *vai*—indeed; *srotasi*—in a flowing river; *etam mantram*—this *mantra; udīrayet*—one should chant.

TRANSLATION

If dirt dug up by a boar is available, on the day of the dark moon one should smear this dirt on his body and then bathe in a flowing river. While bathing, one should chant the following mantra.

TEXT 27

त्वं देव्यादिवराहेण रसायाः स्थानमिच्छता।
उद्धृतासि नमस्तुभ्यं पाप्मानं मे प्रणाशय ॥ २७ ॥

tvaṁ devy ādi-varāheṇa
rasāyāḥ sthānam icchatā
uddhṛtāsi namas tubhyaṁ
pāpmānaṁ me praṇāśaya

tvam—you; *devi*—O mother earth; *ādi-varāheṇa*—by the Supreme Personality of Godhead in the form of a boar; *rasāyāḥ*—from the bottom of the universe; *sthānam*—a place; *icchatā*—desiring; *uddhṛtā asi*—you have been raised; *namaḥ tubhyam*—I offer my respectful obeisances unto you; *pāpmānam*—all sinful activities and their reactions; *me*—of me; *praṇāśaya*—please undo.

TRANSLATION

O mother earth, you were raised by the Supreme Personality of Godhead in the form of a boar because of your desiring to have a place to stay. I pray that you kindly vanquish all the reactions of my sinful life. I offer my respectful obeisances unto you.

TEXT 28

निर्वर्तितात्मनियमो देवमर्चेत् समाहितः ।
अर्चायां स्थण्डिले सूर्ये जले वह्नौ गुरावपि ॥ २८ ॥

nirvartitātma-niyamo
devam arcet samāhitaḥ
arcāyāṁ sthaṇḍile sūrye
jale vahnau gurāv api

nirvartita—finished; *ātma-niyamaḥ*—the daily duties of washing, chanting other *mantras* and so on, according to one's practice; *devam*—the Supreme Personality of Godhead; *arcet*—one should worship; *samāhitaḥ*—with full attention; *arcāyām*—unto the Deities; *sthaṇḍile*—unto the altar; *sūrye*—unto the sun; *jale*—unto the water; *vahnau*—unto the fire; *gurau*—unto the spiritual master; *api*—indeed.

TRANSLATION

Thereafter, one should perform his daily spiritual duties and then, with great attention, offer worship to the Deity of the Supreme Personality of Godhead, and also to the altar, the sun, water, fire and the spiritual master.

TEXT 29

नमस्तुभ्यं भगवते पुरुषाय महीयसे ।
सर्वभूतनिवासाय वासुदेवाय साक्षिणे ॥ २९ ॥

namas tubhyaṁ bhagavate
puruṣāya mahīyase
sarva-bhūta-nivāsāya
vāsudevāya sākṣiṇe

namaḥ tubhyam—I offer my respectful obeisances unto You; *bhagavate*—unto the Supreme Personality of Godhead; *puruṣāya*—the Supreme Person; *mahīyase*—the best of all personalities; *sarva-bhūta-nivāsāya*—the person who lives in everyone's heart; *vāsudevāya*—the Lord who lives everywhere; *sākṣiṇe*—the witness of everything.

TRANSLATION

O Supreme Personality of Godhead, greatest of all, who lives in everyone's heart and in whom everyone lives, O witness of everything, O Vāsudeva, supreme and all-pervading person, I offer my respectful obeisances unto You.

TEXT 30

नमोऽव्यक्ताय सूक्ष्माय प्रधानपुरुषाय च ।
चतुर्विंशद्गुणज्ञाय गुणसंख्यानहेतवे ॥ ३० ॥

namo 'vyaktāya sūkṣmāya
pradhāna-puruṣāya ca
catur-viṁśad-guṇa-jñāya
guṇa-saṅkhyāna-hetave

namaḥ—I offer my respectful obeisances unto You; *avyaktāya*—who are never seen by material eyes; *sūkṣmāya*—transcendental; *pradhāna-puruṣāya*—the Supreme Person; *ca*—also; *catuḥ-viṁśat*—twenty-four; *guṇa-jñāya*—the knower of the elements; *guṇa-saṅkhyāna*—of the *sāṅkhya-yoga* system; *hetave*—the original cause.

TRANSLATION

I offer my respectful obeisances unto You, the Supreme Person. Being very subtle, You are never visible to material eyes. You are the knower of the twenty-four elements, and You are the inaugurator of the sāṅkhya-yoga system.

PURPORT

Catur-viṁśad-guṇa, the twenty-four elements, are the five gross elements (earth, water, fire, air and ether), the three subtle elements (mind, intelligence and false ego), the ten senses (five for working and five for acquiring knowledge), the five sense objects, and contaminated consciousness. These are the subject matter of *sāṅkhya-yoga,* which was inaugurated by Lord Kapiladeva. This *sāṅkhya-yoga* was again propounded by another Kapila, but he was an atheist, and his system is not accepted as bona fide.

TEXT 31

नमो द्विशीर्ष्णे त्रिपदे चतुःशृङ्गाय तन्तवे ।
सप्तहस्ताय यज्ञाय त्रयीविद्यात्मने नमः ॥ ३१ ॥

namo dvi-śīrṣṇe tri-pade
catuḥ-śṛṅgāya tantave
sapta-hastāya yajñāya
trayī-vidyātmane namaḥ

namaḥ—I offer my respectful obeisances unto You; *dvi-śīrṣṇe*—who have two heads; *tri-pade*—who have three legs; *catuḥ-śṛṅgāya*—who have four horns; *tantave*—who expand; *sapta-hastāya*—who have seven hands; *yajñāya*—unto the *yajña-puruṣa,* the supreme enjoyer; *trayī*—the three modes of Vedic ritualistic ceremonies; *vidyā-ātmane*—the Personality of Godhead, the embodiment of all knowledge; *namaḥ*—I offer my respectful obeisances unto You.

TRANSLATION

I offer my respectful obeisances unto You, the Supreme Personality of Godhead, who have two heads [prāyaṇīya and udāyanīya], three legs [savana-traya], four horns [the four Vedas] and seven hands [the seven chandas, such as Gāyatrī]. I offer my obeisances unto You, whose heart and soul are the three Vedic rituals [karma-kāṇḍa, jñāna-kāṇḍa and upāsanā-kāṇḍa] and who expand these rituals in the form of sacrifice.

TEXT 32

नमः शिवाय रुद्राय नमः शक्तिधराय च ।
सर्वविद्याधिपतये भूतानां पतये नमः ॥ ३२ ॥

namaḥ śivāya rudrāya
namaḥ śakti-dharāya ca
sarva-vidyādhipataye
bhūtānāṁ pataye namaḥ

namaḥ—I offer my respectful obeisances unto You; *śivāya*—the incarnation named Lord Śiva; *rudrāya*—the expansion named Rudra; *namaḥ*—obeisances; *śakti-dharāya*—the reservoir of all potencies; *ca*—and; *sarva-vidyā-adhipataye*—the reservoir of all knowledge; *bhūtānām*—of the living entities; *pataye*—the supreme master; *namaḥ*—I offer my respectful obeisances unto You.

TRANSLATION

I offer my respectful obeisances unto You, Lord Śiva, or Rudra, who are the reservoir of all potencies, the reservoir of all knowledge, and the master of everyone.

PURPORT

It is the system for one to offer obeisances unto the expansion or incarnation of the Lord. Lord Śiva is the incarnation of ignorance, one of the material modes of nature.

TEXT 33

नमो हिरण्यगर्भाय प्राणाय जगदात्मने ।
योगैश्वर्यशरीराय नमस्ते योगहेतवे ॥ ३३ ॥

namo hiraṇyagarbhāya
prāṇāya jagad-ātmane
yogaiśvarya-śarīrāya
namas te yoga-hetave

namaḥ—I offer my respectful obeisances unto You; *hiraṇyagarbhāya*—situated as the four-headed Hiraṇyagarbha, Brahmā; *prāṇāya*—the source of everyone's life; *jagat-ātmane*—the Supersoul of the entire universe; *yoga-aiśvarya-śarīrāya*—whose body is full of opulences and mystic power; *namaḥ te*—I offer my respectful obeisances unto You; *yoga-hetave*—the original master of all mystic power.

TRANSLATION

I offer my respectful obeisances unto You, who are situated as Hiraṇyagarbha, the source of life, the Supersoul of every living entity. Your body is the source of the opulence of all mystic power. I offer my respectful obeisances unto You.

TEXT 34

नमस्त आदिदेवाय साक्षिभूताय ते नमः ।
नारायणाय ऋषये नराय हरये नमः ॥ ३४ ॥

namas ta ādi-devāya
sākṣi-bhūtāya te namaḥ
nārāyaṇāya ṛṣaye
narāya haraye namaḥ

namaḥ te—I offer my respectful obeisances unto You; *ādi-devāya*—who are the original Personality of Godhead; *sākṣi-bhūtāya*—the witness of everything within the heart of everyone; *te*—unto You; *namaḥ*—I offer my respectful obeisances; *nārāyaṇāya*—who take the incarnation of Nārāyaṇa; *ṛṣaye*—the sage; *narāya*—the incarnation of a human being; *haraye*—unto the Supreme Personality of Godhead; *namaḥ*—I offer my respectful obeisances.

TRANSLATION

I offer my respectful obeisances unto You, who are the original Personality of Godhead, the witness in everyone's heart, and the incarnation of Nara-Nārāyaṇa Ṛṣi in the form of a human being. O Personality of Godhead, I offer my respectful obeisances unto You.

TEXT 35

नमो मरकतश्यामवपुषेऽधिगतश्रिये ।
केशवाय नमस्तुभ्यं नमस्ते पीतवाससे ॥ ३५ ॥

namo marakata-śyāma-
vapuṣe 'dhigata-śriye
keśavāya namas tubhyaṁ
namas te pīta-vāsase

namaḥ—I offer my respectful obeisances unto You; *marakata-śyāma-vapuṣe*—whose bodily hue is blackish like the *marakata* gem; *adhigata-śriye*—under whose control is mother Lakṣmī, the goddess of fortune; *keśavāya*—Lord Keśava, who killed the Keśī demon; *namaḥ tubhyam*—I offer my respectful obeisances unto You; *namaḥ te*—again I offer my respectful obeisances unto You; *pīta-vāsase*—whose garment is yellow.

TRANSLATION

My Lord, I offer my respectful obeisances unto You, who are dressed in yellow garments, whose bodily hue resembles the marakata gem, and who have full control over the goddess of fortune. O my Lord Keśava, I offer my respectful obeisances unto You.

TEXT 36

त्वं सर्ववरदः पुंसां वरेण्य वरदर्षभ ।
अतस्ते श्रेयसे धीराः पादरेणुमुपासते ॥ ३६ ॥

tvaṁ sarva-varadaḥ puṁsāṁ
vareṇya varadarṣabha
atas te śreyase dhīrāḥ
pāda-reṇum upāsate

tvam—You; *sarva-vara-daḥ*—who can give all kinds of benedictions; *puṁsām*—to all living entities; *vareṇya*—O most worshipable; *vara-da-ṛṣabha*—O most powerful of all givers of benediction; *ataḥ*—for this reason; *te*—Your; *śreyase*—the source of all auspiciousness; *dhīrāḥ*—the most sober; *pāda-reṇum upāsate*—worship the dust of the lotus feet.

TRANSLATION

O most exalted and worshipable Lord, best of those who bestow benediction, You can fulfill the desires of everyone, and therefore those who are sober, for their own welfare, worship the dust of Your lotus feet.

TEXT 37

अन्ववर्तन्त यं देवाः श्रीश्च तत्पादपद्मयोः ।
स्पृहयन्त इवामोदं भगवान्मे प्रसीदताम् ॥ ३७ ॥

anvavartanta yaṁ devāḥ
śrīś ca tat-pāda-padmayoḥ
spṛhayanta ivāmodaṁ
bhagavān me prasīdatām

anvavartanta—engaged in devotional service; *yam*—unto whom; *devāḥ*—all the demigods; *śrīḥ ca*—and the goddess of fortune; *tat-pāda-padmayoḥ*—of the lotus feet of His Lordship; *spṛhayantaḥ*—desiring; *iva*—exactly; *āmodam*—celestial bliss; *bhagavān*—the Supreme Personality of Godhead; *me*—upon me; *prasīdatām*—may be pleased.

TRANSLATION

All the demigods, as well as the goddess of fortune, engage in the service of His lotus feet. Indeed, they respect the fragrance of those lotus feet. May the Supreme Personality of Godhead be pleased with me.

TEXT 38

एतैर्मन्त्रैर्हृषीकेशमावाहनपुरस्कृतम् ।
अर्चयेच्छ्रद्धया युक्तः पाद्योपस्पर्शनादिभिः ॥ ३८ ॥

etair mantrair hṛṣīkeśam
āvāhana-puraskṛtam
arcayec chraddhayā yuktaḥ
pādyopasparśanādibhiḥ

etaiḥ mantraiḥ—by chanting all these *mantras; hṛṣīkeśam*—unto the Supreme Personality of Godhead, the master of all senses; *āvāhana*—calling; *puraskṛtam*—honoring Him in all respects; *arcayet*—one should worship; *śraddhayā*—with faith and devotion; *yuktaḥ*—engaged; *pādya-upasparśana-ādibhiḥ*—with the paraphernalia of worship (*pādya, arghya,* etc.).

TRANSLATION

Kaśyapa Muni continued: By chanting all these mantras, welcoming the Supreme Personality of Godhead with faith and devotion, and offering Him items of worship [such as pādya and arghya], one should worship Keśava, Hṛṣīkeśa, Kṛṣṇa, the Supreme Personality of Godhead.

TEXT 39

अर्चित्वा गन्धमाल्याद्यैः पयसा स्नपयेद् विभुम् ।
वस्त्रोपवीताभरणपाद्योपस्पर्शनैस्ततः ।
गन्धधूपादिभिश्चार्चेद् द्वादशाक्षरविद्यया ॥ ३९ ॥

arcitvā gandha-mālyādyaiḥ
payasā snapayed vibhum
vastropavītābharaṇa-
pādyopasparśanais tataḥ
gandha-dhūpādibhiś cārced
dvādaśākṣara-vidyayā

arcitvā—worshiping in this way; *gandha-mālya-ādyaiḥ*—with incense, flower garlands, etc.; *payasā*—with milk; *snapayet*—should bathe; *vibhum*—the Lord; *vastra*—dress; *upavīta*—sacred thread; *ābharaṇa*—ornaments; *pādya*—water for washing the lotus feet; *upasparśanaiḥ*—touching; *tataḥ*—

thereafter; *gandha*—fragrance; *dhūpa*—incense; *ādibhiḥ*—with all of these; *ca*—and; *arcet*—should worship; *dvādaśa-akṣara-vidyayā*—with the *mantra* of twelve syllables.

TRANSLATION

In the beginning, the devotee should chant the dvādaśākṣara-mantra and offer flower garlands, incense and so on. After worshiping the Lord in this way, one should bathe the Lord with milk and dress Him with proper garments, a sacred thread, and ornaments. After offering water to wash the Lord's feet, one should again worship the Lord with fragrant flowers, incense and other paraphernalia.

PURPORT

The *dvādaśākṣara-mantra* is *oṁ namo bhagavate vāsudevāya.* While worshiping the Deity, one should ring a bell with his left hand and offer *pādya, arghya, vastra, gandha, mālā, ābharaṇa, bhūṣaṇa* and so on. In this way, one should bathe the Lord with milk, dress Him and again worship Him with all paraphernalia.

TEXT 40

शृतं पयसि नैवेद्यं शाल्यन्नं विभवे सति ।
ससर्पिः सगुडं दत्त्वा जुहुयान्मूलविद्यया ॥ ४० ॥

śṛtaṁ payasi naivedyaṁ
śāly-annaṁ vibhave sati
sasarpiḥ saguḍaṁ dattvā
juhuyān mūla-vidyayā

śṛtam—cooked; *payasi*—in milk; *naivedyam*—offering to the Deity; *śāli-annam*—fine rice; *vibhave*—if available; *sati*—in this way; *sa-sarpiḥ*—with ghee (clarified butter); *sa-guḍam*—with molasses; *dattvā*—offering Him; *juhuyāt*—should offer oblations in the fire; *mūla-vidyayā*—with chanting of the same *dvādaśākṣara-mantra*

TRANSLATION

If one can afford to, one should offer the Deity fine rice boiled in milk with clarified butter and molasses. While chanting the same original mantra, one should offer all this to the fire.

TEXT 41

निवेदितं तद्भक्ताय दद्याद्भुञ्जीत वा स्वयम् ।
दत्त्वाचमनमर्चित्वा ताम्बूलं च निवेदयेत् ॥ ४१ ॥

niveditaṁ tad-bhaktāya
dadyād bhuñjīta vā svayam
dattvācamanam arcitvā
tāmbūlaṁ ca nivedayet

niveditam—this offering of *prasāda; tat-bhaktāya*—unto His devotee; *dadyāt*—should be offered; *bhuñjīta*—one should take; *vā*—either; *svayam*—personally; *dattvā ācamanam*—giving water to wash the hands and mouth; *arcitvā*—in this way worshiping the Deity; *tāmbūlam*—betel nuts with spices; *ca*—also; *nivedayet*—one should offer.

TRANSLATION

One should offer all the prasāda to a Vaiṣṇava or offer him some of the prasāda and then take some oneself. After this, one should offer the Deity ācamana and then betel nut and then again worship the Lord.

TEXT 42

जपेदष्टोत्तरशतं स्तुवीत स्तुतिभिः प्रभुम् ।
कृत्वा प्रदक्षिणं भूमौ प्रणमेद् दण्डवन्मुदा ॥ ४२ ॥

japed aṣṭottara-śataṁ
stuvīta stutibhiḥ prabhum
kṛtvā pradakṣiṇaṁ bhūmau
praṇamed daṇḍavan mudā

japet—should silently murmur; *aṣṭottara-śatam*—108 times; *stuvīta*—should offer prayers; *stutibhiḥ*—by various prayers of glorification; *prabhum*—unto the Lord; *kṛtvā*—thereafter doing; *pradakṣiṇam*—circumambulation; *bhūmau*—on the ground; *praṇamet*—should offer obeisances; *daṇḍavat*—straight, with the whole body; *mudā*—with great satisfaction.

TRANSLATION

Thereafter, one should silently murmur the mantra 108 times and offer prayers to the Lord for His glorification. Then one should circumambulate

the Lord and finally, with great delight and satisfaction, offer obeisances, falling straight like a rod [daṇḍavat].

TEXT 43

कृत्वा शिरसि तच्छेषां देवमुद्वासयेत् ततः ।
द्व्यवरान्भोजयेद् विप्रान्पायसेन यथोचितम् ॥ ४३ ॥

kṛtvā śirasi tac-cheṣāṁ
devam udvāsayet tataḥ
dvy-avarān bhojayed viprān
pāyasena yathocitam

kṛtvā—taking; *śirasi*—on the head; *tat-śeṣām*—all the remnants (the water and flowers offered to the Deity); *devam*—unto the Deity; *udvāsayet*—should be thrown into a sacred place; *tataḥ*—thereafter; *dvi-avarān*—a minimum of two; *bhojayet*—should feed; *viprān*—*brāhmaṇas; pāyasena*—with sweet rice; *yathā-ucitam*—as each deserves.

TRANSLATION

After touching to one's head all the flowers and water offered to the Deity, one should throw them into a sacred place. Then one should feed at least two brāhmaṇas with sweet rice.

TEXTS 44-45

भुञ्जीत तैरनुज्ञातः सेष्टः शेषं सभाजितैः ।
ब्रह्मचार्यथ तद्रात्र्यां श्वोभूते प्रथमेऽहनि ॥ ४४ ॥
स्नातः शुचिर्यथोक्तेन विधिना सुसमाहितः ।
पयसा स्नापयित्वार्चेद् यावद्व्रतसमापनम् ॥ ४५ ॥

bhuñjīta tair anujñātaḥ
seṣṭaḥ śeṣaṁ sabhājitaiḥ
brahmacāry atha tad-rātryāṁ
śvo bhūte prathame 'hani

snātaḥ śucir yathoktena
vidhinā susamāhitaḥ

payasā snāpayitvārced
yāvad vrata-samāpanam

bhuñjīta—should take the *prasāda; taiḥ*—by the *brāhmaṇas; anujñātaḥ*—being permitted; *sa-iṣṭaḥ*—with friends and relatives; *śeṣam*—the remnants; *sabhājitaiḥ*—properly honored; *brahmacārī*—observance of celibacy; *atha*—of course; *tat-rātryām*—at night; *śvaḥ bhūte*—at the end of the night, when the morning comes; *prathame ahani*—on the first day; *snātaḥ*—bathing; *śuciḥ*—becoming purified; *yathā-uktena*—as stated before; *vidhinā*—by following the regulative principles; *su-samāhitaḥ*—with great attention; *payasā*—with milk; *snāpayitvā*—bathing the Deity; *arcet*—should offer worship; *yāvat*—as long as; *vrata-samāpanam*—the period of worship is not over.

TRANSLATION

One should perfectly honor the respectable brāhmaṇas one has fed, and then, after taking their permission, one should take prasāda with his friends and relatives. For that night, one should observe strict celibacy, and the next morning, after bathing again, with purity and attention one should bathe the Deity of Viṣṇu with milk and worship Him according to the methods formerly stated in detail.

TEXT 46

पयोभक्षो व्रतमिदं चरेद् विष्णवर्चनादृतः ।
पूर्ववज्जुहुयादग्निं ब्राह्मणांश्चापि भोजयेत् ॥ ४६ ॥

payo-bhakṣo vratam idaṁ
cared viṣṇv-arcanādṛtaḥ
pūrvavaj juhuyād agniṁ
brāhmaṇāṁś cāpi bhojayet

payaḥ-bhakṣaḥ—one who drinks milk only; *vratam idam*—this process of worshiping with a vow; *caret*—one should execute; *viṣṇu-arcana-ādṛtaḥ*—worshiping Lord Viṣṇu with great faith and devotion; *pūrva-vat*—as prescribed previously; *juhuyāt*—one should offer oblations; *agnim*—into the fire; *brāhmaṇān*—unto the *brāhmaṇas; ca api*—as well as; *bhojayet*—should feed.

TRANSLATION

Worshiping Lord Viṣṇu with great faith and devotion and living only by drinking milk, one should follow this vow. One should also offer oblations to the fire and feed the brāhmaṇas as mentioned before.

TEXT 47

एवं त्वहरहः कुर्याद् द्वादशाहं पयोव्रतम् ।
हरेराराधनं होममर्हणं द्विजतर्पणम् ॥ ४७ ॥

evaṁ tv ahar ahaḥ kuryād
dvādaśāhaṁ payo-vratam
harer ārādhanaṁ homam
arhaṇaṁ dvija-tarpaṇam

evam—in this way; *tu*—indeed; *ahaḥ ahaḥ*—day after day; *kuryāt*—should execute; *dvādaśa-aham*—until twelve days; *payaḥ-vratam*—the observance of the *vrata* known as *payo-vrata; hareḥ ārādhanam*—worshiping the Supreme Personality of Godhead; *homam*—by executing a fire sacrifice; *arhaṇam*—worshiping the Deity; *dvija-tarpaṇam*—and satisfying the *brāhmaṇas* by feeding them.

TRANSLATION

In this way, until twelve days have passed, one should observe this payo-vrata, worshiping the Lord every day, executing the routine duties, performing sacrifices and feeding the brāhmaṇas.

TEXT 48

प्रतिपद्दिनमारभ्य यावच्छुक्लत्रयोदशीम् ।
ब्रह्मचर्यमधःस्वप्नं स्नानं त्रिषवणं चरेत् ॥ ४८ ॥

pratipad-dinam ārabhya
yāvac chukla-trayodaśīm
brahmacaryam adhaḥ-svapnaṁ
snānaṁ tri-ṣavaṇaṁ caret

pratipat-dinam—on the day of *pratipat; ārabhya*—beginning; *yāvat*—until; *śukla*—of the bright fortnight; *trayodaśīm*—the thirteenth day of the moon (the second day after Ekādaśī); *brahmacaryam*—observing complete celibacy; *adhaḥ-svapnam*—lying down on the floor; *snānam*—bathing; *tri-savanam*—three times (morning, evening and noon); *caret*—one should execute.

TRANSLATION

From pratipat until the thirteenth day of the next bright moon [śukla-trayodaśī], one should observe complete celibacy, sleep on the floor, bathe three times a day and thus execute the vow.

TEXT 49

वर्जयेदसदालापं भोगानुच्चावचांस्तथा ।
अहिंस्रः सर्वभूतानां वासुदेवपरायणः ॥ ४९ ॥

varjayed asad-ālāpaṁ
bhogān uccāvacāṁs tathā
ahiṁsraḥ sarva-bhūtānāṁ
vāsudeva-parāyaṇaḥ

varjayet—one should give up; *asat-ālāpam*—unnecessary talk on material subject matters; *bhogān*—sense gratification; *ucca-avacān*—superior or inferior; *tathā*—as well as; *ahiṁsraḥ*—without being envious; *sarva-bhūtānām*—of all living entities; *vāsudeva-parāyaṇaḥ*—simply being a devotee of Lord Vāsudeva.

TRANSLATION

During this period, one should not unnecessarily talk of material subjects or topics of sense gratification, one should be completely free from envy of all living entities, and one should be a pure and simple devotee of Lord Vāsudeva.

TEXT 50

त्रयोदश्यामथो विष्णोः स्नपनं पञ्चकैर्विभोः ।
कारयेच्छास्त्रदृष्टेन विधिना विधिकोविदैः ॥ ५० ॥

trayodaśyām atho viṣṇoḥ
snapanaṁ pañcakair vibhoḥ

kārayec chāstra-dṛṣṭena
vidhinā vidhi-kovidaiḥ

trayodaśyām—on the thirteenth day of the moon; *atho*—thereafter; *viṣṇoḥ*—of Lord Viṣṇu; *snapanam*—bathing; *pañcakaiḥ*—by *pañcāmṛta,* five substances; *vibhoḥ*—the Lord; *kārayet*—one should execute; *śāstra-dṛṣṭena*—enjoined in the scripture; *vidhinā*—under regulative principles; *vidhi-kovidaiḥ*—assisted by the priests who know the regulative principles.

TRANSLATION

Thereafter, following the directions of the śāstra with help from brāhmaṇas who know the śāstra, on the thirteenth day of the moon one should bathe Lord Viṣṇu with five substances [milk, yogurt, ghee, sugar and honey].

TEXTS 51-52

पूजां च महतीं कुर्याद् वित्तशाठ्यविवर्जितः ।
चरुं निरूप्य पयसि शिपिविष्टाय विष्णवे ॥ ५१ ॥
सूक्तेन तेन पुरुषं यजेत सुसमाहितः ।
नैवेद्यं चातिगुणवद् दद्यात्पुरुषतुष्टिदम् ॥ ५२ ॥

pūjāṁ ca mahatīṁ kuryād
vitta-śāṭhya-vivarjitaḥ
caruṁ nirūpya payasi
śipiviṣṭāya viṣṇave

sūktena tena puruṣaṁ
yajeta susamāhitaḥ
naivedyaṁ cātiguṇavad
dadyāt puruṣa-tuṣṭidam

pūjām—worship; *ca*—also; *mahatīm*—very gorgeous; *kuryāt*—should do; *vitta-śāṭhya*—miserly mentality (not spending sufficient money); *vivarjitaḥ*—giving up; *carum*—grains offered in the *yajña; nirūpya*—seeing properly; *payasi*—with milk; *śipiviṣṭāya*—unto the Supersoul, who is situated in the heart of every living entity; *viṣṇave*—unto Lord Viṣṇu; *sūktena*—by chanting the Vedic *mantra* known as *Puruṣa-sūkta; tena*—by that; *puruṣam*—the Supreme Personality of Godhead; *yajeta*—one should worship; *su-*

samāhitaḥ—with great attention; *naivedyam*—food offered to the Deity; *ca*—and; *ati-guṇa-vat*—prepared very gorgeously with all varieties of taste; *dadyāt*—should offer; *puruṣa-tuṣṭi-dam*—everything extremely pleasing to the Supreme Personality of Godhead.

TRANSLATION

Giving up the miserly habit of not spending money, one should arrange for the gorgeous worship of the Supreme Personality of Godhead, Viṣṇu, who is situated in the heart of every living entity. With great attention, one must prepare an oblation of grains boiled in ghee and milk and must chant the Puruṣa-sūkta mantra. The offerings of food should be of varieties of tastes. In this way, one should worship the Supreme Personality of Godhead.

TEXT 53

आचार्यं ज्ञानसम्पन्नं वस्त्राभरणधेनुभिः ।
तोषयेदृत्विजश्चैव तद्विद्ध्याराधनं हरेः ॥ ५३ ॥

ācāryaṁ jñāna-sampannaṁ
vastrābharaṇa-dhenubhiḥ
toṣayed ṛtvijaś caiva
tad viddhy ārādhanaṁ hareḥ

ācāryam—the spiritual master; *jñāna-sampannam*—very advanced in spiritual knowledge; *vastra-ābharaṇa-dhenubhiḥ*—with clothing, ornaments and many cows; *toṣayet*—should satisfy; *ṛtvijaḥ*—the priests recommended by the spiritual master; *ca eva*—as well as; *tat viddhi*—try to understand that; *ārādhanam*—worship; *hareḥ*—of the Supreme Personality of Godhead.

TRANSLATION

One should satisfy the spiritual master [ācārya], who is very learned in Vedic literature, and should satisfy his assistant priests [known as hotā, udgātā, adhvaryu and brahma]. One should please them by offering them clothing, ornaments and cows. This is the ceremony called viṣṇu-ārādhana, or worship of Lord Viṣṇu.

TEXT 54

भोजयेत् तान् गुणवता सदन्नेन शुचिस्मिते ।
अन्यांश्च ब्राह्मणाञ्छक्त्या ये च तत्र समागताः ॥ ५४ ॥

bhojayet tān guṇavatā
sad-annena śuci-smite
anyāṁś ca brāhmaṇāñ chaktyā
ye ca tatra samāgatāḥ

bhojayet—should distribute *prasāda; tān*—unto all of them; *guṇa-vatā*—by rich foods; *sat-annena*—with food prepared with ghee and milk, which is supposed to be very pure; *śuci-smite*—O most pious lady; *anyān ca*—others also; *brāhmaṇān*—*brāhmaṇas; śaktyā*—as far as possible; *ye*—all of them who; *ca*—also; *tatra*—there (at the ceremonies); *samāgatāḥ*—assembled.

TRANSLATION

O most auspicious lady, one should perform all the ceremonies under the direction of learned ācāryas and should satisfy them and their priests. By distributing prasāda, one should also satisfy the brāhmaṇas and others who have assembled.

TEXT 55

दक्षिणां गुरवे दद्यादृत्विग्भ्यश्च यथार्हतः ।
अन्नाद्येनाश्वपाकांश्च प्रीणयेत्समुपागतान् ॥ ५५ ॥

dakṣiṇāṁ gurave dadyād
ṛtvigbhyaś ca yathārhataḥ
annādyenāśva-pākāṁś ca
prīṇayet samupāgatān

dakṣiṇām—some contribution of money or gold; *gurave*—unto the spiritual master; *dadyāt*—one should give; *ṛtvigbhyaḥ ca*—and to the priests engaged by the spiritual master; *yathā-arhataḥ*—as far as possible; *anna-adyena*—by distributing *prasāda; āśva-pākān*—even to the *caṇḍālas,* persons habituated to eating the flesh of dogs; *ca*—also; *prīṇayet*—one should please; *samupāgatān*—because they have assembled there for the ceremony.

TRANSLATION

One should satisfy the spiritual master and assistant priests by giving them cloth, ornaments, cows and also some monetary contribution. And by distributing prasāda one should satisfy everyone assembled, including even the lowest of men, the caṇḍālas [eaters of dog flesh].

PURPORT

In the Vedic system, *prasāda* is distributed, as recommended here, without discrimination as to who may take the *prasāda.* Regardless of whether one be a *brāhmaṇa, śūdra, vaiśya, kṣatriya,* or even the lowest of men, a *caṇḍāla,* he should be welcome to accept *prasāda.* However, when the *caṇḍālas,* the lower class or poorer class, are taking *prasāda,* this does not mean that they have become Nārāyaṇa or Viṣṇu. Nārāyaṇa is situated in everyone's heart, but this does not mean Nārāyaṇa is a *caṇḍāla* or poor man. The Māyāvāda philosophy of accepting a poor man as Nārāyaṇa is the most envious and atheistic movement in Vedic culture. This mentality should be completely given up. Everyone should be given the opportunity to take *prasāda,* but this does not mean that everyone has the right to become Nārāyaṇa.

TEXT 56

भुक्तवत्सु च सर्वेषु दीनान्धकृपणादिषु ।
विष्णोस्तत्प्रीणनं विद्वान्भुञ्जीत सह बन्धुभिः ॥ ५६ ॥

bhuktavatsu ca sarveṣu
dīnāndha-kṛpaṇādiṣu
viṣṇos tat prīṇanaṁ vidvān
bhuñjīta saha bandhubhiḥ

bhuktavatsu—after feeding; *ca*—also; *sarveṣu*—everyone present there; *dīna*—very poor; *andha*—blind; *kṛpaṇa*—those who are not *brāhmaṇas; ādiṣu*—and so on; *viṣṇoḥ*—of Lord Viṣṇu, who is situated in everyone's heart; *tat*—that (*prasāda*); *prīṇanam*—pleasing; *vidvān*—one who understands this philosophy; *bhuñjīta*—should take *prasāda* himself; *saha*—with; *bandhubhiḥ*—friends and relatives.

TRANSLATION

One should distribute viṣṇu-prasāda to everyone, including the poor man, the blind man, the nondevotee and the non-brāhmaṇa. Knowing that

Lord Viṣṇu is very pleased when everyone is sumptuously fed with viṣṇu-prasāda, the performer of yajña should then take prasāda with his friends and relatives.

TEXT 57

नृत्यवादित्रगीतैश्च स्तुतिभिः स्वस्तिवाचकैः ।
कारयेत्तत्कथाभिश्च पूजां भगवतोऽन्वहम् ॥ ५७ ॥

nṛtya-vāditra-gītaiś ca
stutibhiḥ svasti-vācakaiḥ
kārayet tat-kathābhiś ca
pūjāṁ bhagavato 'nvaham

nṛtya—by dancing; *vāditra*—by beating the drum; *gītaiḥ*—and by singing; *ca*—also; *stutibhiḥ*—by chanting auspicious *mantras; svasti-vācakaiḥ*—by offering prayers; *kārayet*—should execute; *tat-kathābhiḥ*—by reciting the *Bhāgavatam, Bhagavad-gītā* and similar literature; *ca*—also; *pūjām*—worship; *bhagavataḥ*—of the Supreme Personality of Godhead, Viṣṇu; *anvaham*—every day (from *pratipat* to *trayodaśī*).

TRANSLATION

Every day from pratipat to trayodaśī, one should continue the ceremony, to the accompaniment of dancing, singing, the beating of a drum, the chanting of prayers and all-auspicious mantras, and recitation of Śrīmad-Bhāgavatam. In this way, one should worship the Supreme Personality of Godhead.

TEXT 58

एतत्पयोव्रतं नाम पुरुषाराधनं परम् ।
पितामहेनाभिहितं मया ते समुदाहृतम् ॥ ५८ ॥

etat payo-vrataṁ nāma
puruṣārādhanaṁ param
pitāmahenābhihitaṁ
mayā te samudāhṛtam

etat—this; *payaḥ-vratam*—ceremony known as *payo-vrata; nāma*—by that name; *puruṣa-ārādhanam*—the process of worshiping the Supreme Personality of Godhead; *param*—the best; *pitāmahena*—by my grandfather, Lord Brahmā; *abhihitam*—stated; *mayā*—by me; *te*—unto you; *samudāhṛtam*—described in all details.

TRANSLATION

This is the religious ritualistic ceremony known as payo-vrata, by which one may worship the Supreme Personality of Godhead. I received this information from Brahmā, my grandfather, and now I have described it to you in all details.

TEXT 59

त्वं चानेन महाभागे सम्यक्चीर्णेन केशवम् ।
आत्मना शुद्धभावेन नियतात्मा भजाव्ययम् ॥ ५९ ॥

tvaṁ cānena mahā-bhāge
samyak cīrṇena keśavam
ātmanā śuddha-bhāvena
niyatātmā bhajāvyayam

tvam ca—you also; *anena*—by this process; *mahā-bhāge*—O greatly fortunate one; *samyak cīrṇena*—executed properly; *keśavam*—unto Lord Keśava; *ātmanā*—by oneself; *śuddha-bhāvena*—in a pure state of mind; *niyata-ātmā*—controlling oneself; *bhaja*—go on worshiping; *avyayam*—the Supreme Personality of Godhead, who is inexhaustible.

TRANSLATION

O most fortunate lady, establishing your mind in a good spirit, execute this process of payo-vrata and thus worship the Supreme Personality of Godhead, Keśava, who is inexhaustible.

TEXT 60

अयं वै सर्वयज्ञाख्यः सर्वव्रतमिति स्मृतम् ।
तपःसारमिदं भद्रे दानं चेश्वरतर्पणम् ॥ ६० ॥

ayaṁ vai sarva-yajñākhyaḥ
sarva-vratam iti smṛtam
tapaḥ-sāram idaṁ bhadre
dānaṁ ceśvara-tarpaṇam

ayam—this; *vai*—indeed; *sarva-yajña*—all kinds of religious rituals and sacrifices; *ākhyaḥ*—called; *sarva-vratam*—all religious ceremonies; *iti*—thus; *smṛtam*—understood; *tapaḥ-sāram*—the essence of all austerities; *idam*—this; *bhadre*—O good lady; *dānam*—acts of charity; *ca*—and; *īśvara*—the Supreme Personality of Godhead; *tarpaṇam*—the process of pleasing.

TRANSLATION

This payo-vrata is also known as sarva-yajña. In other words, by performing this sacrifice one can perform all other sacrifices automatically. This is also acknowledged to be the best of all ritualistic ceremonies. O gentle lady, it is the essence of all austerities, and it is the process of giving charity and pleasing the supreme controller.

PURPORT

Ārādhanānāṁ sarveṣāṁ viṣṇor ārādhanaṁ param. This is a statement made by Lord Śiva to Pārvatī. Worshiping Lord Viṣṇu is the supreme process of worship. And how Lord Viṣṇu is worshiped in this *payo-vrata* ceremony has now been fully described. The ultimate goal of life is to please Lord Viṣṇu by *varṇāśrama-dharma.* The Vedic principles of four *varṇas* and four *āśramas* are meant for worship of Viṣṇu (*viṣṇur ārādhyate puṁsāṁ nānyat tat-toṣa-kāraṇam*). The Kṛṣṇa consciousness movement is also *viṣṇu-ārādhanam,* or worship of Lord Viṣṇu, according to the age. The *payo-vrata* method of *viṣṇu-ārādhanam* was enunciated long, long ago by Kaśyapa Muni to his wife, Aditi, in the heavenly planets, and the same process is bona fide on earth even now. Especially for this age of Kali, the process accepted by the Kṛṣṇa consciousness movement is to open hundreds and thousands of Viṣṇu temples (temples of Rādhā-Kṛṣṇa, Jagannātha, Balarāma, Sītā-Rāma, Gaura-Nitāi and so on). Performing prescribed worship in such temples of Viṣṇu and thus worshiping the Lord is as good as performing the *payo-vrata* ceremony recommended here. The *payo-vrata* ceremony is performed from the first to the thirteenth day of the bright fortnight of the moon, but in our Kṛṣṇa consciousness movement Lord Viṣṇu is worshiped in every temple according to a schedule of twenty-four hours of engagement in performing *kīrtana,* chanting the Hare Kṛṣṇa *mahā-mantra,* offering palatable food to Lord Viṣṇu and distributing this food to Vaiṣṇavas and others. These are authorized activities, and if the members of the Kṛṣṇa consciousness movement stick to these principles, they will achieve the same result one gains by observing the *payo-vrata* ceremony. Thus the essence of all auspicious activities, such as performing *yajña,* giving in charity, observing *vratas,* and undergoing austerities, is included in the Kṛṣṇa consciousness movement. The members of this movement should immediately and sincerely follow the processes already recommended. Of course, sacrifice is meant to please Lord Viṣṇu. *Yajñaiḥ saṅkīrtana-prāyair yajanti hi sumedhasaḥ:* in Kali-yuga, those who are intelligent perform the *saṅkīrtana-yajña.* One should follow this process conscientiously.

TEXT 61

त एव नियमाः साक्षात्त एव च यमोत्तमाः ।
तपो दानं व्रतं यज्ञो येन तुष्यत्यधोक्षजः ॥ ६१ ॥

ta eva niyamāḥ sākṣāt
ta eva ca yamottamāḥ
tapo dānaṁ vrataṁ yajño
yena tuṣyaty adhokṣajaḥ

te—that is; *eva*—indeed; *niyamāḥ*—all regulative principles; *sākṣāt*—directly; *te*—that is; *eva*—indeed; *ca*—also; *yama-uttamāḥ*—the best process of controlling the senses; *tapaḥ*—austerities; *dānam*—charity; *vratam*—observing vows; *yajñaḥ*—sacrifice; *yena*—by which process; *tuṣyati*—is very pleased; *adhokṣajaḥ*—the Supreme Lord, who is not perceived by material senses.

TRANSLATION

This is the best process for pleasing the transcendental Supreme Personality of Godhead, known as Adhokṣaja. It is the best of all regulative principles, the best austerity, the best process of giving charity, and the best process of sacrifice.

PURPORT

The Supreme Lord says in *Bhagavad-gītā* (18.66):

sarva-dharmān parityajya
mām ekaṁ śaraṇaṁ vraja
ahaṁ tvāṁ sarva-pāpebhyo
mokṣayiṣyāmi mā śucaḥ

"Abandon all varieties of religion and just surrender unto Me. I shall deliver you from all sinful reaction. Do not fear." Unless one pleases the Supreme

Personality of Godhead according to His demand, no good result will come from any of his actions.

dharmaḥ svanuṣṭhitaḥ puṁsāṁ
viṣvaksena-kathāsu yaḥ
notpādayed yadi ratiṁ
śrama eva hi kevalam

"The occupational activities a man performs according to his own position are only so much useless labor if they do not provoke attraction for the message of the Personality of Godhead." (*Bhāg.* 1.2.8) If one is not interested in satisfying Lord Viṣṇu, Vāsudeva, all his so-called auspicious activities are fruitless. *Moghāśā mogha-karmāṇo mogha-jñānā vicetasaḥ:* because he is bewildered, he is baffled in his hopes, baffled in his activities, and baffled in his knowledge. In this regard, Śrīla Viśvanātha Cakravartī remarks, *napuṁsakam anapuṁsakenety-ādinaikatvam.* One cannot equate the potent and the impotent. Among modern Māyāvādīs it has become fashionable to say that whatever one does or whatever path one follows is all right. But these are all foolish statements. Here it is forcefully affirmed that this is the only method for success in life. *Īśvara-tarpaṇaṁ vinā sarvam eva viphalam.* Unless Lord Viṣṇu is satisfied, all of one's pious activities, ritualistic ceremonies and *yajñas* are simply for show and have no value. Unfortunately, foolish people do not know the secret of success. *Na te viduḥ svārtha-gatiṁ hi viṣṇum*. They do not know that real self-interest ends in pleasing Lord Viṣṇu.

TEXT 62

तस्मादेतद्व्रतं भद्रे प्रयता श्रद्धयाचर ।
भगवान्परितुष्टस्ते वरानाशु विधास्यति ॥ ६२ ॥

tasmād etad vrataṁ bhadre
prayatā śraddhayācara
bhagavān parituṣṭas te
varān āśu vidhāsyati

tasmāt—therefore; *etat*—this; *vratam*—observance of a *vrata* ceremony; *bhadre*—my dear gentle lady; *prayatā*—by observing rules and regulations; *śraddhayā*—with faith; *ācara*—execute; *bhagavān*—the Supreme Personality of Godhead; *parituṣṭaḥ*—being very satisfied; *te*—unto you; *varān*—benedictions; *āśu*—very soon; *vidhāsyati*—will bestow.

TRANSLATION

Therefore, my dear gentle lady, follow this ritualistic vow, strictly observing the regulative principles. By this process, the Supreme Person will very soon be pleased with you and will satisfy all your desires.

Thus end the Bhaktivedanta purports of the Eighth Canto, Sixteenth Chapter, of the Śrīmad-Bhāgavatam, *entitled "Executing the Payo-vrata Process of Worship."*

CHAPTER SEVENTEEN

The Supreme Lord Agrees to Become Aditi's Son

As explained in this chapter, the Supreme Personality of Godhead, being very pleased by the *payo-vrata* ceremony performed by Aditi, appeared before her in full opulence. At her request, the Lord agreed to become her son.

After Aditi performed the *payo-vrata* ceremony for twelve continuous days, the Lord, who was certainly very pleased with her, appeared before her with four hands and dressed in yellow garments. As soon as Aditi saw the Supreme Personality of Godhead present before her, she immediately got up, and with great ecstatic love for the Lord she fell to the ground to offer respectful obeisances. Aditi's throat was choked because of ecstatic feelings, and her entire body trembled with devotion. Although she wanted to offer suitable prayers to the Lord, she could not do anything, and thus she remained silent for some time. Then, feeling solace, observing the beauty of the Lord, she offered her prayers. The Supreme Personality of Godhead, the Supersoul of all living entities, was very pleased with her, and He agreed to become her son by incarnating as a plenary expansion. He was already pleased by Kaśyapa Muni's austerities, and thus He agreed to become their son and maintain the demigods. After giving His word of honor to this effect, the Lord disappeared. Following the order of the Supreme Personality of Godhead, Aditi engaged in the service of Kaśyapa Muni, who could see by *samādhi* that the Lord was within him and who thus placed his semen in the womb of Aditi. Lord Brahmā, who is known as Hiraṇyagarbha, understood that the Supreme Personality of Godhead had entered Aditi's womb. Thus he offered prayers to the Lord.

TEXT 1

श्रीशुक उवाच
इत्युक्ता सादिती राजन्स्वभर्त्रा कश्यपेन वै।
अन्वतिष्ठद् व्रतमिदं द्वादशाहमतन्द्रिता ॥ १ ॥

śrī-śuka uvāca
ity uktā sāditī rājan
sva-bhartrā kaśyapena vai
anv atiṣṭhad vratam idaṁ
dvādaśāham atandritā

śrī-śukaḥ uvāca—Śrī Śukadeva Gosvāmī said; *iti*—thus; *uktā*—being advised; *sā*—that lady; *aditiḥ*—Aditi; *rājan*—O King; *sva-bhartrā*—by her husband; *kaśyapena*—Kaśyapa Muni; *vai*—indeed; *anu*—similarly; *atiṣṭhat*—executed; *vratam idam*—this *payo-vrata* ritualistic ceremony; *dvādaśa-aham*—for twelve days; *atandritā*—without any laziness.

TRANSLATION

Śukadeva Gosvāmī said: O King, after Aditi was thus advised by her husband, Kaśyapa Muni, she strictly followed his instructions without laziness and in this way performed the payo-vrata ritualistic ceremony.

PURPORT

For advancement in anything, especially in spiritual life, one must strictly follow the bona fide instructions of the teacher. Aditi did this. She strictly followed the instructions of her husband and *guru.* As confirmed in the Vedic injunctions, *yasya deve parā bhaktir yathā deve tathā gurau*. One should have complete faith in the *guru,* who helps the disciple make progress in spiritual life. As soon as the disciple thinks independently, not caring for the instructions of the spiritual master, he is a failure (*yasyāprasādān na gatiḥ kuto 'pi*). Aditi very strictly followed the instructions of her husband and spiritual master, and thus she was successful.

TEXTS 2-3

चिन्तयन्त्येकया बुद्ध्या महापुरुषमीश्वरम् ।
प्रगृह्येन्द्रियदुष्टाश्वान्मनसा बुद्धिसारथिः ॥ २ ॥
मनश्चैकाग्रया बुद्ध्या भगवत्यखिलात्मनि ।
वासुदेवे समाधाय चचार ह पयोव्रतम् ॥ ३ ॥

cintayanty ekayā buddhyā
mahā-puruṣam īśvaram
pragṛhyendriya-duṣṭāśvān
manasā buddhi-sārathiḥ

manaś caikāgrayā buddhyā
bhagavaty akhilātmani
vāsudeve samādhāya
cacāra ha payo-vratam

cintayanti—constantly thinking; *ekayā*—with one attention; *buddhyā*—and intelligence; *mahā-puruṣam*—upon the Supreme Personality of Godhead; *īśvaram*—the supreme controller, Lord Viṣṇu; *pragṛhya*—completely controlling; *indriya*—the senses; *duṣṭa*—formidable, powerful; *aśvān*—horses; *manasā*—by the mind; *buddhi-sārathiḥ*—with the help of intelligence, the chariot driver; *manaḥ*—the mind; *ca*—also; *eka-agrayā*—with full attention; *buddhyā*—with the intelligence; *bhagavati*—unto the Supreme Personality of Godhead; *akhila-ātmani*—the Supreme Soul, the Supersoul of all living entities; *vāsudeve*—unto Lord Vāsudeva; *samādhāya*—keeping full attention; *cacāra*—executed; *ha*—thus; *payaḥ-vratam*—the ritualistic ceremony known as *payo-vrata.*

TRANSLATION

With full, undiverted attention, Aditi thought of the Supreme Personality of Godhead and in this way brought under full control her mind and senses, which resembled forceful horses. She concentrated her mind upon the Supreme Lord, Vāsudeva. Thus she performed the ritualistic ceremony known as payo-vrata.

PURPORT

This is the process of *bhakti-yoga.*

anyābhilāṣitā-śūnyaṁ
jñāna-karmādy-anāvṛtam
ānukūlyena kṛṣṇānu-
śīlanaṁ bhaktir uttamā

"One should render transcendental loving service to the Supreme Lord Kṛṣṇa favorably and without desire for material profit or gain through fruitive activities or philosophical speculation. That is called pure devotional service." One simply has to concentrate upon the lotus feet of Vāsudeva, Kṛṣṇa (*sa vai manaḥ kṛṣṇa-padāravindayoḥ*). Then the mind and senses will be controlled, and one can engage himself fully in the devotional service of the Lord. The devotee does not need to practice the *haṭha-yoga* system to control the mind and senses; his mind and senses are automatically controlled because of unalloyed devotional service to the Lord.

TEXT 4

तस्याः प्रादुरभूत्तात भगवानादिपुरुषः ।
पीतवासाश्चतुर्बाहुः शङ्खचक्रगदाधरः ॥ ४ ॥

tasyāḥ prādurabhūt tāta
bhagavān ādi-puruṣaḥ
pīta-vāsāś catur-bāhuḥ
śaṅkha-cakra-gadā-dharaḥ

tasyāḥ—before her; *prādurabhūt*—appeared; *tāta*—my dear King; *bhagavān*—the Supreme Personality of Godhead; *ādi-puruṣaḥ*—the original person; *pīta-vāsāḥ*—dressed in yellow garments; *catuḥ-bāhuḥ*—with four arms; *śaṅkha-cakra-gadā-dharaḥ*—bearing the conchshell, disc, club and lotus flower.

TRANSLATION

My dear King, the original Supreme Personality of Godhead, dressed in yellow garments and bearing a conchshell, disc, club and lotus in His four hands, then appeared before Aditi.

TEXT 5

तं नेत्रगोचरं वीक्ष्य सहसोत्थाय सादरम् ।
ननाम भुवि कायेन दण्डवत्प्रीतिविह्वला ॥ ५ ॥

taṁ netra-gocaraṁ vīkṣya
sahasotthāya sādaram
nanāma bhuvi kāyena
daṇḍavat-prīti-vihvalā

tam—Him (the Supreme Personality of Godhead); *netra-gocaram*—visible by her eyes; *vīkṣya*—after seeing; *sahasā*—all of a sudden; *utthāya*—getting up; *sa-ādaram*—with great respect; *nanāma*—offered respectful obeisances; *bhuvi*—on the ground; *kāyena*—by the whole body; *daṇḍa-vat*—falling like a rod; *prīti-vihvalā*—almost puzzled because of transcendental bliss.

TRANSLATION

When the Supreme Personality of Godhead became visible to Aditi's eyes, Aditi was so overwhelmed by transcendental bliss that she at once stood up and then fell to the ground like a rod to offer the Lord her respectful obeisances.

TEXT 6

सोत्थाय बद्धाञ्जलिरीडितुं स्थिता
नोत्सेह आनन्दजलाकुलेक्षणा ।
बभूव तूष्णीं पुलकाकुलाकृति-
स्तद्दर्शनात्युत्सवगात्रवेपथुः ॥ ६ ॥

sotthāya baddhāñjalir īḍituṁ sthitā
notseha ānanda-jalākulekṣaṇā
babhūva tūṣṇīṁ pulakākulākṛtis
tad-darśanātyutsava-gātra-vepathuḥ

sā—she; *utthāya*—standing up; *baddha-añjaliḥ*—with folded hands; *īḍitum*—to worship the Lord; *sthitā*—situated; *na utsehe*—could not endeavor; *ānanda*—from transcendental bliss; *jala*—with water; *ākula-īkṣaṇā*—her eyes were filled; *babhūva*—remained; *tūṣṇīm*—silent; *pulaka*—with standing of the hairs of the body; *ākula*—overwhelmed; *ākṛtiḥ*—her form; *tat-darśana*—by seeing the Lord; *ati-utsava*—with great pleasure; *gātra*—her body; *vepathuḥ*—began to tremble.

TRANSLATION

Aditi stood silently with folded hands, unable to offer prayers to the Lord. Because of transcendental bliss, tears filled her eyes, and the hairs on her body stood on end. Because she could see the Supreme Personality of Godhead face to face, she felt ecstasy, and her body trembled.

TEXT 7

प्रीत्या शनैर्गद्गदया गिरा हरिं
तुष्टाव सा देव्यदितिः कुरूद्वह ।
उद्वीक्षती सा पिबतीव चक्षुषा
रमापतिं यज्ञपतिं जगत्पतिम् ॥ ७ ॥

prītyā śanair gadgadayā girā hariṁ
tuṣṭāva sā devy aditiḥ kurūdvaha
udvīkṣatī sā pibatīva cakṣuṣā
ramā-patiṁ yajña-patiṁ jagat-patim

prītyā—because of love; *śanaiḥ*—again and again; *gadgadayā*—faltering; *girā*—with a voice; *harim*—unto the Supreme Personality of Godhead; *tuṣṭāva*—pleased; *sā*—she; *devī*—the demigoddess; *aditiḥ*—Aditi; *kuru-udvaha*—O Mahārāja Parīkṣit; *udvīkṣatī*—while staring; *sā*—she; *pibatī iva*—appeared as if she were drinking; *cakṣuṣā*—through the eyes; *ramā-patim*—unto the Lord, the husband of the goddess of fortune; *yajña-patim*—unto the Lord, the enjoyer of all sacrificial ceremonies; *jagat-patim*—the master and Lord of the entire universe.

TRANSLATION

O Mahārāja Parīkṣit, the demigoddess Aditi then began offering her prayers to the Supreme Personality of Godhead in a faltering voice and with great love. She appeared as though drinking through her eyes the Supreme Lord, who is the husband of the goddess of fortune, the enjoyer of all sacrificial ceremonies, and the master and Lord of the entire universe.

PURPORT

After observing the *payo-vrata,* Aditi was certain that the Lord had appeared before her as Ramā-pati, the husband of all good fortune, just to offer her sons all opulences. She had performed the *yajña* of *payo-vrata* under the direction of her husband, Kaśyapa, and therefore she thought of the Lord as Yajña-pati. She was completely satisfied to see the master and Lord of the entire universe come before her to fulfill her desire.

TEXT 8

श्रीअदितिरुवाच
यज्ञेश यज्ञपुरुषाच्युत तीर्थपाद
तीर्थश्रवः श्रवणमङ्गलनामधेय ।
आपन्नलोकवृजिनोपशमोदयाद्य
शं नः कृधीश भगवन्नसि दीननाथः ॥ ८ ॥

śrī-aditir uvāca
yajñeśa yajña-puruṣācyuta tīrtha-pāda
tīrtha-śravaḥ śravaṇa-maṅgala-nāmadheya
āpanna-loka-vṛjinopaśamodayādya
śaṁ naḥ kṛdhīśa bhagavann asi dīna-nāthaḥ

śrī-aditiḥ uvāca—the demigoddess Aditi said; *yajña-īśa*—O controller of all sacrificial ceremonies; *yajña-puruṣa*—the person who enjoys the benefits of all sacrifices; *acyuta*—infallible; *tīrtha-pāda*—at whose lotus feet stand all the holy places of pilgrimage; *tīrtha-śravaḥ*—celebrated as the ultimate shelter of all saintly persons; *śravaṇa*—hearing about whom; *maṅgala*—is auspicious; *nāmadheya*—to chant His name is also auspicious; *āpanna*—surrendered; *loka*—of people; *vṛjina*—dangerous material position; *upaśama*—diminishing; *udaya*—who has appeared; *ādya*—the original Personality of Godhead; *śam*—auspiciousness; *naḥ*—our; *kṛdhi*—kindly bestow upon us; *īśa*—O supreme controller; *bhagavan*—O Lord; *asi*—You are; *dīna-nāthaḥ*—the only shelter of the down trodden.

TRANSLATION

The goddess Aditi said: O master and enjoyer of all sacrificial ceremonies, O infallible and most famous person, whose name, when chanted, spreads all good fortune! O original Supreme Personality of Godhead, supreme controller, shelter of all holy places, You are the shelter of all poor, suffering living entities, and You have appeared to diminish their suffering. Please be kind to us and spread our good fortune.

PURPORT

The Supreme Personality of Godhead is the master of those who observe vows and austerities, and it is He who bestows benedictions upon them. He is worshipable for the devotee throughout the devotee's life, for He never breaks His promises. As He says in *Bhagavad-gītā* (9.31), *kaunteya pratijānīhi na me bhaktaḥ praṇaśyati:* "O son of Kuntī, declare it boldly that My devotee never perishes." The Lord is addressed here as *acyuta,* the infallible, because He takes care of His devotees. Anyone inimical to the devotees is certainly vanquished by the mercy of the Lord. The Lord is the source of the Ganges water, and therefore He is addressed here as *tīrtha-pāda,* indicating that all the holy places are at His lotus feet, or that whatever He touches with His foot becomes a holy place. *Bhagavad-gītā,* for example, begins with the words *dharma-kṣetre kuru-*

kṣetre . Because the Lord was present on the Battlefield of Kurukṣetra, it became a *dharma-kṣetra,* a place of pilgrimage. Therefore the Pāṇḍavas, who were extremely religious, were assured of victory. Any place where the Supreme Personality of Godhead displays His pastimes, such as Vṛndāvana or Dvārakā, becomes a holy place. The chanting of the holy name of the Lord—Hare Kṛṣṇa, Hare Kṛṣṇa, Kṛṣṇa Kṛṣṇa, Hare Hare/ Hare Rāma, Hare Rāma, Rāma Rāma, Hare Hare—is pleasing to the ear, and it expands good fortune to the audience who hears it chanted. Owing to the presence of the Supreme Personality of Godhead, Aditi was fully assured that the troublesome condition created for her by the demons would now be ended.

TEXT 9

विश्वाय विश्वभवनस्थितिसंयमाय
स्वैरं गृहीतपुरुशक्तिगुणाय भूम्ने ।
स्वस्थाय शश्वदुपबृंहितपूर्णबोध-
व्यापादितात्मतमसे हरये नमस्ते ॥ ९ ॥

viśvāya viśva-bhavana-sthiti-saṁyamāya
svairaṁ gṛhīta-puru-śakti-guṇāya bhūmne
sva-sthāya śaśvad-upabṛṁhita-pūrṇa-bodha-
vyāpāditātma-tamase haraye namas te

viśvāya—unto the Supreme Personality of Godhead, who is actually the entire universe; *viśva*—of the universe; *bhavana*—creation; *sthiti*—maintenance; *saṁyamāya*—and annihilation; *svairam*—fully independent; *gṛhīta*—taking in hand; *puru*—completely; *śakti-guṇāya*—controlling the three modes of material nature; *bhūmne*—the supreme great; *sva-sthāya*—who is always situated in His original form; *śaśvat*—eternally; *upabṛṁhita*—achieved; *pūrṇa*—complete; *bodha*—knowledge; *vyāpādita*—completely vanquished; *ātma-tamase*—the illusory energy of Your Lordship; *haraye*—unto the Supreme Lord; *namaḥ te*—I offer my respectful obeisances unto You.

TRANSLATION

My Lord, You are the all-pervading universal form, the fully independent creator, maintainer and destroyer of this universe. Although You engage Your energy in matter, You are always situated in Your original form

and never fall from that position, for Your knowledge is infallible and always suitable to any situation. You are never bewildered by illusion. O my Lord, let me offer my respectful obeisances unto You.

PURPORT

In the *Caitanya-caritāmṛta* (*Ādi* 2.117) it is said:

siddhānta baliyā citte nā kara alasa
ihā ha-ite kṛṣṇe lāge sudṛḍha mānasa

Anyone trying to become fully Kṛṣṇa conscious must know the Lord's glories as far as they are possible to understand. Here Aditi hints at these glories. The universe is nothing but the external potency of the Lord. This is confirmed in *Bhagavad-gītā* (9.4): *mayā tatam idaṁ sarvam.* Whatever we see in this universe is but an expansion of the potency of the Supreme Personality of Godhead, just as the sunshine and heat all over the universe are expansions of the sun. When one surrenders unto the Supreme Personality of Godhead, he surpasses the influence of the illusory energy, for the Supreme Lord, being fully wise and being situated in the heart of everyone, especially in the heart of the devotee, gives one intelligence by which one is sure never to fall into illusion.

TEXT 10

आयुः परं वपुरभीष्टमतुल्यलक्ष्मी-
द्योभूरसाः सकलयोगगुणास्त्रिवर्गः ।
ज्ञानं च केवलमनन्त भवन्ति तुष्टात्
त्वत्तो नृणां किमु सपत्नजयादिराशीः ॥ १० ॥

āyuḥ paraṁ vapur abhīṣṭam atulya-lakṣmīr
dyo-bhū-rasāḥ sakala-yoga-guṇās tri-vargaḥ
jñānaṁ ca kevalam ananta bhavanti tuṣṭāt
tvatto nṛṇāṁ kim u sapatna-jayādir āśīḥ

āyuḥ—duration of life; *param*—as long as that of Lord Brahmā; *vapuḥ*—a particular type of body; *abhīṣṭam*—the goal of life; *atulya-lakṣmīḥ*—unparalleled opulence in material existence; *dyo*—the upper planetary system; *bhū*—Bhūloka; *rasāḥ*—the lower planetary system; *sakala*—all kinds of; *yoga-guṇāḥ*—the eight mystic perfections; *tri-vargaḥ*—the principles of religiosity, economic development and sense gratification; *jñānam*—transcendental knowledge; *ca*—and; *kevalam*—complete; *ananta*—O unlimited one; *bhavanti*—all become possible; *tuṣṭāt*—by Your satisfaction; *tvattaḥ*—from You; *nṛṇām*—of all living entities; *kim u*—what to speak of; *sapatna*—enemies; *jaya*—conquering; *ādiḥ*—and others; *āśīḥ*—such benedictions.

TRANSLATION

O unlimited one, if Your Lordship is satisfied, one can very easily obtain a lifetime as long as that of Lord Brahmā, a body either in the upper, lower or middle planetary systems, unlimited material opulence, religion, economic development and satisfaction of the senses, full transcendental knowledge, and the eight yogic perfections, what to speak of such petty achievements as conquering one's rivals.

TEXT 11

श्रीशुक उवाच
अदित्यैवं स्तुतो राजन्भगवान्पुष्करेक्षणः ।
क्षेत्रज्ञः सर्वभूतानामिति होवाच भारत ॥ ११ ॥

śrī-śuka uvāca
adityaivaṁ stuto rājan
bhagavān puṣkarekṣaṇaḥ
kṣetra-jñaḥ sarva-bhūtānām
iti hovāca bhārata

śrī-śukaḥ uvāca—Śrī Śukadeva Gosvāmī said; *adityā*—by Aditi; *evam*—thus; *stutaḥ*—being worshiped; *rājan*—O King (Mahārāja Parīkṣit); *bhagavān*—the Supreme Personality of Godhead; *puṣkara-īkṣaṇaḥ*—whose eyes are like lotus flowers; *kṣetra-jñaḥ*—the Supersoul; *sarva-bhūtānām*—of all living entities; *iti*—thus; *ha*—indeed; *uvāca*—replied; *bhārata*—O best of the Bharata dynasty.

TRANSLATION

Śukadeva Gosvāmī said: O King Parīkṣit, best of the Bharata dynasty, when the lotus-eyed Lord, the Supersoul of all living entities, was thus worshiped by Aditi, He replied as follows.

TEXT 12

श्रीभगवानुवाच
देवमातर्भवत्या मे विज्ञातं चिरकाङ्क्षितम् ।
यत् सपत्नैर्हृतश्रीणां च्यावितानां स्वधामतः ॥ १२ ॥

śrī-bhagavān uvāca
deva-mātar bhavatyā me
vijñātaṁ cira-kāṅkṣitam
yat sapatnair hṛta-śrīṇāṁ
cyāvitānāṁ sva-dhāmataḥ

śrī-bhagavān uvāca—the Supreme Personality of Godhead said; *deva-mātar*—O mother of the demigods; *bhavatyāḥ*—of you; *me*—by Me; *vijñātam*—understood; *cira-kāṅkṣitam*—what You have desired for a long time; *yat*—because; *sapatnaiḥ*—by the rivals; *hṛta-śrīṇām*—of your sons, who are bereft of all opulences; *cyāvitānām*—vanquished; *sva-dhāmataḥ*—from their own residential quarters.

TRANSLATION

The Supreme Personality of Godhead said: O mother of the demigods, I have already understood your long-cherished desires for the welfare of your sons, who have been deprived of all opulences and driven from their residence by their enemies.

PURPORT

The Supreme Personality of Godhead, being situated in everyone's heart, and especially in the hearts of His devotees, is always ready to help devotees in adversity. Since He knows everything, He knows how things are to be adjusted, and He does the needful to relieve the suffering of His devotee.

TEXT 13

तान्विनिर्जित्य समरे दुर्मदानसुरर्षभान् ।
प्रतिलब्धजयश्रीभिः पुत्रैरिच्छस्युपासितुम् ॥ १३ ॥

tān vinirjitya samare
durmadān asurarṣabhān

pratilabdha-jaya-śrībhiḥ
putrair icchasy upāsitum

tān—them; *vinirjitya*—defeating; *samare*—in the fight; *durmadān*—puffed up by strength; *asura-ṛṣabhān*—the leaders of the demons; *pratilabdha*—getting back; *jaya*—victory; *śrībhiḥ*—as well as the opulence; *putraiḥ*—with your sons; *icchasi*—you are desiring; *upāsitum*—to come together and worship Me.

TRANSLATION

O Devī, O goddess, I can understand that you want to regain your sons and be together with them to worship Me, after defeating the enemies in battle and retrieving your abode and opulences.

TEXT 14

इन्द्रज्येष्ठैः स्वतनयैर्हतानां युधि विद्विषाम् ।
स्त्रियो रुदन्तीरासाद्य द्रष्टुमिच्छसि दुःखिताः ॥ १४ ॥

indra-jyeṣṭhaiḥ sva-tanayair
hatānāṁ yudhi vidviṣām
striyo rudantīr āsādya
draṣṭum icchasi duḥkhitāḥ

indra-jyeṣṭhaiḥ—persons of whom King Indra is the eldest; *sva-tanayaiḥ*—by your own sons; *hatānām*—who are killed; *yudhi*—in the fight; *vidviṣām*—of the enemies; *striyaḥ*—the wives; *rudantīḥ*—lamenting; *āsādya*—coming near the dead bodies of their husbands; *draṣṭum icchasi*—you want to see; *duḥkhitāḥ*—very much aggrieved.

TRANSLATION

You want to see the wives of the demons lamenting for the death of their husbands when those demons, the enemies of your sons, are killed in battle by the demigods, of whom Indra is the chief.

TEXT 15

आत्मजान्सुसमृद्धांस्त्वं प्रत्याहृतयशःश्रियः ।
नाकपृष्ठमधिष्ठाय क्रीडतो द्रष्टुमिच्छसि ॥ १५ ॥

ātmajān susamṛddhāṁs tvaṁ
pratyāhṛta-yaśaḥ-śriyaḥ
nāka-pṛṣṭham adhiṣṭhāya
krīḍato draṣṭum icchasi

ātma-jān—your own sons; *su-samṛddhān*—completely opulent; *tvam*—you; *pratyāhṛta*—having received back; *yaśaḥ*—reputation; *śriyaḥ*—opulence; *nāka-pṛṣṭham*—in the heavenly kingdom; *adhiṣṭhāya*—situated; *krīḍataḥ*—enjoying their life; *draṣṭum*—to see; *icchasi*—you are desiring.

TRANSLATION

You want your sons to regain their lost reputation and opulence and live again on their heavenly planet as usual.

TEXT 16

प्रायोऽधुना तेऽसुरयूथनाथा
अपारणीया इति देवि मे मतिः ।
यत्तेऽनुकूलेश्वरविप्रगुप्ता
न विक्रमस्तत्र सुखं ददाति ॥ १६ ॥

prāyo 'dhunā te 'sura-yūtha-nāthā
apāraṇīyā iti devi me matiḥ
yat te 'nukūleśvara-vipra-guptā
na vikramas tatra sukhaṁ dadāti

prāyaḥ—almost; *adhunā*—at the present moment; *te*—all of them; *asura-yūtha-nāthāḥ*—the chiefs of the demons; *apāraṇīyāḥ*—unconquerable; *iti*—thus; *devi*—O mother Aditi; *me*—My; *matiḥ*—opinion; *yat*—because; *te*—all the demons; *anukūla-īśvara-vipra-guptāḥ*—protected by *brāhmaṇas,* by whose favor the supreme controller is always present; *na*—not; *vikramaḥ*—the use of power; *tatra*—there; *sukham*—happiness; *dadāti*—can give.

TRANSLATION

O mother of the demigods, in My opinion almost all the chiefs of the demons are now unconquerable, for they are being protected by brāhmaṇas, whom the Supreme Lord always favors. Thus the use of power against them now will not at all be a source of happiness.

PURPORT

When a person is favored by *brāhmaṇas* and Vaiṣṇavas, no one can defeat him. Even the Supreme Personality of Godhead does not interfere when one is protected by a *brāhmaṇa.* It is said, *go-brāhmaṇa-hitāya ca.* The Lord's first inclination is to give all benedictions to the cows and *brāhmaṇas.* Therefore if *brāhmaṇas* favor someone, the Lord does not interfere, nor can anyone interfere with the happiness of such a person.

TEXT 17

अथाप्युपायो मम देवि चिन्त्यः
सन्तोषितस्य व्रतचर्यया ते ।
ममार्चनं नार्हति गन्तुमन्यथा
श्रद्धानुरूपं फलहेतुकत्वात् ॥ १७ ॥

athāpy upāyo mama devi cintyaḥ
santoṣitasya vrata-caryayā te
mamārcanaṁ nārhati gantum anyathā
śraddhānurūpaṁ phala-hetukatvāt

atha—therefore; *api*—in spite of this situation; *upāyaḥ*—some means; *mama*—by Me; *devi*—O goddess; *cintyaḥ*—must be considered; *santoṣita-sya*—very pleased; *vrata-caryayā*—observing the vow; *te*—by you; *mama arcanam*—worshiping Me; *na*—never; *arhati*—deserves; *gantum anyathā*—to become otherwise; *śraddhā-anurūpam*—according to one's faith and devotion; *phala*—of the result; *hetukatvāt*—from being the cause.

TRANSLATION

Yet because I have been satisfied by the activities of your vow, O goddess Aditi, I must find some means to favor you, for worship of Me never goes in vain but certainly gives the desired result according to what one deserves.

TEXT 18

त्वयार्चितश्चाहमपत्यगुप्तये
पयोव्रतेनानुगुणं समीडितः ।

स्वांशेन पुत्रत्वमुपेत्य ते सुतान्
गोप्तास्मि मारीचतपस्यधिष्ठितः ॥ १८ ॥

tvayārcitaś cāham apatya-guptaye
payo-vratenānuguṇaṁ samīḍitaḥ
svāṁśena putratvam upetya te sutān
goptāsmi mārīca-tapasy adhiṣṭhitaḥ

tvayā—by you; *arcitaḥ*—being worshiped; *ca*—also; *aham*—I; *apatya-guptaye*—giving protection to your sons; *payaḥ-vratena*—by the *payo-vrata* vow; *anuguṇam*—as far as possible; *samīḍitaḥ*—properly worshiped; *sva-aṁśena*—by My plenary portion; *putratvam*—becoming your son; *upetya*—taking this opportunity; *te sutān*—to your other sons; *goptā asmi*—I shall give protection; *mārīca*—of Kaśyapa Muni; *tapasi*—in the austerity; *adhiṣṭhitaḥ*—situated.

TRANSLATION

You have prayed to Me and properly worshiped Me by performing the great payo-vrata ceremony for the sake of protecting your sons. Because of Kaśyapa Muni's austerities, I shall agree to become your son and thus protect your other sons.

TEXT 19

उपधाव पतिं भद्रे प्रजापतिमकल्मषम् ।
मां च भावयती पत्यावेवंरूपमवस्थितम् ॥ १९ ॥

upadhāva patiṁ bhadre
prajāpatim akalmaṣam
māṁ ca bhāvayatī patyāv
evaṁ rūpam avasthitam

upadhāva—just go worship; *patim*—your husband; *bhadre*—O gentle woman; *prajāpatim*—who is a Prajāpati; *akalmaṣam*—very much purified because of his austerity; *mām*—Me; *ca*—as well as; *bhāvayatī*—thinking of; *patyau*—within your husband; *evam*—thus; *rūpam*—form; *avasthitam*—situated there.

TRANSLATION

Always thinking of Me as being situated within the body of your husband, Kaśyapa, go worship your husband, who has been purified by his austerity.

TEXT 20

नैतत् परस्मा आख्येयं पृष्टयापि कथंचन ।
सर्वं सम्पद्यते देवि देवगुह्यं सुसंवृतम् ॥ २० ॥

naitat parasmā ākhyeyaṁ
pṛṣṭayāpi kathañcana
sarvaṁ sampadyate devi
deva-guhyaṁ susaṁvṛtam

na—not; *etat*—this; *parasmai*—to outsiders; *ākhyeyam*—is to be disclosed; *pṛṣṭayā api*—even though questioned; *kathañcana*—by anyone; *sarvam*—everything; *sampadyate*—becomes successful; *devi*—O lady; *deva-guhyam*—very confidential even to the demigods; *su-saṁvṛtam*—very carefully kept confidential.

TRANSLATION

O lady, even if someone inquires, you should not disclose this fact to anyone. That which is very confidential is successful if kept secret.

TEXT 21

श्रीशुक उवाच
एतावदुक्त्वा भगवांस्तत्रैवान्तरधीयत ।
अदितिर्दुर्लभं लब्ध्वा हरेर्जन्मात्मनि प्रभोः ।
उपाधावत् पतिं भक्त्या परया कृतकृत्यवत् ॥ २१ ॥

śrī-śuka uvāca
etāvad uktvā bhagavāṁs
tatraivāntaradhīyata
aditir durlabhaṁ labdhvā
harer janmātmani prabhoḥ
upādhāvat patiṁ bhaktyā
parayā kṛta-kṛtyavat

śrī-śukaḥ uvāca—Śrī Śukadeva Gosvāmī said; *etāvat*—in this way; *uktvā*—saying (to her); *bhagavān*—the Supreme Personality of Godhead; *tatra eva*—in that very spot; *antaḥ-adhīyata*—disappeared; *aditiḥ*—Aditi; *durlabham*—a very rare achievement; *labdhvā*—getting; *hareḥ*—of the Supreme Personality of Godhead; *janma*—birth; *ātmani*—in herself; *prabhoḥ*—of the Lord; *upādhāvat*—immediately went; *patim*—unto her husband; *bhaktyā*—with devotion; *parayā*—great; *kṛta-kṛtya-vat*—thinking herself very successful.

TRANSLATION

Śukadeva Gosvāmī said: After speaking in this way, the Supreme Personality of Godhead disappeared from that very spot. Aditi, having received the extremely valuable benediction that the Lord would appear as her son, considered herself very successful, and with great devotion she approached her husband.

TEXT 22

स वै समाधियोगेन कश्यपस्तदबुध्यत ।
प्रविष्टमात्मनि हरेरंशं ह्यवितथेक्षणः ॥ २२ ॥

sa vai samādhi-yogena
kaśyapas tad abudhyata
praviṣṭam ātmani harer
aṁśaṁ hy avitathekṣaṇaḥ

saḥ—Kaśyapa Muni; *vai*—indeed; *samādhi-yogena*—by mystic meditation; *kaśyapaḥ*—Kaśyapa Muni; *tat*—then; *abudhyata*—could understand; *praviṣṭam*—entered; *ātmani*—within himself; *hareḥ*—of the Supreme Lord; *aṁśam*—a plenary portion; *hi*—indeed; *avitatha-īkṣaṇaḥ*—whose vision is never mistaken.

TRANSLATION

Being situated in a meditational trance, Kaśyapa Muni, whose vision is never mistaken, could see that a plenary portion of the Supreme Personality of Godhead had entered within him.

TEXT 23

सोऽदित्यां वीर्यमाधत्त तपसा चिरसंभृतम् ।
समाहितमना राजन्दारुण्यग्निं यथानिलः ॥ २३ ॥

so 'dityāṁ vīryam ādhatta
tapasā cira-sambhṛtam
samāhita-manā rājan
dāruṇy agniṁ yathānilaḥ

saḥ—Kaśyapa; *adityām*—unto Aditi; *vīryam*—semen; *ādhatta*—placed; *tapasā*—by austerity; *cira-sambhṛtam*—restrained for long, long years; *samāhita-manāḥ*—being fully in trance upon the Supreme Personality of Godhead; *rājan*—O King; *dāruṇi*—as in firewood; *agnim*—fire; *yathā*—as; *anilaḥ*—wind.

TRANSLATION

O King, as the wind promotes friction between two pieces of wood and thus gives rise to fire, Kaśyapa Muni, whose transcendental position was fully absorbed in the Supreme Personality of Godhead, transferred his potency into the womb of Aditi.

PURPORT

A forest fire begins when two pieces of wood rub against one another, being agitated by the wind. Actually, however, fire belongs neither to the wood nor to the wind; it is always different from both. Similarly, here it is to be understood that the union of Kaśyapa Muni and Aditi was not like the sexual intercourse of ordinary human beings. The Supreme Personality of Godhead has nothing to do with the human secretions of sexual intercourse. He is always completely aloof from such material combinations.

The Lord says in *Bhagavad-gītā* (9.29), *samo 'haṁ sarva-bhūteṣu:* "I am equal toward all living entities." Nonetheless, to protect the devotees and kill the demons, who were a disturbing element, the Lord entered the womb of Aditi. Therefore this is a transcendental pastime of the Lord. This should not be misunderstood. One should not think that the Lord became the son of Aditi the way an ordinary child is born because of sexual intercourse between man and woman.

Here it may also be appropriate to explain, in these days of controversy, the origin of life. The life force of the living entity—the soul—is different from the ovum and semen of the human being. Although the conditioned soul has nothing to do with the reproductive cells of man and woman, he is placed into the proper situation because of his work (*karmaṇā daiva-netreṇa*). Life is not, however, a product of two secretions, but is independent of all material elements. As fully described in *Bhagavad-gītā,* the living entity is not subject to any material reactions. He can neither be burnt by fire, cut by sharp weapons, moistened by water, nor dried by the air. He is completely different from the physical elements, but by a superior arrangement he is put into these material elements. He is always aloof from material contact (*asaṅgo hy ayaṁ puruṣaḥ*) but because he is placed in a material condition, he suffers the reactions of the material modes of nature.

puruṣaḥ prakṛti-stho hi
bhuṅkte prakṛtijān guṇān
kāraṇaṁ guṇa-saṅgo 'sya
sad-asad-yoni-janmasu

"The living entity in material nature thus follows the ways of life, enjoying the three modes of nature. This is due to his association with that material nature. Thus he meets with good and evil amongst various species." (Bg. 13.22) Although the living entity is aloof from the material elements, he is put into material conditions, and thus he must suffer the reactions of material activities.

TEXT 24

अदितेर्धिष्ठितं गर्भं भगवन्तं सनातनम् ।
हिरण्यगर्भो विज्ञाय समीडे गुह्यनामभिः ॥ २४ ॥

aditer dhiṣṭhitaṁ garbhaṁ
bhagavantaṁ sanātanam
hiraṇyagarbho vijñāya
samīḍe guhya-nāmabhiḥ

aditeḥ—into the womb of Aditi; *dhiṣṭhitam*—being established; *garbham*—pregnancy; *bhagavantam*—unto the Supreme Personality of Godhead; *sanātanam*—who is eternal; *hiraṇyagarbhaḥ*—Lord Brahmā; *vijñāya*—knowing this; *samīḍe*—offered prayers; *guhya-nāmabhiḥ*—with transcendental names.

TRANSLATION

When Lord Brahmā understood that the Supreme Personality of Godhead was now within the womb of Aditi, he began to offer prayers to the Lord by reciting transcendental names.

PURPORT

The Supreme Personality of Godhead exists everywhere (*aṇḍāntara-stha-paramāṇu-cayāntara-stham*). Therefore when one chants His transcendental names—Hare Kṛṣṇa, Hare Kṛṣṇa, Kṛṣṇa Kṛṣṇa, Hare Hare/ Hare Rāma, Hare Rāma, Rāma Rāma, Hare Hare—the Supreme Personality of Godhead is automatically pleased by such *saṅkīrtana.* It is not that the Supreme Personality of Godhead is absent; He is present there. And when a devotee utters the transcendental name, it is not a material sound. Therefore, the Supreme Personality of Godhead is naturally pleased. A devotee knows that the Lord is present everywhere and that one can please Him simply by chanting His holy name.

TEXT 25

श्रीब्रह्मोवाच
जयोरुगाय भगवन्नुरुक्रम नमोऽस्तु ते ।
नमो ब्रह्मण्यदेवाय त्रिगुणाय नमो नमः ॥ २५ ॥

śrī-brahmovāca
jayorugāya bhagavann
urukrama namo 'stu te
namo brahmaṇya-devāya
tri-guṇāya namo namaḥ

śrī-brahmā uvāca—Lord Brahmā offered prayers; *jaya*—all glories; *urugāya*—unto the Lord, who is constantly glorified; *bhagavan*—O my Lord; *urukrama*—whose activities are very glorious; *namaḥ astu te*—I offer my respectful obeisances unto You; *namaḥ*—my respectful obeisances; *brahmaṇya-devāya*—unto the Lord of the transcendentalists; *tri-guṇāya*—the controller of the three modes of nature; *namaḥ namaḥ*—I offer my respectful obeisances unto You again and again.

TRANSLATION

Lord Brahmā said: O Supreme Personality of Godhead, all glories unto You, who are glorified by all and whose activities are all uncommon. I offer my respectful obeisances unto You, O Lord of the transcendentalists, controller of the three modes of nature. I offer my respectful obeisances unto You again and again.

TEXT 26

नमस्ते पृश्निगर्भाय वेदगर्भाय वेधसे ।
त्रिनाभाय त्रिपृष्ठाय शिपिविष्टाय विष्णवे ॥ २६ ॥

namas te pṛśni-garbhāya
veda-garbhāya vedhase
tri-nābhāya tri-pṛṣṭhāya
śipi-viṣṭāya viṣṇave

namaḥ te—I offer my respectful obeisances unto You; *pṛśni-garbhāya*—who formerly lived within the womb of Pṛśni (Aditi in her previous birth); *veda-garbhāya*—who always remain within Vedic knowledge; *vedhase*—who are full of knowledge; *tri-nābhāya*—within the stem growing from whose navel live all the three worlds; *tri-pṛṣṭhāya*—who are transcendental to the three worlds; *śipi-viṣṭāya*—who are within the cores of the hearts of all living entities; *viṣṇave*—unto the all-pervading Supreme Personality of Godhead.

TRANSLATION

I offer my respectful obeisances unto You, the all-pervading Lord Viṣṇu, who have entered the cores of the hearts of all living entities. All the three worlds reside within Your navel, yet You are above the three worlds. Formerly You appeared as the son of Pṛśni. To You, the supreme creator, who are understood only through Vedic knowledge, I offer my respectful obeisances.

TEXT 27

त्वमादिरन्तो भुवनस्य मध्य-
मनन्तशक्तिं पुरुषं यमाहुः ।
कालो भवानाक्षिपतीश विश्वं
स्त्रोतो यथान्तःपतितं गभीरम् ॥ २७ ॥

tvam ādir anto bhuvanasya madhyam
ananta-śaktiṁ puruṣaṁ yam āhuḥ
kālo bhavān ākṣipatīśa viśvaṁ
sroto yathāntaḥ patitaṁ gabhīram

tvam—Your Lordship; *ādiḥ*—the original cause; *antaḥ*—the cause of dissolution; *bhuvanasya*—of the universe; *madhyam*—maintenance of the present manifestation; *ananta-śaktim*—the reservoir of unlimited potencies; *puruṣam*—the Supreme Person; *yam*—whom; *āhuḥ*—they say; *kālaḥ*—the principle of eternal time; *bhavān*—Your Lordship; *ākṣipati*—attracting; *īśa*—the Supreme Lord; *viśvam*—the whole universe; *srotaḥ*—waves; *yathā*—as; *antaḥ patitam*—fallen within the water; *gabhīram*—very deep.

TRANSLATION

O my Lord, You are the beginning, the manifestation and the ultimate dissolution of the three worlds, and You are celebrated in the Vedas as the reservoir of unlimited potencies, the Supreme Person. O my Lord, as waves attract branches and leaves that have fallen into deep water, You, the supreme eternal time factor, attract everything in this universe.

PURPORT

The time factor is sometimes described as *kāla-strota,* waves of time. Everything in this material world is within the time factor and is being carried away by waves of attraction, which represent the Supreme Personality of Godhead.

TEXT 28

त्वं वै प्रजानां स्थिरजङ्गमानां
प्रजापतीनामसि सम्भविष्णुः ।
दिवौकसां देव दिवश्च्युतानां
परायणं नौरिव मज्जतोऽप्सु ॥ २८ ॥

tvaṁ vai prajānāṁ sthira-jaṅgamānāṁ
prajāpatīnām asi sambhaviṣṇuḥ
divaukasāṁ deva divaś cyutānāṁ
parāyaṇaṁ naur iva majjato 'psu

tvam—Your Lordship; *vai*—indeed; *prajānām*—of all living entities; *sthira-jaṅgamānām*—either stationary or moving; *prajāpatīnām*—of all the Prajāpatis; *asi*—You are; *sambhaviṣṇuḥ*—the generator of everyone; *diva-okasām*—of the inhabitants of the upper planetary system; *deva*—O Supreme Lord; *divaḥ cyutānām*—of the demigods, who have now fallen from their residential quarters; *parāyaṇam*—the supreme shelter; *nauḥ*—boat; *iva*—like; *majjataḥ*—of one drowning; *apsu*—in the water.

TRANSLATION

My Lord, You are the original generator of all living entities, stationary or moving, and You are also the generator of the Prajāpatis. O my Lord, as a boat is the only hope for a person drowning in the water, You are the only shelter for the demigods, who are now bereft of their heavenly position.

Thus end the Bhaktivedanta purports of the Eighth Canto, Seventeenth Chapter, of the Śrīmad-Bhāgavatam, *entitled "The Supreme Lord Agrees to Become Aditi's Son."*

CHAPTER EIGHTEEN

Lord Vāmanadeva, the Dwarf Incarnation

This chapter describes how Lord Vāmanadeva appeared and how He went to the sacrificial arena of Mahārāja Bali, who received Him well and fulfilled His desire by offering Him benedictions.

Lord Vāmanadeva appeared in this world from the womb of Aditi completely equipped with conchshell, disc, club and lotus. His bodily hue was blackish, and He was dressed in yellow garments. Lord Viṣṇu appeared at an auspicious moment on Śravaṇa-dvādaśī when the Abhijit star had arisen. At that time, in all the three worlds (including the higher planetary system, outer space and this earth), all the demigods, the cows, the *brāhmaṇas* and even the seasons were happy because of God's appearance. Therefore this auspicious day is called Vijayā. When the Supreme Personality of Godhead, who has a *sac-cid-ānanda* body, appeared as the son of Kaśyapa and Aditi, both of His parents were very astonished. After His appearance, the Lord assumed the form of a dwarf (Vāmana). All the great sages expressed their jubilation, and with Kaśyapa Muni before them they performed the birthday ceremony of Lord Vāmana. At the time of Lord Vāmanadeva's sacred thread ceremony, He was honored by the sun-god, Bṛhaspati, the goddess presiding over the planet earth, the deity of the heavenly planets, His mother, Lord Brahmā, Kuvera, the seven *ṛṣis* and others. Lord Vāmanadeva then visited the sacrificial arena on the northern side of the Narmadā River, at the field known as Bhṛgukaccha, where *brāhmaṇas* of the Bhṛgu dynasty were performing *yajñas.* Wearing a belt made of *muñja* straw, an upper garment of deerskin and a sacred thread and carrying in His hands a *daṇḍa,* an umbrella and a waterpot (*kamaṇḍalu*), Lord Vāmanadeva appeared in the sacrificial arena of Mahārāja Bali. Because of His transcendentally effulgent presence, all the priests were diminished in their prowess, and thus they all stood from their seats and offered prayers to Lord Vāmanadeva. Even Lord Śiva accepts on his head the Ganges water generated from the toe of Lord Vāmanadeva. Therefore, after washing the Lord's feet, Bali Mahārāja immediately accepted the water from the Lord's feet on his head and felt that he and his predecessors had certainly been glorified. Then Bali Mahārāja inquired of Lord

Vāmanadeva's welfare and requested the Lord to ask him for money, jewels or anything He might desire.

TEXT 1

श्रीशुक उवाच
इत्थं विरिञ्चस्तुतकर्मवीर्यः
प्रादुर्बभूवामृतभूरदित्याम् ।
चतुर्भुजः शङ्खगदाब्जचक्रः
पिशङ्गवासा नलिनायतेक्षणः ॥ १ ॥

śrī-śuka uvāca
itthaṁ viriñca-stuta-karma-vīryaḥ
prādurbabhūvāmṛta-bhūr adityām
catur-bhujaḥ śaṅkha-gadābja-cakraḥ
piśaṅga-vāsā nalināyatekṣaṇaḥ

śrī-śukaḥ uvāca—Śrī Śukadeva Gosvāmī said; *ittham*—in this way; *viriñca-stuta-karma-vīryaḥ*—the Personality of Godhead, whose activities and prowess are always praised by Lord Brahmā; *prādurbabhūva*—became manifested; *amṛta-bhūḥ*—whose appearance is always deathless; *adityām*—from the womb of Aditi; *catuḥ-bhujaḥ*—having four arms; *śaṅkha-gadā-abja-cakraḥ*—decorated with conchshell, club, lotus and disc; *piśaṅga-vāsāḥ*—dressed in yellow garments; *nalina-āyata-īkṣaṇaḥ*—having blooming eyes like the petals of a lotus.

TRANSLATION

Śukadeva Gosvāmī said: After Lord Brahmā had thus spoken, glorifying the Supreme Lord's activities and prowess, the Supreme Personality of Godhead, who is never subject to death like an ordinary living being, appeared from the womb of Aditi. His four hands were decorated with a conchshell, club, lotus and disc, He was dressed in yellow garments, and His eyes appeared like the petals of a blooming lotus.

PURPORT

The word *amṛta-bhūḥ* is significant in this verse. The Lord sometimes appears like an ordinary child taking birth, but this does not mean that He is subject to birth, death or old age. One must be very intelligent to understand the appearance and activities of the Supreme Lord in His incarnations. This is confirmed in *Bhagavad-gītā* (4.9): *janma karma ca me divyam evaṁ yo vetti tattvataḥ.* One should try to understand that the Lord's appearance and disappearance and His activities are all *divyam,* or transcendental. The Lord has nothing to do with material activities. One who understands the appearance, disappearance and activities of the Lord is immediately liberated. After giving up his body, he never again has to accept a material body, but is transferred to the spiritual world (*tyaktvā dehaṁ punar janma naiti mām eti so 'rjuna*).

TEXT 2

श्यामावदातो झषराजकुण्डल-
त्विषोल्लसच्छ्रीवदनाम्बुजः पुमान् ।
श्रीवत्सवक्षा बलयाङ्गदोल्लस-
त्किरीटकाञ्चीगुणचारुनूपुरः ॥ २ ॥

śyāmāvadāto jhaṣa-rāja-kuṇḍala-
tviṣollasac-chrī-vadanāmbujaḥ pumān
śrīvatsa-vakṣā balayāṅgadollasat-
kirīṭa-kāñcī-guṇa-cāru-nūpuraḥ

śyāma-avadātaḥ—whose body is blackish and free from inebriety; *jhaṣa-rāja-kuṇḍala*—of the two earrings, made in the shape of sharks; *tviṣā*—by the luster; *ullasat*—dazzling; *śrī-vadana-ambujaḥ*—having a beautiful lotus face; *pumān*—the Supreme Person; *śrīvatsa-vakṣāḥ*—with the mark of Śrīvatsa on His bosom; *balaya*—bracelets; *aṅgada*—arm bands; *ullasat*—dazzling; *kirīṭa*—helmet; *kāñcī*—belt; *guṇa*—sacred thread; *cāru*—beautiful; *nūpuraḥ*—ankle bells.

TRANSLATION

The body of the Supreme Personality of Godhead, blackish in complexion, was free from all inebrieties. His lotus face, decorated with earrings resembling sharks, appeared very beautiful, and on His bosom was the mark of Śrīvatsa. He wore bangles on His wrists, armlets on His arms, a helmet on His head, a belt on His waist, a sacred thread across His chest, and ankle bells decorating His lotus feet.

TEXT 3

मधुव्रतव्रातविघुष्टया स्वया
विराजितः श्रीवनमालया हरिः ।
प्रजापतेर्वेश्मतमः स्वरोचिषा
विनाशयन् कण्ठनिविष्टकौस्तुभः ॥ ३ ॥

madhu-vrata-vrāta-vighuṣṭayā svayā
virājitaḥ śrī-vanamālayā hariḥ
prajāpater veśma-tamaḥ svarociṣā
vināśayan kaṇṭha-niviṣṭa-kaustubhaḥ

madhu-vrata—of bees always hankering for honey; *vrāta*—with a bunch; *vighuṣṭayā*—resounding; *svayā*—uncommon; *virājitaḥ*—situated; *śrī*—beautiful; *vana-mālayā*—with a flower garland; *hariḥ*—the Supreme Lord; *prajāpateḥ*—of Kaśyapa Muni, the Prajāpati; *veśma-tamaḥ*—the darkness of the house; *sva-rociṣā*—by His own effulgence; *vināśayan*—vanquishing; *kaṇṭha*—on the neck; *niviṣṭa*—worn; *kaustubhaḥ*—the Kaustubha gem.

TRANSLATION

An uncommonly beautiful garland of flowers decorated His bosom, and because the flowers were extremely fragrant, a large group of bees, making their natural humming sounds, invaded them for honey. When the Lord appeared, wearing the Kaustubha gem on His neck, His effulgence vanquished the darkness in the home of the Prajāpati Kaśyapa.

TEXT 4

दिशः प्रसेदुः सलिलाशयास्तदा
प्रजाः प्रहृष्टा ऋतवो गुणान्विताः ।
द्यौरन्तरीक्षं क्षितिरग्निजिह्वा
गावो द्विजाः संजहृषुर्नगाश्च ॥ ४ ॥

diśaḥ praseduḥ salilāśayās tadā
prajāḥ prahṛṣṭā ṛtavo guṇānvitāḥ
dyaur antarīkṣaṁ kṣitir agni-jihvā
gāvo dvijāḥ sañjahṛṣur nagāś ca

diśaḥ—all directions; *praseduḥ*—became happy; *salila*—of water; *āśayāḥ*—the reservoirs; *tadā*—at that time; *prajāḥ*—all living entities; *prahṛṣṭāḥ*—very happy; *ṛtavaḥ*—the seasons; *guṇa-anvitāḥ*—full of their respective qualities; *dyauḥ*—the upper planetary system; *antarīkṣam*—outer space; *kṣitiḥ*—the surface of the earth; *agni-jihvāḥ*—the demigods; *gāvaḥ*—the cows; *dvijāḥ*—the *brāhmaṇas; sañjahṛṣuḥ*—all became happy; *nagāḥ ca*—and the mountains.

TRANSLATION

At that time, there was happiness in all directions, in the reservoirs of water like the rivers and oceans, and in the core of everyone's heart. The various seasons displayed their respective qualities, and all living entities in the upper planetary system, in outer space and on the surface of the earth were jubilant. The demigods, the cows, the brāhmaṇas and the hills and mountains were all filled with joy.

TEXT 5

श्रोणायां श्रवणद्वादश्यां मुहूर्तेऽभिजिति प्रभुः ।
सर्वे नक्षत्रताराद्याश्चक्रुस्तज्जन्म दक्षिणम् ॥ ५ ॥

śroṇāyāṁ śravaṇa-dvādaśyāṁ
muhūrte 'bhijiti prabhuḥ
sarve nakṣatra-tārādyāś
cakrus taj-janma dakṣiṇam

śroṇāyām—when the moon was situated in the Śravaṇa lunar mansion; *śravaṇa-dvādaśyām*—on the twelfth lunar day of the bright fortnight in the month of Bhādra, the day famous as the Śravaṇa-dvādaśī; *muhūrte*—in the auspicious moment; *abhijiti*—in the first portion of the Śravaṇa lunar mansion known as the Abhijit-*nakṣatra* and in the Abhijit-*muhūrta* (occurring at midday); *prabhuḥ*—the Lord; *sarve*—all; *nakṣatra*—stars; *tārā*—planets; *ādyāḥ*—beginning with the sun and followed by the other planets; *cakruḥ*—made; *tat-janma*—the birthday of the Lord; *dakṣiṇam*—very munificent.

TRANSLATION

On the day of Śravaṇa-dvādaśī [the twelfth day of the bright fortnight in the month of Bhādra], when the moon came into the lunar mansion Śravaṇa, at the auspicious moment of Abhijit, the Lord appeared in this

universe. Considering the Lord's appearance very auspicious, all the stars and planets, from the sun to Saturn, were munificently charitable.

PURPORT

Śrīla Viśvanātha Cakravartī Ṭhākura, an expert astrologer, explains the word *nakṣatra-tārādyāḥ.* The word *nakṣatra* means "the stars," the word *tāra* in this context refers to the planets, and *ādyāḥ* means "the first one specifically mentioned." Among the planets, the first is Sūrya, the sun, not the moon. Therefore, according to the Vedic version, the modern astronomer's proposition that the moon is nearest to the earth should not be accepted. The chronological order in which people all over the world refer to the days of the week—Sunday, Monday, Tuesday, Wednesday, Thursday, Friday and Saturday—corresponds to the Vedic order of the planets and thus circumstantiates the Vedic version. Apart from this, when the Lord appeared the planets and stars became situated very auspiciously, according to astrological calculations, to celebrate the birth of the Lord.

TEXT 6

द्वादश्यां सवितातिष्ठन्मध्यंदिनगतो नृप ।
विजया नाम सा प्रोक्ता यस्यां जन्म विदुर्हरेः ॥ ६ ॥

dvādaśyāṁ savitātiṣṭhan
madhyandina-gato nṛpa
vijayā-nāma sā proktā
yasyāṁ janma vidur hareḥ

dvādaśyām—on the twelfth day of the moon; *savitā*—the sun; *atiṣṭhat*—was staying; *madhyam-dina-gataḥ*—on the meridian; *nṛpa*—O King; *vijayā-nāma*—by the name Vijayā; *sā*—that day; *proktā*—is called; *yasyām*—on which; *janma*—the appearance; *viduḥ*—they know; *hareḥ*—of Lord Hari.

TRANSLATION

O King, when the Lord appeared—on dvādaśī, the twelfth day of the moon—the sun was at the meridian, as every learned scholar knows. This dvādaśī is called Vijayā.

TEXT 7

शङ्खदुन्दुभयो नेदुर्मृदङ्गपणवानकाः ।
चित्रवादित्रतूर्याणां निर्घोषस्तुमुलोऽभवत् ॥ ७ ॥

śaṅkha-dundubhayo nedur
mṛdaṅga-paṇavānakāḥ
citra-vāditra-tūryāṇāṁ
nirghoṣas tumulo 'bhavat

śaṅkha—conchshells; *dundubhayaḥ*—kettledrums; *neduḥ*—vibrated; *mṛdaṅga*—drums; *paṇava-ānakāḥ*—drums named *paṇavas* and *ānakas; citra*—various; *vāditra*—of these vibrations of musical sound; *tūryāṇām*—and of other instruments; *nirghoṣaḥ*—the loud sound; *tumulaḥ*—tumultuous; *abhavat*—became.

TRANSLATION

Conchshells, kettledrums, drums, paṇavas and ānakas vibrated in concert. The sound of these and various other instruments was tumultuous.

TEXT 8

प्रीताश्चाप्सरसोऽनृत्यन्गन्धर्वप्रवरा जगुः ।
तुष्टुवुर्मुनयो देवा मनवः पितरोऽग्नयः ॥ ८ ॥

prītāś cāpsaraso 'nṛtyan
gandharva-pravarā jaguḥ
tuṣṭuvur munayo devā
manavaḥ pitaro 'gnayaḥ

prītāḥ—being very pleased; *ca*—also; *apsarasaḥ*—the celestial dancing girls; *anṛtyan*—danced; *gandharva-pravarāḥ*—the best of the Gandharvas; *jaguḥ*—sang; *tuṣṭuvuḥ*—satisfied the Lord by offering prayers; *munayaḥ*—the great sages; *devāḥ*—the demigods; *manavaḥ*—the Manus; *pitaraḥ*—the inhabitants of Pitṛloka; *agnayaḥ*—the fire-gods.

TRANSLATION

Being very pleased, the celestial dancing girls [Apsarās] danced in jubilation, the best of the Gandharvas sang songs, and the great sages, demigods, Manus, Pitās and fire-gods offered prayers to satisfy the Lord.

TEXTS 9-10

सिद्धविद्याधरगणाः सकिंपुरुषकिन्नराः ।
चारणा यक्षरक्षांसि सुपर्णा भुजगोत्तमाः ॥ ९ ॥
गायन्तोऽतिप्रशंसन्तो नृत्यन्तो विबुधानुगाः ।
अदित्या आश्रमपदं कुसुमैः समवाकिरन् ॥ १० ॥

siddha-vidyādhara-gaṇāḥ
sakimpuruṣa-kinnarāḥ
cāraṇā yakṣa-rakṣāṁsi
suparṇā bhujagottamāḥ

gāyanto 'tipraśaṁsanto
nṛtyanto vibudhānugāḥ
adityā āśrama-padaṁ
kusumaiḥ samavākiran

siddha—the inhabitants of Siddhaloka; *vidyādhara-gaṇāḥ*—the inhabitants of Vidyādhara-loka; *sa*—with; *kimpuruṣa*—the inhabitants of Kimpuruṣa-loka; *kinnarāḥ*—the inhabitants of Kinnaraloka; *cāraṇāḥ*—the inhabitants of Cāraṇaloka; *yakṣa*—the Yakṣas; *rakṣāṁsi*—the Rākṣasas; *suparṇāḥ*—the Suparṇas; *bhujaga-uttamāḥ*—the best of the inhabitants of the serpent *loka; gāyantaḥ*—glorifying the Lord; *ati-praśaṁsantaḥ*—praising the Lord; *nṛtyantaḥ*—dancing; *vibudhānugāḥ*—the followers of the demigods; *adityāḥ*—of Aditi; *āśrama-padam*—the place of residence; *kusumaiḥ*—by flowers; *samavākiran*—covered.

TRANSLATION

The Siddhas, Vidyādharas, Kimpuruṣas, Kinnaras, Cāraṇas, Yakṣas, Rākṣasas, Suparṇas, the best of serpents, and the followers of the demigods all showered flowers on Aditi's residence, covering the entire house, while glorifying and praising the Lord and dancing.

TEXT 11

दृष्ट्वादितिस्तं निजगर्भसम्भवं
परं पुमांसं मुदमाप विस्मिता ।
गृहीतदेहं निजयोगमायया
प्रजापतिश्चाह जयेति विस्मितः ॥ ११ ॥

dṛṣṭvāditis taṁ nija-garbha-sambhavaṁ
paraṁ pumāṁsaṁ mudam āpa vismitā
gṛhīta-dehaṁ nija-yoga-māyayā
prajāpatiś cāha jayeti vismitaḥ

dṛṣṭvā—seeing; *aditiḥ*—mother Aditi; *tam*—Him (the Supreme Personality of Godhead); *nija-garbha-sambhavam*—born of her own womb; *param*—the Supreme; *pumāṁsam*—the Personality of Godhead; *mudam*—great happiness; *āpa*—conceived; *vismitā*—being very much astonished; *gṛhīta*—accepted; *deham*—body, or transcendental form; *nija-yoga-māyayā*—by His own spiritual potency; *prajāpatiḥ*—Kaśyapa Muni; *ca*—also; *āha*—said; *jaya*—all glories; *iti*—thus; *vismitaḥ*—being astonished.

TRANSLATION

When Aditi saw the Supreme Personality of Godhead, who had appeared from her own womb, having accepted a transcendental body by His own spiritual potency, she was struck with wonder and was very happy. Upon seeing the child, Prajāpati Kaśyapa exclaimed, "Jaya! Jaya!" in great happiness and wonder.

TEXT 12

यत् तद् वपुर्भाति विभूषणायुधै-
रव्यक्तचिद्व्यक्तमधारयद्धरिः ।
बभूव तेनैव स वामनो वटुः
सम्पश्यतोर्दिव्यगतिर्यथा नटः ॥ १२ ॥

yat tad vapur bhāti vibhūṣaṇāyudhair
avyakta-cid-vyaktam adhārayad dhariḥ
babhūva tenaiva sa vāmano vaṭuḥ
sampaśyator divya-gatir yathā naṭaḥ

yat—which; *tat*—that; *vapuḥ*—transcendental body; *bhāti*—manifests; *vibhūṣaṇa*—with regular ornaments; *āyudhaiḥ*—and with weapons; *avyakta*—unmanifested; *cit-vyaktam*—spiritually manifested; *adhārayat*—assumed; *hariḥ*—the Lord; *babhūva*—immediately became; *tena*—with that; *eva*—certainly; *saḥ*—He (the Lord); *vāmanaḥ*—dwarf; *vaṭuḥ*—a *brāhmaṇa brahmacārī; sampaśyatoḥ*—while both His father and mother were seeing; *divya-gatiḥ*—whose movements are wonderful; *yathā*—as; *naṭaḥ*—a theatrical actor.

TRANSLATION

The Lord appeared in His original form, with ornaments and weapons in His hands. Although this ever-existing form is not visible in the material world, He nonetheless appeared in this form. Then, in the presence of His father and mother, He assumed the form of Vāmana, a brāhmaṇa-dwarf, a brahmacārī, just like a theatrical actor.

PURPORT

The word *naṭaḥ* is significant. An actor changes dress to play different parts, but is always the same man. Similarly, as described in the *Brahma-saṁhitā* (5.33, 39), the Lord assumes many thousands and millions of forms (*advaitam acyutam anādim ananta-rūpam ādyaṁ purāṇa-puruṣam*). He is always present with innumerable incarnations (*rāmādi-mūrtiṣu kalā-niyamena tiṣṭhan nānāvatāram akarod bhuvaneṣu kintu*). Nonetheless, although He appears in various incarnations, they are not different from one another. He is the same person, with the same potency, the same eternity and the same spiritual existence, but He can simultaneously assume various forms. When Vāmanadeva appeared from the womb of His mother, He appeared in the form of Nārāyaṇa, with four hands equipped with the necessary symbolic weapons, and then immediately transformed Himself into a *brahmacārī* (*vaṭu*). This means that His body is not material. One who thinks that the Supreme Lord assumes a material body is not intelligent. He has to learn more about the Lord's position. As confirmed in *Bhagavad-gītā* (4.9), *janma karma ca me divyam evaṁ yo vetti tattvataḥ.* One has to understand the transcendental appearance of the Lord in His original transcendental body (*sac-cid-ānanda-vigraha*).

TEXT 13

तं वटुं वामनं दृष्ट्वा मोदमाना महर्षयः ।
कर्माणि कारयामासुः पुरस्कृत्य प्रजापतिम् ॥ १३ ॥

taṁ vaṭuṁ vāmanaṁ dṛṣṭvā
modamānā maharṣayaḥ
karmāṇi kārayām āsuḥ
puraskṛtya prajāpatim

tam—Him; *vaṭum*—the *brahmacārī; vāmanam*—dwarf; *dṛṣṭvā*—seeing; *modamānāḥ*—in a happy mood; *mahā-ṛṣayaḥ*—the great saintly persons;

karmāṇi—ritualistic ceremonies; *kārayām āsuḥ*—performed; *puraskṛtya*—keeping in front; *prajāpatim*—Kaśyapa Muni, the Prajāpati.

TRANSLATION

When the great sages saw the Lord as the brahmacārī-dwarf Vāmana, they were certainly very pleased. Thus they placed before them Kaśyapa Muni, the Prajāpati, and performed all the ritualistic ceremonies, such as the birthday ceremony.

PURPORT

According to Vedic civilization, when a child is born in the family of a *brāhmaṇa,* the birthday ceremony, known as *jāta-karma,* is first performed, and then other ceremonies are also gradually performed. But when this *vāmana-rūpa* appeared in the form of a *vaṭu,* or *brahmacārī,* His sacred thread ceremony was also performed immediately.

TEXT 14

तस्योपनीयमानस्य सावित्रीं सविताब्रवीत् ।
बृहस्पतिर्ब्रह्मसूत्रं मेखलां कश्यपोऽददात् ॥ १४॥

tasyopanīyamānasya
sāvitrīṁ savitābravīt
bṛhaspatir brahma-sūtraṁ
mekhalāṁ kaśyapo 'dadāt

tasya—of Lord Vāmanadeva; *upanīyamānasya*—at the time of His being offered the sacred thread ceremony; *sāvitrīm*—the Gāyatrī *mantra; savitā*—the sun-god; *abravīt*—chanted; *bṛhaspatiḥ*—Bṛhaspati, the *guru* of the demigods; *brahma-sūtram*—the sacred thread; *mekhalām*—the belt of straw; *kaśyapaḥ*—Kaśyapa Muni; *adadāt*—offered.

TRANSLATION

At the sacred thread ceremony of Vāmanadeva, the sun-god personally uttered the Gāyatrī mantra, Bṛhaspati offered the sacred thread, and Kaśyapa Muni offered a straw belt.

TEXT 15

ददौ कृष्णाजिनं भूमिर्दण्डं सोमो वनस्पतिः ।
कौपीनाच्छादनं माता द्यौश्छत्रं जगतः पतेः ॥ १५॥

dadau kṛṣṇājinaṁ bhūmir
daṇḍaṁ somo vanaspatiḥ
kaupīnācchādanaṁ mātā
dyauś chatraṁ jagataḥ pateḥ

dadau—gave, offered; *kṛṣṇa-ajinam*—the skin of a deer; *bhūmiḥ*—mother earth; *daṇḍam*—a *brahmacārī's* rod; *somaḥ*—the moon-god; *vanaḥ-patiḥ*—the king of the forest; *kaupīna*—the underwear; *ācchādanam*—covering the body; *mātā*—His mother, Aditi; *dyauḥ*—the heavenly kingdom; *chatram*—an umbrella; *jagataḥ*—of the whole universe; *pateḥ*—of the master.

TRANSLATION

Mother earth gave Him a deerskin, and the demigod of the moon, who is the king of the forest, gave Him a brahma-daṇḍa [the rod of a brahmacārī]. His mother, Aditi, gave Him cloth for underwear, and the deity presiding over the heavenly kingdom offered Him an umbrella.

TEXT 16

कमण्डलुं वेदगर्भः कुशान्सप्तर्षयो ददुः ।
अक्षमालां महाराज सरस्वत्यव्ययात्मनः ॥ १६ ॥

kamaṇḍaluṁ veda-garbhaḥ
kuśān saptarṣayo daduḥ
akṣa-mālāṁ mahārāja
sarasvaty avyayātmanaḥ

kamaṇḍalum—a waterpot; *veda-garbhaḥ*—Lord Brahmā; *kuśān*—*kuśa* grass; *sapta-ṛṣayaḥ*—the seven sages; *daduḥ*—offered; *akṣa-mālām*—a string of Rudrākṣa beads; *mahārāja*—O King; *sarasvatī*—the goddess Sarasvatī; *avyaya-ātmanaḥ*—to the Supreme Personality of Godhead.

TRANSLATION

O King, Lord Brahmā offered a waterpot to the inexhaustible Supreme Personality of Godhead, the seven sages offered Him kuśa grass, and mother Sarasvatī gave Him a string of Rudrākṣa beads.

TEXT 17

तस्मा इत्युपनीताय यक्षराट् पात्रिकामदात् ।
भिक्षां भगवती साक्षादुमादादम्बिका सती ॥ १७ ॥

tasmā ity upanītāya
yakṣa-rāṭ pātrikām adāt
bhikṣāṁ bhagavatī sākṣād
umādād ambikā satī

tasmai—unto Him (Lord Vāmanadeva); *iti*—in this way; *upanītāya*—who had undergone His sacred thread ceremony; *yakṣa-rāṭ*—Kuvera, the treasurer of heaven and King of the Yakṣas; *pātrikām*—a pot for begging alms; *adāt*—delivered; *bhikṣām*—alms; *bhagavatī*—mother Bhavānī, the wife of Lord Śiva; *sākṣāt*—directly; *umā*—Umā; *adāt*—gave; *ambikā*—the mother of the universe; *satī*—the chaste.

TRANSLATION

When Vāmanadeva had thus been given the sacred thread, Kuvera, King of the Yakṣas, gave Him a pot for begging alms, and mother Bhagavatī, the wife of Lord Śiva and most chaste mother of the entire universe, gave Him His first alms.

TEXT 18

स ब्रह्मवर्चसेनैवं सभां संभावितो वटुः ।
ब्रह्मर्षिगणसञ्जुष्टामत्यरोचत मारिषः ॥ १८ ॥

sa brahma-varcasenaivaṁ
sabhāṁ sambhāvito vaṭuḥ
brahmarṣi-gaṇa-sañjuṣṭām
atyarocata māriṣaḥ

saḥ—He (Vāmanadeva); *brahma-varcasena*—by His Brahman effulgence; *evam*—in this way; *sabhām*—the assembly; *sambhāvitaḥ*—having been welcomed by everyone; *vaṭuḥ*—the *brahmacārī; brahma-ṛṣi-gaṇa-sañjuṣṭām*—filled with great *brāhmaṇa* sages; *ati-arocata*—surpassing, appeared beautiful; *māriṣaḥ*—the best of the *brahmacārīs.*

TRANSLATION

Having thus been welcomed by everyone, Lord Vāmanadeva, the best of the brahmacārīs, exhibited His Brahman effulgence. Thus He surpassed in beauty that entire assembly, which was filled with great saintly brāhmaṇas.

TEXT 19

समिद्धमाहितं वह्निं कृत्वा परिसमूहनम् ।
परिस्तीर्य समभ्यर्च्य समिद्भिरजुहोद् द्विजः ॥ १९ ॥

samiddham āhitaṁ vahniṁ
kṛtvā parisamūhanam
paristīrya samabhyarcya
samidbhir ajuhod dvijaḥ

samiddham—blazing; *āhitam*—being situated; *vahnim*—the fire; *kṛtvā*—after making; *parisamūhanam*—properly; *paristīrya*—surpassing; *samabhyarcya*—after offering worship; *samidbhiḥ*—with sacrificial offerings; *ajuhot*—completed the fire sacrifice; *dvijaḥ*—the best of the *brāhmaṇas.*

TRANSLATION

After Lord Śrī Vāmanadeva set a sacrificial fire, He offered worship and performed a fire sacrifice on the sacrificial field.

TEXT 20

श्रुत्वाश्वमेधैर्यजमानमूर्जितं
बलिं भृगूणामुपकल्पितैस्ततः ।
जगाम तत्राखिलसारसंभृतो
भारेण गां सन्नमयन्पदे पदे ॥ २० ॥

śrutvāśvamedhair yajamānam ūrjitaṁ
baliṁ bhṛgūṇām upakalpitais tataḥ
jagāma tatrākhila-sāra-sambhṛto
bhāreṇa gāṁ sannamayan pade pade

śrutvā—after hearing; *aśvamedhaiḥ*—by *aśvamedha* sacrifices; *yajamānam*—the performer; *ūrjitam*—very glorious; *balim*—Bali Mahārāja;

bhṛgūṇām—under the guidance of the *brāhmaṇas* born in the Bhṛgu dynasty; *upakalpitaiḥ*—performed; *tataḥ*—from that place; *jagāma*—went; *tatra*—there; *akhila-sāra-sambhṛtaḥ*—the Supreme Personality of Godhead, the essence of all creation; *bhāreṇa*—with the weight; *gām*—the earth; *sanna-mayan*—depressing; *pade pade*—at every step.

TRANSLATION

When the Lord heard that Bali Mahārāja was performing aśvamedha sacrifices under the patronage of brāhmaṇas belonging to the Bhṛgu dynasty, the Supreme Lord, who is full in every respect, proceeded there to show His mercy to Bali Mahārāja. By His weight, He pushed down the earth with every step.

PURPORT

The Supreme Personality of Godhead is *akhila-sāra-sambhṛta.* In other words, He is the proprietor of everything essential in this material world. Thus although the Lord was going to Bali Mahārāja to beg something, He is always complete and has nothing to beg from anyone. Indeed, He is so powerful that in His full opulence He pressed down the surface of the earth at every step.

TEXT 21

तं नर्मदायास्तट उत्तरे बले-
यं ऋत्विजस्ते भृगुकच्छसंज्ञके ।
प्रवर्तयन्तो भृगवः क्रतूत्तमं
व्यचक्षतारादुदितं यथा रविम् ॥ २१ ॥

taṁ narmadāyās taṭa uttare baler
ya ṛtvijas te bhṛgukaccha-saṁjñake
pravartayanto bhṛgavaḥ kratūttamaṁ
vyacakṣatārād uditaṁ yathā ravim

tam—Him (Vāmanadeva); *narmadāyāḥ*—of the River Narmadā; *taṭe*—on the bank; *uttare*—northern; *baleḥ*—of Mahārāja Bali; *ye*—who; *ṛtvijaḥ*—the priests engaged in ritualistic ceremonies; *te*—all of them; *bhṛgukaccha-saṁjñake*—in the field named Bhṛgukaccha; *pravartayantaḥ*—performing; *bhṛgavaḥ*—all the descendants of Bhṛgu; *kratu-uttamam*—the most important sacrifice, named *aśvamedha; vyacakṣata*—they observed; *ārāt*—nearby; *uditam*—risen; *yathā*—like; *ravim*—the sun.

TRANSLATION

While engaged in performing the sacrifice in the field known as Bhṛgukaccha, on the northern bank of the Narmadā River, the brahminical priests, the descendants of Bhṛgu, saw Vāmanadeva to be like the sun rising nearby.

TEXT 22

ते ऋत्विजो यजमानः सदस्या
हतत्विषो वामनतेजसा नृप ।
सूर्यः किलायात्युत वा विभावसुः
सनत्कुमारोऽथ दिदृक्षया क्रतोः ॥ २२ ॥

te ṛtvijo yajamānaḥ sadasyā
hata-tviṣo vāmana-tejasā nṛpa
sūryaḥ kilāyāty uta vā vibhāvasuḥ
sanat-kumāro 'tha didṛkṣayā kratoḥ

te—all of them; *ṛtvijaḥ*—the priests; *yajamānaḥ*—as well as Bali Mahārāja, who had engaged them in performing the *yajña; sadasyāḥ*—all the members of the assembly; *hata-tviṣaḥ*—decreased in their bodily effulgence; *vāmana-tejasā*—by the brilliant effulgence of Lord Vāmana; *nṛpa*—O King; *sūryaḥ*—the sun; *kila*—whether; *āyāti*—is coming; *uta vā*—either; *vibhāvasuḥ*—the fire-god; *sanat-kumāraḥ*—the Kumāra known as Sanat-kumāra; *atha*—either; *didṛkṣayā*—with a desire to observe; *kratoḥ*—the sacrificial ceremony.

TRANSLATION

O King, because of Vāmanadeva's bright effulgence, the priests, along with Bali Mahārāja and all the members of the assembly, were robbed of their splendor. Thus they began to ask one another whether the sun-god himself, Sanat-kumāra or the fire-god had personally come to see the sacrificial ceremony.

TEXT 23

इत्थं सशिष्येषु भृगुष्वनेकधा
वितर्क्यमाणो भगवान्स वामनः ।
छत्रं सदण्डं सजलं कमण्डलुं
विवेश बिभ्रद्धयमेधवाटम् ॥ २३ ॥

itthaṁ saśiṣyeṣu bhṛguṣv anekadhā
vitarkyamāṇo bhagavān sa vāmanaḥ
chatraṁ sadaṇḍaṁ sajalaṁ kamaṇḍaluṁ
viveśa bibhrad dhayamedha-vāṭam

ittham—in this way; *sa-śiṣyeṣu*—with their disciples; *bhṛguṣu*—among the Bhṛgus; *anekadhā*—in many ways; *vitarkyamāṇaḥ*—being talked and argued about; *bhagavān*—the Supreme Personality of Godhead; *saḥ*—that; *vāmanaḥ*—Lord Vāmana; *chatram*—umbrella; *sadaṇḍam*—with the rod; *sa-jalam*—filled with water; *kamaṇḍalum*—waterpot; *viveśa*—entered; *bibhrat*—taking in hand; *hayamedha*—of the *aśvamedha* sacrifice; *vāṭam*—the arena.

TRANSLATION

While the priests of the Bhṛgu dynasty and their disciples talked and argued in various ways, the Supreme Personality of Godhead, Vāmanadeva, holding in His hands the rod, the umbrella and a waterpot full of water, entered the arena of the aśvamedha sacrifice.

TEXTS 24-25

मौञ्ज्या मेखलया वीतमुपवीताजिनोत्तरम् ।
जटिलं वामनं विप्रं मायामाणवकं हरिम् ॥ २४ ॥
प्रविष्टं वीक्ष्य भृगवः सशिष्यास्ते सहाग्निभिः ।
प्रत्यगृह्णन्समुत्थाय संक्षिप्तास्तस्य तेजसा ॥ २५ ॥

mauñjyā mekhalayā vītam
upavītājinottaram
jaṭilaṁ vāmanaṁ vipraṁ
māyā-māṇavakaṁ harim

praviṣṭaṁ vīkṣya bhṛgavaḥ
saśiṣyās te sahāgnibhiḥ
pratyagṛhṇan samutthāya
saṅkṣiptās tasya tejasā

mauñjyā—made of *muñja* straw; *mekhalayā*—with a belt; *vītam*—circled; *upavīta*—sacred thread; *ajina-uttaram*—wearing a deerskin upper garment; *jaṭilam*—having matted locks of hair; *vāmanam*—Lord Vāmana;

vipram—a *brāhmaṇa; māyā-māṇavakam*—the illusory son of a human being; *harim*—the Supreme Personality of Godhead; *praviṣṭam*—entered; *vīkṣya*—seeing; *bhṛgavaḥ*—the priests who were descendants of Bhṛgu; *sa-śiṣyāḥ*—with their disciples; *te*—all of them; *saha-agnibhiḥ*—with the fire sacrifice; *pratyagṛhṇan*—properly welcomed; *samutthāya*—standing up; *saṅkṣiptāḥ*—being diminished; *tasya*—His; *tejasā*—by brilliance.

TRANSLATION

Appearing as a brāhmaṇa boy, wearing a belt of straw, a sacred thread, an upper garment of deerskin, and matted locks of hair, Lord Vāmanadeva entered the arena of sacrifice. His brilliant effulgence diminished the brilliance of all the priests and their disciples, who thus stood from their seats and welcomed the Lord properly by offering obeisances.

TEXT 26

यजमानः प्रमुदितो दर्शनीयं मनोरमम् ।
रूपानुरूपावयवं तस्मा आसनमाहरत् ॥ २६ ॥

yajamānaḥ pramudito
darśanīyaṁ manoramam
rūpānurūpāvayavaṁ
tasmā āsanam āharat

yajamānaḥ—Bali Mahārāja, who had engaged all the priests in performing the sacrifice; *pramuditaḥ*—being very jubilant; *darśanīyam*—pleasing to see; *manoramam*—so beautiful; *rūpa*—with beauty; *anurūpa*—equal to His bodily beauty; *avayavam*—all the different parts of the body; *tasmai*—unto Him; *āsanam*—a sitting place; *āharat*—offered.

TRANSLATION

Bali Mahārāja, jubilant at seeing Lord Vāmanadeva, whose beautiful limbs contributed equally to the beauty of His entire body, offered Him a seat with great satisfaction.

TEXT 27

स्वागतेनाभिनन्द्याथ पादौ भगवतो बलिः ।
अवनिज्यार्चयामास मुक्तसङ्गमनोरमम् ॥ २७ ॥

svāgatenābhinandyātha
pādau bhagavato baliḥ
avanijyārcayām āsa
mukta-saṅga-manoramam

su-āgatena—by words of welcome; *abhinandya*—welcoming; *atha*—thus; *pādau*—the two lotus feet; *bhagavataḥ*—of the Lord; *baliḥ*—Bali Mahārāja; *avanijya*—washing; *arcayām āsa*—worshiped; *mukta-saṅga-manoramam*—the Supreme Personality of Godhead, who is beautiful to the liberated souls.

TRANSLATION

Thus offering a proper reception to the Supreme Personality of Godhead, who is always beautiful to the liberated souls, Bali Mahārāja worshiped Him by washing His lotus feet.

TEXT 28

तत्पादशौचं जनकल्मषापहं
स धर्मविन्मूर्ध्न्यदधात् सुमङ्गलम् ।
यद् देवदेवो गिरिशश्चन्द्रमौलि-
र्दधार मूर्ध्ना परया च भक्त्या ॥ २८ ॥

tat-pāda-śaucaṁ jana-kalmaṣāpahaṁ
sa dharma-vin mūrdhny adadhāt sumaṅgalam
yad deva-devo giriśaś candra-maulir
dadhāra mūrdhnā parayā ca bhaktyā

tat-pāda-śaucam—the water that washed the lotus feet of the Lord; *jana-kalmaṣa-apaham*—which washes away all the sinful reactions of the people in general; *saḥ*—he (Bali Mahārāja); *dharma-vit*—completely aware of religious principles; *mūrdhni*—on the head; *adadhāt*—carried; *su-maṅgalam*—all-auspicious; *yat*—which; *deva-devaḥ*—the best of the demigods; *giriśaḥ*—Lord Śiva; *candra-mauliḥ*—who carries on his forehead the emblem of the moon; *dadhāra*—carried; *mūrdhnā*—on the head; *parayā*—supreme; *ca*—also; *bhaktyā*—with devotion.

TRANSLATION

Lord Śiva, the best of demigods, who carries on his forehead the emblem of the moon, receives on his head with great devotion the Ganges water emanating from the toe of Viṣṇu. Being aware of religious principles, Bali Mahārāja knew this. Consequently, following in the footsteps of Lord Śiva, he also placed on his head the water that had washed the Lord's lotus feet.

PURPORT

Lord Śiva is known as Gaṅgā-dhara, or one who carries the water of the Ganges on his head. On Lord Śiva's forehead is the emblem of the half-moon, yet to give supreme respect to the Supreme Personality of Godhead, Lord Śiva placed the water of the Ganges above this emblem. This example should be followed by everyone, or at least by every devotee, because Lord Śiva is one of the *mahājanas.* Similarly, Mahārāja Bali also later became a *mahājana.* One *mahājana* follows another *mahājana,* and by following the *paramparā* system of *mahājana* activities one can become advanced in spiritual consciousness. The water of the Ganges is sanctified because it emanates from the toe of Lord Viṣṇu. Bali Mahārāja washed the lotus feet of Vāmanadeva, and the water with which he did so became equal to the Ganges. Bali Mahārāja, who perfectly knew all religious principles, therefore took that water on his head, following in the footsteps of Lord Śiva.

TEXT 29

श्रीबलिरुवाच

स्वागतं ते नमस्तुभ्यं ब्रह्मन्किं करवाम ते ।
ब्रह्मर्षीणां तपः साक्षान्मन्ये त्वार्य वपुर्धरम् ॥ २९ ॥

śrī-balir uvāca
svāgataṁ te namas tubhyaṁ
brahman kiṁ karavāma te
brahmarṣīṇāṁ tapaḥ sākṣān
manye tvārya vapur-dharam

śrī-baliḥ uvāca—Bali Mahārāja said; *su-āgatam*—all welcome; *te*—unto You; *namaḥ tubhyam*—I offer my respectful obeisances unto You; *brahman*—O *brāhmaṇa; kim*—what; *karavāma*—can we do; *te*—for You; *brahma-*

ṛṣīṇām—of the great *brāhmaṇa* sages; *tapaḥ*—austerity; *sākṣāt*—directly; *manye*—I think; *tvā*—You; *ārya*—O noble one; *vapuḥ-dharam*—personified.

TRANSLATION

Bali Mahārāja then said to Lord Vāmanadeva: O brāhmaṇa, I offer You my hearty welcome and my respectful obeisances. Please let us know what we may do for You. We think of You as the personified austerity of the great brāhmaṇa-sages.

TEXT 30

अद्य नः पितरस्तृप्ता अद्य नः पावितं कुलम् ।
अद्य स्विष्टः क्रतुरयं यद् भवानागतो गृहान् ॥ ३० ॥

adya naḥ pitaras tṛptā
adya naḥ pāvitaṁ kulam
adya sviṣṭaḥ kratur ayaṁ
yad bhavān āgato gṛhān

adya—today; *naḥ*—our; *pitaraḥ*—forefathers; *tṛptāḥ*—satisfied; *adya*—today; *naḥ*—our; *pāvitam*—purified; *kulam*—the whole family; *adya*—today; *su-iṣṭaḥ*—properly executed; *kratuḥ*—the sacrifice; *ayam*—this; *yat*—because; *bhavān*—Your Lordship; *āgataḥ*—arrived; *gṛhān*—at our residence.

TRANSLATION

O my Lord, because You have kindly arrived at our home, all my forefathers are satisfied, our family and entire dynasty have been sanctified, and the sacrifice we are performing is now complete because of Your presence.

TEXT 31

अद्याग्नयो मे सुहुता यथाविधि
द्विजात्मज त्वच्चरणावनेजनैः ।
हतांहसो वार्भिरियं च भूरहो
तथा पुनीता तनुभिः पदैस्तव ॥ ३१ ॥

adyāgnayo me suhutā yathā-vidhi
dvijātmaja tvac-caraṇāvanejanaiḥ
hatāṁhaso vārbhir iyaṁ ca bhūr aho
tathā punītā tanubhiḥ padais tava

adya—today; *agnayaḥ*—the sacrificial fires; *me*—executed by me; *su-hutāḥ*—properly offered oblations; *yathā-vidhi*—in terms of the śāstric injunction; *dvija-ātmaja*—O son of a *brāhmaṇa; tvat-caraṇa-avanejanaiḥ*—which washed Your lotus feet; *hata-aṁhasaḥ*—who have become cleansed of all sinful reactions; *vārbhiḥ*—by the water; *iyam*—this; *ca*—also; *bhūḥ*—the surface of the globe; *aho*—oh; *tathā*—as well; *punītā*—sanctified; *tanubhiḥ*—small; *padaiḥ*—by the touch of the lotus feet; *tava*—Your.

TRANSLATION

O son of a brāhmaṇa, today the fire of sacrifice is ablaze according to the injunction of the śāstra, and I have been freed from all the sinful reactions of my life by the water that has washed Your lotus feet. O my Lord, by the touch of Your small lotus feet the entire surface of the world has been sanctified.

TEXT 32

यद् यद् वटो वाञ्छसि तत्प्रतीच्छ मे
त्वामर्थिनं विप्रसुतानुतर्कये ।
गां काञ्चनं गुणवद् धाम मृष्टं
तथान्नपेयमुत वा विप्रकन्याम् ।
ग्रामान् समृद्धांस्तुरगान् गजान् वा
रथांस्तथार्हत्तम सम्प्रतीच्छ ॥ ३२ ॥

yad yad vaṭo vāñchasi tat pratīccha me
tvām arthinaṁ vipra-sutānutarkaye
gāṁ kāñcanaṁ guṇavad dhāma mṛṣṭaṁ
tathānna-peyam uta vā vipra-kanyām
grāmān samṛddhāṁs turagān gajān vā
rathāṁs tathārhattama sampratīccha

yat yat—whatever; *vaṭo*—O *brahmacārī; vāñchasi*—You desire; *tat*—that; *pratīccha*—You may take; *me*—from me; *tvām*—You; *arthinam*—desiring something; *vipra-suta*—O son of a *brāhmaṇa; anutarkaye*—I consider; *gām*—a cow; *kāñcanam*—gold; *guṇavat dhāma*—a furnished residence; *mṛṣṭam*—palatable; *tathā*—as well as; *anna*—food grains; *peyam*—drink; *uta*—indeed; *vā*—either; *vipra-kanyām*—the daughter of a *brāhmaṇa; grāmān*—villages; *samṛddhān*—prosperous; *turagān*—horses; *gajān*—elephants; *vā*—either; *rathān*—chariots; *tathā*—as well as; *arhat-tama*—O best of those who are worshipable; *sampratīccha*—You may take.

TRANSLATION

O son of a brāhmaṇa, it appears that You have come here to ask me for something. Therefore, whatever You want You may take from me. O best of those who are worshipable. You may take from me a cow, gold, a furnished house, palatable food and drink, the daughter of a brāhmaṇa for Your wife, prosperous villages, horses, elephants, chariots or whatever You desire.

Thus end the Bhaktivedanta purports of the Eighth Canto, Eighteenth Chapter, of the Śrīmad-Bhāgavatam, *entitled "Lord Vāmanadeva, the Dwarf Incarnation."*

CHAPTER NINETEEN

Lord Vāmanadeva Begs Charity from Bali Mahārāja

This Nineteenth Chapter describes how Lord Vāmanadeva asked for three paces of land in charity, how Bali Mahārāja agreed to His proposal, and how Śukrācārya forbade Bali Mahārāja to fulfill Lord Vāmanadeva's request.

When Bali Mahārāja, thinking Vāmanadeva to be the son of a *brāhmaṇa,* told Him to ask for anything He liked, Lord Vāmanadeva praised Hiraṇyakaśipu and Hiraṇyākṣa for their heroic activities, and after thus praising the family in which Bali Mahārāja had been born, He begged the King for three paces of land. Bali Mahārāja agreed to give this land in charity, since this was very insignificant, but Śukrācārya, who could understand that Vāmanadeva was Viṣṇu, the friend of the demigods, forbade Bali Mahārāja to give this land. Śukrācārya advised Bali Mahārāja to withdraw his promise. He explained that in subduing others, in joking, in responding to danger, in acting for the welfare of others, and so on, one could refuse to fulfill one's promise, and there would be no fault. By this philosophy, Śukrācārya tried to dissuade Bali Mahārāja from giving land to Lord Vāmanadeva.

TEXT 1

श्रीशुक उवाच
इति वैरोचनेर्वाक्यं धर्मयुक्तं स सूनृतम् ।
निशम्य भगवान्प्रीतः प्रतिनन्द्येदमब्रवीत् ॥ १ ॥

śrī-śuka uvāca
iti vairocaner vākyaṁ
dharma-yuktaṁ sa sūnṛtam
niśamya bhagavān prītaḥ
pratinandyedam abravīt

śrī-śukaḥ uvāca—Śrī Śukadeva Gosvāmī said; *iti*—thus; *vairocaneḥ*—of the son of Virocana; *vākyam*—the words; *dharma-yuktam*—in terms of religious principles; *saḥ*—He; *sū-nṛtam*—very pleasing; *niśamya*—hearing; *bhagavān*—the Supreme Personality of Godhead; *prītaḥ*—completely pleased; *pratinandya*—congratulating him; *idam*—the following words; *abravīt*—said.

TRANSLATION

Śukadeva Gosvāmī continued: When the Supreme Personality of Godhead, Vāmanadeva, heard Bali Mahārāja speaking in this pleasing way, He was very satisfied, for Bali Mahārāja had spoken in terms of religious principles. Thus the Lord began to praise him.

TEXT 2

श्रीभगवानुवाच
वचस्तवैतज्जनदेव सूनृतं
कुलोचितं धर्मयुतं यशस्करम्।
यस्य प्रमाणं भृगवः सांपराये
पितामहः कुलवृद्धः प्रशान्तः ॥ २ ॥

śrī-bhagavān uvāca
vacas tavaitaj jana-deva sūnṛtaṁ
kulocitaṁ dharma-yutaṁ yaśas-karam
yasya pramāṇaṁ bhṛgavaḥ sāmparāye
pitāmahaḥ kula-vṛddhaḥ praśāntaḥ

śrī-bhagavān uvāca—the Supreme Personality of Godhead said; *vacaḥ*—words; *tava*—your; *etat*—this kind of; *jana-deva*—O King of the people; *sū-nṛtam*—very true; *kula-ucitam*—exactly befitting your dynasty; *dharma-yutam*—completely in accord with the principles of religion; *yaśaḥ-karam*—fit for spreading your reputation; *yasya*—of whom; *pramāṇam*—the evidence; *bhṛgavaḥ*—the *brāhmaṇas* of the Bhṛgu dynasty; *sāmparāye*—in the next world; *pitāmahaḥ*—your grandfather; *kula-vṛddhaḥ*—the oldest in the family; *praśāntaḥ*—very peaceful (Prahlāda Mahārāja).

TRANSLATION

The Supreme Personality of Godhead said: O King, you are indeed exalted because your present advisors are the brāhmaṇas who are descendants of Bhṛgu and because your instructor for your future life is your

grandfather, the peaceful and venerable Prahlāda Mahārāja. Your statements are very true, and they completely agree with religious etiquette. They are in keeping with the behavior of your family, and they enhance your reputation.

PURPORT

Prahlāda Mahārāja is a vivid example of a pure devotee. Someone might argue that since Prahlāda Mahārāja, even though very old, was attached to his family, and specifically to his grandson Bali Mahārāja, how could he be an ideal example? Therefore this verse uses the word *praśāntaḥ.* A devotee is always sober. He is never disturbed by any conditions. Even if a devotee remains in *gṛhastha* life and does not renounce material possessions, he should still be understood to be *praśānta,* sober, because of his pure devotion to the Lord. Śrī Caitanya Mahāprabhu therefore said:

kibā vipra, kibā nyāsī, śūdra kene naya
yei kṛṣṇa-tattva-vettā, sei 'guru' haya

"Whether one is a *brāhmaṇa,* a *sannyāsī* or a *śūdra*—regardless of what he is—he can become a spiritual master if he knows the science of Kṛṣṇa." (Cc. *Madhya* 8.128) Anyone completely aware of the science of Kṛṣṇa, regardless of his status in life, is a *guru.* Thus Prahlāda Mahārāja is a *guru* in all circumstances.

Here His Lordship Vāmanadeva also teaches *sannyāsīs* and *brahmacārīs* that one should not ask more than necessary. He wanted only three paces of land, although Bali Mahārāja wanted to give Him anything He wanted.

TEXT 3

न ह्येतस्मिन्कुले कश्चिन्निःसत्त्वः कृपणः पुमान् ।
प्रत्याख्याता प्रतिश्रुत्य यो वादाता द्विजातये ॥ ३ ॥

na hy etasmin kule kaścin
niḥsattvaḥ kṛpaṇaḥ pumān
pratyākhyātā pratiśrutya
yo vādātā dvijātaye

na—not; *hi*—indeed; *etasmin*—in this; *kule*—in the dynasty or family; *kaścit*—anyone; *niḥsattvaḥ*—poor-minded; *kṛpaṇaḥ*—miser; *pumān*—any person; *pratyākhyātā*—refuses; *pratiśrutya*—after promising to give; *yaḥ vā*—either; *adātā*—not being charitable; *dvijātaye*—unto the *brāhmaṇas.*

TRANSLATION

I know that even until now, no one taking birth in your family has been poor-minded or miserly. No one has refused to give charity to brāhmaṇas, nor after promising to give charity has anyone failed to fulfill his promise.

TEXT 4

न सन्ति तीर्थे युधि चार्थिनार्थिताः
पराङ्मुखा ये त्वमनस्विनो नृप।
युष्मत्कुले यद्यशसामलेन
प्रह्लाद उद्भाति यथोडुपः खे ॥ ४ ॥

na santi tīrthe yudhi cārthinārthitāḥ
parāṅmukhā ye tv amanasvino nṛpa
yuṣmat-kule yad yaśasāmalena
prahrāda udbhāti yathoḍupaḥ khe

na—not; *santi*—there are; *tīrthe*—in holy places (where charity is given); *yudhi*—in the battlefield; *ca*—also; *arthinā*—by a *brāhmaṇa* or a *kṣatriya; arthitāḥ*—who have been asked; *parāṅmukhāḥ*—who refused their prayers; *ye*—such persons; *tu*—indeed; *amanasvinaḥ*—such low-minded, low-grade kings; *nṛpa*—O King (Bali Mahārāja); *yuṣmat-kule*—in your dynasty; *yat*—therein; *yaśasā amalena*—by impeccable reputation; *prahrādaḥ*—Prahlāda Mahārāja; *udbhāti*—arises; *yathā*—as; *uḍupaḥ*—the moon; *khe*—in the sky.

TRANSLATION

O King Bali, never in your dynasty has the low-minded King been born who upon being requested has refused charity to brāhmaṇas in holy places or a fight to kṣatriyas on a battlefield. And your dynasty is even more glorious due to the presence of Prahlāda Mahārāja, who is like the beautiful moon in the sky.

PURPORT

The symptoms of a *kṣatriya* are given in *Bhagavad-gītā.* One of the qualifications is the willingness to give charity (*dāna*). A *kṣatriya* does not refuse to give charity when requested by a *brāhmaṇa,* nor can he refuse to fight another *kṣatriya.* A king who does refuse is called low-minded. In the dynasty of Bali Mahārāja there were no such low-minded kings.

TEXT 5

यतो जातो हिरण्याक्षश्चरन्नेक इमां महीम् ।
प्रतिवीरं दिग्विजये नाविन्दत गदायुधः ॥ ५ ॥

yato jāto hiraṇyākṣaś
carann eka imāṁ mahīm
prativīraṁ dig-vijaye
nāvindata gadāyudhaḥ

yataḥ—in which dynasty; *jātaḥ*—was born; *hiraṇyākṣaḥ*—the king named Hiraṇyākṣa; *caran*—wandering; *ekaḥ*—alone; *imām*—this; *mahīm*—surface of the globe; *prativīram*—a rival hero; *dik-vijaye*—for conquering all directions; *na avindata*—could not get; *gadā-āyudhaḥ*—bearing his own club.

TRANSLATION

It was in your dynasty that Hiraṇyākṣa was born. Carrying only his own club, he wandered the globe alone, without assistance, to conquer all directions, and no hero he met could rival him.

TEXT 6

यं विनिर्जित्य कृच्छ्रेण विष्णुः क्ष्मोद्धार आगतम् ।
आत्मानं जयिनं मेने तद्वीर्यं भूर्यनुस्मरन् ॥ ६ ॥

yaṁ vinirjitya kṛcchreṇa
viṣṇuḥ kṣmoddhāra āgatam
ātmānaṁ jayinaṁ mene
tad-vīryaṁ bhūry anusmaran

yam—whom; *vinirjitya*—after conquering; *kṛcchreṇa*—with great difficulty; *viṣṇuḥ*—Lord Viṣṇu in His incarnation as a boar; *kṣmā-uddhāre*—at the time when the earth was delivered; *āgatam*—appeared before Him; *ātmānam*—personally, Himself; *jayinam*—victorious; *mene*—considered; *tat-vīryam*—the prowess of Hiraṇyākṣa; *bhūri*—constantly, or more and more; *anusmaran*—thinking about.

TRANSLATION

When delivering the earth from the Garbhodaka Sea, Lord Viṣṇu, in His incarnation as a boar, killed Hiraṇyākṣa, who had appeared before Him. The fight was severe, and the Lord killed Hiraṇyākṣa with great difficulty. Later, as the Lord thought about the uncommon prowess of Hiraṇyākṣa, He felt Himself victorious indeed.

TEXT 7

निशम्य तद्वधं भ्राता हिरण्यकशिपुः पुरा ।
हन्तुं भ्रातृहणं क्रुद्धो जगाम निलयं हरेः ॥ ७ ॥

niśamya tad-vadhaṁ bhrātā
hiraṇyakaśipuḥ purā
hantuṁ bhrātṛ-haṇaṁ kruddho
jagāma nilayaṁ hareḥ

niśamya—after hearing; *tat-vadham*—the killing of Hiraṇyākṣa; *bhrātā*—the brother; *hiraṇyakaśipuḥ*—Hiraṇyakaśipu; *purā*—formerly; *hantum*—just to kill; *bhrātṛ-haṇam*—the killer of his brother; *kruddhaḥ*—very angry; *jagāma*—went; *nilayam*—to the residence; *hareḥ*—of the Supreme Personality of Godhead.

TRANSLATION

When Hiraṇyakaśipu heard the news of his brother's being killed, with great anger he went to the residence of Viṣṇu, the killer of his brother, wanting to kill Lord Viṣṇu.

TEXT 8

तमायान्तं समालोक्य शूलपाणिं कृतान्तवत् ।
चिन्तयामास कालज्ञो विष्णुर्मायाविनां वरः ॥ ८ ॥

tam āyāntaṁ samālokya
śūla-pāṇiṁ kṛtāntavat
cintayām āsa kāla-jño
viṣṇur māyāvināṁ varaḥ

tam—him (Hiraṇyakaśipu); *āyāntam*—coming forward; *samālokya*—observing minutely; *śūla-pāṇim*—with a trident in his hand; *kṛtānta-vat*—

just like death personified; *cintayām āsa*—thought; *kāla-jñaḥ*—who knows the progress of time; *viṣṇuḥ*—Lord Viṣṇu; *māyāvinām*—of all kinds of mystics; *varaḥ*—the chief.

TRANSLATION

Seeing Hiraṇyakaśipu coming forward bearing a trident in his hand like personified death, Lord Viṣṇu, the best of all mystics and the knower of the progress of time, thought as follows.

TEXT 9

यतो यतोऽहं तत्रासौ मृत्युः प्राणभृतामिव ।
अतोऽहमस्य हृदयं प्रवेक्ष्यामि पराग्दृशः ॥ ९ ॥

yato yato 'haṁ tatrāsau
mṛtyuḥ prāṇa-bhṛtām iva
ato 'ham asya hṛdayaṁ
pravekṣyāmi parāg-dṛśaḥ

yataḥ yataḥ—wheresoever; *aham*—I; *tatra*—there indeed; *asau*—this Hiraṇyakaśipu; *mṛtyuḥ*—death; *prāṇa-bhṛtām*—of all living entities; *iva*—just like; *ataḥ*—therefore; *aham*—I; *asya*—of him; *hṛdayaṁ*—within the core of the heart; *pravekṣyāmi*—shall enter; *parāk-dṛśaḥ*—of a person who has only external vision.

TRANSLATION

Wheresoever I go, Hiraṇyakaśipu will follow Me, as death follows all living entities. Therefore it is better for Me to enter the core of his heart, for then, because of his power to see only externally, he will not see Me.

TEXT 10

एवं स निश्चित्य रिपोः शरीर-
माधावतो निर्विविशेऽसुरेन्द्र ।
श्वासानिलान्तर्हितसूक्ष्मदेह-
स्तत्प्राणरन्ध्रेण विविग्नचेताः ॥ १० ॥

evaṁ sa niścitya ripoḥ śarīram
ādhāvato nirviviśe 'surendra

śvāsānilāntarhita-sūkṣma-dehas
tat-prāṇa-randhreṇa vivigna-cetāḥ

evam—in this way; *saḥ*—He (Lord Viṣṇu); *niścitya*—deciding; *ripoḥ*—of the enemy; *śarīram*—the body; *ādhāvataḥ*—who was running after Him with great force; *nirviviśe*—entered; *asura-indra*—O King of the demons (Mahārāja Bali); *śvāsa-anila*—through the breathing; *antarhita*—invisible; *sūkṣma-dehaḥ*—in his finer body; *tat-prāṇa-randhreṇa*—through the hole of the nostril; *vivigna-cetāḥ*—being very anxious.

TRANSLATION

Lord Vāmanadeva continued: O King of the demons, after Lord Viṣṇu made this decision, He entered the body of His enemy Hiraṇyakaśipu, who was running after Him with great force. In a subtle body inconceivable to Hiraṇyakaśipu, Lord Viṣṇu, who was in great anxiety, entered Hiraṇyakaśipu's nostril along with his breath.

PURPORT

The Supreme Personality of Godhead is already in the core of everyone's heart. *Īśvaraḥ sarva-bhūtānāṁ hṛd-deśe 'rjuna tiṣṭhati* (Bg. 18.61). Logically, therefore, it was not at all difficult for Lord Viṣṇu to enter Hiraṇyakaśipu's body. The word *vivigna-cetāḥ,* "very anxious," is significant. It is not that Lord Viṣṇu was afraid of Hiraṇyakaśipu; rather, because of compassion, Lord Viṣṇu was in anxiety about how to act for his welfare.

TEXT 11

स तन्निकेतं परिमृश्य शून्य-
मपश्यमानः कुपितो ननाद ।
क्ष्मां द्यां दिशः खं विवरान्समुद्रान्
विष्णुं विचिन्वन् न ददर्श वीरः ॥ ११ ॥

sa tan-niketaṁ parimṛśya śūnyam
apaśyamānaḥ kupito nanāda
kṣmāṁ dyāṁ diśaḥ khaṁ vivarān samudrān
viṣṇuṁ vicinvan na dadarśa vīraḥ

saḥ—that Hiraṇyakaśipu; *tat-niketam*—the residence of Lord Viṣṇu; *parimṛśya*—searching; *śūnyam*—vacant; *apaśyamānaḥ*—not seeing Lord

Viṣṇu; *kupitaḥ*—being very angry; *nanāda*—cried very loudly; *kṣmām*—on the surface of the earth; *dyām*—in outer space; *diśaḥ*—in all directions; *kham*—in the sky; *vivarān*—in all the caves; *samudrān*—all the oceans; *viṣṇum*—Lord Viṣṇu; *vicinvan*—searching for; *na*—not; *dadarśa*—did see; *vīraḥ*—although he was very powerful.

TRANSLATION

Upon seeing that the residence of Lord Viṣṇu was vacant, Hiraṇyakaśipu began searching for Lord Viṣṇu everywhere. Angry at not seeing Him, Hiraṇyakaśipu screamed loudly and searched the entire universe, including the surface of the earth, the higher planetary systems, all directions and all the caves and oceans. But Hiraṇyakaśipu, the greatest hero, did not see Viṣṇu anywhere.

TEXT 12

अपश्यन्निति होवाच मयान्विष्टमिदं जगत् ।
भ्रातृहा मे गतो नूनं यतो नावर्तते पुमान् ॥ १२ ॥

apaśyann iti hovāca
mayānviṣṭam idaṁ jagat
bhrātṛ-hā me gato nūnaṁ
yato nāvartate pumān

apaśyan—not seeing Him; *iti*—in this way; *ha uvāca*—uttered; *mayā*—by me; *anviṣṭam*—has been sought; *idam*—the whole; *jagat*—universe; *bhrātṛ-hā*—Lord Viṣṇu, who killed the brother; *me*—my; *gataḥ*—must have gone; *nūnam*—indeed; *yataḥ*—from where; *na*—not; *āvartate*—comes back; *pumān*—a person.

TRANSLATION

Unable to see Him, Hiraṇyakaśipu said, "I have searched the entire universe, but I could not find Viṣṇu, who has killed my brother. Therefore, He must certainly have gone to that place from which no one returns. [In other words, He must now be dead.]"

PURPORT

Atheists generally follow the Bauddha philosophical conclusion that at death everything is finished. Hiraṇyakaśipu, being an atheist, thought this way.

Because Lord Viṣṇu was not visible to him, he thought that the Lord was dead. Even today, many people follow the philosophy that God is dead. But God is never dead. Even the living entity, who is part of God, never dies. *Na jāyate mriyate vā kadācit:* "For the soul there is never birth or death." This is the statement of *Bhagavad-gītā* (2.20). Even the ordinary living entity never takes birth or dies. What then is to be said of the Supreme Personality of Godhead, who is the chief of all living entities? He certainly never takes birth or dies. *Ajo'pi sann avyayātmā* (Bg. 4.6). Both the Lord and the living entity exist as unborn and inexhaustible personalities. Thus Hiraṇyakaśipu's conclusion that Viṣṇu was dead was wrong.

As indicated by the words *yato nāvartate pumān,* there is certainly a spiritual kingdom, and if the living entity goes there, he never returns to this material world. This is also confirmed in *Bhagavad-gītā* (4.9): *tyaktvā dehaṁ punar janma naiti mām eti so'rjuna.* Materially speaking, every living entity dies; death is inevitable. But those who are *karmīs, jñānīs* and *yogīs* return to this material world after death, whereas *bhaktas* do not. Of course, if a *bhakta* is not completely perfect he takes birth in the material world again, but in a very exalted position, either in a rich family or a family of the purest *brāhmaṇas* (*śucīnām śrīmatāṁ gehe*), just to finish his development in spiritual consciousness. Those who have completed the course of Kṛṣṇa consciousness and are free from material desire return to the abode of the Supreme Personality of Godhead (*yad gatvā na nivartante tad dhāma paramaṁ mama*). Here the same fact is stated: *yato nāvartate pumān.* Any person who goes back home, back to Godhead, does not return to this material world.

TEXT 13

वैरानुबन्ध एतावानामृत्योरिह देहिनाम् ।
अज्ञानप्रभवो मन्युरहंमानोपबृंहितः ॥ १३ ॥

vairānubandha etāvān
āmṛtyor iha dehinām
ajñāna-prabhavo manyur
ahaṁ-mānopabṛṁhitaḥ

vaira-anubandhaḥ—enmity; *etāvān*—so great; *āmṛtyoḥ*—up to the point of death; *iha*—in this; *dehinām*—of persons too involved in the bodily concept of life; *ajñāna-prabhavaḥ*—because of the great influence of ignorance; *manyuḥ*—anger; *aham-māna*—by egotism; *upabṛṁhitaḥ*—expanded.

TRANSLATION

Hiraṇyakaśipu's anger against Lord Viṣṇu persisted until his death. Other people in the bodily concept of life maintain anger only because of false ego and the great influence of ignorance.

PURPORT

Generally speaking, even though the conditioned soul is angry, his anger is not perpetual but temporary. It is due to the influence of ignorance. Hiraṇyakaśipu, however, maintained his enmity and his anger against Lord Viṣṇu until the point of death. He never forgot his vengeful attitude toward Viṣṇu for having killed his brother, Hiraṇyākṣa. Others in the bodily concept of life are angry at their enemies but not at Lord Viṣṇu. Hiraṇyakaśipu, however, was everlastingly angry. He was angry not only because of false prestige but also because of continuous enmity toward Viṣṇu.

TEXT 14

पिता प्रह्लादपुत्रस्ते तद्विद्वान्द्विजवत्सलः ।
स्वमायुर्द्विजलिङ्गेभ्यो देवेभ्योऽदात् स याचितः ॥ १४ ॥

pitā prahrāda-putras te
tad-vidvān dvija-vatsalaḥ
svam āyur dvija-liṅgebhyo
devebhyo 'dāt sa yācitaḥ

pitā—father; *prahrāda-putraḥ*—the son of Mahārāja Prahlāda; *te*—your; *tat-vidvān*—although it was known to him; *dvija-vatsalaḥ*—still, because of his affinity for *brāhmaṇas; svam*—his own; *āyuḥ*—duration of life; *dvija-liṅgebhyaḥ*—who were dressed like *brāhmaṇas; devebhyaḥ*—unto the demigods; *adāt*—delivered; *saḥ*—he; *yācitaḥ*—being so requested.

TRANSLATION

Your father, Virocana, the son of Mahārāja Prahlāda, was very affectionate toward brāhmaṇas. Although he knew very well that it was the demigods who had come to him in the dress of brāhmaṇas, at their request he delivered to them the duration of his life.

PURPORT

Mahārāja Virocana, Bali's father, was so pleased with the *brāhmaṇa* community that even though he knew that those approaching him for charity were the demigods in the dress of *brāhmaṇas,* he nonetheless agreed to give it.

TEXT 15

भवानाचरितान्धर्मानास्थितो गृहमेधिभिः ।
ब्राह्मणैः पूर्वजैः शूरैरन्यैश्चोद्दामकीर्तिभिः ॥ १५ ॥

bhavān ācaritān dharmān
āsthito gṛhamedhibhiḥ
brāhmaṇaiḥ pūrvajaiḥ śūrair
anyaiś coddāma-kīrtibhiḥ

bhavān—your good self; *ācaritān*—executed; *dharmān*—religious principles; *āsthitaḥ*—being situated; *gṛhamedhibhiḥ*—by persons in household life; *brāhmaṇaiḥ*—by the *brāhmaṇas; pūrva-jaiḥ*—by your forefathers; *śūraiḥ*—by great heroes; *anyaiḥ ca*—and others also; *uddāma-kīrtibhiḥ*—very highly elevated and famous.

TRANSLATION

You also have observed the principles followed by great personalities who are householder brāhmaṇas, by your forefathers and by great heroes who are extremely famous for their exalted activities.

TEXT 16

तस्मात् त्वत्तो महीमीषद् वृणेऽहं वरदर्षभात् ।
पदानि त्रीणि दैत्येन्द्र संमितानि पदा मम ॥ १६ ॥

tasmāt tvatto mahīm īṣad
vṛṇe 'haṁ varadarṣabhāt
padāni trīṇi daityendra
sammitāni padā mama

tasmāt—from such a person; *tvattaḥ*—from Your Majesty; *mahīm*—land; *īṣat*—very little; *vṛṇe*—am asking for; *aham*—I; *varada-ṛṣabhāt*—from the personality who can give charity munificently; *padāni*—footsteps; *trīṇi*—three; *daitya-indra*—O King of the Daityas; *sammitāni*—to the measurement of; *padā*—by a foot; *mama*—My.

TRANSLATION

O King of the Daityas, from Your Majesty, who come from such a noble family and who are able to give charity munificently, I ask only three paces of land, to the measurement of My steps.

PURPORT

Lord Vāmanadeva wanted three paces of land according to the measurement of His footsteps. He did not want more than necessary. But although He pretended to be an ordinary human child, He actually wanted the land comprising the upper, middle and lower planetary systems. This was just to show the prowess of the Supreme Personality of Godhead.

TEXT 17

नान्यत् ते कामये राजन्वदान्याज्जगदीश्वरात् ।
नैनः प्राप्नोति वै विद्वान्यावदर्थप्रतिग्रहः ॥ १७ ॥

nānyat te kāmaye rājan
vadānyāj jagad-īśvarāt
nainaḥ prāpnoti vai vidvān
yāvad-artha-pratigrahaḥ

na—not; *anyat*—anything else; *te*—from you; *kāmaye*—I beg; *rājan*—O King; *vadānyāt*—who are so munificent; *jagat-īśvarāt*—who are the king of the entire universe; *na*—not; *enaḥ*—distress; *prāpnoti*—gets; *vai*—indeed; *vidvān*—one who is learned; *yāvat-artha*—as much as one needs; *pratigrahaḥ*—taking charity from others.

TRANSLATION

O King, controller of the entire universe, although you are very munificent and are able to give Me as much land as I want, I do not want anything from you that is unnecessary. If a learned brāhmaṇa takes charity from others only according to his needs, he does not become entangled in sinful activities.

PURPORT

A *brāhmaṇa* or *sannyāsī* is qualified to ask charity from others, but if he takes more than necessary he is punishable. No one can use more of the Supreme Lord's property than necessary. Lord Vāmanadeva indirectly indicated to Bali Mahārāja that he was occupying more land than he needed. In the material world, all distresses are due to extravagance. One acquires money extravagantly and also spends it extravagantly. Such activities are sinful. All property belongs to the Supreme Personality of Godhead, and all living beings, who are sons of the Supreme Lord, have the right to use the Supreme Father's property, but one cannot take more than necessary. This principle should especially be followed by *brāhmaṇas* and *sannyāsīs* who live at the cost of others. Thus Vāmanadeva was an ideal beggar, for He asked only three paces of land. Of course, there is a difference between His footsteps and those of an ordinary human being. The Supreme Personality of Godhead, by His inconceivable prowess, can occupy the entire universe, including the upper, lower and middle planetary systems, by the unlimited measurement of His footsteps.

TEXT 18

श्रीबलिरुवाच

अहो ब्राह्मणदायाद वाचस्ते वृद्धसंमताः ।
त्वं बालो बालिशमतिः स्वार्थं प्रत्यबुधो यथा ॥ १८ ॥

śrī-balir uvāca
aho brāhmaṇa-dāyāda
vācas te vṛddha-sammatāḥ
tvaṁ bālo bāliśa-matiḥ
svārthaṁ praty abudho yathā

śrī-baliḥ uvāca—Bali Mahārāja said; *aho*—alas; *brāhmaṇa-dāyāda*—O son of a *brāhmaṇa; vācaḥ*—the words; *te*—of You; *vṛddha-sammatāḥ*—are certainly acceptable to learned and elderly persons; *tvam*—You; *bālaḥ*—a boy; *bāliśa-matiḥ*—without sufficient knowledge; *sva-artham*—self-interest; *prati*—toward; *abudhaḥ*—not knowing sufficiently; *yathā*—as it should have been.

TRANSLATION

Bali Mahārāja said: O son of a brāhmaṇa, Your instructions are as good as those of learned and elderly persons. Nonetheless, You are a boy, and Your intelligence is insufficient. Thus You are not very prudent in regard to Your self-interest.

PURPORT

The Supreme Personality of Godhead, being full in Himself, actually has nothing to want for His self-interest. Lord Vāmanadeva, therefore, had not gone to Bali Mahārāja for His own self-interest. As stated in *Bhagavad-gītā* (5.29), *bhoktāraṁ yajña-tapasāṁ sarva-loka-maheśvaram.* The Lord is the proprietor of all planets, in both the material and spiritual worlds. Why should He be in want of land? Bali Mahārāja rightly said that Lord Vāmanadeva was not at all prudent in regard to His own personal interests. Lord Vāmanadeva had approached Bali not for His personal welfare but for the welfare of His devotees. Devotees sacrifice all personal interests to satisfy the Supreme Personality of Godhead, and similarly the Supreme Lord, although having no personal interests, can do anything for the interests of His devotees. One who is full in himself has no personal interests.

TEXT 19

मां वचोभिः समाराध्य लोकानामेकमीश्वरम् ।
पदत्रयं वृणीते योऽबुद्धिमान् द्वीपदाशुषम् ॥ १९ ॥

māṁ vacobhiḥ samārādhya
lokānām ekam īśvaram
pada-trayaṁ vṛṇīte yo
'buddhimān dvīpa-dāśuṣam

mām—me; *vacobhiḥ*—by sweet words; *samārādhya*—after sufficiently pleasing; *lokānām*—of all the planets in this universe; *ekam*—the one and only; *īśvaram*—master, controller; *pada-trayam*—three feet; *vṛṇīte*—is asking for; *yaḥ*—He who; *abuddhimān*—not very intelligent; *dvīpa-dāśuṣam*—because I can give You an entire island.

TRANSLATION

I am able to give You an entire island because I am the proprietor of the three divisions of the universe. You have come to take something from me

and have pleased me by Your sweet words, but You are asking only three paces of land. Therefore You are not very intelligent.

PURPORT

According to Vedic understanding, the entire universe is regarded as an ocean of space. In that ocean there are innumerable planets, and each planet is called a *dvīpa,* or island. When approached by Lord Vāmanadeva, Bali Mahārāja was actually in possession of all the *dvīpas,* or islands in space. Bali Mahārāja was very pleased to see the features of Vāmanadeva and was ready to give Him as much land as He could ask, but because Lord Vāmanadeva asked only three paces of land, Bali Mahārāja considered Him not very intelligent.

TEXT 20

न पुमान् मामुपव्रज्य भूयो याचितुमर्हति ।
तस्माद् वृत्तिकरीं भूमिं वटो कामं प्रतीच्छ मे ॥ २० ॥

na pumān mām upavrajya
bhūyo yācitum arhati
tasmād vṛttikarīṁ bhūmiṁ
vaṭo kāmaṁ pratīccha me

na—not; *pumān*—any person; *mām*—unto me; *upavrajya*—after approaching; *bhūyaḥ*—again; *yācitum*—to beg; *arhati*—deserves; *tasmāt*—therefore; *vṛtti-karīm*—suitable to maintain Yourself; *bhūmim*—such land; *vaṭo*—O small *brahmacārī*; *kāmam*—according to the necessities of life; *pratīccha*—take; *me*—from me.

TRANSLATION

O small boy, one who approaches me to beg something should not have to ask anything more, anywhere. Therefore, if You wish, You may ask from me as much land as will suffice to maintain You according to Your needs.

TEXT 21

श्रीभगवानुवाच
यावन्तो विषयाः प्रेष्ठास्त्रिलोक्यामजितेन्द्रियम् ।
न शक्नुवन्ति ते सर्वे प्रतिपूरयितुं नृप ॥ २१ ॥

śrī-bhagavān uvāca
yāvanto viṣayāḥ preṣṭhās
tri-lokyām ajitendriyam
na śaknuvanti te sarve
pratipūrayituṁ nṛpa

śrī-bhagavān uvāca—the Supreme Personality of Godhead said; *yāvantaḥ*—as far as possible; *viṣayāḥ*—the objects of sense enjoyment; *preṣṭhāḥ*—pleasing to anyone; *tri-lokyām*—within these three worlds; *ajita-indriyam*—a person who is not self-controlled; *na śaknuvanti*—are unable; *te*—all those; *sarve*—taken together; *pratipūrayitum*—to satisfy; *nṛpa*—O King.

TRANSLATION

The Personality of Godhead said: O my dear King, even the entirety of whatever there may be within the three worlds to satisfy one's senses cannot satisfy a person whose senses are uncontrolled.

PURPORT

The material world is an illusory energy to deviate the living entities from the path of self-realization. Anyone who is in this material world is extremely anxious to get more and more things for sense gratification. Actually, however, the purpose of life is not sense gratification but self-realization. Therefore, those who are too addicted to sense gratification are advised to practice the mystic *yoga* system, or *aṣṭāṅga-yoga* system, consisting of *yama, niyama, āsana, prāṇāyāma, pratyāhāra* and so on. In this way, one can control the senses. The purpose of controlling the senses is to stop one's implication in the cycle of birth and death. As stated by Ṛṣabhadeva:

nūnaṁ pramattaḥ kurute vikarma
yad indriya-prītaya āpṛṇoti
na sādhu manye yata ātmano 'yam
asann api kleśada āsa dehaḥ

"When a person considers sense gratification the aim of life, he certainly becomes mad after materialistic living and engages in all kinds of sinful activity. He does not know that due to his past misdeeds he has already received a body which, although temporary, is the cause of his misery. Actually the living entity should not have taken on a material body, but he has been awarded the material body for sense gratification. Therefore I think it not befitting an intelligent man to involve himself again in the activities of sense gratification, by which he perpetually gets material bodies one after another." (*Bhā*g. 5.5.4) Thus according to Ṛṣabhadeva the human beings in this material world are just like madmen engaged in activities which they should not perform but which they do perform only for sense gratification. Such activities are not good because in this way one creates another body for his next life, as punishment for his nefarious activities. And as soon as he gets another material body, he is put into repeated suffering in material existence. Therefore the Vedic culture or brahminical culture teaches one how to be satisfied with possessing the minimum necessities in life.

To teach this highest culture, *varṇāśrama-dharma* is recommended. The aim of the *varṇāśrama* divisions—*brāhmaṇa, kṣatriya, vaiśya, śūdra, brahmacarya, gṛhastha, vānaprastha* and *sannyāsa*—is to train one to control the senses and be content with the bare necessities. Here Lord Vāmanadeva, as an ideal *brahmacārī,* refuses Bali Mahārāja's offer to give Him anything He might want. He says that without contentment one could not be happy even if he possessed the property of the entire world or the entire universe. In human society, therefore, the brahminical culture, *kṣatriya* culture and *vaiśya* culture must be maintained, and people must be taught how to be satisfied with only what they need. In modern civilization there is no such education; everyone tries to possess more and more, and everyone is dissatisfied and unhappy. The Kṛṣṇa consciousness movement is therefore establishing various farms, especially in America, to show how to be happy and content with minimum necessities of life and to save time for self-realization, which one can very easily achieve by chanting the *mahā-mantra*—Hare Kṛṣṇa, Hare Kṛṣṇa, Kṛṣṇa Kṛṣṇa, Hare Hare/ Hare Rāma, Hare Rāma, Rāma Rāma, Hare Hare.

TEXT 22

त्रिभिः क्रमैरसंतुष्टो द्वीपेनापि न पूर्यते ।
नववर्षसमेतेन सप्तद्वीपवरेच्छया ॥ २२ ॥

tribhiḥ kramair asantuṣṭo
dvīpenāpi na pūryate
nava-varṣa-sametena
sapta-dvīpa-varecchayā

tribhiḥ—three; *kramaiḥ*—by steps; *asantuṣṭaḥ*—one who is dissatisfied; *dvīpena*—by a complete island; *api*—although; *na pūryate*—cannot be satisfied; *nava-varṣa-sametena*—even by possessing nine *varṣas; sapta-dvīpa-vara-icchayā*—by the desire to take possession of seven islands.

TRANSLATION

If I were not satisfied with three paces of land, then surely I would not be satisfied even with possessing one of the seven islands, consisting of nine varṣas. Even if I possessed one island, I would hope to get others.

TEXT 23

सप्तद्वीपाधिपतयो नृपा वैन्यगयादयः ।
अर्थैः कामैर्गता नान्तं तृष्णाया इति नः श्रुतम् ॥ २३ ॥

sapta-dvīpādhipatayo
nṛpā vaiṇya-gayādayaḥ
arthaiḥ kāmair gatā nāntaṁ
tṛṣṇāyā iti naḥ śrutam

sapta-dvīpa-adhipatayaḥ—those who are proprietors of the seven islands; *nṛpāḥ*—such kings; *vaiṇya-gaya-ādayaḥ*—Mahārāja Pṛthu, Mahārāja Gaya and others; *arthaiḥ*—for fulfillment of ambition; *kāmaiḥ*—for satisfying one's desires; *gatāḥ na*—could not reach; *antam*—the end; *tṛṣṇāyāḥ*—of their ambitions; *iti*—thus; *naḥ*—by Us; *śrutam*—has been heard.

TRANSLATION

We have heard that although powerful kings like Mahārāja Pṛthu and Mahārāja Gaya achieved proprietorship over the seven dvīpas, they could not achieve satisfaction or find the end of their ambitions.

TEXT 24

यदृच्छयोपपन्नेन संतुष्टो वर्तते सुखम् ।
नासंतुष्टस्त्रिभिर्लोकैरजितात्मोपसादितैः ॥ २४ ॥

yadṛcchayopapannena
santuṣṭo vartate sukham
nāsantuṣṭas tribhir lokair
ajitātmopasāditaiḥ

yadṛcchayā—as offered by the supreme authority according to one's *karma; upapannena*—by whatever is obtained; *santuṣṭaḥ*—one should be satisfied; *vartate*—there is; *sukham*—happiness; *na*—not; *asantuṣṭaḥ*—one who is dissatisfied; *tribhiḥ lokaiḥ*—even by possessing the three worlds; *ajita-ātmā*—one who cannot control his senses; *upasāditaiḥ*—even though obtained.

TRANSLATION

One should be satisfied with whatever he achieves by his previous destiny, for discontent can never bring happiness. A person who is not self-controlled will not be happy even with possessing the three worlds.

PURPORT

If happiness is the ultimate goal of life, one must be satisfied with the position in which he is placed by providence. This instruction is also given by Prahlāda Mahārāja:

sukham aindriyakaṁ daityā
deha-yogena dehinām
sarvatra labhyate daivād
yathā duḥkham ayatnataḥ

"My dear friends born of demoniac families, the happiness perceived with reference to the sense objects by contact with the body can be obtained in any form of life, according to one's past fruitive activities. Such happiness is automatically obtained without endeavor, just as we obtain distress." (*Bhāg.* 7.6.3) This philosophy is perfect in regard to obtaining happiness.

Real happiness is described in *Bhagavad-gītā* (6.21):

sukham ātyantikaṁ yat tad
buddhi-grāhyam atīndriyam
vetti yatra na caivāyaṁ
sthitaś calati tattvataḥ

"In the spiritually joyous state, one is situated in boundless transcendental happiness and enjoys himself through transcendental senses. Established thus, one never departs from the truth." One has to perceive happiness by the supersenses. The supersenses are not the senses of the material elements. Every one of us is a spiritual being (*ahaṁ brahmāsmi*), and every one of us is an individual person. Our senses are now covered by material elements, and because of ignorance we consider the material senses that cover us to be our real senses. The real senses, however, are within the material covering.

Dehino'smin yathā dehe: within the covering of the material elements are the spiritual senses. *Sarvopādhi-vinirmuktaṁ tat-paratvena nirmalam:* when the spiritual senses are uncovered, by these senses we can be happy. Satisfaction of the spiritual senses is thus described: *hṛṣīkeṇa hṛṣīkeśa-sevanaṁ bhaktir ucyate.* When the senses are engaged in devotional service to Hṛṣīkeśa, then the senses are completely satisfied. Without this superior knowledge of sense gratification, one may try to satisfy his material senses, but happiness will never be possible. One may increase his ambition for sense gratification and even achieve what he desires for the gratification of his senses, but because this is on the material platform, he will never achieve satisfaction and contentment.

According to brahminical culture, one should be content with whatever he obtains without special endeavor and should cultivate spiritual consciousness. Then he will be happy. The purpose of the Kṛṣṇa consciousness movement is to spread this understanding. People who do not have scientific spiritual knowledge mistakenly think that the members of the Kṛṣṇa consciousness movement are escapists trying to avoid material activities. In fact, however, we are engaged in real activities for obtaining the ultimate happiness in life. If one is not trained to satisfy the spiritual senses and continues in material sense gratification, he will never obtain happiness that is eternal and blissful. *Śrīmad-Bhāgavatam* (5.5.1) therefore recommends:

tapo divyaṁ putrakā yena sattvaṁ
śuddhyed yasmād brahma-saukhyaṁ tv anantam

One must practice austerity so that his existential position will be purified and he will achieve unlimited blissful life.

TEXT 25

पुंसोऽयं संसृतेर्हेतुरसंतोषोऽर्थकामयोः ।
यदृच्छयोपपन्नेन संतोषो मुक्तये स्मृतः ॥ २५ ॥

puṁso 'yaṁ saṁsṛter hetur
asantoṣo 'rtha-kāmayoḥ
yadṛcchayopapannena
santoṣo muktaye smṛtaḥ

puṁsaḥ—of the living entity; *ayam*—this; *saṁsṛteḥ*—of the continuation of material existence; *hetuḥ*—the cause; *asantoṣaḥ*—dissatisfaction with his destined achievement; *artha-kāmayoḥ*—for the sake of lusty desires and getting more and more money; *yadṛcchayā*—with the gift of destiny; *upapannena*—which has been achieved; *santoṣaḥ*—satisfaction; *muktaye*—for liberation; *smṛtaḥ*—is considered fit.

TRANSLATION

Material existence causes discontent in regard to fulfilling one's lusty desires and achieving more and more money. This is the cause for the continuation of material life, which is full of repeated birth and death. But one who is satisfied by that which is obtained by destiny is fit for liberation from this material existence.

TEXT 26

यद‍ृच्छालाभतुष्टस्य तेजो विप्रस्य वर्धते ।
तत् प्रशाम्यत्यसंतोषादम्भसेवाशुशुक्षणिः ॥ २६ ॥

yadṛcchā-lābha-tuṣṭasya
tejo viprasya vardhate
tat praśāmyaty asantoṣād
ambhasevāśuśukṣaṇiḥ

yadṛcchā-lābha-tuṣṭasya—who is satisfied by things obtained by the grace of God; *tejaḥ*—the brilliant effulgence; *viprasya*—of a *brāhmaṇa; vardhate*—increases; *tat*—that (effulgence); *praśāmyati*—is diminished; *asantoṣāt*—because of dissatisfaction; *ambhasā*—by pouring of water; *iva*—as; *āśuśukṣaṇiḥ*—a fire.

TRANSLATION

A brāhmaṇa who is satisfied with whatever is providentially obtained is increasingly enlightened with spiritual power, but the spiritual potency of a dissatisfied brāhmaṇa decreases, as fire diminishes in potency when water is sprinkled upon it.

TEXT 27

तस्मात् त्रीणि पदान्येव वृणे त्वद् वरदर्षभात् ।
एतावतैव सिद्धोऽहं वित्तं यावत्प्रयोजनम् ॥ २७ ॥

tasmāt trīṇi padāny eva
vṛṇe tvad varadarṣabhāt
etāvataiva siddho 'haṁ
vittaṁ yāvat prayojanam

tasmāt—because of being satisfied by things easily obtained; *trīṇi*—three; *padāni*—steps; *eva*—indeed; *vṛṇe*—I ask; *tvat*—from your good self; *varada-ṛṣabhāt*—who are a munificent benedictor; *etāvatā eva*—merely by such an endowment; *siddhaḥ aham*—I shall feel full satisfaction; *vittam*—achievement; *yāvat*—as far as; *prayojanam*—is needed.

TRANSLATION

Therefore, O King, from you, the best of those who give charity, I ask only three paces of land. By such a gift I shall be very pleased, for the way of happiness is to be fully satisfied to receive that which is absolutely needed.

TEXT 28

श्रीशुक उवाच
इत्युक्तः स हसन्नाह वाञ्छातः प्रतिगृह्यताम् ।
वामनाय महीं दातुं जग्राह जलभाजनम् ॥ २८ ॥

śrī-śuka uvāca
ity uktaḥ sa hasann āha
vāñchātaḥ pratigṛhyatām
vāmanāya mahīṁ dātuṁ
jagrāha jala-bhājanam

śrī-śukaḥ uvāca—Śrī Śukadeva Gosvāmī said; *iti uktaḥ*—thus being addressed; *saḥ*—he (Bali Mahārāja); *hasan*—smiling; *āha*—said; *vāñchātaḥ*—as You have desired; *pratigṛhyatām*—now take from me; *vāmanāya*—unto Lord Vāmana; *mahīm*—land; *dātum*—to give; *jagrāha*—took; *jala-bhājanam*—the waterpot.

TRANSLATION

Śukadeva Gosvāmī continued: When the Supreme Personality of Godhead had thus spoken to Bali Mahārāja, Bali smiled and told Him, "All right. Take whatever You like." To confirm his promise to give Vāmanadeva the desired land, he then took up his waterpot.

TEXT 29

विष्णवे क्ष्मां प्रदास्यन्तमुशना असुरेश्वरम् ।
जानंश्चिकीर्षितं विष्णोः शिष्यं प्राह विदां वरः ॥ २९ ॥

viṣṇave kṣmāṁ pradāsyantam
uśanā asureśvaram
jānaṁś cikīrṣitaṁ viṣṇoḥ
śiṣyaṁ prāha vidāṁ varaḥ

viṣṇave—unto Lord Viṣṇu (Vāmanadeva); *kṣmām*—the land; *pradāsyantam*—who was ready to deliver; *uśanāḥ*—Śukrācārya; *asura-īśvaram*—unto the King of the demons (Bali Mahārāja); *jānan*—knowing well; *cikīrṣitam*—what was the plan; *viṣṇoḥ*—of Lord Viṣṇu; *śiṣyam*—unto his disciple; *prāha*—said; *vidām varaḥ*—the best of the knowers of everything.

TRANSLATION

Understanding Lord Viṣṇu's purpose, Śukrācārya, the best of the learned, immediately spoke as follows to his disciple, who was about to offer everything to Lord Vāmanadeva.

TEXT 30

श्रीशुक्र उवाच
एष वैरोचने साक्षाद् भगवान्विष्णुरव्ययः ।
कश्यपाददितेर्जातो देवानां कार्यसाधकः ॥ ३० ॥

śrī-śukra uvāca
eṣa vairocane sākṣād
bhagavān viṣṇur avyayaḥ
kaśyapād aditer jāto
devānāṁ kārya-sādhakaḥ

śrī-śukraḥ uvāca—Śukrācārya said; *eṣaḥ*—this (boy in the form of a dwarf); *vairocane*—O son of Virocana; *sākṣāt*—directly; *bhagavān*—the Supreme Personality of Godhead; *viṣṇuḥ*—Lord Viṣṇu; *avyayaḥ*—without deterioration; *kaśyapāt*—from His father, Kaśyapa; *aditeḥ*—in the womb of His mother, Aditi; *jātaḥ*—was born; *devānām*—of the demigods; *kārya-sādhakaḥ*—working in the interest.

TRANSLATION

Śukrācārya said: O son of Virocana, this brahmacārī in the form of a dwarf is directly the imperishable Supreme Personality of Godhead, Viṣṇu. Accepting Kaśyapa Muni as His father and Aditi as His mother, He has now appeared in order to fulfill the interests of the demigods.

TEXT 31

प्रतिश्रुतं त्वयैतस्मै यदनर्थमजानता ।
न साधु मन्ये दैत्यानां महानुपगतोऽनयः ॥ ३१ ॥

pratiśrutaṁ tvayaitasmai
yad anartham ajānatā
na sādhu manye daityānāṁ
mahān upagato 'nayaḥ

pratiśrutam—promised; *tvayā*—by you; *etasmai*—unto Him; *yat anartham*—which is repugnant; *ajānatā*—by you who have no knowledge; *na*—not; *sādhu*—very good; *manye*—I think; *daityānām*—of the demons; *mahān*—great; *upagataḥ*—has been achieved; *anayaḥ*—inauspiciousness.

TRANSLATION

You do not know what a dangerous position you have accepted by promising to give Him land. I do not think that this promise is good for you. It will bring great harm to the demons.

TEXT 32

एष ते स्थानमैश्वर्यं श्रियं तेजो यशः श्रुतम् ।
दास्यत्याच्छिद्य शक्राय मायामाणवको हरिः ॥ ३२ ॥

eṣa te sthānam aiśvaryaṁ
śriyaṁ tejo yaśaḥ śrutam
dāsyaty ācchidya śakrāya
māyā-māṇavako hariḥ

eṣaḥ—this person falsely appearing as a *brahmacārī; te*—of you; *sthānam*—the land in possession; *aiśvaryam*—the riches; *śriyam*—the material beauty; *tejaḥ*—the material power; *yaśaḥ*—the reputation; *śrutam*—the education; *dāsyati*—will give; *ācchidya*—taking from you; *śakrāya*—unto your enemy, Lord Indra; *māyā*—falsely appearing; *māṇavakaḥ*—a *brahmacārī* son of a living being; *hariḥ*—He is actually the Supreme Personality of Godhead, Hari.

TRANSLATION

This person falsely appearing as a brahmacārī is actually the Supreme Personality of Godhead, Hari, who has come in this form to take away all your land, wealth, beauty, power, fame and education. After taking everything from you, He will deliver it to Indra, your enemy.

PURPORT

Śrīla Viśvanātha Cakravartī Ṭhākura explains in this regard that the very word *hariḥ* means "one who takes away." If one connects himself with Hari, the Supreme Personality of Godhead, the Lord takes away all his miseries, and in the beginning the Lord also superficially appears to take away all his material possessions, reputation, education and beauty. As stated in *Śrīmad-Bhāgavatam* (10.88.8), *yasyāham anugṛhṇāmi hariṣye tad-dhanaṁ śanaiḥ.* The Lord said to Mahārāja Yudhiṣṭhira, "The first installment of My mercy toward a devotee is that I take away all his possessions, especially his material opulence, his money." This is the special favor of the Lord toward a sincere devotee. If a sincere devotee wants Kṛṣṇa above everything but at the same time is attached to material possessions, which hinder his advancement in Kṛṣṇa consciousness, by tactics the Lord takes away all his possessions. Here Śukrācārya says that this dwarf *brahmacārī* would take away everything. Thus he indicates that the Lord will take away all one's material possessions and also one's mind. If one delivers his mind to the lotus feet of Kṛṣṇa (*sa vai manaḥ kṛṣṇa-padāravindayoḥ*), one can naturally sacrifice everything to satisfy Him. Although Bali Mahārāja was a devotee, he was attached to material possessions, and therefore the Lord, being very kind to him, showed him special favor by appearing as Lord Vāmana to take away all his material possessions, and his mind as well.

TEXT 33

त्रिभिः क्रमैरिमाल्लोकान्विश्वकायः क्रमिष्यति ।
सर्वस्वं विष्णवे दत्त्वा मूढ वर्तिष्यसे कथम् ॥ ३३ ॥

tribhiḥ kramair imāl lokān
viśva-kāyaḥ kramiṣyati

sarvasvaṁ viṣṇave dattvā
mūḍha vartiṣyase katham

tribhiḥ—three; *kramaiḥ*—by steps; *imān*—all these; *lokān*—three planetary systems; *viśva-kāyaḥ*—becoming the universal form; *kramiṣyati*—gradually He will expand; *sarvasvam*—everything; *viṣṇave*—unto Lord Viṣṇu; *dattvā*—after giving charity; *mūḍha*—O you rascal; *vartiṣyase*—you will execute your means of livelihood; *katham*—how.

TRANSLATION

You have promised to give Him three steps of land in charity, but when you give it He will occupy the three worlds. You are a rascal! You do not know what a great mistake you have made. After giving everything to Lord Viṣṇu, you will have no means of livelihood. How then shall you live?

PURPORT

Bali Mahārāja might argue that he had promised only three steps of land. But Śukrācārya, being a very learned *brāhmaṇa,* immediately understood that this was a plan of Hari, who had falsely appeared there as a *brahmacārī.* The words *mūḍha vartiṣyase katham* reveal that Śukrācārya was a *brāhmaṇa* of the priestly class. Such priestly *brāhmaṇas* are mostly interested in receiving remuneration from their disciples. Therefore when Śukrācārya saw that Bali Mahārāja had risked all of his possessions, he understood that this would cause havoc not only to the King but also to the family of Śukrācārya, who was dependent on Mahārāja Bali's mercy. This is the difference between a Vaiṣṇava and a *smārta-brāhmaṇa.* A *smārta-brāhmaṇa* is always interested in material profit, whereas a Vaiṣṇava is interested only in satisfying the Supreme Personality of Godhead. From the statement of Śukrācārya, it appears that he was in all respects a *smārta-brāhmaṇa* interested only in personal gain.

TEXT 34

क्रमतो गां पदैकेन द्वितीयेन दिवं विभोः ।
खं च कायेन महता तार्तीयस्य कुतो गतिः ॥ ३४ ॥

kramato gāṁ padaikena
dvitīyena divaṁ vibhoḥ
khaṁ ca kāyena mahatā
tārtīyasya kuto gatiḥ

kramataḥ—gradually; *gām*—the surface of the land; *padā ekena*—by one step; *dvitīyena*—by the second step; *divam*—the whole of outer space; *vibhoḥ*—of the universal form; *kham ca*—the sky also; *kāyena*—by the expansion of His transcendental body; *mahatā*—by the universal form; *tārtīyasya*—as far as the third step is concerned; *kutaḥ*—where is; *gatiḥ*—to keep His step.

TRANSLATION

Vāmanadeva will first occupy the three worlds with one step, then He will take His second step and occupy everything in outer space, and then He will expand His universal body to occupy everything. Where will you offer Him the third step?

PURPORT

Śukrācārya wanted to tell Bali Mahārāja how he would be cheated by Lord Vāmana. "You have promised three steps," he said. "But with only two steps, all your possessions will be finished. How then will you give Him a place for His third step?" Śukrācārya did not know how the Lord protects His devotee. The devotee must risk everything in his possession for the service of the Lord, but he is always protected and never defeated. By materialistic calculations, Śukrācārya thought that Bali Mahārāja would under no circumstances be able to keep his promise to the *brahmacārī*, Lord Vāmanadeva.

TEXT 35

निष्ठां ते नरके मन्ये ह्यप्रदातुः प्रतिश्रुतम् ।
प्रतिश्रुतस्य योऽनीशः प्रतिपादयितुं भवान् ॥ ३५ ॥

niṣṭhāṁ te narake manye
hy apradātuḥ pratiśrutam
pratiśrutasya yo 'nīśaḥ
pratipādayituṁ bhavān

niṣṭhām—perpetual residence; *te*—of you; *narake*—in hell; *manye*—I think; *hi*—indeed; *apradātuḥ*—of a person who cannot fulfill; *pratiśrutam*—what has been promised; *pratiśrutasya*—of the promise one has made; *yaḥ anīśaḥ*—one who is unable; *pratipādayitum*—to fulfill properly; *bhavān*—you are that person.

TRANSLATION

You will certainly be unable to fulfill your promise, and I think that because of this inability your eternal residence will be in hell.

TEXT 36

न तद्दानं प्रशंसन्ति येन वृत्तिर्विपद्यते ।
दानं यज्ञस्तपः कर्म लोके वृत्तिमतो यतः ॥ ३६ ॥

na tad dānaṁ praśaṁsanti
yena vṛttir vipadyate
dānaṁ yajñas tapaḥ karma
loke vṛttimato yataḥ

na—not; *tat*—that; *dānam*—charity; *praśaṁsanti*—the saintly persons praise; *yena*—by which; *vṛttiḥ*—one's livelihood; *vipadyate*—becomes endangered; *dānam*—charity; *yajñaḥ*—sacrifice; *tapaḥ*—austerity; *karma*—fruitive activities; *loke*—in this world; *vṛttimataḥ*—according to one's means of livelihood; *yataḥ*—as it is so.

TRANSLATION

Learned scholars do not praise that charity which endangers one's own livelihood. Charity, sacrifice, austerity and fruitive activities are possible for one who is competent to earn his livelihood properly. [They are not possible for one who cannot maintain himself.]

TEXT 37

धर्माय यशसेऽर्थाय कामाय स्वजनाय च ।
पञ्चधा विभजन्वित्तमिहामुत्र च मोदते ॥ ३७ ॥

dharmāya yaśase 'rthāya
kāmāya sva-janāya ca
pañcadhā vibhajan vittam
ihāmutra ca modate

dharmāya—for religion; *yaśase*—for one's reputation; *arthāya*—for increasing one's opulence; *kāmāya*—for increasing sense gratification; *sva-janāya ca*—and for maintaining one's family members; *pañcadhā*—for these five different objectives; *vibhajan*—dividing; *vittam*—his accumulated wealth; *iha*—in this world; *amutra*—the next world; *ca*—and; *modate*—he enjoys.

TRANSLATION

Therefore one who is in full knowledge should divide his accumulated wealth in five parts—for religion, for reputation, for opulence, for sense gratification and for the maintenance of his family members. Such a person is happy in this world and in the next.

PURPORT

The *śāstras* enjoin that if one has money one should divide all that he has accumulated into five divisions—one part for religion, one part for reputation, one part for opulence, one part for sense gratification and one part to maintain the members of his family. At the present, however, because people are bereft of all knowledge, they spend all their money for the satisfaction of their family. Śrīla Rūpa Gosvāmī taught us by his own example by using fifty percent of his accumulated wealth for Kṛṣṇa, twenty-five percent for his own self, and twenty-five percent for the members of his family. One's main purpose should be to advance in Kṛṣṇa consciousness. This will include *dharma, artha* and *kāma.* However, because one's family members expect some profit, one should also satisfy them by giving them a portion of one's accumulated wealth. This is a śāstric injunction.

TEXT 38

अत्रापि बह्वृचैर्गीतं शृणु मेऽसुरसत्तम ।
सत्यमोमिति यत् प्रोक्तं यन्नेत्याहानृतं हि तत् ॥ ३८ ॥

atrāpi bahvṛcair gītaṁ
śṛṇu me 'sura-sattama
satyam om iti yat proktaṁ
yan nety āhānṛtaṁ hi tat

atra api—in this regard also (in deciding what is truth and what is not truth); *bahu-ṛcaiḥ*—by the *śruti-mantras* known as *Bahvṛca-śruti,* which are evidence from the *Vedas; gītam*—what has been spoken; *śṛṇu*—just hear; *me*—from me; *asura-sattama*—O best of the *asuras; satyam*—the truth is; *om iti*—preceded by the word *oṁ; yat*—that which; *proktam*—has been spoken; *yat*—that which is; *na*—not preceded by *oṁ; iti*—thus; *āha*—it is said; *anṛtam*—untruth; *hi*—indeed; *tat*—that.

TRANSLATION

One might argue that since you have already promised, how can you refuse? O best of the demons, just take from me the evidence of the Bahvṛca-śruti, which says that a promise is truthful preceded by the word oṁ and untruthful if not.

TEXT 39

सत्यं पुष्पफलं विद्यादात्मवृक्षस्य गीयते ।
वृक्षेऽजीवति तन्न स्यादनृतं मूलमात्मनः ॥ ३९ ॥

satyaṁ puṣpa-phalaṁ vidyād
ātma-vṛkṣasya gīyate
vṛkṣe 'jīvati tan na syād
anṛtaṁ mūlam ātmanaḥ

satyam—the factual truth; *puṣpa-phalam*—the flower and the fruit; *vidyāt*—one should understand; *ātma-vṛkṣasya*—of the tree of the body; *gīyate*—as described in the *Vedas; vṛkṣe ajīvati*—if the tree is not living; *tat*—that (*puṣpa-phalam*); *na*—not; *syāt*—is possible; *anṛtam*—untruth; *mūlam*—the root; *ātmanaḥ*—of the body.

TRANSLATION

The Vedas enjoin that the factual result of the tree of the body is the good fruits and flowers derived from it. But if the bodily tree does not exist, there is no possibility of factual fruits and flowers. Even if the body is based on untruth, there cannot be factual fruits and flowers without the help of the bodily tree.

PURPORT

This *śloka* explains that in relation to the material body even the factual truth cannot exist without a touch of untruth. The Māyāvādīs say, *brahma satyaṁ jagan mithyā:* "The spirit soul is truth, and the external energy is untruth." The Vaiṣṇava philosophers, however, do not agree with the Māyāvāda philosophy. Even if for the sake of argument the material world is accepted as untruth, the living entity entangled in the illusory energy cannot come out of it without the help of the body. Without the help of the body, one cannot follow a system of religion, nor can one speculate on philosophical perfection. Therefore, the flower and fruit (*puṣpa-phalam*) have to be obtained as a result of the body. Without the help of the body, that fruit cannot be gained. The Vaiṣṇava philosophy therefore recommends *yukta-vairāgya.* It is not that all attention should be diverted for the maintenance of the body, but at the same time one's bodily maintenance should not be neglected. As long as the body exists one can thoroughly study the Vedic instructions, and thus at the end of life one can achieve perfection. This is explained in *Bhagavad-gītā* [8.6]*: yaṁ yaṁ vāpi smaran bhāvaṁ tyajaty ante kalevaram.* Everything is examined at the time of death. Therefore, although the body is temporary, not eternal, one can take from it the best service and make one's life perfect.

TEXT 40

तद् यथा वृक्ष उन्मूलः शुष्यत्युद्वर्ततेऽचिरात् ।
एवं नष्टानृतः सद्य आत्मा शुष्येन्न संशयः ॥ ४० ॥

tad yathā vṛkṣa unmūlaḥ
śuṣyaty udvartate 'cirāt
evaṁ naṣṭānṛtaḥ sadya
ātmā śuṣyen na saṁśayaḥ

tat—therefore; *yathā*—as; *vṛkṣaḥ*—a tree; *unmūlaḥ*—being uprooted; *śuṣyati*—dries up; *udvartate*—falls down; *acirāt*—very soon; *evam*—in this way; *naṣṭa*—lost; *anṛtaḥ*—the temporary body; *sadyaḥ*—immediately; *ātmā*—the body; *śuṣyet*—dries up; *na*—not; *saṁśayaḥ*—any doubt.

TRANSLATION

When a tree is uprooted it immediately falls down and begins to dry up. Similarly, if one doesn't take care of the body, which is supposed to be untruth—in other words, if the untruth is uprooted—the body undoubtedly becomes dry.

PURPORT

In this regard, Śrīla Rūpa Gosvāmī says:

prāpañcikatayā buddhyā
hari-sambandhi-vastunaḥ

mumukṣubhiḥ parityāgo
vairāgyaṁ phalgu kathyate

"One who rejects things without knowledge of their relationship to Kṛṣṇa is incomplete in his renunciation." (*Bhakti-rasāmṛta-sindhu* 1.2.256) When the body is engaged in the service of the Lord, one should not consider the body material. Sometimes the spiritual body of the spiritual master is misunderstood. But Śrīla Rūpa Gosvāmī instructs, *prāpañcikatayā buddhyā hari-sambandhi-vastunaḥ.* The body fully engaged in Kṛṣṇa's service should not be neglected as material. One who does neglect it is false in his renunciation. If the body is not properly maintained, it falls down and dries up like an uprooted tree, from which flowers and fruit can no longer be obtained. The *Vedas* therefore enjoin:

om iti satyaṁ nety anṛtaṁ tad etat-puṣpaṁ phalaṁ vāco yat satyaṁ saheśvaro yaśasvī kalyāṇa-kīrtir bhavitā; puṣpaṁ hi phalaṁ vācaḥ satyaṁ vadaty athaitan-mūlaṁ vāco yad anṛtaṁ yad yathā vṛkṣa āvirmūlaḥ śuṣyati, sa udvartata evaṁ evānṛtaṁ vadann āvirmūlam ātmānaṁ karoti, sa śuṣyati sa udvartate, tasmād anṛtaṁ na vaded dayeta tv etena.

The purport is that activities performed with the help of the body for the satisfaction of the Absolute Truth (*oṁ tat sat*) are never temporary, although performed by the temporary body. Indeed, such activities are everlasting. Therefore, the body should be properly cared for. Because the body is temporary, not permanent, one cannot expose the body to being devoured by a tiger or killed by an enemy. All precautions should be taken to protect the body.

TEXT 41

पराग् रिक्तमपूर्णं वा अक्षरं यत् तदोमिति ।
यत् किञ्चिदोमिति ब्रूयात् तेन रिच्येत वै पुमान् ।
भिक्षवे सर्वमोंकुर्वन्नालं कामेन चात्मने ॥ ४१ ॥

parāg riktam apūrṇaṁ vā
akṣaraṁ yat tad om iti
yat kiñcid om iti brūyāt
tena ricyeta vai pumān
bhikṣave sarvam oṁ kurvan
nālaṁ kāmena cātmane

parāk—that which separates; *riktam*—that which makes one free from attachment; *apūrṇam*—that which is insufficient; *vā*—either; *akṣaram*—this syllable; *yat*—that; *tat*—which; *om*—*oṁkāra; iti*—thus stated; *yat*—which; *kiñcit*—whatever; *oṁ*—this word *oṁ; iti*—thus; *brūyāt*—if you say; *tena*—by such an utterance; *ricyeta*—one becomes free; *vai*—indeed; *pumān*—a person; *bhikṣave*—unto a beggar; *sarvam*—everything; *oṁ kurvan*—giving charity by uttering the word *oṁ; na*—not; *alam*—sufficiently; *kāmena*—for sense gratification; *ca*—also; *ātmane*—for self-realization.

TRANSLATION

The utterance of the word "oṁ" signifies separation from one's monetary assets. In other words, by uttering this word one becomes free from attachment to money because his money is taken away from him. To be without money is not very satisfactory, for in that position one cannot fulfill one's desires. In other words, by using the word "oṁ" one becomes poverty-stricken. Especially when one gives charity to a poor man or beggar, one remains unfulfilled in self-realization and in sense gratification.

PURPORT

Mahārāja Bali wanted to give everything to Vāmanadeva, who had appeared as a beggar, but Śukrācārya, being Mahārāja Bali's familial spiritual master in the line of seminal succession, could not appreciate Mahārāja Bali's promise. Śukrācārya gave Vedic evidence that one should not give everything to a poor man. Rather, when a poor man comes for charity one should untruthfully say, "Whatever I have I have given you. I have no more." It is not that one should give everything to him. Actually the word *oṁ* is meant for *oṁ tat sat,* the Absolute Truth. *Oṁkāra* is meant for freedom from all attachment to money because money should be spent for the purpose of the Supreme. The tendency of modern civilization is to give money in charity to the poor. Such charity has no spiritual value because we actually see that although there are so many hospitals and other foundations and institutions for the poor, according to the three modes of material nature a class of poor men is always destined to continue. Even though there are so many charitable institutions, poverty has not been driven from human society. Therefore it is recommended here, *bhikṣave sarvam oṁ kurvan nālaṁ kāmena cātmane.* One should not give everything to the beggars among the poor.

The best solution is that of the Kṛṣṇa consciousness movement. This movement is always kind to the poor, not only because it feeds them but also because it gives them enlightenment by teaching them how to become Kṛṣṇa conscious. We are therefore opening hundreds and thousands of centers for those who are poor, both in money and in knowledge, to enlighten them in Kṛṣṇa consciousness and reform their character by teaching them how to avoid illicit sex, intoxication, meat-eating and gambling, which are the most sinful activities and which cause people to suffer, life after life. The best way to use money is to open such a center, where all may come live and reform their character. They may live very comfortably, without denial of any of the body's necessities, but they live under spiritual control, and thus they live happily and save time for advancement in Kṛṣṇa consciousness. If one has money, it should not be squandered away on nothing. It should be used to push forward the Kṛṣṇa consciousness movement so that all of human society will become happy, prosperous and hopeful of being promoted back home, back to Godhead. The Vedic *mantra* in this regard reads as follows:

parāg vā etad riktam akṣaraṁ yad etad om iti tad yat kiñcid om iti āhātraivāsmai tad ricyate; sa yat sarvam oṁ kuryād ricyād ātmānaṁ sa kāmebhyo nālaṁ syāt.

TEXT 42

अथैतत् पूर्णमभ्यात्मं यच्च नेत्यनृतं वचः ।
सर्वं नेत्यनृतं ब्रूयात् स दुष्कीर्तिः श्वसन्मृतः ॥ ४२ ॥

athaitat pūrṇam abhyātmaṁ
yac ca nety anṛtaṁ vacaḥ
sarvaṁ nety anṛtaṁ brūyāt
sa duṣkīrtiḥ śvasan mṛtaḥ

atha—therefore; *etat*—that; *pūrṇam*—completely; *abhyātmam*—drawing the compassion of others by presenting oneself as always poverty-stricken; *yat*—that; *ca*—also; *na*—not; *iti*—thus; *anṛtam*—false; *vacaḥ*—words; *sarvam*—completely; *na*—not; *iti*—thus; *anṛtam*—falsity; *brūyāt*—who should say; *saḥ*—such a person; *duṣkīrtiḥ*—infamous; *śvasan*—while breathing or while alive; *mṛtaḥ*—is dead or should be killed.

TRANSLATION

Therefore, the safe course is to say no. Although it is a falsehood, it protects one completely, it draws the compassion of others toward oneself,

and it gives one full facility to collect money from others for oneself. Nonetheless, if one always pleads that he has nothing, he is condemned, for he is a dead body while living, or while still breathing he should be killed.

PURPORT

Beggars always present themselves as possessing nothing, and this may be very good for them because in this way they are assured of not losing their money and of always drawing the attention and compassion of others for the sake of collection. But this is also condemned. If one purposely continues this professional begging, he is supposed to be dead while breathing, or, according to another interpretation, such a man of falsity should be killed while still breathing. The Vedic injunction in this regard is as follows: *athaitat pūrṇam abhyātmaṁ yan neti sa yat sarvaṁ neti brūyāt pāpikāsya kīrtir jāyate. sainaṁ tatraiva hanyāt.* If one continuously poses himself as possessing nothing and collects money by begging, he should be killed (*sainaṁ tatraiva hanyāt*).

TEXT 43

स्त्रीषु नर्मविवाहे च वृत्त्यर्थे प्राणसंकटे ।
गोब्राह्मणार्थे हिंसायां नानृतं स्याज्जुगुप्सितम् ॥ ४३ ॥

strīṣu narma-vivāhe ca
vṛtty-arthe prāṇa-saṅkaṭe
go-brāhmaṇārthe hiṁsāyāṁ
nānṛtaṁ syāj jugupsitam

strīṣu—to encourage a woman and bring her under control; *narma-vivāhe*—in joking or in a marriage ceremony; *ca*—also; *vṛtti-arthe*—for earning one's livelihood, as in business; *prāṇa-saṅkaṭe*—or in time of danger; *go-brāhmaṇa-arthe*—for the sake of cow protection and brahminical culture; *hiṁsāyām*—for any person who is going to be killed because of enmity; *na*—not; *anṛtam*—falsity; *syāt*—becomes; *jugupsitam*—abominable.

TRANSLATION

In flattering a woman to bring her under control, in joking, in a marriage ceremony, in earning one's livelihood, when one's life is in danger,

in protecting cows and brahminical culture, or in protecting a person from an enemy's hand, falsity is never condemned.

Thus end the Bhaktivedanta purports of the Eighth Canto, Nineteenth Chapter, of the Śrīmad-Bhāgavatam, *entitled, "Lord Vāmanadeva Begs Charity from Bali Mahārāja."*

CHAPTER TWENTY

Bali Mahārāja Surrenders the Universe

The summary of this Twentieth Chapter is as follows. Despite his knowledge that Lord Vāmanadeva was cheating him, Bali Mahārāja gave everything to the Lord in charity, and thus the Lord extended His body and assumed a gigantic form as Lord Viṣṇu.

After hearing the instructive advice of Śukrācārya, Bali Mahārāja became contemplative. Because it is the duty of a householder to maintain the principles of religion, economic development and sense gratification, Bali Mahārāja thought it improper to withdraw his promise to the *brahmacārī.* To lie or fail to honor a promise given to a *brahmacārī* is never proper, for lying is the most sinful activity. Everyone should be afraid of the sinful reactions to lying, for mother earth cannot even bear the weight of a sinful liar. The spreading of a kingdom or empire is temporary; if there is no benefit for the general public, such expansion has no value. Previously, all the great kings and emperors expanded their kingdoms with a regard for the welfare of the people in general. Indeed, while engaged in such activities for the benefit of the general public, eminent men sometimes even sacrificed their lives. It is said that one who is glorious in his activities is always living and never dies. Therefore, fame should be the aim of life, and even if one becomes poverty-stricken for the sake of a good reputation, that is not a loss. Bali Mahārāja thought that even if this *brahmacārī,* Vāmanadeva, were Lord Viṣṇu, if the Lord accepted his charity and then again arrested him, Bali Mahārāja would not envy Him. Considering all these points, Bali Mahārāja finally gave in charity everything he possessed.

Lord Vāmanadeva then immediately extended Himself into a universal body. By the mercy of Lord Vāmanadeva, Bali Mahārāja could see that the Lord is all-pervading and that everything rests in His body. Bali Mahārāja could see Lord Vāmanadeva as the supreme Viṣṇu, wearing a helmet, yellow garments, the mark of Śrīvatsa, the Kaustubha jewel, a flower garland, and ornaments decorating His entire body. The Lord gradually covered the entire surface of the world, and by extending His body He covered the entire sky. With His hands He covered all directions, and with His second footstep He covered the entire upper planetary system. Therefore there was no vacant place where He could take His third footstep.

TEXT 1

श्रीशुक उवाच
बलिरेवं गृहपतिः कुलाचार्येण भाषितः ।
तूष्णीं भूत्वा क्षणं राजन्नुवाचावहितो गुरुम् ॥ १ ॥

śrī-śuka uvāca
balir evaṁ gṛha-patiḥ
kulācāryeṇa bhāṣitaḥ
tūṣṇīṁ bhūtvā kṣaṇaṁ rājann
uvācāvahito gurum

śrī-śukaḥ uvāca—Śrī Śukadeva Gosvāmī said; *baliḥ*—Bali Mahārāja; *evam*—thus; *gṛha-patiḥ*—the master of the household affairs, although guided by the priests; *kula-ācāryeṇa*—by the family *ācārya* or guide; *bhāṣitaḥ*—being thus addressed; *tūṣṇīm*—silent; *bhūtvā*—becoming; *kṣaṇam*—for a moment; *rājan*—O King (Mahārāja Parīkṣit); *uvāca*—said; *avahitaḥ*—after full deliberation; *gurum*—unto his spiritual master.

TRANSLATION

Śrī Śukadeva Gosvāmī said: O King Parīkṣit, when Bali Mahārāja was thus advised by his spiritual master, Śukrācārya, his family priest, he remained silent for some time, and then, after full deliberation, he replied to his spiritual master as follows.

PURPORT

Śrīla Viśvanātha Cakravartī Ṭhākura remarks that Bali Mahārāja remained silent at a critical point. How could he disobey the instruction of Śukrācārya, his spiritual master? It is the duty of such a sober personality as Bali Mahārāja to abide by the orders of his spiritual master immediately, as his spiritual master had advised. But Bali Mahārāja also considered that Śukrācarya was no longer to be accepted as a spiritual master, for he had deviated from the duty of a spiritual master. According to *śāstra,* the duty of the *guru* is to take the disciple back home, back to Godhead. If he is unable to do so and instead hinders the disciple in going back to Godhead, he should not be a *guru. Gurur na sa syāt* (*Bhāg.* 5.5.18). One should not become a *guru* if he cannot enable his disciple to advance in Kṛṣṇa consciousness. The goal of life is to become a devotee of Lord Kṛṣṇa so that one may be freed from the bondage of material existence (*tyaktvā dehaṁ punar janma naiti mām eti so 'rjuna*). The spiritual master helps the disciple attain this stage by developing Kṛṣṇa consciousness. Now Śukrācārya has advised Bali Mahārāja to deny the promise to Vāmanadeva. Under the circumstances, therefore, Bali Mahārāja thought that there would be no fault if he disobeyed the order of his spiritual master. He deliberated on this point—should he refuse to accept the advice of his spiritual master, or should he independently do everything to please the Supreme Personality of Godhead? He took some time. Therefore it is said, *tūṣṇīṁ bhūtvā kṣaṇaṁ rajann uvācāvahito gurum.* After deliberating on this point, he decided that Lord Viṣṇu should be pleased in all circumstances, even at the risk of ignoring the *guru's* advice to the contrary.

Anyone who is supposed to be a *guru* but who goes against the principle of *viṣṇu-bhakti* cannot be accepted as *guru.* If one has falsely accepted such a *guru,* one should reject him. Such a *guru* is described as follows (*Mahābhārata, Udyoga* 179.25):

guror apy avaliptasya
kāryākāryam ajānataḥ
utpatha-pratipannasya
parityāgo vidhīyate

Śrīla Jīva Gosvāmī has advised that such a useless *guru,* a family priest acting as *guru,* should be given up, and that the proper, bona-fide *guru* should be accepted.

ṣaṭ-karma-nipuṇo vipro
mantra-tantra-viśāradaḥ
avaiṣṇavo gurur na syād
vaiṣṇavaḥ śvapaco guruḥ

"A scholarly *brāhmaṇa* expert in all subjects of Vedic knowledge is unfit to become a spiritual master without being a Vaiṣṇava, but if a person born in a family of a lower caste is a Vaiṣṇava, he can become a spiritual master." (*Padma Purāṇa*)

TEXT 2

श्रीबलिरुवाच
सत्यं भगवता प्रोक्तं धर्मोऽयं गृहमेधिनाम् ।
अर्थं कामं यशो वृत्तिं यो न बाधेत कर्हिचित् ॥ २ ॥

śrī-balir uvāca
satyaṁ bhagavatā proktaṁ
dharmo 'yaṁ gṛhamedhinām
arthaṁ kāmaṁ yaśo vṛttiṁ
yo na bādheta karhicit

śrī-baliḥ uvāca—Bali Mahārāja said; *satyam*—it is truth; *bhagavatā*—by Your Greatness; *proktam*—what has already been spoken; *dharmaḥ*—a religious principle; *ayam*—that is; *gṛhamedhinām*—especially for the householders; *artham*—economic development; *kāmam*—sense gratification; *yaśaḥ vṛttim*—reputation and means of livelihood; *yaḥ*—which religious principle; *na*—not; *bādheta*—hinders; *karhicit*—at any time.

TRANSLATION

Bali Mahārāja said: As you have already stated, the principle of religion that does not hinder one's economic development, sense gratification, fame and means of livelihood is the real occupational duty of the householder. I also think that this religious principle is correct.

PURPORT

Bali Mahārāja's grave answer to Śukrācārya is meaningful. Śukrācārya stressed that one's material means of livelihood and one's material reputation, sense gratification and economic development must continue properly. To see to this is the first duty of a man who is a householder, especially one who is interested in material affairs. If a religious principle does not affect one's material condition, it is to be accepted. At the present time, in this age of Kali, this idea is extremely prominent. No one is prepared to accept any religious principle if it hampers material prosperity. Śukrācārya, being a person of this material world, did not know the principles of a devotee. A devotee is determined to serve the Supreme Personality of Godhead to His full satisfaction. Anything that hampers such determination should certainly be rejected. This is the principle of *bhakti. Ānukūlyasya saṅkalpaḥ prātikūlyasya varjanam* (*Cc. Madhya* 22.100). To perform devotional service, one must accept only that which is favorable and reject that which is unfavorable. Bali Mahārāja had the opportunity to contribute everything he possessed to the lotus feet of Lord Vāmanadeva, but Śukrācārya was putting forward a material argument to hamper this process of devotional service. Under the circumstances, Bali Mahārāja decided that such hindrances should certainly be avoided. In other words, he decided immediately to reject the advice of Śukrācārya and go on with his duty. Thus he gave all his possessions to Lord Vāmanadeva.

TEXT 3

स चाहं वित्तलोभेन प्रत्याचक्षे कथं द्विजम् ।
प्रतिश्रुत्य ददामीति प्राह्रादिः कितवो यथा ॥ ३ ॥

sa cāhaṁ vitta-lobhena
pratyācakṣe kathaṁ dvijam
pratiśrutya dadāmīti
prāhrādiḥ kitavo yathā

saḥ—such a person as I am; *ca*—also; *aham*—I am; *vitta-lobhena*—for being allured by greed for money; *pratyācakṣe*—I shall cheat or say no when I have already said yes; *katham*—how; *dvijam*—especially to a *brāhmaṇa; pratiśrutya*—after already having promised; *dadāmi*—that I shall give; *iti*—thus; *prāhrādiḥ*—I who am famous as the grandson of Mahārāja Prahlāda; *kitavaḥ*—an ordinary cheater; *yathā*—just like.

TRANSLATION

I am the grandson of Mahārāja Prahlāda. How can I withdraw my promise because of greed for money when I have already said that I shall give this land? How can I behave like an ordinary cheater, especially toward a brāhmaṇa?

PURPORT

Bali Mahārāja had already been blessed by his grandfather Prahlāda Mahārāja. Therefore, he was a pure devotee, although born in a family of demons. There are two kinds of highly elevated devotees, called *sādhana-siddha* and *kṛpā-siddha. Sādhana-siddha* refers to one who has become a devotee by regular execution of the regulative principles mentioned in the *śāstras,* as ordered and directed by the spiritual master. If one regularly executes such devotional service, he will certainly attain perfection in due course of time. But there are other devotees, who may not have undergone all the required details of devotional service but who, by the special mercy of *guru* and Kṛṣṇa—the spiritual master and the Supreme Personality of

Godhead—have immediately attained the perfection of pure devotional service. Examples of such devotees are the *yajña-patnīs,* Mahārāja Bali and Śukadeva Gosvāmī. The *yajña-patnīs* were the wives of ordinary *brāhmaṇas* engaged in fruitive activities. Although the *brāhmaṇas* were very learned and advanced in Vedic knowledge, they could not achieve the mercy of Kṛṣṇa-Balarāma, whereas their wives achieved complete perfection in devotional service, despite their being women. Similarly, Vairocani, Bali Mahārāja, received the mercy of Prahlāda Mahārāja, and by Prahlāda Mahārāja's mercy he also received the mercy of Lord Viṣṇu, who appeared before him as a *brahmacārī* beggar. Thus Bali Mahārāja became a *kṛpā-siddha* because of the special mercy of both *guru* and Kṛṣṇa. Caitanya Mahāprabhu confirms this favor: *guru-kṛṣṇa-prasāde pāya bhakti-latā-bīja* (Cc. *Madhya* 19.151). Bali Mahārāja, by the grace of Prahlāda Mahārāja, got the seed of devotional service, and when that seed developed, he achieved the ultimate fruit of that service, namely love of Godhead (*premā pum-artho mahān*), immediately upon the appearance of Lord Vāmanadeva. Bali Mahārāja regularly maintained devotion for the Lord, and because he was purified, the Lord appeared before him. Because of unalloyed love for the Lord, he then immediately decided, "I shall give this little dwarf *brāhmaṇa* whatever He asks from me." This is a sign of love. Thus Bali Mahārāja is understood to be one who received the highest perfection of devotional service by special mercy.

TEXT 4

न ह्यसत्यात् परोऽधर्म इति होवाच भूरियम् ।
सर्वं सोढुमलं मन्ये ऋतेऽलीकपरं नरम् ॥ ४ ॥

na hy asatyāt paro 'dharma
iti hovāca bhūr iyam
sarvaṁ soḍhum alaṁ manye
ṛte 'līka-paraṁ naram

na—not; *hi*—indeed; *asatyāt*—than compulsion to untruthfulness; *paraḥ*—more; *adharmaḥ*—irreligion; *iti*—thus; *ha uvāca*—indeed had spoken; *bhūḥ*—mother earth; *iyam*—this; *sarvam*—everything; *soḍhum*—to bear; *alam*—I am able; *manye*—although I think; *ṛte*—except; *alīka-param*—the most heinous liar; *naram*—a human being.

TRANSLATION

There is nothing more sinful than untruthfulness. Because of this, mother earth once said, "I can bear any heavy thing except a person who is a liar."

PURPORT

On the surface of the earth there are many great mountains and oceans that are very heavy, and mother earth has no difficulty carrying them. But she feels very much overburdened when she carries even one person who is a liar. It is said that in Kali-yuga lying is a common affair: *māyaiva vyāvahārike* (*Bhā*g.12.2.3). Even in the most common dealings, people are accustomed to speaking so many lies. No one is free from the sinful reactions of speaking lies. Under the circumstances, one can just imagine how this has overburdened the earth, and indeed the entire universe.

TEXT 5

नाहं बिभेमि निरयान्नाधन्यादसुखार्णवात् ।
न स्थानच्यवनान्मृत्योर्यथा विप्रप्रलम्भनात् ॥ ५ ॥

nāhaṁ bibhemi nirayān
nādhanyād asukhārṇavāt
na sthāna-cyavanān mṛtyor
yathā vipra-pralambhanāt

na—not; *aham*—I; *bibhemi*—am afraid of; *nirayāt*—from a hellish condition of life; *na*—nor; *adhanyāt*—from a poverty-stricken condition; *asukha-arṇavāt*—nor from an ocean of distresses; *na*—nor; *sthāna-cyavanāt*—from falling from a position; *mṛtyoḥ*—nor from death; *yathā*—as; *vipra-pralambhanāt*—from the cheating of a *brāhmaṇa.*

TRANSLATION

I do not fear hell, poverty, an ocean of distress, falldown from my position or even death itself as much as I fear cheating a brāhmaṇa.

TEXT 6

यद् यद्धास्यति लोकेऽस्मिन्संपरेतं धनादिकम् ।
तस्य त्यागे निमित्तं किं विप्रस्तुष्येन्न तेन चेत् ॥ ६ ॥

yad yad dhāsyati loke 'smin
samparetaṁ dhanādikam
tasya tyāge nimittaṁ kiṁ
vipras tuṣyen na tena cet

yat yat—whatsoever; *hāsyati*—will leave; *loke*—in the world; *asmin*—in this; *samparetam*—one who is already dead; *dhana-ādikam*—his wealth and riches; *tasya*—of such wealth; *tyāge*—in renunciation; *nimittam*—the purpose; *kim*—what is; *vipraḥ*—the *brāhmaṇa* who is confidentially Lord Viṣṇu; *tuṣyet*—must be pleased; *na*—is not; *tena*—by such (riches); *cet*—if there is a possibility.

TRANSLATION

My lord, you can also see that all the material opulences of this world are certainly separated from their possessor at death. Therefore, if the brāhmaṇa Vāmanadeva is not satisfied by whatever gifts one has given, why not please Him with the riches one is destined to lose at death?

PURPORT

The word *vipra* means *brāhmaṇa,* and at the same time "confidential." Bali Mahārāja had confidentially decided to give the gift to Lord Vāmanadeva without discussion, but because such a decision would hurt the hearts of the *asuras* and his spiritual master, Śukrācārya, he spoke equivocally. Bali Mahārāja, as a pure devotee, had already decided to give all the land to Lord Viṣṇu.

TEXT 7

श्रेयः कुर्वन्ति भूतानां साधवो दुस्त्यजासुभिः ।
दध्यङ्शिबिप्रभृतयः को विकल्पो धरादिषु ॥ ७ ॥

śreyaḥ kurvanti bhūtānāṁ
sādhavo dustyajāsubhiḥ
dadhyaṅ-śibi-prabhṛtayaḥ
ko vikalpo dharādiṣu

śreyaḥ—activities of the utmost importance; *kurvanti*—execute; *bhūtānām*—of the general mass of people; *sādhavaḥ*—the saintly persons; *dustyaja*—which are extremely hard to give up; *asubhiḥ*—by their lives; *dad-*

hyaṁ—Mahārāja Dadhīci; *śibi*—Mahārāja Śibi; *prabhṛtayaḥ*—and similar great personalities; *kaḥ*—what; *vikalpaḥ*—consideration; *dharā-ādiṣu*—in giving the land to the *brāhmaṇa.*

TRANSLATION

Dadhīci, Śibi and many other great personalities were willing to sacrifice even their lives for the benefit of the people in general. This is the evidence of history. So why not give up this insignificant land? What is the serious consideration against it?

PURPORT

Bali Mahārāja was prepared to give everything to Lord Viṣṇu, and Śukrācārya, being a professional priest, might have been anxiously waiting, doubting whether there had been any such instance in history in which one had given everything in charity. Bali Mahārāja, however, cited the tangible examples of Mahārāja Śibi and Mahārāja Dadhīci, who had given up their lives for the benefit of the general public. Certainly one has attachment for everything material, especially one's land, but land and other possessions are forcibly taken away at the time of death, as stated in *Bhagavad-gītā* (*mṛtyuḥ sarva-haraś cāham*). The Lord personally appeared to Bali Mahārāja to take away everything he had, and thus he was so fortunate that he could see the Lord face to face. Nondevotees, however, cannot see the Lord face to face; to such persons the Lord appears as death and takes away all their possessions by force. Under the circumstances, why should we not part with our possessions and deliver them to Lord Viṣṇu for His satisfaction? Śrī Cāṇakya Paṇḍita says in this regard, *san-nimitte varaṁ tyāgo vināśe niyate sati* (*Cāṇakya-śloka* 36). Since our money and possessions do not last but will somehow or other be taken away, as long as they are in our possession it is better to use them for charity to a noble cause. Therefore Bali Mahārāja defied the order of his so-called spiritual master.

TEXT 8

यैरियं बुभुजे ब्रह्मन्दैत्येन्द्रैरनिवर्तिभिः ।
तेषां कालोऽग्रसील्लोकान् न यशोऽधिगतं भुवि ॥ ८ ॥

yair iyaṁ bubhuje brahman
daityendrair anivartibhiḥ
teṣāṁ kālo 'grasīl lokān
na yaśo 'dhigataṁ bhuvi

yaiḥ—by whom; *iyam*—this world; *bubhuje*—was enjoyed; *brahman*—O best of the *brāhmaṇas; daitya-indraiḥ*—by great heroes and kings born in demoniac families; *anivartibhiḥ*—by those who were determined to fight, either to lay down their lives or to win victory; *teṣām*—of such persons; *kālaḥ*—the time factor; *agrasīt*—took away; *lokān*—all possessions, all objects of enjoyment; *na*—not; *yaśaḥ*—the reputation; *adhigatam*—achieved; *bhuvi*—in this world.

TRANSLATION

O best of the brāhmaṇas, certainly the great demoniac kings who were never reluctant to fight enjoyed this world, but in due course of time everything they had was taken away, except their reputation, by which they continue to exist. In other words, one should try to achieve a good reputation instead of anything else.

PURPORT

In this regard, Cāṇakya Paṇḍita (*Cāṇakya-śloka* 34) also says, *āyuṣaḥ kṣaṇa eko 'pi na labhya svarṇa-koṭibhiḥ.* The duration of one's life is extremely short, but if in that short lifetime one can do something that enhances his good reputation, that may continue to exist for many millions of years. Bali Mahārāja therefore decided not to follow his spiritual master's instruction that he deny his promise to Vāmanadeva; instead, he decided to give the land according to the promise and be everlastingly celebrated as one of the twelve *mahājanas* (*balir vaiyāsakir vayam*).

TEXT 9

सुलभा युधि विप्रर्षे ह्यनिवृत्तास्तनुत्यजः ।
न तथा तीर्थ आयाते श्रद्धया ये धनत्यजः ॥ ९ ॥

sulabhā yudhi viprarṣe
hy anivṛttās tanu-tyajaḥ
na tathā tīrtha āyāte
śraddhayā ye dhana-tyajaḥ

su-labhāḥ—very easily obtained; *yudhi*—in the battlefield; *vipra-ṛṣe*—O best of the *brāhmaṇas; hi*—indeed; *anivṛttāḥ*—not being afraid of fighting; *tanu-tyajaḥ*—and thus lay down their lives; *na*—not; *tathā*—as; *tīrthe āyāte*—on the arrival of a saintly person who creates holy places; *śraddhayā*—with faith and devotion; *ye*—those who; *dhana-tyajaḥ*—can give up their accumulated wealth.

TRANSLATION

O best of the brāhmaṇas, many men have laid down their lives on the battlefield, being unafraid of fighting, but rarely has one gotten the chance to give his accumulated wealth faithfully to a saintly person who creates holy places.

PURPORT

Many *kṣatriyas* have laid down their lives on the battlefield for their nations, but hardly a person can be found who has given up all his property and his accumulated wealth in charity to a person worthy of the gift. As stated in *Bhagavad-gītā* (17.20):

dātavyam iti yad dānaṁ
dīyate 'nupakāriṇe
deśe kāle ca pātre ca
tad dānaṁ sāttvikaṁ smṛtam

"That gift which is given out of duty, at the proper time and place, to a worthy person, and without expectation of return is considered to be charity in the mode of goodness." Thus charity given in the proper place is called *sāttvika.* And above this charity in goodness is transcendental charity, in which everything is sacrificed for the sake of the Supreme Personality of Godhead. Vāmanadeva, the Supreme Personality of Godhead, had come to Bali Mahārāja for alms. How could one get such an opportunity to give charity? Therefore, Bali Mahārāja decided without hesitation to give the Lord whatever He wanted. One may get various opportunities to lay down his life on the battlefield, but such an opportunity as this is hardly ever obtained.

TEXT 10

मनस्विनः कारुणिकस्य शोभनं
यदर्थिकामोपनयेन दुर्गतिः ।
कुतः पुनर्ब्रह्मविदां भवादृशां
ततो वटोरस्य ददामि वाञ्छितम् ॥ १० ॥

manasvinaḥ kāruṇikasya śobhanaṁ
yad arthi-kāmopanayena durgatiḥ

kutaḥ punar brahma-vidāṁ bhavādṛśāṁ
tato vaṭor asya dadāmi vāñchitam

manasvinaḥ—of persons who are greatly munificent; *kāruṇikasya*—of persons celebrated as very merciful; *śobhanam*—very auspicious; *yat*—that; *arthi*—of persons in need of money; *kāma-upanayena*—by satisfying; *durgatiḥ*—becoming poverty-stricken; *kutaḥ*—what; *punaḥ*—again (is to be said); *brahma-vidām*—of persons well versed in transcendental science (*brahma-vidyā*); *bhavādṛśām*—like your good self; *tataḥ*—therefore; *vaṭoḥ*—of the *brahmacārī; asya*—of this Vāmanadeva; *dadāmi*—I shall give; *vāñchitam*—whatever He wants.

TRANSLATION

By giving charity, a benevolent and merciful person undoubtedly becomes even more auspicious, especially when he gives charity to a person like your good self. Under the circumstances, I must give this little brahmacārī whatever charity He wants from me.

PURPORT

If one accepts a poverty-stricken position because of losing money in business, gambling, prostitution or intoxication, no one will praise him, but if one becomes poverty-stricken by giving all of his possessions in charity, he becomes adored all over the world. Aside from this, if a benevolent and merciful person exhibits his pride in becoming poverty-stricken by giving his possessions in charity for good causes, his poverty is a welcome and auspicious sign of a great personality. Bali Mahārāja decided that even though he would become poverty-stricken by giving everything to Vāmanadeva, this is what he would prefer.

TEXT 11

यजन्ति यज्ञंक्रतुभिर्यमादृता
भवन्त आम्नायविधानकोविदाः ।
स एव विष्णुर्वरदोऽस्तु वा परो
दास्याम्यमुष्मै क्षितिमीप्सितां मुने ॥ ११ ॥

yajanti yajñaṁ kratubhir yam ādṛtā
bhavanta āmnāya-vidhāna-kovidāḥ

sa eva viṣṇur varado 'stu vā paro
dāsyāmy amuṣmai kṣitim īpsitāṁ mune

yajanti—worship; *yajñam*—who is the enjoyer of sacrifice; *kratubhiḥ*—by the different paraphernalia for sacrifice; *yam*—unto the Supreme Person; *ādṛtāḥ*—very respectfully; *bhavantaḥ*—all of you; *āmnāya-vidhāna-kovidāḥ*—great saintly persons fully aware of the Vedic principles of performing sacrifice; *saḥ*—that; *eva*—indeed; *viṣṇuḥ*—is Lord Viṣṇu, the Supreme Personality of Godhead; *varadaḥ*—either He is prepared to give benedictions; *astu*—He becomes; *vā*—or; *paraḥ*—comes as an enemy; *dāsyāmi*—I shall give; *amuṣmai*—unto Him (unto Lord Viṣṇu, Vāmanadeva); *kṣitim*—the tract of land; *īpsitām*—whatever He has desired; *mune*—O great sage.

TRANSLATION

O great sage, great saintly persons like you, being completely aware of the Vedic principles for performing ritualistic ceremonies and yajñas, worship Lord Viṣṇu in all circumstances. Therefore, whether that same Lord Viṣṇu has come here to give me all benedictions or to punish me as an enemy, I must carry out His order and give Him the requested tract of land without hesitation.

PURPORT

As stated by Lord Śiva:

ārādhanānāṁ sarveṣāṁ
viṣṇor ārādhanaṁ param
tasmāt parataraṁ devi
tadīyānāṁ samarcanam
(*Padma Purāṇa*)

Although in the *Vedas* there are recommendations for worshiping many demigods, Lord Viṣṇu is the Supreme Person, and worship of Viṣṇu is the ultimate goal of life. The Vedic principles of the *varṇāśrama* institution are meant to organize society to prepare everyone to worship Lord Viṣṇu.

varṇāśramācāravatā
puruṣeṇa paraḥ pumān
viṣṇur ārādhyate panthā
nānyat tat-toṣa-kāraṇam

"The Supreme Personality of Godhead, Lord Viṣṇu, is worshiped by the proper execution of prescribed duties in the system of *varṇa* and *āśrama.* There is no other way to satisfy the Supreme Personality of Godhead." (*Viṣṇu Purāṇa* 3.8.9) One must ultimately worship Lord Viṣṇu, and for that purpose the *varṇāśrama* system organizes society into *brāhmaṇas, kṣatriyas, vaiśyas, śūdras, brahmacārīs, gṛhasthas, vānaprasthas* and *sannyāsīs.* Bali Mahārāja, having been perfectly educated in devotional service by his grandfather Prahlāda Mahārāja, knew how things are to be done. He was never to be misguided by anyone, even by a person who happened to be his so-called spiritual master. This is the sign of full surrender. Bhaktivinoda Ṭhākura said:

mārabi rākhabi—yo icchā tohārā
nitya-dāsa-prati tuyā adhikārā

When one surrenders to Lord Viṣṇu, one must be prepared to abide by His orders in all circumstances, whether He kills one or gives one protection. Lord Viṣṇu must be worshiped in all circumstances.

TEXT 12

यद्यप्यसावधर्मेण मां बध्नीयादनागसम् ।
तथाप्येनं न हिंसिष्ये भीतं ब्रह्मतनुं रिपुम् ॥ १२ ॥

yadyapy asāv adharmeṇa
māṁ badhnīyād anāgasam
tathāpy enaṁ na hiṁsiṣye
bhītaṁ brahma-tanuṁ ripum

yadyapi—although; *asau*—Lord Viṣṇu; *adharmeṇa*—crookedly, without reference to the straight way; *mām*—me; *badhnīyāt*—kills; *anāgasam*—although I am not sinful; *tathāpi*—still; *enam*—against Him; *na*—not; *hiṁsiṣye*—I shall take any retaliation; *bhītam*—because He is afraid; *brahma-tanum*—having assumed the form of a *brāhmaṇa-brahmacārī; ripum*—even though He is my enemy.

TRANSLATION

Although He is Viṣṇu Himself, out of fear He has covered Himself in the form of a brāhmaṇa to come to me begging. Under the circumstances, because He has assumed the form of a brāhmaṇa, even if He irreligiously arrests me or even kills me, I shall not retaliate, although He is my enemy.

PURPORT

If Lord Viṣṇu as He is had come to Bali Mahārāja and asked him to do something, Bali Mahārāja certainly would not have refused His request. But to enjoy a little humor between Himself and His devotee, the Lord covered Himself as a *brāhmaṇa-brahmacārī* and thus came to Bali Mahārāja to beg for only three feet of land.

TEXT 13

एष वा उत्तमश्लोको न जिहासति यद् यशः ।
हत्वा मैनां हरेद् युद्धे शयीत निहतो मया ॥ १३ ॥

eṣa vā uttamaśloko
na jihāsati yad yaśaḥ
hatvā maināṁ hared yuddhe
śayīta nihato mayā

eṣaḥ—this (*brahmacārī*); *vā*—either; *uttama-ślokaḥ*—is Lord Viṣṇu, who is worshiped by Vedic prayers; *na*—not; *jihāsati*—desires to give up; *yat*—because; *yaśaḥ*—perpetual fame; *hatvā*—after killing; *mā*—me; *enām*—all this land; *haret*—will take away; *yuddhe*—in the fight; *śayīta*—will lie down; *nihataḥ*—being killed; *mayā*—by me.

TRANSLATION

If this brāhmaṇa really is Lord Viṣṇu, who is worshiped by Vedic hymns, He would never give up His widespread reputation; either He would lie down having been killed by me, or He would kill me in a fight.

PURPORT

Bali Mahārāja's statement that Viṣṇu would lie down having been killed is not the direct meaning, for Viṣṇu cannot be killed by anyone. Lord Viṣṇu can kill everyone, but He cannot be killed. Thus the real meaning of the words "lie down" is that Lord Viṣṇu would reside within the core of Bali Mahārāja's heart. Lord Viṣṇu is defeated by a devotee through devotional service; otherwise, no one can defeat Lord Viṣṇu.

TEXT 14

श्रीशुक उवाच
एवमश्रद्धितं शिष्यमनादेशकरं गुरुः ।
शशाप दैवप्रहितः सत्यसन्धं मनस्विनम् ॥ १४ ॥

śrī-śuka uvāca
evam aśraddhitaṁ śiṣyam
anādeśakaraṁ guruḥ
śaśāpa daiva-prahitaḥ
satya-sandhaṁ manasvinam

śrī-śukaḥ uvāca—Śrī Śukadeva Gosvāmī said; *evam*—thus; *aśraddhitam*—who was not very respectful to the instruction of the spiritual master; *śiṣyam*—unto such a disciple; *anādeśa-karam*—who was not prepared to carry out the order of his spiritual master; *guruḥ*—the spiritual master (Śukrācārya); *śaśāpa*—cursed; *daiva-prahitaḥ*—being inspired by the Supreme Lord; *satya-sandham*—one who was fixed in his truthfulness; *manasvinam*—who was of a highly elevated character.

TRANSLATION

Śrī Śukadeva Gosvāmī continued: Thereafter, the spiritual master, Śukrācārya, being inspired by the Supreme Lord, cursed his exalted disciple Bali Mahārāja, who was so magnanimous and fixed in truthfulness that instead of respecting his spiritual master's instructions, he wanted to disobey his order.

PURPORT

The difference between the behavior of Bali Mahārāja and that of his spiritual master, Śukrācārya, was that Bali Mahārāja had already developed love of Godhead, whereas Śukrācārya, being merely a priest of routine rituals, had not. Thus Śukrācārya was never inspired by the Supreme Personality of Godhead to develop in devotional service. As stated by the Lord Himself in *Bhagavad-gītā* (10.10):

teṣāṁ satata-yuktānāṁ
bhajatāṁ prīti-pūrvakam
dadāmi buddhi-yogaṁ taṁ
yena mām upayānti te

"To those who are constantly devoted and worship Me with love, I give the understanding by which they can come to Me."

Devotees who actually engage in devotional service with faith and love are inspired by the Supreme Personality of Godhead. Vaiṣṇavas are never concerned with ritualistic *smārta-brāhmaṇas.* Śrīla Sanātana Gosvāmī has therefore compiled *Hari-bhakti-vilāsa* to guide the Vaiṣṇavas, who never follow the *smārta-viddhi.* Although the Supreme Lord is situated in the core of everyone's heart, unless one is a Vaiṣṇava, unless one is engaged in devotional service, one does not get sound advice by which to return home, back to Godhead. Such instructions are meant only for devotees. Therefore in this verse the word *daiva-prahitaḥ,* "being inspired by the Supreme Lord," is important. Śukrācārya should have encouraged Bali Mahārāja to give everything to Lord Viṣṇu. This would have been a sign of love for the Supreme Lord. But he did not do so. On the contrary, he wanted to punish his devoted disciple by cursing him.

TEXT 15

दृढं पण्डितमान्यज्ञः स्तब्धोऽस्यस्मदुपेक्षया ।
मच्छासनातिगो यस्त्वमचिराद्भ्रश्यसे श्रियः ॥ १५ ॥

dṛḍhaṁ paṇḍita-māny ajñaḥ
stabdho 'sy asmad-upekṣayā
mac-chāsanātigo yas tvam
acirād bhraśyase śriyaḥ

dṛḍham—so firmly convinced or fixed in your decision; *paṇḍita-mānī*—considering yourself very learned; *ajñaḥ*—at the same time foolish; *stabdhaḥ*—impudent; *asi*—you have become; *asmat*—of us; *upekṣayā*—by disregarding; *mat-śāsana-atigaḥ*—surpassing the jurisdiction of my administration; *yaḥ*—such a person (as you); *tvam*—yourself; *acirāt*—very soon; *bhraśyase*—will fall down; *śriyaḥ*—from all opulence.

TRANSLATION

Although you have no knowledge, you have become a so-called learned person, and therefore you dare be so impudent as to disobey my order. Because of disobeying me, you shall very soon be bereft of all your opulence.

PURPORT

Śrīla Viśvanātha Cakravartī Ṭhākura says that Bali Mahārāja was not *paṇḍita-mānī,* or one who falsely assumes himself learned; rather, he was *paṇḍita-mānya-jñaḥ,* one who is so learned that all other learned persons worship him. And because he was so learned, he could disobey the order of his so-called spiritual master. He had no fear of any condition of material existence. Anyone cared for by Lord Viṣṇu does not need to care about anyone else. Thus Bali Mahārāja could never be bereft of all opulences. The opulences offered by the Supreme Personality of Godhead are not to be compared to the opulences obtained by *karma-kāṇḍa.* In other words, if a devotee becomes very opulent, it is to be understood that his opulence is a gift of the Supreme Personality of Godhead. Such opulence will never be vanquished, whereas the opulence achieved by one's fruitive activity may be vanquished at any moment.

TEXT 16

एवं शप्तः स्वगुरुणा सत्यान्न चलितो महान्।
वामनाय ददावेनामर्चित्वोदकपूर्वकम् ॥ १६ ॥

evaṁ śaptaḥ sva-guruṇā
satyān na calito mahān
vāmanāya dadāv enām
arcitvodaka-pūrvakam

evam—in this way; *śaptaḥ*—being cursed; *sva-guruṇā*—by his own spiritual master; *satyāt*—from truthfulness; *na*—not; *calitaḥ*—who moved; *mahān*—the great personality; *vāmanāya*—unto Lord Vāmanadeva; *dadau*—gave in charity; *enām*—all the land; *arcitvā*—after worshiping; *udaka-pūrvakam*—preceded by offering of water.

TRANSLATION

Śukadeva Gosvāmī continued: Even after being cursed in this way by his own spiritual master, Bali Mahārāja, being a great personality, never deviated from his determination. Therefore, according to custom, he first offered water to Vāmanadeva and then offered Him the gift of land he had promised.

TEXT 17

विन्ध्यावलिस्तदागत्य पत्नी जालकमालिनी।
आनिन्ये कलशं हैममवनेजन्यपां भृतम् ॥ १७ ॥

vindhyāvalis tadāgatya
patnī jālaka-mālinī
āninye kalaśaṁ haimam
avanejany-apāṁ bhṛtam

vindhyāvaliḥ—Vindhyāvali; *tadā*—at that time; *āgatya*—coming there; *patnī*—the wife of Mahārāja Bali; *jālaka-mālinī*—decorated with a necklace of pearls; *āninye*—caused to be brought; *kalaśam*—a waterpot; *haimam*—made of gold; *avanejani-apām*—with water for the sake of washing the Lord's feet; *bhṛtam*—filled.

TRANSLATION

Bali Mahārāja's wife, known as Vindhyāvali, who was decorated with a necklace of pearls, immediately came and had a large golden waterpot brought there, full of water with which to worship the Lord by washing His feet.

TEXT 18

यजमानः स्वयं तस्य श्रीमत् पादयुगं मुदा ।
अवनिज्यावहन्मूर्ध्नि तदपो विश्वपावनीः ॥ १८ ॥

yajamānaḥ svayaṁ tasya
śrīmat pāda-yugaṁ mudā
avanijyāvahan mūrdhni
tad apo viśva-pāvanīḥ

yajamānaḥ—the worshiper (Bali Mahārāja); *svayam*—personally; *tasya*—of Lord Vāmanadeva; *śrīmat pāda-yugam*—the most auspicious and beautiful pair of lotus feet; *mudā*—with great jubilation; *avanijya*—properly washing; *avahat*—took; *mūrdhni*—on his head; *tat*—that; *apaḥ*—water; *viśva-pāvanīḥ*—which gives liberation to the whole universe.

TRANSLATION

Bali Mahārāja, the worshiper of Lord Vāmanadeva, jubilantly washed the Lord's lotus feet and then took the water on his head, for that water delivers the entire universe.

TEXT 19

तदासुरेन्द्रं दिवि देवतागणा
गन्धर्वविद्याधरसिद्धचारणाः ।
तत्कर्म सर्वेऽपि गृणन्त आर्जवं
प्रसूनवर्षैर्ववृषुर्मुदान्विताः ॥ १९ ॥

tadāsurendraṁ divi devatā-gaṇā
gandharva-vidyādhara-siddha-cāraṇāḥ
tat karma sarve 'pi gṛṇanta ārjavaṁ
prasūna-varṣair vavṛṣur mudānvitāḥ

tadā—at that time; *asura-indram*—unto the King of the demons, Bali Mahārāja; *divi*—in the higher planetary system; *devatā-gaṇāḥ*—the residents known as the demigods; *gandharva*—the Gandharvas; *vidyādhara*—the Vidyādharas; *siddha*—the residents of Siddhaloka; *cāraṇāḥ*—the residents of Cāraṇaloka; *tat*—that; *karma*—action; *sarve api*—all of them; *gṛṇantaḥ*—declaring; *ārjavam*—plain and simple; *prasūna-varṣaiḥ*—with a shower of flowers; *vavṛṣuḥ*—released; *mudā-anvitāḥ*—being very pleased with him.

TRANSLATION

At that time, the residents of the higher planetary system, namely the demigods, the Gandharvas, the Vidyādharas, the Siddhas and the Cāraṇas, all being very pleased by Bali Mahārāja's simple, nonduplicitous act, praised his qualities and showered upon him millions of flowers.

PURPORT

Ārjavam—simplicity or freedom from duplicity—is a qualification of a *brāhmaṇa* and a Vaiṣṇava. A Vaiṣṇava automatically acquires all the qualities of a *brāhmaṇa.*

yasyāsti bhaktir bhagavaty akiñcanā
sarvair guṇais tatra samāsate surāḥ
(Bhāg. 5.18.12)

A Vaiṣṇava should possess the brahminical qualities such as *satya, śama, dama, titikṣā* and *ārjava.* There cannot be any duplicity in the character of a Vaiṣṇava. When Bali Mahārāja acted with unflinching faith and devotion unto the lotus feet of Lord Viṣṇu, this was very much appreciated by all the residents of the higher planetary system.

TEXT 20

नेदुर्मुहुर्दुन्दुभयः सहस्रशो
गन्धर्वकिंपूरुषकिन्नरा जगुः ।
मनस्विनानेन कृतं सुदुष्करं
विद्वानदाद् यद् रिपवे जगत्त्रयम् ॥ २० ॥

nedur muhur dundubhayaḥ sahasraśo
gandharva-kimpūruṣa-kinnarā jaguḥ
manasvinānena kṛtaṁ suduṣkaraṁ
vidvān adād yad ripave jagat-trayam

neduḥ—began to beat; *muhuḥ*—again and again; *dundubhayaḥ*—trumpets and kettledrums; *sahasraśaḥ*—by thousands and thousands; *gandharva*—the residents of Gandharvaloka; *kimpūruṣa*—the residents of Kimpuruṣaloka; *kinnarāḥ*—and the residents of Kinnaraloka; *jaguḥ*—began to sing and declare; *manasvinā*—by the most exalted personality; *anena*—by Bali Mahārāja; *kṛtam*—was done; *su-duṣkaram*—an extremely difficult task; *vidvān*—because of his being the most learned person; *adāt*—gave Him a gift; *yat*—that; *ripave*—unto the enemy, Lord Viṣṇu, who was siding with Bali Mahārāja's enemies, the demigods; *jagat-trayam*—the three worlds.

TRANSLATION

The Gandharvas, the Kimpuruṣas and the Kinnaras sounded thousands and thousands of kettledrums and trumpets again and again, and they sang in great jubilation, declaring, "How exalted a person is Bali Mahārāja, and what a difficult task he has performed! Even though he knew that Lord Viṣṇu was on the side of his enemies, he nonetheless gave the Lord the entire three worlds in charity."

TEXT 21

तद् वामनं रूपमवर्धताद्भुतं
हरेरनन्तस्य गुणत्रयात्मकम् ।
भूः खं दिशो द्यौर्विवराः पयोधय-
स्तिर्यङ्नृदेवा ऋषयो यदासत ॥ २१ ॥

tad vāmanaṁ rūpam avardhatādbhutaṁ
harer anantasya guṇa-trayātmakam
bhūḥ khaṁ diśo dyaur vivarāḥ payodhayas
tiryaṅ-nṛ-devā ṛṣayo yad-āsata

tat—that; *vāmanam*—incarnation of Lord Vāmana; *rūpam*—form; *avardhata*—began to increase more and more; *adbhutam*—certainly very wonderful; *hareḥ*—of the Supreme Personality of Godhead; *anantasya*—of the unlimited; *guṇa-traya-ātmakam*—whose body is expanded by the material energy, consisting of three modes (goodness, passion and ignorance); *bhūḥ*—the land; *kham*—the sky; *diśaḥ*—all directions; *dyauḥ*—the planetary systems; *vivarāḥ*—different holes of the universe; *payodhayaḥ*—great seas and oceans; *tiryak*—lower animals, birds and beasts; *nṛ*—human beings; *devāḥ*—demigods; *ṛṣayaḥ*—great saintly persons; *yat*—wherein; *āsata*—lived.

TRANSLATION

The unlimited Supreme Personality of Godhead, who had assumed the form of Vāmana, then began increasing in size, acting in terms of the material energy, until everything in the universe was within His body, including the earth, the planetary systems, the sky, the directions, the various holes in the universe, the seas, the oceans, the birds, beasts, human beings, the demigods and the great saintly persons.

PURPORT

Bali Mahārāja wanted to give charity to Vāmanadeva, but the Lord expanded His body in such a way that He showed Bali Mahārāja that everything in the universe is already in His body. Actually, no one can give anything to the Supreme Personality of Godhead, for He is full in everything. Sometimes we see a devotee offering Ganges water to the Ganges. After taking his bath in the Ganges, a devotee takes a palmful of water and offers it back to the Ganges. Actually, when one takes a palmful of water from the Ganges, the Ganges does not lose anything, and similarly if a devotee offers a palmful of water to the Ganges, the Ganges does not increase in any way. But by such an offering, the devotee becomes celebrated as a devotee of mother Ganges. Similarly, when we offer anything with devotion and faith, what we offer does not belong to us, nor does it enrich the opulence of the Supreme Personality of Godhead. But if one offers whatever he has in his possession, he becomes a recognized devotee. In this regard, the example is given that when one's face is decorated with a garland and sandalwood pulp, the reflection of one's face in a mirror automatically becomes beautiful. The original source of everything is the Supreme Personality of Godhead, who is our original source also. Therefore when the Supreme Personality of Godhead is decorated, the devotees and all living entities are decorated automatically.

TEXT 22

काये बलिस्तस्य महाविभूतेः
सहर्त्विगाचार्यसदस्य एतत् ।
ददर्श विश्वं त्रिगुणं गुणात्मके
भूतेन्द्रियार्थाशयजीवयुक्तम् ॥ २२ ॥

kāye balis tasya mahā-vibhūteḥ
sahartvig-ācārya-sadasya etat
dadarśa viśvaṁ tri-guṇaṁ guṇātmake
bhūtendriyārthāśaya-jīva-yuktam

kāye—in the body; *baliḥ*—Mahārāja Bali; *tasya*—of the Personality of Godhead; *mahā-vibhūteḥ*—of that person who is equipped with all wonderful opulences; *saha-ṛtvik-ācārya-sadasyaḥ*—with all the priests, *ācāryas* and members of the holy assembly; *etat*—this; *dadarśa*—saw; *viśvam*—the whole universe; *tri-guṇam*—made of three modes of material nature; *guṇa-ātmake*—in that which is the source of all such qualities; *bhūta*—with all the gross material elements; *indriya*—with the senses; *artha*—with the sense objects; *āśaya*—with mind, intelligence and false ego; *jīva-yuktam*—with all the living entities.

TRANSLATION

Bali Mahārāja, along with all the priests, ācāryas and members of the assembly, observed the Supreme Personality of Godhead's universal body, which was full of six opulences. That body contained everything within the universe, including all the gross material elements, the senses, the sense objects, the mind, intelligence and false ego, the various kinds of living entities, and the actions and reactions of the three modes of material nature.

PURPORT

In *Bhagavad-gītā*, the Supreme Personality of Godhead says, *ahaṁ sarvasya prabhavo mattaḥ sarvaṁ pravartate:* Kṛṣṇa is the origin of everything. *Vāsudevaḥ sarvam iti:* Kṛṣṇa is everything. *Mat-sthāni sarva-bhūtāni na cāhaṁ teṣv avasthitaḥ:* everything rests in the body of the Lord, yet the Lord is not everywhere. Māyāvādī philosophers think that since the Supreme Personality of Godhead, the Absolute Truth, has become everything, He has no separate existence. Their philosophy is called *advaita-vāda*. Actually, however, their philosophy is not correct. Here, Bali Mahārāja was the seer of the Personality of Godhead's universal body, and that body was that which was seen. Thus there is *dvaita-vāda*; there are always two entities—the seer and the seen. The seer is a part of the whole, but he is not equal to the whole. The part of the whole, the seer, is also one with the whole, but since he is but a part, he cannot be the complete whole at any time. This *acintya-bhedābheda*—simultaneous oneness and difference—is the perfect philosophy propounded by Lord Śrī Caitanya Mahāprabhu.

TEXT 23

रसामचष्टाङ्घ्रितलेऽथ पादयो-
र्महीं महीध्रान्पुरुषस्य जङ्घयोः ।
पतत्त्रिणो जानुनि विश्वमूर्ते-
रूर्वोर्गणं मारुतमिन्द्रसेनः ॥ २३ ॥

rasām acaṣṭāṅghri-tale 'tha pādayor
mahīṁ mahīdhrān puruṣasya jaṅghayoḥ
patattriṇo jānuni viśva-mūrter
ūrvor gaṇaṁ mārutam indrasenaḥ

rasām—the lower planetary system; *acaṣṭa*—observed; *aṅghri-tale*—beneath the feet, or on the sole; *atha*—thereafter; *pādayoḥ*—on the feet; *mahīm*—the surface of the land; *mahīdhrān*—the mountains; *puruṣasya*—of the giant Personality of Godhead; *jaṅghayoḥ*—on the calves; *patattriṇaḥ*—the flying living entities; *jānuni*—on the knees; *viśva-mūrteḥ*—of the form of the gigantic Lord; *ūrvoḥ*—on the thighs; *gaṇam mārutam*—varieties of air; *indra-senaḥ*—Bali Mahārāja, who had obtained the soldiers of King Indra and who was situated in the post of Indra.

TRANSLATION

Thereafter, Bali Mahārāja, who was occupying the seat of King Indra, could see the lower planetary systems, such as Rasātala, on the soles of the feet of the Lord's universal form. He saw on the Lord's feet the surface of the globe, on the surface of His calves all the mountains, on His knees the various birds, and on His thighs the varieties of air.

PURPORT

The universal situation is described herein in regard to the complete constitution of the Lord's gigantic universal form. The study of this universal form begins from the sole. Above the soles are the feet, above the feet are the calves, above the calves are the knees, and above the knees are the thighs. Thus the parts of the universal body, one after another, are described herein. The knees are the place of birds, and above that are varieties of air. The birds can fly over the mountains, and above the birds are varieties of air.

TEXT 24

सन्ध्यां विभोर्वाससि गुह्य ऐक्षत्
प्रजापतीञ्जघने आत्ममुख्यान् ।
नाभ्यां नभः कुक्षिषु सप्तसिन्धू-
नुरुक्रमस्योरसि चर्क्षमालाम् ॥ २४ ॥

sandhyāṁ vibhor vāsasi guhya aikṣat
prajāpatīñ jaghane ātma-mukhyān
nābhyāṁ nabhaḥ kukṣiṣu sapta-sindhūn
urukramasyorasi carkṣa-mālām

sandhyām—the evening twilight; *vibhoḥ*—of the Supreme; *vāsasi*—in the garment; *guhye*—on the private parts; *aikṣat*—he saw; *prajāpatīn*—the various Prajāpatis, who had given birth to all living entities; *jaghane*—on the hips; *ātma-mukhyān*—the confidential ministers of Bali Mahārāja; *nābhyām*—on the navel; *nabhaḥ*—the whole sky; *kukṣiṣu*—on the waist; *sapta*—seven; *sindhūn*—oceans; *urukramasya*—of the Supreme Personality of Godhead, who was acting wonderfully; *urasi*—on the bosom; *ca*—also; *ṛkṣa-mālām*—the clusters of stars.

TRANSLATION

Bali Mahārāja saw beneath the garments of the Lord, who acts wonderfully, the evening twilight. In the Lord's private parts he saw the Prajāpatis, and in the round portion of the waist he saw himself with his confidential associates. In the Lord's navel he saw the sky, on the Lord's waist he saw the seven oceans, and on the Lord's bosom he saw all the clusters of stars.

TEXTS 25-29

हृद्यङ्ग धर्मं स्तनयोर्मुरारे-
ऋतं च सत्यं च मनस्यथेन्दुम् ।
श्रियं च वक्षस्यरविन्दहस्तां
कण्ठे च सामानि समस्तरेफान् ॥ २५ ॥
इन्द्रप्रधानानमरान्भुजेषु
तत्कर्णयोः ककुभो द्यौश्च मूर्ध्नि ।
केशेषु मेघाञ्छ्वसनं नासिकाया-
मक्ष्णोश्च सूर्यं वदने च वह्निम् ॥ २६ ॥
वाण्यां च छन्दांसि रसे जलेशं
भ्रुवोर्निषेधं च विधिं च पक्ष्मसु ।
अहश्च रात्रिं च परस्य पुंसो
मन्युं ललाटेऽधर एव लोभम् ॥ २७ ॥
स्पर्शे च कामं नृप रेतसाम्भः
पृष्ठे त्वधर्मं क्रमणेषु यज्ञम् ।
छायासु मृत्युं हसिते च मायां
तनूरुहेष्वोषधिजातयश्च ॥ २८ ॥
नदीश्च नाडीषु शिला नखेषु
बुद्धावजं देवगणानृषींश्च ।
प्राणेषु गात्रे स्थिरजङ्गमानि
सर्वाणि भूतानि ददर्श वीरः ॥ २९ ॥

hṛdy aṅga dharmaṁ stanayor murārer
ṛtaṁ ca satyaṁ ca manasy athendum
śriyaṁ ca vakṣasy aravinda-hastāṁ
kaṇṭhe ca sāmāni samasta-rephān

indra-pradhānān amarān bhujeṣu
tat-karṇayoḥ kakubho dyauś ca mūrdhni
keśeṣu meghāñ chvasanaṁ nāsikāyām
akṣṇoś ca sūryaṁ vadane ca vahnim

vāṇyāṁ ca chandāṁsi rase jaleśaṁ
bhruvor niṣedhaṁ ca vidhiṁ ca pakṣmasu

ahaś ca rātriṁ ca parasya puṁso
manyuṁ lalāṭe 'dhara eva lobham

sparśe ca kāmaṁ nṛpa retasāmbhaḥ
pṛṣṭhe tv adharmaṁ kramaṇeṣu yajñam
chāyāsu mṛtyuṁ hasite ca māyāṁ
tanū-ruheṣv oṣadhi-jātayaś ca

nadīś ca nāḍīṣu śilā nakheṣu
buddhāv ajaṁ deva-gaṇān ṛṣīṁś ca
prāṇeṣu gātre sthira-jaṅgamāni
sarvāṇi bhūtāni dadarśa vīraḥ

hṛdi—within the heart; *aṅga*—my dear King Parīkṣit; *dharmam*—religion; *stanayoḥ*—on the bosom; *murāreḥ*—of Murāri, the Supreme Personality of Godhead; *ṛtam*—very pleasing words; *ca*—also; *satyam*—truthfulness; *ca*—also; *manasi*—in the mind; *atha*—thereafter; *indum*—the moon; *śriyam*—the goddess of fortune; *ca*—also; *vakṣasi*—on the chest; *aravinda-hastām*—who always carries a lotus flower in her hand; *kaṇṭhe*—on the neck; *ca*—also; *sāmāni*—all the *Vedas* (*Sāma, Yajur, Ṛg* and *Atharva*); *samasta-rephān*—all sound vibrations; *indra-pradhānān*—headed by King Indra; *amarān*—all the demigods; *bhujeṣu*—on the arms; *tat-karṇayoḥ*—on the ears; *kakubhaḥ*—all the directions; *dyauḥ ca*—the luminaries; *mūrdhni*—on the top of the head; *keśeṣu*—within the hair; *meghān*—the clouds; *śvasanam*—breathing air; *nāsikāyām*—on the nostrils; *akṣṇoḥ ca*—in the eyes; *sūryam*—the sun; *vadane*—in the mouth; *ca*—also; *vahnim*—fire; *vāṇyām*—in His speech; *ca*—also; *chandāṁsi*—the Vedic hymns; *rase*—in the tongue; *jala-īśam*—the demigod of the water; *bhruvoḥ*—on the eyebrows; *niṣedham*—warnings; *ca*—also; *vidhim*—regulative principles; *ca*—also; *pakṣmasu*—in the eyelids; *ahaḥ ca*—daytime; *rātrim*—night; *ca*—also; *parasya*—of the supreme; *puṁsaḥ*—of the person; *manyum*—anger; *lalāṭe*—on the forehead; *adhare*—on the lips; *eva*—indeed; *lobham*—greed; *sparśe*—in His touch; *ca*—also; *kāmam*—lusty desires; *nṛpa*—O King; *retasā*—by semen; *ambhaḥ*—water; *pṛṣṭhe*—on the back; *tu*—but; *adharmam*—irreligion; *kramaṇeṣu*—in the wonderful activities; *yajñam*—fire sacrifice; *chāyāsu*—in the shadows; *mṛtyum*—death; *hasite*—in His smiling; *ca*—also; *māyām*—the illusory energy; *tanū-ruheṣu*—in the hair on the body; *oṣadhi-jātayaḥ*—all species of drugs, herbs and plants; *ca*—and; *nadīḥ*—the rivers; *ca*—also; *nāḍīṣu*—in the veins; *śilāḥ*—stones; *nakheṣu*—

in the nails; *buddhau*—in the intelligence; *ajam*—Lord Brahmā; *deva-gaṇān*—the demigods; *ṛṣīn ca*—and the great sages; *prāṇeṣu*—in the senses; *gātre*—in the body; *sthira-jaṅgamāni*—moving and stationary; *sarvāṇi*—all of them; *bhūtāni*—living entities; *dadarśa*—saw; *vīraḥ*—Bali Mahārāja.

TRANSLATION

My dear King, on the heart of Lord Murāri he saw religion; on the chest, both pleasing words and truthfulness; in the mind, the moon; on the bosom, the goddess of fortune, with a lotus flower in her hand; on the neck, all the Vedas and all sound vibrations; on the arms, all the demigods, headed by King Indra; in both ears, all the directions; on the head, the upper planetary systems; on the hair, the clouds; in the nostrils, the wind; on the eyes, the sun; and in the mouth, fire. From His words came all the Vedic mantras, on His tongue was the demigod of water, Varuṇadeva, on His eyebrows were the regulative principles, and on His eyelids were day and night. [When His eyes were open it was daytime, and when they were closed it was night.] On His forehead was anger, and on His lips was greed. O King, in His touch were lusty desires, in His semen were all the waters, on His back was irreligion, and in His wonderful activities or steps was the fire of sacrifice. On His shadow was death, in His smile was the illusory energy, and on the hairs of His body were all the drugs and herbs. In His veins were all the rivers, on His nails were all the stones, in His intelligence were Lord Brahmā, the demigods and the great saintly persons, and throughout His entire body and senses were all living entities, moving and stationary. Bali Mahārāja thus saw everything in the gigantic body of the Lord.

TEXT 30

सर्वात्मनीदं भुवनं निरीक्ष्य
सर्वेऽसुराः कश्मलमापुरङ्ग ।
सुदर्शनं चक्रमसह्यतेजो
धनुश्च शार्ङ्गं स्तनयित्नुघोषम् ॥ ३० ॥

sarvātmanīdaṁ bhuvanaṁ nirīkṣya
sarve 'surāḥ kaśmalam āpur aṅga
sudarśanaṁ cakram asahya-tejo
dhanuś ca śārṅgaṁ stanayitnu-ghoṣam

sarva-ātmani—in the supreme whole, the Supreme Personality of Godhead; *idam*—this universe; *bhuvanam*—the three worlds; *nirīkṣya*—by observing; *sarve*—all; *asurāḥ*—the demons, the associates of Bali Mahārāja; *kaśmalam*—lamentation; *āpuḥ*—received; *aṅga*—O King; *sudarśanam*—named Sudarśana; *cakram*—the disc; *asahya*—unbearable; *tejaḥ*—the heat of which; *dhanuḥ ca*—and the bow; *śārṅgam*—named Śārṅga; *stanayitnu*—the resounding of assembled clouds; *ghoṣam*—sounding like.

TRANSLATION

O King, when all the demons, the followers of Mahārāja Bali, saw the universal form of the Supreme Personality of Godhead, who held everything within His body, when they saw in the Lord's hand His disc, known as the Sudarśana cakra, which generates intolerable heat, and when they heard the tumultuous sound of His bow, all of these caused lamentation within their hearts.

TEXT 31

पर्जन्यघोषो जलजः पाञ्चजन्यः
कौमोदकी विष्णुगदा तरस्विनी ।
विद्याधरोऽसिः शतचन्द्रयुक्त-
स्तूणोत्तमावक्षयसायकौ च ॥ ३१ ॥

parjanya-ghoṣo jalajaḥ pāñcajanyaḥ
kaumodakī viṣṇu-gadā tarasvinī
vidyādharo 'siḥ śata-candra-yuktas
tūṇottamāv akṣayasāyakau ca

parjanya-ghoṣaḥ—having a sound vibration like that of the clouds; *jalajaḥ*—the Lord's conchshell; *pāñcajanyaḥ*—which is known as Pāñcajanya; *kaumodakī*—known by the name Kaumodakī; *viṣṇu-gadā*—the club of Lord Viṣṇu; *tarasvinī*—with great force; *vidyādharaḥ*—named Vidyādhara; *asiḥ*—the sword; *śata-candra-yuktaḥ*—with a shield decorated with hundreds of moons; *tūṇa-uttamau*—the best of quivers; *akṣayasāyakau*—named Akṣayasāyaka; *ca*—also.

TRANSLATION

The Lord's conchshell, named Pāñcajanya, which made sounds like that of a cloud; the very forceful club named Kaumodakī; the sword named

Vidyādhara, with a shield decorated with hundreds of moonlike spots; and also Akṣayasāyaka, the best of quivers—all of these appeared together to offer prayers to the Lord.

TEXTS 32-33

सुनन्दमुख्या उपतस्थुरीशं
पार्षदमुख्याः सहलोकपालाः ।
स्फुरत्किरीटाङ्गदमीनकुण्डलः
श्रीवत्सरत्नोत्तममेखलाम्बरैः ॥ ३२ ॥
मधुव्रतस्रग्वनमालयावृतो
रराज राजन्भगवानुरुक्रमः ।
क्षितिं पदैकेन बलेर्विचक्रमे
नभः शरीरेण दिशश्च बाहुभिः ॥ ३३ ॥

sunanda-mukhyā upatasthur īśaṁ
pārṣada-mukhyāḥ saha-loka-pālāḥ
sphurat-kirīṭāṅgada-mīna-kuṇḍalaḥ
śrīvatsa-ratnottama-mekhalāmbaraiḥ

madhuvrata-srag-vanamālayāvṛto
rarāja rājan bhagavān urukramaḥ
kṣitiṁ padaikena baler vicakrame
nabhaḥ śarīreṇa diśaś ca bāhubhiḥ

sunanda-mukhyāḥ—the associates of the Lord headed by Sunanda; *upatasthuḥ*—began to offer prayers; *īśam*—unto the Supreme Personality of Godhead; *pārṣada-mukhyāḥ*—other chiefs of the associates; *saha-loka-pālāḥ*—with the predominant deities of all the planets; *sphurat-kirīṭa*—with a brilliant helmet; *aṅgada*—bracelets; *mīna-kuṇḍalaḥ*—and earrings in the shape of fish; *śrīvatsa*—the hair named Śrīvatsa on His bosom; *ratna-uttama*—the best of jewels (Kaustubha); *mekhalā*—belt; *ambaraiḥ*—with yellow garments; *madhu-vrata*—of bees; *srak*—in which there was a garland; *vanamālayā*—by a flower garland; *āvṛtaḥ*—covered; *rarāja*—predominantly manifested; *rājan*—O King; *bhagavān*—the Supreme Personality of Godhead; *urukramaḥ*—who is prominent by His wonderful activities; *kṣitim*—the whole surface of the world; *padā ekena*—by one footstep; *baleḥ*—of Bali

Mahārāja; *vicakrame*—covered; *nabhaḥ*—the sky; *śarīreṇa*—by His body; *diśaḥ ca*—and all directions; *bāhubhiḥ*—by His arms.

TRANSLATION

These associates, headed by Sunanda and other chief associates and accompanied by all the predominating deities of the various planets, offered prayers to the Lord, who wore a brilliant helmet, bracelets, and glittering earrings that resembled fish. On the Lord's bosom were the lock of hair called Śrīvatsa and the transcendental jewel named Kaustubha. He wore a yellow garment, covered by a belt, and He was decorated by a flower garland, surrounded by bees. Manifesting Himself in this way, O King, the Supreme Personality of Godhead, whose activities are wonderful, covered the entire surface of the earth with one footstep, the sky with His body, and all directions with His arms.

PURPORT

One might argue, "Since Bali Mahārāja promised Vāmanadeva only the land occupied by His steps, why did Lord Vāmanadeva occupy the sky also?" In this regard, Śrīla Jīva Gosvāmī says that the steps include everything, downward and upward. When one stands up, he certainly occupies certain parts of the sky and certain portions of the earth below his feet. Thus there was nothing uncommon for the Supreme Personality of Godhead when He occupied the entire sky with His body.

TEXT 34

पदं द्वितीयं क्रमतस्त्रिविष्टपं
न वै तृतीयाय तदीयमण्वपि ।
उरुक्रमस्याङ्घ्रिरुपर्युपर्यथो
महर्जनाभ्यां तपसः परं गतः ॥ ३४ ॥

padaṁ dvitīyaṁ kramatas triviṣṭapaṁ
na vai tṛtīyāya tadīyam aṇv api
urukramasyāṅghrir upary upary atho
mahar-janābhyāṁ tapasaḥ paraṁ gataḥ

padam—step; *dvitīyam*—second; *kramataḥ*—advancing; *tri-viṣṭapam*—all of the heavenly planets; *na*—not; *vai*—indeed; *tṛtīyāya*—for the third step; *tadīyam*—of the Lord; *aṇu api*—only a spot of land remained; *urukra-*

masya—of the Supreme Personality of Godhead, who performs uncommon activities; *aṅghriḥ*—steps occupying above and below; *upari upari*—higher and higher; *atho*—now; *mahaḥ-janābhyām*—than Maharloka and Janaloka; *tapasaḥ*—that Tapoloka; *param*—beyond that; *gataḥ*—approached.

TRANSLATION

As the Lord took His second step, He covered the heavenly planets. And not even a spot remained for the third step, for the Lord's foot extended higher and higher, beyond Maharloka, Janaloka, Tapoloka and even Satyaloka.

PURPORT

When the Lord's footstep exceeded the height of all the *lokas,* including Maharloka, Janaloka, Tapoloka and Satyaloka, His nails certainly pierced the covering of the universe. The universe is covered by the five material elements (*bhūmir āpo 'nalo vāyuḥ kham*). As stated in the *śāstra,* these elements are in layers, each ten times thicker than the previous one. Nonetheless, the nails of the Lord pierced through all these layers and made a hole penetrating into the spiritual world. From this hole, the water of the Ganges infiltrated into this material world, and therefore it is said, *pada-nakha-nīra-janita-jana-pāvana* (*Daśāvatāra-stotra* 5). Because the Lord kicked a hole in the covering of the universe, the water of the Ganges came into this material world to deliver all the fallen souls.

Thus end the Bhaktivedanta purports of the Eighth Canto, Twentieth Chapter, of the Śrīmad-Bhāgavatam, *entitled "Bali Mahārāja Surrenders the Universe."*

CHAPTER TWENTY-ONE

Bali Mahārāja Arrested by the Lord

This chapter describes how Lord Viṣṇu, desiring to advertise the glories of Bali Mahārāja, arrested him for not fulfilling his promise in regard to the Lord's third step.

With the second step the Supreme Personality of Godhead reached the topmost planet of the universe, Brahmaloka, which He diminished in beauty by the effulgence of His toenails. Thus Lord Brahmā, accompanied by great sages like Marīci and the predominating deities of all the higher planets, offered humble prayers and worship to the Lord. They washed the Lord's feet and worshiped Him with all paraphernalia. Ṛkṣarāja, Jāmbavān, played his bugle to vibrate the glories of the Lord. When Bali Mahārāja was deprived of all his possessions, the demons were very angry. Although Bali Mahārāja warned them not to do so, they took up weapons against Lord Viṣṇu. All of them were defeated, however, by Lord Viṣṇu's eternal associates, and, in accordance with Bali Mahārāja's order, they all entered the lower planets of the universe. Understanding Lord Viṣṇu's purpose, Garuḍa, the carrier of Lord Viṣṇu, immediately arrested Bali Mahārāja with the ropes of Varuṇa. When Bali Mahārāja was thus reduced to a helpless position, Lord Viṣṇu asked him for the third step of land. Because Lord Viṣṇu appreciated Bali Mahārāja's determination and integrity, when Bali Mahārāja was unable to fulfill his promise, Lord Viṣṇu ascertained that the place for him would be the planet Sutala, which is better than the planets of heaven.

TEXT 1

श्रीशुक उवाच

सत्यं समीक्ष्याब्जभवो नखेन्दुभि-

हतस्वधामद्युतिरावृतोऽभ्यगात् ।

मरीचिमिश्रा ऋषयो बृहद्व्रताः

सनन्दनाद्या नरदेव योगिनः ॥ १ ॥

śrī-śuka uvāca
satyaṁ samīkṣyābja-bhavo nakhendubhir
hata-svadhāma-dyutir āvṛto 'bhyagāt
marīci-miśrā ṛṣayo bṛhad-vratāḥ
sanandanādyā nara-deva yoginaḥ

śrī-śukaḥ uvāca—Śrī Śukadeva Gosvāmī said; *satyam*—the planet Satyaloka; *samīkṣya*—by observing; *abja-bhavaḥ*—Lord Brahmā, who appeared on the lotus flower; *nakha-indubhiḥ*—by the effulgence of the nails; *hata*—having been reduced; *sva-dhāma-dyutiḥ*—the illumination of his own residence; *āvṛtaḥ*—being covered; *abhyagāt*—came; *marīci-miśrāḥ*—with sages like Marīci; *ṛṣayaḥ*—great saintly persons; *bṛhat-vratāḥ*—all of them absolutely *brahmacārī; sanandana-ādyāḥ*—like Sanaka, Sanātana, Sanandana and Sanat-kumāra; *nara-deva*—O King; *yoginaḥ*—greatly powerful mystics.

TRANSLATION

Śukadeva Gosvāmī continued: When Lord Brahmā, who was born of a lotus flower, saw that the effulgence of his residence, Brahmaloka, had been reduced by the glaring effulgence from the toenails of Lord Vāmanadeva, he approached the Supreme Personality of Godhead. Lord Brahmā was accompanied by all the great sages, headed by Marīci, and by yogīs like Sanandana, but in the presence of that glaring effulgence, O King, even Lord Brahmā and his associates seemed insignificant.

TEXTS 2-3

वेदोपवेदा नियमा यमान्विता-
स्तर्केतिहासाङ्गपुराणसंहिताः ।
ये चापरे योगसमीरदीपित-
ज्ञानाग्निना रन्धितकर्मकल्मषाः ॥ २ ॥

ववन्दिरे यत्स्मरणानुभावतः
स्वायम्भुवं धाम गता अकर्मकम् ।
अथाङ्घ्रये प्रोन्नमिताय विष्णो-
रुपाहरत् पद्मभवोऽर्हणोदकम् ।
समर्च्य भक्त्याभ्यगृणाच्छुचिश्रवा
यन्नाभिपङ्केरुहसंभवः स्वयम् ॥ ३ ॥

vedopavedā niyamā yamānvitās
tarketihāsāṅga-purāṇa-saṁhitāḥ
ye cāpare yoga-samīra-dīpita-
jñānāgninā randhita-karma-kalmaṣāḥ

vavandire yat-smaraṇānubhāvataḥ
svāyambhuvaṁ dhāma gatā akarmakam
athāṅghraye pronnamitāya viṣṇor
upāharat padma-bhavo 'rhaṇodakam
samarcya bhaktyābhyagṛṇāc chuci-śravā
yan-nābhi-paṅkeruha-sambhavaḥ svayam

veda—the four *Vedas* (*Sāma, Yajur, Ṛg* and *Atharva*), the original knowledge given by the Supreme Personality of Godhead; *upavedāḥ*—the complementary and supplementary Vedic knowledge, like *Āyur-veda* and *Dhanur-veda; niyamāḥ*—regulative principles; *yama*—controlling processes; *anvitāḥ*—fully expert in such matters; *tarka*—logic; *itihāsa*—history; *aṅga*—Vedic education; *purāṇa*—old history recorded in the stories of the *Purāṇas; saṁhitāḥ*—Vedic complementary studies like the *Brahma-saṁhitā; ye*—others; *ca*—also; *apare*—other than Lord Brahmā and his associates; *yoga-samīra-dīpita*—ignited by the air of mystic *yoga* practice; *jñāna-agninā*—by the fire of knowledge; *randhita-karma-kalmaṣāḥ*—those for whom all pollution of fruitive activities has been stopped; *vavandire*—offered their prayers; *yat-smaraṇa-anubhāvataḥ*—simply by meditating on whom; *svāyambhuvam*—of Lord Brahmā; *dhāma*—the residence; *gatāḥ*—had achieved; *akarmakam*—which cannot be achieved by fruitive activities; *atha*—thereupon; *aṅghraye*—unto the lotus feet; *pronnamitāya*—offered obeisances; *viṣṇoḥ*—of Lord Viṣṇu; *upāharat*—offered worship; *padma-bhavaḥ*—Lord Brahmā, who appeared from the lotus flower; *arhaṇa-udakam*—oblation by water; *samarcya*—worshiping; *bhaktyā*—in devotional service; *abhyagṛṇāt*—pleased him; *śuci-śravāḥ*—the most celebrated Vedic authority; *yat-nābhi-paṅkeruha-sambhavaḥ svayam*—Lord Brahmā, who personally appeared from the lotus in the navel of whom (the Personality of Godhead).

TRANSLATION

Among the great personalities who came to worship the lotus feet of the Lord were those who had attained perfection in self-control and regulative principles, as well as experts in logic, history, general education and the Vedic literature known as kalpa [dealing with old historical incidents].

Others were experts in the Vedic corollaries like Brahma-saṁhitā, all the other knowledge of the Vedas [Sāma, Yajur, Ṛg and Atharva], and also the supplementary Vedic knowledge [Āyur-veda, Dhanur-veda, etc.]. Others were those who had been freed of the reactions to fruitive activities by transcendental knowledge awakened by practice of yoga. And still others were those who had attained residence in Brahmaloka not by ordinary karma but by advanced Vedic knowledge. After devotedly worshiping the upraised lotus feet of the Supreme Lord with oblations of water, Lord Brahmā, who was born of the lotus emanating from Lord Viṣṇu's navel, offered prayers to the Lord.

TEXT 4

धातुः कमण्डलुजलं तदुरुक्रमस्य
पादावनेजनपवित्रतया नरेन्द्र ।
स्वर्धुन्यभून्नभसि सा पतती निमार्ष्टि
लोकत्रयं भगवतो विशदेव कीर्तिः ॥ ४ ॥

dhātuḥ kamaṇḍalu-jalaṁ tad urukramasya
pādāvanejana-pavitratayā narendra
svardhuny abhūn nabhasi sā patatī nimārṣṭi
loka-trayaṁ bhagavato viśadeva kīrtiḥ

dhātuḥ—of Lord Brahmā; *kamaṇḍalu-jalam*—water from the *kamaṇḍalu; tat*—that; *urukramasya*—of Lord Viṣṇu; *pāda-avanejana-pavitratayā*—because of washing the lotus feet of Lord Viṣṇu and thus being transcendentally pure; *nara-indra*—O King; *svardhunī*—the river named Svardhunī of the celestial world; *abhūt*—so became; *nabhasi*—in outer space; *sā*—that water; *patatī*—flowing down; *nimārṣṭi*—purifying; *loka-trayam*—the three worlds; *bhagavataḥ*—of the Supreme Personality of Godhead; *viśadā*—so purified; *iva*—just like; *kīrtiḥ*—the fame or the glorious activities.

TRANSLATION

O King, the water from Lord Brahmā's kamaṇḍalu washed the lotus feet of Lord Vāmanadeva, who is known as Urukrama, the wonderful actor. Thus that water became so pure that it was transformed into the water of the Ganges, which went flowing down from the sky, purifying the three worlds like the pure fame of the Supreme Personality of Godhead.

PURPORT

Here we understand that the Ganges began when the water from Lord Brahmā's *kamaṇḍalu* washed the lotus feet of Lord Vāmanadeva. But in the Fifth Canto it is stated that the Ganges began when Vāmanadeva's left foot pierced the covering of the universe so that the transcendental water of the Causal Ocean leaked through. And elsewhere it is also stated that Lord Nārāyaṇa appeared as the water of the Ganges. The water of the Ganges, therefore, is a combination of three transcendental waters, and thus the Ganges is able to purify the three worlds. This is the description given by Śrīla Viśvanātha Cakravartī Ṭhākura.

TEXT 5

ब्रह्मादयो लोकनाथाः स्वनाथाय समादृताः ।
सानुगा बलिमाजह्रुः संक्षिप्तात्मविभूतये ॥ ५ ॥

brahmādayo loka-nāthāḥ
sva-nāthāya samādṛtāḥ
sānugā balim ājahruḥ
saṅkṣiptātma-vibhūtaye

brahma-ādayaḥ—great personalities, headed by Lord Brahmā; *loka-nāthāḥ*—the predominating deities of various planets; *sva-nāthāya*—unto their supreme master; *samādṛtāḥ*—with great respect; *sa-anugāḥ*—with their respective followers; *balim*—different paraphernalia of worship; *ājahruḥ*—collected; *saṅkṣipta-ātma-vibhūtaye*—unto the Lord, who had expanded His personal opulence but had now reduced His size to the Vāmana form.

TRANSLATION

Lord Brahmā and all the predominating deities of the various planetary systems began to worship Lord Vāmanadeva, their supreme master, who had reduced Himself from His all-pervading form to His original form. They collected all the ingredients and paraphernalia for this worship.

PURPORT

Vāmanadeva first expanded Himself to the universal form and then reduced Himself to the original Vāmana-rūpa. Thus He acted exactly like Lord Kṛṣṇa, who, at the request of Arjuna, first showed His universal form and later resumed His original form as Kṛṣṇa. The Lord can assume any form He likes, but His original form is that of Kṛṣṇa (*kṛṣṇas tu bhagavān svayam*). According to the capacity of the devotee, the Lord assumes various forms so that the devotee can handle Him. This is His causeless mercy. When Lord Vāmanadeva resumed His original form, Lord Brahmā and his associates collected various paraphernalia for worship with which to please Him.

TEXTS 6-7

तोयैः समर्हणैः स्रग्भिर्दिव्यगन्धानुलेपनैः ।
धूपैर्दीपैः सुरभिभिर्लाजाक्षतफलाङ्कुरैः ॥ ६ ॥
स्तवनैर्जयशब्दैश्च तद्वीर्यमहिमाङ्कितैः ।
नृत्यवादित्रगीतैश्च शङ्खदुन्दुभिनिःस्वनैः ॥ ७ ॥

toyaiḥ samarhaṇaiḥ sragbhir
divya-gandhānulepanaiḥ
dhūpair dīpaiḥ surabhibhir
lājākṣata-phalāṅkuraiḥ

stavanair jaya-śabdaiś ca
tad-vīrya-mahimāṅkitaiḥ
nṛtya-vāditra-gītaiś ca
śaṅkha-dundubhi-niḥsvanaiḥ

toyaiḥ—by water required for washing the lotus feet and bathing; *samarhaṇaiḥ*—by *pādya, arghya* and other such items for worshiping the Lord; *sragbhiḥ*—by flower garlands; *divya-gandha-anulepanaiḥ*—by many kinds of pulp, like sandalwood and *aguru,* to smear upon the body of Lord Vāmanadeva; *dhūpaiḥ*—by incense; *dīpaiḥ*—by lamps; *surabhibhiḥ*—all of them extremely fragrant; *lāja*—by fried paddies; *akṣata*—by unbroken grains; *phala*—by fruits; *aṅkuraiḥ*—by roots and sprouts; *stavanaiḥ*—by offering prayers; *jaya-śabdaiḥ*—by saying *"jaya, jaya"; ca*—also; *tat-vīrya-mahimā-aṅkitaiḥ*—which indicated the glorious activities of the Lord; *nṛtya-vāditra-gītaiḥ ca*—by dancing, playing various musical instruments, and singing songs; *śaṅkha*—of vibrating conchshells; *dundubhi*—of the beating on kettledrums; *niḥsvanaiḥ*—by the sound vibrations.

TRANSLATION

They worshiped the Lord by offering fragrant flowers, water, pādya and arghya, sandalwood pulp and aguru pulp, incense, lamps, fused rice, un-

broken grains, fruits, roots and sprouts. While so doing, they offered prayers indicating the glorious activities of the Lord and shouted "Jaya! Jaya!" They also danced, played instruments, sang, sounded conchshells and beat kettledrums, in this way worshiping the Lord.

TEXT 8

जाम्बवानृक्षराजस्तु भेरीशब्दैर्मनोजवः ।
विजयं दिक्षु सर्वासु महोत्सवमघोषयत् ॥ ८ ॥

jāmbavān ṛkṣa-rājas tu
bherī-śabdair mano-javaḥ
vijayaṁ dikṣu sarvāsu
mahotsavam aghoṣayat

jāmbavān—who was named Jāmbavān; *ṛkṣa-rājaḥ tu*—the king in the form of a bear also; *bherī-śabdaiḥ*—by sounding the bugle; *manaḥ-javaḥ*—in mental ecstasy; *vijayam*—victory; *dikṣu*—in all directions; *sarvāsu*—everywhere; *mahā-utsavam*—festival; *aghoṣayat*—declared.

TRANSLATION

Jāmbavān, king of the bears, also joined in the ceremony. Sounding his bugle in all directions, he declared a great festival for Lord Vāmanadeva's victory.

TEXT 9

महीं सर्वां हृतां दृष्ट्वा त्रिपदव्याजयाच्ञया ।
ऊचुः स्वभर्तुरसुरा दीक्षितस्यात्यमर्षिताः ॥ ९ ॥

mahīṁ sarvāṁ hṛtāṁ dṛṣṭvā
tripada-vyāja-yācñayā
ūcuḥ sva-bhartur asurā
dīkṣitasyātyamarṣitāḥ

mahīm—land; *sarvām*—all; *hṛtām*—lost; *dṛṣṭvā*—after seeing; *tri-pada-vyāja-yācñayā*—by simply asking three steps of land; *ūcuḥ*—said; *sva-bhartuḥ*—of their master; *asurāḥ*—the demons; *dīkṣitasya*—of Bali Mahārāja, who was so determined in the sacrifice; *ati*—very much; *amarṣitāḥ*—for whom the function was unbearable.

TRANSLATION

When the demoniac followers of Mahārāja Bali saw that their master, who had been determined in performing sacrifice, had lost all his possessions to Vāmanadeva, who had taken them away on the plea of begging three paces of land, they were very angry and spoke as follows.

TEXT 10

न वायं ब्रह्मबन्धुर्विष्णुर्मायाविनां वरः ।
द्विजरूपप्रतिच्छन्नो देवकार्यं चिकीर्षति ॥ १० ॥

na vāyaṁ brahma-bandhur
viṣṇur māyāvināṁ varaḥ
dvija-rūpa-praticchanno
deva-kāryaṁ cikīrṣati

na—not; *vā*—either; *ayam*—this; *brahma-bandhuḥ*—Vāmanadeva, in the form of a *brāhmaṇa; viṣṇuḥ*—He is Lord Viṣṇu Himself; *māyāvinām*—of all cheaters; *varaḥ*—the greatest; *dvija-rūpa*—by assuming the form of a *brāhmaṇa; praticchannaḥ*—is disguised for the purpose of cheating; *deva-kāryam*—the interest of the demigods; *cikīrṣati*—He is trying for.

TRANSLATION

"This Vāmana is certainly not a brāhmaṇa but the best of cheaters, Lord Viṣṇu. Assuming the form of a brāhmaṇa, He has covered His own form, and thus He is working for the interests of the demigods."

TEXT 11

अनेन याचमानेन शत्रुणा वटुरूपिणा ।
सर्वस्वं नो हृतं भर्तुर्न्यस्तदण्डस्य बर्हिषि ॥ ११ ॥

anena yācamānena
śatruṇā vaṭu-rūpiṇā
sarvasvaṁ no hṛtaṁ bhartur
nyasta-daṇḍasya barhiṣi

anena—by Him; *yācamānena*—who is in the position of a beggar; *śatruṇā*—by the enemy; *vaṭu-rūpiṇā*—in the form of a *brahmacārī; sarvasvam*—

everything; *naḥ*—our; *hṛtam*—has been taken away; *bhartuḥ*—of our master; *nyasta*—had been given up; *daṇḍasya*—of whom the power of giving punishment; *barhiṣi*—because of taking the vow of a ritualistic ceremony.

TRANSLATION

"Our lord, Bali Mahārāja, because of his position in performing the yajña, has given up the power to punish. Taking advantage of this, our eternal enemy, Viṣṇu, dressed in the form of a brahmacārī beggar, has taken away all his possessions."

TEXT 12

सत्यव्रतस्य सततं दीक्षितस्य विशेषतः ।
नानृतं भाषितुं शक्यं ब्रह्मण्यस्य दयावतः ॥ १२ ॥

satya-vratasya satataṁ
dīkṣitasya viśeṣataḥ
nānṛtaṁ bhāṣituṁ śakyaṁ
brahmaṇyasya dayāvataḥ

satya-vratasya—of Mahārāja Bali, who is fixed in truthfulness; *satatam*—always; *dīkṣitasya*—of he who was initiated into performing *yajña; viśeṣataḥ*—specifically; *na*—not; *anṛtam*—untruth; *bhāṣitum*—to speak; *śakyam*—is able; *brahmaṇyasya*—to the brahminical culture, or to the *brāhmaṇa; dayā-vataḥ*—of he who is always kind.

TRANSLATION

"Our lord, Bali Mahārāja, is always fixed in truthfulness, and this is especially so at present, since he has been initiated into performing a sacrifice. He is always kind and merciful toward the brāhmaṇas, and he cannot at any time speak lies."

TEXT 13

तस्मादस्य वधो धर्मो भर्तुः शुश्रूषणं च नः ।
इत्यायुधानि जगृहुर्बलेरनुचरासुराः ॥ १३ ॥

tasmād asya vadho dharmo
bhartuḥ śuśrūṣaṇaṁ ca naḥ

ity āyudhāni jagṛhur
baler anucarāsurāḥ

tasmāt—therefore; *asya*—of this *brahmacārī* Vāmana; *vadhaḥ*—the killing; *dharmaḥ*—is our duty; *bhartuḥ*—of our master; *śuśrūṣaṇam ca*—and it is the way of serving; *naḥ*—our; *iti*—thus; *āyudhāni*—all kinds of weapons; *jagṛhuḥ*—they took up; *baleḥ*—of Bali Mahārāja; *anucara*—followers; *asurāḥ*—all the demons.

TRANSLATION

"Therefore it is our duty to kill this Vāmanadeva, Lord Viṣṇu. It is our religious principle and the way to serve our master." After making this decision, the demoniac followers of Mahārāja Bali took up their various weapons with a view to killing Vāmanadeva.

TEXT 14

ते सर्वे वामनं हन्तुं शूलपट्टिशपाणयः ।
अनिच्छन्तो बले राजन् प्राद्रवञ्जातमन्यवः ॥ १४ ॥

te sarve vāmanaṁ hantuṁ
śūla-paṭṭiśa-pāṇayaḥ
anicchanto bale rājan
prādravañ jāta-manyavaḥ

te—the demons; *sarve*—all of them; *vāmanam*—Lord Vāmanadeva; *hantum*—to kill; *śūla*—tridents; *paṭṭiśa*—lances; *pāṇayaḥ*—all taking in hand; *anicchantaḥ*—against the will; *baleḥ*—of Bali Mahārāja; *rājan*—O King; *prādravan*—they pushed forward; *jāta-manyavaḥ*—aggravated by usual anger.

TRANSLATION

O King, the demons, aggravated by their usual anger, took their lances and tridents in hand, and against the will of Bali Mahārāja they pushed forward to kill Lord Vāmanadeva.

TEXT 15

तानभिद्रवतो दृष्ट्वा दितिजानीकपान् नृप ।
प्रहस्यानुचरा विष्णोः प्रत्यषेधन्नुदायुधाः ॥ १५ ॥

tān abhidravato dṛṣṭvā
ditijānīkapān nṛpa
prahasyānucarā viṣṇoḥ
pratyaṣedhann udāyudhāḥ

tān—them; *abhidravataḥ*—thus going forward; *dṛṣṭvā*—seeing; *ditija-anīka-pān*—the soldiers of the demons; *nṛpa*—O King; *prahasya*—smiling; *anucarāḥ*—the associates; *viṣṇoḥ*—of Lord Viṣṇu; *pratyaṣedhan*—forbade; *udāyudhāḥ*—taking up their weapons.

TRANSLATION

O King, when the associates of Lord Viṣṇu saw the soldiers of the demons coming forward in violence, they smiled. Taking up their weapons, they forbade the demons to continue their attempt.

TEXTS 16-17

नन्दः सुनन्दोऽथ जयो विजयः प्रबलो बलः ।
कुमुदः कुमुदाक्षश्च विष्वक्सेनः पतत्त्रिराट् ॥ १६ ॥
जयन्तः श्रुतदेवश्च पुष्पदन्तोऽथ सात्वतः ।
सर्वे नागायुतप्राणाश्चमूं ते जघ्नुरासुरीम् ॥ १७ ॥

nandaḥ sunando 'tha jayo
vijayaḥ prabalo balaḥ
kumudaḥ kumudākṣaś ca
viṣvaksenaḥ patattrirāṭ

jayantaḥ śrutadevaś ca
puṣpadanto 'tha sātvataḥ
sarve nāgāyuta-prāṇāś
camūṁ te jaghnur āsurīm

nandaḥ sunandaḥ—the associates of Lord Viṣṇu such as Nanda and Sunanda; *atha*—in this way; *jayaḥ vijayaḥ prabalaḥ balaḥ kumudaḥ kumudākṣaḥ ca viṣvaksenaḥ*—as well as Jaya, Vijaya, Prabala, Bala, Kumada, Kumudākṣa and Viṣvaksena; *patattri-rāṭ*—Garuḍa, the king of the birds; *jayantaḥ śrutadevaḥ ca puṣpadantaḥ atha sātvataḥ*—Jayanta, Śrutadeva, Puṣpadanta and Sātvata; *sarve*—all of them; *nāga-ayuta-prāṇāḥ*—as powerful as ten thousand elephants; *camūm*—the soldiers of the demons; *te*—they; *jaghnuḥ*—killed; *āsurīm*—demoniac.

TRANSLATION

Nanda, Sunanda, Jaya, Vijaya, Prabala, Bala, Kumuda, Kumudākṣa, Viṣvaksena, Patattrirāṭ [Garuḍa], Jayanta, Śrutadeva, Puṣpadanta and Sātvata were all associates of Lord Viṣṇu. They were as powerful as ten thousand elephants, and now they began killing the soldiers of the demons.

TEXT 18

हन्यमानान् स्वकान् दृष्ट्वा पुरुषानुचरैर्बलिः ।
वारयामास संरब्धान् काव्यशापमनुस्मरन् ॥ १८ ॥

hanyamānān svakān dṛṣṭvā
puruṣānucarair baliḥ
vārayām āsa saṁrabdhān
kāvya-śāpam anusmaran

hanyamānān—being killed; *svakān*—his own soldiers; *dṛṣṭvā*—after seeing; *puruṣa-anucaraiḥ*—by the associates of the Supreme Person; *baliḥ*—Bali Mahārāja; *vārayām āsa*—forbade; *saṁrabdhān*—even though they were very angry; *kāvya-śāpam*—the curse given by Śukrācārya; *anusmaran*—remembering.

TRANSLATION

When Bali Mahārāja saw that his own soldiers were being killed by the associates of Lord Viṣṇu, he remembered the curse of Śukrācārya and forbade his soldiers to continue fighting.

TEXT 19

हे विप्रचित्ते हे राहो हे नेमे श्रूयतां वचः ।
मा युध्यत निवर्तध्वं न नः कालोऽयमर्थकृत् ॥ १९ ॥

he vipracitte he rāho
he neme śrūyatāṁ vacaḥ
mā yudhyata nivartadhvaṁ
na naḥ kālo 'yam artha-kṛt

he vipracitte—O Vipracitti; *he rāho*—O Rāhu; *he neme*—O Nemi; *śrūyatām*—kindly hear; *vacaḥ*—my words; *mā*—do not; *yudhyata*—fight; *nivar-*

tadhvam—stop this fighting; *na*—not; *naḥ*—our; *kālaḥ*—favorable time; *ayam*—this; *artha-kṛt*—which can give us success.

TRANSLATION

O Vipracitti, O Rāhu, O Nemi, please hear my words! Don't fight. Stop immediately, for the present time is not in our favor.

TEXT 20

यः प्रभुः सर्वभूतानां सुखदुःखोपपत्तये ।
तं नातिवर्तितुं दैत्याः पौरुषैरीश्वरः पुमान् ॥ २० ॥

yaḥ prabhuḥ sarva-bhūtānāṁ
sukha-duḥkhopapattaye
taṁ nātivartituṁ daityāḥ
pauruṣair īśvaraḥ pumān

yaḥ prabhuḥ—that Supreme Person, the master; *sarva-bhūtānām*—of all living entities; *sukha-duḥkha-upapattaye*—for administering happiness and distress; *tam*—Him; *na*—not; *ativartitum*—to overcome; *daityāḥ*—O demons; *pauruṣaiḥ*—by human endeavors; *īśvaraḥ*—the supreme controller; *pumān*—a person.

TRANSLATION

O Daityas, by human efforts no one can supersede the Supreme Personality of Godhead, who can bring happiness and distress to all living entities.

TEXT 21

यो नो भवाय प्रागासीदभवाय दिवौकसाम् ।
स एव भगवानद्य वर्तते तद्विपर्ययम् ॥ २१ ॥

yo no bhavāya prāg āsīd
abhavāya divaukasām
sa eva bhagavān adya
vartate tad-viparyayam

yaḥ—the time factor, which represents the Supreme Personality of Godhead; *naḥ*—of us; *bhavāya*—for the improvement; *prāk*—formerly; *āsīt*—

was situated; *abhavāya*—for the defeat; *diva-okasām*—of the demigods; *saḥ*—that time factor; *eva*—indeed; *bhagavān*—the representative of the Supreme Person; *adya*—today; *vartate*—is existing; *tat-viparyayam*—just the opposite of our favor.

TRANSLATION

The supreme time factor, which represents the Supreme Person, was previously in our favor and not in favor of the demigods, but now that same time factor is against us.

TEXT 22

बलेन सचिवैर्बुद्ध्या दुर्गैर्मन्त्रौषधादिभिः ।
सामादिभिरुपायैश्च कालं नात्येति वै जनः ॥ २२ ॥

balena sacivair buddhyā
durgair mantrauṣadhādibhiḥ
sāmādibhir upāyaiś ca
kālaṁ nātyeti vai janaḥ

balena—by material power; *sacivaiḥ*—by the counsel of ministers; *buddhyā*—by intelligence; *durgaiḥ*—by fortresses; *mantra-auṣadha-ādibhiḥ*—by mystic chanting or the influence of drugs and herbs; *sāma-ādibhiḥ*—by diplomacy and other such means; *upāyaiḥ ca*—by similar other attempts; *kālam*—the time factor, representing the Supreme Lord; *na*—never; *atyeti*—can overcome; *vai*—indeed; *janaḥ*—any person.

TRANSLATION

No one can surpass the time representation of the Supreme Personality of Godhead by material power, by the counsel of ministers, by intelligence, by diplomacy, by fortresses, by mystic mantras, by drugs, by herbs or by any other means.

TEXT 23

भवद्भिर्निर्जिता ह्येते बहुशोऽनुचरा हरेः ।
दैवेनर्द्धैस्त एवाद्य युधि जित्वा नदन्ति नः ॥ २३ ॥

bhavadbhir nirjitā hy ete
bahuśo 'nucarā hareḥ

daivenarddhais ta evādya
yudhi jitvā nadanti naḥ

bhavadbhiḥ—by all of you demons; *nirjitāḥ*—have been defeated; *hi*—indeed; *ete*—all these soldiers of the demigods; *bahuśaḥ*—in great number; *anucarāḥ*—followers; *hareḥ*—of Lord Viṣṇu; *daivena*—by providence; *ṛddhaiḥ*—whose opulence was increased; *te*—they (the demigods); *eva*—indeed; *adya*—today; *yudhi*—in the fight; *jitvā*—defeating; *nadanti*—are vibrating in jubilation; *naḥ*—us.

TRANSLATION

Previously, being empowered by providence, you defeated a great number of such followers of Lord Viṣṇu. But today those same followers, having defeated us, are roaring in jubilation like lions.

PURPORT

Bhagavad-gītā mentions five causes of defeat or victory. Of these five, *daiva* (providence) is the most powerful (*na ca daivāt paraṁ balam*). Bali Mahārāja knew the secret of how he had formerly been victorious because providence was in his favor. Now, since that same providence was not in his favor, there was no possibility of his victory. Thus he very intelligently forbade his associates to fight.

TEXT 24

एतान् वयं विजेष्यामो यदि दैवं प्रसीदति ।
तस्मात् कालं प्रतीक्षध्वं यो नोऽर्थत्वाय कल्पते ॥ २४ ॥

etān vayaṁ vijeṣyāmo
yadi daivaṁ prasīdati
tasmāt kālaṁ pratīkṣadhvaṁ
yo no 'rthatvāya kalpate

etān—all these soldiers of the demigods; *vayam*—we; *vijeṣyāmaḥ*—shall gain victory over them; *yadi*—if; *daivam*—providence; *prasīdati*—is in favor; *tasmāt*—therefore; *kālam*—that favorable time; *pratīkṣadhvam*—wait until; *yaḥ*—which; *naḥ*—our; *arthatvāya kalpate*—should be considered in our favor.

TRANSLATION

Unless providence is in our favor, we shall not be able to gain victory. Therefore we must wait for that favorable time when our defeating them will be possible.

TEXT 25

श्रीशुक उवाच
पत्युर्निगदितं श्रुत्वा दैत्यदानवयूथपाः ।
रसां निर्विविशू राजन् विष्णुपार्षदताडिताः ॥ २५ ॥

śrī-śuka uvāca
patyur nigaditaṁ śrutvā
daitya-dānava-yūthapāḥ
rasāṁ nirviviśū rājan
viṣṇu-pārṣada tāḍitāḥ

śrī-śukaḥ uvāca—Śrī Śukadeva Gosvāmī said; *patyuḥ*—of their master (Bali Mahārāja); *nigaditam*—what had been thus described; *śrutvā*—after hearing; *daitya-dānava-yūtha-pāḥ*—the leaders of the Daityas and demons; *rasām*—the lower regions of the universe; *nirviviśūḥ*—entered; *rājan*—O King; *viṣṇu-pārṣada*—by the associates of Lord Viṣṇu; *tāḍitāḥ*—driven.

TRANSLATION

Śukadeva Gosvāmī continued: O King, in accordance with the order of their master, Bali Mahārāja, all the chiefs of the demons and the Daityas entered the lower regions of the universe, to which they were driven by the soldiers of Viṣṇu.

TEXT 26

अथ तार्क्ष्यसुतो ज्ञात्वा विराट् प्रभुचिकीर्षितम् ।
बबन्ध वारुणैः पाशैर्बलिं सूत्येऽहनि क्रतौ ॥ २६ ॥

atha tārkṣya-suto jñātvā
virāṭ prabhu-cikīrṣitam
babandha vāruṇaiḥ pāśair
baliṁ sūtye 'hani kratau

atha—thereafter; *tārkṣya-sutaḥ*—Garuḍa; *jñātvā*—knowing; *virāṭ*—the king of birds; *prabhu-cikīrṣitam*—the desire of Lord Viṣṇu as Vāmanadeva; *babandha*—arrested; *vāruṇaiḥ*—belonging to Varuṇa; *pāśaiḥ*—by the ropes; *balim*—Bali; *sūtye*—when *soma-rasa* is taken; *ahani*—on the day; *kratau*—at the time of sacrifice.

TRANSLATION

Thereafter, on the day of soma-pāna, after the sacrifice was finished, Garuḍa, king of the birds, understanding the desire of his master, arrested Bali Mahārāja with the ropes of Varuṇa.

PURPORT

Garuḍa, the constant companion of the Supreme Personality of Godhead, knows the confidential part of the Lord's desire. Bali Mahārāja's tolerance and devotion were undoubtedly superexcellent. Garuḍa arrested Bali Mahārāja to show the entire universe the greatness of the King's tolerance.

TEXT 27

हाहाकारो महानासीद् रोदस्योः सर्वतोदिशम् ।
निगृह्यमाणेऽसुरपतौ विष्णुना प्रभविष्णुना ॥ २७ ॥

hāhākāro mahān āsīd
rodasyoḥ sarvato diśam
nigṛhyamāṇe 'sura-patau
viṣṇunā prabhaviṣṇunā

hāhā-kāraḥ—a tumultuous roar of lamentation; *mahān*—great; *āsīt*—there was; *rodasyoḥ*—in both the lower and upper planetary systems; *sarvataḥ*—everywhere; *diśam*—all directions; *nigṛhyamāṇe*—because of being suppressed; *asura-patau*—when Bali Mahārāja, the King of the demons; *viṣṇunā*—by Lord Viṣṇu; *prabhaviṣṇunā*—who is the most powerful everywhere.

TRANSLATION

When Bali Mahārāja was thus arrested by Lord Viṣṇu, who is the most powerful, there was a great roar of lamentation in all directions throughout the upper and lower planetary systems of the universe.

TEXT 28

तं बद्धं वारुणैः पाशैर्भगवानाह वामनः ।
नष्टश्रियं स्थिरप्रज्ञमुदारयशसं नृप ॥ २८ ॥

taṁ baddhaṁ vāruṇaiḥ pāśair
bhagavān āha vāmanaḥ
naṣṭa-śriyaṁ sthira-prajñam
udāra-yaśasaṁ nṛpa

tam—unto him; *baddham*—who was so arrested; *vāruṇaiḥ pāśaiḥ*—by the ropes of Varuṇa; *bhagavān*—the Supreme Personality of Godhead; *āha*—said; *vāmanaḥ*—Vāmanadeva; *naṣṭa-śriyam*—unto Bali Mahārāja, who had lost his bodily luster; *sthira-prajñam*—but was all the same determined in his decision; *udāra-yaśasam*—the most magnanimous and celebrated; *nṛpa*—O King.

TRANSLATION

O King, the Supreme Personality of Godhead, Vāmanadeva, then spoke to Bali Mahārāja, the most liberal and celebrated personality whom He had arrested with the ropes of Varuṇa. Bali Mahārāja had lost all bodily luster, but he was nonetheless fixed in his determination.

PURPORT

When one is bereft of all his possessions, he is certainly reduced in bodily luster. But although Bali Mahārāja had lost everything, he was fixed in his determination to satisfy Vāmanadeva, the Supreme Personality of Godhead. In *Bhagavad-gītā,* such a person is called *sthita-prajña.* A pure devotee is never deviated from the service of the Lord, despite all difficulties and impediments offered by the illusory energy. Generally men who have wealth and opulence are famous, but Bali Mahārāja became famous for all time by being deprived of all his possessions. This is the special mercy of the Supreme Personality of Godhead toward His devotees. The Lord says, *yasyāham anugṛhṇāmi hariṣye tad-dhanaṁ śanaiḥ* . As the first installment of His special favor, the Lord takes away all the possessions of His devotee. A devotee, however, is never disturbed by such a loss. He continues his service, and the Lord amply rewards him, beyond the expectations of any common man.

TEXT 29

पदानि त्रीणि दत्तानि भूमेर्मह्यं त्वयासुर ।
द्वाभ्यां क्रान्ता मही सर्वा तृतीयमुपकल्पय ॥ २९ ॥

padāni trīṇi dattāni
bhūmer mahyaṁ tvayāsura
dvābhyāṁ krāntā mahī sarvā
tṛtīyam upakalpaya

padāni—footsteps; *trīṇi*—three; *dattāni*—have been given; *bhūmeḥ*—of land; *mahyam*—unto Me; *tvayā*—by you; *asura*—O King of the demons; *dvābhyām*—by two steps; *krāntā*—have been occupied; *mahī*—all the land; *sarvā*—completely; *tṛtīyam*—for the third step; *upakalpaya*—now find the means.

TRANSLATION

O King of the demons, you have promised to give Me three steps of land, but I have occupied the entire universe with two steps. Now think about where I should put My third.

TEXT 30

यावत् तपत्यसौ गोभिर्यावदिन्दुः सहोडुभिः ।
यावद् वर्षति पर्जन्यस्तावती भूरियं तव ॥ ३० ॥

yāvat tapaty asau gobhir
yāvad induḥ sahoḍubhiḥ
yāvad varṣati parjanyas
tāvatī bhūr iyaṁ tava

yāvat—as far as; *tapati*—is shining; *asau*—the sun; *gobhiḥ*—by the sunshine; *yāvat*—as long or as far as; *induḥ*—the moon; *saha-uḍubhiḥ*—with the luminaries or stars; *yāvat*—as far as; *varṣati*—are pouring rain; *parjanyaḥ*—the clouds; *tāvatī*—to that much distance; *bhūḥ*—land; *iyam*—this; *tava*—in your possession.

TRANSLATION

As far as the sun and moon shine with the stars and as far as the clouds pour rain, all the land throughout the universe is in your possession.

TEXT 31

पदैकेन मयाक्रान्तो भूर्लोकः खं दिशस्तनोः ।
स्वर्लोकस्ते द्वितीयेन पश्यतस्ते स्वमात्मना ॥ ३१ ॥

padaikena mayākrānto
bhūrlokaḥ khaṁ diśas tanoḥ
svarlokas te dvitīyena
paśyatas te svam ātmanā

padā ekena—by one step only; *mayā*—by Me; *ākrāntaḥ*—have been covered; *bhūrlokaḥ*—the entire planetary system known as Bhūrloka; *kham*—the sky; *diśaḥ*—and all directions; *tanoḥ*—by My body; *svarlokaḥ*—the upper planetary system; *te*—in your possession; *dvitīyena*—by the second step; *paśyataḥ te*—while you were seeing; *svam*—your own; *ātmanā*—by Myself.

TRANSLATION

Of these possessions, with one step I have occupied Bhūrloka, and with My body I have occupied the entire sky and all directions. And in your presence, with My second step, I have occupied the upper planetary system.

PURPORT

According to the Vedic description of the planetary system, all the planets move from east to west. The sun, the moon and five other planets, such as Mars and Jupiter, orbit one above another. Vāmanadeva, however, expanding His body and extending His steps, occupied the entire planetary system.

TEXT 32

प्रतिश्रुतमदातुस्ते निरये वास इष्यते ।
विश त्वं निरयं तस्माद् गुरुणा चानुमोदितः ॥ ३२ ॥

pratiśrutam adātus te
niraye vāsa iṣyate
viśa tvaṁ nirayaṁ tasmād
guruṇā cānumoditaḥ

pratiśrutam—what had been promised; *adātuḥ*—who could not give; *te*—of you; *niraye*—in hell; *vāsaḥ*—residence; *iṣyate*—prescribed; *viśa*—now enter; *tvam*—yourself; *nirayam*—the hellish planet; *tasmāt*—therefore; *guruṇā*—by your spiritual master; *ca*—also; *anumoditaḥ*—approved.

TRANSLATION

Because you have been unable to give charity according to your promise, the rule is that you should go down to live in the hellish planets. Therefore, in accordance with the order of Śukrācārya, your spiritual master, now go down and live there.

PURPORT

It is said:

nārāyaṇa-parāḥ sarve
na kutaścana bibhyati
svargāpavarga-narakeṣv
api tulyārtha-darśinaḥ

"Devotees solely engaged in the devotional service of the Supreme Personality of Godhead, Nārāyaṇa, never fear any condition of life. For them the heavenly planets, liberation and the hellish planets are all the same, for such devotees are interested only in the service of the Lord." (*Bhā*g. 6.17.28) A devotee engaged in the service of Nārāyaṇa is always in equilibrium. A devotee actually lives transcendentally. Although he may appear to have gone to hell or heaven, he does not live in either place; rather, he always lives in Vaikuṇṭha (*sa guṇān samatītyaitān brahma-bhūyāya kalpate*). Vāmanadeva asked Bali Mahārāja to go to the hellish planets, apparently just to show the entire universe how tolerant he was, and Bali Mahārāja did not hesitate to carry out the order. A devotee does not live alone. Of course, everyone lives with the Supreme Personality of Godhead, but because the devotee is engaged in His service, he actually does not live in any material condition. Bhaktivinoda Ṭhākura says, *kīṭa-janma hao yathā tuyā dāsa.* Thus he prays to take birth as an insignificant insect in the association of devotees. Because devotees are engaged in the service of the Lord, anyone who lives with them also lives in Vaikuṇṭha.

TEXT 33

वृथा मनोरथस्तस्य दूरः स्वर्गः पतत्यधः ।
प्रतिश्रुतस्यादानेन योऽर्थिनं विप्रलम्भते ॥ ३३ ॥

vṛthā manorathas tasya
dūraḥ svargaḥ pataty adhaḥ
pratiśrutasyādānena
yo 'rthinaṁ vipralambhate

vṛthā—without any good result; *manorathaḥ*—mental concoction; *tasya*—of him; *dūraḥ*—far away; *svargaḥ*—elevation to the higher planetary system; *patati*—falls down; *adhaḥ*—to a hellish condition of life; *pratiśrutasya*—things promised; *adānena*—being unable to give; *yaḥ*—anyone who; *arthinam*—a beggar; *vipralambhate*—cheats.

TRANSLATION

Far from being elevated to the heavenly planets or fulfilling one's desire, one who does not properly give a beggar what he has promised falls down to a hellish condition of life.

TEXT 34

विप्रलब्धो ददामीति त्वयाहं चाढ्यमानिना ।
तद् व्यलीकफलं भुङ्क्ष्व निरयं कतिचित् समाः ॥ ३४ ॥

vipralabdho dadāmīti
tvayāhaṁ cāḍhya-māninā
tad vyalīka-phalaṁ bhuṅkṣva
nirayaṁ katicit samāḥ

vipralabdhaḥ—now I am cheated; *dadāmi*—I promise I shall give you; *iti*—thus; *tvayā*—by you; *aham*—I am; *ca*—also; *āḍhya-māninā*—by being very proud of your opulence; *tat*—therefore; *vyalīka-phalam*—as a result of cheating; *bhuṅkṣva*—you enjoy; *nirayam*—in hellish life; *katicit*—a few; *samāḥ*—years.

TRANSLATION

Being falsely proud of your possessions, you promised to give Me land, but you could not fulfill your promise. Therefore, because your promise was false, you must live for a few years in hellish life.

PURPORT

The false prestige of thinking "I am very rich, and I possess such vast property" is another side of material life. Everything belongs to the Supreme Personality of Godhead, and no one else possesses anything. This is the real fact. *Īśāvāsyam idaṁ sarvaṁ yat kiñca jagatyāṁ jagat.* Bali Mahārāja was undoubtedly the most exalted devotee, whereas previously he had maintained a misunderstanding due to false prestige. By the supreme will of the Lord, he now had to go to the hellish planets, but because he went there by the order of the Supreme Personality of Godhead, he lived there more opulently than one could expect to live in the planets of heaven. A devotee always lives with the Supreme Personality of Godhead, engaging in His service, and therefore he is always transcendental to hellish or heavenly residences.

Thus end the Bhaktivedanta purports of the Eighth Canto, Twenty-first Chapter, of the Śrīmad-Bhāgavatam, entitled *"Bali Mahārāja Arrested by the Lord"*

CHAPTER TWENTY-TWO

Bali Mahārāja Surrenders His Life

The summary of this Twenty-second Chapter is as follows. The Supreme Personality of Godhead was pleased by the behavior of Bali Mahārāja. Thus the Lord placed him on the planet Sutala, and there, after bestowing benedictions upon him, the Lord agreed to become his doorman.

Bali Mahārāja was extremely truthful. Being unable to keep his promise, he was very much afraid, for he knew that one who has deviated from truthfulness is insignificant in the eyes of society. An exalted person can suffer the consequences of hellish life, but he is very much afraid of being defamed for deviation from the truth. Bali Mahārāja agreed with great pleasure to accept the punishment awarded him by the Supreme Personality of Godhead. In Bali Mahārāja's dynasty there were many *asuras* who because of their enmity toward Viṣṇu had achieved a destination more exalted than that of many mystic *yogīs*. Bali Mahārāja specifically remembered the determination of Prahlāda Mahārāja in devotional service. Considering all these points, he decided to give his head in charity as the place for Viṣṇu's third step. Bali Mahārāja also considered how great personalities give up their family relationships and material possessions to satisfy the Supreme Personality of Godhead. Indeed, they sometimes even sacrifice their lives for the satisfaction of the Lord, just to become His personal servants. Accordingly, by following in the footsteps of previous *ācāryas* and devotees, Bali Mahārāja perceived himself successful.

While Bali Mahārāja, having been arrested by the ropes of Varuṇa, was offering prayers to the Lord, his grandfather Prahlāda Mahārāja appeared there and described how the Supreme Personality of Godhead had delivered Bali Mahārāja by taking his possessions in a tricky way. While Prahlāda Mahārāja was present, Lord Brahmā and Bali's wife, Vindhyāvali, described the supremacy of the Supreme Lord. Since Bali Mahārāja had given everything to the Lord, they prayed for his release. The Lord then described how a nondevotee's possession of wealth is a danger whereas a devotee's opulence is a benediction from the Lord. Then, being pleased with Bali Mahārāja, the Supreme Lord offered His disc to protect Bali Mahārāja and promised to remain with him.

TEXT 1

श्रीशुक उवाच

एवं विप्रकृतो राजन् बलिर्भगवतासुरः ।
भिद्यमानोऽप्यभिन्नात्मा प्रत्याहाविक्लवं वचः ॥ १ ॥

śrī-śuka uvāca
evaṁ viprakṛto rājan
balir bhagavatāsuraḥ
bhidyamāno 'py abhinnātmā
pratyāhāviklavaṁ vacaḥ

śrī-śukaḥ uvāca—Śrī Śukadeva Gosvāmī said; *evam*—thus, as aforementioned; *viprakṛtaḥ*—having been put into difficulty; *rājan*—O King; *baliḥ*—Mahārāja Bali; *bhagavatā*—by the Personality of Godhead Vāmanadeva; *asuraḥ*—the King of the *asuras; bhidyamānaḥ api*—although situated in this uncomfortable position; *abhinna-ātmā*—without being disturbed in body or mind; *pratyāha*—replied; *aviklavam*—undisturbed; *vacaḥ*—the following words.

TRANSLATION

Śukadeva Gosvāmī said: O King, although the Supreme Personality of Godhead was superficially seen to have acted mischievously toward Bali Mahārāja, Bali Mahārāja was fixed in his determination. Considering himself not to have fulfilled his promise, he spoke as follows.

TEXT 2

श्रीबलिरुवाच

यद्युत्तमश्लोक भवान् ममेरितं
वचो व्यलीकं सुरवर्य मन्यते ।
करोम्यृतं तन्न भवेत् प्रलम्भनं
पदं तृतीयं कुरु शीर्ष्णि मे निजम् ॥ २ ॥

śrī-balir uvāca
yady uttamaśloka bhavān mameritaṁ
vaco vyalīkaṁ sura-varya manyate

karomy ṛtaṁ tan na bhavet pralambhanaṁ
padaṁ tṛtīyaṁ kuru śīrṣṇi me nijam

śrī-baliḥ uvāca—Bali Mahārāja said; *yadi*—if; *uttamaśloka*—O Supreme Lord; *bhavān*—Your good self; *mama*—my; *īritam*—promised; *vacaḥ*—words; *vyalīkam*—false; *sura-varya*—O greatest of all *suras* (demigods); *manyate*—You think so; *karomi*—I shall make it; *ṛtam*—truth; *tat*—that (promise); *na*—not; *bhavet*—will become; *pralambhanam*—cheating; *padam*—step; *tṛtīyam*—the third; *kuru*—just do it; *śīrṣṇi*—on the head; *me*—my; *nijam*—Your lotus feet.

TRANSLATION

Bali Mahārāja said: O best Personality of Godhead, most worshipable for all the demigods, if You think that my promise has become false, I shall certainly rectify matters to make it truthful. I cannot allow my promise to be false. Please, therefore, place Your third lotus footstep on my head.

PURPORT

Bali Mahārāja could understand the pretense of Lord Vāmanadeva, who had taken the side of the demigods and come before him as a beggar. Although the Lord's purpose was to cheat him, Bali Mahārāja took pleasure in understanding how the Lord will cheat His devotee to glorify the devotee's position. It is said that God is good, and this is a fact. Whether He cheats or rewards, He is always good. Bali Mahārāja therefore addressed Him as Uttamaśloka. "Your Lordship," he said, "You are always praised with the best of selected verses. On behalf of the demigods, You disguised Yourself to cheat me, saying that You wanted only three paces of land, but later You expanded Your body to such an extent that with two footsteps You covered the entire universe. Because You were working on behalf of Your devotees, You do not regard this as cheating. Never mind. I cannot be considered a devotee. Nonetheless, because although You are the husband of the goddess of fortune You have come to me to beg, I must satisfy You to the best of my ability. So please do not think that I wanted to cheat You; I must fulfill my promise. I still have one possession—my body. When I place my body for Your satisfaction, please put Your third step on my head." Since the Lord had covered the entire universe with two steps, one might ask how Bali Mahārāja's head could be sufficient for His third step? Bali Mahārāja, however, thought that the possessor of wealth must be greater than the possession. Therefore although the Lord had taken all his possessions, the head of Bali Mahārāja, the possessor, would provide adequate place for the Lord's third step.

TEXT 3

बिभेमि नाहं निरयात् पदच्युतो
न पाशबन्धाद् व्यसनाद् दुरत्ययात् ।
नैवार्थकृच्छ्राद् भवतो विनिग्रहा-
दसाधुवादाद् भृशमुद्विजे यथा ॥ ३ ॥

bibhemi nāhaṁ nirayāt pada-cyuto
na pāśa-bandhād vyasanād duratyayāt
naivārtha-kṛcchrād bhavato vinigrahād
asādhu-vādād bhṛśam udvije yathā

bibhemi—I do fear; *na*—not; *aham*—I; *nirayāt*—from a position in hell; *pada-cyutaḥ*—nor do I fear being deprived of my position; *na*—nor; *pāśa-bandhāt*—from being arrested by the ropes of Varuṇa; *vyasanāt*—nor from the distress; *duratyayāt*—which was unbearable for me; *na*—nor; *eva*—certainly; *artha-kṛcchrāt*—because of poverty, or scarcity of money; *bhavataḥ*—of Your Lordship; *vinigrahāt*—from the punishment I am now suffering; *asādhu-vādāt*—from defamation; *bhṛśam*—very much; *udvije*—I become anxious; *yathā*—as.

TRANSLATION

I do not fear being deprived of all my possessions, living in hellish life, being arrested for poverty by the ropes of Varuṇa or being punished by You as much as I fear defamation.

PURPORT

Although Bali Mahārāja fully surrendered to the Supreme Personality of Godhead, he could not tolerate being defamed for cheating a *brāhmaṇa-brahmacārī*. Being quite alert in regard to his reputation, he thought deeply about how to prevent being defamed. The Lord, therefore, gave him the good counsel to prevent defamation by offering his head. A Vaiṣṇava does not fear any punishment. *Nārāyaṇa-parāḥ sarve na kutaścana bibhyati* (*Bhāg.* 6.17.28).

TEXT 4

पुंसां श्लाघ्यतमं मन्ये दण्डमर्हत्तमार्पितम् ।
यं न माता पिता भ्राता सुहृदश्चादिशन्ति हि ॥ ४ ॥

puṁsāṁ ślāghyatamaṁ manye
daṇḍam arhattamārpitam
yaṁ na mātā pitā bhrātā
suhṛdaś cādiśanti hi

puṁsām—of men; *ślāghya-tamam*—the most exalted; *manye*—I consider; *daṇḍam*—punishment; *arhattama-arpitam*—given by You, the supreme worshipable Lord; *yam*—which; *na*—neither; *mātā*—mother; *pitā*—father; *bhrātā*—brother; *suhṛdaḥ*—friends; *ca*—also; *ādiśanti*—offer; *hi*—indeed.

TRANSLATION

Although a father, mother, brother or friend may sometimes punish one as a well-wisher, they never punish their subordinate like this. But because You are the most worshipable Lord, I regard the punishment You have given me as most exalted.

PURPORT

Punishment meted out by the Supreme Personality of Godhead is accepted by the devotee as the greatest mercy.

tat te 'nukampāṁ susamīkṣamāṇo
bhuñjāna evātma-kṛtaṁ vipākam
hṛd-vāg-vapurbhir vidadhan namas te
jīveta yo mukti-pade sa dāya-bhāk

"One who seeks Your compassion and thus tolerates all kinds of adverse conditions due to the *karma* of his past deeds, who engages always in Your devotional service with his mind, words and body, and who always offers obeisances to You is certainly a bona fide candidate for liberation." (*Bhāg.* 10.14.8) A devotee knows that so-called punishment by the Supreme Personality of Godhead is only His favor to correct His devotee and bring him to the right path. Therefore the punishment awarded by the Supreme Personality of Godhead cannot be compared to even the greatest benefit awarded by one's material father, mother, brother or friend.

TEXT 5

त्वं नूनमसुराणां नः पारोक्षः परमो गुरुः ।
यो नोऽनेकमदान्धानां विभ्रंशं चक्षुरादिशत् ॥ ५ ॥

tvaṁ nūnam asurāṇāṁ naḥ
parokṣaḥ paramo guruḥ
yo no 'neka-madāndhānāṁ
vibhraṁśaṁ cakṣur ādiśat

tvam—Your Lordship; *nūnam*—indeed; *asurāṇām*—of the demons; *naḥ*—as we are; *parokṣaḥ*—indirect; *paramaḥ*—the supreme; *guruḥ*—spiritual master; *yaḥ*—Your Lordship; *naḥ*—of us; *aneka*—many; *mada-andhānām*—blinded by material opulences; *vibhraṁśam*—destroying our false prestige; *cakṣuḥ*—the eye of knowledge; *ādiśat*—gave.

TRANSLATION

Since Your Lordship is indirectly the greatest well-wisher of us demons, You act for our best welfare by posing as if our enemy. Because demons like us always aspire for a position of false prestige, by chastising us You give us the eyes by which to see the right path.

PURPORT

Bali Mahārāja considered the Supreme Personality of Godhead a better friend to the demons than to the demigods. In the material world, the more one gets material possessions, the more he becomes blind to spiritual life. The demigods are devotees of the Lord for the sake of material possessions, but although the demons apparently do not have the Supreme Personality of Godhead on their side, He always acts as their well-wisher by depriving them of their positions of false prestige. By false prestige one is misguided, so the Supreme Lord takes away their position of false prestige as a special favor.

TEXTS 6-7

यस्मिन् वैरानुबन्धेन व्यूढेन विबुधेतराः ।
बहवो लेभिरे सिद्धिं यामुहैकान्तयोगिनः ॥ ६ ॥
तेनाहं निगृहीतोऽस्मि भवता भूरिकर्मणा ।
बद्धश्च वारुणैः पाशैर्नातिव्रीडे न च व्यथे ॥ ७ ॥

yasmin vairānubandhena
vyūḍhena vibudhetarāḥ
bahavo lebhire siddhiṁ
yām u haikānta-yoginaḥ

tenāhaṁ nigṛhīto 'smi
bhavatā bhūri-karmaṇā
baddhaś ca vāruṇaiḥ pāśair
nātivrīḍe na ca vyathe

yasmin—unto You; *vaira-anubandhena*—by continuously treating as an enemy; *vyūḍhena*—firmly fixed by such intelligence; *vibudha-itarāḥ*—the demons (those other than the demigods); *bahavaḥ*—many of them; *lebhire*—achieved; *siddhim*—perfection; *yām*—which; *u ha*—it is well known; *ekānta-yoginaḥ*—equal to the achievements of the greatly successful mystic *yogīs; tena*—therefore; *aham*—I; *nigṛhītaḥ asmi*—although I am being punished; *bhavatā*—by Your Lordship; *bhūri-karmaṇā*—who can do many wonderful things; *baddhaḥ ca*—I am arrested and bound; *vāruṇaiḥ pāśaiḥ*—by the ropes of Varuṇa; *na ati-vrīḍe*—I am not at all ashamed of this; *na ca vyathe*—nor am I suffering very much.

TRANSLATION

Many demons who were continuously inimical toward You finally achieved the perfection of great mystic yogīs. Your Lordship can perform one work to serve many purposes, and consequently, although You have punished me in many ways, I do not feel ashamed of having been arrested by the ropes of Varuṇa, nor do I feel aggrieved.

PURPORT

Bali Mahārāja appreciated the Lord's mercy not only upon him but upon many other demons. Because this mercy is liberally distributed, the Supreme Lord is called all-merciful. Bali Mahārāja was indeed a fully surrendered devotee, but even some demons who were not at all devotees but merely enemies of the Lord attained the same exalted position achieved by many mystic *yogīs.* Thus Bali Mahārāja could understand that the Lord had some hidden purpose in punishing him. Consequently he was neither unhappy nor ashamed because of the awkward position in which he had been put by the Supreme Personality of Godhead.

TEXT 8

पितामहो मे भवदीयसंमतः
प्रह्लाद आविष्कृतसाधुवादः ।
भवद्विपक्षेण विचित्रवैशसं
संप्रापितस्त्वंपरमः स्वपित्रा ॥ ८ ॥

pitāmaho me bhavadīya-sammataḥ
prahrāda āviṣkṛta-sādhu-vādaḥ
bhavad-vipakṣeṇa vicitra-vaiśasaṁ
samprāpitas tvaṁ paramaḥ sva-pitrā

pitāmahaḥ—grandfather; *me*—my; *bhavadīya-sammataḥ*—approved by the devotees of Your Lordship; *prahrādaḥ*—Prahlāda Mahārāja; *āviṣkṛta-sādhu-vādaḥ*—famous, being celebrated everywhere as a devotee; *bhavat-vipakṣeṇa*—simply going against You; *vicitra-vaiśasam*—inventing different kinds of harassments; *samprāpitaḥ*—suffered; *tvam*—You; *paramaḥ*—the supreme shelter; *sva-pitrā*—by his own father.

TRANSLATION

My grandfather Prahlāda Mahārāja is famous, being recognized by all Your devotees. Although harassed in many ways by his father, Hiraṇyakaśipu, he still remained faithful, taking shelter at Your lotus feet.

PURPORT

A pure devotee like Prahlāda Mahārāja, although harassed circumstantially in many ways, never gives up the shelter of the Supreme Personality of Godhead to take shelter of anyone else. A pure devotee never complains against the mercy of the Supreme Personality of Godhead. A vivid example is Prahlāda Mahārāja. Examining the life of Prahlāda Mahārāja, we can see how severely he was harassed by his own father, Hiraṇyakaśipu, yet he did not divert his attention from the Lord even to the smallest extent. Bali Mahārāja, following in the footsteps of his grandfather Prahlāda Mahārāja, remained fixed in his devotion to the Lord, despite the Lord's having punished him.

TEXT 9

किमात्मनानेन जहाति योऽन्ततः
किं रिक्थहारैः स्वजनाख्यदस्युभिः ।

किं जायया संसृतिहेतुभूतया
मर्त्यस्य गेहैः किमिहायुषो व्ययः ॥ ९ ॥

kim ātmanānena jahāti yo 'ntataḥ
kiṁ riktha-hāraiḥ svajanākhya-dasyubhiḥ
kiṁ jāyayā saṁsṛti-hetu-bhūtayā
martyasya gehaiḥ kim ihāyuṣo vyayaḥ

kim—what is the use; *ātmanā anena*—of this body; *jahāti*—gives up; *yaḥ*—which (body); *antataḥ*—at the end of life; *kim*—what is the use; *riktha-hāraiḥ*—the plunderers of wealth; *svajana-ākhya-dasyubhiḥ*—they who are actually plunderers but who pass by the name of relatives; *kim*—what is the use; *jāyayā*—of a wife; *saṁsṛti-hetu-bhūtayā*—who is the source of increasing material conditions; *martyasya*—of a person sure to die; *gehaiḥ*—of houses, family and community; *kim*—what is the use; *iha*—in which house; *āyuṣaḥ*—of the duration of life; *vyayaḥ*—simply wasting.

TRANSLATION

What is the use of the material body, which automatically leaves its owner at the end of life? And what is the use of all one's family members, who are actually plunderers taking away money that is useful for the service of the Lord in spiritual opulence? What is the use of a wife? She is only the source of increasing material conditions. And what is the use of family, home, country and community? Attachment for them merely wastes the valuable energy of one's lifetime.

PURPORT

The Supreme Personality of Godhead, Kṛṣṇa, advises, *sarva-dharmān parityajya mām ekaṁ śaraṇaṁ vraja:* "Give up all other varieties of religion and just surrender unto Me." The common man does not appreciate such a statement by the Supreme Personality of Godhead because he thinks that during his lifetime his family, society, country, body and relatives are everything. Why should one give up any one of them and take shelter of the Supreme Personality of Godhead? But from the behavior of great personalities like Prahlāda Mahārāja and Bali Mahārāja we understand that surrendering to the Lord is the right action for an intelligent person. Prahlāda Mahārāja took shelter of Viṣṇu against the will of his father. Similarly, Bali Mahārāja took shelter of Vāmanadeva against the will of his spiritual master, Śukrācārya, and all the leading demons. People may be surprised that devotees like Prahlāda Mahārāja and Bali Mahārāja could seek shelter of the side of the enemy, giving up the natural affinity for family, hearth and home. In this connection, Bali Mahārāja explains that the body, which is the center of all material activities, is also a foreign element. Even though we want to keep the body fit and helpful to our activities, the body cannot continue eternally. Although I am the soul, which is eternal, after using the body for some time I have to accept another body (*tathā dehāntara-prāptiḥ*), according to the laws of nature, unless I render some service with the body for advancement in devotional service. One should not use the body for any other purpose. One must know that if he uses the body for any other purpose he is simply wasting time, for as soon as the time is ripe, the soul will automatically leave the body.

We are very interested in society, friendship and love, but what are they? Those in the garb of friends and relatives merely plunder the hard-earned money of the bewildered soul. Everyone is affectionate toward his wife and is attached to her, but what is this wife? The wife is called *strī,* which means, "one who expands the material condition." If a person lives without a wife, his material conditions are less extensive. As soon as one marries and is connected with a wife, his material necessities increase.

puṁsaḥ striyā mithunī-bhāvam etaṁ
tayor mitho hṛdaya-granthim āhuḥ
ato gṛha-kṣetra-sutāpta-vittair
janasya moho 'yam ahaṁ mameti

"The attraction between male and female is the basic principle of material existence. On the basis of this misconception, which ties together the hearts of the male and female, one becomes attracted to his body, home, property, children, relatives and wealth. In this way one increases life's illusions and thinks in terms of 'I and mine.' " (*Bhā*g. 5.5.8) Human life is meant for self-realization, not for increasing unwanted things. Actually, a wife increases unwanted things. One's lifetime, one's home and everything one has, if not properly used in the service of the Lord, are all sources of material conditions of perpetual suffering under the threefold miseries (*adhyātmika, adhibhautika* and *adhidaivika*). Unfortunately, there is no institution in human society for education on this subject. People are kept in darkness about the goal of life, and thus there is a continuous struggle for existence. We speak of "survival of the fittest," but no one survives, for no one is free under material conditions.

TEXT 10

इत्थं स निश्चित्य पितामहो महा-
नगाधबोधो भवतः पादपद्मम् ।
ध्रुवं प्रपेदे ह्यकुतोभयं जनाद्
भीतः स्वपक्षक्षपणस्य सत्तम ॥ १० ॥

ittham sa niścitya pitāmaho mahān
agādha-bodho bhavataḥ pāda-padmam
dhruvaṁ prapede hy akutobhayaṁ janād
bhītaḥ svapakṣa-kṣapaṇasya sattama

ittham—because of this (as stated above); *saḥ*—he, Prahlāda Mahārāja; *niścitya*—definitely deciding on this point; *pitāmahaḥ*—my grandfather; *mahān*—the great devotee; *agādha-bodhaḥ*—my grandfather, who received unlimited knowledge because of his devotional service; *bhavataḥ*—of Your Lordship; *pāda-padmam*—the lotus feet; *dhruvam*—the infallible, eternal shelter; *prapede*—surrendered; *hi*—indeed; *akutaḥ-bhayam*—completely free of fear; *janāt*—from ordinary common people; *bhītaḥ*—being afraid; *sva-pakṣa-kṣapaṇasya*—of Your Lordship, who kill the demons on our own side; *sat-tama*—O best of the best.

TRANSLATION

My grandfather, the best of all men, who achieved unlimited knowledge and was worshipable for everyone, was afraid of the common men in this world. Being fully convinced of the substantiality afforded by shelter at Your lotus feet, He took shelter of Your lotus feet, against the will of his father and demoniac friends, who were killed by Your own self.

TEXT 11

अथाहमप्यात्मरिपोस्तवान्तिकं
दैवेन नीतः प्रसभं त्याजितश्रीः ।
इदं कृतान्तान्तिकवर्ति जीवितं
ययाध्रुवं स्तब्धमतिर्न बुध्यते ॥ ११ ॥

athāham apy ātma-ripos tavāntikaṁ
daivena nītaḥ prasabhaṁ tyājita-śrīḥ

idaṁ kṛtāntāntika-varti jīvitaṁ
yayādhruvaṁ stabdha-matir na budhyate

atha—therefore; *aham*—I; *api*—also; *ātma-ripoḥ*—who are the traditional enemy of the family; *tava*—of Your good self; *antikam*—the shelter; *daivena*—by providence; *nītaḥ*—brought in; *prasabham*—by force; *tyājita*—bereft of; *śrīḥ*—all opulence; *idam*—this philosophy of life; *kṛta-anta-antika-varti*—always given the facility for death; *jīvitam*—the duration of life; *yayā*—by such material opulence; *adhruvam*—as temporary; *stabdha-matiḥ*—such an unintelligent person; *na budhyate*—cannot understand.

TRANSLATION

Only by providence have I been forcibly brought under Your lotus feet and deprived of all my opulence. Because of the illusion created by temporary opulence, people in general, who live under material conditions, facing accidental death at every moment, do not understand that this life is temporary. Only by providence have I been saved from that condition.

PURPORT

Bali Mahārāja appreciated the actions of the Supreme Personality of Godhead, although all the members of the demoniac families except Prahlāda Mahārāja and Bali Mahārāja considered Viṣṇu their eternal traditional enemy. As described by Bali Mahārāja, Lord Viṣṇu was actually not the enemy of the family but the best friend of the family. The principle of this friendship has already been stated. *Yasyāham anugṛhnāmi hariṣye tad-dhanaṁ śanaiḥ:* the Lord bestows special favor upon His devotee by taking away all his material opulences. Bali Mahārāja appreciated this behavior by the Lord. Therefore he said, *daivena nītaḥ prasabhaṁ tyājita-śrīḥ:* "It is to bring me to the right platform of eternal life that You have put me into these circumstances."

Actually, everyone should fear the so-called society, friendship and love for which he works so hard all day and night. As indicated by Bali Mahārāja by the words *janād bhītaḥ,* every devotee in Kṛṣṇa consciousness should always be afraid of the common man engaged in pursuing material prosperity. Such a person is described as *pramatta,* a madman chasing the will-o'-the-wisp. Such men do not know that after a hard struggle for life one must change his body, with no certainty of what kind of body he will receive next. Those who are completely established in Kṛṣṇa conscious philosophy and who therefore understand the aim of life will never take to the activities of the materialistic dog race. But if a sincere devotee somehow does fall down, the Lord corrects him and saves him from gliding down to the darkest region of hellish life.

adānta-gobhir viśatāṁ tamisraṁ
punaḥ punaś carvita-carvaṇānām

(Bhāg. 7.5.30)

The materialistic way of life is nothing but the repeated chewing of that which has already been chewed. Although there is no profit in such a life, people are enamored of it because of uncontrolled senses. *Nūnaṁ pramattaḥ kurute vikarma* . Because of uncontrolled senses, people fully engage in sinful activities by which they get a body full of suffering. Bali Mahārāja appreciated how the Lord had saved him from such a bewildered life of ignorance. He therefore said that his intelligence had been stunned. *Stabdha-matir na budhyate.* He could not understand how the Supreme Personality of Godhead favors His devotees by forcibly stopping their materialistic activities.

TEXT 12

श्रीशुक उवाच
तस्येत्थं भाषमाणस्य प्रह्रादो भगवत्प्रियः ।
आजगाम कुरुश्रेष्ठ राकापतिरिवोत्थितः ॥ १२ ॥

śrī-śuka uvāca
tasyetthaṁ bhāṣamāṇasya
prahrādo bhagavat-priyaḥ
ājagāma kuru-śreṣṭha
rākā-patir ivotthitaḥ

śrī-śukaḥ uvāca—Śrī Śukadeva Gosvāmī said; *tasya*—Bali Mahārāja; *ittham*—in this way; *bhāṣamāṇasya*—while describing his fortunate position; *prahrādaḥ*—Mahārāja Prahlāda, his grandfather; *bhagavat-priyaḥ*—the most favored devotee of the Supreme Personality of Godhead; *ājagāma*—appeared there; *kuru-śreṣṭha*—O best of the Kurus, Mahārāja Parīkṣit; *rākā-patiḥ*—the moon; *iva*—like; *utthitaḥ*—having risen.

TRANSLATION

Śukadeva Gosvāmī said: O best of the Kurus, while Bali Mahārāja was describing his fortunate position in this way, the most dear devotee of the

Lord, Prahlāda Mahārāja, appeared there, like the moon rising in the nighttime.

TEXT 13

तमिन्द्रसेनः स्वपितामहं श्रिया
विराजमानं नलिनायतेक्षणम् ।
प्रांशुं पिशङ्गाम्बरमञ्जनत्विषं
प्रलम्बबाहुं शुभगर्षभमैक्षत ॥ १३ ॥

tam indra-senaḥ sva-pitāmahaṁ śriyā
virājamānaṁ nalināyatekṣaṇam
prāṁśuṁ piśaṅgāmbaram añjana-tviṣaṁ
pralamba-bāhuṁ śubhagarṣabham aikṣata

tam—that Prahlāda Mahārāja; *indra-senaḥ*—Bali Mahārāja, who now possessed all the military force of Indra; *sva-pitāmaham*—unto his grandfather; *śriyā*—present with all beautiful features; *virājamānam*—standing there; *nalina-āyata-īkṣaṇam*—with eyes as broad as the petals of a lotus; *prāṁśum*—a very beautiful body; *piśaṅga-ambaram*—dressed in yellow garments; *añjana-tviṣam*—with his body resembling black ointment for the eyes; *pralamba-bāhum*—very long arms; *śubhaga-ṛṣabham*—the best of all auspicious persons; *aikṣata*—he saw.

TRANSLATION

Then Bali Mahārāja saw his grandfather Prahlāda Mahārāja, the most fortunate personality, whose dark body resembled black ointment for the eyes. His tall, elegant figure was dressed in yellow garments, he had long arms, and his beautiful eyes were like the petals of a lotus. He was very dear and pleasing to everyone.

TEXT 14

तस्मै बलिर्वारुणपाशयन्त्रितः
समर्हणं नोपजहार पूर्ववत् ।
ननाम मूर्ध्नाश्रुविलोललोचनः
सव्रीडनीचीनमुखो बभूव ह ॥ १४ ॥

tasmai balir vāruṇa-pāśa-yantritaḥ
samarhaṇaṁ nopajahāra pūrvavat
nanāma mūrdhnāśru-vilola-locanaḥ
sa-vrīḍa-nīcīna-mukho babhūva ha

tasmai—unto Prahlāda Mahārāja; *baliḥ*—Bali Mahārāja; *vāruṇa-pāśa-yantritaḥ*—being bound by the ropes of Varuṇa; *samarhaṇam*—befitting respect; *na*—not; *upajahāra*—offered; *pūrva-vat*—like before; *nanāma*—he offered obeisances; *mūrdhnā*—with the head; *aśru-vilola-locanaḥ*—eyes inundated with tears; *sa-vrīḍa*—with shyness; *nīcīna*—downward; *mukhaḥ*—face; *babhūva ha*—he so became.

TRANSLATION

Being bound by the ropes of Varuṇa, Bali Mahārāja could not offer befitting respect to Prahlāda Mahārāja as he had before. Rather, he simply offered respectful obeisances with his head, his eyes being inundated with tears and his face lowered in shame.

PURPORT

Since Bali Mahārāja had been arrested by Lord Vāmanadeva, he was certainly to be considered an offender. Bali Mahārāja seriously felt that he was an offender to the Supreme Personality of Godhead. Certainly Prahlāda Mahārāja would not like this. Therefore Bali Mahārāja was ashamed and hung his head.

TEXT 15

स तत्र हासीनमुदीक्ष्य सत्पतिं
हरिं सुनन्दाद्यनुगैरुपासितम् ।
उपेत्य भूमौ शिरसा महामना
ननाम मूर्ध्ना पुलकाश्रुविक्लवः ॥ १५ ॥

sa tatra hāsīnam udīkṣya sat-patiṁ
hariṁ sunandādy-anugair upāsitam
upetya bhūmau śirasā mahā-manā
nanāma mūrdhnā pulakāśru-viklavaḥ

saḥ—Prahlāda Mahārāja; *tatra*—there; *ha āsīnam*—seated; *udīkṣya*—after seeing; *sat-patim*—the Supreme Personality of Godhead, master of the liberated souls; *harim*—Lord Hari; *sunanda-ādi-anugaiḥ*—by His followers, like Sunanda; *upāsitam*—being worshiped; *upetya*—reaching nearby; *bhūmau*—on the ground; *śirasā*—with his head (bowed down); *mahā-manāḥ*—the great devotee; *nanāma*—offered obeisances; *mūrdhnā*—with his head; *pulaka-aśru-viklavaḥ*—agitated by tears of jubilation.

TRANSLATION

When the great personality Prahlāda Mahārāja saw that the Supreme Lord was sitting there, surrounded and worshiped by His intimate associates like Sunanda, he was overwhelmed with tears of jubilation. Approaching the Lord and falling to the ground, he offered obeisances to the Lord with his head.

TEXT 16

श्रीप्रह्राद उवाच
त्वयैव दत्तं पदमैन्द्रमूर्जितं
हृतं तदेवाद्य तथैव शोभनम् ।
मन्ये महानस्य कृतो ह्यनुग्रहो
विभ्रंशितो यच्छ्रिय आत्ममोहनात् ॥ १६ ॥

śrī-prahrāda uvāca
tvayaiva dattaṁ padam aindram ūrjitaṁ
hṛtaṁ tad evādya tathaiva śobhanam
manye mahān asya kṛto hy anugraho
vibhraṁśito yac chriya ātma-mohanāt

śrī-prahrādaḥ uvāca—Prahlāda Mahārāja said; *tvayā*—by Your Lordship; *eva*—indeed; *dattam*—which had been given; *padam*—this position; *aindram*—of the King of heaven; *ūrjitam*—very, very great; *hṛtam*—has been taken away; *tat*—that; *eva*—indeed; *adya*—today; *tathā*—as; *eva*—indeed; *śobhanam*—beautiful; *manye*—I consider; *mahān*—very great; *asya*—of him (Bali Mahārāja); *kṛtaḥ*—has been done by You; *hi*—indeed; *anugrahaḥ*—mercy; *vibhraṁśitaḥ*—being bereft of; *yat*—because; *śriyaḥ*—from that opulence; *ātma-mohanāt*—which was covering the process of self-realization.

TRANSLATION

Prahlāda Mahārāja said: My Lord, it is Your Lordship who gave this Bali the very great opulence of the post of heavenly king, and now, today, it is

You who have taken it all away. I think You have acted with equal beauty in both ways. Because his exalted position as King of heaven was putting him in the darkness of ignorance, You have done him a very merciful favor by taking away all his opulence.

PURPORT

As it is said, *yasyāham anugṛhṇāmi hariṣye tad-dhanaṁ śanaiḥ* (*Bhāg.* 10.88.8). It is by the mercy of the Lord that one gets all material opulence, but if such material opulence causes one to become puffed up and forget the process of self-realization, the Lord certainly takes all the opulence away. The Lord bestows mercy upon His devotee by helping him find out his constitutional position. For that purpose, the Lord is always ready to help the devotee in every way. But material opulence is sometimes dangerous because it diverts one's attention to false prestige by giving one the impression that he is the owner and master of everything he surveys, although actually this is not the fact. To protect the devotee from such a misunderstanding, the Lord, showing special mercy, sometimes takes away his material possessions. *Yasyāham anugṛhṇāmi hariṣye tad-dhanaṁ śanaiḥ.*

TEXT 17

यया हि विद्वानपि मुह्यते यत-
स्तत् को विचष्टे गतिमात्मनो यथा ।
तस्मै नमस्ते जगदीश्वराय वै
नारायणायाखिललोकसाक्षिणे ॥ १७ ॥

yayā hi vidvān api muhyate yatas
tat ko vicaṣṭe gatim ātmano yathā
tasmai namas te jagad-īśvarāya vai
nārāyaṇāyākhila-loka-sākṣiṇe

yayā—by which material opulence; *hi*—indeed; *vidvān api*—even a person fortunately advanced in education; *muhyate*—becomes bewildered; *yataḥ*—self-controlled; *tat*—that; *kaḥ*—who; *vicaṣṭe*—can search for; *gatim*—the progress; *ātmanaḥ*—of the self; *yathā*—properly; *tasmai*—unto Him; *namaḥ*—I offer my respectful obeisances; *te*—unto You; *jagat-īśvarāya*—unto the Lord of the universe; *vai*—indeed; *nārāyaṇāya*—unto His Lordship Nārāyaṇa; *akhila-loka-sākṣiṇe*—who are the witness of all creation.

TRANSLATION

Material opulence is so bewildering that it makes even a learned, self-controlled man forget to search for the goal of self-realization. But the Supreme Personality of Godhead, Nārāyaṇa, the Lord of the universe, can see everything by His will. Therefore I offer my respectful obeisances unto Him.

PURPORT

The words *ko vicaṣṭe gatim ātmano yathā* indicate that when one is puffed up by the false prestige of possessing material opulence, he certainly neglects the goal of self-realization. This is the position of the modern world. Because of so-called scientific improvements in material opulence, people have entirely given up the path of self-realization. Practically no one is interested in God, one's relationship with God or how one should act. Modern men have altogether forgotten such questions because they are mad for material possessions. If this kind of civilization continues, the time will soon come when the Supreme Personality of Godhead will take away all the material opulences. Then people will come to their senses.

TEXT 18

श्रीशुक उवाच
तस्यानुश‍ृण्वतो राजन् प्रह्लादस्य कृताञ्जलेः ।
हिरण्यगर्भो भगवानुवाच मधुसूदनम् ॥ १८ ॥

śrī-śuka uvāca
tasyānuśṛṇvato rājan
prahrādasya kṛtāñjaleḥ
hiraṇyagarbho bhagavān
uvāca madhusūdanam

śrī-śukaḥ uvāca—Śrī Śukadeva Gosvāmī said; *tasya*—of Prahlāda Mahārāja; *anuśṛṇvataḥ*—so that he could hear; *rājan*—O King Parīkṣit; *prahrādasya*—of Prahlāda Mahārāja; *kṛta-añjaleḥ*—who was standing with folded hands; *hiraṇyagarbhaḥ*—Lord Brahmā; *bhagavān*—the most powerful; *uvāca*—said; *madhusūdanam*—unto Madhusūdana, the Personality of Godhead.

TRANSLATION

Śukadeva Gosvāmī continued: O King Parīkṣit, Lord Brahmā then began to speak to the Supreme Personality of Godhead, within the hearing of Prahlāda Mahārāja, who stood nearby with folded hands.

TEXT 19

बद्धं वीक्ष्य पतिं साध्वी तत्पत्नी भयविह्वला ।
प्राञ्जलिः प्रणतोपेन्द्रं बभाषेऽवाङ्मुखी नृप ॥ १९ ॥

baddhaṁ vīkṣya patiṁ sādhvī
tat-patnī bhaya-vihvalā
prāñjaliḥ praṇatopendraṁ
babhāṣe 'vāṅ-mukhī nṛpa

baddham—arrested; *vīkṣya*—seeing; *patim*—her husband; *sādhvī*—the chaste woman; *tat-patnī*—Bali Mahārāja's wife; *bhaya-vihvalā*—being very disturbed by fear; *prāñjaliḥ*—with folded hands; *praṇatā*—having offered obeisances; *upendram*—unto Vāmanadeva; *babhāṣe*—addressed; *avāk-mukhī*—with face downward; *nṛpa*—O Mahārāja Parīkṣit.

TRANSLATION

But Bali Mahārāja's chaste wife, afraid and aggrieved at seeing her husband arrested, immediately offered obeisances to Lord Vāmanadeva [Upendra]. She folded her hands and spoke as follows.

PURPORT

Although Lord Brahmā was speaking, he had to stop for a while because Bali Mahārāja's wife, Vindhyāvali, who was very agitated and afraid, wanted to say something.

TEXT 20

श्रीविन्ध्यावलिरुवाच

क्रीडार्थमात्मन इदं त्रिजगत् कृतं ते
स्वाम्यं तु तत्र कुधियोऽपर ईश कुर्युः ।
कर्तुः प्रभोस्तव किमस्यत आवहन्ति
त्यक्तह्रियस्त्वदवरोपितकर्तृवादाः ॥ २० ॥

śrī-vindhyāvalir uvāca
krīḍārtham ātmana idaṁ tri-jagat kṛtaṁ te
svāmyaṁ tu tatra kudhiyo 'para īśa kuryuḥ
kartuḥ prabhos tava kim asyata āvahanti
tyakta-hriyas tvad-avaropita-kartṛ-vādāḥ

śrī-vindhyāvaliḥ uvāca—Vindhyāvali, the wife of Bali Mahārāja, said; *krīḍā-artham*—for the sake of pastimes; *ātmanaḥ*—of Yourself; *idam*—this; *tri-jagat*—the three worlds (this universe); *kṛtam*—was created; *te*—by You; *svāmyam*—proprietorship; *tu*—but; *tatra*—thereon; *kudhiyaḥ*—foolish rascals; *apare*—others; *īśa*—O my Lord; *kuryuḥ*—have established; *kartuḥ*—for the supreme creator; *prabhoḥ*—for the supreme maintainer; *tava*—for Your good self; *kim*—what; *asyataḥ*—for the supreme annihilator; *āvahanti*—they can offer; *tyakta-hriyaḥ*—shameless, without intelligence; *tvat*—by You; *avaropita*—falsely imposed because of a poor fund of knowledge; *kartṛ-vādāḥ*—the proprietorship of such foolish agnostics.

TRANSLATION

Śrīmatī Vindhyāvali said: O my Lord, You have created the entire universe for the enjoyment of Your personal pastimes, but foolish, unintelligent men have claimed proprietorship for material enjoyment. Certainly they are shameless agnostics. Falsely claiming proprietorship, they think they can give charity and enjoy. In such a condition, what good can they do for You, who are the independent creator, maintainer and annihilator of this universe?

PURPORT

Bali Mahārāja's wife, who was most intelligent, supported the arrest of her husband and accused him of having no intelligence because he had claimed proprietorship of the property of the Lord. Such a claim is a sign of demoniac life. Although the demigods, who are officials appointed by the Lord for management, are attached to materialistic enjoyment, they never claim to be proprietors of the universe, for they know that the actual proprietor of everything is the Supreme Personality of Godhead. This is the qualification of the demigods. But the demons, instead of accepting the exclusive proprietorship of the Supreme Personality of Godhead, claim the property of the universe for themselves through demarcations of nationalism. "This part is mine, and that part is yours," they say. "This part I can give in charity, and this part I can keep for my enjoyment." These are all demoniac conceptions. This is described in *Bhagavad-gītā* (16.13): *idam adya mayā labdham imaṁ prāpsye manoratham.* "Thus far I have acquired so much money and land. Now I have to add more and more. In this way I shall be the greatest proprietor of everything. Who can compete with me?" These are all demoniac conceptions.

Bali Mahārāja's wife accused Bali Mahārāja by saying that although the Supreme Personality of Godhead had arrested him, showing him extraordinary mercy, and although Bali Mahārāja was offering his body to the Supreme Lord for the Lord's third step, he was still in the darkness of ignorance. Actually the body did not belong to him, but because of his long-standing demoniac mentality he could not understand this. He thought that since he had been defamed for his inability to fulfill his promise of charity, and since the body belonged to him, he would free himself from defamation by offering his body. Actually, however, the body does not belong to anyone but the Supreme Personality of Godhead, by whom the body is given. As stated in *Bhagavad-gītā* (18.61):

īśvaraḥ sarva-bhūtānāṁ
hṛd-deśe 'rjuna tiṣṭhati
bhrāmayan sarva-bhūtāni
yantrārūḍhāni māyayā

The Lord is situated in the core of everyone's heart, and, according to the material desires of the living entity, the Lord offers a particular type of machine —the body—through the agency of the material energy. The body actually does not belong to the living entity; it belongs to the Supreme Personality of Godhead. Under the circumstances, how could Bali Mahārāja claim that the body belonged to him?

Thus Vindhyāvali, Bali Mahārāja's intelligent wife, prayed that her husband be released, by the Lord's causeless mercy. Otherwise, Bali Mahārāja was nothing but a shameless demon, specifically described as *tyakta-hriyas tvad-avaropita-kartṛ-vādāḥ,* a foolish person claiming proprietorship over the property of the Supreme Person. In the present age, Kali-yuga, the number of such shameless men, who are agnostics disbelieving in the existence of God, has increased. Trying to defy the authority of the Supreme Personality of Godhead, so-called scientists, philosophers and politicians manufacture plans and schemes for the destruction of the world. They cannot do anything good for the world, and unfortunately, because of Kali-yuga, they have plunged the affairs of the world into mismanagement. Thus there is a great need for the Kṛṣṇa consciousness movement for the benefit of innocent people who are being carried away by propaganda of such demons. If the present status quo is allowed to continue, people will certainly suffer more and more under the leadership of these demoniac agnostics.

TEXT 21

श्रीब्रह्मोवाच
भूतभावन भूतेश देवदेव जगन्मय ।
मुञ्चैनं हृतसर्वस्वं नायमर्हति निग्रहम् ॥ २१ ॥

śrī-brahmovāca
bhūta-bhāvana bhūteśa
deva-deva jaganmaya
muñcainaṁ hṛta-sarvasvaṁ
nāyam arhati nigraham

śrī-brahmā uvāca—Lord Brahmā said; *bhūta-bhāvana*—O Supreme Being, well-wisher of everyone, who can cause one to flourish; *bhūta-īśa*—O master of everyone; *deva-deva*—O worshipable Deity of the demigods; *jagat-maya*—O all-pervading one; *muñca*—please release; *enam*—this poor Bali Mahārāja; *hṛta-sarvasvam*—now bereft of everything; *na*—not; *ayam*—such a poor man; *arhati*—deserves; *nigraham*—punishment.

TRANSLATION

Lord Brahmā said: O well-wisher and master of all living entities, O worshipable Deity of all the demigods, O all-pervading Personality of Godhead, now this man has been sufficiently punished, for You have taken everything. Now You can release him. He does not deserve to be punished more.

PURPORT

When Lord Brahmā saw that Prahlāda Mahārāja and Vindhyāvali had already approached the Lord to ask mercy for Bali Mahārāja, he joined them and recommended Bali Mahārāja's release on the grounds of worldly calculations.

TEXT 22

कृत्स्ना तेऽनेन दत्ता भूर्लोकाः कर्मार्जिताश्च ये ।
निवेदितं च सर्वस्वमात्माविक्लवया धिया ॥ २२ ॥

kṛtsnā te 'nena dattā bhūr
lokāḥ karmārjitāś ca ye
niveditaṁ ca sarvasvam
ātmāviklavayā dhiyā

kṛtsnāḥ—all; *te*—unto You; *anena*—by Bali Mahārāja; *dattāḥ*—have been given or returned; *bhūḥ lokāḥ*—all land and all planets; *karma-arjitāḥ ca*—whatever he achieved by his pious activities; *ye*—all of which; *niveditam ca*—have been offered to You; *sarvasvam*—everything he possessed; *ātmā*—even his body; *aviklavayā*—without hesitation; *dhiyā*—by such intelligence.

TRANSLATION

Bali Mahārāja had already offered everything to Your Lordship. Without hesitation, he has offered his land, the planets and whatever else he earned by his pious activities, including even his own body.

TEXT 23

यत्पादयोरशठधीः सलिलं प्रदाय
दूर्वाङ्कुरैरपि विधाय सतीं सपर्याम् ।
अप्युत्तमां गतिमसौ भजते त्रिलोकीं
दाश्वानविक्लवमनाः कथमार्तिमृच्छेत् ॥ २३ ॥

yat-pādayor aśaṭha-dhīḥ salilaṁ pradāya
dūrvāṅkurair api vidhāya satīṁ saparyām
apy uttamāṁ gatim asau bhajate tri-lokīṁ
dāśvān aviklava-manāḥ katham ārtim ṛcchet

yat-pādayoḥ—at the lotus feet of Your Lordship; *aśaṭha-dhīḥ*—a great-minded person who is without duplicity; *salilam*—water; *pradāya*—offering; *dūrvā*—with fully grown grass; *aṅkuraiḥ*—and with buds of flowers; *api*—although; *vidhāya*—offering; *satīm*—most exalted; *saparyām*—with worship; *api*—although; *uttamām*—the most highly elevated; *gatim*—destination; *asau*—such a worshiper; *bhajate*—deserves; *tri-lokīm*—the three worlds; *dāśvān*—giving to You; *aviklava-manāḥ*—without mental duplicity; *katham*—how; *ārtim*—the distressed condition of being arrested; *ṛcchet*—he deserves.

TRANSLATION

By offering even water, newly grown grass, or flower buds at Your lotus feet, those who maintain no mental duplicity can achieve the most exalted position within the spiritual world. This Bali Mahārāja, without duplicity, has now offered everything in the three worlds. How then can he deserve to suffer from arrest?

PURPORT

In *Bhagavad-gītā* (9.26) it is stated:

patraṁ puṣpaṁ phalaṁ toyaṁ
yo me bhaktyā prayacchati
tad ahaṁ bhakty-upahṛtam
aśnāmi prayatātmanaḥ

The Supreme Personality of Godhead is so kind that if an unsophisticated person, with devotion and without duplicity, offers at the lotus feet of the Lord a little water, a flower, a fruit or a leaf, the Lord accepts it. Then the devotee is promoted to Vaikuṇṭha, the spiritual world. Brahmā drew the Lord's attention to this subject and requested that He release Bali Mahārāja, who was suffering, being bound by the ropes of Varuṇa, and who had already given everything, including the three worlds and whatever he possessed.

TEXT 24

श्रीभगवानुवाच
ब्रह्मन् यमनुगृह्णामि तद्विशो विधुनोम्यहम् ।
यन्मदः पुरुषः स्तब्धो लोकं मां चावमन्यते ॥ २४ ॥

śrī-bhagavān uvāca
brahman yam anugṛhṇāmi
tad-viśo vidhunomy aham
yan-madaḥ puruṣaḥ stabdho
lokaṁ māṁ cāvamanyate

śrī-bhagavān uvāca—the Supreme Personality of Godhead said; *brahman*—O Lord Brahmā; *yam*—unto anyone to whom; *anugṛhṇāmi*—I show My mercy; *tat*—his; *viśaḥ*—material opulence or riches; *vidhunomi*—take away; *aham*—I; *yat-madaḥ*—having false prestige due to this money; *puruṣaḥ*—such a person; *stabdhaḥ*—being dull-minded; *lokam*—the three worlds; *mām ca*—unto Me also; *avamanyate*—derides.

TRANSLATION

The Supreme Personality of Godhead said: My dear Lord Brahmā, because of material opulence a foolish person becomes dull-witted and mad. Thus he has no respect for anyone within the three worlds and defies even My authority. To such a person I show special favor by first taking away all his possessions.

PURPORT

A civilization that has become godless because of material advancement in opulence is extremely dangerous. Because of great opulence, a materialist becomes so proud that he has no regard for anyone and even refuses to accept the authority of the Supreme Personality of Godhead. The result of such a mentality is certainly very dangerous. To show special favor, the Lord sometimes makes an example of someone like Bali Mahārāja, who was now bereft of all his possessions.

TEXT 25

यदा कदाचिज्जीवात्मा संसरन् निजकर्मभिः ।
नानायोनिष्वनीशोऽयं पौरुषीं गतिमाव्रजेत् ॥ २५ ॥

yadā kadācij jīvātmā
saṁsaran nija-karmabhiḥ
nānā-yoniṣv anīśo 'yaṁ
pauruṣīṁ gatim āvrajet

yadā—when; *kadācit*—sometimes; *jīva-ātmā*—the living entity; *saṁsaran*—rotating in the cycle of birth and death; *nija-karmabhiḥ*—because of his own fruitive activities; *nānā-yoniṣu*—in different species of life; *anīśaḥ*—not independent (completely under the control of material nature); *ayam*—this living entity; *pauruṣīm gatim*—the situation of being human; *āvrajet*—wants to obtain.

TRANSLATION

While rotating in the cycle of birth and death again and again in different species because of his own fruitive activities, the dependent living entity, by good fortune, may happen to become a human being. This human birth is very rarely obtained.

PURPORT

The Supreme Personality of Godhead is fully independent. Thus it is not always a fact that a living being's loss of all opulence is a sign of the Supreme Lord's mercy upon him. The Lord can act any way He likes. He may take away one's opulence, or He may not. There are varieties of forms of life, and the Lord treats them according to the circumstances, as He chooses. Generally it is to be understood that the human form of life is one of great responsibility.

puruṣaḥ prakṛti-stho hi
bhuṅkte prakṛtijān guṇān
kāraṇaṁ guṇa-saṅgo 'sya
sad-asad-yoni-janmasu

'The living entity in material nature follows the ways of life, enjoying the three modes of nature. This is due to his association with that material nature. Thus he meets with good and evil amongst various species." (Bg. 13.22) After thus rotating through many, many forms of life in the cycle of birth and death, the living being gets a chance for a human form. Therefore every human being, especially one belonging to a civilized nation or culture, must be extremely responsible in his activities. He should not risk degradation in the next life. Because the body will change (*tathā dehāntara-prāptir*), we should be extremely careful. To see to the proper use of life is the purpose of Kṛṣṇa consciousness. The foolish living entity declares freedom from all control, but factually he is not free; he is fully under the control of material nature. He must therefore be most careful and responsible in the activities of his life.

TEXT 26

जन्मकर्मवयोरूपविद्यैश्वर्यधनादिभिः ।
यद्यस्य न भवेत् स्तम्भस्तत्रायं मदनुग्रहः ॥ २६ ॥

janma-karma-vayo-rūpa-
vidyaiśvarya-dhanādibhiḥ

yady asya na bhavet stambhas
tatrāyaṁ mad-anugrahaḥ

janma—by birth in an aristocratic family; *karma*—by wonderful activities, pious activities; *vayaḥ*—by age, especially youth, when one is capable of doing many things; *rūpa*—by personal beauty, which attracts everyone; *vidyā*—by education; *aiśvarya*—by opulence; *dhana*—by wealth; *ādibhiḥ*—by other opulences also; *yadi*—if; *asya*—of the possessor; *na*—not; *bhavet*—there is; *stambhaḥ*—pride; *tatra*—in such a condition; *ayam*—a person; *mat-anugrahaḥ*—should be considered to have received My special mercy.

TRANSLATION

If a human being is born in an aristocratic family or a higher status of life, if he performs wonderful activities, if he is youthful, if he has personal beauty, a good education and good wealth, and if he is nonetheless not proud of his opulences, it is to be understood that he is especially favored by the Supreme Personality of Godhead.

PURPORT

When in spite of possessing all these opulences a person is not proud, this means that he is fully aware that all his opulences are due to the mercy of the Supreme Personality of Godhead. He therefore engages all his possessions in the service of the Lord. A devotee knows very well that everything, even his body, belongs to the Supreme Lord. If one lives perfectly in such Kṛṣṇa consciousness, it is to be understood that he is especially favored by the Supreme Personality of Godhead. The conclusion is that one's being deprived of his wealth is not to be considered the special mercy of the Lord. If one continues in his opulent position but does not become unnecessarily proud, falsely thinking that he is the proprietor of everything, this is the Lord's special mercy.

TEXT 27

मानस्तम्भनिमित्तानां जन्मादीनां समन्ततः ।
सर्वश्रेयःप्रतीपानां हन्त मुह्येन्न मत्परः ॥ २७ ॥

māna-stambha-nimittānāṁ
janmādīnāṁ samantataḥ

sarva-śreyaḥ-pratīpānāṁ
hanta muhyen na mat-paraḥ

māna—of false prestige; *stambha*—because of this impudence; *nimittānām*—which are the causes; *janma-ādīnām*—such as birth in a high family; *samantataḥ*—taken together; *sarva-śreyaḥ*—for the supreme benefit of life; *pratīpānām*—which are impediments; *hanta*—also; *muhyet*—becomes bewildered; *na*—not; *mat-paraḥ*—My pure devotee.

TRANSLATION

Although aristocratic birth and other such opulences are impediments to advancement in devotional service because they are causes of false prestige and pride, these opulences never disturb a pure devotee of the Supreme Personality of Godhead.

PURPORT

Devotees like Dhruva Mahārāja, who was given unlimited material opulence, have the special mercy of the Supreme Personality of Godhead. Once Kuvera wanted to give Dhruva Mahārāja a benediction, but although Dhruva Mahārāja could have asked him for any amount of material opulence, he instead begged Kuvera that he might continue his devotional service to the Supreme Personality of Godhead. When a devotee is fixed in his devotional service, there is no need for the Lord to deprive him of his material opulences. The Supreme Personality of Godhead never takes away material opulences achieved because of devotional service, although He sometimes takes away opulences achieved by pious activities. He does this to make a devotee prideless or put him in a better position in devotional service. If a special devotee is meant for preaching but does not give up his family life or material opulences to take to the service of the Lord, the Lord surely takes away his material opulences and establishes him in devotional service. Thus the pure devotee becomes fully engaged in propagating Kṛṣṇa consciousness.

TEXT 28

एष दानवदैत्यानामग्रणीः कीर्तिवर्धनः ।
अजैषीदजयां मायां सीदन्नपि न मुह्यति ॥ २८ ॥

eṣa dānava-daityānām
agranīḥ kīrti-vardhanaḥ

ajaiṣīd ajayāṁ māyāṁ
sīdann api na muhyati

eṣaḥ—this Bali Mahārāja; *dānava-daityānām*—among the demons and unbelievers; *agranīḥ*—the foremost devotee; *kīrti-vardhanaḥ*—the most famous; *ajaiṣīt*—has already surpassed; *ajayām*—the insurmountable; *māyām*—material energy; *sīdan*—being bereft (of all material opulences); *api*—although; *na*—not; *muhyati*—is bewildered.

TRANSLATION

Bali Mahārāja has become the most famous among the demons and nonbelievers, for in spite of being bereft of all material opulences, he is fixed in his devotional service.

PURPORT

In this verse, the words *sīdann api na muhyati* are very important. A devotee is sometimes put into adversity while executing devotional service. In adversity, everyone laments and becomes aggrieved, but by the grace of the Supreme Personality of Godhead, a devotee, even in the worst condition, can understand that he is going through a severe examination by the Personality of Godhead. Bali Mahārāja passed all such examinations, as explained in the following verses.

TEXTS 29-30

क्षीणरिक्थश्च्युतः स्थानात् क्षिप्तो बद्धश्च शत्रुभिः ।
ज्ञातिभिश्च परित्यक्तो यातनामनुयापितः ॥ २९ ॥
गुरुणा भर्त्सितः शप्तो जहौ सत्यं न सुव्रतः ।
छलैरुक्तो मया धर्मो नायं त्यजति सत्यवाक् ॥ ३० ॥

kṣīṇa-rikthaś cyutaḥ sthānāt
kṣipto baddhaś ca śatrubhiḥ
jñātibhiś ca parityakto
yātanām anuyāpitaḥ

guruṇā bhartsitaḥ śapto
jahau satyaṁ na suvrataḥ
chalair ukto mayā dharmo
nāyaṁ tyajati satya-vāk

kṣīṇa-rikthaḥ—although bereft of all riches; *cyutaḥ*—fallen; *sthānāt*—from his superior position; *kṣiptaḥ*—forcefully thrown away; *baddhaḥ ca*—and forcefully bound; *śatrubhiḥ*—by his enemies; *jñātibhiḥ ca*—and by his family members or relatives; *parityaktaḥ*—deserted; *yātanām*—all kinds of suffering; *anuyāpitaḥ*—unusually severely suffered; *guruṇā*—by his spiritual master; *bhartsitaḥ*—rebuked; *śaptaḥ*—and cursed; *jahau*—gave up; *satyam*—truthfulness; *na*—not; *su-vrataḥ*—being fixed in his vow; *chalaiḥ*—pretentiously; *uktaḥ*—spoken; *mayā*—by Me; *dharmaḥ*—the religious principles; *na*—not; *ayam*—this Bali Mahārāja; *tyajati*—does give up; *satya-vāk*—being true to his word.

TRANSLATION

Although bereft of his riches, fallen from his original position, defeated and arrested by his enemies, rebuked and deserted by his relatives and friends, although suffering the pain of being bound and although rebuked and cursed by his spiritual master, Bali Mahārāja, being fixed in his vow, did not give up his truthfulness. It was certainly with pretension that I spoke about religious principles, but he did not give up religious principles, for he is true to his word.

PURPORT

Bali Mahārāja passed the severe test put before him by the Supreme Personality of Godhead. This is further proof of the Lord's mercy toward His devotee. The Supreme Personality of Godhead sometimes puts a devotee to severe tests that are almost unbearable. One could hardly even live under the conditions forced upon Bali Mahārāja. That Bali Mahārāja endured all these severe tests and austerities is the mercy of the Supreme Lord. The Lord certainly appreciates the devotee's forbearance, and it is recorded for the future glorification of the devotee. This was not an ordinary test. As described in this verse, hardly anyone could survive such a test, but for the future glorification of Bali Mahārāja, one of the *mahājanas,* the Supreme Personality of Godhead not only tested him but also gave him the strength to tolerate such adversity. The Lord is so kind to His devotee that when severely testing him the Lord gives him the necessary strength to be tolerant and continue to remain a glorious devotee.

TEXT 31

एष मे प्रापितः स्थानं दुष्प्रापममरैरपि ।
सावर्णेरन्तरस्यायं भवितेन्द्रो मदाश्रयः ॥ ३१ ॥

eṣa me prāpitaḥ sthānaṁ
duṣprāpam amarair api
sāvarṇer antarasyāyaṁ
bhavitendro mad-āśrayaḥ

eṣaḥ—Bali Mahārāja; *me*—by Me; *prāpitaḥ*—has achieved; *sthānam*—a place; *duṣprāpam*—extremely difficult to obtain; *amaraiḥ api*—even by the demigods; *sāvarṇeḥ antarasya*—during the period of the Manu known as Sāvarṇi; *ayam*—this Bali Mahārāja; *bhavitā*—will become; *indraḥ*—the lord of the heavenly planet; *mat-āśrayaḥ*—completely under My protection.

TRANSLATION

The Lord continued: Because of his great tolerance, I have given him a place not obtainable even by the demigods. He will become King of the heavenly planets during the period of the Manu known as Sāvarṇi.

PURPORT

This is the mercy of the Supreme Personality of Godhead. Even if the Lord takes away a devotee's material opulences, the Lord immediately offers him a position of which the demigods cannot even dream. There are many examples of this in the history of devotional service. One of them is the opulence of Sudāmā Vipra. Sudāmā Vipra suffered severe material scarcity, but he was not disturbed and did not deviate from devotional service. Thus he was ultimately given an exalted position by the mercy of Lord Kṛṣṇa. Here the word *mad-āśrayaḥ* is very significant. Because the Lord wanted to give Bali Mahārāja the exalted position of Indra, the demigods might naturally have been envious of him and might have fought to disturb his position. But the Supreme Personality of Godhead assured Bali Mahārāja that he would always remain under the Lord's protection (*mad-āśrayaḥ*).

TEXT 32

तावत् सुतलमध्यास्तां विश्वकर्मविनिर्मितम् ।
यदाधयो व्याधयश्च क्लमस्तन्द्रा पराभवः ।
नोपसर्गा निवसतां संभवन्ति ममेक्षया ॥ ३२ ॥

tāvat sutalam adhyāstāṁ
viśvakarma-vinirmitam

yad ādhayo vyādhayaś ca
klamas tandrā parābhavaḥ
nopasargā nivasatāṁ
sambhavanti mamekṣayā

tāvat—as long as you are not in the post of Lord Indra; *sutalam*—in the planet known as Sutala; *adhyāstām*—go live there and occupy the place; *viśvakarma-vinirmitam*—which is especially created by Viśvakarmā; *yat*—wherein; *ādhayaḥ*—miseries pertaining to the mind; *vyādhayaḥ*—miseries pertaining to the body; *ca*—also; *klamaḥ*—fatigue; *tandrā*—dizziness or laziness; *parābhavaḥ*—becoming defeated; *na*—not; *upasargāḥ*—symptoms of other disturbances; *nivasatām*—of those who live there; *sambhavanti*—become possible; *mama*—of Me; *īkṣayā*—by the special vigilance.

TRANSLATION

Until Bali Mahārāja achieves the position of King of heaven, he shall live on the planet Sutala, which was made by Viśvakarmā according to My order. Because it is especially protected by Me, it is free from mental and bodily miseries, fatigue, dizziness, defeat and all other disturbances. Bali Mahārāja, you may now go live there peacefully.

PURPORT

Viśvakarmā is the engineer or architect for the palatial buildings in the heavenly planets. Therefore, since he was engaged to construct the residential quarters of Bali Mahārāja, the buildings and palaces on the planet Sutala must at least equal those on the heavenly planets. A further advantage of this place designed for Bali Mahārāja was that he would not be disturbed by any outward calamity. Moreover, he would not be disturbed by mental or bodily miseries. These are all extraordinary features of the planet Sutala, where Bali Mahārāja would live.

In the Vedic literatures we find descriptions of many different planets where there are many, many palaces, hundreds and thousands of times better than those of which we have experience on this planet earth. When we speak of palaces, this naturally includes the idea of great cities and towns. Unfortunately, when modern scientists try to explore other planets they see nothing but rocks and sand. Of course, they may go on their frivolous excursions, but the students of the Vedic literature will never believe them or give them any credit for exploring other planets.

TEXT 33

इन्द्रसेन महाराज याहि भो भद्रमस्तु ते ।
सुतलं स्वर्गिभिः प्रार्थ्यं ज्ञातिभिः परिवारितः ॥ ३३ ॥

indrasena mahārāja
yāhi bho bhadram astu te
sutalaṁ svargibhiḥ prārthyaṁ
jñātibhiḥ parivāritaḥ

indrasena—O Mahārāja Bali; *mahārāja*—O King; *yāhi*—better go; *bhoḥ*—O King; *bhadram*—all auspiciousness; *astu*—let there be; *te*—unto you; *sutalam*—in the planet known as Sutala; *svargibhiḥ*—by the demigods; *prārthyam*—desirable; *jñātibhiḥ*—by your family members; *parivāritaḥ*—surrounded.

TRANSLATION

O Bali Mahārāja [Indrasena], now you may go to the planet Sutala, which is desired even by the demigods. Live there peacefully, surrounded by your friends and relatives. All good fortune unto you.

PURPORT

Bali Mahārāja was transferred from the heavenly planet to the planet Sutala, which is hundreds of times better than heaven, as indicated by the words *svargibhiḥ prārthyam.* When the Supreme Personality of Godhead deprives His devotee of material opulences, this does not mean that the Lord puts him into poverty; rather, the Lord promotes him to a higher position. The Supreme Personality of Godhead did not ask Bali Mahārāja to separate from his family; instead, the Lord allowed him to stay with his family members (*jñātibhiḥ parivāritaḥ*).

TEXT 34

न त्वामभिभविष्यन्ति लोकेशाः किमुतापरे ।
त्वच्छासनातिगान् दैत्यांश्चक्रं मे सूदयिष्यति ॥ ३४ ॥

na tvām abhibhaviṣyanti
lokeśāḥ kim utāpare
tvac-chāsanātigān daityāṁś
cakraṁ me sūdayiṣyati

na—not; *tvām*—unto you; *abhibhaviṣyanti*—will be able to conquer; *loka-īśāḥ*—the predominating deities of the various planets; *kim uta apare*—what to speak of ordinary people; *tvat-śāsana-atigān*—who transgress your rulings; *daityān*—such demons; *cakram*—disc; *me*—My; *sūdayiṣyati*—will kill.

TRANSLATION

On the planet Sutala, not even the predominating deities of other planets, what to speak of ordinary people, will be able to conquer you. As far as the demons are concerned, if they transgress your rule, My disc will kill them.

TEXT 35

रक्षिष्ये सर्वतोऽहं त्वां सानुगं सपरिच्छदम्।
सदा सन्निहितं वीर तत्र मां द्रक्ष्यते भवान् ॥ ३५ ॥

rakṣiṣye sarvato 'haṁ tvāṁ
sānugaṁ saparicchadam
sadā sannihitaṁ vīra
tatra māṁ drakṣyate bhavān

rakṣiṣye—shall protect; *sarvataḥ*—in all respects; *aham*—I; *tvām*—you; *sa-anugam*—with your associates; *sa-paricchadam*—with your paraphernalia; *sadā*—always; *sannihitam*—situated nearby; *vīra*—O great hero; *tatra*—there, in your place; *mām*—Me; *drakṣyate*—will be able to see; *bhavān*—you.

TRANSLATION

O great hero, I shall always be with you and give you protection in all respects along with your associates and paraphernalia. Moreover, you will always be able to see Me there.

TEXT 36

तत्र दानवदैत्यानां सङ्गात् ते भाव आसुरः ।
दृष्ट्वा मदनुभावं वै सद्यः कुण्ठो विनङ्क्ष्यति ॥ ३६ ॥

tatra dānava-daityānāṁ
saṅgāt te bhāva āsuraḥ

dṛṣṭvā mad-anubhāvaṁ vai
sadyaḥ kuṇṭho vinaṅkṣyati

tatra—in that place; *dānava-daityānām*—of the demons and the Dānavas; *saṅgāt*—because of the association; *te*—your; *bhāvaḥ*—mentality; *āsuraḥ*—demoniac; *dṛṣṭvā*—by observing; *mat-anubhāvam*—My superexcellent power; *vai*—indeed; *sadyaḥ*—immediately; *kuṇṭhaḥ*—anxiety; *vinaṅkṣyati*—will be destroyed.

TRANSLATION

Because there you will see My supreme prowess, your materialistic ideas and anxieties that have arisen from your association with the demons and Dānavas will immediately be vanquished.

PURPORT

The Lord assured Bali Mahārāja of all protection, and finally the Lord assured him of protection from the effects of bad association with the demons. Bali Mahārāja certainly became an exalted devotee, but he was somewhat anxious because his association was not purely devotional. The Supreme Personality of Godhead therefore assured him that his demoniac mentality would be annihilated. In other words, by the association of devotees, the demoniac mentality is vanquished.

satāṁ prasaṅgān mama vīrya-saṁvido
bhavanti hṛt-karṇa-rasāyanāḥ kathāḥ
(*Bhāg.* 3.25.25)

When a demon associates with devotees engaged in glorifying the Supreme Personality of Godhead, he gradually becomes a pure devotee.

Thus end the Bhaktivedanta purports of the Eighth Canto, Twenty-second Chapter, of the Śrīmad-Bhāgavatam, *entitled "Bali Mahārāja Surrenders His Life."*

CHAPTER TWENTY-THREE

The Demigods Regain the Heavenly Planets

This chapter describes how Bali Mahārāja, along with his grandfather Prahlāda Mahārāja, entered the planet Sutala and how the Supreme Personality of Godhead allowed Indra to reenter the heavenly planet.

The great soul Bali Mahārāja experienced that the highest gain in life is to attain devotional service under the shelter of the Lord's lotus feet in full surrender. Being fixed in this conclusion, his heart full of ecstatic devotion and his eyes full of tears, he offered obeisances to the Personality of Godhead and then, with his associates, entered the planet known as Sutala. Thus the Supreme Personality of Godhead satisfied the desire of Aditi and reinstalled Lord Indra. Prahlāda Mahārāja, being aware of Bali's release from arrest, then described the transcendental pastimes of the Supreme Personality of Godhead in this material world. Prahlāda Mahārāja praised the Supreme Lord for creating the material world, for being equal to everyone and for being extremely liberal to the devotees, just like a desire tree. Indeed, Prahlāda Mahārāja said that the Lord is kind not only to His devotees but also to the demons. In this way he described the unlimited causeless mercy of the Supreme Personality of Godhead. Then, with folded hands, he offered his respectful obeisances unto the Lord, and after circumambulating the Lord he also entered the planet Sutala in accordance with the Lord's order. The Lord then ordered Śukrācārya to describe Bali Mahārāja's faults and discrepancies in executing the sacrificial ceremony. Śukrācārya became free from fruitive actions by chanting the holy name of the Lord, and he explained how chanting can diminish all the faults of the conditioned soul. He then completed Bali Mahārāja's sacrificial ceremony. All the great saintly persons accepted Lord Vāmanadeva as the benefactor of Lord Indra because He had returned Indra to his heavenly planet. They accepted the Supreme Personality of Godhead as the maintainer of all the affairs of the universe. Being very happy, Indra, along with his associates, placed Vāmanadeva before him and reentered the heavenly planet in their airplane. Having seen the wonderful activities of Lord Viṣṇu in the sacrificial arena of Bali Mahārāja, all the demigods, saintly persons, Pitās, Bhūtas and Siddhas glorified the Lord again and again. The chapter concludes by saying that the most auspicious function of the conditioned soul is to chant and hear about the glorious activities of Lord Viṣṇu.

TEXT 1

श्रीशुक उवाच

इत्युक्तवन्तं पुरुषं पुरातनं
महानुभावोऽखिलसाधुसंमतः ।
बद्धाञ्जलिर्बाष्पकलाकुलेक्षणो
भक्त्युत्कलो गद्गदया गिराब्रवीत्॥ १ ॥

śrī-śuka uvāca
ity uktavantaṁ puruṣaṁ purātanaṁ
mahānubhāvo 'khila-sādhu-sammataḥ
baddhāñjalir bāṣpa-kalākulekṣaṇo
bhakty-utkalo gadgadayā girābravīt

śrī-śukaḥ uvāca—Śrī Śukadeva Gosvāmī said; *iti*—thus; *uktavantam*—upon the order of the Supreme Personality of Godhead; *puruṣam*—unto the Supreme Personality of Godhead; *purātanam*—the oldest of everyone; *mahā-anubhāvaḥ*—Bali Mahārāja, who was a great and exalted soul; *akhila-sādhu-sammataḥ*—as approved by all saintly persons; *baddha-añjaliḥ*—with folded hands; *bāṣpa-kala-ākula-īkṣaṇaḥ*—whose eyes were filled with tears; *bhakti-utkalaḥ*—full of ecstatic devotion; *gadgadayā*—which were faltering in devotional ecstasy; *girā*—by such words; *abravīt*—said.

TRANSLATION

Śukadeva Gosvāmī said: When the supreme, ancient, eternal Personality of Godhead had thus spoken to Bali Mahārāja, who is universally accepted as a pure devotee of the Lord and therefore a great soul, Bali Mahārāja, his eyes filled with tears, his hands folded and his voice faltering in devotional ecstasy, responded as follows.

TEXT 2

श्रीबलिरुवाच

अहो प्रणामाय कृतः समुद्यमः
प्रपन्नभक्तार्थविधौ समाहितः ।

यल्लोकपालैस्त्वदनुग्रहोऽमरै-
रलब्धपूर्वोऽपसदेऽसुरेऽर्पितः ॥ २ ॥

śrī-balir uvāca
aho praṇāmāya kṛtaḥ samudyamaḥ
prapanna-bhaktārtha-vidhau samāhitaḥ
yal loka-pālais tvad-anugraho 'marair
alabdha-pūrvo 'pasade 'sure 'rpitaḥ

śrī-baliḥ uvāca—Bali Mahārāja said; *aho*—alas; *praṇāmāya*—to offer my respectful obeisances; *kṛtaḥ*—I did; *samudyamaḥ*—only an endeavor; *prapanna-bhakta-artha-vidhau*—in the regulative principles observed by pure devotees; *samāhitaḥ*—is capable; *yat*—that; *loka-pālaiḥ*—by the leaders of various planets; *tvat-anugrahaḥ*—Your causeless mercy; *amaraiḥ*—by the demigods; *alabdha-pūrvaḥ*—not achieved previously; *apasade*—unto a fallen person like me; *asure*—belonging to the *asura* community; *arpitaḥ*—endowed.

TRANSLATION

Bali Mahārāja said: What a wonderful effect there is in even attempting to offer respectful obeisances to You! I merely endeavored to offer You obeisances, but nonetheless the attempt was as successful as those of pure devotees. The causeless mercy You have shown to me, a fallen demon, was never achieved even by the demigods or the leaders of the various planets.

PURPORT

When Vāmanadeva appeared before Bali Mahārāja, Bali Mahārāja immediately wanted to offer Him respectful obeisances, but he was unable to do so because of the presence of Śukrācārya and other demoniac associates. The Lord is so merciful, however, that although Bali Mahārāja did not actually offer obeisances but only endeavored to do so within his mind, the Supreme Personality of Godhead blessed him with more mercy than even the demigods could ever expect. As confirmed in *Bhagavad-gītā* (2.40), *svalpam apy asya dharmasya trāyate mahato bhayāt:* "Even a little advancement on this path can protect one from the most dangerous type of fear." The Supreme Personality of Godhead is known as *bhāva-grāhī janārdana* because He takes only the essence of a devotee's attitude. If a devotee sincerely surrenders, the

Lord, as the Supersoul in everyone's heart, immediately understands this. Thus even though, externally, a devotee may not render full service, if he is internally sincere and serious the Lord welcomes his service nonetheless. Thus the Lord is known as *bhāva-grāhī janārdana* because He takes the essence of one's devotional mentality.

TEXT 3

श्रीशुक उवाच
इत्युक्त्वा हरिमानत्य ब्रह्माणं सभवं ततः ।
विवेश सुतलं प्रीतो बलिर्मुक्तः सहासुरैः ॥ ३ ॥

śrī-śuka uvāca
ity uktvā harim ānatya
brahmāṇaṁ sabhavaṁ tataḥ
viveśa sutalaṁ prīto
balir muktaḥ sahāsuraiḥ

śrī-śukaḥ uvāca—Śrī Śukadeva Gosvāmī said; *iti uktvā*—saying this; *harim*—unto the Supreme Personality of Godhead, Hari; *ānatya*—offering obeisances; *brahmāṇam*—unto Lord Brahmā; *sa-bhavam*—with Lord Śiva; *tataḥ*—thereafter; *viveśa*—he entered; *sutalam*—the planet Sutala; *prītaḥ*—being fully satisfied; *baliḥ*—Bali Mahārāja; *muktaḥ*—thus released; *saha asuraiḥ*—with his *asura* associates.

TRANSLATION

Śukadeva Gosvāmī continued: After speaking in this way, Bali Mahārāja offered his obeisances first to the Supreme Personality of Godhead, Hari, and then to Lord Brahmā and Lord Śiva. Thus he was released from the bondage of the nāga-pāśa [the ropes of Varuṇa], and in full satisfaction he entered the planet known as Sutala.

TEXT 4

एवमिन्द्राय भगवान् प्रत्यानीय त्रिविष्टपम् ।
पूरयित्वादितेः काममशासत् सकलं जगत् ॥ ४ ॥

evam indrāya bhagavān
pratyānīya triviṣṭapam

pūrayitvāditeḥ kāmam
aśāsat sakalaṁ jagat

evam—in this way; *indrāya*—unto King Indra; *bhagavān*—the Supreme Personality of Godhead; *pratyānīya*—giving back; *tri-viṣṭapam*—his supremacy in the heavenly planets; *pūrayitvā*—fulfilling; *aditeḥ*—of Aditi; *kāmam*—the desire; *aśāsat*—ruled; *sakalam*—complete; *jagat*—universe.

TRANSLATION

Thus having delivered the proprietorship of the heavenly planets to Indra and having fulfilled the desire of Aditi, mother of the demigods, the Supreme Personality of Godhead ruled the affairs of the universe.

TEXT 5

लब्धप्रसादं निर्मुक्तं पौत्रं वंशधरं बलिम् ।
निशाम्य भक्तिप्रवणः प्रह्लाद इदमब्रवीत् ॥ ५ ॥

labdha-prasādaṁ nirmuktaṁ
pautraṁ vaṁśa-dharaṁ balim
niśāmya bhakti-pravaṇaḥ
prahrāda idam abravīt

labdha-prasādam—who had achieved the blessings of the Lord; *nirmuktam*—who was released from bondage; *pautram*—his grandson; *vaṁśa-dharam*—the descendant; *balim*—Bali Mahārāja; *niśāmya*—after overhearing; *bhakti-pravaṇaḥ*—in fully ecstatic devotion; *prahrādaḥ*—Prahlāda Mahārāja; *idam*—this; *abravīt*—spoke.

TRANSLATION

When Prahlāda Mahārāja heard how Bali Mahārāja, his grandson and descendant, had been released from bondage and had achieved the benediction of the Lord, he spoke as follows in a tone of greatly ecstatic devotion.

TEXT 6

श्रीप्रह्लाद उवाच
नेमं विरिञ्चो लभते प्रसादं
न श्रीर्न शर्वः किमुतापरेऽन्ये ।

यन्नोऽसुराणामसि दुर्गपालो
विश्वाभिवन्द्यैरभिवन्दिताङ्घ्रिः ॥ ६ ॥

śrī-prahrāda uvāca
nemaṁ viriñco labhate prasādaṁ
na śrīr na śarvaḥ kim utāpare 'nye
yan no 'surāṇām asi durga-pālo
viśvābhivandyair abhivanditāṅghriḥ

śrī-prahrādaḥ uvāca—Prahlāda Mahārāja said; *na*—not; *imam*—this; *viriñcaḥ*—even Lord Brahmā; *labhate*—can achieve; *prasādam*—benediction; *na*—nor; *śrīḥ*—the goddess of fortune; *na*—nor; *śarvaḥ*—Lord Śiva; *kim uta*—what to speak of; *apare anye*—others; *yat*—which benediction; *naḥ*—of us; *asurāṇām*—the demons; *asi*—You have become; *durga-pālaḥ*—the maintainer; *viśva-abhivandyaiḥ*—by personalities like Lord Brahmā and Lord Śiva, who are worshiped all over the universe; *abhivandita-aṅghriḥ*—whose lotus feet are worshiped.

TRANSLATION

Prahlāda Mahārāja said: O Supreme Personality of Godhead, You are universally worshiped; even Lord Brahmā and Lord Śiva worship Your lotus feet. Yet although You are such a great personality, You have kindly promised to protect us, the demons. I think that such kindness has never been achieved even by Lord Brahmā, Lord Śiva or the goddess of fortune, Lakṣmī, what to speak of other demigods or common people.

PURPORT

The word *durga-pāla* is significant. The word *durga* means "that which does not go very easily." Generally *durga* refers to a fort, which one cannot very easily enter. Another meaning of *durga* is "difficulty." Because the Supreme Personality of Godhead promised to protect Bali Mahārāja and his associates from all dangers, He is addressed here as *durga-pāla,* the Lord who gives protection from all miserable conditions.

TEXT 7

यत्पादपद्ममकरन्दनिषेवणेन
ब्रह्मादयः शरणदाश्नुवते विभूतीः ।

कस्माद् वयं कुसृतयः खलयोनयस्ते
दाक्षिण्यदृष्टिपदवीं भवतः प्रणीताः ॥ ७ ॥

yat-pāda-padma-makaranda-niṣevaṇena
brahmādayaḥ śaraṇadāśnuvate vibhūtīḥ
kasmād vayaṁ kusṛtayaḥ khala-yonayas te
dākṣiṇya-dṛṣṭi-padavīṁ bhavataḥ praṇītāḥ

yat—of whom; *pāda-padma*—of the lotus flower of the feet; *makaranda*—of the honey; *niṣevaṇena*—by tasting the sweetness of rendering service; *brahma-ādayaḥ*—great personalities like Lord Brahmā; *śaraṇa-da*—O my Lord, supreme shelter of everyone; *aśnuvate*—enjoy; *vibhūtīḥ*—benedictions given by You; *kasmāt*—how; *vayam*—we; *ku-sṛtayaḥ*—all the rogues and thieves; *khala-yonayaḥ*—born of an envious dynasty, namely that of the demons; *te*—those *asuras; dākṣiṇya-dṛṣṭi-padavīm*—the position bestowed by the merciful glance; *bhavataḥ*—of Your Lordship; *praṇītāḥ*—have achieved.

TRANSLATION

O supreme shelter of everyone, great personalities like Brahmā enjoy their perfection simply by tasting the honey of rendering service at Your lotus feet. But as for us, who are all rogues and debauchees born of an envious family of demons, how have we received Your mercy? It has been possible only because Your mercy is causeless.

TEXT 8

चित्रं तवेहितमहोऽमितयोगमाया-
लीलाविसृष्टभुवनस्य विशारदस्य ।
सर्वात्मनः समदृशोऽविषमः स्वभावो
भक्तप्रियो यदसि कल्पतरुस्वभावः ॥ ८ ॥

citraṁ tavehitam aho 'mita-yogamāyā-
līlā-visṛṣṭa-bhuvanasya viśāradasya
sarvātmanaḥ samadṛśo 'viṣamaḥ svabhāvo
bhakta-priyo yad asi kalpataru-svabhāvaḥ

citram—very wonderful; *tava īhitam*—all Your activities; *aho*—alas; *amita*—unlimited; *yogamāyā*—of Your spiritual potency; *līlā*—by the pastimes; *visṛṣṭa-bhuvanasya*—of Your Lordship, by whom all the universes have been created; *viśāradasya*—of Your Lordship, who are expert in all respects; *sarva-ātmanaḥ*—of Your Lordship, who pervade all; *sama-dṛśaḥ*—and who are equal toward all; *aviṣamaḥ*—without differentiation; *svabhāvaḥ*—that is Your characteristic; *bhakta-priyaḥ*—under the circumstances You become favorable to the devotees; *yat*—because; *asi*—You are; *kalpataru-svabhāvaḥ*—having the characteristic of a desire tree.

TRANSLATION

O my Lord, Your pastimes are all wonderfully performed by Your inconceivable spiritual energy; and by her perverted reflection, the material energy, You have created all the universes. As the Supersoul of all living entities, You are aware of everything, and therefore You are certainly equal toward everyone. Nonetheless, You favor Your devotees. This is not partiality, however, for Your characteristic is just like that of a desire tree, which yields everything according to one's desire.

PURPORT

The Lord says in *Bhagavad-gītā* (9.29):

samo 'haṁ sarva-bhūteṣu
na me dveṣyo 'sti na priyaḥ
ye bhajanti tu māṁ bhaktyā
mayi te teṣu cāpy aham

"I envy no one, nor am I partial to anyone. I am equal to all. But whoever renders service unto Me in devotion is a friend, is in Me, and I am also a friend to him." The Supreme Personality of Godhead is certainly equal toward all living entities, but a devotee who fully surrenders at the lotus feet of the Lord is different from a nondevotee. In other words, everyone can take shelter at the lotus feet of the Lord to enjoy equal benedictions from the Lord, but nondevotees do not do so, and therefore they suffer the consequences created by the material energy. We can understand this fact by a simple example. The king or government is equal to all citizens. Therefore, if a citizen capable of receiving special favors from the government is offered such favors, this does not mean that the government is partial. One who knows how to receive favors from the authority can receive them, but one who does not neglects these favors and does not receive them. There are two classes of men—the demons and the demigods. The demigods are fully aware of the Supreme Lord's position, and therefore they are obedient to Him, but even if demons know about the supremacy of the Lord they purposely defy His authority. Therefore, the Lord makes distinctions according to the mentality of the living being, but otherwise He is equal to everyone. Like a desire tree, the Lord fulfills the desires of one who takes shelter of Him, but one who does not take such shelter is distinct from the surrendered soul. One who takes shelter at the lotus feet of the Lord is favored by the Lord, regardless of whether such a person is a demon or a demigod.

TEXT 9

श्रीभगवानुवाच
वत्स प्रह्लाद भद्रं ते प्रयाहि सुतलालयम् ।
मोदमानः स्वपौत्रेण ज्ञातीनां सुखमावह ॥ ९ ॥

śrī-bhagavān uvāca
vatsa prahrāda bhadraṁ te
prayāhi sutalālayam
modamānaḥ sva-pautreṇa
jñātīnāṁ sukham āvaha

śrī-bhagavān uvāca—the Personality of Godhead said; *vatsa*—O My dear son; *prahrāda*—O Prahlāda Mahārāja; *bhadram te*—all auspiciousness unto you; *prayāhi*—please go; *sutala-ālayam*—to the place known as Sutala; *modamānaḥ*—in a spirit of jubilation; *sva-pautreṇa*—with your grandson (Bali Mahārāja); *jñātīnām*—of your relatives and friends; *sukham*—happiness; *āvaha*—just enjoy.

TRANSLATION

The Supreme Personality of Godhead said: My dear son Prahlāda, all good fortune unto you. For the time being, please go to the place known as Sutala and there enjoy happiness with your grandson and your other relatives and friends.

TEXT 10

नित्यं द्रष्टासि मां तत्र गदापाणिमवस्थितम् ।
मद्दर्शनमहाह्लादध्वस्तकर्मनिबन्धनः ॥ १० ॥

nityaṁ draṣṭāsi māṁ tatra
gadā-pāṇim avasthitam
mad-darśana-mahāhlāda-
dhvasta-karma-nibandhanaḥ

nityam—constantly; *draṣṭā*—the seer; *asi*—you shall be; *mām*—unto Me; *tatra*—there (in Sutalaloka); *gadā-pāṇim*—with a club in My hand; *avasthitam*—situated there; *mat-darśana*—by seeing Me in that form; *mahā-āhlāda*—by the great transcendental bliss; *dhvasta*—having been vanquished; *karma-nibandhanaḥ*—the bondage of fruitive activities.

TRANSLATION

The Supreme Personality of Godhead assured Prahlāda Mahārāja: You shall be able to see Me there in My usual feature with conchshell, disc, club and lotus in My hand. Because of your transcendental bliss due to always personally seeing Me, you will have no further bondage to fruitive activities.

PURPORT

Karma-bandha, the bondage of fruitive activities, entails the repetition of birth and death. One performs fruitive activities in such a way that he creates another body for his next life. As long as one is attached to fruitive activities, he must accept another material body. This repeated acceptance of material bodies is called *saṁsāra-bandhana.* To stop this, a devotee is advised to see the Supreme Lord constantly. The *kaniṣṭha-adhikārī,* or neophyte devotee, is therefore advised to visit the temple every day and see the form of the Lord regularly. Thus the neophyte devotee can be freed from the bondage of fruitive activities.

TEXTS 11-12

श्रीशुक उवाच
आज्ञां भगवतो राजन्प्रह्लादो बलिना सह ।
बाढमित्यमलप्रज्ञो मूर्ध्न्याधाय कृताञ्जलिः ॥ ११ ॥
परिक्रम्यादिपुरुषं सर्वासुरचमूपतिः ।
प्रणतस्तदनुज्ञातः प्रविवेश महाबिलम् ॥ १२ ॥

śrī-śuka uvāca
ājñāṁ bhagavato rājan
prahrādo balinā saha
bāḍham ity amala-prajño
mūrdhny ādhāya kṛtāñjaliḥ

parikramyādi-puruṣaṁ
sarvāsura-camūpatiḥ
praṇatas tad-anujñātaḥ
praviveśa mahā-bilam

śrī-śukaḥ uvāca—Śrī Śukadeva Gosvāmī said; *ājñām*—the order; *bhagavataḥ*—of the Supreme Personality of Godhead; *rājan*—O King (Mahārāja Parīkṣit); *prahrādaḥ*—Mahārāja Prahlāda; *balinā saha*—accompanied by Bali Mahārāja; *bāḍham*—yes, sir, what You say is all right; *iti*—thus; *amala-prajñaḥ*—Prahlāda Mahārāja, who had clear intelligence; *mūrdhni*—on his head; *ādhāya*—accepting; *kṛta-añjaliḥ*—with folded hands; *parikramya*—after circumambulating; *ādi-puruṣam*—the supreme original person, Bhagavān; *sarva-asura-camūpatiḥ*—the master of all the chiefs of the demons; *praṇataḥ*—after offering obeisances; *tat-anujñātaḥ*—being permitted by Him (Lord Vāmana); *praviveśa*—entered; *mahā-bilam*—the planet known as Sutala.

TRANSLATION

Śrīla Śukadeva Gosvāmī said: Accompanied by Bali Mahārāja, my dear King Parīkṣit, Prahlāda Mahārāja, the master of all the chiefs of the demons, took the Supreme Lord's order on his head with folded hands. After saying yes to the Lord, circumambulating Him and offering Him respectful obeisances, he entered the lower planetary system known as Sutala.

TEXT 13

अथाहोशनसं राजन् हरिर्नारायणोऽन्तिके ।
आसीनमृत्विजां मध्ये सदसि ब्रह्मवादिनाम् ॥ १३ ॥

athāhośanasaṁ rājan
harir nārāyaṇo 'ntike

āsīnam ṛtvijāṁ madhye
sadasi brahma-vādinām

atha—thereafter; *āha*—said; *uśanasam*—unto Śukrācārya; *rājan*—O King; *hariḥ*—the Supreme Personality of Godhead; *nārāyaṇaḥ*—the Lord; *antike*—nearby; *āsīnam*—who was sitting; *ṛtvijām madhye*—in the group of all the priests; *sadasi*—in the assembly; *brahma-vādinām*—of the followers of Vedic principles.

TRANSLATION

Hari, the Supreme Personality of Godhead, Nārāyaṇa, thereafter addressed Śukrācārya, who was sitting nearby in the midst of the assembly with the priests [brahma, hotā, udgātā and adhvaryu]. O Mahārāja Parīkṣit, these priests were all brahma-vādīs, followers of the Vedic principles for performing sacrifices.

TEXT 14

ब्रह्मन् संतनु शिष्यस्य कर्मच्छिद्रं वितन्वतः ।
यत् तत् कर्मसु वैषम्यं ब्रह्मदृष्टं समं भवेत् ॥ १४ ॥

brahman santanu śiṣyasya
karma-cchidraṁ vitanvataḥ
yat tat karmasu vaiṣamyaṁ
brahma-dṛṣṭaṁ samaṁ bhavet

brahman—O *brāhmaṇa; santanu*—please describe; *śiṣyasya*—of your disciple; *karma-chidram*—the discrepancies in the fruitive activities; *vitanvataḥ*—of he who was performing sacrifices; *yat tat*—that which; *karmasu*—in the fruitive activities; *vaiṣamyam*—discrepancy; *brahma-dṛṣṭam*—when it is judged by the *brāhmaṇas; samam*—equipoised; *bhavet*—it so becomes.

TRANSLATION

O best of the brāhmaṇas, Śukrācārya, please describe the fault or discrepancy in your disciple Bali Mahārāja, who engaged in performing sacrifices. This fault will be nullified when judged in the presence of qualified brāhmaṇas.

PURPORT

When Bali Mahārāja and Prahlāda Mahārāja had departed for the planet Sutala, Lord Viṣṇu asked Śukrācārya what the fault was in Bali Mahārāja for which Śukrācārya had cursed him. It might be argued that since Bali Mahārāja had now left the scene, how could his faults be judged? In reply to this, Lord Viṣṇu informed Śukrācārya that there was no need for Bali Mahārāja's presence, for his faults and discrepancies could be nullified if judged before the *brāhmaṇas.* As will be seen in the next verse, Bali Mahārāja had no faults; Śukrācārya had unnecessarily cursed him. Nonetheless, this was better for Bali Mahārāja. Being cursed by Śukrācārya, Bali Mahārāja was deprived of all his possessions, with the result that the Supreme Personality of Godhead favored him for his strong faith in devotional service. Of course, a devotee is not required to engage in fruitive activities. As stated in the *śāstra, sarvārhaṇam acyutejyā* (*Bhāg.* 4.31.14). By worshiping Acyuta, the Supreme Personality of Godhead, one satisfies everyone. Because Bali Mahārāja had satisfied the Supreme Personality of Godhead, there were no discrepancies in his performance of sacrifices.

TEXT 15

श्रीशुक्र उवाच
कुतस्तत्कर्मवैषम्यं यस्य कर्मेश्वरो भवान् ।
यज्ञेशो यज्ञपुरुषः सर्वभावेन पूजितः ॥ १५ ॥

śrī-śukra uvāca
kutas tat-karma-vaiṣamyaṁ
yasya karmeśvaro bhavān
yajñeśo yajña-puruṣaḥ
sarva-bhāvena pūjitaḥ

śrī-śukraḥ uvāca—Śrī Śukrācārya said; *kutaḥ*—where is that; *tat*—of him (Bali Mahārāja); *karma-vaiṣamyam*—discrepancy in discharging fruitive activities; *yasya*—of whom (Bali Mahārāja); *karma-īśvaraḥ*—the master of all fruitive activities; *bhavān*—Your Lordship; *yajña-īśaḥ*—You are the enjoyer of all sacrifices; *yajña-puruṣaḥ*—You are the person for whose pleasure all sacrifices are offered; *sarva-bhāvena*—in all respects; *pūjitaḥ*—having worshiped.

TRANSLATION

Śukrācārya said: My Lord, You are the enjoyer and lawgiver in all performances of sacrifice, and You are the yajña-puruṣa, the person to whom all sacrifices are offered. If one has fully satisfied You, where is the chance of discrepancies or faults in his performances of sacrifice?

PURPORT

In *Bhagavad-gītā* (5.29) the Lord says, *bhoktāraṁ yajña-tapasāṁ sarva-loka-maheśvaram:* the Lord, the supreme proprietor, is the actual person to be satisfied by the performance of *yajñas.* The *Viṣṇu Purāṇa* (3.8.9) says:

varṇāśramācāravatā
puruṣeṇa paraḥ pumān
viṣṇur ārādhyate panthā
nanyat tat-toṣa-kāraṇam

All the Vedic ritualistic sacrifices are performed for the purpose of satisfying Lord Viṣṇu, the *yajña-puruṣa.* The divisions of society—*brāhmaṇa, kṣatriya, vaiśya, śūdra, brahmacarya, gṛhastha, vānaprastha* and *sannyāsa*—are all meant to satisfy the Supreme Lord, Viṣṇu. To act according to this principle of the *varṇāśrama* institution is called *varṇāśramācaraṇa.* In *Śrīmad-Bhāgavatam* (1.2.13), Sūta Gosvāmī says:

ataḥ pumbhir dvija-śreṣṭhā
varṇāśrama-vibhāgaśaḥ
svanuṣṭhitasya dharmasya
saṁsiddhir hari-toṣaṇam

"O best among the twice-born, it is therefore concluded that the highest perfection one can achieve by discharging his prescribed duties according to caste divisions and orders of life is to please the Personality of Godhead." Everything is meant to satisfy the Supreme Personality of Godhead. Therefore, since Bali Mahārāja had satisfied the Lord, he had no faults, and Śukrācārya admitted that cursing him was not good.

TEXT 16

मन्त्रतस्तन्त्रतश्छिद्रं देशकालार्हवस्तुतः ।
सर्वं करोति निश्छिद्रमनुसंकीर्तनं तव ॥ १६ ॥

mantratas tantrataś chidraṁ
deśa-kālārha-vastutaḥ
sarvaṁ karoti niśchidram
anusaṅkīrtanaṁ tava

mantrataḥ—in pronouncing the Vedic *mantras* improperly; *tantrataḥ*—in insufficient knowledge for following regulative principles; *chidram*—discrepancy; *deśa*—in the matter of country; *kāla*—and time; *arha*—and recipient; *vastutaḥ*—and paraphernalia; *sarvam*—all these; *karoti*—makes; *niśchidram*—without discrepancy; *anusaṅkīrtanam*—constantly chanting the holy name; *tava*—of Your Lordship.

TRANSLATION

There may be discrepancies in pronouncing the mantras and observing the regulative principles, and, moreover, there may be discrepancies in regard to time, place, person and paraphernalia. But when Your Lordship's holy name is chanted, everything becomes faultless.

PURPORT

Śrī Caitanya Mahāprabhu has recommended:

harer nāma harer nāma
harer nāmaiva kevalam
kalau nāsty eva nāsty eva
nāsty eva gatir anyathā

"In this age of quarrel and hypocrisy the only means of deliverance is chanting the holy name of the Lord. There is no other way. There is no other way. There is no other way." (*Bṛhan-nāradīya Purāṇa* 38.126) In this age of Kali, it is extremely difficult to perform Vedic ritualistic ceremonies or sacrifices perfectly. Hardly anyone can chant the Vedic *mantras* with perfect pronunciation or accumulate the paraphernalia for Vedic performances. Therefore the sacrifice recommended in this age is *saṅkīrtana,* constant chanting of the holy name of the Lord. *Yajñaiḥ saṅkīrtana-prāyair yajanti hi sumedhasaḥ* (*Bhāg.* 11.5.29). Instead of wasting time performing Vedic sacrifices, those who are intelligent, those who possess good brain substance, should take to the chanting of the Lord's holy name and thus perform sacrifice perfectly. I have seen that many religious leaders are addicted to performing *yajñas* and spending hundreds and thousands of rupees for imperfect sacrificial performances. This is a lesson for those who unnecessarily execute such imperfect sacrifices. We should take the advice of Śrī Caitanya Mahāprabhu (*yajñaiḥ saṅkīrtana-prāyair yajanti hi sumedhasaḥ*). Although Śukrācārya was a strict *brāhmaṇa* addicted to ritualistic activities, he also admitted, *niśchidram anusaṅkīrtanaṁ tava:* "My Lord, constant chanting of the holy name of Your Lordship makes everything perfect." In Kali-yuga the Vedic ritualistic ceremonies cannot be performed as perfectly as before. Therefore Śrīla Jīva Gosvāmī has recommended that although one should take care to follow all the principles in every kind of spiritual activity, especially in worship of the Deity, there is still a chance of discrepancies, and one should compensate for this by chanting the holy name of the Supreme Personality of Godhead. In our Kṛṣṇa consciousness movement we therefore give special stress to the chanting of the Hare Kṛṣṇa *mantra* in all activities.

TEXT 17

तथापि वदतो भूमन् करिष्याम्यनुशासनम् ।
एतच्छ्रेयः परं पुंसां यत् तवाज्ञानुपालनम् ॥ १७ ॥

tathāpi vadato bhūman
kariṣyāmy anuśāsanam
etac chreyaḥ paraṁ puṁsāṁ
yat tavājñānupālanam

tathāpi—although there was no fault on the part of Bali Mahārāja; *vadataḥ*—because of your order; *bhūman*—O Supreme; *kariṣyāmi*—I must execute; *anuśāsanam*—because it is Your order; *etat*—this is; *śreyaḥ*—that which is the most auspicious; *param*—supreme; *puṁsām*—of all persons; *yat*—because; *tava ājñā-anupālanam*—to obey Your order.

TRANSLATION

Lord Viṣṇu, I must nonetheless act in obedience to Your order because obeying Your order is most auspicious and is the first duty of everyone.

TEXT 18

श्रीशुक उवाच
प्रतिनन्द्य हरेराज्ञामुशना भगवानिति ।
यज्ञच्छिद्रं समाधत्त बलेर्विप्रर्षिभिः सह ॥ १८ ॥

śrī-śuka uvāca
pratinandya harer ājñām
uśanā bhagavān iti
yajña-cchidraṁ samādhatta
baler viprarṣibhiḥ saha

śrī-śukaḥ uvāca—Śrī Śukadeva Gosvāmī said; *pratinandya*—offering all obeisances; *hareḥ*—of the Personality of Godhead; *ājñām*—the order; *uśanāḥ*—Śukrācārya; *bhagavān*—the most powerful; *iti*—thus; *yajña-chidram*—discrepancies in the performance of sacrifices; *samādhatta*—made it a point to fulfill; *baleḥ*—of Bali Mahārāja; *vipra-ṛṣibhiḥ*—the best *brāhmaṇas*; *saha*—along with.

TRANSLATION

Śukadeva Gosvāmī continued: In this way, the most powerful Śukrācārya accepted the order of the Supreme Personality of Godhead with full respect. Along with the best brāhmaṇas, he began to compensate for the discrepancies in the sacrifices performed by Bali Mahārāja.

TEXT 19

एवं बलेर्महीं राजन् भिक्षित्वा वामनो हरिः ।
ददौ भ्रात्रे महेन्द्राय त्रिदिवं यत् परैर्हृतम् ॥ १९ ॥

evaṁ baler mahīṁ rājan
bhikṣitvā vāmano hariḥ
dadau bhrātre mahendrāya
tridivaṁ yat parair hṛtam

evam—thus; *baleḥ*—from Bali Mahārāja; *mahīm*—the land; *rājan*—O King Parīkṣit; *bhikṣitvā*—after begging; *vāmanaḥ*—His Lordship Vāmana; *hariḥ*—the Supreme Personality of Godhead; *dadau*—delivered; *bhrātre*—unto His brother; *mahā-indrāya*—Indra, the King of heaven; *tridivam*—the planetary system of the demigods; *yat*—which; *paraiḥ*—by others; *hṛtam*—was taken.

TRANSLATION

O King Parīkṣit, thus having taken all the land of Bali Mahārāja by begging, the Supreme Personality of Godhead, Lord Vāmanadeva, delivered to His brother Indra all the land taken away by Indra's enemy.

TEXTS 20-21

प्रजापतिपतिर्ब्रह्मा देवर्षिपितृभूमिपैः ।
दक्षभृग्वङ्गिरोमुख्यैः कुमारेण भवेन च ॥ २० ॥
कश्यपस्यादितेः प्रीत्यै सर्वभूतभवाय च ।
लोकानां लोकपालानामकरोद् वामनं पतिम् ॥ २१ ॥

prajāpati-patir brahmā
devarṣi-pitṛ-bhūmipaiḥ
dakṣa-bhṛgv-aṅgiro-mukhyaiḥ
kumāreṇa bhavena ca

kaśyapasyāditeḥ prītyai
sarva-bhūta-bhavāya ca
lokānāṁ loka-pālānām
akarod vāmanaṁ patim

prajāpati-patiḥ—the master of all Prajāpatis; *brahmā*—Lord Brahmā; *deva*—with the demigods; *ṛṣi*—with the great saintly persons; *pitṛ*—with the inhabitants of Pitṛloka; *bhūmipaiḥ*—with the Manus; *dakṣa*—with Dakṣa; *bhṛgu*—with Bhṛgu Muni; *aṅgiraḥ*—with Aṅgirā Muni; *mukhyaiḥ*—with all the chiefs of the various planetary systems; *kumāreṇa*—with Kārttikeya; *bhavena*—with Lord Śiva; *ca*—also; *kaśyapasya*—of Kaśyapa Muni; *aditeḥ*—of Aditi; *prītyai*—f or the pleasure; *sarva-bhūta-bhavāya*—for the auspiciousness of all living entities; *ca*—also; *lokānām*—of all planetary systems; *loka-pālānām*—of the predominating persons in all planets; *akarot*—made; *vāmanam*—Lord Vāmana; *patim*—the supreme leader.

TRANSLATION

Lord Brahmā [the master of King Dakṣa and all other Prajāpatis], accompanied by all the demigods, the great saintly persons, the inhabitants of Pitṛloka, the Manus, the munis, and such leaders as Dakṣa, Bhṛgu and Aṅgirā, as well as Kārttikeya and Lord Śiva, accepted Lord Vāmanadeva as the protector of everyone. He did this for the pleasure of Kaśyapa Muni and his wife Aditi and for the welfare of all the inhabitants of the universe, including their various leaders.

TEXTS 22-23

वेदानां सर्वदेवानां धर्मस्य यशसः श्रियः ।
मङ्गलानां व्रतानां च कल्पं स्वर्गापवर्गयोः ॥ २२ ॥
उपेन्द्रं कल्पयांचक्रे पतिं सर्वविभूतये ।
तदा सर्वाणि भूतानि भृशं मुमुदिरे नृप ॥ २३ ॥

vedānāṁ sarva-devānāṁ
dharmasya yaśasaḥ śriyaḥ
maṅgalānāṁ vratānāṁ ca
kalpaṁ svargāpavargayoḥ

upendraṁ kalpayāṁ cakre
patiṁ sarva-vibhūtaye
tadā sarvāṇi bhūtāni
bhṛśaṁ mumudire nṛpa

vedānām—(for the protection) of all the *Vedas; sarva-devānām*—of all the demigods; *dharmasya*—of all principles of religion; *yaśasaḥ*—of all fame; *śriyaḥ*—of all opulences; *maṅgalānām*—of all auspiciousness; *vratānām ca*—and of all vows; *kalpam*—the most expert; *svarga-apavargayoḥ*—of elevation to the heavenly planets or liberation from material bondage; *upendram*—Lord Vāmanadeva; *kalpayām cakre*—they made it the plan; *patim*—the master; *sarva-vibhūtaye*—for all purposes; *tadā*—at that time; *sarvāṇi*—all; *bhūtāni*—living entities; *bhṛśam*—very much; *mumudire*—became happy; *nṛpa*—O King.

TRANSLATION

O King Parīkṣit, Indra was considered the King of all the universe, but the demigods, headed by Lord Brahmā, wanted Upendra, Lord Vāmanadeva, as the protector of the Vedas, the principles of religion, fame, opulence, auspiciousness, vows, elevation to the higher planetary system, and liberation. Thus they accepted Upendra, Lord Vāmanadeva, as the supreme master of everything. This decision made all living entities extremely happy.

TEXT 24

ततस्त्विन्द्रः पुरस्कृत्य देवयानेन वामनम् ।
लोकपालैर्दिवं निन्ये ब्रह्मणा चानुमोदितः ॥ २४ ॥

tatas tv indraḥ puraskṛtya
deva-yānena vāmanam
loka-pālair divaṁ ninye
brahmaṇā cānumoditaḥ

tataḥ—thereafter; *tu*—but; *indraḥ*—the King of heaven; *puraskṛtya*—keeping forward; *deva-yānena*—by an airplane used by the demigods; *vāmanam*—Lord Vāmana; *loka-pālaiḥ*—with the chiefs of all other planets; *divam*—to the heavenly planets; *ninye*—brought; *brahmaṇā*—by Lord Brahmā; *ca*—also; *anumoditaḥ*—being approved.

TRANSLATION

Thereafter, along with all the leaders of the heavenly planets, Indra, the King of heaven, placed Lord Vāmanadeva before him and, with the approval of Lord Brahmā, brought Him to the heavenly planet in a celestial airplane.

TEXT 25

प्राप्य त्रिभुवनं चेन्द्र उपेन्द्रभुजपालितः ।
श्रिया परमया जुष्टो मुमुदे गतसाध्वसः ॥ २५ ॥

prāpya tri-bhuvanaṁ cendra
upendra-bhuja-pālitaḥ
śriyā paramayā juṣṭo
mumude gata-sādhvasaḥ

prāpya—after obtaining; *tri-bhuvanam*—the three worlds; *ca*—also; *indraḥ*—the King of heaven; *upendra-bhuja-pālitaḥ*—being protected by the arms of Vāmanadeva, Upendra; *śriyā*—by opulence; *paramayā*—by supreme; *juṣṭaḥ*—thus being served; *mumude*—enjoyed; *gata-sādhvasaḥ*—without fear of the demons.

TRANSLATION

Indra, King of heaven, being protected by the arms of Vāmanadeva, the Supreme Personality of Godhead, thus regained his rule of the three worlds and was reinstated in his own position, supremely opulent, fearless and fully satisfied.

TEXTS 26-27

ब्रह्मा शर्वः कुमारश्च भृग्वाद्या मुनयो नृप ।
पितरः सर्वभूतानि सिद्धा वैमानिकाश्च ये ॥ २६ ॥
सुमहत् कर्म तद् विष्णोर्गायन्तः परमद्भुतम् ।
धिष्ण्यानि स्वानि ते जग्मुरदितिं च शशंसिरे ॥ २७ ॥

brahmā śarvaḥ kumāraś ca
bhṛgv-ādyā munayo nṛpa
pitaraḥ sarva-bhūtāni
siddhā vaimānikāś ca ye

sumahat karma tad viṣṇor
gāyantaḥ param adbhutam
dhiṣṇyāni svāni te jagmur
aditiṁ ca śaśaṁsire

brahmā—Lord Brahmā; *śarvaḥ*—Lord Śiva; *kumāraḥ ca*—also Lord Kārttikeya; *bhṛgu-ādyāḥ*—headed by Bhṛgu Muni, one of the seven *ṛṣis; munayaḥ*—the saintly persons; *nṛpa*—O King; *pitaraḥ*—the inhabitants of Pitṛloka; *sarva-bhūtāni*—other living entities; *siddhāḥ*—the residents of Siddhaloka; *vaimānikāḥ ca*—human beings who can travel everywhere in outer space by airplane; *ye*—such persons; *sumahat*—highly praiseworthy; *karma*—activities; *tat*—all those (activities); *viṣṇoḥ*—done by Lord Viṣṇu; *gāyantaḥ*—glorifying; *param adbhutam*—uncommon and wonderful; *dhiṣṇyāni*—to their respective planets; *svāni*—own; *te*—all of them; *jagmuḥ*—departed; *aditim ca*—as well as Aditi; *śaśaṁsire*—praised all these activities of the Lord.

TRANSLATION

Lord Brahmā, Lord Śiva, Lord Kārttikeya, the great sage Bhṛgu, other saintly persons, the inhabitants of Pitṛloka and all other living entities present, including the inhabitants of Siddhaloka and living entities who travel in outer space by airplane, all glorified the uncommon activities of Lord Vāmanadeva. O King, while chanting about and glorifying the Lord, they returned to their respective heavenly planets. They also praised the position of Aditi.

TEXT 28

सर्वमेतन्मयाख्यातं भवतः कुलनन्दन ।
उरुक्रमस्य चरितं श्रोतॄणामघमोचनम् ॥ २८ ॥

sarvam etan mayākhyātaṁ
bhavataḥ kula-nandana
urukramasya caritaṁ
śrotṝṇām agha-mocanam

sarvam—all; *etat*—these incidents; *mayā*—by me; *ākhyātam*—have been described; *bhavataḥ*—of you; *kula-nandana*—O Mahārāja Parīkṣit, the pleasure of your dynasty; *urukramasya*—of the Supreme Personality of Godhead; *caritam*—activities; *śrotṝṇām*—of the audience; *agha-mocanam*—such hearing of the Lord's activities certainly vanquishes the results of sinful activities.

TRANSLATION

O Mahārāja Parīkṣit, pleasure of your dynasty, I have now described to you everything about the wonderful activities of the Supreme Personality of Godhead Vāmanadeva. Those who hear about this are certainly freed from all the results of sinful activities.

TEXT 29

पारं महिम्न उरुविक्रमतो गृणानो
यः पार्थिवानि विममे स रजांसि मर्त्यः ।
किं जायमान उत जात उपैति मर्त्य
इत्याह मन्त्रदृगृषिः पुरुषस्य यस्य ॥ २९ ॥

pāraṁ mahimna uruvikramato gṛṇāno
yaḥ pārthivāni vimame sa rajāṁsi martyaḥ
kim jāyamāna uta jāta upaiti martya
ity āha mantra-dṛg ṛṣiḥ puruṣasya yasya

pāram—the measurement; *mahimnaḥ*—of the glories; *uruvikramataḥ*—of the Supreme Personality of Godhead, who acts wonderfully; *gṛṇānaḥ*—can count; *yaḥ*—a person who; *pārthivāni*—of the whole planet earth; *vimame*—can count; *saḥ*—he; *rajāṁsi*—the atoms; *martyaḥ*—a human being who is subject to death; *kim*—what; *jāyamānaḥ*—one who will take birth in the future; *uta*—either; *jātaḥ*—one who is already born; *upaiti*—can do; *martyaḥ*—a person subject to death; *iti*—thus; *āha*—said; *mantra-dṛk*—who could foresee the Vedic *mantras; ṛṣiḥ*—the great saintly Vasiṣṭha Muni; *puruṣasya*—of the supreme person; *yasya*—of whom.

TRANSLATION

One who is subject to death cannot measure the glories of the Supreme Personality of Godhead, Trivikrama, Lord Viṣṇu, any more than he can count the number of atoms on the entire planet earth. No one, whether born already or destined to take birth, is able to do this. This has been sung by the great sage Vasiṣṭha.

PURPORT

Vasiṣṭha Muni has given a *mantra* about Lord Viṣṇu: *na te viṣṇor jāyamāno na jāto mahimnaḥ pāram anantam āpa.* No one can estimate the extent of the uncommonly glorious activities of Lord Viṣṇu. Unfortunately, there are so-called scientists who are subject to death at every moment but are trying to understand by speculation the wonderful creation of the cosmos. This is a foolish attempt. Long, long ago, Vasiṣṭha Muni said that no one in the past could measure the glories of the Lord and that no one can do so in the future. One must simply be satisfied with seeing the glorious activities of the Supreme Lord's creation. The Lord therefore says in *Bhagavad-gītā* (10.42), *viṣṭabhyāham idaṁ kṛtsnam ekāṁśena sthito jagat:* "With a single fragment of Myself, I pervade and support this entire universe." The material world consists of innumerable universes, each one full of innumerable planets, which are all considered to be products of the Supreme Personality of Godhead's material energy. Yet this is only one fourth of God's creation. The other three fourths of creation constitute the spiritual world. Among the innumerable planets in only one universe, the so-called scientists cannot understand even the moon and Mars, but they try to defy the creation of the Supreme Lord and His uncommon energy. Such men have been described as crazy. *Nūnaṁ pramattaḥ kurute vikarma* (*Bhāg.* 5.5.4). Such crazy men unnecessarily waste time, energy and money in attempting to defy the glorious activities of Urukrama, the Supreme Personality of Godhead.

TEXT 30

य इदं देवदेवस्य हरेरद्भुतकर्मणः ।
अवतारानुचरितं शृण्वन् याति परां गतिम् ॥ ३० ॥

ya idaṁ deva-devasya
harer adbhuta-karmaṇaḥ
avatārānucaritaṁ
śṛṇvan yāti parāṁ gatim

yaḥ—anyone who; *idam*—this; *deva-devasya*—of the Supreme Personality of Godhead, who is worshiped by the demigods; *hareḥ*—of Lord Kṛṣṇa, Hari; *adbhuta-karmaṇaḥ*—whose activities are all wonderful; *avatāra-anucaritam*—activities performed in His different incarnations; *śṛṇvan*—if one continues to hear; *yāti*—he goes; *parām gatim*—to the supreme perfection, back home, back to Godhead.

TRANSLATION

If one hears about the uncommon activities of the Supreme Personality of Godhead in His various incarnations, he is certainly elevated to the higher planetary system or even brought back home, back to Godhead.

TEXT 31

क्रियमाणे कर्मणीदं दैवे पित्र्येऽथ मानुषे।
यत्र यत्रानुकीर्त्येत तत् तेषां सुकृतं विदुः ॥ ३१ ॥

kriyamāṇe karmaṇīdaṁ
daive pitrye 'tha mānuṣe
yatra yatrānukīrtyeta
tat teṣāṁ sukṛtaṁ viduḥ

kriyamāṇe—upon the performance; *karmaṇi*—of a ritualistic ceremony; *idam*—this description of the characteristics of Vāmanadeva; *daive*—to please the demigods; *pitrye*—or to please the forefathers, as in a *śrāddha* ceremony; *atha*—either; *mānuṣe*—for the pleasure of human society, as in marriages; *yatra*—wherever; *yatra*—whenever; *anukīrtyeta*—is described; *tat*—that; *teṣām*—for them; *sukṛtam*—auspicious; *viduḥ*—everyone should understand.

TRANSLATION

Whenever the activities of Vāmanadeva are described in the course of a ritualistic ceremony, whether the ceremony be performed to please the demigods, to please one's forefathers in Pitṛloka, or to celebrate a social

event like a marriage, that ceremony should be understood to be extremely auspicious.

PURPORT

There are three kinds of ceremonies—specifically, ceremonies to please the Supreme Personality of Godhead or the demigods, those performed for social celebrations like marriages and birthdays, and those meant to please the forefathers, like the *śrāddha* ceremony. In all these ceremonies, large amounts of money are spent for various activities, but here it is suggested that if along with this there is recitation of the wonderful activities of Vāmanadeva, certainly the ceremony will be carried out successfully and will be free of all discrepancies.

Thus end the Bhaktivedanta purports of the Eighth Canto, Twenty-third Chapter, of the Śrīmad-Bhāgavatam, *entitled "The Demigods Regain the Heavenly planets."*

CHAPTER TWENTY-FOUR

Matsya, the Lord's Fish Incarnation

This chapter describes the Supreme Personality of Godhead's incarnation as a fish, and it also describes the saving of Mahārāja Satyavrata from an inundation.

The Supreme Personality of Godhead expands Himself by *svāṁśa* (His personal expansions) and *vibhinnāṁśa* (His expansions as the living entities). As stated in *Bhagavad-gītā* (*4.8*), *paritrāṇāya sādhūnāṁ vināśāya ca duṣkṛtām:* the Supreme Personality of Godhead appears on this planet for the protection of the *sādhus,* or devotees, and for the destruction of the miscreants, or nondevotees. He especially descends to give protection to the cows, the *brāhmaṇas,* the demigods, the devotees and the Vedic system of religion. Thus He appears in various forms—sometimes as a fish, sometimes a boar, sometimes Nṛsiṁhadeva, sometimes Vāmanadeva and so on—but in any form or incarnation, although He comes within the atmosphere of the material modes of nature, He is unaffected. This is a sign of His supreme controlling power. Although He comes within the material atmosphere, *māyā* cannot touch Him. Therefore, no material qualities can be attributed to Him in any degree.

Once, at the end of the previous *kalpa,* a demon named Hayagrīva wanted to take the Vedic knowledge away from Lord Brahmā at the time of annihilation. Therefore the Supreme Personality of Godhead took the incarnation of a fish at the beginning of the period of Svāyambhuva Manu and saved the *Vedas.* During the reign of Cākṣuṣa Manu there was a king named Satyavrata, who was a great pious ruler. To save him, the Lord appeared as the fish incarnation for a second time. King Satyavrata later became the son of the sun-god and was known as Śrāddhadeva. He was established as Manu by the Supreme Personality of Godhead.

To receive the favor of the Supreme Personality of Godhead, King Satyavrata engaged in the austerity of subsisting only by drinking water. Once, while performing this austerity on the bank of the Kṛtamālā River and offering oblations of water with the palm of his hand, he found a small fish. The fish appealed to the King for protection, asking the King to keep Him in a safe place. Although the King did not know that the small fish was the

Supreme Personality of Godhead Himself, as a king he gave shelter to the fish and kept Him in a water jug. The fish, being the Supreme Personality of Godhead, wanted to show His potency to King Satyavrata, and thus He immediately expanded His body in such a way that He could no longer be kept in the jug of water. The King then put the fish in a big well, but the well was also too small. Then the King put the fish in a lake, but the lake was also unsuitable. Finally the King put the fish in the sea, but even the sea could not accommodate Him. Thus the King understood that the fish was no one else but the Supreme Personality of Godhead, and he requested the Lord to describe His incarnation as a fish. The Personality of Godhead, being pleased with the King, informed him that within a week there would be an inundation throughout the universe and that the fish incarnation would protect the King, along with the *ṛṣis,* herbs, seeds and other living entities, in a boat, which would be attached to the fish's horn. After saying this, the Lord disappeared. King Satyavrata offered respectful obeisances to the Supreme Lord and continued to meditate upon Him. In due course of time, annihilation took place, and the King saw a boat coming near. After getting aboard with learned *brāhmaṇas* and saintly persons, he offered prayers to worship the Supreme Personality of Godhead. The Supreme Lord is situated in everyone's heart, and thus he taught Mahārāja Satyavrata and the saintly persons about Vedic knowledge from the core of the heart. King Satyavrata took his next birth as Vaivasvata Manu, who is mentioned in *Bhagavad-gītā. Vivasvān manave prāha:* the sun-god spoke the science of *Bhagavad-gītā* to his son Manu. Because of being the son of Vivasvān, this Manu is known as Vaivasvata Manu.

TEXT 1

श्रीराजोवाच
भगवञ्छ्रोतुमिच्छामि हरेरद्भुतकर्मणः ।
अवतारकथामाद्यां मायामत्स्यविडम्बनम् ॥ १ ॥

śrī-rājovāca
bhagavañ chrotum icchāmi
harer adbhuta-karmaṇaḥ
avatāra-kathām ādyāṁ
māyā-matsya-viḍambanam

śrī-rājā uvāca—King Parīkṣit said; *bhagavan*—O most powerful; *śrotum*—to hear; *icchāmi*—I desire; *hareḥ*—of the Supreme Personality of Godhead, Hari; *adbhuta-karmaṇaḥ*—whose activities are wonderful; *avatāra-kathām*—pastimes of the incarnation; *ādyām*—first; *māyā-matsya-viḍambanam*—which is simply an imitation of a fish.

TRANSLATION

Mahārāja Parīkṣit said: The Supreme Personality of Godhead, Hari, is eternally situated in His transcendental position, yet He descends to this material world and manifests Himself in various incarnations. His first incarnation was that of a great fish. O most powerful Śukadeva Gosvāmī, I wish to hear from you the pastimes of that fish incarnation.

PURPORT

The Supreme Personality of Godhead is all-powerful, yet He accepted the form of an uncommon fish. This is one of the ten original incarnations of the Lord.

TEXTS 2-3

यदर्थमदधाद् रूपं मात्स्यं लोकजुगुप्सितम् ।
तमःप्रकृति दुर्मर्षं कर्मग्रस्त इवेश्वरः ॥ २ ॥
एतन्नो भगवन् सर्वं यथावद् वक्तुमर्हसि ।
उत्तमश्लोकचरितं सर्वलोकसुखावहम् ॥ ३ ॥

yad-artham adadhād rūpaṁ
mātsyaṁ loka-jugupsitam
tamaḥ-prakṛti-durmarṣaṁ
karma-grasta iveśvaraḥ

etan no bhagavan sarvaṁ
yathāvad vaktum arhasi
uttamaśloka-caritaṁ
sarva-loka-sukhāvaham

yat-artham—for what purpose; *adadhāt*—accepted; *rūpam*—form; *mātsyam*—of a fish; *loka-jugupsitam*—which is certainly not very favorable in this world; *tamaḥ*—in the mode of ignorance; *prakṛti*—such behavior; *durmarṣam*—which is certainly very painful and condemned; *karma-grastaḥ*—

one who is under the laws of *karma; iva*—like; *īśvaraḥ*—the Supreme Personality of Godhead; *etat*—all these facts; *naḥ*—unto us; *bhagavan*—O most powerful sage; *sarvam*—everything; *yathāvat*—properly; *vaktum arhasi*—kindly describe; *uttamaśloka-caritam*—the pastimes of the Supreme Personality of Godhead; *sarva-loka-sukha-āvaham*—by hearing of which everyone becomes happy.

TRANSLATION

What was the purpose for which the Supreme Personality of Godhead accepted the abominable form of a fish, exactly as an ordinary living being accepts different forms under the laws of karma? The form of a fish is certainly condemned and full of terrible pain. O my lord, what was the purpose of this incarnation? Kindly explain this to us, for hearing about the pastimes of the Lord is auspicious for everyone.

PURPORT

Parīkṣit Mahārāja's question to Śukadeva Gosvāmī was based on this principle stated by the Lord Himself in *Bhagavad-gītā* (4.7):

yadā yadā hi dharmasya
glānir bhavati bhārata
abhyutthānam adharmasya
tadātmānaṁ sṛjāmy aham

"Whenever and wherever there is a decline in religious practice, O descendant of Bharata, and a predominant rise of irreligion—at that time I descend Myself." The Lord appears in each incarnation to save the world from irreligious principles and especially to protect His devotees (*paritrāṇāya sādhūnām*). Vāmanadeva, for example, appeared to save the devotee Bali Mahārāja. Similarly, when the Supreme Personality of Godhead accepted the abominable form of a fish, He must have done so to favor some devotee. Parīkṣit Mahārāja was eager to know about the devotee for whom the Supreme Lord accepted this form.

TEXT 4

श्रीसूत उवाच
इत्युक्तो विष्णुरातेन भगवान् बादरायणिः ।
उवाच चरितं विष्णोर्मत्स्यरूपेण यत् कृतम् ॥ ४ ॥

śrī-sūta uvāca
ity ukto viṣṇu-rātena
bhagavān bādarāyaṇiḥ
uvāca caritaṁ viṣṇor
matsya-rūpeṇa yat kṛtam

śrī-sūtaḥ uvāca—Śrī Sūta Gosvāmī said; *iti uktaḥ*—thus being questioned; *viṣṇu-rātena*—by Mahārāja Parīkṣit, known as Viṣṇurāta; *bhagavān*—the most powerful; *bādarāyaṇiḥ*—the son of Vyāsadeva, Śukadeva Gosvāmī; *uvāca*—said; *caritam*—the pastimes; *viṣṇoḥ*—of Lord Viṣṇu; *matsya-rūpeṇa*—by Him in the form of a fish; *yat*—whatever; *kṛtam*—was done.

TRANSLATION

Sūta Gosvāmī said: When Parīkṣit Mahārāja thus inquired from Śukadeva Gosvāmī, that most powerful saintly person began describing the pastimes of the Lord's incarnation as a fish.

TEXT 5

श्रीशुक उवाच
गोविप्रसुरसाधूनां छन्दसामपि चेश्वरः ।
रक्षामिच्छंस्तनूर्धत्ते धर्मस्यार्थस्य चैव हि ॥ ५ ॥

śrī-śuka uvāca
go-vipra-sura-sādhūnāṁ
chandasām api ceśvaraḥ
rakṣām icchaṁs tanūr dhatte
dharmasyārthasya caiva hi

śrī-śukaḥ uvāca—Śrī Śukadeva Gosvāmī said; *go*—of the cows; *vipra*—of the *brāhmaṇas; sura*—of the demigods; *sādhūnām*—and of the devotees; *chandasām api*—even of the Vedic literature; *ca*—and; *īśvaraḥ*—the supreme controller; *rakṣām*—the protection; *icchan*—desiring; *tanūḥ dhatte*—accepts the forms of incarnations; *dharmasya*—of the principles of religion; *arthasya*—of the principles of the purpose of life; *ca*—and; *eva*—indeed; *hi*—certainly.

TRANSLATION

Śrī Śukadeva Gosvāmī said: O King, for the sake of protecting the cows, brāhmaṇas, demigods, devotees, the Vedic literature, religious principles,

and principles to fulfill the purpose of life, the Supreme Personality of Godhead accepts the forms of incarnations.

PURPORT

The Supreme Personality of Godhead generally appears in various types of incarnations to give protection to the cows and *brāhmaṇas.* The Lord is described as *go-brāhmaṇa-hitāya ca;* in other words, He is always eager to benefit the cows and *brāhmaṇas.* When Lord Kṛṣṇa appeared, He purposefully became a cowherd boy and showed personally how to give protection to the cows and calves. Similarly, He showed respect to Sudāmā Vipra, a real *brāhmaṇa.* From the Lord's personal activities, human society should learn how to give protection specifically to the *brāhmaṇas* and cows. Then the protection of religious principles, fulfillment of the aim of life and protection of Vedic knowledge can be achieved. Without protection of cows, brahminical culture cannot be maintained; and without brahminical culture, the aim of life cannot be fulfilled. The Lord, therefore, is described as *go-brāhmaṇa-hitāya* because His incarnation is only for the protection of the cows and *brāhmaṇas.* Unfortunately, because in Kali-yuga there is no protection of the cows and brahminical culture, everything is in a precarious position. If human society wants to be exalted, the leaders of society must follow the instructions of *Bhagavad-gītā* and give protection to the cows, the *brāhmaṇas* and brahminical culture.

TEXT 6

उच्चावचेषु भूतेषु चरन् वायुरिवेश्वरः ।
नोच्चावचत्वं भजते निर्गुणत्वाद्धियो गुणैः ॥ ६ ॥

uccāvaceṣu bhūteṣu
caran vāyur iveśvaraḥ
noccāvacatvaṁ bhajate
nirguṇatvād dhiyo guṇaiḥ

ucca-avaceṣu—having higher or lower bodily forms; *bhūteṣu*—among the living entities; *caran*—behaving; *vāyuḥ iva*—exactly like the air; *īśvaraḥ*—the Supreme Lord; *na*—not; *ucca-avacatvam*—the quality of higher or lower grades of life; *bhajate*—accepts; *nirguṇatvāt*—because of being transcendental, above all material qualities; *dhiyaḥ*—generally; *guṇaiḥ*—by the modes of material nature.

TRANSLATION

Like the air passing through different types of atmosphere, the Supreme Personality of Godhead, although appearing sometimes as a human being and sometimes as a lower animal, is always transcendental. Because He is above the material modes of nature, He is unaffected by higher and lower forms.

PURPORT

The Supreme Personality of Godhead is the master of the material nature (*mayādhyakṣeṇa prakṛtiḥ sūyate sacarācaram*). Therefore, being the supreme controller of the laws of nature, the Lord cannot be under their influence. An example given in this regard is that although the wind blows through many places, the air is not affected by the qualities of these places. Although the air sometimes carries the odor of a filthy place, the air has nothing to do with such a place. Similarly, the Supreme Personality of Godhead, being all-good and all-auspicious, is never affected by the material qualities like an ordinary living entity. *Puruṣaḥ prakṛti-stho hi bhuṅkte prakṛtijān guṇān* [*Bg.* 13.21]. When the living entity is in the material nature, he is affected by its qualities. The Supreme Personality of Godhead, however, is not affected. Disrespectfully, one who does not know this considers the Supreme Personality of Godhead an ordinary living being (*avajānanti māṁ mūḍhāḥ*). *Paraṁ bhāvam ajānantaḥ:* such a conclusion is reached by the unintelligent because they are unaware of the transcendental qualities of the Lord.

TEXT 7

आसीदतीतकल्पान्ते ब्राह्मो नैमित्तिको लयः ।
समुद्रोपप्लुतास्तत्र लोका भूरादयो नृप ॥ ७ ॥

āsīd atīta-kalpānte
brāhmo naimittiko layaḥ
samudropaplutās tatra
lokā bhūr-ādayo nṛpa

āsīt—there was; *atīta*—past; *kalpa-ante*—at the end of the *kalpa; brāhmaḥ*—of Lord Brahmā's day; *naimittikaḥ*—because of that; *layaḥ*—inundation; *samudra*—in the ocean; *upaplutāḥ*—were inundated; *tatra*—there; *lokāḥ*—all the planets; *bhūḥ-ādayaḥ*—Bhūḥ, Bhuvaḥ and Svaḥ, the three *lokas; nṛpa*—O King.

TRANSLATION

O King Parīkṣit, at the end of the past millennium, at the end of Brahmā's day, because Lord Brahmā sleeps during the night, annihilation took place, and the three worlds were covered by the water of the ocean.

TEXT 8

कालेनागतनिद्रस्य धातुः शिशयिषोर्बली ।
मुखतो निःसृतान् वेदान् हयग्रीवोऽन्तिकेऽहरत् ॥ ८ ॥

kālenāgata-nidrasya
dhātuḥ śiśayiṣor balī
mukhato niḥsṛtān vedān
hayagrīvo 'ntike 'harat

kālena—because of time (the end of Brahmā's day); *āgata-nidrasya*—when he felt sleepy; *dhātuḥ*—of Brahmā; *śiśayiṣoḥ*—desiring to lie down to sleep; *balī*—very powerful; *mukhataḥ*—from the mouth; *niḥsṛtān*—emanating; *vedān*—the Vedic knowledge; *hayagrīvaḥ*—the great demon named Hayagrīva; *antike*—nearby; *aharat*—stole.

TRANSLATION

At the end of Brahmā's day, when Brahmā felt sleepy and desired to lie down, the Vedas were emanating from his mouth, and the great demon named Hayagrīva stole the Vedic knowledge.

TEXT 9

ज्ञात्वा तद् दानवेन्द्रस्य हयग्रीवस्य चेष्टितम् ।
दधार शफरीरूपं भगवान् हरिरीश्वरः ॥ ९ ॥

jñātvā tad dānavendrasya
hayagrīvasya ceṣṭitam
dadhāra śapharī-rūpaṁ
bhagavān harir īśvaraḥ

jñātvā—after understanding; *tat*—that; *dānava-indrasya*—of the great demon; *hayagrīvasya*—of Hayagrīva; *ceṣṭitam*—activity; *dadhāra*—accepted; *śapharī-rūpam*—the form of a fish; *bhagavān*—the Supreme Personality of Godhead; *hariḥ*—the Lord; *īśvaraḥ*—the supreme controller.

TRANSLATION

Understanding the acts of the great demon Hayagrīva, the Supreme Personality of Godhead, Hari, who is full of all opulences, assumed the form of a fish and saved the Vedas by killing the demon.

PURPORT

Because everything was inundated by water, to save the *Vedas* it was necessary for the Lord to assume the form of a fish.

TEXT 10

तत्र राजऋषिः कश्चिन्नाम्ना सत्यव्रतो महान्।
नारायणपरोऽतपत् तपः स सलिलाशनः ॥ १० ॥

tatra rāja-ṛṣiḥ kaścin
nāmnā satyavrato mahān
nārāyaṇa-paro 'tapat
tapaḥ sa salilāśanaḥ

tatra—in that connection; *rāja-ṛṣiḥ*—a king equally qualified as a great saintly person; *kaścit*—someone; *nāmnā*—by the name; *satyavrataḥ*—Satyavrata; *mahān*—a great personality; *nārāyaṇa-paraḥ*—a great devotee of Lord Nārāyaṇa, the Supreme Personality of Godhead; *atapat*—performed austerities; *tapaḥ*—penances; *saḥ*—he; *salila-āśanaḥ*—only drinking water.

TRANSLATION

During the Cākṣuṣa-manvantara there was a great king named Satyavrata who was a great devotee of the Supreme Personality of Godhead. Satyavrata performed austerities by subsisting only on water.

PURPORT

The Lord assumed one fish incarnation to save the *Vedas* at the beginning of the Svāyambhuva-*manvantara*, and at the end of the Cākṣuṣa-*manvantara* the Lord again assumed the form of a fish just to favor the great king named Satyavrata. As there were two incarnations of Varāha, there were also two incarnations of fish. The Lord appeared as one fish incarnation to save the *Vedas* by killing Hayagrīva, and He assumed the other fish incarnation to show favor to King Satyavrata.

TEXT 11

योऽसावस्मिन् महाकल्पे तनयः स विवस्वतः ।
श्राद्धदेव इति ख्यातो मनुत्वे हरिणार्पितः ॥ ११ ॥

yo 'sāv asmin mahā-kalpe
tanayaḥ sa vivasvataḥ
śrāddhadeva iti khyāto
manutve hariṇārpitaḥ

yaḥ—one who; *asau*—He (the Supreme Person); *asmin*—in this; *mahā-kalpe*—great millennium; *tanayaḥ*—son; *saḥ*—he; *vivasvataḥ*—of the sun-god; *śrāddhadevaḥ*—by the name Śrāddhadeva; *iti*—thus; *khyātaḥ*—celebrated; *manutve*—in the position of Manu; *hariṇā*—by the Supreme Personality of Godhead; *arpitaḥ*—was situated.

TRANSLATION

In this [the present] millennium King Satyavrata later became the son of Vivasvān, the king of the sun planet, and was known as Śrāddhadeva. By the mercy of the Supreme Personality of Godhead, he was given the post of Manu.

TEXT 12

एकदा कृतमालायां कुर्वतो जलतर्पणम् ।
तस्याञ्जल्युदके काचिच्छफर्येकाभ्यपद्यत ॥ १२ ॥

ekadā kṛtamālāyāṁ
kurvato jala-tarpaṇam
tasyāñjaly-udake kācic
chaphary ekābhyapadyata

ekadā—one day; *kṛtamālāyām*—on the bank of the Kṛtamālā River; *kurvataḥ*—executing; *jala-tarpaṇam*—the offering of oblations of water; *tasya*—his; *añjali*—palmful; *udake*—in the water; *kācit*—some; *śapharī*—a small fish; *ekā*—one; *abhyapadyata*—was generated.

TRANSLATION

One day while King Satyavrata was performing austerities by offering water on the bank of the River Kṛtamālā, a small fish appeared in the water in his palms.

TEXT 13

सत्यव्रतोऽञ्जलिगतां सह तोयेन भारत।
उत्ससर्ज नदीतोये शफरीं द्रविडेश्वरः ॥ १३ ॥

satyavrato 'ñjali-gatāṁ
saha toyena bhārata
utsasarja nadī-toye
śapharīṁ draviḍeśvaraḥ

satyavrataḥ—King Satyavrata; *añjali-gatām*—in the water held in the palms of the King; *saha*—with; *toyena*—water; *bhārata*—O King Parīkṣit; *utsasarja*—threw; *nadī-toye*—in the water of the river; *śapharīm*—that small fish; *draviḍa-īśvaraḥ*—Satyavrata, the King of Draviḍa.

TRANSLATION

Satyavrata, the King of Draviḍadeśa, threw the fish into the water of the river along with the water in his palm, O King Parīkṣit, descendant of Bharata.

TEXT 14

तमाह सातिकरुणं महाकारुणिकं नृपम् ।
यादोभ्यो ज्ञातिघातिभ्यो दीनां मां दीनवत्सल ।
कथं विसृजसे राजन् भीतामस्मिन् सरिज्जले ॥१४॥

tam āha sātikaruṇaṁ
mahā-kāruṇikaṁ nṛpam
yādobhyo jñāti-ghātibhyo
dīnāṁ māṁ dīna-vatsala
kathaṁ visṛjase rājan
bhītām asmin sarij-jale

tam—unto him (Satyavrata); *āha*—said; *sā*—that small fish; *ati-karuṇam*—extremely compassionate; *mahā-kāruṇikam*—extremely merciful; *nṛpam*—unto King Satyavrata; *yādobhyaḥ*—to the aquatics; *jñāti-ghātibhyaḥ*—who are always eager to kill the smaller fish; *dīnām*—very poor; *mām*—me; *dīna-vatsala*—O protector of the poor; *katham*—why; *visṛjase*—you are throwing; *rājan*—O King; *bhītām*—very much afraid; *asmin*—within this; *sarit-jale*—in the water of the river.

TRANSLATION

With an appealing voice, the poor small fish said to King Satyavrata, who was very merciful: My dear King, protector of the poor, why are you throwing Me in the water of the river, where there are other aquatics who can kill Me? I am very much afraid of them.

PURPORT

In the *Matsya Purāṇa* it is said:

ananta-śaktir bhagavān
matsya-rūpī janārdanaḥ
krīḍārthaṁ yācayām āsa
svayaṁ satyavrataṁ nṛpam

"The Supreme Personality of Godhead possesses unlimited potency. Nonetheless, in His pastime in the form of a fish He begged protection from King Satyavrata."

TEXT 15

तमात्मनोऽनुग्रहार्थं प्रीत्या मत्स्यवपुर्धरम् ।
अजानन् रक्षणार्थाय शफर्याः स मनो दधे ॥ १५ ॥

tam ātmano 'nugrahārthaṁ
prītyā matsya-vapur-dharam
ajānan rakṣaṇārthāya
śapharyāḥ sa mano dadhe

tam—unto the fish; *ātmanaḥ*—personal; *anugraha-artham*—to show favor; *prītyā*—very much pleased; *matsya-vapuḥ-dharam*—the Supreme Personality of Godhead, who had assumed the form of a fish; *ajānan*—without knowledge of this; *rakṣaṇa-arthāya*—just to give protection; *śapharyāḥ*—of the fish; *saḥ*—the King; *manaḥ*—mind; *dadhe*—decided.

TRANSLATION

To please himself, King Satyavrata, not knowing that the fish was the Supreme Personality of Godhead, decided with great pleasure to give the fish protection.

PURPORT

Here is an example of giving service to the Supreme Personality of Godhead even without knowledge. Such service is called *ajñāta-sukṛti.* King Satyavrata wanted to show his own mercy, not knowing that the fish was Lord Viṣṇu. By such unknowing devotional service, one is favored by the Supreme Personality of Godhead. Service rendered to the Supreme Lord, knowingly or unknowingly, never goes in vain.

TEXT 16

तस्या दीनतरं वाक्यमाश्रुत्य स महीपतिः ।
कलशाप्सु निधायैनां दयालुर्निन्य आश्रमम् ॥ १६ ॥

tasyā dīnataraṁ vākyam
āśrutya sa mahīpatiḥ
kalaśāpsu nidhāyaināṁ
dayālur ninya āśramam

tasyāḥ—of the fish; *dīna-taram*—pitiable; *vākyam*—words; *āśrutya*—hearing; *saḥ*—that; *mahī-patiḥ*—the King; *kalaśa-apsu*—in the water contained in the water jug; *nidhāya*—taking; *enām*—the fish; *dayāluḥ*—merciful; *ninye*—brought; *āśramam*—to his residence.

TRANSLATION

The merciful King, being moved by the pitiable words of the fish, placed the fish in a water jug and brought Him to his own residence.

TEXT 17

सा तु तत्रैकरात्रेण वर्धमाना कमण्डलौ ।
अलब्ध्वात्मावकाशं वा इदमाह महीपतिम् ॥ १७ ॥

sā tu tatraika-rātreṇa
vardhamānā kamaṇḍalau
alabdhvātmāvakāśaṁ vā
idam āha mahīpatim

sā—that fish; *tu*—but; *tatra*—therein; *eka-rātreṇa*—in one night; *vardhamānā*—expanding; *kamaṇḍalau*—in the waterpot; *alabdhvā*—without attaining; *ātma-avakāśam*—a comfortable position for His body; *vā*—either; *idam*—this; *āha*—said; *mahī-patim*—unto the King.

TRANSLATION

But in one night that fish grew so much that He could not move His body comfortably in the water of the pot. He then spoke to the King as follows.

TEXT 18

नाहं कमण्डलावस्मिन् कृच्छ्रं वस्तुमिहोत्सहे ।
कल्पयौकः सुविपुलं यत्राहं निवसे सुखम् ॥ १८ ॥

nāhaṁ kamaṇḍalāv asmin
kṛcchraṁ vastum ihotsahe
kalpayaukaḥ suvipulaṁ
yatrāhaṁ nivase sukham

na—not; *aham*—I; *kamaṇḍalau*—in this waterpot; *asmin*—in this; *kṛcchram*—with great difficulty; *vastum*—to live; *iha*—here; *utsahe*—like; *kalpaya*—just consider; *okaḥ*—residential place; *su-vipulam*—more expanded; *yatra*—wherein; *aham*—I; *nivase*—can live; *sukham*—in pleasure.

TRANSLATION

O My dear King, I do not like living in this waterpot with such great difficulty. Therefore, please find some better reservoir of water where I can live comfortably.

TEXT 19

स एनां तत आदाय न्यधादौदञ्चनोदके ।
तत्र क्षिप्ता मुहूर्तेन हस्तत्रयमवर्धत ॥ १९ ॥

sa enāṁ tata ādāya
nyadhād audañcanodake
tatra kṣiptā muhūrtena
hasta-trayam avardhata

saḥ—the King; *enām*—unto the fish; *tataḥ*—thereafter; *ādāya*—taking out; *nyadhāt*—placed; *audañcana-udake*—in a well of water; *tatra*—therein; *kṣiptā*—being thrown; *muhūrtena*—within a moment; *hasta-trayam*—three cubits; *avardhata*—immediately developed.

TRANSLATION

Then, taking the fish out of the waterpot, the King threw Him in a large well. But within a moment the fish developed to the length of three cubits.

TEXT 20

न म एतदलं राजन् सुखं वस्तुमुदञ्चनम् ।
पृथु देहि पदं मह्यं यत् त्वाहं शरणं गता ॥ २० ॥

na ma etad alaṁ rājan
sukhaṁ vastum udañcanam
pṛthu dehi padaṁ mahyaṁ
yat tvāhaṁ śaraṇaṁ gatā

na—not; *me*—unto Me; *etat*—this; *alam*—fit; *rājan*—O King; *sukham*—in happiness; *vastum*—to live; *udañcanam*—reservoir of water; *pṛthu*—very great; *dehi*—give; *padam*—a place; *mahyam*—unto Me; *yat*—which; *tvā*—unto you; *aham*—I; *śaraṇam*—shelter; *gatā*—have taken.

TRANSLATION

The fish then said: My dear King, this reservoir of water is not fit for My happy residence. Please give Me a more extensive pool of water, for I have taken shelter of you.

TEXT 21

तत आदाय सा राज्ञा क्षिप्ता राजन् सरोवरे।
तदावृत्यात्मना सोऽयं महामीनोऽन्ववर्धत ॥ २१ ॥

tata ādāya sā rājñā
kṣiptā rājan sarovare
tad āvṛtyātmanā so 'yaṁ
mahā-mīno 'nvavardhata

tataḥ—from there; *ādāya*—taking away; *sā*—the fish; *rājñā*—by the King; *kṣiptā*—being thrown; *rājan*—O King (Mahārāja Parīkṣit); *sarovare*—in a lake; *tat*—that; *āvṛtya*—covering; *ātmanā*—by the body; *saḥ*—the fish; *ayam*—this; *mahā-mīnaḥ*—gigantic fish; *anvavardhata*—immediately developed.

TRANSLATION

O Mahārāja Parīkṣit, the King took the fish from the well and threw Him in a lake, but the fish then assumed a gigantic form exceeding the extent of the water.

TEXT 22

नैतन्मे स्वस्तये राजन्नुदकं सलिलौकसः ।
निधेहि रक्षायोगेन ह्रदे मामविदासिनि ॥ २२ ॥

naitan me svastaye rājann
udakaṁ salilaukasaḥ
nidhehi rakṣā-yogena
hrade mām avidāsini

na—not; *etat*—this; *me*—unto Me; *svastaye*—comfortable; *rājan*—O King; *udakam*—water; *salila-okasaḥ*—because I am a big aquatic; *nidhehi*—put; *rakṣā-yogena*—by some means; *hrade*—in a lake; *mām*—Me; *avidāsini*—perpetual.

TRANSLATION

The fish then said: O King, I am a large aquatic, and this water is not at all suitable for Me. Now kindly find some way to save Me. It would be better to put Me in the water of a lake that will never reduce.

TEXT 23

इत्युक्तः सोऽनयन्मत्स्यं तत्र तत्राविदासिनि ।
जलाशयेऽसंमितं तं समुद्रे प्राक्षिपज्झषम् ॥ २३ ॥

ity uktaḥ so 'nayan matsyaṁ
tatra tatrāvidāsini
jalāśaye 'sammitaṁ tam
samudre prākṣipaj jhaṣam

iti uktaḥ—thus being requested; *saḥ*—the King; *anayat*—brought; *matsyam*—the fish; *tatra*—therein; *tatra*—therein; *avidāsini*—where the water never diminishes; *jala-āśaye*—in the reservoir of water; *asammitam*—unlimited; *tam*—unto the fish; *samudre*—in the ocean; *prākṣipat*—threw; *jhaṣam*—the gigantic fish.

TRANSLATION

When thus requested, King Satyavrata took the fish to the largest reservoir of water. But when that also proved insufficient, the King at last threw the gigantic fish into the ocean.

TEXT 24

क्षिप्यमाणस्तमाहेदमिह मां मकरादयः ।
अदन्त्यतिबला वीर मां नेहोत्स्त्रष्टुमर्हसि ॥ २४ ॥

kṣipyamāṇas tam āhedam
iha māṁ makarādayaḥ
adanty atibalā vīra
māṁ nehotsraṣṭum arhasi

kṣipyamāṇaḥ—being thrown in the ocean; *tam*—unto the King; *āha*—the fish said; *idam*—this; *iha*—in this place; *mām*—Me; *makara-ādayaḥ*—dangerous aquatics like sharks; *adanti*—will eat; *ati-balāḥ*—because of being too powerful; *vīra*—O heroic King; *mām*—Me; *na*—not; *iha*—in this water; *utsraṣṭum*—to throw; *arhasi*—you deserve.

TRANSLATION

While being thrown in the ocean, the fish said to King Satyavrata: O hero, in this water there are very powerful and dangerous sharks that will eat Me. Therefore you should not throw Me in this place.

TEXT 25

एवं विमोहितस्तेन वदता वल्गुभारतीम् ।
तमाह को भवानस्मान् मत्स्यरूपेण मोहयन् ॥ २५ ॥

evaṁ vimohitas tena
vadatā valgu-bhāratīm
tam āha ko bhavān asmān
matsya-rūpeṇa mohayan

evam—thus; *vimohitaḥ*—bewildered; *tena*—by the fish; *vadatā*—speaking; *valgu-bhāratīm*—sweet words; *tam*—unto him; *āha*—said; *kaḥ*—who; *bhavān*—You; *asmān*—us; *matsya-rūpeṇa*—in the form of a fish; *mohayan*—bewildering.

TRANSLATION

After hearing these sweet words from the Supreme Personality of Godhead in the form of a fish, the King, being bewildered, asked Him: Who are You, sir? You simply bewilder us.

TEXT 26

नैवंवीर्यो जलचरो दृष्टोऽस्माभिः श्रुतोऽपि वा।
यो भवान् योजनशतमह्नाभिव्यानशे सरः ॥ २६ ॥

naivaṁ vīryo jalacaro
dṛṣṭo 'smābhiḥ śruto 'pi vā
yo bhavān yojana-śatam
ahnābhivyānaśe saraḥ

na—not; *evam*—thus; *vīryaḥ*—powerful; *jala-caraḥ*—aquatic; *dṛṣṭaḥ*—seen; *asmābhiḥ*—by us; *śrutaḥ api*—nor heard of; *vā*—either; *yaḥ*—who; *bhavān*—Your Lordship; *yojana-śatam*—hundreds of miles; *ahnā*—in one day; *abhivyānaśe*—expanding; *saraḥ*—water.

TRANSLATION

My Lord, in one day You have expanded Yourself for hundreds of miles, covering the water of the river and the ocean. Before this I had never seen or heard of such an aquatic animal.

TEXT 27

नूनं त्वं भगवान् साक्षाद्धरिर्नारायणोऽव्ययः।
अनुग्रहाय भूतानां धत्से रूपं जलौकसाम् ॥ २७ ॥

nūnaṁ tvaṁ bhagavān sākṣād
dharir nārāyaṇo 'vyayaḥ
anugrahāya bhūtānāṁ
dhatse rūpaṁ jalaukasām

nūnam—certainly; *tvam*—You (are); *bhagavān*—the Supreme Personality of Godhead; *sākṣāt*—directly; *hariḥ*—the Lord; *nārāyaṇaḥ*—the Personality of Godhead; *avyayaḥ*—inexhaustible; *anugrahāya*—to show mercy; *bhūtānām*—to all living entities; *dhatse*—You have assumed; *rūpam*—a form; *jala-okasām*—like an aquatic.

TRANSLATION

My Lord, You are certainly the inexhaustible Supreme Personality of Godhead, Nārāyaṇa, Śrī Hari. It is to show Your mercy to the living entities that You have now assumed the form of an aquatic.

TEXT 28

नमस्ते पुरुषश्रेष्ठ स्थित्युत्पत्त्यप्ययेश्वर ।
भक्तानां नः प्रपन्नानां मुख्यो ह्यात्मगतिर्विभो ॥ २८ ॥

namas te puruṣa-śreṣṭha
sthity-utpatty-apyayeśvara
bhaktānāṁ naḥ prapannānāṁ
mukhyo hy ātma-gatir vibho

namaḥ—I offer my respectful obeisances; *te*—unto You; *puruṣa-śreṣṭha*—the best of all living entities, the best of all enjoyers; *sthiti*—of maintenance; *utpatti*—creation; *apyaya*—and destruction; *īśvara*—the Supreme Lord; *bhaktānām*—of Your devotees; *naḥ*—like us; *prapannānām*—those who are surrendered; *mukhyaḥ*—the supreme; *hi*—indeed; *ātma-gatiḥ*—the supreme destination; *vibho*—Lord Viṣṇu.

TRANSLATION

O my Lord, master of creation, maintenance and annihilation, O best of enjoyers, Lord Viṣṇu, You are the leader and destination of surrendered devotees like us. Therefore let me offer my respectful obeisances unto You.

TEXT 29

सर्वे लीलावतारास्ते भूतानां भूतिहेतवः ।
ज्ञातुमिच्छाम्यदो रूपं यदर्थं भवता धृतम् ॥ २९ ॥

sarve līlāvatārās te
bhūtānāṁ bhūti-hetavaḥ
jñātum icchāmy ado rūpaṁ
yad-arthaṁ bhavatā dhṛtam

sarve—everything; *līlā*—pastimes; *avatārāḥ*—incarnations; *te*—of Your Lordship; *bhūtānām*—of all living entities; *bhūti*—of a flourishing condition; *hetavaḥ*—the causes; *jñātum*—to know; *icchāmi*—I wish; *adaḥ*—this; *rū-*

pam—form; *yat-artham*—for what purpose; *bhavatā*—by Your Lordship; *dhṛtam*—assumed.

TRANSLATION

All Your pastimes and incarnations certainly appear for the welfare of all living entities. Therefore, my Lord, I wish to know the purpose for which You have assumed this form of a fish.

TEXT 30

न तेऽरविन्दाक्ष पदोपसर्पणं
मृषा भवेत् सर्वसुहृत्प्रियात्मनः ।
यथेतरेषां पृथगात्मनां सता-
मदीदृशो यद् वपुरद्भुतं हि नः ॥ ३० ॥

na te 'ravindākṣa padopasarpaṇaṁ
mṛṣā bhavet sarva-suhṛt-priyātmanaḥ
yathetareṣāṁ pṛthag-ātmanāṁ satām
adīdṛśo yad vapur adbhutaṁ hi naḥ

na—never; *te*—of Your Lordship; *aravinda-akṣa*—My Lord, whose eyes are like the petals of a lotus; *pada-upasarpaṇam*—worship of the lotus feet; *mṛṣā*—useless; *bhavet*—can become; *sarva-suhṛt*—the friend of everyone; *priya*—dear to everyone; *ātmanaḥ*—the Supersoul of everyone; *yathā*—as; *itareṣām*—of others (the demigods); *pṛthak-ātmanām*—living entities who have material bodies different from the soul; *satām*—of those who are spiritually fixed; *adīdṛśaḥ*—You have manifested; *yat*—that; *vapuḥ*—body; *adbhutam*—wonderful; *hi*—indeed; *naḥ*—unto us.

TRANSLATION

O my Lord, possessing eyes like the petals of a lotus, the worship of the demigods, who are in the bodily concept of life, is fruitless in all respects. But because You are the supreme friend and dearmost Supersoul of everyone, worship of Your lotus feet is never useless. You have therefore manifested Your form as a fish.

PURPORT

The demigods like Indra, Candra and Sūrya are ordinary living entities who are differentiated parts and parcels of the Supreme Personality of Godhead.

The Lord expands Himself through the living beings (*nityo nityānāṁ cetanaś cetanānām*). His personal *viṣṇu-tattva* forms, which are all spiritual, are called *svāṁśa,* and the living entities who are differentiated parts are called *vibhinnāṁśa.* Some of the *vibhinnāṁśa* forms are spiritual, and some are a combination of matter and spirit. The conditioned souls in the material world are different from their external bodies made of material energy. Thus the demigods living in the upper planetary systems and the living entities living in the lower planetary system are of the same nature. Nonetheless, those living as human beings on this planet are sometimes attracted to worshiping the demigods in the higher planetary systems. Such worship is temporary. As the human beings on this planet have to change their bodies (*tathā dehāntara-prāptiḥ*), the living entities known as Indra, Candra, Varuṇa and so on will also have to change their bodies in due course of time. As stated in *Bhagavad-gītā, antavat tu phalaṁ teṣāṁ tad bhavaty alpa-medhasām:* "Men of small intelligence worship the demigods, and their fruits are limited and temporary." *Kāmais tais tair hṛta jñānāḥ prapadyante 'nya-devatāḥ:* those who do not know the position of the demigods are inclined to worship the demigods for some material purpose, but the results of such worship are never permanent. Consequently, here it is said, *yathetareṣāṁ pṛthag-ātmanāṁ satām, padopasarpaṇaṁ mṛṣā bhavet.* In other words, if one is to worship someone else, he must worship the Supreme Personality of Godhead. Then his worship will never be fruitless. *Svalpam apy asya dharmasya trāyate mahato bhayāt:* even a slight attempt to worship the Supreme Personality of Godhead is a permanent asset. Therefore, as recommended in *Śrīmad-Bhāgavatam, tyaktvā sva-dharmaṁ caraṇāmbujaṁ hareḥ.* One should take to the worship of the lotus feet of Hari, even if this means giving up the so-called occupational duty assigned because of the particular body one has accepted. Because worship in terms of the body is temporary, it does not bear any permanent fruit. But worship of the Supreme Personality of Godhead gives immense benefit.

TEXT 31

श्रीशुक उवाच

इति ब्रुवाणं नृपतिं जगत्पतिः
सत्यव्रतं मत्स्यवपुर्युगक्षये ।
विहर्तुकामः प्रलयार्णवेऽब्रवी-
च्चिकीर्षुरेकान्तजनप्रियः प्रियम् ॥ ३१ ॥

śrī-śuka uvāca
iti bruvāṇaṁ nṛpatiṁ jagat-patiḥ
satyavrataṁ matsya-vapur yuga-kṣaye
vihartu-kāmaḥ pralayārṇave 'bravīc
cikīrṣur ekānta-jana-priyaḥ priyam

śrī-śukaḥ uvāca—Śrī Śukadeva Gosvāmī said; *iti*—thus; *bruvāṇam*—speaking like that; *nṛpatim*—unto the King; *jagat-patiḥ*—the master of the entire universe; *satyavratam*—unto Satyavrata; *matsya-vapuḥ*—the Lord, who had assumed the form of a fish; *yuga-kṣaye*—at the end of a *yuga; vihartu-kāmaḥ*—to enjoy His own pastimes; *pralaya-arṇave*—in the water of inundation; *abravīt*—said; *cikīrṣuḥ*—desiring to do; *ekānta-jana-priyaḥ*—most beloved by the devotees; *priyam*—something very beneficial.

TRANSLATION

Śukadeva Gosvāmī said: When King Satyavrata spoke in this way, the Supreme Personality of Godhead, who at the end of the yuga had assumed the form of a fish to benefit His devotee and enjoy His pastimes in the water of inundation, responded as follows.

TEXT 32

श्रीभगवानुवाच
सप्तमेह्यद्यतनादूर्ध्वमहन्येतदरिन्दम ।
निमङ्क्ष्यत्यप्ययाम्भोधौ त्रैलोक्यं भूर्भुवादिकम् ॥ ३२ ॥

śrī-bhagavān uvāca
saptame hy adyatanād ūrdhvam
ahany etad arindama
nimaṅkṣyaty apyayāmbhodhau
trailokyaṁ bhūr-bhuvādikam

śrī-bhagavān uvāca—the Supreme Personality of Godhead said; *saptame*—on the seventh; *hi*—indeed; *adyatanāt*—from today; *ūrdhvam*—forward; *ahani*—on the day; *etat*—this creation; *arimdama*—O King who can subdue your enemies; *nimaṅkṣyati*—shall be inundated; *apyaya-ambhodhau*—in the ocean of destruction; *trailokyam*—the three *lokas; bhūḥ-bhuva-ādikam*—namely Bhūrloka, Bhuvarloka and Svarloka.

TRANSLATION

The Supreme Personality of Godhead said: O King, who can subdue your enemies, on the seventh day from today the three worlds—Bhūḥ, Bhuvaḥ and Svaḥ—will all merge into the water of inundation.

TEXT 33

त्रिलोक्यां लीयमानायां संवर्ताम्भसि वै तदा ।
उपस्थास्यति नौः काचिद् विशाला त्वां मयेरिता ॥ ३३ ॥

tri-lokyāṁ līyamānāyāṁ
saṁvartāmbhasi vai tadā
upasthāsyati nauḥ kācid
viśālā tvāṁ mayeritā

tri-lokyām—the three *lokas; līyamānāyām*—upon being merged; *saṁvarta-ambhasi*—in the water of destruction; *vai*—indeed; *tadā*—at that time; *upasthāsyati*—will appear; *nauḥ*—boat; *kācit*—one; *viśālā*—very big; *tvām*—unto you; *mayā*—by Me; *īritā*—sent.

TRANSLATION

When all the three worlds merge into the water, a large boat sent by Me will appear before you.

TEXTS 34-35

त्वं तावदोषधीः सर्वा बीजान्युच्चावचानि च ।
सप्तर्षिभिः परिवृतः सर्वसत्त्वोपबृंहितः ॥ ३४ ॥
आरुह्य बृहतीं नावं विचरिष्यस्यविक्लवः ।
एकार्णवे निरालोके ऋषीणामेव वर्चसा ॥ ३५ ॥

tvaṁ tāvad oṣadhīḥ sarvā
bījāny uccāvacāni ca
saptarṣibhiḥ parivṛtaḥ
sarva-sattvopabṛṁhitaḥ

āruhya bṛhatīṁ nāvaṁ
vicariṣyasy aviklavaḥ
ekārṇave nirāloke
ṛṣīṇām eva varcasā

tvam—you; *tāvat*—until that time; *oṣadhīḥ*—herbs; *sarvāḥ*—all kinds of; *bījāni*—seeds; *ucca-avacāni*—lower and higher; *ca*—and; *sapta-ṛṣibhiḥ*—by the seven *ṛṣis; parivṛtaḥ*—surrounded; *sarva-sattva*—all kinds of living entities; *upabṛṁhitaḥ*—surrounded by; *āruhya*—getting on; *bṛhatīm*—very large; *nāvam*—boat; *vicariṣyasi*—shall travel; *aviklavaḥ*—without moroseness; *eka-arṇave*—in the ocean of inundation; *nirāloke*—without being illuminated; *ṛṣīṇām*—of the great *ṛṣis; eva*—indeed; *varcasā*—by the effulgence.

TRANSLATION

Thereafter, O King, you shall collect all types of herbs and seeds and load them on that great boat. Then, accompanied by the seven ṛṣis and surrounded by all kinds of living entities, you shall get aboard that boat, and without moroseness you shall easily travel with your companions on the ocean of inundation, the only illumination being the effulgence of the great ṛṣis.

TEXT 36

दोधूयमानां तां नावं समीरेण बलीयसा ।
उपस्थितस्य मे शृङ्गे निबध्नीहि महाहिना ॥ ३६ ॥

dodhūyamānāṁ tāṁ nāvaṁ
samīreṇa balīyasā
upasthitasya me śṛṅge
nibadhnīhi mahāhinā

dodhūyamānām—being tossed about; *tām*—that; *nāvam*—boat; *samīreṇa*—by the wind; *balīyasā*—very powerful; *upasthitasya*—situated nearby; *me*—of Me; *śṛṅge*—to the horn; *nibadhnīhi*—bind; *mahā-ahinā*—by the large serpent (Vāsuki).

TRANSLATION

Then, as the boat is tossed about by the powerful winds, attach the vessel to My horn by means of the great serpent Vāsuki, for I shall be present by your side.

TEXT 37

अहं त्वामृषिभिः सार्धं सहनावमुदन्वति ।
विकर्षन् विचरिष्यामि यावद् ब्राह्मी निशा प्रभो ॥ ३७ ॥

ahaṁ tvām ṛṣibhiḥ sārdhaṁ
saha-nāvam udanvati
vikarṣan vicariṣyāmi
yāvad brāhmī niśā prabho

aham—I; *tvām*—unto you; *ṛṣibhiḥ*—with all the saintly persons; *sārdham*—all together; *saha*—with; *nāvam*—the boat; *udanvati*—in the water of devastation; *vikarṣan*—contacting; *vicariṣyāmi*—I shall travel; *yāvat*—as long as; *brāhmī*—pertaining to Lord Brahmā; *niśā*—night; *prabho*—O King.

TRANSLATION

Pulling the boat, with you and all the ṛṣis in it, O King, I shall travel in the water of devastation until the night of Lord Brahmā's slumber is over.

PURPORT

This particular devastation actually took place not during the night of Lord Brahmā but during his day, for it was during the time of Cākṣuṣa Manu. Brahmā's night takes place when Brahmā goes to sleep, but in the daytime there are fourteen Manus, one of whom is Cākṣuṣa Manu. Therefore, Śrīla Viśvanātha Cakravartī Ṭhākura comments that although it was daytime for Lord Brahmā, Brahmā felt sleepy for a short time by the supreme will of the Lord. This short period is regarded as Lord Brahmā's night. This has been elaborately discussed by Śrīla Rūpa Gosvāmī in his *Laghu-bhāgavatāmṛta.* The following is a summary of his analysis. Because Agastya Muni cursed Svāyambhuva Manu, during the time of Svāyambhuva Manu a devastation took place. This devastation is mentioned in the *Matsya Purāṇa.* During the time of Cākṣuṣa Manu, by the supreme will of the Lord, there was suddenly another *pralaya,* or devastation. This is mentioned by Mārkaṇḍeya Ṛṣi in the *Viṣṇu-dharmottara.* At the end of Manu's time there is not necessarily a devastation, but at the end of the Cākṣuṣa-*manvantara,* the Supreme Personality of Godhead, by His illusory energy, wanted to show Satyavrata the effects of devastation. Śrīla Śrīdhara Svāmī also agrees with this opinion. The *Laghu-bhāgavatāmṛta* says:

madhye manvantarasyaiva
muneḥ śāpān manuṁ prati
pralayo 'sau babhūveti
purāṇe kvacid īryate

ayam ākasmiko jātaś
cākṣuṣasyāntare manoḥ
pralayaḥ padmanābhasya
līlayeti ca kutracit

sarva-manvantarasyānte
pralayo niścitaṁ bhavet
viṣṇu-dharmottare tv etat
mārkaṇḍeyeṇa bhāṣitam

manor ante layo nāsti
manave 'darśi māyayā
viṣṇuneti bruvāṇais tu
svāmibhir naiṣa manyate

TEXT 38

मदीयं महिमानं च परं ब्रह्मेति शब्दितम् ।
वेत्स्यस्यनुगृहीतं मे संप्रश्नैर्विवृतं हृदि ॥ ३८ ॥

madīyaṁ mahimānaṁ ca
paraṁ brahmeti śabditam
vetsyasy anugṛhītaṁ me
sampraśnair vivṛtaṁ hṛdi

madīyam—pertaining to Me; *mahimānam*—glories; *ca*—and; *param brahma*—the Supreme Brahman, the Absolute Truth; *iti*—thus; *śabditam*—celebrated; *vetsyasi*—you shall understand; *anugṛhītam*—being favored; *me*—by Me; *sampraśnaiḥ*—by inquiries; *vivṛtam*—thoroughly explained; *hṛdi*—within the heart.

TRANSLATION

You will be thoroughly advised and favored by Me, and because of your inquiries, everything about My glories, which are known as paraṁ brahma, will be manifest within your heart. Thus you will know everything about Me.

PURPORT

As stated in *Bhagavad-gītā* (15.15), *sarvasya cāhaṁ hṛdi sanniviṣṭo mattaḥ smṛtir jñānam apohanaṁ ca:* the Supreme Personality of Godhead,

Paramātmā, is situated in everyone's heart, and from Him come remembrance, knowledge and forgetfulness. The Lord reveals Himself in proportion to one's surrender to Him. *Ye yathā māṁ prapadyante tāṁs tathaiva bhajāmy aham*. In responsive cooperation, the Lord reveals Himself in proportion to one's surrender. That which is revealed to one who fully surrenders is different from what is revealed to one who surrenders partially. Everyone naturally surrenders to the Supreme Personality of Godhead, either directly or indirectly. The conditioned soul surrenders to the laws of nature in material existence, but when one fully surrenders to the Lord, material nature does not act upon him. Such a fully surrendered soul is favored by the Supreme Personality of Godhead directly. *Mām eva ye prapadyante māyām etāṁ taranti te*. One who has fully surrendered to the Lord has no fear of the modes of material nature, for everything is but an expansion of the Lord's glories (*sarvaṁ khalv idaṁ brahma*), and these glories are gradually revealed and realized. The Lord is the supreme purifier (*paraṁ brahma paraṁ dhāma pavitraṁ paramaṁ bhavān*). The more one is purified and the more he wants to know about the Supreme, the more the Lord reveals to him. Full knowledge of Brahman, Paramātmā and Bhagavān is revealed to the pure devotees. The Lord says in *Bhagavad-gītā* (10.11):

teṣām evānukampārtham
aham ajñāna-jaṁ tamaḥ
nāśayāmy ātma-bhāvastho
jñāna-dīpena bhāsvatā

"Out of compassion for them, I, dwelling in their hearts, destroy with the shining lamp of knowledge the darkness born of ignorance."

TEXT 39

इत्थमादिश्य राजानं हरिरन्तरधीयत ।
सोऽन्ववैक्षत तं कालं यं हृषीकेश आदिशत् ॥ ३९ ॥

ittham ādiśya rājānaṁ
harir antaradhīyata
so 'nvavaikṣata taṁ kālaṁ
yaṁ hṛṣīkeśa ādiśat

ittham—as aforementioned; *ādiśya*—instructing; *rājānam*—the King (Satyavrata); *hariḥ*—the Supreme Personality of Godhead; *antaradhīyata*—

disappeared from that place; *saḥ*—he (the King); *anvavaikṣata*—began to wait for; *tam kālam*—that time; *yam*—which; *hṛṣīka-īśaḥ*—Lord Hṛṣīkeśa, the master of all the senses; *ādiśat*—instructed.

TRANSLATION

After thus instructing the King, the Supreme Personality of Godhead immediately disappeared. Then King Satyavrata began to wait for that time of which the Lord had instructed.

TEXT 40

आस्तीर्य दर्भान् प्राक्कूलान् राजर्षिः प्रागुदङ्मुखः ।
निषसाद हरेः पादौ चिन्तयन् मत्स्यरूपिणः ॥ ४० ॥

āstīrya darbhān prāk-kūlān
rājarṣiḥ prāg-udaṅ-mukhaḥ
niṣasāda hareḥ pādau
cintayan matsya-rūpiṇaḥ

āstīrya—spreading; *darbhān*—*kuśa* grass; *prāk-kūlān*—the upper portion facing east; *rāja-ṛṣiḥ*—Satyavrata, the saintly King; *prāk-udak-mukhaḥ*—looking toward the northeast (*īśāna*); *niṣasāda*—sat down; *hareḥ*—of the Supreme Personality of Godhead; *pādau*—upon the lotus feet; *cintayan*—meditating; *matsya-rūpiṇaḥ*—who had assumed the form of a fish.

TRANSLATION

After spreading kuśa with its tips pointing east, the saintly King, himself facing the northeast, sat down on the grass and began to meditate upon the Supreme Personality of Godhead, Viṣṇu, who had assumed the form of a fish.

TEXT 41

ततः समुद्र उद्वेलः सर्वतः प्लावयन् महीम् ।
वर्धमानो महामेघैर्वर्षद्भिः समदृश्यत ॥ ४१ ॥

tataḥ samudra udvelaḥ
sarvataḥ plāvayan mahīm
vardhamāno mahā-meghair
varṣadbhiḥ samadṛśyata

tataḥ—thereafter; *samudraḥ*—the ocean; *udvelaḥ*—overflowing; *sarvataḥ*—everywhere; *plāvayan*—inundating; *mahīm*—the earth; *vardhamānaḥ*—increasing more and more; *mahā-meghaiḥ*—by gigantic clouds; *varṣadbhiḥ*—incessantly pouring rain; *samadṛśyata*—King Satyavrata saw it.

TRANSLATION

Thereafter, gigantic clouds pouring incessant water swelled the ocean more and more. Thus the ocean began to overflow onto the land and inundate the entire world.

TEXT 42

ध्यायन् भगवदादेशं ददृशे नावमागताम्।
तामारुरोह विप्रेन्द्रैरादायौषधिवीरुधः ॥ ४२ ॥

dhyāyan bhagavad-ādeśaṁ
dadṛśe nāvam āgatām
tām āruroha viprendrair
ādāyauṣadhi-vīrudhaḥ

dhyāyan—remembering; *bhagavat-ādeśam*—the order of the Supreme Personality of Godhead; *dadṛśe*—he saw; *nāvam*—a boat; *āgatām*—coming near; *tām*—aboard the boat; *āruroha*—got up; *vipra-indraiḥ*—with the saintly *brāhmaṇas; ādāya*—taking; *auṣadhi*—herbs; *vīrudhaḥ*—and creepers.

TRANSLATION

As Satyavrata remembered the order of the Supreme Personality of Godhead, he saw a boat coming near him. Thus he collected herbs and creepers, and, accompanied by saintly brāhmaṇas, he got aboard the boat.

TEXT 43

तमूचुर्मुनयः प्रीता राजन् ध्यायस्व केशवम्।
स वै नः संकटादस्मादविता शं विधास्यति॥ ४३ ॥

tam ūcur munayaḥ prītā
rājan dhyāyasva keśavam
sa vai naḥ saṅkaṭād asmād
avitā śaṁ vidhāsyati

tam—unto the King; *ūcuḥ*—said; *munayaḥ*—all the saintly *brāhmaṇas; prītāḥ*—being pleased; *rājan*—O King; *dhyāyasva*—meditate; *keśavam*—upon the Supreme Lord, Keśava; *saḥ*—His Lordship; *vai*—indeed; *naḥ*—us; *saṅkaṭāt*—from the great danger; *asmāt*—as now visible; *avitā*—will save; *śam*—auspiciousness; *vidhāsyati*—He will arrange.

TRANSLATION

The saintly brāhmaṇas, being pleased with the King, said to him: O King, please meditate upon the Supreme Personality of Godhead, Keśava. He will save us from this impending danger and arrange for our well-being.

TEXT 44

सोऽनुध्यातस्ततो राज्ञा प्रादुरासीन्महार्णवे ।
एकशृङ्गधरो मत्स्यो हैमो नियुतयोजनः ॥ ४४ ॥

so 'nudhyātas tato rājñā
prādurāsīn mahārṇave
eka-śṛṅga-dharo matsyo
haimo niyuta-yojanaḥ

saḥ—the Lord; *anudhyātaḥ*—being meditated upon; *tataḥ*—thereafter (hearing the words of the saintly *brāhmaṇas*); *rājñā*—by the King; *prādurāsīt*—appeared (before him); *mahā-arṇave*—in the great ocean of inundation; *eka-śṛṅga-dharaḥ*—with one horn; *matsyaḥ*—a big fish; *haimaḥ*—made of gold; *niyuta-yojanaḥ*—eight million miles long.

TRANSLATION

Then, while the King constantly meditated upon the Supreme Personality of Godhead, a large golden fish appeared in the ocean of inundation. The fish had one horn and was eight million miles long.

TEXT 45

निबध्य नावं तच्छृङ्गे यथोक्तो हरिणा पुरा ।
वरत्रेणाहिना तुष्टस्तुष्टाव मधुसूदनम् ॥ ४५ ॥

nibadhya nāvaṁ tac-chṛṅge
yathokto hariṇā purā

varatreṇāhinā tuṣṭas
tuṣṭāva madhusūdanam

nibadhya—anchoring; *nāvam*—the boat; *tat-śṛṅge*—onto the horn of the big fish; *yathā-uktaḥ*—as advised; *hariṇā*—by the Supreme Personality of Godhead; *purā*—before; *varatreṇa*—used as a rope; *ahinā*—by the great serpent (of the name Vāsuki); *tuṣṭaḥ*—being pleased; *tuṣṭāva*—he satisfied; *madhusūdanam*—the Supreme Lord, the killer of Madhu.

TRANSLATION

Following the instructions formerly given by the Supreme Personality of Godhead, the King anchored the boat to the fish's horn, using the serpent Vāsuki as a rope. Thus being satisfied, he began offering prayers to the Lord.

TEXT 46

श्रीराजोवाच
अनाद्यविद्योपहतात्मसंविद-
स्तन्मूलसंसारपरिश्रमातुराः ।
यदृच्छयोपसृता यमाप्नुयु-
र्विमुक्तिदो नः परमो गुरुर्भवान् ॥ ४६ ॥

śrī-rājovāca
anādy-avidyopahatātma-saṁvidas
tan-mūla-saṁsāra-pariśramāturāḥ
yadṛcchayopasṛtā yam āpnuyur
vimuktido naḥ paramo gurur bhavān

śrī-rājā uvāca—the King offered prayers as follows; *anādi*—from time immemorial; *avidyā*—by ignorance; *upahata*—has been lost; *ātma-saṁvidaḥ*—knowledge about the self; *tat*—that is; *mūla*—the root; *saṁsāra*—material bondage; *pariśrama*—full of miserable conditions and hard work; *āturāḥ*—suffering; *yadṛcchayā*—by the supreme will; *upasṛtāḥ*—being favored by the *ācārya; yam*—the Supreme Personality of Godhead; *āpnuyuḥ*—can achieve; *vimukti-daḥ*—the process of liberation; *naḥ*—our; *paramaḥ*—the supreme; *guruḥ*—spiritual master; *bhavān*—Your Lordship.

TRANSLATION

The King said: By the grace of the Lord, those who have lost their self-knowledge since time immemorial, and who because of this ignorance are involved in a material, conditional life full of miseries, obtain the chance to meet the Lord's devotee. I accept that Supreme Personality of Godhead as the supreme spiritual master.

PURPORT

The Supreme Personality of Godhead is actually the supreme spiritual master. The Supreme Lord knows everything about the suffering of the conditioned soul, and therefore He appears in this material world, sometimes personally, sometimes by an incarnation and sometimes by authorizing a living being to act on His behalf. In all cases, however, He is the original spiritual master who enlightens the conditioned souls who are suffering in the material world. The Lord is always busy helping the conditioned souls in many ways. Therefore He is addressed here as *paramo gurur bhavān.* The representative of the Supreme Personality of Godhead who acts to spread Kṛṣṇa consciousness is also guided by the Supreme Lord to act properly in executing the Lord's order. Such a person may appear to be an ordinary human being, but because he acts on behalf of the Supreme Personality of Godhead, the supreme spiritual master, he is not to be neglected as ordinary. It is therefore said, *ācāryaṁ māṁ vijānīyāt:* an *ācārya* who acts on behalf of the Supreme Personality of Godhead should be understood to be as good as the Supreme Lord Himself.

sākṣād dharitvena samasta-śāstrair
uktas tathā bhāvyata eva sadbhiḥ
kintu prabhor yaḥ priya eva tasya
vande guroḥ śrī-caraṇāravindam

Viśvanātha Cakravartī Ṭhākura has advised that the spiritual master acting on the Supreme Lord's behalf must be worshiped as being as good as the Supreme Lord, for he is the Lord's most confidential servant in broadcasting the Lord's message for the benefit of the conditioned souls involved in the material world.

TEXT 47

जनोऽबुधोऽयं निजकर्मबन्धनः
सुखेच्छया कर्म समीहतेऽसुखम् ।

यत्सेवया तां विधुनोत्यसन्मतिं
ग्रन्थिं स भिन्द्याद् धृदयं स नो गुरुः ॥ ४७ ॥

jano 'budho 'yaṁ nija-karma-bandhanaḥ
sukhecchayā karma samīhate 'sukham
yat-sevayā tāṁ vidhunoty asan-matiṁ
granthiṁ sa bhindyād dhṛdayaṁ sa no guruḥ

janaḥ—the conditioned soul subjected to birth and death; *abudhaḥ*—most foolish because of accepting the body as the self; *ayam*—he; *nija-karma-bandhanaḥ*—accepting different bodily forms as a result of his sinful activities; *sukha-icchayā*—desiring to be happy within this material world; *karma*—fruitive activities; *samīhate*—plans; *asukham*—but it is for distress only; *yat-sevayā*—by rendering service unto whom; *tām*—the entanglement of *karma; vidhunoti*—clears up; *asat-matim*—the unclean mentality (accepting the body as the self); *granthim*—hard knot; *saḥ*—His Lordship the Supreme Personality of Godhead; *bhindyāt*—being cut off; *hṛdayaṁ*—in the core of the heart; *saḥ*—He (the Lord); *naḥ*—our; *guruḥ*—the supreme spiritual master.

TRANSLATION

In hopes of becoming happy in this material world, the foolish conditioned soul performs fruitive activities that result only in suffering. But by rendering service to the Supreme Personality of Godhead, one becomes free from such false desires for happiness. May my supreme spiritual master cut the knot of false desires from the core of my heart.

PURPORT

For material happiness, the conditioned soul involves himself in fruitive activities, which actually put him into material distress. Because the conditioned soul does not know this, he is said to be in *avidyā,* or ignorance. Because of a false hope for happiness, the conditioned soul becomes involved in various plans for material activity. Here Mahārāja Satyavrata prays that the Lord sever this hard knot of false happiness and thus become his supreme spiritual master.

TEXT 48

यत्सेवयाग्नेरिव रुद्ररोदनं
पुमान् विजह्यान्मलमात्मनस्तमः ।

भजेत वर्णं निजमेष सोऽव्ययो
भूयात् स ईशः परमो गुरोर्गुरुः ॥ ४८ ॥

yat-sevayāgner iva rudra-rodanaṁ
pumān vijahyān malam ātmanas tamaḥ
bhajeta varṇaṁ nijam eṣa so 'vyayo
bhūyāt sa īśaḥ paramo guror guruḥ

yat-sevayā—the Supreme Personality of Godhead, by serving whom; *agneḥ*—in touch with fire; *iva*—as it is; *rudra-rodanam*—a block of silver or gold becomes purified; *pumān*—a person; *vijahyāt*—can give up; *malam*—all the dirty things of material existence; *ātmanaḥ*—of one's self; *tamaḥ*—the mode of ignorance, by which one performs pious and impious activities; *bhajeta*—may revive; *varṇam*—his original identity; *nijam*—one's own; *eṣaḥ*—such; *saḥ*—He; *avyayaḥ*—inexhaustible; *bhūyāt*—let Him become; *saḥ*—He; *īśaḥ*—the Supreme Personality of Godhead; *paramaḥ*—the supreme; *guroḥ guruḥ*—the spiritual master of all other spiritual masters.

TRANSLATION

One who wants to be free of material entanglement should take to the service of the Supreme Personality of Godhead and give up the contamination of ignorance, involving pious and impious activities. Thus one regains his original identity, just as a block of gold or silver sheds all dirt and becomes purified when treated with fire. May that inexhaustible Supreme Personality of Godhead become our spiritual master, for He is the original spiritual master of all other spiritual masters.

PURPORT

In human life one is meant to undergo austerity to purify one's existence. *Tapo divyaṁ putrakā yena sattvaṁ śuddhyet*. Because of contamination by the modes of material nature, one continues in the cycle of birth and death (*kāraṇaṁ guṇa-saṅgo 'sya sad-asad-yoni janmasu*). Therefore the purpose of human life is to purify oneself of this contamination so that one can regain his spiritual form and not undergo this cycle of birth and death. The recommended process of decontamination is devotional service to the Lord. There are various processes for self-realization, such as *karma, jñāna* and *yoga,* but none of them is equal to the process of devotional service. As gold and silver can be freed from all dirty contamination by being put into a fire but not merely by being washed, the living entity can be awakened to his own identity by performing devotional service (*yat-sevayā*), but not by *karma, jñāna* or *yoga.* Cultivation of speculative knowledge or practice of yogic gymnastics will not be helpful.

The word *varṇam* refers to the luster of one's original identity. The original luster of gold or silver is brilliant. Similarly, the original luster of the living being, who is part of the *sac-cid-ānanda-vigraha,* is the luster of *ānanda,* or pleasure. *Ānandamayo bhyāsāt.* Every living entity has the right to become *ānandamaya,* joyful, because he is part of the *sac-cid-ānanda-vigraha,* Kṛṣṇa. Why should the living being be put into tribulation because of dirty contamination by the material modes of nature? The living entity should become purified and regain his *svarūpa,* his original identity. This he can do only by devotional service. Therefore, one should adopt the instructions of the Supreme Personality of Godhead, who is described here as *guror guruḥ,* the spiritual master of all other spiritual masters.

Even though we may not have the fortune to contact the Supreme Lord personally, the Lord's representative is as good as the Lord Himself because such a representative does not say anything unless it is spoken by the Supreme Personality of Godhead. Śrī Caitanya Mahāprabhu therefore gives a definition of *guru. Yāre dekha, tāre kaha 'kṛṣṇa'-upadeśa:* the bona fide *guru* is he who advises his disciples exactly in accordance with the principles spoken by Kṛṣṇa. The bona fide *guru* is he who has accepted Kṛṣṇa as *guru.* This is the *guru-paramparā* system. The original *guru* is Vyāsadeva because he is the speaker of *Bhagavad-gītā* and *Śrīmad-Bhāgavatam,* wherein everything spoken relates to Kṛṣṇa. Therefore *guru-pūjā* is known as Vyāsa-pūjā. In the final analysis, the original *guru* is Kṛṣṇa, His disciple is Nārada, whose disciple is Vyāsa, and in this way we gradually come in touch with the *guru-paramparā.* One cannot become a *guru* if he does not know what the Personality of Godhead Kṛṣṇa or His incarnation wants. The mission of the *guru* is the mission of the Supreme Personality of Godhead: to spread Kṛṣṇa consciousness all over the world.

TEXT 49

न यत्प्रसादायुतभागलेश-
मन्ये च देवा गुरवो जनाः स्वयम् ।
कर्तुं समेताः प्रभवन्ति पुंस-
स्तमीश्वरं त्वां शरणं प्रपद्ये ॥ ४९ ॥

na yat-prasādāyuta-bhāga-leśam
anye ca devā guravo janāḥ svayam
kartuṁ sametāḥ prabhavanti puṁsas
tam īśvaraṁ tvāṁ śaraṇaṁ prapadye

na—not; *yat-prasāda*—of the mercy of the Supreme Personality of Godhead; *ayuta-bhāga-leśam*—only one ten-thousandth; *anye*—others; *ca*—also; *devāḥ*—even the demigods; *guravaḥ*—the so-called *gurus; janāḥ*—the total population; *svayam*—personally; *kartum*—to execute; *sametāḥ*—all together; *prabhavanti*—can become equally able; *puṁsaḥ*—by the Supreme Personality of Godhead; *tam*—unto Him; *īśvaram*—unto the Supreme Personality of Godhead; *tvām*—unto You; *śaraṇam*—shelter; *prapadye*—let me surrender.

TRANSLATION

Neither all the demigods, nor the so-called gurus nor all other people, either independently or together, can offer mercy that equals even one ten-thousandth of Yours. Therefore I wish to take shelter of Your lotus feet.

PURPORT

It is said, *kāmais tais tair hṛta jñānāḥ prapadyante 'nya-devatāḥ:* people in general, being motivated by material desires, worship the demigods to get fruitive results very quickly. People generally do not become devotees of Lord Viṣṇu, since Lord Viṣṇu never becomes the order-supplier of His devotee. Lord Viṣṇu does not give a devotee benedictions that will create a further demand for benedictions. By worshiping the demigods one may get results, but, as described in *Bhagavad-gītā, antavat tu phalaṁ teṣāṁ tad bhavaty alpa-medhasām:* whatever great benedictions one may achieve from the demigods are all temporary. Because the demigods themselves are temporary, their benedictions are also temporary and have no permanent value. Those who aspire for such benedictions have a poor fund of knowledge (*tad bhavaty alpa-medhasām*). The benedictions of Lord Viṣṇu are different. By the mercy of the Lord Viṣṇu, one can be completely freed from material contamination and go back home, back to Godhead. Therefore the benedictions offered by the demigods cannot compare to even one ten-thousandth of the Lord's benedictions. One should not, therefore, try to obtain benedictions from the demigods or false *gurus.* One should aspire only for the benediction offered by the Supreme Personality of Godhead. As the Lord says in *Bhagavad-gītā* (18.66):

sarva-dharmān parityajya
mām ekaṁ śaraṇaṁ vraja
ahaṁ tvāṁ sarva-pāpebhyo
mokṣayiṣyāmi mā śucaḥ

"Abandon all varieties of religion and just surrender unto Me. I shall deliver you from all sinful reaction. Do not fear." This is the greatest benediction.

TEXT 50

अचक्षुरन्धस्य यथाग्रणीः कृत-
स्तथा जनस्याविदुषोऽबुधो गुरुः ।
त्वमर्कदृक् सर्वदृशां समीक्षणो
वृतो गुरुर्नः स्वगतिं बुभुत्सताम् ॥ ५० ॥

acakṣur andhasya yathāgraṇīḥ kṛtas
tathā janasyāviduṣo 'budho guruḥ
tvam arka-dṛk sarva-dṛśāṁ samīkṣaṇo
vṛto gurur naḥ sva-gatiṁ bubhutsatām

acakṣuḥ—one who does not have his power of sight; *andhasya*—for such a blind person; *yathā*—as; *agraṇīḥ*—the leader, who goes first; *kṛtaḥ*—accepted; *tathā*—similarly; *janasya*—such a person; *aviduṣaḥ*—who has no knowledge of the goal of life; *abudhaḥ*—a foolish rascal; *guruḥ*—the spiritual master; *tvam*—Your Lordship; *arka-dṛk*—appear like the sun; *sarva-dṛśām*—of all sources of knowledge; *samīkṣaṇaḥ*—the complete seer; *vṛtaḥ*—accepted; *guruḥ*—the spiritual master; *naḥ*—our; *sva-gatim*—one who knows his real self-interest; *bubhutsatām*—such an enlightened person.

TRANSLATION

As a blind man, being unable to see, accepts another blind man as his leader, people who do not know the goal of life accept someone as a guru who is a rascal and a fool. But we are interested in self-realization. Therefore we accept You, the Supreme Personality of Godhead, as our spiritual master, for You are able to see in all directions and are omniscient like the sun.

PURPORT

The conditioned soul, being wrapped in ignorance and therefore not knowing the goal of life, accepts a *guru* who can juggle words and make some display of magic that is wonderful to a fool. Sometimes a foolish person accepts someone as a *guru* because he can manufacture a small quantity of gold by mystic yogic power. Because such a disciple has a poor fund of knowledge, he cannot judge whether the manufacture of gold is the criterion for a *guru.* Why should one not accept the Supreme Personality of Godhead, Kṛṣṇa, from whom unlimited numbers of gold mines come into being? *Ahaṁ sarvasya prabhavo mattaḥ sarvaṁ pravartate*. All the gold mines are created by the energy of the Supreme Personality of Godhead. Therefore, why should one accept a magician who can manufacture only a small portion of gold? Such *gurus* are accepted by those who are blind, not knowing the goal of life. Mahārāja Satyavrata, however, knew the goal of life. He knew the Supreme Personality of Godhead, and therefore he accepted the Lord as his *guru.* Either the Supreme Lord or His representative can become *guru.* The Lord says, *mām eva ye prapadyante māyām etāṁ taranti te:* "One can get relief from the clutches of *māyā* as soon as he surrenders unto Me." Therefore it is the *guru's* business to instruct his disciple to surrender to the Supreme Personality of Godhead if he wants relief from the material clutches. This is the symptom of the *guru.* This same principle was instructed by Śrī Caitanya Mahāprabhu: *yāre dekha, tāre kaha 'kṛṣṇa'-upadeśa*. In other words, one is advised not to accept a *guru* who does not follow the path of instruction given by Lord Kṛṣṇa.

TEXT 51

जनो जनस्यादिशतेऽसतीं गतिं
यया प्रपद्येत दुरत्ययं तमः ।
त्वं त्वव्ययं ज्ञानममोघमञ्जसा
प्रपद्यते येन जनो निजं पदम् ॥ ५१ ॥

jano janasyādiśate 'satīṁ gatiṁ
yayā prapadyeta duratyayaṁ tamaḥ
tvaṁ tv avyayaṁ jñānam amogham añjasā
prapadyate yena jano nijaṁ padam

janaḥ—a person who is not a bona fide *guru* (an ordinary person); *janasya*—of an ordinary person who does not know the goal of life; *ādiśate*—instructs; *asatīm*—impermanent, material; *gatim*—the goal of life; *yayā*—by such knowledge; *prapadyeta*—he surrenders; *duratyayam*—insurmountable; *tamaḥ*—to ignorance; *tvam*—Your Lordship; *tu*—but; *avyayam*—indestructible; *jñānam*—knowledge; *amogham*—without material contamination; *añjasā*—very soon; *prapadyate*—achieves; *yena*—by such knowledge; *janaḥ*—a person; *nijam*—his own; *padam*—original position.

TRANSLATION

A materialistic so-called guru instructs his materialistic disciples about economic development and sense gratification, and because of such instructions the foolish disciples continue in the materialistic existence of ignorance. But Your Lordship gives knowledge that is eternal, and the intelligent person receiving such knowledge is quickly situated in his original constitutional position.

PURPORT

So-called *gurus* instruct their disciples for the sake of material profit. Some *guru* advises that one meditate in such a way that his intelligence will increase in regard to keeping his body fit for sense gratification. Another *guru* advises that sex is the ultimate goal of life and that one should therefore engage in sex to the best of his ability. These are the instructions of foolish *gurus.* In other words, because of the instructions of a foolish *guru* one remains perpetually in material existence and suffers its tribulations. But if one is intelligent enough to take instructions from the Supreme Personality of Godhead, as enunciated in *Bhagavad-gītā* or the Sāṅkhya philosophy of Kapiladeva, one can very soon attain liberation and be situated in his original position of spiritual life. The words *nijaṁ padam* are significant. The living entity, being part and parcel of the Supreme Personality of Godhead, has the birthright to a position in Vaikuṇṭhaloka, or the spiritual world, where there is no anxiety. Therefore, one should follow the instructions of the Supreme Personality of Godhead. Then, as stated in *Bhagavad-gītā, tyaktvā dehaṁ punar janma naiti mām eti so 'rjuna:* after giving up one's body, one will return home, back to Godhead. The Lord lives in the spiritual world in His original personality, and a devotee who follows the instructions of the Lord approaches Him (*mām eti*). As a spiritual person, such a devotee returns to the Personality of Godhead and plays and dances with Him. That is the ultimate goal of life.

TEXT 52

त्वं सर्वलोकस्य सुहृत् प्रियेश्वरो
ह्यात्मा गुरुर्ज्ञानमभीष्टसिद्धिः ।
तथापि लोको न भवन्तमन्धधी-
र्जानाति सन्तं हृदि बद्धकामः ॥ ५२ ॥

tvaṁ sarva-lokasya suhṛt priyeśvaro
hy ātmā gurur jñānam abhīṣṭa-siddhiḥ
tathāpi loko na bhavantam andha-dhīr
jānāti santaṁ hṛdi baddha-kāmaḥ

tvam—You, my dear Lord; *sarva-lokasya*—of all planets and their inhabitants; *suhṛt*—the most well-wishing friend; *priya*—the most dear; *īśvaraḥ*—the supreme controller; *hi*—also; *ātmā*—the supreme soul; *guruḥ*—the supreme teacher; *jñānam*—the supreme knowledge; *abhīṣṭa-siddhiḥ*—the fulfillment of all desires; *tathā api*—still; *lokaḥ*—persons; *na*—not; *bhavantam*—unto You; *andha-dhīḥ*—because of blind intelligence; *jānāti*—can know; *santam*—situated; *hṛdi*—in his heart; *baddha-kāmaḥ*—because of being bewildered by material lusty desires.

TRANSLATION

My Lord, You are the supreme well-wishing friend of everyone, the dearmost friend, the controller, the Supersoul, the supreme instructor and the giver of supreme knowledge and the fulfillment of all desires. But although You are within the heart, the foolish, because of lusty desires in the heart, cannot understand You.

PURPORT

Herein the reason for foolishness is described. Because the conditioned soul in this material world is full of materialistic lusty desires, he cannot understand the Supreme Personality of Godhead, although the Lord is situated in everyone's heart (*īśvaraḥ sarva-bhūtānāṁ hṛd-deśe 'rjuna tiṣṭhati*). It is because of this foolishness that one cannot take instructions from the Lord, although the Lord is ready to instruct everyone both externally and internally. The Lord says, *dadāmi buddhi-yogaṁ tam yena mām upayānti te.* In other words, the Lord can give instructions on devotional service by which one can return home, back to Godhead. Unfortunately, however, people do not take this devotional service. The Lord, being situated in everyone's heart, can give one complete instructions on going back to Godhead, but because of lusty desires one engages himself in materialistic activities and does not render service to the Lord. Therefore one is bereft of the value of the Lord's instructions. By mental speculation one can understand that one is not the body but a spirit soul, but unless one engages in devotional service, the real purpose of life is never fulfilled. The real purpose of life is to go back home, back to Godhead, and live with the Supreme Personality of Godhead, play with the Supreme Personality of Godhead, dance with the Supreme Personality of Godhead and eat with the Supreme Personality of Godhead. These are different items of *ānanda,* spiritual happiness in spiritual variegatedness. Even though one may come to the platform of *brahma-bhūta* and understand his spiritual identity by speculative knowledge, one cannot enjoy spiritual life without understanding the Supreme Personality of Godhead. This is indicated here by the word *abhīṣṭa-siddhiḥ.* One can fulfill the ultimate goal of life only by engaging in devotional service to the Lord. Then the Lord will give one proper instructions on how to go back home, back to Godhead.

TEXT 53

त्वं त्वामहं देववरं वरेण्यं
प्रपद्य ईशं प्रतिबोधनाय ।
छिन्ध्यर्थदीपैर्भगवन् वचोभि-
र्ग्रन्थीन् हृदय्यान् विवृणु स्वमोकः ॥ ५३ ॥

tvaṁ tvām ahaṁ deva-varaṁ vareṇyaṁ
prapadya īśaṁ pratibodhanāya
chindhy artha-dīpair bhagavan vacobhir
granthīn hṛdayyān vivṛṇu svam okaḥ

tvam—how exalted You are; *tvām*—unto You; *aham*—myself; *deva-varam*—worshiped by the demigods; *vareṇyam*—the greatest of all; *prapadye*—fully surrendering; *īśam*—unto the supreme controller; *pratibodhanāya*—for understanding the real purpose of life; *chindhi*—cut off; *artha-dīpaiḥ*—by the light of purposeful instruction; *bhagavan*—O Supreme Lord; *vacobhiḥ*—by Your words; *granthīn*—knots; *hṛdayyān*—fixed within the core of the heart; *vivṛṇu*—kindly explain; *svam okaḥ*—my destination in life.

TRANSLATION

O Supreme Lord, for self-realization I surrender unto You, who are worshiped by the demigods as the supreme controller of everything. By Your instructions, exposing life's purpose, kindly cut the knot from the core of my heart and let me know the destination of my life.

PURPORT

Sometimes it is argued that people do not know who is a spiritual master and that finding a spiritual master from whom to get enlightenment in regard to the destination of life is very difficult. To answer all these questions, King Satyavrata shows us the way to accept the Supreme Personality of Godhead as the real spiritual master. The Supreme Lord has given full directions in *Bhagavad-gītā* about how to deal with everything in this material world and how to return home, back to Godhead. Therefore, one should not be misled by so-called *gurus* who are rascals and fools. Rather, one should directly see the Supreme Personality of Godhead as the *guru* or instructor. It is difficult, however, to understand *Bhagavad-gītā* without the help of the *guru.* Therefore the *guru* appears in the *paramparā* system. In *Bhagavad-gītā* (4.34) the Supreme Personality of Godhead recommends:

tad viddhi praṇipātena
paripraśnena sevayā
upadekṣyanti te jñānaṁ
jñāninas tattva-darśinaḥ

"Just try to learn the truth by approaching a spiritual master. Inquire from him submissively and render service unto him. The self-realized soul can impart knowledge unto you because he has seen the truth." Lord Kṛṣṇa directly instructed Arjuna. Arjuna is therefore *tattva-darśī* or *guru.* Arjuna accepted the Supreme Personality of Godhead (*paraṁ brahma paraṁ dhāma pavitraṁ paramaṁ bhavān*). Similarly, following in the footsteps of Śrī Arjuna, who is a personal devotee of the Lord, one should accept the supremacy of Lord Kṛṣṇa, as supported by Vyāsa, Devala, Asita, Nārada and later by the *ācāryas* Rāmānujācārya, Madhvācārya, Nimbārka and Viṣṇusvāmī and still later by the greatest *ācārya,* Śrī Caitanya Mahāprabhu. Where, then, is the difficulty in finding a *guru*? If one is sincere he can find the *guru* and learn everything. One should take lessons from the *guru* and find out the goal of life. Mahārāja Satyavrata, therefore, shows us the way of the *mahājana. Mahājano yena gataḥ sa panthāḥ* . One should surrender to the Supreme Personality of

Godhead (*daśāvatāra*) and learn from Him about the spiritual world and the goal of life.

TEXT 54

श्रीशुक उवाच
इत्युक्तवन्तं नृपतिं भगवानादिपूरुषः ।
मत्स्यरूपी महाम्भोधौ विहरंस्तत्त्वमब्रवीत् ॥ ५४ ॥

śrī-śuka uvāca
ity uktavantaṁ nṛpatiṁ
bhagavān ādi-pūruṣaḥ
matsya-rūpī mahāmbhodhau
viharaṁs tattvam abravīt

śrī-śukaḥ uvāca—Śrī Śukadeva Gosvāmī said; *iti*—thus; *uktavantam*—being addressed by Mahārāja Satyavrata; *nṛpatim*—unto the King; *bhagavān*—the Supreme Personality of Godhead; *ādi-pūruṣaḥ*—the original person; *matsya-rūpī*—who had assumed the form of a fish; *mahā-ambhodhau*—in that water of inundation; *viharan*—while moving; *tattvam abravīt*—explained the Absolute Truth.

TRANSLATION

Śukadeva Gosvāmī continued: When Satyavrata had thus prayed to the Supreme Personality of Godhead, who had assumed the form of a fish, the Lord, while moving in the water of inundation, explained to him the Absolute Truth.

TEXT 55

पुराणसंहितां दिव्यां सांख्ययोगक्रियावतीम् ।
सत्यव्रतस्य राजर्षेरात्मगुह्यमशेषतः ॥ ५५ ॥

purāṇa-saṁhitāṁ divyāṁ
sāṅkhya-yoga-kriyāvatīm
satyavratasya rājarṣer
ātma-guhyam aśeṣataḥ

purāṇa—the subject matter explained in *the Purāṇas,* the old histories, especially the *Matsya Purāṇa; saṁhitām*—the Vedic instructions contained in *Brahma-saṁhitā* and other *saṁhitās; divyām*—all transcendental literatures; *sāṅkhya*—the philosophical way of *sāṅkhya-yoga; yoga*—the science of self-realization or *bhakti-yoga; kriyāvatīm*—practically applied in life; *satyavratasya*—of King Satyavrata; *rāja-ṛṣeḥ*—the great king and saint; *ātma-guhyam*—all the mysteries of self-realization; *aśeṣataḥ*—including all branches.

TRANSLATION

The Supreme Personality of Godhead thus explained to King Satyavrata the spiritual science known as sāṅkhya-yoga, the science by which one distinguishes between matter and spirit [in other words, bhakti-yoga], along with the instructions contained in the Purāṇas [the old histories] and the saṁhitās. The Lord explained Himself in all these literatures.

TEXT 56

अश्रौषीदृषिभिः साकमात्मतत्त्वमसंशयम् ।
नाव्यासीनो भगवता प्रोक्तं ब्रह्म सनातनम् ॥ ५६ ॥

aśrauṣīd ṛṣibhiḥ sākam
ātma-tattvam asaṁśayam
nāvy āsīno bhagavatā
proktaṁ brahma sanātanam

aśrauṣīt—he heard; *ṛṣibhiḥ*—the great saintly persons; *sākam*—with; *ātma-tattvam*—the science of self-realization; *asaṁśayam*—without any doubt (because it was spoken by the Supreme Lord); *nāvi āsīnaḥ*—sitting in the boat; *bhagavatā*—by the Supreme Personality of Godhead; *proktam*—explained; *brahma*—all transcendental literatures; *sanātanam*—eternally existing.

TRANSLATION

While sitting in the boat, King Satyavrata, accompanied by the great saintly persons, listened to the instructions of the Supreme Personality of Godhead in regard to self-realization. These instructions were all from the eternal Vedic literature [brahma]. Thus the King and sages had no doubt about the Absolute Truth.

TEXT 57

अतीतप्रलयापाय उत्थिताय स वेधसे ।
हत्वासुरं हयग्रीवं वेदान् प्रत्याहरद्धरिः ॥ ५७ ॥

atīta-pralayāpāya
utthitāya sa vedhase
hatvāsuraṁ hayagrīvaṁ
vedān pratyāharad dhariḥ

atīta—passed; *pralaya-apāye*—at the end of the inundation; *utthitāya*—to bring him to his senses after sleeping; *saḥ*—the Supreme Lord; *vedhase*—unto Lord Brahmā; *hatvā*—after killing; *asuram*—the demon; *hayagrīvam*—by the name Hayagrīva; *vedān*—all the Vedic records; *pratyāharat*—delivered; *hariḥ*—the Supreme Personality of Godhead.

TRANSLATION

At the end of the last inundation [during the period of Svāyambhuva Manu] the Supreme Personality of Godhead killed the demon named Hayagrīva and delivered all the Vedic literatures to Lord Brahmā when Lord Brahmā awakened from sleeping.

TEXT 58

स तु सत्यव्रतो राजा ज्ञानविज्ञानसंयुतः ।
विष्णोः प्रसादात् कल्पेऽस्मिन्नासीद् वैवस्वतो मनुः ॥ ५८ ॥

sa tu satyavrato rājā
jñāna-vijñāna-saṁyutaḥ
viṣṇoḥ prasādāt kalpe 'sminn
āsīd vaivasvato manuḥ

saḥ—he; *tu*—indeed; *satyavrataḥ*—Satyavrata; *rājā*—the King; *jñāna-vijñāna-saṁyutaḥ*—enlightened in full knowledge and its practical use; *viṣṇoḥ*—of Lord Viṣṇu; *prasādāt*—by the mercy; *kalpe asmin*—in this period (ruled by Vaivasvata Manu); *āsīt*—became; *vaivasvataḥ manuḥ*—Vaivasvata Manu.

TRANSLATION

King Satyavrata was illuminated with all Vedic knowledge by the mercy

of Lord Viṣṇu, and in this period he has now taken birth as Vaivasvata Manu, the son of the sun-god.

PURPORT

Śrīla Viśvanātha Cakravartī Ṭhākura gives his verdict that Satyavrata appeared in the Cākṣuṣa-*manvantara.* When the Cākṣuṣa-*manvantara* ended, the period of Vaivasvata Manu began. By the grace of Lord Viṣṇu, Satyavrata received instructions from the second fish incarnation and was thus enlightened in all spiritual knowledge.

TEXT 59

सत्यव्रतस्य राजर्षेर्मायामत्स्यस्य शार्ङ्गिणः ।
संवादं महदाख्यानं श्रुत्वा मुच्येत किल्बिषात् ॥ ५९ ॥

satyavratasya rājarṣer
māyā-matsyasya śārṅgiṇaḥ
saṁvādaṁ mahad-ākhyānaṁ
śrutvā mucyeta kilbiṣāt

satyavratasya—of King Satyavrata; *rāja-ṛṣeḥ*—of the great king; *māyā-matsyasya*—and the fish incarnation; *śārṅgiṇaḥ*—who had one horn on His head; *saṁvādam*—the description or dealings; *mahat-ākhyānam*—the great story; *śrutvā*—by hearing; *mucyeta*—is delivered; *kilbiṣāt*—from all sinful reactions.

TRANSLATION

This story concerning the great King Satyavrata and the fish incarnation of the Supreme Personality of Godhead, Viṣṇu, is a great transcendental narration. Anyone who hears it is delivered from the reactions of sinful life.

TEXT 60

अवतारं हरेर्योऽयं कीर्तयेदन्वहं नरः ।
सङ्कल्पास्तस्य सिध्यन्ति स याति परमां गतिम् ॥ ६० ॥

avatāraṁ harer yo 'yaṁ
kīrtayed anvahaṁ naraḥ
saṅkalpās tasya sidhyanti
sa yāti paramāṁ gatim

avatāram—incarnation; *hareḥ*—of the Supreme Personality of Godhead; *yaḥ*—whoever; *ayam*—he; *kīrtayet*—narrates and chants; *anvaham*—daily; *naraḥ*—such a person; *saṅkalpāḥ*—all ambitions; *tasya*—of him; *sidhyanti*—become successful; *saḥ*—such a person; *yāti*—goes back; *paramām gatim*—back home to Godhead, the supreme place.

TRANSLATION

One who narrates this description of the Matsya incarnation and King Satyavrata will certainly have all his ambitions fulfilled, and he will undoubtedly return home, back to Godhead.

TEXT 61

प्रलयपयसि धातुः सुप्तशक्तेर्मुखेभ्यः
श्रुतिगणमपनीतं प्रत्युपादत्त हत्वा ।
दितिजमकथयद् यो ब्रह्म सत्यव्रतानां
तमहमखिलहेतुं जिह्ममीनं नतोऽस्मि ॥ ६१ ॥

pralaya-payasi dhātuḥ supta-śakter mukhebhyaḥ
śruti-gaṇam apanītaṁ pratyupādatta hatvā
ditijam akathayad yo brahma satyavratānāṁ
tam aham akhila-hetuṁ jihma-mīnaṁ nato 'smi

pralaya-payasi—in the water of inundation; *dhātuḥ*—from Lord Brahmā; *supta-śakteḥ*—who was inert because of sleeping; *mukhebhyaḥ*—from the mouths; *śruti-gaṇam*—Vedic records; *apanītam*—stolen; *pratyupādatta*—gave back to him; *hatvā*—by killing; *ditijam*—the great demon; *akathayat*—explained; *yaḥ*—one who; *brahma*—Vedic knowledge; *satyavratānām*—for the enlightenment of Satyavrata and the great saintly persons; *tam*—unto Him; *aham*—I; *akhila-hetum*—unto the cause of all causes; *jihma-mīnam*—appearing as and pretending to be a great fish; *nataḥ asmi*—I offer my respectful obeisances.

TRANSLATION

I offer my respectful obeisances unto the Supreme Personality of Godhead, who pretended to be a gigantic fish, who restored the Vedic literature to Lord Brahmā when Lord Brahmā awakened from sleep, and who explained the essence of Vedic literature to King Satyavrata and the great saintly persons.

PURPORT

Here is a summary of Satyavrata's meeting with the fish incarnation of Lord Viṣṇu. Lord Viṣṇu's purpose was to take back all the Vedic literatures from the demon Hayagrīva and restore them to Lord Brahmā. Incidentally, by His causeless mercy, the Lord spoke with Satyavrata. The word *satyavratānām* is significant because it indicates that those on the level of Satyavrata can take knowledge from the *Vedas* delivered by the Supreme Personality of Godhead. Whatever is spoken by the Supreme Lord is accepted as *Veda.* As stated in *Bhagavad-gītā, vedānta-kṛd veda-vit:* the Supreme Personality of Godhead is the compiler of all Vedic knowledge, and He knows the purport of the *Vedas.* Therefore, anyone who takes knowledge from the Supreme Personality of Godhead, Kṛṣṇa, or from *Bhagavad-gītā* as it is, knows the purpose of the *Vedas* (*vedaiś ca sarvair aham eva vedyaḥ*). One cannot understand Vedic knowledge from the *veda-vāda-ratās,* who read the *Vedas* and misconstrue their subject matter. One has to know the *Vedas* from the Supreme Personality of Godhead.

Thus end the Bhaktivedanta purports of the Eighth Canto, Twenty-fourth Chapter, of the Śrīmad-Bhāgavatam, *entitled "Matsya, the Lord's Fish Incarnation."*

—This commentation has been finished in our New Delhi center today, the first of September, 1976, the day of Rādhāṣṭamī, by the grace of the Supreme Personality of Godhead and the *ācāryas.* Śrīla Narottama dāsa Ṭhākura says, *tāṅdera caraṇa sevi bhakta-sane vāsa janame janame haya, ei abhilāṣa.* I am attempting to present *Śrīmad-Bhāgavatam* in the English language by the order of my spiritual master, Śrīmad Bhaktisiddhānta Sarasvatī Ṭhākura, and by his grace the work of translation is gradually progressing, and the European and American devotees who have joined the Kṛṣṇa consciousness movement are helping me considerably. Thus we have expectations of finishing the great task before my passing away. All glories to Śrī Guru and Gaurāṅga.

END OF THE EIGHTH CANTO

Appendixes

About the Author

His Divine Grace A.C. Bhaktivedanta Swami Prabhupāda appeared in this world in 1896 in Calcutta, India. He first met his spiritual master, Śrīla Bhaktisiddhānta Sarasvatī Gosvāmi, in Calcutta in 1922. Śrīla Bhaktisiddhānta Sarasvatī, a prominent religious scholar and the founder of sixty-four Gauḍīya Maṭhas (Vedic institutes) in India, liked this educated young man and convinced him to dedicate his life to teaching Vedic knowledge. Śrīla Prabhupāda became his student and, in 1933, his formally initiated disciple.

At their first meeting, Śrīla Bhaktisiddhānta Sarasvatī requested Śrīla Prabhupāda to broadcast Vedic knowledge in English. In the years that followed, Śrīla Prabhupāda wrote a commentary on the *Bhagavad-gītā,* assisted the Gauḍīya Maṭha in its work, and, in 1944, started *Back to Godhead,* an English fortnightly magazine. Single-handedly, Śrīla Prabhupāda edited it, typed the manuscripts, checked the galley proofs, and even distributed the individual copies. The magazine is now being continued by his disciples all over the world.

In 1950 Śrīla Prabhupāda retired from married life, adopting the *vānaprastha* (retired) order to devote more time to his studies and writing. He traveled to the holy city of Vṛndāvana, where he lived in humble circumstances in the historic temple of Rādhā-Dāmodara. There he engaged for several years in deep study and writing. He accepted the renounced order of life (*sannyāsa*) in 1959. At Rādhā-Dāmodara, Śrīla Prabhupāda began work on his life's masterpiece: a multivolume commentated translation of the eighteen-thousand-verse *Śrīmad-Bhāgavatam* (*Bhāgavata Purāṇa*). He also wrote *Easy Journey to Other Planets.*

After publishing three volumes of the *Bhāgavatam,* Śrīla Prabhupāda came to the United States, in September 1965, to fulfill the mission of his spiritual master. Subsequently, His Divine Grace wrote more than sixty volumes of authoritative commentated translations and summary studies of the philosophical and religious classics of India.

When he first arrived by freighter in New York City, Śrīla Prabhupāda was practically penniless. It was after almost a year of great difficulty that he established the International Society for Krishna Consciousness in July of 1966. Before he passed away on November 14, 1977, he had guided the Society and seen it grow to a worldwide confederation of more than one hundred *ashrams,* schools, temples, institutes, and farm communities.

In 1972 His Divine Grace introduced the Vedic system of primary and secondary education in the West by founding the *gurukula* school in Dallas, Texas. Since then his disciples have established similar schools throughout the United States and the rest of the world.

Śrīla Prabhupāda also inspired the construction of several large international cultural centers in India. The center at Śrīdhāma Māyāpur is the site for a planned spiritual city, an ambitious project for which construction will extend over many years to come. In Vṛndāvana are the magnificent Kṛṣṇa-Balarāma Temple and International Guesthouse, *gurukula* school, and Śrīla Prabhupāda Memorial and Museum. There is also a major cultural and educational center in Mumbai. There are beautiful temples in Delhi, Bangalore, Ahmedabad and Vadodara besides many other centers throughout India.

Śrīla Prabhupāda's most significant contribution, however, is his books. Highly respected by scholars for their authority, depth, and clarity, they are used as textbooks in numerous college courses. His writings have been translated into over fifty languages. The Bhaktivedanta Book Trust, established in 1972 exclusively to publish the works of His Divine Grace, has thus become the world's largest publisher of books in the field of Indian religion and philosophy.

In just twelve years, despite his advanced age, Śrīla Prabhupāda circled the globe fourteen times on lecture tours that took him to six continents. In spite of such a vigorous schedule, Śrīla Prabhupāda continued to write prolifically. His writings constitute a veritable library of Vedic philosophy, religion, literature, and culture.

References

The purports of *Śrīmad-Bhāgavatam* are all confirmed by standard Vedic authorities. The following authentic scriptures are cited in this volume. For specific page references, consult the general index.

Aitareya Upaniṣad

Bahvṛca-śruti

Bhagavad-gītā

Bhāgavata-candra-candrikā

Bhakti-rasāmṛta-sindhu

Brahma-saṁhitā

Brahma-vaivarta Purāṇa

Brahma-yāmala

Bṛhan-nāradīya Purāṇa

Caitanya-candrodaya-nāṭaka

Caitanya-caritāmṛta

Chāndogya Upaniṣad

Daśāvatāra-stotra

Gautamīya Tantra

Gopāla-tāpanī Upaniṣad

Īśopaniṣad

Laghu-bhāgavatāmṛta

Mahābhārata

Manu-saṁhitā

Matsya Purāṇa

Padma Purāṇa

Śikṣāṣṭaka

Śrīmad-Bhāgavatam

Śvetāśvatara Upaniṣad

Taittirīya Upaniṣad

Vedānta-sūtra

Viṣṇu-dharmottara

Viṣṇu Purāṇa

Glossary

A

Ācamana—a ritual of purification in which one sips water and simultaneously chants names of the Supreme Lord.

Ācārya—a spiritual master who teaches by his own example, and who sets the proper religious example for all human beings.

Acit—the inert material nature; without life or consciousness

Ārati— a ceremony in which one greets and worships the Lord in His form of a Deity by offerings such as incense, a flame, water, a fine cloth, a fragrant flower, a peacock-feather, and yak-tail whisk, accompanied by ringing of a bell and chanting of *mantras*.

Arcana—the procedures followed for worshiping the *arcā-vigraha*, the Deity in the temple; engaging all the senses in the service of the Lord.

Arghya—a ceremonial offering, in a conch shell, of water and other auspicious items.

Artha—economic development.

Asat—not eternal, temporary.

Āśrama—a spiritual order of life. The four *āśramas* are *brahmacārī* or student life, *gṛhastha* or married life, *vānaprastha* or retired life, and *sannyāsa* or the renounced order of life; the home of the spiritual master, a place where spiritual practices are executed.

Asura—demon, one who does not follow the principles of scripture, an atheist, a gross materialist. One who is envious of God, and is averse to the supremacy and service of the Supreme Lord, Viṣṇu.

Avatāra—literally "one who descends." A partially or fully empowered incarnation of Lord Kṛṣṇa who descends from the spiritual sky to the material universe with a particular mission described in scriptures. Lord Śrī Kṛṣṇa is the original Personality of Godhead from whom all *avatāras* originate. There are two broad categories of *avatāras*. Some, like Śrī Kṛṣṇa, Śrī Rāma and Śrī Nṛsiṁha, are Viṣṇu-tattva, i.e. direct forms of God Himself, the source of all power. Others are ordinary souls (*jīva-tattva*) who are called *śaktyāveśa avatāras*, and are empowered by the Lord to execute a certain purpose.

B

Bhagavad-gītā—a seven-hundred verse record of a conversation between Lord Kṛṣṇa and His disciple, Arjuna, from the *Bhīṣma Parva* of the *Mahābhārata* of Vedavyāsa. The conversation took place between two armies minutes before the start of an immense fratricidal battle. Kṛṣṇa teaches the science of the Absolute Truth and the importance of devotional service to the despondent Arjuna, and it contains the essence of all Vedic wisdom. Śrīla Prabhupāda's annotated English translation is called *Bhagavad-gītā As It Is*; This most essential text of spiritual knowledge, The Song of the Lord, contains Kṛṣṇa's instructions to Arjuna at Kurukṣetra. It is found in the *Mahābhārata*. The *Mahābhārata* is classified as *smṛti-śāstra*, a supplement of the *śruti-śāstra*. *Śruti*, the core Vedic literature, includes the four *Vedas* (*Ṛg, Sāma, Yajur* and *Atharva*) and the *Upaniṣads*. *Śruti* advances the understanding of the absolute. B*hagavad-gītā* is also known as *Gītopaniṣad*, or a *śruti* text spoken by the Supreme Personality of Godhead Himself. Therefore, Śrīla Prabhupāda wrote in a letter, the *Gītā* should be taken as *śruti*. But they take it as smṛti because it is part of the *smṛti* (*Mahābhārata*). In one sense it is both *śruti* and *smṛti*. In only 700 verses, the *Bhagavad-gītā* summarizes all Vedic knowledge about the soul, God, *sanātana-dharma*, sacrifice, *yoga*, *karma*, reincarnation, the modes of material nature, *Vedānta* and pure devotion.

Bhakta—a devotee of the Lord; one who performs devotional service (*bhakti*).

Bhakti-mārga—the path of developing devotion to Kṛṣṇa.

Bhakti-yoga—the system of cultivation of pure devotional service to the Supreme Personality of Godhead, Lord Kṛṣṇa, which is not tinged by sense gratification or philosophical speculation. It consists of nine *aṅgas* or parts: (1) *śravaṇaṁ*–hearing about the transcendental holy name, form, and other qualities of the Lord (2) *kīrtanaṁ*– chanting about these qualities, (3) *viṣṇoḥ smaraṇaṁ*–remembering them, (4) *pāda-sevanam*–serving the lotus feet of the Lord, (5) *arcanaṁ*–worshipping the Deity of the Lord, (6) *vandanaṁ*–offering prayers to the Lord, (7) *dāsyaṁ* –serving His mission, (8) *sakhyam*–making friends with the Lord, and (9) *ātma-nivedanam*–surrendering everything unto Him.

Brahmacarya—celibate student life, the first order of Vedic spiritual life; the vow of strict abstinence from sex indulgence.

Brahmajyoti—the impersonal bodily effulgence emanating from the transcendental body of the Supreme Lord Kṛṣṇa, which constitutes the brilliant illumination of the spiritual sky; From Kṛṣṇa's transcendental personal form of eternity, knowledge and bliss emanates a shining effulgence called the *brahmajyoti* (light of Brahman). The material *prakṛti*, the souls or *jīvas* who desire to enjoy matter, and *kāla* (time), are situated within this *brahmajyoti*, which is pure existence devoid of difference and activity. It is the impersonal Brahman of the Mayavādīs, and the Clear Light of some Buddhist sects. For many mystics and philosophers the world over, the *brahmajyoti* is the indefinable One from which all things emerge in the beginning and merge into at the end. The *brahmajyoti* is Kṛṣṇa's feature of *sat* (eternality) separated from *cit* (knowledge) and *ānanda* (bliss).

Brahman—(1) the infinitesimal spiritual individual soul, (2) the impersonal, all-pervasive aspect of the Supreme, (3) the Supreme Personality of Godhead and (4) the *mahat-tattva*, or total material substance; this Sanskrit term comes from the root *bṛh*, which means to grow or to evolve. The *Cāndogya Upaniṣad* describes Brahman as *tajjalān*, as that (*tat*) from which the world arises (*ja*), into which it returns (*la*), and by which is supported and lives (*an*). Impersonalists equate Brahman with the *brahmajyoti*. But in its fullest sense, Brahman is the *vastu*, the actual substance of the world: (1) Viṣṇu as the Supreme Soul (*paraṁ brahman*), (2) the individual self as the subordinate soul (*jīva-brahman*), and (3) matter as creative nature (*mahad-brahman*). Viṣṇu is accepted by all schools of Vaiṣṇava *Vedānta* as the transcendental, unlimited *Puruṣottama* (Supreme Person), while the individual souls and matter are His conscious and unconscious energies (*cid-acid-śakti*).

Brahmāstra—a nuclear weapon produced by chanting a *mantra*, more powerful than many atomic bombs. It could be used only on a person of equal or superior strength. This weapon was given by Droṇa to Arjuna.

C

Cakra (Sudarśana)—the personal disc weapon of the Supreme Lord, Viṣṇu. On the top of Viṣṇu temples there is usually a cakra.

Chandas—the different meters of Vedic hymns.

Cit—alive and conscious; unlimited knowledge.

D

Daityas—demons; a race of demons descending from Diti.

Dama—controlling the senses and not deviating from the Lord's service.

Demigods—universal controllers and residents of the higher planets, and also known as *deva* or *devata*. Demigods are *jīvas* whom the Supreme Lord Kṛṣṇa or Viṣṇu empowers to represent Him in the management of the universe. The first of the demigods is Brahmā. Some of the principal demigods are Indra—demigod of rain, Sūrya—of sunshine, Vāyu—of wind, Candra—of moonshine and Varuṇa—of water. There are thirty-three million demigods in all. Demigods live in the upper regions of the universe called *svarga*, or heaven. Less intelligent people worship the demigods through *karma-kāṇḍa* rituals to get material blessings in this life, and to be granted entrance into *svarga* in the next life. In the *Bhagavad-gītā*, Lord Kṛṣṇa condemns demigod worship as being *avidhi-pūrvaka*, against the true purpose of the *Vedas*.

Deva—a demigod or godly person.

Dharma—religious principles; one's natural occupation; the quality of rendering service, which is the essential, eternal quality of the soul, regarded as inseparable from it. The Sanskrit term *dharma* is variously translated as duty, virtue, morality, righteousness, or religion, but no single English word conveys the actual import of *dharma*. Dharma ultimately means to surrender to the Supreme Lord, as Lord Kṛṣṇa commands Arjuna in the *Gīta*.

Dvādaśī—the twelfth day after the full or new moon, thus the day after Ekādaśī, when one breaks one's fast by eating grains.

Dvija—a *brāhmaṇa*, or twice-born person.

E

Ekādaśī—directly presided over by Lord Hari, Ekādaśī is a holy day for Vaiṣṇavas. It falls on the eleventh day after both the full and new moon days. Abstinence from grains and beans is prescribed. One should utilize this day for fasting and increasing one's devotion to Lord Kṛṣṇa by intensifying the chanting of the Hare Kṛṣṇa *mantra* and other devotional activities.

G

Gadā—the club held by Lord Viṣṇu.

Goloka Vṛndāvana (Kṛṣṇaloka)—the highest spiritual planet in the kingdom of God, Lord Kṛṣṇa's personal abode.

Gopīs—the cowherd girls of Vraja, who are generally the counterparts of Śrī Kṛṣṇa's *hlādini-sākti*, Śrīmatī Rādhārāṇī, and His most surrendered and confidential devotees. They assist Her as maidservants in her conjugal pastimes with the Supreme Personality of Godhead.

Gṛhastha—regulated householder life. One who leads a God conscious married life and raises a family in Kṛṣṇa consciousness according to the Vedic social system; the second order of Vedic spiritual life.

Guṇa-avatāras—the presiding deities of the three modes of nature: Viṣṇu, Brahmā and Śiva. They control the modes of goodness, passion and ignorance respectively.

Guru—spiritual master; one of the three spiritual authorities for a Vaiṣṇava. Literally, this term means heavy. The spiritual master is heavy with knowledge.

Guru-pūjā—worship of the spiritual master.

H

Hare Kṛṣṇa mantra—a sixteen-word prayer composed of the names Hare, Kṛṣṇa, and Rāma: Hare Kṛṣṇa, Hare Kṛṣṇa, Kṛṣṇa Kṛṣṇa, Hare Hare, Hare Rāma, Hare Rāma, Rāma Rāma, Hare Hare. Hare is an address to Harā, another name for His eternal consort, Śrīmatī Rādhārāṇī. Kṛṣṇa, "the all-attractive one," and Rāma, "the all-pleasing one," are names of God. The chanting of this *mantra* is the most recommended means for spiritual progress in this age of Kali, as it cleanses the mind of all impurities, and helps to understand one's true identity as an eternal spiritual being. Lord Caitanya personally designated it as the *mahā-mantra* and practically demonstrated the effects of the chanting.

J

Jagat—the material universe.

Jaya—an exclamation meaning "All victory to you!" or "All glories to you!"

Jīva (jīvātmā)—the living entity, vital force in the body who is an eternal individual soul, part and parcel of the Supreme Lord; one of the five *tattvas* or Vedic ontological truths.

Jīva-tattva—the living entities, atomic parts of the Supreme Lord.

Jñāna—knowledge. Material *jñāna* does not go beyond the material body and its expansions. Transcendental *jñāna* discriminates between matter and spirit. Perfect *jñāna* is knowledge of the body, the soul and the Supreme Lord.

Jñāna-kāṇḍa—One of the three divisions of the *Vedas*, which deals with empirical speculation in pursuit of truth; also such speculation itself; the portions of the *Vedas* containing knowledge of Brahman or spirit.

Jñānī—one who is engaged in the cultivation of knowledge (especially by philosophical speculation). Upon attaining perfection, a *jñānī* surrenders to Kṛṣṇa.

K

Kali-yuga—the present age, the Age of Kalī, the Age of Quarrel and Hypocrisy. The fourth and last age in the cycle of a *mahā-yuga*. It began 5,000 years ago, and lasts for a total of 432,000 years. It is characterized by irreligious practice and stringent material miseries.

Kalpa—Brahmā's daytime: 4,320,000,000 years.

Kāma—lust; the desire to gratify one's own senses; desire, especially material desire and sexual desire; lust, as opposed to *prema*, or love of God.

Kamaṇḍalu—the water-pot carried by *sannyāsīs*.

Karatālas—hand cymbals used in *kīrtana*.

Karma—1. material action performed according to scriptural regulations; 2. action pertaining to the development of the material body; 3. any material action which will incur a subsequent reaction and 4. the material reaction one incurs due to fruitive activities. The soul receives due reaction to work by taking his next birth in a lower species, or the human species, or a higher species. Or the soul may be liberated from birth and death altogether. All this depends upon whether the *karma* performed within this lifetime is ignorant, passionate, good or transcendental.

Karma-kāṇḍa—the division of the *Vedas* which deals with fruitive activities performed for the purpose of gradual purification of the grossly entangled materialist; the path of fruitive work.

Karmī—a fruitive laborer, one who is attached to the fruits of work, a materialist who works hard to enjoy material life.

Kīrtana—glorification of the Supreme Lord; narrating or singing the glories of the Supreme Personality of Godhead and His Holy Names; the devotional process of chanting the names and glories of the Supreme Lord.

Kṛṣṇaloka—*See:* Goloka Vṛndāvana.

Kṣatriya—second of the four social orders of the *varṇāśrama* system; a warrior who is inclined to fight and lead others; the administrative or protective occupation.

Kuśa—an auspicious grass used in Vedic rituals and sacrifices.

L

Līlā-avatāras—innumerable incarnations, like Matsya, Kurma, Rāma and Nṛsiṁha, who descend to display the spiritual pastimes of the Personality of Godhead in the material world.

Loka—planet.

M

Mahājana—one of the twelve great self-realized souls, an authority in the science of Kṛṣṇa Consciousness, who preaches the path of devotional service to the people in general; one who understands the Absolute Truth.

Mahā-mantra— *See:* Hare Kṛṣṇa mantra

Mahat-tattva—the original, undifferentiated form of the total material energy, from which the material world is manifested when the three modes of material nature are activated by the glance of Mahā-Viṣṇu.

Mantra—A transcendental sound or Vedic hymn, a prayer or chant; a pure sound vibration when repeated over and over delivers the mind from its material inclinations and illusion. The Vedic scriptures are composed of many thousands of *mantras.*

Manu—son of Brahmā who is the original father and lawgiver of the human race; a generic name for any of the fourteen universal rulers also known as Manvantara-avataras who appear in each day of Lord Brahmā. Their names are (1) Svāyambhuva; (2) Svārociṣa; (3) Uttama; (4) Tāmasa; (5) Raivata; (6) Cākṣusa; (7) Vaivasvata; (8) Sāvarṇi; (9) Dakṣa-sāvarṇi; (10) Brahma-sāvarṇi; (11) Dharma-sāvarṇi; (12) Rudra-sāvarṇi; (13) Deva-sāvarni; (14) Indra-sāvarṇi.

Manvantara—duration of each Manu' s reign, comprising 306,720,000 years.

Manvantara-avatāras—the incarnations of the Supreme Lord who appear during the reign of each Manu.

Mathurā—Lord Kṛṣṇa's abode, and birth place, surrounding Vṛndāvana. Lord Krsṇa displayed many of His pastimes here after leaving Vṛndāvana. At the end of Lord Kṛṣṇa's manifest *līlā*, Vajranābha, His grandson, was put in charge of this sacred city.

Māyā—Māyāvāda philosophy. Māyāvāda in Sanskrit means doctrine of illusion. In India, the philosophies of the Buddha and of Śaṅkarācārya are called Māyāvāda. The second grew out of the first. The fundamental principles accepted by both are the following: (1) name, form, individuality, thoughts, desires and words arise from *māyā* or illusion, not God; (2) *māyā* cannot be rationally explained, since the very idea that anything needs explaining is itself *māyā*; (3) the individual self or soul is not eternal, because upon liberation it ceases to exist; (4) like *māyā*, the state of liberation is beyond all explanation. The main difference between the two is that Śaṅkarācārya's Māyāvāda asserts that beyond *māyā* is an eternal impersonal monistic reality, Brahman, the nature of which is the self. Buddhism, however, aims at extinction (*nirodha*) as the final goal. Of the two, Śaṅkarācārya's Māyāvāda is more dangerous, as it apparently derives its authority from the *Vedas*. Much word-jugglery is employed to defend the Vedic origins of Śaṅkarācārya's Māyāvāda. But ultimately Māyāvādīs dispense with Vedic authority by concluding that the Supreme cannot be known through *śabda*, that the name of Kṛṣṇa is a material vibration, that the form of Kṛṣṇa is illusion, and so on. The Śaṅkarites agree with the Buddhists that *nāma-rūpa* (name and form) must always be *māyā*. Therefore Vaiṣṇavas reject both kinds of Māyāvāda as atheism. Buddhists generally do not deny that they are atheists, whereas the Śaṅkarite Māyāvādīs claim to be theists. But actually they are monists and pantheists. Their claim to theism is refuted by their belief that the Supreme Self is overcome by *māyā* and becomes the bound soul. Śaṅkarācārya's Māyāvāda is similar in significant ways to the Western doctrine of solipsism. Like solipsism, it arrives at a philosophical dead end. The questions that remain unanswered are: If my consciousness is the only reality, why can't I change the universe at will, simply by thought? And if my own self is the only reality, why am I dependent for my life, learning and happiness upon a world full of living entities that refuse to acknowledge this reality?

Māyā—illusion; an energy of Krṣna's which deludes the living entity into forgetfulness of the Supreme Lord. That which is not, unreality, deception, forgetfulness, material illusion. Under illusion a man thinks he can be happy in this temporary material world. The nature of the material world is that the more a man tries to exploit the material situation, the more he is bound by *māyā's* complexities; This is a Sanskrit term of many meanings. It may mean energy; *yoga-māyā* is the spiritual energy sustaining the transcendental manifestation of the spiritual Vaikuṇṭha world, while the reflection, *mahā-māyā*, is the energy of the material world. The Lord's twofold *māyā* bewilders the jīva, hence *māyā* also means bewilderment or illusion. Transcendental bewilderment is in love, by which the devotee sees God as his master, friend, dependent or amorous beloved. The material bewilderment of the living entity begins with his attraction to the glare of the brahmajyoti. That attraction leads to his entanglement in the modes of material nature. According to Bhaktisiddhānta Sarasvatī Ṭhākura, *māyā* also means that which can be measured. This is the feature of Lord Kṛṣṇa's *prakṛti* that captures the minds of scientific materialists. The Vaiṣṇava and Māyāvāda explanations of *māyā* are not the same.

Māyāvāda—the impersonal philosophy propounded by Śaṅkarācārya, which proposes the unqualified oneness of God and the living entities (who are both conceived of as being ultimately formless) and the non-reality of manifest nature; the philosophy that everything is one and that the Absolute Truth is not a person.

Mayāvādī—one who propounds the impersonal philosophy of Māyāvāda.

Mokṣa—liberation from material bondage.

Mṛdaṅga—a two-headed clay drum used for *kīrtana* performances and congregational chanting.

Muni—a sage.

N

Nirguṇa—without material qualities; uncontaminated by the three modes of material nature.

O

Oṁkāra—oṁ, the root of Vedic knowledge; known as the *mahā-vākya*, the supreme sound; the transcendental syllable which represents Kṛṣṇa, and which is vibrated by transcendentalists for attainment of the Supreme while undertaking sacrifices, charities and penances; it denotes the Personality of Godhead as the root of the creation, maintenance and destruction of the cosmic manifestation.

P

Padma—the lotus flower held by Lord Viṣṇu.

Pādya—water ceremoniously offered for washing feet.

Paramahaṁsa—a topmost, God-realized, swanlike devotee of the Supreme Lord; the highest stage of *sannyāsa*.

Paramparā—the disciplic succession, beginning with Kṛṣṇa, through which spiritual knowledge is transmitted by bonafide spiritual masters; literally, one after the other.

Prajāpatis—the progenitors of living entities, chief of whom is Lord Brahmā; the demigods in charge of populating the universe.

Prasāda, or prasādam—"the mercy of Lord Kṛṣṇa." Food spiritualized by being prepared for the pleasure of Kṛṣṇa, and by offering with love and devotion. Ordinary food subjects one to karmic reactions, one of the reasons being the many living entities that gave up their lives during the preparation. But food offered to Kṛṣṇa is freed of sin and invokes an attraction to Him.

Puruṣa—the enjoyer, or male; the living entity or the Supreme Lord; Viṣṇu, the incarnation of the Lord for material creation; the male or controlling principle. This term may be applied to both, the individual living being and the Supreme Personality of Godhead.

R

Rasa—relationship between the Lord and the living entities; mellow, or the sweet taste of a relationship, especially between the Lord and the living entities. There are five principal varieties of *rasa*—neutral relationship (*śānta-rasa*), relationship as servant (*dāsya-rasa*), as friend (*sākhya-rasa*), as parent (*vātsalya-rasa*) and conjugal lover (*mādhurya-rasa*). Just as our present material body permits us to engage in karma (physical activities), the spiritual *rasa*-body permits us to engage in *līlā*, Kṛṣṇa's endlessly expanding spiritual activities.

Ṛṣi—a sage who performs austerities.

S

Sac-cid-ānanda-vigraha—the Lord's transcendental form, which is eternal and full of knowledge and bliss; the eternal transcendental form of the living entity.

Śakti-tattva—plenary expansions of the Lord's internal potency; the various energies of the Lord.

Sama—control of the mind.

Saṁhitās—supplementary Vedic literatures expressing the conclusions of self-realized authorities.

Sampradāya—a disciplic succession of spiritual masters, along with the followers in that tradition, through which spiritual knowledge is transmitted; school of thought.

Śaṅkha—a son of King Viraṭa. He was killed by Droṇa during the Kurukṣetra war; the conchshell held by Lord Viṣṇu.

Saṅkīrtana— congregational or public glorification of the Supreme Lord Kṛṣṇa through chanting of His holy names, and glorification of His fame and pastimes.

Sannyāsa—the renounced order, the fourth stage of Vedic spiritual life in the Vedic system of *varṇāsrama-dharma*, which is free from family relationships, and in which all activities are completely dedicated to Kṛṣṇa. It is the order of ascetics who travel and constantly preach the message of Godhead for the benefit of all. It is usually accepted at age fifty, after a man has fulfilled his household responsibilities.

Śāstra—the revealed scriptures, obeyed by all those who follow the Vedic teachings. Śās means "to regulate and direct" and tra means "an instrument"; Vedic literature; The Vedic scriptures; one of the three authorities for a Vaiṣṇava. In his purport to *Cc.*, *Ādi-līlā* 17.157, Śrīla Prabhupāda writes: The word *śāstra* is derived from the dhātu, or verbal root, śas. *Sas-dhātu* pertains to controlling or ruling. A government's ruling through force or weapons is called *śastra*. Thus whenever there is ruling, either by weapons or by injunctions, the *śas-dhātu* is the basic principle. Between *śastra* (ruling through weapons) and *śāstra* (ruling through the injunctions of the scriptures), the better is *śāstra*. Our Vedic scriptures are not ordinary law books of human common sense; they are the statements of factually liberated persons unaffected by the imperfectness of the senses. *Śāstra* must be correct always, not sometimes correct and sometimes incorrect. In the Vedic scriptures, the cow is described as a mother. Therefore she is a mother for all time; it is not, as some rascals say, that in the Vedic age she was a mother but she is not in this age. If *śāstra* is an authority, the cow is a mother always; she was a mother in the Vedic age, and she is a mother in this age also. If one acts according to the injunctions of *śāstra*, he is freed from the reactions of sinful activity. For example, the propensities for eating flesh, drinking wine and enjoying sex life are all natural to the conditioned soul. The path of such enjoyment is called *pravṛtti-mārga*. The *śāstra* says, *pravṛttir eṣāṁ bhūtānāṁ nivṛttis tu mahā-phalā:* one should not be carried away by the propensities of defective conditioned life; one should be guided by the principles of the *śāstras*. A child's propensity is to play all day long, but it is the injunction of the *śāstras* that the parents should take care to educate him. The *śāstras* are there just to guide the activities of human society. But because people do not refer to the instructions of *śāstras*, which are free from defects and imperfections, they are therefore misguided by so-called educated teachers and leaders who are full of the deficiencies of conditioned life.

Sat—eternal, unlimited existence.

Satya-yuga—the first and best of the four cyclic ages of a *mahā-yuga* in the progression of universal time. Satya-yuga is characterized by virtue, wisdom and religion. It is known as the golden age, when people lived as long as one hundred thousand years. It lasts 1,728,000 solar years.

Śloka—a Sanskrit verse.

Smārta-brāhmaṇa—a *brāhmaṇa* interested more in the external performance of the rules and rituals of the *Vedas* than in attaining Lord Kṛṣṇa who is the goal of the *Vedas*; one who strictly follows the Vedic principles on the mundane platform.

Smṛti—remembrance, a *vyabhicāri-bhāva*; revealed scriptures supplementary to the *śruti*, or original Vedic scriptures, which are the *Vedas* and *Upaniṣads*; scriptures compiled by living entities under transcendental direction; the corollaries of the *Vedas*; one of the five functions of *buddhi*.

Soma-rasa—a life-extending heavenly beverage available on the moon to demigods on the higher planets.

Sravaṇam kīrtanaṁ viṣṇoḥ—the devotional process of hearing and chanting about Lord Viṣṇu, or Kṛṣṇa.

Śruti—knowledge via hearing; the original Vedic scriptures (the *Vedas* and *Upaniṣads*) given directly by the Supreme Lord.

Śruti-mantras—the hymns of the *Vedas*.

Stotra—a prayer.

Śūdra—a member of the fourth social order, laborer class, in the traditional Vedic social system They render service to the three higher classes, namely the *brāhmaṇas*, the *kṣatriyas*, and the *vaiśyas*.

Svāmī—*See:* Gosvāmī.

T

Tantras—minor scriptures describing various rituals, mostly for persons in the mode of ignorance; also refer to Vedic literatures consisting mostly of dialogues between Lord Śiva and Durgā which contain instructions on Deity worship and other aspects of spiritual practice; many *tantras* have special hymns for conjuring magic or producing mystical effects.

Tapasya—the voluntary acceptance of hardships for spiritual realization, such as rising early in the morning and taking a bath, fasting on certain days of the month etc.

Tattva—truth, reality. According to Baladeva Vidyābhūṣaṇa, Vedic knowledge categorizes reality into five *tattvas*, or ontological truths: *īśvara* (the Supreme Lord), *jīva* (the living entity), *prakṛti* (nature), *kāla* (eternal time) and *karma* (activity).

Tilaka—sacred clay markings placed on the forehead and other parts of the body to designate one as a follower of Viṣṇu, Rāma, Śiva etc.

Titikṣā—tolerance; endurance of unhappiness.

U

Upāsanā-kāṇḍa—portions of the *Vedas* dealing with ceremonies of worship, especially demigod worship; one of the three departments of Vedic knowledge.

V

Vaikuṇṭha—the eternal planets of the spiritual world, the abode of Lord Nārāyaṇa, which lies beyond the coverings of the material universe. Literally, "the place with no anxiety."

Vaiṣṇava—a devotee of the Supreme Lord, Viṣṇu, or Kṛṣṇa.

Vaiśya—member of the mercantile and agricultural class in the Vedic *varṇāśrama* system; the third Vedic social order.

Vānaprastha—A retired householder, a member of the third Vedic spiritual order or *āśrama*, who quits home to cultivate renunciation and travels to holy places, in preparation for the renounced order of life.

Varṇa—the four socio-occupational divisions of Vedic society. Contrary to popular misconception, *varṇas* are nor fixed by birth, but are determined by a person's inclination toward different types of work and his psychological qualities. The four *varṇas* are *brāhmaṇas*, *kṣatriyas*, *vaiśyas* and *śūdras*.

Varṇāśrama-dharma—the system of four social and four spiritual orders of Vedic society, based on the individual's psycho-physical qualities and tendencies toward particular types of work.

Veda-vāda-rata—one who gives his own explanation of the *Vedas*; a smārta; fruitive workers who become entangled in material activities disguised as spiritual activities.

Vedas—the original *Veda* was divided into four by Śrīla Vyāsadeva. The four original Vedic scriptures, *Saṁhitās* (*Ṛg, Sāma, Atharva* and *Yajur*) and the 108 *Upaniṣads, Mahābhārata, Vedānta-sūtra*, etc. The system of eternal wisdom compiled by Śrīla Vyāsadeva, the literary incarnation of the Supreme Lord, for the gradual upliftment of all mankind from the state of bondage to the state of liberation. The word *veda* literally means "knowledge", and thus in a wider sense it refers to the whole body of Indian Sanskrit religious literature that is in harmony with the philosophical conclusions found in the original four Vedic *Saṁhitās* and *Upaniṣads*. The message of the transcendental realm that has come down to this phenomenal world through the medium of sound is known as the *Veda*. Being the very words of Godhead Himself, the *Vedas* have existed from eternity. Lord Kṛṣṇa originally revealed the *Vedas* to Brahmā, the first soul to appear in the realm of physical nature, and by him they were subsequently made available to other souls through the channel of spiritual disciplic succession; *Veda, Vedas,* Vedic knowledge. The Sanskrit root of the word *Veda* is *vid*, knowledge. This root is widespread even in modern Western language: e.g. *video* (from the Latin word to see) and idea (Gr. *ida*). The term Vedic refers to the teachings of the Vedic literatures. From these literatures we learn that this universe, along with countless others, was produced from the breath of Mahā-Viṣṇu some 155,250,000,000,000 years ago. The Lord's divine breath simultaneously transmitted all the knowledge mankind requires to meet his material needs and revive his dormant God consciousness. This knowledge is called *Veda*. Caturmukha (four-faced) Brahmā, the first created being within this universe, received *Veda* from Viṣṇu. Brahmā, acting as an obedient servant of the Supreme Lord, populated the planetary systems with all species of life. He spoke four *Vedas*, one from each of his mouths, to guide human beings in their spiritual and material progress. The *Vedas* are thus traced to the very beginning of the cosmos. Some of the most basic Vedic teachings are: (1) every living creature is an eternal soul covered by a material body; (2) as long as the souls are bewildered by *māyā* (the illusion of identifying the self with the body) they must reincarnate from body to body, life after life; (3) to accept a material body means to suffer the four-fold pangs of birth, old age, disease and death; (4) depending upon the quality of work (*karma*) in the human form, a soul may take its next birth in a subhuman species, or the human species, or a superhuman species, or it may be freed from birth and death altogether; (5) *karma* dedicated in sacrifice to Viṣṇu as directed by Vedic injunctions elevates and liberates the soul.

Virāṭ-rupa—the universal form of the Supreme Lord containing the totality of the entire material manifestation.

Viṣṇu— literally, the all-pervading God; the Supreme Personality of Godhead in His four-armed expansion in Vaikuṇṭha. A plenary expansion of the original Supreme Personality of Godhead, Śrī Kṛṣṇa, He supervises the maintenance of the created universe, and enters into the material universe before creation. He is worshiped by all the demigods and sages, and described throughout the *Vedas* as the summum bonum of all knowledge.

Viṣṇu bhakti—devotional service to Lord Viṣṇu.

Viṣṇu tattva—a primary expansion of Kṛṣṇa having full status as Godhead. The term also applies to primary expansions of the Supreme Lord such as Rāma, Nṛsiṁha etc.

Vṛndāvana—Kṛṣṇa's eternal abode, where He fully manifests His quality of sweetness; the village on this earth in which He enacted His childhood pastimes five thousand years ago; the topmost transcendental abode of the Supreme Lord. It is His personal spiritual abode descended to the earthly plane. It is situated on the western bank of the river Yamunā.

Vyāsa-pūjā—worship of Vyāsadeva or the bona fide spiritual master, as the representative of Vyāsadeva, on the spiritual master's appearance day.

Vyāsadeva—the literary incarnation of God, and the greatest philosopher of ancient times. The son of Parāśara Muni and Satyavatī devī, he rendered the *Vedas* into written texts some 5000 years ago. He divided the *Veda* into four parts, the Ṛg, *Yajur*, *Sāma* and *Atharva Veda*, and also compiled the supplementary Vedic literature such as the eighteen *Purāṇas*, *Vedānta-sūtra*, and the *Mahābhārata*. He played a very important part in guiding the Pāṇḍavas during crucial times. He gave the vision of the battle of Kurukṣetra to Sañjaya so that he could relate it to Dhṛtarāṣṭra. He is still living in this world; he is also known as Vedavyāsa, Bādarāyaṇa and Dvaipāyana Vyāsa.

Y

Yajña—a Vedic sacrifice; also a name for the Supreme Lord meaning "the personification of sacrifice"; the goal and enjoyer of all sacrifices.

Yoga—literally, connection; the discipline of self-realization, a spiritual discipline meant for linking one's consciousness with the Supreme Lord, Kṛṣṇa; one of the six systems of Vedic philosophy, taught by Patañjali. Through the process of *bhakti-yoga*, the consciousness of the individual soul connects with its source, Kṛṣṇa.

Yoga-siddhis—mystic perfections or mystic powers.

Yogamāyā—the internal, spiritual energy of the Supreme Lord, to which the external energy, *mahāmayā*, is subordinate, and which hides Him from non-devotees..

Yogī—a transcendentalist who practices one of the many authorized forms of *yoga* or processes of spiritual purification; one who practices the eightfold mystic *yoga* process to gain mystic *siddhis* or Paramātmā realization.

Yuga-avatāra—an incarnation of the Lord in each millennium who prescribes the appropriate process of self-realization for that age.

Yuga—one of the four ages of the universe; they differ in length and rotate like calendar months.

Yukta-vairāgya—befitting, real renunciation, in which one utilizes everything in the service of the Supreme Lord.

Sanskrit Pronunciation Guide

Throughout the centuries, the Sanskrit language has been written in a variety of alphabets. The mode of writing most widely used throughout India, however, is called *devanāgarī*, which means, literally, the writing used in "the cities of the demigods." The *devanāgarī* alphabet consists of forty-eight characters: thirteen vowels and thirty-five consonants. Ancient Sanskrit grammarians arranged this alphabet according to practical linguistic principles, and this order has been accepted by all Western scholars. The system of transliteration used in this book conforms to a system that scholars have accepted to indicate the pronunciation of each Sanskrit sound.

Vowels

अ a आ ā इ i ई ī उ u ऊ ū ऋ ṛ ॠ ṝ ऌ ḷ

ए e ऐ ai ओ o औ au

Consonants

Guttarals:	क ka	ख kha	ग ga	घ gha	ङ ṅa
Palatals:	च ca	छ cha	ज ja	झ jha	ञ ña
Cerebrals:	ट ṭa	ठ ṭha	ड ḍa	ढ ḍha	ण ṇa
Dentals:	त ta	थ tha	द da	ध dha	न na
Labials:	प pa	फ pha	ब ba	भ bha	म ma
Semivowels:	य ya	र ra	ल la	व va	
Sibilants:	श śa	ष ṣa	स sa		
Aspirate :	ह ha	Anusvāra : ं ṁ	Visarga : ः ḥ		

Numerals

०–0 १–1 २–2 ३–3 ४–4 ५–5 ६–6 ७–7 ८–8 ९–9

The vowels are written as follows after a consonant:

ा ā ि i ी ī ु u ू ū ृ ṛ ॄ ṝ े e ै ai ो o ौ au

For example : क ka का kā कि ki की kī कु ku कू kū
कृ kṛ कॄ kṝ के ke कै kai को ko कौ kau

Generally two or more consonants in conjunction are written together in a special form, as for example: क्ष **kṣa** त्र **tra**

The vowel "a" is implied after a consonant with no vowel symbol.

The symbol virāma (्) indicates that there is no final vowel: क्

The vowels are pronounced as follows:.

a	—	as in b**u**t	o	—	as in **go**
ā	—	as in f**a**r but held twice as long as **a**	ṛ	—	as in **ri**m
ai	—	as in **ai**sle	ṝ	—	as in **ree**d but held twice as long as **ṛ**
au	—	as in h**ow**	u	—	as in p**u**sh
e	—	as in th**ey**	ū	—	as in r**u**le but held twice as long as **u**
i	—	as in p**i**n			
ī	—	as in p**i**que but held twice as long as **i**			
ḷ	—	as in **lree**			

The consonants are pronounced as follows:

Gutterals
(pronounced from the throat)

k	—	as in **k**ite
kh	—	as in Ec**kh**art
g	—	as in **g**ive
gh	—	as in di**g-h**ard
ṅ	—	as in si**ng**

Labials
(pronounced with the lips)

p	—	as in **p**ine
ph	—	as in u**p-h**ill
b	—	as in **b**ird
bh	—	as in ru**b-h**ard
m	—	as in **m**other

Cerebrals
(pronounced with the tip of the tongue against the roof of the mouth)

ṭ	—	as in **t**ub
ṭh	—	as in ligh**t-h**eart
ḍ	—	as in **d**ove
ḍh	—	as in re**d-h**ot
ṇ	—	as in si**ng**

Palatals
(pronounced with the middle of the tongue against the palate)

c	—	as in **ch**air
ch	—	as in staun**ch-h**eart
j	—	as in **j**oy
jh	—	as in he**dgeh**og
ñ	—	as in ca**ny**on

Dentals
(pronounced like the cerebrals but with the tongue against the teeth)

t	—	as in **t**ub
th	—	as in ligh**t-h**eart
d	—	as in **d**ove
dh	—	as in re**d-h**ot
n	—	as in **n**ut

Semivowels

y	—	as in **y**es
r	—	as in **r**un
l	—	as in **l**ight
v	—	as in **v**ine, except when preceded in the same syllable by a consonant, then like in s**w**an

Sibilants

ś	—	as in the German word *sprechen*
ṣ	—	as in **sh**ine
s	—	as in **s**un

Aspirate

h	—	as in **h**ome

Anusvāra

ṁ	—	a resonant nasal sound as in the French word *bon*

Visarga

ḥ	—	a final **h**-sound: **aḥ** is pronounced like **aha**; **iḥ** like **ihi**.

There is no strong accentuation of syllables in Sanskrit, or pausing between words in a line, only a flowing of short and long syllables (the long twice as long as the short). A long syllable is one whose vowel is long (**ā, ai, au, e , ī, o, ṝ, ū**) or whose short vowel is followed by more than one consonant (including **ḥ** and **ṁ**). Aspirated consonants (consonants followed by an **h**) count as single consonants.

Index of Sanskrit Verses

This index constitutes a complete listing of the first and third lines of each of the Sanskrit poetry verses of this volume of *Śrīmad-Bhāgavatam*, arranged in English alphabetical order. The first column gives the Sanskrit transliteration; the second, the chapter-verse reference. Apostrophes are alphabetized as a's.

A

O

P

R

S

T

U

Y

Index of Verses Quoted

This index lists the verses quoted in the purports of this volume of *Śrīmad-Bhāgavatam*. Numerals in boldface type refer to the first or third lines of verses quoted in full; numerals in roman type refer to partially quoted verses.

General Index

The references to the translations and purports of the verses of *Śrīmad-Bhāgavatam* are presented in the following format: "xx.yy (para n)", where 'xx' is the chapter number, 'yy' is the verse number (text number) and 'n' is the paragraph number in the purport. Numerals in the boldface type indicate the translations and those in regular type indicate the purports. Numerals in the mixed type indicate both translation and purports. While counting the paragraphs in the purports, please remember that, the new paragraph begins (in the purport) only where the first word is indented.

A

Abhiṣeka ceremony
  for goddess of fortune, 8.15
  ingredients for, 8.15
Abhramu, **8.5**
Absolute Truth
  devotional service reveals, 12.8 (para 3)
  Lord as, 1.12, **1.13**, 5.28, **12.5**, 12.5, 12.36, 20.22
  as one & different, 12.5
  pāñcarātrikī-vidhi reveals, 12.10 (para 1)
  as personal, 3.2 (para 2)
  philosophers can't find, 14.10
  spiritual master sees, 6.9
  surrender reveals, 12.10 (para 2)
  Vaiśeṣika philosophers misunderstand, 12.8 (para 2)
  See also: Kṛṣṇa; Supreme Lord; Truth
Ācārya(s). See: Spiritual master(s)
Acintya-bhedābheda
  Absolute Truth as, 12.5
  defined, 1.12
  Lord as, 12.7
  philosophy of, 20.22
Activities
  in base modes of nature, 12.10 (para 1)
  bondage to, 1.14 (para 1), 1.15 (para 1)
  fruitful, compared with futile, 16.61
  fruitive. *See:* Fruitive activities
  impersonalist falls to materialistic, 4.13 (para 2)
  of Kṛṣṇa. *See:* Incarnation(s) of Supreme Lord; Supreme Lord, pastime(s) of in Kṛṣṇa consciousness, 1.14 (para 2)
  Lord beyond, 18.1
Activities *(continued)*
  of Lord. *See:* Incarnations of Supreme Lord; Supreme Lord, pastime(s) of
  Lord's pleasure measure of, 16.61
  lusty desires cause, 24.52
  of *mahājanas,* 18.28
  material, compared with spiritual, 1.14 (para 1), 3.11 (para 2), **9.28**, **9.29**
  for sense gratification, 19.21 (para 1)
  sinful, four listed, 19.41 (para 2)
  spiritual, 19.40
  as suffering, 17.23 (para 3)
  time controls, **11.7**, 11.7, **11.8**
  by Viṣṇu, via Śiva, 7.22
  See also: Fruitive activities; *Karma*
Actor compared to Lord, **18.12**
Adbhuta, **13.19**, **13.20**
Aditi
  as *arta,* 16.22
  blissful at Lord's appearance, **17.5**, **17.6–7**, **18.11**
  concentrates on Lord, **17.2–3**
  as demigods' mother, 16.15, **17.12**, **23.3–4**
  as householder, **16.5**, 16.5
  Kaśyapa
    begged by, for instructions, **16.22**, **16.23**
    begged by, for protection, **16.15–16**, **16.18**
    instructs on devotional service, **16.20**, 16.20 (para 3), **16.21**
    instructs on *payo-vrata,* **16.25–58**, **17.1**, 17.7
    queried, **16.5**, **16.6**, **16.8**, 16.9
    reassured by, about household, **16.11**, **16.12–13**

Anger
in conditioned soul, 19.13
of demons toward Vāmana, **21.8–14**
of Hiraṇyakaśipu toward Viṣṇu, **19.7–8, 19.11, 19.13**
ignorance causes, **19.13**
in Lord's universal form, **20.25–29**
as self-defeating, **6.24**
Aṅgirā, **8.27, 23.20–21**
Animal(s)
bodily conception for, 16.19
compared to wild women, **9.10**
in demigod-demon battle, **10.6–12, 10.25, 10.36–37, 10.41, 10.47, 10.56–**57, **11.14–**16
on higher planets, 2.6
humans under bodily conception as, 3.17 (para 2), 5.23 (para 7)
in Indra's city, **15.10–11, 15.13, 15.20**
killing of. *See:* Animal slaughter
materialists as, 2.6
in Milk Ocean, **7.13, 7.18**
poisonous, **7.46**
as sexually fickle, **9.10**
of Trikūṭa Mountain, **2.6, 2.7, 2.14–19**
See also: specific animals
Animal slaughter
devotees shun, 8.21 (para 1)
in Kali-yuga, 6.12 (para 3)
natural reactions to, 8.11
peace prevented via, 8.11
by sectarian religionists, 8.21 (para 1)
society ruined by, 8.11
Annihilation of universe(s)
in Brahmā's day, 24.37
in Brahmā's night, **24.7**
in Cākṣuṣa-manvantara, 24.37
as darkness, **3.5**
living entities at, 1.9, 1.9
Lord foretells, **24.32, 24.33–35**
at Manu's finish, 24.37
by Śiva, 7.21, **7.32**
in Svāyambhuva-manvantara, 24.37
by water, **24.7, 24.32, 24.33–35, 24.41–42**
Anxiety
spiritual world free of, 24.51
of Viṣṇu for Hiraṇyakaśipu, 19.10
See also: Suffering
Aparājita, **10.30–31**
Appearance of Lord. *See:* Supreme Lord, advent(s) of
Apsarās, **2.5, 18.8**
in heavenly planets, **8.7**
Apsarās *(continued)*
in Indra's city, **15.19**
Indra's triumph gladdened, **11.40**
from Lord's universal form, **5.40**
from Milk Ocean, **8.7**
Āpyas, **5.8**
Araṇi wood, living entities compared to, 3.16
Arcanā-paddhati defined, 4.6
Arcanā. See: Deity worship to Supreme Lord
Arcira, **5.36**
Arcirādi-vartma defined, **5.36**
Ariṣṭa, **10.19–25**
Ariṣṭanemi, **6.31, 10.19–25**
Ārjavam defined, 20.19
Arjuna, 1.12
as *guru,* 24.53
Kṛṣṇa compared with, 1.11 (para 2)
Kṛṣṇa instructed, 1.16 (para 1), 24.53
universal form shown to, 21.5
Arjuna (son of Raivata Manu), **5.2**
Artha defined, 12.6
Artist, Lord compared to, **3.6**
Āryaka, **13.26**
Asat defined, 9.29
Asita, 24.53
Āśrama(s)
of Aditi forlorn, **16.1**
as battle positions, 2.30 (para 1), 2.30 (para 2)
of Indradyumna, **4.8**
See also: Brahmacārī(s); Gṛhastha(s); Sannyāsa
Association with devotees, value of, 21.32, 22.36
Astagiri Hill, **11.46, 11.47**
Aṣṭāṅga-yoga, processes of, 19.21 (para 1)
Astrologer, Viśvanātha Cakravartī as, 18.5
Astronomy, 18.5
Asuras. See: Atheist(s); Demon(s); Nondevotee(s); Rākṣasa(s)
Aśvamedha sacrifices, **18.19–20**
Bali performed, **15.34**
Indra performed, **15.34, 15.34**
Asvini-kumāras, **10.30–31**
Atheist(s)
creator denied by, 3.27 (para 1)
as demons, 7.3 (para 1)
devotees compared with, 9.28
devotee's worship misunderstood by, 3.2 (para 2)
Hiraṇyakaśipu as, 5.31, 19.12 (para 1)
incarnations of God enlighten, 3.12 (para 2)
incarnations of Lord cheat, 9.11
karma binds, 9.28

B

Bali Mahārāja *(continued)*
as Indra, **13.12**, 15.31
Indra enemy of, **19.32**
Indra's truce proposals accepted by, **6.31**
Indra vs., **10.27–28**, **10.41–45**, **11.2–3**, 11.7, **11.8–12**, **15.3**, **15.8–9**, **15.23**
as king of heaven, **22.16**, **22.29–31**
as *kṛpā-siddha,* 20.3
lamentation absent in, **11.48**
as learned, 20.15
Lord
blessed, **13.14**
favored, 23.14
loved by, 20.3
praised, **19.2**
protected, 20.15, 22.31, **22.33**, **22.35**, 23.6
punished, **22.3–4**, **22.6–7**, 22.8
tested, 22.29–30
took charity from, **13.13**, **15.1–2**
See also: Bali Mahārāja, Vāmana & . . .
Lord's
mercy on, 22.6–7, **22.11**, 22.11 (para 1), **22.16**, 22.20 (para 2), 22.24, 22.29–30, **23.1–2**
purpose understood by, 22.2, 22.6–7, 22.11 (para 1)
universal form seen by, **20.22**, **20.25–29**
as *mahājana,* 18.28, 20.8, 22.29–30
material attachment shucked by, 22.9 (para 1)
as materially attached, 19.32
as moonlike, **10.16–18**, **15.35**
as munificent, **19.16**
power of, **15.26**, **15.34**
Prahlāda beheld by, **22.13–14**
Prahlāda garlanded, **15.6**
as Prahlāda's grandson, **19.2**, **20.3**, 20.11, **22.8**, **22.10**, **23.5**
pride &, **21.33–34**
as pure devotee, 20.3, 20.6, 21.34, 22.36, **23.1**
quoted. *See:* Bali Mahārāja quoted
religious, **18.28**, **19.1**, **19.2**, **22.29–30**
sacrifices of, Śukrācārya corrected, **23.17–18**
Śiva's example followed by, **18.28**
suffering of, 22.23, **22.29–30**
Śukrācārya
advises, on charity promises, **19.36**, **19.38–39**, **19.41**, 19.41 (para 1), **19.42**, **19.43**

Bali Mahārāja
Śukrācārya *(continued)*
curses, **20.14**, **20.15**, 23.14, 23.15
defied by, 15.31
rejected by, 20.1 (para 1), 20.2, 20.6, **20.14–16**, 22.9 (para 1)
revives, **11.47**, **15.1–2**
vs., **20.14**
warns, about Vāmana, **19.29–35**
as Śukrācārya's disciple, **15.3**, **15.23**, 15.28, 15.31, 19.41 (para 1), 20.6, **20.14**, **21.32**
Śukrācārya's gifts to, **15.6**, **15.8–9**, **15.23**
as surrendered soul, 20.11, 22.3, 22.6–7, 22.9 (para 1)
as tolerant, 21.25–26, 21.32, **22.29–31**
as truthful, **21.11–12**, **22.29–30**
Uccaiḥśravā claimed by, **8.3**
universe conquered by, **15.33**
Vāmana
arrested, **21.27**, **21.28**, 22.14
assigned, to Sutala, **22.32**
begged land from, **19.17**, **19.17**, **19.19**, **19.27**, 20.12, **21.8–9**, **23.19**
"cheated," 22.2
criticized by, **19.18**, **19.19**
given land by, **20.16**, **20.20**
offered charity by, **18.32**, **19.20**, **19.28**, **19.33**, **22.2**, 22.2, 22.20 (para 2), **22.21–22**, **22.23**, 22.23
outshone, **18.22**
pleased by, 15.31
praised, **19.17**
sanctified, **18.31**
saved, 24.2–3
sent, to hell, **21.32**, **21.33–34**, 21.34
welcomed by, **18.24–26**
worshiped by, **20.17–18**
Varuṇa arrested, **22.6–7**
Vindhyāvali prayed for, 22.20 (para 3)
as Virocana's son, **19.14**
Viśvajit-yajña performed by, **15.4**, **15.7**
weapons of, **15.8–9**
wife of, **20.17–18**, **22.18**, 22.20 (para 2)
Bali Mahārāja quoted
on his promise to Lord, **22.2**
on Lord's mercy, **23.1–2**
on religious principles, **20.2**
on time, **11.7**
on Vāmana, **18.29–30**, **19.18**
Bāṇa, **10.19–25**, **10.30–31**

C

Demon(s) *(continued)*
Kaśyapa father of, **16.14**
Lord
baffles, 5.31, 6.31
defeats, **10.56**–57
defied by, 23.8
denied by, 6.38, 6.39
kills, 17.23 (para 3)
misunderstood by, 7.8
pacified, **7.4**
revealed Himself to, **9.27**
revives, **6.37**, **7.11**
Lord's mercy on, **22.5**, **22.6–7**, **23.6**, **23.7–8**, 23.8
Lord's universal form seen by, **20.30**
Mandara Mountain smashed, **6.35**–37
mentality of, devotee's association dispels, 22.36
Milk Ocean churned by, **7.1**, **7.5**, **7.13**, **7.16**, **8.1**, **8.31**
in modes of nature, **16.14**
Mohinī
captivated, **8.41–46**
cautioned, **9.9**
cheated, **9.11–13**, **9.19**, **9.21**, 9.21, **12.15**
enchanted, **9.2–9**, **9.11–13**, **9.18**, **9.23**, 12.15
requested by, to settle nectar dispute, **9.6**, **9.7**
nectar denied to, **10.1**, **10.19**–25
nectar stolen by, **8.35**, **8.37**
in passion, **7.11**
in passion & ignorance, **12.10**
proprietorship pretended by, 22.20 (para 1), 22.20 (para 2)
qualifications of, 7.3 (para 2)
quarreled over nectar, **8.38**, **8.39–40**, **9.1**, **9.6**
quoted. *See:* Demon(s) quoted
ritualistic ceremonies by, **9.14–15**, **9.16–17**
as snakelike, **9.19**
suffering due to, 22.20 (para 3)
suffering misunderstood by, 7.8
Śukrācārya revived, **11.47**
as Śukrācārya's disciples, 6.19
surabhi cow neglected by, 8.2
surrender shunned by, 2.33 (para 1), 7.3 (para 2)
time initially favored, **6.19**
Vāmana angered, **21.8–14**
Vāruṇī claimed by, **8.30**
Vāsuki weakens, **7.14**

Demon(s) *(continued)*
Vedas rejected by, 6.38
Viṣṇu's associates vs., **21.15–26**
weak & strong, **8.39–40**
women bewilder, 12.15
world disturbed by, 5.19–20
world ruined by, 22.20 (para 3)
See also: Atheist(s); Nondevotee(s); *specific demons*
Demon-demigod battle. *See:* Battle between demigods & demons
Demon(s) quoted
on beautiful woman, **9.2–3**
on Mohinī, **9.13**
on nectar, **8.38**, **8.39–40**
on Vāmana, **21.10**
Desire(s)
of Aditi, **17.12**
bhakta free of, 16.21 (para 1)
body according to, 1.10 (para 4), 22.20 (para 2)
in conditioned soul, 24.52
demigod worship for, 7.35
of devotee purified by Lord, 16.21 (para 2)
devotional service dispels, 16.21 (para 2)
devotional service fulfills, 3.19 (para 1), 5.48 (para 2), **12.16**, 16.21 (para 2)
freedom from, 19.12 (para 2)
futility of, 19.24 (para 2)
karmīs afflicted by, 16.21 (para 1)
Lord free of, **1.16**, 12.7
Lord fulfills, 3.15 (para 3), 3.19 (para 1), 5.48 (para 2), **16.21**, 16.21 (para 2), 16.22, **16.35–36**, **23.8**
material activities caused by, 24.52
material life continued by, **19.25–26**
for opulences, 8.9
pārijāta flower fulfills, **8.6**
pure devotees free of, 12.6
Śiva above, 7.33
See also: Attachment, material; Lust
Desire tree, Lord compared to, **23.8**
Destiny
satisfaction with, **19.23**, **19.25–26**
See also: Karma
Detachment. *See:* Renunciation
Deva(s)
defined, 4.1, 12.5
Lord as, 15.36
See also: Demigod(s)
Devaguhya, **13.17**
Devahotra, **13.32**
Devahūti, **1.5**, **1.6**
Devala, 24.53

Disciple succession(s) *(continued)*
spiritual power via, 15.28
Vivasvān in, 14.5
Vyāsa in, 24.48 (para 3)
Disease
cause of, 8.11
Lord free of, 18.1
Dissolution of universe by fire, **10.50**
Diṣṭa, **13.2–3**
Distress. *See:* Suffering
Divaspati, **13.32**
Divyam defined, 18.1
Draviḍa province, **4.7**
Dream(s)
bad, 4.15 (para 2)
as illusory, **10.55**
material life as, 1.9, 5.30
Dress
in demigod-demon battle, **10.13–15**
of Lord, **10.54**, **16.35–36**, **16.39–40**, **17.2–3**, **18.1**, **20.32–33**
of Mohinī, **12.18–21**, **12.24**
of Prahlāda, **22.13–14**
for ritualistic ceremony, 9.14–15
of Vāmana, **18.24–26**
Drinking intoxicants, 11.5
Duality, material
devotee &, 11.8
Lord free of, **1.12**, 12.5, **12.8**
modes of nature cause, 12.8 (para 3)
pure devotees free of, 12.6
See also: Bodily concept of life; *Māyā*
Durga defined, 23.6
Durgā, Goddess, 5.49
as co-creator, **12.28**
Niśumbha vs., **10.30–31**
as Śiva's wife, 12.15, 12.40
See also: Māyā
Durmarṣa, **10.32–34**
Durvāsā Muni, Indra cursed by, 5.15–16 (para 1)
Duṣkṛtī
defined, 2.33 (para 1)
See also: Atheist(s); Demon(s)
Dust clouds in demon-demigod battle, **10.38**
Duty
of *brāhmaṇas,* 16.5
of devotees, 1.15 (para 2), 7.39
devotional service as, 6.14
of *guru,* 20.1 (para 1)
of Hare Kṛṣṇa movement, 5.23 (para 7), 6.14
of householder, 16.6, **20.2**, 20.2
of human being, 14.4
Duty *(continued)*
in Kṛṣṇa consciousness, 11.48
Manus reestablish, **14.5**
occupational, 24.30
perfection of, 23.15
pleasing Kṛṣṇa as, 1.14 (para 2)
preaching as, 5.23 (para 7)
of saints, 14.4
of society, 14.8
to Viṣṇu, **23.17–18**
See also: Occupational duty; *Sanātana-dharma*
Dvādaśākṣara-mantra identified, 16.39
Dvādaśī
defined, **18.6**
Lord appeared on, **18.5**, **18.6**
milk diet on, **16.25**
vijayā, **18.6**
Dvaita-vāda compared with *advaita-vāda,* 20.22
Dvāpara-yuga, 5.23 (para 2), **5.27**
as half religious, 14.4
Dvārakā as holy place, 17.8
Dvija-deva, brāhmaṇas as, 15.36
Dvijas as *brāhmaṇas,* 6.15 (para 1)
Dvimūrdhā, **10.19–25**
Dvīpa
defined, 19.19
See also: Planet(s)
Dwarf incarnation. *See:* Vāmana
Dynasty of Bali praised by Vāmana, **19.2**, **19.14**

E

Earthen pot compared to energy, 3.3, 6.10
Earth planet
bodily conception on, 16.19
compared to Lord, 3.3, **6.10**
food from, 6.12 (para 4)
heavenly planets compared with, 22.32 (para 1)
liars burden, **20.4**
as mother, **18.14–15**, **20.4**
sun's position relative to, 10.38
in universal perspective, 2.14–19
Vāmana's footstep covered, **20.32–33**
Vāmana stepped down on, **18.19–20**, 18.20
Varāha rescued, **16.26–27**, **19.6**
Eclipses, Rāhu causes, **9.24**, 10.6
Economic development, 1.10 (para 6)
Ecstasy. *See:* Bliss
Education
godless, as demoniac, 7.3 (para 2)

Education *(continued)*
spiritual
in *Bhagavad-gītā,* 16.19
modern society lacks, 16.19, 19.21 (para 2), 22.9 (para 2)
Vedic civilization based on, 16.19
Effulgence, Brahman. *See:* Brahman effulgence
Ego, false, **19.13**
Ekādaśi, grains not eaten on, 16.25
Elements, material
body consists of, **16.19**
in body wheel, **5.28**
life independent of, 17.23 (para 3)
Lord manufactures, 1.10 (para 5)
as Lord's energy, 12.5
senses covered by, 19.24 (para 1)
types of, listed, 1.10 (para 5), 5.32, 16.30
universe covered by, 20.34
See also: Energy, material; *specific elements*
Elephant(s)
goddess of fortune bathed by, **8.14**
Indradyumna as, **4.10**, **4.11–12**
king of. *See:* Airāvata; Gajendra
as less intelligent, 4.10
from Milk Ocean, **8.4**, **8.5**
Mohinī compared to, **12.27**, **12.29–30**, **12.32**
Śiva compared to, **12.27**, **12.29–30**, **12.32**
Enemies
etiquette among, off battlefield, 6.28
as guest, 16.6
internal & external, 5.24 (para 1)
truce among, **6.20**
Energy (energies) of Supreme Lord
as all-pervading, 7.31 (para 1)
cosmos rests on, 3.3, **3.4**
external, 6.11, 7.22, 8.8, 12.21, **12.28**, 17.9
gold by, 24.50
hlādinī, 12.11 (para 1)
illusory, 3.29, 9.12, 12.15, **12.39**, **12.43**, **14.10**, **16.18**, 17.9, 21.28
See also: Māyā
internal, **12.21**, 12.31
as limitless, 3.22–24, **3.28**
as Lord Himself, 12.8 (para 1), 12.8 (para 2)
Lord's work done by, 5.26 (para 2), 5.44
marginal, 12.8
material, 12.5, 12.8, 12.8 (para 1), 12.15, **12.40**, **23.7–8**, 23.8, 23.29
as Bhadra Kālī, **10.30–31**
compared with spiritual, **1.13**, 1.13 (para 2)
as insurmountable, **5.30**
Energy (energies) of Supreme Lord
material, *(continued)*
under Lord's direction, 12.40
See also: Elements, material; *Māyā;* Material nature
spiritual, 12.8 (para 1), 12.8 (para 3), **23.7–8**
as wonderful, 12.31
See also: Māyā; Yoga-māyā
Enjoyment, material
demigods attached to, 22.20 (para 1)
objects of, listed, 8.9
See also: Happiness, material
Entity(entities), individual. *See:* Living entity (entities)

F

False ego, 19.13
Falsity
Śukrācārya &, **19.42**, **19.43**
See also: Liars
Family
of Bali praised by Vāmana, **19.2**, **19.14**
of elephant king, **2.26**
Indradyumna renounced, **4.8**
man attached to, 22.9 (para 1)
money share for, **19.37**
preaching more important than, 22.27
pure devotee in, 19.2 (para 1)
sex life for, 2.30 (para 2)
See also: Householder(s)
Farms in Hare Kṛṣṇa movement, 19.21 (para 2)
Fasting
by demigods & demons, **9.14–15**
from grains on Ekādaśi, 16.25
Fear
Bali &, 11.7, **20.5**, **22.3–4**
Bali free of, 20.15
of death, 2.33 (para 2)
devotees free of, 21.32, 22.3
of elephant king by animals, **2.21**
of materialism advised, 22.11 (para 2)
protection from, 23.2
surrender dispels, 24.38
Female-male attraction
material life as, 22.9 (para 2)
See also: Sex life
Festivals, requirements for, 16.9
Fire
Agni as, 7.26
in body, **5.35**

G

H

I

M

Milk Ocean *(continued)*
gems from, 6.25, **8.6**
goddess of fortune from, **8.8**, 8.17, 8.19
hearing about churning of, recommended, **12.46**
Lord churned, **7.16**
Mandara Mountain sank in, **7.6**
nectar from, **5.10**, **5.11–12**, **6.22–23**, 6.25
pārijāta flower from, **8.6**
poison from, 6.25, **7.18**, **7.43**
surabhi cow from, **8.1**
Śvetadvīpa in, **5.24**
Trikūṭa Mountain in, **2.1**, **2.2–4**
Uccaiḥśravā from, **8.3**
Vāruṇi from, **8.30**
wealth from, 6.25
women from, 6.25
Mimāṁsaka philosophers, **12.9**
Mind
devotional service disciplines, 17.2–3
sacrificed to Kṛṣṇa, 19.32
Misery. *See:* Suffering
Mitra, Lord, **10.28**
Modes of material nature
base symptoms of, 12.10 (para 1)
in body wheel, 5.28
Brahman effulgence above, **7.31**
competition among, 16.20 (para 1)
as controller, 11.7
demigods under, 11.8, **16.14**
demons under, **16.14**
devotional service above, 16.20 (para 1)
duality caused by, 12.8 (para 3)
freedom from, 24.38
goodness. *See:* Goodness, mode of
ignorance. *See:* Ignorance, mode of
living entities under, 3.16, **8.21**
Lord
above, **1.10**, 1.11 (para 1), 3.8–9, **3.18**, 5.29, **5.50**, **6.8**, **12.7**, 12.7
incarnates in, **5.22**, 5.22, 5.50
as Lord's eyes, **7.30**
passion. *See:* Passion, mode of
philosophers under, 12.10 (para 1)
suffering in, 17.23 (para 3)
transcendentalist above, 11.8
wise men tolerate, 11.8
world conducted via, 5.23 (para 1), 7.11
See also: Material nature; *specific modes of nature*
Mohinī-mūrti
as all-attractive, 12.14, **12.20–22**
beauty of, **8.41–46**, **9.1**, **9.4–8**, **9.16–17**, **9.18**, **12.18–24**, **12.26**, **12.29–30**
Mohinī-mūrti *(continued)*
as Buddhalike, 9.11
chastity of, **9.4**
demigods
not bewildered by, 12.15, 12.16
enchanted by, **9.18**
received nectar from, **9.21**, 9.21
demons
cautioned by, **9.9**
cheated by, **9.11–13**, **9.19**, **9.21**, 9.21, **12.15**
desired, **8.41–46**
enchanted by, **9.2–9**, **9.11–13**, **9.18**, **9.23**, **12.15**
requested, to settle nectar dispute, **9.6**, **9.7**
dress of, **8.41–46**, **12.18–21**, **12.24**
goddess of fortune excelled by, 9.18
quoted on demons & nectar, **9.12**
quoted on woman, **9.9**
Rāhu beheaded by, 9.25
sages instructed by, 12.34
Śiva beheld, **12.18**, **12.21–25**
Śiva captivated by, **12.21–34**
as *yoga-māyā*, **12.29–30**
Mokṣa
defined, 12.6
See also: Liberation
Mokṣa-kāma defined, 16.21 (para 1)
Monarchy
as good government, 1.16 (para 1)
as lost in time, 1.7
See also: Government(s); King(s)
Money
ceremonies require, 23.31
for charity, 20.7
extravagance with, sinful, 19.17
family's share of, **19.37**
as Kṛṣṇa's property, 1.10 (para 6)
material uses compared with spiritual uses of, 19.41 (para 1)
spending divisions of, five listed, **19.37**
Śukrācārya quoted on, **19.41**
See also: Opulence, material; Wealth
Monists. *See:* Impersonalist(s); *Jñānī(s)*
Month
of Bhādra, **18.5**
of Caitra, **8.11**
of Phālguna, **16.25**
of Vaiśākha, **8.11**
Moon
Bali compared to, **10.16–18**, **15.35**
demigods sustained by, **5.34**, 5.34
Earth expeditions to, as failures, 2.14–19

Moon *(continued)*
food sustained by light of, 5.34
god of, **10.30–31**, **18.14–15**
as Lord's mind, **5.34**, **7.27**
in Lord's universal form, **20.25–29**
orbit of, 21.31
in *payo-vrata* calculation, **16.25**, **16.48–49**, 16.60
position of
at Lord's advent, **18.5**, **18.6**
relative to Earth, 10.38, 18.5
Prahlāda compared to, **19.5**, **22.12**
Rāhu detected by, **9.24**
Rāhu harasses, **9.26**, 9.26, 10.6
scientists' perception of, 5.34, 23.29
space travel to, 10.38, 11.5
sun's position relative to, 10.38, 18.5
Moon god, **10.30–31**, **18.14–15**
Mountain(s)
in demigod-demon battle, **10.45**, **10.46**
flying, **11.11–12**, **11.34**
Lord's advent gladdened, **18.4**
in Lord's universal fonn, **20.23**
Mūḍhas defined, 2.32
Muktātmā defined, 3.18
"Mukti-pade"
in Bhaṭṭācārya-Caitanya debate, 12.6
See also: Supreme Lord, lotus feet of
Mukti. See: Liberation
Munayaḥ
defined, 12.6
See also: Devotee(s); Sage(s); Wise men
Musical instruments, playing of
Bali honored by, **20.20**
in demigod-demon battle, **10.7**, **10.19–25**, **11.41**
in Indra's city, **15.21**
Lord's advent hailed by, **18.7**
Vāmana honored by, **21.6–7**
Muslims, 8.21 (para 1)
Mysticism
of false *guru,* 24.50
Viṣṇu master of, **19.7–8**
yogic
demons achieved, **22.6–7**
processes of, 19.21 (para 1)
See also: Kṛṣṇa consciousness; Meditation; *Yoga*
Mystic power(s)
in demigod-demon battle, **11.4**
for heavenly elevation condemned, **11.5**
of Lord, 12.14, **16.33–34**
types of, eight, 13.13
See also: Illusion; Mysticism; *Yoga-siddhis*
Mystics. *See:* Devotee(s); Sage(s); Transcendentalists
Mythology, 6.38

N

Nābhāga, 13.2–3
Nāga-pāśa defined, **23.3–4**
Nāgas, **8.16**
Naimiṣāraṇya, 1.14 (para 2)
Naiṣkarmya
defined, 3.11 (para 2)
as impractical without Kṛṣṇa consciousness, 1.14 (para 2)
Names of Supreme Lord. *See:* Supreme Lord, name(s) of
Namuci
Aparājita vs., **10.30–31**
Indra vs., **11.19**, **11.20**, **11.23**, **11.30**, 11.33, **11.37–40**
Nandana garden, **15.10–11**
Nara, **1.27**
Nārada Muni
curse by, as benediction, 4.1
demigods obeyed, **11.46**
in disciplic succession, 24.48 (para 3)
Kṛṣṇa's supremacy accepted by, 24.53
pāñcarātrikī-vidhi from, 12.10 (para 1)
quoted
on demigods, **11.43**
on proprietorship, 1.10 (para 6)
Nara-devas, kṣatriyas as, 15.36
Narakāsura, **10.32–34**
Nārāyaṇa, Lord
Ajāmila saved by name of, 3.1 (para 2), 3.8–9, 5.48 (para 1)
Gajendra rescued by, **3.32**
as Ganges, 21.4
as Lakṣmī's Lord, 8.9, 8.17, 8.19, 8.25
as soul of universe, 3.30 (para 1)
Vāmana as, 18.12
See also: Supreme Lord; Viṣṇu
Nārāyaṇa, "poor," 16.55
Nariṣyanta, **13.2–3**
Narmadā River, **18.21**
Narottama dāsa Ṭhākura
quoted on spiritual master, 15.28
songs by, 5.25 (para 2)
Nationalism as demoniac, 22.20 (para 2)
Nature, material. *See:* Material nature
Nectar
demigods drank, **9.27**, **9.28**
demigods enlivened by, **10.4**
demons deprived of, **10.1**, **10.19–25**

Nectar *(continued)*
demons quarreled over, **8.38**, **8.39–40**, **9.1**, **9.6**
demons stole, **8.35**, **8.36**
Dhanvantari carried, **8.35**
for immortality, 6.22–23
Lord fed, to demigods, **10.2**, **12.47**
from Milk Ocean, **5.10**, **5.11–12**, **6.22–23**, 6.25
as miracle potion, **9.21**, 9.25
Mohinī cheated demons out of, **9.11**, **9.12**, **9.19**, **9.21**, 9.21
Mohinī gave, to demigods, **9.21**, 9.21
Rāhu immortalized by, **9.26**
Rāhu sneaked, **9.24**
Nectar of Devotion as auspicious, 1.32
Nighttime in Lord's universal form, **20.25–29**
Nimbārka, 24.53
Nirāśiṣaḥ defined, 12.7
Nirguṇa defined, 3.8–9
Nirvāṇa. See: Liberation
Niśumbha, **10.19–25**, **10.30–31**
Nityānanda, Lord, as Caitanya's associate, 5.27 (para 3)
Nivātakavaca, **10.19–25**, **10.32–34**
Nondevotee(s)
creator denied by, 3.27 (para 1)
devotees compared with, 8.38, 23.8
as failures, 9.29
Lord destroys, 20.7
Lord disfavors, 3.28
sense gratification pursued by, 8.38
suffering of, 23.8
See also: Atheist(s); Demon(s); Materialist(s)
Nṛsiṁha-deva, Lord, Hiraṇyakaśipu killed by, 5.31, 8.21 (para 2)
Nṛsiṁha prayer recommended, 3.1 (para 2)

O

Obeisances, *daṇḍavat*, 16.42–43
Obeisances offered to Lord, benefit of, **23.1–2**
Occupational duty
for liberation, 16.5
for pleasing Lord, 16.61
See also: Dharma; Duty; Religious principles
Ocean(s)
fire in, **5.35**
goddess of fortune served by, **8.15**
of inundation, **24.7**, **24.32**, **24.33–35**, **24.41–42**
in Lord's universal form, **20.24**
of Milk. *See:* Milk Ocean
Ocean(s) *(continued)*
in universe, **2.4**
Offense(s)
to Deity, 3.2 (para 1)
by demigods during Gajendra's plight, 3.31
to spiritual master, 3.2 (para 1)
Offerings to Supreme Lord
by devotee, 20.21
spiritual world reached via, **22.23**
See also: Devotional service
Old age, Lord free of, 18.1
Oṁ (oṁkāra)
chanting, for detachment from money, **19.41**
letters in, **7.25**
Lord as, **5.29**, **7.25**
as Lord's sound representation, 3.2 (para 2)
Māyāvādīs misunderstand, 3.2 (para 2)
in promise-making, **19.38–39**
Vedic *mantras* begun by, 3.2 (para 2)
Oṁ tat sat
defined, 19.40
See also: Absolute Truth
Oneness. *See:* Impersonalist(s); Liberation
Opulence(s)
in Bali, Lord removed, **22.16**
dangerous, **22.17**, **22.23–24**–24
death nullifies, **20.6**
of demigods lost to demons, 5.15–16 (para 1), **17.12**
of devotee, Lord removes, 19.32, 22.27, 22.33 (para 1)
devotee's, compared with *karmī's,* 8.25
devotional service hindered by, **22.27**
Dhruva indifferent to, 22.27
from goddess of fortune, **8.9**, 8.14, **8.24**
illusory, **22.11**
of Indra's city, **15.10–11**
of Lord, 18.20
as Lord's mercy, 22.26
as Lord's property, 8.8
of Lord's universal form, **20.22**
material, compared with spiritual, 20.15
people desire, 8.9
pride due to, **22.27**
pure devotee indifferent to, **22.27**
as risky, 5.15–16 (para 2)
self-realization hindered by, **22.17**
Śiva worship for, 12.33
types of, six listed, **22.26**
See also: Goddess of fortune; Gold; Money; Possessions, material; Wealth

P

Q

R

S

Sannyāsa (renounced life)
Caitanya in, 2.30 (para 2)
in Kali-yuga risky, 2.30 (para 2)
for preaching, 2.30 (para 2)
premature, condemned, 2.30 (para 2)
sex forbidden in, 2.30 (para 2)
Sannyāsī(s) (renunciants)
ceremonial dress for, 9.14–15
charity quota for, 19.17
in Hare Kṛṣṇa movement, 1.32
naiṣkarmya dissatisfies, 3.11 (para 2)
Vāmana's teachings to, 19.2 (para 1)
Sarasvatī, Goddess, **8.16**, **13.17**, **18.16–17**
Sārūpya-mukti
defined, 4.10, 4.13 (para 2)
Gajendra attained, **4.6**, **4.13**
Sārvabhauma Bhaṭṭācārya
Caitanya cautioned by, 2.30 (para 2)
Caitanya instructs, 12.6
quoted on Caitanya, 1.16 (para 3)
Sārvabhauma, Lord, parents of, **13.17**
Sarva-kāma defined, 16.21 (para 1)
Śaryāti, **13.2–3**
Śāstras (scriptures)
foretell future, 13.11
householders guided by, 16.5, 16.11
See also: Vedas; specific Vedic scriptures
Śatarūpa, **1.7**
Satī, **7.36**
Satisfaction
in *brāhmaṇa*, **19.25–26**
happiness by, **19.27**
liberation by, **19.25–26**
via sense control, 19.21 (para 2), 19.24 (para 2)
Vāmana quoted on, **19.21**, **19.22**, **19.25–26**
See also: Happiness
Satrāyaṇa, **13.35**
Sattva-guṇa. See: Goodness, mode of
Saturn, **10.32–34**, **13.10**, **18.5**
Satyajit, **1.24**, **1.26**
Satyakas, **1.28**
Satyaloka, **20.34**
Satyas, **1.24**
Satyasahā, **13.29**
Satya-saṅkalpa
defined, 16.22
See also: Desires, Lord fulfills
Satyasena, Lord, **1.25**
Satyavrata, King
austerities by, **24.10**, **24.12–13**
boat boarded by, **24.41–42**
in Cākṣuṣa-manvantara, 24.58
Satyavrata, King *(continued)*
devotional service by, 24.15
Lord instructed on
Absolute Truth, **24.54–55**, **24.56**, **24.60–61**
surviving water devastation, **24.33–35**
as Lord's disciple, **24.50**
Lord's mercy on, **24.11**
as *mahājana* follower, 24.53
as Manu, **24.11**
Matsya (fish incarnation)
appeared in palms of, **24.12–13**
begged protection of, **24.14**
favored, 24.10
instructed, 24.58
let loose by, **24.12–13**
protected by, **24.15**, **24.16–17**
recognized by, **24.27–28**
transferred by, to wider waters, **24.18–23**
unrecognized by, **24.15**
meditates on Lord, **24.39–40**, **24.44–45**
merciful, **24.14–17**
narration about Matsya &, recommended, **24.59**, **24.60–61**
prays to Lord, **24.46**, **24.47**, **24.48**, **24.49–53**
quoted on Lord, **24.46**, **24.47**, **24.48**, **24.49–53**
as Śrāddhadeva, **24.11**
as sun god's son, **24.11**, **24.57–58**
Satya-yuga
Lord advents in, **5.27**
as religious, 14.4
Science of Kṛṣṇa. *See:* Kṛṣṇa consciousness
Scientist(s), material
astronomical, 18.5, 23.29
in bodily concept, 5.23 (para 7)
destructive, 22.20 (para 3)
extraterrestrial exploration by, 22.32 (para 2)
as limited, 2.4, 2.6
Lord challenged by, 23.29
Lord's creation immeasurable by, 23.29
moon & planets misunderstood by, 5.35, 23.29
understandings of, 2.6, 5.33, 18.5, 23.29
universe misunderstood by, 2.6, 23.29
water misunderstood by, 5.33
Self-realization
via chanting Hare Kṛṣṇa, 19.21 (para 2)
via devotional service, 24.48 (para 1), 24.48 (para 2)
God realization above, 1.14 (para 2)

Supreme Lord *(continued)*
atheists baffled by, 3.28, 5.31
atheists deny, 3.27 (para 1)
in atom, **5.26**
authorities reveal, 5.25 (para 2), 5.26 (para 3)
as authority, **2.33**, 3.30 (para 1)
as *avyaya,* 12.5
Bali &. *See:* Bali Mahārāja, Lord &
beauty of, **7.17**, 9.18, **10.54**, **18.1**
before Vāmana's appearance, **18.12**
as benefactor, 17.8
Bhagavad-gītā as instructions of, 7.3 (para 2), 24.53
as *bhāva-grāhī janārdana,* 23.2
as birthless, **1.13**, 3.8–9, **6.8**, 6.8, 17.23 (para 3), 18.1, 19.12 (para 2)
as bliss, **6.8**
bodily color of, **16.35–36**
body of
beauty of, **6.3–7**, **18.1**
cosmos as, **1.13**
demigods dazzled by, **6.2**, **6.3–7**
as eternal, 1.3
purifying power of, 4.6
as sunlike, **6.1**
transcendental, 6.8, **18.11**, 18.12
universe included in, **20.21**
See also: Supreme Lord, form(s) of; Universal form of Lord
as body's owner, 22.20 (para 2)
brāhmaṇas favored by, **17.16**, **24.5**
Brahmā &. *See:* Brahmā, Lord &
Caitanya as, 5.27 (para 3)
as cause of all causes, 1.12, 3.3, 3.15 (para 1), **3.20–21**, 3.30 (para 2), **5.26**, 5.27 (para 1), 5.32, 7.24, **12.4**, 12.5, **12.7**, 12.7, **12.8**, 14.10
as changeless, **12.5**, 12.5
chanting Hare Kṛṣṇa pleases, 17.24
as complete, 12.5, **12.7**, 18.20, 20.21
as complete whole, 3.15 (para 1)
conchshell of, **20.31**
conditioned souls. *See:* Conditioned soul(s)
as controller, 3.2 (para 2), 3.3, 3.5, **3.22–24**, **5.43**, **6.10**, **6.11**, 6.12 (para 1), 7.8, 7.22, 8.20, **12.4**, 12.7, **16.14**, **16.22**, **17.8**, **17.25**
cow protection advocated by, 8.11
cows favored by, 17.16
cows protected by, **24.5**
as creator, **1.3**, **1.9**, **1.13**, **1.15**, 3.3, **3.4**, **3.22–24**, **6.10**, **6.11**, 6.12 (para 1), **7.23**, **7.25**, 12.40, **17.26**, **17.28**

Supreme Lord *(continued)*
as creator, maintainer, & destroyer, **17.9**, **17.27**, **22.20**
crocodile killed by, **3.33**
as death, 2.33 (para 2), 5.31, 8.21 (para 2)
death fears, 2.33 (para 2)
as deathless, **18.1**, 18.1, 19.12 (para 2)
demigods &. *See:* Demigod(s), Lord &
demons &. *See:* Demon(s), Lord &
as desireless, 12.7
desires fulfilled by, 3.15 (para 3), 3.19 (para 3), 5.48 (para 2), **16.21**, 16.21 (para 2), 16.22, **16.35–36**, **23.8**
desire tree, compared to, **23.8**
as detached, **5.44**, 5.44, 7.31 (para 2)
as Devakī-nandana, 1.13 (para 1)
in devotee role, 5.27 (para 3)
devotee &. *See:* Devotee(s), Lord &
devotional service to. *See:* Devotional service
Dhruva blessed by, 3.19 (para 3), 4.6
Dhruva saw, 5.48 (para 2), 6.13
as *dīna-anukampana,* 16.21 (para 2)
disinterested in Brahmān, 7.31 (para 2)
dress of, **6.3–7**, **10.54**, **16.33–34**, **16.39–40**, **17.2–3**, **18.1**, **20.32–33**
duality absent in, **1.12**, 12.5, **12.8**
as *durga-pāla,* 23.6
duty toward, 1.14 (para 2)
effulgence of, **18.4**
energy of. *See:* Energies of Supreme Lord
as enjoyer, 1.14 (para 1), 8.9, 9.29
as equally disposed, 5.22, **16.14**, 16.14, 17.23 (para 2), **23.8**
as eternal, 1.3, 1.11 (para 2), 5.26 (para 1), 5.27 (para 1), **5.50**
as everything, 12.5, 12.8 (para 1), 12.8 (para 3), 20.22
as everywhere, 17.24, 17.24
expansions of, **17.22**, 24.30
See also: Incarnation(s) of Supreme Lord
as father of all, 3.13 (para 2), **5.48**, 7.22, 7.2G, **8.25**
as firelike, **6.15**
flower shower(s) for. *See:* Flower(s), shower(s) of, for Lord
following, recommended, 1.15 (para 1), **1.16**, 1.16 (para 1), 1.16 (para 3)
form(s) of
devotees eager to see, 5.45, 5.46
impersonal, compared with personal, 5.45
as lotuslike, 5.45

Supreme Lord
mercy of *(continued)*
as causeless, 12.7, **23.7–8**
demigods' blessings compared with, **24.49**
on demons, **22.5**, **22.6–7**, **23.6**, **23.7–8**, 23.8
on devotee, 4.11–12, 19.32, 21.5, 21.28, 22.4, 22.16, 22.27, 22.29–30
devotee sees danger as, 3.32
on Hūhū, **4.3–4**, **4.3–4–5**
liberation via, 12.7
as limitless, 3.17 (para 3), **3.19**
on materialist, **22.23–24**
opulence as, 22.26
pure devotee at, 3.20–21
pure devotees accept, 22.8
pure devotional service via, 20.3
on Satyavrata, **24.11**
self-realization via, 3.16
on society, 14.8
on Sudāmā Vipra, 22.31
superexcellence of, **24.49**
Milk Ocean churned by, **7.16**
mission of, 24.48 (para 3)
modern civilization ignores, 22.17
modes of nature under, 5.50, 6.8, **12.7**
as Mukunda, **8.23**, 12.6
as mystic master, **3.27**, 12.14, **16.33–34**
name(s) of
for creation, maintenance, & annihilation, **7.23**
as God Himself, 3.8–9
pastimes according to, 1.13 (para 1)
potency of, 1.13 (para 1)
transcendental, 17.24
See also: Chanting holy name(s) of Lord; Hare Kṛṣṇa *mantra; specific names of Lord*
as Nārāyaṇa, **3.32**
nature under, 2.4, 3.13 (para 1), 5.26 (para 2), 5.44, 6.11, 6.39, **24.6**
as *nirguṇa,* 3.8–9, 6.12 (para 1)
nondevotees deny, 3.27 (para 1)
nondevotees disfavored by, 3.28
numberless incarnations of, 18.12
offerings to. *See:* Offerings to Supreme Lord
as omnipotent, 6.38, 6.39, 12.31, **12.36**, 12.44
as omniscient, **5.27**, 5.50, **6.14**, **6.36**, 7.31 (para 2), **12.11**, 12.11 (para 1), 12.44
oṁ represents, 3.2 (para 2), **7.25**
as one & different, 1.12, **12.7**

Supreme Lord *(continued)*
as one without a second, **12.8**, 12.8 (para 3)
opulence of, 5.27 (para 3), 5.32, 8.8, 18.20
original form of, as Kṛṣṇa, 21.5
as origin of all, 20.21, 20.22
as origin of species, 3.13 (para 2)
Pāṇḍavas' victory assured by, 17.8
as Parabrahman, 1.14 (para 2), **7.24**
as Paramātmā. *See:* Supersoul
parts & parcels of. *See:* Living entities
pastime(s) of
names of Lord according to, 1.13 (para 1)
places of, as holy, 17.8
purpose of, **24.29**
as transcendental, 3.8–9, 6.8, 17.23 (para 2)
as wonderful, **23.7–8**
See also: Incarnations of Supreme Lord
philosophers baffled by, 3.6
pious people seek, 2.31
pleasing
as life's purpose, 7.44
as measure of action, 16.61
plenary portions of. *See:* Supreme Lord, expansions of
power of, 18.20
as power source, 15.28
Prahlāda &. *See:* Prahlāda, Lord &
prasāda distribution pleases, **16.56**
preacher dear to, 7.44
pride-free people favored by, **22.26**
as proprietor, 1.10 (para 3–6), 3.13 (para 1), 8.8, 9.28, 9.29, **15.1–2**, 18.20, 19.17, 19.18, 21.34, **22.20**, 22.20 (para 3), 23.15
protection by. *See:* Protection, Lord &
protects devotees, 12.47
pure devotees realize, **3.11**, 3.27 (para 2)
quoted. *See:* Supreme Lord quoted
Rāhu beheaded by, **9.25**
Rākṣasas killed by, **1.18**, **1.26**
as Ramāpati, 17.7
as reality, **3.14**
reciprocates one's surrender, 9.28, 9.28, 16.14, 23.8, 24.38
remembering. *See:* Remembering Supreme Lord
remembers everything, 1.11 (para 2)
sacrifices for, **23.15**
sages baffled by, 3.6
sages take shelter of, 16.20 (para 3)
as Śārṅgadhanvā, **12.45**

T

U

W

Worship *(continued)*
payo-vrata. See: Payo-vrata sacrifice
via preaching, 7.44
to sacrificial fire, **16.9**, 16.9
via *saṅkīrtana,* 5.27 (para 3)
to Śiva, 12.33
by impersonalists, 7.31 (para 1)
to spiritual master, 24.46
to Vāmana, **21.5, 21.6–7**
by Bali, **18.27, 20.17–18**
by Brahmā, **21.2–3, 21.5**
via *varṇāśrama-dharma,* 16.60
to Viṣṇu, 5.49, **16.53–54**, 16.60, **20.11**
via Śiva, 7.21, 7.22, 7.24
See also: Deity worship to Supreme Lord

Y

Yajña(s)
defined, 1.14 (para 1)
See also: Ritualistic ceremony; Sacrifice
Yajña-hotra, **1.23**
Yajña, Lord
as Ākūti's son, **1.5, 1.6**
as Indra, **1.18**
subjects taught by, 1.5
Yajña-patnīs as *kṛpā-siddhas,* 20.3
Yajñavalkya, Lord, **14.8**
Yakṣas
as fallible, **8.19**
Kuvera king of, **18.16–17**
Lord's appearance honored by, **18.9–10**
Satyasena killed, **1.26**
Yamarāja, Lord
Bali compared to, **15.29**
Kālanābha vs., **10.29**
from universal form of Lord, **5.42**
wife of, **1.25**
Yāmas, **1.18**
Yamunā River
purification via bathing in, 9.14–15
served goddess of fortune, **8.10**
Yoga
aṣṭāṅga-, processes of, 19.21 (para 1)
bogus, compared with bona fide, 3.27 (para 2)
of devotion, 3.18
See also: Devotional service
devotional service compared with, 24.48 (para 1)
haṭha-, 17.2–3
knowledge via, **21.2–3**
in Kṛṣṇa consciousness, 3.20–21
Lord teaches, **14.8**, 14.8
Yoga (continued)
mystic
nowadays anomalous, 3.27 (para 2)
processes of, 19.21 (para 1)
See also: Mysticism; Mystic power
sāṅkhya-, **16.30**, 16.30
as sense control, 5.29
sense control via, 19.21 (para 1)
sense gratification cured via, 19.21 (para 1)
Śiva performed, **12.44**
See also: Devotional service; Kṛṣṇa consciousness; *Yogī(s)*
Yoga-māyā
creations of, in material world, **5.43**
Mohinī as, 12.31
Yoga-siddhis. See: Mystic power(s)
Yogī(s)
bogus, condemned, 3.27 (para 2)
in devotion as best, 3.18
as failures, 9.28
fate of, 19.12 (para 2)
householders as, 16.5
Lord baffles, 3.6
Lord compared with, 12.14
in meditation, 3.27 (para 2)
mystic, demons became, **22.6–7**
See also: Devotee(s); Sage(s); *specific* yogīs
Yudhiṣṭhira Mahārāja, 4.15 (para 1)
Yuga(s)
Kali. *See:* Kali-yuga
Lord's advent in, **5.27**
in Manu's life, 1.2, 13.11
religion deteriorates during, 14.4
Tretā. *See:* Tretā-yuga